1881
Michigan begins child protection with
the Michigan Public Acts of 1881.

1884
The state assumes the authority to take
neglected children and place them in
an institution. See *Reynolds v. Howe*, 51
Conn. 472, 478 (1884).

1886
First neglect case is heard in
Massachusetts.

1889
Board of children's guardians is
established in Indiana and given
jurisdiction over neglected and
dependent children.

1866
Massachusetts establishes that the state
has power over children under 16 whose
parents are "unfit."

1868
Passage of the Fourteenth Amendment to
the U.S. Constitution

1890
Children's Aid Society of
Pennsylvania, a foster home for
the juvenile delinquent used
as an alternative to reform schools,
is established.

1870
Illinois Supreme Court reverses Dan
O'Connell's vagrancy sentence to the
Chicago Reform School due to lack of due
process procedures in *People v. Turner*.

1891
Supreme Court of Minnesota
establishes the doctrine of
parental immunity.

1875–1900
Case Law begins to deal with protective statutes.

1897
Ex Parte Becknell, a
California decision that
reverses the sentence of
a juvenile who has not
been given a jury trial

1899
Illinois Juvenile
Court Act

1860   1870   1880   1890   **1900**

1903–1905
Many other states pass juvenile court acts.

1905
Commonwealth v. Fisher—Pennsylvania
Court upholds the constitutionality of
the Juvenile Court Act.

1906
Massachusetts passes an act to provide for
the treatment of children not as criminals
but as children in need of guidance and aid.

1908
Ex Parte Sharpe defines more clearly
the role of the juvenile court to include
parens patriae.

Legislation establishes juvenile justice
in Canada (*Juvenile Delinquents Act*)
and in England (*Children Act*)

1910
Compulsory school acts

1918
Chicago area studies are conducted by
Shaw and McKay.

1924
Federal Probation Act

1930
Children's Charter

continued on back inside cover …

1900   1910   1920   1930   1940

Juvenile Delinquency
Theory, Practice, and Law

EIGHTH EDITION

Larry J. Siegel
University of Massachusetts–Lowell

Brandon C. Welsh
University of Massachusetts–Lowell

Joseph J. Senna
Northeastern University

THOMSON
WADSWORTH

Australia • Canada • Mexico • Singapore • Spain • United Kingdom • United States

THOMSON

WADSWORTH

Senior Executive Editor, Criminal Justice: Sabra Horne
Development Editor: Julie Sakaue
Assistant Editor: Dawn Mesa
Editorial Assistant: Lee McCracken
Technology Project Manager: Susan DeVanna
Marketing Manager: Dory Schaeffer
Marketing Assistant: Neena Chandra
Advertising Project Manager: Bryan Vann
Project Manager, Editorial Production: Jennie Redwitz
Print/Media Buyer: Karen Hunt
Permissions Editor: Bob Kauser
Production Service: Linda Jupiter, Jupiter Productions

Text Designer: Jennifer Dunn
Photo Researcher: Linda Rill
Copy Editor: Judith Brown
Proofreader: M. Kate St.Clair
Illustrator: John and Judy Waller, Scientific Illustrators
Cover Designer: Yvo Riezebos
Cover Image: Painting by Nathan Oliveira, "Cobalt Racer," 2001. Copyright held by the Irv Weissman Collection. Use of image courtesy of the Marsha Mateyka Gallery, Washington, D.C.
Compositor: R&S Book Composition
Text and Cover Printer: Transcontinental/Beauceville

Printed in Canada
1 2 3 4 5 6 7 06 05 04 03 02

For more information about our products, contact us at:
Thomson Learning Academic Resource Center
1-800-423-0563

For permission to use material from this text, contact us by:
Phone: 1-800-730-2214
Fax: 1-800-730-2215
Web: http://www.thomsonrights.com

Library of Congress Control Number: 2002105118

Student Edition ISBN 0-534-57808-X
Instructor Edition ISBN 0-534-57830-6

Wadsworth/Thomson Learning
10 Davis Drive
Belmont, CA 94002-3098
USA

Asia
Thomson Learning
5 Shenton Way #01-01
UIC Building
Singapore 068808

Australia
Nelson Thomson Learning
102 Dodds Street
South Melbourne, Victoria 3205
Australia

Canada
Nelson Thomson Learning
1120 Birchmount Road
Toronto, Ontario M1K 5G4
Canada

Europe/Middle East/Africa
Thomson Learning
High Holborn House
50/51 Bedford Row
London WC1R 4LR
United Kingdom

Latin America
Thomson Learning
Seneca, 53
Colonia Polanco
11560 Mexico D.F.
Mexico

Spain
Paraninfo Thomson Learning
Calle/Magallanes, 25
28015 Madrid, Spain

To my wife, Therese J. Libby, and my children, Julie, Andrew, Eric, and Rachel

—L.J.S.

To my wife, Jennifer, and our son, Ryan

—B.C.W.

To my wife, Janet, and my children, Christian, Stephen, Peter, and Joseph

—J.J.S.

About the Authors

LARRY J. SIEGEL was born in the Bronx in 1947. While attending City College of New York in the 1960s he was introduced to the study of crime and justice in courses taught by sociologist Charles Winick. After graduation he attended the newly opened program in criminal justice at the State University of New York at Albany, where he earned both his M.A. and Ph.D. and studied with famed scholars such as Michael Hindelang, Gilbert Geis, and Donald Newman. After completing his graduate work, Dr. Siegel began his teaching career at Northeastern University, where he worked closely with colleague Joseph Senna on a number of texts and research projects. After leaving Northeastern, he held teaching positions at the University of Nebraska–Omaha and Saint Anselm College in New Hampshire. He is currently a professor at the University of Massachusetts–Lowell.

Dr. Siegel has written extensively in the area of crime and justice, including books on juvenile law, delinquency, criminology, and criminal procedure. He is a court-certified expert on police conduct and has testified in numerous legal cases. He resides in Bedford, New Hampshire, with his wife Therese J. Libby, Esq. and their children.

BRANDON C. WELSH was born in Canada. He received his undergraduate and M.A. degrees at the University of Ottawa and his Ph.D. from the University of Cambridge in England. Dr. Welsh is currently an assistant professor at the University of Massachusetts–Lowell. He teaches graduate and undergraduate courses on crime prevention, juvenile delinquency, policing, and international criminology.

His research interests include the prevention of crime and delinquency and the economic analysis of crime prevention programs. Dr. Welsh has published extensively in these areas, including two books with Drs. David Farrington and Lawrence Sherman. He lives in Brookline, New Hampshire, with his wife and son.

JOSEPH J. SENNA was born in Brooklyn, New York. He graduated from Brooklyn College, Fordham University Graduate School of Social Service, and Suffolk University Law School. Mr. Senna has spent over fourteen years teaching law and justice courses at Northeastern University. In addition, he has served as an Assistant District Attorney, Director of Harvard Law School Prosecutorial Program, and consultant to numerous criminal justice organizations.

His academic specialities include the areas of Criminal Law, Constitutional Due Process, Criminal Justice, and Juvenile Law. Mr. Senna lives with his wife and sons outside of Boston. He is currently working on a criminal law textbook.

Brief Contents

Contents

Part Three
Social, Community, and Environmental Influences on Delinquency *163*

6 Gender and Delinquency 164

7 The Family and Delinquency 192

Preface

Northern New Hampshire is known for its beautiful scenery and laid-back lifestyle, not violent crime. So when two Dartmouth College professors— Half Zantop, 62, an economic geologist, and his wife, Susanne, 55, who chaired the German Studies department—were found dead in their home on January 27, 2001, the killings rocked the state. The murders had been carried out in a particularly grisly fashion: Each had been stabbed repeatedly in the neck, chest, and head with a military-style knife. Police quickly traced the weapons used in the killings to Robert Tulloch, 17, and James Parker, 16, who lived in Chelsea, Vermont, a town of about 1,200 people located about 20 miles northwest of the Zantop's home in Etna, New Hampshire.

The murders seemed to make no sense to the people who knew the boys. Chelsea is a peaceful village. Robert Tulloch was a student council president, champion debater, and a good student who did well in tough courses, such as precalculus and physics. James Parker, 16, played on the high school basketball team and was known as a fun-loving jokester. Both Parker and Tulloch came from families who were well respected in the community.

The Zantop murders raise many issues concerning youth crime and juvenile delinquency. What could possibly motivate two young people with no history of violent crimes to commit such ghastly acts? They were not inner-city youths growing up in poverty and despair. Those familiar with the case seemed baffled by their outburst of violence. And, considering their youth and immaturity, what would be a fitting punishment for their act: life in an adult prison? the death penalty? On April 4, 2002, the boys pled guilty to murder. Robert Tulloch received a mandatory sentence of life without parole, while James Parker was sentenced to 25 years to life as an accomplice to murder (Parker had struck a deal and agreed to testify against Tulloch).

Cases such as the Zantop murders have sparked interest in the study of juvenile delinquency, and it is not surprising, considering the national concern with the problems of youth, that courses on juvenile delinquency have become popular offerings on the nation's college campuses. We wrote *Juvenile Delinquency: Theory, Practice, and Law* to help students understand the nature of juvenile delinquency and its causes and correlates, as well as the current strategies being used to prevent or control its occurrence. The text also reviews the legal rules that have been set down either to protect innocent minors or control adolescent misconduct. Thus the text addresses such questions as these: Can children be required to submit to drug testing in school? Can teachers search suspicious students or use corporal punishment as a method of discipline? Should children be allowed to testify on closed-circuit TV in child abuse cases? Should a minor be given a death penalty sentence?

Because the study of juvenile delinquency is a dynamic, ever-changing field of scientific inquiry and because the theories, concepts, and processes of this area of study are constantly evolving, we have updated *Juvenile Delinquency: Theory, Practice, and Law,* Eighth Edition, to reflect the changes that have taken place in the study of delinquent behavior during the past few years.

Like its predecessors, the eighth edition includes a review of recent legal cases, research studies, and policy initiatives. Also like earlier editions, its aim is to provide a foundation for the study of juvenile delinquency by analyzing and describing the nature and extent of delinquency, the suspected causes of delinquent behavior, and the environmental influences on youthful misbehavior. It also covers what most experts believe are the critical issues in juvenile delinquency and analyzes crucial policy issues, including the use of pretrial detention, waiver to adult court, and restorative justice programs. This edition adds three new chapters—one on developmental views of delinquency, another on delinquency prevention, and a third on delinquency and juvenile justice abroad—to reflect the growing interest in these important topics.

Goals and Objectives

Our primary goals in writing this Eighth Edition remain the same as that for previous editions:

1. To be as objective as possible, presenting the many diverse views and perspectives that characterize the study of juvenile delinquency and reflect its interdisciplinary nature.
2. To maintain a balance of theory, law, policy, and practice. It is essential that a book on delinquency address the juvenile justice system when discussing theory and include legal issues and cases when covering current policies.
3. To be as thorough and up-to-date as possible. We have attempted to include the most current data and information available.
4. To make the study of delinquency interesting as well as informative. We want readers to become interested in the study of delinquency so that they will pursue it on an undergraduate or graduate level.

We have tried to provide a book that is both scholarly and informative, comprehensive yet interesting, well organized and objective, yet provocative and thought provoking. We hope you agree that we have been successful in reaching our goals.

Organization of the Text

The Eighth Edition of *Juvenile Delinquency* is divided into four main sections.

Part One examines the concept of delinquency and status offending, the measurement of delinquency, and the trends and patterns in the delinquency rate. Chapter 1 contains extensive material on the history of childhood and the legal concept of delinquency and status offending. This material enables the reader to understand how the concept of adolescence evolved over time and how that evolution influenced the development of the juvenile court and the special status of delinquency. Chapter 2 covers the measurement of delinquent behavior, the trends and patterns in teen crime, and also discusses the correlates of delinquency, including race, gender, class, age, and chronic offending.

Part Two describes the various theoretical models that have been used to explain the onset of delinquent behavior. Chapter 3 covers recent individual-level views that focus on choice, biological, and psychological theories. Chapter 4 looks at theories that hold that economic, cultural, and environmental influences control delinquent behavior. Chapter 5 covers the newly emerging developmental theories of delinquency, including such issues as the onset, continuity, paths, and desistance of a delinquent career.

Part Three covers the environmental and individual correlates of delinquency. It begins with Chapter 6 on gender and delinquency, which explores the sex-based differences that are thought to account for gender patterns in the delinquency rate. Also in Part Three are chapters that cover the influence of families (Chapter 7), peers (Chapter 8), schools (Chapter 9), and drugs (Chapter 10). Part Three concludes with a new chapter, Chapter 11, that addresses social and developmental perspectives on delinquency prevention. It examines a wide range of innovative programs and policies applicable during the childhood and teenage years to prevent young people's involvement in delinquency.

Part Four addresses juvenile justice advocacy. It covers both the history of juvenile justice and the philosophy and practice of today's juvenile justice system. Chapter 12 gives extensive coverage to the emergence of state control over children in need and the development of the juvenile justice system. It covers the contemporary juvenile justice system, the major stages in the justice process, the role of the federal government in the juvenile justice system, and an analysis of the differences between the adult and juvenile justice systems. It also provides extensive coverage of the legal rights of children, including a new time line of constitutional cases. Chapter 13 discusses the role of police in delinquency prevention. It covers legal issues such as major court decisions on school searches and *Miranda* rights of juveniles. It also examines how race and gender affect police discretion, as well as efforts by police departments to control delinquent behavior. Chapter 14, which covers the juvenile trial process through sentencing, includes coverage of plea bargaining in juvenile court, the use of detention, and transfer to adult jails. It also contains an analysis of the critical factors that influence the waiver decision.

Chapter 15's coverage of juvenile corrections includes material on probation and other community dispositions, including restorative justice programs and secure juvenile corrections, with an emphasis on legal issues such as the right to treatment and controversial programs such as boot camps. The final chapter, Chapter 16, looks at juvenile delinquency abroad and examines how juvenile justice systems in other nations compare with the system used in the United States.

What's New in This Edition

We have added a number of important new features to this edition. On the author team, we are joined by a new colleague, Dr. Brandon Welsh, who contributes his expertise on delinquency prevention and international delinquency. We are very pleased that Brandon has joined our team.

Each chapter now begins with a real-life vignette illustrating an actual dilemma that highlights issues relevant to the chapter's study of juvenile delinquency and helps draw students immediately into the chapter. Also included are InfoTrac® College Edition exercises—scattered throughout each chapter and at the end of the boxed features—that direct students to a variety of relevant articles supplementing the material found in the chapter itself. InfoTrac College Edition is an online library containing hundreds of thousands of current articles, many related to juvenile delinquency. To encourage students to think critically, we have added critical-thinking questions at the end of each boxed feature, where we take a look at specific topics or events in greater detail.

We have thoroughly updated each chapter in this new edition. Following are a few of the more important changes and updates we have made.

We begin Chapter 1 with an analysis of the 2001 case of 14-year-old Nathaniel Brazill, who killed his teacher in Florida. In the chapter itself, we updated data on the state of America's children, including the latest statistics on adolescent poverty. We also added new information on why kids take risks, and we address the results of a national police survey on the use of juvenile curfews in the new *Policy and Practice* box, "Keeping Truants in School."

In Chapter 2 we added a new discussion on the youngest victims as well as new material on the background of chronic offenders. We also incorporated a new section on the relationship between gun possession and juvenile delinquency. In this chapter, you will see two new boxes: The first, *Focus on Delinquency:* "Delinquent and Victim: One and the Same?" looks at the relationship between delinquents and victims, while the second, *Focus on Delinquency:* "Internet Victimization," reviews this growing national phenomenon.

Chapter 3 includes a new box, *Focus on Delinquency:* "Delinquency as Problem Solving," which shows how kids may turn to delinquency to deal with personal issues. A second box, *Focus on Delinquency:* "Diet and Delinquency," reviews research indicating that aggression may be linked to food intake. We also added new sections on the relationship between lead exposure and homicide, female violence and personality, and the continuing debate over birth order, family size, and intelligence.

Sociological views of delinquency are reviewed in Chapter 4. We added new data on the key national indicators of well-being to the chapter, which now also covers such topics as economic deprivation and changes in homicide arrest rates; the concept of collective efficacy; and the political, economic, and social consequences that influence children when prisoners return to communities. There is new evidence on how the ethnic composition of neighborhoods is related to perceived risk of crime, and other new sections include discussions on whether disorder in urban neighborhoods leads to crime, the association between adolescent religious commitment and crime, and the impact of maternal employment on delinquency.

Chapter 5 is new to this edition. Topics include life transitions, problem behavior syndrome, pathways to crime and delinquency, delinquent trajectories, continuity of crime and delinquency, age-graded theories, and the concept of latent traits. Among the boxes included in this new chapter are *Focus on Delinquency:* "The Cambridge Youth Study" and *Focus on Delinquency:* "Five Hundred Delinquent Boys in the New Millennium."

The association between gender and delinquency is the topic of Chapter 6. In it, we included new material on girls in the juvenile justice system and how gender relates to delinquency in the everyday lives of high-risk youths. There is also a new *Focus on Delinquency* box, "Girls on the Run," which deals with the lives of runaway teens.

Chapter 7 has been fully updated. We added new data on the changing American family, as well as on the sexual exploitation of children. We also included recent surveys of child abuse, child maltreatment, and child abuse cases reported to the police, and added a new section on parental efficacy and delinquent behavior. You will find two new *Focus on Delinquency* boxes: "Does Divorce Matter? Two Opposing Views on Families in Crisis" and "Relationship between Substance Abuse and Child Maltreatment."

We updated Chapter 8 with data from the most recent youth gang surveys and added two new boxes, *Policy and Practice:* "Boston's Youth Violence Strike Force (YVSF)" and *Focus on Delinquency:* "Gang Boys and Guns."

In Chapter 9 we added new data on school-based crime, including school shootings and a discussion on bullying in the new *Focus on Delinquency* box, "Bullying in School." We also updated the legal component with cases such as *Good News Club v. Milford Central School* (2001) on school prayer.

Chapter 10 now covers the relationship between mental health and substance abuse among adolescents. You will also see that it reviews the new (2001) D.A.R.E. curriculum, and the relationship between alcohol and interpersonal aggression during adolescence. There are new sections on prevention, including breaking the juvenile drug/crime cycle and preventing and reducing substance use among institutionalized adolescents.

Brand new for this edition, Chapter 11 provides an overview of current efforts to prevent delinquency before it occurs. It looks at the financial costs of delinquency as a justification for prevention. It covers what works and what doesn't in preventing delinquency in childhood and adolescent years. It also presents the policy implications of early delinquency prevention programs.

Chapter 12 was updated with new material on the history of the House of Refuge movement. We also added new perspectives on the future of juvenile justice, going into further depth on specific aspects of the topic in boxes such as *Policy and Practice:* "Teen Courts" and *Policy and Practice:* "Abolish the Juvenile Court?"

We thoroughly revamped Chapter 13. We now look at what works and what doesn't in policing for delinquency prevention and cover such topics as aggressive law enforcement, community-based policing services, and police in schools. We examine integrated policing models and look at new research on police discretion.

In this edition, we streamlined the discussion on the juvenile court process by combining two chapters—one on pretrial procedure and another on trials and sentencing—into one that covers all three phases. Chapter 14 contains new data on court case flow and changes in the pretrial detention of children, as well as new material that supports the waiver of children to adult court. Finally, we added a new box, *Policy and Practice:* "The Detention Diversion Advocacy Program," that discusses efforts to reduce reliance on detention.

Instead of addressing juvenile probation and community treatment in one chapter and institutions for juveniles in another as we did in the previous edition, we now address all three topics in a single chapter: Chapter 15. To this chapter, we added new material on innovations in correctional treatment for juveniles, up-to-date research on the effectiveness of boot camps, and an assessment of new data on disproportionate minority confinement.

Chapter 16 is a brand-new chapter. In it, we compare the juvenile delinquency rates across a variety of countries and examine why the rate has or has not climbed in certain instances, including a closer look at a rising rate in Japan in the *Focus on Delinquency* box, "Youth Violence on the Rise in Japan." We also examine the juvenile justice systems across countries. We address how they are managed, as well as how special issues, such as the use of juvenile courts and transfers to adult courts, are handled abroad. We end the chapter with a special profile on juvenile justice in England and how it compares with the system in the United States.

Learning Tools

The text contains the following features designed to help students learn and comprehend the material:

1. Each chapter begins with a chapter outline.
2. The book contains more than 200 photos, tables, figures, and exhibits.
3. The book is now more closely linked to the Internet. Numerous research exercises in each chapter, called *A Closer View*, direct students to important articles and sources on InfoTrac College Edition, the comprehensive Web-based database. There are also Web-link features throughout each chapter. These provide Web site addresses that can be accessed for more information on topics covered in the text. Keep in mind, however, that although we have attempted to select stable sites, URLs frequently change over the course of time.
4. As in previous editions, we have included *Focus on Delinquency* boxes that address topics of special importance and concern. For example, in Chapter 3, a box called "Diet and Delinquency" discusses whether children's food intake can affect their behavior.
5. *Juvenile Law in Review* boxes include major Supreme Court cases that influence and control the juvenile justice system. For example, *In re Gault*, which defines the concept of due process for youthful offenders, is covered in a box in Chapter 14.
6. *Policy and Practice* boxes discuss major initiatives and programs. For example, in Chapter 16, the box "Precourt Diversion Programs around the World" tells

how keeping youths who have become involved in minor delinquent acts from being formally processed through the juvenile justice system has become a top priority of many countries.

7. Each of the boxes—*Focus on Delinquency, Juvenile Law in Review,* and *Policy and Practice*—includes critical-thinking questions and InfoTrac College Edition references intended to motivate students to develop their ability to apply the concepts covered in the text, as well as cultivate a critical perspective.

8. Each chapter ends with a *Viewpoint* feature that uses material found in articles from InfoTrac College Edition to lead students to research ideas contained within the chapter.

9. Key terms are defined throughout the text as they appear in each chapter.

10. Each chapter ends with thought-provoking discussion questions to help students review and gain a deeper understanding of the material covered in the chapter.

11. A glossary sets out and defines the key terms used in the text.

Supplements

Juvenile Delinquency, Eighth Edition, is accompanied by a wide array of supplements prepared for both the instructor and student to create the best learning environment inside as well as outside the classroom. All the continuing supplements for *Juvenile Delinquency,* Eighth Edition, have been thoroughly revised and updated, and several are new to this edition. Especially noteworthy are the new media- and Internet-based supplements. We invite you to examine and take full advantage of the teaching and learning tools available to you.

For the Instructor

Instructor's Resource Manual   This revised and updated Instructor's Resource Manual includes the following for every chapter: learning objectives, key terms with definitions, detailed chapter outlines, chapter summaries, and a test bank. The completely new test bank features the following for each chapter: 25 multiple choice, 20 true/false, 15 fill-in-the-blank, and 3 essay questions.

ExamView® Computerized Testing   ExamView helps you create and customize tests in minutes. You can easily edit and import your own questions and graphics, edit and maneuver existing questions, and change test layouts. Tests appear on screen just as they will when printed. ExamView offers flexible delivery and the ability to test and grade online.

InfoTrac® College Edition   With InfoTrac College Edition, the premier online library of current publications, instructors can ignite discussions and augment lectures with the latest developments in corrections and criminal justice. Available free with this newly purchased book, InfoTrac College Edition gives you and your students four months of free access to an extensive online database of reliable, full-length articles (not just abstracts) from hundreds of top academic journals and popular sources that goes back as far as 1980. By entering a single keyword, users instantly search the entire InfoTrac College Edition database for related articles that can be read online or printed. This is available only to colleges and universities.

Classroom Presentation Tools for the Instructor

Juvenile Delinquency 2003: A Microsoft® PowerPoint® Presentation Tool This set of over 500 slides will help you enhance your classroom presentations quickly and easily.

Transparency Acetates for *Juvenile Delinquency* This set of 50 full-color transparencies will help you enhance your discussion of key concepts and research findings effortlessly.

CNN™ Today: Criminal Justice Video Series Now you can integrate the up-to-the-minute programming power of CNN and its affiliate networks right into your course. These videos feature short, high-interest clips perfect for launching your lectures. A current new volume is available to adopters each year. Ask your Thomson/ Wadsworth representative about our video policy by adoption size.

> Juvenile Delinquency: Vol. I: 0-534-55733-3. Vol. II: 0-534-55753-8.
> Vol. III: 0-534-55754-6. Vol. IV: 0-534-55763-5

The Wadsworth Custom Videos for Criminal Justice Produced by Wadsworth and *Films for the Humanities,* these videos include 5- to 10-minute segments that encourage classroom discussion. Topics include white-collar crime, domestic violence, forensics, suicide and the police officer, the court process, the history of corrections, prison society, and juvenile justice. Vol. I: 0-534-52528-5. Vol. II: 0-534-57335-5

The Wadsworth Criminal Justice Video Library So many exciting, new videos... so many great ways to enrich your lectures and spark discussion of the material in this book. Your Thomson/Wadsworth representative will be happy to provide details on our video policy by adoption size. The library includes these selections and many others:

- *Court TV* **videos:** one-hour videos presenting seminal and high-profile court cases
- **Plus** videos from the *A&E American Justice Series, Films for the Humanities,* and the *National Institute of Justice Crime File Videos*

For the Student

Study Guide For each chapter of the book, this helpful guide contains learning objectives, detailed chapter outlines, key terms with definitions, critical-thinking exercises, and a practice test. The practice test questions include 35 multiple choice, 25 true/false, 20 fill-in-the-blank, and 5 essay questions.

Internet Activities for Criminal Justice, Second Edition This completely updated booklet shows how to best utilize the Internet for research through interesting and informative exercises, searches, and activities.

Internet Guide for Criminal Justice, Second Edition Intended for the less-experienced Internet user, the first part of this completely revised booklet explains the background and vocabulary necessary for navigating the Internet, while the second part focuses on Internet applications in criminal justice, doing criminal justice research online, and criminal justice career information on the Web.

InfoTrac College Edition Student Guide for Criminal Justice This booklet provides detailed user guidelines for students, illustrating how to use the InfoTrac College Edition database. Special features include log-in help, a complete search tips worksheet, and a topic list of suggested keyword search terms for criminal justice.

***The Criminal Justice Internet Investigator,* Third Edition** This colorful trifold brochure lists some of the most popular Internet addresses for criminal justice–related Web sites.

Internet-Based Supplements

WebTutor® Advantage This Web-based software for students and instructors takes a course beyond the classroom to an anywhere, anytime environment. Students gain access to a full array of study tools, including chapter outlines, chapter-specific quizzing material, interactive games and maps, and videos. With WebTutor Advantage, instructors have access to an assortment of communication and class management tools. Instructors can provide virtual office hours, post syllabi, track student progress with the quizzing material, and even customize the content to suit their needs. They can also set up threaded discussions and conduct real-time chats. "Out of the box" or customized, WebTutor Advantage provides powerful tools for instructors and students alike.

Criminal Justice Resource Center at **http://cj.wadsworth.com** This Web site provides instructors and students with a wealth of *free* information and resources, such as:

- The Criminal Justice Timeline
- What Americans Think
- BookFinder
- Terrorism: An Interdisciplinary Perspective
- National Criminal Justice Reference Service Calendar of Events

and so much more!

The Criminal Justice Resource Center also includes text-specific Web sites with chapter-specific resources for instructors and students. For instructors, the Web sites offer password-protected instructor's manuals, Microsoft PowerPoint presentation slides, and more. For students, there is a multitude of text-specific study aids. These chapter-specific features are available for students using many of Wadsworth's criminal justice and criminology textbooks:

- Tutorial practice quizzes that can be scored and emailed to the instructor
- Internet links and exercises
- InfoTrac College Edition exercises
- Flashcards
- Crossword puzzles
- MicroCase Exercises. On the text-specific Web site for *Juvenile Delinquency,* Eighth Edition, the activities for Chapters 2, 7, 10, and 12 (chapters particularly amenable to statistical research) include exercises with real data and corresponding questions that give students the opportunity to extend their exploration and analysis of the criminal justice issues and principles presented in the text. Basic univariate statistics, mapping, and cross-tabulations give students a chance to discover criminal justice by using the same data and methods utilized by professional researchers.

To access all these exciting text-specific Web resources, go to The Wadsworth Criminal Justice Resource Center at **http://cj.wadsworth.com** and follow these steps:

1. Click either Student Resources or Instructor Resources on the left navigation bar. If you are an instructor, you will be prompted to enter a user name and password.
2. Click the cover of the text that you use.

Acknowledgments

The preparation of this text would not have been possible without the aid of our colleagues who helped by reviewing the previous editions and giving us important suggestions for improvement.

Reviewers of the Eighth Edition are

Randy Blazak, *Portland State University*

Dr. Darl H. Champion, Sr., *Methodist College*

Steve Christiansen, *Green River Community College*

Richard Lawrence, *St. Cloud State University*

Clayton Mosher, *Washington State University, Vancouver*

Theresa A. Severance, *Eastern Connecticut State University*

Robert W. Winslow, *San Diego State University*

Reviewers of the previous editions include Fred Andes, Robert Agnew, Richard Ball, Sarah Boggs, Thomas Calhoun, Scott Decker, Steven Frazier, Fred Hawley, Tonya Hilligoss, Vincent Hoffman, David Horton, Fred Jones, Irwin Kantor, James Larson, Elizabeth McConnell, Harold Osborne, Barbara Owen, Ray Paternoster, Joseph Rankin, Studipto Roy, Jeff Rush, Thomas Segady, Richard Siebert, Paul Steele, Leslie Sue, Stanley Swart, Pam Tontodonato, Paul Tracy, William Waegel, Bill Wagner, Kim Weaver, Mervin White, and Michael Wiatrowski.

In addition, important information was provided by the following individuals and institutions: Marcus Felson, Marty Schwartz, George Knox, G. David Curry, Joan McDermott, Helene Raskin White, Joe Sanborn, Jim Inciardi, Vic Streib, Malcom Klein, Robert Agnew, Eve Buzawa, Meda Chesney-Lind, Gerald Hotaling, Marv Zalman, John Laub, Rob Sampson, David Farrington, Rolf Loeber, Larry Sherman, Anthony Braga, Carol Petrie, Mark Irving, Deborah Denno, James A. Fox, Jack McDevitt, Robert Worden, Lee Ellis, Stephen Schoenthaler; the staff at the Institute for Social Research at the University of Michigan; the National Center for State Courts; the Police Foundation; the Sentencing Project; Kathleen Maguire and the staff of the Hindelang Research Center at State University of New York–Albany; the National Criminal Justice Reference Service; Deborah Daro and Karen McCurdy of the National Committee for Prevention of Child Abuse; and Terence Thornberry and the researchers at the Rochester Youth Study, Albany, New York.

And, of course, our colleagues at Wadsworth did their usual outstanding job of aiding us in the preparation of the text. Sabra Horne, our editor, did her usual fine job. Julie Sakaue is more than a developmental editor, she is a friend. Linda Rill was her awesome self as photo researcher and honorary family member. Linda Jupiter was a joy to work with as production manager and psychotherapist. Judith Brown was a terrific copyeditor; we are really indebted to her. Karen Austin Keith worked diligently to keep things in order and everything moving toward production. Jennie Redwitz, who oversees the production, never once lost patience with me and my cover neuroses, and Dory Schaeffer, who works tirelessly on the marketing front, has and will continue to make a huge difference.

Many thanks to all!

Larry Siegel
Bedford, New Hampshire

Part One The Concept of Delinquency

The field of juvenile delinquency has been an important area of study since the turn of the twentieth century. Academicians, practitioners, policy makers, and legal scholars have devoted their attention to basic questions about the nature of youth crime: How should delinquency be defined? Who commits delinquent acts? How much delinquency occurs each year? Is the rate of delinquent activity increasing or decreasing? What can we do to prevent delinquency?

Part One reviews these basic questions in detail. Chapter 1 discusses the current state of American youth and the challenges they face. It covers the origins of society's concern for children and the development of the concept of delinquency. It shows how the definition of delinquency was developed and how the legal definition has evolved. While society has chosen to treat adult and juvenile law violators separately, it has also expanded the definition of youthful misbehaviors eligible for social control; these are referred to as *status offenses*. Status offenses include such behaviors as truancy, running away, and incorrigibility. Critics suggest that juveniles' noncriminal behavior is probably not a proper area of concern for law enforcement agencies.

Chapter 2 examines the nature and extent of delinquent behavior. It discusses how social scientists gather information on juvenile delinquency and provides an overview of some of the major trends in juvenile crime. Chapter 2 also discusses some of the critical factors related to delinquency, such as race, gender, class, and age. It covers the concept of the chronic delinquent, those who continually commit delinquent acts in their youth and continue to offend as adults.

1   **Childhood and Delinquency**

2   **The Nature and Extent of Delinquency**

1 Childhood and Delinquency

As the governor of a large southern state, you have been asked to grant a pardon to a young man by his family and friends. Nathaniel B. was convicted of second-degree murder in 1995 and received a sentence of 28 years in the state penal system. Tried as an adult, he was found guilty of murder for intentionally killing Mr. Barry G., his English teacher, because he was angry over receiving a failing grade and being suspended for throwing water balloons. During trial, Nathaniel's attorney claimed that the gun Nathaniel brought to school had gone off accidentally after he pointed it at Mr. G. in an attempt to force him to let him talk to two girls in the classroom.

"As he's holding the gun up, he's overwhelmed with tears," Nathaniel's lawyer told the jury. "His hand begins to shake, and the gun discharges. The gun discharged in the hands of an inexperienced 13-year-old with a junk gun." The prosecutor countered that Nathaniel's act was premeditated. He was frustrated because he was receiving an F in the class, and he was angry because he was being barred from talking to the girls. His victim "had no idea of the rage, hate, the anger, the frustration" filling the young man. There was also damaging information from police, who reported that Nathaniel told a classmate he was going to return to school and shoot the teacher; he said he'd be "all over the news."

At his sentencing hearing, Nathaniel read a statement: "Words cannot really explain how sorry I am, but they're all I have." His mother, Polly, blamed herself for her son's actions, claiming that he was surrounded by domestic abuse and alcoholism at home.

Now that he has served seven years in prison, Nathaniel's case has come to your attention. As governor, you recognize that his conviction and punishment raise a number of important issues. His mother claims that his actions were a product of abuse and violence in the home. You have read research showing that many habitually aggressive children have been raised in homes in which they are physically brutalized by their parents; this violence then persists into adulthood.[1] Even though he was only

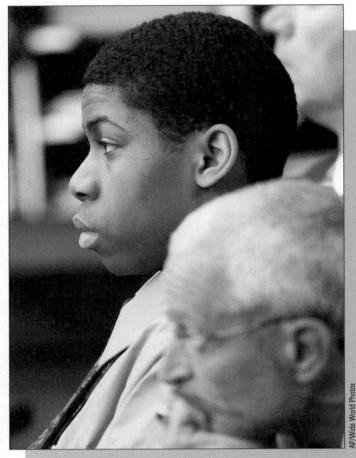

NATHANIEL BRAZILL, shown here with his attorney Robert Udell, was convicted of second-degree murder in 2001 for intentionally killing Mr. Barry Grunow, his English teacher. Nathaniel received a sentence of 28 years in the Florida penal system. Is it appropriate to give minors harsh criminal penalties in adult prisons, or would they be better served by treatment in a separate juvenile justice system dedicated to their eventual rehabilitation and release? Many juvenile court judges today base their sentencing decisions on the need to punish offenders and are more concerned about protecting the rights of victims of crime than rehabilitating juvenile offenders. Can a juvenile who commits a serious violent crime be "rehabilitated"? Should a juvenile be treated differently from an adult who commits the same crime?

13 at the time of the crime, he has been sentenced to more than 20 years in an adult prison.

- Should children who are subject to brutal treatment, such as Nathaniel, be punished again by the justice system?

- Should Nathaniel be held personally responsible for actions that may in fact have been caused by a home life beyond his control?

- Even though he was only 13 years old when he committed his crime, Nathaniel's case was heard in an adult court, and he received a long sentence to an adult prison. Should minor children who commit serious crimes, as Nathaniel did, be treated as an adult, or should they be tried within an independent juvenile justice system oriented to treatment and rehabilitation?

- Would you pardon Nathaniel now that he has served more than seven years in prison?

The Adolescent Dilemma

The case of Nathaniel B. is not unique. In fact it is based on an actual Florida case that occurred in 2001.[2]

The questions raised by this case have become highly pertinent in a nation in which crimes involving gang violence and school shootings have made Americans quite concerned about their youth. His mother claims that his actions were a product of abuse and violence in the home. Research indicates that many habitually aggressive children have been raised in homes in which they are physically brutalized by their parents; this violence then persists into adulthood.[3] Should children subject to such brutal treatment then be punished again by the justice system? Should they be held responsible for actions that may in fact spring from a home life beyond their control? And, even though he was only 13 years old when he committed his crime, Nathaniel's case was heard in an adult court and he received a long sentence to an adult prison. Should minor children who commit serious crimes, as Nathaniel did, be treated as an adult, or should they be tried within an independent juvenile justice system oriented to treatment?

This latest generation of adolescents has been described as cynical and preoccupied with material acquisitions.[4] By age 18, American youth have spent more time in front of a television set than in the classroom; each year they may see up to 1,000 rapes, murders, and assaults on TV. Can such prolonged exposure to violence have an impact on child development?

And why does America, considered the richest country on Earth, come up short in many areas of child welfare? As Exhibit 1.1 shows, problems exist in important areas of childcare and protection, despite the fact that the United States has the highest rate of gross domestic product in the world.[5]

Such complex questions are the subjects of debates among academicians, policy makers, and juvenile justice officials, as well as ordinary citizens concerned about public safety and the health and well-being of children.

Adolescent Stress

The problems of American society and the daily stress of modern life have had a significant effect on our nation's youth, who are going through their tumultuous teenage years. Adolescence is unquestionably a time of transition. During this period, the self,

Exhibit 1.1 The State of America's Children

- 1 in 2 will live in a single-parent family at some point in childhood.
- 1 in 3 is born to unmarried parents.
- 1 in 3 will be poor at some point in their childhood.
- 1 in 3 is behind a year or more in school.
- 1 in 4 lives with only one parent.
- 2 in 5 never complete a single year of college.
- 1 in 5 was born poor.
- 1 in 5 is born to a mother who did not graduate from high school.
- 1 in 5 has a foreign-born mother.
- 3 in 5 preschoolers have their mother in the labor force.
- 1 in 6 is poor now.
- 1 in 6 is born to a mother who did not receive prenatal care in the first three months of pregnancy.
- 1 in 7 has no health insurance.
- 1 in 7 has a worker in their family but still is poor.
- 1 in 8 lives in a family receiving food stamps.
- 1 in 8 never graduates from high school.
- 1 in 8 is born to a teenage mother.
- 1 in 12 has a disability.
- 1 in 13 was born with low birth weight.
- 1 in 15 lives at less than half the poverty level.
- 1 in 24 lives with neither parent.
- 1 in 26 is born to a mother who received late or no prenatal care.
- 1 in 60 sees their parents divorce in any year.
- 1 in 139 will die before their first birthday.
- 1 in 1,056 will be killed by guns before age 20.

Source: The Children's Defense Fund, *The State of America's Children Yearbook 2001* (Washington, DC, 2001).

ego identity   According to Erik Erickson, ego identity is formed when persons develop a firm sense of who they are and what they stand for.

role diffusion   According to Erik Erikson, role diffusion occurs when youths spread themselves too thin, experience personal uncertainty, and place themselves at the mercy of leaders who promise to give them a sense of identity they cannot develop for themselves.

at-risk youth   Young people who are extremely vulnerable to the negative consequences of school failure, substance abuse, and early sexuality.

or basic personality, is still undergoing a metamorphosis and is vulnerable to a host of external determinants as well as internal physiological changes.[6]

Adolescence is a time of trial and uncertainty for many youths. They may become extremely vulnerable to emotional turmoil and experience anxiety, humiliation, and mood swings. Adolescents also undergo a period of biological development that proceeds at a far faster pace than at any other time in their lives except infancy. Over a period of a few years, their height, weight, and sexual characteristics change dramatically. The average age at which girls reach puberty today is 12.5 years; whereas 150 years ago, girls matured sexually at age 16. But while they may become biologically mature and capable of having children as early as 14, many youngsters remain emotionally and intellectually immature.[7] By the time they reach 15, a significant number of teenagers are approaching adulthood unable to adequately meet the requirements and responsibilities of the workplace, family, and neighborhood. Many suffer from health problems, are educational underachievers, and are already skeptical about their ability to enter the American mainstream.[8]

In later adolescence (ages 16 to 18), youths may experience a life crisis that famed psychologist Erik Erikson labeled the struggle between **ego identity** and **role diffusion.** Ego identity is formed when youths develop a firm sense of who they are and what they stand for; role diffusion occurs when they experience personal uncertainty, spread themselves too thin, and place themselves at the mercy of leaders who promise to give them a sense of identity they cannot mold for themselves.[9] Psychologists also find that late adolescence is a period dominated by the yearning for independence from parental domination.[10] Given this explosive mixture of biological change and desire for autonomy, it isn't surprising that the teenage years are a time of rebelliousness and conflict with authority at home, at school, and in the community.

Youth in Crisis

There are approximately 71 million children in the United States, a number that is projected to increase to 77.6 million in 2020.[11] During the "baby boom" (1946 to 1964), the number of children grew rapidly; then, after declining in the 1970s and 1980s, the number of children began to increase again in 1990. Children are projected to remain a fairly stable percentage of the total population, making up about 24 percent of the population by the year 2020.

Problems in the home, the school, and the neighborhood, coupled with health and developmental hazards, have placed a significant portion of American youth "at risk." Youths considered at risk are those dabbling in various forms of dangerous conduct such as drug abuse, alcohol use, and precocious sexuality. They are living in families that, because of economic, health, or social problems, are unable to provide adequate care and discipline. Though it is impossible to determine precisely the number of **at-risk youth** in the United States, one estimate is that 25 percent of the population under 17, or about 15 million youths, are vulnerable to the negative consequences of school failure, substance abuse, and early sexuality; of these, 7 million are extremely vulnerable to delinquency and gang activity. An additional 7 million adolescents can be classified as at "moderate risk."[12]

Adolescent Poverty   According to the U.S. Census Bureau, the poverty rate has been declining. As of 2000, about 11 percent of all Americans were considered poor, which was almost an all-time low.[13] Nonetheless, more than 30 million Americans still live in poverty, which the Census Bureau defines as an income below $13,700 a year for a family of three. Included within this group of poor Americans are almost 12 million indigent children. As Figure 1.1 indicates, about 16 percent of children are living in impoverished families today. The likelihood of a child under 18 years old living in poverty is greater than that of any other age group.

Figure 1.1
Poverty Rates by Age: 1959 to 2000
While poverty rate trends have moved downward, the Tufts University Center on Hunger, Poverty, and Nutrition Policy estimates that by the year 2012, 20.7 million, or 28 percent, of all minor children will be living in poverty.[14]
Source: U.S. Census Bureau (September 25, 2001).

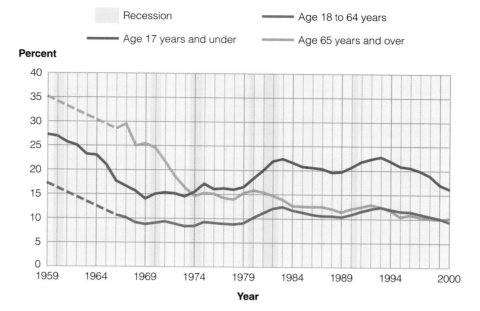

Family Problems   Divorce strikes about half of all new marriages; many families sacrifice time with each other to afford better housing and lifestyles. Research shows that children in the United States are being polarized into two distinct economic groups: those born into affluent, two-earner, married-couple households and those residing in impoverished, single-parent households.[15]

Urban Decay   The destructive environment of deteriorated urban areas prevents too many adolescents from having productive, fulfilling, or happy lives. Many face an early death from random bullets and drive-by shootings. Some are homeless, living desperate lives on the street, where they are at risk for drug addiction and sexually transmitted diseases, including AIDS. One study of 425 homeless street kids in New York City found that 37 percent earn money through prostitution and almost one-third had contracted an STD.[16]

Inadequate Educational Opportunity   The U.S. educational system, once the envy of the world, now seems to be failing many young people. We are lagging behind other developed nations in such critical areas as science and mathematics achievement. The rate of *retention*—being forced to repeat a grade—is far higher than it should be in most communities. Retention rates are associated with another major educational problem—dropping out. Between 1979 and 1992, the dropout rate fell from 14.6 percent to 11 percent but has remained at that level ever since; in 2001, about 11 percent of all eligible youths did not finish high school.[17] Despite this improvement, some large cities have extremely low graduation rates. In Cleveland, just 28 percent of the class of 1998 earned a diploma. Cleveland is one of five large school districts in America that has an overall graduation rate below 50 percent, joined by Memphis (42%), Milwaukee (43%), Columbus, Ohio (45%), and Chicago (47%).[18]

Although all young people face stress in the education system, the risks are greatest for the poor, members of racial and ethnic minorities, and recent immigrants. These children usually attend the most underfunded schools, receive inadequate educational opportunities, and have the fewest opportunities to achieve conventional success.

Considering that youth are at risk during the most tumultuous time of their lives, it comes as no surprise that they are willing to engage in risky, destructive behavior, as the Focus on Delinquency box entitled "Risky Business" suggests.

The Eisenhower National Clearinghouse's mission is to identify effective curriculum resources, create high-quality professional development materials, and disseminate useful information and products to improve K–12 mathematics and science teaching and learning. For more information, go to *http://www.enc.org/* For an up-to-date list of Web links, go to *http://info.wadsworth.com/siegel*

The mission of the Children's Defense Fund is to "Leave No Child Behind"; to ensure every child a Healthy Start, a Head Start, a Fair Start, a Safe Start, and a Moral Start in life; and a successful passage to adulthood with the help of caring families and communities. The CDF tries to provide a strong, effective voice for kids who cannot vote, lobby, or speak for themselves. Visit their Web site at *http://www.childrensdefense.org/* For an up-to-date list of Web links, go to *http://info.wadsworth.com/siegel*

Risky Business

The Center for Disease Control reports that in the United States, 73 percent of all deaths among youths and young adults 10–24 years of age result from only four causes: motor vehicle crashes, other unintentional injuries, homicide, and suicide. It appears that many high school students engage in risky behaviors that increase their likelihood of death from violence, accident, or self-destruction. A survey conducted by the center found that about 20 percent of youths rarely or never wore a seat belt; 37 percent had ridden with a driver who had been drinking alcohol; 18 percent had carried a weapon; 50.8 percent had drunk alcohol; 26 percent had used marijuana. About 8 percent had attempted suicide during the 12 months preceding the survey. The CDC survey found that about half of all high school students had sexual intercourse; 43 percent of sexually active students had not used a condom; about 36 percent of high school students had smoked cigarettes during the prior month.

Why do youths take such chances? Criminologist Nanette Davis suggests that merely trying to survive the adolescent experience in America makes kids prone to take risks. Risk behaviors are emotionally edgy, dangerous, exciting, hazardous, challenging, and volatile. Youths are forced into risky behavior as they try to negotiate the hurdles of adolescent life—learning to drive, date, drink, work, relate, and live. Davis finds that social developments in the United States have increased the risks of growing up for all children. It is a society that is prone to suffer severe economic upswings and downturns. Planning a future is problematic when job elimination and corporate downsizing are accepted business practices and divorce and family restructuring are epidemic. It is a culture that overemphasizes consumerism with often troubling results. In high schools, peer respect is "bought" through the accumulation of material goods; the right clothes, electronic gear, and car are required for popularity. Underprivileged youths are driven to illegal behavior in an effort to gain the material goods they can't afford. Drug deals and theft may be a shortcut to acquiring coveted name-brand clothes and athletic shoes. Kids learn to be part of the "cult of individualism," which makes them self-involved and self-centered. Children are taught to put their own interests above those of others. People occupy their own private worlds without caring for the rights of others. In an effort to fit into this fast-paced environment, some kids become risk takers who engage in chancy behaviors.

Some adolescents may not choose to take risks but rather are forced into them in order to survive in a hostile environment. For example, while joining gangs may put kids at risk for drug use and violence, in some neighborhoods choosing not to join may put them in even greater peril. The benefits of protection and respect outweigh the dangers of arrest and punishment.

Adulthood may not bring a respite from risk taking. The uncertainties of modern society may prolong risk-taking behavior. Jobs have become unpredictable, and many undereducated and undertrained youths find themselves competing with hundreds of other applicants for the same low-paying job; they are a "surplus product." Under these circumstances, continued risk taking may be a plausible alternative for fitting into our consumer-oriented society.

Critical Thinking

1. Do kids engage in risky behavior because they feel there is nothing to lose as an adolescent? Would a campaign to inform them of the danger of taking risks, such as early sex, help reduce risky behaviors?
2. What are the benefits of risk taking? Millions of people take risks every day and get involved in risky activities ranging from mountain climbing to diving in shark-filled waters. Why do people take such risks?

InfoTrac College Edition Research

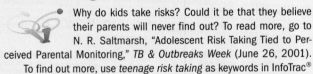

Why do kids take risks? Could it be that they believe their parents will never find out? To read more, go to N. R. Saltmarsh, "Adolescent Risk Taking Tied to Perceived Parental Monitoring," *TB & Outbreaks Week* (June 26, 2001). To find out more, use *teenage risk taking* as keywords in InfoTrac® College Edition.

Sources: Laura Kann et al., "Youth Risk Behavior Surveillance—United States, 1997 (Atlanta: Center for Disease Control, August 14, 1998); Nanette Davis, *Youth Crisis: Growing Up in the High-Risk Society* (New York: Praeger, Greenwood Publishing, 1998).

Are There Reasons for Hope?

Despite the many hazards faced by teens, there are some bright spots on the horizon. Teenage birthrates nationwide have declined substantially (22%) during the past decade.[19] The birthrate for young teenagers aged 15–17 (29%) and African American girls (31%) has shown the greatest decline. The data indicate that more young girls are using birth control and practicing safe sex. There are other signs of improvement in adolescent health care. Fewer children with health risks are being born today than in 1990. This probably means that fewer women are drinking alcohol during pregnancy, smoking cigarettes, or receiving late or no prenatal care. Since 1990 the number of children immunized against disease has also increased.[20] Due in large part to improvements in medical technology, the infant mortality rate—or the number of children who die before their first birthday—has declined about 30 percent during the past decade (from 10.6 to 7.6 per 1,000 births).[21]

Exhibit 1.2   Positive Trends in the Well-Being of American Youth

- The poverty rate for children living with family members continued to decline from 18 percent in 1998 to 16 percent in 1999. The poverty rate for children has fluctuated since the early 1980s: It reached a high of 22 percent in 1993 and has since decreased to the lowest rate since 1979.
- The percentage of children who had health insurance coverage increased from 85 percent in 1998 to 86 percent in 1999.
- In 1999, 78 percent of children 19 to 35 months of age had completed the combined series of vaccinations (DTP, polio, measles, and *Haemophilus influenzae* type b), up from 69 percent in 1994.
- In 1999, the adolescent birthrate was at a record low, at 29 births per 1,000 young women ages 15 to 17.
- Cigarette use among adolescents shows indications of decline.

- The percentage of high school graduates who had taken advanced courses has increased dramatically since 1982.
- Long-term trend mathematics and reading assessment scores show improvements in mathematics since 1982.
- The percentage of high school graduates who went on to earn a bachelor's degree or higher increased to an all-time high of 33 percent in 2000, up from 26 percent in 1980. Among black, non-Hispanic high school graduates, this percentage increased from 17 percent in 1999 to 21 percent in 2000.

Source: Federal Interagency Forum on Child and Family Statistics, *America's Children: Key National Indicators of Well-Being, 2001* (Washington, DC, 2001).

Although education is still a problem area, more parents are reading to their young children, and math achievement is rising in grades 4–12. More students are receiving degrees in math and science.[22]

There are also indications that youngsters may be rejecting hard drugs. While teen smoking and drinking rates remain unacceptably high, fewer kids are getting involved in heroin and crack cocaine use.[23]

Some of the most important trends in the well-being of youth are listed in Exhibit 1.2. While these signs are encouraging, many problem areas remain, and the continued improvement of adolescent life must remain a national goal.

The Study of Juvenile Delinquency

juvenile delinquency Participation in illegal behavior by a minor who falls under a statutory age limit.

chronic delinquent offenders (also known as chronic juvenile offenders, chronic delinquents, or chronic recidivists) Youths who have been arrested four or more times during their minority and perpetuate a striking majority of serious criminal acts; this small group, known as the "chronic 6 percent," is believed to engage in a significant portion of all delinquent behavior; these youths do not age out of crime but continue their criminal behavior into adulthood.

The problems of youth in modern society are both a major national concern and an important subject for academic study. This text focuses on one area of particular concern: **juvenile delinquency,** or criminal behavior committed by minors. The study of juvenile delinquency is important both because of the damage suffered by its victims and the problems faced by its perpetrators.

More than 2 million youths are now arrested each year for crimes ranging in seriousness from loitering to murder.[24] Though most juvenile law violations are minor, some young offenders are extremely dangerous and violent. More than 800,000 youths belong to street gangs and groups that can put fear into an entire city. Youths involved in multiple serious criminal acts—referred to as lifestyle, repeat, or **chronic delinquent offenders**—are now recognized as a serious social problem. State juvenile authorities must deal with these offenders, along with responding to a range of other social problems, including child abuse and neglect, school crime and vandalism, family crises, and drug abuse.

Given the diversity and gravity of these problems, there is an urgent need for strategies to combat such a complex social phenomenon as juvenile delinquency. But formulating effective strategies demands a solid understanding of delinquency's causes and prevention. Is delinquency a function of psychological abnormality? A collective reaction by youths against destructive social conditions? The product of a disturbed home life and disrupted socialization? Does serious delinquent behavior occur only in large urban areas among lower-class youths? Or is it spread throughout the entire social structure? What impact do family life, substance abuse, school

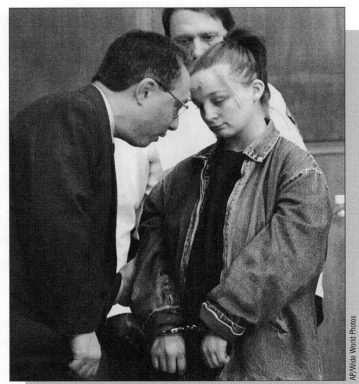

IN 1999 JULIE ANN BARNES, a homeless teen, was living in a cold-storage warehouse in Worcester, Massachusetts, with her 37-year-old boyfriend, when they started a fire by knocking over a candle during an argument. They left the building without reporting the fire and went to a nearby mall to hang out. Six firefighters died while fighting the blaze. Ms. Barnes was initially vilified for having caused one of the most devastating fires in state history, but public sentiment changed when it became known that she was developmentally disabled, neglected by her parents, left to wander the streets, and most likely the victim of sexual abuse. Rather than face manslaughter charges, she was placed in the custody of a foster family. Should adolescents with such troubled pasts be held accountable for their actions?

aging-out process (also known as desistance or spontaneous remission) The tendency for youths to reduce the frequency of their offending behavior as they age; aging out is thought to occur among all groups of offenders.

persistence The process by which juvenile offenders continue to persist in their delinquent careers rather than aging out of crime.

desistance Termination of delinquent careers.

juvenile justice system The segment of the justice system including law enforcement officers, the courts, and correctional agencies, designed to treat youthful offenders.

experiences, and peer relations have on youth and their law-violating behaviors? We know that most youthful law violators do not go on to become adult criminals (what is known as the **aging-out process**). Yet we do not know why some youths become chronic delinquents whose careers begin early and persist into their adulthood. Why does the onset of delinquency begin so early in some children? Why does the severity of their offenses escalate? What factors predict the **persistence,** or continuation, of delinquency, and conversely, what are the factors associated with its **desistance,** or termination? Unless the factors that control the onset and termination of a delinquent career are studied in an orderly and scientific manner, developing effective prevention and control efforts will be difficult.

The study of delinquency also involves the analysis of the law enforcement, court, and correctional agencies designed to treat youthful offenders who fall into the arms of the law—known collectively as the **juvenile justice system.** How should police deal with minors who violate the law? What are the legal rights of children? For example, should minors who commit murder receive the death penalty? What kind of correctional programs are most effective with delinquent youths? How useful are educational, community, counseling, and vocational development programs? Is it true, as some critics claim, that most efforts to rehabilitate young offenders are doomed to failure?[25] Should we adopt a punishment or a treatment orientation to combat delinquency, or something in between?

In sum, the scientific study of delinquency requires understanding the nature, extent, and cause of youthful law violations and the methods devised for their control. We also need to study important environmental and social issues associated with delinquent behavior, including substance abuse, child abuse and neglect, education, and peer relations. This text investigates these aspects of juvenile delinquency along with the efforts being made to treat problem youths and prevent the spread of delinquent behavior. Our study begins with a look back to the development of the concept of childhood and how children were first identified as a unique group with its own special needs and behaviors.

The Development of Childhood

The treatment of children as a distinct social group with special needs and behavior is, in historical terms, a relatively new concept. It is only for the past 350 years or so that any mechanism existed to care for even the most needy children, including those left orphaned and destitute. How did this concept of concern for children develop?

In Europe, during the Middle Ages (1500 A.D. to 700 A.D.), the concept of childhood as we know it today did not exist. In the **paternalistic family** of the time, the father was the final authority on all family matters and exercised complete control over the social, economic, and physical well-being of his wife and children.[26] Children who did not obey were subject to severe physical punishment, even death.

For children of medieval times, the passage into adulthood was abrupt. As soon as they were physically capable, children of all classes were expected to engage in adult roles. Among the working classes, males engaged in peasant farming and/or learning a skilled trade, such as masonry or metalworking; females aided in food preparation or household maintenance.[27] Some peasant youths went into domestic or agricultural service on the estate of a powerful landowner or in trades or crafts such as a blacksmith or farrier (horseshoe maker).[28]

Children of the affluent landholding classes also assumed adult roles at an early age. Girls born into aristocratic families were educated at home and married in their early teens. A few were taught to read, write, and do sufficient mathematics to handle household accounts in addition to typical female duties such as supervising servants and ensuring the food supply of the manor.

At age 7 or 8, boys born to landholding families were either sent to a monastery or cathedral school to be trained for lives in the church or selected to be a member of the warrior class and sent to serve a term as a squire—an apprentice and assistant to an experienced knight. At age 21, young men of the knightly classes completed their term as squire, received their own knighthood, and returned home to live with their parents. Most remained single because it was widely believed there should only be one married couple residing in a manor and/or castle. To pass the time and maintain their fighting edge, many entered the tournament circuit, engaging in melees and jousts to win fame and fortune. Upon the death of their fathers, young nobles assumed their inherited titles, married, and began their own families.

paternalistic family A family style wherein the father is the final authority on all family matters and exercises complete control over his wife and children.

For more information on the early history of childhood and the development of education, go to the Web site of The History of Education and Childhood at Nijmegen University, the Netherlands: *http://www.socsci. kun.nl/ped/whp/histeduc/* For an up-to-date list of Web links, go to *http://info.wadsworth.com/siegel*

Custom and Practice in the Middle Ages

primogeniture During the Middle Ages, the right of the first-born sons to inherit lands and titles, leaving their brothers the option of a military or religious career.

Custom and practice greatly amplified the hardships suffered by many children during the Middle Ages. Among the landholding classes, **primogeniture** required that the oldest surviving male child inherit family lands and titles. He could then distribute them as he saw fit to younger siblings. There was no absolute requirement, however, that portions of the estate be distributed equally; so many youths who received no lands were forced to enter religious orders, become soldiers, or seek wealthy patrons. Primogeniture often caused intense family rivalry that led to blood feuds and tragedy.

AS SOON AS they were physically capable, children of the Middle Ages were expected to engage in adult roles. Among the working classes, males engaged in peasant farming or learned a skilled trade, such as masonry or metalworking; females aided in food preparation or household maintenance. Some peasant youth went into domestic or agricultural service on the estate of a powerful landowner or into trades or crafts, such as blacksmith or farrier (horseshoer).

A CLOSER VIEW
To learn more about primogeniture, use it as a key term on InfoTrac College Edition.

Dower The *dower system* mandated that a woman's family bestow money, land, or other wealth (called a *dowery*) on a potential husband or his family in exchange for his marriage to her. In return, the young woman received a promise of financial assistance, called a *jointure,* from the groom's family. Jointure provided a lifetime income if a wife outlived her mate. The dower system had a significant impact on the role of women in medieval society and consequently on the role of children. Within this system, a father or male guardian had the final say in his daughter's choice of marital partner since he could threaten to withhold her dowery. Some women were denied access to marriage simply because of their position in a family. A father with many daughters and few sons might find himself financially unable to obtain suitable marriages. Consequently, the youngest girls in many families were forced either to enter convents or stay at home, with few prospects for marriage and family.

The dower system had far-reaching effects on the position of women in society, forcing them into the role of second-class citizens dependent upon their fathers, brothers, and guardians. It established a pattern in which females who did not conform to what males considered to be acceptable standards of feminine behavior could receive harsh sanctions; it established a sexual double standard that in part still exists today.

Childrearing The harshness of medieval life influenced childrearing practices during the fifteenth and sixteenth centuries. For instance, newborns were almost immediately handed over to *wet nurses,* who fed and cared for them during the first two years of their life. These women often lived away from the family so that parents had little contact with their children. Even the wealthiest families employed wet nurses, because it was considered demeaning for a noblewoman to nurse. Wrapping a newborn entirely in bandages, or **swaddling,** was a common practice. The bandages prevented any movement and enabled the wet nurse to manage the child easily. This practice was thought to protect the child, but it most likely contributed to high infant mortality rates because the child could not be kept clean.

swaddling The practice during the Middle Ages of completely wrapping newborns in long bandagelike clothes in order to restrict their movements and make them easier to manage.

Discipline was severe during this period. Young children of all classes, both peasant and wealthy, were subjected to stringent rules and regulations. They were beaten severely for any sign of disobedience or ill temper. Many children of this time would be considered abused by today's standards. The relationship between parent and child was remote. Children were expected to enter the world of adults and to undertake responsibilities early in their lives, sharing in the work of siblings and parents. Children thought to be suffering from disease or retardation were often abandoned to churches, orphanages, or foundling homes.[29]

The roots of the impersonal relationship between parent and child can be traced to high mortality rates, which made sentimental and affectionate relationships risky. Parents were reluctant to invest emotional effort in relationships that could so easily be terminated by violence, accidents, or disease. Many believed that children must be toughened to ensure their survival in a hostile world. Close family relationships were viewed as detrimental to this process. Also, since the oldest male child was viewed as the essential player in a family's well-being, younger male and female siblings were considered economic and social liabilities.

The Development of Concern for Children

Throughout the seventeenth and eighteenth centuries, a number of developments in England heralded the march toward the recognition of children's rights. Some of these events eventually affected the juvenile legal system as it emerged in America. They include (1) changes in family style and childcare, (2) the English Poor Laws, (3) the apprenticeship movement, and (4) the role of the chancery court.[30]

Changes in Family Structure Family structure and the role of children began to change after the Middle Ages. Extended families, which were created over centuries, gave way to the nuclear family structure with which we are familiar today. It became more common for marriage to be based on love and mutual attraction between men and women rather than on parental consent and paternal dominance. The changing concept of marriage—from an economic arrangement to an emotional commitment—also began to influence the way children were treated within the family structure. Though parents still rigidly disciplined their children, they formed closer parental ties and greater concerns for their offsprings' well-being.

To provide more controls over children, grammar and boarding schools were established and began to flourish in many large cities during this time.[31] Children studied grammar, Latin, law, and logic, often beginning at a young age. Teachers in these institutions regularly ruled by fear, and flogging was their main method of discipline. Students were beaten for academic mistakes as well as moral lapses. Such brutal treatment fell on both the rich and the poor throughout all levels of educational life, including boarding schools and universities. This treatment abated in Europe with the rise of the Enlightenment, but it remained in full force in Great Britain until late in the nineteenth century. Although this brutal approach to children may be difficult to understand now, the child in that society was a second-class citizen.

Toward the close of the eighteenth century, the work of such philosophers as Voltaire, Rousseau, and Locke launched a new age for childhood and the family.[32] Their vision produced a period known as the Enlightenment, which stressed a humanistic view of life, freedom, family, reason, and law. The ideal person was sympathetic to others and receptive to new ideas. These new beliefs influenced both the structure and lifestyle of the family. The father's authority was tempered, discipline in the home became more relaxed, and the expression of love and affection became more commonplace among family members. Upper- and middle-class families began to devote attention to childrearing, and the status of children was advanced.

As a result of these changes, in the nineteenth century children began to emerge as a readily distinguishable group with independent needs and interests. Parents often took greater interest in their upbringing. In addition, serious questions arose over the treatment of children in school. Public outcries led to a decrease in excessive physical discipline. Restrictions were placed on the use of the whip, and in some schools, the imposition of academic assignments or the loss of privileges replaced corporal punishment. Despite such reforms, many children still led harsh lives. Girls were still undereducated, punishment was still primarily physical, and schools continued to mistreat children.

Poor Laws   Government action to care for needy children can be traced to the **Poor Laws** of Great Britain. As early as 1535, the English passed statutes allowing for the appointment of overseers to place destitute or neglected children as servants in the homes of the affluent.[33] The Poor Laws forced children to serve during their minority in the care of families who trained them in agricultural, trade, or domestic services. The Elizabethan Poor Laws of 1601 were a model for dealing with poor children for more than 200 years. These laws created a system of church wardens and overseers who, with the consent of justices of the peace, identified vagrant, delinquent, and neglected children and took measures to put them to work. Often this meant placing them in poorhouses or workhouses, or apprenticing them to masters.

The Apprenticeship Movement   Under the apprenticeship concept, children were placed in the care of adults who trained them to discharge various duties and obtain different skills. Voluntary apprentices were bound out by parents or guardians who wished to secure training for their children. Involuntary apprentices were compelled by the authorities to serve until they were 21 or older. The master-apprentice relationship was similar to the parent-child relationship in that the master had complete responsibility for and authority over the apprentice. If an apprentice was unruly, a complaint could be made and the apprentice could be punished. Incarcerated apprentices were often placed in rooms or workshops apart from other prisoners and were generally treated differently from those charged with a criminal offense. Even at this early stage, the conviction was growing that the criminal law and its enforcement should be applied differently to children.

Chancery Court   Throughout the Middle Ages, Great Britain relied on a system of **chancery courts.** They were established primarily to protect property rights, although their authority extended to the welfare of children generally. The major issues in medieval cases that came before the chancery courts concerned guardianship of children who were orphaned, their property and inheritance rights, and the appointment of guardians to protect them until they reached the age of majority and could care for themselves.

Chancery courts were founded on the proposition that children and other incompetents were under the protective control of the king; thus, the Latin phrase

Poor Laws   English statutes that allowed the courts to appoint overseers over destitute and neglected children, allowing placement of these children as servants in the homes of the affluent.

A CLOSER VIEW
To read more about the history of the Poor Laws and their effect on society, go to InfoTrac College Edition and read Graham Goodlad, "From Old to New Poor Law," *History Review* (December 2000): 15.

chancery courts   Court proceedings created in fifteenth-century England to oversee the lives of high-born minors who were orphaned or otherwise could not care for themselves.

parens patriae Power of the
state to act in behalf of the child
and provide care and protection
equivalent to that of a parent.

parens patriae was used, referring to the role of the king as the father of his country. The concept was first used by English kings to establish their right to intervene in the lives of the children of their vassals—children whose position and property were of direct concern to the monarch.[34] The concept of *parens patriae* became the theoretical basis for the protective jurisdiction of the chancery courts acting as part of the crown's power. As time passed, the monarchy used *parens patriae* more and more to justify its intervention in the lives of families and children by its interest in their general welfare.[35]

The chancery courts dealt with the property and custody problems of the wealthier classes. They did not have jurisdiction over children charged with criminal conduct. Juveniles who violated the law were handled within the framework of the regular criminal court system. Nonetheless, the concept of *parens patriae,* which was established within the English chancery court system, grew to refer primarily to the responsibility of the courts and the state to act in the best interests of the child.

Childhood in America

While England was using its chancery courts and Poor Laws to care for children in need, the American colonies were developing similar concepts. The colonies were a haven for poor and unfortunate people looking for religious and economic opportunities denied them in England and Europe. Along with early settlers, many children came not as citizens but as indentured servants, apprentices, or agricultural workers. They were recruited from the various English workhouses, orphanages, prisons, and asylums that housed vagrant and delinquent youths during the sixteenth and seventeenth centuries.[36]

At the same time, the colonies themselves produced illegitimate, neglected, abandoned, and delinquent children. The colonies' initial response to caring for such unfortunate children was to adopt court and Poor Laws systems similar to those in England. Involuntary apprenticeship, indenture, and binding out of children became integral parts of colonization in America. For example, Poor Law legislation requiring poor and dependent children to serve apprenticeships was passed in Virginia in 1646 and in Massachusetts and Connecticut in 1673.[37]

The master in colonial America acted as a surrogate parent, and in certain instances, apprentices would actually become part of the nuclear family structure. If they disobeyed their masters, apprentices were punished by local tribunals. If masters abused apprentices, courts would make them pay damages, return the children to the parents, or find new guardians. Maryland and Virginia developed an orphan's court that supervised the treatment of youth placed with guardians and ensured that they were not mistreated or taken advantage of by their masters. These courts did not supervise children living with their natural parents, leaving intact the parents' right to care for their children.[38]

By the beginning of the nineteenth century, as the agrarian economy began to be replaced by industry, the apprenticeship system gave way to the factory system. Yet the problems of how to deal effectively with growing numbers of dependent youths increased. Early American settlers believed that hard work, strict discipline, and rigorous education were the only reliable means to salvation. A child's life was marked by work alongside parents, some schooling, prayer, more work, and further study. Work in the factories, however, often taxed young laborers by placing demands on them that they were too young to endure. To alleviate a rapidly developing problem, the Factory Act of the early nineteenth century limited the hours children were permitted to work and the age at which they could begin to work. It also prescribed a minimum amount of schooling to be provided by factory owners.[39] This and related statutes were often violated, and conditions of work and school remained troublesome issues well into the twentieth century. Nevertheless, the statutes were a step in the direction of reform.

Controlling Children   In America, as in England, moral discipline was rigidly enforced. "Stubborn child" laws were passed that required children to obey their parents.[40] It was not uncommon in the colonies for children who were disobedient or disrespectful to their families to be whipped or otherwise physically chastised. Children were often required to attend public whippings and executions because these events were thought to be important forms of moral instruction. Parents often referred their children to published works and writings on behavior and discipline and expected them to follow their precepts carefully. The early colonists, however, viewed family violence as a sin, and child protection laws were passed as early as 1639 (in New Haven, Connecticut). These laws were generally symbolic and rarely enforced. They expressed the community's commitment to God to oppose sin; offenders usually received lenient sentences.[41]

While most colonies adopted a protectionist stance, few cases of child abuse were actually brought before the courts. There are several explanations for this neglect. The absence of child abuse cases may reflect the nature of life in what were essentially extremely religious households. Children were productive laborers and respected by their parents. In addition, large families provided many siblings and kinfolk who could care for children and relieve stress-producing burdens on parents.[42]

Another view is that though many children were harshly punished in Early American families, the acceptable limits of discipline were so high that few parents were charged with assault. Any punishment that fell short of maiming or permanently harming a child was considered within the sphere of parental rights.[43]

The Concept of Delinquency

Considering the rough treatment handed out to children who misbehaved at home or at school, it should come as no surprise that children who actually broke the law and committed serious criminal acts were dealt with harshly. Before the twentieth century, little distinction was made between adult and juvenile offenders. Although judges considered the age of an offender when deciding punishments, both adults and children were often eligible for the same forms of punishment—prison, corporal punishment, and even the death penalty. In fact, children were treated with extreme cruelty at home, at school, and by the law.[44]

child savers   Nineteenth-century reformers who developed programs for troubled youth and influenced legislation creating the juvenile justice system; today some critics view them as being more concerned with control of the poor than with their welfare.

Over the years, this treatment changed, as society became sensitive to the special needs of children. Beginning in the mid-nineteenth century, as immigrant youth poured into America, there was official recognition that children formed a separate group with its own separate needs. Around the nation, in cities such as New York, Boston, and Chicago, groups known as **child savers** were being formed to assist children in need. They created community programs to service needy children, and lobbied for a separate legal status for children, which ultimately led to the development of a formal juvenile justice system. The child saving movement will be discussed more fully in Chapter 12.

Delinquency and *Parens Patriae*

The current treatment of juvenile delinquents is a byproduct of this developing national consciousness. The designation *delinquent* became popular at the onset of the twentieth century when the first separate juvenile courts were instituted. The child savers believed that treating minors and adults equivalently violated the humanitarian ideals of American society. Consequently, the newly emerging juvenile justice system operated under the *parens patriae* philosophy. Minors who engaged in extralegal behavior were viewed as victims of improper care, custody, and treatment at home. Illegal behavior was a sign that the state should step in and take control of the youths

best interests of the child
A philosophical viewpoint that encourages the state to take control of wayward children and provide care, custody, and treatment to remedy delinquent behavior.

before they committed more serious crimes. The state, through its juvenile authorities, should act in the **best interests of the child.** This means that children should not be punished for their misdeeds but instead should be given the care and custody necessary to remedy and control wayward behavior. It makes no sense to find children guilty of specific crimes, such as burglary or petty larceny, because that stigmatizes them and labels them as thieves or burglars. Instead, the catchall term *juvenile delinquency* should be used since it indicates that the child needs the care, custody, and treatment of the state.

The Legal Status of Delinquency

Though the child savers fought hard for a separate legal status of "juvenile delinquent" early in the twentieth century, the concept that children could be treated differently before the law can actually be traced back much farther to its roots in the British legal tradition. Early English jurisprudence held that children under the age of 7 were legally incapable of committing crimes. Children between the ages of 7 and 14 were responsible for their actions, but their age might be used to excuse or lighten their punishment. Our legal system still recognizes that many young people are incapable of making mature judgments and that responsibility for their acts should be limited. Children can intentionally steal cars and know full well that the act is illegal, but they may be incapable of fully understanding the consequences of their behavior and the harm it may cause. Therefore, the law does not punish a youth as it would an adult, and it sees youthful misconduct as evidence of unreasoned or impaired judgment.

Today, the legal status of "juvenile delinquent" refers to a minor child who has been found to have violated the penal code. Most states define "minor child" as an individual who falls under a statutory age limit, most commonly 17 or 18 years of age. Because of their minority status, juveniles are usually kept separate from adults and receive different consideration and treatment under the law. For example, most large police departments employ officers whose sole responsibility is youth crime and delinquency. Every state has some form of separate juvenile court with its own judges, probation department, and other facilities. Terminology is also different: Adults are tried in court; children are adjudicated. Adults can be punished; children are treated. If treatment is mandated, children can be sent to secure detention facilities; they cannot normally be committed to adult prisons.

Children also have their own unique legal status. Minors apprehended for a criminal act are usually charged with being a "juvenile delinquent" regardless of the crime they commit. These charges are usually confidential, trial records are kept secret, and the name, behavior, and background of delinquent offenders are sealed. Eliminating specific crime categories and maintaining secrecy are efforts to shield children from the stigma of a criminal conviction and to prevent youthful misdeeds from becoming a lifelong burden.

Legal Responsibility of Youth

In our society the actions of adults are controlled by two types of law: criminal and civil. Criminal laws prohibit activities that are injurious to the well-being of society and threaten the social order, for example, drug use, theft, and rape; they are legal actions brought by state authorities against private citizens. Civil laws, on the other hand, control interpersonal or private activities and are usually initiated by individual citizens. The ownership and transfer of property, contractual relationships, and personal conflicts (torts) are the subject of the civil law. Also covered under the civil law are provisions for the care and custody of those people who cannot care for themselves—the mentally ill, incompetent, or infirm.

Today, the juvenile delinquency concept occupies a legal status falling somewhere between the criminal and civil law. Under *parens patriae,* delinquent acts are not considered criminal violations, nor are delinquents considered "criminals." Children cannot be found "guilty" of a crime and punished like adult criminals; the legal action against them is considered more similar (though not identical) to a civil action that determines their "need for treatment." This legal theory recognizes that children who violate the law are in need of the same care and treatment as are law-abiding citizens who cannot care for themselves and require state intervention into their lives.

Delinquent behavior is sanctioned less heavily than criminality because the law considers juveniles as being less responsible for their behavior than adults. As a class, adolescents are believed to (1) have a stronger preference for risk and novelty; (2) assess the potentially negative consequences of risky conduct less unfavorably than adults; (3) have a tendency to be impulsive and more concerned with short-term than long-term consequences; (4) have a different appreciation of time and self-control; and (5) be more susceptible to peer pressure.[45] Although many adolescents may be more responsible and calculating than adults, under normal circumstances the law is willing to recognize age as a barrier to having full responsibility over one's actions.

Although youths share a lesser degree of legal responsibility than adults, they are in fact also subject to arrest, trial, and incarceration. Their legal predicament has prompted the courts to grant them many of the same legal protections granted to adults accused of criminal offenses. These legal protections include the right to consult an attorney, to be free from self-incrimination, and to be protected from illegal searches and seizures. In addition, state legislatures are toughening legal codes and making them more punitive in an effort to "get tough" on dangerous youth.

While appreciation of the criminal nature of the delinquency concept has helped increase the legal rights of minors, it has also allowed state authorities to declare that some offenders are "beyond control" and cannot be treated as children. This recognition has prompted the policy of **waiver,** or transferring legal jurisdiction over the most serious and experienced juvenile offenders to the adult court for criminal prosecution. So while the *parens patriae* concept is still applied to children whose law violations are considered not to be serious, the more serious juvenile offenders can be declared "legal adults" and placed outside the jurisdiction of the juvenile court.

waiver (also known as bindover or removal) Transferring legal jurisdiction over the most serious and experienced juvenile offenders to the adult court for criminal prosecution.

Status Offenders

status offenses Conduct that is illegal only because the child is under age.

In contrast to serious offenses that lead to prosecution of minors as adults, a child can also be sent to the juvenile court for behavior as frivolous as cutting class!

A child can also become subject to state authority for committing **status offenses**— actions that would not be considered if perpetrated by an adult; such conduct is illegal only because the child is under age. Figure 1.2 illustrates some typical status offenses. It is extremely difficult to evaluate the annual number of status offenses since most cases escape police detection, and those that do not are more often than not handled informally. Yet, according to data compiled by the Federal Bureau of Investigation, more than 300,000 juveniles are arrested each year for such status type offenses as running away from home, breaking curfew, and violating liquor laws.[46]

State control over a child's noncriminal behavior supports the *parens patriae* philosophy since it is assumed to be in the best interests of the child. Usually, status offenders are directed to the juvenile court when it is determined that their parents are unable or unwilling to care for or control them and that the offender's behavior is self-destructive or harmful to society.

A historical basis exists for status offense statutes. It was common practice early in the nation's history to place disobedient or runaway youths in orphan asylums, residential homes, or houses of refuge.[47] When the first juvenile courts were established in Illinois, the Chicago Bar Association described part of their purpose as follows:

Figure 1.2
Status Offenses

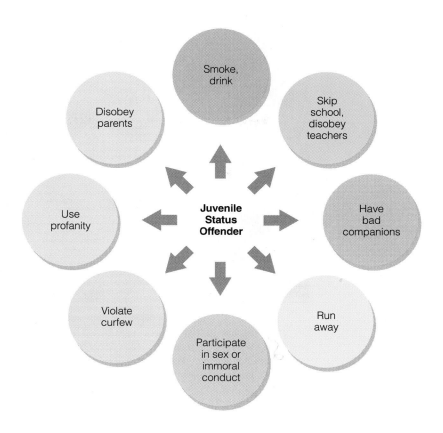

> *The whole trend and spirit of the [1889 Juvenile Court Act] is that the State, acting through the Juvenile Court, exercises that tender solicitude and care over its neglected, dependent wards that a wise and loving parent would exercise with reference to his own children under similar circumstances.*[48]

wayward minors Early legal designation of youths who violate the law because of their minority status; now referred to as status offenders.

Until relatively recently, however, almost every state treated status offenders and juvenile delinquents alike, referring to them as either **wayward minors** or delinquent children. A trend begun in the 1960s has resulted in the creation of separate status offense categories—children, minors, persons, youths, or juveniles in need of supervision (CHINS, MINS, PINS, YINS, or JINS)—which vary from state to state. The purpose of creating separate status offender categories was to shield noncriminal youths from the stigma attached to the label "juvenile delinquent" and to signify that they were troubled youths who had special needs and problems (as Exhibit 1.3 on page 21 shows). Wisconsin's code seems more oriented toward protective services than Louisiana's and encompasses more areas of child neglect.

Most states now have separate categories for juvenile conduct that would not be considered criminal if committed by an adult; these sometimes pertain to neglected or dependent children as well.[49] Of these, 11 states use the term "child in need of supervision," while the remainder use such terms as "unruly child," "incorrigible child," and "minor in need of supervision."[50]

Even where there are separate legal categories for delinquents and status offenders, the distinction between them has become blurred. Some noncriminal conduct may be included in the definition of delinquency, and some less serious criminal offenses occasionally may be included within the status offender.[51]

In some states, the juvenile court judge is granted discretion to substitute a status offense for a delinquency charge.[52] Replacing a juvenile delinquency charge with a status offense charge can be used as a bargaining chip to encourage youths to admit to the charges against them in return for a promise of being treated as a (less stigmatized) status offender receiving less punitive treatment.

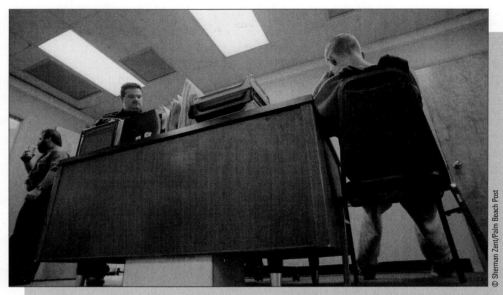

A CHILD can also become subject to state authority for committing status offenses—conduct that is illegal only because the child is under age. Should noncriminal youths who have run away from home or broken curfew be kept in secure detention before trial? Some experts believe that many status offenders have histories of drug and delinquency problems and are little different from kids arrested on criminal charges. Consequently, such confinement may be warranted. Do you agree?

The Status Offender in the Juvenile Justice System

To learn more about the efforts to remove status offenders from secure lockups, go to Gwen A. Holden and Robert A. Kapler, "Deinstitutionalizing Status Offenders: A Record of Progress": *http://www.ncjrs.org/txtfiles/jjjf95.txt* For an up-to-date list of Web links, go to *http://info.wadsworth.com/siegel*

truancy Staying out of school without permission.

Office of Juvenile Justice and Delinquency Prevention (OJJDP) Branch of the U.S. Justice Department charged with shaping national juvenile justice policy through disbursement of federal aid and research funds.

Separate status offense categories may avoid some of the stigma associated with the delinquency label, but they can have relatively little practical effect on the child's treatment. Youths in either category can be picked up by the police and brought to a police station. They can be petitioned to the same juvenile court, where they have a hearing before the same judge and come under the supervision of the probation department, the court clinic, and the treatment staff. At a hearing, status offenders may see little difference between the treatment they receive and the treatment of the delinquent offenders sitting across the room. Although status offenders are usually not detained or incarcerated with delinquents, they can be transferred to secure facilities if they are repeatedly unruly and considered uncontrollable. Some states are more likely to prosecute status offenses formally in the juvenile court, while others handle most cases informally. Within individual states, some courts make a habit of prosecuting status offenders, while others will divert most cases to treatment institutions.[53]

Efforts have been ongoing to reduce the penalties and stigma borne by status offenders and help kids avoid becoming status offenders. The Policy and Practice box, on page 22, entitled "Keeping Truants in School" illustrates how government agencies are focusing on one type of status offense—school **truancy**.

The federal government's **Office of Juvenile Justice and Delinquency Prevention (OJJDP)**, an agency created to identify the needs of youths and fund policy initiatives in the juvenile justice system, made it a top priority to encourage the removal of status offenders from secure lockups, detention centers, and postdisposition treatment facilities that also house delinquent offenders.[54] States in violation of the initiative are ineligible to receive part of the $76 million in direct grants for local juvenile justice annually awarded by the federal government. In the year 2000, grants ranged from $638,000 (Washington, D.C.) to $8.4 million (California).[55] This initiative has been responsible for significantly lowering the number of status offenders kept in secure confinement.

Despite this mandate, juvenile court judges in many states can still detain status offenders in secure lockups if the youths are found in "contempt of court." The act

Exhibit 1.3   Status Offense Laws: Wisconsin and Louisiana

Louisiana

"Child in need of supervision" means a child who needs care or rehabilitation because:

1. Being subject to compulsory school attendance, he is habitually truant from school or willfully violates the rules of the school;

2. He habitually disobeys the reasonable and lawful demands of his parents, and is ungovernable and beyond their control;

3. He absents himself from his home or usual place of abode without the consent of his parent;

4. He purposefully, intentionally and willfully deceives, or misrepresents the true facts to any person holding a retail dealer's permit, or his agent, associate, employee or representative, for the purposes of buying or receiving alcoholic beverages or beer, or visiting or loitering in or about any place where such beverages are the principal commodities sold or handled;

5. His occupation, conduct, environment or associations are injurious to his welfare; or

6. He has committed an offense applicable only to children.

Wisconsin

The court has exclusive original jurisdiction over a child alleged to be in need of protection or services which can be ordered by the court, and:

1. Who is without a parent or guardian;

2. Who has been abandoned;

3. Who has been the victim of sexual or physical abuse including injury which is self-inflicted or inflicted by another by other than accidental means;

4. Whose parent or guardian signs the petition requesting jurisdiction and states that he or she is unable to care for, control or provide necessary special care or special treatment for the child;

5. Who has been placed for care or adoption in violation of law;

6. Who is habitually truant from school, after evidence is provided by the school attendance officer that the activities under s. 118.16(5) have been completed;

7. Who is habitually truant from home and either the child or a parent, guardian or a relative in whose home the child resides signs the petition requesting jurisdiction and attests in court that reconciliation efforts have been attempted and have failed;

8. Who is receiving inadequate care during the period of time a parent is missing, incarcerated, hospitalized or institutionalized;

9. Who is at least age 12, signs the petition requesting jurisdiction and attests in court that he or she is in need of special care and treatment which the parent, guardian or legal custodian is unwilling to provide;

10. Whose parent, guardian or legal custodian neglects, refuses or is unable for reasons other than poverty to provide necessary care, food, clothing, medical or dental care or shelter so as to seriously endanger the physical health of the child;

11. Who is suffering emotional damage for which the parent or guardian is unwilling to provide treatment, which is evidenced by one or more of the following characteristics, exhibited to a severe degree: anxiety, depression, withdrawal or outward aggressive behavior;

12. Who, being under 12 years of age, has committed a delinquent act as defined in s. 48.12;

13. Who has not been immunized as required by s. 140.05(16) and not exempted under s. 140.05(16)(c); or

14. Who has been determined, under s. 48.30(5)(c), to be not responsible for a delinquent act by reason of mental disease or defect.

Source: LA. Code Juv. Proc. Ann. art. 13 § 12 (West 1979, amended 1987) and Wis. Stat. Ann. § 48.13 (West 1979, amended 1987).

A CLOSER VIEW

There is quite a bit of information on the Office of Juvenile Justice and Delinquency Prevention on InfoTrac College Edition. To access it, use the full name as a key term.

that created the OJJDP was amended in 1987 to allow status offenders to be detained and incarcerated for violations of "valid court orders."[56] Children have been detained for such behavior as wearing shorts to court, throwing paper on the floor, and, in one Florida case involving a pregnant teenager, for not keeping a doctor's appointment.[57] Activists have attempted to outlaw such practices because it puts noncriminal youth in jeopardy; the Florida State Supreme Court forbade the practice in the case of *A. A. v. Rolle* (1992).[58] Several studies have found that as a result of deinstitutionalization, children who could no longer be detained are being recycled or "relabeled" as delinquent offenders so they could be housed in secure facilities. Even more troubling is the charge that some minors no longer subject to detention as status offenders were being committed involuntarily and inappropriately to in-patient drug treatment facilities and psychiatric hospitals.[59]

Keeping Truants in School

Every day, hundreds of thousands of youth are absent from school; many are absent without an excuse and deemed truant. Some large cities report that unexcused absences can number in the thousands on certain days

In general, the proportion of truancy cases handled in juvenile court is relatively small. However, the juvenile justice system is increasingly serving as the final stop for truants and as a mechanism for intervening with chronic truants. Recent statistics available on the extent of truancy cases in juvenile court clearly demonstrate how important it is for schools and communities to confront this issue. Truancy accounts for 26 percent of all formally handled status offense cases, representing an 85 percent increase in truancy cases in juvenile court since 1989. What causes truancy? Among the factors identified are the following:

- **Family factors** These include lack of guidance or parental supervision, domestic violence, poverty, drug or alcohol abuse in the home, lack of awareness of attendance laws, and differing attitudes toward education.
- **School factors** These include school climate issues—such as school size and attitudes of teachers, other students, and administrators—and inflexibility in meeting the diverse cultural and learning styles of the students.
- **Economic influences** These include employed students, single-parent homes, high mobility rates, parents who hold multiple jobs, and a lack of affordable transportation and childcare.
- **Student variables** These include drug and alcohol abuse, lack of understanding of attendance laws, lack of social competence, mental health difficulties, and poor physical health.

The Costs of Truancy

Truancy places significant social burdens on society. Students with the highest truancy rates have the lowest academic achievement rates and have high dropout rates as well. Truancy can also be linked to juvenile delinquency in several ways. Kids who are chronically truant seem at high risk to future criminality and drug abuse. There is also evidence that high rates of truancy can be linked to high rates of daytime burglary and vandalism. In some jurisdictions, a significant portion of all burglaries and aggravated assaults occurring between 8:00 A.M. and 1:00 P.M. on weekdays are committed by juveniles.

Combating Truancy

Because of the social cost of truancy, local jurisdictions, with the aid of the federal government, are sponsoring truancy control efforts. A few significant efforts are described below:

1. The State Attorney's Office, Jacksonville, Florida, provides a precourt diversion program for truant youths and their families. The school district refers families to the program when chronic truancy has not been solved by school-based intervention. Following the referral, a hearing is conducted with the parent, youth, school attendance social worker, and volunteer hearing officer. A contract is negotiated that includes plans for reducing truancy and accessing services and community supports. A case manager makes home visits and monitors the family's compliance with the plan. In the fall of 2000, a school-based component was added to address prevention and early intervention at two elementary schools, where an onsite case manager monitors attendance and provides early outreach.

Change in the treatment of status offenders reflects the current attitude toward children who violate the law. On the one hand, there appears to be a national movement to severely sanction youths who commit serious, violent offenses. On the other hand, a great effort has been made to remove nonserious cases, such as those involving status offenders, from the official agencies of justice and place these youths in informal, community-based treatment programs.

Reforming Status Offense Laws

For the past two decades national commissions have called for reform of status offense laws. More than 20 years ago, the National Council on Crime and Delinquency, an influential privately funded think tank, recommended removing status offenders from the juvenile court.[60] In 1976, the federal government's National Advisory Commission on Criminal Justice Standards and Goals, a task force created to develop a national crime policy, opted for the nonjudicial treatment of status offenders: "The only conduct that should warrant family court intervention is conduct that is clearly self-destructive or otherwise harmful to the child." To meet this standard, the commission suggested that the nation's juvenile courts confine themselves to controlling five status offenses: habitual truancy, repeated disregard for parental authority, repeated running away, repeated use of intoxicating beverages, and delinquent acts by youths under the age of 10.[61] The American Bar Association's Na-

2. The University of Hawaii in Honolulu is building on a previous program to prevent truancy in the Wai'anae area. Attendance officers in two elementary schools work to provide early outreach to young students and their families when absences become chronic. Community resources are used to address the issues that may prevent youths from attending school regularly. In addition, the schools work with the Honolulu police department to provide Saturday truancy workshops for youths with chronic truancy problems and their families.

3. The Suffolk County Probation Department's (Yaphank, New York) South County Truancy Reduction Program builds on community policing efforts, targeting elementary and middle school students who have illegal absences. A probation officer monitors attendance in collaboration with school personnel, facilitates access to school- and community-based services needed by the student and family to establish regular school attendance, and observes attendance and other school-based indicators to ensure that the student's attendance and engagement at school are improving. A similar model is in existence at the local high school.

4. The mayor's Anti-Gang Office in Houston, Texas, places an experienced case manager in one high school to identify students with chronic truancy patterns. Through home visits and school-based supports, students and their families are provided with services, support, and resources to address truancy. The program also works with community police officers, who provide a "knock and talk" service for youths and their families when truancy continues to be an issue. The officers assess family functioning and deliver information about the law and truancy outcomes; they also issue the official summons to court for a truancy petition.

5. King County Superior Court, Seattle, Washington, offers families three options after a truancy petition is filed: attending an evening workshop, participating in a community truancy board hearing, or proceeding to court on the charges. The workshop includes education about truancy law and outcomes and facilitates planning between the parent and youth for addressing the cause of truancy. Community truancy boards composed of local community members hear the case, develop a plan for use with the youth and family, and monitor compliance with the stipulated agreement. In the fall of 2000, a school-based component was added to address prevention and early intervention.

Critical Thinking

1. Some kids are persistently truant and do not wish to attend school. Should the educational system provide support for these children or simply let them skip classes and then formally drop out once they are of legal age? Is there any purpose to devoting limited resources to kids who simply do not want to learn?

InfoTrac College Edition Research

For some children, school attendance is so distressing that they have difficulty attending school, a problem that often results in prolonged absence and truancy. To find out why this phenomenon occurs, go to Neville J. King and Gail A. Bernstein, "School Refusal in Children and Adolescents: A Review of the Past 10 Years," *Journal of the American Academy of Child and Adolescent Psychiatry* 40(2):197 (February 2001).

Source: Myriam Baker, Jane Nady Sigmon, and M. Elaine Nugent, *Truancy Reduction: Keeping Students in School* (Washington, DC: Office of Juvenile Justice and Delinquency Prevention, 2001).

tional Juvenile Justice Standards Project, designed to promote significant improvements in the way children are treated by the police and the courts, called for the end of juvenile court jurisdiction over status offenders: "A juvenile's acts of misbehavior, ungovernability or unruliness which do not violate the criminal law should not constitute a ground for asserting juvenile court jurisdiction over the juvenile committing them."[62]

These calls for reform prompted a number of states, including New York, to experiment with replacing juvenile court jurisdiction over most status offenders with community-based treatment programs.[63] A few states, such as Maine, Delaware, Idaho, and Washington, have attempted to eliminate status offense laws and treat these youths as neglected or dependent children, giving child protective services the primary responsibility for their care. However, juvenile court judges strongly resist removal of status jurisdiction since they believe that reducing their authority over children leads to limiting juvenile court jurisdiction to only the most hard-core juvenile offenders and interferes with their ability to help youths before they commit serious antisocial acts.[64] Legislative changes may be cosmetic because when efforts to remedy the child's problems through a social welfare approach fail, the case may be referred to the juvenile court for more formal processing.[65]

Those who favor removing status offenders from juvenile court authority charge that their experience with the legal system further stigmatizes these already troubled youths, exposes them to the influence of "true" delinquents, and enmeshes them in a system that cannot really afford to help them.[66] Reformer Ira Schwartz, for

Increasing Social Control over Juveniles

Those in favor of retaining the status offense category point to society's responsibility to care for troubled youths. Others maintain that the status offense should remain a legal category so that juvenile courts can force a youth to receive treatment. Although it is recognized that a court appearance can produce a stigma, the taint may be less important than the need for treatment. Many state jurisdictions, prompted by concern over serious delinquency, have enacted laws that actually expand social control over juveniles.

Curfew Laws

Beginning in 1990 there has been an explosion in the passage of curfew laws aimed at restricting the opportunity kids have for getting in trouble. A survey of 77 large U.S. cities found that 59 of them have curfew laws.

As a general rule, the courts have upheld the use of juvenile curfew laws as long as (a) the language of the statute shows a compelling government interest for use of the curfew and (b) the language of the curfew law is consistent with this narrowly defined interest. Curfew ordinances must also allow youth to be out during curfew hours under certain circumstances (for example, in the company of their parents, coming or going to work/school, in the event of an emergency).

Evaluations of the benefits of curfews yield mixed results. Andra Bannister and her associates surveyed more than 400 police agencies and found that most had curfew ordinances in effect for several years.

In the majority of cases, police felt that curfew was an effective tool to control vandalism, graffiti, nighttime burglary, and auto theft. Those jurisdictions that did not have curfew laws reported that their absence was a result of political objections rather than perceived ineffectiveness.

Contrary to these findings, other research efforts find that both juvenile victimization and juvenile arrest rates do not seem to decrease significantly during curfew hours; effects, if any, seem modest. Some research efforts have even found that after curfews were implemented, victimization levels increased significantly during noncurfew hours, an indication that rather than suppressing delinquency, curfews merely shift the time of occurrence of the offenses.

Parental Responsibility Laws

Since the early twentieth century, there have been laws aimed at disciplining parents for *contributing to the delinquency of a minor*. The first of these was enacted in Colorado in 1903, and today 42 states and the District of Columbia maintain similar laws. Such laws allow parents to be sanctioned in juvenile courts for behaviors associated with their child's misbehavior. Some states (Florida, Idaho, Virginia) require parents to reimburse the government for the costs of detention or care of their children. Others (Maryland, Missouri, Oklahoma) demand that parents make restitution payments, for example, paying for damage caused by their children who vandalized a school. All states except New Hampshire have incorporated parental liability laws

one, argues that status offenders "should be removed from the jurisdiction of the courts altogether."[67] Schwartz maintains that status offenders would best be served not by juvenile courts but by dispute resolution and mediation programs designed to strengthen family ties, since "status offense cases are often rooted in family problems."[68]

Increasing Social Control

Do curfew laws work in reducing the rate of youth crime? To find out, visit the following site at the Justice Policy Institute: *http://www.cjcj.org/jpi/curfewex.html*
For an up-to-date list of Web links, go to *http://info.wadsworth.com/siegel*

Those in favor of retaining the status offense category point to society's responsibility to care for troubled youths. Some have suggested that the failure of the courts to extend social control over wayward youths neglects the rights of concerned parents who are not able to care for and correct their children.[69] Others maintain that the status offense should remain a legal category so that juvenile courts can "force" a youth into receiving treatment.[70] While it is recognized that a court appearance can produce negative "stigma," the taint may be less important than the need for treatment.[71] Many state jurisdictions, prompted by concern over serious delinquency, have enacted laws that actually expand social control over juveniles.[72] The Policy and Practice box entitled "Increasing Social Control over Juveniles" discusses this issue in greater detail.

Research shows that a majority of youth routinely engage in some form of status offenses and that those who refrain form an atypical minority.[73] "Illegal" acts such as teen sex and substance abuse have become normative and commonplace. It makes little sense to have the juvenile court intervene with kids who are caught in within their statutes, though most recent legislation places limits on recovery somewhere between $250 (Vermont) and $15,000 (Texas); the average is $2,500. Other states (Colorado, Texas, Louisiana) require parents as well as children to participate in counseling and community service activities.

Parents may also be held civilly liable, under the concept of *vicarious liability,* for the damages caused by a child. In some states, parents are responsible for up to $300,000 in damages; in others the liability cap is $3,500 (sometimes home-owner's insurance covers at least some of liability). Parents can also be charged with civil negligence if they should have known of the damage a child was about to inflict but did nothing to stop the child—for example, when they give a weapon to an emotionally unstable youth. Juries have levied awards of up to $500,000 in such cases.

An extreme form of discipline for parents makes them criminally liable for the illegal acts of their children. Since 1990 there have been more than 18 cases in which parents have been ordered to serve time in jail because their children have been truant from school. Civil libertarians charge that these laws violate the constitutional right to due process and seem to be used only against lower-class parents. They find little evidence that punishing parents can deter delinquency. State laws of this kind have been successfully challenged in the lower courts.

Critical Thinking

1. Is it fair to punish parents for the misdeeds of their children? What happens if parents tried to control their teenager and failed? Should they be held liable?

2. Why should all youths be forced to meet a curfew simply because a few are rowdy and get in trouble with the law? Is it fair to punish the innocent for the acts of the guilty?

InfoTrac College Edition Research

To learn more about the legal and social effects of curfews, use *curfews* as a keyword on InfoTrac College Edition.

Sources: Andra Bannister, David Carter, and Joseph Schafer, "A National Police Survey on the Use of Juvenile Curfews," *Journal of Criminal Justice* 29:233–40 (2001); Mike Reynolds, Ruth Seydlitz, and Pamela Jenkins, "Do Juvenile Curfew Laws Work? A Time-Series Analysis of the New Orleans Law," *Justice Quarterly* (2000); Mike Males and Dan Macallair, "An Analysis of Curfew Enforcement and Juvenile Crime in California," *Western Criminology Review* (September 1999); Joannie M. Schrof, "Who's Guilty?" *U.S. News & World Report* 126:60 (May 17, 1999); William Ruefle and Kenneth Mike Reynolds, "Curfews and Delinquency in Major American Cities," *Crime and Delinquency* 41:347–63 (1995); *Federal Bureau of Investigation Uniform Crime Report, 1999* (Washington, DC: FBI, 2000) p. 213; *Juvenile Justice Reform Initiatives in the States* (Washington, DC: Office of Juvenile Justice and Delinquency Prevention, 1997); Gilbert Geis and Arnold Binder, "Sins of Their Children: Parental Responsibility for Juvenile Delinquency," *Notre Dame Journal of Law, Ethics, and Public Policy* 5:303–22 (1991); David McDowall and Colin Loftin, "The Impact of Youth Curfew Laws on Juvenile Crime Rates," *Crime and Delinquency* 46:76–92 (2000).

what has become routine teenage behavior. In contrast, juvenile court jurisdiction over status offenders may be defended if in fact the youths' offending patterns are similar to those of delinquents. Is their current offense only the tip of an antisocial iceberg, or are they actually noncriminal youths who need only the loving hand of a substitute parent-figure interested in their welfare? Some find that status offenders are quite different from delinquents, but others note that many status offenders also had prior arrests for delinquent acts and that many delinquents exhibited behaviors that would define them as status offenders.[74]

These disparate findings may be explained in part by the fact that there may be different types of status offenders, some similar to delinquents and others who are quite different.[75] It might be more realistic to divide status offenders into three groups: (1) first-time status offenders, (2) those with prior status offenses, and (3) those with both a delinquent record and a status offense record.[76] The fact that many young offenders have mixed delinquent–status offender records indicates that these legal categories are not entirely independent. It is also recognized that some "pure" first-time status offenders are quite different from delinquents and that a juvenile court experience can be harmful to them and escalate the frequency and seriousness of their law-violating behaviors.[77]

The removal of these status offenders from the juvenile court is an issue that continues to be debated. The predominant view today is that many status offenders and delinquents share similar social and developmental problems and that consequently both categories should fall under the jurisdiction of the juvenile court. Not surprisingly, research does show that the legal processing of delinquents and status offenders remains quite similar.[78]

SUMMARY

The study of delinquency is concerned with a number of different issues: the nature and extent of the criminal behavior of youths; the causes of youthful law violations; the legal rights of juveniles; and prevention and treatment techniques.

The problems of American youth have become a national concern and an important subject of academic study. The dynamic nature of adolescence and the stress American youth are under are considered. Drugs, pregnancy, suicide, and social conflict are all taking their toll on youth.

The concept of a separate status of "childhood" has developed slowly over the centuries. Early family life included such practices as dower and primogeniture. Punishment was severe, and children were expected to take on adult roles early in their lives.

With the start of the seventeenth century came greater recognition of the needs of children. In Great Britain, the chancery court movement, the Poor Laws, and apprenticeship programs greatly affected the lives of children. In colonial America, many of the characteristics of English family living were adopted.

In the nineteenth century, neglected, delinquent, and dependent or runaway children were treated no differently than criminal defendants. Children were often charged and convicted of crimes. During this time, however, because of philosophical shifts in the areas of crime and delinquency, as well as a change in the emphasis of the concept of *parens patriae*, steps were taken to reduce the responsibility of children under the criminal law in both Great Britain and the United States.

The concept of delinquency was developed in the early twentieth century. Before that, criminal youths and adults were treated in almost the same fashion. A group of reformers, referred to as *child savers*, helped create a separate delinquency category to insulate juvenile offenders from the influence of adult criminals.

The separate status of juvenile delinquency is still based on the *parens patriae* philosophy, which holds that children have the right to care and custody and that if parents are not capable of providing that care, the state must step in to take control.

Juvenile courts also have jurisdiction over noncriminal status offenders. Status offenses are illegal only because of the minority status of the offender. They include such misbehavior as truancy, running away, and sexual misconduct. Some experts have called for an end to juvenile court control over status offenders, charging that it merely further stigmatizes already troubled youths. Some research indicates that status offenders are harmed by juvenile court processing. Other efforts indicate that status offenders and delinquents are actually quite similar.

The treatment of juveniles is an ongoing dilemma in American society. Still uncertain is whether young law violators respond better to harsh punishments or benevolent treatment.

KEY TERMS

ego identity	persistence	Poor Laws	status offenses
role diffusion	desistance	chancery courts	wayward minors
at-risk youth	juvenile justice system	*parens patriae*	truancy
juvenile delinquency	paternalistic family	child savers	Office of Juvenile Justice and Delinquency Prevention (OJJDP)
chronic delinquent offenders	primogeniture	best interests of the child	
aging-out process	swaddling	waiver	

QUESTIONS FOR DISCUSSION

1. Is it fair to have a separate legal category for youths? Considering how dangerous young people can be, does it make more sense to group offenders on the basis of what they have done and not their age?

2. At what age are juveniles truly capable of understanding the seriousness of their actions?

3. Is it fair to institutionalize a minor simply for being truant or running away from home? Should the jurisdiction of status offenders be removed from juvenile court and placed with the state department of social services or some other welfare organization?

4. Should delinquency proceedings be secretive? Does the public have the right to know who juvenile criminals are?

5. Can a "get tough" policy help control juvenile misbehavior, or should *parens patriae* remain the standard?

6. Should juveniles who commit felonies such as rape or robbery be treated as adults?

VIEWPOINT

Children in the colonial period were seen as beings who should adopt adult behavior and assume adult responsibilities as soon as possible. They were dressed as adults as early as 7 or 8. By age 10, children often lived with other families and worked for them as hired laborers or servants.

Analysis of the history of childhood provides an important glimpse into the forces that shape contemporary culture. To read more about this fascinating topic, go to InfoTrac College Edition: Elizabeth H. Pleck, *The Reader's Companion to American History,* 3rd ed. (1991), p. 163.

NOTES

1. For a thorough review, see Robin Malinosky-Rummell and David Hansen, "Long-Term Consequences of Childhood Physical Abuse," *Psychological Bulletin* 114:68–79 (1993).

2. Associated Press Florida Teenager May Face Life for Shooting," *New York Times,* 2 May 2001, A3; Tim Roche, "Nate Brazill, Sentenced to Grow Up in Prison: The Florida Teen Gets 28 Years for Shooting His Teacher," *Time,* 27 July 2001, p. 19.

3. Robin Malinosky-Rummell and David Hansen, "Long-Term Consequences of Childhood Physical Abuse," *Psychological Bulletin* 114:68–79 (1993).

4. Nanette Davis, *Youth Crisis: Growing Up in the High-Risk Society* (New York: Praeger, Greenwood Publishing, 1998).

5. Children's Defense Fund, *The State of America's Children Yearbook 2001* (Washington, DC: Children's Defense Fund, 2001).

6. Susan Crimmins and Michael Foley, "The Threshold of Violence in Urban Adolescents." Paper presented at the annual meeting of the American Society of Criminology, Reno, Nevada, November 1989.

7. Ibid., p. 21.

8. Task Force on Education of Young Adolescents, *Turning Points, Preparing American Youth for the 21st Century* (New York: Carnegie Council on Adolescent Development, 1989). Hereinafter cited as *Turning Points.*

9. Erik Erikson, *Childhood and Society* (New York: W. H. Norton, 1963).

10. Roger Gould, "Adult Life Stages: Growth toward Self-Tolerance," *Psychology Today* 8:74–78 (1975).

11. U.S. Bureau of the Census, *Population Estimates and Projections* (Washington, DC, 2001).

12. *Turning Points,* p. 27.

13. U.S. Bureau of the Census, *Poverty in the United States, 2000* (Washington, DC: U.S. Census Bureau, 2001).

14. John Cook and Larry Brown, *Two Americas: Alternative Future for Child Poverty in America* (Medford, MA: Tufts University Center on Hunger, Poverty and Nutrition, 1993).

15. David Eggebeen and Daniel Lichter, "Race, Family Structure, and Changing Poverty among American Children," *American Sociological Review* 56:801–17 (1991).

16. W. Rees Davis and Michael Clatts, "High Risk Youth and the N.Y.C. Street Economy: Policy Implications." Paper presented at the American Society of Criminology meeting, Boston, November 1995.

17. National Center for Education Statistics, *Fast Facts* (Washington, DC: U.S. Department of Education, 2001).

18. Jay P. Greene, *High School Graduation Rates in the United States* (The Manhattan Institute for Policy Research Report, November 2001).

19. Center for Disease Control news release, "New CDC Report Shows Teen Birth Rate Hits Record Low: U.S. Births Top 4 Million in 2000 (Atlanta, Tuesday, July 24, 2001).

20. National Education Goals Panel, *The National Education Goals Report, Building a Nation of Learners* (Washington, DC: U.S. Government Printing Office, 1997), pp.111–1V.

21. News release, "Kids Count Survey, 1998" (Annie E. Casey Foundation, Baltimore, May 5, 1998).

22. National Education Goals Panel, *The National Education Goals Report.*

23. Bruce Johnson, George Thomas, and Andrew Golub, "Trends in Heroin Use among Manhattan Arrestees from the Heroin and Crack Era," in James Inciardi and Lana Harrison, eds., *Heroin in the Age of Crack-Cocaine* (Thousand Oaks, CA.: Sage, 1998), pp. 108–30.

24. Federal Bureau of Investigation, *Crimes in the United States, 1999* (Washington, DC: Government Printing Office, 2000), p. 228.

25. John Whitehead and Steven Lab, "A Meta-Analysis of Juvenile Correctional Treatment," *Journal of Research in Crime and Delinquency* 26:276–95 (1989).

26. See Lawrence Stone, *The Family, Sex, and Marriage in England: 1500–1800* (New York: Harper & Row, 1977).

27. This section relies on Jackson Spielvogel, *Western Civilization* (St. Paul: West, 1991), pp. 279–86.

28. Ibid.

29. See Philipe Aries, *Century of Childhood: A Social History of Family Life* (New York: Vintage, 1962).

30. See Douglas R. Rendleman, "Parens Patriae: From Chancery to the Juvenile Court," *South Carolina Law Review* 23:205 (1971).

31. See Stone, *The Family, Sex, and Marriage in England,* and Lawrence Stone, ed., *Schooling and Society: Studies in the History of Education* (Baltimore: John Hopkins University Press, 1970).

32. Ibid.

33. See Wiley B. Sanders, *Some Early Beginnings of the Children's Court Movement in England,* National Probation Association Yearbook (New York: National Council on Crime and Delinquency, 1945).

34. Douglas Besharov, *Juvenile Justice Advocacy—Practice in a Unique Court* (New York: Practicing Law Institute, 1974), p. 2.

35. Rendleman, "Parens Patriae," p. 209.

36. See Anthony Platt, "The Rise of the Child Saving Movement: A Study in Social Policy and Correctional Reform," *Annals of the American Academy of Political and Social Science* 381:21–38 (1969).

37. Robert Bremmer, ed., and John Barnard, Hareven Tamara, and Robert Mennel, asst. eds., *Children and Youth in America* (Cambridge: Harvard University Press, 1970), p. 64.

38. Elizabeth Pleck, "Criminal Approaches to Family Violence, 1640–1980," in Lloyd Ohlin and Michael Tonry, eds., *Family Violence* (Chicago: University of Chicago Press, 1989), pp. 19–58.

39. Ibid.

40. John R. Sutton, *Stubborn Children: Controlling Delinquency in the United States, 1640–1981* (Berkeley: University of California Press, 1988).

41. Pleck, "Criminal Approaches to Family Violence," p. 29.

42. John Demos, *Past, Present and Personal* (New York: Oxford University Press, 1986), pp. 80–88.

43. Elizabeth Pleck, *Domestic Tyranny: The Making of Social Policy against Family Violence from Colonial Times to the Present* (New York: Oxford University Press, 1987), p. 28–30.

44. Graeme Newman, *The Punishment Response* (Philadelphia: J. B. Lippincott, 1978), pp. 53–79; Philip Aries, *Centuries of Childhood* (New York: Knopf, 1962). The history of childhood juvenile justice is discussed in detail in Chapter 13.

45. Stephen J. Morse, "Immaturity and Irresponsibility," *Journal of Criminal Law and Criminology* 88:15–67 (1997).

46. FBI, *Crime in the United States, 1999* (Washington, DC: U.S. Government Printing Office, 2000), p. 222.

47. See, generally, David Rothman, *The Discovery of the Asylum* (Boston: Little, Brown, 1971).

48. Reports of the Chicago Bar Association Committee, 1899, cited in Anthony Platt, *The Child Savers* (Chicago: University of Chicago Press, 1969), p. 119.

49. John L. Hutzler, *Juvenile Court Jurisdiction over Children's Conduct: 1982 Comparative Analysis of Juvenile and Family Codes and National Standards* (Pittsburgh: National Center for Juvenile Justice, 1982), p. 2.

50. Ibid.

51. Susan Datesman and Mikel Aickin, "Offense Specialization and Escalation among Status Offenders," *Journal of Criminal Law and Criminology* 75:1246–75 (1985).

52. Ibid.

53. David J. Steinharthe, *Status Offenses: The Future of Children 6(3)* (The David and Lucile Packard Foundation, Winter 1996).

54. See, generally, Solomon Kobrin and Malcolm Klein, *National Evaluation of the Deinstitutionalization of Status Offender Programs—Executive Summary* (Los Angeles: Social Science Research Institute, University of Southern California, 1982).

55. OJJDP Annual Report 2000 (June 2001).

56. 42 U.S.C.A. 5601–5751 (1983 & Supp. 1987).

57. Claudia Wright, "Contempt No Excuse for Locking Up Status Offenders, Says Florida Supreme Court," *Youth Law News* 13:1–3 (1992).

58. *A.A. v. Rolle,* 604 So. 2d 813 (1992).

59. Steinharthe, *Status Offenses,* p. 5.

60. National Council on Crime and Delinquency, "Juvenile Curfews—A Policy Statement," *Crime and Delinquency* 18:132–33 (1972).

61. National Advisory Commission on Criminal Justice Standards and Goals, *Juvenile Justice and Delinquency Prevention* (Washington, DC: Government Printing Office, 1977), p. 311.

62. American Bar Association Joint Commission on Juvenile Justice Standards, *Summary and Analysis* (Cambridge, MA: Ballinger, 1977), sect. 1.1.

63. Martin Rouse, "The Diversion of Status Offenders, Criminalization, and the New York Family Court," rev. version. Paper presented at the American Society of Criminology, Reno Nevada, November 1989), p. 12.

64. Barry Feld, "Criminalizing the American Juvenile Court," in Michael Tonry, ed., *Crime and Justice, A Review of Research* (Chicago: University of Chicago Press, 1993), p. 232.

65. Marc Miller, "Changing Legal Paradigms in Juvenile Justice," in Peter Greenwood, ed., *The Juvenile Rehabilitation Reader* (Santa Monica, CA: Rand Corporation, 1985) p. V.44.

66. Thomas Kelley, "Status Offenders Can Be Different: A Comparative Study of Delinquent Careers," *Crime and Delinquency* 29:365–80 (1983).

67. Ira Schwartz, *(In) Justice for Juveniles: Rethinking the Best Interests of the Child* (Lexington, MA: Lexington Books, 1989), p. 171.

68. Ibid.

69. Lawrence Martin and Phyllis Snyder, "Jurisdiction over Status Offenses Should Not Be Removed from the Juvenile Court," *Crime and Delinquency* 22:44–47 (1976).

70. Lindsay Arthur, "Status Offenders Need a Court of Last Resort," *Boston University Law Review* 57:631–44 (1977).

71. Ibid.

72. David McDowall and Colin Loftin, "The Impact of Youth Curfew Laws on Juvenile Crime Rates." *Crime and Delinquency* 46:76–92 (2000).

73. Carolyn Smith, "Factors Associated with Early Sexual Activity among Urban Adolescents," *Social Work* 42:334–46 (1997).

74. Charles Thomas, "Are Status Offenders Really So Different?" *Crime and Delinquency* 22:438–55 (1976); Howard Snyder, *Court Careers of Juvenile Offenders* (Washington, DC: Office of Juvenile Justice and Delinquency Prevention, 1988), p. 65.

75. Randall Shelden, John Horvath, and Sharon Tracy, "Do Status Offenders Get Worse? Some Clarifications on the Question of Escalation," *Crime and Delinquency 35*: 202–16 (1989).

76. Solomon Kobrin, Frank Hellum, and John Peterson, "Offense Patterns of Status Offenders," in D. Schichor and D. Kelly, eds., *Critical Issues in Juvenile Delinquency* (Lexington, MA: Lexington Books, 1980), pp. 203–35.

77. Schwartz, *(In) Justice for Juveniles*, pp. 378–79.

78. Chris Marshall, Ineke Marshall, and Charles Thomas, "The Implementation of Formal Procedures in Juvenile Court Processing of Status Offenders," *Journal of Criminal Justice 11*:195–211 (1983).

2 The Nature and Extent of Delinquency

As a juvenile court judge, you are forced to make a tough decision during a hearing to decide whether a juvenile should be waived to the adult court. It seems that gang activity has become a way of life for residents living in local public housing projects. The Bloods sell crack, and the Wolfpack controls the drug market. When the rivalry between the two gangs explodes, 16-year-old Shatiek Johnson, a Wolfpack member, shoots and kills a member of the Bloods; in retaliation the Bloods put out a contract on his life. While in hiding, Shatiek is confronted by two undercover detectives who recognize the young fugitive. Fearing for his life, Shatiek pulls a pistol and begins firing, fatally wounding one of the officers. During the hearing you learn that Shatiek's story is not dissimilar from that of many other children raised in housing projects. With an absent father and a single mother who could not control her five sons, Shatiek lived in a world of drugs, gangs, and shootouts long before he was old enough to vote. By age 13, Shatiek had been involved in the gang beating death of a homeless man in a dispute over $10, for which he was given a one-year sentence at a youth detention center and released after six months. Now charged with a crime that could be considered first-degree murder if committed by an adult, Shatiek could—if waived to the adult court—be sentenced to life in prison or even face the death penalty.

At the hearing, Shatiek seems like a lost soul. He claims he thought the police officers were killers out to collect the bounty put on his life by the Bloods. He says that killing the rival gang boy was an act of self-defense. The DA confirms that the victim was in fact a known gang assassin with numerous criminal convictions. Shatiek's mother begs you to consider the fact that her son is only 16 years old, that he has had a very difficult childhood, and that he is a victim of society's indifference to the poor.

- Would you treat Shatiek as a juvenile and see if a prolonged stay in a youth facility could help this troubled young man?

- Would you bind him over to the adult system?

- Does a 16-year-old like Shatiek deserve a second chance?

- Is Shatiek's behavior common among adolescent boys?

- Is this case just the tip of a rising tide of juvenile violence?

social class

II offenses

To get the UCR online, as well as to access other important information, go to
http://www.fbi.gov/
For an up-to-date list of Web links, go to
http://info.wadsworth.com/siegel

Federal Bureau of Investigation (FBI) Arm of the U.S. Department of Justice that investigates violations of federal law, gathers crime statistics, runs a comprehensive crime laboratory, and helps train local law enforcement officers.

Cases like that of Shatiek Johnson are all too common today. (The scenario is based on an actual case that occurred in New York City in 1998.[1]) Is it accurate to say that these cases are common? Just how common *are* serious acts of juvenile delinquency? Who commits delinquent acts, and where are these acts most likely to occur? Is the juvenile crime rate increasing or decreasing? Are juveniles more likely than adults to become the victims of crime?[2] To understand the causes of delinquent behavior and to devise effective means to reduce their occurrence, we must seek answers to these questions.

Delinquency experts have devised a variety of methods to measure the nature and extent of delinquency (Exhibit 2.1). We begin with a description of the most widely used sources of data on crime and delinquency. We also examine the information these resources furnish on juvenile crime rates and trends. These data sources will then be used to provide information on the characteristics of adolescent law violators.

Official Statistics

Uniform Crime Report (UCR) Compiled by the FBI, the UCR is the most widely used source of national crime and delinquency statistics.

Part I offenses (also known as index crimes) Offenses including homicide and nonnegligent manslaughter, forcible rape, robbery, aggravated assault, burglary, larceny, arson, and motor vehicle theft; recorded by local law enforcement officers, these crimes are tallied quarterly and sent to the FBI for inclusion in the UCR.

Each year the U.S. Justice Department's **Federal Bureau of Investigation (FBI)** compiles information gathered by police departments on the number of criminal acts reported by citizens and the number of persons arrested. This information is published in the *Uniform Crime Report* **(UCR),** which is the most widely used source of national crime and delinquency statistics.

The UCR is compiled from statistics sent to the FBI from more than 16,000 police departments. It groups offenses into two categories. **Part I offenses,** also known as **index crimes,** include homicide and non-negligent manslaughter, forcible rape, robbery, aggravated assault, burglary, larceny, arson, and motor vehicle theft. Police record every reported incident of these offenses and report them on a quarterly basis to the FBI. Data are broken down by city, county, metropolitan area, and geographical divisions. In addition, the UCR provides information on individuals who have been arrested for these and all other criminal offenses, including vandalism, liquor law violations, and drug trafficking. These are known as **Part II offenses.** The arrest data are presented by age, sex, and race.

Exhibit 2.1   Sources of Delinquency Data

Official Data

Official data is based on the criminal incidents reported to the nation's police departments. This information is collected and disseminated on an annual basis by the Federal Bureau of Investigation (FBI) in their Uniform Crime Report (UCR) program. The UCR records both the total number of crimes reported to the police for major offense categories such as murder and rape, and the total number of arrests made for *any crime* that is cleared or solved. Because the age of arrestees is recorded, official data can be used to study trends and patterns in the delinquency rate. Youths with an arrest record are referred to as "official delinquents"; their actions are considered recorded or **official delinquency;** their behavior becomes part of the "official statistics."

Self-Report Data

Self-report data are obtained from anonymous surveys or interviews, often conducted in schools, which query adolescents about their participation in illegal acts such as drug abuse and vandalism. Self-report data are aimed at assessing criminal acts that have gone undetected by the police either because victims fail to report crime or because the crime is victimless, for example, drug abuse. They measure the extent of unrecorded juvenile delinquency, the so-called **dark figures of crime.** These data can also be used to compare the personal characteristics, such as race and gender, of official delinquents with those youths whose criminal activity remains undetected.

Victim Data

Victim surveys ask those who have experienced crime first-hand to tell about the episode. Victim data includes crimes reported to the police as well as crimes that the victim failed to report. They provide important information on where victimization takes place, the likelihood of victimization, and the kinds of personal behaviors and lifestyle that increase the chances of becoming a crime victim. The most widely used of these is the federally sponsored National Crime Victimization Survey (NCVS), an annual survey of thousands of citizens selected in communities across the nation.

Part II offenses All crimes other than Part I offenses; recorded by local law enforcement officers, arrests for these crimes are tallied quarterly and sent to the FBI for inclusion in the UCR.

The UCR expresses crime data in three ways. First, the number of crimes reported to the police and the arrests made are given as raw figures (for example, 15,517 murders occurred in 2000). Second, crime rates per 100,000 people are computed. That is, when the UCR indicates that the murder rate was 5.7 in 2000, it means that about 6 people in every 100,000 were murdered between January 1 and December 31, 2000.

Crime Trends in the United States

official delinquency Delinquent acts that result in arrest by local police. These are included in the FBI's arrest data.

dark figures of crime Incidents of crime and delinquency that go undetected by police.

The U.S. crime rate skyrocketed between 1960, when 3.3 million crimes were reported to police agencies, and 1981, when more than 13 million crimes were recorded. The crime rate began to decline in the 1990s. (See Figure 2.1.) Though the change between 1999 and 2000 was negligible, the Crime Index total was 16 percent less than in 1995 and 20 percent less than in 1990. Nevertheless, the FBI estimates that about 11.6 million serious crimes occurred in 2000, more than 4,000 per 100,000 inhabitants.[3] So, while the number and rate of crime has undergone a dramatic decline, millions of serious criminal incidents still occur each year.

Measuring Official Delinquency

disaggregated Analyzing the relationship between two or more independent variables (such as murder convictions and death sentence) while controlling for the influence of a dependent variable (such as race).

> **A CLOSER VIEW**
> To learn more about the *Uniform Crime Report* and how it may be used, employ it as a key term on InfoTrac College Edition.

Because the UCR arrest statistics are **disaggregated** (broken down) by age of suspects, they can be used to estimate adolescent crime. Juvenile arrest data must be interpreted with caution, however. First, the number of teenagers arrested does not represent the actual number of youths who have committed delinquent acts. Some offenders are never counted because they are never caught. Others are counted more than once because multiple arrests of the same individual for different crimes are counted separately in the UCR. Consequently, the total number of arrests does not equal the number of people who have been arrested. Put another way, if 2 million arrests of youths under 18 years of age were made in a given year, we could not be sure if 2 million individuals had been arrested once or if 500,000 chronic offenders had been arrested four times each. In addition, when an arrested offender commits multiple crimes, only the most serious one is recorded. Therefore, if 2 million juveniles are arrested, the number of crimes committed is at least 2 million, but it may be much higher.

Figure 2.1
Crime Rate Trends, 1960–2001
Source: FBI, *Uniform Crime Report,* 2001, preliminary estimates.

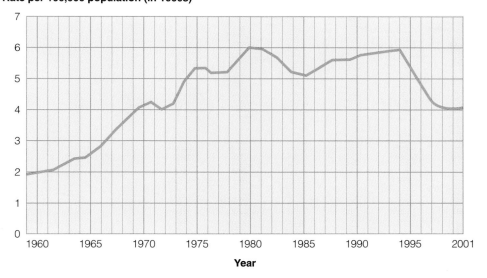

Rate per 100,000 population (in 1000s)

Year

Table 2.1   Persons Arrested, by Age

	Under 15	Under 18	Over 18
Index violent crime	5%	16%	84%
Index property crime	12%	32%	68%
Index total	10%	28%	72%
Total all crimes	6%	17%	83%

Source: FBI, *Crime in the United States*, 2000, p. 226.

Despite these limitations, the nature of arrest data remains constant over time. Consequently, arrest data can provide some indication of the nature and trends in juvenile crime. What does the UCR tell us about delinquency?

Official Delinquency   In 2000 (the latest data available), 14 million arrests were made, or about 5,000 per 100,000 population. Of these, about 2 million were for serious Part I crimes and 12 million for less serious Part II crimes. About 17 percent of all arrests were juveniles under age 18. Juveniles accounted for about 28 percent of all index crime arrests. A disproportionate number of violent crime arrests involve young people. The under-18 population is about 8 percent of the U.S. population but is responsible for about 16 percent of the violent crime arrests (65,000) and about one-third of the property crime arrests (345,000). (See Table 2.1.)

About 1.1 million juvenile arrests were made in 2000 for Part II offenses. Included in this total were more than 300,000 arrests for status offenses, including 93,000 arrests for running away from home, 106,000 for curfew violations, and 101,000 for liquor law violations.

It comes as no surprise, then, that crime is a young person's game. As Figure 2.2 shows, most serious property crime activity peaks at age 16, and the peak for violent crime arrests is age 18. Age-level crime rates decline after these years, and by age 24 violent crime arrests are about 64 percent and property crime arrests 31 percent of what they were at their peak.

Juvenile Crime Trends   Juvenile crime continues to have a significant influence on the nation's overall crime statistics. Arrests for violent juvenile crime began to increase in 1989, peaked in 1994, and then began to fall. Juvenile murder rates more than doubled between the early 1980s and their peak in 1993; they have since been in decline.[4] For example, 1,700 youths were arrested for murder in 1997, a number

Figure 2.2
The Relationship between Age and Serious Crime Arrests
Source: FBI, *Uniform Crime Report*, 2000, pp. 232–33.

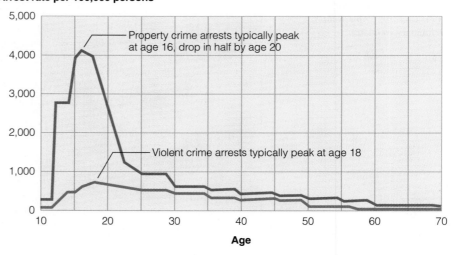

Arrest rate per 100,000 persons

Property crime arrests typically peak at age 16, drop in half by age 20

Violent crime arrests typically peak at age 18

Part One   The Concept of Delinquency

that by 2000 had declined by less than half to 806. Similarly, 3,800 juveniles were arrested for rape in 1997, and 2,937 in 2000. This dramatic decline in juvenile violence is especially welcome considering that its rate was approaching epidemic proportions.

The official data tell us that juvenile crime rates ebb and flow. What factors account for change in the juvenile crime rate? This is the topic of the accompanying Focus on Delinquency box entitled "The Rise and Fall of Juvenile Crime Rates."

What the Future Holds

A CLOSER VIEW
Can future crime trends be predicted? To find out, go to InfoTrac College Edition and use *crime trends* as a subject.

Want to find out more about world population trends? Go to the Population Reference Bureau's home page:
http://www.prb.org/
For an up-to-date list of Web links, go to
http://info.wadsworth.com/siegel

Some experts, such as criminologist James A. Fox, predict a significant increase in teen violence if current population trends persist. The nation's teenage population will increase by 15 percent, or more than 9 million, between now and 2010; the number in the high-risk ages between 15 and 17 will increase by more than 3 million, or 31 percent. There are approximately 50 million school-age children in the United States, many under age 10—more than we have had for decades. While many come from stable homes, others lack stable families and adequate supervision; these are some of the children who will soon enter their prime crime years. As a result, Fox predicts a wave of youth violence even greater than that of the past 10 years.[5]

While Fox's predictions may be persuasive, not all delinquency experts believe that we are in for an age-driven crime wave. Some, like Steven Levitt, dispute the fact that the population's age makeup contributes as much to the crime rate as suggested by Fox and others.[6] Levitt finds that even if the rising number of teens will contribute heavily to the total crime rate, their effect will be offset by the equally growing number of senior citizens, a group with a relatively low crime rate. The crime rate effect of these two growing segments of the population should neutralize one another, creating a more stable crime rate. While such prognostication is reassuring, there is no accurate way to foretell the factors that influence crime rates to go either up or down.

Is the UCR Data Valid?

Go to the Siegel/Welsh/Senna *Juvenile Delinquency* book-specific Web site for MicroCase exercises about this material:

http://info.wadsworth.com/siegel

Questions have been raised about the validity and accuracy of UCR's "official" crime data. Victim surveys show that less than half of all victims report the crime to police. Because official data are derived entirely from police records, we can assume that a significant number of crimes are not accounted for in the UCR. There are also concerns that police departments make systematic errors in recording crime data. In addition, some police commanders may manipulate crime data.[7] In New York, Atlanta, and Boca Raton, Florida, charges of falsely reporting crime statistics have resulted in the resignation or demotion of police commanders.

Using official arrest data to measure delinquency rates is particularly problematic. Arrest records only count adolescents who have been *caught*, and these youths may be different from those who evade capture. In addition, victimless crimes such as drug and alcohol use are significantly undercounted using this measure.

Arrest decision criteria vary among police agencies. Some police agencies may practice full enforcement, arresting all teens who violate the law, whereas others may follow a policy of discretion that encourages unofficial handling of juvenile matters through social service agencies.

While these questions are troubling, the problems associated with collecting and verifying the official UCR data are consistent and stable over time. This means that while the absolute accuracy of the data can be questioned, the trends and patterns they show are probably reliable. Although we cannot be absolutely sure about the actual number of adolescents who commit crime, it is likely that the teen crime rate has been in a significant decline.

The Rise and Fall of Juvenile Crime Rates

Crime rates climb and fall, reflecting a variety of social and economic conditions. Although there is still disagreement over what causes crime rate fluctuations, the following factors are considered to play a major role in determining patterns and trends.

Age

Change in the age distribution of the population deeply influences crime and delinquency rates. Since juvenile males commit more crimes than any other population segment, as a general rule the crime rate follows the proportion of young males in the population. The postwar baby-boom generation reached their teenage years in the 1960s, just as the crime rate began a sharp increase. With the graying of society and a decline in the birthrate, it is not surprising that the overall crime rate began to decline in the mid-1990s. Some criminologists fear crime rates will begin to climb when (and if) the number of juveniles in the population begins to increase.

Economy

In the short term, a poor economy may actually help lower crime rates. Unemployed parents are at home to supervise children and guard their homes. Because there is less to spend, a poor economy means that there are actually fewer valuables worth stealing. However, long-term periods of economic weakness and unemployment eventually raise crime rates. Chronic teenage unemployment rates may produce a perception of hopelessness that leads to crime and delinquency. Violence may be a function of urban problems and the economic deterioration in the nation's inner cities. Our nation's economy is now fueled by the service and technology industries. Youths who at one time might have obtained low-skill jobs in factories and shops find that these legitimate economic opportunities no longer exist. Low-skill manufacturing jobs have been dispersed to overseas plants; most new jobs that don't require specialized skills are in the low-paying service area. Lack of real economic opportunity may encourage drug dealing, theft, and violence. Experts fear that a long-term economic downturn coupled with a relatively large number of teens in the population will produce the high delinquency rates of the late eighties and early nineties.

Drugs

Drug use has been linked to fluctuations in the crime and delinquency rate. Abusers are particularly crime-prone, so as drug use levels increase, so too do crime rates. When teen violence skyrocketed in the 1980s, it was no coincidence that this period also witnessed increases in drug trafficking and arrests for drug crimes. Teenage substance abusers commit a significant portion of all serious crimes, and inner-city drug-abuse problems may account in part for the persistently high violent-crime rate. Groups and gangs that are involved in the urban drug trade recruit juveniles because they work cheaply, are immune from heavy criminal penalties, and are daring and willing to take risks. Arming themselves for protection, these youthful dealers pose a threat to neighborhood adolescents, who in turn arm themselves for self-protection. The result is an arms race that produces an increasing spiral of violence.

Drug abuse may also have a more direct influence on teen crime patterns—for example, when alcohol-abusing kids engage in acts of senseless violence. Users may turn to theft and violence for money to purchase drugs and support drug habits. Increases in teenage drug use may be a precursor to higher violence rates in the future.

Social Problems

As the level of social problems increases so too does the crime rate. Increases in the number of single-parent families, dropout rates, and teen pregnancies may also influence crime rates. Cross-national research indicates that child homicide rates are greatest in those nations, including the United States, that have the highest rates of teenage mothers and children born out of wedlock.

In spite of a strong economy, millions of youth now live in poverty, and those numbers are expected to increase dramatically over the next 15 years. Children living in single-parent homes are twice as likely to be impoverished than those in two-parent homes. Such children are especially at risk to juvenile delinquency, foretelling an increasing crime rate. Kathleen Heide has identified some of the social problems associated with teen violence, listed in Table A.

Table A Social Problems Associated with Teen Violence

Child abuse and neglect

Lack of role models

Crisis in leadership

Witnessing violence

Access to guns

Substance abuse

Poverty and lack of resources

Low self-esteem

Self-Reported Delinquency

self-reports Questionnaire or survey technique that asks subjects to reveal their own participation in delinquent or criminal acts.

Official statistics are useful for examining general trends, but they cannot tell us how many youths commit crimes but are never arrested. Nor do they reveal much about the personality, attitudes, and behavior of individual delinquents. To get information at this level, criminologists have developed alternative sources of delinquency statistics, the most commonly used source being **self-reports** of delinquent behavior.

The inability to deal with strong negative feelings

Boredom and lack of fun activities

Poor judgment and lack of boundaries

Prejudice and intolerance

Feelings that there is nothing left to lose

Abortion

In a controversial work, John J. Donohue III and Steven D. Levitt found empirical evidence that the recent drop in the crime rate can be attributable to the availability of legalized abortion. In 1973, *Roe v. Wade* legalized abortion nationwide. Within a few years of *Roe v. Wade*, more than 1 million abortions were being performed annually, or roughly one abortion for every three live births. Donohue and Levitt suggest that the decrease in the crime rate that began approximately 18 years later, in 1991, can be related to the fact that the first group of potential offenders affected by the abortion decision began reaching the peak age of criminal activity. It is possible that the link between crime rates and abortion is the result of two mechanisms: (1) selective abortion on the part of women most at risk to have children who would engage in delinquent activity, and (2) improved childrearing or environmental circumstances caused by better maternal, familial, or fetal circumstances because women are having fewer children. If abortion were illegal, these researchers find, crime rates might be 10–20 percent higher than they currently are with abortion.

Guns

Another important influence on violence rates is the number of weapons in the hands of teens. In 2000, 28,000 kids were arrested on weapons-related charges. More than 60 percent of the homicides committed by juveniles involve firearms. Guns can turn a schoolyard fight into a homicide. Their presence creates a climate in which kids who would otherwise shun firearms begin to carry them to "protect" themselves. As the number of guns in the hands of children increases, so do juvenile violence rates.

Gangs

The explosive growth in teenage gangs has also contributed to teen violence rates. Surveys indicate that there are about one-half million gang members in the United States. A large and growing number of juveniles who kill do so in groups of two or more; multiple-offender killings have doubled since the mid-1980s. Gang-related violence is frequently compounded by the use of firearms. Research indicates that in major cities about one-third of kids who are gang members carry a gun all or most of the time.

Juvenile Justice Policy

Some law enforcement experts have suggested that a reduction in crime rates may be attributed to a recent "get tough" attitude toward delinquency and drug abuse. Police have become more aggressive. New laws call for mandatory incarceration for juvenile offenders. Juveniles may even be eligible for the death penalty. Putting potentially high-rate offenders behind bars may help to stabilize crime rates.

Critical Thinking

1. Is it possible that most delinquents are suffering from some mental or physical handicap if factors such as justice policy, drug use, and the economy influence delinquency rates? It would seem that if delinquency is a function of some physical/mental trait, rates would not be influenced by social phenomena.
2. Considering current conditions in the United States and abroad, what is your prediction for future delinquency rates?

InfoTrac College Edition Research

 The abortion–delinquency rate association is quite controversial. To read more of the research, go to InfoTrac College Edition and search for John J. Donohue and Steven D. Levitt, "The Impact of Legalized Abortion on Crime," *Quarterly Journal of Economics* 116(2):379 (May 2001). For an opposing opinion, read George F. Will, "Abortions Don't Mean Drop in Crime," *The Human Life Review* 27(2):127 (Spring 2001).

Sources: Kathleen Heide, "Why Kids Keep Killing: The Correlates, Causes and Challenge of Juvenile Homicide." Paper presented at the American Society of Criminology meeting, Boston, November 1995; John J. Donohue III and Steven D. Levitt, "Legalized Abortion and Crime" (June 24, 1999, unpublished paper, University of Chicago); Donald Green, Dara Strolovitch, and Janelle Wong, "Defended Neighborhoods, Integration, and Racially Motivated Crime," *American Journal of Sociology* 104:372–403 (1998); Robert O'Brien, Jean Stockard, and Lynne Isaacson, "The Enduring Effects of Cohort Characteristics on Age-Specific Homicide Rates, 1960–1995," *American Journal of Sociology* 104:1061–95 (1999); Darrell Steffensmeier and Miles Harer, "Making Sense of Recent U.S. Crime Trends, 1980 to 1996/1998: Age Composition Effects and Other Explanations," *Journal of Research in Crime and Delinquency* 36:235–74 (1999); Rosemary Gartner, "Family Structure, Welfare Spending, and Child Homicide in Developed Democracies," *Journal of Marriage and the Family* 53:231–40(1991); Scott Decker and Susan Pennell, *Arrestees and Guns: Monitoring the Illegal Firearms Market* (Washington, DC: National Institute of Justice, 1995); G. David Curry, Richard Ball, and Scott Decker, "Estimating the National Scope of Gang Crime from Law Enforcement Data," in C. Ronald Huff, ed., *Gangs in America*, 2nd ed. (Newbury Park, CA: Sage, 1996).

Self-report studies are designed to obtain information from youthful subjects about their violations of the law. Youths arrested by police may be interviewed at the station house; an anonymous survey can be distributed to every student in a high school; boys in a detention center may be asked to respond to a survey; or, youths randomly selected from the population of teenagers can be questioned in their homes. Self-report information can be collected in one-to-one interviews or through a self-administered questionnaire, but more commonly this information is gathered through a mass distribution of anonymous questionnaires.

Exhibit 2.2   Self-Report Survey Questions

Please indicate how often in the past 12 months you did each act. (Check the best answer.)

	Never Did Act	One Time	2–5 Times	6–9 Times	10+ Times
Stole something worth less than $50	___	___	___	___	___
Stole something worth more than $50	___	___	___	___	___
Used cocaine	___	___	___	___	___
Been in a fistfight	___	___	___	___	___
Carried a weapon such as a gun or knife	___	___	___	___	___
Fought someone using a weapon	___	___	___	___	___

Self-report surveys can include all segments of the population. They provide information on offenders who have never been arrested and are therefore not part of the official data. They also measure behavior that is rarely detected by police, such as drug abuse, because their anonymity allows youths freely to describe their illegal activities. Surveys can also include items measuring personality characteristics, behavior, and attitudes.

Exhibit 2.2 shows one format for asking self-report questions. Youths are asked to indicate how many times they have participated in illegal or deviant behavior. Other formats allow subjects to record the precise number of times they engaged in each delinquent activity. Note that the reporting period is limited to the previous 12 months; some surveys question lifetime activity.

Questions not directly related to delinquent activity are often included on self-report surveys. Information on self-image, intelligence, personality, leisure activities, school activities, attitudes toward family, friends, and school may be collected. Self-report surveys also gather information on family background, social status, race, and sex. Reports of delinquent acts can be correlated with this information to create a much more complete picture of delinquent offenders than official statistics can provide.

Criminologists have used self-report studies of delinquency for more than 40 years.[8] And though there are always questions about the validity of answers, studies designed to test the accuracy of self-reports indicate that they may be a valuable source of information on the activities of youths who have had contact with the juvenile justice system as well as on the dark figures of crime—that is, those who have escaped official notice.[9]

A CLOSER VIEW
To see how self-report data is used in social science research, use the term *self-report data* as a subject guide on InfoTrac College Edition.

Self-Report Data

Most self-report studies indicate that the number of children who break the law is far greater than official statistics would lead us to believe.[10] In fact, when truancy, alcohol consumption, petty theft, and recreational drug use are included in self-report scales, delinquency appears to be almost universal. The most common offenses are truancy, drinking alcohol, using a false ID, shoplifting or larceny under five dollars, fighting, using marijuana, and damaging the property of others. In Chapter 10, self-report data will be used to gauge trends in adolescent drug abuse.

Researchers at the University of Michigan's Institute for Social Research (ISR)[11] conduct an annual national self-report survey, called Monitoring the Future (MTF), that involves a sample of about 3,000 youths selected randomly from schools around the nation. Table 2.2 contains some of the data from the 2000 MTF survey. A surprising number of these *typical* teenagers reported involvement in serious criminal behavior: About 12 percent reported hurting someone badly enough that the victim needed medical care (6 percent said they did it more than once); about 30 percent reported stealing something worth less than $50, and another 13 percent stole some-

Table 2.2 Self-Reported Delinquent Activity

Percentage of High School Seniors, Class of 2000, Engaging in Offenses during the Past 12 Months		
Crime Category	At Least One Offense	Multiple Offenses
Serious fight	7	5
Gang fight	11	9
Hurt someone badly	7	5
Used a weapon to steal	1	2
Stole less than $50	12	18
Stole more than $50	6	7
Shoplift	11	17
Breaking and entering	10	12
Arson	1	2
Damaged school property	7	6

Source: *Monitoring the Future, 2000* (Ann Arbor, MI: Institute of Social Research, 2001).

thing worth more than $50; 28 percent reported shoplifting; 13 percent had damaged school property.

If the ISR data are accurate, the juvenile crime problem is much greater than official statistics would lead us to believe. There are approximately 14 million youths between the ages of 14 and 17. Extrapolating from the MTF findings, this group accounts for more than 100 percent of all theft offenses reported in the UCR (about 8 million). About 3 percent of the students said they used a knife or a gun in a robbery. At this rate, high school students commit 1.05 million armed robberies per year. In comparison, the UCR tallies about 400,000 armed robberies for *all* age groups annually.

Although these statistics show that the delinquency problem is far greater than indicated by the national arrest statistics, self-reports rarely show the delinquency rate climbing. Over the past decade, the MTF surveys indicate that teenager participation in theft, violence, and damage-related crimes seems to be stable.

To find out more about the Institute of Social Research's Monitoring the Future program, go to their Web page at *http://monitoringthefuture.org/* For an up-to-date list of Web links, go to *http://info.wadsworth.com/siegel*

Correlates of Delinquency

An important aspect of delinquency research is measurement of the personal traits and social characteristics associated with adolescent misbehavior. If, for example, a strong association exists between delinquent behavior and family income, then poverty and economic deprivation must be considered in any explanation of the onset of adolescent criminality. If the delinquency-income association is not present, other forces may be responsible for producing antisocial behavior. It would be fruitless to concentrate delinquency control efforts in areas such as job creation and vocational training if social status were found to be unrelated to delinquent behavior. Similarly, if only a handful of delinquents are responsible for most serious crimes, crime control policies might be made more effective by identifying and treating these offenders. The next sections discuss the relationship between delinquency and the characteristics of gender, race, social class, and age.

MC MicroCase CORPORATION

Go to the Siegel/Welsh/Senna *Juvenile Delinquency* book-specific Web site for MicroCase exercises about this material:

http://info.wadsworth.com/siegel

Gender and Delinquency

Official arrest statistics, victim data, and self-reports indicate that males are significantly more criminal than females. The teenage gender ratio for serious violent crime is approximately 6 to 1, and for property crime, approximately 2.5 to 1, male to female.

One relationship reverses this general pattern: Girls (58 percent) are more likely than boys (42 percent) to be arrested as runaways. There are two possible explanations for this: Girls could be more likely than boys to run away from home, or police

IN RECENT YEARS, arrests of female delinquents have been increasing faster than those for males. Here, girls from the 18th Street Gang pose in South Central L.A. Between 1990 and 2000, the number of arrests of male delinquents actually decreased by about 3 percent, whereas the number of female delinquents arrested increased about 25 percent.

may view the female runaway as the more serious problem and therefore be more likely to process females through official justice channels. This may reflect paternalistic attitudes toward girls, who are viewed as likely to "get in trouble" if they are on the street.[12]

Gender-Based Rate Changes In recent years arrests of female delinquents have been increasing faster than those for males. Between 1990 and 2000, the number of arrests of male delinquents actually decreased by about 3 percent, whereas the number of female delinquents arrested increased about 25 percent. The change in serious violent crime arrests was even more striking: Males decreased 23 percent, while females' violent-crime arrests increased about 28 percent.

Self-report data also seem to show that the incidence of female delinquency is much higher than believed earlier, and that the most common crimes committed by males are also the ones most female offenders commit.[13] Table 2.3 shows the percentages of males and females who admitted engaging in delinquent acts during the past 12 months in the latest MTF survey. As Table 2.3 indicates, about 33 percent of boys and 24 percent of girls admit to shoplifting, 19 percent of boys and 6 percent of girls said they stole something worth more than $50, and 20 percent of boys and 4 percent of girls said they hurt someone badly enough that they required medical care. Although self-report studies indicate that the content of girls' delinquency is similar to boys', the few adolescents who reported engaging frequently in serious violent crime are still predominantly male.[14] Because the relationship between gender and delinquency rate is so apparent, this topic will be discussed further in Chapter 6.

A CLOSER VIEW
Studies indicate that sexual and physical abuse, especially incest, are significant factors in explaining gender differences in offending. To read more, go to InfoTrac College Edition and look up Joanne Belknap, Kristi Holsinger, and Melissa Dunn, "Understanding Incarcerated Girls: The Results of a Focus Group Study," *Prison Journal* 77(4):381 (December 1997).

Racial Patterns in Delinquency

There are approximately 38 million white and 7.5 million African American youths ages 5 to 17, a ratio of about 5 to 1. Yet racial minorities are disproportionately represented in the arrest statistics. African American youths are arrested for a dispro-

Table 2.3 Delinquent Acts by Gender

Percentage of High School Seniors Admitting to at Least One Offense during the Past 12 Months		
Crime Category	Males	Females
Serious fight	17	14
Gang fight	25	15
Hurt someone badly	20	4
Used a weapon to steal	4	1
Stole less than $50	39	24
Stole more than $50	19	6
Shoplift	33	24
Breaking and entering	29	17
Arson	5	1
Damaged school property	21	7

Source: *Monitoring the Future, 2000* (Ann Arbor, MI: Institute for Social Research, 2001).

portionate number of murders, rapes, robberies, and assaults, while white youths are arrested for a disproportionate share of arsons. Among Part II crimes, white youths are disproportionately arrested for alcohol-related violations.

The racial gap in the juvenile arrest rate has widened during the past decade. African American youths have experienced a steady increase in their arrest rates, whereas rates for other groups have remained stable.

Self-Report Differences Official statistics show that minority youths are much more likely than white youths to be arrested for serious criminal behavior. To many delinquency experts, this pattern reflects discrimination in the juvenile justice system. In other words, African American youths are more likely to be formally arrested by the police, who, in contrast, will treat white youths informally. One way to examine this issue is to compare the racial differences in self-reported data with those found in the official delinquency records. Given the disproportionate numbers of African Americans arrested, charges of racial discrimination would be supported if we found little difference between the number of self-reported minority and white crimes.

Early researchers found that the relationship between race and self-reported delinquency was virtually nonexistent.[15] This suggests that racial differences in the official crime data may reflect the fact that African American youths have a much greater chance of being arrested and officially processed.[16] Self-report studies also suggest that the delinquent behavior rates of African American and white teenagers are generally similar and that differences in arrest statistics may indicate discrimination by police.[17] The MTF survey, for example, generally shows that offending differences between African American and white youths are marginal.[18] However, some experts warn that African American youths may underreport more serious crimes, limiting the ability of self-reports to be a valid indicator of racial differences in the crime rate.[19]

Are the Data Valid? The view that the disproportionate amount of African American official delinquency is a result of bias has found some support in research studies. For example, recent research shows that juvenile suspects belonging to ethnic minorities who are male, and are poor, are more likely to be formally arrested than suspects who are white, female, and affluent.[20]

Juvenile court judges may see the offenses committed by African American youths as more serious than those committed by white offenders.[21] Judges seem more willing to give white defendants lenient sentences if, for example, they show strong family ties or live in two-parent households.[22] Any form of racial bias is crucial because possession of a prior record increases the likelihood that upon subsequent contact, police will formally arrest a suspect rather than release the individual with a warning.[23]

Although evidence of racial bias does exist in the justice system, there is enough correspondence between official and self-report data to conclude that racial differences in the crime rate are real.[24] Samuel Walker, Cassia Spohn, and Miriam DeLone found that African American youths are arrested at a disproportionately high rate, and that for crimes such as robbery and assault, this is a result of offending rates rather than bias on the part of the criminal justice system.[25]

Explaining Racial Patterns   If, in fact, the racial differences in the delinquency rate recorded by official data are valid, one view is that they are a function of the institutionalized racism that is present in the United States. African Americans have suffered through a long history of discrimination, which has produced lasting emotional scars.[26]

Racism is still an element of daily life in the African American community, a factor that undermines faith in social and political institutions and weakens confidence in the justice system. These learned attitudes are supported by empirical evidence that, in at least some jurisdictions, young African American males are treated more harshly by the justice system than members of any other group.[27] There is evidence that in some legal jurisdictions African Americans, especially those who are indigent or unemployed, receive longer sentences than whites. It is possible that some judges view poor blacks as antisocial, considering them more dangerous and likely to recidivate than white offenders.[28] Yet when African Americans are the victims of crime, their predicament receives less public concern and media attention than that afforded white victims.[29]

Racial differentials in the crime rate may also be tied to frustrations over perceived racism, discrimination, and economic disparity. Even during times of economic growth, many economically disadvantaged African Americans believe they are being left out of the mainstream and feel a growing sense of frustration.[30] Such frustration may be magnified by frequent exposure to violence. African Americans who live in poor areas with high crime rates may be disproportionately violent because they are exposed to more violence in their daily lives than other racial and economic groups. Research has shown that such exposure is a significant risk factor for violent behavior.[31]

The burden of social and economic marginalization may be compounded by the weakening of the African American family structure. Family dissolution is tied to low employment rates among minority males, which places a strain on marriages. When families are weakened or disrupted, their ability to act as social control agents is compromised. It is not surprising that divorce and separation rates are significantly associated with homicide rates in the African American community.[32]

In summary, official data indicate that African American youths are arrested for more serious crimes than whites. However, self-report studies show that the differences in the rate of delinquency between the races is insignificant and that official differences are an artifact of bias in the justice system: Police are more likely to arrest and courts are more likely to convict young African Americans.[33] To those who believe that the official data have validity, the participation of African American youths in serious criminal behavior is generally viewed as a function of their socioeconomic position and the racism they face.

If you want to learn more
about race-related issues in America, check out the NAACP Web site at
http://www.naacp.org/
For an up-to-date list of Web links, go to
http://info.wadsworth.com/siegel

A CLOSER VIEW
Is the nation still plagued by racism and racial discrimination? To find an answer, go to InfoTrac College Edition and use these terms as keywords.

Social Class and Delinquency

Defining the relationship between economic status and delinquent behavior is a key element in the study of delinquency. If youth crime is purely a lower-class phenomenon, its cause must be rooted in the social forces that are found solely in lower-class areas: poverty, unemployment, social disorganization, culture conflict, and alienation.[34] However, if delinquent behavior is spread throughout the social structure, its cause must be related to some noneconomic factor: intelligence, personality, socialization, family dysfunction, educational failure, or peer influence. According to

To get information on the economic status of America's children, go to the federal government's Web site on children at *http://www.childstats.gov/* For an up-to-date list of Web links, go to *http://info.wadsworth.com/siegel*

this line of reasoning, providing jobs or economic incentives would have little effect on the crime rate.

At first glance, the relationship between class and crime seems clear. Youths who lack wealth or social standing are the most likely to use criminal means to achieve their goals. Communities that lack economic and social opportunities produce high levels of frustration. Kids who live in these areas believe that they can never compete socially or economically with adolescents being raised in more affluent areas. They may turn to criminal behavior for monetary gain and psychological satisfaction.[35] Family life is disrupted in these low-income areas, and law-violating youth groups thrive in a climate that undermines and neutralizes adult supervision.[36]

Research on Social Class and Delinquency The social class–delinquency relationship was challenged by pioneering self-report studies, specifically those that revealed no direct relationship between social class and the commission of delinquent acts.[37] Instead, socioeconomic class was related to the manner of official processing by police, court, and correctional agencies.[38] In other words, while both poor and affluent kids get into fights, shoplift, and take drugs, only the indigent are likely to be arrested and sent to juvenile court.[39]

Those who fault self-report studies point to the inclusion of trivial offenses, for example, using a false ID, in most self-report instruments. Although middle- and upper-class youths may appear to be as delinquent as those in the lower class, it is because they engage in significant amounts of status offenses. Lower-class youths are more likely to engage in serious delinquent acts.[40]

In sum, there are those experts who believe that antisocial behavior occurs at all levels of the social strata. Other experts argue that while some middle- and upper-class youths engage in some forms of minor illegal activity and theft offenses, it is members of the underclass who are responsible for the majority of serious delinquent acts.[41] The prevailing wisdom is that kids who engage in the most serious forms of delinquency (for example, gang violence) are more likely to be members of the lower class.

Age and Delinquency

Age is inversely related to criminality: As youthful offenders mature, their offending rates decline.[42] Official statistics tell us that young people are arrested at a disproportionate rate to their numbers in the population, and this finding is supported by victim surveys. Youths, 17 and under, make up about 10 percent of the total U.S. population, but they account for 27 percent of the index crime arrests and 17 percent of the arrests for all crimes. In contrast, adults, 50 and older, who make up 32 percent of the population, account for only about 10 percent of arrests. Self-report studies also indicate that rates for crimes such as assault, robbery, and trespass decline substantially between the ages of 17 and 23; the incidence of some illegal acts, such as substance abuse, may increase.[43]

Why Does Crime Decline with Age? Why do people commit less crime as they age? One view is that the relationship is constant: Regardless of race, sex, social class, intelligence, or any other social variable, people commit less crime as they age.[44] As mentioned in Chapter 1, this is referred to as the aging-out process, sometimes called desistance from crime, or **spontaneous remission**. According to this view, even the most chronic juvenile offenders will commit less crime as they age.[45]

Delinquency experts have developed a number of reasons for the aging-out process:

spontaneous remission (also known as desistance or aging-out process) The tendency for youths to reduce the frequency of their offending behavior as they age; aging out is thought to occur among all groups of offenders.

- Growing older means having to face the future. Young people, especially the indigent and antisocial, tend to "discount the future."[46] Why should they delay gratification when faced with an uncertain future?
- With maturity comes the ability to resist the "quick fix" to problems.[47] Research shows that some kids may turn to crime as a way to solve the problems

WHY DOES CRIME DECLINE WITH AGE? One reason may be that with maturity comes an increased level of responsibility. Crime may be an exciting social activity that provides adventure, but such risky behavior is inconsistent with the responsibilities of young people who marry, enlist in the armed services, or enroll in vocational training courses. It is unlikely that the teen father shown here would risk committing a foolish crime.

of adolescence, loneliness, frustration, and fear of peer rejection. As they mature, conventional means of problem solving become available. Life experience helps former delinquents seek nondestructive solutions to their personal problems.[48]

- Maturation coincides with increased levels of responsibility. Petty crimes are a risky and exciting social activity that provides adventure in an otherwise boring world. As youths grow older, they take on new responsibilities that are inconsistent with criminality.[49] For example, young people who marry, enlist in the armed services, or enroll in vocational training courses are less likely to pursue criminal activities.[50]
- Personalities can change with age. As youths mature, rebellious youngsters may develop increased self-control and be able to resist antisocial behavior.[51]
- Young adults become more aware of the risks that accompany crime. As adults, they are no longer protected by the kindly arms of the juvenile justice system.[52]

Does Age Matter?   There are also those experts who disagree with the concept of spontaneous remission. They suggest that age is one important determinant of crime but that other factors directly associated with a person's lifestyle, such as peer relations, also affect offending rates.[53] Evidence exists, for example, that the **age of onset** of a delinquent career has an important effect on its length: Those who demonstrate antisocial tendencies at a very early age are more likely to commit more crime for a longer duration. According to this view, there are two classes of offenders. The first begin committing crime in late adolescence, typically with their peers, and then cease offending as they mature and enter young adulthood. These juvenile criminals desist when they begin to realize that crime is too dangerous, physically taxing, and unrewarding, and punishments too harsh and long lasting, to become a way of life.[54] The second group of delinquents are those who begin their offending careers early

age of onset Age at which youths begin their delinquent careers; early onset is believed to be linked with chronic offending patterns.

in life and maintain a high rate of offending throughout their lifespan. Early onset of crime is a marker for their chronic offending patterns. The phenomenon of chronic offending is discussed in more detail next.

Chronic Offending: Careers in Delinquency

early onset The outbreak of deviant or delinquent behavior in preadolescence, which is generally viewed as a precursor of chronic offending in adolescence and which generally continues into adulthood.

A CLOSER VIEW
What factors predict the onset of chronic offending? One suspected cause is dysfunctional family life. To find out more, go to InfoTrac College Edition and read Deborah Gorman-Smith, Patrick H. Tolan, Rolf Loeber, and David B. Henry, "Relation of Family Problems to Patterns of Delinquent Involvement among Urban Youth," *Journal of Abnormal Child Psychology* 26(5): 319 (October 1998).

Although most adolescents age out of crime, a relatively small number of youths begin to violate the law early in their lives (**early onset**) and continue at a high rate well into adulthood (persistence).[55] The association between early onset and high-rate persistent offending has been demonstrated in samples drawn from a variety of cultures, time periods, and offender types.[56] These offenders are resistant to change and seem immune to the effects of punishment. Arrest, prosecution, and conviction do little to slow down their offending careers. These so-called chronic offenders are responsible for a significant amount of all delinquent and criminal activity.

Current interest in the delinquent life cycle was also prompted by the "discovery" in the 1970s of the chronic delinquent offender. According to this view, a relatively small number of youthful offenders commit a significant percentage of all serious crimes, and many of these same offenders grow up to become chronic adult criminals.

Chronic offenders can be distinguished from other delinquent youths. Many youthful law violators are apprehended for a single instance of criminal behavior such as shoplifting or joyriding. Chronic offenders begin their delinquent careers at a young age (under 10 years old, referred to as early onset), have serious and persistent brushes with the law, and may be excessively violent and destructive. They do not age out of crime but continue their law-violating behavior into adulthood.[57] Most research shows that early and repeated delinquent activity is the best predictor of future adult criminality.

A number of research efforts have set out to chronicle the careers of serious delinquent offenders. The next sections describe these initiatives.

Landmark Study: *Delinquency in a Birth Cohort*

chronic recidivists (also known as chronic juvenile offenders, chronic delinquent offenders, or chronic delinquents) Youths who have been arrested four or more times during their minority and perpetuate a striking majority of serious criminal acts; this small group, known as the "chronic 6 percent," is believed to engage in a significant portion of all delinquent behavior; these youths do not age out of crime but continue their criminal behavior into adulthood.

The concept of the chronic career offender is most closely associated with the research efforts of Marvin Wolfgang.[58] In 1972, Wolfgang, Robert Figlio, and Thorsten Sellin published a landmark study, *Delinquency in a Birth Cohort*. They followed the delinquent careers of a cohort of 9,945 boys born in Philadelphia from birth until they reached age 18. Data were obtained from police files and school records. Socioeconomic status was determined by locating the residence of each member of the cohort and assigning him the median family income for that area. About one-third of the boys (3,475) had some police contact. The remaining two-thirds (6,470) had none. Those boys who had at least one contact with the police committed a total of 10,214 offenses.

The most significant discovery of Wolfgang and his associates was that of the so-called chronic offender. The data indicated that 54 percent (1,862) of the sample's delinquent youths were repeat offenders. The repeaters could be further categorized as nonchronic recidivists and **chronic recidivists.** Nonchronic recidivists had been arrested more than once but fewer than five times. The 627 boys labeled chronic recidivists had been arrested five times or more. Although these offenders accounted for only 18 percent of the delinquent population (6 percent of the total sample), they were responsible for 52 percent of all offenses. Known today as the "chronic 6 percent," this group perpetrated 71 percent of the homicides, 82 percent of the robberies, and 64 percent of the aggravated assaults.

Arrest and juvenile court experience did little to deter chronic offenders. In fact, the greater the punishment, the more likely they were to engage in repeat delinquent behavior. Strict punishment also increased the probability that further court action would be taken. Two factors stood out as encouraging recidivism: the seriousness of the original offense and the severity of the punishment. The researchers concluded that efforts of the juvenile justice system to eliminate delinquent behavior may be futile.

Wolfgang and his colleagues conducted a second cohort study with children born in 1958 and substantiated the finding that a relatively few chronic offenders are responsible for a significant portion of all delinquent acts.[59] Wolfgang's results have been duplicated in a number of research studies conducted in locales across the United States and also in Great Britain.[60]

Who Becomes a Chronic Delinquent?

Who is at risk of becoming a chronic offender? As might be expected, kids who have been exposed to a variety of personal and social problems at an early age are the most at risk for repeat offending. One important study of delinquent offenders in Orange County, California, conducted by Michael Schumacher and Gwen Kurz, found that seven factors (see Exhibit 2.3) could predict chronic offending and that those youths who manifested these problems in the home and at school were at high risk for repeat offending.[61]

Other research studies have found that early involvement in criminal activity (for example, getting arrested before age 15), relatively low intellectual development, and parental drug involvement were the key predictive factors for chronicity.[62]

Stability in Crime: From Delinquent to Criminal

Do chronic juvenile offenders grow up to become chronic adult criminals? One study that followed a sample (approximately 10%) of the original Philadelphia cohort (974 subjects) to age 30 found that 70 percent of the "persistent" adult offenders had also been chronic juvenile offenders. Chronic juvenile offenders had an 80 percent chance of becoming adult offenders and a 50 percent chance of being arrested four or more

Exhibit 2.3   Characteristics That Predict Chronic Offending

School Behavior/Performance Factor

- Attendance problems (truancy or a pattern of "skipping" school)
- Behavior problems (recent suspensions or expulsion)
- Poor grades (failing two or more classes)

Family Problem Factor

- Poor parental supervision and control
- Significant family problems (illness, substance abuse, discord)
- Criminal family members
- Documented child abuse, neglect, or family violence

Substance Abuse Factor

- Alcohol or drugs by minors in any way but experimentation

Delinquency Factor

- Stealing pattern of behavior
- Runaway pattern of behavior
- Gang member or associate

Source: Michael Schumacher and Gwen Kurz, *The 8% Solution: Preventing Serious Repeat Juvenile Crime* (Thousand Oaks, CA: Sage Publications, 1999).

times as adults.[63] Paul Tracy and Kimberly Kempf-Leonard conducted a follow-up study of all subjects in the second 1958 cohort study by Wolfgang and his associates. By age 26, Cohort II subjects were displaying the same behavior patterns as their older peers. Kids who started their delinquent careers early, committed a violent crime, and continued offending throughout adolescence were most likely to persist in criminal behavior as adults. Delinquents who began their offending careers with serious offenses or who quickly increased the severity of their offending early in life were most likely to persist in their criminal behavior into adulthood. Severity of offending rather than frequency of criminal behavior had the greatest impact on later adult criminality.[64] Using data from the second birth cohort, Kempf-Leonard and her associates found that delinquents can be divided into different subgroups based on the seriousness of their offending, and that those falling into the most serious category (chronic delinquents who commit violent acts) have a much greater chance of becoming an adult offender than other delinquent youths (see Table 2.4).[65]

Children who are found to be disruptive and antisocial as early as age 5 or 6 are the most likely to exhibit stable, long-term patterns of disruptive behavior through adolescence.[66] They have measurable behavior problems in areas such as learning and motor skills, cognitive abilities, family relations, and other areas of social, psychological, and physical functioning.[67] Youthful offenders who persist are more likely to abuse alcohol, get into trouble while in military service, become economically dependent, have lower aspirations, get divorced or separated, and have a weak employment record.[68] They do not specialize in one type of crime; rather, they engage in a variety of criminal acts, including theft, drugs, and violent offenses. Apprehension and punishment seem to have little effect on their offending behavior. A recent study that followed the offending careers of nearly 2,000 serious, chronic youthful offenders for 10 years after their release from the California Youth Authority found they were arrested on 24,615 occasions over the following decade—an average of 22 arrests each. More than 90 percent had been rearrested during the following decade, and their arrests were for an average of nine property crimes, four violent offenses, three drug crimes, and six other type crimes.[69] This recent research suggests the axiom, "The best predictor of future behavior is past behavior."

Policy Implications

Efforts to chart the life cycle of crime and delinquency will have a major influence on both theory and policy. Rather than simply asking why youths become delinquent or commit antisocial acts, theorists are charting the onset, escalation, frequency, and cessation of delinquent behavior. Research on delinquent careers has also influenced

Table 2.4 Delinquency Types and Probability of Becoming an Adult Offender

Delinquent Type	Probability of Becoming an Adult Offender	
	Male	Female
Nondelinquent	14%	2.5%
Total all delinquents	42%	12%
Serious delinquent	52%	25%
Violent delinquent	56%	26%
Chronic delinquent	63%	29%
Serious and chronic	64%	44%
Violent and chronic	64%	44%

Source: Kimberly Kempf-Leonard, Paul Tracy, and James Howell, "Serious, Violent, and Chronic Juvenile Offenders: The Relationship of Delinquency Career Types to Adult Criminality," *Justice Quarterly* 18:449–78 (2001).

policy. If a relatively few offenders commit a great proportion of all delinquent acts and then persist as adult criminals, it follows that steps should be taken to limit their criminal opportunities.[70] One approach is to identify persistent offenders at the beginning of their offending careers and provide early treatment.[71] This might be facilitated by research aimed at identifying traits (for example, impulsive personalities) that can be used to classify high-risk offenders.[72] Because many of these youths suffer from a variety of problems, treatment must be aimed at a broad range of educational, family, vocational, and psychological problems. Focusing on a single problem, such as a lack of employment, may be ineffective.[73]

Juvenile Victimization

Juveniles are also victims of crime, and data from victim surveys can help us understand the nature of juvenile victimization. Most of what is known about juvenile victimization comes from an ongoing cooperative effort of the Bureau of Justice Statistics of the U.S. Department of Justice and the U.S. Census Bureau, called the National Crime Victimization Survey (NCVS). The NCVS is a household survey of victims of criminal behavior that measures the nature of the crime and the characteristics of victims.

The total annual sample size of the NCVS has been about 43,000 households containing about 80,000 individuals. The sample is broken down into subsamples of 10,000 households, and each group is interviewed twice a year. The NCVS has been conducted annually for more than 15 years.

Victimization in the United States

victimizations The number of people who are victims of criminal acts; young teens are fifteen times more likely than older adults (age 65 and over) to be victims of crimes.

The NCVS provides estimates of the total number of personal contact crimes (assault, rape, robbery) and household **victimizations** (burglary, larceny, vehicle theft). The survey indicates that currently about 25 million criminal incidents occur each

© Michael Newman/ Photo Edit

JUVENILES ARE MUCH more likely to become crime victims than adults. They have a more dangerous lifestyle, which places them at risk for crime. They spend a great deal of time in one of the most dangerous areas in the community, the local school, and hang out with the most dangerous people, fellow teenagers!

year. Being the target or victim of rape, robbery, or assault is a terrible burden and one that can have considerable long-term consequences. If we translate the value of pain, emotional trauma, disability, and risk of death into dollar terms, the cost is $450 billion, or $1,800 for every person in the United States.[74] At first glance these figures seem overwhelming, but victimization rates are stable or declining for most crime categories.

Many of the differences between NCVS data and official statistics can be attributed to the fact that victimizations are frequently not reported. More than half the crimes of violence, three-quarters of personal crimes of theft, and two-thirds of household crimes go unreported to the police.

Young Victims NCVS data indicate that young people are much more likely to be the victims of crime than adults (Table 2.5).[75]

The chance of victimization declines with age. The difference is particularly striking when we compare teens under age 19 with people over age 65—teens are more than 20 times as likely to become victims than their grandparents. Children ages 17 and under make up about 10 percent of the population and are the victims of more than 20 percent of all violent crimes. In contrast, people over age 50—more than 30 percent of the population—account for about 7 percent of all victimization.

The victim data also show that male teenagers have a significantly higher chance than females of becoming victims of violent crime, and that African American youth have a greater chance of becoming victims of violent crimes than white teenagers of the same age.[76]

As part of their Monitoring the Future program, the Institute for Social Research also collects data on teen victimization. The most recent data available (2000)

Table 2.5 **Number of Violent Crimes per 1,000 Persons Age 12 or Older**

Age	1999	2000	% Change
12–15 years	74.4	60.1	–19.2*
16–19 years	77.4	64.3	–16.9*
20–24 years	68.5	49.4	–27.9*
25–34 years	36.3	34.8	–4.1
35–49 years	25.2	21.8	–13.5*
50–64 years	14.4	13.7	–4.9
65+ years	3.8	3.7	–2.6

Source: Callie Marie Rennison, *Criminal Victimization 2000, Changes 1999–2000, with Trends 1993–2000* (Washington, DC: Bureau of Justice Statistics, 2001), p. 4.

Table 2.6 **Juvenile Victimization: Percentage of Youth Who Have Been Victimized, by Gender and Race**

Crime Category	Total	Males	Female	Black	White
Something stolen < $50	45	50	41	54	43
Something stolen > $50	26	29	22	39	22
Deliberately damaged property	30	37	24	28	30
Injured with a weapon	4	7	2	4	5
Threatened with a weapon	16	23	9	19	14
Injured without a weapon	14	18	11	14	14
Threatened without weapon	28	36	21	28	29

Source: *Monitoring the Future, 2001* (Ann Arbor, MI: Institute for Social Research, 2002).

indicate that each year a significant number of adolescents become crime victims (Table 2.6). This and other self-report surveys reveal that the NCVS seriously *underreports* juvenile victimization, and that the true rate of juvenile victimization may actually be several times higher.[77]

Who Victimizes Youth?

NCVS data can also tell us something about the relationship between victims and offenders. This information is available because victims of violent personal crimes, such as assault and robbery, can identify the age, sex, and race of their attackers.

In general, teens tend to be victimized by their peers. A majority of teens were shown to have been victimized by other teens, whereas victims age 20 and over identified their attackers as being 21 or older. However, people in almost all age groups who were victimized by *groups* of offenders identified their attackers as teenagers. Violent crime victims report that a disproportionate number of their attackers are young, ranging in age from 16 to 25.

The data also tell us that victimization is intraracial (within race). White teenagers tend to be victimized by white teens, and African American teenagers tend to be victimized by African American teens.

Most teens are victimized by people with whom they are acquainted, and their victimization is more likely to occur during the day. In contrast, adults are more often victimized by strangers, and at night. One explanation for this pattern is that youths are at greatest risk from their own family and relatives. (Chapter 7 deals with the issue of child abuse and neglect.) Another possibility is that many teenage victimizations occur at school. About 10 percent of all crimes of violence take place in school buildings or on school grounds.

While most teens are victimized by someone they know, there is a frightening new phenomenon that may alter that pattern: Internet victimization. This new threat is discussed in the accompanying Focus on Delinquency box.

Victimization Risk

Children who have high-risk lifestyles—drinking, taking drugs, getting involved in crime—maintain a much greater chance of victimization.[78] For example, young runaways are at high risk for victimization; the more time they are exposed to street life, the greater their risk of becoming crime victims.[79] Teenage males have an extremely high victimization risk because their lifestyle places them at risk both at school and once they leave school grounds. They spend a great deal of time hanging out with their friends and pursuing recreational fun. Their friends may give them a false ID so they can go drinking in the neighborhood bar; or they may hang out in taverns at night, which places them at risk because many fights and assaults occur in places that serve liquor. Those who have histories of engaging in serious delinquency, getting involved in gangs, carrying guns, and selling drugs have an increased chance of being shot and killed themselves.[80]

As they mature, kids with high-risk lifestyles continue to have a high victimization risk, which continues into young adulthood. College students who spend several nights each week partying and who take recreational drugs are much more likely to suffer violent crime than those who avoid such risky academic lifestyles.[81]

The association between lifestyle and juvenile victimization may be explained in part by the fact that kids who bear a number of risk factors for crime, such as carrying guns, and engage in delinquent and other antisocial activity, may be at the highest risk for victimization. This phenomenon is explored further in the Focus on Delinquency box entitled "Delinquent and Victim: One and the Same?"

Focus on Delinquency

Internet Victimization

Today some predators are using modern Internet technology to prey on innocent victims. Recent years have seen a great increase in access to and use of the Internet. By the end of 1998, more than 40 percent of all American homes had computers, and 25 percent had Internet access. As of 2002, about 45 million children are online, and by 2005 the number is expected to grow to 77 million.

Predatory criminals use the Internet to victimize children in a number of different ways:

- Enticing them through online contact for the purpose of engaging them in sexual acts.
- Using the Internet for the production, manufacture, and distribution of child pornography.
- Using the Internet to expose youths to child pornography and encourage them to exchange pornography.
- Enticing and exploiting children for the purpose of sexual tourism (travel with the intent to engage in sexual behavior) for commercial gain and/or personal gratification.

Several characteristics distinguish Internet crimes from other crimes committed against children:

- Physical contact between the child and the perpetrator does not need to occur for a child to become a victim or for a crime to be committed. Innocent pictures or images of children can be digitally transformed into pornographic material and distributed across the Internet without the victims' knowledge.
- The Internet provides a source for repeated, long-term victimization of a child that can last for years, often without the victim's knowledge. Once a child's picture is displayed on the Internet, it can remain there forever. Images can stay on the Internet indefinitely without damage to the quality of the image.
- These crimes transcend jurisdictional boundaries, often involving multiple victims from different communities, states, and countries. The geographic location of a child is not a primary concern for perpetrators who target victims over the Internet. Often, perpetrators travel hundreds of miles to different states and countries to engage in sexual acts with children they met over the Internet. Many of these cases involve local, state, federal, and international law enforcement entities in multiple jurisdictions.
- Many victims of Internet crimes do not disclose their victimization or even realize that they have been victims of a crime. Whereas children who experience physical or sexual abuse may disclose the abuse to a friend, teacher, or parent, many victims of Internet crimes remain anonymous until pictures or images are discovered by law enforcement during an investigation. The presumed anonymity of Internet activities often provides a false sense of security and secrecy for both the perpetrator and the victim.

A recent study by sociologist David Finkelhor sampled 1,501 youths, aged 10 to 17, who used the Internet regularly (at least once a month for the previous six months on a computer at home, at school, in a library, at someone else's home, or in some other place). Finkelhor found that 1 in 5 youths received a sexual approach or solicitation over the Internet during the prior 12 months. About 1 in 33 youths received an aggressive sexual solicitation during which a predator asked a young person to meet somewhere, called a young person on the phone, and/or sent the young person correspondence, money, or gifts through the U.S. postal service. One in 4 youths had an unwanted exposure in the past year to pictures of naked people or people having sex, and 1 in 17 youths were threatened or harassed in the past year.

Most of the young victims were not extremely disturbed about their experiences, and only a fraction of all episodes was reported to authorities such as the police, an Internet service provider, or a hotline. About 25 percent of the youths who encountered a sexual approach or solicitation told a parent. Almost 40 percent of those reporting an unwanted exposure to sexual material told a parent.

The survey results show that the Internet can be very dangerous. One in 5 youths who regularly use the Internet received sexual solicitations or approaches during a one-year period. In addition to pedophiles, other predators use the Internet. Nearly half (48%) of the offenders were other youths, and one-fourth of the aggressive episodes were initiated by females. Further, 77 percent of targeted youths were age 14 or older—not an age characteristically targeted by pedophiles. And though most youths reported not being distressed by sexual exposures online, 23 percent reported being very or extremely upset, 20 percent reported being very or extremely embarrassed, and 20 percent reported at least one symptom of stress.

Critical Thinking

1. Considering the danger posed by Internet victimization, should the Net be more closely regulated by the government?

InfoTrac College Edition Research

 To learn more about how the Internet has been used to exploit and victimize youth, use *Internet sex* and *Internet victimization* as key terms on InfoTrac College Edition.

Source: Office for Victims of Crime, Internet Crimes against Children Training Bulletin (Washington, DC: Office of Justice Programs, February 2001).

The Youngest Victims

Children under age 6 are often the target of criminal and sexual assaults. In the majority of instances, parents and other family members are the perpetrators (parents in about 36 percent of all instances, and nonparental family offenders another 17 percent).[82] A recent study finds that babysitters make up a relatively small portion

Delinquent and Victim: One and the Same?

Are adolescents with a high-risk lifestyle who commit delinquent acts themselves at great risk to become crime victims? This question intrigued researchers who have been conducting longitudinal studies in Denver and Pittsburgh.

To address this question they used data gathered in the Denver and Pittsburgh Youth Studies. The Denver Youth Survey began in 1987 and is based on a sample of 1,527 girls and boys ages 7, 9, 11, 13, and 15, randomly selected from more than 20,000 households, and repeatedly measured over time. The Pittsburgh Youth Study consisted of a random sample of 1,517 boys in the first, fourth, and seventh grades in inner-city public schools in 1987 and also subject to repeated contacts by the research team. The study employed a sample of nonvictims for means of comparison.

The researchers attempted to show whether kids who had a variety of personal and social risk factors were more likely to become crime victims than those who were risk free. They looked at a number of potential risk factors. Family risk factors included having a low socioeconomic status, being raised by parents who committed crimes, living in a single-parent household, and receiving poor parental supervision. Individual risk factors included receiving poor school grades; being involved in gang or group fights; carrying weapons; participating in serious assault, drug usage, and sales; associating with delinquent peers; and having a personality that could be labeled oppositional, hyperactive, or impulsive.

Delinquency and Victimization

The research team found that a striking percentage of youths in the two samples were crime victims and had suffered serious injury as a result of assaults or robberies. Among males, 11 percent in Pittsburgh and 20 percent in Denver reported having been a victim, as did 10 percent of the females in Denver.

Several risk factors were significantly related to victimization at both sites and for both genders. Kids who became victims of serious crime were more likely than nonvictims to have participated in gang/group fights, carried a weapon, committed a serious assault, sold drugs, and associated with delinquent peers. Youths characterized by any one of these risk factors were generally two to four times more likely to become a crime victim than a youth who did not have the risk factor. For example, between 24 and 40 percent of males involved in gang/group fights had themselves been seriously injured; among females, 27 percent of those involved in gang/group fights had been seriously injured.

Carrying a weapon was another surefire way to become a crime victim. Males who carried weapons were approximately three times more likely to be victimized than those who did not carry weapons—27 percent to 33 percent of the weapons carriers became victims, as opposed to only 10 percent who did not carry weapons. To a somewhat lesser extent, family and other risk factors were associated with elevated levels of victimization. These included coming from a single-parent household, having an oppositional and hyperactive personality, and using drugs. Among males only, risk factors also included having poor school grades, being impulsive, and having parents involved in criminal activities.

There was a direct correlation between number of risk factors youths had and their victimization potential. For example, only 6–8 percent of males with no risk factors were victimized compared with 50–70 percent who had four or more risk factors. Among females, those with no risk factors had a 5 percent chance of becoming victims; among those with two or more risk factors, 42 percent became victims. One of the most striking findings was that kids who carried a weapon and engaged in fights were the ones most prone to becoming victims themselves. Among males, 40–46 percent of those individuals who carried weapons and were assaultive were themselves victims; among females who carried weapons and were assaultive, 30 percent were victims.

Analysis of the data drawn from the Denver and Pittsburgh cohort studies shows that maintaining a high-risk lifestyle is a key factor in juvenile victimization. For the majority of victims, successful delinquency prevention procedures are likely to prevent victimization because most victims are themselves involved in delinquency.

Critical Thinking

1. Analysis of the data drawn from the Denver and Pittsburgh cohort studies shows that maintaining a high-risk lifestyle is a key factor in juvenile victimization. Is it possible to conclude, therefore, that successful delinquency prevention programs are likely to reduce juvenile victimization because most victims are themselves involved in delinquency?

InfoTrac College Edition Research

Though the present research shows a clear link between engaging in risky behaviors and victimization, not all studies have reached the same result or conclusion. To read a study conducted in Canada with dissimilar findings, go to InfoTrac College Edition and look up Wendy C. Regoeczi, "Adolescent Violent Victimization and Offending: Assessing the Extent of the Link," *Canadian Journal of Criminology* 42(4):493 (October 2000).

Source: Rolf Loeber, Larry Kalb, and David Huizinga, *Juvenile Delinquency and Serious Injury Victimization* (Washington, DC: Office of Juvenile Justice and Delinquency Prevention, 2001).

of offenders (0.5%) who commit violent crimes against all children but somewhat more (about 4%) of those who committed crimes against young children (those under age 6).

Complete strangers accounted for 11 percent of those arrested for offenses against juveniles and 5.6 percent against young children. Despite some sensational cases, the number of children seriously harmed (abducted or murdered) by strangers is less than commonly thought.[83] Each year there are about 50 cases in which it can be verified that a child was abducted and killed by a stranger; in another 100 cases the circumstances remain unknown, except that a child was killed by a stranger. Although stranger victimizations may be less common than once thought, the fact that as many as three children are abducted and killed by strangers every week is extremely disturbing.

SUMMARY

Official delinquency refers to youths who are arrested. What is known comes from the FBI's *Uniform Crime Report* (UCR), an annual tally of crimes reported to police by citizens. In addition, the FBI gathers arrest statistics from local police departments. From these, it is possible to determine the number of youths who are arrested each year, along with their age, race, and gender.

About 2 million youths are arrested annually. There has been an increase in the number of juveniles arrested for violent crimes. Though it is not certain why this trend has developed, possible explanations include involvement in gang activity, drug abuse, and teen gun ownership.

Dissatisfaction with the UCR prompted criminologists to develop other means of measuring delinquent behavior. Self-reports are surveys in which subjects are asked to describe their misbehavior. Although self-reports indicate that many more crimes are committed than are known to the police, they also show that the delinquency rate is rather stable.

The third method of gathering information on delinquency involves victim surveys. The National Crime Victimization Survey (NCVS) is an annual national survey of the victims of crime conducted by agencies of the federal government. Teenagers are much more likely to become victims of crime than are people in other age groups. All three sources of crime statistics agree that young people commit more crimes than adults.

Delinquents are disproportionately male, although female delinquency rates are rising faster than those for males. Minority youths are overrepresented in the delinquency rate, especially for violent crime. Experts are split on the cause of racial differences. Some believe the differences are a function of system bias; others see them as representing actual differences in the delinquency rate. Disagreement also exists over the relationship between class position and delinquency. Some hold that adolescent crime is a lower-class phenomenon, whereas others see it throughout the social structure. Problems in methodology have obscured the true class-crime relationship. However, official statistics indicate that lower-class youths are responsible for the most serious criminal acts.

There is general agreement that delinquency rates decline with age. Some experts believe this phenomenon is universal, whereas others believe a small group of offenders persists in crime at a high rate. The age-crime relationship has spurred research on the nature of delinquency over the life course. One discovery is the chronic persistent offender, who begins his or her offending career early in life and persists as an adult. Wolfgang and his colleagues identified chronic offenders in a series of cohort studies conducted in Philadelphia. Ongoing research has identified the characteristics of persistent offenders as they mature, and both personality and social factors help predict long-term offending patterns.

KEY TERMS

Federal Bureau of Investigation (FBI)	Part I offenses, index crimes	dark figures of crime	age of onset
		disaggregated	early onset
Uniform Crime Report (UCR)	Part II offenses	self-reports	chronic recidivists
	official delinquency	spontaneous remission	victimizations

QUESTIONS FOR DISCUSSION

1. What factors contribute to the aging-out process?

2. Why are males more delinquent than females? Is it a matter of lifestyle, culture, or physical properties?

3. Discuss the racial differences found in the crime rate. What factors account for differences in the African American and white crime rates?

4. Should kids who have been arrested more than three times be given mandatory incarceration sentences?

5. Do you believe that self-reports are an accurate method of gauging the nature and extent of delinquent behavior?

VIEWPOINT

"Kids are also victimized at a higher rate than adults—most are attacked by acquaintances. Such statistics on youth violence and media portrayals of the incidents they represent have produced a tremendous climate of fear in our nation and a super-predator mentality that is changing the way policies are made and the way people live.

"I think it's time for us to shift how we are framing the problem of juvenile violence. While it is true that we need to be vigilant in ensuring our immediate safety through our law enforcement and correctional efforts, it is also true that if we are to find long-lasting solutions, we must explore the predator theme from a different vantage point."

So says Shay Bilchick, director of the Office of Juvenile Justice and Delinquency Prevention. To learn more, go to InfoTrac College Edition, and look at Shay Bilchik, "Prevention and Teamwork Key to Fighting Juvenile Crime," *Corrections Today* 59:42 (1997). To see more on this topic, use *juvenile violence* as a key term.

NOTES

1. Jim Yardley, "A Violent Life: Gangs and Guns Shaped a Suspect in the Death of an Officer," *New York Times,* 10 August 1998, p. A16; Mayor Rudolph W. Giuliani, "Early Release from Prison Causes Another Preventable Tragedy," Mayor's WINS radio address, 2 August 1998.

2. Howard Snyder and Melissa Sickmund, *Juvenile Offenders and Victims: A National Report* (Washington, DC: National Center for Juvenile Justice, 1995).

3. Federal Bureau of Investigation, *Crime in the United States, 1999* (Washington, DC: U.S. Government Printing Office, 2000). Hereinafter cited as FBI, UCR, 1999.

4. Thomas Bernard, "Juvenile Crime and the Transformation of Juvenile Justice: Is There a Juvenile Crime Wave?" *Justice Quarterly* 16:336–56 (1999).

5. James A. Fox, *Trends in Juvenile Violence: A Report to the United States Attorney General on Current and Future Rates of Juvenile Offending* (Boston: Northeastern University, 1996).

6. Steven Levitt, "The Limited Role of Changing Age Structure in Explaining Aggregate Crime Rates," *Criminology* 37:581–99 (1999).

7. Fox Butterfield, "Possible Manipulation of Crime Data Worries Top Police," *New York Times,* 3 August 1998, p.1.

8. A pioneering effort of self-report research is A. L. Porterfield's *Youth in Trouble* (Fort Worth, TX: Leo Potishman Foundation, 1946); for a review, see Robert Hardt and George Bodine, *Development of Self-Report Instruments in Delinquency Research: A Conference Report* (Syracuse, NY: Syracuse University Youth Development Center, 1965); see also Fred Murphy, Mary Shirley, and Helen Witmer, "The Incidence of Hidden Delinquency," *American Journal of Orthopsychiatry* 16:686–96 (1946).

9. Mallie Paschall, Miriam Ornstein, and Robert Flewelling, "African-American Male Adolescents' Involvement in the Criminal Justice System: The Criterion Validity of Self-Report Measures in a Prospective Study," *Journal of Research in Crime and Delinquency* 38:174–87 (2001).

10. For example, the following studies have noted the great discrepancy between official statistics and self-report studies: Maynard Erickson and LaMar Empey, "Court Records, Undetected Delinquency, and Decision-Making," *Journal of Criminal Law, Criminology, and Police Science* 54:456–69 (1963); Martin Gold, "Undetected Delinquent Behavior," *Journal of Research in Crime and Delinquency* 3:27–46 (1966); James Short and F. Ivan Nye, "Extent of Unrecorded Delinquency, Tentative Conclusions," *Journal of Criminal Law, Criminology, and Police Science* 49: 296–302 (1958).

11. Jerald Bachman, Lloyd Johnston, and Patrick O'Malley, *Monitoring the Future: Questionnaire Responses from the Nation's High School Seniors, 2000* (Ann Arbor, MI:

Institute for Social Research, 2001). Hereinafter cited as Monitoring the Future, 2000.

12. For a discussion of sex bias, see Meda Chesney-Lind, "Guilty by Reason of Sex: Young Women and the Criminal Justice System." Paper presented at the American Society of Criminology meeting, Toronto, 1980.

13. Michael Hindelang, Travis Hirschi, and Joseph Weis, *Measuring Delinquency* (Beverly Hills: Sage, 1981); Gary Jensen and Raymond Eve, "Sex Differences in Delinquency: An Examination of Popular Sociological Explanation," *Criminology* 13:427–48 (1976); Michael Hindelang, "Age, Sex, and the Versatility of Delinquent Involvements," *Social Problems* 18:522–35 (1979); James Short and F. Ivan Nye, "Extent of Unrecorded Juvenile Delinquency, Tentative Conclusions," *Journal of Criminal Law, Criminology, and Police Science* 49:296–302 (1958).

14. For a review, see Meda Chesney-Lind and Randall Shelden, *Girls, Delinquency and Juvenile Justice* (Pacific Grove, CA: Brooks/Cole, 1992), pp. 7–14.

15. Leroy Gould, "Who Defines Delinquency? A Comparison of Self-Report and Officially Reported Indices of Delinquency for Three Racial Groups," *Social Problems* 16:325–36 (1969); Harwin Voss, "Ethnic Differentials in Delinquency in Honolulu," *Journal of Criminal Law, Criminology, and Police Science* 54:322–27 (1963); Ronald Akers, Marvin Krohn, Marcia Radosevich, and Lonn Lanza-Kaduce, "Social Characteristics and Self-Reported Delinquency," in Gary Jensen, ed., *Sociology of Delinquency* (Beverly Hills: Sage, 1981), pp. 48–62.

16. David Huizinga and Delbert Elliott, "Juvenile Offenders: Prevalence, Offender Incidence, and Arrest Rates by Race," *Crime and Delinquency* 33:206–23 (1987); see also Dale Dannefer and Russell Schutt, "Race and Juvenile Justice Processing in Court and Police Agencies," *American Journal of Sociology* 87:1113–32 (1982).

17. Paul Tracy, "Race and Class Differences in Official and Self-Reported Delinquency," in Marvin Wolfgang, Terrence Thornberry, and Robert Figlio, eds., *From Boy to Man, from Delinquency to Crime* (Chicago: University of Chicago Press, 1987), p. 120.

18. Monitoring the Future, pp. 102–104.

19. Samuel Walker, Cassia Spohn, and Miriam DeLone, *The Color of Justice: Race, Ethnicity and Crime in America* (Belmont, CA: Brooks/Cole, 1992), pp. 46–47.

20. Miriam Sealock and Sally Simpson, "Unraveling Bias in Arrest Decisions: The Role of Juvenile Offender Typescripts," *Justice Quarterly* 15:427–57 (1998).

21. Christina Polsenberg and Kenneth Jackson, "Putting Race into Context: Race, Juvenile Justice Processing and Urbanization." Paper presented at the American Society of Criminology meeting, Boston, November 1995 (updated version, 1996); for a general review, see Carl Pope and William Feyerherm, "Minority Status and Juvenile Justice Processing (Part I)," *Criminal Justice Abstracts* 22:327–35 (1990); see also Douglas Smith and Jody Klein, "Police Control of Interpersonal Disputes," *Social Problems* 31:468–81 (1984).

22. Christina DeJong and Kenneth Jackson, "Putting Race into Context: Race, Juvenile Justice Processing, and Urbanization," *Justice Quarterly* 15:487–504 (1998).

23. Donna Bishop and Charles Frazier, "The Influence of Race in Juvenile Justice Processing," *Journal of Research in Crime and Delinquency* 25:242–63 (1989).

24. For a general review, see William Wilbanks, *The Myth of a Racist Criminal Justice System* (Pacific Grove, CA: Brooks/Cole, 1987).

25. Walker, Spohn, and DeLone, *The Color of Justice,* pp. 47–48.

26. Fox Butterfield, *All God's Children: The Bosket Family and the American Tradition of Violence* (New York: Avon, 1996).

27. Michael Leiber and Jayne Stairs, "Race, Contexts and the Use of Intake Diversion," *Journal of Research in Crime and Delinquency* 36:56–86 (1999); Darrell Steffensmeier, Jeffery Ulmer, and John Kramer, "The Interaction of Race, Gender, and Age in Criminal Sentencing: The Punishment Cost of Being Young, Black, and Male," *Criminology* 36:763–98 (1998).

28. Tracy Nobiling, Cassia Spohn, and Miriam DeLone, "A Tale of Two Counties: Unemployment and Sentence Severity," *Justice Quarterly* 15:459–86(1998).

29. Alexander Weiss and Steven Chermak, "The News Value of African-American Victims: An Examination of the Media's Presentation of Homicide," *Journal of Crime and Justice* 21:71–84 (1998).

30. Melvin Thomas, "Race, Class and Personal Income: An Empirical Test of the Declining Significance of Race Thesis, 1968–1988," *Social Problems* 40:328–39 (1993).

31. Mallie Paschall, Robert Flewelling, and Susan Ennett, "Racial Differences in Violent Behavior among Young Adults: Moderating and Confounding Effects," *Journal of Research in Crime and Delinquency* 35:148–65 (1998).

32. Julie Phillips, "Variation in African-American Homicide Rates: An Assessment of Potential Explanations," *Criminology* 35:527–59 (1997).

33. Carl Pope and William Feyerherm, "Minority Status and Juvenile Processing: An Assessment of the Research Literature." Paper presented at the American Society of Criminology meeting, Reno, Nevada, November 1989.

34. Jefferey Fagan, Elizabeth Piper, and Melinda Moore, "Violent Delinquents and Urban Youths," *Criminology* 24:439–71 (1986).

35. Robert Agnew, "A General Strain Theory of Community Differences in Crime Rates," *Journal of Research in Crime and Delinquency* 36:123–55 (1999).

36. Bonita Veysey and Steven Messner, "Further Testing of Social Disorganization Theory: An Elaboration of Sampson and Groves's 'Community Structure and Crime'," *Journal of Research in Crime and Delinquency* 36:156–74 (1999).

37. James Short and Ivan Nye, "Reported Behavior as a Criterion of Deviant Behavior," *Social Problems* 5:207–13 (1958).

38. Classic studies include Ivan Nye, James Short, and Virgil Olsen, "Socio-economic Status and Delinquent Behavior," *American Journal of Sociology* 63:381–89 (1958); Robert Dentler and Lawrence Monroe, "Social Correlates of Early Adolescent Theft," *American Sociological Review* 26:733–43 (1961); Charles Tittle, Wayne Villemez, and Douglas Smith, "The Myth of Social Class and Criminality: An Empirical Assessment of the Empirical Evidence," *American Sociological Review* 43:643–56 (1978).

39. R. Gregory Dunaway, Francis Cullen, Velmer Burton, and T. David Evans, "The Myth of Social Class and Crime Revisited: An Examination of Class and Adult Criminality," *Criminology* 38:589–632 (2000).

40. Delbert Eliott and Suzanne Ageton, "Reconciling Race and Class Differences in Self-Reported and Official Estimates of Delinquency," *American Sociological Review* 45:95–110 (1980); for a similar view, see John Braithwaite, "The Myth of Social Class and Criminality Reconsidered," *American*

Sociological Review 46:35–58 (1981); Margaret Farnworth, Terence Thornberry, Marvin Krohn, and Alan Lizotte, *Measurement in the Study of Class and Delinquency: Integrating Theory and Research,* working paper no. 4, rev. (Albany, NY: Rochester Youth Development Survey, 1992), p. 19.

41. G. Roger Jarjoura and Ruth Triplett, "Delinquency and Class: A Test of the Proximity Principle," *Justice Quarterly* 14:765–92 (1997).

42. See, generally, David Farrington, "Age and Crime," in Michael Tonry and Norval Morris, eds., *Crime and Justice, An Annual Review,* vol. 7 (Chicago: University of Chicago Press, 1986), pp. 189–250.

43. Patrick O'Malley, Jerald Bachman, and Lloyd Johnston, "Period, Age and Cohort Effects on Substance Abuse among Young Americans: A Decade of Change, 1976–1986," *American Journal of Public Health* 78:1315–21 (1989); Darrell Steffensmeier, Emilie Allan, Miles Harer, and Cathy Streifel, "Age and the Distribution of Crime," *American Journal of Sociology* 94:803–31 (1989); Alfred Blumstein and Jacqueline Cohen, "A Characterizing Criminal Careers," *Science* 237:985–91 (1987).

44. Travis Hirschi and Michael Gottfredson, "Age and the Explanation of Crime," *American Journal of Sociology* 89:552–84 (1983).

45. Michael Gottfredson and Travis Hirschi, "The True Value of Lambda Would Appear to Be Zero: An Essay on Career Criminals, Criminal Careers, Selective Incapacitation, Cohort Studies, and Related Topics," *Criminology* 24:213–34 (1986); further support for their position can be found in Lawrence Cohen and Kenneth Land, "Age Structure and Crime," *American Sociological Review* 52:170–83 (1987).

46. Edward Mulvey and John LaRosa, "Delinquency Cessation and Adolescent Development: Preliminary Data," *American Journal of Orthopsychiatry* 56:212–24 (1986).

47. Margo Wilson and Martin Daly, "Life Expectancy, Economic Inequality, Homicide, and Reproductive Timing in Chicago Neighbourhoods," *British Journal of Medicine* 31:1271–74 (1997).

48. Timothy Brezina, "Delinquent Problem-Solving: An Interpretive Framework for Criminological Theory and Research," *Journal of Research in Crime and Delinquency* 37:3–30 (2000).

49. Gordon Trasler, "Cautions for a Biological Approach to Crime," in Sarnoff Mednick, Terrie Moffitt, and Susan Stack, eds., *The Causes of Crime, New Biological Approaches* (Cambridge: Cambridge University Press, 1987), pp. 7–25.

50. Alicia Rand, "Transitional Life Events and Desistance from Delinquency and Crime," in Marvin Wolfgang, Terence Thornberry, and Robert Figlio, eds., *From Boy to Man, from Delinquency to Crime* (Chicago: University of Chicago Press, 1987), pp. 134–63.

51. Marc Le Blanc, "Late Adolescence Deceleration of Criminal Activity and Development of Self- and Social-Control," *Studies on Crime and Crime Prevention* 2:51–68 (1993).

52. Barry Glassner, Margaret Ksander, Bruce Berg, and Bruce Johnson, "Note on the Deterrent Effect of Juvenile vs. Adult Jurisdiction," *Social Problems* 31:219–21 (1983).

53. David Greenberg, "Age, Crime and Social Explanation," *American Journal of Sociology* 91:1–21 (1985).

54. Neal Shover and Carol Thompson, "Age, Differential Expectations, and Crime Desistance," *Criminology* 30:89–104 (1992).

55. D. Wayne Osgood, "The Covariation among Adolescent Problem Behaviors." Paper presented at the American Society of Criminology meeting, Baltimore, November 1990.

56. Stephen Tibbetts, "Low Birth Weight, Disadvantaged Environment and Early Onset: A Test of Moffitt's Interactional Hypothesis." Paper presented at the American Society of Criminology meeting, Boston, November 1995.

57. Arnold Barnett, Alfred Blumstein, and David Farrington, "A Prospective Test of a Criminal Career Model," *Criminology* 27:373–88 (1989).

58. Marvin Wolfgang, Robert Figlio, and Thorsten Sellin, *Delinquency in a Birth Cohort* (Chicago: University of Chicago Press, 1972).

59. Paul Tracy, Marvin Wolfgang, and Robert Figlio, *Delinquency in Two Birth Cohorts, Executive Summary* (Washington, DC: U.S. Department of Justice, 1985).

60. Shannon, *Assessing the Relationship of Adult Criminal Careers to Juvenile Careers*; Howard Snyder, *Court Careers of Juvenile Offenders* (Washington, DC: Office of Juvenile Justice and Delinquency Prevention, 1988); D. J. West and David P. Farrington, *The Delinquent Way of Life* (London: Heinemann, 1977); Donna Hamparian, Richard Schuster, Simon Dinitz, and John Conrad, *The Violent Few* (Lexington, MA: Lexington Books, 1978).

61. Michael Schumacher and Gwen Kurz, *The 8% Solution: Preventing Serious Repeat Juvenile Crime* (Thousand Oaks, CA, Sage Publications, 1999).

62. Peter Jones, Philip Harris, James Fader, and Lori Grubstein, "Identifying Chronic Juvenile Offenders," *Justice Quarterly* 18: 478-507 (2001).

63. See, generally, Marvin Wolfgang, Terence Thornberry, and Robert Figlio, eds., *From Boy to Man, from Delinquency to Crime* (Chicago: University of Chicago Press, 1987).

64. Paul Tracy and Kimberly Kempf-Leonard, *Continuity and Discontinuity in Criminal Careers* (New York: Plenum Press, 1996).

65. Kimberly Kempf-Leonard, Paul Tracy, James Howell, "Serious, Violent, and Chronic Juvenile Offenders: The Relationship of Delinquency Career Types to Adult Criminality," *Justice Quarterly* 18: 449–78 (2001).

66. R. Tremblay et al., "Disruptive Boys with Stable and Unstable High Fighting Behavior Patterns during Junior Elementary School," *Journal of Abnormal Child Psychology* 19:285–300 (1991).

67. Jennifer White, Terrie Moffitt, Felton Earls, Lee Robins, and Phil Silva, "How Early Can We Tell? Predictors of Childhood Conduct Disorder and Adolescent Delinquency," *Criminology* 28: 507–35 (1990).

68. John Laub and Robert Sampson, "Unemployment, Marital Discord, and Deviant Behavior: The Long-Term Correlates of Childhood Misbehavior." Paper presented at the annual meeting of the American Society of Criminology, Baltimore, November 1990; rev. version.

69. Michael Ezell and Amy D'Unger, "Offense Specialization among Serious Youthful Offenders: A Longitudinal Analysis of a California Youth Authority Sample" (unpublished report, Durham, NC: Duke University, 1998.

70. Kimberly Kempf, "Crime Severity and Criminal Career Progression," *Journal of Criminal Law and Criminology* 79:524–40 (1988).

71. Jeffrey Fagan, "Social and Legal Policy Dimensions of Violent Juvenile Crime," *Criminal Justice and Behavior* 17:93–133 (1990).

72. Peter Greenwood, *Selective Incapacitation* (Santa Monica: Rand, 1982).

73. Terence Thornberry, David Huizinga, and Rolf Loeber, "The Prevention of Serious Delinquency and Violence," in James Howell, Barry Krisberg, J. David Hawkins, and John Wilson, eds., *Sourcebook on Serious, Violent, and Chronic Juvenile Offenders* (Thousand Oaks, CA: Sage, 1995).

74. Ted Miller, Mark Cohen, and Brian Wiersema, *The Extent and Costs of Crime Victimization: A New Look* (Washington, DC: National Institute of Justice, 1995).

75. Callie Marie Rennison, *Criminal Victimization 1999, Changes 1998–99, with Trends 1993–99* (Washington, DC: Bureau of Justice Statistics, 2000).

76. Craig A. Perkins, *Age Patterns of Victims of Serious Violent Crime* (Washington, DC: Bureau of Justice Statistics, 1997).

77. L. Edward Wells and Joseph Rankin, "Juvenile Victimization: Convergent Validation of Alternative Measurements," *Journal of Research in Crime and Delinquency* 32:301–304 (1995).

78. Lening Zhang, John W. Welte, and William F. Wieczorek, "Deviant Lifestyle and Crime Victimization," *Journal of Criminal Justice* 29:133-43 (2001).

79. Dan Hoyt, Kimberly Ryan, and Mari Cauce, "Personal Victimization in a High-Risk Environment: Homeless and Runaway Adolescents," *Journal of Research in Crime and Delinquency* 36:371-92 (1999).

80. Rolf Loeber et al., "Gun Injury and Mortality: The Delinquent Backgrounds of Juvenile Offenders," *Violence and Victims* 14: 339–51 (1999).

81. Bonnie Fisher, John Sloan, Francis Cullen, and Chunmeng Lu, "Crime in the Ivory Tower: The Level and Sources of Student Victimization," *Criminology* 36:671–710 (1998).

82. David Finkelhor and Richard Ormrod, "Crimes against Children by Babysitters," *Juvenile Justice Bulletin* (Office of Juvenile Justice and Delinquency Prevention, U.S. Department of Justice, September 2001).

83. Gerald Hotaling and David Finkelhor, "Estimating the Number of Stranger Abduction Homicides of Children: A Review of Available Evidence," *Journal of Criminal Justice* 18:385–99 (1990).

Part Two Theories of Delinquency

What causes delinquent behavior? Why do some youths enter a life of crime that persists into their adulthood? Are people products of their environment, or is the likelihood of their becoming a delinquent determined at birth?

Social scientists have speculated on the cause of delinquency for 200 years. They have observed facts about delinquent behavior and organized them into complex theoretical models. A *theory* is a statement that explains the relationship between abstract concepts in a meaningful way. For example, if scientists observe that delinquency rates are usually higher in neighborhoods with high unemployment rates, poor housing, and inadequate schools, they might theorize that environmental conditions influence delinquent behavior. This theory suggests that social conditions can exert a powerful influence on human behavior.

Since the study of delinquency is essentially interdisciplinary, it is not surprising that a variety of theoretical models have been formulated to explain juvenile misbehavior. Each reflects the training and orientation of its creator. Consequently, theories of delinquency reflect many different avenues of inquiry, including biology, psychology, sociology, political science, and economics. Chapter 3 reviews theories that hold that delinquency is essentially caused by individual-level factors, such as personal choices and decision making or by psychological and biological factors. Chapter 4 reviews social theories of delinquency that hold that youthful misbehavior is either caused by children's place in the social structure, their relationships with social institutions and processes, or their reaction to the effects of social conflict. Chapter 5 discusses those theories of delinquency that regard it as a developmental process, reflecting the changes that occur in young people's lives as they evolve during their life course.

Many students regard this variety of delinquency theories as confusing and contradictory. Logic dictates that the competing theoretical models presented here cannot all be correct and that most delinquency efforts may be barking up the wrong tree! Yet every branch of social science—sociology, psychology, political science, economics—contains competing theoretical models. Why people behave the way they do and how society functions are issues that are far from settled. So do not lose patience! Recognize that there are different explanations for similar phenomena because it is possible and even common for people to view the world in different ways. One person's necessary governmental program is another person's waste of public funds. Explaining delinquency is no different. It is a highly complex phenomenon with many different explanations.

3 Individual Views of Delinquency

© Catherine Leroy/Sipa Press

You are a state legislator who is a member of the subcommittee on juvenile justice. Your committee has been asked to redesign the state's juvenile code because of public outrage over serious juvenile crime. At an open hearing, a professor from the local university testifies that she has devised a surefire test to predict violence-prone delinquents. The procedure involves brain scans, DNA testing, and blood analysis. Used with samples of incarcerated adolescents, her procedure has been able to distinguish with 90 percent accuracy between youths with a history of violence and those who are exclusively property offenders. The professor testifies that if each juvenile offender were tested with her techniques, the violence-prone career offender could easily be identified and given special treatment.

Opponents argue that this type of testing is unconstitutional because it violates the Fifth Amendment protection against self-incrimination and can unjustly label nonviolent offenders. Any attempt to base policy on biosocial makeup seems inherently wrong and unfair. Those who favor the professor's approach maintain that it is not uncommon to single out the insane or mentally incompetent for special treatment and that these conditions often have a biological basis. It is better that a few delinquents be unfairly labeled than seriously violent offenders be ignored until it is too late.

theory

- Is it possible that some kids are born to be delinquents? Or, do kids "choose" crime?

- Is it fair to test kids to see if they have biological traits related to crime, even if they have never committed a single offense?

- Should special laws be created to deal with the potentially dangerous offender?

- Should offenders be typed on the basis of their biological characteristics?

psychopathic

Some experts believe that delinquent behavior is a function of individual traits: selfish temperament, impulsive personality, abnormal hormones, genetic characteristics, and so on. They reject the notion that delinquents are a "product of their environment." If social and economic factors alone determine behavior, how is it that many youths residing in the most dangerous and deteriorated neighborhoods live law-abiding lives? Conversely, why are so many middle-class youths involved in delinquency? Research indicates that relatively few youths in any population, even the most economically disadvantaged, actually become hard-core, chronic delinquents.[1] Most kids age out of crime regardless of whether they become financially successful or move to a more affluent community. The quality of neighborhood and family life may have little impact on the choices individuals make.[2]

If social factors are not responsible for the onset of delinquency, what is? To some theorists, the locus of delinquency is rooted in the *individual*: how the individual makes decisions, the quality of his or her biological makeup, and the personality and psychological profile.

There is more than one explanation for why individuals become crime prone. One position, referred to as **choice theory**, suggests that young offenders choose to engage in antisocial activity because they believe their actions will be beneficial and profitable. Whether they join a gang, steal cars, or sell drugs, their delinquent acts are motivated by the reasoned belief that crime can be a relatively risk-free way to better their personal situation. They have little fear of getting caught or of the consequences of punishment. Some are motivated by fantasies of riches, while others may simply enjoy the excitement and short-term gratification produced by criminal acts such as beating up an opponent or stealing a car.

All youthful misbehavior, however, cannot be traced to rational choice, profit motive, and criminal entrepreneurship. Some delinquent acts, especially violent ones, seem irrational, selfish, and/or hedonistic. Many forms of delinquency, such as substance abuse and vandalism, appear more impulsive than rational. It is believed that these antisocial behaviors may be inspired by aberrant physical or psychological traits that govern behavioral choices. While some youths may choose to commit crime simply because they desire conventional luxuries and power, others may be driven by constitutional abnormalities, such as hyperactivity, low intelligence, biochemical imbalance, or genetic defects. This view of delinquency is referred to here generally as **trait theory** because it links delinquency to biological and psychological traits that control human development.

Choice and trait theories share common ground because they focus on the individual's mental and behavioral processes. All people are different, so that each person reacts to the same set of environmental and social conditions in a unique way. Faced with extreme stress and economic hardship, one person will seek employment, borrow money, save for the future, and live a law-abiding life; another will use antisocial or violent behavior to satisfy his needs.

This chapter first covers those theoretical models that focus on individual choice. Then it discusses the view that biological and psychological development controls youngsters' ability to make choices, rendering some of them violent, aggressive, and antisocial.

choice theory Holds that youths will engage in delinquent and criminal behavior after weighing the consequences and benefits of their actions; delinquent behavior is a rational choice made by a motivated offender who perceives that the chances of gain outweigh any possible punishment or loss.

trait theory Holds that youths engage in delinquent or criminal behavior due to aberrant physical or psychological traits that govern behavioral choices; delinquent actions are impulsive or instinctual rather than rational choices.

Choice Theory and Classical Criminology

free will View that youths are in charge of their own destinies and are free to make personal behavior choices unencumbered by environmental factors.

The first formal explanations of crime and delinquency held that human behavior was a matter of choice. Since it was assumed that people had **free will** to choose their behavior, those who violated the law were motivated by personal needs: greed, revenge, survival, hedonism. Over 200 years ago, **utilitarian** philosophers Cesare Beccaria and Jeremy Bentham argued that people weigh the benefits and consequences

utilitarians Those who believe that people weigh the benefits and consequences of their future actions before deciding on a course of behavior.

classical criminology Holds that decisions to violate the law are weighed against possible punishments, and to deter crime the pain of punishment must outweigh the benefit of illegal gain; led to graduated punishments based on seriousness of the crime (let the punishment fit the crime).

A CLOSER VIEW
If you wish to read more about Beccaria's views, go to InfoTrac College Edition and access Richard Bellamy, "Crime and Punishment," *History Review* 28(2):24 (September 1997).

of their future actions before deciding on a course of behavior.[3] Their writings formed the core of what is referred to today as **classical criminology.**

The classical view of crime and delinquency holds that the decision to violate the law comes after a careful weighing of the benefits and costs of criminal behaviors. Most potential law violators would cease their actions if the potential pain associated with a behavior outweighed its anticipated gain; conversely, law-violating behavior seems attractive if the future rewards seem far greater than the potential punishment.[4]

According to the classical view, youths who decide to become drug dealers weigh and compare the possible benefits, such as cash to buy cars, clothes, and other luxury items, with the potential penalties, such as arrest followed by a long stay in a juvenile facility. If they believe that drug dealers are rarely caught and even then usually avoid severe punishments, the youths will more likely choose to become dealers than if they believe that dealers are almost always caught and punished by lengthy prison terms. They may know or hear about criminals who make a significant income from their illegal activities and want to follow in their footsteps.[5] Put simply, in order to deter or prevent crime, the pain of punishment must outweigh the benefit of illegal gain.[6]

The classical criminologists argued that punishment should be only severe enough to deter a particular offense and that punishments should be graded according to the seriousness of particular crimes: "Let the punishment fit the crime." For example, Beccaria argued that it would be foolish to punish pickpockets and murderers in a similar fashion because this would encourage thieves to kill the victims or witnesses to their crimes.[7]

The popularity of the classical approach was in part responsible for the development of the prison as an alternative to physical punishment and the eventual creation of criminal sentences geared to the seriousness of crimes.[8] The choice approach dominated the policy of the U.S. justice system for about 150 years.

The Rational Delinquent

The view that delinquents are rational decision makers who *choose* to violate the law remains a popular theoretical approach to the study and control of delinquency. Its current popularity is in part due to the disappointing results of rehabilitative categories. Past efforts to treat known delinquents by treatment, counseling, and other rehabilitation techniques, have been regarded by some experts as noble failures.[9] This failure, they argue, is a signal that delinquency is not merely a function of social ills, such as a lack of economic opportunity or family dysfunction. If it were, then educational enrichment, family counseling, job training programs, and the like should be more effective alternatives to crime. In reality, some affluent youths from "good" families choose to break the law, while most indigent adolescents are law abiding. The reasoning goes then that rich or poor, some youths choose crime and their behavior can only be controlled by the punishments severe enough to convince them to choose conventional over criminal behaviors.[10] Those who subscribe to the rational choice model believe that the decision to commit a specific type of crime and the subsequent entry into a criminal lifestyle are a matter of personal decision making based on a weighing of available information; hence, the term *rational choice.*

The well-publicized resurgence of youthful gang activity has also lent credence to the rational choice explanations. (See Chapter 8 for more on gangs.) The emergence of gangs and their involvement in the drug trade strengthens the case for rational choice: These young, well-armed entrepreneurs are seeking to cash in on a lucrative, albeit illegal, "business enterprise." Gang leaders are surely "rational decision makers," constantly processing information during their criminal transactions: Who are my enemies? How can I make more money? What are the chances of getting caught? Where can I find a good lawyer?[11] Contemporary gang boys involved in drug trafficking have been found to act like employers, who can provide their business

Delinquency as Problem Solving

If delinquents are rational decision makers, it stands to reason that their behavior may be designed to overcome problems they face in their daily lives. In this sense, delinquency can be viewed as problem-solving behavior designed to cope with the stresses of daily life.

Sociologist Timothy Brezina has identified some of the problems that delinquent behavior may address or improve.

- *Perceived control:* Brezina finds that a fundamental need of humans is to maintain a sense of mastery over their environment. Kids may turn to delinquent behaviors to restore control over their lives when conventional alternatives are unavailable. Adolescents may find themselves feeling "out of control" because society limits their opportunities and resources. They may also find themselves in the ironic situation of being forced to obey parents, teachers, and other authority figures while being socialized to be independent and self-regulating. Delinquency may allow some adolescents to exert control over their own lives and destinies, by helping them to avoid situations they find uncomfortable or repellant (for example, by cutting school or running away from an abusive home) or to obtain resources for desired activities and commodities (for example, by stealing or selling drugs to buy stylish outfits).

- *Positive self-evaluation:* According to Brezina, some delinquents are motivated to improve their self-evaluations. Adolescence is a time when peer evaluations are critical for feelings of self-worth. Kids who are not in the right clique or are socially isolated may suffer acute psychological distress. Delinquency may provide a means of countering negative evaluations, to attack symbolically or otherwise the source of the youths' self-rejecting attitudes.

Delinquency may also provide a path for enhancing self-feelings, for example, by becoming part of a close-knit gang.

- *Negative affect:* Kids may sometimes feel they have been the target of undue punishment, sanctions, negative evaluations, and other hurtful experiences that cause them severe emotional distress. Drinking and drug taking may allow some kids to ward off depression and compensate for a lack of positive experiences: a form of self-medication. Some, angry at their mistreatment, may turn to violence to satisfy a desire for revenge or retaliation.

Brezina finds that there is a great deal of evidence that kids engage in antisocial acts in order to solve problems. The literature on drug and alcohol abuse is replete with examples of research showing that kids turn to substance abuse to increase their sense of personal power, to become more assertive, and to reduce tension and anxiety. Others may embrace deviant lifestyles such as the punk culture to offend conventional society and overcome their own ordinariness. Engaging in risky behavior helps some kids to feel alive and competent. There is also evidence that antisocial acts can provide positive solutions to problems. Violent kids, for example, may have learned that being aggressive with others is a good means to control the situation and get what they want; counterattacks may be one means of controlling people who are treating them poorly.

Just because an adolescent faces social problems does not necessarily mean he or she will turn to antisocial behavior to solve them. Most kids are faced with adverse situations while growing up, and relatively few deal with them by turning to violence or drug abuse. Why do some kids turn to antisocial acts to solve their life's problems?

associates with security and the know-how to conduct business deals. Gang membership helps kids achieve financial success that would otherwise be impossible. Like legitimate business enterprises, some gangs actively recruit new personnel and cut deals with rivals over products and territory.[12] Similarly, drug dealers have been observed to carefully evaluate the desirability of their "sales area" before getting ready to "deal."[13] Geography is an important issue: Dealers usually choose the middle of a long street in order to conduct transactions because of the good visibility in both directions; police raids can then be spotted before they occur.[14]

Such illustrations support the belief that law-violating behavior occurs when a reasoning offender decides to take the chance of violating the law after considering his or her personal situation (need for money, learning experiences, opportunities for conventional success), values (conscience, moral values, need for peer approval), and situational factors (how well the target is protected, whether people are at home, how wealthy the neighborhood is, the likelihood of getting caught, the punishment if apprehended). Conversely, the decision to forgo law-violating behavior may be based on the growing perception that the economic benefits are no longer there or the probability of successfully completing a crime is less than the chances of being caught and punished. In this sense, delinquent behavior may be viewed as a form of problem-solving behavior that helps kids deal with the difficulties of negotiating their environment. The Focus on Delinquency box entitled "Delinquency as Problem Solving" looks at this issue in more depth.

- *Lack of conventional problem-solving alternatives:* Problem-solving techniques normally available to adults are generally denied adolescents, for example, borrowing money from a bank. Some youths may feel there is no escape from their problems and that there are few options open to them. When they have conflict with adults, they may turn to vandalism rather than to an attorney. They may engage in antisocial acts because they simply could not think of anything else to do. Some may lack self-control and act on impulse rather than reasoned thought.
- *Positive outcome expectancies:* Kids are more likely to commit delinquent acts to solve their problems if they perceive a positive outcome from their actions. They may have a here-and-now orientation and fail to realize that what may work in the short run, such as quitting school, will have long-term negative consequences.
- *The efficacy of delinquent adaptations:* Prior experiences with delinquent problem solving will enhance the likelihood of future experiences. Some kids have been successful at using antisocial methods to solve problems; they will turn to these successful strategies when similar situations arise. Once committed to delinquent strategies, kids may feel they have little to lose by using them again and again. Their commitment to conformity becomes weak and attenuated.

Brezina argues that viewing delinquency as a problem-solving device can help explain the aging-out phenomenon. As people mature, the level and intensity of the problems they face may diminish. The Sturm und Drang of adolescence gives way to the relative tranquility of adulthood, without the worries of school and peer group approval. Family conflict is diminished as young adults find their own place in the world. Young adults have more power to control their own destiny and have acquired the skills through experience to become better problem solvers. At the same time, short-term solutions, appealing as they are to adolescents, may be far less so to adults who have reached a more mature life view. Going to a drunken frat party may sound appealing to sophomores, but the risks involved make them off-limits to grads. As people mature, their thinking extends farther into the future, and risky behavior is a threat to long-range plans. Not all delinquents develop the capacity to apply mature evaluations. Some remain impulsive, and lack self-control. Those who have experienced overwhelming social problems may find it difficult to develop long-range thinking, but the majority can and will choose not to commit crimes.

Critical Thinking

1. Brezina claims that for a small group of offenders, the value associated with developing delinquent coping techniques remains compelling and contributes to their long-term involvement in crime. What can be done to convince such youth that they have chosen an inappropriate strategy?
2. Have you changed your problem-solving methods during your lifetime? Have your life experiences shaped your coping techniques?

InfoTrac College Edition Research

 How do kids solve problems? To find out more about this topic, go to InfoTrac College Edition and use *problem solving* as a subject guide; then click on the subcategory of Problem Solving in Children.

Source: Timothy Brezina, "Delinquent Problem-Solving: An Interpretive Framework for Criminological Theory and Research," *Journal of Research in Crime and Delinquency* 37:3–30 (2000).

Choosing Delinquent Acts

How are crimes planned? What makes one target inviting and another forbidding? The rational choice theory views the concepts of crime and criminality as two separate issues. Criminality is the propensity to engage in criminal or delinquent acts; crimes are events that are in violation of the criminal law.[15] There will always be a population of criminally motivated adolescents; unless they have criminal opportunities they will not be able to act upon their inclinations. Similarly, given an open opportunity for illegal gain, even the least criminally inclined youth may be motivated to act. Crime, after all, can be very exciting—even seductive. See the Focus on Delinquency box entitled "Is Crime Seductive?" The explanation for the reasons why a child eventually becomes a delinquent then is quite distinct from the reasons an individual delinquent decides to break into a particular house one day or sell narcotics the next. The decision to "choose" crime occurs when an offender decides to take the chance of violating the law after considering his or her situation (for example, need for money, opportunities for conventional success), values (for example, conscience, need for peer approval), and situational factors (for example, the likelihood of getting caught, the punishment if apprehended). Conversely, the decision to forgo law-violating behavior may be based on the perception that the benefits are no longer worthwhile, or the probability of successfully completing a crime is less than the chance of being caught. For example, aging out may occur because as delinquents

Focus on Delinquency

Is Crime Seductive?

Sociologist Jack Katz makes the provocative argument that violating the law can be exciting and even "seductive" for those willing to take the risk; the "seductions of crime" result from the thrills and kicks associated with successful involvement in delinquent acts.

The key to understanding why young people engage in crime is not as mysterious as some experts make it seem. Delinquency has a here-and-now orientation. Kids become involved in provocative situations that influence their behavior choices: Someone challenges their authority, heritage, or reputation, and they vanquish this opponent with a beating; they want to maximize their pleasure by doing something exciting, so they break into and vandalize a school building. Crime then is a pleasurable exercise that can relieve tension, increase self-esteem, and even, in the case of drug use, provide pleasurable physical sensations.

According to Katz, choosing crime satisfies the need to relieve emotional upheavals brought about by moral challenges. Gang boys are rejecting society's expectations that they become conventional adults. They violently defend meaningless turf boundaries and get into brawls in an effort to show their indifference to social expectations. Young gang members carry on like the avenging gods of mythology, electing to have life-or-death control over their victims.

Theft crimes bring what Katz calls "sneaky thrills." For many youngsters, shoplifting and theft are attractive because "getting away with it" is a thrilling demonstration of personal competence, especially when the crime is consummated under the eyes of an adult. Getting away with crime is especially thrilling, not so much because it brings material goods, but because it shows how competent the young thief is and how he or she can flaunt the moral and legal code with impunity.

Katz finds that the central theme in the choice to commit crime is perceived emotional upheaval: humiliation, righteousness, arrogance, ridicule, cynicism, defilement, and vengeance. For example, the assailant interprets the victim's behavior as disrespectful and humiliating, and violence is a way of expressing her resulting rage. When the drunk at a party is told to "shut up and go home" because she is disturbing people, she responds, "So, I'm acting like a fool, am I?" goes

home and returns with a gun: She must "sacrifice" or injure the body of the victim to maintain her "honor."

There is growing evidence that immediate events do in fact play an important role in adolescent misbehavior. People committed to criminal careers seem to take an intrinsic pleasure in their own behavior; they enjoy taking risks. Kids are most likely to be "seduced" if they neither fear the risk of apprehension nor its social consequences, such as losing the respect of their peers; fear of punishment then may help neutralize the attractions of crime. Whether it is violent or profit oriented, crime has an allure that some people cannot resist. Delinquency may produce a natural high and other positive sensations that are instrumental in maintaining and reinforcing delinquent behavior.

Critical Thinking

1. Do you think crime is seductive and alluring? What is it about drinking and/or taking drugs that gets people to engage in such risky activities? And, how can we convince them that while seductive, such behavior is eventually destructive?

InfoTrac College Edition Research

Are some kids thrill seekers? To find out, use *thrill seeking* as a key term on InfoTrac College Edition.

Sources: Jack Katz, *Seductions of Crime* (New York: Basic Books, 1988); Peter Wood, Walter Gove, James Wilson, and John Cochran, "Nonsocial Reinforcement and Habitual Criminal Conduct: An Extension of Learning," *Criminology* 35:335–66 (1997); Bill McCarthy, "Not Just 'For the Thrill of It': An Instrumentalist Elaboration of Katz's Explanation of Sneaky Thrill Property Crime," *Criminology* 33:519–39 (1995); Bill McCarthy and John Hagan, "Mean Streets: The Theoretical Significance of Situational Delinquency among Homeless Youths," *American Journal of Sociology* 3:597–627 (1992).

mature they begin to realize that the risks of crime are greater than the potential profits. The solution to crime, therefore, may be formulating policies that will cause the potential criminal to choose conventional behaviors.[16]

Routine Activities

To some crime experts, the concept of the "motivated offender" is insufficient to explain patterns in the delinquency rate. If the number of motivated delinquents is a constant, why do crime rates rise and fall? Why are some areas more crime ridden than others? To answer these questions, attention must be paid to fluctuations in the *opportunity to commit crimes*, controlled in part by both the behavior of potential victims and those charged with their protection, such as police officers.[17] Delinquency may occur not only because a juvenile decides to break the law but also because victims place themselves at risk and no one is around to protect them.[18]

routine activities theory View that crime is a "normal" function of the routine activities of modern living; offenses can be expected if there is a motivated offender and a suitable target that is not protected by capable guardians.

predatory crime Violent crimes against persons, and crimes in which an offender attempts to steal an object directly from its holder.

One of the most prominent statements of this view is **routine activities theory,** developed by Lawrence Cohen and Marcus Felson.[19] At the heart of this theory is the assumption that certain activities or settings lend themselves to conditions that are conducive to the occurrence of crimes. According to Cohen and Felson's vision, the volume and distribution of **predatory crime** (violent crimes against the person and crimes in which an offender attempts to steal an object directly from its holder) are influenced by the interaction of three variables that reflect the routine activities found in everyday American life: the availability of *suitable targets* (such as homes containing easily salable goods); the absence of *capable guardians* (such as home owners and their neighbors, friends, and relatives); and the presence of *motivated offenders* (such as unemployed teenagers). If each of these components is present, there is greater likelihood that a predatory crime will take place. (See Figure 3.1.)

The routine activities approach gives equal weight to the role of both the victim and the offender in the crime process. Criminal opportunity is significantly influenced by the victim's lifestyle and behavior. The greater the opportunity for criminals and victims to interact, the greater the probability of crime; reduce the interaction, and the opportunity for crime will decline.[20]

Lack of Capable Guardians According to the routine activities approach, general social change can filter down to influence delinquency rates and patterns. For example,

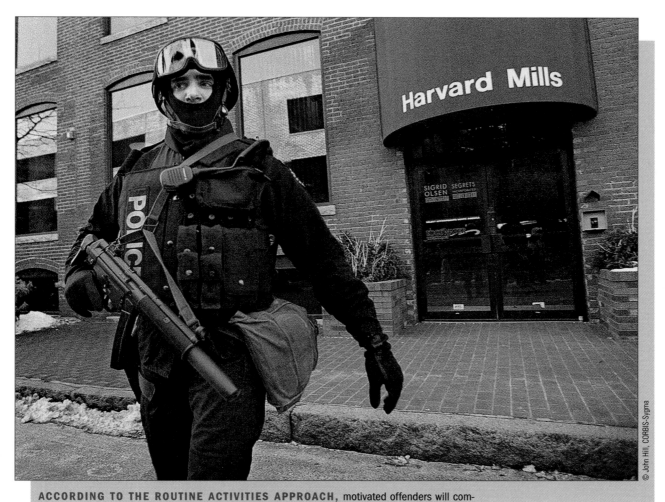

ACCORDING TO THE ROUTINE ACTIVITIES APPROACH, motivated offenders will commit criminal acts if suitable targets exist in the absence of capable guardians, such as police and security guards. Would you commit a crime if the police officer shown in the photo here was on guard?

Figure 3.1
Routine Activities Theory Posits the Interaction of Three Factors Help Explain Fluctuations in the Delinquency Rate

Lack of capable guardians
• Police officers
• Home owners
• Security systems

Motivated offenders
• Teenage boys
• Unemployed
• Addict population

Delinquency

Suitable targets
• Unlocked homes
• Expensive cars
• Easily transportable goods

Sometimes people who cannot perform the duty themselves hire capable guardians. Wackenhut provides capable guardians, such as uniformed security personnel, who can complement and even replace sworn police officers in many situations. See their Web site at
http://www.wackenhut.com/security.htm
For an up-to-date list of Web links, go to
http://info.wadsworth.com/siegel

one reason the delinquency rate may have trended upward between 1970 and 1990 is because the number of adult caretakers at home during the day (guardians) decreased as more women entered the workforce. Since mothers are at work and children are in daycare, homes are left unguarded and become more suitable targets. Similarly, with the growth of suburbia and the decline of the traditional neighborhood, the number of such familiar guardians as family, neighbors, and friends has diminished.[21] Research shows that crime levels are relatively low in neighborhoods where residents keep a watchful eye on their neighbor's property.[22]

Suitable Targets Routine activities theory suggests that the availability of suitable targets such as easily transportable commodities will increase delinquency rates. Research has generally supported the fact that the more wealth a home contains, the more likely it will become a target.[23] As computers, stereo systems, and TVs become more commonplace, burglary rates should rise, simply because the more these high-priced and easily sold goods are available, the more offenders will be motivated to steal.[24]

Routine activities also recognizes that behavior and lifestyle will influence the nature and likelihood of victimization risk. Delinquents do not like to travel to commit crimes, and targets are generally found close to their homes.[25] People who routinely go out to public places are the ones most likely to be victimized by strangers; "stay at homes" are the ones most likely to be harmed by family or friends.[26] Maintaining a high-risk lifestyle by frequenting dangerous hot spots, such as bars and taverns, increases the likelihood of victimization.[27]

Motivated Offenders Routine activities theory also links the delinquency rates to general social changes that increase the number and motivation of offenders. Structural changes in the population can have an impact on crime rates. Delinquency rates will increase if there is a surplus of youths of the same age category competing for a limited number of jobs and educational opportunities. If during any given period, the number of teenagers exceeds the available part-time and after-school jobs, the supply of motivated offenders may be increased simply because many potential offenders are competing for a limited number of legitimate resources.[28]

A CLOSER VIEW
Is it possible that a routine activity such as watching a hockey game can influence the likelihood of committing suicide? To find out, go to InfoTrac College Edition and read Frank Trovato, "The Stanley Cup of Hockey and Suicide in Quebec, 1951–1992," *Social Forces* 77(1):105 (September 1998).

Lifestyle also affects delinquent motivation. Adolescents who spend much time socializing with peers in the absence of authority figures—riding around in cars, going to parties, going out at night for fun—are also the ones most likely to engage in deviant behaviors.[29] In the presence of "motivated peers," the lack of structure and guardianship leaves more opportunity for antisocial behaviors, including substance abuse, crime, and dangerous driving. Participation in unstructured activities helps explain the association between crime rates and gender, age, and status: Teenage boys have the highest crime rates because they are the group most likely to engage in unsupervised socialization. Even when adolescents engage in what should be character-building activities, such as having a part-time job after school, the opportunity to socialize with deviant peers combined with lack of parental supervision increases criminal motivation.[30]

Preventing Delinquency

If delinquency is a rational choice and a routine activity, as some believe, then delinquency prevention is a matter of three general strategies: (1) It stands to reason that it can be prevented by convincing potential delinquents that they will be severely punished for committing delinquent acts; and then (2) they must be punished so severely that they never again commit crimes, or (3) it must be so difficult to commit crimes that the potential gain is not worth the risk. The first of these strategies is called *general deterrence,* the second is *specific deterrence,* and the third, *situational crime prevention.* Each is discussed below.

General Deterrence

general deterrence Crime control policies that depend on the fear of criminal penalties, such as long prison sentences for violent crimes; the aim is to convince law violators that the pain outweighs the benefit of criminal activity.

The **general deterrence** concept holds that the choice to commit delinquent acts can be controlled or structured by the threat of punishment. If people fear the power of the law, believing that illegal behavior will result in certain and severe sanctions, they will choose not to commit crimes.[31]

One of the guiding principles of deterrence theory is that *the more severe, certain, and swift the punishment, the greater its deterrent effect will be.*[32] Even if a particular crime carries a severe punishment, there will be relatively little deterrent effect if most people do not believe they will be caught.[33] Conversely, even a mild sanction may be sufficient to deter crime if people believe that punishment is certain. And even the most severe sanctions will have little deterrent effect if they are slow, delayed, or easily put off.

Traditionally, juvenile justice authorities have been reluctant to incorporate deterrence-based punishments on the grounds that they interfere with the stated *parens patriae* philosophy. Children are punished less severely than adults, which limits the power of the law to deter juvenile crime. Yet, in recent years, the increase in teenage violence, gang activity, and drug abuse has prompted a reevaluation of deterrence strategies. Some juvenile courts have shifted from an emphasis on treatment to concerns with public safety.[34] Police are now more willing to use aggressive tactics, such as gang-busting units, to deter membership in drug-trafficking gangs; youthful-looking officers have been sent undercover into high schools in order to identify, contact, and arrest student drug dealers.[35]

Many courts have also attempted to initiate a deterrence strategy. Juvenile court judges have been willing to waive youths to adult courts; prior record may outweigh an offender's need for services in making this decision.[36] Legislators seem willing to pass more restrictive juvenile codes featuring mandatory incarceration sentences in juvenile facilities; the number of incarcerated juveniles continues to increase. Adolescents

CAN DELINQUENCY AND DRUG ABUSE be deterred when so many teens consider it fun and socially acceptable? High school student Cathy, left, parties with other rave fans at an abandoned warehouse in Portland, Oregon. Oregon's rave scene is an escape for teens, a worry for parents, and a worrisome new challenge to law enforcement officials.

are not even spared capital punishment; the U.S. Supreme Court has upheld the use of the death penalty for youths over 16.[37] The trend toward a more punitive, deterrence-based juvenile process will be discussed further in Chapters 12–15.

Do General Deterrence Strategies Work? The effectiveness of deterrence strategies is a topic of considerable debate. A number of studies have contributed data supporting deterrence concepts. Evidence indicates that the threat of police arrest can deter property crimes.[38] Areas of the country in which punishment is more certain seem to have lower delinquency rates; the more likely people are to anticipate punishment, the less likely they are to commit crimes.[39]

While these findings are persuasive, there is actually little conclusive evidence that the threat of apprehension and punishment alone can deter crime.[40] More evidence exists that fear of social disapproval and informal penalties, criticisms, and punishments from parents and friends may actually be a greater deterrent to crime than legal punishments.[41]

Since deterrence strategies are based on the idea of a rational, calculating offender, they may not be effective when applied to immature young people. Minors tend to be less capable of making mature judgments about their behavior choices. For example, many younger offenders are unaware of the content of juvenile legal codes, so that imposition of a deterrence policy, such as mandatory waiver to the adult court for violent crimes, will have little effect on delinquency rates.[42] It seems futile, therefore, to try to deter delinquency through fear of legal punishment. Teens seem more fearful of being punished by their parents or of being the target of disapproval from their friends than they are of the police.[43]

It is also possible that for the highest-risk group of young offenders—teens living in economically depressed neighborhoods—the deterrent threat of formal sanctions may be irrelevant. Inner-city youngsters may not have internalized the norms of society, which hold that getting arrested is wrong. (See Chapter 4 for more on inner-city norms and values.) Young people in these areas have less to lose if arrested; they have a limited stake in society and are not worried about their future. They also may not make connections between their illegal behavior and punishment since they see many people in their neighborhood commit crimes and not get caught or punished.[44]

Research also shows that many juvenile offenders are under the influence of drugs and/or alcohol when they break the law, a condition that might impair their decision-making ability.[45] Similarly, juveniles often commit crimes in groups, and peer pressure can outweigh the deterrent effect of the law.

In sum, deterring delinquency through the fear of punishment may be of limited value because children may neither fully comprehend the seriousness of their acts nor the consequences they may face.[46] While on the surface deterrence appears to have benefit as a delinquency control device, there is also reason to believe that it has limited demonstrable effectiveness.

Specific Deterrence

For a review of the deterrence concept, go to *http://www.umsl.edu/~rkeel/200/ratchoc.html* For an up-to-date list of Web links, go to *http://info.wadsworth.com/siegel*

specific deterrence Sending convicted offenders to secure incarceration facilities so that punishment is severe enough to convince offenders not to repeat their criminal activity.

The theory of **specific deterrence** holds that if offenders are punished severely, the experience will convince them not to repeat their illegal acts. While general deterrence focuses on potential offenders, specific deterrence targets offenders who have already been convicted. Juveniles are sent to secure incarceration facilities with the understanding that their ordeal will deter future misbehavior.

Specific deterrence is a popular approach to crime control today. The admissions rate to confinement facilities has increased sharply during the past decade. Unfortunately, relying on punitive measures may expand rather than reduce future delinquency. Institutions quickly become overcrowded, and chronic violent offenders are packed into swollen facilities with juveniles who have committed nonserious and nonviolent crimes. The use of mandatory sentences for some crimes (usually violent crimes or drug dealing) means that all kids who are found to have committed those crimes must be institutionalized; first offenders may be treated the same as chronic recidivists.

Some believe that rather than reducing delinquency, increased use of punitive measures may increase its frequency. Research shows that arrest and punishment may even increase the likelihood that inexperienced or first-time offenders will commit new crimes.[47] Similarly, chronic offender research indicates that a stay in a juvenile justice facility has little deterrent effect on the likelihood that a persistent delinquent will become an adult criminal.[48] A history of prior arrest, conviction, and punishment has proven to be the *best predictor* of rearrest among young offenders released from a correctional institution. Rather than deter future offending, punishment may in fact encourage reoffending.[49]

Why does punishment encourage rather than reduce delinquency? According to some experts, institutionalization cuts youth off from prosocial supports in the community, making them more reliant on deviant peers. Incarceration may also diminish chances for successful future employment, reducing access to legitimate opportunities. While some researchers have found that punishment may reduce the frequency of future offending, the weight of the evidence suggests that time served has little impact on recidivism.[50] The failure of specific deterrence might help explain why delinquency rates are increasing at the same time that incarceration rates are at an all-time high.

To find situational crime prevention resources, go to this Web site maintained by Rutgers University: *http://crimeprevention.rutgers.edu/resources/resources.htm* For an up-to-date list of Web links, go to *http://info.wadsworth.com/siegel*

Situational Crime Prevention

Rather than deterring or punishing individuals in order to reduce delinquency rates, **situational crime prevention** strategies aim to reduce the opportunities people have to commit particular crimes. The idea is to make it so difficult to commit specific criminal acts that would-be delinquent offenders will be convinced that the risks of crime are greater than the rewards.[51] Controlling the situation of crime can be accomplished

situational crime prevention
Crime prevention method that relies on reducing the opportunity to commit criminal acts by (1) making them more difficult to perform, (2) reducing their reward, and (3) increasing their risks.

target-hardening technique
Crime prevention technique that makes it more difficult for a would-be delinquent to carry out the illegal act, for example, by a security device in a home.

by either (a) increasing the effort (b) increasing the risks, and/or (c) reducing the rewards attached to delinquent acts.

Increasing the effort might involve **target-hardening techniques** such as placing steering locks on cars and putting unbreakable glass on storefronts. *Access control* can be maintained by locking gates and fencing yards.[52] The *facilitators of crime* can be controlled by such measures as banning the sale of spray paint to adolescents in an effort to cut down on graffiti, or having photos put on credit cards to reduce their value if stolen.

Increasing the risks of crime might involve such measures as improving surveillance lighting, creating neighborhood watch programs, controlling building entrances and exits, installing burglar alarms and security systems, and increasing the number of private security officers and police patrols.

Reducing the rewards of crime could include strategies such as making car radios removable so they can be kept at home at night, marking property so that it is more difficult to sell when stolen, and having gender-neutral phone listings to discourage obscene phone calls. Tracking systems, such as those made by the LoJack Corporation, help police locate and return stolen vehicles.

Do Delinquents Choose Crime?

All the delinquency control methods based on choice theory assume the delinquent to be a motivated offender who breaks the law because he or she perceives an abundance of benefits and an absence of threat. Increase the threat and reduce the benefits, and the delinquency rate should decline.

This logic is hard to refute. After all, by definition, a person who commits an illegal act but is not rational cannot be considered a criminal or delinquent but instead is "not guilty by reason of insanity." To say that delinquents choose their crimes is for the most part entirely logical. Yet several questions remain unanswered by choice theorists. First, why do some people continually choose to break the law, even after suffering its consequences, while others are content with living law-abiding yet indigent lives; that is, how can "the good boy in the high crime area" be explained?[53] Conversely, why do affluent youth break the law when they have everything to lose and little more to gain?

Choice theorists also have problems explaining seemingly irrational crimes, such as vandalism, arson, and even drug abuse. To say a teenager painted swastikas on a synagogue after making a "rational choice" seems inadequate to explain such a destructive, nonbeneficial act.

The relationships observed by rational choice theorists can also be explained in other ways. For example, while the high victimization rates in lower-class neighborhoods can be explained by an oversupply of "motivated offenders," they may also be due to other factors, such as social conflict and disorganization.[54]

In sum, although choice theories can contribute to understanding criminal events and victim patterns, they leave a major question unanswered: Why do some people choose crime over legal activities? (See Exhibit 3.1 for a summary of the different choice theories and concepts.)

A CLOSER VIEW
Does installing a mechanical device such as LoJack deter kids from stealing cars? To find out, read Ian Ayres and Steven D. Levitt, "Measuring Positive Externalities from Unobservable Victim Precaution: An Empirical Analysis of Lojack," *Quarterly Journal of Economics* 113(1):43 (February 1998) on InfoTrac College Edition.

Trait Theories: Biosocial and Psychological Views

Why, then, do delinquents choose crime over law-abiding behavior? A faithful and loyal choice theorist believes that selecting crime is usually part of an economic strategy, a function of carefully weighing the benefits of criminal over legal behavior. For example, youths decide to commit a robbery if they believe they will make a good

Exhibit 3.1 Choice Theories and Strategies

Choice Theories	Major Premise	Strengths
Rational choice	Law-violating behavior is an event that occurs after offenders weigh information on their personal needs and the situational factors involved in the difficulty and risk of committing a crime.	Explains why high-risk youth do not constantly engage in delinquent acts. Relates theory to delinquency control policy. It is not limited by class or other social variables.
Routine activities	Crime and delinquency are functions of the presence of motivated offenders, the availability of suitable targets, and the absence of capable guardians.	Can explain fluctuations in crime and delinquency rates. Shows how victim behavior influences criminal choice.
Choice Theory Strategies		
General deterrence	People will commit crime and delinquency if they perceive that the benefits outweigh the risks. Crime is a function of the severity, certainty, and speed of punishment.	Shows the relationship between delinquency and punishment. Suggests a real solution to crime: Increases the certainty and severity of punishment
Specific deterrence	Punishing people severely will prevent future law violations. People learn from punishment that "crime does not pay."	Provides a simple solution to the crime problem. Punishment can be made proportionate to the seriousness of the crime. Increasing the severity of punishment will reduce delinquency.
Situational crime prevention	Crime can be controlled by increasing the effort, increasing the risks, and reducing the rewards attached to committing offenses.	Shows the importance of situational factors or the specific circumstances surrounding crimes. Offers concrete crime prevention alternatives.

profit, have a good chance of getting away with it, and, even if caught, stand little chance of being severely punished.

A number of delinquency experts believe that this model is incomplete. They believe it is wrong to infer that all youths choose crime simply because they believe its advantages outweigh its risks. If that were the case, how could senseless and profit-less crimes such as vandalism and random violence be explained? These experts argue that human behavioral choices are a function of an individual's mental and/or physical makeup. Most law-abiding youths have personal traits that keep them within the mainstream of conventional society. In contrast, youths who choose to engage in repeated aggressive, antisocial, or conflict-oriented behavior manifest abnormal traits that influence their behavior choices.[55] Uncontrollable, impulsive behavior patterns place some youths at odds with society, and they soon find themselves in trouble with the law. Although delinquents may choose their actions, the decision is a product of all but uncontrollable mental and physical properties and traits.

The view that delinquents are somehow "abnormal" is not a new one. Some of the earliest theories of criminal and delinquent behavior stressed that crime was a product of personal traits and that measurable physical and mental conditions, such as IQ and body build, determined behavior. This view is generally referred to today as *positivism*. Positivists believe that the scientific method can be used to measure the causes of human behavior and that behavior is a function of often uncontrollable factors, such as mental illness.

The source of behavioral control is one significant difference between trait and choice theories: While the former reasons that behavior is controlled by personal traits, the latter views behavior as purely a product of human reasoning. To a choice theorist, reducing the benefits of crime by increasing the likelihood and severity of punishment will eventually lower the crime rate; biosocial, or trait, theory focuses less on the effects of punishment and more on the treatment of abnormal mental and physical conditions as a crime-reduction method.

In the following section, the primary components of trait theory are reviewed.

Origins of Trait Theory

criminal atavism The idea that delinquents manifest physical anomalies that make them biologically and physiologically similar to our primitive ancestors, savage throwbacks to an earlier stage of human evolution.

For a complete list of the crime-producing physical traits identified by Lombroso, go to *http://www.d.umn.edu/~jhamlin1/lombroso.html* For an up-to-date list of Web links, go to *http://info.wadsworth.com/siegel*

The first attempts to discover why criminal tendencies develop focused on the physical makeup of offenders. Biological traits present at birth were thought to predetermine whether people would live a life of crime.

The origin of this school of thought is generally credited to the Italian physician Cesare Lombroso (1835–1909).[56] Known as the father of criminology, Lombroso put his many years of medical research to use in his theory of **criminal atavism**.[57] Lombroso found that delinquents manifest physical anomalies that make them biologically and physiologically similar to our primitive ancestors. These atavistic individuals are savage throwbacks to an earlier stage of human evolution. Because of this link, the "born criminal" has such physical traits as enormous jaws, strong canines, a flattened nose, and supernumerary teeth (double rows, as in snakes). Lombroso made such statements as "It was easy to understand why the span of the arms in criminals so often exceeds the height, for this is a characteristic of apes, whose forelimbs are used in walking and climbing."[58]

Contemporaries of Lombroso refined the notion of a physical basis of crime. Raffaele Garofalo (1851–1934) shared Lombroso's belief that certain physical characteristics indicate a criminal or delinquent nature.[59] Enrico Ferri (1856–1929), a student of Lombroso, believed that a number of biological, social, and organic factors caused delinquency and crime.[60]

These early views portrayed delinquent behavior as a function of a single factor or trait, such as body build or defective intelligence. They had a significant impact on early American criminology, which relied heavily on developing a science of "criminal anthropology."[61] Eventually, these views evoked criticism for their unsound methodology and lack of proper scientific controls. Some researchers used captive offender populations and failed to compare experimental subjects with control groups of nondelinquents or undetected delinquents. These methodological flaws made it impossible to determine whether biological traits produce delinquency. It is equally plausible that police are more likely to arrest, and courts convict, the mentally and physically abnormal. By the middle of the twentieth century, biological theories had fallen out of favor as an explanation of delinquency.

Contemporary Biosocial Theory

equipotentiality View that all people are equal at birth and are thereafter influenced by their environment.

For most of the twentieth century, delinquency experts scoffed at the notion that a youth's behavior was controlled by physical conditions present at birth. During this period, the majority of delinquency research focused on social factors, such as poverty and family life, that were believed to be responsible for law-violating behavior. However, a small group of criminologists and penologists kept alive the biological approach.[62] Some embraced sociobiology, a perspective that suggests behavior will adapt to the environment in which it evolved.[63] Creatures of all species are influenced by their genetic inheritance and their innate need to survive and dominate others. Sociobiology had a tremendous effect on reviving interest in a biological basis for crime and delinquency, because if biological (genetic) makeup controls all human behavior, it follows that a person's genes should also be responsible for determining whether he or she chooses law-violating or conventional behavior.[64]

Today, those who embrace trait theory reject the traditional assumptions that all humans are born with equal potential to learn and achieve (**equipotentiality**) and that thereafter their behavior is controlled by external or social forces.[65] While traditional criminologists suggest (either explicitly or implicitly) that all people are born equal and that parents, schools, neighborhoods, and friends control subsequent development, trait theorists argue that no two people (with rare exceptions, such as identical twins) are alike, and therefore each will react to environmental stimuli in a distinct way. They assume that a combination of personal traits and the environment produces individual behavior patterns. People with pathological traits such as brain damage, an abnormal personality, or a low IQ may have a heightened risk for crime; this risk is elevated by environmental stresses such as poor family life, educational failure, substance abuse, and exposure to delinquent peers. For example, low-birth-weight babies have been found to suffer poor educational achievement later in life; academic deficiency has been linked to delinquency and drug abuse.[66] The reverse may also apply: A supportive environment may be strong enough to counteract adverse biological and psychological traits.[67]

biosocial theory The view that both thought and behavior have biological and social bases.

Biosocial theorists believe that it is the interaction between predisposition and environment that produces delinquency. For example, children born into a disadvantaged environment often do not get the social and familial support they need to overcome their handicaps. Lack of family support can have long-term physical consequences. For example, a child's neural pathways may be damaged by repeated child neglect or abuse. Once experiences are ingrained, the brain "remembers," and a pattern of electrochemical activation is established, which remains present across the lifespan.[68] The relatively small number of youths who suffer both physical and social handicaps, and who also lack social supports, are the ones who become early onset offenders and persist in a life of crime.[69]

Contemporary biosocial theorists seek to explain the onset of antisocial behaviors, such as aggression and violence, by focusing on the physical qualities of the offenders.[70] The majority of major research efforts appear to be concentrated in three distinct areas of study: biochemical factors, neurological dysfunction, and genetic influences. These three views are discussed in some detail below.

Biochemical Factors

This area of biosocial research concerns the suspected relationship between antisocial behavior and biochemical makeup.[71] For example, research indicates that environmental contaminants that alter body chemistry can influence behavior.[72] When criminologists Paul Stretesky and Michael Lynch examined lead concentrations in air across counties in the United States, they found that areas with the highest concentrations of lead also reported the highest level of homicide.[73]

There is also evidence that diet may influence behavior through its impact on body chemistry. Of particular concern is an unusually high intake of such items as artificial food coloring, milk, and sweets. Some scientists believe that chronic under- or oversupply of vitamins, such as C and B3 and B6, may be related to restlessness and antisocial behavior in youths. Evidence also exists that allergies to foods can influence mood and behavior, resulting in personality swings between hyperactivity and depression.[74] This relationship is further explored in the Focus on Delinquency box entitled "Diet and Delinquency."

While this evidence seems persuasive, the relationship between biochemical intake and abnormal behavior is far from settled. A number of controlled experiments have failed to substantiate any real link between the two variables.[75] Despite these criticisms, the relationship between diet and delinquency remains unresolved. Further replication and research to study this relationship is certainly warranted.

Hormonal Levels   Hormonal levels are another area of biochemical research. Antisocial behavior allegedly peaks in the teenage years because hormonal activity is at its greatest level during this period. It is argued that increased levels of the male androgen testosterone are responsible for excessive levels of violence among teenage boys. Adolescents who experience more intense moods, mood swings, anxiety, and restlessness than people at other points in development also have the highest crime rates.[76] These mood and behavior changes have been associated with family conflict and antisocial behavior.

Focus on Delinquency

Diet and Delinquency

Stephen Schoenthaler, a well-known biocriminologist, has conducted a number of studies that substantiate his belief that there is a significant association between individuals' diets and their aggressive behavior patterns. In some cases the relationship is direct, while in others a poor diet may compromise individual functioning, which in turn produces aggressive behavior responses. For example, a poor diet may inhibit school performance, and kids who fail at school are at risk for delinquent behavior and criminality.

In one study of 803 New York City public schools, Schoenthaler found academic performance of 1.1 million schoolchildren rose 16 percent after their diets were modified. The number of "learning disabled" children fell from 125,000 to 74,000 in one year. No other changes in school programs for the learning disabled were initiated that year. In a similar experiment conducted in a correctional institution, violent and nonviolent antisocial behavior fell, on average, 48 percent among 8,047 offenders after dietary changes were implemented. In both these studies the improvements in behavior and academic performance were attributed to diets containing more vitamins and minerals as compared with the old diets. The greater amounts of these essential nutrients in the new diets were believed to have corrected impaired brain function caused by poor nutrition.

More recently, Schoenthaler conducted three randomized controlled studies in which 66 elementary school children, 62 confined teenage delinquents, and 402 confined adult felons, received dietary supplements that were the equivalent of a diet providing more fruit, vegetables, and whole grains. In order to remove experimental bias, neither subjects nor researchers knew who received the supplement and who received a placebo. In each study, the subjects receiving the dietary supplement demonstrated significantly less violent and nonviolent antisocial behavior when compared to the control subjects who received placebos. The carefully collected data verified that a very good diet, as defined by the World Health Organization, has significant behavioral benefits beyond its health effects.

Schoenthaler and his associates have also evaluated the relationship between nutrition and intelligence. These studies involved 1,753 children and young adults in California, Arizona, Oklahoma, Missouri, England, Wales, Scotland, and Belgium. In each study, the IQ of subjects taking dietary supplements rose higher, on average 16 points, than the placebo control group. Furthermore, the differences in IQ could be attributed to about 20 percent of the children who were presumably inadequately nourished prior to supplementation. The IQ research was expanded to include academic performance in two studies of over 300 schoolchildren aged 6 to 14 years in Arizona and California. In both studies, children who received daily supplements at school for three months achieved significantly higher gains in grade level compared to the matched control group taking placebos. The children taking a supplement improved academically at twice the rate of the children who took placebos.

Schoenthaler finds that parents with a child who behaves badly, or does poorly in school, might benefit from having their child take a blood test to determine whether concentrations of certain nutrients are below the reference norms; if so, a dietary supplement may correct the child's conduct and performance. There is evidence that 19 nutrients may be critical, and low levels appear to adversely affect brain function, academic performance, intelligence, and conduct. When attempting to improve IQ or conduct, it is critical to assess all these nutrients and correct deficiencies as needed. If blood nutrient concentrations are consistently in the normal range, physicians and parents may consider looking elsewhere for the cause of a child's difficulties.

Though more research is needed before the scientific community reaches a consensus on how low is "too low," Schoenthaler finds that the evidence that vitamins, minerals, chemicals, and other nutrients from a diet rich in fruits, vegetables, and whole grains can improve brain function, basic intelligence, and academic performance. These are all variables that have been linked to antisocial behavior.

Critical Thinking

1. If Schoenthaler is correct in his assumptions, should schools be required to provide a proper lunch for all children?
2. How would Schoenthaler explain the aging-out process? Hint: Do people develop better eating habits as they mature? What about after they get married?

InfoTrac College Edition Research

To read more about the relationship of nutrition and behavior, use *nutrition and behavior* as key terms on InfoTrac College Edition.

Sources: Stephen Schoenthaler, *Intelligence, Academic Performance, and Brain Function* (California State University Stanislaus, 2000); see also, S. Schoenthaler and I. Bier, "The Effect of Vitamin-Mineral Supplementation on Juvenile Delinquency among American Schoolchildren: A Randomized Double-Blind Placebo-Controlled Trial," *The Journal of Alternative and Complementary Medicine: Research on Paradigm, Practice, and Policy* 6:7–18 (2000).

An association between hormonal activity and antisocial behavior is suggested because rates of both factors peak in adolescence.[77] Hormonal sensitivity may begin at the very early stages of life when the fetus can be exposed to abnormally high levels of testosterone while in the uterus. This may trigger a heightened response to the release of testosterone when an adolescent male reaches puberty. Although testosterone levels appear normal, the young male is at risk for overaggressive behavior responses.[78]

Hormonal activity as an explanation of gender differences in the delinquency crime rate will be discussed further in Chapter 6.

Neurological Dysfunction

neurological The brain and nervous system structure.

Another focus of biosocial theory is the **neurological,** or brain and nervous system, structure of offenders. Studies measure indicators of system functioning, such as brain waves, heart rate, arousal levels, skin conductance and attention span, cognitive ability, and spatial learning, and then compare them to measures of antisocial behavior.

One view is that the neuroendocrine system, which controls brain chemistry, is the key to understanding violence and aggression. Imbalance in the central nervous system's chemical and hormonal activity has been linked to antisocial behavior and drug abuse. Research shows that persistent abnormality in the way the brain metabolizes glucose can be linked to substance abuse.[79] The National Center on Addiction and Substance Abuse at Columbia University recently released findings, illustrated in Exhibit 3.2, that show how learning disabilities are linked to substance abuse.

minimal brain dysfunction (MBD) Damage to the brain itself that causes antisocial behavior injurious to the individual's lifestyle and social adjustment.

Another view is that neurological dysfunction, commonly measured with an electroencephalogram (EEG), a CAT scan, or performance indicators (gross motor functions, visual processing, auditory-language functioning), is the key factor in causing aggression and violence. Children who manifest behavior disturbances may have identifiable neurological deficits, such as damage to the hemispheres of the brain.[80] This is sometimes referred to as **minimal brain dysfunction (MBD),** defined as an abnormality in the cerebral or brain structure that causes behavior injurious to a person's lifestyle and social adjustment. Impairment is produced by such factors as low birth weight, brain injury, birth complications, and inherited abnormality.[81] Research indicates that children exhibiting neurological impairment also have an increased risk for a garden variety of developmental problems, such as low IQ scores and cognitive impairment, which have been associated with delinquency.[82]

A number of research efforts have attempted to substantiate a link between neurological impairment and crime. There is evidence that this relationship can be detected quite early and that children who suffer from measurable neurological deficits at birth are more likely to become criminals later in life.[83] For example, low-birth-weight children are also likely to be early onset delinquents; low birth weight is highly correlated with neurological impairment.[84] Clinical analysis of death row inmates found that a significant number had suffered head injuries as children, resulting in damage to their central nervous system and neurological impairment.[85] Measurement of the brain activity of antisocial youths has revealed impairments that might cause them to experience otherwise unexplainable outbursts of anger, hostility, and aggression.[86] Evidence has been found linking the brain damage to mental disorders

Exhibit 3.2   Factors Linking Learning Disabilities and Substance Abuse

- Risk factors for adolescent substance abuse are very similar to the behavioral effects of learning disabilities—reduced self-esteem, academic difficulty, loneliness, depression, and the desire for social acceptance. Thus, learning disabilities may indirectly lead to substance abuse by generating types of behavior that typically lead adolescents to abuse drugs.
- A child with a learning disability is twice as likely to suffer attention deficit disorder (ADD) as a member of the general population, and there is a high incidence of ADD among individuals who abuse alcohol and drugs. It is known that as many as half of those suffering ADD self-medicate with drugs and alcohol.
- Children who are exposed to alcohol, tobacco, and illicit drugs in the womb are at higher risk for various developmental disorders, including learning disabilities. A mother using drugs while pregnant may be a predictor that the child will grow up in a home with a parent who is a substance abuser. This will also increase the risk that the child will abuse drugs or alcohol.

Source: National Center for Addiction and Substance Abuse (CASA) at Columbia University, *Substance Abuse and Learning Disabilities: Peas in a Pod or Apples and Oranges?* (New York: 2000).

such as schizophrenia and depression.[87] Cross-national studies also support a link between neurological dysfunction and antisocial behavior.[88]

A number of research studies have used an electroencephalogram to measure the brain waves and activity of delinquents and then compared them with those of law-abiding adolescents. In what is considered the most significant investigation of EEG abnormality and delinquency, 335 violent delinquents were classified on the basis of their antisocial activities and measured on an EEG.[89] While youths who committed a single violent act had a 12 percent abnormality rate—the same as the general population—the habitually aggressive youths tested at a 57 percent abnormality rate, almost five times normal. Behaviors believed to be highly correlated with abnormal EEG functions include poor impulse control, inadequate social ability, hostility, temper tantrums, destructiveness, and hyperactivity.[90]

The Focus on Delinquency box entitled "Attention Deficit/Hyperactivity Disorder (ADHD)" discusses this neurological condition associated with antisocial behavior in some detail.

The Learning Disabilities One specific type of MBD that has generated considerable interest is **learning disability (LD)**, a term that has been defined by the National Advisory Committee on Handicapped Children:

learning disability (LD) Neurological dysfunction that prevents an individual from learning to his or her potential.

> *Children with special learning disabilities exhibit a disorder in one or more of the basic psychological processes involved in understanding or using spoken or written languages. They may be manifested in disorders of listening, thinking, talking, reading, writing or arithmetic. They include conditions which have been referred to as perceptual handicaps, brain injury, minimal brain dysfunction, dyslexia, developmental aphasia, etc. They do not include learning problems which are due to visual, hearing or motor handicaps, to mental retardation, emotional disturbance, or to environmental disadvantages.*[91]

Learning disabled kids usually exhibit poor motor coordination (for example, problems with poor hand-eye coordination, trouble climbing stairs, clumsiness); have behavior problems (lack of emotional control, hostility, cannot stay on task); and improper auditory and vocal responses (do not seem to hear, cannot differentiate sounds and noises).

The relationship between learning disabilities and delinquency has been highlighted by studies showing that arrested and incarcerated children have a far higher LD rate than do children in the general population.[92] While learning disabilities are quite common (approximately 10% of all youths have some form of learning disorders), estimates of LD among adjudicated delinquents range from 26 percent to 73 percent.[93] Do these statistics necessarily mean that learning disabilities somehow cause delinquent behavior?

Typically, there are two possible explanations of the link between learning disabilities and delinquency.[94] One view, known as the *susceptibility rationale,* argues that the link is caused by certain side effects of learning disabilities, such as impulsiveness, poor ability to learn from experience, and inability to take social cues. In contrast, the *school failure rationale* assumes that the frustration caused by the LD child's poor school performance will lead to a negative self-image and acting-out behavior.

A number of recent research efforts have found that the LD child may not be any more susceptible to delinquent behavior than the non-LD child and that the proposed link between learning disabilities and delinquency may be an artifact of bias in the way the juvenile justice system treats LD youths.[95] Because of social bias, LD kids are more likely to get arrested, and if petitioned to juvenile court, their poor school record can influence the outcome of the case. LD youths bring with them to court a record of school problems and low grades and a history of frustrating efforts by agents of the educational system to help them. When information is gleaned from the school personnel at juvenile trials, LD children's poor performance may work

Attention Deficit/Hyperactivity Disorder (ADHD)

Many parents have noticed that their children do not pay attention to them—they run around and do things in their own way. Sometimes this inattention is a function of age; in other instances, it is a symptom of a common learning disability referred to as attention deficit/hyperactivity disorder (ADHD), a condition in which a child shows a developmentally inappropriate lack of attention, distractibility, impulsivity, and hyperactivity. No one is really sure how ADHD develops, but some psychologists believe it is tied to dysfunction in a section of the lower portion of the brain known as the reticular activating system. This area keeps the higher brain centers alert and ready for input. There is some evidence that this area is not working properly in ADHD kids and that their behavior is really the brain's attempt to generate new stimulation to maintain alertness. Other suspected origins are neurological damage to the frontal lobes of the brain, prenatal stress, and even food additives and chemical allergies. Some experts suggest that the condition might be traced to the neurological effects of abnormal levels of the chemicals dopamine and norepinephrine.

Children from any background can develop ADHD, but it is five to seven times more common in boys than girls. It does not affect intelligence, and ADHD children often show considerable ability with artistic endeavors. More common in the United States than elsewhere, ADHD tends to run in families, and there is some suggestion of an association with a family history of alcoholism and/or depression.

Estimates of ADHD in the general population range from 3 percent to 12 percent, but it is much more prevalent in adolescence, where some estimates reach as high as one third of the population. ADHD children are most often treated by giving them doses of stimulants, most commonly Ritalin and Dexedrine (or Dextroamphetamine), that, ironically, help these children to control their emotional and behavioral outbursts. The antimanic/anticonvulsant drug Tegretol has also been used effectively.

The condition usually results in poor school performance, including high dropout rates, bullying, stubbornness, mental disorder, and a lack of response to discipline; these conditions are highly correlated with delinquent behavior. A series of research studies now link ADHD to the onset and sustenance of a delinquent career and increased risk for antisocial behavior and substance abuse in adulthood. ADHD children are more likely to be arrested, charged with a felony, and have multiple arrests than non-ADHD youth. There is also evidence that ADHD youths who *also* exhibit early signs of MBD and conduct disorder, such as fighting, are the most at risk for persistent antisocial behaviors, continuing into adulthood. Many children who are diagnosed with ADHD engage in delinquent behavior, and new treatment techniques featuring behavior modification and/or drug therapies are constantly being developed to help children who have attention and/or hyperactivity problems.

The various symptoms of ADHD are described in Table A.

Table A   **Symptoms of ADHD**

Lack of Attention
Frequently fails to finish projects
Does not seem to pay attention
Does not sustain interest in play activities
Cannot sustain concentration on schoolwork or related tasks
Constantly runs around and climbs on things
Cannot organize tasks or work

Impulsivity
Frequently acts without thinking
Often "calls out" in class
Does not want to wait his or her turn in line or games
Shifts from activity to activity
Requires constant supervision

Hyperactivity
Shows excessive motor activity while asleep
Cannot sit still; is constantly fidgeting
Does not remain in his or her seat in class
Is easily distracted
Is constantly on the go like a "motor"
Difficulty regulating emotions
Difficulty getting started
Difficulty staying on track
Difficulty adjusting to social demands

Critical Thinking

1. Should youngsters suffering from ADHD be given mood-altering drugs, or are there dangers in this approach to treatment?
2. Should kids who suffer from ADHD be tried in juvenile court if they commit delinquent behaviors, or should their condition exempt them from official avenues of social control?

InfoTrac College Edition Research

 To learn more about attention deficit/hyperactivity disorder, use it as a subject guide on InfoTrac College Edition.

Sources: Kimberly Barletto, "Who's at Risk: Delinquent Trajectories of Children with Attention and Conduct Problems," Paper presented at the American Society of Criminology meeting, San Diego, 1997; Harry Wexler, "Attention Deficit Disorder, Drugs and Crime: The Dangerous Mixture," Paper presented at the American Society of Criminology meeting, Boston, November 1995; Terrie Moffitt and Phil Silva, "Self-Reported Delinquency, Neuropsychological Deficit, and History of Attention Deficit Disorder," *Journal of Abnormal Child Psychology* 16:553–69 (1988); American Psychiatric Association, *Diagnostic and Statistical Manual of the Mental Disorders*, 3rd ed. (Washington, DC: American Psychiatric Press, 1987), pp. 50–53.

against them in the court. Consequently, the view that learning disabilities cause delinquency has been questioned, and the view that LD children are more likely to be arrested and officially labeled delinquent demands further inquiry. Self-reports show little differences between the behavior of LD and non-LD youth, a finding that supports the social bias view.[96]

Despite this evidence, some scholars continue to affirm the presence of an LD-JD link. Psychologist Terrie Moffitt has evaluated the relevant literature on the connection between LD and delinquency and concludes that LD is a significant correlate of persistent antisocial behavior (*conduct disorders*).[97] She finds that neurological symptoms, such as LD and MBD, correlate highly with factors that create high risk for persistent antisocial behavior: early onset of deviance, hyperactivity, and aggressiveness. Moffitt's review indicates further research is needed on the cause and impact of neurological dysfunction: When do such problems begin? Are they the result of injury during birth? Or of child abuse and neglect?[98] Is there a continuum of learning disabilities, and are the most severely disabled also the most prone to delinquency?[99] Efforts are being made to introduce new technologies in the measurement of brain function and behavior to investigate early detection, prevention, and control of maladapted behaviors.[100]

Arousal Theory It has long been suspected that obtaining "thrills" is a motivator of crime. Adolescents may engage in such crimes as shoplifting and vandalism simply because they offer the attraction of "getting away with it"; delinquency is a thrilling demonstration of personal competence.[101] Is it possible that "thrill seekers" are people who have some form of abnormal brain functioning that directs their behavior?

Arousal theorists believe that for a variety of genetic and environmental reasons, some people's brains function differently in response to environmental stimuli. All of us seek to maintain a preferred or optimal level of arousal: Too much stimulation

arousal theorists Delinquency experts who believe that aggression is a function of the level of an individual's need for stimulation or arousal from the environment. Those who require more stimulation may act in an aggressive manner to meet their needs.

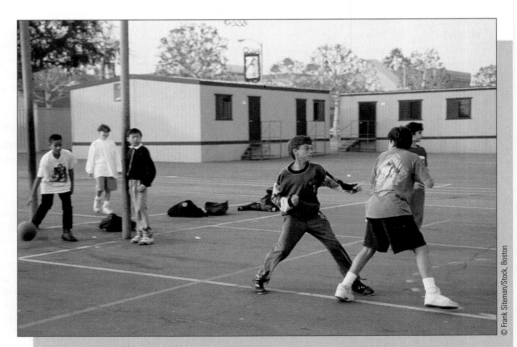

AROUSAL THEORISTS believe that, for a variety of genetic and environmental reasons, some people's brains function differently in response to environmental stimuli. All of us seek to maintain a preferred or optimal level of arousal. Too much stimulation may leave us anxious and stressed out; too little may make us bored and weary. Some kids may need the rush that comes from getting into scrapes and conflicts in order to feel relaxed and at ease.

leaves us anxious and stressed out; too little makes us feel bored and weary. There is, however, variation in the way children's brains process sensory input. Some nearly always feel comfortable with little stimulation, while others require a high degree of environmental input to feel comfortable. The latter group become "sensation seekers," who seek out stimulating activities that may include aggressive, violent behavior patterns.[102]

The factors that determine a person's level of arousal have not been fully determined. Suspected sources include brain chemistry (for example, serotonin levels) and brain structure. The number of nerve cells with receptor sites for neurotransmitters in the brain differs among people; some have many more than others. Another view is that adolescents with low heart rates are more likely to commit crimes because they seek stimulation to increase their arousal levels to normal levels.[103]

Genetic Influences

Individuals who share genes are alike in personality regardless of how they are reared, whereas rearing environment induces little or no personality resemblance.[104]

Biosocial theorists also study the genetic makeup of delinquents.[105] It has been hypothesized that some youths inherit a genetic configuration that predisposes them to violence and aggression.[106] Biosocial theorists believe that in the same way that people inherit genes for height and eye color, antisocial behavior characteristics and mental disorders may be passed down.[107]

Early theories of heredity suggested that delinquency-proneness ran in families. More recent research shows a significant association in sibling behavior: Brothers and sisters seem to share antisocial lifestyles.[108] However, most families share a similar lifestyle as well as a similar gene pool, making it difficult to determine whether behavior is a function of heredity or the environment. To establish the influence of environment and genetics independently, criminologists have employed samples of twins and adopted children.

Twin Studies   One method of studying the genetic basis of delinquency is to compare the behavior of twins to non-twin siblings. If criminal behavior is an inherited trait, identical twins should be quite similar in their behavior because they share a common genetic makeup.

Because twins are usually brought up in the same household and share common life experiences, however, any similarity in their delinquent behavior might be a function of comparable environmental influences and not genetics at all. To guard against this, biosocial theorists have compared the behavior of identical monozygotic (MZ) twins with fraternal dizygotic (DZ) twins; while the former have an identical genetic makeup, the latter share only about 50 percent of their genetic combinations. Research has shown that MZ twins are significantly closer in their personal characteristics, such as intelligence, than are DZ twins.[109] Reviews of twin studies found that in almost all cases, MZ twins have delinquent and antisocial behavior patterns more similar than that of DZ twins.[110]

While this seems to support a connection between genetic makeup and delinquency, little conclusive evidence exists of such an actual link. MZ twins are more likely to look alike and to share physical traits than DZ twins, and they are more likely to be treated similarly. Shared behavior patterns may therefore be a function of socialization and not heredity. Critics have also challenged the methodology of these studies and suggest that those that show a conclusive genetic link to behavior use faulty data.[111]

Against this interpretation is research evidence that identical twins reared apart are quite as similar in many traits, including personality, intelligence, and attitudes, as twins who live in the same household.[112] The Minnesota study of twins reared

To learn more about twin research, go to University of Minnesota–Twin Cities Department of Psychology, Minnesota Twin Family Study, What's Special about Twins to Science? http://www.psych.umn.edu/psylabs/mtfs/special.htm For an up-to-date list of Web links, go to http://info.wadsworth.com/siegel

apart found that MZ twins who were separated at birth shared many similarities in personal style and behavior; in contrast, the DZ twins reared apart seldom produced similar behavior patterns.[113] Such findings support a genetic basis of behavior.

Adoption Studies   Another way to determine whether delinquency is an inherited trait is to compare the behavior of adopted children with that of their biological parents. If the criminal behavior of children is more like that of their biological parents (whom they have never met) than that of their adopted parents (who brought them up), it would indicate that the tendency toward delinquency is inherited, rather than shaped by the environment.

Studies of this kind have generally supported the hypothesis that there is a link between genetics and behavior.[114] Adoptees share many of the behavioral and intellectual characteristics of their biological parents despite the social and environmental conditions found in their adoptive homes. Genetic makeup is sufficient to counteract and/or negate even the most extreme environmental conditions, such as malnutrition and abuse.[115]

Some of the most influential research in this area has been conducted by Sarnoff Mednick. In one study, Mednick and Bernard Hutchings found that while only 13 percent of the adoptive fathers of a sample of adjudicated delinquent youths had criminal records, 31 percent of their biological fathers had criminal records.[116] Analysis of a control group's background indicated that about 11 percent of all fathers will have criminal records. Hutchings and Mednick were forced to conclude that genetics played at least some role in creating delinquent tendencies, because the biological fathers of delinquents were much more likely than the fathers of noncriminal youths to be criminals.[117]

In addition to a direct link between heredity and delinquency, the literature also shows that behavior traits indirectly linked to delinquency may be at least in part inherited. Biological parents of adopted hyperactive children are more likely to show symptoms of hyperactivity than are the adoptive parents.[118] Several studies have reported a higher incidence of psychological problems in parents of hyperactive children when compared to control groups. While all hyperactive children do not become delinquent, the link between this neurological condition and delinquency has long been suspected.

Similarly, there is evidence (disputed) that intelligence is related to heredity and that low intelligence is a cause of impulsive delinquent acts that are easier to detect and more likely to result in arrest.[119] This connection can create the appearance of a relationship between heredity and delinquency. (See later in the chapter for more on IQ and delinquency.)

Connecting delinquent behavior to heredity is quite controversial since it implies that the cause of delinquency is (a) present at birth, and (b) "transmitted" from one generation to the next and immune to treatment efforts (since genes cannot be altered). Recent evaluations of the gene-crime relationship find that though a relationship can be detected, the better-designed research efforts provide less support than earlier and weaker studies.[120] If there is a genetic basis of delinquency, it is likely that genetic factors contribute to certain individual differences that interact with specific social and environmental conditions to bring about antisocial behavior.[121]

Evolutionary Theory

Some theorists have speculated that the human traits producing violence and aggression have been nurtured and produced through the long process of human evolution.[122] According to this **evolutionary theory,** the competition for scarce resources has influenced and shaped the human species.[123] Over the course of human existence, people have been shaped to engage in actions that promote their well-being and ensure the survival and reproduction of their genetic line. Males who are impulsive risk takers may be able to father more children; impulsive behavior is inher-

Exhibit 3.3 **Biosocial Theories**

	Major Premise	Strengths
Biochemical	Crime, especially violence, is a function of diet, vitamin intake, hormonal imbalance, and/or food allergies.	Explains irrational violence. Shows how the environment interacts with personal traits to influence behavior.
Neurological	Criminals and delinquents often suffer brain impairment, as measured by the EEG. Learning disabilities such as attention deficit hyperactive disorder and minimum brain dysfunction are related to antisocial behavior.	Helps explain relationship between child abuse and crime, and why there is a relationship between victimization and violence (i.e., people who suffer head trauma may become violent).
Genetic	Delinquent traits and predispositions are inherited. Criminality of parents can predict the delinquency of children.	Explains why only a small percentage of youths in a high-crime area become chronic offenders.
Evolutionary	Behavior patterns and reproductive traits, developed over the millennia, control behavior.	Explains male aggressiveness.

evolutionary theory Explaining the existence of aggression and violent behavior as positive adaptive behaviors in human evolution; these traits allowed their bearers to reproduce disproportionately, which has had an effect on the human gene pool.

ited and becomes intergenerational. It is not surprising that human history has been marked by war, violence, and aggression.

Crime rate differences between the genders then are less a matter of socialization than inherent differences in the mating patterns that have developed between the sexes over time.[124] Among young men, reckless, life-threatening "risk-proneness" is especially likely to evolve in societies where choosing not to compete means the inability to find suitable mates and to reproduce.[125] Aggressive males have had the greatest impact on the gene pool. The descendants of these aggressive males now account for the disproportionate amount of male aggression and violence.[126]

This evolutionary model suggests that a subpopulation of men has evolved with genes that incline them toward extremely low parental involvement. Sexually aggressive, they use their cunning to gain sexual conquests with as many females as possible. Since females would not willingly choose them as mates, they use stealth to gain sexual access—cheating—including such tactics as mimicking the behavior of more stable males.[127] Psychologist Byron Roth notes that these flamboyant, sexually aggressive males are especially attractive to younger, less intelligent women who begin having children at a very early age.[128] Their fleeting courtship process produces children with low IQs, aggressive personalities, and little chance of proper socialization in father-absent families. Because the criminal justice system treats them leniently, argues Roth, sexually irresponsible men are free to prey upon young girls. Over time, their offspring will yield an ever-expanding supply of offspring who are both antisocial and sexually aggressive.

Exhibit 3.3 offers a summary of the major biosocial theories of delinquency.

Psychological Theories of Delinquency

Some experts view the cause of delinquency as essentially psychological.[129] After all, most behaviors labeled delinquent—for example, violence, theft, sexual misconduct—seem to be symptomatic of some underlying psychological problem. Psychologists point out that many delinquent youths have poor home lives, destructive relationships with neighbors, friends, and teachers, and conflicts with authority figures in general. These relationships seem to indicate a disturbed personality structure. Furthermore, numerous studies of incarcerated youths indicate that the youths' personalities are marked by negative, antisocial behavior characteristics. And since delinquent behavior occurs among youths in every racial, ethnic, and socioeconomic

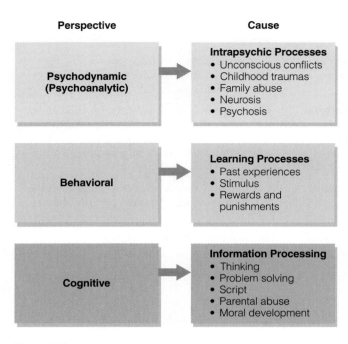

Perspective · Cause

Psychodynamic (Psychoanalytic)
Intrapsychic Processes
• Unconscious conflicts
• Childhood traumas
• Family abuse
• Neurosis
• Psychosis

Behavioral
Learning Processes
• Past experiences
• Stimulus
• Rewards and punishments

Cognitive
Information Processing
• Thinking
• Problem solving
• Script
• Parental abuse
• Moral development

Figure 3.2
Psychological Perspectives of Delinquency

psychodynamic theory Branch of psychology that holds that the human personality is controlled by unconscious mental processes developed early in childhood.

For a collection of links to libraries, museums, and biographical materials related to Sigmund Freud and his works, go to *http://users.rcn.com/brill/freudarc.html* For an up-to-date list of Web links, go to *http://info.wadsworth.com/siegel*

group, psychologists view it as a function of emotional and mental disturbance, rather than purely a result of social factors, such as racism, poverty, and class conflict. While many delinquents do not manifest significant psychological problems, enough do to give clinicians a powerful influence on delinquency theory.

Because psychology is a complex and diversified discipline, more than one psychological perspective on crime exists. Three prominent psychological perspectives on delinquency are the psychodynamic, the behavioral, and the cognitive.[130] (See Figure 3.2.)

Psychodynamic Theory

According to **psychodynamic theory,** which originated with the pioneering work of the Austrian physician Sigmund Freud (1856–1939), law violations are a product of an abnormal personality structure formed early in life and which thereafter controls human behavior choices.[131] In extreme cases, mental torment drives people into violence and aggression. The basis of psychodynamic theory is the assumption that human behavior is controlled by unconscious mental processes developed early in childhood.

Psychodynamic theory argues that the human personality contains three major components. The *id* is the unrestrained, primitive, pleasure-seeking component with which each child is born. The *ego* develops through the reality of living in the world and helps manage and restrain the id's need for immediate gratification. The *superego* develops through interactions with parents and other significant people and represents the development of conscience and the moral rules shared by most adults.

Psychodynamic theory suggests that unconscious motivations for behavior come from the id's action in response to two primal needs—sex and aggression. Human behavior is often marked by symbolic actions that reflect hidden feelings about these needs. For example, stealing a car may reflect a person's unconscious need for shelter and mobility to escape from hostile enemies (aggression) or perhaps an urge to enter a closed, dark, womblike structure that reflects the earliest memories (sex).

All three segments of the personality operate simultaneously. The id dictates needs and desires, the superego counteracts the id by fostering feelings of morality and righteousness, and the ego evaluates the reality of a position between these two extremes. If these components are properly balanced, the individual can lead a normal life. If one aspect of the personality becomes dominant at the expense of the others, the individual exhibits abnormal personality traits. (See Figure 3.3.)

Furthermore, the theory suggests that an imbalance in personality traits caused by a traumatic early childhood can result in long-term psychological difficulties. For example, if neglectful parents fail to develop a child's superego adequately, the child's id may become the predominant personality force; the absence of a strong superego results in an inability to distinguish clearly between right and wrong. Later, the youth may demand immediate gratification, lack compassion and sensitivity for the needs of others, disassociate feelings, act aggressively and impulsively, and demonstrate other psychotic symptoms. Antisocial behavior then may be the result of conflict or trauma occurring early in a child's development, and delinquent activity may become an outlet for violent and antisocial feelings.

Neuroses and Psychosis According to Freud's version of psychodynamic theory, people who experience feelings of anxiety and are afraid that they are losing control of their personalities are said to be suffering from a form of *neuroses* and are referred to as *neurotics.* People who have lost total control and who are dominated

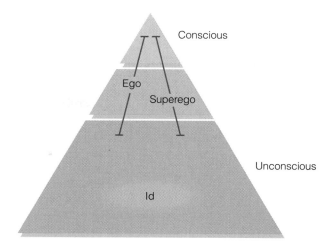

Figure 3.3
The Structure of the Id, Ego, and Superego

Conscious

Ego

Superego

Unconscious

Id

by their primitive id are known as *psychotics*. Their behavior may be marked by bizarre episodes, hallucinations, and inappropriate responses. *Psychosis* takes many forms, the most common being labeled *schizophrenia,* a condition marked by illogical thought processes, distorted perceptions, and abnormal emotional expression. According to the classical psychoanalytic view, the most serious types of youthful antisocial behavior, such as murder, might be motivated by psychosis, while neurotic feelings would be responsible for less serious delinquent acts and status offenses, such as petty theft and truancy.[132]

Contemporary psychologists generally no longer use the term neuroses to describe all forms of unconscious conflict. It is now more common to characterize people with more specific types of *disorders,* including anxiety disorder, mood disorder, sleep disorder, and so on.

The Psychodynamic Tradition and Delinquency A number of psychoanalysts have expanded upon Freud's original model to explain the onset of antisocial behaviors. Erik Erickson speculated that many adolescents experience a life crisis in which they feel emotional, impulsive, and uncertain of their role and purpose.[133] He coined the phrase **identity crisis** to denote this period of inner turmoil and confusion. Erickson's approach might characterize the behavior of youthful drug abusers as an expression of confusion over their place in society, their inability to direct behavior toward useful outlets, and perhaps their dependency on others to offer them solutions to their problems.

Psychoanalysts view youth crime as a result of unresolved mental anguish and internal conflict. Some children, especially those who have been abused or mistreated, may experience unconscious feelings associated with resentment, fear, and hatred. If this conflict cannot be reconciled, the children may regress to a state in which they become id dominated. This regression may be considered responsible for a great number of mental diseases, from neuroses to psychoses, and in many cases it may be related to criminal behavior.[134]

Another psychoanalytic view is that delinquents are id-dominated people who suffer from the inability to control impulsive drives. Perhaps because they suffered unhappy experiences in childhood or had families who could not provide proper love and care, delinquents suffer from weak or damaged egos that make them unable to cope with conventional society.[135] In its most extreme form, delinquency may be viewed as a form of psychosis that prevents delinquent youths from appreciating the feelings of their victims or controlling their own impulsive needs for gratification. For example, in his classic work, psychoanalyst August Aichorn found that social stress alone could not produce such an emotional state. He identifies **latent delinquents**—youths whose troubled family life leads them to seek immediate gratification without consideration of right and wrong or the feelings of others.[136]

identity crisis Psychological state, identified by Erikson, in which youth face inner turmoil and uncertainty about life roles.

latent delinquents Youths whose troubled family life leads them to seek immediate gratification without consideration of right and wrong or the feelings of others.

Others have viewed adolescent antisocial behavior as a consequence of feeling unable to cope with feelings of oppression. Criminality actually allows youths to strive by producing positive psychic results: helping them to feel free and independent; giving them the possibility of excitement and the chance to use their skills and imagination; providing the promise of positive gain; allowing them to blame others for their predicament (for example, the police); and giving them a chance to rationalize their own sense of failure ("If I hadn't gotten into trouble, I could have been a success").[137]

The psychodynamic view is supported by research that shows that a number of serious, violent juvenile offenders suffer from some sort of personality disturbance. Violent youths have been clinically diagnosed as "overtly hostile," "explosive or volatile," "anxious," and "depressed."[138] As many as 75 percent of a sample of male adolescents accused of murder could be classified as having some mental illness, including schizophrenia.[139] Abused, depressed, and suicidal children may grow up to vent their feelings in a homicidal rage.[140]

Family Life   The psychodynamic approach places heavy emphasis on the family's role in producing a delinquent child. Antisocial youths frequently come from families in which parents are unable to give love, set consistent limits, and provide the controls that allow children to develop the necessary personal tools to cope with the world in which they live.[141] The exploitive, destructive behavior of a youth may actually be a symbolic call for help. In fact, some psychoanalysts view delinquents' behavior as being motivated by an unconscious urge to be punished. These children who feel unloved at home assume the reason must be their own inadequacy—hence, they deserve punishment.

Behavioral Theory

behaviorism   Branch of psychology concerned with the study of observable behavior rather than unconscious processes; focuses on particular stimuli and responses to them.

Not all psychologists agree that behavior is controlled by unconscious mental processes determined by parental relationships developed early in childhood. Behavioral psychologists argue that a person's personality is learned throughout life during interaction with others. Based primarily on the works of the American psychologist John B. Watson (1878–1958) and popularized by Harvard professor B. F. Skinner (1904–1990), **behaviorism** concerns itself solely with measurable events and not the unobservable psychic phenomena described by psychoanalysts.

Behaviorists suggest that individuals learn by observing how people react to their behavior. Behavior is triggered initially by a stimulus or change in the environment. If a particular behavior is reinforced by some positive reaction or event, that behavior will be continued and eventually learned. However, behaviors that are not reinforced or are punished will be extinguished or become extinct. For example, if children are given a reward (ice cream for dessert) for eating their entire dinner, eventually they will learn to eat properly as a matter of habit. Conversely, if children are punished for some misbehavior, they will eventually learn to associate disapproval with that act and avoid it.

social learning theory   The view that behavior is modeled through observation, either directly through intimate contact with others, or indirectly through media; interactions that are rewarded are copied, whereas those that are punished are avoided.

Social Learning Theory   Not all behaviorists follow the teachings of Watson and Skinner strictly. Some hold that a person's learning and social experiences, coupled with his or her values and expectations, determine behavior. This is known as the **social learning** approach. The most widely read social learning theorists are Albert Bandura, Walter Mischel, and Richard Walters.[142] In general, they hold that children will model their behavior according to the reactions they receive from others, either positive or negative; the behavior of those adults they are in close contact with, especially parents; and the behavior they view on television and in movies. If children observe aggression and see that the aggressive behavior, such as an adult slapping or punching someone during an argument, is approved or rewarded, they will likely react violently during a similar incident. Eventually, the children will master the techniques of aggression and become more confident that their behavior will bring tangible rewards.[143]

By implication, social learning suggests that children who grow up in a home where violence is a way of life may learn to believe that such behavior is acceptable and rewarding. Even if parents tell children not to be violent and punish them if they are, the children will still model their behavior on the observed parental violence. Thus, children are more likely to heed what parents *do* than what they *say*. By midchildhood, some children have already acquired an association between their use of aggression against others and the physical punishment they receive at home. Often their aggressive responses are directed at other family members and siblings. The family may serve as a training ground for violence since the child perceives physical punishment as the norm during conflict situations with others.[144]

Adolescent aggression is a result of disrupted dependency relations with parents. This refers to the frustration and anger a child feels when parents provide poor role models and hold back affection and nurturing. Children who lack close dependent ties to their parents may have little opportunity or desire to model themselves after them or to internalize their standards of behavior. In the absence of such internalized controls, the child's aggression is likely to be expressed in an immediate, direct, and socially unacceptable fashion such as violence and aggression.[145]

The Media and Delinquency   One aspect of social learning theory that has received a great deal of attention is the belief that children will model their behavior after characters they observe on TV or see in movies. Many parents are concerned about the effects of their children's exposure to violence in the mass media. Often the violence is of a sexual nature, and some experts fear that there is a link between sexual violence and the viewing of pornography.[146]

Children are particularly susceptible to TV imagery. It is believed that many children consider television images to be real, especially when the images are authoritatively presented by an adult (as in a commercial). Some children, especially those who are considered "emotionally disturbed," may be unable to distinguish between fantasy and reality when watching TV shows.[147] Studies have found that frequent viewing of TV begins at 2.5 years of age and continues at a high level during the preschool and early school years. It has been estimated that children ages 2 to 5 watch TV 27.8 hours each week; children 6 to 11, 24.3 hours per week; and teens, 23 hours per week.[148] But what do they watch? Marketing research indicates that adolescents aged 11 to 14 rent violent horror movies at a higher rate than any other age group; kids this age use older peers and siblings and apathetic parents to gain access to R-rated films. More than 40 percent of U.S. households now have cable TV, which features violent films and shows. Even children's programming is saturated with violence.

What are the alternatives to violent programming? A well-publicized study conducted by researchers at UCLA found that at least 10 network shows made heavy use of violence. Of the 161 television movies monitored (every one that aired that season), 23 raised concerns from viewers about their use of violence, violent theme, violent title, or inappropriate graphicness of a scene. Of the 118 theatrical films monitored, 50 raised concerns about their use of violence. Some television series may contain limited depictions of violence, each of which may be appropriate in its context. However, it was found that commercials for these programs emphasized only the violent scenes with little in the way of context. Even some children's television programs were found to feature "sinister combat" as the theme of the show. The characters were portrayed as happy to fight with little provocation.[149] It is estimated that the average child views 8,000 TV murders before finishing elementary school.

TV and Violence   A number of research methods have been used to measure the effect of TV viewing on violent behavior. One method is to expose groups of subjects to violent TV shows in a laboratory setting and then compare their behavior to control groups who viewed nonviolent programming; observations have also been made in playgrounds, athletic fields, and residences. Other experiments require subjects to answer attitude surveys after watching violent TV shows. Still another approach is to use aggregate measures of TV viewing; for example, the number of violent TV shows on the air during a given time period is compared to crime rates during the same period.

Most evaluations of experimental data gathered using these techniques indicate that watching violence on TV is correlated to aggressive behaviors.[150] Such august bodies as the American Psychological Association and the National Institute of Mental Health support the TV-violence link.[151] Subjects who view violent TV shows are likely to commence aggressive behavior almost immediately. This phenomenon is demonstrated by numerous reports of copycat behavior after a particularly violent film or TV show is aired.

According to a recent analysis of all scientific data since 1975, Brad Bushman and Craig Anderson found that the weight of the evidence is that watching violence on TV is correlated to aggressive behaviors and that the newest, most methodologically sophisticated work shows the greatest amount of association. Put another way, the weight of the experimental results indicates that violent media have an immediate impact on people with a preexisting tendency toward crime and violence. A study conducted by researchers at Columbia University found that kids who watched more than an hour of TV each day showed an increase in assaults, fights, robberies, and other acts of aggression later in life. About 6 percent of 14-year-olds who watched less than an hour of television a day became involved in aggressive acts between the ages of 16 and 22. The rate of aggressive acts skyrocketed to 22.5 percent when kids watched between one to three hours of TV. For kids who viewed more than three hours of TV per day, 28.8 percent were later involved in aggressive acts as adults. This association remained significant after previous aggressive behavior, childhood neglect, family income, neighborhood violence, parental education, and psychiatric disorders were controlled statistically. This research provides a direct link between TV viewing in adolescence and later aggressive behavior in adulthood.[152]

Though this evidence is persuasive, the relationship between TV viewing and violence is still uncertain. A number of critics claim that the evidence simply does not support the claim that TV viewing is related to antisocial behavior.[153] Some critics assert that experimental results are inconclusive and short-lived. Kids may have an immediate reaction to viewing violence on TV, but aggression is quickly extinguished once the viewing ends.[154] Experiments showing that kids act aggressively after watching violent TV shows fail to link aggression to actual criminal behaviors, such as rape or assault. Aggregate data is also inconclusive. Little evidence exists that areas with the highest levels of violent TV viewing also have rates of violent crime that are above the norm.[155] Millions of children watch violence every night yet fail to become violent criminals. And even if a violent behavior–TV link could be established, it would be difficult to show that antisocial people develop aggressive traits merely from watching TV. Aggressive youths may simply enjoy watching TV shows that conform to and support their behavioral orientation.

Cognitive Theory

cognitive theory The branch of psychology that studies the perception of reality and the mental processes required to understand the world we live in.

A third area of psychology that has received increasing recognition in recent years has been **cognitive theory.** Psychologists with a cognitive perspective focus on mental processes—the way people perceive and mentally represent the world around them, and how they solve problems. The pioneers of this school were Wilhelm Wundt (1832–1920), Edward Titchener (1867–1927), and William James (1842–1920). The cognitive perspective contains several subgroups. Perhaps the most important for criminological theory is the moral and intellectual development branch, which is concerned with how people morally represent and reason about the world.

Jean Piaget (1896–1980), the founder of this approach, hypothesized that a child's reasoning processes develop in an orderly fashion, beginning at birth and continuing until age 12 and older.[156] At first, during the *sensorimotor stage,* children respond to the environment in a simple manner, seeking interesting objects and developing their reflexes. By the fourth and final stage, the *formal operational stage*, they have developed into mature adults who can use logic and abstract thought.

Lawrence Kohlberg applied the concept of developmental stages to issues in criminology.[157] He suggested that people travel through stages of moral development, during which the basis for moral and ethical decision making changes. It is possible that serious offenders have a moral orientation that differs from that of law-abiding citizens. Kohlberg's stages of development are as follows:

Stage 1: Right is obedience to power and avoidance of punishment.

Stage 2: Right is taking responsibility for oneself, meeting one's own needs, and leaving to others the responsibility for themselves.

Stage 3: Right is being good in the sense of having good motives, having concern for others, and "putting yourself in the other person's shoes."

Stage 4: Right is maintaining the rules of a society and serving the welfare of the group or society.

Stage 5: Right is based on recognized individual rights within a society with agreed-upon rules—a social contract.

Stage 6: Right is an assumed obligation to principles applying to all humankind—principles of justice, equality, and respect for human personality.

Kohlberg classified people according to the stage on this continuum at which their moral development has ceased to grow. In studies conducted by Kohlberg and his associates, criminals were found to be significantly lower in their moral judgment development than noncriminals of the same social background.[158] The majority of noncriminals were classified in stages three and four, while a majority of criminals were in stages one and two. Moral development theory, then, suggests that people who obey the law simply to avoid punishment or who have outlooks mainly characterized by self-interest are more likely to commit crimes than those who view the law as something that benefits all of society and who honor the rights of others. Subsequent research with delinquent youths has found that a significant number were in the first two moral development categories, while nondelinquents were ranked higher.[159] In addition, higher stages of moral reasoning are associated with such behaviors as honesty, generosity, and nonviolence, which are considered incompatible with delinquency.[160]

Information Processing   Cognitive theorists who study information processing try to explain antisocial behavior in terms of perception and analysis of data. When people make decisions, they engage in a sequence of cognitive thought processes. They first *encode* information so that it can be interpreted. They then search for a proper response and decide upon the most appropriate action; finally, they act on their decision.[161]

According to this approach, adolescents who use information properly, who are better conditioned to make reasoned judgments, and who can make quick and reasoned decisions when facing emotion-laden events are the ones best able to avoid antisocial behavior choices.[162] In contrast, violence-prone adolescents may be using information incorrectly or too slowly when making decisions. They have difficulty making the "right decision" while under stress. One reason is that they may be relying on mental "scripts" learned in their early childhood that tell them how to interpret events, what to expect, how they should react, and what the outcome of the interaction should be.[163] Hostile children may have learned improper scripts by observing how others react to events; their own parents' aggressive and inappropriate behavior would have considerable impact. Some children may have had early and prolonged exposure to violence, such as child abuse, which increases their sensitivity to teasing and maltreatment. Oversensitivity to rejection by their peers is a continuation of sensitivity to rejection by parents.[164] Violence becomes a stable behavior because the scripts that emphasize aggressive responses are repeatedly rehearsed as the child matures.

SOME TEENS MAY COMMIT VIOLENT acts because they misread situations and use faulty information when making decisions. Here Hallie Gnatovich of Lexington, Mass., performs an educational play called "The Yellow Dress" during a teen dating violence workshop at Ashland High School in Ashland, Mass. She portrays a character battered to death by an abusive boyfriend.

Violence-prone kids perceive people as more aggressive than they actually are and may feel that when there is no reason for alarm. As these children mature, they use fewer cues than most people to process information. Some use violence in a calculating fashion as a means of getting what they want; others react in an overly volatile fashion to the slightest provocation. When they attack victims, they may believe they are defending themselves, even though they are misreading the situation.[165] Adolescents who use violence as a coping technique with others are also more likely to exhibit other social problems, such as drug and alcohol abuse.[166]

There is also evidence that delinquent boys who engage in theft are more likely to exhibit cognitive deficits than nondelinquent youth. For example, they have a poor sense of time, leaving them incapable of dealing with or solving social problems in an effective manner.[167]

Personality and Delinquency

Personality can be defined as the reasonably stable patterns of behavior, including thoughts and emotions, that distinguish one person from another.[168] An individual's personality reflects characteristic ways of adapting to life's demands and problems. The way we behave is a function of how our personality enables us to interpret life events and make appropriate behavioral choices.

Can the cause of delinquency be linked to personality? There has been a great deal of research on this subject and an equal amount of controversy and debate over the findings.[169] In their early work, Sheldon Glueck and Eleanor Glueck identified a number of personality traits that characterize delinquents:

self-assertiveness	extroversion
defiance	ambivalence
impulsiveness	feeling unappreciated
narcissism	distrust of authority
suspicion	poor personal skills
destructiveness	mental instability
sadism	hostility
lack of concern for others	resentment[170]

The Gluecks' research is representative of the view that delinquents maintain a distinct personality whose characteristics increase the probability that (a) they will be aggressive and antisocial and (b) their actions will involve them with agents of social control, ranging from teachers to police. A number of personality deficits have been identified in the delinquent population.

Personality and Antisocial Behaviors   Since the Gluecks' findings were published, other research efforts have attempted to identify personality traits that would increase the chances for a delinquent career.[171] A common theme is that delinquents are hyperactive, impulsive individuals with short attention spans (attention deficit disorder), who frequently manifest conduct disorders, anxiety disorders, and depression.[172] These traits make them prone to problems ranging from psychopathology to drug abuse, sexual promiscuity, and violence.[173] Suspected traits include impulsivity, hostility, and aggressiveness.[174] The psychologist Hans Eysenck identified two important personality traits that he associated with antisocial behavior: extraversion and neuroticism. Eysenck defines **extraverts** as impulsive individuals who lack the ability to examine their own motives and behaviors; **neuroticism** produces anxiety, tension, and emotional instability.[175] Youths who lack self-insight and are impulsive and emotionally unstable are likely to interpret events differently than youths who are able to give reasoned judgments to life events. While the former may act destructively, for example, by using drugs, the latter will be able to reason that such behavior is ultimately self-defeating and life threatening.

In a recent study evaluating the most widely used measures of personality, Joshua Miller and Donald Lynam found that variance within two dimensions—agreeableness and conscientiousness—seems most closely related to antisocial behaviors. Agreeableness involves the ability to use appropriate interpersonal strategies when dealing with others; conscientiousness involves the ability to control impulses, carry out plans and tasks, maintain organizational skills, and follow one's internal moral code.[176] Miller and Lynam found that personality researchers now link antisocial behaviors to such traits as hostility, self-centeredness, spitefulness, jealousy, and indifference to others. Law violators tend to lack ambition, motivation, and perseverance, have difficulty controlling their impulses, and hold unconventional values and beliefs. While Miller and Lynam show that these personality traits are linked to crime, there is still some question about the direction of the linkage. On the one hand, it is possible that kids with these personality traits are programmed to commit crimes. On the other hand, it is possible that personality traits interact with environmental factors to alter behavior. For example, kids who are low in conscientiousness will most likely have poor educational and occupational histories, which limit their opportunity for advancement; this blocked opportunity renders them crime-prone.[177]

The Antisocial Personality   It has also been suggested that chronic delinquency may result from a personality pattern or syndrome commonly referred to as the **psychopathic** or **sociopathic personality** (the terms are used interchangeably). Though no more than 3 percent of the male offending population may be classified as sociopathic, it is possible that a large segment of the persistent chronic offenders share this trait.[178]

Psychopathic (sociopathic) youths exhibit a low level of guilt and anxiety and persistently violate the rights of others. Although they may exhibit superficial charm and above-average intelligence, these often mask a disturbed personality that makes them incapable of forming enduring relationships with others. Frequently involved in such deviant behaviors as truancy, running away, lying, substance abuse, and impulsivity, psychopaths lack the ability to empathize with others. From an early age, the psychopath's home life was filled with frustrations, bitterness, and quarreling. Consequently, throughout life, the sociopath is unreliable, unstable, demanding, and egocentric. Hervey Cleckley, a leading authority on psychopathy, uses this definition:

> *[Psychopaths are] chronically antisocial individuals who are always in trouble, profiting neither from experience nor punishment, and maintaining no real*

extravert   A person who behaves impulsively and doesn't have the ability to examine motives and behavior.

neuroticism   A personality trait marked by unfounded anxiety, tension, and emotional instability.

psychopathic personality (also known as sociopathic personality)   A person lacking in warmth and affection, exhibiting inappropriate behavior responses, and unable to learn from experience.

loyalties to any person, group, or code. They are frequently callous and hedonistic, showing marked emotional immaturity, with lack of responsibility, lack of judgment, and an ability to rationalize their behavior so that it appears warranted, reasonable, and justified.[179]

Youths diagnosed as psychopaths are believed to be thrill seekers who engage in violent, destructive behavior. Some become gang members and engage in violent and destructive sexual escapades to compensate for a fear of responsibility and an inability to maintain interpersonal relationships.[180] Delinquents have been described as sensation seekers who desire a hedonistic pursuit of pleasure, an extraverted lifestyle, partying, drinking, and a variety of sexual partners.[181]

A number of factors have been found to contribute to the development of psychopathic/sociopathic personalities. They include having an emotionally disturbed parent, a lack of love, parental rejection during childhood, and inconsistent discipline.[182] Another view is that psychopathy has its basis in a measurable physical condition—psychopaths suffer from levels of arousal that are lower than those of the general population. Consequently, psychopathic youths may need greater-than-average stimulation to bring them up to comfortable levels. Psychologists have attempted to treat patients diagnosed as psychopaths by giving them adrenaline, which increases their arousal levels.

Intelligence and Delinquency

Psychologists have long been concerned with the development of intelligence and its subsequent relationship to behavior. It has been charged that children with low IQs are responsible for a disproportionate share of delinquency.

Early criminologists believed that low intelligence was a major cause of delinquency. They thought that if it could be determined which individuals were less intelligent, it might be possible to identify potential delinquents before they committed socially harmful acts.[183] Since social scientists had a captive group of subjects in training schools and penal institutions, studies began to appear that measured the correlation between IQ and crime by testing adjudicated juvenile delinquents. Delinquent juveniles were believed to be inherently substandard in intelligence and thus naturally inclined to commit more crimes than more intelligent persons. Thus, juvenile delinquents were used as a test group around which numerous theories about intelligence were built.

Nature Theory   When the newly developed IQ tests were administered to inmates of prisons and juvenile training schools in the first decades of the twentieth century, a large proportion of the inmates scored low on the tests. Henry Goddard found in his studies in 1920 that many institutionalized persons were what he considered "feeble-minded" and thus concluded that at least half of all juvenile delinquents were mental defectives.[184]

Similarly, in 1926, William Healy and Augusta Bronner tested a group of delinquents in Chicago and Boston and found that 37 percent were subnormal in intelligence.[185] They concluded that delinquents were 5 to 10 times more likely to be mentally deficient than nondelinquent boys.

These and other early studies were embraced as proof that low IQ scores indicated potentially delinquent children and that a correlation existed between innate low intelligence and deviant behavior. IQ tests were believed to measure the inborn genetic makeup of individuals, and many criminologists accepted the predisposition of substandard individuals toward delinquency. This view is referred to as **nature theory** of intelligence.

nature theory   Holds that low intelligence is genetically determined and inherited.

nurture theory Holds that intelligence is partly biological but mostly sociological; negative environmental factors encourage delinquent behavior and depress intelligence scores for many youths.

Nurture Theory   Changing and more culturally sensitive explanations of human behavior in the 1930s led to the **nurture theory** of intelligence. This school of thought holds that intelligence must be viewed as partly biological but primarily sociological. Nurture theory argues that intelligence is not inherited and that low-IQ parents do not necessarily produce low-IQ children.[186] It discredits the notion that people commit crimes because they have low IQ scores. Instead, it holds that environmental stimulation from parents, relatives, schools, peer groups, and innumerable others creates a child's IQ level and that low IQs result from an environment that also encourages delinquent and criminal behavior.[187] For example, if educational environments could be improved, the result might be both an elevation in IQ scores and a decrease in delinquency.[188]

Studies challenging the assumption that people automatically committed delinquent acts because they had below-average IQs began to appear as early as the 1920s. John Slawson's study of 1,543 delinquent boys in New York institutions found that although 80 percent of the delinquents achieved lower scores in abstract verbal intelligence than the general population, delinquents were about normal in mechanical aptitude and nonverbal intelligence. Slawson found no relationship between the number of arrests, the types of offenses, and IQ.[189] In 1931, Edwin Sutherland also evaluated IQ studies of criminals and delinquents and found evidence disputing the association between intelligence and criminality.[190] These findings did much to discredit the notion that a strong relationship existed between IQ and criminality, and for many years the IQ-delinquency link was ignored.

IQ and Delinquency Today   A study published in the 1970s by Travis Hirschi and Michael Hindelang revived interest in the association between IQ and delinquency.[191] After conducting a thorough statistical analysis of IQ and delinquency data sets, Hirschi and Hindelang concluded both that IQ tests are a valid predictor of intelligence and that "the weight of evidence is that IQ is more important than race and social class" for predicting delinquent involvement. They argued that a low IQ increases the likelihood of delinquent behavior through its effect on school performance: Youths with low IQs do poorly in school, and school failure and academic incompetence are highly related to delinquency.

The Hirschi-Hindelang findings have been supported by a number of research efforts.[192] In their widely read *Crime and Human Nature,* James Q. Wilson and Richard Herrnstein concluded

> . . . *there appears to be a clear and consistent link between criminality and low intelligence. That is, taking all offenders as a group, and ignoring differences among kinds of crime, criminals seem, on the average, to be a bit less bright and to have a different set of intellectual strengths and weaknesses than do noncriminals as a group.*[193]

Contemporary research efforts have continued to uncover an association between low IQ scores and antisocial behavior. Scores on intelligence tests have been used to predict violent behavior and used to distinguish between groups of violent and nonviolent offenders.[194] However, among those social scientists who believe that IQ scores predict criminality, there is still disagreement on the direction of the association. Some believe that IQ has an *indirect* influence on delinquency. Children with a low IQ are more likely to engage in delinquent behavior because their poor verbal ability creates a frustrating school experience. According to this view, low IQ leads to school failure, and academic deficiency has consistently been associated with delinquency.[195] In contrast, some experts believe that IQ may have a *direct* influence on the onset of delinquent involvement. The key linkage between IQ and delinquency is the ability to manipulate abstract concepts. Low intelligence limits adolescents' ability to "foresee the consequences of their offending and to appreciate the feelings of victims."[196] Therefore, youths with limited intelligence are more likely to misinterpret events and gestures, act foolishly, take risks, and engage in harmful behavior.

IQ and Delinquency Controversy   The relationship between IQ and delinquency is extremely controversial. It implies there is a condition present at birth that accounts for a child's delinquent behavior throughout the life cycle and that this condition is not easily changed or improved.[197] By implication, if delinquency is not spread evenly through the social structure, neither is intelligence.

The controversy has been fueled by charges that tests are culturally biased and invalid, which makes any existing evidence at best inconclusive. There is also research indicating that IQ level has negligible influence on delinquent behavior.[198] If, as some believe, the linkage between IQ and crime is indirect, then delinquency may be a reflection of poor school performance and educational failure.[199] As Wilson and Herrnstein put it, "A child who chronically loses standing in the competition of the classroom may feel justified in settling the score outside, by violence, theft, and other forms of defiant illegality."[200] Since the relationship runs from low IQ to poor school performance to frustration to delinquency, school officials need to recognize the problem and plan programs to help underachievers perform better in school. Since the hypothesized relationship between IQ and delinquency, even if proved to be valid, is an indirect one, educational enrichment programs can help counteract any influence intellectual impairment has on the predilection of young people to commit crime.

Critiquing Individual-Level Theories

Individual-level studies have been criticized on a number of grounds. One view is that the research methodologies they employ are weak and invalid. Most research efforts use adjudicated or incarcerated offenders. It is often difficult to determine whether findings represent the delinquent population or merely those most likely to be arrested and adjudicated by officials of the justice system. For example, some critics have described the methods used in heredity studies as "poorly designed, ambiguously reported and exceedingly inadequate in addressing the relevant issues."[201]

Some critics also fear that individual-level research can be socially and politically damaging. If an above-average number of indigent youth become delinquent offenders, can it be assumed that the less affluent are impulsive, greedy, have low IQs, or are genetically inferior? To many social scientists, the implications of this conclusion are unacceptable in light of what is known about race, gender, and class bias.

Critics also suggest that individual-level theory is limited as a generalized explanation of delinquent behavior because it fails to account for the known patterns of criminal behavior. Delinquent behavior trends seem to conform to certain patterns linked to social-ecological rather than individual factors—social class, seasonality, population density, and gender roles. Social forces that appear to be influencing the onset and maintenance of delinquent behavior are not accounted for by explanations of delinquency that focus on the individual. If, as is often the case, the delinquent rate is higher in one neighborhood than another, are we to conclude that youths in the high-crime area are more likely to be watching violent TV shows or eating more sugar-coated cereals than those in low-crime neighborhoods? How can individual traits explain the fact that crime rates vary between cities and between regions?

Defending Individual-Level Theory   The legitimization of social-psychological, psychiatric, and biosocial approaches to explaining deviant behavior may prove to be an important and productive paradigm shift in the decades ahead.[202]

Theorists who focus on individual behavior contend that critics overlook the fact that their research often gives equal weight to environmental and social as well as mental and physical factors.[203] For example, some people may have particular developmental problems that place them at a disadvantage in society, limit their chances of conventional success, and heighten their feelings of anger, frustration, and rage.

Though the incidence of these personal traits may be spread evenly across the social structure, families in one segment of the population have the financial wherewithal to help treat the problem, while families in another segment may lack the economic means and the institutional support needed to help their children. Delinquency rate differences may be a result of differential access to opportunities either to commit crime or receive the care and treatment needed to correct and compensate for developmental problems.

In addition, individual-level theorists believe that, like it or not, youths are in fact different and may have differing potentials for antisocial acts. For example, gender differences in the violence rate may be explained by the fact that after centuries of aggressive mating behavior, males have become naturally more violent than females.[204] Male aggression may be more a matter of genetic transfer than socialization or cultural patterns.

Trait Theory and Delinquency Prevention

Since many individual-oriented theorists are also practitioners and clinicians, it is not surprising that a great deal of delinquency prevention efforts are based in psychological and biosocial theory.

As a group, individual perspectives on delinquency suggest that prevention efforts should be directed at strengthening a youth's home life and personal relationships. Almost all of these theoretical efforts point to the child's home life as a key factor in delinquent behavior. If parents cannot supply proper nurturing, love, care, discipline, nutrition, and so on, the child cannot develop properly. Whether one believes that delinquency has a biosocial basis, a psychological basis, or a combination of both, it is evident that delinquency prevention efforts should be oriented to reach children early in their development.

It is, therefore, not surprising that county welfare agencies and privately funded treatment centers have offered counseling and other mental health services to families referred by schools, welfare agents, and juvenile court authorities. In some instances, intervention is focused on a particular family problem that has the potential for producing delinquent behavior, for example, alcohol and drug problems, child abuse, and sexual abuse. In other situations, intervention is more generalized and oriented toward developing the self-image of parents and children or improving discipline in the family. These programs are covered in Chapter 11.

In addition, individual approaches have been used to prevent court-adjudicated youths from engaging in further criminal activities. It has become almost universal practice for incarcerated and court-adjudicated youths to be given some form of mental and physical evaluation before they begin their term of correctional treatment. Such rehabilitation methods as psychological counseling and psychotropic medication (involving such drugs as Valium or Ritalin) are often prescribed. In some instances, rehabilitation programs are provided through drop-in centers that service youths unable to remain in their homes, while more intensive programs require residential care and treatment. The creation of such programs illustrates how agents of the juvenile justice system believe that many delinquent youths and status offenders have psychological or physical problems and that their successful treatment can help reduce repeat criminal behavior. Faith in this treatment approach suggests widespread agreement among juvenile justice system professionals that the cause of delinquency can be traced to individual pathology; if not, why else bother treating them?

Some questions remain about the effectiveness of individual treatment as a delinquency prevention technique. Little hard evidence exists that clinical treatment alone can prevent delinquency or rehabilitate known delinquents. It is possible that programs designed to help youths may actually stigmatize and label them, hindering their efforts to live conventional lives.[205] Because this issue is so critical, it will be discussed further in Chapter 15.

SUMMARY

Delinquency theories that focus on the individual can be classified according to two major groups—choice theories and trait theories.

Choice theory holds that people have free will to control their actions. Delinquency is a product of the weighing of the risks of crime against its benefits. If the risk is greater than the gain, people will choose not to commit crime. One way of creating a greater risk is to make sure that the punishments associated with delinquency are severe, certain, and fast.

The routine activities theory maintains that a pool of motivated offenders exists and that they will take advantage of unguarded, suitable targets.

Deterrence theory holds that if delinquents are indeed rational, an inverse relationship should exist between punishment and crime. Deterrence theory has been criticized on the grounds that it wrongfully assumes that delinquents make a rational choice before committing crimes and does not take into account the social and psychological factors that may influence delinquency. Research designed to test the validity of the deterrence concept has not indicated that deterrent measures actually reduce the delinquency rate.

Specific deterrence theory holds that the delinquency rate can be reduced if known offenders are punished so severely that they never commit crimes again. There is little evidence that harsh punishments actually reduce the crime rate. Incapacitation theory maintains that if deterrence does not work, the best course of action is to incarcerate known offenders for long periods of time so that they lack criminal opportunity. Research efforts have not provided clear-cut proof that experiencing punishment actually will reduce crime rates.

Choice theorists argue that delinquent behavior can be prevented if youths can be deterred from illegal acts. Consequently, they agree that the punishment for delinquency should be increased. One method is to transfer youths to the criminal courts or to grant the adult justice system original jurisdiction over serious juvenile cases. Similarly, some delinquency experts advocate the use of incapacitation for serious juvenile offenders—for example, using mandatory, long-term sentences for chronic delinquents.

Trait theories hold that personal and environmental factors dictate behavior choices—that delinquents do not choose to commit crimes freely but are influenced by forces beyond their control.

One of the earliest branches of biosocial theory focused on the biological bases of delinquency. Cesare Lombroso originated the concept of the "born criminal" and linked delinquency to inborn traits. Following his lead were theories based on genetic inheritance and body build. While biological theory was in disrepute for many years, it has recently reemerged in importance. Biochemical, neurological, and genetic factors have been linked to aggressiveness and violence in youth. However, because biosocial theory has not been subjected to methodologically sound tests, the results remain problematic.

Another type of individual-level theory has a psychological orientation. Some theorists rely on Freud's psychoanalytic theory and link delinquency to ego development and personality. Others use a behavioral perspective. Social-learning theorists hold that children imitate the adult behavior they observe firsthand or on television. Children who are exposed to violence and see it rewarded may become violent as adults. Cognitive psychology is concerned with human development and how people perceive the world. Criminality is viewed as a function of improper information processing and/or moral development.

Psychological traits, such as personality and intelligence, have been linked to delinquency. One important area of study has been the psychopath, a person who lacks emotion and concern for others. The controversial issue of the relationship of IQ to delinquency has received new interest with the publication of research studies purporting to show that delinquents have lower IQs than nondelinquents.

Many delinquency prevention efforts are based on psychological theory. Judges commonly order delinquent youths to receive counseling and other mental health care. Recently, some adjudicated delinquent offenders have been given biochemical therapy.

KEY TERMS

choice theory	predatory crime	criminal atavism	arousal theorists
trait theory	general deterrence	equipotentiality	evolutionary theory
free will	specific deterrence	biosocial theory	psychodynamic theory
utilitarians	situational crime prevention	neurological	identity crisis
classical criminology		minimal brain dysfunction (MBD)	latent delinquents
routine activities theory	target-hardening technique	learning disability (LD)	behaviorism

| social learning theory | extravert | psychopathic or sociopathic personality | nature theory |
| cognitive theory | neuroticism | | nurture theory |

QUESTIONS FOR DISCUSSION

1. Is there such a thing as the "born criminal"? Are some people programmed to commit crime at birth?

2. Is crime psychologically abnormal? Can there be "normal" crimes?

3. Apply psychodynamic theory to such delinquent acts as shoplifting and breaking and entering a house.

4. Can delinquent behavior be deterred by the threat of punishment? If not, how can it be controlled?

5. Should we incapacitate violent juvenile offenders for long periods of time—10 years or more?

6. Does watching violent TV and films encourage youth to be aggressive and antisocial? Do advertisements for beer featuring attractive, provocatively dressed young men and women encourage drinking and precocious sex? If not, why bother advertising?

7. Discuss the characteristics of psychopaths. Do you know anyone who fits the description?

VIEWPOINT

Americans now spend twice the money on video games as on going to the movies. The core gaming audience is 8- to 14-year-old males. Eighty percent of the games produced are violent. Blood, decapitation, guns, knives, mutilation, and death are presented in color, sound, and ever-more realistic graphics. If imitation or modeling is a problem with television, as social learning research has shown, extrapolate this to the more immersible media, where visually, auditorily, and physically the audience becomes embedded in its context. Piaget has shown how learning/assimilation is enhanced with sensorimotor activity—using a joystick or mouse. These actions become habits and are further reinforced. As Jane Healy has said, "Habits of the mind become structures of the brain."

Does playing with violent video games increase a child's chances of becoming violent? To find out, go to Michael Brody, "Playing with Death," *The Brown University Child and Adolescent Behavior Letter* 16:8 (2000), on InfoTrac College Edition. Use *violence in the mass media* as a subject guide to learn more about the topic.

NOTES

1. Marvin Wolfgang, Robert Figlio, and Thorsten Sellin, *Delinquency in a Birth Cohort* (Chicago: University of Chicago Press, 1972).

2. Alan Lizotte, Terence Thornberry, Marvin Krohn, Deborah Chard-Wierschem, and David McDowall, "Neighborhood Context and Delinquency: A Longitudinal Analysis," in H. J. Kerner and E. Weitekamp, eds., *Cross-National Longitudinal Research on Human Development and Criminal Behavior* (Dordrecht, The Netherlands: Kluwer Academic Publishers, 1993), pp. 11–15.

3. Jeremy Bentham, *A Fragment on Government and an Introduction to the Principles of Morals and Legislation,* ed. Wilfred Harrison (Oxford: Basic Blackwell, 1967).

4. See, generally, Ernest Van den Haag, *Punishing Criminals* (New York: Basic Books, 1975).

5. Pierre Tremblay and Carlo Morselli, "Patterns in Criminal Achievement: Wilson and Abrahamsen Revisited," *Criminology* 38:633–60 (2000).

6. See, generally, James Q. Wilson, *Thinking about Crime* (New York: Basic Books, 1975).

7. Cesare Beccaria, *On Crimes and Punishments,* 6th ed., trans. Henry Paolucci (Indianapolis: Bobbs-Merrill, 1977), p. 43.

8. F. E. Devine, "Cesare Beccaria and the Theoretical Foundations of Modern Penal Jurisprudence," *New England Journal on Prison Law* 7:8–21 (1982).

9. See, generally, Morgan Reynolds, *Crime and Punishment in America* (Washington, DC: National Center for Policy Analysis, 1995).

10. James Q. Wilson and Richard Herrnstein, *Crime and Human Nature* (New York: Simon and Schuster, 1985), p. 396.

11. Mary Tuck and David Riley, "The Theory of Reasoned Action: A Decision Theory of Crime," in D. Cornish and R. Clarke, eds., *The Reasoning Criminal* (New York: Springer-Verlag, 1986), pp. 156–69.

12. Felix Padilla, *The Gang as an American Enterprise* (New Brunswick, NJ: Rutgers University Press, 1992); see also Martin Sanchez-Jankowski, *Islands in the Street: Gangs and American Urban Society* (Berkeley: University of California Press, 1991).

13. Bruce Jacobs, "Crack Dealers' Apprehension Avoidance Techniques: A Case of Restrictive Deterrence," *Justice Quarterly* 13:359-81 (1996).

14. Ibid., p. 367.

15. Travis Hirschi, "Rational Choice and Social Control Theories of Crime," in D. Cornish and R. Clarke, eds., *The Reasoning Criminal* (New York: Springer-Verlag, 1986), p. 114.

16. See, generally, Derek Cornish and Ronald Clarke, eds., *The Reasoning Criminal* (New York: Springer-Verlag, 1986); see also Philip Cook, "The Demand and Supply of Criminal Opportunities," in Michael Tonry and Norval Morris, eds., *Crime and Justice,* vol. 7 (Chicago: University of Chicago Press, 1986), pp. 1–28; Ronald Clarke and Derek Cornish, "Modeling Offenders' Decisions: A Framework for Research and Policy," in Michael Tonry and Norval Morris, eds., *Crime and Justice,* vol. 6 (Chicago: University of Chicago Press, 1985), pp. 147–87; Morgan Reynolds, *Crime by Choice: An Economic Analysis* (Dallas: Fisher Institute, 1985).

17. Michael Hindelang, Michael Gottfredson, and James Garofalo, *Victims of Personal Crime: An Empirical Foundation for a Theory of Personal Victimization* (Cambridge, MA: Ballinger, 1978).

18. James Massey, Marvin Krohn, and Lisa Bonati, "Property Crime and the Routine Activities of Individuals," *Journal of Research in Crime and Delinquency* 26:378–400 (1989).

19. Lawrence Cohen and Marcus Felson, "Social Change and Crime Rate Trends: A Routine Activities Approach," *American Sociological Review* 44:588–608 (1979).

20. David Maume, "Inequality and Metropolitan Rape Rates: A Routine Activity Approach," *Justice Quarterly* 6:513–27 (1989).

21. Denise Osborn, Alan Trickett, and Rob Elder, "Area Characteristics and Regional Variates as Determinants of Area Property Crime Levels," *Journal of Quantitative Criminology* 8:265–82 (1992).

22. Paul Bellair, "Informal Surveillance and Street Crime: A Complex Relationship," *Criminology* 38:137–67 (2000).

23. Massey, Krohn, and Bonati, "Property Crime and Routine Activities of Individuals," p. 397.

24. Lawrence Cohen, Marcus Felson, and Kenneth Land, "Property Crime Rates in the United States: A Macrodynamic Analysis, 1947–1977, with Ex-Ante Forecasts for the Mid-1980's," *American Journal of Sociology* 86:90–118 (1980).

25. William Smith, Sharon Glave Frazee, and Elizabeth Davison, "Furthering the Integration of Routine Activity and Social Disorganization Theories: Small Units of Analysis and the Study of Street Robbery as a Diffusion Process," *Criminology* 38:489–521 (2000).

26. Steven Messner and Kenneth Tardiff, "The Social Ecology of Urban Homicide: An Application of the 'Routine Activities' Approach," *Criminology* 23:241–67 (1985).

27. Leslie Kennedy and David Forde, "Routine Activities and Crime: An Analysis of Victimization in Canada," *Criminology* 28:137–52 (1990).

28. Robert O'Brien, "Relative Cohort Sex and Age-Specific Crime Rates: An Age-Period-Relative-Cohort-Size Model," *Criminology* 27:57–78 (1989).

29. D. Wayne Osgood, Janet Wilson, Patrick O'Malley, Jerald Bachman, and Lloyd Johnston, "Routine Activities and Individual Deviant Behavior," *American Sociological Review* 61:635-55 (1996).

30. Matthew Ploeger, "Youth Employment and Delinquency: Reconsidering A Problematic Relationship," *Criminology* 35:659-75 (1997).

31. Ernest Van den Haag, "The Criminal Law as a Threat System," *Journal of Criminal Law and Criminology* 73:709–85 (1982).

32. Beccaria, *On Crimes and Punishments.*

33. For the classic analysis on the subject, see Johannes Andenaes, *Punishment and Deterrence* (Ann Arbor: University of Michigan Press, 1974).

34. Gordon Bazemore and Mark Umbreit, "Rethinking the Sanctioning Function in Juvenile Court: Retributive or Restorative Responses to Youth Crime," *Crime and Delinquency* 41:296–316 (1995).

35. Bruce Jacobs, "Anticipatory Undercover Targeting in High Schools," *Journal of Criminal Justice* 22:445–57 (1994).

36. Leona Lee, "Factors Determining Waiver in a Juvenile Court," *Journal of Criminal Justice* 22:329–39 (1994).

37. *Wilkins v. Missouri; Stanford v. Kentucky,* 109 S.Ct. 2969 (1989).

38. Carol Kohfeld and John Sprague, "Demography, Police Behavior, and Deterrence," *Criminology* 28:111–36 (1990).

39. Steven Klepper and Daniel Nagin, "The Deterrent Effect of Perceived Certainty and Severity of Punishment Revisited," *Criminology* 27:721–46 (1989).

40. See, generally, Raymond Paternoster, "The Deterrent Effect of Perceived Certainty and Severity of Punishment: A Review of the Evidence and Issues," *Justice Quarterly* 42:173–217 (1987); idem, "Absolute and Restrictive Deterrence in a Panel of Youth: Explaining the Onset, Persistence/Desistance, and Frequency of Delinquent Offending," *Social Problems* 36:289–307 (1989).

41. Wanda Foglia, "Perceptual Deterrence and the Mediating Effect of Internalized Norms among Inner-City Teenagers," *Journal of Research in Crime and Delinquency* 34:414–42 (1997); Donald Green, "Measures of Illegal Behavior in Individual-Level Deterrence Research," *Journal of Research in Crime and Delinquency* 26:253–75 (1989); Charles Tittle, *Sanctions and Social Deviance: The Question of Deterrence* (New York: Praeger, 1980).

42. Eric Jensen and Linda Metsger, "A Test of the Deterrent Effect of Legislative Waiver on Violent Juvenile Crime," *Crime and Delinquency* 40:96–104 (1994).

43. Foglia, "Perceptual Deterrence and the Mediating Effect of Internalized Norms among Inner-City Teenagers."

44. Ibid.

45. Bureau of Justice Statistics, *Prisoners and Drugs* (Washington, DC: Government Printing Office, 1983); idem, *Prisoners and Alcohol* (Washington, DC: Government Printing Office, 1983).

46. Maynard Erickson and Jack Gibbs, "Punishment, Deterrence, and Juvenile Justice," in D. Shichor and D. Kelly, eds., *Critical Issues in Juvenile Justice* (Lexington, MA: Lexington Books, 1980), pp. 183–202.

47. Christina Dejong, "Survival Analysis and Specific Deterrence: Integrating Theoretical and Empirical Models of Recidivism," *Criminology* 35:561–76 (1997).

48. Paul Tracy and Kimberly Kempf-Leonard, *Continuity and Discontinuity in Criminal Careers* (New York: Plenum Press, 1996).

49. Pamela Lattimore, Christy Visher, and Richard Linster, "Predicting Rearrest for Violence among Serious Youthful Offenders," *Journal of Research in Crime and Delinquency* 32:54–83 (1995).

50. David Altschuler, "Juveniles and Violence: Is There an Epidemic and What Can Be Done." Paper presented at the American Society of Criminology meeting, Boston, November 1995; Charles Murray and Louis B. Cox, *Beyond Probation* (Beverly Hills: Sage, 1979).

51. Marcus Felson, "Routine Activities and Crime Prevention," in National Council for Crime Prevention, *Studies on Crime and Crime Prevention, Annual Review,* vol. 1 (Stockholm: Scandinavian University Press, 1992), pp. 30–34.

52. Barry Webb, "Steering Column Locks and Motor Vehicle Theft: Evaluations for Three Countries," in Ronald Clarke, ed., *Crime Prevention Studies* (Monsey, NY: Criminal Justice Press, 1994), pp. 71–89.

53. Taken from the famous title of an article by Walter Reckless, Simon Dinitz, and Ellen Murray: "The Good Boy in a High Delinquency Area," *Journal of Criminal Law, Criminology, and Police Science* 48:18–26 (1957).

54. Massey, Krohn, and Bonati, "Property Crime and the Routine Activities of Individuals."

55. David Shantz, "Conflict, Aggression, and Peer Status: An Observational Study," *Child Development* 57:1322–32 (1986).

56. For an excellent review of Lombroso's work, as well as that of other well-known theorists, see Randy Martin, Robert Mutchnick, and W. Timothy Austin, *Criminological Thought, Pioneers Past and Present* (New York: Macmillan, 1990).

57. Marvin Wolfgang, "Cesare Lombroso," in Herman Mannheim, ed., *Pioneers in Criminology* (Montclair, NJ: Patterson Smith, 1970), pp. 232–71.

58. Gina Lombroso-Ferrero, *Criminal Man According to the Classification of Cesare Lombroso* (1911; reprint, Montclair, NJ: Patterson Smith, 1972), p. 7.

59. Edwin Driver, "Charles Buckman Goring," in Herman Mannheim, ed., *Pioneers in Criminology* (Montclair, NJ: Patterson Smith, 1970), pp. 429–42.

60. See, generally, Thorsten Sellin, "Enrico Ferri," in Herman Mannheim, ed., *Pioneers in Criminology* (Montclair, NJ: Patterson Smith, 1970), pp. 361–84.

61. Nicole Hahn Rafter, "Criminal Anthropology in the United States," *Criminology* 30:525–47 (1992).

62. Edmond O. Wilson, *Sociobiology: The New Synthesis* (Cambridge: Harvard University Press, 1975).

63. For a general review, see John Archer, "Human Sociobiology: Basic Concepts and Limitations," *Journal of Social Issues* 47:11–26 (1991).

64. Arthur Caplan, *The Sociobiology Debate: Readings on Ethical and Scientific Issues* (New York: Harper & Row, 1978).

65. See C. Ray Jeffrey, "Criminology as an Interdisciplinary Behavioral Science," *Criminology* 16:149–67 (1978).

66. Dalton Conley and Neil Bennett, "Is Biology Destiny? Birth Weight and Life Chances," *American Sociological Review* 654:458–67 (2000).

67. Diana Fishbein, "Selected Studies on the Biology of Antisocial Behavior," in John Conklin, ed., *New Perspectives in Criminology* (Needham Heights, MA: Allyn and Bacon, 1996), pp. 26–38.

68. Anthony Walsh and Lee Ellis, "Shoring Up the Big Three: Improving Criminological Theories with Biosocial Concepts." Paper presented at the annual Society of Criminology Meeting, San Diego, November 1997, p. 15.

69. Terrie Moffitt, "Adolescence-Limited and Life-Course Persistent Antisocial Behavior: A Developmental Taxonomy," *Psychological Review* 100:674–701 (1993).

70. For a thorough review of the biosocial perspective, see Diana Fishbein, "Biological Perspectives in Criminology," *Criminology* 28:27–72 (1990); idem, "Selected Studies on the Biology of Antisocial Behavior," in John Conklin, ed., *New Perspectives in Criminology* (Needham Heights, MA: Allyn and Bacon, 1996), 26–38.

71. See, generally, Adrian Raine, *The Psychopathology of Crime* (San Diego: Academic Press, 1993); see also Leonard Hippchen, *The Ecologic-Biochemical Approaches to Treatment of Delinquents and Criminals* (New York: Van Nostrand Reinhold, 1978).

72. Alexander Schauss, *Diet, Crime and Delinquency* (Berkeley: Parker House, 1980).

73. Paul Stretesky and Michael Lynch, "The Relationship between Lead Exposure and Homicide," *Archives of Pediatric Adolescent Medicine* 155:579–82 (2001).

74. Paul Marshall, "Allergy and Depression: A Neurochemical Threshold Model of the Relation between the Illnesses," *Psychological Bulletin* 113:23–29 (1993).

75. Mark Wolraich et al., "Effects of Diets High in Sucrose or Aspartame on the Behavior and Cognitive Performance of Children," *The New England Journal of Medicine* 330:303–6 (1994).

76. Christy Miller Buchanan, Jacquelynne Eccles, and Jill Becker, "Are Adolescents the Victims of Raging Hormones? Evidence for Activational Effects of Hormones on Moods and Behavior at Adolescence," *Psychological Bulletin* 111:62–107 (1992).

77. Alex Piquero and Timothy Brezina, "Testing Moffitt's Account of Adolescent-Limited Delinquency," *Criminology* 39:353–70 (2001).

78. Fishbein, "Selected Studies on the Biology of Antisocial Behavior."

79. Diana Fishbein, "Neuropsychological Function, Drug Abuse, and Violence, a Conceptual Framework," *Criminal Justice and Behavior* 27:139–59 (2000).

80. Kytja Voeller, "Right-Hemisphere Deficit Syndrome in Children," *American Journal of Psychiatry* 143:1004–9 (1986).

81. Moffitt, "Adolescence-Limited and Life-Course Persistent Antisocial Behavior."

82. Leila Beckwith and Arthur Parmelee, "EEG Patterns of Preterm Infants, Home Environment, and Later IQ," *Child Development* 57:777–89 (1986).

83. Adrian Raine, Patricia Brennan, Brigitte Mednick, and Sarnoff Mednick, "High Rates of Violence, Crime, Academic Problems, and Behavioral Problems in Males with Both Early Neuromotor Deficits and Unstable Family Environments," *Archives of General Psychiatry* 53:544–49 (1966).

84. Stephen Tibbetts, "Low Birth Weight, Disadvantaged Environment and Early Onset: A Test of Moffitt's Interactional Hypothesis." Paper presented at the American Society of Criminology meeting, Boston, November 1995.

85. Dorothy Otnow Lewis, Jonathan Pincus, Marilyn Feldman, Lori Jackson, and Barbara Bard, "Psychiatric, Neurological, and Psychoeducational Characteristics of 15 Death Row Inmates in the United States," *American Journal of Psychiatry* 143:838–45 (1986).

86. See, generally, R. R. Monroe, *Brain Dysfunction in Aggressive Criminals* (Lexington, MA: D.C. Heath, 1978).

87. Adrian Raine et al., "Interhemispheric Transfer in Schizophrenics, Depressives and Normals with Schizoid Tendencies," *Journal of Abnormal Psychology* 98:35–41 (1989).

88. Jean Seguin, Robert Pihl, Philip Harden, Richard Tremblay, and Bernard Boulerice, "Cognitive and Neuropsychological Characteristics of Physically Aggressive Boys," *Journal of Abnormal Psychology* 104:614–24 (1995).

89. D. Williams, "Neural Factors Related to Habitual Aggression—Consideration of Differences between Habitual Aggressives and Others Who Have Committed Crimes of Violence," *Brain* 92:503–20 (1969).

90. Charlotte Johnson and William Pelham, "Teacher Ratings Predict Peer Ratings of Aggression at 3-Year Follow-Up in Boys with Attention Deficit Disorder with Hyperactivity," *Journal of Consulting and Clinical Psychology* 54:571–72 (1987).

91. Cited in Charles Post, "The Link between Learning Disabilities and Juvenile Delinquency: Cause, Effect, and 'Present Solutions,'" *Juvenile and Family Court Journal* 31:59 (1981).

92. For a general review, see Concetta Culliver, "Juvenile Delinquency and Learning Disability: Any Link?" Paper presented at the Academy of Criminal Justice Sciences, San Francisco, April 1988.

93. Joel Zimmerman, William Rich, Ingo Keilitz, and Paul Broder, "Some Observations on the Link between Learning Disabilities and Juvenile Delinquency," *Journal of Criminal Justice* 9:9–17 (1981); J. W. Podboy and W. A. Mallory, "The Diagnosis of Specific Learning Disabilities in a Juvenile Delinquent Population," *Juvenile and Family Court Journal* 30:11–13 (1978).

94. Charles Murray, *The Link between Learning Disabilities and Juvenile Delinquency: A Current Theory and Knowledge* (Washington, DC: Government Printing Office, 1976).

95. Robert Pasternak and Reid Lyon, "Clinical and Empirical Identification of Learning Disabled Juvenile Delinquents," *Journal of Correctional Education* 33:7–13 (1982).

96. Zimmerman et al., "Some Observations on the Link between Learning Disabilities and Juvenile Delinquency."

97. Terrie Moffitt, "The Neuropsychology of Conduct Disorder" (University of Wisconsin-Madison, mimeo, 1992).

98. Elizabeth Kandel and Sarnoff Mednick, "Perinatal Complications Predict Violent Offending," *Criminology* 29:519–30 (1991).

99. James Creechan, "The Masking of Learning Disabilities and Juvenile Delinquency: The Learning Disabilities–Juvenile Delinquency Amplification Model." Paper presented at the annual meeting of the American Society of Criminology, New Orleans, November 1992.

100. Diana Fishbein and Robert Thatcher, "New Diagnostic Methods in Criminology: Assessing Organic Sources of Behavioral Disorder," *Journal of Research in Crime and Delinquency* 23:240–67 (1986).

101. Jack Katz, *Seduction of Crime: Moral and Sensual Attractions of Doing Evil* (New York: Basic Books, 1988), pp. 12–15.

102. Lee Ellis, "Arousal Theory and the Religiosity-Criminality Relationship, in Peter Cordella and Larry Siegel, eds., *Contemporary Criminological Theory* (Boston: Northeastern University, 1996), pp. 65–84.

103. Adrian Raine, Peter Venables, and Sarnoff Mednick, "Low Resting Heart Rate at Age 3 Years Predisposes to Aggression at Age 11 Years: Evidence from the Mauritius Child Health Project," *Journal of the American Academy of Adolescent Psychiatry* 36:1457–64 (1997).

104. David Rowe, *The Limits of Family Influence: Genes, Experiences and Behavior* (New York: Guilford Press, 1995), p. 64.

105. For a review, see Lisabeth Fisher DiLalla and Irving Gottesman, "Biological and Genetic Contributors to Violence—Widom's Untold Tale," *Psychological Bulletin* 109:125–29 (1991).

106. Ibid.

107. L. Erlenmeyer-Kimling, Robert Golden, and Barbara Cornblatt, "A Taxometric Analysis of Cognitive and Neuromotor Variables in Children in Risk for Schizophrenia," *Journal of Abnormal Psychology* 98:203–8 (1989).

108. David Rowe, Joseph Rogers, and Sylvia Meseck-Bushey, "Sibling Delinquency and the Family Environment: Shared and Unshared Influences," *Child Development* 63:59–67 (1992).

109. David Rowe, "Sibling Interaction and Self-Reported Delinquent Behavior: A Study of 265 Twin Pairs," *Criminology* 23:223–40 (1985); Nancy Segal, "Monozygotic and Dizygotic Twins: A Comparative Analysis of Mental Ability Profiles," *Child Development* 56:1051–58 (1985).

110. Mednick and Volavka, "Biology and Crime," in Norval Morris and Michael Tonry, eds., *Crime and Justice* vol. 1 (Chicago: University of Chicago Press, 1980), pp. 85–159; Lee Ellis, "Genetics and Criminal Behavior," *Criminology* 10:43–66 (1982); Karl O. Christiansen, "A Preliminary Study of Criminality among Twins," in S. A. Mednick and Karl O. Christiansen, eds., *The Biosocial Bases of Criminal Behavior* (New York: Gardner Press, 1977).

111. Glenn Walters, "A Meta-Analysis of the Gene-Crime Relationship," *Criminology* 30:595–613 (1992).

112. T. J. Bouchard, D. T. Lykken, D. T. McGue, N. L. Segal, and A. Tellegen, "Sources of Human Psychological Differences: The Minnesota Study of Twins Reared Apart," *Science* 250:223–28 (1990).

113. D. T. Lykken, M. McGue, A. Tellegen, and T. J. Bouchard, Jr., "Emergenesis, Genetic Traits That May Not Run in Families," *American Psychologist* 47:1565–77 (1992).

114. Remi Cadoret, Colleen Cain, and Raymond Crowe, "Evidence for a Gene-Environment Interaction in the Development of Adolescent Antisocial Behavior," *Behavior Genetics* 13:301–10 (1983).

115. Rowe, *The Limits of Family Influence,* p. 110.

116. Bernard Hutchings and Sarnoff Mednick, "Criminality in Adoptees and Their Adoptive and Biological Parents: A Pilot Study," in S. A. Mednick and Karl O. Christiansen, eds., *Biosocial Bases of Criminal Behavior* (New York: Gardner Press, 1977).

117. For similar findings, see William Gabrielli and Sarnoff Mednick, "Urban Environment, Genetics, and Crime," *Criminology* 22:645–53 (1984).

118. Jody Alberts-Corush, Philip Firestone, and John Goodman, "Attention and Impulsivity Characteristics of the Biological and Adoptive Parents of Hyperactive and Normal Control Children," *American Journal of Orthopsychiatry* 56:413–23 (1986).

119. Wilson and Herrnstein, *Crime and Human Nature,* p. 131.

120. Walters, "A Meta-Analysis of the Gene-Crime Relationship."

121. Ibid., p. 108.

122. Lawrence Cohen and Richard Machalek, "A General Theory of Expropriative Crime: An Evolutionary Ecological Approach," *American Journal of Sociology* 94:465–501 (1988).

123. For a general review, see Martin Daly and Margo Wilson, "Crime and Conflict: Homicide in Evolutionary Psychological Theory," in Michael Tonry, ed., *Crime and Justice, An Annual Edition* (Chicago: University of Chicago Press, 1997), pp. 51–100.

124. David Rowe, Alexander Vazsonyi, and Aurelio Jose Figuerdo, "Mating-Effort in Adolescence: A Conditional of Alternative Strategy," *Personal Individual Differences* 23:105–15 (1997).

125. Ibid.

126. Lee Ellis, "The Evolution of Violent Criminal Behavior and Its Nonlegal Equivalent," in Harry Hoffman, ed., *Crime in Biological, Social, and Moral Contexts* (New York: Praeger, 1990), pp. 61–81.

127. Ellis and Walsh, "Gene-Based Evolutionary Theories of Criminology."

128. Byron Roth, "Crime and Child Rearing," *Society* 34:39–45 (1996).

129. For a thorough review of this issue, see David Brandt and S. Jack Zlotnick, *The Psychology and Treatment of the Youthful Offender* (Springfield, IL: Charles C. Thomas, 1988).

130. Spencer Rathus, *Psychology* (New York: Holt, Rinehart & Winston, 1996), pp. 11–21.

131. See, generally, Sigmund Freud, *An Outline of Psychoanalysis,* trans. James Strachey (New York: Norton, 1963).

132. Seymour Halleck, *Psychiatry and the Dilemmas of Crime* (Berkeley: University of California Press, 1971).

133. See, generally, Erik Erickson, *Identity, Youth, and Crisis* (New York: Norton, 1968).

134. David Abrahamsen, *Crime and Human Mind* (New York: Columbia University Press, 1944), p. 137.

135. See, generally, Fritz Redl and Hans Toch, "The Psychoanalytic Perspective," in Hans Toch, ed., *Psychology of Crime and Criminal Justice* (New York: Holt, Rinehart & Winston, 1979), pp. 193–95.

136. August Aichorn, *Wayward Youth* (New York: Viking Press, 1935).

137. Halleck, *Psychiatry and the Dilemmas of Crime.*

138. James Sorrells, "Kids Who Kill," *Crime and Delinquency* 23:312–20 (1977).

139. Richard Rosner et al., "Adolescents Accused of Murder and Manslaughter: A Five-Year Descriptive Study," *Bulletin of the American Academy of Psychiatry and the Law* 7:342–51 (1979).

140. Milton Rosenbaum and Binni Bennet, "Homicide and Depression," *American Journal of Psychiatry* 143:367–70 (1986).

141. Brandt and Zlotnick, *The Psychology and Treatment of the Youthful Offender,* pp. 72–73.

142. See Albert Bandura and Frances Menlove, "Factors Determining Vicarious Extinction of Avoidance Behavior through Symbolic Modeling," *Journal of Personality and Social Psychology* 8:99–108 (1965); and Albert Bandura and Richard Walters, *Social Learning and Personality Development* (New York: Holt, Rinehart & Winston, 1963).

143. David Perry, Louise Perry, and Paul Rasmussen, "Cognitive Social Learning Mediators of Aggression," *Child Development* 57:700–11 (1986).

144. Bonnie Carlson, "Children's Beliefs about Punishment," *American Journal of Orthopsychiatry* 56:308–12 (1986).

145. Albert Bandura and Richard Walters, *Adolescent Aggression* (New York: Ronald Press, 1959), p. 32.

146. Edward Donnerstein and Daniel Linz, "The Question of Pornography," *Psychology Today* 20:56–59 (1986).

147. Joyce Sprafkin, Kenneth Gadow, and Monique Dussault, "Reality Perceptions of Television: A Preliminary Comparison of Emotionally Disturbed and Nonhandicapped Children," *American Journal of Orthopsychiatry* 56:147–52 (1986).

148. Daniel Anderson, Elizabeth Pugzles Lorch, Diane Field, Patricia Collins, and John Nathan, "Television Viewing at Home: Age Trends in Visual Attention Time with TV," *Child Development* 57:1024–33 (1986).

149. UCLA Center for Communication Policy, Television Violence Monitoring Project (Los Angeles, 1995); Associated Press, "Hollywood Is Blamed in Token Booth Attack," *Boston Globe,* 28 November 1995, p. 30.

150. Wendy Wood, Frank Wong, and J. Gregory Chachere, "Effects of Media Violence on Viewers' Aggression in Unconstrained Social Interaction," *Psychological Bulletin* 109:371–83 (1991); Lynette Friedrich-Cofer and Aletha Huston, "Television Violence and Aggression: The Debate Continues," *Psychological Bulletin* 100:364–71 (1986).

151. American Psychological Association, *Violence on TV.* A social issue release from the Board of Social and Ethical Responsibility for Psychology (Washington, DC: APA, 1985).

152. Brad Bushman and Craig Anderson, "Media Violence and the American Public," *American Psychologist* 56:477–89

(2001); Jeffrey Johnson, Patricia Cohen, Elizabeth Smailes, Stephanie Kasen, and Judith Brook, "Television Viewing and Aggressive Behavior During Adolescence and Adulthood," *Science* 295:2468–71 (2002).

153. Jonathon Freedman, "Television Violence and Aggression: What the Evidence Shows," in S. Oskamp, ed., *Applied Social Psychology Annual: Television as a Social Issue* (Newbury Park, CA: Sage, 1988), pp. 144–62.

154. Jonathon Freedman, "Effect of Television Violence on Aggressiveness," *Psychological Bulletin* 96:227–46 (1984); idem, "Television Violence and Aggression: A Rejoinder," *Psychological Bulletin* 100:372–78 (1986).

155. Steven Messner, "Television Violence and Violent Crime: An Aggregate Analysis," *Social Problems* 33:218–35 (1986).

156. See, generally, Jean Piaget, *The Moral Judgement of the Child* (London: Keagan Paul, 1932).

157. Lawrence Kohlberg, *Stages in the Development of Moral Thought and Action* (New York: Holt, Rinehart and Winston, 1969).

158. L. Kohlberg, K. Kauffman, P. Scharf, and J. Hickey, *The Just Community Approach in Corrections: A Manual* (Niantic, CT: Connecticut Department of Corrections, 1973).

159. Scott Henggeler, *Delinquency in Adolescence* (Newbury Park, CA: Sage, 1989), p. 26.

160. Ibid.

161. K. A. Dodge, "A Social Information Processing Model of Social Competence in Children," in M. Perlmutter, ed., *Minnesota Symposium in Child Psychology*, vol. 18 (Hillsdale, NJ: Erlbaum, 1986), pp. 77–125.

162. Adrian Raine, Peter Venables, and Mark Williams, "Better Autonomic Conditioning and Faster Electrodermal Half-Recovery Time at Age 15 Years as Possible Protective Factors Against Crime at Age 29 Years," *Developmental Psychology* 32:624–30 (1996).

163. L. Huesman and L. Eron, "Individual Differences and the Trait of Aggression," *European Journal of Personality* 3:95–106 (1989).

164. Rolf Loeber and Dale Hay, "Key Issues in the Development of Aggression and Violence from Childhood to Early Adulthood," *Annual Review of Psychology* 48:371–410 (1997).

165. J. E. Lochman, "Self and Peer Perceptions and Attributional Biases of Aggressive and Nonaggressive Boys in Dyadic Interactions," *Journal of Consulting and Clinical Psychology* 55:404–10 (1987).

166. Kathleen Cirillo et al., "School Violence: Prevalence and Intervention Strategies for At-Risk Adolescents," *Adolescence* 33:319–31 (1998).

167. Leilani Greening, "Adolescent Stealers' and Nonstealers' Social Problem-Solving Skills," *Adolescence* 32:51–56 (1997).

168. See, generally, Walter Mischel, *Introduction to Personality*, 4th ed. (New York: Holt, Rinehart and Winston, 1986).

169. D. A. Andrews and J. Stephen Wormith, "Personality and Crime: Knowledge and Construction in Criminology," *Justice Quarterly* 6:289–310 (1989); Donald Gibbons, "Comment—Personality and Crime: Non-Issues, Real Issues, and a Theory and Research Agenda," *Justice Quarterly* 6:311–24 (1989).

170. Sheldon Glueck and Eleanor Glueck, *Unraveling Juvenile Delinquency* (Cambridge: Harvard University Press, 1950).

171. See, generally, Hans Eysenck, *Personality and Crime* (London: Routledge and Kegan Paul, 1977).

172. David Farrington, "Psychobiological Factors in the Explanation and Reduction of Delinquency," *Today's Delinquent* 7:37–51 (1988).

173. Laurie Frost, Terrie Moffitt, and Rob McGee, "Neuropsychological Correlates of Psychopathology in an Unselected Cohort of Young Adolescents," *Journal of Abnormal Psychology* 98:307–13 (1989).

174. Edelyn Verona and Joyce Carbonell, "Female Violence and Personality," *Criminal Justice and Behavior* 27:176–95 (2000).

175. Hans Eysenck and M. W. Eysenck, *Personality and Individual Differences* (New York: Plenum, 1985).

176. Joshua Miller and Donald Lynam, "Personality and Antisocial Behavior," *Criminology* 39:765–99 (2001).

177. Ibid., pp. 781–82.

178. Linda Mealey, "The Sociobiology of Sociopathy: An Integrated Evolutionary Model," *Behavioral and Brain Sciences* 18:523–40 (1995).

179. Harvey Cleckley, "Psychopathic States," in S. Aneti, ed., *American Handbook of Psychiatry* (New York: Basic Books, 1959), pp. 567–69.

180. Lewis Yablonsky, *The Violent Gang* (Baltimore: Penguin, 1971), pp. 195–205.

181. Helen Raskin White, Erich Labouvie, and Marsha Bates, "The Relationship between Sensation Seeking and Delinquency: A Longitudinal Analysis," *Journal of Research in Crime and Delinquency* 22:197–211 (1985).

182. Rathus, *Psychology*, p. 452.

183. L. M. Terman, "Research on the Diagnosis of Predelinquent Tendencies," *Journal of Delinquency* 9:124–30 (1925); idem, *Measurement of Intelligence* (Boston: Houghton-Mifflin, 1916). For example, see M. G. Caldwell, "The Intelligence of Delinquent Boys Committed to Wisconsin Industrial School," *Journal of Criminal Law and Criminology* 20:421–28 (1929); and C. Murcheson, *Criminal Intelligence* (Worcester, MA: Clark University, 1926), pp. 41–44.

184. Henry Goddard, *Efficiency and Levels of Intelligence* (Princeton, NJ: Princeton University Press, 1920).

185. William Healy and Augusta Bronner, *Delinquency and Criminals: Their Making and Unmaking* (New York: Macmillan, 1926).

186. Joseph Lee Rogers, H. Harrington Cleveland, Edwin van den Oord, and David Rowe, "Resolving the Debate over Birth Order, Family Size, and Intelligence," *American Psychologist* 55:599–612 (2000).

187. Kenneth Eels, *Intelligence and Cultural Differences* (Chicago: University of Chicago Press, 1951), p. 181.

188. Sorel Cahahn and Nora Cohen, "Age versus Schooling Effects on Intelligence Development," *Child Development* 60:1239–49 (1989).

189. John Slawson, *The Delinquent Boys* (Boston: Budget Press, 1926).

190. Edwin Sutherland, "Mental Deficiency and Crime," in Kimball Young, ed., *Social Attitudes* (New York: Henry Holt, 1973), chap. 15.

191. Travis Hirschi and Michael Hindelang, "Intelligence and Delinquency: A Revisionist Review," *American Sociological Review* 42:471–586 (1977).

192. Terrie Moffitt and Phil Silva, "IQ and Delinquency: A Direct Test of the Differential Detection Hypothesis," *Journal of Abnormal Psychology* 97:1–4 (1988); E. Kandel et al., "IQ as a Protective Factor for Subjects at a High Risk for Antisocial Behavior," *Journal of Consulting and Clinical Psychology* 56:224–26 (1988); Christine Ward and Richard McFall, "Further Validation of the Problem Inventory for Adolescent Girls: Comparing Caucasian and Black Delinquents and Nondelinquents," *Journal of Consulting and Clinical Psychology* 54:732–33 (1986).

193. Wilson and Herrnstein, *Crime and Human Nature* p. 148.

194. Alex Piquero, "Frequency, Specialization, and Violence in Offending Careers," *Journal of Research in Crime and Delinquency* 37:392-418 (2000).

195. Terrie Moffitt, William Gabrielli, Sarnoff Mednick, and Fini Schulsinger, "Socioeconomic Status, IQ, and Delinquency," *Journal of Abnormal Psychology* 90:152–56 (1981); for a similar finding, see L. Hubble and M. Groff, "Magnitude and Direction of WISC-R Verbal Performance IQ Discrepancies among Adjudicated Male Delinquents," *Journal of Youth and Adolescence* 10:179–83 (1981).

196. David Farrington, "Juvenile Delinquency," in John C. Coleman, ed., *The School Years* (London: Routledge: 1992), p. 137.

197. Robert McCall and Michael Carriger, "A Meta-Analysis of Infant Habituation and Recognition Memory Performance as Predictors of Later IQ," *Child Development* 64:57–79 (1993).

198. H. D. Day, J. M. Franklin and D. D. Marshall, "Predictors of Aggression in Hospitalized Adolescents," *Journal of Psychology* 132:427–35 (1998).

199. Deborah Denno, "Sociological and Human Developmental Explanations of Crime: Conflict or Consensus," *Criminology* 23:141–74 (1985).

200. Ibid., p. 171.

201. Glenn Walters and Thomas White, "Heredity and Crime: Bad Genes or Bad Research," *Justice Quarterly* 27:455–85 (1989), at 478.

202. John Cochran, Peter Wood, and Bruce Arneklev, "Is the Religiosity-Delinquency Relationship Spurious? A Test of Arousal and Social Control Theories," *Journal of Research in Crime and Delinquency* 31:92–113 (1994).

203. Lee Ellis, "Genetics and Criminal Behavior," *Criminology* 10:43–66 (1982) at 58.

204. Lee Ellis, "The Evolution of the Nonlegal Equivalent of Aggressive Criminal Behavior," *Aggressive Behavior* 12:57–71 (1986).

205. Edwin Schur, *Radical Nonintervention: Rethinking the Delinquency Problem* (Englewood Cliffs, NJ: Prentice-Hall, 1973).

4 Sociological Views of Delinquency

Social Structure Theories
- **Social Structure/Social Problems**
- **Structure, Culture, and Delinquency**
- **Social Disorganization Theory**
- **Anomie/Strain**
- **Cultural Deviance Theory**

Social Process Theories
- **Socialization and Crime**
- **Theories of Socialization**
- **Learning Theories**
- **Control Theories**

Social Reaction Theories
- **The Labeling Process**
- **The Effect of Labeling**
- **The Juvenile Justice Process and Labeling**
- **Evaluating Labeling Theory**

Social Conflict Theory
- **Law and Justice**
- **The Conflict Concept of Delinquency**

Sociological Theories and Social Policy
- **Social Structure Theories and Social Policy**
- **Socialization and Social Policy**
- **Social Reaction and Social Policy**
- **Social Conflict and Social Policy**

© Felicia Martinez/Photo Edit

You have just been appointed as a presidential adviser on urban problems. The president informs you that he wants to initiate a demonstration project in a major city aimed at showing that government can do something to reduce poverty, crime, and drug abuse. The area he has chosen for development is a large inner-city neighborhood with more than 100,000 residents. The neighborhood suffers from disorganized community structure, poverty, and hopelessness. Predatory delinquent gangs run free and terrorize local merchants and citizens. The school system has failed to provide opportunities and education experiences sufficient to dampen enthusiasm for gang recruitment. Stores, homes, and public buildings are deteriorated and decayed. Commercial enterprise has fled the area, and civil servants are reluctant to enter the neighborhood. There is an uneasy truce among the various ethnic and racial groups that populate the area. Residents feel that little can be done to bring the neighborhood back to life.

You are faced with suggesting an urban redevelopment program that can revitalize the area and eventually bring down the crime rate. You can bring any element of the public and private sector to bear on this rather overwhelming problem—including the military! You can also ask private industry to help in the struggle, promising them tax breaks for their participation.

- Do you believe that living in such an area contributes to high delinquency rates? Or is poverty merely an excuse and delinquency a matter of personal choice?

- What programs do you feel could break the cycle of urban poverty?

- Would reducing the poverty rate produce a lowered delinquency rate?

- What role does the family play in creating delinquent behaviors?

conflict
dramatization
of evil

Many delinquency experts believe it would be a mistake to ignore social and environmental factors in trying to understand the cause of adolescent misbehavior.[1] Most delinquents are indigent and desperate, not calculating or evil. Most grew up in deteriorated parts of town and lack the social support and economic resources familiar to more affluent members of society. Understanding delinquent behavior, then, requires us to account for the destructive influence these social forces have on human behavior.

According to this view, explanations of delinquency as an individual-level phenomenon fail to account for the consistent social patterns found in delinquency. If delinquency was in fact related to rational decision making, how could we explain the ecological differences routinely found in the delinquency rate? We know that youths are more likely to commit crimes if they live in the poorest neighborhoods within large urban areas; the South and/or West have higher delinquency rates than the Northeast and/or Midwest. It seems unlikely that a majority of kids who "choose" crime all live in a particular neighborhood or that kids in one state are more likely to choose crime, while those in another choose conventional activities. It seems equally unlikely that most kids with physical or mental problems live in a particular section of town and/or that some regions of the nation produce children with higher rates of biological and/or psychological abnormality than others. As you have learned, some experts believe that watching violent TV shows and films contributes to adolescent aggression. If this were so, how can regional differences in the delinquency rate be explained? Adolescents watch similar TV shows and films in all regions of the country and all parts of the city. If violence has a biological or psychological origin, should it not be distributed more evenly throughout the social structure? The fact that crime rates are highest in the poorest neighborhoods seems more than a coincidence.

To some delinquency experts, these facts can only mean one thing: The cause of delinquency rests within the dynamics of the social world. They point to cultural norms, social processes, and social institutions as the key elements that shape human behavior. When these elements are strained, crime rates increase. Political unrest and mistrust, economic stress, and family disintegration are social changes that have been found to precede sharp increases in crime rates; when traditional social institutions and values predominate, the crime rate declines.[2]

Another important social change has been the rapid advance in technology and its influence on the social system. People who lack the requisite social and educational training have found that the road to success is almost impassable. The lack of opportunity for upward mobility may make drug dealing and other crimes an attractive solution to socially deprived but economically enterprising people.[3]

The shape of intergroup and interpersonal relationships may also be a source of delinquent behavior. The dynamics of interactions between individuals and important social institutions—families, peers, schools, jobs, criminal justice agencies, and the like—are believed to be important for understanding the cause of delinquency.[4] The relationship of one social class or group to another or to the power structure that controls the nation's legal and economic system may also be closely related to delinquency. It seems logical that people on the lowest rung of the economic ladder will have the greatest incentive to commit crimes: They may be either enraged and frustrated by their lack of economic success, or simply financially desperate and disillusioned. In either instance, crime may appear to be an attractive means to financial success.

This chapter reviews the most prominent social theories of delinquency. They are divided into four groups: (1) social structure theories, which hold that delinquency is a function of a person's place in the economic structure; (2) social process theories, which view delinquency as a result of poor socialization or upbringing; (3) social reaction theories, which view delinquent careers as a function of stigma; and (4) social conflict theories, which consider delinquent behavior to be a product of economic inequality.

A CLOSER VIEW
To learn more about cultural norms and values, use these terms as keywords on InfoTrac College Edition.

Social Structure Theories

culture of poverty View that lower-class people form a separate culture with their own values and norms, which are sometimes in conflict with conventional society.

In 1966, sociologist Oscar Lewis coined the phrase "**culture of poverty**" to describe the crushing burden faced by the urban poor.[5] According to Lewis, the culture of poverty is marked by apathy, cynicism, helplessness, and mistrust of institutions such as police and government. Mistrust of authority prevents the impoverished from taking advantage of the few conventional opportunities available to them. The result is a permanent underclass whose members have little chance of upward mobility or improvement. This extreme level of economic and social hardship has been related to psychological adjustment: People who live in poverty are more likely to suffer low self-esteem, depression, and loneliness.[6]

Social Structure/Social Problems

A CLOSER VIEW
Can poverty actually affect a person's mental health? To find out, go to InfoTrac College Edition and read Keya Acharya, "Poverty and Mental Health in the Developing World," *Contemporary Review* 279:136 (2001).

Nowhere are social problems more pressing than in the inner-city neighborhoods that experience constant population turnover as their more affluent residents move to stable communities or suburbs. While the American economy has been generally robust, social conditions have worsened in many blighted urban areas during the past decade, and their residents have suffered.[7] As a city becomes *hollowed out,* with a deteriorated inner core surrounded by less devastated communities, delinquency rates spiral upward.[8] Those remaining are forced to live in communities with poorly organized social networks, alienated populations, and high crime.[9] The impoverished are deprived of a standard of living enjoyed by most other citizens, and their children suffer from much more than financial hardship. They attend poor schools, live in substandard housing, and lack good health care. More than half of families in poverty are fatherless and husbandless; many are supported entirely by government aid despite a concerted national effort to limit eligibility for public assistance.

Chronic Unemployment Neighborhoods that provide few employment opportunities are the most vulnerable to predatory crime. Unemployment destabilizes households, and unstable families are more likely to produce children who choose aggression as a means of dealing with limited opportunity.[10] Lack of employment opportunity also limits the authority of parents, reducing their ability to influence children. Because adults cannot serve as role models, local culture is dominated by gangs whose members are both feared and respected. Predatory crime increases to levels that cannot easily be controlled by police. Hundreds of studies have documented the association between family poverty and children's health, achievement, and behavior.[11] Children in poor families suffer many problems, including inadequate education. They are less likely to achieve in school and to complete their schooling than are children with more affluent parents.[12]

Kids Count, a project of the Annie E. Casey Foundation, is a national and state-by-state effort to track the relative status of children in the United States: *http://www.aecf.org/kidscount* For an up-to-date list of Web links, go to *http://info.wadsworth.com/siegel*

Child Poverty Child poverty rates are now in decline. The poverty rate for children living with family members declined from 18 percent in 1998 to 16 percent in 1999. The poverty rate for children reached a high of 22 percent in 1993 and has since decreased to the lowest rate since 1979.[13]

However, because there are more than 70 million children in the United States, these data mean that almost 13 million kids are living in poverty and suffering its consequences. Poor children are also more likely to suffer from health problems and to receive inadequate health care. Many lack health care coverage, which almost guarantees that they will suffer health problems that will impede their long-term development. Poor children are much more likely than the wealthy to suffer social ills ranging from low birth weight to never earning a college degree. The cycle of poverty can lead to a variety of adverse outcomes, including life- and health-endangering

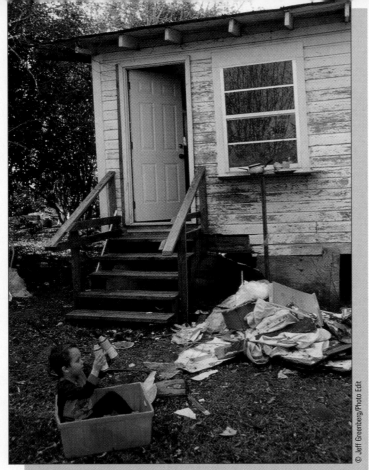

THERE ARE MORE THAN 13 MILLION KIDS living in poverty in the United States. Poor children, such as the one shown here, are also more likely to suffer from health problems and to receive inadequate health care. As a result they will suffer health problems that will impede their long-term development. Children living in poverty are much more likely than the wealthy to suffer social ills ranging from low birth weight to never earning a college degree. They are at great risk for crime and delinquency.

underclass Group of urban poor whose members have little chance of upward mobility or improvement.

truly disadvantaged According to William Julius Wilson, those people who are left out of the economic mainstream and reduced to living in the most deteriorated inner-city areas.

The Northwestern University/ University of Chicago Joint Center for Poverty Research examines what it means to be poor and live in America: *http://www.jcpr.org/* For an up-to-date list of Web links, go to *http://info.wadsworth.com/siegel*

conditions (Figure 4.1). Providing adequate care to children under these circumstances can be an immense undertaking.

Racial Disparity Members of the urban **underclass,** typically minority group members, are referred to as the **truly disadvantaged.**[14] Race-based economic disparity haunts these members of the underclass and their children over the course of their lifespan. Even if they value education and other middle-class norms, their desperate life circumstances (for example, high unemployment and nontraditional family structures) may prevent them from developing the skills, habits, and styles that lead first to educational success and later to success in the workplace.

Racial disparity has been linked to the onset of delinquency and drug abuse. As a result, minority males are often overrepresented in the arrest statistics, and in some jurisdictions, a significant portion of all minority males are under criminal justice system control.[15] Research shows that states with a substantial minority population have a much higher imprisonment rate than those with predominantly Caucasian populations.[16] The collateral costs of this injustice, such as paying for lawyers and court costs, perpetuate poverty by absorbing what money there is and depriving families and children of the support it could otherwise bring.[17] Racial disparity in the justice system has been linked to the fear Caucasians have of young black men, which in most instances is disproportionate to the amount of crime African Americans actually commit.[18]

Race and Economic Disparity William Julius Wilson is one of the nation's most prominent experts on race and its effect on poverty. In his most recent book, *The Bridge over the Racial Divide: Rising Inequality and Coalition Politics,* Wilson argues that despite economic gains, there is a growing inequality in American society, and ordinary families, of all races and ethnic origins, are suffering. Whites, Latinos, African Americans, Asians, and Native Americans must therefore begin to put aside their differences and concentrate more on what they have in common—their aspirations, problems, and hopes. There needs to be mutual cooperation across racial lines.[19] Despite its continuing presence, Wilson finds that racism is becoming more subtle and hard to detect. Whites believe that African Americans are responsible for their own inferior economic status because of their cultural traits. Because even affluent whites fear corporate downsizing, they are unwilling to vote for governmental assistance to the poor. Whites are continuing to be suburban dwellers, further isolating poor minorities in central cities and making their problems distant and unimportant. Wilson continues to believe that the changing marketplace, with its reliance on sophisticated computer technologies, is continually decreasing demand for low-skilled workers, which impacts African Americans more negatively than other better-educated and affluent groups.

Economic disparity will continually haunt members of the underclass and their children over the course of their lifespan. About 26 percent of African Americans and 27 percent of Hispanic Americans still live in poverty as compared to 8.6 percent of the white population. According to the U.S. Census Bureau, the median fam-

Figure 4.1

Examples of Documented Pathways from Poverty to Adverse Child Outcomes

Source: Arloc Sherman, *Poverty Matters* (Washington, DC: Children's Defense Fund, 1997), p. 23.

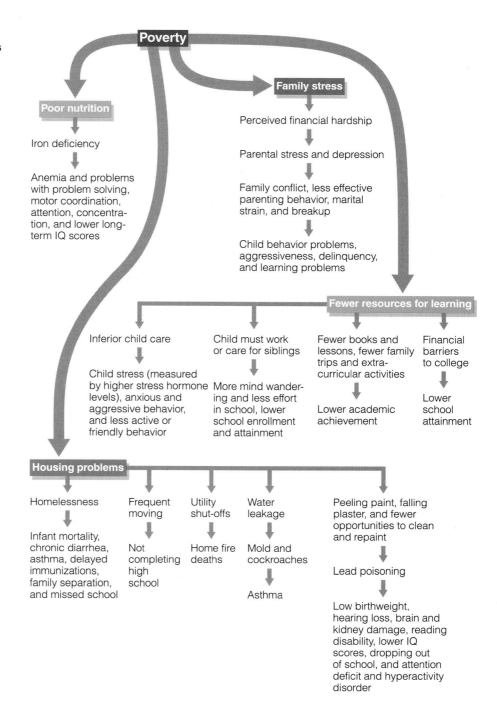

ily income for white families is about $37,000, while African Americans and Hispanic families earned about $24,000.[20]

Structure, Culture, and Delinquency

Some delinquency experts tie delinquency rates to socioeconomic conditions and cultural values. According to this view, neighborhoods that experience high levels of poverty will also have high delinquency rates. Long-term, unremitting poverty undermines a community and its residents, instilling within them a sense of hopelessness that makes antisocial forms of behavior seem attractive.

This structural theory of delinquency finds delinquency is a consequence of the inequalities built into the social structure. Kids growing up in disadvantaged areas are at risk for delinquency because they find little hope that they can be successful in the conventional world. Areas that experience high levels of poverty, in which the basic stabilizing forces of society—the family, school, and neighborhood—have become ineffective, also have high delinquency rates. Residents of such areas are frustrated by their inability to become part of the "American Dream." There are actually a number of different structural theories of crime, and these will now be discussed in some detail.

Social Disorganization Theory

Social disorganization theory was first recognized early in the twentieth century by sociologists Clifford Shaw and Henry McKay. These Chicago-based scholars found that delinquency rates were high in what they called **transitional neighborhoods**—areas that had changed from affluence to decay. Here, factories and commercial establishments were interspersed with private residences. In such environments, teenage gangs developed as a means of survival, defense, and friendship. Gang leaders recruited younger members, passing on delinquent traditions and ensuring survival of the gang from one generation to the next, a process referred to as **cultural transmission**.

While mapping delinquency rates in Chicago, Shaw and McKay noted that distinct ecological areas had developed that could be visualized as a series of concentric zones, each with a stable delinquency rate (Figure 4.2).[21] The areas of heaviest delinquency concentration appeared to be the poverty-stricken, transitional, inner-city zones. The zones farthest from the city's center were the least prone to delinquency. Analysis of these data indicated a stable pattern of delinquent activity in the ecological zones over a 65-year period.[22]

According to their social disorganization view, a healthy, organized community has the ability to regulate itself so that common goals (such as living in a crime-free area) can be achieved; this is referred to as **social control**.[23] Those neighborhoods that become disorganized are incapable of social control because they are wracked by deterioration and economic failure.[24] Though the evidence that crime rates soar during periods of high unemployment is inconclusive, Shaw and McKay claimed that areas continually hurt by poverty and long-term unemployment also experience social disorganization.[25] (See Figure 4.3.)

Consequences of Disorganization Social disorganization is related to a long list of collateral social problems, residential instability, family disruption, and ethnic/racial conflict.[26] Social institutions such as schools and churches cannot work effectively in the climate of alienation and mistrust that characterizes disorganized areas. Typically, the absence of political power limits access to external funding and protection; without outside re-

Figure 4.2
Shaw and McKay's Concentric Zones Map of Chicago
Source: Clifford R. Shaw et al., *Delinquency Areas* (Chicago: University of Chicago Press, 1929), p. 99. Reprinted with permission. Copyright 1929 by the University of Chicago. All rights reserved.
Note: Arabic numbers represent the rate of male delinquency.

Figure 4.3
Social Disorganization Theory

Poverty
• Development of isolated poor neighborhoods.
• Lack of conventional social opportunities.
• Racial and ethnic discrimination.

Social Disorganization
• Breakdown of social institutions and organizations such as school and family.
• Lack of informal social control.

Breakdown of Social Control
• Development of gangs, groups.
• Peer group replaces family and social institutions.

Criminal Areas
• Neighborhood becomes crime-prone.
• Stable pockets of delinquency develop.
• Lack of external support and investment.

Cultural Transmission
• Older youths pass their norms (focal concerns) to younger generation.

Criminal Careers
• Most youths "age out" of delinquency, marry, and raise families. A few remain in a life of crime.

social disorganization theory Posits that delinquency is a product of the social forces existing in inner-city, low-income areas.

transitional neighborhood Area undergoing a shift in population and structure, usually from middle-class residential to lower-class mixed use.

cultural transmission Cultural norms and values that are passed down from one generation to the next.

social control Ability of social institutions to influence human behavior; the justice system is the primary agency of formal social control.

gentrified The process of transforming a lower-class area into a middle-class enclave through property rehabilitation.

poverty concentration effect According to sociologist William Julius Wilson, the consolidation of poor minority group members in urban areas.

sources and financial aid, the neighborhood cannot get back on its feet.[27] Children who reside in these disorganized neighborhoods find that involvement with conventional social institutions, such as schools and afternoon programs, is either absent or blocked, which puts them at risk for recruitment into gangs.[28] These problems are stubborn and difficult to overcome. Even when an attempt is made to revitalize a disorganized neighborhood by creating institutional support programs such as community centers and better schools, the effort may be countered by the ongoing drain of deep-rooted economic and social deprivation.[29] Some of the factors that create and maintain social disorganization are discussed next.

Community Change Urban areas have a life cycle during which they undergo significant change: from affluent to impoverished, from impoverished to rehabilitated or **gentrified,** from residential to commercial, from stable to transient. As communities go through these changes, levels of delinquency also change.[30] Neighborhood change precedes increasing rates of delinquency.[31]

Communities on the downswing are likely to experience increases in the number of single-parent families, changes in housing from owner- to renter-occupied units, a loss of semiskilled and unskilled jobs, and a growth in numbers of discouraged, unemployed workers who are no longer seeking jobs.[32] These communities also tend to develop mixed-use areas in which commercial and residential properties stand side by side. Areas in which retail establishments are abandoned have the highest crime rates.[33]

The changing racial makeup of communities may also influence delinquency rates. Areas undergoing change in their racial composition will experience increases in delinquency rates.[34] This may reflect fear of racial conflict. Adults may encourage teens to terrorize the newcomers; the result is conflict, violence, and disorder.

Poverty Concentration William Julius Wilson describes how white working and middle-class families flee inner-city poverty areas, resulting in a **poverty concentration effect,** in which elements of the most disadvantaged population are consolidated in urban ghettos. As the working and middle classes move out, they take with them their financial and institutional resources and support. Businesses are disinclined to locate in poverty areas; banks become reluctant to lend money for new housing or businesses.[35] Poverty concentration may motivate young African American males to enter the drug trade, an enterprise that increases the likelihood they will become involved in violent crimes.[36] Minority group members living in these areas also suffer other forms of race-based inequality, such as institutional racism.[37] Psychologists warn that under these circumstances, young males will envy people they perceive as doing much better socially and financially than themselves. If they fail to take aggressive tactics, they are going to lose out in social competition.[38]

A CLOSER VIEW
To learn how social disorganization variables influence crime rates in other nations, go to InfoTrac College Edition and read Marc Ouimet, "Aggregation Bias in Ecological Research: How Social Disorganization and Criminal Opportunities Shape the Spatial Distribution of Juvenile Delinquency in Montreal," *Canadian Journal of Criminology* 24:135 (2000).

Neighborhood Instability Neighborhoods may become unstable when they become a "magnet" for people who hold unconventional values and desire to engage in deviant behaviors with impunity. Criminologist Joan Petersilia has warned that as a result of America's two-decade-long imprisonment boom, more than 500,000 inmates are now being released back into the community each year. Many of them have not received adequate treatment and are unprepared for life in conventional society. They provide a significant risk to the communities; these risks include increases in child abuse, family violence, the spread of infectious diseases, homelessness, and community disorganization.[39] For example, only 13 percent of inmates who suffer addiction receive any kind of drug abuse treatment in prison. Petersilia argues that once back in the community, offenders may increase their criminal activity because they want to "make up for lost time" and resume their criminal careers. The majority leave prison with no savings, no immediate entitlement to unemployment benefits, and few employment prospects. One year after release, as many as 60 percent of former inmates are not employed in the regular labor market, and there is increasing reluctance among employers to hire ex-offenders. Unemployment is closely related to drug and alcohol abuse. Losing a job can lead to substance abuse, which in turn is related to child and family violence. Mothers released from prison have difficulty finding services such as housing, employment, and childcare, and this causes stress for them and their children. Children of incarcerated and released parents often suffer confusion, sadness, and social stigma, and these feelings often result in school-related difficulties, low self-esteem, aggressive behavior, and general emotional dysfunction. If the parents are negative role models, children fail to develop positive attitudes about work and responsibility. Children of incarcerated parents are five times more likely to serve time in prison than are children whose parents are not incarcerated.

The situation will become more serious as more and more parolees are released back into the disorganized communities whose deteriorated conditions may have motivated their original crimes.

Community Fear Unstable and disorganized neighborhoods suffer social incivility—trash and litter, graffiti, burned-out buildings, drunks, vagabonds, loiterers, prostitutes, noise, congestion, angry words. This evidence of incivility convinces residents that their neighborhood is dangerous; not surprisingly, when crime rates are high in these areas, fear levels undergo a dramatic increase.[40] As crime flourishes, neighborhood fear increases, which in turn decreases a community's cohesion and thwarts its ability to exert social control over its residents.[41] Fear of crime is much higher in disorganized neighborhoods than in affluent suburbs.[42] Members of the underclass fear crime and have little confidence that the government can do anything to counter the drug dealers and gangs that terrorize the neighborhood.[43] People tell others of their experiences of being victimized, spreading the word that the neighborhood is dangerous. Such fear is not the property of any single racial or ethnic group but can paralyze members of any population, especially when they believe that they are in the minority and vulnerable to attack.[44]

People living in neighborhoods with high levels of crime and civil disorder become suspicious and mistrusting.[45] They report being fatalistic, and they anticipate a relatively short life expectancy. Why plan for the future when there is a significant likelihood that they may never see it? In such areas young boys and girls may adjust psychologically by taking risks and discounting the future. Teenage birth rates soar, and so do violence rates.[46]

When fear grips a neighborhood, people do not want to leave their homes at night, so they withdraw from community life. Fear has been related to distress, inactivity, and decline in health.[47] High levels of fear are also related to deteriorating business conditions, increased population mobility, and the domination of street life by violent gangs.

Weak Social Controls Most neighborhood residents share the goal of living in a crime-free area. Some communities rely on institutions such as families and schools to regulate behavior. When these efforts are blunted, delinquency rates increase and neighborhood cohesiveness is weakened, setting the stage for deterioration.

Neighborhoods maintain a variety of agencies of social control. Some operate on the personal level and involve peers, families, and relatives. These sources exert informal control over behavior by either awarding or withholding approval and respect. Informal control mechanisms include criticism, ridicule, ostracism, and physical punishment.[48] Communities also use local institutions to control delinquency; these include business associations, schools, churches, and voluntary organizations.[49]

Disorganized neighborhoods cannot mount an effective social control effort. Because the population is transient, interpersonal relationships tend to be superficial and cannot help to reduce deviant behavior. Social institutions cannot work effectively in a climate of mistrust. In such neighborhoods, the absence of political power brokers limits access to external funding and police protection. In contrast, areas that can draw on outside help and secure external resources—a process referred to as public social control—are better able to reduce the effects of disorganization and maintain lower levels of crime and victimization.[50]

Social control is also weakened because unsupervised peer groups, which flourish in disorganized areas, disrupt the influence of neighborhood control agents.[51] Children in disorganized areas report that they are unable to become involved with conventional social institutions and are therefore vulnerable to aggression and delinquency.[52]

Rage, Distrust, and Hopelessness Kids in disorganized areas are socialized in a world where adults maintain a siege mentality, sometimes believing there are government plots to undermine the neighborhood ("the AIDS virus was created to kill us off"; "the government brings drugs into the neighborhood to keep people under control").[53] Young people growing up in these areas become angry, convinced that no one cares about their plight. There is free-floating anger, which causes adolescents to strike out at the merest hint of provocation.[54]

Children living in these conditions become "crusted over"; they do not let people get close to them. Their peer relations are exploitive, and they develop a sense of hopelessness. Parents and teachers seem to focus on children's failures rather than on their achievements, leaving them vulnerable to the lure of delinquent groups.[55]

Collective Efficacy Communities that are cohesive and maintain high levels of social control develop **collective efficacy**—mutual trust and a willingness to intervene in the supervision of children and the maintenance of public order.[56] It is the cohesion among neighborhood residents combined with a shared interest in maintaining social control over public space within the neighborhood that promotes collective efficacy.[57]

Local organizations designed to control crime, such as neighborhood associations, may only be effective if they promote a sense of collective efficacy.[58] As they learn to increase levels of collective efficacy they may be better equipped to draw on resources from their neighbors in more affluent surrounding communities.[59] The plight of poor neighborhoods, which lack the means of forming collective efficacy, is exacerbated because they are cut off from outside areas for support.[60]

Communities with high collective efficacy generally experience low violence rates and low levels of physical and social disorder (for example, drinking in the street, spray-painting graffiti, and breaking windows). In contrast, neighborhoods with low collective efficacy suffer high rates of violence and significant physical and social disorder.

Summary of Social Disorganization Theory In sum, according to social disorganization theory: (1) Disorganized areas cannot exert social control over acting-out youth; (2) these areas can be identified by their relatively high levels of change, fear, instability, incivility, poverty, and deterioration; and (3) these factors have a direct influence on the area's delinquency rate. It is not, then, some individual property or trait that is the cause of delinquency, but the quality and ambience of the community in

Want to know how to improve community crime control efforts? Then go to *http://www. ncja.org/Policies/improving.htm* For an up-to-date list of Web links, go to *http://info.wadsworth.com/siegel*

collective efficacy The ability of communities to regulate the behavior of their residents through the influence of community institutions, such as the family and school. Residents in these communities share mutual trust and a willingness to intervene in the supervision of children and the maintenance of public order.

which adolescents are forced to reside. In areas where there is a sense of collective efficacy, delinquency rates will be controlled no matter what the immediate economic situation.

Anomie/Strain

strain theory Links delinquency to the strain of being locked out of the economic mainstream, which creates the anger and frustration that lead to delinquent acts.

Strain theory, the second branch of social structure theory, holds that crime is a function of the conflict between the goals people have and the means they can use to legally obtain them. Strain theorists argue that while social and economic goals are common to people in all economic strata, the ability to obtain these goals is class dependent. Most people in the United States desire wealth, material possessions, power, prestige, and other life comforts. Members of the lower class are unable to achieve these symbols of success through conventional means. Consequently, they feel anger, frustration, and resentment, which is referred to as strain. Lower-class citizens can either accept their condition and live out their days as socially responsible, if unrewarded, citizens, or they can choose an alternative means of achieving success, such as theft, violence, or drug trafficking.

According to sociologist Robert Merton, although most people share common values and goals, the means for legitimate economic and social success are stratified by socioeconomic class.[61] Upper-class kids can achieve success because they have ready access to good education and prestigious jobs; kids in the lower class rarely have such opportunities. Without acceptable means for obtaining success, individuals feel social and psychological strain; Merton called this condition **anomie.** Consequently, these youths may either (1) use deviant methods to achieve their goals (for example, stealing money), or (2) reject socially accepted goals and substitute deviant ones (for example, becoming drug users or alcoholics). (See Figure 4.4.)

anomie Normlessness produced by rapidly shifting moral values; according to Merton, anomie occurs when personal goals cannot be achieved using available means.

Relative Deprivation Feelings of anomie/strain are not typically found in middle- and upper-class communities, where education and prestigious occupations are readily obtainable. In lower-class areas, however, strain occurs because legitimate avenues for success are closed. One reason is that in these areas residents may experience **relative deprivation,** a pervasive, strain-producing sense of injustice that develops in communities in which the poor and the wealthy live in close proximity to one another.[62] In these areas, kids who feel they are less well off than others begin to form negative self-feelings and hostility, which motivates them to engage in delinquent and antisocial behaviors.[63] There is ample evidence that neighborhoods that experience high levels of relative deprivation have significantly higher rates of crime and delinquency.[64] The effect of inequality may be felt the most among minority kids

relative deprivation Condition that exists when people of wealth and poverty live in close proximity to one another; the relatively deprived are apt to have feelings of anger and hostility, which may produce criminal behavior.

Figure 4.4
Strain Theory

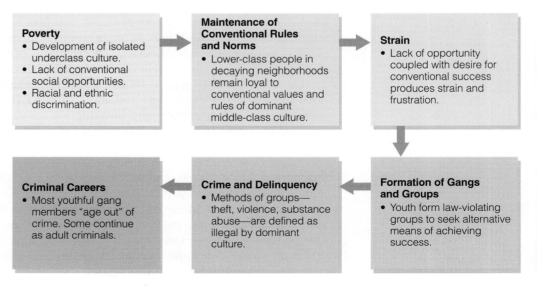

Poverty
- Development of isolated underclass culture.
- Lack of conventional social opportunities.
- Racial and ethnic discrimination.

Maintenance of Conventional Rules and Norms
- Lower-class people in decaying neighborhoods remain loyal to conventional values and rules of dominant middle-class culture.

Strain
- Lack of opportunity coupled with desire for conventional success produces strain and frustration.

Formation of Gangs and Groups
- Youth form law-violating groups to seek alternative means of achieving success.

Crime and Delinquency
- Methods of groups—theft, violence, substance abuse—are defined as illegal by dominant culture.

Criminal Careers
- Most youthful gang members "age out" of crime. Some continue as adult criminals.

Crime and the American Dream

In their important book, *Crime and the American Dream,* Steven Messner and Richard Rosenfeld share their vision that cultural and institutional influences in American society are the reason why American crime and delinquency rates are so high.

Messner and Rosenfeld agree with Merton's view that the success goal is pervasive in American culture. They refer to this as the "American Dream," a term that they employ as both a goal and a process. As a goal, the American Dream involves the accumulation of material goods and wealth under conditions of open individual competition. As a process, it involves the socialization of youth to pursue material success above all else and to believe that prosperity is a universally achievable goal in the American culture. The desire to succeed at any cost drives people apart, weakens the collective sense of community, fosters ambition, and restricts the desirability of other kinds of achievement, such as a "good name" and respected reputation.

That Americans are conditioned to succeed "at all costs" should come as no surprise because the capitalist system encourages innovation in the pursuit of monetary rewards. Billionaire businessmen such as Michael Bloomberg, Ross Perot, Bill Gates, and Donald Trump are considered national heroes whose wealth and lifestyle are universally admired. They have become cultural icons and leaders who many believe deserve to be elected president because of their business success. Bloomberg allegedly spent $45 million of his own money in his successful 2001 campaign to become mayor of New York City.

What is distinct about American society, according to Messner and Rosenfeld, and what most likely determines our exceedingly high national crime rate, is that institutions that might otherwise control the exaggerated emphasis on financial success have been rendered powerless or obsolete. There are three reasons social institutions have been undermined:

1. Noneconomic functions and roles have been devalued. Performance in other institutional settings—the family, school, or community—is assigned a lower priority than the goal of financial success. Human service jobs such as social work and teaching are considered significantly less important than entertainment or sports. Consider the following: Why does it seem normal and rational in American society for citizens to demand that the board of education ask public school teachers to take pay cuts or go for years without a raise, while the same people complain when the owner of a local baseball team allows a slugger to sign with another team rather than pay him $10 million per year?
2. When conflicts emerge, noneconomic roles become subordinate to and must accommodate economic roles. The schedules, routines, and demands of the workplace take priority over those of

the home, the school, the community, and other aspects of social life. For example, many parents are willing to leave very young children in daycare for 10 hours or more per day in order to pursue the careers that can bring them increased levels of luxury.
3. Economic standards and norms penetrate into noneconomic realms. Economic terms become part of the common language: People want you to get to the "bottom line"; spouses view themselves as "partners" who "manage" the household. Business leaders run for public office promising to "run the country like a corporation."

According to Messner and Rosenfeld, the relatively high American delinquency rates can be explained by the interrelationship between culture and institutions. At the cultural level, the dominance of the American Dream mythology ensures that a great many kids will hunger for material goods that simply cannot be satisfied by legitimate means. Kids feel strain because no matter how much the typical American has, it's never enough: Kids always want the most stylish fashions, newest music, and hottest car. As soon as cultural values change, so does their need for material possessions.

At the institutional level, the dominance of economic concerns weakens the informal social control exerted by the family and school. Parents lose their authority when they cannot provide children with economic luxuries. Teachers lose their influence when adolescents no longer believe that education will get them what they want. Because the message "to succeed by any means necessary" has become a national icon, the result is high rates of theft and violence.

Critical Thinking

1. Can you identify cultural values that indicate the importance of the success goal in American society? Do you believe these are appropriate, or do they undercut the quality of life?
2. What role does the media play in promoting the American Dream? Do TV advertisements glorifying luxury items such as cars and clothes encourage antisocial behaviors?

InfoTrac College Edition Research

Use *American Dream* as keywords on InfoTrac College Edition. Can these various writings help us identify the core values of American culture?

Source: Steven Messner and Richard Rosenfeld, *Crime and the American Dream,* 3rd ed. (Belmont, CA: Wadsworth, 2001).

who believe they are losing out in a society where the balance of economic and social power is shifting further toward the already affluent white middle class. Under these conditions, the likelihood that relatively poor kids will choose illegitimate life-enhancing activities will increase.[65]

Considering the economic stratification of U.S. society, and the general emphasis on economic success above all else, anomie predicts that crime will prevail in lower-class culture, which it does. The infusion of the success goal in American culture and its effect on crime is discussed in the Focus on Delinquency box entitled "Crime and the American Dream."

A CLOSER VIEW
To learn more about the concept of anomie, use it as a keyword on InfoTrac College Edition.

General Strain Theory (GST)   An important reformulation of the strain concept is found in sociologist Robert Agnew's General Strain Theory (GST). Agnew has attempted to explain why kids who feel stress and strain are more likely to commit crimes, by offering a more general explanation of criminal activity among all elements of society rather than restricting his views to lower-class crime.[66]

Agnew suggests that criminality is the direct result of *negative affective states*—the anger, frustration, and adverse emotions that emerge in the wake of negative and destructive social relationships. He finds that negative affective states are produced by a variety of sources of strain:

- *Strain caused by the failure to achieve positively valued goals:* This category of strain, similar to what Merton speaks of in his theory of anomie, is a result of the disjunction between aspirations and expectations. This type of strain occurs when a youth aspires to wealth and fame but, lacking financial and educational resources, assumes that such goals are impossible to achieve.
- *Strain caused by the disjunction of expectations and achievements:* Strain can also be produced when there is a disjunction between expectations and achievements. When people compare themselves to peers who seem to be doing a lot better financially or socially (such as making more money or getting better grades), even those doing relatively well feel strain. For example, when a high school senior is accepted at a good college, but not a "prestige school" like some of her friends, she will feel strain. Perhaps she is not being treated fairly because the "playing field" is tilted against her: "Other kids have connections," she may say.
- *Strain as the removal of positively valued stimuli from the individual:* Strain may occur because of the actual or anticipated removal or loss of a positively valued stimuli from the individual.[67] For example, the loss of a girl- or boyfriend can produce strain, as can the death of a loved one, moving to a new neighborhood or school, and the divorce or separation of parents. The loss of positive stimuli may lead to delinquency as the adolescent tries to prevent the loss, retrieve what has been lost, obtain substitutes, or seek revenge against those responsible for the loss.
- *Strain as the presentation of negative stimuli:* Strain may also be caused by the presence of negative or noxious stimuli. Included within this category are such pain-inducing social interactions as child abuse and neglect, crime victimization, physical punishment, family and peer conflict, school failure, and interaction with stressful life. Children who are abused at home may take their rage out on younger children at school or become involved in violent delinquency.[68] (See Figure 4.5.)

According to Agnew, the greater the intensity and frequency of strain experiences, the greater their impact and the more likely they are to cause delinquency.

Each type of strain will increase the likelihood of experiencing negative emotions as disappointment, depression, fear, and, most importantly, anger. Anger increases perceptions of being wronged and produces a desire for revenge, energizes individuals to take action, and lowers inhibitions. Violence and aggression seem justified if you have been wronged and are righteously angry.

There are a variety of sources of strain. Sometimes, a particular individual may be causing problems, such as an abusive parent or peer group rival. There are also social sources of strain. Kids may begin to feel strain because their membership in a

Figure 4.5
General Strain Theory (GST)

Sources of Strain	Negative Affective States	Antisocial Behavior
• Failure to achieve goals • Removal of positive stimuli • Presentation of negative stimuli • Disjunction of expectations and achievements	• Anger • Frustration • Disappointment • Depression • Fear	• Drug abuse • Delinquency • Violence • Dropping out

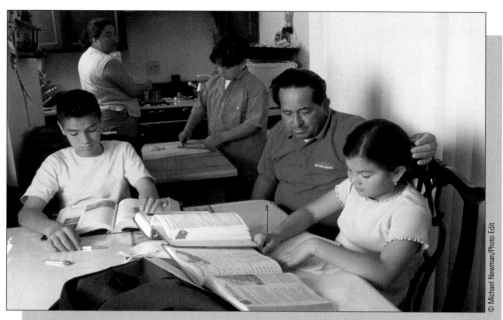

ACCORDING TO AGNEW, strain may be caused by the presence of negative pain-inducing social interactions within the family, such as child abuse and neglect. Children who are abused at home may take their rage out on younger children at school or become involved in violent delinquency. On the other hand, a warm, supportive family life, such as that shown here, can help kids cope with delinquency-producing environmental strain.

peer or social group forces them into unwanted behavior patterns, such as using drugs.[69] These feelings may become magnified as compliance with peer group demands forces them to escalate their risky behaviors, for example, getting involved in a shoplifting spree to pay for drugs.[70]

Not all people who experience strain eventually resort to criminality. Some are able to marshal their emotional, mental, and behavioral resources to cope with the anger and frustration produced by strain. However, some cannot learn to cope effectively, and instead, these youths develop what Agnew calls **negative affective states,** as described earlier. The greater the intensity and frequency of strain experiences, the greater their impact and the more likely they are to cause delinquency. Research supports many of Agnew's claims: Kids who report feelings of stress and anger and have negative emotions are also more likely to engage in criminal behaviors;[71] people who fail to meet success goals are more likely to engage in illegal activities.[72]

Agnew's vision of strain seems particularly useful for explaining why crime rates peak during late adolescence. During this portion of the life course, social stress is maximized as parental supervision weakens and is replaced by relationships with a diverse peer group. Many kids going through the trauma of family breakup and frequent changes in family structure find themselves feeling a high degree of strain. For example, research shows that young girls of any social class are more likely to bear out-of-wedlock children if they themselves experienced an unstable family life.[73] Adolescence is also a period during which hormone levels peak and the behavior-moderating aspects of the brain have not fully developed, two factors that make adolescent males susceptible to environmental sources of strain.[74] They may react by becoming involved in precocious sexuality or by turning to substance abuse to mask the strain.

As they mature, children's expectations increase; some find that they are unable to meet academic and social demands. Adolescents are very concerned about their standing with peers. Those deficient in these areas may find they are social outcasts, another source of strain. In adulthood, crime rates drop because these sources of strain are reduced. New sources of self-esteem emerge, and adults seem more likely to bring their goals in line with reality.

negative affective states Anger, depression, disappointment, fear, and other adverse emotions that derive from strain.

Figure 4.6
Cultural Deviance Theory

Poverty
• Lack of opportunity.
• Feeling of oppression.

Culture
• Inner-city youths are socialized to value middle-class goals and ideas.

Subculture
• Blocked opportunities prompt formation of groups with alternative lifestyles and values.

Criminal Careers
• Some gang boys can parlay their status into criminal careers. Others become drug users or violent assaulters.

Crime and Delinquency
• New methods of gaining success involve law-violating behavior.

Success Goal
• Gangs provide alternative methods of gaining success for some, venting anger for others.

Cultural Deviance Theory

cultural deviance theory Links delinquent acts to the formation of independent subcultures with a unique set of values that clash with the mainstream culture.

culture conflict When the values of a subculture clash with those of the dominant culture.

A third branch of structural theory, **cultural deviance theory,** holds that delinquency is a result of youths' desire to conform to lower-class neighborhood cultural values that conflict with those of the greater society. (See Figure 4.6.) Lower-class values include being tough, never showing fear, living for today, and disrespecting authority. In a socially disorganized neighborhood, conventional values such as honesty, obedience, and hard work make little sense to youths whose role models may include the neighborhood gunrunner, drug dealer, or pimp. Those adolescents who share lower-class values and admire criminals, drug dealers, and pimps find it difficult to impress authority figures such as teachers or employers. They experience a form of **culture conflict** and are rendered incapable of achieving success in a legitimate fashion; as a result, they join together in gangs and engage in behavior that is malicious and negativistic.[75]

Both legitimate and illegitimate opportunities are closed to youths in the most disorganized inner-city areas.[76] Consequently, they may join violent gangs to defend their turf, displaying their bravery and fighting prowess.[77] Instead of aspiring to be "preppies" or "yuppies," they want to be considered tough and street smart.

Youths living in disorganized areas consider themselves part of an urban underclass whose members must use their wits to survive or they will succumb to poverty, alcoholism, and drug addiction.[78] Exploitation of women abounds in a culture wracked by limited opportunity. Sexual conquest is one of the few areas open to lower-class males for achieving self-respect. The absence of male authority figures contributes to the fear that marriage will limit freedom. Peers heap scorn on anyone who allows himself to get "trapped" by a female, fueling the number of single-parent households. Youths who are committed to the norms of this deviant subculture are also more likely to disparage agents of conventional society such as police and teachers.[79] By joining gangs and committing crimes, lower-class youths are rejecting the culture that has already rejected them; they may be failures in conventional society, but they are the kings and queens of the neighborhood.

Social Process Theories

Not all sociologists believe that merely living in an impoverished, deteriorated, lower-class area is a determinant of a delinquent career. Instead they argue that the root cause of delinquency may be traced to learning delinquent attitudes from peers, becoming detached from school, or experiencing conflict in the home. Although social position is important, socialization is considered to be the key determinant of behavior. If the *socialization* The process of learning the values and norms of the society or the subculture to which the individual belongs.

socialization process is incomplete or negatively focused, it can produce an adolescent with a poor self-image who is alienated from conventional social institutions.

Socialization is the process of guiding people into acceptable behavior patterns through information, approval, rewards, and punishments. It involves learning the techniques needed to function in society. Socialization is a developmental process that is influenced by family and peers, neighbors, teachers, and other authority figures.

Socialization and Crime

A CLOSER VIEW
To find out more about socialization, use it as a keyword on InfoTrac College Edition.

Early socialization experiences have a lifelong influence on self-image, values, and behavior. Even children living in the most deteriorated inner-city environments will not get involved in delinquency if their socialization experiences are positive.[80] After all, most inner-city youths do not commit serious crimes, and relatively few of those who do become career criminals.[81] More than 14 million youths live in poverty, but the majority do not become chronic offenders. Only those who experience improper socialization are at risk for crime. Research consistently shows a relationship between the elements of socialization and delinquency.

Family The primary influence on children is the family. When parenting is inadequate, a child's maturational processes will be interrupted and damaged. Although much debate still occurs over which elements of the parent-child relationship are most critical, there is little question that family relationships have a significant influence on behavior.[82] One view is that youths socialized in families wracked by conflict and abuse are at risk for delinquency. For example, there is now evidence that children who grow up in homes where parents use severe discipline, yet lack warmth and are less involved in their children's lives, are prone to antisocial behavior.[83] In contrast, parents who are supportive and effectively control their children in a noncoercive fashion—*parental efficacy*—are more likely to raise children who refrain from delinquency.[84] Delinquency will be reduced if parents provide the type

SOCIAL STRUCTURE–BASED DELINQUENCY prevention programs aim to improve conditions within broad areas of the city in order to reduce delinquency rates. Here, a police officer participates in a neighborhood program in Redlands, California, which targets at-risk kids for weekly play dates. According to this view, changing the climate of a neighborhood environment can help reduce crime rates.

of structure that integrates children into families while giving them the ability to assert their individuality and regulate their own behavior.[85] Children who have warm and affectionate ties to their parents report greater levels of self-esteem beginning in adolescence and extending into their adulthood; high self-esteem is inversely related to criminal behavior.[86] Conversely, when a parent exhibits deviant behavior, his or her children are more likely to follow suit. In fact, parental deviance has been linked to a child's criminal behavior.

Schools The literature linking delinquency to poor school performance and inadequate educational facilities is extensive. Youths who feel that teachers do not care, who consider themselves failures, and who do poorly in school are more likely to become involved in a delinquent way of life than adolescents who are educationally successful. Research findings based on studies done over the past two decades indicate that many school dropouts, especially those who have been expelled, face a significant chance of entering a criminal career.[87] In contrast, doing well in school and developing attachments to teachers has been linked to crime resistance.[88]

Peer Relations Still another suspected element of deviant socialization is peer group relations. Youths who become involved with peers who engage in antisocial behavior may learn the attitudes that support delinquency and soon find themselves cut off from conventional associates and institutions.[89] Chronic offenders surround themselves with peers who share their antisocial activities, and these relationships seem to be stable over time. People who maintain close relations with antisocial peers will sustain their own criminal behavior into their adulthood. When peer influence diminishes, so does delinquent activity.[90]

Religion It has also been suggested that youths who are taught to hold high moral values and beliefs, who have learned to distinguish "right from wrong," and who regularly attend religious services should also eschew crime and other antisocial behaviors.[91] Religion binds people together and forces them to confront the consequences of their behavior. Committing crimes would violate the principles of all organized religions. Kids living in disorganized high-crime areas who attend religious services are better able to resist illegal drug use and delinquency.[92] Interestingly, participation seems to be a more significant inhibitor of crime than merely having religious beliefs and values.[93] Cross-national research shows that countries with high rates of church membership and attendance have lower crime rates than less "devout" nations.[94]

learning theory Posits that delinquency is learned through close relationships with others; asserts that children are born "good" and learn to be "bad" from others.

Theories of Socialization

Sociologists believe that the socialization process impacts delinquency in two ways. The first, **learning theory,** holds that delinquency is learned through close relationships with others. Both the techniques of crime and the attitudes necessary to support delinquency are learned. Learning theories assume that children are born "good" and then learn to be "bad."

The second, **control theory,** views delinquency as a result of a weakened commitment to family, peers, and school. Because their bonds to these institutions of informal social control are severed, some adolescents feel free to exercise antisocial behavior. Unlike learning theories, control theories assume that people are born "bad" and then must be taught to control themselves through the efforts of parents and teachers.

control theory Posits that delinquency results from a weakened commitment to the major social institutions (family, peers, and school); lack of such commitment allows youths to exercise antisocial behavioral choices.

Learning Theories

Learning theories hold that children living in even the most deteriorated areas can resist inducements to crime if they have learned proper values and behaviors. Delinquency, by contrast, develops by learning the values and behaviors associated with criminal activity (Figure 4.7). Kids can learn deviant values from their parents, relatives, or peers. Social learning can involve the techniques of crime (how to hot-wire

Figure 4.7
Learning Theory of Delinquency

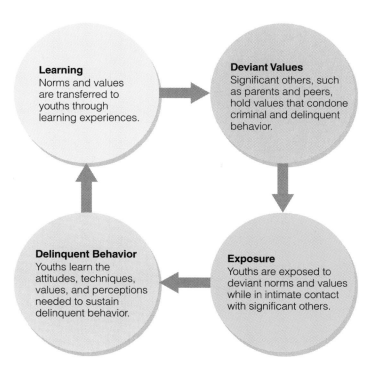

Learning
Norms and values are transferred to youths through learning experiences.

Deviant Values
Significant others, such as parents and peers, hold values that condone criminal and delinquent behavior.

Delinquent Behavior
Youths learn the attitudes, techniques, values, and perceptions needed to sustain delinquent behavior.

Exposure
Youths are exposed to deviant norms and values while in intimate contact with significant others.

differential association theory
Asserts that criminal behavior is learned primarily within interpersonal groups and that youths will become delinquent if definitions they have learned favorable to violating the law exceed definitions favorable to obeying the law within that group.

a car) as well as the psychological aspects (how to deal with guilt). The former are needed to commit crimes, whereas the latter are required to cope with the emotional turmoil that follows.

The best-known learning theory is Edwin Sutherland's **differential association theory,** which he first articulated in 1939 in *Principles of Criminology.*[95] Sutherland believed that as children are socialized, they are exposed to and learn prosocial and antisocial attitudes and behavior. Simply put, if the prodelinquency definitions they have learned outweigh the antidelinquency definitions, they will be vulnerable to choosing criminal behaviors over conventional ones. The basic principles of differential association theory are set out in Exhibit 4.1.

Exhibit 4.1   Principles of Differential Association

1. Criminal behavior is learned. Learning criminal behavior involves all the mechanisms and techniques involved in any other learning.

2. Crime is learned in interactions with others, in a process of communication.

3. Learning occurs within close personal groups such as peers, families, work, sports, and so on. Observational learning in the media is not that important.

4. Learning includes the techniques, motives, drives, rationalizations, and attitudes that support behavior.

5. The specific direction of motives, drives, rationalizations, and attitudes is learned from legal codes as being favorable or unfavorable.

6. Kids engage in crime because of an excess of definitions favorable to law violation over definitions unfavorable to law breaking. This is the principle of differential association.

7. Differential association may vary in frequency, duration, priority, and intensity. For example, definitions acquired from parents may have a higher priority than those acquired from distant relatives; definitions that are constantly repeated over a long period of time are more important than those that occur in a single instance.

Source: Edwin Sutherland, *Principles of Criminology* (Philadelphia: Lippincott, 1939).

Figure 4.8
Techniques of Neutralization

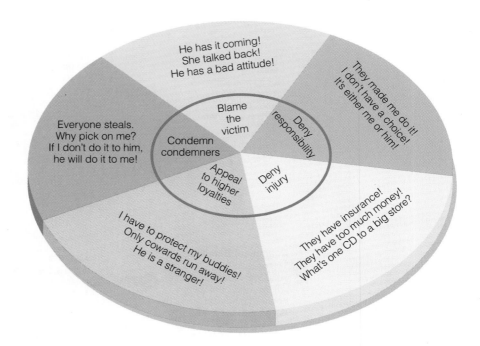

drift   Idea that youths move in and out of delinquency and that their lifestyles can embrace both conventional and deviant values.

neutralization techniques   A set of attitudes or beliefs that allow would-be delinquents to negate any moral apprehension they may have about committing crime so that they may freely engage in antisocial behavior without regret.

Another prominent learning approach, identified with David Matza and Gresham Sykes, suggests that delinquents hold values similar to those of law-abiding citizens, but they learn techniques that enable them to neutralize those values and drift back and forth between legitimate and delinquent behavior.[96] **Drift** is the process by which an individual moves from one behavioral extreme to another, behaving sometimes in an unconventional manner and at other times with constraint.

Sykes and Matza suggest that juveniles develop a distinct set of justifications for their behavior when it violates accepted social rules and norms. These **neutralization techniques** allow youths to drift away from the rules of the normative society and participate in delinquent behaviors. While most adolescents accept the rules of society, they learn these techniques to release themselves temporarily from moral constraints. The most prominent techniques of neutralization are described in Figure 4.8.[97]

Learning theory, then, portrays the delinquent as someone who, during the socialization process, has been consistently exposed not only to people who teach that "crime pays" but also to the techniques for becoming a successful criminal. Conversely, children living in the most highly disorganized neighborhood will be able to avoid the temptations of the streets if they are socialized in a warm, supportive family and have law-abiding peers.

Control Theories

Control theories argue that delinquency can be pleasurable and exciting. Kids may enjoy flaunting the rules of society and engaging in antisocial behavior. According to control theorists, kids who obey the law and engage in conventional activities have been socialized to control their behavior. Maintaining control is a function of the close relationships with parents, friends, and teachers, which help them form the ability to resist the lure of deviant behaviors. Kids who are socialized to develop a strong "commitment to conformity" will be able to resist pressures to violate the law.

The most prominent control theory is one developed by sociologist Travis Hirschi. In his classic book *Causes of Delinquency,* Hirschi argues that the cause of delinquency lies in the strength of the relationships or **social bonds** a child forms with conventional individuals and groups.[98] If these bonds to society become fractured or broken, youths will feel free to violate the law; if caught, they have nothing to lose

social bond   Ties a person to the institutions and processes of society; elements of the bond include attachment, commitment, involvement, and belief.

Figure 4.9
Elements of the Social Bond

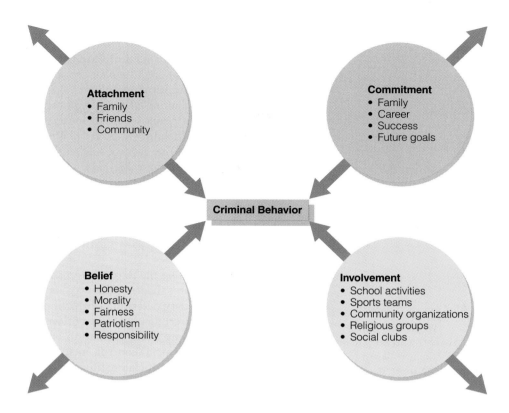

(Figure 4.9). The youthful law violator, then, is someone who lacks a real commitment to social norms. The major elements of Hirschi's argument are (1) all people have the potential to commit crimes—for example, underage drinking—because they are pleasurable; (2) people are kept in check by their social bonds or attachments to society; and (3) weakened social bonds free people to engage in antisocial but personally desirable behaviors. Hirschi argues that the social bond a person maintains with society is divided into four main elements:

- *Attachment* to parents, peers, and schools
- *Commitment* to the pursuit of conventional activities, such as getting an education and saving for the future
- *Involvement* in conventional activities such as school, sports, and religion
- *Belief* in values such as sensitivity to the rights of others and respect for the legal code

Hirschi suggests that the elements of the social bond may be interrelated. For example, boys or girls who are attached to their parents and friends are also more likely to be committed to future goals. Youths who are unattached may lack commitment to conventional goals and are more likely to be involved in unconventional activities. Hirschi's vision of delinquency causation is one of the most influential of recent times.[99] There has been significant empirical support for Hirschi's work. For example, research shows that positive attachments help control delinquency.[100] Kids who fail at school and are detached from the educational experience are at risk of criminality; those who do well and are committed to school are less likely to engage in delinquent acts.[101]

Evaluating Social Control Theory While many research efforts support Hirschi's ideas, some important questions are still being raised about his views. For example, Hirschi argues that commitment to future success, such as an exciting career, reduces delinquent involvement. Research indicates that kids who are committed to success but actually fail to achieve it may be crime-prone.[102] Perhaps their failures produce feelings of strain that counterbalance the control of commitment. Questions have also been raised about the social relations of delinquents. Hirschi portrays them as "lone wolves," detached from family and friends. A number of research efforts show that delinquents do maintain close peer group ties.[103] Their friendship patterns seem similar to those of conventional youths.[104] In fact, there is some evidence that drug abusers maintain even more intimate relations with peers than do nonabusers.[105] Attachment to deviant peers seems to motivate the decision to commit crime; deviant friends facilitate delinquent acts.[106] While the issue of peer relations is troublesome, Hirschi's vision of control has remained one of the most influential models of delinquency for the past 25 years.

Social Reaction Theories

stigmatized People who have been negatively labeled because of their participation, or alleged participation, in deviant or outlawed behaviors.

Social reaction theories are the third type of sociological theories of delinquency. According to social reaction theories, the way society reacts to individuals and the way individuals react to society determines behavior. Social reactions determine which behaviors are considered criminal or conventional; they also determine individual behavior and can contribute to the formation of delinquent careers. Being **stigmatized,** or labeled, by agents of social control, including official institutions such as the police and the courts, and unofficial institutions, such as parents and neighbors, is what sustains delinquent careers.[107]

The Labeling Process

labeling theory Posits that society creates deviance through a system of social control agencies that designate (or label) certain individuals as delinquent, thereby stigmatizing youths and encouraging them to accept this negative personal identity.

According to this view, also known as **labeling theory,** youths may violate the law for a variety of reasons, including poor family relationships, peer pressure, psychological abnormality, and prodelinquent learning experiences. Regardless of the cause, if individuals' delinquent behaviors are detected, the offenders will be given a negative label that can follow them throughout life. These labels include "troublemaker," "juvenile delinquent," "mentally ill," "junkie," and many more.

The way labels are applied is likely to have important consequences for the delinquent. The degree to which youngsters are perceived as deviants may affect their treatment at home and at school. Parents may consider them a detrimental influence on younger brothers and sisters. Neighbors may tell their children to avoid the "troublemaker." Teachers may place them in classes reserved for students with behavior problems, minimizing their chances of obtaining higher education. The delinquency label may also affect the attitudes of society in general, and youthful offenders are subjected to sanctions ranging from mild reprimands to incarceration.

Beyond these results, and depending on the visibility of the label and the manner in which it is applied, youths will have an increasing commitment to delinquent careers. As the negative feedback of law enforcement agencies, teachers, and other figures strengthens their commitment, delinquents may come to see themselves as "screwups." Thus, through a process of identification and sanctioning, reidentification, and increased sanctioning, young offenders are transformed. They are no longer children in trouble; they are "delinquents," and they accept that label as a personal identity—a process called **self-labeling** (Figure 4.10).[108]

self-labeling The process by which a person who has been negatively labeled accepts the label as a personal role or identity.

The Effect of Labeling

We often form opinions of others based on first impressions.[109] If interactions involve perceptions of deviance, individuals may be assigned informal labels—"loser," "slut"—that both harm their social relationships and damage their self-image. Kids

Figure 4.10
Labeling Theory

Initial Delinquent Act
Youths commit crimes for a number of reasons.

Detection by the Justice System
Arrest is influenced by racial, economic, and power relations.

Decision to Label
Some youths are labeled "official" delinquents by police and court authorities.

Deviance Amplification
The outcast youths are now locked into delinquent careers.

Acceptance of Labels
The labeled youths begin to see themselves as outsiders. Secondary deviance. Self-labeling.

Creation of a New Identity
The labeled youths are known as troublemakers, criminals, and so on, and shunned by conventional society.

who are suspected of harboring such behavior problems are scrutinized by those with whom they interact; people search for signs of deviance, or simply shun them.[110]

When kids who have been rejected by society violate the criminal law, they may be given official labels, applied in "ceremonies"—for example, during trials or expulsion hearings in schools—that are designed to redefine the deviant's identity.[111] The effect of this process is a durable negative label and an accompanying loss of status. The labeled deviant becomes a social outcast who is prevented from enjoying higher education, well-paying jobs, and other societal benefits. Because this label is "official," few question the accuracy of the assessment. People who may have been merely suspicious now feel justified in their assessments: "I always knew he was a bad kid."

A good example of the labeling ceremony occurs in juvenile courts. Here offenders find (perhaps for the first time) that authority figures consider them incorrigible outcasts who must be separated from the right-thinking members of society. To reach that decision, the judge relies on the testimony of witnesses—parents, teachers, police officers, social workers, and psychologists—who may testify that the offender is unfit to be part of conventional society.[112] As the label "juvenile delinquent" is conferred on offenders, their identities may be transformed from kids who have done something bad, to "bad kids."[113]

self-fulfilling prophecy Deviant behavior patterns that are a response to an earlier labeling experience; youths act out these social roles even if they were falsely bestowed.

The Self-Fulfilling Prophecy The labeling process helps create a **self-fulfilling prophecy**.[114] If children continually receive negative feedback from parents, teachers, and others whose opinion they take to heart, they will interpret this rejection as accurate. Their behavior will begin to conform to the negative expectations; they will become the person others perceive them to be ("Teachers already think I'm stupid, so why should I bother to study"). The self-fulfilling prophecy leads to a damaged self-image and an increase in antisocial behaviors.[115]

Self-Rejection Labeling helps create a deviant identity. Those exposed to negative sanctions experience both self-rejection and lowered self-image. Self-rejecting attitudes result in both a weakened commitment to conventional values and the acquisition of motives to deviate from social norms.[116] This transformation is amplified by the bonds social outcasts form with peers.[117] Labeled delinquents will seek out others who are similarly stigmatized.[118] Associating with deviant peers helps reinforce conventional society's negative evaluations: "We were right all along about him, look who his friends are!" (See Figure 4.11.)

Delinquent peers may help labeled youths "reject their rejectors." Teachers are "stupid"; cops are "dishonest"; parents "just don't understand."[119] Group identity enables outcast youths to show contempt for the sources of the labels and to distance themselves. These actions help solidify both the grip of deviant peers and the impact of the labels.[120]

Figure 4.11
Lemert's Cycle of Secondary Deviance
According to sociologist Edwin Lemert, people who bear negative labels become secondary deviants—their label becomes a master status by which they are defined.

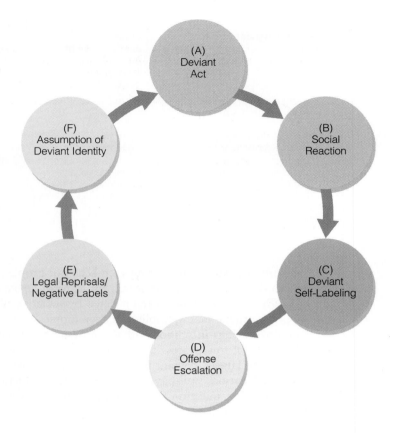

The Juvenile Justice Process and Labeling

dramatization of evil The process of social typing that transforms an offender's identity from a doer of evil to an evil person.

The justice system has long been accused of bestowing destructive labels on children who are suspected of being delinquents. Frank Tannenbaum first suggested that social typing, which he called **"dramatization of evil,"** transforms the offender's identity from a doer of evil to an "evil person."[121] Delinquents, the argument goes, are the products of the juvenile justice assembly line.[122] Although youths enter as children in trouble, they emerge as bearers of criminal histories, which are likely to reinvolve them in criminal activity. Authority figures anticipate that these troublemakers will continue their life of crime.[123] Labeled delinquents are assumed to engage in a full range of violence, theft, and drug abuse. Although they have not necessarily demonstrated these characteristics, they become perennial suspects.[124] The system designed to reduce delinquency may help produce young criminals.

degradation ceremony Going to court, being scolded by a judge, or being found delinquent after a trial are examples of public ceremonies that can transform youthful offenders by degrading their self-image.

According to the social reaction perspective, the actions of the juvenile justice system turn the self-perception of a youthful suspect into that of a delinquent.[125] Harold Garfinkel addressed the reason this occurs when he described what he called a **"degradation ceremony,"** where the public identity of an offender is transformed in a solemn ritual during which the targeted person is thrust outside the social mainstream.[126] This process may be seen in juvenile court when a youngster goes before the court, is scolded by a judge, has charges read, and is officially labeled a delinquent; this process contains all the conditions for "successful degradation." Recognizing the role stigma plays in developing a delinquent career has prompted some juvenile justice agencies to create programs designed to limit delinquent labels.

Evaluating Labeling Theory

Enthusiasm for the labeling approach diminished when its validity was heavily criticized. Some critics argued that the crime-controlling effects of punishment more than made up for the crime-producing effects of stigma. In *Beyond Delinquency,* Charles Murray and Louis Cox found that youths assigned to a program designed to reduce labels were more likely later to commit delinquent acts than a comparison group who were placed in a more punitive state training school. The implication was that the threat of punishment was deterrent and that the crime-producing influence of labels was minimal.[127]

While these criticisms were damaging, other experts suggest that the labeling perspective can offer important insights:

- It identifies the role played by social control agents in the process of delinquency causation; delinquent behavior cannot be fully understood if the agencies empowered to control it are ignored.
- It recognizes that delinquency is not a pathological behavior; it focuses on the social interactions that shape behavior.
- It distinguishes between delinquent acts and delinquent careers and shows that they must be treated differently.[128]

Labeling theory may help explain why some youths continue down the path of antisocial behaviors (they are labeled), whereas most are able to desist from crime (they are free of stigma).

Social Conflict Theory

social conflict theory Asserts that society is in a state of constant internal conflict, and focuses on the role of social and governmental institutions as mechanisms for social control.

The final branch of sociological theory, **social conflict theory,** finds that society is in a constant state of internal conflict, and different groups strive to impose their will on others. Those with money and power succeed in shaping the law to meet their needs and maintain their interests. Those adolescents whose behavior cannot conform to the needs of the power elite are defined as delinquents and criminals.

According to this view, those in power use the justice system to maintain their status while keeping others subservient: Men use their economic power to subjugate women; members of the majority want to stave off the economic advancement of minorities; capitalists want to reduce the power of workers to ensure they are willing to accept low wages. Conflict theory thus centers around a view of society in which an elite class uses the law as a means of meeting threats to its status. The ruling class is a self-interested collective whose primary interest is self-gain.[129]

Law and Justice

The conflict view of delinquency is rooted in the political philosophy of Karl Marx. To learn more about his viewpoints, go to *http://www.anu.edu. au/polsci/marx/marx.html* For an up-to-date list of Web links, go to *http://info.wadsworth.com/siegel*

Social conflict theorists view the law and the justice system as vehicles for controlling the have-not members of society; legal institutions help the powerful and rich to impose their standards of good behavior on the entire society. The law protects the property and physical safety of the haves from attack by the have-nots, and helps control the behavior of those who might otherwise threaten the status quo.[130] The ruling elite draws the lower-middle class into this pattern of control, leading it to believe it has a stake in maintaining the status quo.[131] According to social conflict theory, the poor may or may not commit more crimes than the rich, but they certainly are arrested more often. Police may act more forcefully in areas where class conflict creates the perception that extreme forms of social control are needed to maintain order.[132] It is not surprising to conflict theorists that complaints of police brutality are highest in minority neighborhoods, especially those that experience relative deprivation. (African American residents earn significantly less money than the majority and therefore have less political and social power.[133]) Police misbehavior, which is routine in minority neighborhoods, would never be tolerated in affluent white areas. Consequently, a

Figure 4.12
Social Conflict Theory

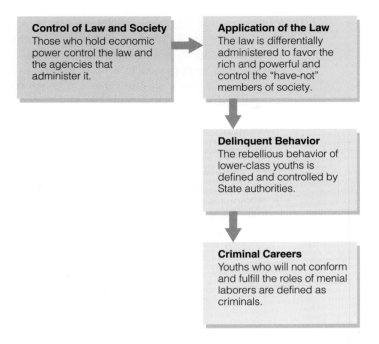

Control of Law and Society
Those who hold economic power control the law and the agencies that administer it.

Application of the Law
The law is differentially administered to favor the rich and powerful and control the "have-not" members of society.

Delinquent Behavior
The rebellious behavior of lower-class youths is defined and controlled by State authorities.

Criminal Careers
Youths who will not conform and fulfill the roles of menial laborers are defined as criminals.

deep-rooted hostility is generated among members of the lower class toward a social order they may neither shape nor share.[134] (See Figure 4.12.)

The Conflict Concept of Delinquency

Conflict theorists view delinquency as a normal response to the conditions created by capitalism.[135] In fact, the creation of a legal category, delinquency, is a function of the class consciousness that occurred around the turn of the twentieth century.[136] In *The Child Savers,* Anthony Platt documented the creation of the delinquency concept and the role played by wealthy child savers in forming the philosophy of the juvenile court. Platt believed the child-saving movement's real goal was to maintain order and control while preserving the existing class system.[137] He and others have concluded that the child savers were powerful citizens who aimed to control the behavior of disenfranchised youths.[138]

Conflict theorists still view delinquent behavior as a function of the capitalist system's inherent inequity. They argue that capitalism accelerates the trend toward replacing human labor with machines so that youths are removed from the labor force.[139] From early childhood, the values of capitalism are reinforced. Social control agencies such as schools prepare youths for placement in the capitalist system by presenting them with behavior models that will help them conform to later job expectations. For example, rewards for good schoolwork correspond to the rewards a manager uses with employees. In fact, most schools are set up to reward youths who show promise in self-discipline and motivation and are therefore judged likely to perform well in the capitalist system. Youths who are judged inferior as potential job prospects become known as losers and punks and wind up in delinquent roles.[140]

Class and Delinquency   The capitalist system affects youths differently at each level of the class structure. In the lowest classes, youths form gangs, which can be found in the most desolate ghetto areas. These gangs serve as a means of survival in a system that offers no reasonable alternative. Lower-class youths who live in more stable areas are on the fringe of criminal activity because the economic system excludes them from meaningful opportunity.

Conflict theory also acknowledges middle-class delinquency. The alienation of individuals from one another, the competitive struggle, and the absence of human feeling, all qualities of capitalism, contribute to middle-class delinquency. Because capitalism is dehumanizing, it is not surprising that even middle-class youths turn to drugs, gambling, and illicit sex to find escape.

Controlling Delinquents   Conflict theorists suggest that, rather than inhibiting delinquent behavior, the justice system may help to sustain such behavior. They claim that the capitalist state fails to control delinquents because it is in the state's interest to maintain a large number of outcast deviant youths. These youths can be employed as marginal workers, willing to work for minimum wage in jobs no one else wants. Thus, labeling by the justice system fits within the capitalist managers' need to maintain an underclass of cheap labor.

Sociological Theories and Social Policy

Each of the various branches of sociological theory has had an impact on social policy designed to reduce or eliminate delinquency. The following sections describe a few of these efforts.

Social Structure Theories and Social Policy

Social structure–based delinquency prevention programs aim to improve conditions within broad areas of the community in order to reduce delinquency rates. The most prominent contemporary manifestation of a program based on social structure theory is Operation Weed and Seed, the federal multilevel action plan for revitalizing communities.[141] The concept of this program is that no single approach can reduce crime rates and that social service and law enforcement agencies must cooperate to be effective. Therefore there are four basic elements in this plan: law enforcement; community policing; prevention, intervention, and treatment; and neighborhood restoration. The last element, neighborhood restoration, is the one most closely attached to the social structure theory because it is designed to revitalize distressed neighborhoods and improve the quality of life in the target communities. The neighborhood restoration element focuses on economic development activities, such as economic opportunities for residents, improved housing conditions, enhanced social services, and improved public services in the target area. Programs are being developed that will improve living conditions; enhance home security; allow for low-cost physical improvements; develop long-term efforts to renovate and maintain housing; and provide educational, economic, social, recreational, and other vital opportunities. A key feature is the fostering of self-worth and individual responsibility among community members.

Socialization and Social Policy

Social process theories suggest that delinquency can be prevented by strengthening the socialization process. One approach has been helping social institutions improve their outreach. Educational programs have been improved by expanding preschool programs, developing curricula relevant to students' lives, and stressing teacher development. Counseling and remedial services have been aimed at troubled youth.

Prevention programs have also been aimed at strengthening families in crisis. Because attachment to parents is a cornerstone of all social process theories, developing good family relations is an essential element of delinquency prevention. Programs have been developed that encourage families to help children develop the positive self-image necessary to resist the forces promoting delinquency.[142]

Prevention programs have also focused on providing services for youngsters who have been identified as delinquents or predelinquents. Such services usually include counseling, job placement, legal assistance, and more. Their aim is to reach out to troubled youths and provide them with the skills necessary to function in their environment before they get in trouble with the law. In addition to these local efforts, the federal government has sponsored several delinquency-prevention efforts using the principles of social process theory. These include vocational training programs, such as the Comprehensive Employment Training Act, as well as educational enrichment programs, such as Head Start for preschoolers. See Chapter 11 for more on these programs.

Social Reaction and Social Policy

As the dangers of labeling became known, a massive effort was made to limit the interface of youths with the juvenile justice system. One approach was to divert youths from official processing at the time of their initial contact with police. The usual practice is to have police refer children to treatment facilities rather than to the juvenile court. In a similar vein, children who were petitioned to juvenile court might be eligible for alternative programs rather than traditional juvenile justice processing. For example, restitution allows children to pay back the victims of their crimes for the damage (or inconvenience) they have caused instead of receiving an official delinquency label.

If a youth was found delinquent, efforts were made to reduce stigma by using alternative programs such as boot camp or intensive probation monitoring. Alternative community-based sanctions substituted for state training schools, a policy known as **deinstitutionalization.** Whenever possible, anything producing stigma was to be avoided, a philosophy referred to as nonintervention.

deinstitutionalization Removing juveniles from adult jails and placing them in community-based programs to avoid the stigma attached to these facilities.

While these programs were initially popular, critics claimed that the nonintervention movement created a new class of juvenile offenders who heretofore might have avoided prolonged contact with juvenile justice agencies; they referred to this phenomenon as widening the net.[143] Evaluation of existing programs did not indicate that they could reduce the recidivism rate of clients.[144] While these criticisms proved damaging, many nonintervention programs still operate.

Social Conflict and Social Policy

restorative justice Nonpunitive strategies for dealing with juvenile offenders that make the justice system a healing process rather than a punishment process.

If conflict is the source of delinquency, conflict resolution may be the key to its demise. This is the aim of **restorative justice,** an approach that relies on nonpunitive strategies for delinquency control.[145] The restorative justice movement has a number of sources. Negotiation, mediation, and peacemaking have been part of the dispute resolution process in European and Asian communities for centuries.[146] Native American and Native Canadian people have long used participation of community members in the adjudication process (sentencing circles, panels of elders).[147]

Restoration involves turning the justice system into a healing process rather than a distributor of retribution. Most people involved in offender-victim relationships actually know one another or are related. Restorative justice attempts to address the issues that produced conflict between these people rather than to treat one as a victim deserving sympathy and the other as a delinquent deserving punishment. Rather than choose whom to punish, society should try to reconcile the parties.[148] Hence, it relies on such techniques as victim-offender reconciliation programs, which bring victims and offenders together so that offenders can understand the damage they caused and what they can do to change their behaviors.[149] Restorative justice stands in opposition to views of juvenile justice that limit consideration of the personal and social qualities of offenders.

Even the most effective restorative justice programs will be unable to reach those who are disengaged from community institutions. Therefore, community involvement is an essential ingredient of the restorative justice approach. Gordon Bazemore and other policy experts helped formulate a version of restorative justice known as the balanced approach, which emphasizes that victims, offenders, and the community should all benefit from interactions with the justice system.[150]

SUMMARY

Social structure theories hold that delinquent behavior is an adaptation to conditions that predominate in lower-class environments. The social disorganization view suggests that economically deprived areas lose their ability to control the behavior of residents. Gangs flourish in these areas. Delinquency is a product of the socialization mechanisms within a neighborhood: Unstable neighborhoods have the greatest chance of producing delinquents. More recent ecological theories have shown how fear, unemployment, change, and attitudes influence behavior patterns.

Strain theories hold that lower-class youths may desire legitimate goals but that their unavailability causes frustration and deviant behavior. Robert Merton linked strain to anomie, a condition caused when there is a disjunction between goals and means. In his General Strain Theory, Robert Agnew identifies two more sources of strain: the removal of positive reinforcements and the addition of negative ones. He shows how strain causes delinquent behavior by creating negative affective states, and he outlines the means adolescents employ to cope with strain.

The third branch of structural theory is cultural deviance, or subcultural, theory. This maintains that the re-

sult of social disorganization and strain is the development of subcultures that hold values in opposition to mainstream society.

Social process theories hold that improper socialization is the key to delinquency. One branch called learning theories holds that kids learn deviant behaviors and attitudes during interaction with family and peers. In contrast, control theories suggest that kids are prone to delinquent behavior when they have not been properly socialized and lack a strong bond to society.

According to social reaction theories, labeling and stigma may also reinforce delinquency.

Social conflict theory views delinquency as an inevitable result of the class and racial conflict that pervades society. Delinquents are members of the have-not class that is shut out of the mainstream. The law benefits the wealthy over the poor.

Sociological views of delinquency have had a great deal of influence on social policy. Programs have been designed to improve neighborhood conditions, help children be properly socialized, and reduce conflict.

KEY TERMS

culture of poverty

underclass

truly disadvantaged

social disorganization theory

transitional neighborhood

cultural transmission

social control

gentrified

poverty concentration effect

collective efficacy

strain theory

anomie

relative deprivation

negative affective states

cultural deviance theory

culture conflict

socialization

learning theory

control theory

differential association
    theory

drift

neutralization techniques

social bond

stigmatized

labeling theory

self-labeling

self-fulfilling prophecy

dramatization of evil

degradation ceremony

social conflict theory

deinstitutionalization

restorative justice

QUESTIONS FOR DISCUSSION

1. Is there a transitional area in your town or city?

2. Is it possible that a distinct lower-class culture exists? Are lower-class values different from those of the middle class?

3. Have you ever perceived anomie? What causes anomie? Is there more than one cause of strain?

4. How does poverty cause delinquency?

5. Do middle-class youths become delinquent for the same reasons as lower-class youths?

6. Does relative deprivation produce delinquency?

VIEWPOINT

"Reintegrative shaming communicates disapproval within a continuum of respect for the offender; the offender is treated as a good person who has done a bad deed. Stigmatization is disrespectful shaming; the offender is treated as a bad person. Stigmatization is unforgiving—the offender is left with the stigma permanently, whereas reintegrative shaming is forgiving—ceremonies to certify deviance are terminated by ceremonies to decertify deviance. Put another way, societies that are forgiving and respectful while taking crime seriously have low crime rates; societies that degrade and humiliate criminals have higher crime rates."

John Braithwaite's concept of reintegrative shaming is an important concept within the restorative justice movement. Read more about this concept on InfoTrac College Edition: John Braithwaite, "Shame and Criminal Justice," *Canadian Journal of Criminology* 42:281 (2000).

NOTES

1. Steven Messner and Richard Rosenfeld, *Crime and the American Dream* (Belmont, CA: Wadsworth, 1994), p. 11.

2. Gary LaFree, *Losing Legitimacy: Street Crime and the Decline of Social Institutions in America* (Boulder, CO: Westview, 1998).

3. Emilie Andersen Allan and Darrell Steffensmeier, "Youth, Underemployment, and Property Crime: Differential Effects of Job Availability and Job Quality on Juvenile and Young Adult Arrest Rates," *American Sociological Review* 54:107–23 (1989).

4. Edwin Lemert, *Human Deviance, Social Problems and Social Control* (Englewood Cliffs, NJ: Prentice-Hall, 1967).

5. Oscar Lewis, "The Culture of Poverty," *Scientific American* 215:19–25 (1966).

6. Laura G. De Haan and Shelley MacDermid, "The Relationship of Individual and Family Factors to the Psychological Well-Being of Junior High School Students Living in Urban Poverty," *Adolescence* 33:73–90 (1998).

7. Julian Chow and Claudia Coulton, "Was There a Social Transformation of Urban Neighborhoods in the 1980s?" *Urban Studies* 35:135–75 (1998).

8. Rodrick Wallace, "Expanding Coupled Shock Fronts of Urban Decay and Criminal Behavior: How U.S. Cities Are Becoming 'Hollowed Out'," *Journal of Quantitative Criminology* 7:333–55 (1991).

9. Ken Auletta, *The Under Class* (New York: Random House, 1982).

10. Richard McGahey, "Economic Conditions, Organization, and Urban Crime," in Albert Reiss and Michael Tonry, eds., *Communities and Crime* (Chicago: University of Chicago Press, 1986), pp. 231–70.

11. Jeanne Brooks-Gunn and Greg J. Duncan, "The Effects of Poverty on Children," *The Future of Children* 7:34–39 (1997).

12. Greg Duncan, W. Jean Yeung, Jeanne Brooks-Gunn, and Judith Smith, "How Much Does Childhood Poverty Affect the Life Chances of Children?" *American Sociological Review* 63:406–23 (1998).

13. Federal Interagency Forum on Child and Family Statistics, *America's Children: Key National Indicators of Well-Being* (Washington, DC: Federal Interagency Forum on Child and Family Statistics, 2001).

14. William Julius Wilson, *The Truly Disadvantaged* (Chicago: University of Chicago Press, 1987).

15. James Ainsworth-Darnell and Douglas Downey, "Assessing the Oppositional Culture Explanation for Racial/Ethnic Differences on School Performances," *American Sociological Review* 63:536–53 (1998).

16. David Greenberg and Valerie West, "State Prison Populations and Their Growth, 1971–1991 *Criminology* 39:615–54 (2001).

17. Eric Lotke, "Hobbling a Generation: Young African-American Men in Washington, D.C.'s Criminal Justice System—Five Years Later," *Crime and Delinquency* 44:355–66 (1998).

18. Greenberg and West, "State Prison Populations and their Growth, 1971–1991," pp. 615–54.

19. William Julius Wilson, *The Bridge over the Racial Divide: Rising Inequality and Coalition Politics* (Wildavsky Forum Series, 2) (Berkeley: University of California Press, 1999).

20. Children's Defense Fund, *The State of America's Children, 1998* (Washington, DC: Children's Defense Fund, 1998); U.S. Bureau of Census Data, Race and Income (Washington, DC: U.S. Census Bureau, 1998).

21. Ibid., p. 355.

22. Frederick Thrasher, *The Gang* (Chicago: University of Chicago Press, 1927).

23. Robert Bursik and Harold Grasmick, "The Multiple Layers of Social Disorganization." Paper presented at the annual meeting of the American Society of Criminology, New Orleans, November 1992; Robert Bursik and Harold Grasmick, "Longitudinal Neighborhood Profiles in Delinquency: The Decomposition of Change," *Journal of Quantitative Criminology* 8:247–56 (1992).

24. Clifford R. Shaw and Henry D. McKay, *Juvenile Delinquency and Urban Areas*, rev. ed. (Chicago: University of Chicago Press, 1972).

25. Steven Messner, Lawrence Raffalovich, and Richard McMillan, "Economic Deprivation and Changes in Homicide Arrest Rates for White and Black Youths, 1967–1998: A National Time Series—Analysis, *Criminology* 39:591–614 (2001).

26. D. Wayne Osgood and Jeff Chambers, "Social Disorganization outside the Metropolis: An Analysis of Rural Youth Violence," *Criminology* 38:81–117 (2000).

27. Robert Bursik and Harold Grasmick, "Economic Deprivation and Neighborhood Crime Rates, 1960–1980," *Law and Society Review* 27:263–78 (1993).

28. Robert Sampson and W. Byron Groves, "Community Structure and Crime: Testing Social Disorganization Theory," *American Journal of Sociology* 94:774–802 (1989); Denise Gottfredson, Richard McNeill, and Gary Gottfredson, "Social Area Influences on Delinquency: A Multilevel Analysis," *Journal of Research in Crime and Delinquency* 28:197–206 (1991).

29. Ruth Peterson, Lauren Krivo, and Mark Harris, "Disadvantage and Neighborhood Violent Crime: Do Local Institutions Matter?" *Journal of Research in Crime and Delinquency* 37:31–63 (2000).

30. Ora Simcha-Fagan and Joseph Schwartz, "Neighborhood and Delinquency: An Assessment of Contextual Effects," *Criminology* 24:667–703 (1986).

31. Leo Scheurman and Solomon Kobrin, "Community Careers in Crime," in Albert Reiss and Michael Tonry, eds., *Communities and Crime* (Chicago: University of Chicago Press, 1986), pp. 67–100.

32. Ibid., p. 96.

33. Ellen Kurtz, Barbara Koons, and Ralph Taylor, "Land Use, Physical Deterioration, Resident-Based Control, and Calls for Service on Urban Streetblocks," *Justice Quarterly* 15:121–49 (1998).

34. Janet Heitgerd and Robert Bursik Jr., "Extracommunity Dynamics and the Ecology of Delinquency," *American Journal of Sociology* 92:775–87 (1987).

35. Jeffrey Morenoff, Robert Sampson, and Stephen Raudenbush, "Neighborhood Inequality, Collective Efficacy, and the Spatial Dynamics of Urban Violence," *Criminology* 39:517–60 (2001).

36. Richard Fowles and Mary Merva, "Wage Inequality and Criminal Activity: An Extreme Bounds Analysis for the United States 1975–1990," *Criminology* 34:163–82 (1996).

37. Karen Parker and Matthew Pruitt, "Poverty, Poverty Concentration, and Homicide," *Social Science Quarterly* 81:555–82 (2000).

38. Margo Wilson and Martin Daly, "Life Expectancy, Economic Inequality, Homicide, and Reproductive Timing in Chicago Neighbourhoods," *British Journal of Medicine* 314:1271–74 (1997).

39. Joan Petersilia, When Prisoners Return to Communities: Political, Economic, and Social Consequences" *Federal Probation*, 65:3–9 (2001).

40. Pamela Wilcox Rountree and Kenneth Land, "Burglary Victimization, Perceptions of Crime Risk, and Routine Ac-

tivities: A Multilevel Analysis across Seattle Neighborhoods and Census Tracts," *Journal of Research in Crime and Delinquency* 33:147–80 (1996).

41. Fred Markowitz, Paul Bellair, Allen Liska, Jianhong Liu, "Extending Social Disorganization Theory: Modeling the Relationships between Cohesion, Disorder, and Fear," *Criminology* 39:293–320 (2001).

42. See, generally, Wesley Skogan, "Fear of Crime and Neighborhood Change," in Albert Reiss and Michael Tonry, eds., *Communities and Crime* (Chicago: University of Chicago Press, 1986), pp. 191–232; Stephanie Greenberg, "Fear and Its Relationship to Crime, Neighborhood Deterioration, and Informal Social Control," in James Byrne and Robert Sampson, eds., *The Social Ecology of Crime* (New York: Springer-Verlag, 1985), pp. 47–62.

43. Jeffery Will and John McGrath, "Crime, Neighborhood Perceptions, and the Underclass: The Relationship between Fear of Crime and Class Position," *Journal of Criminal Justice* 23:163–76 (1995).

44. Ted Chiricos, Ranee Mcentire, and Marc Gertz, "Social Problems, Perceived Racial and Ethnic Composition of Neighborhood and Perceived Risk of Crime," *Social Problems* 48:322–41 (2001).

45. Catherine E. Ross, John Mirowsky, and Shana Pribesh, "Powerlessness and the Amplification of Threat: Neighborhood Disadvantage, Disorder, and Mistrust," *American Sociological Review* 66:568–80 (2001).

46. Wilson and Daly, "Life Expectancy, Economic Inequality, Homicide, and Reproductive Timing in Chicago Neighborhoods."

47. Catherine Ross, "Fear of Victimization and Health," *Journal of Quantitative Criminology* 9:159–65 (1993).

48. Donald Black, "Social Control as a Dependent Variable," in D. Black, ed., *Toward a General Theory of Social Control* (Orlando, FL: Academic, 1990).

49. Bursik and Grasmick, "The Multiple Layers of Social Disorganization," pp. 8–10.

50. Maria Velez, "The Role of Public Social Control in Urban Neighborhoods: A Multi-Level Analysis of Victimization Risk," *Criminology* 39:837–64 (2001).

51. Sampson and Groves, "Community Structure and Crime: Testing Social Disorganization Theory," pp. 774–802.

52. Gottfredson, McNeill, and Gottfredson, "Social Area Influences on Delinquency: A Multilevel Analysis," pp. 197–206.

53. Elijah Anderson, *Streetwise: Race, Class and Change in an Urban Community* (Chicago: University of Chicago Press, 1990), pp. 243–44.

54. Michael Greene, "Chronic Exposure to Violence and Poverty: Interventions that Work for Youth," *Crime and Delinquency* 39:106–24 (1993).

55. Ibid., pp. 110–11.

56. Felton Earls, *Linking Community Factors and Individual Development* (Washington, DC: National Institute of Justice, 1998).

57. Robert J. Sampson and Stephen W. Raudenbush, *Disorder in Urban Neighborhoods: Does It Lead to Crime?* (Washington, DC: National Institute of Justice, 2001).

58. Morenoff, Sampson, and Raudenbush, "Neighborhood Inequality, Collective Efficacy, and the Spatial Dynamics of Urban Violence," pp. 550–51.

59. Robert Sampson, Jeffrey Morenoff, and Felton Earls, "Beyond Social Capital: Spatial Dynamics of Collective Efficacy for Children," *American Sociological Review* 64:633–60 (1999).

60. Thomas McNulty, "Assessing the Race-Violence Relationship at the Macro Level: The Assumption of Racial Invariance and the Problem of Restricted Distribution," *Criminology* 39:467–90 (2001).

61. Robert Merton, *Social Theory and Social Structure* (Glencoe, IL: Free Press, 1957).

62. Judith Blau and Peter Blau, "The Cost of Inequality: Metropolitan Structure and Violent Crime," *American Sociological Review* 147:114–29 (1982).

63. Beverly Stiles, Xiaoru Liu, and Howard Kaplan, "Relative Deprivation and Deviant Adaptations: The Mediating Effects of Negative Self-Feelings," *Journal of Research in Crime and Delinquency* 37:64–90 (2000).

64. Morenoff, Sampson, and Raudenbush, "Neighborhood Inequality, Collective Efficacy, and the Spatial Dynamics of Urban Violence."

65. Tomislav Kovandzic, Lynne Vieraitis, and Mark Yeisley, "The Structural Covariates of Urban Homicide: Reassessing the Impact of Income Inequality and Poverty in the Post-Reagan Era," *Criminology* 36:569–600 (1998); Scott South and Steven Messner, "Structural Determinants of Intergroup Association," *American Journal of Sociology* 91:1409–30 (1986); Steven Messner and Scott South, "Economic Deprivation, Opportunity Structure and Robbery Victimization," *Social Forces* 64:975–91 (1986).

66. Robert Agnew, "Foundation for a General Strain Theory of Crime and Delinquency," *Criminology* 30:47–87 (1992).

67. Ibid., p. 57.

68. Timothy Brezina, "Adolescent Maltreatment and Delinquency: The Question of Intervening Processes," *Journal of Research in Crime and Delinquency* 35:71–99 (1998).

69. Paul Mazerolle, Velmer Burton, Francis Cullen, T. David Evans, and Gary Payne, "Strain, Anger, and Delinquent Adaptations Specifying General Strain Theory," *Journal of Criminal Justice* 28:89–101 (2000); Paul Mazerolle and Alex Piquero, "Violent Responses to Strain: An Examination of Conditioning Influences, *Violence and Victimization* 12:323–45 (1997).

70. George E. Capowich, Paul Mazerolle, and Alex Piquero, "General Strain Theory, Situational Anger, and Social Networks: An Assessment of Conditioning Influences," *Journal of Criminal Justice* 29:445–61 (2001).

71. Mazerolle, Burton, Cullen, Evans, and Payne, "Strain, Anger, and Delinquent Adaptations Specifying General Strain Theory."

72. Stephen Cernkovich, Peggy Giordano, and Jennifer Rudolph, "Race, Crime and the American Dream," *Journal of Research in Crime and Delinquency* 37:131–70 (2000).

73. Lawrence Wu, "Effects of Family Instability, Income and Income Instability on the Risk of Premarital Birth," *American Sociological Review* 61:386–406 (1996).

74. Anthony Walsh, "Behavior Genetics and Anomie/Strain Theory," *Criminology* 38:1075–108 (2000).

75. Albert Cohen, *Delinquent Boys* (New York: Free Press, 1955).

76. Richard Cloward and Lloyd Ohlin, *Delinquency and Opportunity* (New York: Free Press, 1960).

77. See, for example, Irving Spergel, *Racketville, Slumtown, and Haulburg* (Chicago: University of Chicago Press, 1964).

78. James Short, "Gangs, Neighborhoods, and Youth Crime," *Criminal Justice Research Bulletin* 5:1–11 (1990).

79. Michael Leiber, Mahesh Nalla, and Margaret Farnworth, "Explaining Juveniles' Attitudes toward the Police," *Justice Quarterly* 15:151–73 (1998).

80. A. Leigh Ingram, "Type of Place, Urbanism, and Delinquency: Further Testing of the Determinist Theory," *Journal of Research in Crime and Delinquency* 30:192–212 (1993).

81. Alan Lizotte, Terence Thornberry, Marvin Krohn, Deborah Chard-Wierschem, and David McDowall, "Neighborhood Context and Delinquency: A Longitudinal Analysis," in H. J. Kerner and E. Weitekamp, eds., *Cross-National Longitudinal Research on Human Development and Criminal Behavior* (Dordrecht, The Netherlands: Kluwer Academic Publishers, 1993), pp. 1–11.

82. Lawrence Rosen, "Family and Delinquency: Structure or Function," *Criminology* 23:553–73 (1985).

83. Ronald Simons, Chyi-In Wu, Kuei-Hsiu Lin, Leslie Gordon, and Rand Conger, "A Cross-Cultural Examination of the Link between Corporal Punishment and Adolescent Antisocial Behavior," *Criminology* 38:47–79 (2000).

84. John Paul Wright and Francis Cullen, "Parental Efficacy and Delinquent Behavior: Do Control and Support Matter?" *Criminology* 39:677–706 (2001).

85. Carter Hay, "Parenting, Self-Control, and Delinquency: A Test of Self-Control Theory," *Criminology* 39:707–36 (2001).

86. Robert Roberts and Vern Bengston, "Affective Ties to Parents in Early Adulthood and Self-Esteem Across 20 Years," *Social Psychology Quarterly* 59:96–106 (1996).

87. G. Roger Jarjoura, "Does Dropping Out of School Enhance Delinquent Involvement? Results from a Large-Scale National Probability Sample," *Criminology* 31:149–72 (1993); Terence Thornberry, Melaine Moore, and R. L. Christenson, "The Effect of Dropping Out of High School on Subsequent Criminal Behavior," *Criminology* 233–18 (1985).

88. Carolyn Smith, Alan Lizotte, Terence Thornberry, and Marvin Krohn, *Resilient Youth: Identifying Factors That Prevent High-Risk Youth from Engaging in Delinquency and Drug Use* (Albany, NY: Rochester Youth Development Study, 1994), pp. 19–21.

89. Thomas Berndt, "The Features and Effects of Friendship in Early Adolescence," *Child Development* 53:1447–60 (1982).

90. David Fergusson, L. John Horwood, and Daniel Nagin, "Offending Trajectories in a New Zealand Birth Cohort," *Criminology* 38:525–51 (2000).

91. Colin Baier and Bradley Wright, "If You Love Me, Keep My Commandments": A Meta-Analysis of the Effect of Religion on Crime," *Journal of Research in Crime and Delinquency* 38:3–21 (2001); Byron Johnson, Sung Joon Jang, David Larson, and Spencer De Li, "Does Adolescent Religious Commitment Matter? A Reexamination of the Effects of Religiosity on Delinquency," *Journal of Research in Crime and Delinquency* 38:22–44 (2001).

92. Sung Joon Jang and Byron Johnson, "Neighborhood Disorder, Individual Religiosity, and Adolescent Use of Illicit Drugs: A Test of Multilevel Hypothesis," *Criminology* 39:109–44 (2001).

93. T. David Evans, Francis Cullen, R. Gregory Dunaway, and Velmer Burton, Jr., "Religion and Crime Reexamined: The Impact of Religion, Secular Controls, and Social Ecology on Adult Criminality," *Criminology* 33:195–224 (1995).

94. Lee Ellis and James Patterson, "Crime and Religion: An International Comparison among Thirteen Industrial Nations," *Personal Individual Differences* 20:761–68 (1996).

95. Edwin Sutherland, *Principles of Criminology* (Philadelphia: Lippincott, 1939).

96. Gresham Sykes and David Matza, "Techniques of Neutralization: A Theory of Delinquency," *American Sociological Review* 22:664–70 (1957); David Matza, *Delinquency and Drift* (New York: Wiley, 1964).

97. Ibid.

98. Travis Hirschi, *Causes of Delinquency* (Berkeley: University of California Press, 1969).

99. For a review of existing research, see Kimberly Kempf, "The Empirical Status of Hirschi's Control Theory," in Bill Laufer and Freda Adler, eds., *Advances in Criminological Theory* (New Brunswick, NJ: Transaction, 1992).

100. Bobbi Jo Anderson, Malcolm Holmes, and Erik Ostresh, "Male and Female Delinquent's Attachments and Effects of Attachments on Severity of Self-Reported Delinquency," *Criminal Justice and Behavior* 26:425–52 (1999).

101. Thomas Vander Ven, Francis Cullen, Mark Carrozza, John Paul Wright, "Home Alone: The Impact of Maternal Employment on Delinquency," *Social Problems* 48:236–57 (2001); Patricia Jenkins, "School Delinquency and the School Social Bond," *Journal of Research in Crime and Delinquency* 34:337–67 (1997).

102. Stephen Cernkovich, Peggy Giordano, and Jennifer Rudolph, "Race, Crime and the American Dream," *Journal of Research in Crime and Delinquency* 37:131–70 (2000).

103. Richard Lawrence, "Parents, Peers, School and Delinquency." Paper presented at the American Society of Criminology meeting, Boston, November 1995.

104. Peggy Giordano, Stephen Cernkovich, and M. D. Pugh, "Friendships and Delinquency," *American Journal of Sociology* 91:1170–1202 (1986).

105. Denise Kandel and Mark Davies, "Friendship Networks, Intimacy, and Illicit Drug Use in Young Adulthood: A Comparison of Two Competing Theories," *Criminology* 29:441–67 (1991).

106. Leslie Samuelson, Timothy Hartnagel, and Harvey Krahn, "Crime and Social Control among High School Dropouts," *Journal of Crime and Justice* 18:129–61 (1990).

107. For a review of this position, see Anne R. Mahoney, "The Effect of Labeling upon Youths in the Juvenile Justice System: A Review of the Evidence," *Law and Society Review* 8:583–614 (1974); see also David Matza, *Becoming Deviant* (Englewood Cliffs, NJ: Prentice-Hall, 1974).

108. The self-labeling concept originated in Edwin Lemert, *Social Pathology* (New York: McGraw-Hill, 1951); see also Frank Tannenbaum, *Crime and the Community* (Boston: Ginn, 1936).

109. Nalini Ambady and Robert Rosenthal, "Half a Minute: Predicting Teacher Evaluations from Thin Slices of Nonverbal Behavior and Physical Attractiveness," *Journal of Personality and Social Psychology* 64:431–41 (1993).

110. Monica Harris, Richard Milich, Elizabeth Corbitt, Daniel Hoover, and Marianne Brady, "Self-Fulfilling Effects of Stigmatizing Information on Children's Social Interactions," *Journal of Personality and Social Psychology* 33:41–50 (1992).

111. Harold Garfinkel, "Conditions of Successful Degradation Ceremonies," *American Journal of Sociology* 61:420–24 (1956)

112. M. A. Bortner, *Inside a Juvenile Court: The Tarnished Ideal of Individualized Justice* (New York: NYU Press, 1982).

113. Edwin Lemert, *Human Deviance, Social Problems, and Social Control* (Englewood Cliffs, NJ: Prentice-Hall, 1967), p. 15.

114. Charles H. Cooley, *Human Nature and the Social Order* (New York: Scribner's, 1902).

115. Ross Matsueda, "Reflected Appraisals, Parental Labeling, and Delinquency: Specifying a Symbolic Interactionist Theory," *American Journal of Sociology* 97:1577–1611 (1992).

116. Howard Kaplan and Hiroshi Fukurai, "Negative Social Sanctions, Self-Rejection, and Drug Use," *Youth and Society* 23:275–98 (1992).

117. Howard Kaplan, *Toward a General Theory of Deviance: Contributions from Perspectives on Deviance and Criminality* (College Station, TX: Texas A & M University, n.d.).

118. Harris et al., "Self-Fulfilling Effects of Stigmatizing Information on Children's Social Interactions," pp. 48–50.

119. Kaplan, *Toward a General Theory of Deviance*.

120. Howard Kaplan, Robert Johnson, and Carol Bailey, "Deviant Peers and Deviant Behavior: Further Elaboration of a Model," *Social Psychology Quarterly* 30:277–84 (1987).

121. Tannenbaum, *Crime and the Community*.

122. Aaron Cicourel, *The Social Organization of Juvenile Justice* (New York: Wiley, 1968).

123. Matza, *Becoming Deviant*.

124. Ibid., p. 78.

125. Stanton Wheeler and Leonard Cottrell, "Juvenile Delinquency: Its Prevention and Control," in Donald Cressey and David Ward, eds., *Delinquency, Crime, and Social Processes* (New York: Harper & Row, 1969), p. 609.

126. Garfinkel, *Conditions of Successful Degradation Ceremonies*, p. 424.

127. Charles Murray and Lewis Cox, *Beyond Probation* (Beverly Hills: Sage, 1979).

128. Raymond Paternoster and Leeann Iovanni, "The Labeling Perspective and Delinquency: An Elaboration of the Theory and an Assessment of the Evidence," *Justice Quarterly* 6:358–94 (1989).

129. Meier, "The New Criminology," p. 463.

130. Sykes, "The Rise of Critical Criminology," pp. 211–13.

131. Ibid.

132. David Jacobs and David Britt, "Inequality and Police Use of Deadly Force: An Empirical Assessment of a Conflict Hypothesis," *Social Problems* 26:403–12 (1979).

133. Malcolm Homes, "Minority Threat and Police Brutality: Determinants of Civil Rights Criminal Complaints in U.S. Municipalities," *Criminology* 38:343–68 (2000).

134. Ibid.

135. Robert Gordon, "Capitalism, Class, and Crime in America," *Crime and Delinquency* 19:174 (1973).

136. Richard Quinney, *Class, State, and Crime* (New York: Longman, 1977), p. 52.

137. Anthony Platt, "The Triumph of Benevolence: The Origins of the Juvenile Justice System in the United States," in Richard Quinney, ed., *Criminal Justice in America: A Critical Understanding* (Boston: Little, Brown, 1974), p. 367; see also Anthony Platt, *The Child Savers* (Chicago: University of Chicago Press, 1969).

138. Barry Krisberg and James Austin, *Children of Ishmael* (Palo Alto, CA.: Mayfield, 1978), p. 2.

139. Herman Schwendinger and Julia Schwendinger, "Delinquency and Social Reform: A Radical Perspective," in Lamar Empey, ed., *Juvenile Justice* (Charlottesville: University of Virginia Press, 1979), p. 250.

140. Ibid., p. 252.

141. Operation Weed and Seed Executive Offices, U.S. Department of Justice, Washington, DC, 1998; Executive Office for Weed and Seed, Weed and Seed In-sites, Series: Volume VI, Number 5, August/September 1998.

142. Terence Thornberry, David Huizinga, and Rolf Loeber, "The Prevention of Serious Delinquency and Violence," in James Howell, Barry Krisberg, J. David Hawkins, and John Wilson, eds., *Sourcebook on Serious, Violent, and Chronic Juvenile Offenders* (Thousand Oaks, CA: Sage, 1995).

143. James Austin and Barry Krisberg, "The Unmet Promise of Alternatives to Incarceration," *Crime and Delinquency* 28:3–19 (1982).

144. William Selke, "Diversion and Crime Prevention," *Criminology* 20:395–406 (1982).

145. Kathleen Daly and Russ Immarigeon, "The Past, Present, and Future of Restorative Justice: Some Critical Reflections," *Contemporary Justice Review* 1:21–45 (1998).

146. Kay Pranis, "Peacemaking Circles: Restorative Justice in Practice Allows Victims and Offenders to Begin Repairing the Harm," *Corrections Today* 59:72–76 (1997).

147. Carol LaPrairie, "The 'New' Justice: Some Implications for Aboriginal Communities," *Canadian Journal of Criminology* 40:61–79 (1998).

148. Gene Stephens, "The Future of Policing: From a War Model to a Peace Model," in Brendan Maguire and Polly Radosh, eds., *The Past, Present and Future of American Criminal Justice* (Dix Hills, NY: General Hall, 1996), pp. 77–93.

149. Peter Cordella, "Justice." Unpublished paper, St. Anselm College, Manchester, NH, 1997; see also Herbert Bianchi, *Justice as Sanctuary* (Bloomington: Indiana University Press, 1994); Nils Christie, "Conflicts as Property," *The British Journal of Criminology* 17:1–15 (1977); L. Hulsman, "Critical Criminology and the Concept of Crime," *Contemporary Crises* 10:63–80 (1986).

150. Gordon Bazemore, "What's New about the Balanced Approach?" *Juvenile and Family Court Journal* 48:1–23 (1997); Gordon Bazemore and Mara Schiff, "Community Justice/Restorative Justice: Prospects for a New Social Ecology for Community Corrections," *International Journal of Comparative and Applied Criminal Justice* 20:311–35 (1996).

5 Developmental Views of Delinquency

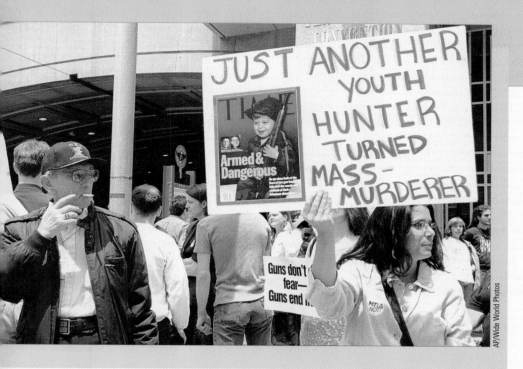

AP/Wide World Photos

You are the governor of your state. In 1991, when Steven B. was a 16-year-old high school wrestler, he and a teammate raped and severely beat a young girl who asked them for a ride home from a party. Though never in serious trouble before the attack, Steven was involved in an ongoing pattern of school misbehavior, substance abuse, and petty scrapes with the law. Those who knew him recognized that he had a short attention span and poor study habits, and he seemed to be impulsive and lacking in self-control. There were allegations that he was sexually aggressive and tried to force himself on young girls, but no formal charges were ever made.

While out on bail, Steven escaped to Europe with the help of his wealthy parents. After wandering the continent for two years, he settled in a small French town. There, Steven, now known as "Paul," established a thriving wine shop, became a respected community member, married a local woman, and fathered two children. He even served on the town council. However, after more than a decade abroad, Steven's true identity became known when he was involved in a minor traffic accident. After some negotiation, French authorities turned him over to American authorities, and he has been returned home to face the outstanding charges.

Steven now asks that you pardon him so he can return to his home and family. He argues that his friend, who was convicted of rape and served time in prison, was the one who actually attacked the girl. Steven claims he merely held her down and prevented her from escaping; his friend substantiates the story. He now realizes he was wrong, but he points out that he has lived an exemplary life for the last 10 years, that his family needs him, and that he poses no danger to society. He has offered to apologize to the victim and make financial restitution before returning to France.

- Do you believe that Steven is unlikely to commit another violent act as an adult, even though he did so as a juvenile?

- Is it possible, now that Steven is an adult, that his impulsive personality has moderated and he has regained the ability to control his own behavior? Or do you believe that behavior patterns originating in childhood, such as lack of self-control, persist into adulthood?

- Should the justice system distinguish between a young man who commits a single act of violence and a chronic offender who is repeatedly involved in criminal acts?

developmental theories Assert that personal characteristics guide human development and influence behavioral choices, but that these choices may change over the life course.

life-course theory The view that people change as they mature and that the quality of their personal development shapes their behavior choices.

latent trait view The view that a master trait, developed at birth or soon after, influences behavior across the life course. People who have this trait are crime-prone throughout their lives.

Interested in the concept of human development? Then access the United Nations Web site on the topic at *http://www.undp.org/hdro/* For an up-to-date list of Web links, go to *http://info.wadsworth.com/siegel*

Cases such as Steven B., though unusual, raise important questions about young people's antisocial activities. Why do some kids become delinquents and then abandon the delinquent way of life as they mature? Why do others persist into their adulthood? Why do some offenders escalate their delinquent activities, while others decrease or limit their law violations? Why do some delinquents turn away from criminal activity for a short period of time, only to resume it later in life? Research now shows that some offenders begin their delinquent careers at a very early age, whereas others begin later. How can this phenomenon of early- and late-onset delinquency be explained?[1] Focusing attention on these questions has produced what is known as the **developmental theory** of delinquency, which views a delinquent career as a dynamic process, influenced by both internal and external factors, with pauses, escalations, and changes of direction along the way.

There are actually two distinct developmental views. The first, referred to as the **life-course theory,** suggests that delinquent behavior is a dynamic process, influenced by individual characteristics as well as social experiences, and that the factors that cause antisocial behaviors change dramatically over a person's lifespan. However, while their position is growing increasingly popular, the life-course theorists are challenged by another group of scholars who suggest that human development is controlled by a "master trait" that remains stable and unchanging throughout a person's lifetime. Rather than focusing on human change and development, the **latent trait view** regards the opportunities people have to commit crime at various stages of their life as critical. They believe that "people don't change, opportunities do."

In the sections below, we will review the history, basic concepts, and theoretical models of the developmental, or life-course, approach. We will then turn to the latent trait view that challenges its validity.

Origins of Developmental Theories

Current developmental research was inspired by the early efforts of Sheldon and Eleanor Glueck. Working at Harvard University in the 1930s, the Gluecks popularized research on the life cycle of delinquent careers. In a series of longitudinal research studies, making extensive use of interviews and records, they followed the careers of known delinquents to determine the factors that predicted persistent offending.[2]

The Gluecks' research focused on early onset of delinquency as a harbinger of a delinquent career: "...the deeper the roots of childhood maladjustment, the smaller the chance of adult adjustment."[3] They also noted the stability of offending careers. Children who are antisocial early in life are the most likely to continue their offending careers into adulthood. The Gluecks identified a number of personal and social factors related to persistent offending, the most important of which was family relations. The adolescent raised in a large, single-parent family of limited economic means and educational achievement was the most vulnerable to delinquency. However, the Gluecks did not restrict their analysis to social variables but included such biological and psychological traits as body type, intelligence, and personality in their analysis. They found that physical and mental factors also played a role in determining behavior, and that children with low intelligence and a background of mental disease were the most likely to become persistent offenders. The Glueck research indicated that both physical and social factors shaped the direction of children's behavior and that these factors changed over the life course.

Although it was popular during their lifetime, the Gluecks' research was attacked after their deaths and disputed by social scientists who believed any effort to link physical and psychological traits to delinquency was spurious. For many years delinquency experts believed that the root cause of adolescent misbehavior could be traced to purely social constructs such as poverty and improper socialization. However, in the late 1980s, a series of research papers published by well-known criminologists John Laub

The Murray Research Center at Radcliffe College sponsors an ongoing Crime Causation Study: Unraveling Juvenile Delinquency 1940–1963, based on the work of the Gluecks. You can visit their site at *http://www.radcliffe. edu/murray/data/ds/ds0896.htm* For an up-to-date list of Web links, go to *http://info.wadsworth.com/siegel*

and Robert Sampson rekindled interest in the Gluecks' vision of delinquency.[4] Other prominent researchers followed suit and began to call for a rethinking of the directions taken by delinquency theory.[5] It was proposed that delinquency experts devote time and effort to understanding some basic questions about the evolution of delinquent careers: Why do kids begin committing antisocial acts? Why do some stop while others continue? Why do some escalate the severity of their criminality (that is, go from shoplifting to drug dealing to armed robbery), while others de-escalate and commit less serious crimes as they mature? If some terminate their delinquent activity, what, if anything, causes them to begin again? Why do some delinquents specialize in certain types of crime, whereas others are generalists engaging in a variety of antisocial behavior?

Contemporary Developmental Concepts

These pioneering efforts have produced views of delinquency causation that integrate both social and personal factors and also recognize that the factors that produce crime and delinquency are multidimensional and dynamic. Crime-producing elements that affect people at one point in the life cycle may not be relevant at another.[6] People may show a propensity to offend early in their lives, but the nature and frequency of their activities are affected by outside forces beyond their control.[7] Although one factor may dominate, the cause of delinquency is essentially multidimensional. The next sections review some of the more important concepts associated with the developmental perspective.

Age of Onset

Most life-course theories assume that the seeds of a criminal career are planted early in life and that early onset of deviance strongly predicts later criminality. Research supports this by showing that children who will later become delinquents begin their deviant careers at a very early (preschool) age, and the earlier the onset of criminality, the more frequent, varied, and sustained the criminal career.[8] In a thorough review of this issue, Rolf Loeber and David Farrington have found that the youngest criminals typically have a long history of disruptive behavior beginning in early childhood with truancy, cruelty to animals, lying, and theft.[9] Though most commit less serious forms of delinquency, since 1980 more than 600 murders have been committed by youngsters aged 12 or under; between 12 percent and 14 percent of all juveniles arrested for rape are between 7 and 12 years old.

Life Transitions

A CLOSER VIEW
What's age got to do with it? To find out, read Benjamin B. Lahey et al., "Relation of Age of Onset to the Type and Severity of Child and Adolescent Conduct Problems," *Journal of Abnormal Child Psychology* 27(4):247 (August 1999) on Info-Trac College Edition.

Developmental theories focus attention on the chronic or persistent offender. Although the concept of chronic offenders, who begin their offending careers as children and persist into adulthood, is now an accepted fact, delinquency experts are still struggling to understand why this is so. They do not fully understand why, when faced with a similar set of life circumstances (poverty and family dysfunction, for example), one youth becomes a chronic offender while another may commit an occasional illegal act but later desists from crime. One possibility is that when faced with important life transitions such as becoming a student or getting a job, some kids have what it takes to succeed, while others are incapable of maturing in a reasonable and timely fashion because of family, environmental, or personal problems.

According to developmental theory, even as toddlers, people begin relationships and behaviors that will determine their adult life course. At first they must learn to conform to social rules and function effectively in society. Later they are expected to begin thinking about careers, leave their parental homes, find permanent relationships, and eventually marry and begin their own families.[10] These transitions are expected to take place in order: completing education, entering the workforce, getting married,

A CLOSER VIEW
How does pregnancy influence the self-feelings of adolescent girls? To find out, read Carol Cowley and Tillman Farley, "Adolescent Girls' Attitudes toward Pregnancy," *Journal of Family Practice* 50(7):603 (July 2001) on InfoTrac College Edition.

and having children. In some cases transitions can occur too early—for example, when an adolescent girl engages in precocious sex and has a child while still enrolled in school. In other cases transitions may occur too late, such as when a student fails to graduate on time because of bad grades or too many incompletes. Sometimes disruption of one trajectory can harm another. For example, teenage childbirth will most likely disrupt educational and career development.

Disruptions in life's major transitions can be destructive and, ultimately, may promote criminality. Those who are already at risk because of socioeconomic problems or family dysfunction are the most susceptible to these awkward transitions. The cumulative impact of these disruptions sustains criminality from childhood into adulthood.

Because a transition from one stage of life to another can be a bumpy ride, the propensity to commit delinquent acts is neither stable nor constant; it is a *developmental process*. A positive life experience may help some delinquents desist from crime for a while, whereas a negative one may cause them to resume their activities. Delinquent careers are also said to be developmental because people are influenced by the behavior of those around them and, in turn, influence others' behavior. For example, a youth's antisocial behavior may turn his more conventional friends against him; their rejection solidifies and escalates his antisocial behavior.

Changing Life Experiences   As people mature, the factors that influence their behavior change.[11] At first, family relations may be most influential; in later adolescence, school and peer relations predominate; in adulthood, vocational achievement and marital relations may be the most critical influences. For example, some antisocial children who are in trouble throughout their adolescence may manage to find stable work and maintain intact marriages as adults; these life events help them desist from crime. In contrast, the less-fortunate adolescents who develop arrest records and get involved with the wrong crowd may find themselves limited to menial jobs and at risk for delinquent careers. Because people are influenced by different factors as they mature, a factor that may have an important influence at one stage of life (like delinquent peers) may have little influence later on.[12]

Problem Behavior Syndrome

problem behavior syndrome (PBS)   Convergence of a variety of psychological problems and family dysfunctions, including substance abuse and criminality.

Some developmental advocates believe that delinquency may best be understood as one of many social problems faced by at-risk youth. Referred to as **problem behavior syndrome (PBS)**, developmental theorists realize that crime occurs among a group of antisocial behaviors that cluster together and typically involve family dysfunction, substance abuse, smoking, precocious sexuality and early pregnancy, educational underachievement, suicide attempts, sensation seeking, and unemployment.[13]

People who suffer from one of these conditions typically exhibit many symptoms of the others.[14] All varieties of delinquent behavior, including violence, theft, and drug offenses, may be part of a generalized PBS, indicating that all forms of antisocial behavior have similar developmental patterns (Exhibit 5.1).[15] Those who suffer PBS are prone to more difficulties than the general population.[16] They find themselves with a range of personal dilemmas, from drug abuse, to being accident-prone, to requiring more health care and hospitalization, to becoming teenage parents. Problem behavior syndrome has been linked to personality problems (rebelliousness, low ego), family problems (intrafamily conflict, parental mental disorder), and educational failure.[17] Multisite research has shown that PBS is not unique to any single area of the country and that children who suffer PBS, including drug use, delinquency, and precocious sexuality, display symptoms at an early age.[18]

PBS can manifest itself in many different ways. For example, one study of youth in Pittsburgh found that kids who became fathers before their 19th birthday were much more likely to get into trouble with the law (72%) compared to youths who did not have children out of wedlock (41%). About 40 percent of the fathers were involved in frequent alcohol use and drug dealing, compared to about 20 percent for

A CLOSER VIEW
Do prior problems predict future ones? To find out, read Thomas C. Harford and Bengt O. Muthen, "Alcohol Use among College Students: The Effects of Prior Problem Behaviors and Change of Residence," *Journal of Studies on Alcohol* 62(3):306 (May 2001) on InfoTrac College Edition.

Exhibit 5.1 Problem Behaviors

Social	• Family dysfunction
	• Unemployment
	• Educational underachievement
	• School misconduct
Personal	• Substance abuse
	• Suicide attempts
	• Early sexuality
	• Sensation seeking
	• Early parenthood
	• Accident-prone
	• Medical problems
	• Mental disease
	• Anxiety
	• Eating disorders (bulimia, anorexia)
Environmental	• High-crime area
	• Disorganized area
	• Racism
	• Exposure to poverty

A CLOSER VIEW
To read more about Rolf Loeber's view of the problem of serious and violent juvenile offenders and how they should be treated, read his paper on InfoTrac College Edition: Rolf Loeber, "Early Intervention Can Work for Serious and Violent Juvenile Offenders," *The Brown University Child and Adolescent Behavior Letter* 16:1 (May 2000).

nonfathers. Similarly, while 60 percent of the fathers dropped out of school, only 21 percent of the nonfathers failed to complete their education. Fathers were also more likely to use drugs and become high-rate chronic offenders. A similar study using samples of youth from Rochester, New York, also found that teenage fatherhood was related to antisocial behavior, delinquency, and drug abuse.[19]

While not all delinquents have multiple social problems, kids who suffer from PBS are more likely to become delinquent and later criminal offenders. Data from Pittsburgh and Rochester show that kids with two or more persistent social problems (substance abuse, school failure, mental health problems) are significantly more likely to be persistent delinquent offenders than youths who are problem free.[20] These problems affect behavior throughout the offending cycle. Studies of inmates show that many of them have had mental health problems and were also undereducated, unemployed, and have had histories of alcohol, marijuana, cocaine, and heroin abuse.[21]

Pathways to Crime and Delinquency

Developmental theorists recognize that career delinquents may travel more than a single road: Some may specialize in violence and extortion; some may be involved in theft and fraud; others may engage in a variety of delinquent acts. Some offenders may begin their careers early in life, whereas others are late bloomers who begin committing crime when most people desist.

Are there different pathways to crime? Using data from a longitudinal cohort study conducted in Pittsburgh, Rolf Loeber and his associates have identified three distinct paths to a delinquent career (Figure 5.1):[22]

authority-conflict pathway
The developmental path taken to delinquency that begins with stubborn and defiant behavior.

covert pathway The developmental path taken to delinquency that begins with sneaky, deceitful, and underhanded behavior.

1. The **authority-conflict pathway** begins at an early age with stubborn behavior. This leads to defiance (doing things one's own way, disobedience) and then to authority avoidance (staying out late, truancy, running away).
2. The **covert pathway** begins with minor, underhanded behavior (lying, shoplifting) that leads to property damage (setting nuisance fires, damaging property). This behavior eventually escalates to more serious forms of criminality, ranging from joyriding, pocket picking, larceny, and fencing to passing bad checks, using stolen credit cards, stealing cars, dealing drugs, and breaking and entering.

Figure 5.1
Loeber's Pathways to Crime
Source: "Serious and Violent Offenders," *Juvenile Justice Bulletin*, May 1998.

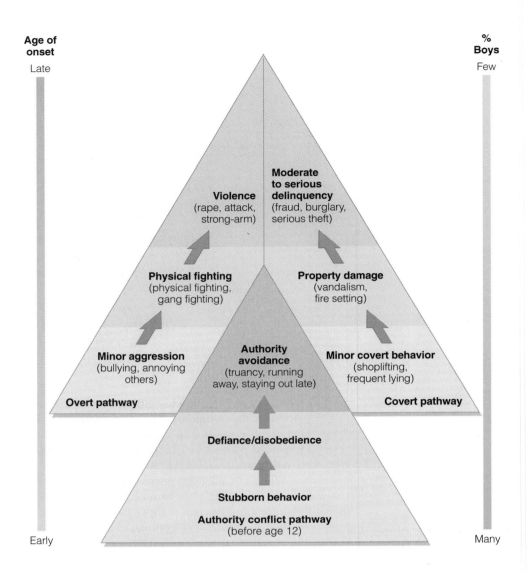

Age of onset
Late

Early

% Boys
Few

Many

Moderate to serious delinquency (fraud, burglary, serious theft)

Violence (rape, attack, strong-arm)

Physical fighting (physical fighting, gang fighting)

Property damage (vandalism, fire setting)

Minor aggression (bullying, annoying others)

Authority avoidance (truancy, running away, staying out late)

Minor covert behavior (shoplifting, frequent lying)

Overt pathway

Covert pathway

Defiance/disobedience

Stubborn behavior

Authority conflict pathway (before age 12)

overt pathway The developmental path taken to delinquency that begins with violent outbursts and bullying.

The developmental path to delinquency begins with violent outbursts and bullying. To read about the highlights of the Pittsburgh Youth Study, directed by Rolf Loeber, go to *http://www.ncjrs.org/txtfiles1/fs9995.txt* For an up-to-date list of Web links, go to *http://info.wadsworth.com/siegel*

3. The **overt pathway** escalates to aggressive acts beginning with aggression (annoying others, bullying), and leading to physical (and gang) fighting and then to violence (attacking someone, forced theft).

The Loeber research indicates that each of these paths may lead to a sustained deviant career. Some people enter two and even three paths simultaneously: They are stubborn, lie to teachers and parents, are bullies, and commit petty thefts. These adolescents are the most likely to become persistent offenders as they mature. Although some persistent offenders may specialize in one type of behavior, others engage in varied delinquent acts and antisocial behaviors as they mature. For example, they cheat on tests, bully kids in the school yard, take drugs, commit burglary, steal a car, and then shoplift from a store.

Some recent support for Loeber's "pathways" model was encountered by Sheila Royo Maxwell and Christopher Maxwell in their study of the career paths of young female offenders. One distinct group was made up of substance abusers who used drugs and engaged in a variety of illegal activities, including theft and prostitution, to generate capital for further drug purchases. The second group specialized in drug selling and avoided prostitution and other illegal activities.[23] The Maxwell research suggests the existence of a multitude of criminal career subgroupings with their own distinctive career paths.

Delinquent Trajectories

adolescent-limiteds Delinquent youths who begin their offending career in their late teens and soon desist from crime.

life-course persisters Delinquent youths who begin their offending career quite early and persist into their adulthood.

A CLOSER VIEW
Early onset of sexuality linked to environmental contaminants is becoming a troubling phenomenon. Read more on Infotrac College Edition: Peter Montague, "The Obscenity of Accelerated Child Development," *The Ecologist* 28(3):140, (May-June 1998).

In addition to taking different paths to criminality, people may begin their journey at different times: Some are precocious, beginning their delinquent careers early, while others stay out of trouble until their teenage years. Some offenders may peak at an early age, whereas others persist into adulthood. Research shows that there are a number of categories of delinquent careers that seem to reflect changes in the life course. Some youths maximize their offending rates at a relatively early age and then reduce their delinquent activity; others persist into their 20s. Some are high-rate offenders, whereas others offend at relatively low rates.[24]

According to psychologist Terrie Moffitt, although the prevalence and frequency of antisocial behavior peak in adolescence and then diminish for most offenders (she labels these **adolescent-limiteds**), a small group of **life-course persisters** offend well into adulthood.[25] Life-course persisters combine family dysfunction with severe neurological problems that predispose them to antisocial behavior patterns. These afflictions can be the result of maternal drug abuse, poor nutrition, or exposure to toxic agents such as lead. Life-course persisters may have low verbal ability, which inhibits reasoning skills, learning ability, and school achievement. They seem to mature faster and engage in early sexuality and drug use, referred to as *pseudomaturity*.[26] There may be more than one subset of life-course persisters. One begins acting out during the preschool years; these youths show signs of ADHD and do not outgrow the levels of disobedience typical of the preschool years. The second group shows few symptoms of ADHD but, from an early age, is aggressive, underhanded, and in constant opposition to authority.[27]

In contrast, adolescent-limited delinquents reduce the frequency of their offending as they mature to around age 18.[28] These kids may be considered "typical teenagers," who get into minor scrapes and engage in what might be considered rebellious teenage behavior with their friends.[29] They are deeply influenced by the misbehavior of their friends and peers up to around age 16; then peer group influence begins to decline.[30] Adolescent-limited delinquents tend to focus on a specific type of misbehavior, such as drug abuse, while life-course persisters (both males and females) are more likely to engage in a variety of antisocial behaviors.[31]

Why do some kids embark on a path to crime later rather than sooner? Early starters, who begin offending before age 14, experience (1) poor parenting, which leads them into (2) deviant behaviors, and (3) involvement with delinquent groups. In contrast, late starters, who begin offending after age 14, follow a somewhat different path: (1) Poor parenting leads to (2) identification with delinquent groups, and to (3) deviant involvement. By implication, adolescents who suffer poor parenting and are at risk for deviant careers can avoid criminality if they can bypass involvement with delinquent peers.[32]

Continuity of Crime and Delinquency

The Program of Research on the Causes and Correlates of Delinquency, sponsored by the federal government, comprises three coordinated longitudinal projects that are often referred to in this text. You can reach their Web site at http://ojjdp.ncjrs.org/ccd/oview.html
For an up-to-date list of Web links, go to http://info.wadsworth.com/siegel

Another aspect of developmental theory is the continuity of crime: The best predictor of future criminality is past criminality. Children who are repeatedly in trouble during early adolescence will generally still be antisocial in their middle and late teens and as adults.[33] For example, using samples of Philadelphia youth, Alex Piquero and He-Len Chung found that males who began their offending career before age 14 were the most likely to begin serious offending by age 18, with the earliest onset ages relating to the most severe delinquency patterns.[34]

Early delinquent activity is likely to be sustained because these offenders seem to lack the social survival skills necessary to find work or to develop the interpersonal relationships that will allow them to drop out of crime.[35] One explanation for this phenomenon suggests that delinquent propensity may be "contagious": Kids at risk for crime may be located in families and neighborhoods in which they are constantly exposed to deviant behavior. As they mature, having brothers, fathers, neighbors, and friends who engage in and support their activities reinforces their deviance.[36]

The Cambridge Youth Study

One of the most important longitudinal studies tracking persistent offenders is the Cambridge Study in Delinquent Development, which has followed the offending careers of 411 London boys born in 1953. This cohort study, directed since 1982 by David Farrington, is one of the most serious attempts to isolate the factors that predict lifelong continuity of criminal behavior. The study uses self-report data as well as in-depth interviews and psychological testing. The boys have been interviewed eight times over 24 years, beginning at age 8 and continuing to age 32.

The results of the Cambridge study show that many of the same patterns found in the United States are repeated in a cross-national sample: the existence of chronic offenders, the continuity of offending, and early onset of criminal activity. Each of these patterns leads to persistent criminality.

Farrington found that the traits present in persistent offenders can be observed as early as age 8. The chronic criminal begins as a property offender; is born into a large low-income family headed by parents who have criminal records; and has delinquent older siblings. The future criminal receives poor parental supervision, including the use of harsh or erratic punishment and childrearing techniques; the parents are likely to divorce or separate. The chronic offender tends to associate with friends who are also future criminals. By age 8, the child exhibits antisocial behavior, including dishonesty and aggressiveness; at school the chronic offender tends to have low educational achievement and is restless, troublesome, hyperactive, impulsive, and often truant. After leaving school at age 18, the persistent criminal tends to take a relatively well paid but low-status job and is likely to have an erratic work history and periods of unemployment.

Farrington found that deviant behavior tends to be versatile rather than specialized. That is, the typical offender not only commits property offenses, such as theft and burglary, but also engages in violence, vandalism, drug use, excessive drinking, drunk driving, smoking, reckless driving, and sexual promiscuity—evidence of a generalized problem behavior syndrome. Chronic offenders are more likely to live away from home and have conflicts with their parents. They wear tattoos, go out most evenings, and enjoy hanging out with groups of their friends. They are much more likely than nonoffenders to get involved in fights, to carry weapons, and to use them in violent encounters. The frequency of offending reaches a peak in the teenage years (about 17 or 18) and then declines in the 20s, when offenders marry or live with a significant other.

By the 30s, the former delinquent is likely to be separated or divorced and be an absent parent. His employment record remains spotty, and he moves often between rental units. His life is still characterized by evenings out, heavy drinking, substance abuse, and more violent behavior than his contemporaries. Because the typical offender provides the same kind of deprived and disrupted family life for his own children that he experienced, the social experiences and conditions that produce delinquency are carried on from one generation to the next. Table A summarizes the specific risk factors that Farrington associates with forming a delinquent career.

Nonoffenders and Desisters

Farrington has also identified factors that predict the discontinuity of criminal offenses. He found that people who exhibit these factors have backgrounds that put them at risk of becoming offenders; however, either they are able to remain nonoffenders, or they begin a criminal career and then later desist. The factors that protected high-risk youths from beginning criminal careers include having a somewhat shy personality, having few friends (at age 8), having nondeviant families, and being highly regarded by their mothers. Shy children with few friends avoided damaging relationships with other adolescents (members of a high-risk group) and were therefore able to avoid criminality.

What Caused Offenders to Desist?

Holding a relatively good job helped reduce criminal activity. Conversely, unemployment seemed to be related to the escalation of theft offenses; violence and substance abuse were unaffected by unemployment. In a similar vein, getting married also helped diminish criminal activity. However, finding a spouse who was also involved in criminal activity and had a criminal record increased criminal involvement. Physical relocation also helped some offenders desist because they were forced to sever ties with co-offenders. For this reason, leaving the city for a rural or suburban area was linked to reduced criminal activity.

Although employment, marriage, and relocation helped potential offenders desist, not all desisters found success. At-risk youths who managed to avoid criminal convictions were unlikely to avoid other social problems. Rather than becoming prosperous home owners with

---

One of the most important studies of the continuity of crime is the Cambridge Youth Survey conducted in England by David Farrington. The results of this important project are described in the accompanying Focus on Delinquency box.

Theories of Delinquent Development

An ongoing effort has been made to track persistent offenders over their life course.[37] The early data seem to support what is already known about delinquent and criminal career patterns: Early onset predicts more lasting crime; there is continuity in crime (juvenile offenders are likely to become adult criminals); and chronic offenders commit a significant portion of all crimes.[38] Based on these findings, a number flourishing careers, they tended to live in unkempt homes and have large debts and low-paying jobs. They were also more likely to remain single and live alone. Youths who experienced social isolation at age 8 were also found to experience it at age 32.

Farrington's theory suggests that life experiences shape the direction and flow of behavior choices. He finds that while there may be continuity in offending, the factors that predict criminality at one point in the life course may not be the ones that predict criminality at another. Although most adult criminals begin their careers in childhood, life events may help some children forgo criminality as they mature.

Table A   Risk Factors for a Delinquent Career

Prenatal and perinatal: Early childbearing increases the risk of such undesirable outcomes for children as low school attainment, antisocial behavior, substance use, and early sexual activity. An increased risk of offending among children of teenage mothers is associated with low income, poor housing, absent fathers, and poor childrearing methods.

Personality: Impulsiveness, hyperactivity, restlessness, and limited ability to concentrate are associated with low attainment in school and a poor ability to foresee the consequences of offending.

Intelligence and attainment: Low intelligence and poor performance in school, although important statistical predictors of offending, are difficult to disentangle from each other. One plausible explanation of the link between low intelligence and crime is its association with a poor ability to manipulate abstract concepts and to appreciate the feelings of victims.

Parental supervision and discipline: Harsh or erratic parental discipline and cold or rejecting parental attitudes have been linked to delinquency and are associated with children's lack of internal inhibitions against offending. Physical abuse by parents has been associated with an increased risk of the children themselves becoming violent offenders in later life.

Parental conflict and separation: Living in a home affected by separation or divorce is more strongly related to delinquency than when the disruption has been caused by the death of one parent. However, it may not be a "broken home" that creates an increased risk of offending so much as the parental conflict that leads to the separation.

Socioeconomic status: Social and economic deprivation are important predictors of antisocial behavior and crime, but low family income and poor housing are better measurements than the prestige of parents' occupations.

Delinquent friends: Delinquents tend to have delinquent friends. But it is not certain whether membership in a delinquent peer group leads to offending or whether delinquents simply gravitate toward each other's company (or both). Breaking up with delinquent friends often coincides with desisting from crime.

School influences: The prevalence of offending by pupils varies widely between secondary schools. But it is not clear how far schools themselves have an effect on delinquency (for example, by paying insufficient attention to bullying or providing too much punishment and too little praise), or whether it is simply that troublesome children tend to go to high-delinquency-rate schools.

Community influences: The risks of becoming criminally involved are higher for young people raised in disorganized inner-city areas, characterized by physical deterioration, overcrowded households, publicly subsidized renting, and high residential mobility. It is not clear, however, whether this is due to a direct influence on children, or whether environmental stress causes family adversities, which in turn cause delinquency.

Critical Thinking

1. Farrington finds that the traits present in persistent offenders can be observed as early as age 8. Should such young children be observed and monitored, even though they have not actually committed crimes? Would such monitoring create a self-fulfilling prophecy?

InfoTrac College Edition Research

Use the term *child development* as a subject guide on InfoTrac College Edition. A number of periodical articles provide information on development issues that influence behavior over the life course.

Sources: David Farrington, "The Development of Offending and Anti-Social Behavior from Childhood: Key Findings from the Cambridge Study of Delinquent Development," *Journal of Child Psychology and Psychiatry* 36:2–36 (1995); idem, "Understanding and Preventing Youth Crime" (London: Joseph Rowntree Foundation, 1996).

of systematic theories that account for the onset, continuance, and desistance from crime have been formulated. The following sections discuss a number of developmental theories.

The Social Development Model (SDM)

social development model (SDM)
An array of personal, psychological, and community-level risk factors that make some children susceptible to development of antisocial behaviors.

In their **social development model (SDM),** Joseph Weis, Richard Catalano, J. David Hawkins, and their associates show how different factors affecting children's social development over their life course influence their delinquent behavior patterns.[39] As children mature within their environment, elements of socialization control their developmental process. Children are socialized and develop bonds to their families through four distinct interactions and processes:

1. The perceived opportunities for involvement in activities and interactions with others
2. The degree of involvement and interaction with parents
3. The children's ability to participate in these interactions
4. The reinforcement (such as feedback) they perceive for their participation

prosocial bonds The attachment a child has with positive elements of society such as schools, parents, and peers.

To control the risk of antisocial behavior, a child must maintain **prosocial bonds.** These are developed within the context of family life, which not only provides prosocial opportunities but also reinforces them by consistent, positive feedback. Parental attachment affects a child's behavior for life, determining both school experiences and personal beliefs and values. For those with strong family relationships, school will be a meaningful experience marked by academic success and commitment to education. Youths in this category are likely to develop conventional beliefs and values, become committed to conventional activities, and form attachments to conventional others.

Children's antisocial behavior also depends on the quality of their attachments to parents and other influential relations. If they remain unattached or develop attachments to deviant others, their behavior may become deviant as well. The SDM suggests that interaction with antisocial peers and adults promotes participation in delinquency and substance abuse.[40]

As Figure 5.2 shows, the SDM suggests that involvement in prosocial or antisocial behavior determines the quality of attachments. Adolescents who perceive op-

The Seattle Social Development Project (SSDP) is a longitudinal study of youth and young adult development based on the SDM. Visit their Web site at *http://depts.washington.edu/ssdp/* For an up-to-date list of Web links, go to *http://info.wadsworth.com/siegel*

Figure 5.2
The Social Development Model of Antisocial Behavior
Source: Adapted from Seattle Social Development Project.

ACCORDING TO CRIMINOLOGIST TERENCE THORNBERRY, the onset of crime can be traced to a deterioration of the social bond during adolescence, marked by a weakening of attachment to parents, commitment to school, and belief in conventional values. Delinquent youths seek the company of other kids who share their interests and who are likely to reinforce their beliefs about the world and support their delinquent behavior.

portunities and rewards for antisocial behavior will form deep attachments to deviant peers and will become committed to a delinquent way of life. In contrast, those who perceive opportunities for prosocial behavior will take a different path, getting involved in conventional activities and forming attachments to others who share their conventional lifestyle.

The SDM holds that commitment and attachment to conventional institutions, activities, and beliefs insulates youths from the crimogenic influences of their environment. The prosocial path inhibits deviance by strengthening bonds to prosocial others and activities. Without the proper level of bonding, adolescents can succumb to the influence of deviant others.

Many of the core assumptions of the SDM have been tested and verified empirically.[41] The path predicted by the SDM seems an accurate picture of the onset and continuation of violent and antisocial behavior, both for early onset offenders and later onset offenders who begin offending in their teens.[42] Kids who (a) learn deviant attitudes and behaviors, (b) have weak ties to conventional institutions, and (c) perceive that antisocial behaviors are "cool" and rewarding seem to be the ones most likely to engage in criminal behaviors.[43]

Interactional Theory

interactional theory Asserts that youths' interactions with institutions and events over the life course determine criminal behavior patterns and that these patterns of behavior evolve over time.

Terence Thornberry has proposed a developmental view of crime that he calls **interactional theory** (Figure 5.3).[44] He also finds that the onset of crime can be traced to a deterioration of the social bond during adolescence, marked by weakened attachment to parents, commitment to school, and belief in conventional values. Interactional theory also holds that seriously delinquent youths form belief systems that are consistent with their deviant lifestyle. They seek out the company of other kids who share their interests and who are likely to reinforce their beliefs about the world and support their delinquent behavior. According to interactional theory, delinquents find a delinquent peer group in the same way that chess buffs look for others who share their passion for the game; hanging out with other chess players helps improve their game. Similarly, deviant peers do not turn an otherwise innocent boy into a delinquent; they support and amplify the behavior of kids who have already accepted a delinquent way of life.[45]

Chapter 5 Developmental Views of Delinquency   **149**

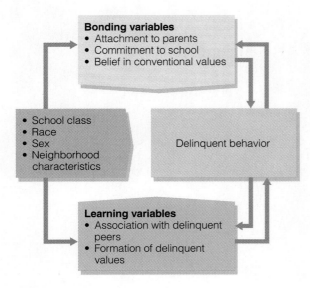

Bonding variables
- Attachment to parents
- Commitment to school
- Belief in conventional values

- School class
- Race
- Sex
- Neighborhood characteristics

Delinquent behavior

Learning variables
- Association with delinquent peers
- Formation of delinquent values

Figure 5.3
Overview of the Interactional Theory of Delinquency
Source: Terence Thornberry, Margaret Farnworth, Alan Lizotte, and Susan Stern, "A Longitudinal Examination of the Causes and Correlates of Delinquency," working paper No. 1, Rochester Youth Development Study (Albany, NY: Hindelang Criminal Justice Research Center, 1987), p. 11.

The key idea here is that causal influences are bidirectional. Weak bonds lead kids to develop friendships with deviant peers and get involved in delinquency. Frequent delinquency involvement further weakens bonds and makes it difficult to reestablish conventional ones. Delinquency-promoting factors tend to reinforce one another and sustain a chronic delinquent career.

Thornberry suggests that criminality is a developmental process that takes on different meaning and form as a person matures. According to Thornberry, the causal process is a dynamic one and develops over a person's life.[46] During early adolescence, attachment to the family is the single most important determinant of whether a youth will adjust to conventional society and be shielded from delinquency. By midadolescence the influence of the family is replaced by the "world of friends, school and youth culture."[47] By adulthood, individuals' behavioral choices are shaped by their place in conventional society and their own nuclear family.

In sum, interactional theory suggests that criminality is *part* of a dynamic social process and not just an outcome of that process. Although crime is influenced by social forces, it also influences these processes and associations to create behavioral trajectories toward increasing law violations for some people.[48] Interactional theory integrates elements of social disorganization, social control, social learning, and cognitive theories into a powerful model of the development of a delinquent career.

Sampson and Laub: Age-Graded Theory

turning points According to Laub and Sampson, life events, such as marriage, that help a person desist from crime.

age-graded theory Identifies turning points (such as marriage and career) that can cause delinquents to reverse course and desist from further criminal behavior.

If there are various pathways to crime and delinquency, are there trails back to conformity? In an important 1993 work, *Crime in the Making,* Robert Sampson and John Laub identify the **turning points** in a delinquent career.[49] Laub and Sampson reanalyzed the data originally collected by the Gluecks more than 40 years ago. Using modern statistical analysis, Laub and Sampson found evidence supporting the developmental view. Their theory is known as **age-graded theory** because they recognize that different factors influence people as they go through the life course.

Life's Turning Points Laub and Sampson's most important contribution is identifying the life events that enable young offenders to desist from crime as they mature (Figure 5.4). Two critical turning points are marriage and career. For example, adolescents who are at risk for crime can live conventional lives if they can find good jobs and/or achieve successful careers. Their success may hinge on a lucky break. Even those who have been in trouble with the law may turn from crime if employers are willing to give them a chance despite their records. When they achieve adulthood, adolescents who had significant problems with the law are able to desist from crime if they become attached to a spouse who supports and sustains them, even when the spouse knows about their earlier trouble. Happy marriages are life sustaining, and marital quality improves over time (as people work less and have fewer parental responsibilities).[50] Spending time in marital and family activities also reduces exposure to deviant peers, which in turn reduces the opportunity to become involved in delinquent activities.[51] People who cannot sustain secure marital relations are less likely to desist from crime (see Figure 5.4).

Sampson and Laub's age-graded theory is also supported by research that shows children who grow up in two-parent families are likely to have happier marriages than children who are the product of divorced or never-married parents.[52] This finding suggests that the marriage-crime association may be intergenerational: If people with marital problems are more crime-prone, their children will suffer a greater long-term risk of marital failure and antisocial activity.

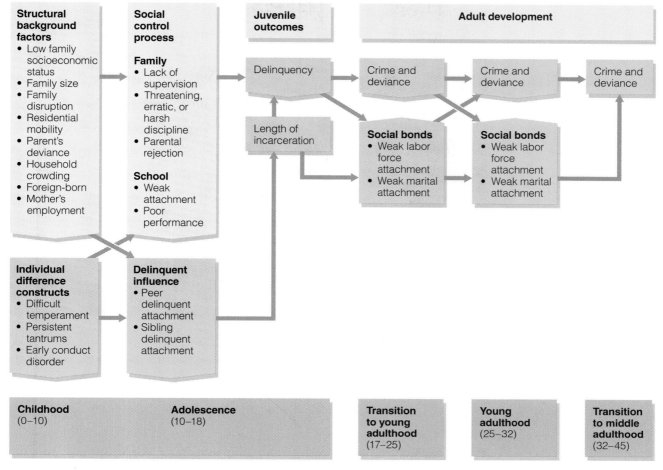

Figure 5.4
Sampson and Laub's Age-Graded Theory
Source: Robert Sampson and John Laub, *Crime in the Making: Pathways and Turning Points through Life* (Cambridge, MA: Harvard University Press, 1993), pp. 244–45.

social capital The positive relationships people develop that help them succeed in life and avoid criminal behaviors.

Social Capital   Social scientists recognize that people build **social capital**—that is, positive relations with individuals and institutions that are life sustaining. In the same manner that building financial capital improves the chances for personal success, building social capital supports conventional behavior and inhibits deviant behavior. For example, a successful marriage creates social capital when it improves a person's stature, creates feelings of self-worth, and encourages people to trust the individual. A successful career inhibits crime by creating a stake in conformity; why commit crimes when you are doing well at your job? The relationship is reciprocal. If people are chosen to be employees, they return the favor by doing the best job possible; if they are chosen as spouses, they blossom into devoted partners. In contrast, moving to a new city reduces social capital by closing people off from long-term relationships.[53]

Sampson and Laub's research indicates that building social capital and strong social bonds reduces the likelihood of long-term deviance. This finding suggests that, in contrast to latent trait theories, events that occur in later adolescence and adulthood do in fact influence the direction of delinquent careers. Life events can either help to terminate or sustain deviant careers. For example, getting arrested and punished may have little direct effect on future criminality, but it can help sustain a delinquent career because it reduces the chances of employment and job stability, two factors that are directly related to crime.[54]

ACCORDING TO DEVELOPMENTAL THEORIES, people change as they go through critical life transitions such as having a child and becoming a parent. Fifteen-month-old Brian Vides is held by his mother, Jasira Perlera, as they attend a rally March 14, 2001, at the Statehouse in Boston, in support of increased funding for teen parent families. Legislators and family advocate organizations say increased funding is necessary to reduce the level of homelessness among teen parents.

Testing Age-Graded Theory   Several indicators support the validity of age-graded theory.[55] Evidence now shows that delinquent career trajectories can be reversed if life conditions improve, an outcome predicted by age-graded theory.[56] For example, employment status affects behavior—men who are unemployed or underemployed report higher delinquent participation rates than employed men. Similarly, men released from prison on parole who obtain jobs are less likely to recidivate than those who lack or lose employment.[57]

Research has been directed at identifying the sources of social capital and determining whether and how it is related to crime. For example, youths who accumulate social capital in childhood (doing well in school, having a tightly knit family) are also the most likely to maintain steady work as adults; employment may help insulate them from crime.[58] People who maintain a successful marriage in their 20s and become parents are the most likely to mature out of crime.[59] Although it is possible that marriage stabilizes people and helps them build social capital, it is also likely that marriage may discourage crime by reducing contact with delinquent peers.[60]

A number of research efforts have supported the Sampson and Laub association between social capital and crime. For example, delinquents who enter the military, serve overseas, and receive veterans' benefits enhance their occupational status (social capital) while reducing delinquent involvement.[61] In contrast, research shows that people who are self-centered and present oriented are less likely to accumulate social capital and more prone to commit delinquent acts.[62]

In an important new study, Laub and Sampson have recontacted subjects from the original Glueck sample to find out how they fared as adults. Now in their 60s and 70s, these men provide an important source of information on what happens to former delinquents as they go through the life cycle. Some of Sampson and Laub's findings are discussed in the Focus on Delinquency box "Five Hundred Delinquent Boys in the New Millennium."

Five Hundred Delinquent Boys in the New Millennium

Why, and when, do most juvenile delinquents stop offending? Are some delinquents destined to become persistent criminals as adults? John Laub and Robert Sampson are now conducting a follow-up to their reanalysis of Sheldon and Eleanor Glueck's study, which matched 500 delinquents with 500 nondelinquents. The original sample was reinterviewed by the Gluecks at age 25 and later at age 32. Now Sampson and Laub have located the survivors, the oldest subject being 70 years old and the youngest 62!

Persistence and Desistance

Laub and Sampson find that delinquency and other forms of antisocial conduct in childhood are strongly related to adult crime and to drug and alcohol abuse. Former delinquents also suffer consequences in other areas of social life, such as school, work, and family life. For example, they are far less likely to finish high school than nondelinquents and subsequently more likely to be unemployed, receive welfare, and experience separation or divorce as adults.

In their latest research, Laub and Sampson address one of the key questions posed by developmental theories: Is it possible for former delinquents to rehabilitate themselves as adults? They found that most antisocial children do not remain antisocial as adults. Of those men who survived to age 50, 24 percent had no arrests for crimes of violence and property after age 17 (6% had no arrests for total crime); 48 percent had no arrests for these predatory crimes after age 25 (19% for total crime); 60 percent had no arrests for predatory crime after age 31 (33% for total crime); and 79 percent had no arrests for predatory crime after age 40 (57% for total crime). The researchers conclude that desistance from crime is the norm and that most, if not all, serious delinquents eventually desist from crime.

Why Do Delinquents Desist?

Laub and Sampson's earlier research indicated that building social capital through marriage and job is a key component of desistance from crime. However, in this new round of research, they were able to find out more about long-term desistance by interviewing 52 men as they approached age 70. Drawing on the men's own words, they find that one important element for going straight is "knifing off" individuals from their immediate environment, offering them a new script for the future. Joining the military can provide this knifing-off effect, as does marriage, and changing one's residence. One former delinquent (age 69) told them:

> I'd say the turning point was, number one, the Army. You get into an outfit, you had a sense of belonging, you made your friends. I think I became a pretty good judge of character. In the Army, you met some good ones, you met some foul balls. Then I met the wife. I'd say probably that would be the turning point. Got married, then naturally, kids come. So now you got to get a better job, you got to make more money. And that's how I got to the Navy Yard and tried to improve myself.

Former delinquents who "went straight" were able to put structure into their lives. Structure often led the men to disassociate from delinquent peers, reducing the opportunity to get into trouble. Getting mar-

ried, for example, may limit the number of nights men can "hang with the guys." As one wife of a former delinquent said, "It is not how many beers you have, it's who you drink with." Even multiple offenders who did time in prison were able to desist with the help of a stabilizing marriage.

The former delinquents who can turn their life around, who have acquired a degree of maturity by taking on family and work responsibilities, and who have forged new commitments are the ones most likely to make a fresh start and find new direction and meaning in life. It seems that men who desisted changed their identity as well, and this in turn affected their outlook and sense of maturity and responsibility. The ability to change was not related to the type of crimes committed in their youth; violent offenders followed the same path as property offenders.

Policy Implications

Laub and Sampson find that youth problems—delinquency, substance abuse, violence, dropping out, teen pregnancy—often share common risk characteristics. Intervention strategies therefore should consider a broad array of antisocial, criminal, and deviant behaviors, and not just limit the focus to one subgroup or crime type. Because delinquency and other social problems are linked, early prevention efforts that reduce crime will probably also reduce alcohol abuse, drunk driving, drug abuse, sexual promiscuity, and family violence, and perhaps school failure, unemployment, marital disharmony, and divorce. The best way to achieve these goals is through four significant life-changing events: getting married, joining the military, getting a job, and changing one's environment or neighborhood. What appears to be important about these processes is that they all involve, to varying degrees, the following items: a knifing off of the past from the present; new situations that provide both supervision and monitoring as well as new opportunities of social support and growth; and new situations that provide the opportunity for transforming identity. Prevention of crime must therefore be a policy at all times and at all stages of life.

Critical Thinking

1. Laub and Sampson believe that a military experience helps kids build social capital and knife off from a criminal way of life. Would compulsory military service help bring crime rates down?

InfoTrac College Edition Research

 For a review comparing and contrasting Laub and Sampson's work with other contemporary theoretical models, read Augustine Brannigan, "Self-Control, Social Control and Evolutionary Psychology: Towards an Integrated Perspective on Crime," *Canadian Journal of Criminology* 39(4):403–31 (Oct 1997) on InfoTrac College Edition.

Source: John Laub, "Crime over the Life Course," *Poverty Research News* 4(3) (the newsletter of the Northwestern University/University of Chicago Joint Center for Poverty Research, May-June 2000).

The Concept of Latent Traits

Developmental theories all suggest that people constantly change as they travel over the life cycle and that change affects crime and delinquency. Some criminologists challenge that assumption when they suggest that hard-core criminals possess a master trait or personal attribute that controls their inclination or propensity to commit crimes.[63] This latent trait may be either present at birth or established early in life, and it remains stable over time. Suspected latent traits include defective intelligence, impulsive personality, genetic abnormalities, the physical-chemical functioning of the brain, and environmental influences on brain function such as drugs, chemicals, and injuries.[64] Those who carry one of these latent traits are in danger of becoming career delinquents; those who lack the traits have a much lower risk.[65]

The latent trait view can be contrasted with previously discussed developmental theories on the basis of human growth and maturation. According to developmental theory, people are constantly changing, and so too is their propensity to commit crime. According to the latent trait view, there is an unchanging master trait that remains stable over time and influences all other aspects of a person's life. Consequently, the *propensity* to commit crime is actually quite stable, but other factors such as the *opportunity* to commit crime fluctuate over time. People age out of crime because, as they mature, there are simply fewer opportunities to violate the law and greater inducements to remain "straight." They may marry, have children, and obtain jobs. The former delinquents' newfound adult responsibilities leave them little time to hang out with their friends, abuse substances, and get into scrapes with the law.

Michael Gottfredson and Travis Hirschi's General Theory of Crime, probably the most prominent latent trait view, is discussed in some detail in the following section.

General Theory of Crime (GTC)

Michael Gottfredson and Travis Hirschi's General Theory of Crime (GTC) is probably the most prominent latent trait view. It modifies and redefines some of the principles articulated in Hirschi's social control theory (Chapter 4) by integrating the concepts of control with those of biosocial, psychological, routine activities, and rational choice theories.[66]

The Act and the Offender In their General Theory of Crime, Gottfredson and Hirschi consider the delinquent offender and the delinquent act as separate concepts (Figure 5.5). On the one hand, delinquent acts, such as robberies or burglaries, are illegal events or deeds that people engage in when they perceive them to be advantageous. For example, burglaries are typically committed by young males looking for cash, liquor, and entertainment; the crime provides "easy, short-term gratification."[67] Crime is rational and predictable; people commit a crime when it promises rewards with minimal threat of pain; the threat of punishment can deter crime. If targets are well guarded, crime rates diminish. Only the truly irrational offender would dare to strike under those circumstances.

On the other hand, delinquent offenders are predisposed to commit crimes. They are not robots who commit crime without restraint; their days are also filled with conventional behaviors, such as going to school, parties, concerts, and church. But given the same set of delinquent opportunities, such as having a lot of free time for mischief and living in a neighborhood with unguarded homes containing valuable merchandise, crime-prone people have a much higher probability of violating the law than do nondelinquents. The propensity to commit crimes remains stable throughout a person's life. Change in the frequency of delinquent activity is purely a function of change in criminal opportunity.

By recognizing that there are stable differences in people's propensity to commit crime, the GTC adds a biosocial element to the concept of social control. The bio-

A CLOSER VIEW
Do people who are crime-prone engage in a garden variety of criminal behaviors? To find out, read Marc LeBlanc and Stephane Girard, "The Generality of Deviance: Replication over Two Decades with a Canadian Sample of Adjudicated Boys," *Canadian Journal of Criminology* 39(2):171–83 (April 1997) on InfoTrac College Edition.

self-control Ability to control impulsive and often imprudent behaviors that offer immediate, short-term gratification.

logical and psychological factors that make people impulsive and crime-prone may be inherited or may develop through incompetent or absent parenting.

What Makes Kids Delinquency-Prone? What, then, causes kids to become excessively crime-prone? Gottfredson and Hirschi attribute the tendency to commit crimes to an adolescent's level of **self-control**. People with limited self-control tend to be impulsive; they are insensitive to other people's feelings, physical (rather than mental) risk takers, shortsighted, and nonverbal.[68] They have a here-and-now orientation and refuse to work for distant goals; they lack diligence, tenacity, and persistence. Adolescents lacking self-control tend to be adventuresome, active, physical, and self-centered. As they mature, they often have unstable marriages, jobs, and friendships.[69] They are less likely to feel shame if they engage in deviant acts and are more likely to find them pleasurable.[70] As they mature they are also more likely to engage in dangerous behaviors such as drinking, smoking, and reckless driving; all of these behaviors are associated with criminality.[71]

Because those with low self-control enjoy risky, exciting, or thrilling behaviors with immediate gratification, they are more likely to enjoy delinquent acts, which require stealth, agility, speed, and power, than conventional acts, which demand long-term study and cognitive and verbal skills. They enjoy taking risks and consequently are more likely to get involved in accidents and suffer injuries than people who maintain self-control.[72] As Gottfredson and Hirschi put it, they derive satisfaction from "money without work, sex without courtship, revenge without court delays."[73] Many of these individuals who have a propensity for committing crime also take part in other behaviors such as smoking, drinking, gambling, and immoral sexuality.[74] Although these acts are not illegal, they too provide immediate, short-term gratification. Figure 5.5 lists the elements of low self-control.

Gottfredson and Hirschi trace the root cause of poor self-control to inadequate childrearing practices. Parents who refuse or are unable to monitor a child's behavior, to recognize deviant behavior when it occurs, and to punish that behavior will produce children who lack self-control. Children who are not attached to their parents, who are poorly supervised, and whose parents are criminal or deviant themselves are the most likely to develop poor self-control. In a sense, lack of self-control occurs naturally when steps are not taken to stop its development.[75] Low self-control develops early in life and remains stable into and through adulthood.[76]

Self-Control and Delinquency Gottfredson and Hirschi claim that the principles of self-control theory can explain all varieties of delinquent behavior and all the social and behavioral correlates of crime. That is, such widely disparate crimes as burglary, robbery, embezzlement, drug dealing, murder, rape, and insider trading all stem from a deficiency of self-control. Likewise, gender, racial, and ecological differences in crime rates can be explained by discrepancies in self-control. Put another way, the male crime rate is higher than the female crime rate because males have lower levels of self-control. Although the delinquent activity of individuals with low self-control also declines as those individuals mature, they maintain an offense rate that remains consistently higher than those with strong self-control.

By integrating the concepts of socialization and criminality, Gottfredson and Hirschi help explain why kids who lack self-control can escape criminality and, conversely, why others who have self-control might not escape criminality. Adolescents who are at risk because they have impulsive personalities may forgo delinquent careers because there are no delinquent opportunities that satisfy their impulsive needs; instead, they may find other outlets for their impulsive personalities. In contrast, if the opportunity is strong enough, even people with relatively strong self-control may be tempted to violate the law; the incentives to commit crimes may overwhelm self-control.

Evaluating the General Theory Following the publication of the General Theory of Crime, dozens of research efforts have tested the validity of Gottfredson and Hirschi's

Impulsive personality
- Physical
- Insensitive
- Risk-taking
- Short-sighted
- Nonverbal

Low self-control
- Poor parenting
- Deviant parents
- Lack of supervision
- Active
- Self-centered

Weakening of social bonds
- Attachment
- Involvement
- Commitment
- Belief

Criminal opportunity
- Gangs
- Free time
- Drugs
- Suitable targets

Crime and deviance
- Delinquency
- Smoking
- Drinking
- Sex
- Crime

Figure 5.5
The General Theory of Crime

theoretical views. One approach involves identifying indicators of impulsiveness and self-control to determine whether scales measuring these factors correlate with measures of delinquent activity; a number of studies conducted both in the United States and abroad have successfully showed this type of association.[77] Supporting research seems to show that young offenders, lacking in self-control, commit a garden variety of criminal acts.[78] Kids whose problems develop early in life are the most resistant to change in treatment and rehabilitation programs.[79] Conversely, delinquency can be suppressed by parents who manage their children's behavior and help increase their self-control.[80] Having parents (or stepparents) available to control behavior may reduce the opportunity to commit crime.[81] In an important study, Alexander Vazsonyi and his associates analyzed self-control and deviant behavior with samples drawn from four different countries (Hungary, Switzerland, the Netherlands, and the United States).[82] Their findings indicate that as predicted by Gottfredson and Hirschi, low self-control is significantly related to antisocial behavior, and the association stands up regardless of culture and/or national settings.

Although there has been quite a bit of supporting evidence, several questions and criticisms remain unanswered. Some critics argue that the theory is tautological (involves circular reasoning): How do we know when people are impulsive? When they commit crimes, are all delinquents impulsive? Of course, or else they would not have broken the law![83]

The GTC also fails to address distinct gender differences in the crime rate. For example, while the male delinquency rate is higher than the female rate, there is little evidence that males are more impulsive than females (although females and males differ in many other personality traits).[84] Similarly, Gottfredson and Hirschi explain racial differences in the crime rate as a failure of childrearing practices in the African American community.[85] In so doing, they overlook issues of institutional racism, poverty, and relative deprivation, which have been shown to significantly impact crime rate differentials.

Do Kids Change? In contrast to life-course theories, the GTC assumes that while the opportunity to commit crime constantly fluctuates, delinquent propensity does not change. Here the criticism of the GTC is most pointed: A number of research efforts show that factors that help control delinquent behavior, such as peer relations and school performance, vary over time. Consequently, the ability to exert self-control may vary with age. Research shows that kids who lack self-control also have trouble maintaining relationships with law-abiding peers. They may either choose (or be forced) to seek out friends who are also limited in their ability to maintain self-control. Establishing relationships with low self-control peers tends to enhance the likelihood that an adolescent will become involved in delinquent behaviors.[86] This finding contradicts the GTC, which suggests the influence of friends should be stable and unchanging and that a relationship established later in life— peer relations—should not influence criminal propensity.

Research also indicates that as people mature, they may be better able to control their impulsive behavior.[87] Social influences, which are dominant in early adolescence, may fade and be replaced by others in adulthood.[88] These data also seem to contradict the GTC, which suggests that people's ability to change is quite limited.

Although questions like these remain, the strength of the General Theory lies in its scope and breadth; it attempts to explain all forms of crime and deviance, from lower-class gang delinquency to sexual harassment in the business community.[89] By integrating concepts of delinquent choice, delinquent opportunity, socialization, and personality, Gottfredson and Hirschi make a plausible argument that all deviant behaviors may originate at the same source. And even if maintaining low self-control alone cannot predict the onset of a criminal or deviant career, it certainly appears to be an important causal factor.[90]

Continued efforts are needed to test the GTC and establish the validity of its core concepts. It remains one of the key developments of modern criminological theory.

THE GENERAL THEORY OF CRIME assumes that the opportunity to commit crime constantly fluctuates while delinquent propensity remains the same. Yet treatment programs typically assume that they can help youngsters change. Lorain County Judge Paulette Lilly laughs as the first juvenile to graduate from the Lorain County Domestic Relations and Juvenile Drug Court program shows her his new tattoo, Oct. 26, 2000, in Elyria, Ohio.

Commonalities and Distinctions

Although the differences between the developmental and latent trait views may seem irreconcilable, they do in fact share some common ground. They indicate that a criminal career must be understood as a passage along which people travel, that it has a beginning and an end, and that events and life circumstances influence the journey. They both agree that diverse factors affect a delinquent career, including structural factors, such as income and status; socialization factors, such as family and peer relations; biological factors, such as size and strength; psychological factors, including intelligence and personality; and situational factors, such as the availability of legitimate opportunities.

These perspectives differ in their view of human development. Developmental theories emphasize the fact that people are changed by their life experiences (that is, experiences change people); latent trait theories assume that it is not people but criminal opportunities that change (that is, people do not change, but their experiences alter their behaviors).

Do people change, as developmental theories suggest, or are they stable, constant, and changeless, as the latent trait view indicates? It is actually possible that both positions may make a notable contribution to understanding the onset and continuity of a criminal career. For example, recent research by Bradley Entner Wright and his associates found evidence supporting both the latent trait and developmental theories.[91]

Their research, conducted with subjects in New Zealand, indicates that low self-control in childhood predicts disrupted social bonds and criminal offending later in life, a finding that supports latent trait theory. They also found that maintaining positive social bonds helps reduce delinquency and that maintaining prosocial bonds counteracts the effect of low self-control. Their findings indicate that while latent traits are an important influence on crime, social relationships that form later in life appear to influence criminal behavior "above and beyond" individuals' preexisting characteristics. There may in fact be two classes of antisocial people, a less serious group who are influenced by life events and a more chronic group whose latent trait insulates them from any positive prosocial relationships.[92]

SUMMARY

Developmental theories look at multiple factors derived from a number of structural and process theories. Examples include the social development model, interactional theory, and age-graded theory. These theories find that events that take place over the life course influence delinquent choices. The cause of crime constantly changes as people mature. At first, the nuclear family influences behavior; during adolescence, the peer group dominates; in adulthood, marriage and career are critical. There are a variety of pathways to crime: Some kids are sneaky, others hostile, and still others defiant. Crime may be part of a variety of social problems, including health, physical, and interpersonal troubles.

Latent trait theories hold that some underlying condition present at birth or soon after controls behavior. Suspect traits include low IQ, impulsivity, and personality structure. This underlying trait explains the continuity of offending because, once present, it remains with individuals throughout their lives. The latent trait theory developed by Gottfredson and Hirschi integrates choice theory concepts: People with latent traits choose crime over noncrime. The opportunity for crime mediates their choice.

KEY TERMS

developmental theory

life-course theory

latent trait view

problem behavior
   syndrome (PBS)

authority-conflict
   pathway

covert pathway

overt pathway

adolescent-limiteds

life-course persisters

social development
   model (SDM)

prosocial bonds

interactional theory

turning points

age-graded theory

social capital

self-control

QUESTIONS FOR DISCUSSION

1. Do you consider yourself the holder of social capital? If so, what form does it take?

2. A person gets 1600 on the SATs. Without knowing him or her, what personal, family, and social characteristics do you think he or she must have? Another person becomes a serial killer. Without knowing him or her, what personal, family, and social characteristics must he or she have? If "bad behavior" is explained by multiple problems, is "good behavior" explained by multiple strengths?

3. Do you believe there is a latent trait that makes a person crime-prone, or is crime a function of environment and socialization?

4. Do you agree with Loeber's multiple-pathway model? Do you know people who have traveled down those paths?

VIEWPOINT

"Serious and violent juvenile (SVJ) offenders comprise a troubled and often dangerous population. Although their numbers are small, they are responsible for a disproportionate amount of crime. To know what to do about this difficult problem and to garner the necessary financial, political, and public support to deal with it effectively, policymakers need a solid research foundation. To build this research base, the Office of Juvenile Justice and Delinquency Prevention (OJJDP) convened the Study Group on Serious and Violent Juvenile Offenders. The findings of this panel are hopeful and compelling. Perhaps the panel's most important findings are that it's never too early to begin efforts to prevent SVJ offending, and it's never too late to intervene with known serious and violent juvenile offenders."

To read more about Rolf Loeber's view of the problem of serious and violent juvenile offenders and how they should be treated, read his paper on InfoTrac College Edition: Rolf Loeber, "Early Intervention Can Work for Serious and Violent Juvenile Offenders," *The Brown University Child and Adolescent Behavior Letter* 16:1 (May 2000).

NOTES

1. Gerald Patterson and Karen Yoeger, "Developmental Models for Delinquent Behavior," in Sheilagh Hodgins, ed., *Mental Disorder and Crime* (Newbury Park, CA: Sage, 1993), pp. 150–59.

2. See, generally, Sheldon Glueck and Eleanor Glueck, *Unraveling Juvenile Delinquency* (Cambridge: Harvard University Press, 1950); Sheldon Glueck and Eleanor Glueck, *500 Criminal Careers* (New York: Knopf, 1930); idem, *One Thousand Juvenile Delinquents* (Cambridge: Harvard University Press, 1934); idem, *Predicting Delinquency and Crime* (Cambridge: Harvard University Press, 1967), pp. 82–83.

3. Glueck and Glueck, *Unraveling Juvenile Delinquency,* p. 48.

4. John Laub and Robert Sampson, "Unraveling Families and Delinquency: A Reanalysis of the Gluecks' Data." *Criminology* 26:355–80 (1988).

5. Rolf Loeber and Marc LeBlanc, "Toward a Developmental Criminology," in Norval Morris and Michael Tonry, eds., *Crime and Justice,* vol. 12 (Chicago: University of Chicago Press, 1990), pp. 375–473; Rolf Loeber and Marc Leblanc, "Developmental Criminology Updated," in Michael Tonry, ed., *Crime and Justice,* vol. 23 (Chicago: University of Chicago Press, 1998), pp. 115–98.

6. G. R. Patterson, L. Crosby, and S. Vuchinich, "Predicting Risk for Early Police Arrest," *Journal of Quantitative Criminology* 8:335–55 (1992); Rolf Loeber, Magda Stouthamer-Loeber, Welmoet Van Kammen, and David Farrington, "Initiation, Escalation, and Desistance in Juvenile Offending and Their Correlates," *Journal of Criminal Law and Criminology* 82:36–82 (1991).

7. Raymond Paternoster, Charles Dean, Alex Piquero, Paul Mazerolle, and Robert Brame, "Generality, Continuity, and Change in Offending," *Journal of Quantitative Criminology* 13:231–66 (1997).

8. David Nurco, Timothy Kinlock, and Mitchell Balter, "The Severity of Preaddiction Criminal Behavior among Urban, Male Narcotic Addicts and Two Nonaddicted Control Groups," *Journal of Research in Crime and Delinquency* 30:293–316 (1993).

9. Rolf Loeber and David Farrington, "Young Children Who Commit Crime: Epidemiology, Developmental Origins, Risk Factors, Early Interventions, and Policy Implications," *Development and Psychopathology* 12:737–62 (2000).

10. Marvin Krohn, Alan Lizotte, and Cynthia Perez, "The Interrelationship between Substance Use and Precocious Transitions to Adult Sexuality," *Journal of Health and Social Behavior* 38:87–103 at 88 (1997).

11. G. R. Patterson, Barbara DeBaryshe, and Elizabeth Ramsey, "A Developmental Perspective on Antisocial Behavior," *American Psychologist* 44:329–35 (1989).

12. Paul Mazerolle, "Delinquent Definitions and Participation Age: Assessing the Invariance Hypothesis," *Studies on Crime and Crime Prevention* 6:151–68 (1997).

13. Magda Stouthamer-Loeber and Evelyn Wei, "The Precursors of Young Fatherhood and Its Effect on Delinquency of Teenage Males," *Journal of Adolescent Health* 22:56–65 (1998); Richard Jessor, John Donovan, and Francis Costa, *Beyond Adolescence: Problem Behavior and Young Adult Development* (New York: Cambridge University Press, 1991).

14. Krohn, Lizotte, and Perez, "The Interrelationship between Substance Use and Precocious Transitions to Adult Sexuality"; Richard Jessor, "Risk Behavior in Adolescence: A Psychosocial Framework for Understanding and Action," in. D. E. Rogers and E. Ginzburg, eds., *Adolescents at Risk:*

Medical and Social Perspectives (Boulder, CO: Westview, 1992).

15. Deborah Capaldi and Gerald Patterson, "Can Violent Offenders Be Distinguished from Frequent Offenders: Prediction from Childhood to Adolescence," *Journal of Research in Crime and Delinquency* 33:206–31 (1996); D. Wayne Osgood, "The Covariation among Adolescent Problem Behaviors." Paper presented at the annual meeting of the American Society of Criminology, Baltimore, November 1990.

16. Terence Thornberry, Carolyn Smith, and Gregory Howard, "Risk Factors for Teenage Fatherhood," *Journal of Marriage and the Family* 59:502–22 (1997); Todd Miller, Timothy Smith, Charles Turner, Margarita Guijarro, and Amanda Hallet, "A Meta-Analytic Review of Research on Hostility and Physical Health," *Psychological Bulletin* 119:322–48 (1996); Marianne Junger, "Accidents and Crime," in T. Hirschi and M. Gottfredson, eds., *The Generality of Deviance* (New Brunswick, NJ: Transaction Press, 1993).

17. Robert Johnson, S. Susan Su, Dean Gerstein, Hee-Choon Shin, and John Hoffman, "Parental Influences on Deviant Behavior in Early Adolescence: A Logistic Response Analysis of Age- and Gender-Differentiated Effects," *Journal of Quantitative Criminology* 11:167–92 (1995); Judith Brooks, Martin Whiteman, and Patricia Cohen, "Stage of Drug Use, Aggression, and Theft/Vandalism," in Howard Kaplan, ed., *Drugs, Crime and Other Deviant Adaptations: Longitudinal Studies* (New York: Plenum Press, 1995), pp. 83–96; Robert Hoge, D. A. Andrews, and Alan Leschied, "Tests of Three Hypotheses Regarding the Predictors of Delinquency," *Journal of Abnormal Child Psychology* 22:547–59 (1994).

18. David Huizinga, Rolf Loeber, and Terence Thornberry, "Longitudinal Study of Delinquency, Drug Use, Sexual Activity, and Pregnancy among Children and Youth in Three Cities," *Public Health Reports* 108:90–96 (1993).

19. Terence Thornberry, Evelyn Wei, Magda Stouthamer-Loeber, and Joyce Van Dyke, *Teenage Fatherhood and Delinquent Behavior* (Washington, DC: Office of Juvenile Justice and Delinquency Prevention, 2000).

20. David Huizinga, Rolf Loeber, Terence Thornberry, and Lynn Cothern, "Co-Occurrence of Delinquency and Other Problem Behaviors," *Juvenile Justice Bulletin,* November 2000 (Washington, DC: Office of Juvenile Justice and Delinquency Prevention, 2000).

21. Angela Maitland and Richard Sluder, "Victimization and Youthful Prison Inmates: An Empirical Analysis," *Prison Journal* 77:55–74 (1998).

22. Rolf Loeber et al., "Developmental Pathways in Disruptive Behavior," *Development and Psychopathology* 23:12–48 (1993).

23. Sheila Royo Maxwell and Christopher Maxwell, "Examining the 'Criminal Careers' of Prostitutes within the Nexus of Drug Use, Drug Selling, and Other Illicit Activities," *Criminology* 38:787–809 (2000).

24. Amy D'Unger, Kenneth Land, Patricia McCall, and Daniel Nagin, "How Many Latent Classes of Delinquent/Criminal Careers? Results from Mixed Poisson Regression Analyses," *American Journal of Sociology* 103:1593–1630 (1998).

25. Terrie Moffitt, "Natural Histories of Delinquency," in Elmar Weitekamp and Hans-Jurgen Kerner, eds., *Cross-National Longitudinal Research on Human Development and Criminal Behavior* (Dordrecht, Netherlands: Kluwer, 1994), pp. 3–65.

26. Michael Newcomb, "Pseudomaturity among Adolescents: Construct Validation, Sex Differences, and Associations in Adulthood," *Journal of Drug Issues* 26:477–504 (1996).

27. Rolf Loeber and Magda Stouthamer-Loeber, "Development of Juvenile Aggression and Violence," *American Psychologist* 53:242–59 (1998).

28. Terrie Moffitt, "Adolescence-Limited and Life-Course Persistent Antisocial Behavior: A Developmental Taxonomy," *Psychological Review* 100:674–701 (1993).

29. Alex Piquero and Timothy Brezina, "Testing Moffitt's Account of Adolescent-Limited Delinquency," *Criminology* 39:353–70 (2001).

30. David Fergusson, L. John Horwood, and Daniel Nagin, "Offending Trajectories in a New Zealand Birth Cohort," *Criminology* 38:525–51 (2000).

31. Paul Mazerolle, Robert Brame, Ray Paternoster, Alex Piquero, and Charles Dean, "Onset Age, Persistence, and Offending Versatility: Comparisons across Gender," *Criminology* 38:1143–72 (2000).

32. Ronald Simons, Chyi-In Wu, Rand Conger, and Frederick Lorenz, "Two Routes to Delinquency: Differences between Early and Later Starters in the Impact of Parenting and Deviant Careers," *Criminology* 32:247–75 (1994).

33. Mark Lipsey and James Derzon, "Predictors of Violent or Serious Delinquency in Adolescence and Early Adulthood: A Synthesis of Longitudinal Research," in Rolf Loeber and David Farrington, eds., *Serious and Violent Juvenile Offenders: Risk Factors and Successful Interventions* (Thousand Oaks, CA: Sage, 1998).

34. Alex Piquero and He-Len Chung, "On the Relationships between Gender, Early Onset, and the Seriousness of Offending," *Journal of Criminal Justice* 29:189–206 (2001).

35. G.R. Patterson and Karen Yoerger, "Differentiating Outcomes and Histories for Early and Late Onset Arrests." Paper presented at the annual meeting of the American Society of Criminology, Phoenix, November 1993.

36. Marshall Jones and Donald Jones, "The Contagious Nature of Antisocial Behavior," *Criminology* 38:25–46 (2000).

37. See, for example, the Rochester Youth Development Study, Hindelang Criminal Justice Research Center, 135 Western Avenue, Albany, New York 12222.

38. David Farrington, "The Development of Offending and Antisocial Behavior from Childhood to Adulthood." Paper presented at the Congress on Rethinking Delinquency, University of Minho, Braga, Portugal, July 1992.

39. Joseph Weis and J. David Hawkins, *Reports of the National Juvenile Assessment Centers, Preventing Delinquency* (Washington, DC: U.S. Department of Justice, 1981); Joseph Weis and John Sederstrom, *Reports of the National Juvenile Justice Assessment Centers, The Prevention of Serious Delinquency: What to Do* (Washington, DC: U.S. Department of Justice, 1981).

40. Julie O'Donnell, J. David Hawkins, and Robert Abbott, "Predicting Serious Delinquency and Substance Use among Aggressive Boys," *Journal of Consulting and Clinical Psychology* 63:529–37 (1995).

41. Ibid., pp. 534–36; Richard Catalano, Rick Kosterman, J. David Hawkins, Michael Newcomb, and Robert Abbott, "Modeling the Etiology of Adolescent Substance Use: A Test of the Social Development Model," *Journal of Drug Issues* 26:429–55 (1996).

42. Todd Herrenkohl et al., "A Comparison of Social Development Processes Leading to Violent Behavior in Late Adolescence for Childhood Initiators and Adolescent Initiators of Violence," *Journal of Research in Crime and Delinquency* 38:45-63 (2001).

43. Bu Huang, Rick Kosterman, Richard Catalano, J. David Hawkins, and Robert Abbott, "Modeling Mediation in the Etiology of Violent Behavior in Adolescence: A Test of the Social Development Model," *Criminology* 39:75–107 (2001).

44. Terence Thornberry, "Toward an Interactional Theory of Delinquency," *Criminology* 25:863–91 (1987).

45. Ross Matsueda and Kathleen Anderson, "The Dynamics of Delinquent Peers and Delinquent Behavior," *Criminology* 36:269–308 (1998).

46. Thornberry, "Toward an Interactional Theory of Delinquency."

47. Ibid., p. 863.

48. Terence Thornberry, Alan Lizotte, Marvin Krohn, Margaret Farnworth, and Sung Joon Jang, "Delinquent Peers, Beliefs, and Delinquent Behavior: A Longitudinal Test of Interactional Theory," *Criminology* 32:601-37 (1994).

49. Robert Sampson and John Laub, *Crime in the Making: Pathways and Turning Points through Life* (Cambridge: Harvard University Press, 1993); John Laub and Robert Sampson, "Turning Points in the Life Course: Why Change Matters to the Study of Crime." Paper presented at the annual meeting of the American Society of Criminology, New Orleans, November 1992.

50. Terri Orbuch, James House, Richard Mero, and Pamela Webster, "Marital Quality over the Life Course," *Social Psychology Quarterly* 59:162–71 (1996); Lee Lillard and Linda Waite, "'Til Death Do Us Part: Marital Disruption and Mortality," *American Journal of Sociology* 100:1131–56 (1995).

51. Mark Warr, "Life-Course Transitions and Desistance from Crime," *Criminology* 36:183–216 (1998).

52. Pamela Webster, Terri Orbuch, and James House, "Effects of Childhood Family Background on Adult Marital Quality and Perceived Stability," *American Journal of Sociology* 101:404–32 (1995).

53. John Hagan, Ross MacMillan, and Blair Wheaton, "New Kid in Town: Social Capital and the Life Course Effects of Family Migration on Children," *American Sociological Review* 61:368–85 (1996).

54. Sampson and Laub, *Crime in the Making*, p. 249.

55. Raymond Paternoster and Robert Brame, "Multiple Routes to Delinquency? A Test of Developmental and General Theories of Crime," *Criminology* 35:49–84 (1997).

56. Robert Hoge, D. A. Andrews, and Alan Leschied, "An Investigation of Risk and Protective Factors in a Sample of Youthful Offenders," *Journal of Child Psychology and Psychiatry* 37:419–24 (1996).

57. Candace Kruttschnitt, Christopher Uggen, and Kelly Shelton, "Individual Variability in Sex Offending and Its Relationship to Informal and Formal Social Controls." Paper presented at the American Society of Criminology meeting, San Diego, 1997; Mark Collins and Don Weatherburn, "Unemployment and the Dynamics of Offender Populations," *Journal of Quantitative Criminology* 11:231–45 (1995).

58. Avshalom Caspi, Terrie Moffitt, Bradley Entner Wright, and Phil Silva, "Early Failure in the Labor Market: Childhood and Adolescent Predictors of Unemployment in the Transition to Adulthood," *American Sociological Review* 63:424–51 (1998).

59. Erich Labouvie, "Maturing Out of Substance Use: Selection and Self-Correction," *Journal of Drug Issues* 26:457–74 (1996).

60. Warr, "Life-Course Transitions and Desistance from Crime."

61. Robert Sampson and John Laub, "Socioeconomic Achievement in the Life Course of Disadvantaged Men: Military Service as a Turning Point, circa 1940–1965," *American Sociological Review* 61:347–67 (1996).

62. Daniel Nagin and Raymond Paternoster, "Personal Capital and Social Control: The Deterrence Implications of a Theory of Criminal Offending," *Criminology* 32:581–606 (1994).

63. David Rowe, D. Wayne Osgood, and W. Alan Nicewander, "A Latent Trait Approach to Unifying Criminal Careers," *Criminology* 28:237–70 (1990).

64. Lee Ellis, "Neurohormonal Bases of Varying Tendencies to Learn Delinquent and Criminal Behavior," in E. Morris and C. Braukmann, eds., *Behavioral Approaches to Crime and Delinquency* (New York: Plenum, 1988), pp. 499–518.

65. David Rowe, Alexander Vazsonyi, and Daniel Flannery, "Sex Differences in Crime: Do Means and Within-Sex Variation Have Similar Causes?" *Journal of Research in Crime and Delinquency* 32:84–100 (1995).

66. Michael Gottfredson and Travis Hirschi, *A General Theory of Crime* (Stanford, CA: Stanford University Press, 1990).

67. Ibid., p. 27.

68. Ibid., p. 90.

69. Ibid., p. 89.

70. Alex Piquero and Stephen Tibbetts, "Specifying the Direct and Indirect Effects of Low Self-Control and Situational Factors in Offenders' Decision Making: Toward a More Complete Model of Rational Offending," *Justice Quarterly* 13:481–508 (1996).

71. David Forde and Leslie Kennedy, "Risky Lifestyles, Routine Activities, and the General Theory of Crime," *Justice Quarterly* 14:265–94 (1997).

72. Marianne Junger and Richard Tremblay, "Self-Control, Accidents, and Crime," *Criminal Justice and Behavior* 26:485–501 (1999).

73. Gottfredson and Hirschi, *A General Theory of Crime*, p. 112.

74. Ibid.

75. Dennis Giever, "An Empirical Assessment of the Core Elements of Gottfredson and Hirschi's General Theory of Crime." Paper presented to the American Society of Criminology, Boston, November 1995.

76. Robert Agnew, "The Contribution of Social-Psychological Strain Theory to the Explanation of Crime and Delinquency," *Advances in Criminological Theory* 6 (1994).

77. David Brownfield and Ann Marie Sorenson, "Self-Control and Juvenile Delinquency: Theoretical Issues and an Empirical Assessment of Selected Elements of a General Theory of Crime," *Deviant Behavior* 14:243–64 (1993); Harold Grasmick, Charles Tittle, Robert Bursik, and Bruce Arneklev, "Testing the Core Empirical Implications of Gottfredson and Hirschi's General Theory of Crime," *Journal of Research in Crime and Delinquency* 30:5–29 (1993); John Cochran, Peter Wood, and Bruce Arneklev, "Is the Religiosity–Delinquency Relationship Spurious? A Test of

Arousal and Social Control Theories," *Journal of Research in Crime and Delinquency* 31:92–123 (1994); Marc LeBlanc, Marc Ouimet, and Richard Tremblay, "An Integrative Control Theory of Delinquent Behavior: A Validation 1976–1985," *Psychiatry* 51:164–76 (1988).

78. Xiaogang Deng and Lening Zhang, "Correlates of Self-Control: An Empirical Test of Self-Control Theory," *Journal of Crime and Justice* 21:89–103 (1998).

79. Linda Pagani, Richard Tremblay, Frank Vitaro, and Sophie Parent, "Does Preschool Help Prevent Delinquency in Boys with a History of Perinatal Complications?" *Criminology* 36:245–68 (1998).

80. John Gibbs, Dennis Giever, and Jamie Martin, "Parental Management and Self-Control: An Empirical Test of Gottfredson and Hirschi's General Theory," *Journal of Research in Crime and Delinquency* 35:40–70 (1998).

81. Vic Bumphus and James Anderson, "Family Structure and Race in a Sample of Offenders," *Journal of Criminal Justice* 27:309–20 (1999).

82. Alexander Vazsonyi, Lloyd Pickering, Marianne Junger, and Dick Hessing, "An Empirical Test of a General Theory of Crime: A Four-Nation Comparative Study of Self-Control and the Prediction of Deviance," *Journal of Research in Crime and Delinquency* 38:91–131 (2001).

83. Ronald Akers, "Self-Control as a General Theory of Crime," *Journal of Quantitative Criminology* 7:201–11 (1991).

84. Alan Feingold, "Gender Differences in Personality: A Meta Analysis," *Psychological Bulletin* 116:429–56 (1994).

85. Gottfredson and Hirschi, *A General Theory of Crime*, p. 153.

86. Bradley Entner Wright, Avashalom Caspi, Terrie Moffitt, and Phil Silva, "The Effects of Social Ties on Crime Vary by Criminal Propensity: A Life-Course Model of Interdependence," *Criminology* 39:321–52 (2001).

87. Charles R. Tittle and Harold G. Grasmick, "Criminal Behavior and Age: A Test of Three Provocative Hypotheses," *Journal of Criminal Law and Criminology* 88:309–42 (1997).

88. Scott Menard, Delbert Elliott, and Sharon Wofford, "Social Control Theories in Developmental Perspective," *Studies on Crime and Crime Prevention* 2:69–87 (1993).

89. Kevin Thompson, "Sexual Harassment and Low Self-Control: An Application of Gottfredson and Hirschi's General Theory of Crime." Paper presented at the annual meeting of the American Society of Criminology, Phoenix, November 1993.

90. Carter Hay, "Parenting, Self-Control, and Delinquency: A Test of Self-Control Theory," *Criminology* 39:707–36 (2001).

91. Bradley Entner Wright, Avashalom Caspi, Terrie Moffitt, and Phil Silva, "Low Self-Control, Social Bonds, and Crime: Social Causation, Social Selection, or Both?" *Criminology* 37:479–514 (1999).

92. Stephen Cernkovich and Peggy Giordano, "Stability and Change in Antisocial Behavior: The Transition from Adolescence to Early Adulthood," *Criminology* 39:371–410 (2001).

Part Three Social, Community, and Environmental Influences on Delinquency

A child's social, community, and environmental relations are thought to exert a powerful influence on their involvement in delinquent activities. Kids who fail at home, at school, and in the neighborhood are considered prone to sustaining delinquent careers over the life course. Research indicates that chronic, persistent offenders are the ones most likely to experience educational failure, poor home life, substance abuse, and unsatisfactory peer relations.

Social, community and environmental relations can also have a positive influence and shield or insulate at-risk children from involvement in a delinquent way of life. Consequently, many delinquency prevention efforts focus on improving family relations, supporting educational achievement, and utilizing community resources. If the family is believed to be a cause of delinquency, family counseling and therapy may be used to prevent delinquency. Similarly, gang control efforts have been made to counteract the influence of peer group pressure toward delinquency.

Part Three contains six chapters devoted to the influences critical social forces have on delinquency. Chapter 6 explores gender relations and their relationship to delinquency. Chapter 7 is devoted to the family; Chapter 8 looks at peer relations and juvenile groups and gangs; Chapter 9 examines the relationship between education and delinquency; and Chapter 10 concerns substance abuse. A new chapter, Delinquency Prevention, looks at how the community environment is being used to help youth avoid involvement in delinquent behaviors.

6 Gender and Delinquency

© Michael Newman/Photo Edit

As the principal of a Northeast junior high school, you get a call from a parent who is disturbed because he has heard a rumor that the student literary digest will carry a story with a sexual theme. The work is written by a junior high school girl who became pregnant during the year and underwent an abortion. You ask for and receive a copy of the narrative.

The girl's theme is actually a cautionary tale of young love that results in an unwanted pregnancy. The author details her abusive home life that led her to engage in an intimate relationship with another student, her pregnancy, her conflict with her parents, her decision to abort, and the emotional turmoil that the incident created. She tells students to use contraception if they are sexually active and recommends appropriate types of birth control. There is nothing provocative or sexually explicit in the work.

Some teachers argue that girls should not be allowed to read this material because it has a sexual content that they must be protected from, and that in a sense it advocates defiance of parents. Also, some parents may object to a story about precocious sexuality because they fear that it may encourage their children to "experiment." Such behavior is linked to delinquency and drug abuse. Those who advocate publication believe that girls have a right to read about such important issues and decide on their own course of action. Censorship would also be a violation of the author's First Amendment rights.

- Should you force the story's deletion because its theme is essentially sexual and controversial?

- Should you allow publication because it deals with the subject matter in a mature fashion?

- Do you think reading and learning about sexual matters encourages or discourages experimentation in sexuality?

differences

sexuality

masculinity

hypothesis

A CLOSER VIEW
What free speech rights do students have while in school? To read an informative article, go to Info-Trac College Edition and read Marc Rohr, "How Free Is the Speech of Public School Students?" *Florida Bar Journal* 74(6):79 (June 2000).

masculinity hypothesis View that women who commit crimes have biological and psychological traits similar to those of men.

A CLOSER VIEW
To read a little about the history of feminism, go to InfoTrac College Edition and look up: "Feminism 1960 to the Present," *The 1993 Information Please Almanac Annual* 2:446 (1992).

Traditionally, girls were restricted and prevented from enjoying the same privileges as males. Though such distinctions do not exist in modern society, vestiges of male domination have not evaporated. It should come as no surprise then that beyond their obvious biological differences, there are still inequalities in the way boys and girls are socialized by their parents and treated by social institutions. Do these differences also manifest themselves in their delinquency rate? How do gender roles impact illegal behavior choices?

As you saw in Chapter 2, significant gender differences in the delinquency rate exist: Males are much more likely than females to engage in repeat and serious offending. Official statistics show that girls are arrested far less often than boys and then for relatively minor offenses; correctional data show that about 95 percent of incarcerated inmates are males.

Nor is this relationship a recent occurrence. To early criminologists, the female offender was an aberration who engaged in crimes that usually had a sexual connotation—prostitution, running away (which presumably leads to sexual misadventure), engaging in premarital sex, incorrigibility, and, later, crimes of sexual passion (killing a boyfriend or husband).[1] Delinquency experts often ignored female offenders, assuming either that they rarely violated the law or, if they did, that their illegal acts were status-type offenses. Female delinquency was viewed as moral, emotional, or family related, and such problems were not an important concern of traditional criminologists. In fact, the few "true" female delinquents were considered anomalies whose criminal or delinquent activity was a function of their abandoning accepted feminine roles and taking on masculine characteristics, a concept referred to as the "**masculinity hypothesis**."[2]

Because female delinquency was considered unimportant, most early theories of delinquency focused on male misconduct and were tested with samples of male delinquents. Quite often these models did not adequately explain gender differences in the delinquency rate. For example, strain theory (Chapter 4) holds that delinquency results from the failure to achieve socially desirable material goals. Using this logic, females should be more criminal than males, because they face *gender discrimination*, a barrier to success unknown to males. Some criminologists interpret such exceptions to the rules as an indication that theoretical explanations of male criminality do not apply to females, and separate explanations for male and female delinquency are required.[3]

Today the interest in the association between gender and delinquency has been fueled by the observation that while the female delinquency rate is still much lower than the male rate, it is now growing at a faster pace. Moreover, female delinquency patterns seem remarkably similar to those of males: Larceny and aggravated assault, the crimes for which most males are arrested (as measured by the UCR), are also the most common offenses for which females are arrested. While young girls still commit less crime than young boys, members of both sexes are quite similar in the onset, development, and dynamic of their offending careers.[4] In societies and groups where there are high rates of male crime and delinquency, so too are there high rates of female crime and delinquency. It appears that the factors influencing male arrest rates also influence female arrest rates; over time both seem to rise and fall in a parallel fashion.[5]

Another reason for the interest in gender studies is that conceptions of gender differences have been altered. A feminist approach to understanding crime is now firmly established. The stereotype of the female delinquent as a purely sexual deviant is no longer taken seriously.[6] The result has been an increased effort to conduct gender-related research in order to adequately understand and explain differences and similarities in male and female offending patterns.

This chapter provides an overview of gender factors in delinquency. First we discuss some of the gender differences in development and offending patterns. We then turn to a more detailed discussion of the explanations of these differences referred to here as the (1) trait view, (2) socialization view, (3) liberal feminist view, and (4) radical feminist view.

Gender Differences in Development

Research on the developmental differences between adolescent males and females is actually a relatively new area of study. But from the information now available we know that gender differences may exist as early as infancy, when boys are able to express positive and negative emotions at higher rates. Infant girls have greater self-control over their emotions, while boys, more easily angered, depend more on inputs from their mothers.[7] There are indications that (a) gender differences in socialization and development do exist, and (b) these differences may in fact have an effect on juvenile offending patterns.[8]

Socialization Differences

To find information on the state of adolescent girls and the risks they face, go to the Web site of the Commonwealth Fund at *http://www.cmwf.org/ programs/women/adoleshl. asp#RISKY* For an up-to-date list of Web links, go to *http://info.wadsworth.com/siegel*

The significant differences in the ways females and males are socialized affect their development. While males learn to value separation and independence, females are taught that their self-worth depends on their ability to sustain relationships. Girls therefore run the risk of losing themselves in their relationships with others, while boys may experience a chronic sense of alienation. Yet, because so many personal and romantic relationships go sour, females also run the risk of feeling alienated and strained because of the failure to achieve relational success.[9]

Although there are few gender-based differences in aggression during the first few years of life, girls are socialized to be less aggressive than boys; they are supervised more closely by parents.[10] Differences in aggression become noticeable between ages 3 and 6, when children are first socialized into organized peer groups such as the day-care center or school. Boys are more likely to display physical aggression, while girls display relational aggression—for example, excluding disliked peers from play groups, gossiping, and interfering with social relationships.[11]

As they mature, girls learn to respond to provocation by feeling anxious and depressed, unlike boys, who are encouraged to retaliate.[12] Overall, women are much more likely to feel distressed than men, experiencing sadness, anxiety, and uneasiness.[13] While females get angry as often as males, many have been taught to blame themselves for harboring such negative feelings. Females are therefore much more likely than males to respond to anger with feelings of depression, anxiety, fear, and shame. Females are socialized to fear that their anger will harm valued relationships, whereas males react with "moral outrage," looking to blame others for their discomfort.[14]

Females are also more likely than males to be the target of sexual and physical abuse. Female victims have been shown to suffer more seriously from these attacks, sustaining long-term damage to self-image; victims of sexual abuse find it difficult to build autonomy and life skills.

Cognitive Differences

There are also measurable cognitive differences between adolescent males and females. Girls have been found to be superior to boys in verbal ability; boys test higher in visual-spatial performance. Girls acquire language faster, learning to speak earlier and faster with better pronunciation. Girls are far less likely to have reading problems than boys, while boys do much better on standardized math tests, attributed by some experts to their strategies for approaching math problems. In most cases cognitive differences are small, narrowing, and usually attributed to cultural expectations. When given training, girls increase visual-spatial skills, making their abilities indistinguishable from boys.

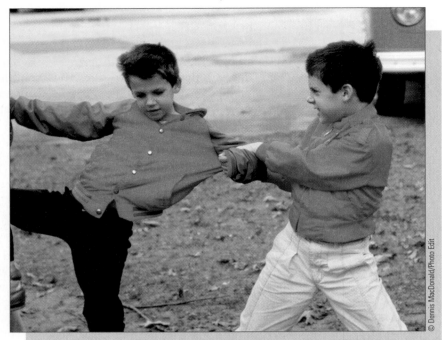

RESEARCH SHOWS that males are more likely than females to behave in an aggressive manner. Biosocial theorists find that qualities of male biological traits make males "naturally" more aggressive than females and therefore more likely to commit violent acts.

Personality Differences

Girls are often stereotyped as talkative, but research shows that males in many situations spend more time talking than females. Females are more willing to reveal their feelings and more likely than boys to express concern for the well-being of others. They are more concerned about finding the "meaning of life" and less interested in competing for material success.[15] Males are more likely to introduce new topics and interrupt conversations.

Adolescent females use different knowledge than males and have different ways of interpreting their lives and interactions with others. These gender differences in achieving self-understanding may later impact self-esteem and self-concept. Research shows that as adolescents develop through the life course, males continually raise their self-esteem and self-concept, whereas female self-confidence is lowered.[16] However, females display more self-control than males, a factor which has been related to criminality.[17]

What Causes Gender Differences?

A CLOSER VIEW
To find out more about the formation of gender roles, use the term *gender roles* as a subject guide on InfoTrac College Edition.

What causes these gender differences to occur? Some experts suggest that the reason may be neurological—males and females have somewhat different brain organizations. Females are more "left brain"–oriented and males "right brain." (The left brain is believed to control language and the right, spatial relations.) Other experts point to the hormonal and biochemical differences between the sexes as the key to understanding their behavior.

A third, nonbiological view is that gender differences are a result of the interaction of socialization, learning, and enculturation. Boys and girls may behave differently because they have been exposed to different styles of socialization, have learned different values, and have been given different cultural experiences. It follows then that if members of both sexes were treated evenly, and equally exposed to the factors that produce delinquency, their delinquency rates would be equivalent.[18]

gender-schema theory Asserts that American culture polarizes males and females, forcing them into exclusive gender roles of "feminine" or "masculine"; these gender scripts provide the basis for deviant behaviors.

Gender Identity   Another explanation of gender differences, referred to as **gender-schema theory**, recognizes the different socialization process of males and females. According to psychologist Sandra Bem, American culture polarizes males and females by forcing them to obey mutually exclusive gender roles, or scripts. Girls are expected to be "feminine" and admire such traits as being tender, sympathetic, understanding, and gentle. In contrast, boys are expected to be "masculine": assertive, forceful, competitive, and dominant. Children internalize these scripts and accept gender polarization as normal behavior. Children's self-esteem becomes wrapped up in how closely their behavior conforms to the proper sex-role stereotype. When children begin to perceive themselves as either boys or girls (which occurs at about age 3), they actively search for information that helps them define their role; they begin to learn what behavior is appropriate for their sex and what is gender-inconsistent behavior.[19] Girls are expected to behave according to the appropriate "script" and seek approval of their behavior (that is, are they acting as a girl should at that age?); masculine behavior is to be avoided. In contrast, males look for cues from their peers to define their masculinity; aggressive behavior may be rewarded with peer approval, while sensitivity is viewed as nonmasculine.[20]

There are a number of institutes at major universities devoted to the study of women's issues. You can visit the site of the one at the University of Michigan: *http://www.umich.edu/~womenstd* For an up-to-date list of Web links, see *http://info.wadsworth.com/siegel*

Gender Differences and Delinquency

There appears then to be measurable differences in the personality, cognitive ability, and socialization of males and females. These distinctions may explain in part the significant gender differences in the delinquency rate.

Males seem more aggressive and assertive and less likely to form attachments to others, factors which might increase their crime rates. They view their aggression as an appropriate means to gain status and power. Boys are also more likely than girls to socialize with deviant peers, and when they do, they display personality traits that make them more susceptible to delinquency. Boys have a more cavalier attitude and are more concerned with their own self-interests. Girls are shielded by their moral sense, which directs them to care about people and avoid harming others. Their moral sensitivity may help counterbalance the effects of poverty and family problems.[21] Females are more verbally proficient, a skill which may help them deal with conflict without resorting to violence. Females are taught to be less aggressive and view belligerence as a lack of self-control; males view aggression as an appropriate way to gain status and power.[22] When girls are aggressive they are more likely than boys to hide their behavior from adults; girls who "bully" others are less likely to admit their behavior than boys.[23]

Cognitive and personality differences are magnified when, at an early age, children begin to internalize gender-specific behaviors. Boys who aren't tough and aggressive are labeled "sissies"

© Michael Newman/Photo Edit

ACCORDING TO GENDER-SCHEMA THEORY, American culture polarizes males and females by forcing them to obey mutually exclusive gender roles or scripts. Girls are expected to be "feminine" and admire such traits as being tender, sympathetic, understanding, and gentle; in contrast, boys are expected to be "masculine"—assertive, forceful, competitive, and dominant.

and "cry babies." In contrast, girls are given different messages; they are expected to form closer bonds with their friends and share feelings. Recent research by Stacey Nofziger finds that grasp of one's *gender identity* is the most important predictor of intersex differences in the delinquency rate. Members of both sexes who identify with "masculine traits," such as dominance and forcefulness, are more likely to engage in delinquent acts than those who admire "feminine traits," such as affection and compassion. Because boys are more likely to identify with masculine traits, their crime rates are higher. Sex may only impact delinquency, she concludes, to the extent that females learn to be "feminine" and males "masculine."[24]

Gender Patterns in Delinquency

The mission of the National Council for Research on Women is to enhance the connections among research, policy analysis, advocacy, and innovative programming on behalf of women and girls. Visit their site at http://www.ncrw.org/ For an up-to-date list of Web links, go to http://info.wadsworth.com/siegel

The crime rate has been in a general decline for most of the past decade (1991–2000), but the number of young females arrested has actually *increased* (25%), while the number of teenage male arrestees has declined (-3%).[25] In other words, more girls but far fewer boys are being arrested today than in 1991. FBI data also indicate that juvenile females make up a greater percentage of the arrest statistics today than 30 years ago. In 1967 females constituted 13 percent of all juvenile crime arrests; today they make up 28 percent of the total. Females are now becoming involved in the most serious offenses, including murder, armed robbery, and aggravated assault.[26] In 1967 about 5 percent of all female index crime arrests were for violent crime; today the percentage has doubled to about 10 percent.

The *patterns* of male and female criminality also appear to be converging. Self-report data indicate that the rank ordering of male and female deviant behaviors are quite similar: The illegal acts most common for boys—petty larceny, using a false ID, and smoking marijuana—are also the ones most frequently committed by girls.

While gender differences in the delinquency rate may be narrowing, there is little question that males continue to be overrepresented in arrests for the most violent crimes. For example, almost all homicide offenders are males. In 2000, of the 806 juveniles arrested for murder, 91 were female.[27] However, the number of juvenile males arrested for homicide decreased by more than two thirds (–67%) between 1991 and 2000, but the number of females arrested did not appreciably decline (–1%).

The New York Public Library maintains a research site for those interested in conducting scholarship on gender issues. Go to http://www.nypl.org/research/ chss/grd/resguides/womhist.html For an up-to-date list of Web links, go to http://info.wadsworth.com/siegel

Why do these differences occur, and why are girls increasing their involvement in most delinquent activities at a faster pace than boys? The wide range of opinions on these important questions will be presented in the remaining sections of this chapter.

Trait Views of Female Delinquency

There has been a long tradition of tracing the onset of gender differences in the delinquency rate to physical and mental traits that are either uniquely male or female. The argument that biological and psychological differences between males and females can explain differences in their crime rates is not a new one. The earliest criminologists, such as Cesare Lombroso, whose theories were introduced in Chapter 3, focused their attention on physical characteristics believed to be precursors of crime. Lombroso's concept of the "born criminal" rested upon male-oriented physical and mental traits such as extraordinary strength and agility, lack of emotion, and insensibility to pain. In contrast, female delinquents were treated as a bizarre aberration. Since the female crime rate was so low and most girls were not delinquents, those whose behavior deviated from what was considered appropriate for females were believed to be inherently evil or physically maladapted.

Biological Explanations: The Female Offender

With the publication in 1895 of his book *The Female Offender,* Lombroso (with William Ferrero) extended his pioneering work on criminality to females.[28] Lombroso maintained that women were lower on the evolutionary scale than men, more childlike, less sensitive, and less intelligent.[29] Women who committed crimes (most often prostitution and other sex-related offenses) could be distinguished from "normal" women by physical characteristics—excessive body hair, wrinkles, crow's feet, and an abnormal cranium, for example.[30] In physical appearance, delinquent females appeared closer both to criminal and noncriminal men than to other women. The masculinity hypothesis suggested that delinquent girls have excessive male characteristics.[31]

Lombroso's suggestion that women were lower on the evolutionary scale than men is puzzling because he viewed atavism or primitivism as the key element in producing criminal behavior, yet the crime rate of females is lower than that of males. Lombroso explained this apparent inconsistency by arguing that most girls are restrained from committing delinquent acts by such counterbalancing traits as "piety, maternity, want of passion, sexual coldness, weakness, and undeveloped intelligence."[32] The delinquent female lacks these traits and is therefore "unrestrained in her childlike, unreasoned passions." Lombroso also believed that much female delinquency is masked and hidden.

Lombroso did recognize, however, that there were far fewer female than male delinquents. He suggested that this was a function of the relative homogeneity and uniformity among females; the female "born criminal" was indeed a rare creature. But he also believed that if a girl did become a delinquent, her behavior might become even more vicious than that of males.[33]

Lombroso's early work on the physical abnormalities of deviant girls portrayed female offenders as suffering from weak egos, abnormal or impulsive personalities, and other psychological problems. Another theme, begun by Lombroso, was that female delinquency was almost always linked to anatomy and sexuality.

Lombroso's Influence   Lombrosian thought had a significant influence on how the female delinquent was viewed for much of the twentieth century. Delinquency rate differentials were explained in terms of gender-based physical differences. For example, Cyril Burt in 1925 linked female delinquency to menstruation.[34] Similarly, William Healy and Augusta Bronner's research suggested that males' physical superiority enhanced their criminality. Their research showed that about 70 percent of the delinquent girls they studied had abnormal, masculine weight and size characteristics, a finding that supported the masculinity hypothesis.[35] In a later work (1950), *The Criminality of Women,* Otto Pollak linked the onset of female criminality to the impact of biological conditions—menstruation, pregnancy, and menopause:[36]

> *Thefts, particularly shoplifting, arson, homicide, and resistance against public officials seem to show a significant correlation between the menstruation of the offender and the time of the offense. The turmoil of the onset of menstruation and the puberty of girls appears to express itself in the relatively high frequency of false accusations and—where cultural opportunities permit—of incendiarism. Pregnancy in its turn is a crime-promoting influence with regard to attacks against the life of the fetus and the newborn. The menopause finally seems to bring about a distinct increase in crime, especially in offenses resulting from irritability such as arson, breaches of the peace, perjury, and insults.*[37]

chivalry hypothesis (also known as paternalism hypothesis)   View that low female crime and delinquency rates are a reflection of the leniency with which police treat female offenders.

Pollak argued that most female delinquency goes unrecorded because the female is the instigator, rather than the perpetrator, of illegal behavior.[38] Females first use their sexual charms to instigate crime and then beguile males in the justice system in order to obtain deferential treatment. This observation is referred to as the **chivalry hypothesis,** which holds that gender differences in the delinquency rate can be explained by the fact that female criminality is overlooked or forgiven by male agents of the criminal justice system. Those who believe in the chivalry hypothesis point to data showing that while women make up about 20 percent of all arrestees, they account for less than 5 percent of all inmates. Police and other justice system personnel may still be less willing to arrest and penalize female offenders than they are to arrest and penalize males.[39]

Psychological Explanations

penis envy According to Freud, women are envious of the male sex organ and unconsciously wish that they were men.

As is the case with biological theorists, psychologists viewed the physical differences between male and female as a basis for behavior differentials. Sigmund Freud maintained that girls interpret their lack of a penis as a sign that they have been punished. Boys fear that they also can be punished by having their penis cut off and thus learn to fear women. From this conflict comes **penis envy** and the girl's wish to become a boy. Penis envy often produces an inferiority complex in girls, forcing them to make an effort to compensate for their "defect." One way to compensate is to identify with their mother and accept a maternal role as wife and childbearer. Also, girls may become narcissistic and attempt to compensate for their lack of a penis by dressing well and beautifying themselves.[40]

Freud also claimed that if a young girl does not overcome her penis envy, neurotic episodes may follow: "If a little girl persists in her first wish—to grow into a boy—in extreme cases she will end as a manifest homosexual, and otherwise she will exhibit markedly masculine traits in the conduct of her later life, will choose a masculine vocation, and so on."[41]

Freud's concept of penis envy has been strongly questioned by contemporary psychoanalysts and psychologists, who scoff at the notion that little girls feel inferior to little boys and charge that Freud's thinking was influenced by the sexist culture of his age.[42] At midcentury, psychodynamic theorists suggested that girls are socialized to be passive and to need affection, which helps explain their low crime rate. However, this personality condition also makes some females susceptible to being manipulated by men; hence, their participation in sex-related crimes, such as prostitution. A girl's wayward behavior, psychoanalysts suggested, was restricted to neurotic theft (kleptomania) and to overt sexual acts that were a symptom of some unresolved personality maladaption.[43]

According to these early versions of the psychoanalytic approach, gender differences in the delinquency rate can be traced to differences in psychological orientation. Male delinquency reflects aggressive personality traits, while female delinquency is a product of young girls' psychosexual development, a function of repressed sexuality, gender conflict, and abnormal socialization.

Contemporary Trait Views

Contemporary biosocial and psychological theorists have continued the tradition of attributing gender differences in delinquency to physical and emotional traits. These more contemporary views recognize that it is the *interaction* of physical and psychological traits with the social environment that produces delinquency. The Focus on Delinquency box entitled "The Biosocial Study of Female Delinquency" describes a major study of the biological and social factors that influence the formation of delinquency.[44]

Precocious Sexuality

precocious sexuality Sexual experimentation in early adolescence.

Early theorists linked female sexuality and delinquency to the effects of early or **precocious sexuality**. According to this view, girls who experience an early onset of physical maturity are most likely to engage in antisocial behavior.[45] Female delinquents were

The Biosocial Study of Female Delinquency

The Biosocial Study followed nearly 1,000 Philadelphia residents from birth through early adulthood. Participants came from families involved in the Philadelphia Collaborative Perinatal Project at Pennsylvania Hospital between 1959 and 1966. This was part of a nationwide study of biological and environmental influences upon the pregnancies of 60,000 women, as well as the physical, neurological, and psychological development of their children. Upon registration for the Perinatal Project, each mother underwent a battery of interviews and physical examinations that provided data for each pregnancy, including the mother's reproductive history, recent and past medical history, and labor and delivery events. Data recorded for each child included information on neurological examinations conducted at birth, throughout the hospital stay, at 4 months, and at ages 1 and 7. Additionally, the children had their speech, language, and hearing examined at ages 3 and 8. Philadelphia public school records were used to collect data on academic achievement and evidence of learning or disciplinary problems. In addition, official police records were collected for all subjects from ages 7 to 22.

The Biosocial Study found that nine factors, some social and some biological, had an important impact on the likelihood that a female would engage in delinquent behavior: disciplinary problems in school, lack of foster parents, abnormal movement, neurological abnormalities, left foot preference, father absence, low language achievement, normal intellectual status, and right eye preference.

The data yielded a number of surprises, including the discovery that foster care had a more positive effect on behavior than keeping a child with her own family! Many of the children who were placed in foster care in the Biosocial Study came from disruptive and abusive homes where at least one parent was absent. It appears then that their early family experiences had a significant effect on their later delinquency. This conclusion is confirmed by the significant association found between father absence and delinquency.

The Biosocial Study also assessed neurological impairment and its relationship to delinquency. A number of different tests were used to measure abnormality. Researchers would ask a test child to hold out both arms horizontally for 30 seconds to ease the detection of abnormal posture, chorea (rapid involuntary jerks), and athetosis (slow, spasmodic repetitions). They recorded many different types of abnormal movements, including tremors, tics, and mirror movements. They also noted neurological abnormalities, which are conditions often related to central nervous system disorders, such as abnormalities of skull size and shape, spinal anomalies, and primary muscle disease. Neurological abnormalities and factors associated with attention deficit disorder were found to be important predictors of female delinquency and violence. Those physical factors—number of neurological abnormalities, mixed cerebral dominance as indicated by left-footedness and right-eyedness, and abnormal movements—can interfere with language achievement. Poor language skills were found to have a positive correlation with female delinquency.

The study found that for females, delinquency and violence are associated with learning difficulties and low achievement, but not with the more serious types of mental impairment such as mental retardation or abnormal intellectual status. This finding is consistent with other analyses, which indicate generally that the more violent and chronic delinquents had lower achievement test scores, but that they are not significantly represented in programs for the mentally retarded.

Which juvenile female delinquents later became adult offenders? Four factors showed direct effects on the number of adult offenses among females: seriousness of juvenile offenses, number of disciplinary problems in school, low number of juvenile offenses, and father's low educational level. As with males, the seriousness of delinquent offenses was significant; however, unlike males, those most apt to continue to commit crime during adulthood were not always those who committed the most crime during their youth. This result is not surprising, however, since females commit a relatively larger number of petty or status offenses, like shoplifting. Therefore, unlike males, chronic female offenders were not always the most serious offenders. In addition, disciplinary problems in school had a long-term effect on adult offending. This is evidence that early problem behavior is predictive of problems in adulthood.

Critical Thinking

1. The Biosocial Study is important because it involves careful and precise measurements of physical traits and conditions. It shows that both social factors and physical traits have important effects on female delinquency and, later, on their adult criminality. Can such physical traits be neutralized by social support, or do you believe that we cannot overcome our biological limitations?

InfoTrac College Edition Research

Is it possible that the traits that predispose people to crime may be developed before birth? To read about this process, go to InfoTrac College Edition, and access Amy Conseur, Frederick P. Rivara, Robert Barnoski, and Irvin Emanuel, "Maternal and Perinatal Risk Factors for Later Delinquency," *Pediatrics* 99(6):785 (June 1997).

Sources: Deborah W. Denno, *Biology and Violence: From Birth to Adulthood* (London: Cambridge University Press, 1990); idem, "Gender, Crime, and the Criminal Law Defenses," *Journal of Criminal Law and Criminology* 85:80–180 (1994).

believed to be promiscuous and somewhat more sophisticated and mature than male delinquents.[46] Linking female delinquency to sexuality was responsible in part for the view that female delinquency is symptomatic of maladjustment and social isolation.[47]

While equating female delinquency purely with sex activity is no longer taken seriously, early sexuality has been linked to other social problems such as a higher risk of teen pregnancy and sexually transmitted diseases.[48] Empirical evidence suggests that girls who reach puberty at an early age are in fact at the highest risk for delinquency.[49] One reason is that "early bloomers" may be more attractive to older adolescent boys, and increased contact with this high-risk group places them in jeopardy for antisocial behavior. The delinquency gap between "early" and "late" bloomers narrows when girls in the latter group reach sexual maturity and increase their exposure to boys.[50] Biological and social factors seem to interact to postpone or accelerate female delinquent activity.

Hormonal Differences

androgen The principal male sex hormone.

As you may recall (Chapter 3), some biosocial theorists link antisocial behavior to hormonal influences.[51] The argument is that male sex hormones (**androgen**) account for their more aggressive behavior and that gender-related hormonal differences can also explain the gender gap in delinquency.[52] Females may be biologically "protected" from deviant behavior in the same way they are immune from some diseases that strike males. Sensation seeking, impulsivity, aggression, dominance, and lesser verbal skills are androgen-related male traits, all of which are related to antisocial behaviors.

Gender differences in the crime rate then may be a function of androgen levels. These hormones cause areas of the brain to become less sensitive to environmental stimuli, making males more likely to seek high levels of stimulation, such as the "rush" that accompanies crime, and to tolerate more pain in the process.[53] Androgens are also linked to brain seizures, which result in greater emotional volatility, especially when stresses are present. Some experts believe that androgens affect the brain structure itself (the left hemisphere of the neocortex), which effectively reduces sympathetic feelings toward others that help to inhibit the urge to victimize.[54]

A great deal of research has been done on the relationship of hormonal levels and aggression. In general, females who test higher on testosterone are more likely to engage in stereotypical male behaviors.[55] Females who have naturally low androgen levels are less aggressive than males, while those who have elevated levels will take on characteristically male traits, including aggression.[56]

Some females are overexposed to male hormones in utero. Females affected this way may become "constitutionally masculinized" and at risk for delinquency. They may develop abnormal hair growth, large musculature, low voice, irregular menstrual cycle, fertility disorders, and hyperaggressiveness; this condition can also develop as a result of steroid use and certain medical disorders.[57] Diana Fishbein has reviewed the literature in this area and finds that after holding constant a variety of factors, including IQ, age, and environment, females exposed to male hormones in utero are more likely to engage in physically aggressive behavior later in life.[58]

Premenstrual Syndrome

premenstrual syndrome (PMS) A set of symptoms related to hormonal changes just prior to menstruation that may contribute to mood swings in women.

Early biotheorists suspected that **premenstrual syndrome (PMS)** was a direct cause of the relatively rare instances of female violence and aggression:

> *For several days prior to and during menstruation, the stereotype has been that "raging hormones" doom women to irritability and poor judgment—two facets of premenstrual syndrome.*[59]

The link between PMS and delinquency was popularized by Katharina Dalton, whose studies of English women led her to conclude that females are more likely to commit suicide and be aggressive and otherwise antisocial before or during menstruation.[60]

Today, there is conflicting evidence on the relationship between PMS and female delinquency. Diana Fishbein, a noted expert on biosocial theory, concludes that there is in fact an association between elevated levels of female aggression and menstruation. Research efforts show that (a) a significant number of incarcerated females committed their crimes during the premenstrual phase, and (b) at least a small percentage of women appear vulnerable to cyclical hormonal changes, which makes them more prone to anxiety and hostility.[61] Nonetheless, the majority of females who suffer anxiety and hostility prior to and during menstruation do not actually engage in criminal behavior.[62]

Existing research has been criticized on the basis of methodological inadequacy.[63] A valid test of the association must consider its time-ordering: It is possible that the psychological and physical stress of antisocial behavior produces early menstruation and not vice versa.[64]

Aggression

Males and females differ with respect to biological vulnerabilities, reflected in consistent findings that males are inherently more likely to aggress.[65]

According to some biosocial theorists, gender differences in the delinquency rate can be explained by inborn differences between males and females in aggression.[66] Some psychologists have suggested that these gender-based differences in aggression are present very early in life, before socialization can influence behavior. Males seem to be more aggressive in all human societies for which data are available; gender differences in aggression can even be found in subhuman primates.[67]

Some biosocial theorists argue that gender-based differences in aggression reflect the essential physical dissimilarities in the male and female reproductive systems. Males are naturally more aggressive because they wish to *possess and control* as many sex partners as possible to increase their chances of producing offspring. Females have learned to control their aggressive impulses because multiple mates do not increase their chances of conception. They instead concentrate their efforts on acquiring things that will help them to successfully rear their offspring, such as a reliable mate who will supply material resources.[68]

Female Aggression   The weight of the evidence is that males are more aggressive than females. However, evidence also exists that females are more likely to act aggressively under some circumstances than others:

- Males are more likely than females to report physical aggression in their behavior, intentions, and dreams.
- Females are more likely to feel anxious or guilty about behaving aggressively, and these feelings tend to inhibit aggression.
- Females behave as aggressively as males when they have the means to do so and believe that their behavior is justified.
- Females are more likely to empathize with the victim—to put themselves in the victim's place.
- Sex differences in aggression decrease when the victim is anonymous. Anonymity may prevent females from empathizing with the victim.[69]
- Females may feel more freedom than males to express anger and aggression in the family setting.[70]

In sum, biosocial theorists find that qualities of male biological traits make males "naturally" more aggressive than females; under some circumstances females may actually be more aggressive than males.

Socialization Views

Socialization views are based on the idea that a child's social development, influenced and controlled by family, peers, teachers, and society, may be the key to understanding delinquent behavior. If children experience impairment, trauma, family disruption, and so on, they will be more susceptible to delinquent associations and criminality.

To read about the socialization of female delinquents, go to *http://ojjdp.ncjrs.org/pubs/principles/ch1_4.html* For an up-to-date list of Web links, go to *http://info.wadsworth.com/siegel*

Linking crime rate variations to gender differences in socialization is not a recent discovery. In a 1928 work, *The Unadjusted Girl,* W. I. Thomas forged a link between socialization, sexuality, and delinquency. He suggested that some impoverished girls who have not been socialized under middle-class family controls can become impulsive thrill seekers. According to Thomas, female delinquency is linked to the "wish" for luxury and excitement.[71] Inequities in the social class system condemned poor girls from demoralized families to use sex as a means to gain amusement, adventure, pretty clothes, and other luxuries. Precocious sexuality makes these disadvantaged girls vulnerable to older men who, taking advantage of their naivete, lead them down the path to crime and decadence.[72]

Socialization and Delinquency

Scholars concerned with gender differences in the crime rate are interested in the distinction between the lifestyles of males and females. Girls may be supervised more closely than boys and are expected to stay at home more often. If girls behave in a socially disapproved fashion, their parents may be more likely to notice and take action. Adults may be more tolerant of deviant behavior in boys than in girls and expect the former to act tough and take risks.[73] Closer supervision restricts the opportunity for crime and the time available to mingle with delinquent peers. It follows, then, that the adolescent girl who is growing up in a troubled home or one marked by abuse, conflict, or neglect and who lacks concern and supervision may be more prone to delinquency.[74]

Focus on Socialization

In the middle of the last century, a number of writers began to focus on gender-specific socialization patterns as a key determinant of antisocial behavior. This view held to three assumptions about gender differences in socialization: (1) families exerted a more powerful influence on girls than on boys; (2) girls did not form close same-sex friendships and generally competed with their peers; and (3) female criminals were primarily sexual offenders. The first assumption was that parents were stricter with girls, whom they perceived as vulnerable and in need of control. In some families, adolescent girls rebelled against strict controls, while in others, where parents were absent or unavailable, they turned to the streets for support and companionship. Girls rarely formed close relationships with female peers whom they viewed as rivals for the few males who would make eligible marriage partners.[75] Instead, girls entered into sexual affairs with older men who would exploit them, involve them in sexual deviance, and father their illegitimate children.[76] The result was prostitution, petty theft, drug abuse, and marginal lives. Their daughters then would repeat this pattern in a never-ending cycle of despair and exploitation.

Perhaps the best-known work of this type focusing on gender differences as a cause of delinquency is Gisela Konopka's *The Adolescent Girl in Conflict* (1966). More than 30 years ago, Konopka integrated psychoanalytic views with sociological concepts, in an effort to explain the onset of deviant behavior in girls.[77]

Konopka suggested that female delinquency has its roots in a girl's feeling of uncertainty and loneliness. During her adolescence, a girl's major emotional need is to be accepted by members of the opposite sex. If normal channels for receiving such approval—family, friends, relatives—are impaired, she may fight isolation by joining a "crowd" or engaging in gratuitous sexual relationships. This behavior eventually leads to "rejection by the community, general experience of having no recognized success . . . and more behavior which increases the feeling of worthlessness."[78]

Konopka identified a number of factors that produced the onset of female delinquent behavior:[79] The onset of puberty in girls is traumatic because of the often cruel

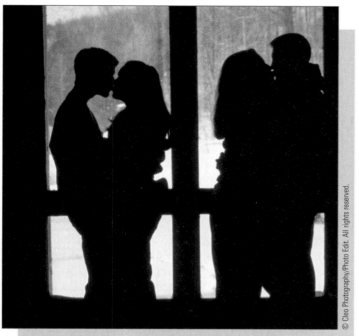

ACCORDING TO CONTEMPORARY SOCIALIZATION VIEWS, if a girl grows up in an atmosphere of sexual tension, where hostility exists between her parents or where the parents are absent, she likely will turn to outside sources for affection and support. In their reaction to loneliness, frustration, and parental hostility, girls begin to engage in the same activities as boys: staying out late at night, drinking, partying, and riding around with their friends.

way in which it is received by parents and the fear it creates in girls. The social identification process can be dramatic and difficult because of a girl's competitiveness with her mother. In fatherless homes, girls have an especially hard time, since "the road to a healthy development toward womanhood through affection for the male and identification with the female simply does not exist."[80] The absence of socioeconomic mobility can also create problems. Delinquent girls are believed to suffer from a lack of training and education. This locks them into low-paying jobs with little hope for advancement. These conditions lead girls to relieve their thwarted ambition through aggressive or destructive behavior. The world then presents a hostile environment to some girls; adult authority figures tell them what to do, but no one is there to listen to their needs.

Broken Homes/Fallen Women At midcentury, a number of experts shared Konopka's emphasis on the family and society as a primary influence on delinquent behavior. Male delinquents were typically portrayed as rebels, who, testing their masculinity, esteemed "toughness," "excitement," and other lower-class values. Males succumbed to the lure of gang delinquency when they perceived few legitimate opportunities. In contrast, female delinquents were portrayed as troubled adolescents, suffering inadequate home lives, and more often than not, being the victims of sexual and physical abuse. Ruth Morris described delinquent girls as unattractive, poorly groomed youths who reside in homes marked by family tensions or absent parents.[81] In an oft-cited work, *The Delinquent Girl* (1970), Clyde Vedder and Dora Somerville suggested that female delinquency is usually a problem of adjustment to family and social pressure; an estimated 75 percent of institutionalized girls have family problems.[82] They also suggest that girls have serious problems in a male-dominated culture with rigid and sometimes unfair social practices.

Eleanor Glueck and Sheldon Glueck also distinguished between the causes of male and female delinquency. They linked male delinquency to muscular body type, impulsive personality, a hostile, defiant attitude, destructive traits, and a poor home life.[83] Delinquent males had been reared in homes of "little understanding or affection, stability or moral fibre," by parents who were unfit to be role models.[84] In contrast, when the Gluecks examined the life histories of institutionalized female offenders in their classic work *Five Hundred Delinquent Women*, they found that a majority of the subjects had been involved in sexual deviance that began early in their teens.[85] The Gluecks concluded that sexual delinquency and general behavior maladjustment developed in girls simultaneously with unstable home lives.[86]

Other early efforts linked "rebellious" or sexually precocious behavior to sexual conflicts in the home and incestuous relationships.[87] Broken or disrupted homes were found to predict female delinquency.[88] Females petitioned to juvenile court were more likely than boys to be charged with ungovernable behavior, running away, and sex offenses and were more likely to reside in a single-parent home.[89] Studies of incarcerated juveniles found that most of the male delinquents were incarcerated for burglary, robbery, and other theft-related offenses, but girls tended to be involved in incorrigibility, sex offenses, and truancy. The conclusion: Boys became delinquent in order to gain status and demonstrate their masculinity by adventurous behavior; girls

A CLOSER VIEW

For an interesting and informative account of the lives of incarcerated girls, on InfoTrac College Edition, read Joanne Belknap, Kristi Holsinger, and Melissa Dunn, "Understanding Incarcerated Girls: The Results of a Focus Group Study," *Prison Journal* 77:381 (1997).

were delinquent because of hostility toward parents and a consequent need to obtain gratification and attention from others.[90]

Contemporary Socialization Views

The view that females are more deeply affected than males by family disruption and conflict has not been abandoned. Investigators continue to support the view that female delinquents have more dysfunctional home lives than male offenders.[91] Institutionalized girls tell of lives filled with severe physical and sexual abuse. Females who are "official" delinquents openly discuss being survivors of rape and incest. In addition to tragic home lives, delinquent girls report social and community experiences that were frustrating or even degrading.[92] The Focus on Delinquency box entitled "Girls on the Run" explores this topic in greater detail.

Girls seem to be more deeply affected than boys by child abuse, and the link between abuse and female delinquency seems stronger than it is for male delinquency.[93] A significant amount of female delinquency can be traced to physical and sexual abuse in the home.[94] Meda Chesney-Lind, a prominent feminist scholar, has described this association: "Young women on the run from homes characterized by sexual abuse and parental neglect are forced, by the very statutes designed to protect them, into the life of an escaped convict."[95]

Joan Moore's analysis of gang girls in East Los Angeles found that many came from troubled homes. Sixty-eight percent of the girls she interviewed were afraid of their fathers, and 55 percent reported fear of their mothers. One girl told Moore about the abuse she received from her mother:

She would hit me, pinch me, and pull my hair, and then she'd have my brother— the oldest one—get a whip, and whip me, and then I'd have stripes all over my body like a zebra, and I went to school like that.[96]

Many of the girls Moore spoke with reported that parents were overly strict and controlling despite the fact that they engaged in drug abuse and criminality themselves. Moore also details accounts of incest and sexual abuse; about 30 percent of the gang girls reported that family members made sexual advances. Considering the restrictions placed on these girls and the high incidence of incest, it comes as no surprise that three quarters reported having run away at least once. Moore concludes:

...clearly more women than men came from troubled families. They were more likely to have been living with a chronically sick relative, one who died, one who was a heroin addict, or one who was arrested....This seems on the face of it to imply that the gang represents [for girls]...a refuge from family problems...[97]

In sum, the socialization approach holds that family interaction and child-parent relations are the key to understanding female delinquency. If a girl grows up in an atmosphere of sexual tension, where hostility exists between her parents or where the parents are absent, she likely will turn to outside sources for affection and support. Unlike boys, girls are expected to follow very narrowly defined behavioral patterns. In contrast, it is not unusual or unexpected for boys to stay out late at night, drive around with friends, and get involved in other unstructured behaviors linked to delinquency. If, in their reaction to loneliness, frustration, and parental hostility, girls begin to engage in the same "routine activities" as boys (staying out late at night, drinking, partying, and riding around with their friends), they run the risk of engaging in similar types of delinquent or wayward behavior.[98]

The socialization approach holds that the psychological pressure of a poor home life is likely to have an even more damaging effect on females than males. Because girls are less likely than boys to have the support of close-knit peer associations, they are more likely to need close parental relationships to retain emotional stability. In fact, girls may become sexually involved with boys to receive support from them, a practice that tends only to magnify their problems.

A CLOSER VIEW
To read a study showing how family problems and improper socialization impacts gender differences in antisocial behaviors, go to InfoTrac College Edition and read Stephen T. Chermack, Scott F. Stoltenberg, Bret E. Fuller, and Frederic C. Blow, "Gender Differences in the Development of Substance-Related Problems: The Impact of Family History of Alcoholism, Family History of Violence and Childhood Conduct," *Journal of Studies on Alcohol* 61(6):845 (November 2000).

Girls on the Run

On any given night in the United States, there are at least a million adolescent runaways; about 1 in 8 American adolescents have run away at least once before the age of 18. Runaways emerge from the full range of American families: black, white, Hispanic, Native American, and Asian families; "broken" homes and homes with intact marriages; and privileged, middle-class, working-class, and low-income families. Over half of teenagers who run away from home are girls.

Sociologist Laurie Schaffner studied young runaways from a variety of backgrounds who were being held in a short-term residential facility in Massachusetts. She found that rather than being rebellious and antisocial, (1) adolescents actually resisted running away—it was actually a last option for them; and (2) each runaway had a plan of action that included "running to somebody" in search of the love and protection they needed from other people. She also found that running away can be viewed as a "fixable" problem—that healing and reconciliation does take place and running away was not necessarily a permanently disabling rupture for every family.

The adolescent girls in her sample actually resisted running away, resisted fighting back with their parents, and resisted breaking family rules. They seemed to struggle against running away, preferring instead to try to remain socially attached to intact family bonds. Runaways expressed resentment and hurt feelings at the loss of an interconnection between themselves and their parents. While many told of the rage and anger that precipitated their escape, the young women also expressed fear, hurt, and pain over their fractured family relations.

Fourteen-year-old Amy, typical of the girls interviewed by Schaffner, was an articulate dark-haired youth who had been physically abused by her mother. Amy was from a white, low-income family; her mother had dropped out of high school and was currently working as a nursing aide in a convalescent home. Her 6-year-old brother still lived at home with her mom. Amy was in the shelter awaiting her dispositional hearing on a charge of possession of a stolen vehicle. Amy said that she ran away from home because her mother didn't want her "running around" with the friends that Amy selected, because Amy had an 18-year-old boyfriend whom her mother wanted to "put statutory rape charges on," and because of the "physical fights" she constantly had with her mom:

> I ran away from home because—I have a lot of problems with my mom, we fight a lot. And we get in physical fights and I don't hit her because she's my mom, but—she—'cause I respect her for that, 'cause she's my mom, but she just—we have really different viewpoints. (Amy)

Another runaway, Gretchen, shared the disappointment and anger she felt toward physically abusive parents that motivated her to "keep running away from all my problems." Sixteen-year-old Gretchen was severely abused physically by both her father and mother. She ran away from her family home in the rural region near the shelter, leaving a younger brother still living there. Tall and slight, from a white, working-class background, Gretchen was confused about her role as a daughter. Although she believed that "daughters should not physically strike their mothers," this became an impossibility because Gretchen's parents were abusing her physically and she had to be disobedient in order to survive. She talked about the dilemma of not wanting to hit her mother back, even when her mother was choking her:

> My mother, she beat me—but I'm not afraid of my mother! The last time she beat me up—I had respect—I did not hit her back—until the day she got arrested. She was beating the s_ _t out of me and I would not hit her back! I cried, I felt so sorry for myself, but I didn't hit her back!

Gretchen fought against her inclination to strike her mother back, but her angry running-away survival behavior won out in the end. Gretchen resolved her moral and emotional dilemma by initiating self-protective "last resort" behavior that consisted of running away.

According to Schaffner, the vision of runaways as incorrigible delinquents is a popular misconception. She found, instead, a much more complex picture of children who find it impossible to conform and comply with unevenly applied family rules and proscriptions; these emotionally abused girls use their running away as a desperate survival strategy. Runaway girls perceived their living arrangements as being so bad that they felt forced to run away, forced to go against what they really wished for or wanted: warm relationships with parents who could be trusted. Not surprisingly, Schaffner also found that in families where emotional and relational dynamics are deeply problematic, but not physical, youths often recounted wishful hopes for reconciliation.

Critical Thinking

1. Schaffner found that except for families where severe and persistent physical and sexual abuse has been occurring, children who have run away from home can be reunited with family members. Do you believe that this is a reasonable solution, or is it merely putting a child back into the situation that created her need to run away in the first place? What would you suggest is the best course to help runaways?

InfoTrac College Edition Research

 To read an article on the topic of teen runaways, go to Laurie Schaffner, "Searching for Connection: A New Look at Teenaged Runaways," *Adolescence* 33(131): 619 (Fall 1998).

Source: Laurie Schaffner, *Teenage Runaways: Broken Hearts and "Bad Attitudes"* (New York: Haworth Press, 1999).

Liberal Feminist Views

All of us, despite our differences, are constantly growing and trying to understand each other's oppression, be it as working class women, black or brown women, gay women or middle class women. We are, by struggling, finding new ways of caring about each other, and it is this that gives us hope of having a movement, finally, which will provide for all of our needs.[99]

This statement represents the sentiments of women who were active participants in the feminist movement in its formative years. Feminist leaders have fought to help women break away from their traditional roles of homemaker and mother and secure for themselves economic, professional, educational, and social advancement. There is little question that the women's movement has revised the way women perceive their roles in society and significantly altered the relationships of women to many important social institutions.

Liberal feminism also has influenced thinking about the nature and extent of delinquency. A number of scholars, including Rita Simon and Freda Adler, have drawn national attention to the changing pattern of female criminality and offered new explanations for the differences between male and female delinquency rates.[100] Their position is that economic conditions and sex role differences are a greater influence than socialization on delinquency rates. After all, improper socialization affects both males and females and therefore cannot be the sole explanation for gender differences in the crime rate.

According to liberal feminists, females are less delinquent than males because their social roles provide them with fewer opportunities to commit crime. As the roles of girls and women become more similar to those of males, so too will their crime patterns. Female criminality is actually motivated by the same crime-producing influences as male criminality. This view was spelled out most clearly more than 25 years ago in Freda Adler's book *Sisters in Crime* (1975), which showed how sex role differences influence crime and delinquency.

For more than 20 years, the Center for Research on Women has been in the forefront of research in which the central questions are shaped by the experiences and perspectives of women. Their Web site can be accessed at *http://www.wellesley.edu/WCW/crwsub.html* For an up-to-date list of Web links, go to *http://info.wadsworth.com/siegel*

Sisters in Crime

Adler's major thesis is that by striving for social and economic independence, women have begun to alter social institutions, which had protected males in their traditional positions of power. "The phenomenon of female criminality," she claims, "is but one wave in this rising tide of female assertiveness."[101]

Adler argued that female delinquency patterns and rates would be affected by the changing role of women in society. As females entered new occupations and participated in sports, education, politics, and other traditionally male endeavors, they would also become involved in crimes that had heretofore been male oriented; delinquency rates would converge. She noted that girls were already becoming increasingly involved in traditionally masculine crimes, such as stealing, gang activity, and fighting.

Adler predicted that in the future, the women's liberation movement would produce even steeper increases in the rate of female delinquency because it would create an environment in which the social roles of girls and boys converge. Boys, she argued, have traditionally entered puberty ill prepared for the world of aggression and competition they encounter in the activities of their peer groups. The consequent emotional strain leads them to engage in delinquent activities. Girls, on the other hand, have always maintained traditional, relatively static behavior patterns. These patterns protected them from the pressures of transition into the adult world. However, Adler argued, "the modern girl... is passing from childhood to adulthood via a new and uncharted course.... She is partly pushed and partly impelled into fields previously closed to women.... Clearly, the developmental difficulties which encouraged male delinquency in the past are exerting a similar influence on girls."[102]

Adler proclaimed that the changing female role will eventually produce female delinquents and criminals who are quite similar to their male counterparts:

> *Women are no longer behaving like subhuman primates with only one option. Medical, educational, political and technological advances have freed women from unwanted pregnancies, provided them with male occupational skills, and equalized their strengths with weapons. Is it any wonder that once women were armed with male opportunities, they should strive for status, criminal as well as civil, through established male hierarchial channels.*
>
> *In the cities... young girls are now taking to the streets just as boys have traditionally done. It has now become quite common for adolescent girls to participate in muggings, burglaries, and extortion rings which prey on schoolmates.*[103]

Support for Liberal Feminism

A number of well-known studies supported the feminist view of gender differences in the delinquency rate.[104] More than 25 years ago, Rita Simon explained how the consistent increase in female criminality is a function of the changing role of women. She claimed that as women were empowered economically and socially they would be less likely to feel victimized, dependent, and oppressed. Consequently, they would be less likely to attack their traditional targets: their husbands, lovers, pimps (that is, men with whom they are emotionally involved and dependent upon), and their babies (those recently born and those not yet delivered).[105] Instead, their new role as family breadwinner might encourage them to engage in traditional male economic crimes, such as larceny and car theft.

Simon's view has been supported in part by Roy Austin's analysis of the effect the women's liberation and economic emancipation movement has had on the female crime rate.[106] Using 1966 as a jumping-off point (because the National Organization for Women was founded in that year), Austin's research shows that patterns of serious female crime (robbery and auto theft) correlate with indicators of female emancipation (namely, the divorce rate and participation in the labor force). While, as Austin admits, this research does not conclusively prove that female crime is related to economic and social change, it certainly identifies behavior patterns that support that hypothesis.

In addition to these efforts, a number of self-report studies have supported the liberal feminist view by showing that gender differences in delinquency *patterns* are fading. That is, the delinquent acts committed most (petty larceny) and least often (heroin addiction, armed robbery) by girls are nearly identical to those reported most and least often by boys.[107] The pattern of female delinquency, if not the extent, is now similar to that of male delinquency.[108] And with few exceptions the factors that seem to motivate both male and female criminality (family dysfunction, educational failure, impulsive personality) seem quite similar.[109]

According to this view then, as the sex roles of males and females become more equivalent, their offending patterns also have become more similar. Girls may be joining gangs and committing crimes in order to gain economic advancement and not because they perceive a lack of parental support and affection. Both these patterns are predicted by liberal feminists.

Critiques of Liberal Feminism

Not all delinquency experts believe that changing sex roles actually influence female crime rates. Some argue that the delinquent behavior patterns of girls have remained static and have not been influenced by the women's movement. Females involved in violent crime more often than not have some connection to a male business or intimate partner who influences their behavior. One recent study of women who kill in the course of their involvement in the drug trade found that rather than act in their own self-interest, they kill on behalf of a man or out of fear of a man.[110]

Others dispute whether overall changes in the female delinquency rate correspond to the feminist movement. They argue that self-report studies show that female participation in most crime patterns has remained stable for the past 10 years, with increases in the area of drug use and alcohol abuse.[111] It is possible that the women's movement has not influenced female crime rates as much as previously thought.[112] Perhaps the greater participation by females in the UCR arrest data is more a function of how police are treating females (the end of "chivalry") and does not reflect actual change in female behavior patterns.

In sum, the evidence indicates that gender differences in the crime rate have not changed as much as liberal feminist writers had predicted.[113] Consequently, the argument that female crime and delinquency will be elevated by the women's movement has not been given unqualified support.

Is Convergence Possible?

Will the gender differences in the delinquency crime rate eventually disappear as liberal feminists have predicted? Are gender differences permanent and unchanging? Not all experts have abandoned the convergence argument, suggesting that in the long run, male and female delinquency rates will become quite similar.[114] Females, for example, have increased gang membership and gang activity, which is associated with increased levels of crime and drug abuse.[115] Crime convergence may be delayed by a slower-than-expected change in gender roles; the women's movement has not yet achieved its full impact on social life.[116] One reason is that while expanding their economic role, women have not abandoned their conventional role as family caretaker and home provider; women today are being forced to cope with added financial and social burdens. Recent research by Jean Bottcher found that young boys still perceive their roles as being more dominant than do young girls. Boys are more likely to be sexually adventuresome while less likely to take on the role of child caregiver. Male power—their ability to have freedom and hang with their friends—helped explain the gender differences in delinquency.[117]

If gender roles were truly equivalent, then crime rates may eventually converge; as our society shifts toward more balanced gender roles, there may be significant changes in female delinquency rates.

Radical Feminist Views

radical or Marxist feminists
Hold that gender inequality stems from the unequal power of men and women and the subsequent exploitation of women by men; the cause of female delinquency originates with the onset of male supremacy and the efforts of males to control females' sexuality.

A number of feminist writers take a more revolutionary view of gender differences in crime. These scholars, who can be categorized as socialist, **radical,** or **Marxist feminists,** believe gender inequality stems from the unequal power of men and women in a capitalist society and the exploitation of females by fathers and husbands: Women are considered a commodity worth possessing, like land or money.[118] The cause of female delinquency originates with the onset of male supremacy (patriarchy), the subsequent subordination of women, male aggression, and the efforts of men to control females sexually.[119]

Radical feminists focus on the social forces that shape girls' lives and experiences to explain female criminality.[120] They attempt to show how the sexual victimization of girls is often a function of male socialization and that young males learn to be aggressive and exploitive of women. James Messerschmidt, an influential feminist scholar, has formulated complex theoretical models that show how misguided concepts of what is "masculinity" flow from the inequities built into "patriarchal capitalism." Men dominate business and power in capitalist societies, and males who cannot function well within its parameters are at risk for crime. Women are inherently powerless in such a male-dominated society, and their crimes reflect the limitations they experience on legitimate as well as illegitimate opportunity.[121] This view is supported by a national survey conducted by the Center for Research on Women at Wellesley College, which found that 90 percent of adolescent girls are sexually harassed in school, with almost 30 percent reporting having been psychologically pressured to "do something sexual" and 10 percent physically forced into sexual behaviors.[122]

According to the radical view, male exploitation acts as a trigger for female delinquent behavior and status offending. Female delinquents have told of their being so severely sexually harassed at school that they were forced to carry knives for their own safety. Some have reported much older boyfriends, sometimes in their 30s, who "knew how to treat a girl," but who often drew these women into criminal acitivity such as drug trafficking, which eventually entangled them in the juvenile justice system.[123]

So when female victims run away and use drugs, they may be reacting to abuse at home and at school. Their attempts at survival are then labeled deviant or delinquent; victim blaming is not uncommon.[124] Research shows that a significant number of girls who require emergency room treatment for sexual abuse later engage in violence as a teen or as an adult; many of these abused girls actually form a romantic attachment with the abusive partner.[125] The Wellesley survey of sexual harassment found that teachers and school officials ignore about 45 percent of the complaints made by female students. Because agents of social control often choose to ignore reports of abuse and harassment, young girls may feel trapped and desperate.

Crime and Patriarchy

A number of theoretical models have attempted to use a radical or Marxist feminist perspective to explain gender differences in the delinquency rate. For example, in *Capitalism, Patriarchy, and Crime*, Marxist James Messerschmidt argues that capitalist society is marked by both patriarchy and class conflict. Capitalists control the labor of workers, while men control women both economically and biologically.[126] This "double marginality" explains why females in a capitalist society commit fewer crimes than males: They are isolated in the family and have fewer opportunities to engage in elite deviance (white-collar and economic crimes); they are also denied access to male-dominated street crimes. Since capitalism renders women powerless, they are forced to commit less serious, nonviolent, and self-destructive crimes, such as abusing drugs.

Power-Control Theory

power-control theory Holds that gender differences in the delinquency rate are a function of class differences and economic conditions that influence the structure of family life.

egalitarian families Husband and wife share power at home; daughters gain a kind of freedom similar to that of sons, and their law-violating behaviors mirror those of their brothers.

In one prominent radical feminist work, John Hagan and his associates have speculated that gender differences in the delinquency rate are a function of class differences and economic conditions that in turn influence the structure of family life. Hagan calls his view **power-control theory**.[127] According to this view, class position influences delinquency by controlling the quality of family life. In paternalistic families, fathers assume the traditional role of breadwinners, while mothers have menial jobs or remain at home. In these homes, mothers are expected to control the behavior of their daughters while granting greater freedom to sons. The parent-daughter relationship can be viewed as a preparation for the "cult of domesticity," which makes daughters' involvement in delinquency unlikely; hence, males exhibit a higher degree of delinquent behavior than their sisters.

On the other hand, in **egalitarian families**—those in which the husband and the wife share similar positions of power at home and in the workplace—daughters gain a kind of freedom that reflects reduced parental control. These families produce daughters whose law-violating behavior mirrors that of their brothers. Ironically,

ACCORDING TO POWER-CONTROL THEORY, when girls grow up in egalitarian families, where the husband and the wife share similar positions of power at home and in the workplace, they achieve freedom and independence.

these kinds of relationships also occur in female-headed households with absent fathers. Similarly, Hagan and his associates found that when both fathers and mothers hold equally valued managerial positions, the similarity between the rates of their daughters' and sons' delinquency is greatest. By implication, middle-class girls are the most likely to violate the law because they are less closely controlled than their lower-class sisters.

Some of the power-control theory's basic premises, such as the relationship between social class and delinquency, have been challenged. For example, the theory holds that upper-class youths may engage in more petty delinquency than lower-class youths because they are brought up to be "risk takers" who do not fear the consequences of their misdeeds; such relationships may not exist.[128] However, ongoing research by Hagan and his colleagues has tended to support the core relationship between family structure and gender differences in the delinquency rate.[129] Other research efforts have also found support for the theory. For example, Brenda Sims Blackwell's research found support for a key element of power-control theory: Females in paternalistic households have been socialized to fear legal sanctions more so than their brothers.[130]

Power-control theory is important because it encourages a new approach to the study of delinquency, one that addresses gender differences, class position, and family structure. It also helps to explain the relative increase in female delinquency by stressing the significance of changing feminine roles in modern society. With the increase in single-parent homes brought about by the significant numbers of unwed teenage mothers and the high divorce rate, the patterns Hagan has identified may also undergo change. The decline of the patriarchal family may produce looser family ties on girls, changing sex roles, and increased delinquency. Ironically, this raises an interesting dilemma: The belief that daughters of successful and powerful mothers are more at risk for delinquency than the daughters of stay-at-home moms may be viewed as an implicit critique of feminist goals. However, as sociologist Christopher Uggen points out, there may be a bright side to this aspect of the theory: Not only are they more likely to commit delinquent acts, but daughters of powerful mothers may also be encouraged to take prosocial risks such as competing in more athletic events and breaking into traditional male-dominated occupations such as policing and the military.[131]

Gender and the Juvenile Justice System

Not only do gender differences have an effect on juvenile crime rates and patterns, but they may also have a significant impact on the way children are treated by the juvenile justice system when and if they are apprehended. Several feminist scholars argue that girls are not only the victims of injustice at home but also risk being victimized by agents of the juvenile justice system.

In the early juvenile justice system, girls were considered sexual deviants who needed to be controlled. At the turn of the century, what appeared to be "scientific proof" showed that there was a connection between intelligence, delinquency, and sexual activity. Juvenile justice reformers believed that the best way to protect feeble-minded girls was to remove them from society and place them in state institutions. Eugenicists believed that females arrested for prostitution and other forms of delinquency should be prohibited from reproducing because they were degenerate, immoral, and feebleminded. As a consequence, the cruel practice of forced sterilization of girls who were labeled amoral by the courts became common. Even social workers, nominally charged with helping young women in need, played a significant role in the criminalization of female sexuality. They considered this an important step in protecting the sanctity of women and the purity of society.[132] In many respects, the treatment girls receive today is not too dissimilar from the "sexualization" of female delinquency of the 1920s. (See the Focus on Delinquency box entitled "Guardians of Virtue" for more on this topic.) Paternalistic attitudes and the sexual double standard increase the likelihood that girls will be referred to juvenile court for status offenses.

Are girls "victims" of the juvenile justice system? In her classic 1973 study, Meda Chesney-Lind found that police in Honolulu were likely to arrest female adolescents for sexual activity and to ignore the same behavior among male delinquents.[133] Some 74 percent of the females in Chesney-Lind's sample were charged with sexual activity or incorrigibility; in comparison, only 27 percent of the boys were so charged. Similar to 1920 Los Angeles practices described in the Focus on Delinquency box, the court ordered 70 percent of the females to undergo physical examinations, while requiring only 15 percent of the males to undergo this embarrassing procedure. Girls were also more likely to be sent to a detention facility before trial, and the length of their detention averaged three times that of the boys.

Chesney-Lind concluded that female adolescents are granted a much narrower range of acceptable behavior than male adolescents. Any sign of misbehavior in girls is seen as a substantial challenge to authority and to the viability of the sexual double standard.

Are Standards Changing?

More than 30 years after the Chesney-Lind research brought attention to the gender "double standard" in juvenile court, distinctions are still being made between male and female offenders. Girls are still being incarcerated if their behavior does not measure up to (male) decision makers' concepts of proper female behavior.[134] Females considered immoral or out of control are more likely to be punished than males.[135] Recent research conducted by John MacDonald and Meda Chesney-Lind found that girls are still receiving more punitive treatment than boys in the latter stages of the juvenile justice process. They reason that the juvenile justice system still categorizes female offenders into two distinct groups: One group is considered to have momentarily strayed from the "good girl" path and is therefore deserving of solicitous, humanitarian treatment; a second group of dangerously wayward girls have serious problems and must therefore be kept under strict control lest they stray further.[136]

Girls may also be feeling the brunt of the more punitive policies now being used in the juvenile justice system. For example, when Chesney-Lind and Vickie Paramore

Focus on Delinquency

Guardians of Virtue

The view that female delinquency is sexual in nature and that the majority of female delinquents' troubles can be linked to their sexual precociousness influenced the treatment of young female offenders in the first juvenile courts. Mary Odem and Steven Schlossman explored this "sexualization" of female delinquency in their study of more than 200 girls petitioned to the Los Angeles Juvenile Court in 1920.

Odem and Schlossman argue that in the first decades of the twentieth century, delinquency "experts" identified young female "sex delinquents" as a major social problem that required a forceful public response. These experts spoke of a rise in illicit sexual activity among young working-class females. This phenomenon was perceived in part as a product of newfound freedoms enjoyed by girls after the turn of the century. Young females were getting jobs in stores and offices, where they were more likely to meet eligible young men. Recreation now included dance halls, movie theaters, beaches, and amusement parks—areas fraught with the danger of "sexual experimentation." Civic leaders concerned about immorality mounted a social hygiene campaign that identified the "sex delinquent" as a moral and sexual threat to American society and advocated a policy of *eugenics*—sterilization to prevent these inferior individuals from having children.

The juvenile justice system also responded to this "epidemic" of sexuality by targeting the lower-class female population in Los Angeles. At first, to prevent "moral ruin," female civic leaders and social workers campaigned for special attention to be given to female delinquency in an effort to combat "moral ruin." Los Angeles responded by hiring the first female police officers in the nation to deal with girls under arrest, and female judges to hear girls' cases in juvenile court. The city also developed a nationally recognized female detention center and a girl's reformatory.

The first female officer in the country was Alice Stebbins Wells, appointed on September 13, 1910. A social worker, Wells argued that she could better serve her clients if she had full police powers. She and her fellow female officers inspected dance halls, cafes, theaters, and other public amusement places to ferret out girls who were in danger of moral ruin, sending some home and bringing the incorrigible to the detention center.

Female "referees" were appointed to hear cases involving girls, and female probation officers were assigned to supervise them. The influx of new cases prompted the county to open custodial institutions for girls, including the El Retiro School, which was considered the latest in modern rehabilitative treatment.

When Odem and Schlossman evaluated the juvenile court records of delinquent girls who entered the Los Angeles Juvenile Court in 1920, they found that the majority were petitioned for either suspected sexual activity or behavior that placed them at risk for sexual relations. Despite the limited seriousness of these charges, the majority of girls were detained prior to their trials, and while in Juvenile Hall, all were given a compulsory pelvic exam. Girls adjudged sexually delinquent on the basis of the exam were segregated from the merely incorrigible girls to prevent moral corruption. Those testing positive for venereal disease were confined in Juvenile Hall Hospital, usually for one to three months.

After trial, *29 percent* of these female adolescents were committed to custodial institutions, a high price to pay for moral transgressions. While society was undergoing a sexual revolution, the juvenile court seemed wedded to a philosophy of controlling "immoral" young women, a policy that was to last more than 30 years.

Critical Thinking

1. Has the system changed since this research was carried out? Are girls still being treated differently than boys in the juvenile justice system? Will gender differences in society and its institutions ever be eradicated?

InfoTrac College Edition Research

 What is it like to be a young woman in the juvenile justice system today? Use *juvenile justice females* as keywords on InfoTrac College Edition to find out.

Source: Mary Odem and Steven Schlossman, "Guardians of Virtue: The Juvenile Court and Female Delinquency in Early 20th-Century Los Angeles," *Crime and Delinquency* 37:186–203 (1991).

---

analyzed data from the city and county of Honolulu, they found that tougher juvenile justice standards have led to less serious offenses being handled formally within the juvenile justice system.[137] While girls are actually committing fewer violent crimes, they are more likely to become enmeshed within the grasp of the more punitive juvenile justice system.

Girls may still be subject to harsh punishments if they are considered dangerously immoral. Girls arrested on status offense charges are more likely than boys to have descriptions of their physical attractiveness placed in case files. There still appears to be an association between male standards of beauty and sexual behavior: Judges, social workers, and other criminal justice professionals may look upon attractive girls who engage in sexual behavior more harshly, punishing them while overlooking some of the same behaviors in less attractive girls. Once in the system, girls may receive fewer benefits and services than their male counterparts. Institutionalized girls report that they receive fewer privileges, less space, equipment, programs, and treatment than institutionalized boys.[138] They resent the fact that boys have more educational, recreational, and occupational opportunities. Why do these differences persist? Because juvenile correctional authorities continue to subscribe to stereotyped beliefs about the needs of young girls, which have little to do with reality.

While these arguments are persuasive, some recent national data gathered for the federal government by the Pittsburgh-based National Center for Juvenile Justice shows that today there is little gender-based difference in state processing of status offenders. Both girls and boys seem to have an equal chance of proceeding to formal adjudication and being sent to out-of-the-home placements for status offenses.[139] This evidence seems to suggest that the gender bias in some areas of the juvenile justice process may be in decline.

SUMMARY

The relationship between gender and delinquency has become a topic of considerable interest to criminologists and other experts interested in youth crimes. At one time attention was directed solely at male offenders, and the rare female delinquent was considered an oddity. The nature and extent of female delinquent activities have changed, and it appears that girls are now engaging in more frequent and serious illegal activity. Consequently, there is ever greater interest in gender issues in delinquency.

Sociologists and psychologists now recognize that there are distinct differences between boys and girls in attitude, values, and behavior. Females process information differently than males and have different cognitive and physical strengths. These differences may explain in part gender differences in the delinquency rate.

Theories that seek to explain the cause of these gender differences fit several major categories. Trait views are concerned with biological and psychological differences between the sexes. Early efforts by Cesare Lombroso and his followers place the blame for delinquency on physical differences between males and females. Girls who were delinquent had inherent male characteristics. Later, biosocial theorists viewed a girl's psychological makeup, hormonal, and physical characteristics as key to delinquent behavior.

Socialization has also been identified as a cause of delinquency. Males are socialized to be tough and aggressive, while females are instructed to be more passive and obedient. The adolescent female offender was portrayed as a troubled girl who lacked love at home and supportive peer relations. These theories treated female delinquents as sexual offenders whose criminal activities were linked to destructive relationships with men.

More recent views of gender and delinquency incorporate the changes brought about by the women's movement. It is argued that as the social and economic roles of women change, so will their crime patterns. While a number of research studies support this view, some theorists question its validity. Though the female crime rate has increased and female delinquency patterns now resemble those of male delinquency, the gender gap has not narrowed after more than three decades since the women's rights movement began. Hagan's power-control theory helps us understand why these differences exist and whether change may be forthcoming.

The treatment girls receive by the juvenile justice system has also been the subject of debate. Originally, it was thought that police treated girls with chivalry and protected them from the stigma of a delinquency label. Contemporary criminologists charge, however, that girls are actually discriminated against by agents of the justice system.

KEY TERMS

masculinity hypothesis	penis envy	premenstrual syndrome (PMS)	power-control theory
gender-schema theory	precocious sexuality		egalitarian families
chivalry hypothesis	androgen	radical or Marxist feminists	

QUESTIONS FOR DISCUSSION

1. Are girls delinquent for different reasons than boys? Do they have a unique set of problems?

2. Do you believe that as sex roles become more homogenous, female delinquency will become identical to male delinquency in rate and type?

3. Does the sexual double standard still exist?

4. Are lower-class girls more strictly supervised than upper- and middle-class girls? Is control stratified across class lines?

5. Are girls the victims of unfairness at the hands of the justice system, or do they benefit from "chivalry"?

VIEWPOINT

The revival of feminism in the sixties is often dated from the appearance of Betty Friedan's The Feminine Mystique. *This 1963 best-seller found a receptive audience among middle- and upper-class women whose experiences Friedan captured. Although her book was important for its challenge to the ideology of domesticity, other factors also contributed to the re-emergence of feminism. Unprecedented numbers of married women were being drawn into the job market—albeit on unequal terms—as the service sector of the economy expanded and consumerism fueled the desire of many families for second income. Both the growing numbers of women graduating from college and the availability of the birth-control pill (which accelerated the already noticeable decline in the birthrate) further encouraged women's entry into the work force.*

Many delinquency experts believe that the changing role of women, inspired by the feminist movement, has changed women's roles and also their patterns of criminal behavior. Go to InfoTrac College Edition and read about the recent history of this movement and the forces that helped shape its appeal in "Feminism 1960 to the Present," *The 1993 Information Please Almanac* 2:446 (1992). To read about the early history of the movement, go to Nancy Woloch and Alice Echols, "Feminist Movement," *The Reader's Companion to American History* 7:391 (1991).

NOTES

1. Cesare Lombroso, *The Female Offender* (New York: Appleton, 1920); W. I. Thomas, *The Unadjusted Girl* (New York: Harper & Row, 1923).

2. Cesare Lombroso and William Ferrero, *The Female Offender* (New York: Philosophical Library, 1895).

3. James Messerschmidt, *Masculinities and Crime* (Lanham, MD: Rowman and Littlefield, 1993).

4. Paul Mazerole, Robert Brame, Ray Paternoster, Alex Piquero, and Charles Dean, "Onset Age, Persistence, and Offending Versatility: Comparisons across Sex." Paper presented at the Annual Society of Criminology meeting, San Diego, November, 1997.

5. Kathleen Daly, "From Gender Ratios to Gendered Lives: Women Gender in Crime and Criminological Theory," in Michael Tonry, ed., *The Handbook of Crime and Punishment* (New York: Oxford University Press, 1998).

6. Rita James Simon, *The Contemporary Woman and Crime* (Washington, DC: Government Printing Office, 1975).

7. Rolf Loeber and Dale Hay, "Key Issues in the Development of Aggression and Violence from Childhood to Early Adulthood," *Annual Review of Psychology* 48:371–410 (1997).

8. This section relies on Spencer Rathus, *Psychology in the New Millennium* (Fort Worth, TX: Harcourt, Brace College Publishers, 1996); see also Darcy Miller, Catherine Trapani, Kathy Fejes-Mendoza, Carolyn Eggleston, and Donna Dwiggins, "Adolescent Female Offenders: Unique Considerations," *Adolescence* 30:429–35 (1995).

9. Allison Morris, *Women, Crime and Criminal Justice* (Oxford, England: Basil Blackwell, 1987).

10. Dennis Giever, "An Empirical Assessment of the Core Elements of Gottfredson and Hirschi's General Theory of Crime." Paper presented at the American Society of Criminology meeting, Boston, November 1995.

11. Loeber and Hay, "Key Issues in the Development of Aggression and Violence," p. 378.

12. John Mirowsky and Catherine Ross, "Sex Differences in Distress: Real or Artifact?" *American Sociological Review* 60:449–68 (1995).

13. Ibid., pp. 460–65.

14. For a review of this issue, see Anne Campbell, *Men, Women and Aggression* (New York: Basic Books, 1993).

15. Ann Beutel and Margaret Mooney Marini, "Gender and Values," *American Sociological Review* 60:436–48 (1995).

16. American Association of University Women, *Shortchanging Girls, Shortchanging America* (Washington, DC: American Association of University Women, 1991).

17. John Gibbs, Dennis Giever, and Jamie Martin, "Parental Management and Self-Control: An Empirical Test of Gottfredson and Hirschi's General Theory," *Journal of Research in Crime and Delinquency* 35:40–70 (1998); Velmer Burton, Francis Cullen, T. David Evans, Leanne Fiftal Alarid, and R. Gregory Dunaway, "Gender, Self-Control, and Crime," *Journal of Research in Crime and Delinquency* 35:123–47 (1998).

18. David Rowe, Alexander Vazsonyi, and Daniel Flannery, "Sex Differences in Crime: Do Means and Within-Sex Variation Have Similar Causes?" *Journal of Research in Crime and Delinquency* 32:84–100 (1995).

19. Sandra Bem, *The Lenses of Gender* (New Haven: Yale University Press, 1993).

20. Walter DeKeseredy and Martin Schwartz, "Male Peer Support and Woman Abuse," *Sociological Spectrum* 13:393–413 (1993).

21. Daniel Mears, Matthew Ploeger, and Mark Warr, "Explaining the Gender Gap in Delinquency: Peer Influence and Moral Evaluations of Behavior," *Journal of Research in Crime and Delinquency* 35:251–66 (1998).

22. Messerschmidt, *Masculinities and Crime.*

23. D. J. Pepler and W. M. Craig, "A Peek behind the Fence: Naturalistic Observations of Aggressive Children with Remote Audiovisual Recording," *Developmental Psychology* 31:548–53 (1995).

24. Stacey Nofziger, "Sex and Gender Identity: A Gendered Look at Delinquency." Paper presented at the American Society of Criminology meeting, Boston, November 1995 (revised version, January, 1996).

25. Data in this section comes from the Federal Bureau of Investigation, *Crime in the United States, 2000* (Washington, DC: United States Government Printing Office, 2001), pp. 228–30.

26. George Calhoun, Janelle Jurgens, and Fengling Chen, "The Neophyte Female Delinquent: A Review of the Literature," *Adolescence* 28:461–71 (1993).

27. *Crime in the United States, 1997,* p. 22.

28. Lombroso and Ferrero, *The Female Offender.*

29. Ibid., p. 122.

30. Ibid., pp. 51–52.

31. For a review, see Anne Campbell, *Girl Delinquents* (Oxford: Basic Blackwell, 1981), pp. 41–48.

32. Ibid., p. 151.

33. Ibid., pp. 150–52.

34. Cyril Burt, *The Young Delinquent* (New York: Appleton, 1925); see also Warren Middleton, "Is There a Relation between Kleptomania and Female Periodicity in Neurotic Individuals?" *Psychology Clinic* 232–47 (December 1933).

35. William Healy and Augusta Bronner, *Delinquents and Criminals, Their Making and Unmaking* (New York: Macmillan, 1926).

36. Otto Pollak, *The Criminality of Women* (Philadelphia: University of Pennsylvania Press, 1950).

37. Ibid., p. 158.

38. Ibid., p. 10.

39. Miriam Sealock and Sally Simpson, "Unraveling Bias in Arrest Decisions: The Role of Juvenile Offender Type-Scripts," *Justice Quarterly* 15:427–57 (1998); Christina Polsenberg and Kenneth Jackson, "Putting Race into Context: Race, Juvenile Justice Processing and Urbanization." Paper presented at the American Society of Criminology meeting, Boston, November 1995 (updated version, 1996). For a general review, see Carl Pope and William Feyerherm, "Minority Status and Juvenile Justice Processing (Part I)," *Criminal Justice Abstracts* 22:327–35 (1990); see also Douglas Smith and Jody Klein, "Police Control of Interpersonal Disputes," *Social Problems* 31:468–81 (1984).

40. Sigmund Freud, *An Outline of Psychoanalysis,* trans. James Strachey (New York: Norton, 1949), p. 278.

41. Dorie Klein, "The Etiology of Female Crime: A Review of the Literature," in Freda Adler and Rita Simon, eds., *The Criminology of Deviant Women* (Boston: Houghton Mifflin, 1979), pp. 69–71.

42. Phyliss Chesler, *Women and Madness* (Garden City, NY: Doubleday, 1972); Karen Horney, *Feminine Psychology* (New York: Norton, 1967).

43. Peter Blos, "Preoedipal Factors in the Etiology of Female Delinquency," *Psychoanalytic Studies of the Child* 12:229–42 (1957).

44. See, generally, Ralph Weisheit and Sue Mahan, *Women, Crime and Criminal Justice* (Cincinnati: Anderson Publishing, 1988).

45. Sheldon Glueck and Eleanor Glueck, *Five Hundred Delinquent Women* (New York: Knopf, 1934).

46. J. Cowie, V. Cowie, and E. Slater, *Delinquency in Girls* (London: Heinemann, 1968).

47. Anne Campbell, "On the Invisibility of the Female Delinquent Peer Group," *Women and Criminal Justice* 2:41–62 (1990).

48. Carolyn Smith, "Factors Associated with Early Sexual Activity among Urban Adolescents," *Social Work* 42:334–46 (1997).

49. For a review, see Christy Miller Buchanan, Jacquelynne Eccles, and Jill Becker, "Are Adolescents the Victims of Raging Hormones? Evidence for Activational Effects of Hormones on Moods and Behavior at Adolescence," *Psychological Bulletin* 111:63–107 (1992). Herein cited as "Raging Hormones."

50. Avshalom Caspi, Donald Lyman, Terrie Moffitt, and Phil Silva, "Unraveling Girl's Delinquency: Biological, Dispositional, and Contextual Contributions to Adolescent Misbehavior," *Developmental Psychology* (1993).

51. Eleanor Maccoby and Carol Jacklin, *The Psychology of Sex Differences* (Palo Alto, CA: Stanford University Press, 1974).

52. Alan Booth and D. Wayne Osgood, "The Influence of Testosterone on Deviance in Adulthood: Assessing and Explaining the Relationship," *Criminology* 31:93–118 (1993).

53. Walter Gove, "The Effect of Age and Gender on Deviant Behavior: A Biopsychosocial Perspective," in A. S. Rossi, ed., *Gender and the Life Course* (New York: Aldine, 1985), pp. 115–44.

54. Lee Ellis, "Evolutionary and Neurochemical Causes of Sex Differences in Victimizing Behavior: Toward a Unified Theory of Criminal Behavior and Social Stratification," *Social Science Information* 28:625–26 (1989).

55. D. H. Baucom, P. K. Besch, and S. Callahan, "Relationship between Testosterone Concentration, Sex Roles Identity, and Personality among Females," *Journal of Personality and Social Psychology* 48:1218–26 (1985).

56. Lee Ellis, "Evidence of Neuroandrogenic Etiology of Sex Roles from a Combined Analysis of Human, Nonhuman Primate and Nonprimate Mammalian Studies," *Personality and Individual Differences* 7:519–52 (1986).

57. Diana Fishbein, "Selected Studies on the Biology of Antisocial Behavior," in John Conklin, ed., *New Perspectives in Criminology* (Needham Heights, MA: Allyn and Bacon, 1996), pp. 26–38.

58. Idem, "The Psychobiology of Female Aggression," *Criminal Justice and Behavior* 19:99–126 (1992).

59. Spencer Rathus, *Psychology*, 3rd ed. (New York: Holt, Rinehart and Winston, 1987), p. 88.

60. See, generally, Katharina Dalton, *The Premenstrual Syndrome* (Springfield, IL: Charles C. Thomas, 1971).

61. Fishbein, "Selected Studies on the Biology of Antisocial Behavior."

62. Ibid.; Karen Paige, "Effects of Oral Contraceptives on Affective Fluctuations Associated with the Menstrual Cycle," *Psychosomatic Medicine* 33:515–37 (1971).

63. B. Harry and C. Balcer, "Menstruation and Crime: A Critical Review of the Literature from the Clinical Criminology Perspective," *Behavioral Sciences and the Law* 5:307–22 (1987).

64. Julie Horney, "Menstrual Cycles and Criminal Responsibility," *Law and Human Nature* 2:25–36 (1978).

65. Ibid., p. 116.

66. Lee Ellis, "The Victimful-Victimless Crime Distinction and Seven Universal Demographic Correlates of Victimful Criminal Behavior," *Personality and Individual Differences* 9:525–48 (1988).

67. Maccoby and Jacklin, *The Psychology of Sex Differences.*

68. Ellis, "Evolutionary and Neurochemical Causes of Sex Differences in Victimizing Behavior," pp. 605–36.

69. Ann Frodi, J. Maccauley, and P. R. Thome, "Are Women Always Less Aggressive Than Men? A Review of the Experimental Literature," *Psychological Bulletin* 84:634–60 (1977).

70. Buchanan, Eccles, and Becker, "Raging Hormones," p. 94.

71. William I. Thomas, *The Unadjusted Girl* (New York: Harper & Row, 1928).

72. Ibid., p. 109.

73. David Farrington, "Juvenile Delinquency," in John Coleman, ed., *The School Years* (London: Routledge, 1992), p. 133.

74. Sylvia Johnson, "Girls Are in Trouble: Do We Care?" *Corrections Today* 60:136–43 (1998).

75. Ruth Morris, "Female Delinquents and Relational Problems," *Social Forces* 43:82-89 (1964).

76. Cowie, Cowie, and Slater, *Delinquency in Girls,* p. 27.

77. Gisela Konopka, *The Adolescent Girl in Conflict* (Englewood Cliffs, NJ: Prentice-Hall, 1966).

78. Ibid., p. 40.

79. Peter Kratcoski and Lucille Kratcoski, *Juvenile Delinquency* (Englewood Cliffs, NJ: Prentice-Hall, 1979), pp. 146–47.

80. Konopka, *The Adolescent Girl in Conflict,* p. 50.

81. Ruth Morris, "Female Delinquency and Relational Problems," *Social Forces* 43:82–89 (1964).

82. Clyde Vedder and Dora Somerville, *The Delinquent Girl* (Springfield, IL: Charles C. Thomas, 1970).

83. Sheldon and Eleanor Glueck, *Unraveling Juvenile Delinquency* (Cambridge: Harvard University Press, 1950).

84. Ibid., pp. 281–82.

85. Glueck and Glueck, *Five Hundred Delinquent Women.*

86. Ibid., p. 90.

87. Ames Robey, Richard Rosenwal, John Small, and Ruth Lee, "The Runaway Girl: A Reaction to Family Stress," *American Journal of Orthopsychiatry* 34:763–67 (1964).

88. William Wattenberg and Frank Saunders, "Sex Differences among Juvenile Court Offenders," *Sociology and Social Research* 39:24–31 (1954).

89. Don Gibbons and Manzer Griswold, "Sex Differences among Juvenile Court Referrals," *Sociology and Social Research* 42:106–10 (1957).

90. Gordon Barker and William Adams, "Comparison of the Delinquencies of Boys and Girls," *Journal of Criminal Law, Criminology, and Police Science* 53:470–75 (1962).

91. George Calhoun, Janelle Jurgens, and Fengling Chen, "The Neophyte Female Delinquent: A Review of the Literature," *Adolescence* 28:461–71 (1993).

92. Joanne Belknap, Kristi Holsinger, and Melissa Dunn, "Understanding Incarcerated Girls: The Results of a Focus Group Study" *Prison Journal* 77:381–405 (1997).

93. Kimberly Barletto, "Who's at Risk: Delinquent Trajectories of Children with Attention and Conduct Problems." Paper presented at the American Society of Criminology meeting, San Diego, November 1997; Veronica Herrera, "Equals in Risk? The Differential Impact of Family Violence on Male and Female Delinquency." Paper presented at the American Society of Criminology meeting, San Diego, November 1997.

94. Meda Chesney-Lind, "Girls' Crime and Women's Place: Toward a Feminist Model of Female Delinquency." Paper presented at the American Society of Criminology meeting, Montreal, November 1987.

95. Ibid., p. 20.

96. Joan Moore, *Going Down to the Barrio: Homeboys and Homegirls in Change* (Philadelphia: Temple University Press, 1991), p. 93.

97. Ibid., p. 101.

98. D. Wayne Osgood, Janet Wilson, Patrick O'Malley, Jerald Bachman, and Lloyd Johnston, "Routine Activities and Individual Deviant Behaviors," *American Sociological Review* (1996).

99. Deborah Babcox and Madeline Belken, *Liberation: NOW* (New York: Dell, 1971).

100. Simon, *The Contemporary Woman and Crime*; Freda Adler, *Sisters in Crime* (New York: McGraw-Hill, 1975).

101. Adler, *Sisters in Crime.*

102. Ibid., p. 104.

103. Ibid., pp. 10–11.

104. Rita James Simon, "Women and Crime Revisited," *Social Science Quarterly* 56:658–63 (1976).

105. Ibid., pp. 660–61.

106. Roy Austin, "Women's Liberation and Increase in Minor, Major, and Occupational Offenses," *Criminology* 20:407–30 (1982).

107. Michael Hindelang, "Age, Sex, and the Versatility of Delinquency Involvements," *Social Forces* 14:525–34 (1971).

108. Martin Gold, *Delinquent Behavior in an American City* (Belmont, CA: Brooks/Cole, 1970), p. 118; John Clark and Edward Haurek, "Age and Sex Roles of Adolescents and Their Involvement in Misconduct: A Reappraisal," *Sociology and Social Research* 50:495–508 (1966); Nancy Wise, "Juvenile Delinquency in Middle-Class Girls," in E. Vaz, ed., *Middle Class Delinquency* (New York: Harper & Row, 1967), pp. 179-88; Gary Jensen and Raymond Eve, "Sex Differences in Delinquency: An Examination of Popular Sociological Explanations," *Criminology* 13:427–48 (1976).

109. Beth Bjerregaard and Carolyn Smith, "Gender Differences in Gang Participation and Delinquency," *Journal of Quantitative Criminology* 9:329–50 (1993).

110. Henry Brownstein, Barry Spunt, Susan Crimmins, and Sandra Langley, "Women Who Kill in Drug Market Situations," *Justice Quarterly* 12:472–98 (1995).

111. Jerald Bachman, Lloyd Johnston, and Patrick O'Malley, *Monitoring the Future: Questionnaire Responses from the Nation's High School Seniors, 2000* (Ann Arbor, MI: Institute for Social Research, 2001).

112. Darrell Steffensmeier, "National Trends in Female Arrests, 1960–1990: Assessment and Recommendations for Research" *Journal of Quantitative Criminology* 9:411–37 (1993).

113. Carol Smart, "The New Female Offender: Reality or Myth?" *British Journal of Criminology* 19:50–59 (1979).

114. Roy Austin, "Recent Trends in Official Male and Female Crime Rates: The Convergence Controversy," *Journal of Criminal Justice* 21:447–66 (1993).

115. Beth Bjerregaard and Carolyn Smith, "Gender Differences in Gang Participation, Delinquency, and Substance Abuse," *Journal of Quantitative Criminology* 9:329–55 (1993).

116. Austin, "Recent Trends in the Male and Female Crime Rate," p. 464.

117. Jean Bottcher, "Social Practices of Gender: How Gender Relates to Delinquency in the Everyday Lives of High-Risk Youths," *Criminology* 39:893–932 (2001).

118. Julia Schwendinger and Herman Schwendinger, *Rape and Inequality* (Beverly Hills: Sage, 1983).

119. For a review of feminist theory, see Sally Simpson, "Feminist Theory, Crime and Justice," *Criminology* 27:605–32 (1989).

120. Ibid., p. 611.

121. Messerschmidt, *Masculinities and Crime.*

122. Center for Research on Women, *Secrets in Public: Sexual Harassment in Our Schools* (Wellesley, MA: Wellesley College, 1993).

123. Belknap, Holsinger, and Dunn, "Understanding Incarcerated Girls."

124. Kathleen Daly and Meda Chesney-Lind, "Feminism and Criminology," *Justice Quarterly* 5:497–538 (1988).

125. Jane Siegel and Linda Meyer Williams, "Aggressive Behavior among Women Sexually Abused as Children." Paper

presented at the American Society of Criminology meeting, Phoenix, 1993. Revised version.

126. James Messerschmidt, *Capitalism, Patriarchy and Crime* (Totowa, NJ: Rowman and Littlefield, 1986); for a critique of this work, see Herman Schwendinger and Julia Schwendinger, "The World According to James Messerschmidt," *Social Justice* 15:123–45 (1988).

127. John Hagan, A. R. Gillis, and John Simpson, "The Class Structure and Delinquency: Toward a Power-Control Theory of Common Delinquent Behavior," *American Journal of Sociology* 90:1151–78 (1985); John Hagan, John Simpson, and A. R. Gillis, "Class in the Household: A Power-Control Theory of Gender and Delinquency," *American Journal of Sociology* 92:788–816 (1987).

128. Gary Jensen and Kevin Thompson, "What's Class Got to Do with It? A Further Examination of Power-Control Theory," *American Journal of Sociology* 95:1009–23 (1990); Kevin Thompson, "Gender and Adolescent Drinking Problems: The Effects of Occupational Structure," *Social Problems* 36:30–44 (1989). For some critical research, see Simon Singer and Murray Levine, "Power Control Theory, Gender and Delinquency: A Partial Replication with Additional Evidence on the Effects of Peers," *Criminology* 26:627–48 (1988).

129. John Hagan, A. R. Gillis, and John Simpson, "Clarifying and Extending Power Control Theory," *American Journal of Sociology* 95:1024–37 (1990).

130. Brenda Sims Blackwell, "Perceived Sanction Threats, Gender, and Crime: A Test and Elaboration of Power-Control Theory," *Criminology* 38:439–88 (2000).

131. Christopher Uggen, "Class, Gender, and Arrest: An Intergenerational Analysis of Workplace Power and Control," *Criminology* 38:835–62 (2001).

132. Laura Abrams and Laura Curran, "Wayward Girls and Virtuous Women: Social Workers and Female Juvenile Delinquency in the Progressive Era," *Journal of Women & Social Work* 15:49–65 (2000).

133. Meda Chesney-Lind, "Judicial Enforcement of the Female Sex Role: The Family Court and the Female Delinquent," *Issues in Criminology* 8:51–59 (1973).

134. Jill Leslie Rosenbaum and Meda Chesney-Lind, "Appearance and Delinquency: A Research Note," *Crime and Delinquency* 40:250–61 (1994).

135. Sealock and Simpson, "Unraveling Bias in Arrest Decisions."

136. John MacDonald and Meda Chesney-Lind, "Gender Bias and Juvenile Justice Revisited: A Multiyear Analysis," *Crime and Delinquency* 47:173–95 (2001).

137. Meda Chesney-Lind and Vickie Paramore, "Are Girls Getting More Violent? Exploring Juvenile Robbery Trends," *Journal of Contemporary Criminal Justice* 17:142–66 (2001).

138. Belknap, Holsinger, and Dunn, "Understanding Incarcerated Girls."

139. *Juvenile Justice: Minimal Gender Bias Occurred in Processing Noncriminal Juveniles* (Gaithersburg, MD: General Accounting Office, 1995).

7 The Family and Delinquency

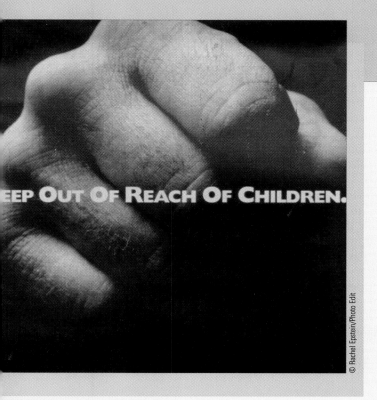

EEP OUT OF REACH OF CHILDREN.

© Rachel Epstein/Photo Edit

Y ou are an investigator with the county bureau of social services. A case has been referred to you by a middle school's head guidance counselor. It seems that a young girl, Emily M., has been showing up to school in a dazed and listless condition. She has had a hard time concentrating in class and seems withdrawn and uncommunicative. The 13-year-old has missed more than a normal share of school days and has often been late to class. Last week, she seemed so lethargic that her homeroom teacher sent her to the school nurse. A physical examination revealed that she was malnourished and in poor physical health. She also had evidence of bruising that could only come from a severe beating. Emily told the nurse that she had been punished by her parents for doing poorly at school and for failing to do her chores at home.

When her parents were called to school to meet with the principal and guidance counselor, they claimed to be members of a religious order that believes children should be punished severely for their misdeeds. Emily had been placed on a restricted diet as well as beaten with a belt to correct her misbehavior. When the guidance counselor asked them if they would be willing to go into family therapy, they were furious and told her to "mind her own business." "It's a sad day," they said, "when God-fearing American citizens cannot bring up their children according to their religious beliefs." The girl is in no immediate danger insofar as her punishment has not been life threatening.

The case is then referred to your office. When you go to see the parents at home, they refuse to make any change in their behavior and claim they are in the right and you represent all that is wrong with society. The "lax" discipline you suggest leads to drugs, sex, and other teenage problems.

- Would you get a court order removing Emily from her house and requiring the parents to go into counseling?

- Would you report the case to the district attorney's office so that criminal action could be taken against her parents under the state's Child Protection Act?

- Would you take no further action, reasoning that Emily's parents have the right to discipline their child as they see fit?

- Would you talk with Emily and see what she wants to happen?

syndrome

abuse

familicide

nuclear family A family unit composed of parents and their children; this smaller family structure is subject to great stress due to the intense, close contact between parents and children.

Cases like Emily's illustrate the often volatile family relationships that many experts believe are the key ingredients in the development of the emotional deficits eventually leading to long-term social problems.[1] Interactions between parents and children, and between siblings, provide opportunities for children to acquire or inhibit antisocial behavior patterns.[2] Children living in high-crime areas are able to resist the temptation of the streets if they receive fair discipline and support from parents who provide them with positive role models.[3] However, children in affluent families who are being raised in a household characterized by abuse and conflict, or whose parents are absent or separated, will still be at risk for delinquency.[4] Nor is the relationship between family life and delinquency unique to U.S. culture; cross-national data support a significant association between family variables and delinquency.[5]

The assumed relationship between delinquency and family life is critical today because the American family is changing. Extended families, once common, are now for the most part anachronisms. In their place is the **nuclear family,** described as a "dangerous hot-house of emotions" because of the close contact between parents and children; in these families problems are unrelieved by contact with other kin living nearby.[6]

The nuclear family is showing signs of breakdown. Much of the responsibility for childrearing is delegated to television and daycare providers. Despite these changes, some families are able to continue functioning as healthy units, producing well-adjusted children. Others have crumbled under the stress, severely damaging their children.[7] This is particularly true when child abuse and neglect become part of family life.

Because these issues are critical for understanding delinquency, this chapter is devoted to an analysis of the family's role in producing or inhibiting delinquency. First, the changing face of the American family is covered; followed by a review of the way family structure and function influence delinquent behavior. The relationship between child abuse, neglect, and delinquency is covered in some depth. Finally, programs designed to improve family functioning are briefly reviewed.

The Changing American Family

The so-called traditional family, with a male breadwinner and a female who cares for the home, is a thing of the past. No longer can this family structure be considered the norm. Changing sex roles have created a family in which women play a much greater role in the economic process; this has created a more egalitarian family structure. About three quarters of all mothers of school-age children are employed, up from 50 percent in 1970 and 40 percent in 1960. The changing economic structure may be reflected in shifting sex roles. Fathers are now spending more time with their children on workdays than they did 20 years ago (2.3 hours versus 1.8), and women are spending somewhat less time (3.3 hours versus 3.0).[8] On their days off, both working men and women spend about an hour more with their children than they did 20 years ago, with women devoting about 8 hours, and men 6. So, although the time spent with children may be less than would be desirable, it has increased over the past 20 years.

Family Makeup

The proportion of American households that have children living with both parents has declined substantially. The number of single mothers increased from 3 million to

10 million between 1970 and 2000; over the same time frame, the number of single fathers increased also, from 393,000 to 2 million.[9] The percentage of children living in two-parent families has declined from 76 percent in 1980 to 68 percent today, while the percentage of kids living with one parent increased from 20 percent to 27 percent over the same period. Today about 23 percent of youth live in mother-only families, as compared to 4 percent living in father-only families (5% live with neither parent).

Family disruption takes its greatest toll on minority youth. Over half of all black children (51%) live in mother-only families, compared with 27 percent of Hispanic children, 16 percent of non-Hispanic white children, and 15 percent of Asian children.[10] Since 1980, the number of children in African American families living with two parents has declined from 64 percent to 35 percent; during the same period, the percentage of white children living with two parents has declined from 90 percent to 74 percent. As many as 40 percent of white children and 75 percent of African American children will experience parental separation or divorce before they reach age 16, and many of these children will experience multiple family disruptions over time.[11]

One reason that the number of children living in mother-only homes is on the rise is simply because more single women than ever are deciding to keep and raise their children; about 30 percent of all births are to unmarried women. Although the teen birthrate has been declining, more than 500,000 babies are born to teenage mothers every year, about 200,000 to girls under age 18.

Childcare

Charged with caring for children is a daycare system whose workers are often paid minimum wage. Of special concern are "family daycare homes," in which a single provider takes care of three to nine children. Several states neither license nor monitor these private providers. Even in states that mandate registration and inspection of daycare providers, it is estimated that 90 percent or more of the facilities operate "underground." It is not uncommon for one adult to care for eight infants, an impossible task regardless of training or concern.

Children from working poor families are most likely to suffer from inadequate childcare; these children often spend time in makeshift arrangements that allow their parents to work but lack the stimulating environment children need to thrive.[12] About 3.5 million children under age 13 spend some time at home alone each week while their parents are at work.

Economic Stress

The family is also undergoing economic stress. The majority of indigent families live in substandard housing without adequate health care, nutrition, or childcare. Those whose incomes place them above the poverty line are deprived of government assistance. Recent political trends suggest that the social "safety net" is under attack, and poor families can expect less government aid in the coming years.

Will this economic pressure be reduced in the future? The number of senior citizens is on the rise. As people retire, there will be fewer workers to cover the costs of Social Security, medical care, and nursing home care. These costs will put greater economic stress on families. Voter sentiment has an impact on the allocation of public funds, and there is concern that an older generation, worried about health care costs, may be reluctant to spend tax dollars on at-risk kids.

The Family's Influence on Delinquency

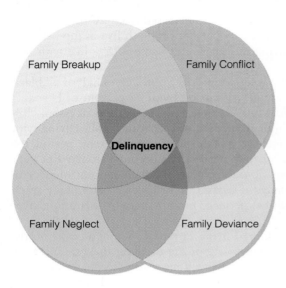

Figure 7.1
Family Influences on Behavior
Each of these four factors has been linked to antisocial behavior and delinquency. Interaction between these factors may escalate delinquent activity.

broken home Home in which one or both parents are absent due to divorce or separation; children in such an environment may be prone to antisocial behavior.

blended families Nuclear families that are the product of divorce and remarriage; blending one parent from each of two families and their combined children into one family unit.

Most experts believe a disturbed home environment can have a significant impact on delinquency. The family is the primary unit in which children learn the values and attitudes that guide their actions throughout their lives. Family disruption or change can have a long-lasting effect on children.

Four categories of family dysfunction seem to promote delinquent behavior: families disrupted by spousal conflict or breakup, families involved in interpersonal conflict, negligent parents who are not attuned to their children's behavior and emotional problems, and families that contain deviant parents who may transmit their behavior to their children (Figure 7.1).[13] These factors may interact; for example, drug-abusing parents may be more likely to engage in family conflict, child neglect, and marital breakup. We now turn to the specific types of family problems that have been linked to delinquent behavior.

Family Breakup

One of the most enduring controversies in the study of delinquency is the relationship between a parent absent from the home and the onset of delinquent behavior. Research indicates that parents whose marriage is secure produce children who are secure and independent.[14] In contrast, children growing up in homes with one or both parents absent may be prone to antisocial behavior.

A number of experts contend that a **broken home** is a strong determinant of a child's law-violating behavior. The connection seems self-evident because a child is first socialized at home. Any disjunction in an orderly family structure could be expected to have a negative impact on the child.

The suspected broken home–delinquency relationship is important because, if current trends continue, less than half of all children born today will live continuously with their own mother and father throughout childhood. And because stepfamilies, or so-called **blended families,** are less stable than families consisting of two biological parents, an increasing number of children will experience family breakup two or even three times during childhood.[15]

A number of studies indicate that children who have experienced family breakup are more likely to demonstrate behavior problems and hyperactivity than children in intact families.[16] Family breakup is often associated with conflict, hostility, and aggression; children of divorce are suspected of having lax supervision, weakened attachment, and greater susceptibility to peer pressure.[17] And, as a recent study of more than 4,000 youths in Denver, Pittsburgh, and Rochester found, the more often children are forced to go through family transitions, the more likely they are to engage in delinquent activity.[18]

Effects of Divorce The relationship between broken homes and delinquency was established in early research, which suggested that a significant association existed between parental absence and youthful misconduct.[19] Other efforts showed that parental absence seemed to affect girls, white youths, and the affluent more than it did males, minorities, and the indigent.[20] But the link was clear: Children growing up in broken homes were much more likely to fall prey to delinquency than those who lived in two-parent households. Considering this view, it is not surprising that as the number of single-parent households in the population surged, so too did the juvenile crime rate.[21]

MILLIONS OF CASES OF ABUSE are reported to child protection agencies each year. Children who are without proper care and support are at risk for abuse. Here the Rev. Joseph Combs (left) and his wife, Evangeline, await sentencing in Sullivan County Criminal Court in Blountville, Tenn., April 25, 2000. Joseph Combs was sentenced to 114 years in prison for aggravated kidnapping, aggravated assault, perjury, and multiple rape counts. Mrs. Combs was sentenced to 65 years in prison for kidnapping and aggravated child abuse. The couple was convicted of abusing a girl they took from an orphanage but never adopted. Mrs. Combs' attorney, Joe Harrison, is in background.

A CLOSER VIEW

What is the effect of an absent father on family functioning? To find out, go to Linda J. Pfiffner, Keith McBurnett, and Paul J. Rathouz, "Father Absence and Familial Antisocial Characteristics," *Journal of Abnormal Child Psychology* 29(5):357 (October 2001) on Info-Trac College Edition.

Not all delinquency experts concur on the divorce-delinquency link. Some argue that the studies that show an association between broken homes and delinquency used the records of police, courts, and correctional institutions.[22] This research may be tainted by sampling bias. Youths from broken homes may get arrested more often than youths from intact families, but this does not necessarily mean they engage in more frequent and serious delinquent behavior. Official statistics may reflect the fact that agents of the justice system treat children from disrupted households more severely because they cannot call on parents for support. The *parens patriae* philosophy of the juvenile courts calls for official intervention when parental supervision is considered inadequate.[23] Researchers concluded that the absence of parents has a greater effect on agents of the justice system than it does on the behavior of children.[24]

These suspicions are substantiated by numerous studies, using self-report data, that have failed to establish any clear-cut relationship between broken homes and delinquent behavior.[25] Boys and girls from intact families seem as likely to self-report delinquency as those whose parents are divorced or separated. And even when self-reports do show that children from intact homes commit less crime, there is evidence that their responses may be invalid: Kids from intact homes tend to underreport their antisocial activity, while kids from single-parent homes are more honest and accurate.[26]

Divorce Reconsidered Though some researchers still question the divorce-delinquency link, there is growing sentiment that family breakup is traumatic and most likely has a direct influence on factors related to adolescent misbehavior.[27] In her study of the effects of parental absence on children, sociologist Sara McLanahan finds that children who grow up apart from their biological fathers typically do less well than children who grow up with both biological parents. They are less likely to finish high school and attend college, less likely to find and keep a steady job, and more likely to become teen mothers. Although most children who grow up with a single parent do quite well, differences between children in one- and two-parent families are significant, and there is fairly good evidence that father absence per se is responsible for some social problems.[28] The traumas resulting from divorce are the subject of a widely read book, *The Unexpected Legacy of Divorce*, which is profiled in the accompanying Focus on Delinquency box.

Family Conflict

intrafamily conflict An environment of discord and conflict within the family; children who grow up in dysfunctional homes often exhibit delinquent behaviors, having learned at a young age that aggression pays off.

Not all unhappy marriages end in divorce; some continue in an atmosphere of conflict. **Intrafamily conflict** is a common experience in many American families.[29] The link between parental conflict and delinquency was established almost 40 years ago when F. Ivan Nye found that a child's perception of his or her parents' marital happiness was a significant predictor of delinquency.[30] Contemporary studies have also found that children who grow up in maladapted homes and witness discord or violence later exhibit emotional disturbance and behavior problems.[31] There seems to be little difference between the behavior of children who merely *witness* intrafamily violence and those who are its *victims*.[32] In fact, some research efforts show that observing the abuse of a parent (mother) is a more significant determinant of delinquency than being the target of child abuse.[33]

Research efforts have consistently supported the relationship between family conflict, hostility, and delinquency.[34] Adolescents who are incarcerated report growing up in dysfunctional homes.[35] Parents of beyond-control youngsters have been found to be inconsistent rule setters, to be less likely to show interest in their children, and to display high levels of hostile detachment.[36]

Although damaged parent-child relationships are associated with delinquency, it is difficult to assess the relationship. It is often assumed that preexisting family problems

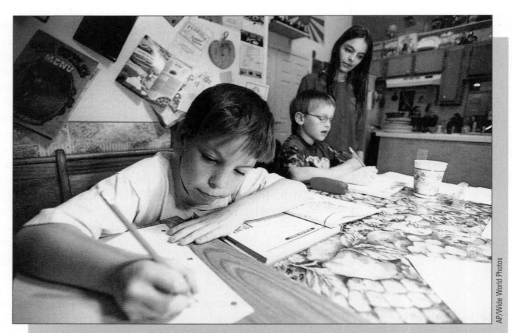

IMPROVED PARENTING SKILLS may be key to reducing the incidence of child abuse. Here, Nicholas, 9 (left), and his brother, Jared, 7, get help with homework from their mom, Wendy Hastie, at their home in Nashville, Tenn. Wendy Hastie and her husband recently completed a Youth Village treatment program so they could learn to cope better with behavioral and health problems experienced by Jared. The program stresses early intervention in an attempt to head off problems before a juvenile breaks the law.

Does Divorce Matter? Two Opposing Views on Families in Crisis

Does divorce matter? Are the children of divorced couples more at risk for antisocial behavior than those who reside in intact homes? Two recent and well-received books reach startlingly opposite conclusions on this important matter.

In their 2000 book, *The Unexpected Legacy of Divorce*, Judith Wallerstein, Julia M. Lewis, and Sandra Blakeslee report on the findings of a longitudinal study, begun in the early 1970s, with 131 children whose parents divorced during their adolescence. Wallerstein and her associates check in with 93 of the original 131 children and extensively profile 5 children who most embody the common life experiences of the larger group. They follow their lives in detail through adolescence, delving into their love affairs, their marital successes and failures, and the parenting of their own children.

The researchers find that the effects of divorce on children are not short term and transient but long lasting and cumulative. Children of divorce develop lingering fears about their *own* ability to develop long-term relationships; these fears often impede their ability to marry and raise families. While most spouses are able to reduce their emotional pain and get on with their lives a few years after they divorce, this is not true of their children, whose emotional turmoil may last for decades. The children often find it emotionally draining to spend time with their noncustodial parents and resent the disruption for years afterward. Some of the children in the study felt they had been an "inconvenience" and that their parents fit them in around their schedules. Considering their emotional turmoil, it is not surprising that these kids exhibit high levels of drug and alcohol abuse and, for girls, precocious sexuality. Consequently, only 40 percent of the kids they follow, many in their late 20s to early 30s, have ever married (compared to 81% of men and 87% of women in the general population). Some subjects told the researchers that marriage seemed impossible because their traumatic home life gave them no clue what a loving relationship was actually like.

In some cases, the parents' intense love/hate relationship that developed during marriage never ends, and parents continue to battle for years after separating; some collapse emotionally and physically. The authors document how some kids cope with long-term psychological turmoil by taking on the job of family caregiver. They become nurse, analyst, mentor, and confidant to their parents. One told them how, at 10 years old, she would spend time with her insomniac mother watching television and drinking beer at midnight. She frequently stayed home from school to make sure that her mother would not become depressed and suicidal or take the car out when she was drinking. Such personal burdens compromise the child's ability to develop friendships and personal interests. Such children may feel both trapped and guilty when they put their own needs ahead of the needy parent.

Wallerstein and her associates find that adolescents who grew up in homes where they experienced divorce are now struggling with the fear that their relationships will fail like those of their parents. Lacking guidance and experience, they must invent their own codes of behavior in a culture that offers few guidelines on how to become successful, protective parents themselves. This development has serious consequences, considering the theoretical importance placed on the development of positive family relationships as an inhibitor of delinquency and adult criminality.

For Better or for Worse

In 2002, award-winning psychologist E. Mavis Hetherington and writing partner John Kelly presented data from her study conducted over a 30-year period of more than 1,400 families and 2,500 children. Rather than the tumultuous event described by Wallerstein, Hetherington sees divorce as part of a series of a life transitions that can be destructive in the short term but actually have positive benefits in the long run. Divorce creates an opportunity for long-term personal growth. If the ex-partners can bring a sense of maturity to the dissolution of their relationship and have enough material and personal strength to become autonomous, they will be able to weather the short-term upheaval of separation. Within five or six years of separating they stand a good chance of becoming much happier than they were while married. Of course, those ex-partners whose personalities render them impulsive and antisocial have a diminished chance of turning their lives around.

Hetherington finds that children of divorce may undergo some trauma, but for the most part they are much better off than those Wallerstein encountered. While children in single-parent families and stepfamilies have more psychological problems than those in intact families, more than 75 percent ultimately do as well as children from intact families. Though divorce is a painful experience, most go on to establish careers, create intimate relationships, and build meaningful lives.

Although Hetherington's picture of the aftermath of divorce is somewhat rosier than Wallerstein's, she too finds peril in family breakup. After six years, about one quarter of her sample had contact with their noncustodial father once a year or less. Many women report anxiety six years after the breakup, and stepfathers often find it difficult to connect with the kids in their blended families; many stop trying after a few years of frustration.

Critical Thinking

1. Considering the long-term effects of divorce, should we make it more difficult to dissolve marriages—for example, by doing away with the concept of no-fault divorce and requiring stringent reasons for obtaining a separation?
2. Should it be more difficult to get married? Should couples be forced to go through counseling and education programs before being granted a marriage license? We do it for driving, why not marriage?
3. Which researcher, Wallerstein or Hetherington, paints a more accurate picture of the aftermath of family dissolution?

InfoTrac College Edition Research

Use *divorce* as a keyword on InfoTrac College Edition in order to conduct research on its effect on children.

Source: Judith S. Wallerstein, Julia M. Lewis, and Sandra Blakeslee, *The Unexpected Legacy of Divorce* (New York: Hyperion, 2000); E. Mavis Hetherington and John Kelly, *For Better or for Worse: Divorce Reconsidered* (New York: W. W. Norton, 2002).

A CLOSER VIEW

Does family conflict cause delinquency? To find out, go to InfoTrac College Edition and read Deborah Gorman-Smith, Patrick H. Tolan, Rolf Loeber, and David B. Henry, "Relation of Family Problems to Patterns of Delinquent Involvement among Urban Youth," *Journal of Abnormal Child Psychology* 26(5):319 (October 1998).

cause delinquency, but it may also be true that children who act out put enormous stress on a family. Kids who are conflict-prone may actually help to destabilize households. To avoid escalation of a child's aggression, these parents may give in to their children's demands. The children learn that aggression pays off.[37]

Parents may feel overwhelmed and shut their child out of their lives. Adolescent misbehavior may be a precursor of family conflict; strife leads to more adolescent misconduct, producing an endless cycle of family stress and delinquency.[38]

Family Conflict vs. Broken Homes   Which is worse, growing up in a home marked by conflict or growing up in a broken home? Research shows that children in both broken homes and high-conflict intact homes are worse off than children in low-conflict intact families.[39] However, children in high-conflict intact families appear to exhibit lower levels of adjustment than children in families where the parents had divorced. See Exhibit 7.1 for other key findings on divorce.

Family Neglect/Support

parental efficacy   The ability of parents to effectively raise their children in a noncoercive fashion.

Many experts believe children need a warm, supportive relationship with their parents.[40] Parents who are supportive and effectively control their children in a noncoercive fashion—**parental efficacy**—are more likely to raise children who refrain from delinquency.[41] Delinquency will be reduced if parents provide the type of structure that integrates children into families while giving them the ability to assert their individuality and regulate their own behavior.[42]

Evidence of the link between the quality of family life and delinquency comes in many forms. Children who feel inhibited with their parents and refuse to discuss important issues with them are more likely to engage in deviant activities. Poor child-parent communications have been related to dysfunctional activities such as running away, and in all too many instances these children enter the ranks of homeless street youths who get involved in theft and prostitution to survive.[43] In contrast, even children who appear to be at risk are better able to resist involvement in delinquent activity when they report a strong attachment to their parents.[44] The importance of close relations with the family may diminish as children reach late adolescence and develop stronger peer-group relations, but most experts believe family influence remains considerable throughout life.[45]

Inconsistent Discipline   Studies show that the parents of delinquent youths tend to be inconsistent disciplinarians, either overly harsh or extremely lenient.[46] But what conclusions can we draw from this observation?

The link between discipline and deviant behavior is uncertain. Most Americans still support the use of corporal punishment to discipline children. The use of phys-

Exhibit 7.1   The Family Structure–Delinquency Link

- Children growing up in families disrupted by parental death are better adjusted than children of divorce. Parental absence is not per se a cause of antisocial behavior.
- Remarriage does not mitigate the effects of divorce on youth: Children living with a stepparent exhibit (a) as many problems as youths in divorce situations and (b) considerably more problems than do children living with both biological parents.
- Continued contact with the noncustodial parent has little effect on a child's well-being.
- Evidence that the behavior of children of divorce improves over time is inconclusive.
- Postdivorce conflict between parents is related to child maladjustment.

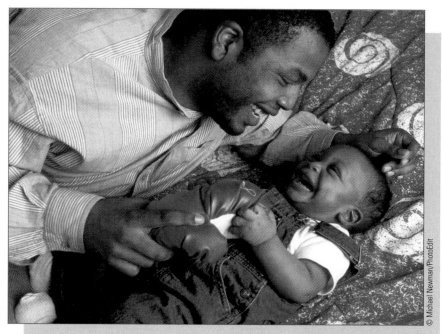

EFFECTIVE CHILDREARING PRACTICES must begin early in the life course. Parents who are supportive and effectively control their children in a noncoercive fashion are more likely to raise children who refrain from delinquency; this is referred to as *parental efficacy*. Delinquency will be reduced if parents provide the type of structure that integrates children into families while giving them the ability to assert their individuality and regulate their own behavior.

ical punishment cuts across racial, ethnic, and religious groups.[47] However, despite this public support, there is growing evidence of a "violence begetting violence" cycle. Children who are subject to even minimal amounts of physical punishment may be more likely to use violence themselves. Murray Straus reviewed the concept of discipline in a series of surveys and found a powerful relationship between exposure to physical punishment and later aggression.[48] Physical punishment weakens the bond between parents and children, lowers the children's self-esteem, and undermines their faith in justice. It is not surprising, then, that Straus finds a high correlation between physical discipline and street crime. It is possible that physical punishment encourages children to become more secretive and dishonest.[49] Overly strict discipline may have an even more insidious link to antisocial behaviors: Abused children have a higher risk of neurological dysfunction than the nonabused, and brain abnormalities have been linked to violent crime.[50]

The corporal punishment–crime relationship has been supported by cross-national research studies. Nonviolent societies are also ones in which parents rarely punish their children physically; there is a link between corporal punishment, delinquency, spousal abuse, and adult crime.[51] Research conducted in 10 European countries shows that the degree to which parents and teachers approve of corporal punishment is related to the homicide rate.[52]

Although the evidence linking corporal punishment to delinquency seems overwhelming, recent research by Ronald Simons and his associates indicates that the effects may be mitigated if parents are otherwise warm and supportive. Using samples from the United States and Taiwan, Simons found that kids who are routinely physically punished are no more likely to engage in antisocial behavior than those who are never so punished, if parents also provide support, warmth, and care. When kids experience physical punishment in the absence of parental involvement, they feel angry and unjustly treated and are more willing to defy their parents and engage in antisocial behavior.[53]

Supervision   Evidence also exists that inconsistent supervision can promote delinquency. F. Ivan Nye found that mothers who threatened discipline but failed to carry it out were more likely to have delinquent children than those who were consistent in their discipline.[54] Contemporary research supports this finding with evidence that assaultive boys tend to grow up in homes in which there is inconsistent discipline.[55]

There is ample evidence that effective supervision can reduce children's involvement in delinquency. Youths who believe their parents care little about their activities are more likely to engage in criminal acts than those who believe their actions will be closely monitored.[56] But simply having parents present in the household is not enough. Effective supervision is not a function of the number of parents in the home but reflects the style and quality of parenting.[57] For example, some critics have suggested that working mothers are unable to adequately supervise their children, leaving them prone to delinquency. However, recent research by Thomas Vander Ven and his associates found that having a mother who is employed has little if any effect on youthful misbehavior, especially if the children are adequately supervised.[58] Parents who closely supervise their children, and have close ties with them, help to reduce the likelihood of adolescent delinquent behavior.[59]

Family Size   Parents may find it hard to control their children because they have such large families that resources, such as time, are spread too thin (referred to as **resource dilution**). Larger families are more likely than smaller ones to produce delinquents, and middle children are more likely than first- or last-born children to engage in delinquent acts.

Some sociologists assume that large family size has a direct effect on delinquency, attributing this phenomenon to stretched resources and the relatively limited supervision parents can provide for each child.[60] It is also possible that the relationship is indirect, caused by the connection of family size to some external factor; for example, resource dilution has been linked to educational underachievement, long considered a correlate of delinquency.[61] Middle children may suffer because they are most likely to be home when large numbers of siblings are also at home and economic resources are most stretched.[62]

The current trend is that affluent, two-wage-earner families are having fewer children, whereas indigent, single-parent households are growing larger. Children are at a greater risk of being both poor and delinquent because indigent families are the ones most likely to have more children.[63]

resource dilution   As the number of children in a family increases, the social and economic resources available to raise them are spread thinner and become less effective.

Family Deviance

A number of studies have found that parental deviance has a powerful influence on delinquent behavior.[64] Parental deviance disrupts the family's role as an agent of social control.[65] Some of the most important data on parental deviance were gathered by Donald J. West and David P. Farrington as part of the Cambridge Youth Survey. Their data (see Chapter 5) indicate that a significant number of delinquent youths have criminal fathers.[66] About 8 percent of the sons of noncriminal fathers became chronic offenders, compared to 37 percent of youths with criminal fathers.[67] In another analysis, Farrington found that one type of parental deviance, bullying, may be both inter- and intragenerational. Bullies have children who bully others, and these "second-generation bullies" grow up to become the fathers of children who are also bullies.[68] (See Chapter 9 for more on bullying.)

The cause of intergenerational deviance is uncertain. Genetic, environmental, psychological, and childrearing factors may all play a role. One finding that supports a genetic basis is that fathers of youths who suffer attention deficit hyperactivity disorder (ADHD), a condition linked to delinquency, are five times more likely to suffer antisocial personality disorder (APD) than fathers of non-ADHD youths.[69] This linkage may be evidence that aggressive tendencies are inherited. Similarly, research on the sons of alcoholics shows that they suffer from neurological impairments related to delinquency.[70] It is possible that parental alcoholism causes genetic problems related to developmental impairment or that the children of substance-abusing parents are more prone to neurological impairment.

As with other forms of contributors to delinquency, the quality of family life may also be key. Criminal parents may be least likely to have close relationships with their offspring, and research confirms that substance-abusing or criminal parents are more likely to use harsh and inconsistent discipline, a factor linked to delinquent behavior.[71] This association may be reinforced by stigmatization of children of known deviants. Social control agents may be quick to fix a "delinquent" label on the children of known law violators.[72] In sum, though there is some agreement that criminal parents produce delinquent offspring, the specific nature of the relationship is unknown.[73]

contagion effect The negative, crime-promoting influence of deviant siblings on their brothers and sisters.

Sibling Influences   Evidence exists that siblings may also influence behavior; this is referred to as the **contagion effect**.[74] Siblings who report warm relationships and share friends are the most likely to behave in a similar fashion; those who maintain a close relationship also report similar rates of drug abuse and delinquency.[75]

A number of interpretations of this data are possible. Siblings who live in the same environment are influenced by similar social and economic factors. Another possibility is that deviant siblings grow closer because of shared interests. It is possible that the relationship is due to personal interactions: Younger siblings imitate older siblings.

The contagion effect may explain in part the higher concordance of deviant behaviors found in identical twins as compared to fraternal twins or mere siblings. (See Chapter 3.) The relationship between identical twins may be stronger and more enduring than the one between other sibling pairs so that contagion and not genetics explains their behavioral similarities. According to Marshall Jones and Donald Jones, the contagion effect may also help explain aspects of the aging-out process.[76] They suggest that a great deal of offending is done with peers, and peer influence has a significant effect on juvenile offending rates. Boys who commit delinquent acts with their friends may desist as adults because as people mature, they marry, get jobs, and their social group dissolves. If peer influence shapes delinquency, its effect wanes as youth groups and cliques split up in adulthood. In contrast, twin relationships are everlasting, and one twin's antisocial behavior legitimizes and supports the criminal behavior of the other twin, an effect which may grow even stronger in adulthood. What seems to be a genetic effect may actually be the result of sibling interaction with a brother or sister who engages in antisocial activity.

In summary, the research on delinquency and family relationships offers ample evidence that family life can be a potent force in a child's development. The delinquent child is likely to grow up in a large family with parents who may drink, participate in criminal acts, be harsh and inconsistent in their discipline, be cold and unaffectionate, have marital conflicts, and be poor role models. Overall, the quality of a child's family life seems to be more important than its structure.

A provocative new book by psychologist Judith Rich Harris challenges the prevailing wisdom that family life is a critical determinant of a child's behavior. Harris's concepts are discussed in the Focus on Delinquency, "Do Families Matter?"

Child Abuse and Neglect

Family violence is a critical priority for criminal justice officials, political leaders, and the public.[77] Concern about the quality of family life has increased because of reports that many children are physically abused or neglected by their parents and that this treatment has serious consequences for their behavior. Because of this topic's importance, the remainder of this chapter is devoted to the issue of child abuse and neglect and its relationship to delinquent behavior.

Do Families Matter?

The prevailing wisdom is that the family is the key determinant of a child's attitudes, values, and behavior. However, in a controversial book, *The Nature Assumption,* psychologist Judith Rich Harris questions the cherished belief that parents play an important, if not the most important, role in a child's upbringing. Instead of family influence, Harris claims that genetics and environment determine, to a large extent, how a child turns out. Children's own temperament and peer relations shape their behavior and modify the characteristics they were born with; their interpersonal relations determine the kind of people they will be when they mature.

Harris reasons that parenting skills may be irrelevant to children's future success. Most parents don't have a single childrearing style, and they may treat each child in the family independently. They are more permissive with their mild-mannered kids and more strict and punitive with those who are temperamental or defiant. Even if every child were treated the same in a family, this would not explain why siblings raised in the same family under relatively similar conditions turn out so differently. Those sent to daycare are quite similar to those who remain at home; having working parents seems to have little long-term effect. Family structure also does not seem to matter: Adults who grew up in one-parent homes are as likely to be successful as those who were raised in two-parent households.

If parenting has little direct influence on children's long-term development, what does? While Harris concedes that genetics plays the most important role in behavior, she asserts that the child's total social environment is the other key influence that shapes behavior. Kids who act one way at home may be totally different at school or with their peers. Some who are mild mannered around the house are hell-raisers in the schoolyard, whereas others who bully their siblings are docile with friends. Children may conform to parental expectations at home but leave those expectations behind in their own social environment. Children develop their own culture with unique traditions, words, rules, and activities, which often conflict with parental and adult values. What parents encourage their children to pierce their bodies or get tattoos? If we are to accept Harris's vision, parents should

become close to their children because they want to have them as companions and friends and not because it will improve their life chances.

Even those who disagree vehemently with Harris's research findings—and there are many—have been influenced by her book, which forced them to develop valid counterarguments. Some, such as the distinguished psychologist Eleanor MacCoby, now see parenting less in terms of one-parent-to-child influence, and more as a set of interactive processes during which parents and children react to each other and influence each other from the moment a child is born. It is foolish, MacCoby claims, to distinguish between genetics and environment, because in reality they are intertwined from the moment of birth.

Critical Thinking

1. Some studies now show that a given parenting style can have different effects on children with different temperaments. The result is that parenting can function to make children in the same family different rather than alike. From your own experiences, do parents treat all siblings in the family in a similar fashion, or are there clear intersibling differences? How might parenting style influence children's behavior within a family?

InfoTrac College Edition Research

 To find out whether Harris's analysis of family functioning is correct, use *family* as a keyword on InfoTrac College Edition.

Sources: Judith Rich Harris, *The Nature Assumption, Why Children Turn Out the Way They Do* (New York: Free Press, 1998); also Beth Azar, "A Forthcoming Book Details Evidence of How, When and in What Context Parents Influence Child Development—and Where They Might Not," *APA Monitor on Psychology* 31 (2000); Eleanor MacCoby, *The Two Sexes: Growing Up Apart, Coming Together* (Cambridge, MA: Belknap Press, 1999).

A Historical Perspective

Parental abuse and neglect are not modern phenomena. Maltreatment of children has occurred throughout history. Some concern for the negative effects of such maltreatment was voiced in the eighteenth century in the United States, but concerted efforts to deal with the problem did not begin until 1874. In that year, residents of a New York City apartment building reported to a public health nurse, Etta Wheeler, that a child in one of the apartments was being abused by her stepmother. The nurse found a young child named Mary Ellen Wilson, who had been repeatedly beaten and was malnourished from a diet of bread and water. Even though the child was seriously ill, the police agreed that the law entitled the parents to raise Mary Ellen as they saw fit. The New York City Department of Charities claimed it had no custody rights over Mary Ellen.

According to legend, Mary Ellen's removal from her parents had to be arranged through the Society for the Prevention of Cruelty to Animals (SPCA) on the grounds that she was a member of the animal kingdom. The truth, however, is less sensational:

American Humane Society

IN 1874 HENRY BUGH AND ETTA ANGELL WHEELER persuaded a New York court to take a child, Mary Ellen, away from her mother on the grounds of child abuse. This is the first recorded case in which a court was used to protect a child. Mary Ellen is shown at age 9 when she appeared in court showing bruises from a whipping and several gashes from a pair of scissors. The other photograph shows her a year later.

Mary Ellen's case was heard by a judge. Because the child needed protection, she was placed in an orphanage.[78] The SPCA was actually founded the following year.[79]

Little research into the problems of maltreated children occurred before that of C. Henry Kempe, at the University of Colorado. In 1962, Kempe reported the results of a survey of medical and law enforcement agencies that indicated the child abuse rate was much higher than had been thought. He coined a term, **battered child syndrome,** which he applied to cases of nonaccidental injury of children by their parents or guardians.[80]

battered child syndrome
Nonaccidental physical injury of children by their parents or guardians.

Defining Abuse and Neglect

child abuse Any physical, emotional, or sexual trauma to a child, including neglecting to give proper care and attention, for which no reasonable explanation can be found.

neglect Passive neglect by a parent or guardian, depriving children of food, shelter, health care, and love.

Kempe's pioneering work has been expanded in a more generic expression of **child abuse** that includes neglect as well as physical abuse. Specifically, it describes any physical or emotional trauma to a child for which no reasonable explanation, such as an accident, can be found. Child abuse is generally seen as a pattern of behavior rather than a single act. The effects of a pattern of behavior are cumulative. That is, the longer the abuse continues, the more severe the effect will be.[81]

Although the terms *child abuse* and **neglect** are sometimes used interchangeably, they represent different forms of maltreatment. Neglect refers to deprivations children suffer at the hands of their parents (lack of food, shelter, health care, love). Abuse is a more overt form of aggression against the child, one that often requires medical attention. The distinction between the terms is often unclear because, in many cases, both abuse and neglect occur simultaneously.

Physical abuse includes throwing, shooting, stabbing, burning, drowning, suffocating, biting, or deliberately disfiguring a child. The greatest number of injuries result from beatings. *Physical neglect* results from parents' failure to provide adequate food, shelter, or medical care for their children, as well as failure to protect them from physical danger.

Emotional abuse or neglect is manifested by constant criticism and rejection of the child.[82] Those who suffer emotional abuse have significantly lower self-esteem as adults.[83] *Emotional neglect* includes inadequate nurturing, inattention to a child's emotional development, and lack of concern about maladaptive behavior.

Sexual abuse refers to the exploitation of children through rape, incest, and molestation by parents, family members, friends, or legal guardians. Finally, **abandonment** refers to the situation in which parents leave their children with the intention of severing the parent-child relationship.[84]

There are a variety of legal definitions of abuse, but almost all contain concepts such as nonaccidental physical injury, physical neglect, emotional abuse or neglect, sexual abuse, and abandonment.[85]

abandonment Parents physically leave their children with the intention of completely severing the parent-child relationship.

Sexual Abuse

Sexual abuse can vary in content and style. It may range from rewarding children for sexual behavior that is inappropriate for their level of development to using force or the threat of force for the purposes of sex. It can involve children who are aware of the sexual content of their actions and others too young to have any idea what their actions mean. It can involve a variety of acts, from inappropriate touching to forcible sexual penetration.

The effects of sexual abuse can be devastating. Abused children suffer disrupted ego and personality development.[86] Guilt and shame are common. The ego of the victim may be overwhelmed by rage and horror over the incident, and the experience can have long-lasting repercussions.

Research indicates a correlation between the severity of abuse and its long-term effects: The less serious the abuse, the more quickly the child can recover.[87] Children who are frequently abused over long periods and suffer actual sexual penetration are most likely to experience long-term trauma, including post-traumatic stress disorder (PTSD), precocious sexuality, and poor self-esteem.[88] Some victims find themselves sexualizing their own children in ways that lead those children to sexual or physical abuse. Several studies have found a close association between sexual abuse and adolescent prostitution.[89] Finally, girls who were sexually and physically abused as children are more often suicidal as adults than the nonabused.[90]

A recent national survey on the sexual exploitation of children conducted by researchers at the University of Pennsylvania indicates that the problem may be much more widespread than previously thought. The Focus on Delinquency box entitled "The Sexual Exploitation of Children" looks at their research in depth.

The Extent of Child Abuse

It is almost impossible to estimate the extent of child abuse. Many victims are so young that they have not learned to communicate. Some are too embarrassed or afraid. Many incidents occur behind closed doors, and even when another adult witnesses inappropriate or criminal behavior, the adult may not want to get involved in a "family matter." There are a number of different ways of measuring the extent of child abuse, and some of the most important ones are discussed next.

Survey Data   Some indications of the severity of the problem came from a 1980 survey conducted by sociologists Richard Gelles, Murray Straus, and Suzanne Steinmentz.[91] Gelles and Straus estimated that between 1.4 and 1.9 million children in the

The Sexual Exploitation of Children

In a detailed study of child sexual exploitation in North America, Richard J. Estes and Neil Alan Weiner found that the problem of child sexual abuse is much more widespread than has been previously believed or documented. Estes and Weiner, two researchers at the School of Social Welfare at the University of Pennsylvania, relied on interviews with victims, child welfare workers, and law enforcement officials in 28 cities in the United States, Mexico, and Canada from January 1999 through March 2001. They also used the latest estimates on the number of runaway and homeless youths in the three countries and on estimates by law enforcement officials and child welfare authorities of the estimated number of sexually exploited children.

Their research indicated that each year in the United States 325,000 children are subjected to some form of sexual exploitation, including sexual abuse, prostitution, use in pornography, and molestation by adults. Most are likely to be white and middle class. Equal numbers of boys and girls are involved, but the activities of boys generally receive less attention from authorities. Many of these kids are runaways (more than 120,000), while others had fled mental hospitals and foster homes. More than 50,000 had been thrown out of their home by a parent or guardian.

Who were the sexual exploiters? Most of the sexual assaults had been committed by relatives and acquaintances, such as a teacher, coach, or a neighbor; and only 4 percent by strangers. Abusers were nearly all men and about a quarter of them were married with children.

Once they fled an abusive situation at home, the kids become vulnerable to life on the streets. Some get hooked into the sex trade, starting as strippers and lap dancers, and drifting into prostitution and pornography. Some meet pimps, who quickly turn them to a life of prostitution and beat them if they do not make their daily financial quotas. Others who fled to the streets exchange sex for money, food, and shelter. Some have been traded between prostitution rings, while others are shipped from city to city and even sent overseas as prostitutes. About 20 percent of sexually exploited children were involved in prostitution rings that worked across state lines. Table A lists some of the sexual exploitation endured by these children.

Table A **Exploitation of Children**

Girls	Boys	Both Sexes
Stripping, topless dancing	Gay sex paid for by adult males	Sexual molestation by family and acquaintances
Sex exploitations in gangs	Commercial sex, hustling	Pornography
Pimp-controlled prostitution		Participation in national and international crime networks that transport children for sexual purposes

Critical Thinking

1. Estes and Weiner maintain that there are serious gaps in policies and services to combat sexual exploitation and provide help to victims. They suggest increasing penalties, enforcing existing laws more vigorously, and expanding the federal government's role in combating abuse. Should special laws be created that would punish those who traffic in children more harshly than if their victims were adults? For example, would you recommend a life sentence for someone who exploits children in a prostitution ring?
2. Is the sexual exploitation of children essentially a hate crime?

InfoTrac College Edition Research

Juvenile prostitution and sexual exploitation are worldwide phenomena. To read more about them, use *Prostitution, juvenile* as a subject guide on InfoTrac College Edition.

Source: Richard J. Estes and Neil Alan Weiner, *The Commercial Sexual Exploitation of Children in the U.S., Canada and Mexico* (Philadelphia: University of Pennsylvania, 2001).

United States were subject to physical abuse from their parents. This abuse was rarely a one-time act. The average number of assaults per year was 10.5, and the median was 4.5. Gelles and Straus also found that 16 percent of the couples in their sample reported spousal abuse; 50 percent of the multichild families reported attacks between siblings; 20 percent of the families reported incidents in which children attacked parents.[92]

The Gelles and Straus survey was a milestone in identifying child abuse as a national phenomenon. Surveys conducted in 1985 and 1992 indicated that the incidence of severe violence toward children had declined.[93] One reason was that parental approval of corporal punishment, which stood at 94 percent in 1968, decreased to 68 percent by 1994.[94] Recognition of the problem may have helped moderate cultural values and awakened parents to the dangers of physically disciplining children. Nonetheless, more than 1 million children were still being subjected to severe violence annually. If the definition of "severe abuse" used in the survey had included hitting with objects such as a stick or a belt, the number of child victims would have been closer to 7 million per year.

Cases Reported to Child Protection Services   Not all child abuse and neglect cases are reported to authorities, but those that are become the focus of state action. Child protective services (CPS) agencies receive referrals from educators, law enforcement personnel, social workers, parents, and concerned neighbors alleging that children have been abused or neglected. While some reports are considered unfounded, many others are "screened in" and investigated, indicating that the referral was deemed appropriate for investigation or assessment. The U.S. Department of Health and Human Services conducts annual surveys of CPS agencies in order to assess the nature and trends in reported abuse.[95] The most recent survey indicates that approximately 3 million referrals are received each year, and about 60 percent are transferred for investigation. Of these, slightly less than one-third of investigations (29%) resulted in a disposition of either substantiated or indicated child maltreatment. Consequently, there were an estimated 826,000 substantiated victims of maltreatment nationwide in 1999, a rate of victimization of 11.8 per 1,000 children (a decline from the rate of 12.6 per 1,000 recorded in 1998). While the data indicate that child abuse may be in decline, the total number of reports nationwide has increased more than 40 percent since 1988.[96] The number of substantiated cases corresponds with the results of the surveys conducted by Gelles, Straus, and their associates.

Though abuse rates may now be in decline, an estimated 1,100 children died of abuse and neglect, a rate of approximately 1.62 deaths per 100,000 children in the general population. Children younger than a year old accounted for 42.6 percent of the fatalities, and 86.1 percent were younger than 6 years of age. Some of the most important findings from the CPS survey are listed in Exhibit 7.2.

Cases Reported to the Police   There have also been attempts to review cases of child abuse reported to local police departments. Using data from 12 states, David Finkelhor and Richard Ormrod found that child abuse constituted a significant portion of all crimes against children and that parents and caretakers were responsible for the majority of these cases.[97] Their data show that large numbers of parental child abuse cases are, in fact, reported to the police. These incidents are predominantly

Exhibit 7.2   Findings from the National Survey of Child Protective Services

Victims

- Almost three-fifths of all victims (58.4%) suffered neglect, while one-fifth (21.3%) suffered physical abuse; 11.3 percent were sexually abused. More than one-third (35.9%) of all victims were reported to be victims of other or additional types of maltreatment.
- The highest victimization rates were for the 0–3 age group (13.9 maltreatments per 1,000 children of this age in the population), and rates declined as age increased.
- Rates of many types of maltreatment were similar for male and female children, but the sexual abuse rate for female children (1.6 female children for every 1,000 female children in the population) was higher than the sexual abuse rate for male children (0.4 male children per 1,000).
- Victimization rates by race/ethnicity ranged from a low of 4.4 Asian/Pacific Islander victims per 1,000 children of the same race in the population to 25.2 African American victims per 1,000.
- Children who had been victimized prior to 1999 were almost three times more likely to experience recurrence during the six months following their first victimization

in 1999 than children without a prior history of victimization.

Perpetrators

- Three-fifths (61.8%) of perpetrators were female. Female perpetrators were typically younger than their male counterparts—41.5 percent were younger than 30 years of age, compared to 31.2 percent of male perpetrators.
- Almost nine-tenths (87.3%) of all victims were maltreated by at least one parent. The most common pattern of maltreatment was a child victimized by a female parent acting alone (44.7%).
- Female parents were identified as the perpetrators of neglect and physical abuse for the highest percentage of child victims. In contrast, male parents were identified as the perpetrators of sexual abuse for the highest percentage of victims.

Source: U.S. Department of Health and Human Services, Administration on Children, Youth and Families, *Child Maltreatment 1999* (Washington, DC: U.S. Government Printing Office, 2001).

Exhibit 7.3   Child Abuse Cases Reported to the Police

- Incidents of child abuse committed by parents and other caretakers make up about one-fifth (19%) of violent crimes against juveniles (ages 0–17) reported to the police and 4 percent of violent crimes against persons of any age.
- The majority (73%) of these parent and other caretaker crimes are physical assaults, and 23 percent are cases of sexual abuse.
- Child abuse constitutes more than one-half of the crimes against children age 2 or younger reported to the police.
- Male offenders are responsible for three-quarters of the child abuse incidents reported to the police, including 92 percent of sexual assaults and 68 percent of physical assaults.
- Thirteen percent of the episodes of parental assault against a child reported to the police are associated with an assault against a spouse or former spouse.
- In spite of protocols in some states that require police notification about child maltreatment, there is evidence that police data tally only a fraction of physical and sexual abuse investigated and substantiated by child welfare authorities.

Source: David Finkelhor and Richard Ormrod, "Child Abuse Cases Reported to the Police," *Juvenile Justice Bulletin* (Washington, DC: Office of Juvenile Justice and Delinquency Prevention, 2001).

physical assaults, involve more older than younger children, and involve more male than female caretakers. Only about one-half of these cases are associated with any recorded injury to the victim. The most important of Finkelhor and Ormrod's findings are contained in Exhibit 7.3.

Reports of Sexual Abuse   Attempts to determine the extent of sexual abuse indicate that perhaps 1 in 10 boys and 1 in 3 girls have been the victims of some form of sexual exploitation. An oft-cited survey by Diana Russell found that 16 percent of women reported sexual abuse by a relative, and 4.5 percent reported abuse by a father or stepfather.[98] It has been estimated that 30 percent to 75 percent of women in treatment for substance-abuse disorders experienced childhood sexual abuse.[99]

While sexual abuse is still quite prevalent, the number of reported cases has been in a significant decline. Research by Lisa Jones and David Finkelhor of the University of New Hampshire's Crimes Against Children Research Center shows that after a 15-year increase, substantiated child sexual-abuse cases in the United States dropped 31 percent between 1992 to 1998. Most states (36 out of the 47 they reviewed) showed declines of at least 30 percent.[100] This data could mean that the actual number of cases is truly in decline because of the effectiveness of prevention programs, increased prosecution, and public awareness campaigns. It could also mean that more cases are getting overlooked because of (1) increased evidentiary requirements to substantiate cases, (2) increased caseworker caution due to new legal rights for caregivers, and (3) increasing limitations on the types of cases that agencies accept for investigation.[101]

Causes of Child Abuse and Neglect

Maltreatment of children is a complex problem with neither a single cause nor a single solution. It cuts across racial, ethnic, religious, and socioeconomic lines. Abusive parents cannot be categorized by sex, age, or educational level.

Of all factors associated with child abuse, three are discussed most often: (1) parents who themselves suffered abuse tend to abuse their own children; (2) the presence of an unrelated adult increases the risk of abuse; and (3) isolated and alienated families tend to become abusive. A cyclical pattern of violence seems to be perpetuated from one generation to another. Evidence indicates that a large number of abused and neglected children grow into adulthood with a tendency to engage in violent behavior. The behavior of abusive parents can often be traced to negative experiences in their own childhood—physical abuse, emotional neglect, and incest. These parents become unable to separate their own childhood traumas from their relationships with their children. Abusive parents often have unrealistic perceptions of normal development. When their children are unable to act appropriately—when they cry or strike their parents—the parents may react in an abusive manner.[102] Parents may also become abusive if they are isolated from friends, neighbors, or relatives.

Many abusive parents describe themselves as alienated from their extended families, and they lack close relationships with persons who could provide help in stressful situations.[103] The relationship between alienation and abuse may be particularly acute in homes where there has been divorce or separation, or in which parents have never actually married; abusive punishment in single-parent homes has been found to be twice that of two-parent families.[104] Parents who are unable to cope with stressful events—divorce, financial stress, recurring mental illness, drug addiction—are most at risk.[105]

Substance Abuse and Child Abuse   Abusive families suffer from severe stress, and it is therefore not surprising that they frequently harbor members who turn to drugs and alcohol. Studies have found a strong association between child abuse and parental alcoholism.[106]

In addition, evidence exists of a significant relationship between cocaine and heroin abuse and neglect and abuse of children. Because this relationship is so important, it is explored further in the Focus on Delinquency box entitled "Relationship between Substance Abuse and Child Maltreatment."

Stepparents and Abuse   Research indicates that stepchildren share a greater risk for abuse than do biological offspring.[107] Stepparents may have less emotional attachment to someone else's children. Often the biological parent has to choose between the new mate and the child, sometimes even becoming an accomplice in the abuse.[108]

familicide Mass murders in which a spouse and one or more children are slain.

Stepchildren are overrepresented in cases of **familicide,** mass murders in which a spouse and one or more children are slain. It is also more common for fathers who kill their biological children to commit suicide than those who kill stepchildren, an indication that the biological parent's act was motivated by despair, the stepparent's by hostility.[109]

Social Class and Abuse   Surveys indicate a high rate of reported abuse and neglect among people in lower economic classes. Children from families earning less than $15,000 per year experience more abuse than children living in more affluent homes.[110] More than 40 percent of CPS workers indicate that most of their clients either live in poverty or face increased financial stress due to unemployment and economic recession.[111] These findings suggest that parental maltreatment of children is predominantly a lower-class problem. Is this conclusion valid?

It is possible that the statistics are generally accurate. Low-income families, especially those headed by a single parent, are often subject to greater environmental stress and have fewer resources for dealing with such stress than families with higher incomes.[112] A relationship seems to exist between the burdens of raising a child without adequate resources and the use of excessive force. Self-report surveys do show that indigent parents are more likely than affluent parents to hold attitudes that condone physical chastisement of children.[113]

Higher rates of maltreatment in low-income families reflect the stress caused by the limited resources lower-class parents have to help them in raising their children; in contrast, middle-class parents devote a smaller percentage of their total resources to raising a family.[114] This burden becomes especially onerous in families with emotionally and physically handicapped children. Stressed-out parents may consider special-needs children a drain on the family's finances with little potential for future success; research finds that children with disabilities are maltreated at a rate almost double that of other children.[115]

Relationship between Substance Abuse and Child Maltreatment

The relationship between parental alcohol or other drug problems and child maltreatment is becoming increasingly evident. It is a serious problem because substance abuse is so widespread: An estimated 14 million adult Americans abuse alcohol, and there may be more than 12 million illicit drug users. With more than 6 million children under the age of 18 living in alcoholic households, and an additional number living in households where parents have problems with illicit drugs, it is evident that a significant number of children in this country are being raised by addicted parents.

Do Parental Alcohol or Other Drug Problems Cause Child Maltreatment?

Recent research on the connection between these problems and child maltreatment clearly indicates a connection between the two behaviors. Among confirmed cases of child maltreatment, 40 percent involve the use of alcohol or other drugs. This suggests that of the almost 1 million confirmed victims of child maltreatment each year, an estimated 480,000 children are mistreated by a caretaker with alcohol or other drug problems. Additionally, research suggests that alcohol and other drug problems are factors in a majority of cases of emotional abuse and neglect. In fact, neglect is the major reason that children are removed from a home in which parents have alcohol or other drug problems. Children in these homes suffer from a variety of physical, mental, and emotional health problems at a greater rate than do children in the general population. Children of alcoholics suffer more injuries and poisonings than do children in the general population. Alcohol and other substances may act as disinhibitors, lessening impulse control and allowing parents to behave abusively. Children in this environment often demonstrate behavioral problems and are diagnosed as having conduct disorders. This may result in provocative behavior. Increased stress resulting from preoccupation with drugs on the part of the parent combined with behavioral problems exhibited by the child increases the likelihood of maltreatment. Frequently, these parents suffer from depression, anxiety, and low self-esteem. They live in an atmosphere of stress and family conflict. Children raised in these types of households are themselves more likely to have problems with alcohol and other drugs.

How Does a Parent's Alcohol or Other Drug Problem Affect Children?

Children of alcoholics are more likely than children in the general population to suffer a variety of physical, mental, and emotional health problems. They often have feelings of low self-esteem and failure and suffer from depression and anxiety. It is thought that exposure to violence in both alcohol-abusing and child-maltreating households increases the likelihood that the children will commit, and be recipients

of, acts of violence. The effects don't end when these children reach adulthood; they may have difficulty with coping and with establishing healthy relationships as adults. In addition to suffering from all the effects of living in a household where alcohol or child-maltreatment problems exist, children whose parents abuse illicit drugs live with the knowledge that their parents' actions are illegal. While research is in its infancy, clinical evidence shows that children of parents who have problems with illicit drug use may suffer from an inability to trust legitimate authority because of fear of discovery of a parent's illegal habits.

As they mature, many fall victim to the same patterns exhibited by their parents. Those who have been severely physically abused often have symptoms of post-traumatic stress disorder and dissociation. Individuals suffering from mental health disorders may use alcohol and illicit drugs to decrease or mitigate their psychological distress. Research suggests that adults who were abused as children may be more likely to abuse their own children than adults who were not abused as children.

Can child maltreatment, when alcohol or other drugs are a problem, be successfully treated? Research has shown that when families exhibit both of these behaviors, the problems must be treated simultaneously in order to ensure a child's safety. Although ending the drug dependency does not automatically end child maltreatment, very little can be done to improve parenting skills until this step is taken. The withdrawal experienced by parents who cease using alcohol or other drugs presents specific risks. The effects of withdrawal often cause a parent to experience intense emotions, which may increase the likelihood of child maltreatment. During this time, lasting as long as two years, it is especially important that resources be available to the family.

Critical Thinking

1. While it would seem that parental substance abuse is a significant cause of child maltreatment, is it possible that the relationship is spurious? Is it possible that the same factors causing substance abuse also produce maltreatment? Consequently, might not abusive parents continue their violence, even if they did not drink or take drugs?

InfoTrac College Edition Research

 To learn more about the damaging effects of parental substance abuse on children, use the term as a subject guide on InfoTrac College Edition.

Source: "The Relationship between Parental Alcohol or Other Drug Problems and Child Maltreatment" (Chicago: Prevent Child Abuse America, 2000).

The Child Protection System: Philosophy and Practice

To access the Child Abuse Prevention and Treatment Act (CAPTA), go to *http://www.acf. dhhs.gov/programs/cb/policy/ capta.htm* For an up-to-date list of Web links, go to *http://info.wadsworth.com/siegel*

For most of the nation's history, courts have assumed that parents have the right to bring up their children as they see fit. In the 2000 case *Troxel v. Granville*, the Supreme Court ruled that the due process clause of the Constitution protects against government interference with certain fundamental rights and liberty interests, including parents' fundamental right to make decisions concerning the care, custody, and control of their children.[116] If the care a child receives falls below reasonable standards, the state may take action to remove a child from the home and place her or him in a less threatening environment. In these extreme circumstances, the rights of both parents and children are constitutionally protected. In the cases of *Lassiter v. Department of Social Services* and *Santosky v. Kramer,* the U.S. Supreme Court recognized the child's right to be free from parental abuse and set down guidelines for a termination-of-custody hearing, including the right to legal representation.[117] States provide a guardian *ad litem* (a lawyer appointed by the court to look after the interests of those who do not have the capacity to assert their own rights). States also ensure confidentiality of reporting.[118]

Though child protection agencies have been dealing with abuse and neglect since the late nineteenth century, recent awareness of the problem has prompted judicial authorities to take increasingly bold steps to ensure the safety of children.[119] The assumption that the parent-child relationship is inviolate has been challenged. In 1974 Congress passed the Child Abuse Prevention and Treatment Act (CAPTA), which provides funds to states to bolster their services for maltreated children and their parents.[120] The act provides federal funding to states in support of prevention, investigation, and treatment. It also provides grants to public agencies and nonprofit organizations for demonstration programs.

The Child Abuse Prevention and Treatment Act has been the impetus for the states to improve the legal frameworks of their child protection systems. Abusive parents are subject to prosecution under statutes against assault, battery, and homicide. Many states have child abuse statutes that make it a felony to injure and abuse children.

Investigating and Reporting Abuse   Maltreatment of children can easily be hidden from public view. Although state laws require doctors, teachers, and others who work with children to report suspected cases to child protection agencies, many maltreated children are out of the law's reach because they are too young for school or because their parents do not take them to a doctor or a hospital. Parents abuse their children in private and, even when confronted, often accuse their children of lying, or blame the children's medical problems on accidents. Social service agencies must find more effective ways to locate abused children and to handle such cases once found.

All states have statutes requiring that persons suspected of abuse and neglect be reported. Many have made failure to report child abuse a criminal offense. Though such statutes are rarely enforced, teachers have been criminally charged for failing to report abuse or neglect cases.[121]

Once reported to a child protection agency, the case is screened by an intake worker and then turned over to an investigative caseworker. Protective service workers often work with law enforcement officers. If the caseworker determines that the child is in imminent danger of severe harm, the caseworker may immediately remove the child from the home. A court hearing must be held shortly after to approve the custody. Stories abound of children erroneously taken from their homes, but it is much more likely that these "gatekeepers" will consider cases unfounded and take no action. More than 50 percent of all reported cases are so classified.[122] Among the most common reasons for screening out cases is that the reporting party is involved in a child custody case.[123]

Even when there is compelling evidence of abuse, most social service agencies will try to involve the family in voluntary treatment. Case managers will do periodic follow-ups to determine whether treatment plans are being followed. If parents are uncooperative or if the danger to the children is so great that they must be removed from the home, a complaint will be filed in the criminal, family, or juvenile court system.

The Process of State Intervention   Although procedures vary from state to state, most follow a similar legal process once a social service agency files a court petition alleging abuse or neglect.[124] This process is diagrammed in Figure 7.2.

If the allegation of abuse is confirmed, the child may be placed in protective custody. Most state statutes require that the court be notified "promptly" or "immediately" if the child is removed; some states, including Arkansas, North Carolina, and Pennsylvania, have gone as far as requiring that no more than 12 hours elapse before official action is taken. If the child has not been removed from the home, state authorities are given more time to notify the court of suspected abuse. For example, Louisiana and Maryland set a limit of 30 days to take action, whereas Wisconsin mandates that state action take no more than 20 days once the case has been investigated.

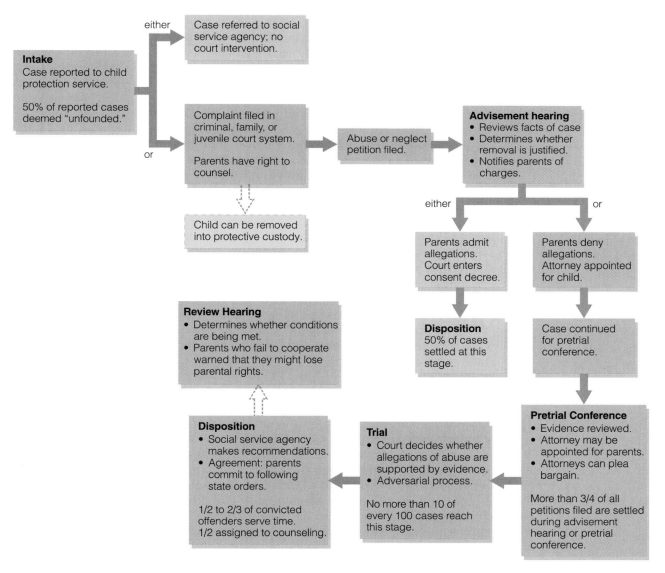

Figure 7.2
The Process of State Intervention in Cases of Abuse and Neglect

advisement hearing A preliminary protective or temporary custody hearing in which the court will review the facts and determine whether removal of the child is justified and notify parents of the charges against them.

pretrial conference The attorney for the social services agency presents an overview of the case, and a plea bargain or negotiated settlement can be agreed to in a consent decree.

disposition hearing The social service agency presents its case plan and recommendations for care of the child and treatment of the parents, including incarceration and counseling or other treatments.

balancing-of-the-interest approach Efforts of the courts to balance the parents' natural right to raise a child with the child's right to grow into adulthood free from physical abuse or emotional harm.

review hearing Periodic meetings to determine whether the conditions of the case plan for an abused child are being met by the parents or guardians of the child.

When an abuse or neglect petition is prosecuted, an **advisement hearing** (also called a *preliminary protective hearing* or *temporary custody hearing*) is held. The court will review the facts of the case, determine whether removal is justified, and notify the parents of the charges against them. Parents have the right to counsel in all cases of abuse and neglect, and many states require the court to appoint an attorney for the child as well. If the parents admit the allegations, the court enters a consent decree, and the case is continued for disposition. Approximately one-half of all cases are settled by admission at the advisement hearing. If the parents deny the petition, an attorney is appointed for the child and the case is continued for a pretrial conference.

At the **pretrial conference,** the attorney for the social service agency presents an overview of the case and the evidence. Such matters as admissibility of photos and written reports are settled. At this point the attorneys can negotiate a settlement of the case. About three-fourths of the cases that go to pretrial conference are settled by a consent decree. About 85 out of every 100 petitions filed will be settled at either the advisement hearing or the pretrial conference.

Of the 15 remaining cases, 5 will generally be settled before trial. Usually no more than 10 cases out of every 100 actually reach the trial stage of the process. This is an adversarial hearing designed to prove the state's allegations.

Disposition   The most crucial part of an abuse or neglect proceeding is the **disposition hearing.** The social service agency presents its case plan, which includes recommendations such as conditions for returning the child to the parents or a visitation plan if the child is to be taken from the parents. An agreement is reached by which the parents commit themselves to following the state orders. Between one-half and two-thirds of all convicted parents will be required to serve time in incarceration; almost half will be assigned to a form of treatment. As far as the children are concerned, some may be placed in temporary care; in other cases, parental rights are terminated and the child is placed in the custody of the child protective service. Legal custody can then be assigned to a relative or some other person.

In making their decisions, courts are guided by three interests: the role of the parents, protection for the child, and the responsibility of the state. Frequently, these interests conflict. In fact, at times even the interests of the two parents are not in harmony. The state attempts to balance the parents' natural right to control their child's upbringing with the child's right to grow into adulthood free from harm. This is referred to as the **balancing-of-the-interest approach.**

Periodically, **review hearings** are held to determine whether the conditions of the case plan are being met. Parents who fail to cooperate are warned that they may lose their parental rights. Most abuse and neglect cases are concluded within a year. Either the parents lose their rights and the child is given a permanent placement, or the child is returned to the parents and the court's jurisdiction ends.

The Abused Child in Court

One of the most significant problems associated with abuse cases is the trauma a child must go through in a court hearing. Children get confused and frightened and may change their testimony. Much controversy has arisen over the accuracy of children's reports of family violence and sexual abuse, resulting in hung juries in some well-known cases, including the McMartin Day Care case in California.[125]

State jurisdictions have instituted procedures to minimize the trauma to the child. Most have enacted legislation allowing videotaped statements, or interviews with child witnesses, taken at a preliminary hearing or at a formal deposition, to be admissible in court. Videotaped testimony spares child witnesses the trauma of testifying in open court. States that allow videotaped testimony usually put some restrictions on its use: Some prohibit the government from calling the child to testify at trial if the videotape is used; some states require a finding that the child is "medically unavailable" because of the trauma of the case before videotaping can be used; some require that the defendant be present during the videotaping; a few specify that the child not be able to see or hear the defendant.[126]

More than two-thirds of the states now allow a child's testimony to be given on closed-circuit television (CCTV). The child is able to view the judge and attorneys, and the courtroom participants are able to observe the child. The standards for CCTV testimony vary widely. Some states, such as New Hampshire, assume that any child witness under age 12 would benefit from not having to appear in court. Others require an independent examination by a mental health professional to determine whether there is a "compelling need" for CCTV testimony.

In addition to innovative methods of testimony, children in sexual abuse cases have been allowed to use anatomically correct dolls to demonstrate happenings that they cannot describe verbally. The Victims of Child Abuse Act of 1990 allows children to use these dolls when testifying in federal courts; at least eight states have passed similar legislation.[127] Similarly, states have relaxed their laws of evidence to allow out-of-court statements by the child to a social worker, teacher, or police officer to be used as evidence (such statements would otherwise be considered **hearsay**). Typically, corroboration is required to support these statements if the child does not also testify.

The prevalence of sexual abuse cases has created new problems for the justice system. Often accusations are made in conjunction with marital disputes. The fear is growing that children may become pawns in custody battles; the mere suggestion of sexual abuse is enough to affect the outcome of a divorce action. The justice system must develop techniques that can get at the truth without creating a lifelong scar on the child's psyche.

hearsay Out-of-court statements made by one person and recounted in court by another; such statements are generally not allowed as evidence except in child abuse cases wherein a child's statements to social workers, teachers, or police may be admissible.

Legal Issues   A number of cases have been brought before the Supreme Court, testing the right of children to present evidence at trial using nontraditional methods. Two issues stand out. One is the ability of physicians and mental health professionals to testify about statements made to them by children, especially when the children are incapable of testifying. The second concerns the way children testify in court.

In a 1992 case, *White v. Illinois*, the Court ruled that the state's attorney is required neither to produce young victims at trial nor to demonstrate the reason they were unavailable to serve as witnesses.[128] *White* involved statements given by the child to the child's babysitter and mother, a doctor, a nurse, and a police officer concerning the alleged assailant in a sexual assault case. The prosecutor twice tried to call the child to testify, but both times the 4-year-old experienced emotional difficulty and could not appear in court. The outcome hinged solely on the testimony of the five witnesses.

By allowing others to testify as to what the child said, *White* removed the requirement that prosecutors produce child victims in court. This facilitates the prosecution of child abusers in cases where a court appearance by a victim would prove too disturbing or where the victim is too young to understand the court process.[129] The Court noted that statements made to doctors during medical exams or those made when a victim is upset carry more weight than ones made after careful reflection. The Court ruled that such statements can be repeated during trial because the circumstances in which they were made could not be duplicated simply by having the child testify to them in court.

In-Court Statements   Children who are victims of sexual or physical abuse often make poor witnesses. Yet their testimony may be crucial. In a 1988 case, *Coy v. Iowa*, the Court placed limitations on efforts to protect child witnesses in court. During a sexual assault case, a one-way glass screen was set up so that the child victims would not be able to view the defendant (the defendant, however, could view the witnesses).[130] The Iowa statute that allowed the protective screen assumed that children would be traumatized by their courtroom experience. The Court ruled that unless there was a finding that the child witness needs special protection, the Sixth Amendment of the Constitution grants defendants "face-to-face" confrontation with their accusers. In her dissenting opinion, Justice Sandra Day O'Connor suggested that if courts found it necessary, it would be appropriate to allow children to testify via CCTV or videotape.

Justice O'Connor's views became law in *Craig v. Maryland*.[131] In this case a daycare operator was convicted of sexually abusing a 6-year-old child; one-way CCTV testimony was used during the trial. The decision was overturned in the Maryland Court of Appeals on the ground that the procedures used were insufficient to show that the child could only testify in this manner because a trial appearance would be too traumatic. On appeal, the Court ruled that the Maryland statute that allows CCTV testimony is sufficient because it requires a determination that the child will suffer distress if forced to testify. The Court noted that CCTV could serve as the equivalent of in-court testimony and would not interfere with the defendant's right to confront witnesses.

The American Bar Association maintains a Web site that has information on legal rights of children in abuse cases. Go to *http://www.abanet.org/child/capta.html* For an up-to-date list of Web links, go to *http://info.wadsworth.com/siegel*

Disposition of Abuse and Neglect Cases

There is considerable controversy over what forms of intervention are helpful in abuse and neglect cases. Today, social service agents avoid removing children from the home whenever possible and instead try to employ techniques to control abusive relationships. In serious cases, the state may remove children from their parents and place them in shelter care or foster homes. Placement of children in foster care is intended to be temporary, but it is not uncommon for children to remain in foster care for three years or more.

Ultimately, the court has the power to terminate the rights of parents over their children, but because the effects of destroying the family unit are far-reaching, the court does so only in the most severe cases. Judicial hesitancy is illustrated in a Virginia appellate case in which grandparents contested a father's being awarded custody of his children. Even though he had a history of alcohol abuse, had already been found to be an unfit parent, and was awaiting appeal of his conviction for killing the children's mother, the trial court claimed that he had turned his life around and granted him custody.[132]

Despite such occurrences, efforts have been ongoing to improve the child protection system. Jurisdictions have expedited case processing, instituted procedures designed not to frighten child witnesses, coordinated investigations between social service and law enforcement agencies, and assigned an advocate or guardian *ad litem* to children in need of protection. Efforts are also being made to help prosecutors handle abuse cases. The Office of Juvenile Justice and Delinquency Prevention (OJJDP) now funds the National Center for Prosecution of Child Abuse (the Center) to enhance investigators' and prosecutors' skills and help them handle child and adolescent abuse cases. First established in 1985, by the National District Attorneys Association, the Center serves as the nation's main resource for training, expert legal assistance, court reform, and state-of-the-art information on criminal child abuse investigations and prosecutions.[133]

Abuse, Neglect, and Delinquency

Because the effects of child abuse are long term, delinquency experts fear that abused kids will experience mental and social problems across their lifespan. For example, victims of abuse are prone to suffer mental illness such as dissociative identity disorder (DID), formerly known as multiple personality disorder (MPD); research shows that child abuse is present in the histories of the vast majority of DID subjects.[134]

One particular area of concern is the child's own personal involvement with violence. Psychologists suggest that maltreatment encourages children to use aggression as a means of solving problems and prevents them from feeling empathy for others. It diminishes their ability to cope with stress and makes them vulnerable to the violence in the culture. Abused children have fewer positive interactions with peers, are less well liked, and are more likely to have disturbed social interactions.[135]

The link between maltreatment and delinquency is also supported by a number of criminological theories. For example:

- *Social control theory* By disrupting normal relationships and impeding socialization, maltreatment reduces the social bond and frees individuals to become involved in deviance.
- *Social learning theory* Maltreatment leads to delinquency because it teaches children that aggression and violence are justifiable forms of behavior.
- *General Strain Theory* Maltreatment creates the "negative affective states" that are related to strain, anger, and aggression.

A significant amount of literature suggests that abuse may have a profound effect on behavior in later years. Exposure to abuse in early life provides a foundation for violent and antisocial behavior.[136] Delinquent behavior is the means by which many abused children act out their hostility toward their parents. Some join gangs, which furnish a sense of belonging and allow pent-up anger to be expressed in group-approved delinquent acts.

Case Studies of the Effects of Child Abuse

Studies of juvenile offenders have confirmed that between 70 percent and 80 percent may have had abusive backgrounds. Many of these juveniles reported serious injury, including bruises, lacerations, fractures, and being knocked unconscious, by a parent or guardian. Several studies have examined the incarcerated delinquent and criminal population and found that adult and juvenile inmates report much higher rates of childhood abuse and neglect than the general population.[137] National estimates indicate that approximately 4–8 percent of all children are reported to child welfare agencies as alleged victims of abuse or neglect, while more than 50 percent of court-referred juveniles have experienced abuse. For example, one study of high-risk male juvenile parolees in three states revealed that the proportion of juveniles who had allegedly been victims of abuse or neglect ranged from 29 percent in Virginia to 45 percent in Colorado to 53 percent in Nevada. Findings are similar for adult offenders. A recent study of adult offenders found that 16 percent of males and 57 percent of females in state prisons had experienced childhood physical or sexual abuse.[138]

Involvement in delinquent activity is not the only social problem for which abused kids are at risk. Compared with nonmaltreated matched control groups, abused or neglected children are significantly more likely to engage in violent behavior, become pregnant during adolescence, use drugs, have lower GPAs, and/or experience mental health problems.[139] For example, girls who are psychologically, sexually, or physically abused as children are more likely to have lower self-esteem and be more suicidal as adults than those who were not abused.[140] Kids who are victimized in the home are more likely to run away in order to escape their environment, an action which puts them at risk for juvenile arrest and involvement with the justice system.[141]

Cohort Studies of the Effects of Child Abuse

These findings do not necessarily prove that maltreatment causes delinquency. It is possible that child abuse is a reaction to misbehavior and not vice versa. In other words, it is possible that angry parents attack their delinquent and drug-abusing children and that child abuse is a *result* of delinquency, not its cause.

One way of solving this dilemma is to follow a cohort of youths who had been reported as victims of abuse and compare them with a similar cohort of nonabused youths. A classic study conducted by Jose Alfaro in New York found that about half of all children reported to area hospitals as abused children later acquired arrest records. Conversely, a significant number of boys (21%) and girls (29%) petitioned to juvenile court had prior histories as abuse cases. Children treated for abuse were disproportionately involved in violent offenses.[142]

Cathy Spatz Widom followed the offending careers of 908 youths reported as abused from 1967 to 1971 and compared them with a control group of 667 nonabused youths. Widom found that the abuse involved a variety of perpetrators, including parents, relatives, strangers, and even grandparents. Twenty-six percent of the abused sample had juvenile arrests, compared to 17 percent of the comparison group; 29 percent of those who were abused had adult criminal records, compared to 21 percent of the control group. Race, gender, and age also affected the probability that abuse would lead to delinquency. The highest-risk group comprised older black males who had suffered abuse; about 67 percent of this group went on to become adult criminals. In contrast, only 4 percent of young, white, nonabused females became adult offenders.[143] Widom's conclusion: Being abused increased the likelihood of arrest both as a juvenile and as an adult.[144]

Widom and her colleagues are now conducting a second phase of research in order to determine why some victims of childhood abuse and neglect fare well, while others experience long-term negative consequences. They located a large number of subjects 20 to 25 years after they experienced childhood victimization. Interviews with formerly abused and neglected youths have found that child abuse in early life is related to the following negative outcomes over the life course:

- Mental health concerns (suicide attempts and post-traumatic stress disorder)
- Educational problems (extremely low IQ scores and reading ability)
- Occupational difficulties (lack of work, high rates of unemployment, and employment in low-level service jobs)
- Public health and safety issues (prostitution in males and females, and alcohol problems in females)[145]

Cohort research also shows that sexually abused youths are much more likely to suffer an arrest than nonabused children. The risk is greatest if the abuse took place when the child was less than 7 years of age and the offense was committed by a male.[146] Sexually abused girls share a significant risk of becoming violent over the life course. There is also evidence that sexual abuse victims are more likely to abuse others, especially if they were exposed to other forms of family violence.[147] Self-report studies also confirm that child maltreatment increases the likelihood of delinquency. The most severely abused youths are at the greatest risk for long-term serious delinquency.[148]

The Abuse-Delinquency Link

These findings do not necessarily mean that most abused children become delinquent. Many do not, and many delinquent youths come from what appear to be model homes. Though Widom found that more abused than nonabused children in her cohort became involved in delinquency, the majority of *both* groups did not.[149]

Although these studies suggest an abuse-delinquency link, others find that the association is either nonsignificant or inconsistent (for example, having a greater influence on girls than boys).[150] Abused adolescents seem to get involved in more status offenses than delinquent acts—perhaps indicating that abused children are more likely to "flee than fight."[151] Some researchers also suggest that if there is a link between abuse and antisocial behavior later in life, the connection is shaped by the nature and type of abuse. For example, research shows that sexual offenders have suffered a history of sexual abuse but that sexual abuse may not be related to other

THIS IS A SANTA CLARA COUNTY SHERIFF BOOKING PHOTO of Rosemarie Randovan taken Nov. 6, 2000, in San Jose, Calif. Randovan was arraigned in a San Jose court-room Nov. 8, 2000, on two felony counts of child abuse. Over a period of four months, Randovan allegedly locked her sons in the trunk of her car while she worked. Police say Randovan was having trouble finding daycare for her two sons, ages 5 and 7. One of Randovan's coworkers called police after hearing moaning coming from the back of Randovan's car. What can be done to help women such as Randovan so that they do not have to resort to such desperate measures?

types of offenses; in contrast, physical abuse seems a significant variable in the history of nonsexual offenders.[152]

The Family and Delinquency Control Policy

Since the family is believed to play such an important role in the production of youth crime, it follows that improving family functioning can help prevent delinquency. Counselors commonly work with the families of antisocial youths as part of a court-ordered treatment strategy. Family counseling and therapy are almost mandatory when the child's acting-out behavior is suspected to be the result of family-related problems such as child abuse or neglect.[153] Some jurisdictions have integrated family counseling services into the juvenile court.[154]

Another approach to involving the family in delinquency prevention is to attack the problem before it occurs. Early childhood prevention programs that target at-risk youths can relieve some of the symptoms associated with delinquency.[155] Frequent home visits by trained nurses and social service personnel help reduce child abuse and other injuries to infants.[156] Evidence suggests that early intervention may be the most effective method and that the later the intervention, the more difficult the change process.[157]

Because the family plays such an important role in delinquency prevention and control policies, it is one of the focus areas in Chapter 11's discussion of delinquency prevention strategies.

SUMMARY

Poor family relationships have been linked to juvenile delinquency. Early theories viewed the broken home as a cause of youthful misconduct, but some subsequent research reached the conclusion that divorce, separation, or parental death actually plays a smaller role than was previously thought. The divorce-delinquency connection remains controversial, as more recently, experts have suggested that broken homes may indeed have a significant effect on delinquency. They argue that it is more difficult for one parent to provide the same degree of discipline and support as two. The quality of family life also has a great influence on a child's behavior. Studies have explored the effects of discipline, parental misconduct, and family harmony on youth crime.

Concern over the relationship between family life and delinquency has been heightened by reports of widespread child abuse. Cases of abuse and neglect have been found in every social class. It has been estimated that there are 3 million reported cases of child abuse each year, of which almost 1 million are confirmed by child welfare investigators. Two factors are seen as causing child abuse. First, parents who themselves suffered abuse

as children tend to abuse their own children. Second, isolated and alienated families tend to become abusive.

Local, state, and federal governments have attempted to alleviate the problem of child abuse. The major issue has been state interference in the family structure. All 50 states have statutes requiring that suspected cases of abuse be reported.

A number of studies have linked abuse to delinquency. They show that a disproportionate number of court-adjudicated youths had been abused or neglected. Although the evidence is not conclusive, it suggests that a strong relationship exists between child abuse and delinquent behavior. To make it easier to prosecute abusers, the Supreme Court has legalized the use of closed-circuit TV in some cases. Most states allow children to use anatomically correct dolls when testifying in court.

The role of the family in delinquency formation has been addressed in various prevention efforts. Family counseling and therapy are often used in cases involving antisocial youths. Some programs are geared to helping children before they engage in delinquent activities.

KEY TERMS

nuclear family	resource dilution	abandonment	balancing-of-the-interest approach
broken home	contagion effect	familicide	
blended families	battered child syndrome	advisement hearing	review hearings
intrafamily conflict	child abuse	pretrial conference	hearsay
parental efficacy	neglect	disposition hearing	

QUESTIONS FOR DISCUSSION

1. What is the meaning of the terms *child abuse* and *child neglect*?

2. Social agencies, police departments, and health groups all indicate that child abuse and neglect are increasing. What is the incidence of such action by

parents against children? Are the definitions of child abuse and child neglect the key elements in determining the volume of child abuse cases in various jurisdictions?

3. What causes parents to abuse their children?

4. What is meant by the child protection system? Do courts act in the best interest of the child when they allow an abused child to remain with the family?

5. Should children be allowed to testify in court via closed-circuit TV? Does this approach prevent defendants in child abuse cases from confronting their accusers?

6. Is corporal punishment ever permissible as a disciplinary method?

VIEWPOINT

Pedophiles and child molesters share some characteristics. Most are male, and they can be heterosexual, homosexual, or bisexual. Some prefer adult sex partners but choose children because they are available and vulnerable. The sexual abuse perpetrated may be a one-time incident and may consist only of fondling. Penetration is unlikely with young children. Perpetrators' ages range from teens to midlife. Most victims are girls, and the perpetrator usually is a relative, friend, or neighbor. The home of the victim is often the setting for the incident. When boys are victims, sexual abuse may take place outside the home, and perpetrators may be strangers. Perpetrators of sexual abuse of children often claim that they themselves were victims of childhood sexual abuse.

Who commits child sexual abuse, and what are their personal characteristics? To find out, go to the following on InfoTrac College Edition: John B. Murray, "Psychological Profile of Pedophiles and Child Molesters," *The Journal of Psychology* 134:211 (2000). For further information, use *child abuse* as a subject.

NOTES

1. Paul Amato and Bruce Keith, "Parental Divorce and the Well-Being of Children: A Meta-Analysis," *Psychological Bulletin* 110:26–46 (1991).

2. Rolf Loeber and Magda Stouthamer-Loeber, "Development of Juvenile Aggression and Violence," *American Psychologist* 53:242–59 (1998), at 250.

3. Joan McCord, "Family Relationships, Juvenile Delinquency, and Adult Criminality," *Criminology* 29:397–417 (1991); Scott Henggeler, ed., *Delinquency and Adolescent Psychopathology: A Family Ecological Systems Approach* (Littleton, MA: Wright–PSG, 1982).

4. For a general review of the relationship between families and delinquency, see Alan Jay Lincoln and Murray Straus, *Crime and the Family* (Springfield, IL: Charles C. Thomas, 1985); Rolf Loeber and Magda Stouthamer-Loeber, "Family Factors as Correlates and Predictors of Juvenile Conduct Problems and Delinquency," in Michael Tonry and Norval Morris, eds., *Crime and Justice*, vol. 7 (Chicago: University of Chicago Press, 1986), pp. 29–151.

5. David Farrington, "Juvenile Delinquency," in John Coleman, ed., *The School Years* (London: Routledge, 1992), pp. 139–40.

6. Ruth Inglis, *Sins of the Fathers: A Study of the Physical and Emotional Abuse of Children* (New York: St. Martin's Press, 1978), p. 131.

7. See Joseph J. Costa and Gordon K. Nelson, *Child Abuse and Neglect: Legislation, Reporting, and Prevention* (Lexington, MA: D.C. Heath, 1978), p. xiii.

8. Tamar Lewin, "Men Assuming Bigger Role at Home, New Survey Shows," *New York Times*, 15 April 1998, p. A18.

9. America's Families and Living Arrangements, U.S. Census Bureau, Washington, DC, 2001.

10. U.S. Census Bureau, 2000 Current Population Survey.

11. Terence P. Thornberry, Carolyn A. Smith, Craig Rivera, David Huizinga, and Magda Stouthamer-Loeber, *Family Disruption and Delinquency, Juvenile Justice Bulletin*, Sept. 1999 (Washington, DC: Office of Juvenile Justice and Delinquency Prevention, 1999).

12. News Release, "Kids Count Survey 1998," Annie E. Casey Foundation, Baltimore, May 5, 1998.

13. Loeber and Stouthamer-Loeber, "Family Factors," pp. 39–41.

14. Paul Howes and Howard Markman, "Marital Quality and Child Functioning: A Longitudinal Investigation," *Child Development* 60:1044–51 (1989).

15. Barbara Dafoe Whitehead, "Dan Quayle Was Right," *Atlantic Monthly* 271:47–84 (1993).

16. C. Patrick Brady, James Bray, and Linda Zeeb, "Behavior Problems of Clinic Children: Relation to Parental Marital

Status, Age, and Sex of Child," *American Journal of Orthopsychiatry* 56:399–412 (1986).

17. Scott Henggeler, *Delinquency in Adolescence* (Newbury Park, CA: Sage, 1989), p. 48.

18. Thornberry et al., *Family Disruption and Delinquency*.

19. Sheldon Glueck and Eleanor Glueck, *Unraveling Juvenile Delinquency* (Cambridge: Harvard University Press, 1950); Ashley Weeks, "Predicting Juvenile Delinquency," *American Sociological Review* 8:40–46 (1943).

20. Jackson Toby, "The Differential Impact of Family Disorganization," *American Sociological Review* 22:505–512 (1957); Ruth Morris, "Female Delinquency and Relation Problems," *Social Forces* 43:82–89 (1964); Roland Chilton and Gerald Markle, "Family Disruption, Delinquent Conduct, and the Effects of Sub-Classification," *American Sociological Review* 37:93–99 (1972).

21. Jukka Savolainen, "Relative Cohort Size and Age-Specific Arrest Rates: A Conditional Interpretation of the Easterlin Effect," *Criminology* 38:117–36 (2000).

22. For a review of these early studies, see Thomas Monahan, "Family Status and the Delinquent Child: A Reappraisal and Some New Findings," *Social Forces* 35:250–58 (1957).

23. Clifford Shaw and Henry McKay, *Report on the Causes of Crime, Social Factors in Juvenile Delinquency*, vol. 2 (Washington, DC: U.S. Government Printing Office, 1931), p. 392.

24. Christina DeJong and Kenneth Jackson, "Putting Race into Context: Race, Juvenile Justice Processing, and Urbanization," *Justice Quarterly* 15:487–504 (1998).

25. John Laub and Robert Sampson, "Unraveling Families and Delinquency: A Reanalysis of the Gluecks' Data," *Criminology* 26:355–80 (1988); Lawrence Rosen, "The Broken Home and Male Delinquency," in M. Wolfgang, L. Savitz, and N. Johnston, eds., *The Sociology of Crime and Delinquency* (New York: Wiley, 1970), pp. 489–95.

26. Julia Yun Soo Kim, Michael Fendrich, and Joseph Wislar, "The Validity of Juvenile Arrestees' Drug Use Reporting: A Gender Comparison," *Journal of Research in Crime and Delinquency* 37:419–32 (2000).

27. Robert Johnson, John Hoffman, and Dean Gerstein, *The Relationship between Family Structure and Adolescent Substance Abuse* (Washington, DC: Office of Applied Studies, Substance Abuse and Mental Health Services Administration, 1996); Cesaro Rebellon, "Reconsidering the Broken Homes/Delinquency Relationship and Exploring Its Mediating Mechanism(s)," *Criminology* 40:103–35 (2002).

28. Sara McLanahan, "Father Absence and the Welfare of Children." Working paper prepared for the John D. and Catherine MacArthur Research Foundation, Chicago, 1998.

29. Judith Smetena, "Adolescents' and Parents' Reasoning about Actual Family Conflict," *Child Development* 60:1052–67 (1989).

30. F. Ivan Nye, "Child Adjustment in Broken and Unhappy Unbroken Homes," *Marriage and Family* 19:356–61 (1957); idem, *Family Relationships and Delinquent Behavior* (New York: Wiley, 1958).

31. Michael Hershorn and Alan Rosenbaum, "Children of Marital Violence: A Closer Look at the Unintended Victims," *American Journal of Orthopsychiatry* 55:260–66 (1985).

32. Peter Jaffe, David Wolfe, Susan Wilson, and Lydia Zak, "Similarities in Behavior and Social Maladjustment among Child Victims and Witnesses to Family Violence," *American Journal of Orthopsychiatry* 56:142–46 (1986).

33. Veronica Herrera, "Equals in Risk? The Differential Impact of Family Violence on Male and Female Delinquency." Paper presented at the Annual Society of Criminology meeting, San Diego, November 1997.

34. Henggeler, *Delinquency in Adolescence*, p. 39.

35. Jill Leslie Rosenbaum, "Family Dysfunction and Female Delinquency," *Crime and Delinquency* 35:31–44 (1989), at 41.

36. Paul Robinson, "Parents of 'Beyond Control' Adolescents," *Adolescence* 13:116–19 (1978).

37. Loeber and Stouthamer-Loeber, "Development of Juvenile Aggression and Violence," p. 251.

38. Carolyn Smith, Sung Joon Jang, and Susan Stern, "The Effect of Delinquency on Families," *Family and Corrections Network Report* 13:1–11 (1997).

39. Amato and Keith, "Parental Divorce and the Well-Being of Children."

40. Adrian Raine, Patricia Brennan, and Sarnoff Mednick, "Interaction between Birth Complications and Early Maternal Rejection in Predisposing Individuals to Adult Violence: Specificity to Serious, Early-Onset Violence," *American Journal of Psychiatry* 154:1265–71 (1997).

41. John Paul Wright and Francis Cullen, "Parental Efficacy and Delinquent Behavior: Do Control and Support Matter," *Criminology* 39:677–706 (2001).

42. Carter Hay, "Parenting, Self-Control, and Delinquency: A Test of Self-Control Theory," *Criminology* 39:707–36 (2001).

43. Bill McCarthy and John Hagan, "Mean Streets: The Theoretical Significance of Situational Delinquency among Homeless Youth," *American Journal of Sociology* 98:597–627 (1992).

44. Carolyn Smith, Alan Lizotte, Terence Thornberry, and Marvin Krohn, "Resilience to Delinquency," *The Prevention Researcher* 4:4–7 (1997).

45. Sung Joon Jang and Carolyn Smith, "A Test of Reciprocal Causal Relationships among Parental Supervision, Affective Ties, and Delinquency," *Journal of Research in Crime and Delinquency* 34:307–36 (1997).

46. Gerald Patterson and Magda Stouthamer-Loeber, "The Correlation of Family Management Practices and Delinquency," *Child Development* 55:1299–1307 (1984); Gerald R. Patterson, *A Social Learning Approach: Coercive Family Process*, vol. 3 (Eugene, OR: Castalia, 1982).

47. Christopher Ellison and Darren Sherkat, "Conservative Protestantism and Support for Corporal Punishment," *American Sociological Review* 58:131–44 (1993).

48. Murray Straus, "Discipline and Deviance: Physical Punishment of Children and Violence and Other Crime in Adulthood," *Social Problems* 38:101–23 (1991).

49. Loeber and Stouthamer-Loeber, "Development of Juvenile Aggression and Violence," p. 251.

50. Nathaniel Pallone and James Hennessy, "Brain Dysfunction and Criminal Violence," *Society* 35:21–27 (1998).

51. Murray A. Straus, "Spanking and the Making of a Violent Society: The Short- and Long-Term Consequences of Corporal Punishment," *Pediatrics* 98:837–43 (1996).

52. Ibid.

53. Ronald Simons, Chyi-In Wu, Kuei-Hsiu Lin, Leslie Gordon, and Rand Conger, "A Cross-Cultural Examination of the Link between Corporal Punishment and Adolescent Antisocial Behavior," *Criminology* 38:47–79 (2000).

54. Nye, *Family Relationships and Delinquent Behavior.*

55. Rolf Loeber and Thomas Dishion, "Boys Who Fight at Home and School: Family Conditions Influencing Cross-Setting Consistency," *Journal of Consulting and Clinical Psychology* 52:759–68 (1984).

56. Lisa Broidy, "Direct Supervision and Delinquency: Assessing the Adequacy of Structural Proxies," *Journal of Criminal Justice* 23:541–54 (1995).

57. Stephen Cernkovich and Peggy Giordano, "Family Relationships and Delinquency," *Criminology* 25:295–321 (1987).

58. Thomas Vander Ven, Francis Cullen, Mark Carrozza, and John Paul Wright, "Home Alone: The Impact of Maternal Employment on Delinquency," *Social Problems* 48:236–57 (2001).

59. Jang and Smith, "A Test of Reciprocal Causal Relationships among Parental Supervision, Affective Ties, and Delinquency."

60. Linda Waite and Lee Lillard, "Children and Marital Disruption," *American Journal of Sociology* 96:930–53 (1991).

61. Douglas Downey, "Number of Siblings and Intellectual Development," *American Psychologist* 56:497–504 (2001); idem, "When Bigger Is Not Better: Family Size, Parental Resources, and Children's Educational Performance," *American Sociological Review* 60:746–61 (1995).

62. G. Rahav, "Birth Order and Delinquency," *British Journal of Criminology* 20:385–95 (1980); D. Viles and D. Challinger, "Family Size and Birth Order of Young Offenders," *International Journal of Offender Therapy and Comparative Criminology* 25:60–66 (1981).

63. David Eggebeen and Daniel Lichter, "Race, Family Structure, and Changing Poverty among American Children," *American Sociological Review* 56:801–17 (1991).

64. For an early review, see Barbara Wooton, *Social Science and Social Pathology* (London: Allen and Unwin, 1959).

65. Laub and Sampson, "Unraveling Families and Delinquency," p. 375.

66. D. J. West and D. P. Farrington, eds., "Who Becomes Delinquent?" in *The Delinquent Way of Life* (London: Heinemann, 1977); D. J. West, *Delinquency, Its Roots, Careers, and Prospects* (Cambridge, MA: Harvard University Press, 1982).

67. West, *Delinquency,* p. 114.

68. David Farrington, "Understanding and Preventing Bullying," in Michael Tonry, ed., *Crime and Justice,* vol. 17 (Chicago: University of Chicago Press, 1993), pp. 381–457.

69. Leonore Simon, "Does Criminal Offender Treatment Work?" *Applied and Preventive Psychology,* Summer:1–22 (1998).

70. Philip Harden and Robert Pihl, "Cognitive Function, Cardiovascular Reactivity, and Behavior in Boys at High Risk for Alcoholism," *Journal of Abnormal Psychology* 104:94–103 (1995).

71. Laub and Sampson, "Unraveling Families and Delinquency," p. 370.

72. D. P. Farrington, Gwen Gundry, and D. J. West, "The Familial Transmission of Criminality," in Alan Lincoln and Murray Straus, eds., *Crime and the Family* (Springfield, IL: Charles C. Thomas, 1985), pp. 193–206.

73. See, generally, Wooton, *Social Science and Social Pathology*; H. Wilson, "Juvenile Delinquency, Parental Criminality, and Social Handicaps," *British Journal of Criminology* 15:241–50 (1975).

74. Marshall Jones and Donald Jones, "The Contagious Nature of Antisocial Behavior," *Criminology* 38:25–46 (2000).

75. David Rowe and Bill Gulley, "Sibling Effects on Substance Use and Delinquency," *Criminology* 30:217–32 (1992); see also David Rowe, Joseph Rogers, and Sylvia Meseck-Bushey, "Sibling Delinquency and the Family Environment: Shared and Unshared Influences," *Child Development* 63:59–67 (1992).

76. Jones and Jones, "The Contagious Nature of Antisocial Behavior," p. 31.

77. Charles De Witt, director of the National Institute of Justice, quoted in National Institute of Justice, Research in Brief, *The Cycle of Violence* (Washington, DC: National Institute of Justice, 1992), p. 1.

78. Richard Gelles and Claire Pedrick Cornell, *Intimate Violence in Families,* 2nd ed. (Newbury Park, CA: Sage, 1990), p. 33.

79. Lois Hochhauser, "Child Abuse and the Law: A Mandate for Change," *Harvard Law Journal* 18:200 (1973); see also Douglas J. Besharov, "The Legal Aspects of Reporting Known and Suspected Child Abuse and Neglect," *Villanova Law Review* 23:458 (1978).

80. C. Henry Kempe, F. N. Silverman, B. F. Steele, W. Droegemueller, and H. K. Silver, "The Battered-Child Syndrome," *Journal of the American Medical Association* 181:17–24 (1962).

81. Brian G. Fraser, "A Glance at the Past, a Gaze at the Present, a Glimpse at the Future: A Critical Analysis of the Development of Child Abuse Reporting Statutes," *Chicago-Kent Law Review* 54:643 (1977–78).

82. See, especially, Inglis, *Sins of the Fathers,* ch. 8.

83. William Downs and Brenda Miller, "Relationships between Experiences of Parental Violence during Childhood and Women's Self-Esteem," *Violence and Victims* 13:63–78 (1998).

84. Ruth S. Kempe and C. Henry Kempe, *Child Abuse* (Cambridge: Harvard University Press, 1978), pp. 6–7.

85. Ibid.

86. Herman Daldin, "The Fate of the Sexually Abused Child," *Clinical Social Work Journal* 16:20–26 (1988).

87. Judith Herman, Diana Russell, and Karen Trocki, "Long-Term Effects of Incestuous Abuse in Childhood," *American Journal of Psychiatry* 143:1293–96 (1986).

88. Kathleen Kendall-Tackett, Linda Meyer Williams, and David Finkelhor, "Impact of Sexual Abuse on Children: A Review and Synthesis of Recent Empirical Studies," *Psychological Bulletin* 113:164–80 (1993).

89. Magnus Seng, "Child Sexual Abuse and Adolescent Prostitution: A Comparative Analysis," *Adolescence* 24:665–75 (1989); Dorothy Bracey, *Baby Pros: Preliminary Profiles of Juvenile Prostitutes* (New York: John Jay Press, 1979).

90. Xavier Coll, Fergus Law, Aurelio Tobias, Keith Hawton, Josep Tomas, "Abuse and Deliberate Self-Poisoning in Women: A Matched Case-Control Study," *Child Abuse and Neglect* 25:1291–93 (2001).

91. Murray Straus, Richard Gelles, and Suzanne Steinmentz, *Behind Closed Doors: Violence in the American Family* (Garden City, NY: Anchor Books, 1980); Richard Gelles and Murray Straus, "Violence in the American Family," *Journal of Social Issues* 35:15–39 (1979).

92. Gelles and Straus, "Violence in the American Family," p. 24.

93. Gelles and Straus, *Intimate Violence*, pp. 108–109; Murray A. Straus and Glenda Kaufman Kantor, "Trends in Physical Abuse by Parents from 1975 to 1992: A Comparison of Three National Surveys." Paper presented at the Annual Meeting of the American Society of Criminology, Boston, 1995.

94. Murray A. Straus and Anita K. Mathur, "Social Change and Trends in Approval of Corporal Punishment by Parents from 1968 to 1994," in D. Frehsee, W. Horn, and K. Bussman, eds., *Violence against Children* (New York: de Gruyter, 1996), pp. 91–105.

95. U.S. Department of Health and Human Services, Administration on Children, Youth and Families. Child Maltreatment 1999 (Washington, DC: U.S. Government Printing Office, 2001).

96. Ching-Tung Wang and Deborah Daro, *Current Trends in Child Abuse Reporting and Fatalities: The Results of the 1997 Annual Fifty State Survey* (Chicago: The Center on Child Abuse Prevention Research, National Committee to Prevent Child Abuse, 1998).

97. David Finkelhor and Richard Ormrod, "Child Abuse Cases Reported to the Police," *Juvenile Justice Bulletin* (Washington, DC: Office of Juvenile Justice and Delinquency Prevention, 2001).

98. Diana Russell, *Sexual Exploitation: Rape, Child Sexual Abuse, and Workplace Harassment* (Beverly Hills: Sage, 1984).

99. Maria Root, "Treatment Failures: The Role of Sexual Victimization in Women's Addictive Behavior," *American Journal of Orthopsychiatry* 59:543–49 (1989).

100. Lisa Jones and David Finkelhor, *The Decline in Child Sexual Abuse Cases* (Washington, DC: Office of Juvenile Justice and Delinquency Prevention, 2001).

101. Lisa Jones, David Finkelhor, Kathy Kopie, "Why Is Sexual Abuse Declining? A Survey of State Child Protection Administrators," *Child Abuse and Neglect* 25:1139–41 (2001).

102. Carolyn Webster-Stratton, "Comparison of Abusive and Nonabusive Families with Conduct-Disordered Children," *American Journal of Orthopsychiatry* 55:59–69 (1985); Brandt F. Steele and Carl B. Pollock, "A Psychiatric Study of Parents Who Abuse Infants and Small Children," in Ray Helfer and C. Henry Kempe, eds., *The Battered Child* (Chicago: University of Chicago Press, 1968), pp. 103–45.

103. Brandt F. Steele, "Violence within the Family," in Ray E. Helfer and C. Henry Kempe, eds., *Child Abuse and Neglect: The Family and the Community* (Cambridge, MA: Ballinger, 1976), p. 13.

104. William Sack, Robert Mason, and James Higgins, "The Single-Parent Family and Abusive Punishment," *American Journal of Orthopsychiatry* 55:252–59 (1985).

105. Fontana, "The Maltreated Children of Our Times," pp. 450–51; see also Blair Justice and Rita Justice, *The Abusing Family* (New York: Human Sciences Press, 1976); Steele, "Violence within the Family," p. 12; Nanette Dembitz, "Preventing Youth Crime by Preventing Child Neglect," *American Bar Association Journal* 65:920–23 (1979).

106. Douglas Ruben, *Treating Adult Children of Alcoholics: A Behavioral Approach* (New York: Academic, 2000).

107. Martin Daly and Margo Wilson, "Violence against Stepchildren," *Current Directions in Psychological Science* 5:77–81 (1996).

108. Ibid.

109. Margo Wilson, Martin Daly, and Atonietta Daniele, "Familicide: The Killing of Spouse and Children," *Aggressive Behavior* 21:275–91 (1995).

110. Wang and Daro, *Current Trends in Child Abuse*, p. 10.

111. Ibid., p. 12.

112. Richard Gelles, "Child Abuse and Violence in Single-Parent Families: Parent Absence and Economic Deprivation," *American Journal of Orthopsychiatry* 59:492–501 (1989).

113. Susan Napier and Mitchell Silverman, "Family Violence as a Function of Occupation Status, Socioeconomic Class, and Other Variables." Paper presented at the American Society of Criminology meeting, Boston, November 1995.

114. Robert Burgess and Patricia Draper, "The Explanation of Family Violence," in Ohlin and Tonry, eds., *Family Violence* (Chicago: University of Chicago Press, 1989), pp. 59–117.

115. Ibid., pp. 103–104.

116. *Troxel et vir. v. Granville* No. 99–138 (June 5, 2000).

117. 452 U.S. 18, 101 S.Ct. 2153 (1981); 455 U.S. 745, 102 S.Ct. 1388 (1982).

118. For a survey of each state's reporting requirements, abuse and neglect legislation, and available programs and agencies, see Costa and Nelson, *Child Abuse and Neglect.*

119. Linda Gordon, "Incest and Resistance: Patterns of Father-Daughter Incest, 1880–1930," *Social Problems* 33:253–67 (1986).

120. P.L. 93B247 (1974); P.L. 104B235 (1996).

121. Martha Brannigan, "Arrests Spark Furor over the Reporting of Suspected Abuse," *Wall Street Journal*, 7 June 1989, p. B8.

122. Debra Whitcomb, *When the Victim Is a Child* (Washington, DC: National Institute of Justice, 1992), p. 5.

123. "False Accusations of Abuse Devastating to Families," *Crime Victims Digest* 6(2):4–5 (1989).

124. This section relies heavily on Shirley Dobbin, Sophia Gatowski, and Margaret Springate, "Child Abuse and Neglect," *Juvenile and Family Court Journal* 48:43–54 (1997).

125. For an analysis of the accuracy of children's recollections of abuse, see Candace Kruttschnitt and Maude Dornfeld, "Will They Tell? Assessing Preadolescents' Reports of Family Violence," *Journal of Research in Crime and Delinquency* 29:136–47 (1992).

126. Ibid.

127. Whitcomb, *When the Victim Is a Child*, p. 33.

128. *White v. Illinois*, 502 U.S. 346; 112 S.Ct. 736 (1992).

129. Myrna Raeder, "*White's* Effect on the Right to Confront One's Accuser," *Criminal Justice*, Winter:2–7 (1993).

130. *Coy v. Iowa*, 487 U.S. 1012 (1988).

131. *Maryland v. Craig*, 110 S.Ct. 3157 (1990).

132. *Walker v. Fagg*, 400 S.E. 2d 708 (Va. App. 1991).

133. Robin V. Delany-Shabazz and Victor Vieth, "The National Center for Prosecution of Child Abuse" (Washington, DC: Office of Juvenile Justice and Delinquency Prevention, 2001).

134. Wendy Fisk, "Childhood Trauma and Dissociative Identity Disorder," *Child and Adolescent Psychiatric Clinics of North America* 5:431–47 (1996).

135. Mary Haskett and Janet Kistner, "Social Interactions and Peer Perceptions of Young Physically Abused Children," *Child Development* 62:679–90 (1991).

136. Gelles and Straus, "Violence in the American Family."

137. This section is based on Richard Wiebush, Raelene Freitag, and Christopher Baird, *Preventing Delinquency through Improved Child Protection Services* (Washington, DC: Office of Juvenile Justice and Delinquency Prevention, 2001).

138. Caroline Wolf Harlow, "Prior Abuse Reported by Inmates and Probationers" (Washington, DC: U.S. Bureau of Justice Statistics, 1999).

139. Wiebush, Freitag, and Baird, *Preventing Delinquency through Improved Child Protection Services*.

140. Michael Wiederman, Randy Sansone, and Lori Sansone, "History of Trauma and Attempted Suicide among Women in a Primary Care Setting," *Violence and Victims* 13:3–11 (1998); Susan Leslie Bryant and Lillian Range, "Suicidality in College Women Who Were Sexually and Physically Abused and Physically Punished by Parents," *Violence and Victims* 10:195–215 (1995); William Downs and Brenda Miller, "Relationships between Experiences of Parental Violence during Childhood and Women's Self-Esteem," *Violence and Victims* 13:63–78 (1998); Sally Davies-Netley, Michael Hurlburt, and Richard Hough, "Childhood Abuse as a Precursor to Homelessness for Homeless Women with Severe Mental Illness," *Violence and Victims* 11:129–42 (1996).

141. Jeanne Kaufman and Cathy Spatz Widom, "Childhood Victimization, Running Away, and Delinquency," *Journal of Research in Crime and Delinquency* 36:347–70 (1999).

142. Jose Alfaro, "Report of the Relationship between Child Abuse and Neglect and Later Socially Deviant Behavior." Unpublished paper (Albany, NY: n.d.), pp. 175–219.

143. Cathy Spatz Widom, "Child Abuse, Neglect, and Violent Criminal Behavior," *Criminology* 27:251–71 (1989).

144. Cathy Spatz Widom, "The Cycle of Violence," *Science* 244:160–66 (1989).

145. Cathy Widom and Michael Maxfield, *An Update on the "Cycle of Violence"* (Washington, DC: National Institute of Justice, 2001).

146. Jane Siegel and Linda Meyer Williams, "Violent Behavior among Men Abused as Children." Paper presented at the American Society of Criminology meeting, Boston, November 1995; Jane Siegel and Linda Meyer Williams, "Aggressive Behavior among Women Sexually Abused as Children." Paper presented at the American Society of Criminology meeting, Phoenix, 1993 (rev. version).

147. David Skuse, Arnon Bentovim, Jill Hodges, Jim Stevenson, Chriso Andreou, Monica Lanyado, Michelle New, Bryn Williams, and Dean McMillan, "Risk Factors for Development of Sexually Abusive Behaviour in Sexually Victimised Adolescent Boys: Cross Sectional Study," *British Medical Journal* 317:175–80 (1998).

148. Carolyn Smith and Terence Thornberry, "The Relationship between Childhood Maltreatment and Adolescent Involvement in Delinquency," *Criminology* 33:451–77 (1995).

149. Widom, "Child Abuse, Neglect, and Violent Criminal Behavior," p. 267.

150. Bruce Rind, Philip Tromovitch, and Robert Bauserman, "A Meta-Analytic Examination of Assumed Properties of Child Sexual Abuse Using College Samples," *Psychological Bulletin* 124:22–53 (1998); Kimberly Barletto, "Who's at Risk: Delinquent Trajectories of Children with Attention and Conduct Problems." Paper presented at the American Society of Criminology meeting, San Diego, 1997; Veronica Herrera, "Equals in Risk? The Differential Impact of Family Violence on Male and Female Delinquency." Paper presented at the Annual Society of Criminology meeting, San Diego, November, 1997.

151. Matthew Zingraff, "Child Maltreatment and Youthful Problem Behavior," *Criminology* 31:173–202 (1993).

152. William Lindsay, Jacqueline Law, Kathleen Quinn, Nicola Smart, Anne H.W. Smith, "A Comparison of Physical and Sexual Abuse: Histories of Sexual and Non-Sexual Offenders with Intellectual Disability," *Child Abuse and Neglect*, 25:989–996 (2001).

153. Leonard Edwards and Inger Sagatun, "Dealing with Parent and Child in Serious Abuse Cases," *Juvenile and Family Court Journal* 34:9–14 (1983).

154. Susan McPherson, Lance McDonald, and Charles Ryer, "Intensive Counseling with Families of Juvenile Offenders," *Juvenile and Family Court Journal* 34:27–34 (1983).

155. The programs in this section are described in Edward Zigler, Cara Taussig, and Kathryn Black, "Early Childhood Intervention, a Promising Preventative for Juvenile Delinquency," *American Psychologist* 47:997–1006 (1992).

156. Lawrence W. Sherman, Denise C. Gottfredson, Doris L. MacKenzie, John Eck, Peter Reuter, and Shawn D. Bushway, *Preventing Crime: What Works, What Doesn't, What's Promising* (Washington, DC: National Institute of Justice, 1998).

157. Zigler, Taussig, and Black, "Early Childhood Intervention: A Promising Preventative for Juvenile Delinquency," pp. 1000–1004.

8 Peers and Delinquency: Juvenile Gangs and Groups

© Michael Newman/Photo Edit

You are a professor who teaches courses on delinquent behavior at a local state university. One day you are approached by the director of the President's National Task Force on Gangs (NTFG). This group has been formed to pool resources from a variety of federal agencies, ranging from the FBI to Health and Human Services, in order to provide local jurisdictions with a comprehensive plan for fighting gangs. The director claims that the gang problem is big and becoming bigger. Thousands of gangs, with hundreds of thousands of members, are operating around the country. Government sources, he claims, indicate that there has been a significant growth in gang membership over the past 20 years. So far the government has not been able to do anything at either a state or national level to stem this growing tide of organized criminal activity. They would like you to be part of the team that provides state and local jurisdictions with a gang control activity model, which, if implemented, would provide a cost-effective means of reducing both gang membership and gang activity.

- Would you recommend that police employ anti-gang units that use tactics developed in the fight against organized crime families?

- Would you recommend the redevelopment of deteriorated neighborhoods in which gangs flourish?

- Would you try to educate kids about the dangers of gang membership?

- Would you tell the director that gangs have always existed and there is probably not much the government can do to reduce their numbers?

slum

Few issues in the study of delinquency are more important today than the problems presented by law-violating gangs and groups.[1] Although some gangs are made up of only a few loosely organized neighborhood youths, others have thousands of members who cooperate in complex illegal enterprises. A significant portion of all drug distribution in the nation's inner cities is believed to be gang controlled; gang violence accounts for hundreds of homicides each year.[2] There has been an outcry from politicians to increase punishment for the "little monsters" and to save the "fallen angels," or the victimized youths, who are being threatened by gang members.[3]

Social service and law enforcement groups have made a concerted effort to contain gangs and reduce their criminal activity. Approaches range from introducing treatment-oriented settlement houses to deploying tactical gang control units. The problem of gang control is a difficult one: Gangs flourish in inner-city areas that offer lower-class youths few conventional opportunities. Members are resistant to the offers of help that cannot deliver legitimate economic hope. Though gang members may be subject to arrest, prosecution, and incarceration, a new crop of young recruits is always ready to take the place of their fallen comrades. Those sent to prison find that upon release, their former gangs are only too willing to have them return to action.

This chapter discusses the nature and extent of gang and group delinquency. It begins with a discussion of peer relations and shows how group relations influence delinquent behavior. It then explores the definition, nature, and structure of delinquent gangs. In addition, theories of gang formation, the extent of gang activity, and gang-control efforts are presented.

Adolescent Peer Relations

A CLOSER VIEW
How do you survive the cliques that form in high school? To find out, use *high school cliques* as keywords on InfoTrac College Edition.

cliques Small groups of friends who share intimate knowledge and confidences.

crowds Loosely organized groups who share interests and activities.

A CLOSER VIEW
Forming self-identity is a critical element of adolescence. To find out more about this process, go to Barbara M. Newman and Philip R. Newman, "Group Identity and Alienation: Giving the We Its Due," *Journal of Youth and Adolescence* 30(5):515 (October 2001) on InfoTrac College Edition.

Psychologists have long recognized that as children mature, the nature of their friendship patterns also evolves. While parents are the primary source of influence and attention in children's early years, between ages 8 and 14, children seek out a stable peer group; both the number and the variety of friendships increase as children go through adolescence. Friends soon begin having a greater influence over decision making than parents.[4] By their early teens, children report that their friends give them emotional support when they are feeling bad and that they can confide intimate feelings to peers without worrying about their confidences being betrayed.[5]

As they go through adolescence, children form **cliques**—small groups of friends who share activities and confidences.[6] They also belong to **crowds,** which are loosely organized groups of children who share interests and activities. While clique members share intimate knowledge, crowds are brought together by mutually shared activities, such as sports, religion, and hobbies. Popular youths can be members of a variety of same-sex cliques and crowds, while also joining groups containing members of the opposite sex. Intimate friends play an important role in social development, but adolescents are also deeply influenced by this wider circle of friends. Adolescent self-image is in part formed by individuals' perceptions of their place in the social world, whether they are considered as an accepted insider or an unpopular outcast.[7]

In later adolescence, acceptance by peers has a major impact on socialization. Popular youths do well in school and are socially astute. In contrast, children who are rejected by their peers are more likely to display aggressive behavior and disrupt group activities by bickering or behaving antisocially.[8] Lower-class youths, lacking in educational and vocational opportunities, may place even greater emphasis on friendship than middle-class youths, who can easily replace friends as they change locale and involvements, for example, when they go off to college.[9]

Peer relations, then, are a significant aspect of maturation. Some experts, such as Judith Rich Harris (see Chapter 7), believe that peers exert a powerful influence on youths and pressure them to conform to group values; peer influence may be more important than parental nurturance in the development of long-term behavior.[10] Peers guide children and help them learn to share and cooperate, cope with aggressive impulses, and discuss feelings they would not dare bring up at home. With peers, youths can compare their own experiences and learn that others have similar concerns and problems; they realize that they are not alone.[11]

Peer Relations and Delinquency

Experts have long debated the exact relationship between peer group interaction and delinquency. Research shows that peer group relationships are closely tied to delinquent behaviors: Kids who report inadequate or strained peer relations, who say they are not popular with the "opposite sex," are the ones most likely to become delinquent.[12] The weight of the empirical evidence indicates that youths who are loyal to delinquent friends, belong to gangs, and have "bad companions" are the ones most likely to commit crimes and engage in violence.[13] Reviews of the research show that delinquent acts tend to be committed in small groups, rather than alone; a process called **co-offending**.[14] The group process may involve family members as well as peers; brothers are likely to commit offenses with brothers of a similar age.[15]

co-offending Committing criminal acts in groups.

Delinquent groups tend to be small and transitory.[16] Kids often belong to more than a single deviant group or clique and develop an extensive *network* of delinquent associates. Multiple memberships are desirable because delinquent groups tend to "specialize" in different types of delinquent activity: One group may concentrate on shoplifting, while another performs home invasions. Group roles can vary: An adolescent who assumes a leadership role in one group may be a follower in another.[17] A youth who may instigate the group to commit a criminal act in one context will be a follower in another.

The Impact of Peer Relations

Does having antisocial peers cause delinquency, or are delinquents antisocial youths who seek like-minded companions? Three opposing viewpoints exist on this question (Figure 8.1). Control theorists, such as Travis Hirschi, argue that delinquents are as detached from their peers as they are from other elements of society. Although delinquent youths may acknowledge that they have "friends," their actual personal relationships are cold and exploitative. In an oft-cited work, James Short and Fred Strodtbeck describe the importance delinquent youths attach to their peer groups, but at the same time they observe how delinquents lack the social skills to make their peer relations rewarding or fulfilling.[18] According to this view, antisocial adolescents seek like-minded peers for criminal associations. If delinquency is committed in groups, it is because "birds of a feather flock together," and not because deviant peers cause otherwise law-abiding youths to commit crimes.

Structural and learning theorists view the delinquency experience as one marked by close peer group support. They link delinquency to the rewards gained by associating with like-minded youths, learning deviant values and behaviors from peers, and being influenced by "peer pressure." Kids who maintain friendships with antisocial friends are more likely to become delinquent regardless of their own personality makeup or the type of supervision they receive at home.[19] Even previously law-abiding kids are more likely to get involved in delinquency

Figure 8.1
Three Versions of the Peer-Delinquency Relationship

Antisocial kids
"Birds of a feather"

Social kids
"Peer pressure"

Co-offending peer groups

Interactive kids
"Mutual aid"

and substance abuse if they become associated with antisocial friends who initiate them into a delinquent career.[20]

A third view is that peers and delinquency are mutually supporting. Antisocial kids join with like-minded friends; deviant peers sustain and amplify delinquent careers.[21] The more antisocial the peer group, the more likely its members will engage in delinquency; nondelinquent friends will help moderate delinquency.[22] As children move through the life course, friends will influence their behavior, and their behavior will influence their friends.[23] These antisocial friends help delinquent careers to withstand the aging-out process.[24] People who maintain close relations with antisocial peers will sustain their own criminal behavior into their adulthood. If adulthood brings close and sustaining ties to marriage and family, and the time spent with peers declines, so too will the level of deviant behavior.[25] The aging-out process may possibly be neutralized by maintaining delinquent friends who reinforce patterns of delinquent behavior.

Delinquent Peers   The weight of the empirical evidence indicates that youths who are loyal to delinquent friends, belong to a gang, have "bad companions," and are otherwise involved with deviant peers are the ones most likely to commit crimes.[26] Nonetheless, having deviant peers does not necessarily mean that the relationships are close, intimate, and influential. Are delinquents actually close to their peers?

Research shows that both delinquents and nondelinquents actually had similar types of friendship patterns.[27] Delinquent youths reported that their peer relations contained elements of caring and trust and that they could be open and intimate with their friends. Delinquent youths also reported getting more intrinsic rewards from their peers than did nondelinquents. However, there were some differences between the peer relations of delinquents and nondelinquents: The former reported more conflict than the latter with their friends, more feelings of jealousy and competition, and, not unexpectedly, more pronounced feelings of loyalty in the face of trouble. These findings support the view that delinquents' peer group relations play an important part in their lifestyle and stand in contrast to the viewpoint that youthful law violators are loners without peer group support.

Comparable relationships have been found in studies of peer relations among young drug-involved males.[28] Alcohol and marijuana users have friendships that are more intimate and varied than those of nonusers.[29]

These findings seem to contradict the control theory model, which holds that delinquents are loners who are detached from their peers, and support the structural theory view that delinquents form close-knit peer groups and cliques that sustain their behavior. Adolescents are influenced by social relationships as they go through their life cycle, and these relationships can influence behavior patterns.

A CLOSER VIEW
Use *delinquent peers* as a subject guide on InfoTrac College Edition to get more information on this subject.

Youth Gangs

As youths move through adolescence, they gravitate toward cliques that provide them with support, assurance, protection, and direction. Peer group membership allows them to devalue enemies, achieve status, and develop self-assurance. In some instances, the peer group provides the social and emotional basis for antisocial activity, including crime and substance abuse. In this instance, the clique is transformed into a *gang*.

Although the youth gang is sometimes viewed as a uniquely American phenomenon, youth gangs have also been reported in England, Germany, Italy, New Zealand, Australia, and other nations.[30] Nor are gangs a recent phenomenon. In the 1600s, London was terrorized by organized gangs who called themselves "Hectors," "Bugles," "Dead Boys," and other colorful names. In the seventeenth and eighteenth centuries, English gangs wore distinctive belts and pins marked with serpents, animals, stars, and so on.[31]

Today, the delinquent gang is a topic of considerable interest to many Americans. Such a powerful mystique has grown up around gangs that mere mention of the word *gang* evokes images of black-jacketed youths roaming the streets at night in groups bearing such colorful names as Latin Kings, Mafia Crips, Bounty Hunters, and Savage Skulls. Films, television shows, novels, and even Broadway musicals, such as *Menace II Society, Boyz N the Hood, New Jack City, Trespass, Fresh, Clockers, Outsiders, West Side Story*, and *Colors* have popularized the youth gang.[32]

Considering the suspected role gangs play in violent crime and drug activity, it is not surprising that they have recently become the target of a great deal of research interest.[33] The secretive, constantly changing nature of juvenile gangs makes them a difficult focus of study. Nonetheless, important attempts have been made to gauge their size, location, makeup, and activities.

A CLOSER VIEW
Use the term *youth gangs* on InfoTrac College Edition.

What Are Gangs?

gangs Groups of youths who collectively engage in delinquent behaviors.

What exactly are delinquent gangs? **Gangs** are groups of youths who collectively engage in delinquent behaviors. Yet there is a distinction between *group delinquency* and *gang delinquency*. The former consists of a short-lived alliance created to commit a particular crime or engage in a random violent act. In contrast, gang delinquency involves long-lived, complex institutions that have a distinct structure and organization, including identifiable leadership, division of labor (some members are fighters, others burglars, while some are known as deal makers), rules, rituals, and possessions (such as a headquarters and weapons).

Despite the familiarity of gangs to the American public, delinquency experts are often at odds over the precise definition of a gang. The term is sometimes used broadly to describe any congregation of youths who have joined together to engage in delinquent acts. Some police departments use narrower definitions, designating as gangs only cohesive groups that hold and defend territory, or turf.[34]

interstitial group Delinquent group that fills a crack in the social fabric and maintains standard group practices.

Academic experts have also created a variety of definitions to distinguish delinquent gangs from groups and cliques. One of the core elements generally included in the concept of the gang is that it is an **interstitial group**, a phrase coined by pioneering gang expert Frederick Thrasher. He used the term to refer to the fact that gangs fill the "cracks" in the fabric of society. To be considered a gang, a group must maintain standard group processes, such as recruiting new members, setting goals (such as controlling the neighborhood drug trade), assigning roles (appointing someone to negotiate with rivals), and developing status (grooming young members for leadership roles).[35] Exhibit 8.1 provides definitions of teen gangs by leading experts on delinquency.

Although a great deal of divergence over the definition of *gang* exists, Malcolm Klein argues that two factors stand out as part of the concept of the youth gang:

To view current examples of gang graffiti, go to http://www.streetgangs.com/graffiti/pics/
For an up-to-date list of Web links, go to http://info.wadsworth.com/siegel

- Members have self-recognition of their gang status, and use special vocabulary, clothing, signs, colors, graffiti, and names. Members set themselves apart from the community and are viewed as a separate entity by others. Once they get the label of gang, members eventually accept and take pride in their status.
- There is a commitment to criminal activity, though even the most criminal gang members spend the bulk of their time in noncriminal activities.[36]

The Study of Juvenile Gangs and Groups

The study of juvenile gangs and groups was prompted by the Chicago School sociologists in the 1920s. Researchers such as Clifford Shaw and Henry McKay were concerned about the nature of the urban environment and how it influenced young

Exhibit 8.1   Definitions of Teen Gangs

Frederick Thrasher

An interstitial group originally formed spontaneously and then integrated through conflict. It is characterized by the following types of behavior: meeting face to face, milling, movement through space as a unit, conflict, and planning. The result of this collective behavior is the development of tradition, unreflective internal structure, esprit de corps, solidarity, morale, group awareness, and attachment to local territory.

Malcolm Klein

Any denotable adolescent group of youngsters who (a) are generally perceived as a distinct aggregation by others in their neighborhood; (b) recognize themselves as a denotable group (almost invariably with a group name); and (c) have been involved in a sufficient number of delinquent incidents to call forth a consistent negative response from neighborhood residents and/or law enforcement agencies.

Desmond Cartwright

An interstitial and integrated group of persons who meet face to face more or less regularly and whose existence and activities are considered an actual or potential threat to the prevailing social order.

Walter Miller

A self-formed association of peers, bound together by mutual interests, with identifiable leadership, well-developed lines of authority, and other organizational features, who act in concert to achieve a specific purpose or purposes, which generally include the conduct of illegal activity and control over a particular territory, facility, or type of enterprise.

G. David Curry and Irving Spergel

Groups containing law-violating juveniles and adults that are complexly organized, although sometimes diffuse, and sometimes cohesive, with established leadership and membership rules. The gang also engages in a range of crime (but with significantly more violence) within a framework of norms and values in respect to mutual support, conflict relations with other gangs, and a tradition of turf, colors, signs, and symbols. Subgroups of the gang may be deferentially committed to various delinquent or criminal patterns, such as drug trafficking, gang fighting, or burglary.

James Short

Gangs are groups of young people whose members meet together with some regularity, over time, on the basis of group-defined criteria of membership and group-defined organizational characteristics. In the simplest terms, gangs are unsupervised (by adults), self-determining groups that demonstrate continuity over time.

Sources: Frederick Thrasher, *The Gang* (Chicago: University of Chicago Press, 1927), p. 57; Malcolm Klein, *Street Gangs and Street Workers* (Englewood Cliffs, NJ: Prentice Hall, 1971), p. 13; Desmond Cartwright, Barbara Tomson, and Hersey Schwarts, eds., *Gang Delinquency* (Pacific Grove, CA: Brooks/Cole, 1975), pp. 149–50; Walter Miller, "Gangs, Groups, and Serious Youth Crime," in David Schicor and Delos Kelly, eds., *Critical Issues in Juvenile Delinquency* (Lexington, MA: Lexington Books, 1980); G. David Curry and Irving Spergel, "Gang Homicide, Delinquency, and Community," *Criminology* 26:382 (1988); James Short, "The Level of Explanation Problem Revisited—The American Society of Criminology 1997 Presidential Address," *Criminology* 36:3–36 (1998), p. 16.

people. Delinquency was believed to be a product of unsupervised groups made up of children of the urban poor and immigrants.

Frederick Thrasher initiated the study of the modern gang in his analysis of more than 1,300 youth groups in Chicago. His report on this effort, *The Gang*, was published in 1927.[37] Thrasher found that the social, economic, and ecological processes that affect the structure of great metropolitan cities create interstitial areas, or cracks, in the normal fabric of society, characterized by weak family controls, poverty, and social disorganization. According to Thrasher, groups of youths develop spontaneously to meet such childhood needs as play, fun, and adventure—activities that sometimes lead to delinquent acts.

The slum area presents many opportunities for conflict between groups of youths and between the groups and adult authority. If this conflict continues, the groups become more solidified, and their activities become primarily illegal. The groups thus develop into gangs, with a name and a structure oriented toward delinquent behavior.

To Thrasher, the gang provides the young, lower-class boy with an opportunity for success. Since adult society does not meet the needs of slum dwellers, the gang solves the problem by offering what society fails to provide—excitement, fun, and opportunity. The gang is not a haven for disturbed youths but rather an alternative lifestyle for normal boys.

Thrasher's work has had an important influence on the accepted view of the gang. Recent studies of delinquent gang behavior are similar to Thrasher's in their emphasis on the gang as a means for lower-class boys to achieve advancement and opportunity as well as to defend themselves and attack rivals.

Gangs in the 1950s and 1960s In the 1950s and early 1960s, the threat of gangs and gang violence swept the public consciousness. Rarely did a week go by without a major city newspaper featuring a story on the violent behavior of fighting gangs and their colorful leaders and names—the Egyptian Kings, the Vice Lords, the Blackstone Rangers. Social service and law enforcement agencies directed major efforts to either rehabilitate or destroy the gangs. Movies, such as *The Wild Ones* and *Blackboard Jungle,* were made about gangs, and the Broadway musical *West Side Story* romanticized violent gangs.

In his classic 1967 work, *Juvenile Gangs in Context,* Malcolm Klein summarized existing knowledge about gangs.[38] He concluded that gang membership was a way for individual boys to satisfy certain personal needs that were related to the development of youths caught up in the emotional turmoil typical of the period between adolescence and adulthood. A natural inclination to form gangs is reinforced by the perception that the gang represents a substitute for unattainable middle-class rewards. The experience of being a member of a gang will dominate a youngster's perceptions, values, expectations, and behavior. Finally, the gang is self-reinforcing: It is within the gang more than anywhere else that a youngster may find forms of acceptance for delinquent behavior—rewards instead of negative sanctions. And as the gang strives for internal cohesion, the negative sanctions of the "outside world" become interpreted as threats to cohesion, thus providing secondary reinforcement for the values central to the legitimization of gang behavior.[39]

By the mid-1960s, the gang menace seemed to have disappeared. Some experts attribute the decline of gang activity to successful gang-control programs.[40] They believed that gangs were eliminated because police gang-control units infiltrated gangs, arrested leaders, and constantly harassed members.[41] Gang boys were more likely to be sanctioned by the juvenile justice system and receive more severe sentences than nongang youths.[42] Another explanation for the decline in gang activity was the increase in political awareness that developed during the 1960s. Many gang leaders became involved in the social or political activities of ethnic pride, civil rights, and antiwar groups. In addition, many gang members were drafted. Still another explanation is that gang activity diminished during the 1960s because many gang members became active users of heroin and other drugs, which curtailed their group-related criminal activity.[43]

Gangs Reemerge Interest in gang activity began anew in the early 1970s. Walter Miller comments on the New York scene:

> All was quiet on the gang front for almost 10 years. Then, suddenly and without advance warning, the gangs reappeared. Bearing such names as Savage Skulls and Black Assassins, they began to form in the South Bronx in the spring of 1971, quickly spread to other parts of the city, and by 1975 comprised 275 police-verified gangs with 11,000 members. These new and mysteriously merging gangs were far more lethal than their predecessors—heavily armed, incited and directed by violence-hardened older men, and directing their lethal activities far more to the victimization of ordinary citizens than to one another.[44]

Gang activity also reemerged in other major cities, including Detroit, El Paso, Los Angeles, and Chicago. Today, the number of gang youths appears, at least in these major cities, to be at an all-time high.[45] In addition, such cities as Cleveland and Columbus, Ohio, and Milwaukee, Wisconsin, which had not experienced serious gang problems before, saw the development of local gangs.[46] Large urban gangs sent representatives to organize chapters in distant areas or take over existing gangs.

For example, Chicago gangs moved into Dade County, Florida, and demanded co-operation and obedience from local gangs. Two major Chicago gangs, the Gangster Disciples and their rivals, the Vice Lords, established branches in Milwaukee.[47] Members of the two largest gangs in Los Angeles, the Crips and the Bloods, began operations in Midwest cities with the result that local police departments with little experience in gang control were confronted with well-organized, established gang activities. Even medium-sized cities, such as Columbus, Ohio, saw gangs emerge from local dance and "rap" groups and neighborhood street-corner groups.[48]

In 1975, sociologist Walter Miller conducted the first national survey of gang membership, and estimated that 55,000 adolescents were members of youth gangs and groups; a second survey conducted in 1982 raised the number to 98,000.[49] This explosion of gang activities in the 1980s was reflected in the renewed media interest in gang activity. The *Los Angeles Times* printed 36 gang-related stories in 1977 and 15 in 1978; by 1988, 69 articles appeared, and in 1989, the number of stories concerning police sweeps, revenge shootings, and murder trials had risen to 267.[50] In some communities the fear of gangs, fanned by media attention, created a "moral panic," which prompted increased funding for police and prosecutors.[51] Clearly, gangs had captured the national attention.

Gangs Today   How many gangs are there in the United States, and how many members do they contain? To answer these questions, the federal government sponsors an annual national assessment of gang activity. The most recent one available (2000) indicates that while gang membership has held steady, the proportion of jurisdictions that report youth gangs actually declined from 53 percent in 1996 to 40 percent in 2000. Larger cities with a population of more than 250,000 were the most likely to report persistent gang activity, while smaller cities with populations of between 25,000 and 50,000 experienced some decline in gang numbers.[52]

While these signs are encouraging, gangs continue to have an enormous presence in the United States. The national survey estimates that more than 24,500 gangs were active in the United States in 2000. These gangs contain an estimated 772,500 gang members. While the number of gang members in smaller cities seems to be on the decline, membership is still rising in larger communities where the bulk of gang members reside. Gang-problem cities are concentrated in a relatively small group of counties with high populations: Cook County, Illinois, reported the largest number of gang cities, followed by Los Angeles County, California; Riverside and Orange Counties in California also reported high concentrations of gang cities. So while the national assessment finds that the number of gangs has declined somewhat, gang membership has been stable, possibly because kids are staying in gangs longer and swelling their membership roles.[53]

Why Did Gang Activity Increase?

One compelling reason for the increase in gang activity may be the involvement of youth gangs in distribution and sales of illegal drugs.[54] While early gangs relied on group loyalty and protection of turf to encourage membership, modern gang boys are lured by the quest for drug profits. In some areas, gangs have replaced traditional organized crime families as the dominant suppliers of cocaine and crack. The traditional weapons of gangs—chains, knives, and homemade guns—have been replaced by the "heavy artillery" drug money can buy: Uzi and AK-47 automatic weapons. Felix Padilla studied a Latino gang in Chicago and found that the gang represents a viable and persistent business enterprise within the U.S. economy, with its own culture, logic, and systematic means of transmitting and reinforcing its fundamental business virtues.[55]

Ironically, efforts by the FBI and other federal agencies to crack down on traditional organized crime families in the 1980s have opened the door to more violent

To access a thorough bibliography that includes books and government documents dealing with juvenile gangs dating from 1985 to the present, go to *http://www.lib.usc.edu/~anthonya/gang.htm*
For an up-to-date list of Web links, go to *http://info.wadsworth.com/siegel*

The purpose of the National Youth Gang Center is to expand and maintain the body of critical knowledge about youth gangs and effective responses to them. To learn more about its activities, go to *http://www.iir.com/nygc/PublicationLinks.htm#Surveys, Statistics, and Analysis*
For an up-to-date list of Web links, go to *http://info.wadsworth.com/siegel*

GANG ACTIVITY by such groups as the Savage Skulls (pictured) reemerged in the 1970s in major cities, including New York, Detroit, El Paso, Los Angeles, and Chicago. In addition, such cities as Cleveland and Columbus, Ohio, and Milwaukee, Wisconsin, which had not experienced serious gang problems before, saw the development of local gangs.

youth gangs that control the drug trade on a local level and will not hesitate to use violence to maintain and expand their authority. The division between organized crime and gang crime is becoming increasingly narrow.

Economic Conditions   Drug trafficking may be an important reason for gang activity, but it is by no means the only one: Not all gang boys sell or use drugs, and many dealers are not gang members. Gang activity may also be on the rise because of economic and social dislocation. In her analyses of gangs in postindustrial America, Pamela Irving Jackson found that gang formation is the natural consequence of the evolution from a manufacturing economy with a surplus of relatively high-paying jobs to a low-wage service economy.[56] The American city, which traditionally required a large population base for its manufacturing plants, now faces incredible economic stress as these plants shut down. In this uneasy economic climate, gangs form and flourish while the moderating influence of successful adult role models and stable families declines.

Family Crisis   The ongoing crisis in the American family was discussed earlier in Chapter 7. Many commentators link gang membership to the disorganization of the American family. Gang members come from families that are torn by parental absence, substance abuse, poverty, and criminality.[57] To some experts, the gang serves as a substitute family that contributes the same kind of support, security, and caring that the "traditional," intact nuclear family is supposed to provide.

This is a compelling argument, but at the same time, a sizable number of gang boys come from stable and adequate families, while a significant number of youths from dysfunctional families avoid gang involvement. In some families one brother or sister is ganged up (a member of a gang), while another evades gang membership. The gang may be a substitute family for some members, but it clearly does not have that appeal for all.

Contemporary Gangs

Thousands of gangs are operating around the country today with hundreds of thousands of members. The gang, however, cannot be viewed as a uniform or homogenous social concept. Gangs vary by activity, makeup, location, leadership style, and age. The following sections attempt to describe some of the most salient features of this heterogeneous social phenomenon.

Gang Names

When the early gangs were formed, they took their names from the neighborhoods where they started and carried on their activities (for example, Southside Raiders, Twelfth Street Locos, Jackson Park Boys).[58] Some used more colorful, non-locality-based names of their own choosing (Cobras, Warriors, Los Diablos, Mafia Emperors). During the 1960s, gang branches became popular in some cities, so local gangs used a variant of a common gang name. For example, many gangs in Chicago employed a variation of the Vicelord name—the California Lords, War Lords, Fifth Avenue Lords, and Maniac Lords—so that they could claim to be part of and loyal to a common organization—the Vicelord Nation. Beginning in the 1980s, gang federations expanded, and the two most prominent organizations—the Los Angeles–based Crips and Bloods—eventually spread. More than 1,100 gangs in 115 cities around the nation had Bloods or Crips in their names, with locality designations reflecting city neighborhoods (for example, Hoover Crips, East Side 40th Street Gangster Crips, Hacienda Village Bloods, and 42nd Street Piru Bloods).

Gang Types

retreatists Gangs whose members actively engage in substance abuse.

Gangs have been categorized by their activity: Some are devoted to violence and protecting their neighborhood boundaries, or turf; others are devoted to theft; some specialize in drug trafficking; others are primarily social groups concerned with recreation, rather than crime.[59]

In their early work, Richard Cloward and Lloyd Ohlin recognized that some gangs specialized in violent behavior; others were **retreatists,** whose members actively engaged in substance abuse; while a third type were criminal gangs that devoted their energy to crime for profit.[60] It has become increasingly difficult to make the *criminal-retreatist-conflict* distinction since so many gang members are involved in all three behaviors, but experts continue to find that on an aggregate level gangs can be characterized according to dominant behavioral activities. For example, Jeffrey Fagan analyzed gang behavior in Chicago, San Diego, and Los Angeles and found that most gangs fall into one of four categories:

- The *social gang* is involved in few delinquent activities and little drug use other than alcohol and marijuana. Membership is more interested in the social aspects of group behavior.
- The *party gang* concentrates on drug use and sales, forgoing most delinquent behavior except vandalism. Drug sales are designed to finance members' personal drug use.
- The *serious delinquent gang* engages in serious delinquent behavior while eschewing most drug use. Drugs are used only on social occasions.
- The *organized gang* is heavily involved in criminality and drug use and sales. Drug use and sales reflect a systemic relationship with other criminal acts. For example, violent acts are used to establish control over drug sale territories. Highly cohesive and organized, this gang is on the verge of becoming a formal criminal organization.[61]

Exhibit 8.2   Maxson's Gang Typology

- **Traditional gangs:** In existence for 20 years or more. Contain clear subgroups based on age. Sometimes subgroups are separated by neighborhoods rather than age. Have wide age range (members ages are from 10 to 30) and are very large, with hundreds of members. Territorial, with well-defined home turf.
- **The neotraditional gang:** A territorial gang, smaller and newer than the traditional gang, which may evolve into a traditional gang over time.
- **The compressed gang:** A smaller gang, with less than 50 members, a short history, no subgroups, narrow age range, and less defined territory.
- **The collective gang:** A larger group resembling a "shapeless mass" of adolescent and young adult members that has not developed the distinguishing characteristics of other gangs.
- **The specialty gang:** A crime-focused gang that is more criminal than social and is smaller in size and age range than other gangs. It has a well-defined territory that can be based either on neighborhoods or the particular form of crime it specializes in, such as drug territories.

Source: Cheryl Maxson, "Investigating Gang Structures," *Journal of Gang Research* 3:33–40 (1995).

Fagan's findings have been duplicated by other gang observations around the United States. After observing gangs in the Columbus, Ohio, area, C. Ronald Huff found that they could be organized into "hedonistic gangs" (similar to the party gangs), "instrumental gangs" (similar to the serious delinquent gang) and "predatory gangs," whose heavy crime and crack use make them similar to the organized gang found by Fagan in Chicago and on the West Coast.[62] Carl Taylor adds the *scavenger gang,* a group of impulsive kids who have no common bond beyond surviving in a tough urban environment. These kids are typically low achievers who prey on any target they encounter. Taylor contrasts the scavenger gang with the *organized/ corporate gang,* whose structure and goal orientation make it similar to a Fortune 500 company in its relentless pursuit of profit and market share.[63]

Cheryl Maxson, a noted gang researcher, finds that gangs can be organized into groups based on their size, age range, duration of existence, territory, and criminal acts. Maxson's findings are illustrated in Exhibit 8.2.[64]

By far the most common gang is the compressed structure; the collective gang is the least common, followed by specialty gangs. Contrary to public opinion, less than half of the specialty gangs are involved in drug distribution.[65]

These more recent observations seem to validate Cloward and Ohlin's research findings from 40 years ago indicating that many gangs specialize in their activities. However, many gangs engage in a variety of criminal activities, ranging from violent turf battles to drug dealing, as well as social activities, including helping members' families and organizing parties.[66]

For an analysis of youth gang drug dealing, go to *http://www.ncjrs.org/pdffiles1/ ojjdp/178282.pdf* For an up-to-date list of Web links, go to *http://info.wadsworth.com/siegel*

Location

The gang problem has traditionally been considered an urban, lower-class phenomenon. Two types of urban areas are gang-prone. The first is the transitional neighborhood, which is marked by rapid population change in which diverse ethnic and racial groups find themselves living side by side and in competition with one another.[67] Intergang conflict and homicide rates are high in these areas, which house the so-called urban underclass.[68]

The second gang area is the **stable slum,** a neighborhood where population shifts have slowed down, permitting patterns of behavior and traditions to develop over a number of years. Most typical of these areas are the slums in New York and Chicago and the Mexican-American barrios of the Southwest and California.[69] The stable slum more often contains the large, structured gang clusters that are the most

stable slum   A neighborhood where population shifts have slowed down, permitting patterns of behavior and traditions to develop over a number of years.

resistant to attempts by law enforcement and social service agencies to modify or disband them.

Shifting Gang Locales   Transitional neighborhoods and the stable slum are not the only environments that produce gangs. In recent years, there has been a massive movement of people out of the central city into outlying communities and suburbs. Many of these people have been from the upper or middle class, but lower-income residents have also been affected. In some cities, once-fashionable outlying neighborhoods have declined, and downtown, central city areas have undergone extensive urban renewal. Central, inner-city districts of major cities such as New York and Chicago have become devoted to finance, retail stores, restaurants, and entertainment.[70] Two aspects of this development inhibit gang formation—first, there are few residential areas and thus few adolescent recruits, and second, there is intensive police patrol. In some areas, such as Miami and Boston, gang areas have shifted from the downtown areas to outer-city, ring-city, or suburban areas—that is, to formerly middle-class areas now in decay. Some midsize cities now contain the type of gangs that only a few years ago were restricted to large metropolitan areas.

Suburban housing projects are also gang-prone. Thus, while gangs are still located in areas of urban blight today, these neighborhoods are often at some distance from their traditional inner-city locations.[71]

Migration   Gang migration may also help to account for the national growth in gang activity. The National Gang Survey estimates that 18 percent of gang members were migrants from another jurisdiction. In rural areas, 34 percent of members had come from elsewhere; in small cities, 27 percent, and in suburban counties, 20 percent were outsiders. Larger cities had the smallest percentage of migrants (17%), indicating that the flow of gang members was from more- to less-populated areas, and not vice versa. Not surprisingly, law enforcement agents report that the appearance of gang members outside of large cities in the 1990s was caused by the migration of young people from central cities.[72]

About 700 U.S. cities have experienced some form of gang migration during the past decade, either short term—for example, to sell drugs—or long term to form permanent gangs. Most of the new arrivals were from Los Angeles gangs, though Chicago, New York, and Detroit are also the source of migrators. The most common motive for gang members to migrate was actually social: Their family relocated; they came to stay with relatives. Others had a specific criminal purpose, such as expanding drug sales and markets. Most of the migrators were African American or Hispanic males who maintained close ties with members of their original gangs "back home."[73] Although retention of gang identity is important, some migrants join local gangs, shedding old ties and gaining new affiliations. And while gang migration remains a serious problem, most cities had local gangs before the onset of migration and most likely would have had a gang problem regardless of migration. The number of migrants is relatively small in proportion to the overall gang population, supporting the contention that most gangs are actually "homegrown."

Neighborhood Reactions   The presence of gangs in areas unaccustomed to delinquent group activity can have a devastating effect on community life. In his famous study of Milwaukee gangs, John Hagedorn found that a great deal of neighborhood hostility was evoked when gangs formed in this Midwestern city.[74] Community resistance to gangs arose for a number of reasons. First, Milwaukee's gangs had little neighborhood turf affiliation and were formed solely to profit from illegal gain and criminal activity. Second, the gangs were formed at the same time minority students were being bused to implement desegregation. Gang recruitment took place on the buses and in schools and not on neighborhood streets. Gang membership, therefore, cut across neighborhoods, rendering local social control ineffective. Finally, the neighborhoods most likely to be plagued by gang violence were strained economically. Residential segregation and a lack of affordable housing prevented many working-class residents from leaving. The result was mixed neighborhoods of struggling working-class and poor families coexisting with drug houses, gangs, and routine violence. Frightened residents had little recourse but to call police when they heard gunshots; neighborhoods became uneasy and unstable.

Hagedorn's study illustrates the dreadful impact gang activity can have on a neighborhood. As Lawrence Rosenthal points out, unlike any other crime, gang activity is frequently undertaken out in the open, on the public ways, and in full view of the rest of the community.[75] Brazen criminal activity undermines community solidarity because it signals that the police must be either corrupt or inept. The fact that gangs are willing to openly engage in drug sales and other types of criminal activity shows their confidence that they have silenced or intimidated law-abiding persons in their midst. The police and community alike become hopeless about their ability to restore community stability.

Age

The ages of gang members range widely, perhaps from as young as 8 to as old as 55.[76] However, members of offending groups are usually no more than a few years apart in age, with a leader, or instigator, who may be more experienced and a few years older.[77]

A recent survey of 3,348 youths, including almost 2,000 gang members, conducted by the National Gang Crime Research Center, found that kids first hear about gangs at around 9 years old, get involved in violence at age 10–11, and join their first gang at age 12. By age 13, half of the gang boys interviewed had (a) fired a pistol, (b) seen someone killed or seriously injured by gang violence, (c) gotten a permanent gang tattoo, and (d) been arrested.[78]

Gang experts believe the average age of gang members has been increasing yearly, a phenomenon explained in part by the changing structure of the U.S. economy.[79] About half of all gang members today are ages 18 to 24, an increase from 46 percent in 1998 and 37 percent in 1996. In contrast, the proportion of gang members ages 15 to 17 decreased to 26 percent from a high of 34 percent in 1996.[80]

Why are gang members' ages increasing? Though the economy was robust during the 1990s, desirable unskilled factory jobs that would entice older boys to leave the gang have been lost to overseas competition. Replacing these legitimate jobs are low-level drug dealing opportunities that require a gang affiliation. William Julius Wilson found that the inability of inner-city males to obtain adequate employment prevents them from attaining adult roles; for example, they cannot afford to marry and raise families. Criminal records acquired at an early age quickly lock them out of the job market. Remaining in a gang into their adulthood has become an economic necessity.[81] The weakening economy should prolong gang membership even further.

In his Milwaukee research, John Hagedorn also found that economic deterioration has had an important impact on the age structure of gang membership. In the past, gangs had a shifting membership because older members could easily slip into the economic mainstream. Good-paying manufacturing jobs that required little education and few skills were an attractive alternative to gang activity. These jobs are simply no longer available, with the result that the economic lure of gangs continues past adolescence into young adulthood. Less than one in five founding members of the youth gangs Hagedorn studied were able to find full-time employment by their mid-20s; 86 percent had spent considerable time in prison. *Old heads*—older members with powerful street reputations—were held in high esteem by young gang boys. In the past, ex-members served as a moderating influence, helping steer gang boys into conventional roles and jobs. Today, young adults continue relationships with their old gangs and promote values of hustling, drug use, and sexual promiscuity. As a result, gang affiliations can last indefinitely, and it is not unusual to see intergenerational membership, with the children and even grandchildren of gang members

A CLOSER VIEW
To read an article by Hagedorn and his colleagues about drug abuse in Milwaukee gangs, go to InfoTrac College Edition, and get John M. Hagedorn, Jose Torres, Greg Giglio, "Cocaine, Kicks, and Strain: Patterns of Substance Use in Milwaukee Gangs," *Contemporary Drug Problems* 25(1): 113–45 (Spring 1998).

affiliating with the same gang.[82] When Hagedorn and his associates interviewed 101 older gang members from 14 Milwaukee area gangs, they found that there are actually four types of adult gang members:

- *Legits* have left the gang and 'hood behind.
- *Dope fiends* are addicted to cocaine and need drug treatment.
- *New Jacks* have given up on the legitimate economy and see nothing wrong in selling cocaine to anyone.
- *Homeboys,* who are a majority of all adult gang members, work regular jobs, but when they cannot make enough money, they sell cocaine. They want out of the drug trade and wish to have a "normal" life, but believe that ganging is the only way to make ends meet.[83]

Gender

Of the more than 1,000 groups included in Thrasher's original survey, only half a dozen were female gangs. Females have traditionally been involved in gang activities in one of three ways: as auxiliaries, or branches, of male gangs; as part of sexually mixed gangs; and as autonomous gangs. Auxiliaries are a feminized version of the male gang name, such as the Lady Disciples of the Devil's Disciples. Some gangs are integrated, containing both male and female members. For example, Mary Glazier's study of a small-town Pennsylvania gang, "The Hit and Run," found that girls were invited to become gang members because it was considered unacceptable for male members to fight with females who gave them trouble; girl members were given that responsibility.[84]

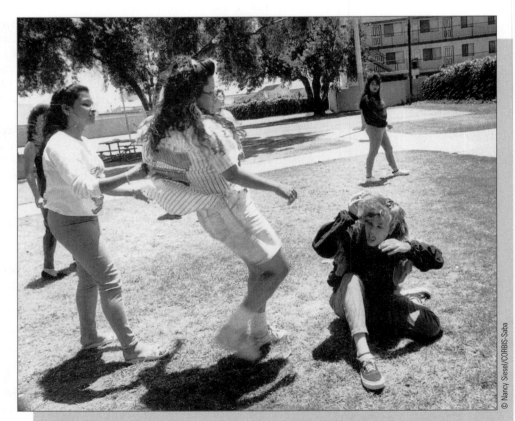

© Nancy Siesel/CORBIS-Saba

THE NUMBER AND EXTENT OF GIRL GANGS IS INCREASING. In the Grape Street area of Los Angeles, a female gang member is about to kick another young woman. This is not a random or spontaneous attack but part of the "court in" ceremony in which new members are initiated into the gang.

Independent or autonomous female gangs are now becoming more common.[85] While initial female gang participation may be forged by links to male gang members, once in gangs, girls form close ties with other female members. Peer interactions form the basis for independent female gangs and group criminal activity.[86]

There is also some question about the benefits of gang membership for females. According to the *liberation view,* ganging can provide girls a sense of sisterhood, independence, and solidarity as well as a chance to earn profit through illegal activity such as drug dealing. In contrast, the *social injury view* suggests that the deficits of gang membership are greater than its benefits. Female members are still sexually exploited by males and are sometimes forced to exploit other females. Girls who are members of male gang auxiliaries may be particularly prone to exploitation. They report that males in the gang not only control the girls in the auxiliary gangs by determining the arenas within which they can operate (for example, the extent to which they are allowed to become involved in intergang violence), but also play a divisive role in the girls' relationships with each other. This manipulation is absent for girls in independent gangs.[87]

Females then join gangs in an effort to cope with a bleak and harsh life and the prospects of an equally dismal future.[88] Girls in gangs seem less violent than boys and more likely to engage in theft offenses than violent crimes.[89] This may indicate the desire for female gang members to use their status for economic gain in order to improve their lifestyle and enhance their future.

It is still difficult to determine the precise number of female gangs or the size of their membership. The 2000 gang assessment found that 94 percent of gang members were male and 6 percent were female; only 2 percent of gangs were identified as predominantly female. However, about 39 percent of all gangs had female members.[90]

Some local gang surveys that rely on interview and self-report data, however, indicate that the number of female gang members may be on the rise in some areas of the country.[91] Carl Taylor's analysis of Detroit gangs found that girls were very much involved in gang activity.[92] And an important analysis of Denver youth found that the number of female gang members is higher than previously thought: Approximately 25 percent of the gang members they surveyed were female.[93] A recent survey of almost 6,000 youths in 42 schools located in 11 cities found that almost 40 percent of the gang members were females.[94] It is possible that law enforcement agencies undercount female gang membership and that in actuality more young girls are gang affiliated than previously believed.[95] See the Focus on Delinquency box entitled "Girls in the Gang."

Formation

It has long been suggested that gangs form in order to defend their turf from outsiders; thus, gang formation involves a sense of territoriality. Most gang members live in close proximity to one another, and their sense of belonging and loyalty extends only to their small area of the city. At first, a gang may form when members of an ethnic minority newly settled in the neighborhood join together for self-preservation. As the group gains numerical domination over an area, it may view the neighborhood as its territory or turf, which needs to be defended. Defending turf involves fighting rivals who want to make the territory their own.

Once formed, gangs grow when youths who admire the older gang boys and wish to imitate their lifestyle "apply" and are accepted for membership. Sometimes, the new members will be given a special, diminished identity within the gang that reflects their inexperience and apprenticeship status. Joan Moore and her associates found that once formed, youth cliques (*klikas*) in Hispanic gangs remain together as unique groups with separate names (for example, the Termites), separate identities, and distinct experiences; they also have more intimate relationships among themselves than among the general gang membership.[96] She likens *klikas* to a particular

klikas Subgroups of same-aged youths in Hispanic gangs that remain together and have separate names and a unique identity within the gang.

Girls in the Gang

A recent review by gang experts Joan Moore and John Hagedorn summarizes both past and current research on female gangs and examines how ethnicity and gender norms may influence female gang behavior. Some of their most significant findings are discussed below.

Being in a Gang

Though most females join gangs for friendship and self-affirmation, economic and social reasons also structure their choices. In the 1980s and early 1990s, the loss of hundreds of thousands of factory jobs made conditions even worse in America's inner cities and encouraged girls to join gangs. Hagedorn's own research on gang formation in Milwaukee, Wisconsin—a city then suffering economic decline—shows that although the parents of most gang members usually held good jobs, these jobs had disappeared by the time their children were grown. It is not surprising that gangs proliferated rapidly during this period, not only in Milwaukee but throughout the nation. An informal economy flourished. Although much of the work associated with this economy was legal, a substantial portion involved drug dealing and other illicit activities, and gang members joined in. In Chicago, for example, economically successful gangs—female and male—became significant community institutions, sometimes offering resources and protection to neighbors.

Female gang members have been affected not only by these economic shifts but by recent changes in the welfare system, which is an important economic resource. In Los Angeles, for example, Mexican-American gang members active in the 1950s and 1970s became pregnant, on average, at age 18. They tended to rely on welfare, combined with work and help from their families, to survive. Similar patterns were found in Milwaukee in the 1990s. However, welfare reforms introduced in the mid-1990s have reduced or eliminated welfare payments. Because female gang members often face significant barriers to legitimate employment, it is unclear what they will do to replace welfare support.

Family Influences

There is one aspect of female gang life that does not seem to be changing—the gang as a refuge for young women who have been victimized at home. The available research consistently shows that high proportions of female gang members have experienced sexual abuse at home. In Los Angeles, for example, 29 percent of a large representative sample of Mexican-American female gang members had been sexually abused at home, and their homes were more likely than those of male gang members to include drug users and persons arrested for crimes. Almost two-thirds of female gang members interviewed in Hawaii had been sexually abused at home. Many had run away and had joined gangs to obtain protection from abusive families.

Joining a gang can be an assertion of independence not only from family, but also from cultural and class constraints. In joining a gang, young Puerto Rican women in New York felt that they would be able to express themselves as assimilated Americans, spending money freely and standing up for themselves. In Los Angeles, Mexican-American gangs were described as a substitute institution that can provide meaning and identity in their lives.

Sex: Stereotyping and Victimization

"Sex object" was one of the early stereotypes of female gang members, and the interest in the sex lives of female gang members still persists. Early reports about the easy sexual availability of female gang members came almost exclusively from male gang members. Even some recent reports present similar male perceptions as fact, with no attempt at verification. However, male gang members may be indulging their own fantasies. While male gang members often claim that group sex is an initiation ritual for female gang members, female gang members dismiss the idea as ludicrous.

There are disparate views of gender relations within gangs. In Los Angeles, one-half of male gang members claim that female members

class in a university, such as the class of '94, not a separate organization but one that has its own unique experiences.

Moore also found that gangs can expand by including members' kin, even if they do not live in the immediate neighborhood, and rival gang members who wish to join because they admire the gang's way of doing things. Adding outsiders gives the gang the ability to take over new territory. However, it also brings with it new problems, since outsider membership and the grasp for new territory usually result in greater conflicts with rival gangs.

Leadership

Most experts describe gang leaders as cool characters who have earned their position by demonstrating a variety of abilities—fighting prowess, verbal quickness, athletic distinction, and so on.[97] Experts emphasize that gang leadership is held by one person and varies with particular activities, such as fighting, sex, and negotiations. In fact, in some gangs, each age level of the gang has its own leaders. Older memare "possessions." This response not only referred to the females' sexual exploitation but also reflected the males' general need to be in charge. The other half of the male members felt that female members were respected and treated like family. (About two-thirds of the female members vehemently deny that they were treated like possessions.) In San Antonio, where there are many Mexican-American gangs but few female gangs or gang members, most females who associate with male gang members are respected. But "hoodrats"—females involved in "frequent partying, drug using, participation in illegal activities and multiple sexual encounters"—are not deemed worthy of respect.

Although male gang members may exaggerate their sexual domination over female members, there are reports from females that they have been sexually exploited by males within gangs. In San Francisco, females from an immigrant Salvadoran gang were sexually victimized by male gang members, although this rarely happened in a nearby Mexican-American gang. Sexual abuse and exploitation by male gang members were also reported by female gang members in Columbus, Ohio; Milwaukee; Phoenix; Chicago; and Los Angeles. Some of these reports may have been from females who were only marginal to the gang. In Milwaukee, Hagedorn found that females controlled admission to their gang (a female auxiliary to the male gang), but female "wannabes" seeking to become members thought that males controlled admission. The male members tricked some female wannabes into group sex by telling them it was an initiation ritual. It was not, and females who participated in the group sex did not become members of the gang. Evidence of sexual exploitation of female gang members at home and within their gangs is one reason for considering female gang membership a serious social concern.

Changing Female Roles

The role of females in gangs may be changing, due in part to a shifting social climate. For example, the number of gangs declined sharply in New York in the 1980s and early 1990s when members began going to prison in large numbers. New gangs emerged in prison and on the streets. These new gangs included the Puerto Rican gang, the Latin Kings. Preliminary research on the Latin Queens (the female counter-part to the Latin Kings) indicated that male domination in Puerto Rican gangs tends to control and isolate females. However, in the mid-1990s, when increasing numbers of Latin Kings were imprisoned, the females' roles changed dramatically. The Latin Queens who remained in the neighborhood became leaders, maintaining communication between incarcerated Kings and gang members still on the streets. The street branches of the Latin Kings became distinct from the prison branches. As females became more important, these street branches became more likely to emphasize community problem solving and to discourage violence.

Critical Thinking

1. Do you think that welfare reform plus a slowing economy will encourage more females to join and stay in gangs? Is the fact that female gang members rely on welfare a reason to support the argument that public assistance should be ended or curtailed?
2. Do you think that girls join gangs to avoid sexual and physical abuse at home, or are they motivated by the excitement and profits that gang membership may bring?

InfoTrac College Edition Research

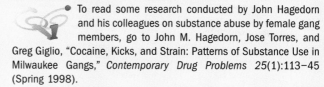

To read some research conducted by John Hagedorn and his colleagues on substance abuse by female gang members, go to John M. Hagedorn, Jose Torres, and Greg Giglio, "Cocaine, Kicks, and Strain: Patterns of Substance Use in Milwaukee Gangs," *Contemporary Drug Problems* 25(1):113–45 (Spring 1998).

Source: Adapted from Joan Moore and John Hagedorn, *Female Gangs: A Focus on Research* (Washington, DC: Office of Juvenile Justice and Delinquency Prevention, 2001).

bers may be looked up to, but they are not necessarily considered leaders by younger members. In his analysis of Los Angeles gangs, Malcolm Klein observed that many gang leaders shrink from taking a leadership role and actively deny leadership. Klein overheard one gang boy claim, "We got no leaders, man. Everybody's a leader, and nobody can talk for nobody else."[98] The most plausible explanation of this ambivalence is the boy's fear that during times of crisis, his decisions will conflict with those of other leaders and he will lose status and face.

There appears then to be a diverse concept of leadership depending on the organizational structure of the gang. Less organized gangs are marked by diffuse and shifting leadership. Larger and more organized gangs have a clear chain of command and leaders who are supposed to give orders, plan activities, and control members' behavior.[99]

Communications

Gangs today seek recognition both from their rivals and the community as a whole. Image and reputation depend on a gang's ability to communicate to the rest of the

Figure 8.2
Gang Symbols Used in Graffiti
Source: Illinois State Police, Springfield, IL, 2001.

graffiti Inscriptions or drawings made on a wall or structure and used by delinquents for gang messages and turf definition.

world. One major source of gang communication is **graffiti.** (See Figure 8.2.) These wall writings are especially elaborate among Latino gangs, who call their inscriptions *placasos* or *placa,* meaning sign or plaque.[100] Latino gang graffiti will usually contain the writer's street name and the name of the gang. Strength or power is frequently asserted through the use of the term *rifa,* which means to rule, and *controllo,* indicating that the gang controls the area. Another common inscription is "p/v," meaning *por vida*; this refers to the fact that the gang expects to control the area "for life." If the numeral 13 is used, it signifies that the gang is *loco,* or "wild."

Crossed-out graffiti indicates that a territory is being contested by a rival gang, while undisturbed writing indicates that the gang's power has gone unchallenged.

Gangs also communicate by ritualistic argot (speech patterns). *Gangbangers* may refer to their *crew, posse, troop,* or *tribe.* Within larger gangs are *sets,* which hang in particular neighborhoods, and *tips,* which are small groups formed for particular purposes. Table 8.1 illustrates a variety of gang argot.

Flashing or tossing gang signs in the presence of rivals is often viewed as a direct challenge that can escalate into a verbal or physical confrontation. In Chicago, gangs call this **representing.** Gang boys will proclaim their affiliation ("Latin King Love!" "Stone Killers!") and ask victims, "Who do you ride?" or "What do you be about?"; an incorrect response will provoke an attack.[101] False representing can be used to intentionally misinform witnesses and victims; it can be used to expose imposters or neutrals trying to make safe passage through gang-controlled territory.

representing Tossing or flashing gang signs in the presence of rivals, often escalating into a verbal or physical confrontation.

Still another method of communication is clothing. In some areas, gang members communicate their membership by wearing jackets with the name of their gang embroidered on the back. In Boston neighborhoods, certain articles of clothing, for ex-

Table 8.1 Gang Slang

Busted/popped a cap: Shot at someone	**Colors:** Gang colors (on shoes, rag, shoelaces, etc.)
Buster: Youngster trying to be a gang member/Fake gang member	**O.G.:** Original gangster, which you are considered to be when you have killed someone; true; original; someone who is true to the game, who never sold out
Camarada: Friend	**Peace out:** Bye
Cap: A retort or to shoot at	**Peace-N:** Not looking for trouble
Carnal: Brother	**Pedo:** Fight
Carnala: Sister	**Phat, that's:** Incredible; great
Chale: No	**Piedra:** Rock cocaine, crack
Chavala: Little girl	**Popo:** Police
Check it out: Listen to what I have to say	**Por vida (P/V):** Forever
Chill out: Stop it/ Don't do that/ Calm down	**Put in some work:** Do a shooting
Chingasos: Fighting	**Quette:** Gun
Chiva: Heroin	**Rock star:** Cocaine prostitute or user
Chivero: Heroin addict	**Rooster:** Piru blood street gang
Chota: Police	**Ruka:** Gang chick
C.K.: Crip killer	**Salty, you:** Think you know everything
Click up: To get along well with a homeboy	
Cluck: Cocaine smoker	Source: Austin, Texas, Police Department Gang Control Unit, 1998.

ample, sneakers or sports jackets with a particular team logo, are worn to identify gang membership.[102] In Los Angeles, the two major black gangs are the Crips and the Bloods, each containing many thousands of members. Crips are identified with the color blue and will wear some article of blue clothing—hat, belt, or jacket—to communicate their allegiance; their rivals, the Bloods, identify with the color red.[103]

Criminality

In the 1600s English gangs broke windows, demolished taverns, assaulted local watchmen, and fought intergang battles (dressed in colored ribbons so they could tell who was on their side).[104] Today, gang criminality has numerous patterns.[105] Some gangs specialize; for example, drug-oriented gangs concentrate on the sale of marijuana, PCP, cocaine, crack, and amphetamines. Other gangs are eclectic, engaging in a wide range of criminal activity from felony assaults to drug dealing.[106]

The 1999 National Youth Gang Survey found that offense types reported to be most prevalent among gang members are larceny/theft, aggravated assault, and burglary/breaking and entering, and estimated that 46 percent of youth gang members are involved in street drug sales to generate profits for the gang.[107] The percentage of youth gangs that specialized in drug trafficking increased from 34 percent in 1998 to 40 percent in 1999. But not all gangs are major players in drug trafficking, and those that are tend to distribute small amounts of drugs at the street level. The world of major dealing belongs to adults, not to gang youths.[108]

Regardless of their type, gang members typically commit more crimes than any other youths in the social environment; gang membership enhances any preexisting propensity to commit crime.[109] Data from the Rochester Youth Development Study (RYDS), a longitudinal cohort study of 1,000 youths in upstate New York, supports the gang-crime association survey. As Figure 8.3 shows, while 30 percent of the youths in the sample report being a gang member, they account for 65 percent of all reported delinquent acts. The RYDS data show that gang members account for 86 percent of all serious crimes, 63 percent of the alcohol use, and 61 percent of the drug abuse.[110]

Gang Violence Research indicates that gang violence is impulsive and emotional and therefore comes in spurts. It typically involves defense of the gang and the gang memberships' reputation.[111] Once a spurt ends, the level of violence may recede, but

Figure 8.3
Percentage of Crimes Reported by Gang Members in the Rochester Youth Development Study
Source: Terence Thornberry and James Burch, "Gang Members and Delinquent Behavior," *Juvenile Justice Bulletin* (Office of Juvenile Justice and Delinquency Prevention, June 1997); created by Center for Substance Abuse Research, University of Maryland, 1997.
Note: All data are based on self-reported behaviors. The question asked to determine gang membership was, "Are you a member of a street gang or a posse?"

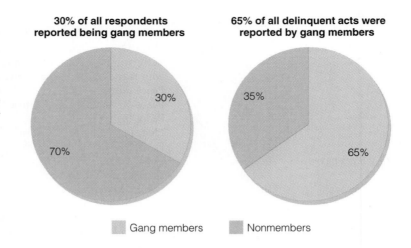

30% of all respondents reported being gang members

65% of all delinquent acts were reported by gang members

Gang members   Nonmembers

it remains at a level higher than it was previously, constantly escalating with each battle. Spurts usually are not citywide but occur in specific neighborhoods during periods of intense competition over the expansion and defense of gang territory. Peaks in gang homicides tend to correspond to a series of escalating confrontations, usually over control of territory—either traditional street gang turf or an entrepreneurial drug market.[112] Violence often takes the form of boundary disputes. The most dangerous areas are along disputed boundaries where a drug hot spot intersects with a turf hot spot. There are also "marauder" patterns in which members of rival gangs travel to the hub of their enemy's territory in search of potential victims.[113]

Because of the violent nature of their vocation, gang boys are heavily armed, dangerous, and more violent than nonmembers. It should come as no surprise that a nationwide survey of arrestees found that half of those who owned or carried guns claimed to be gang members.[114]

Violence is a core factor of gang formation and life; it is what causes gangs to spread from one neighborhood to another.[115] Gang members are always feeling threatened by other gangs and are wary of encroachments on their turf. It is not surprising that gang members are likely to increase gun ownership and possession once they join gangs.[116] Considering that gang boys are well armed and wary, it should come as no surprise that members face a far greater chance of death at an early age than nongang boys.[117]

Those who are members of gangs are much more likely to carry weapons and to have peers—also gang members—who own guns for protection. Gun ownership is related to a wide range of undesirable delinquent behaviors, including gun carrying, gun crime, gang membership, and drug selling.[118] In the Focus on Delinquency box "Gang Boys and Guns," the Rochester study data is used to analyze an important question: Do gangs recruit boys who carry guns, or does joining a gang require members to begin carrying weapons?

Honor, Courage, and Prestige Scott Decker has studied gangs in St. Louis, Missouri, and found that violence is a central feature of gang life, essential to the transformation of a peer group into a gang. When asked why he calls the groups he belongs to a gang, one member replied, "Violence, I guess. There is more violence than a family. With a gang it's like fighting all the time, killing, shooting."[119] Decker found that gang violence can take on a number of different forms. When joining the gang, members may be forced to participate in violent rituals to prove their courage and reliability. Gang members are ready to fight when others attack them and/or when they believe their territory or turf is being encroached upon. Defacing gang

Gang Boys and Guns

The general public and the media equate gang membership with youths who routinely carry guns and are not afraid to use them. Do gangs recruit youths who are already involved with guns, or does gang membership lead to gun ownership? Past research has usually indicated that gangs and guns go hand in hand. Members fear that sudden violence may be perpetrated against them. Since most gang activity takes place outside the realm of police protection, gang members see a need to protect themselves from others who are just like them. Most research efforts show that as members of one gang arm themselves for self-protection, rivals begin to carry guns for the same reason.

Data from the Rochester Youth Study enables researchers to determine whether gun ownership (for sport or protection) occurs prior to, during, or after gang participation. To examine this relationship, researchers compared gang members with nonmembers. Table A shows the percentage of nonmembers and future, current, and past members who reported owning guns for sport and protection, carrying guns, and having peers who owned guns for protection.

Table A **Percentage of Boys Engaging in Gun-Related Behaviors, by Gang Membership Status**

	Gang Membership Status (%)			
Gun behavior	Nonmember ($n = 548$)	Future member ($n = 39$)	Current member ($n = 81$)	Past member ($n = 32$)
Owns gun for sport	8.4	12.8	9.9	7.5
Owns gun for protection[a,b]	14.2	23.1	30.9	13.2
Carries a gun[a,b]	8.6	12.8	21.0	5.7
Peers own guns for protection[a,b,c]	55.1	53.8	77.8	52.8

Note: Nonmembers were never in a gang. Future members were not in a gang in a preceding interview wave but joined a gang in a subsequent wave. Current members belonged to a gang at the time of the current wave. Past members belonged to a gang in a preceding wave but not in the current wave.

Significance tests are for 0.5-level 1-tail tests. The superscripts indicate statistically significant differences for the following comparisons:

[a]Current with Past

[b]Nonmember with Current

[c]Current with Future

There were no statistically significant differences by gang status in the percentage of boys owning guns for sport. That is, gang membership neither enhanced nor diminished the likelihood of owning a gun for sport. However, gang membership did enhance the likelihood of owning a gun for protection. Future gang members were somewhat more likely than nonmembers to own guns for protection (23.1% versus 14.2%), but current gang members were clearly more likely than nonmembers to own guns for protection (30.9% versus 14.2%).

The rate of owning illegal guns was not significantly higher for future gang members than for those who did not join gangs. This finding suggests that gangs are not particularly likely to recruit boys who already own and carry guns for protection. Furthermore, among boys who had left gangs, the rate of gun ownership for protection dropped to a level similar to that of boys who had never belonged to a gang (13.2% for past members versus 14.2% for nonmembers). These findings suggest that boys who do not want to participate in the violence and gun carrying associated with gangs leave the gangs. The findings might also suggest that when youths leave gangs, they feel less need to carry guns because they are no longer in a climate of conflict and violence. Statistically, past gang members look like nonmembers in terms of owning guns for protection and carrying guns on the street. Thus, it appears that gangs cause new members to obtain and then carry guns, but they do not recruit boys who already carry guns.

Critical Thinking

1. Gun control advocates believe that harsh penalties should be adapted for the possession and sale of unregistered firearms. Gun advocates believe that controlling the right to bear arms is a violation of rights affirmed by the U.S. Constitution. Would gun control help reduce gang violence, or would gang boys carry weapons no matter what the penalties?

InfoTrac College Edition Research

 How can gang boys be weaned away from violence? One approach is peer mentoring. To find out about this technique, read Karen Sheehan, Joseph A. DiCara, Susan LeBailly, and Katherine Kaufer Christoffel, "Adapting the Gang Model: Peer Mentoring for Violence Prevention," *Pediatrics* 104(1):50 (July 1999).

Source: Alan Lizotte and David Sheppard, *Gun Use by Male Juveniles* (Washington, DC: Office of Juvenile Justice and Delinquency Prevention, 2001).

signs or graffiti will demand a violent response. Retaliatory violence may be directed against rival gang boys accused of insults or who are involved in personal disputes. Gang boys also expect to fight when they go to certain locations that are off limits or attend events such as house parties where violence is routine.

Gang members are sensitive to any rivals who question their honor or courage. Once an insult is perceived or a challenge is offered, the gang's honor cannot be restored until the "debt" is repaid. Police efforts to cool down gang disputes only delay the inevitable revenge—a beating, or a drive-by shooting. Random acts of revenge have become so common that physicians now consider the consequences of drive-by shootings as a significant health problem, one that is a major contributor to early morbidity and mortality among adolescents and children in Los Angeles and other major gang cities.[120]

Retaliation is often directed against gang members who step out of line. If subordinates disobey orders, perhaps by using rather than selling drugs, they may be subject to harsh disciplinary action by other gang members. Violence is used to maintain the gang's internal discipline and security.

Another common gang crime is extortion, called "turf tax," which involves forcing people to pay the gang to be protected from dangerous neighborhood youths (presumably themselves). **Prestige crimes** occur when a gang boy steals or assaults someone, even a police officer, to gain prestige in the gang and neighborhood. These crimes may be part of an initiation rite or an effort to establish a special reputation, a position of responsibility, or a leadership role; to prevail in an internal power struggle, or to respond to a challenge from a rival (proving the youth is not chicken).

prestige crimes Stealing or assaulting someone to gain prestige in the neighborhood; often part of gang initiation rites.

Ethnic and Racial Composition

The most recent National Youth Gang Survey data (Figure 8.4) found that the race/ethnicity composition of gangs is as follows: Hispanic (47%), African American (31%), Caucasian (13%), Asian (7%), and other (2%).

The majority of gang observers view gangs as racially homogeneous groups: all white (English, Italian, Irish, and/or Slavic origin), all black (African origin), all Hispanic/Latino (Mexican, Puerto Rican, Panamanian, Colombian, and other Spanish-speaking people), or all Asian (Chinese, Japanese, Korean, Taiwanese, Samoan, and Vietnamese).[121] Most intergang conflict appears to be among groups of the same ethnic and racial background.[122]

The ethnic distribution of gangs corresponds to their geographic location. For example, in Philadelphia and Detroit, the overwhelming number of gang members are African American. In New York and Los Angeles, Latino gangs predominate, and San Francisco's small gang population is mostly Asian.[123] Newly emerging immigrant goups are making their presence felt in gangs. Authorities in Buffalo, New York, estimate that 10 percent of their gang population are Jamaicans. Cambodian and Haitian youths are joining gangs in Boston. A significant portion of Honolulu's gangs are Samoans (19%) and Filipinos (46%).[124]

Figure 8.4
Race/Ethnicity of Youth Gang Members, 1996 and 1999
Source: National Youth Gang Survey, 1999.

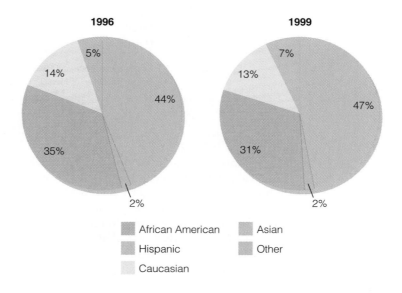

1996: 5%, 14%, 44%, 35%, 2%

1999: 7%, 13%, 47%, 31%, 2%

African American   Asian
Hispanic   Other
Caucasian

African American Gangs The first black youth gangs were organized in the early 1920s and specialized in common street crime activities.[125] Since they had few rival organizations in their inner-city locales, they were able to concentrate on criminal activity, rather than defending their turf. By the 1930s, the expanding number of rival gangs spawned competition, and inner-city gang warfare became commonplace.

In Los Angeles, which is today a hot spot of gang activity, the first black youth gang formed in the 1920s was the Boozies, named after a family that provided a significant portion of its membership. This gang virtually ran the inner city until the 1930s, when rivals began to challenge its criminal monopoly. In the next 20 years, a number of black gangs, including the Businessmen, Home Street, Slauson, and Neighborhood, emerged and met with varying degrees of criminal success.

In the 1970s, the dominant Crips gang was formed and began to spread over much of Los Angeles. Other neighborhood gangs merged into the Crips or affiliated with it by adding "Crips" to their name, so that the Main Street gang became the Main Street Crips. The Crips' dominance has since been challenged by its archrivals, the Bloods. Both of these groups, whose total membership exceeds 25,000 youths, have an organization that resembles an organized crime family and are heavily involved in drug trafficking.

In Chicago, The Blackstone Rangers dominated illicit activities for almost 25 years beginning in the 1960s and until the early 1990s, when their leader, Jeff Fort, and many of his associates were indicted and imprisoned.[126] The Rangers, who later evolved into the El Rukin gang, worked with "legitimate" businessmen to import and sell heroin. Earning millions in profits, they established businesses that helped them launder drug money. Among their enterprises was a security company, which allowed members to carry guns legally. Though many of the convictions were later overturned, the power of El Rukin was ended. (Fort remains in a high-security prison.)

The Rangers' chief rivals, the Black Gangster Disciples, are now the dominant gang in Chicago. While most street gangs are too disorganized to become stable crime groups, the Gangster Disciples have a structure, activities, and relationships similar to traditional organized gangs, such as the Mafia. Gangster Disciple members are actively involved in politics in an effort to gain power and support. Members meet together regularly, commit crime as a group, and maintain ongoing relationships with other street gangs and also with prison-based gangs. The Gangster Disciples have extensive ownership of "legitimate" private businesses and dealings with other businessmen. They offer protection against rival gangs and supply stolen merchandise to customers and employees.[127]

African American gang members, especially those in Los Angeles, have some unique behavioral characteristics. They frequently use nicknames to identify themselves, often based on a behavioral trait: "Little .45" might be used by someone whose favorite weapon is a large handgun. Although TV shows portray gangs as wearing distinctive attire and jackets, in reality, members usually favor nondescript attire in order to reduce police scrutiny; after all, a routine police search can turn up narcotics or weapons. However, gang boys do frequently use distinctive hairstyles, featuring shaving, cornrows, shaping, and/or braids, that are designed to look like their leaders. Tattooing is popular, and members often wear colored scarves or "rags" to identify their gang affiliation. In Los Angeles, Crips use blue or black rags, while Bloods normally carry red.

It is also common for black gang members to mark their territory with distinctive graffiti. The messages are crude, rather than sophisticated: drawings of guns, dollar signs, proclamations of individual power, and profanity.

barrio A Latino term meaning neighborhood.

Hispanic Gangs Latin or **barrio** gangs are not a recent development. Aggressive male youth groups have been a feature of the Mexican community in Los Angeles as far back as the nineteenth century.[128] The early barrio gangs were made up of young laborers whose behavior was more oriented around sports and socializing than criminality. Today these gangs are made up of kids whose ethnic ancestry can be traced to one of several Spanish-speaking cultures, such as Puerto Rico and Mexico. They are known for their fierce loyalty to their original or "home" gang; this affiliation is maintained, even if they move to a new neighborhood that contains a rival gang. Admission to the gang usually involves an initiation ritual in which boys are required to show their fearlessness and prove their *machismo,* or manliness. The most common test requires novices to fight several established members or commit some crime, such as a purse snatching or robbery. The code of conduct associated with membership means never ratting on a brother or even a rival, facing death or prison without betraying their sense of honor.

Latino barrio gangs have evolved over time, sustained by continuous waves of immigrants from Mexico and Latin and South America. Some of these gangs are ethnically distinct—Dominican, Salvadoran, Mexican—while others may have members from a variety of nations. Each new wave of immigrants settles in existing barrios or creates new ones. There, youngsters subscribe to the **cholo** (marginalized) subculture, with its own set of slang, clothing, style, and values. The *cholo* subculture places a high value on friendship, often imputing family and kinship relationships to peers (by calling them "brother" or "cousin"). Scholastic achievement is devalued and replaced with "partying." Employment is valued only if it requires little effort and brings in enough cash to party. An important aspect of the culture is demonstrating *machismo,* or manliness. Barrio youths try to impress their peers and rivals with their ability to drink more than others, their fighting and sexual prowess, and their heart.

In some areas, such as Miami, Hispanic gangs are rigidly organized with a fixed leadership hierarchy. However, in Southern California, which has the largest concentration of Hispanic youth gangs, leadership is fluid. No youth is elected to a post such as president or warlord. During times of crisis, those with particular skills will assume command on a situational basis.[129] For example, one boy will lead in combat, while another will negotiate drug deals.

In the 1940s, the *pachuco* fad swept through the Latino community; its advocates wore outlandish outfits (zoot suits) and spoke a unique Spanish-English slang. A well-publicized murder case and some urban disturbances helped brand the *pachucos* as vicious "rat packs." Though most zoot-suiters (who can be compared to members of the heavy metal music culture today) were not gang members or necessarily involved in crime, the press focused attention on them as a major social problem, and a popular stereotype was created. Hispanic gang boys are still known for their distinctive dress codes. Some wear knit, dark-colored watch caps pulled down over the ears with a small roll at the bottom. Others wear a folded bandana over the forehead and tied in back. Another popular headpiece is the "stingy brim" fedora or a baseball cap with the wearer's nickname and gang affiliation written on the cap's turned up bill. Members favor tank-style T-shirts or an open Pendleton shirt, which gives them quick access to weapons.

Members also proclaim their affiliations by marking off territory with colorful and intricate graffiti. Hispanic gang graffiti has very stylized lettering, frequently uses three-dimensional designs, and proclaims members' organizational pride and power.

Hispanic gangs have a strong sense of territory, or turf, and a great deal of gang violence is directed at warding off any threat to their control. Slights by rivals, including put-downs, stare-downs ("mad-dogging"), defacing gang insignia, and territorial intrusions, can set off a violent and bloody gang confrontation. Newer gangs will carry out this violence with high-powered automatic weapons, a far cry from the zip guns and gravity knives of the past.

Asian Gangs   Asian gangs are prominent in such cities as New York, Los Angeles, San Francisco, Seattle, and Houston. The earliest gangs, *Wah Ching,* were formed in the nineteenth century by Chinese youth affiliated with adult crime groups (*tongs*). In the 1960s, two other gangs formed in San Francisco, the Joe Boys and Yu Li,

cholo   A member of the Hispanic subculture of marginalized, antisocial youth.

now operate, along with the Wah Ching, in many major U.S. cities. National attention focused on the activities of these Chinese gangs in 1977, when a shootout in the Golden Dragon restaurant in San Francisco left 5 dead and 11 wounded. On the East Coast, prominent Asian gangs include Flying Dragon, Green Dragon, Ghost Shadows, Fu Ching, So on Leong, Tong So on, and Born to Kill (a Vietnamese gang).[130]

In an important work, Ko-Lin Chin has described the inner workings of Chinese youth gangs today.[131] Chin finds that these gangs have unique properties, such as their reliance on raising capital from the Chinese community through extortion and then investing this money in legitimate business enterprises. Chinese gangs recruit new members from the pool of disaffected youth who have problems at school and consider themselves among the few educational failures in a culture that prizes academic achievement.

In addition to Chinese gangs, Samoan gangs, primarily the Sons of Samoa, have operated on the West Coast, as have Vietnamese gangs whose influence has been felt in Los Angeles, New York, and Boston. James Diego Vigil and Steve Chong Yun studied Vietnamese gangs and found that their formation can be tied to such external factors as racism, economic problems, and school failure and such internal problems as family stress and failure to achieve the level of success enjoyed by other Asians. Vietnamese gangs are formed when youths feel they need their *ahns,* or brothers, for protection and have unsatisfied needs for belonging.[132]

Asian gangs tend to victimize members of their own ethnic group. Because of group solidarity and distrust of outside authorities, little is known about their activities.

Anglo Gangs The first American youth gangs were made up of white ethnic youths of European ancestry, especially Irish and Italian immigrants. During the 1950s such ethnic youth gangs commonly competed with African American and Hispanic gangs in the nation's largest cities.

skinhead Member of white supremacist gang, identified by a shaved skull and Nazi or Ku Klux Klan markings.

Today, Anglo gang activity is not uncommon, especially in smaller towns.[133] Many are organized as derivatives of the English punk and **skinhead** movement of the 1970s. In England, these youths, generally the daughters and sons of lower-class parents, sported wildly dyed hair, often shaved into "mohawks," military clothes, iron cross earrings, and high-topped military boots. Music was a big part of their lives, and the band that characterized their lifestyle was the punk band the Sex Pistols, led by Johnny Rotten and Sid Vicious. Their creed was antiestablishment, and their anger was directed toward foreigners, who they believed were taking their jobs.

The punker-skinhead style was brought over to the States by bands that replicated the Sex Pistols' antisocial music, stage presence, and dress. The music, philosophy, and lifestyle of these rock bands inspired the formation of a variety of white youth gangs. However, unlike their British brothers, American white gang members are often alienated middle-class youths, rather than poor, lower-class kids who are out of society's mainstream. These gang members include "punkers" or "stoners" who dress in the latest heavy metal rock fashions and engage in drug- and violence-related activities. Some of these gangs espouse religious beliefs involving the occult and satanic worship.[134] There are also skinhead groups that are devoted to racist, white supremacist activities. These kids are being actively recruited by adult hate groups. Another variety of white youth gang engages in satanic rituals and becomes obsessed with occult themes, suicide, ritual killings, and animal mutilations. Members of these gangs get seriously involved in devil worship, tattoo themselves with occult symbols, and gouge their bodies to draw blood for satanic rituals.

While national surveys do not show an upsurge in Anglo gang activity, a recent survey of almost 6,000 youths in 42 schools located in 11 cities found that about 25 percent of the kids who claimed to be gang members are white, a far higher number than found in national surveys.[135]

GANGS POSE A SERIOUS PROBLEM in inner-city areas. Here Ishan Garrett watches as marchers pass through his neighborhood during a rally to take back the neighborhood in Las Vegas, March 24, 2001. More than 200 residents joined together in support of the Coalition for Community Peace to voice their opposition to the recent series of gang slayings. Garrett's neighborhood is one of eight places where gang-related slayings have occurred in the past 30 days.

Why Do Youths Join Gangs?

Though gangs flourish in lower-class, inner-city areas, gang membership cannot be assumed to be solely a function of lower-class subcultural identity: Many lower-class youths do not join gangs, and middle-class kids are found in suburban skinhead and stoner groups. What are some of the suspected causes of gang delinquency?

Anthropological View

Writing about gangs in the 1950s, Herbert Block and Arthur Niederhoffer suggested that gangs appeal to adolescents' deep-seated longing for the tribal group process that sustained and nurtured their ancestors.[136] Block and Niederhoffer found that gang processes and functions do seem similar to the puberty rites of some tribal cultures; like their ancient counterparts, gang rituals help the child bridge the gap between childhood and adulthood. For example, uniforms, tattoos, and other identifying marks are an integral part of gang culture. Gang initiation ceremonies are similar to activities of young men in Pacific island cultures. Many gangs put new members through a hazing as an initiation to make sure they have "heart," a feature similar to tribal rites. In tribal societies, initiation into a cult is viewed as the death of childhood. By analogy, younger boys in lower-class urban areas yearn for the time when they can join the gang and really start to live. Membership in the adolescent gang "means the youth gives up his life as a child and assumes a new way of life."[137] Gang names are suggestive of "totemic ancestors" because they usually are symbolic (Cobras, Jaguars, and Kings, for example).

Evidence exists that contemporary gangs continue these traditions. The Gang Prevention and Intervention survey found that over two-thirds of gang kids have family members who are or were in gangs, and fully two-thirds of the gang kids reported having members in their gang whose parents are also active members. These data indicate that ganging has become a cultural family tradition passed on as a rite of passage from one generation to the next.[138] James Diego Vigil has described the rituals of gang initiation, which include physical pummeling to show that the gang boy is brave and ready to leave his matricentric (mother-dominated) household; this process seems reminiscent of tribal initiation rights.[139] For gang members, these rituals become an important part of gang activities. Hand signs and graffiti have a tribal flavor. Gang members adopt nicknames and street identities that reflect personality or physical traits: The more volatile are called "Crazy," "Loco," or "Psycho," while those who wear glasses or read books are dubbed "Professor."[140]

Social Disorganization/Sociocultural View

Sociologists have commonly viewed the shattering, destructive sociocultural forces in socially disorganized inner-city slum areas as the major cause of gang formation. Thrasher introduced this concept in his pioneering work on gangs, and it is a theme found in the classic studies of Richard Cloward and Lloyd Ohlin and of Albert K. Cohen.[141] Irving Spergel's consummate study *Racketville, Slumtown, and Haulburg,* found that Slumtown, the area with the lowest income and the largest population, also had the highest number of violent gangs.[142] According to Spergel, the gang gives lower-class youths a means of attaining personal reputations and peer group status. Malcolm Klein's oft-cited research of the late 1960s and 1970s again found that typical gang members came from dysfunctional and destitute families, had family members with criminal histories, and lacked adequate educational and vocational role models.[143]

The social disorganization/sociocultural view retains its prominent position today. Vigil paints a vivid picture of the forces that drive kids into gangs in his well-respected work *Barrio Gangs.*[144] Vigil's gang kids are pushed into membership because of poverty and minority status. Those who join gangs are the most marginal youths in their neighborhoods and are outcasts in their own families. Vigil finds that all barrio dwellers experience some forms of psychological, economic, cultural, or social "stressors," which hinder their lives. Gang kids are usually afflicted with more than one of these problems, causing them to suffer from "multiple marginality." Barrio youths join gangs because they seek a sense of belonging; gangs offer a set of peers with whom friendship and family-like relationships are expected.[145]

Overall, the sociocultural view assumes that gangs are a natural and normal response to the privations of lower-class life and that gangs are a status-generating medium for boys whose aspirations cannot be realized by legitimate means. Kids who join gangs may hold conventional values, such as the desire to become a financial success, but are either unwilling or unable to accomplish this goal through conventional means, such as schooling.[146] Gangs then are not solely made up of kids from dysfunctional families who seek deviant peers in order to compensate for parental brutality or incompetence. Gangs form in poor neighborhoods and recruit youths from many different kinds of families. Rather than an alternate family, the gang is a coalition of troubled kids who are socialized mainly by the streets rather than by conventional institutions.[147]

Anomie   In his book on gangs, Irving Spergel suggests that youths are encouraged to join gangs during periods of social, economic, and cultural turmoil; conditions that are thought to produce anomie-like conditions.[148] For example, gangs were present during the Russian Revolution of 1917 and then again during the chaos following the crumbling of the Soviet Union in the early 1990s. The rise of right-wing youth gangs in Germany is associated with social and political change brought about by the unification of East and West Germany. Skinhead groups have formed in response to the immigrants coming from Turkey and North Africa. In the United States, Spergel makes note, gangs have formed in areas where rapid population changes have unsettled community norms.

Immigration or emigration, rapidly expanding or contracting populations, and/or the incursion of different racial/ethnic groups or even different segments or generations of the same racial/ethnic population, can create fragmented communities and gang problems.[149]

Psychological View

A minority position on the formation of gangs is that they serve as an outlet for psychologically diseased youths. One proponent of this view is Lewis Yablonsky, whose theory of violent-gang formation holds that violent gangs recruit their members among the more sociopathic youths living in disorganized slum communities.[150] Yablonsky views the sociopathic youth as one who lacks "social feelings." He "has not been trained to have human feelings or compassion or responsibility for another."[151] Yablonsky supports this contention by pointing to the eccentric, destructive, and hostile sexual attitudes and behavior of gang youths, who are often violent and sadistic. He sums up the sociopathic character traits of gang boys as (1) a defective social conscience marked by limited feelings of guilt for destructive acts against others; (2) limited compassion or empathy for others; (3) behavior dominated by egocentrism and self-seeking goals; and (4) the manipulation of others for immediate self-gratification (for example, sexually exploitative modes of behavior) without any moral concern or responsibility. Yablonsky's view is substantiated by cross-cultural studies, which have also found that gang members suffer from psychological deficits, including impulsivity and poor personality control.[152]

Malcolm Klein's more recent analysis of Los Angeles gangs finds that many street gang members suffer from psychological and neuropsychological deficits, including low self-concept, social disabilities or deficits, poor impulse control, and limited life skills. Adolescents who display conduct disorders, early onset of antisocial behavior, and violent temperaments are at the greatest risk for later gang membership.[153] Yet, Klein does not consider most gang youths to be abnormal or pathological. To help them, he believes that psychological therapy is less important than providing gang members with vocational training, educational skills, and improving their chances for legitimate opportunities.[154]

Rational Choice View

Some youths may join gangs after making the rational choice that gang membership may benefit their law-violating careers and be a source of income. Members of the underclass, who perceive few opportunities in the legitimate economic structure, will turn to gangs as a way of obtaining desired goods and services, either directly through theft and extortion or indirectly through the profits generated by drug dealing and weapon sales. Joining a gang then can be viewed as an "employment decision": the gang can provide its "partners" with the security of knowing they can call on the services of talented "associates" to successfully carry out business ventures. Mercer Sullivan's study of Brooklyn gangs found that members call success at crime "getting paid," a term that imparts an economic edge to gang activity. Gang boys also refer to the rewards of crime as "getting over," which refers to their triumph and pride at "beating the system" and succeeding, even though they are way out of the economic mainstream.[155]

According to this view, the gang boy has long been involved in criminal activity *prior* to his gang membership and joins the gang as a means of improving his illegal "productivity."[156] Gang membership is *not* a necessary precondition for delinquency; kids who are already delinquent may join gangs because membership facilitates or enhances their criminal careers.

Felix Padilla found this when he studied the Diamonds, a Latino gang in Chicago.[157] Joining the gang was a decision made after a careful assessment of legitimate economic opportunities. The gang represented a means of achieving aspirations that were otherwise closed off. The Diamonds made collective business decisions; individuals who made their own deals were severely penalized. The gang maintained a distinct organizational structure and carried out other functions similar to those of legitimate enterprises, including personnel recruitment and financing business ventures with internal and external capital.

The rational choice view is also endorsed by Martin Sanchez-Jankowski in his important book *Islands in the Street*.[158] Sanchez-Jankowski found gangs to be organizations made up of adolescents who maintain a "defiant individualist character." These individuals maintain distinct personality traits: wariness or mistrust of the outside world; self-reliance; isolation from society; good survival instincts; defiance against authority; and a strong belief in the survival of the fittest, that only the strong survive. Kids holding these views and possessing these character traits make a rational decision to join a gang because the gang presents an opportunity to improve the quality of their lives. The gang offers otherwise unobtainable economic and social opportunities, including both support for crime and access to parties, social events, and sexual outlets. Gangs that last the longest and are the most successful are the ones that can offer incentives to these ambitious but destitute youths and can control their behaviors. Sanchez-Jankowski's views, important for understanding the economic and social incentives of gang membership, have been supported by independent research data.[159]

The rational choice view holds that gangs provide support for criminal opportunities that might not otherwise be available. Some recent research by Terence Thornberry and his colleagues at the Rochester Youth Development Study support this model. They found that before kids become gang members, their substance abuse and delinquency rates are no higher than nongang members. When they are in the gang, their crime and drug abuse rates increase significantly, only to decrease when they leave the gang. Thornberry concludes that gangs facilitate criminality, rather than provide a haven for youth who are disturbed or already highly delinquent. This research is also important because it lends support to the life course model: Events that take place during the life cycle, such as joining a gang, have significant impact on criminal behavior and drug abuse.[160] Criminal behavior is not determined solely by factors that are present at birth or soon after.

Personal Safety According to Spergel, some adolescents choose to join gangs from a "rational calculation" to achieve personal safety rather than profit.[161] Youths who are new to a community may believe they will become the targets of harassment or attack if they remain "unaffiliated." Motivation may have its roots in interracial or interethnic rivalry: Youths who are white, African American, Asian, or Hispanic who reside in an area dominated by a different racial or ethnic group may be persuaded that gang membership is an efficient means of collective protection. Ironically, gang members are more likely to be attacked than nonmembers.

Fun and Support Some youths join gangs simply to party and have fun.[162] They want to enjoy hanging out with kids like themselves and getting involved in exciting experiences. Kids can learn the meaning of friendship and loyalty through gang membership. There is evidence that kids learn pro-gang attitudes from their peers and that these attitudes direct them to join gangs.[163]

Some experts suggest that kids join gangs in an effort to obtain the family-like atmosphere all too often absent from their own homes. Many gang members report that they have limited contact with their fathers and mothers, many of whom are unskilled laborers or unemployed and battling with substance abuse problems.[164]

Controlling Gang Activity

Two basic methods are used to control gang activity. The first involves priority targeting by local criminal justice agencies; the second operates through a variety of social service efforts. Each of these methods will be discussed below.

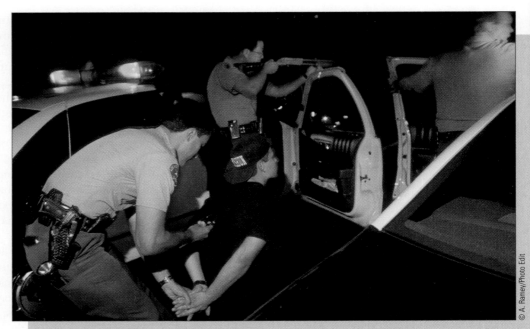

LAW ENFORCEMENT OFFICERS arresting gang members during a sweep in California. Can police actions be an effective deterrent to gang activities or would social services be a more effective alternative?

Law Enforcement Efforts

In recent years, gang control has often been left to local police departments. Gang control takes three basic forms:

1. The youth service program, in which traditional police personnel, usually from the youth unit, are given responsibility for gang control. No personnel are assigned exclusively or mainly to gang-control work.
2. The gang detail, in which one or more police officers, usually from youth or detective units, are assigned exclusively to gang-control work.
3. The gang unit, established solely to deal with gang problems, to which one or more officers are assigned exclusively to gang-control work.[165]

The National Assessment found that 53 of the 72 police departments surveyed maintained separate gang-control units. They are involved in such activities as processing information on youth gangs and gang leaders; prevention efforts, such as mediation programs; enforcement efforts to suppress criminal activity and apprehend those who are believed to have committed crimes; and follow-up investigations directed at apprehending gang members alleged to have committed crimes. About 85 percent of these units have special training in gang control for their personnel, 73 percent have specific policies directed at dealing with gang boys, and 62 percent enforce special laws designed to control gang activity.[166]

A good example of these units is the Chicago Police Department's 400 plus officer gang crime section that maintains intelligence on gang problems and trains officers in dealing with gang problems. Through its gang target program, it identifies street gang members and enters their names in a computer bank that is programmed to alert the unit if the youths are picked up or arrested. Some departments also sponsor general prevention programs that can help control gang activities, including school-based lectures, police-school liaisons, information dissemination, recreation programs, and street worker programs that offer counseling, assistance to parents, and community organization, among other services.

Some police departments engage in *gang-breaking* activities, in which police will focus on the gang leaders and make special efforts to arrest, prosecute, convict, and

Boston's Youth Violence Strike Force (YVSF)

The Youth Violence Strike Force (YVSF) is one of the primary enforcement strategies that Boston is pursuing to combat youth gang violence. The YVSF is a multiagency coordinated task force made up of 45–50 full-time Boston police officers and 15 officers from outside agencies. The membership of the YVSF includes the Massachusetts State Police, the Department of Treasury's Bureau of Alcohol, Tobacco, and Firearms (ATF), police departments from neighboring jurisdictions, Massachusetts Corrections, Probation, Parole, and Division of Youth Service (juvenile corrections) officers, and other agencies as appropriate. It works closely with the Suffolk County District Attorney's and State Attorney General's offices, and participates in the Department of Justice's Anti-Violent Crime Initiative (AVCI) led locally by the U.S. Attorney. The YVSF investigates youth crimes, arrests those responsible, and breaks up the environment for crime. One important accomplishment of the YVSF was the creation of a comprehensive computer database, which has allowed tough enforcement efforts against the leaders of gangs, and positive intervention in the lives of those who are at risk for becoming hard-core gang members.

In addition, the Youth Violence Strike Force, in cooperation with the city of Boston and the Department of Justice, has used criminal and civil forfeiture laws to help secure the safety of the community by taking over drug dens and renovating them as new homes. Over 150 drug dens have been closed through joint federal-state-local cooperation, and nearly 50 are being renovated, including one in the Dorchester neighborhood of Boston, which will provide low-income elderly housing.

The Youth Violence Strike Force takes tough action every day against gangs and gang members across Boston. Yet many of the strike force officers view their work in prevention as equally important, and many of these officers help to sponsor numerous prevention activities in the community. For example, members of the YVSF have been working in partnership with several law enforcement, social service, and private institutions to raise funds for a series of "Kids at Risk" programs provided to youth during the summer. These include professionally run camping programs, membership at the Boys and Girls Clubs and YMCAs, and attendance at basketball camp or the Boston Police's Teen Summer Academy. Another program, called Operation Night Light, puts the YVSF together with concerned clergy members, youth outreach workers, and social service professionals to prevent youth and gang violence of probationers by regularly visiting their homes.

Critical Thinking

1. Is it possible to reduce gang membership without providing youth with a reasonable legitimate alternative, including first-rate schools and job opportunities?

InfoTrac College Edition Research

To read more about Operation Night Light, read James T. Jordan, "Boston's Operation Night Light: New Roles, New Rules," *The FBI Law Enforcement Bulletin* 67(5):1 (August 1998).

Source: "Youth Violence: A Community-Based Response—One City's Success Story" (Washington, DC: Office of the Attorney General, 1996); updated, personal communication Boston Police Department (October 26, 2001).

---

incarcerate them whenever possible. For example, Los Angeles police conduct intensive anti-gang sweeps, in which more than 1,000 officers are put on the street to round up and intimidate gang boys. Police say that the sweeps let the gangs know "who the streets belong to" and show neighborhood residents that someone cares.[167] Despite such efforts, the police response to the gang and youth group problem seems fragmented at best; even in Los Angeles, gang membership and violence remain at all-time highs. Few departments have written policies or procedures on how to deal with youths, and many do not provide gang-control training.

Gang sweeps and other traditional police tactics may not work on today's drug gangs. It might be more appropriate to view gangs as organized criminal enterprises and deal with them as traditional organized crime families. It might be useful to (1) develop informants through criminal prosecutions, payments, and witness protection programs; (2) rely heavily on electronic surveillance and long-term undercover investigations; and (3) use special statutes that create criminal liabilities for conspiracy, extortion, or engaging in criminal enterprises.[168] Of course, such policies are expensive and difficult to implement because they may be needed only against the most sophisticated gangs. However, the gangs that present the greatest threat to urban life may be suitable targets for more intensive police efforts. In addition, as new community-policing strategies are implemented in which police officers are assigned to keep the peace in local neighborhoods (see Chapter 13 for more on community policing), it may be possible to garner sufficient local support and information to counteract gang influences. The Policy and Practice box entitled "Boston's Youth Violence Strike Force" describes one of the more successful police-sponsored gang control efforts.

Once apprehended by police, how are gang boys prosecuted? To find out, go to
http://www.ncjrs.org/txtfiles/pgang.txt
For an up-to-date list of Web links, go to
http://info.wadsworth.com/siegel

Community Control Efforts

detached street workers Social workers who go out into the community and establish close relationships with juvenile gangs with the goal of modifying gang behavior to conform to conventional behaviors and to help gang members get jobs and educational opportunities.

In addition to law enforcement activities, there have been a number of community-based gang-control efforts. Some have involved directing social intervention efforts at gang members. In these programs, social welfare professionals offer direct assistance to at-risk youth. This is actually not a new initiative. During the late nineteenth century, social workers of the YMCA worked with youths in Chicago gangs.[169] During the 1950s, at the height of perceived gang activity, the **detached street worker** program was developed in major centers of gang activity.[170] This unique approach sent social workers into the community to work with gangs on their own turf. The worker attached him- or herself to a gang, participated in its activities, and tried to get to know its members. The purpose was to act as an advocate of the youths, to provide them with a positive role model, to help orient their activities in a positive direction, and to treat individual problems.

Detached street worker programs are sometimes credited with curbing gang activities in the 1950s and 1960s, although their effectiveness has been challenged on the ground that they helped legitimize delinquent groups by turning them into neighborhood organizations.[171] Some critics believed that the detached street workers helped maintain group solidarity, and as a result, new members were drawn to gangs.

Today there are numerous community-level programs designed to limit gang activity. Some, such as the Neutral Zone in Mountlake Terrace, Washington (a Seattle suburb), open recreation areas in the evening hours to provide supervised activities as an alternative to street life.[172] In some areas, citywide coordinating groups help orient gang-control efforts. For example, the Chicago Intervention Network operates field offices around the city in low-income, high-crime areas that provide a variety of services, including neighborhood watches, parent patrols, alternative youth programming, and family support efforts.

Some community efforts are partnerships with juvenile justice agencies. In Los Angeles County the Gang Alternative Prevention Program (GAPP) provides intensive supervision of at-risk juveniles who are on probation for relatively minor crimes. GAPP provides prevention services to juveniles before they become entrenched in gangs. GAPP's services include individual and group counseling; bicultural and bilingual services that are not being provided in the community for adolescents and their parents; and special programs such as tutoring, parent training, job development, and recreational, educational, and cultural experiences.[173]

Sociologist Irving Spergel, a leading expert on gangs, has developed a model for helping communities deal with gang-involved youth that has become the basis for gang-control efforts around the nation. His model includes the five distinct strategies contained in Exhibit 8.3.

Exhibit 8.3   Elements of Spergel's Community Gang-Control Program

1. Community mobilization, including citizens, youth, community groups, and agencies.

2. Provision of academic, economic, and social opportunities. Special school training and job programs are especially critical for older gang members who are not in school but may be ready to leave the gang or decrease participation in criminal gang activity for many reasons, including maturation and the need to provide for family.

3. Social intervention, using street outreach workers to engage gang-involved youth.

4. Gang suppression, including formal and informal social control procedures of the juvenile and criminal justice systems and community agencies and groups. Community-based agencies and local groups must collaborate with juvenile and criminal justice agencies in the surveillance and sharing of information under conditions that protect the community and the civil liberties of youth.

5. Organizational change and development, that is, the appropriate organization and integration of the above strategies and potential reallocation of resources.

Sources: Irving Spergel and Candice Kane, *Community-Based Youth Agency Model* (Washington, DC: Office of Juvenile Justice and Delinquency Prevention, 1990); Jim Burch and Candice Kane, *Implementing the OJJDP Comprehensive Gang Model* (Washington, DC: Office of Juvenile Justice and Delinquency Prevention, 1999).

Community-Based Anti-Gang Programs

Mesa Gang Intervention Project (Mesa, AZ)

The Mesa Gang Intervention Project (MGIP) has targeted 125 youths who are involved in gangs or at high risk for gang involvement and who either reside in or are known to be active within the target area. Key collaborators in the project, which is overseen by a steering committee made up of agency and grassroots executives, are the city of Mesa, the Mesa Police Department, the Maricopa County Adult and Juvenile Probation Departments, Prehab of Arizona, the Mesa Boys and Girls Club, Arizona State University, the United Way, and others.

A team of two gang detectives, one adult and two juvenile probation officers, a youth intervention specialist, and two full-time and two part-time street outreach workers works with and monitors the youths on a daily basis. The team is located in a storefront office within the target community. The MGIP gang detectives and probation officers provide monitoring and surveillance of youth in the program while supporting street outreach workers and staff from other community-based agencies. The MGIP team uses a team problem-solving approach to ensure that progress is made with each youth in the program. The team also provides community assistance, including educating residents about local gang problems and hearing their concerns regarding the neighborhood. Gang education is provided to community members through various professional, neighborhood, and civic groups within the target area.

A computer literacy lab was recently added to the MGIP office, through the support of the Arizona Superior Court. The state of Arizona recently provided additional support to the city of Mesa and MGIP for a mentoring component, and MGIP is supporting a Gang Prevention through Targeted Outreach program at the Mesa Boys and Girls Club.

Other services provided include a cognitive restructuring class for gang-involved youth; parenting classes; services for gang-involved girls; an arts program; a summer camp program focusing on cultural diversity; and tattoo removal services following community service, an educational session, and an agreement not to get any new tattoos for two years. Looking toward the prospect of sustaining local support for project activities, the Mesa Police Department has shifted administrative oversight of the project to the police department's gang unit.

Tucson Gang Project (OUR Town Family Center, Tucson, AZ)

The Tucson Gang Project focused on the Vistas neighborhoods on the south side of Tucson, which have approximately four main gangs with an estimated 350 members. The project served more than 100 youths. Its outreach component operated out of the local Boys and Girls Club in the target area. The primary partners in the project included the Tucson Police Department, Pima County Juvenile Probation and Parole, the Tucson Unified School District, the Tucson Boys and Girls Club, Quail Enterprises (a research and evaluation firm), and a treatment agency known as La Frontera. The project collaborated with, received referrals from, and made referrals to a number of other local agencies. Street outreach workers, probation officers, a police gang unit officer, and others worked to provide services and opportunities on a daily basis to youths targeted by the project and held them accountable for their negative behavior using a range of graduated sanctions. Weekly staff meetings with other agency representatives were supplemented by weekly meetings among project team members to review client and community progress and needs. A community mobilizer on the project staff worked with community agencies and residents of the target neighborhood to keep attention focused on gang issues, and completed a community member survey on the gang problem. The Gang Prevention through Targeted Outreach program was integrated into the project's overall strategy and focused on younger at-risk youth. Where possible, staff from other programs joined gang project staff meetings to share information and coordinate efforts. Project staffing was supplemented by the use of AmeriCorps volunteers.

Critical Thinking

1. What community outreach programs would you suggest to reduce the threat of gang delinquency?
2. Should gang delinquency be considered a health risk, and turned over to medical services rather than law enforcement personnel?

InfoTrac College Edition Research

To read about gang control from a public health perspective, see Allen L. Hixon, "Preventing Street Gang Violence," *American Family Physician* 59(8):2121 (April 15, 1999).

Source: Office of Juvenile Justice and Delinquency Prevention, Washington, DC, August 2000.

The Spergel model is now being tested in a number of communities around the country. The Policy and Practice box entitled "Community-Based Anti-Gang Programs," describes a number of these demonstration programs.

Why Gang Control Is Difficult

The era of the massive urban-based opportunity program has ended in the face of budget shortfalls and the deficit economy. Experts have charged that the lack of legitimate economic opportunity for unskilled adolescents creates a powerful incentive for them to become involved in the illegal economy. To reduce the gang problem, hundreds of thousands of high-paying jobs are needed. Economic opportunities might prove to be particularly effective because surveys of gang boys reveal that many might leave gangs if education and vocational opportunities existed.[174]

This solution does not seem practical or probable. As you may recall (Chapter 4), the more embedded youth become in criminal enterprise, the less likely they are to find meaningful adult work. It is unlikely that gang youth can suddenly be transformed into highly paid professionals. A more reasonable and effective alternative would be to devote a greater degree of available resources to the most deteriorated urban areas, even if it requires pulling funds from groups that have traditionally been recipients of government aid, such as the elderly.[175]

While social solutions to the gang problem seem elusive, the evidence shows that gang involvement is a socio-ecological phenomenon and must therefore be treated as such. Kids join gangs when they live in deteriorated areas, where their need for economic growth and self-fulfillment cannot be met by existing social institutions, and when gang members are there to recruit them at home or at school.[176] Social causes demand social solutions. Programs that enhance the lives of adolescents at school or in the family are the key to reducing gang delinquency.

SUMMARY

Gangs are a serious problem in many cities, yet little is known about them. Most gang members are males, aged 14 to 21, who live in urban ghetto areas. Ethnic minorities make up the majority of gang members. Gangs can be classified by their structure, behavior, or status. Some are believed to be social groups, others are criminally oriented, and still others are violent.

Gangs developed early in the nation's history and reached their heyday in the 1950s and early 1960s. After a lull of 10 years, gang operations began to increase in the late 1970s. Today more than 800,000 youths belong to gangs. Hundreds of thousands of crimes, including drive-by shootings, are believed to be committed by gangs annually. While most members are male, the number of females in gangs is growing at a faster pace.

African American and Hispanic gangs predominate, but Anglo and Asian gangs are also quite common.

We are still not sure what causes gangs. One view is that they serve as a bridge between adolescence and adulthood in communities where adult control is lacking. Another view suggests that gangs are a product of lower-class social disorganization and serve as an alternative means of advancement for disadvantaged boys. Still another view is that some gangs are havens for psychotic and disturbed youths.

Police departments have tried a number of gang-control techniques, but the efforts have not been well organized. A recent national survey found relatively few training efforts designed to help police officers deal with the gang problem.

KEY TERMS

cliques	interstitial group	graffiti	*cholo*
crowds	retreatists	representing	skinhead
co-offending	stable slum	prestige crimes	detached street worker
gangs	*klikas*	barrio	

QUESTIONS FOR DISCUSSION

1. Do gangs serve a purpose? Differentiate between a gang and a fraternity.

2. Discuss the differences between violent, criminal, and drug-oriented gangs.

3. How do gangs in suburban areas differ from inner-city gangs?

4. Do delinquents have cold and distant relationships with their peers?

5. Can gangs be controlled without changing the economic opportunity structure of society? Are there any truly meaningful alternatives to gangs today for lower-class youths?

6. Can you think of other rituals in society that reflect an affinity or longing for more tribal times? Hint: Have you ever pledged a fraternity or sorority, gone to a wedding, or attended a football game?

VIEWPOINT

Community program directors, educators, and other knowledgeable persons need to recognize the attraction that gangs have for children who fit the criteria of high-risk factors of gang involvement. If we address these issues with children who fit the profile of someone likely to be attracted to gangs before they join one, we will make great steps toward eliminating gangs altogether.

There is a tremendous need for prevention programs. To make them available, we need the cooperation of corrections professionals, educators, families, and the community. Children considered or identified as at-risk for gang involvement need mentors, tutors, after-school programs, and counseling. Their families often need counseling and help from social workers as well. As a community, we need to provide hope and show children that success and fulfillment are within their grasp.

To read more about gang prevention efforts, go to Info-Trac College Edition and check out Lonnie Jackson, "Understanding and Responding to Youth Gangs: a Juvenile Corrections Approach," *Corrections Today* 16:62 (August 1999). To do more research on gangs, use *gangs* as a keyword.

NOTES

1. For a general review, see Scott Cummings and Daniel Monti, *Gangs: The Origin and Impact of Contemporary Youth Gangs in the United States* (Albany, NY: State University of New York Press, 1993); this chapter also makes extensive use of George Knox et al., *Gang Prevention and Intervention: Preliminary Results from the 1995 Gang Research Task Force* (National Gang Crime Research Center, 9501 S. King Drive, Chicago, Ill., 1995).

2. George Knox et al., *Preliminary Results of the 1995 Adult Corrections Survey* (Chicago, IL: National Gang Research Center, 1995); G. David Curry, Robert J. Fox, Richard Ball, and Daryl Stone, *National Assessment of Law Enforcement Anti-Gang Information Resources, Final Report* (Morgantown, WV: National Assessment Survey, 1992), Table 6, pp. 36–37. Hereinafter cited as *National Assessment*.

3. Paul Perrone and Meda Chesney-Lind, "Representations of Gangs and Delinquency: Wild in the Streets?" *Social Justice* 24:96–117 (1997).

4. Thomas Berndt, "The Features and Effects of Friendships in Early Adolescence," *Child Development* 53:1447–69 (1982).

5. Thomas Berndt and T. B. Perry, "Children's Perceptions of Friendships as Supportive Relationships," *Developmental Psychology* 22:640–48 (1986).

6. Spencer Rathus, *Understanding Child Development* (New York: Holt, Rinehart and Winston, 1988), p. 462.

7. Peggy Giordano, "The Wider Circle of Friends in Adolescence," *American Journal of Sociology* 101:661–97 (1995).

8. Judith Rich Harris, *The Nurture Assumption: Why Children Turn Out the Way They Do* (New York: Free Press, 1998).

9. See, generally, Penelope Eckert, *Jocks and Burnouts: Social Categories and Identity in the High School* (New York: Teachers College Press, 1989).

10. Harris, *The Nurture Assumption.*

11. Ibid.

12. Robert Agnew and Timothy Brezina, "Relational Problems with Peers, Gender and Delinquency," *Youth and Society* 29:84-111 (1997).

13. David Farrington and Rolf Loeber, "Epidemiology of Juvenile Violence," *Child and Adolescent Psychiatric Clinics of North America* 9:733-48 (2000); Cindy Hanson, Scott Henggeler, William Haefele, and J. Douglas Rodick, "Demographic, Individual, and Family Relationship Correlates of Serious Repeated Crime among Adolescents and Their Siblings," *Journal of Consulting and Clinical Psychology* 52:528-38 (1984).

14. Albert Reiss, "Co-Offending and Criminal Careers," in Michael Tonry and Norval Morris, eds., *Crime and Justice,* vol. 10 (Chicago: University of Chicago Press, 1988).

15. David Farrington and Donald West, "The Cambridge Study in Delinquent Development: A Long-Term Follow-Up of 411 London Males," in H. J. Kerner and G. Kaiser, eds., *Criminality: Personality, Behavior, and Life History* (Berlin: Springer-Verlag, 1990).

16. Mark Warr, "Organization and Instigation in Delinquent Groups" *Criminology* 34:11-37 (1996).

17. Ibid., pp. 31-33.

18. James Short and Fred Strodtbeck, *Group Process and Gang Delinquency* (Chicago: Aldine, 1965).

19. Kate Keenan, Rolf Loeber, Quanwu Zhang, Magda Stouthamer-Loeber, and Welmoet Van Kammen, "The Influence of Deviant Peers on the Development of Boys' Disruptive and Delinquent Behavior: A Temporal Analysis," *Development and Pyschopathology* 7:715-26 (1995).

20. John Cole, Robert Terry, Shari-Miller Johnson, and John Lochman, "Longitudinal Effects of Deviant Peers Groups on Criminal Offending in Late Adolescence." Paper presented at the American Society of Criminology meeting, Boston, November 1995.

21. Terence Thornberry and Marvin Krohn, "Peers, Drug Use and Delinquency," in David Stoff, James Breiling, and Jack Maser, eds. *Handbook of Antisocial Behavior* (New York: Wiley, 1997), pp. 218-33; Thomas Dishion, Deborah Capaldi, Kathleen Spracklen, and Fuzhong Li, "Peer Ecology of Male Adolescent Drug Use," *Development and Psychopathology* 7:803-24 (1995).

22. Sara Battin, Karl Hill, Robert Abbott, Richard Catalano, and J. David Hawkins, "The Contribution of Gang Membership to Delinquency Beyond Delinquent Friends," *Criminology* 36:93-116 (1998).

23. Terence Thornberry, Alan Lizotte, Marvin Krohn, Margaret Farnworth, and Sung Joon Jang, "Delinquent Peers, Beliefs, and Delinquent Behavior: A Longitudinal Test of Inter-actional Theory" (Working Paper no. 6, rev.; Albany, NY: Rochester Youth Development Study, Hindelang Criminal Justice Research Center, 1992), pp. 8-30.

24. Mark Warr, "Age, Peers and Delinquency," *Criminology* 31:17-40 (1993).

25. Mark Warr, "Life-Course Transitions and Desistance from Crime," *Criminology* 36 (1998):502-36.

26. Cindy Hanson, Scott Henggeler, William Haefele, and J. Douglas Rodick, "Demographic, Individual, and Family Relationship Correlates of Serious Repeated Crime among Adolescents and Their Siblings," *Journal of Consulting and Clinical Psychology* 52:528-38 (1984).

27. Peggy Giordano, Stephen Cernkovich, and M. D. Pugh, "Friendships and Delinquency," *American Journal of Sociology* 91:1170-1202 (1986).

28. Denise Kandel, "Friendship Networks, Intimacy and Illicit Drug Use in Young Adulthood: A Comparison of Two Competing Theories," *Criminology* 29:441-69 (1991).

29. Marvin Krohn and Terence Thornberry, "Network Theory: A Model for Understanding Drug Abuse among African-American and Hispanic Youth" (Working Paper no. 10; Albany, NY: Rochester Youth Development Study, Hindelang Criminal Justice Research Center, 1991).

30. Irving Spergel, *The Youth Gang Problem, A Community Approach* (New York: Oxford University Press, 1995). Herein cited as *Youth Gang Problem.*

31. Ibid., p.3.

32. Other well-known movie representations of gangs include *The Wild Ones* and *Hell's Angels on Wheels,* which depicted motorcycle gangs, and *Saturday Night Fever,* which focused on neighborhood street toughs. See also David Dawley, *A Nation of Lords* (Garden City, NY: Anchor, 1973).

33. For a recent review of gang research, see James Howell, "Recent Gang Research: Program and Policy Implications," *Crime and Delinquency* 40:495-515 (1994).

34. Walter Miller, *Violence by Youth Gangs and Youth Groups as a Crime Problem in Major American Cities* (Washington, DC: Government Printing Office, 1975). Hereinafter cited as *Violence by Youth Gangs.*

35. Ibid., p. 20.

36. Malcolm Klein, *The American Street Gang, Its Nature, Prevalence and Control* (New York: Oxford University Press, 1995), p. 30.

37. Frederic M. Thrasher, *The Gang: A Study of 1,313 Gangs in Chicago* (Chicago: University of Chicago Press, 1927).

38. Malcolm Klein, ed., *Juvenile Gangs in Context* (Englewood Cliffs, NJ: Prentice-Hall, 1967), pp. 1-12.

39. Ibid., p. 6.

40. Irving Spergel, *Street Gang Work: Theory and Practice* (Reading, MA: Addison-Wesley, 1966).

41. Miller, *Violence by Youth Gangs,* p. 2.

42. Marjorie Zatz, "*Los Cholos:* Legal Processing of Chicago Gang Members," *Social Problems* 33:13-30 (1985).

43. Miller, *Violence by Youth Gangs,* pp. 1-2.

44. Ibid.

45. "LA Gang Warfare Called Bloodiest in 5 Years," *Boston Globe,* 18 December 1986, p. A4.

46. John Hagedorn, *People and Folks: Gangs, Crime and the Underclass in a Rustbelt City* (Chicago: Lake View Press, 1988).

47. National School Safety Center, *Gangs in Schools, Breaking Up Is Hard to Do* (Malibu, CA: Pepperdine University, 1988), p. 8. Hereinafter cited as *Gangs in Schools.*

48. C. Ronald Huff, "Youth Gangs and Public Policy," *Crime and Delinquency* 35:524-37 (1989).

49. Miller, *Violence by Youth Gangs*; idem, *Crime by Youth Gangs and Groups in the United States* (Washington, DC: Office of Juvenile Justice Delinquency Prevention, 1982).

50. Joan Moore, *Going Down to the Barrio: Homeboys and Homegirls in Change* (Philadelphia: Temple University Press, 1991), p. 3.

51. Richard McCorkle and Terance Miethe, "The Political and Organizational Response to Gangs: An Examination of a "Moral Panic" in Nevada," *Justice Quarterly* 15(9):41–64 (1998).

52. Arlen Egley, Jr., *National Youth Gang Survey Trends from 1996 to 2000* (Washington, DC: Office of Juvenile Justice and Delinquency Prevention, 2002); for more, see Walter Miller, *The Growth of the Youth Gang Problem in the United States, 1970–1998* (Washington, DC: Office of Juvenile Justice and Delinquency Prevention, 2001).

53. Arlen Egley, Jr., and Mehala Arjunan, *Highlights of the 2000 National Youth Gang Survey* (Washington, DC: Office of Juvenile Justice and Delinquency Prevention, 2002).

54. Irving Spergel, *Youth Gangs: Problem and Response* (Chicago: University of Chicago, School of Social Service Administration, 1989).

55. Felix Padilla, *The Gang as an American Enterprise* (New Brunswick, NJ: Rutgers University Press, 1992), p. 3.

56. Pamela Irving Jackson, "Crime, Youth Gangs, and Urban Transition: The Social Dislocations of Postindustrial Economic Development," *Justice Quarterly* 8:379–97 (1991).

57. Moore, *Going Down to the Barrio*, pp. 89–101.

58. Walter B. Miller, *The Growth of Youth Gang Problems in the United States*.

59. Jeffery Fagan, "The Social Organization of Drug Use and Drug Dealing among Urban Gangs," *Criminology* 27:633–69 (1989).

60. Richard Cloward and Lloyd Ohlin, *Delinquency and Opportunity* (New York: Free Press) pp. 1–12.

61. Fagan, "The Social Organization of Drug Use and Drug Dealing among Urban Gangs."

62. Huff, "Youth Gangs and Public Policy," pp. 528–29.

63. Carl Taylor, *Dangerous Society* (East Lansing: Michigan State University Press, 1990).

64. Cheryl Maxson, "Investigating Gang Structures," *Journal of Gang Research* 3:33–40 (1995).

65. Personal communication, Malcolm Klein, 12/12/95.

66. Scott Decker, Tim Bynum, and Deborah Weisel, "A Tale of Two Cities: Gangs and Organized Crime Groups," *Justice Quarterly* 15:395–425 at 410 (1998).

67. Saul Bernstein, *Youth in the Streets: Work with Alienated Youth Gangs* (New York: Associated Press, 1964).

68. William Julius Wilson, *The Truly Disadvantaged* (Chicago: University of Chicago Press, 1987).

69. James Diego Vigil, *Barrio Gangs: Street Life and Identity in Southern California* (Austin: University of Texas Press, 1988).

70. Miller, *Violence by Youth Gangs*, pp. 17–20.

71. Jerome Needle and W. Vaughan Stapleton, *Reports of the National Juvenile Justice Assessment Centers, Police Handling of Youth Gangs* (Washington, DC: Office of Juvenile Justice and Delinquency Prevention, 1983), p. 12.

72. 1999 National Youth Gang Survey.

73. Cheryl Maxson, Kristi Woods, and Malcolm Klein, *Street Migration in the United States: Executive Summary* (Los Angeles: Center for the Study of Crime and Social Control, University of Southern California, 1995).

74. John Hagedorn, "Gangs, Neighborhoods and Public Policy," *Social Problems* 20:529–41 (1991).

75. Lawrence Rosenthal, "Gang Loitering and Race," *Journal of Criminal Law and Criminology,* 91:99–160 (2000).

76. *Gangs in Schools,* p. 7.

77. Warr, "Organization and Instigation in Delinquent Groups."

78. *Gang Prevention and Intervention,* p. vii.

79. Wilson, *The Truly Disadvantaged.*

80. 1999 Youth Gang Survey.

81. Wilson, *The Truly Disadvantaged.*

82. *Gangs in Schools,* p. 7.

83. John Hagedorn, Jerome Wonders, Angelo Vega, and Joan Moore, *The Milwaukee Drug Posse Study* (Unpublished leaflet, undated).

84. Mary Glazier, "Small Town Delinquent Gangs: Origins, Characteristics and Activities." Paper presented at the American Society of Criminology meeting, Boston, November 1995.

85. G. David Curry, "Female Gang Involvement," *Journal of Research in Crime and Delinquency,* 35:100–19 (1998).

86. Moore, *Going Down to the Barrio*; Anne Campbell, *The Girls in the Gang* (Cambridge, MA: Basil Blackwood, 1984).

87. Karen Joe Laidler and Geoffrey Hunt, "Violence and Social Organization in Female Gangs," *Social Justice,* 24:148–87 (1997).

88. Karen Joe and Meda Chesney-Lind, "'Just Every Mother's Angel': An Analysis of Gender and Ethnic Variations in Youth Gang Membership," *Gender and Society* 9:408–30 (1995).

89. Curry, "Female Gang Involvement."

90. Egley, *National Youth Gang Survey Trends from 1996 to 2000.*

91. Gary Jensen, "Defiance and Gang Identity: Quantitative Tests of Qualitative Hypothesis." Paper presented at the American Society of Criminology meeting, Boston, 1995.

92. Taylor, *Dangerous Society*, p. 109.

93. Finn-Aage Esbensen and David Huizinga, "Gangs, Drugs and Delinquency in a Survey of Urban Youth," *Criminology* 31:565–87 (1993).

94. Finn-Aage Esbensen, "Race and Gender Differences between Gang and Nongang Youths: Results from a Multisite Survey" *Justice Quarterly* 15:504–25 (1998).

95. Curry, "Female Gang Involvement."

96. Joan Moore, James Diego Vigil, and Robert Garcia, "Residence and Territoriality in Chicano Gangs," *Social Problems* 31:182–94 (1983).

97. William F. Whyte, *Street Corner Society* (Chicago: University of Chicago Press, 1955).

98. Malcolm Klein, "Impressions of Juvenile Gang Members," *Adolescence* 3:59 (1968).

99. Decker, Bynum, and Weisel, "A Tale of Two Cities."

100. Los Angeles County Sheriff's Department, *Street Gangs of Los Angeles County, White Paper* (Los Angeles: LACSD, n.d.), p. 14.

101. LeRoy Martin, *Collecting, Organizing and Reporting Street Gang Crime* (Chicago: Chicago Police Department, 1988).

102. Patricia Wen, "Boston Gangs: A Hard World," *Boston Globe* 10 May 1988, p. 1.

103. Rick Graves and Ed Allen, *Black Gangs and Narcotics and Black Gangs* (Los Angeles: Los Angeles County Sheriff's Department, n.d.).

104. *Youth Gang Problem*, p. 3.

105. Joseph Sheley, Joshua Zhang, Charles Brody, and James Wright, "Gang Organization, Gang Criminal Activity, and Individual Gang Members' Criminal Behavior," *Social Science Quarterly* 76:53–68 (1995).

106. Kevin Thompson, David Brownfield, and Ann Marie Sorenson, "Specialization Patterns of Gang and Nongang Offending: A Latent Structure Analysis" *Journal of Gang Research* 3:25–35 (1996).

107. 1999 National Youth Gang Survey.

108. Thompson, Brownfield, and Sorenson, "Specialization Patterns of Gang and Nongang Offending."

109. Sara Battin, Karl Hill, Robert Abbott, Richard Catalano, and J. David Hawkins, "The Contribution of Gang Membership to Delinquency Beyond Delinquent Friends," *Criminology* 36:93–116 (1998).

110. Terence Thornberry and James Burch, *Gang Members and Delinquent Behavior* (Washington, DC: Office of Juvenile Justice and Delinquency Prevention, 1997).

111. James C. Howell, "Youth Gang Drug Trafficking and Homicide: Policy and Program Implications," *Juvenile Justice Journal* 4:3–5 (1997).

112. Ibid.

113. Ibid.

114. Scott Decker, Susan Pennell, and Ami Caldwell, *Arrestees and Guns: Monitoring the Illegal Firearms Market* (Washington, DC: National Institute of Justice, 1996).

115. Scott Decker, "Collective and Normative Features of Gang Violence," *Justice Quarterly* 13:243–64 (1996).

116. Beth Bjerregaard and Alan Lizotte, "Gun Ownership and Gang Membership," *Journal of Criminal Law and Criminology* 86:37–53 (1995).

117. Pamela Lattimore, Richard Linster, and John MacDonald, "Risk of Death among Serious Young Offenders," *Journal of Research in Crime and Delinquency* 34:187–209 (1997).

118. Alan Lizotte and David Sheppard, *Gun Use by Male Juveniles* (Washington, DC: Office of Juvenile Justice and Delinquency Prevention, 2001).

119. Decker, "Collective and Normative Features of Gang Violence," p. 253.

120. H. Range Hutson, Deirdre Anglin, and Michale Pratts, Jr., "Adolescents and Children Injured or Killed in Drive-By Shootings in Los Angeles," *The New England Journal of Medicine* 330:324–27 (1994).

121. Miller, *Violence by Youth Gangs*, pp. 2–26.

122. Malcolm Klein, "Violence in American Juvenile Gangs," in Donald Muvihill, Melvin Tumin, and Lynn Curtis, eds., *Crimes of Violence, National Commission on the Causes and Prevention of Violence*, vol. 13 (Washington, DC: U.S. Government Printing Office, 1969), p. 1429.

123. Kevin Cullen, "Gangs Are Seen as Carefully Organized," *Boston Globe,* 7 January 1987, p. 17

124. *National Assessment,* pp. 60–61.

125. The following description of ethnic gangs leans heavily on the material developed in *Gangs in Schools,* pp. 11–23.

126. *The Youth Gang Problem*, pp. 136–37.

127. Decker, Bynum, and Weisel, "A Tale of Two Cities."

128. See generally, Joan Moore, "Isolation and Stigmatization in the Development of an Underclass: The Case of Chicano Gangs in East Los Angeles," *Social Problems* 33:1–12 (1985); idem, *Homeboys: Gangs, Drugs and Prison in the Barrios of Los Angeles* (Philadelphia: Temple University Press, 1979); idem, *Going Down to the Barrio: Homeboys and Homegirls in Change* (Philadelphia: Temple University Press 1991); James Diego Vigil, *Barrio Gangs: Street Life and Identity in Southern California* (Austin: University of Texas Press, 1988); James Diego Vigil and John Long, "Emic and Etic Perspectives on Gang Culture: The Chicano Case," in C. Ronald Huff, ed., *Gangs in America* (Newbury Park, CA: Sage, 1990), pp. 55–70; James Diego Vigil, "*Cholos* and Gangs: Culture Change and Street Youth in Los Angeles," in C. Ronald Huff, ed., *Gangs in America* (Newbury Park, CA: Sage, 1990), pp. 116–28.

129. Los Angeles County Sheriff's Department, *Street Gangs of Los Angeles County.*

130. Zheng Wang, Indiana University of Pennsylvania, personal communication, 3 February 1993.

131. Ko-Lin Chin, *Chinese Subculture and Criminality: Non-Traditional Crime Groups in America* (Westport, CO: Greenwood Press, 1990).

132. James Diego Vigil and Steve Chong Yun, "Vietnamese Youth Gangs in Southern California," in C. Ronald Huff, ed., *Gangs in America* (Newbury Park, CA: Sage, 1990), pp. 146–63.

133. See Glazier, "Small Town Delinquent Gangs."

134. For a review, see Lawrence Trostle, *The Stoners, Drugs, Demons and Delinquency* (New York: Garland, 1992).

135. Esbensen, "Race and Gender Differences between Gang and Nongang Youths."

136. Herbert Block and Arthur Niederhoffer, *The Gang: A Study in Adolescent Behavior* (New York: Philosophical Library, 1958).

137. Ibid., p. 113.

138. *Gang Prevention and Intervention,* p. 44.

139. James Diego Vigil, "Group Processes and Street Identity: Adolescent Chicano Gang Members," *Ethos* 16:421–45 (1988).

140. James Diego Vigil and John Long, "Emic and Etic Perspectives on Gang Culture: The Chicano Case," in C. Ronald Huff, ed., *Gangs in America* (Newbury Park, CA: Sage, 1990), p. 66.

141. Albert Cohen, *Delinquent Boys* (New York: Free Press, 1955), pp. 1–19.

142. Irving Spergel, *Racketville, Slumtown, and Haulburg: An Exploratory Study of Delinquent Subcultures* (Chicago: University of Chicago Press, 1964).

143. Malcolm Klein, *Street Gangs and Street Workers* (Englewood Cliffs, NJ: Prentice-Hall, 1971) pp. 12–15.

144. Vigil, *Barrio Gangs.*

145. Vigil and Long, "Emic and Etic Perspectives on Gang Culture," p. 61.

146. David Brownfield, Kevin Thompson, and Ann Marie Sorenson, "Correlates of Gang Membership: A Test of Strain, Social Learning, and Social Control," *Journal of Gang Research* 4:11–22 (1997).

147. John Hagedorn, Jose Torres, Greg Giglio, "Cocaine, Kicks, and Strain: Patterns of Substance Use in Milwaukee Gangs," *Contemporary Drug Problems,* 25:113–45 (1998).

148. Spergel, *The Youth Gang Problem,* pp. 4–5.

149. Ibid.

150. Lewis Yablonsky, *The Violent Gang* (Baltimore: Penguin Books, 1984), p. 237.

151. Ibid., pp. 239–41.

152. Marc Le Blanc and Nadine Lanctot, "Social and Psychological Characteristics of Gang Members According to the Gang Structure and Its Subcultural and Ethnic Making." Paper presented at the American Society of Criminology meeting, Miami, 1994.

153. Malcom Klein, *The American Street Gang* (New York: Oxford, 1995).

154. Ibid., p. 163.

155. Mercer Sullivan, *"Getting Paid: Youth Crime and Work in the Inner City* (Ithaca, NY: Cornell University Press, 1989), pp. 244–45.

156. Esbensen and Huizinga, "Gangs, Drugs and Delinquency in a Survey of Urban Youth," p. 583; G. David Curry and Irving Spergel, "Gang Involvement and Delinquency among Hispanic and African-American Adolescent Males," *Journal of Research in Crime and Delinquency* 29:273–91 (1992).

157. Padilla, *The Gang as an American Enterprise*, p. 103.

158. Martin Sanchez-Jankowski, *Islands in the Street: Gangs and American Urban Society* (Berkeley: University of California Press, 1991).

159. Jensen, "Defiance and Gang Identity: Quantitative Tests of Qualitative Hypothesis."

160. Terence Thornberry, Marvin Krohn, Alan Lizotte, and Deborah Chard-Wierschem, "The Role of Juvenile Gangs in Facilitating Delinquent Behavior," *Journal of Research in Crime and Delinquency* 30:55–87 (1993).

161. *The Youth Gang Problem*, pp. 93–94.

162. Ibid., p. 93.

163. L. Thomas Winfree, Jr., Teresa Vigil Backstrom, and G. Larry Mays, "Social Learning Theory, Self-Reported Delinquency and Youth Gangs, A New Twist on a General Theory of Crime and Delinquency," *Youth and Society* 26:147–77 (1994).

164. Karen Joe Laidler and Geoffrey Hunt, "Violence and Social Organization in Female Gangs," *Social Justice* 24:148–87 (1997).

165. Needle and Stapleton, *Police Handling of Youth Gangs,* p. 19.

166. *National Assessment,* p. 65.

167. Scott Armstrong, "Los Angeles Seeks New Ways to Handle Gangs," *Christian Science Monitor,* 23 April 1988, p. 3.

168. Mark Moore and Mark A. R. Kleiman, *The Police and Drugs* (Washington, DC: National Institute of Justice, 1989), p. 8.

169. Barry Krisberg, "Preventing and Controlling Violent Youth Crime: The State of the Art," in Ira Schwartz, ed., *Violent Juvenile Crime* (Minneapolis: University of Minnesota, Hubert Humphrey Institute of Public Affairs, n.d.).

170. See, generally, Spergel, *Street Gang Work.*

171. For a revisionist view of gang delinquency, see Hedy Bookin-Weiner and Ruth Horowitz, "The End of the Youth Gang," *Criminology* 21:585–602 (1983).

172. Quint Thurman, Andrew Giacomazzi, Michael Reisig, and David Mueller, *Crime and Delinquency* 42:279–96 (1996).

173. Michael Agopian, "Evaluation of the Gang Alternative Prevention Program." Paper presented at the American Society of Criminology meeting, Boston, November 1995.

174. James Houston, "What Works: The Search for Excellence in Gang Intervention Programs." Paper presented at the American Society of Criminology meeting, Boston, November 1995.

175. Hagedorn, "Gangs, Neighborhoods and Public Policy."

176. Curry and Spergel, "Gang Involvement and Delinquency among Hispanic and African-American Adolescent Males."

9 Schools and Delinquency

On March 16, 2001, Security Officer Cathy Jones was patrolling the halls of a Los Angeles high school between classes when she noticed that two students were standing in an area off-limits to students. When Jones approached the pair, one student named Randy G., put his hand in his pocket and appeared nervous. Jones asked if the two were OK and told them to go to class. Randy G. finished adjusting his pocket and went to class. Jones followed Randy because she felt he was acting "very paranoid and nervous." Jones notified her supervisor and summoned another security officer to the scene. The officers then went to Randy G.'s classroom and asked him to step outside into the hallway. They asked if he had any weapons in his possession. Randy said that he did not have weapons and consented to a search of his bag and a pat-down search of his person. The officers found a knife in the student's pocket.

When Randy was charged with possession of a knife on school property, his attorney claimed that the evidence of the knife should be excluded because the officers who discovered the knife had violated the Fourth Amendment, which provides for freedom from unlawful search and seizure. The defense claimed that the discovery of the knife was unreasonable because Officer Jones had no reasonable suspicion that the student had a knife or had violated a criminal statute or a school rule. Merely looking "nervous" is not reasonable grounds to search a person.

- Should the search of Randy be permitted?

- Should the evidence seized be used against Randy in a court of law?

- Should schools employ security guards such as Officer Jones, who act as cops on campus?

I f you answered yes to this case, you would be in agreement with the California Supreme Court, which upheld the search in a case with similar facts, *The People v. Randy G.*[1] The court ruled that school administrators have broad authority over student behavior and school safety.... School officials have the power to stop a minor student in order to ask questions or conduct an investigation even in the absence of reasonable suspicion, so long as such authority is not exercised in an arbitrary, capricious, or harassing manner."[2]

This case illustrates the varied and complex issues schools must face in modern society. School officials whose interest and training may be focused on education and learning must make daily decisions on discipline and crime prevention. Because the schools are responsible for educating virtually everyone during most of their formative years and because so much of an adolescent's time is spent in school, some relationship would seem logical between delinquent behavior and what is happening—or not happening—in classrooms throughout the United States. This relationship was pointed out as early as 1939, when a study by the New Jersey Delinquency Commission found that of 2,021 inmates of prisons and correctional institutions in that state, two out of every five had first been committed for truancy.[3]

academic achievement
Being successful in a school environment.

Numerous studies have confirmed that delinquency is related to **academic achievement,** and experts have concluded that many of the underlying problems of delinquency, as well as their prevention and control, are intimately connected with the nature and quality of the school experience.[4] Some find that school-related variables are more important contributing factors to delinquent behavior than the effects of either family or friends.[5] Although there are differences of opinion, most theorists agree that the educational system bears some responsibility for the high rate of juvenile crime.

This chapter examines the relationship between the school and delinquency. The first part explores how educational achievement and delinquency are related and what factors in the school experience appear to contribute to delinquent behavior. Next, delinquency within the school setting itself—vandalism, theft, violence, and so on—is discussed. The final sections cover the educational system's attempts to prevent and control delinquency.

The School in Modern American Society

The school plays a significant role in shaping the values and norms of American children.[6] In contrast to earlier periods, when formal education was a privilege of the upper classes, the American system of compulsory public education has made schooling a legal obligation. Today more than 90 percent of the school-age population attends school, compared with only 7 percent in 1890.[7] In contrast to the earlier, agrarian days of U.S. history, when most adolescents shared in the work of the family and became socialized into adulthood as part of the workforce, today's young people, beginning as early as age 3 or 4, spend most of their time in school. The school has become the primary instrument of socialization, the "basic conduit through which the community and adult influences enter into the lives of adolescents."[8]

Because young people spend a longer time in school, the period of their adolescence is prolonged. As long as students are still economically dependent on their families and have not entered the work world, they are not considered adults, either in their own minds or in the estimation of the rest of society. The responsibilities of adulthood come later to modern-day youths than those in earlier generations, and some experts see this prolonged childhood as a factor that contributes to the irresponsible, childish, often irrational behavior of many juveniles who commit delinquent acts.

Socialization and Status

Another significant aspect of the educational experience of American youths is that it is overwhelmingly a peer encounter. Children spend their school hours with their peers, and most of their activities after school take place with school friends. Young people rely increasingly on school friends and consequently become less and less interested in adult role models. The norms and values of the peer culture are often at odds with those of adult society, and a pseudoculture with a distinct social system develops, offering a united front to the adult world. Law-abiding behavior or conventional norms may not be among the values promoted in such an atmosphere. Youth culture may instead admire bravery, defiance, and having fun much more.

In addition to its role as an instrument of socialization, the school has become a primary determinant of economic and social status in American society. In this highly technological age, education is the key to a job that will mark its holder as successful. No longer can parents ensure the status of their children through social-class origin alone. Educational achievement has become of equal, if not greater, importance as a determinant of economic success.

Schools, then, are geared toward success defined in terms of academic achievement, which provides the key to profit and position in society. Adolescents derive much of their identity out of what happens to them in school. Virtually all adolescents must participate in the educational system, not only because it is required by law but also because the notion of success is defined in terms of the possession of a technical or professional skill that can be acquired only through formal education.

The value of education is fostered by parents, the media, and the schools themselves. Regardless of their social or economic background, most children grow up believing that education is the key to success. Despite their apparent acceptance of the

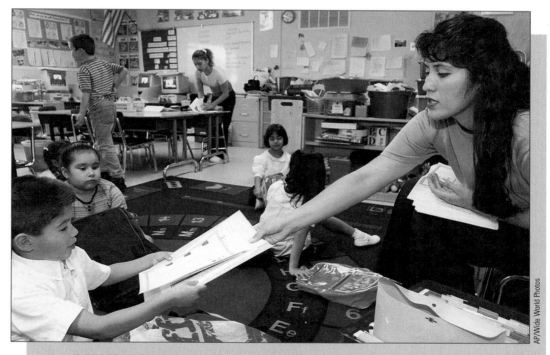

BUDGET CUTTING has severely reduced educational resources in many communities and curtailed state support for local school systems. Some systems are finding it difficult to recruit qualified teachers. Some districts now employ dedicated people who lack the proper qualifications, such as Xochitl Rodriguez, shown here, handing back homework to her students in Sepulveda, California. Rodriguez left her job in human services and was hired by the school district, even though she lacked experience and had not taken teaching courses. In this case, dedication and hard work have been a plus for the district.

value of education, many youths do not meet acceptable standards of school achievement. Whether failure is measured by test scores, not being promoted, or dropping out, its incidence continues to be a major social problem of American society. A single school failure often leads to patterns of chronic academic failure. The links between school failure, academic and social aspirations, and delinquency will be explored more fully in the following sections.

Education in Crisis

The critical role schools play in adolescent development is underscored by the problems faced by the American education system. Budget cutting has severely reduced educational resources in many communities and curtailed state support for local school systems. Spending in the United States on elementary and secondary education (as a percentage of the gross national product) trails that of other nations.

Though there has been some improvement in measured performance in reading, math, and science achievement during the past decade, the United States still lags behind many nations in key educational achievement measures. The results of the Third International Mathematics and Science Study (TIMSS), conducted in 1999, found that on average, eighth-grade students in the United States performed lower than the international average in mathematics and higher than the international average in science. For 12th-graders, however, the average mathematics and science scores in the United States were lower than those of students in their final year of secondary school in the majority of other countries. On the assessments in physics and advanced mathematics, the United States was among the lowest scoring countries. Eighth-graders in the United States lag behind students in less affluent nations in science achievement (for example, Hungary, Slovak Republic, and Bulgaria) and math achievement (for example, Thailand, Slovenia, Russia). (See Figure 9.1.) One reason for the lack of achievement may be that many secondary school math and science teachers did not major or even minor in the subjects they teach. For example, less than half the math teachers in California, Delaware, Washington, and Alaska have at least a minor in mathematics.[9]

The Third International Mathematics and Science Study-Repeat (TIMSS-R) compares various nations with jurisdictions in the United States on students' ability in math and science. To see the full report, go to its site at *http://nces.ed.gov/ timss/timss-r/index.asp* For an up-to-date list of Web links, go to *http://info.wadsworth.com/siegel*

Academic Performance and Delinquency

The general path towards occupational prestige is education, and when youth are deprived of this avenue of success through poor school performance there is a greater likelihood of delinquent behavior.[10]

Poor academic performance has been directly linked to delinquent behavior: There is general consensus that students who are chronic underachievers in school are also among the most likely to be delinquent.[11] In fact, researchers commonly find that school failure is a stronger predictor of delinquency than such personal variables as economic class membership, racial or ethnic background, or peer group relations. Studies that compare the academic records of delinquents and nondelinquents, including their scores on standardized tests of basic skills, failure rate, teacher ratings, and other academic measures, have found that delinquents are often academically deficient, a condition that may lead to their leaving school and becoming involved in antisocial activities. Kids who report that they do not like school, do not do well in school, and do not concentrate on their homework are also the ones most likely to self-report delinquent acts.[12] In contrast, at-risk kids, even those with histories of abuse and neglect, who do well in school are often able to avoid delinquent involvement.[13]

Source: Martin et al., *TIMSS 1999
International Science Report: Find-
ings from IEA's Repeat of the Third
International Mathematics and
Science Study at the Eighth Grade.*
Exhibit 1.1 (Chestnut Hill, MA:
Boston College, 2000); Mullis et al.,
*TIMSS 1999 International Mathe-
matics Report: Findings from IEA's
Repeat of the Third International
Mathematics and Science Study at
the Eighth Grade.* Exhibit 1.1
(Chestnut Hill, MA: Boston
College, 2000).

Mathematics	
Nation	**Average**
Singapore	604
Korea, Republic of	587
Chinese Taipei	585
Hong Kong SAR	582
Japan	579
Belgium-Flemish	558
Netherlands	540
Slovak Republic	534
Hungary	532
Canada	531
Slovenia	530
Russian Federation	526
Australia	525
Finland[1]	520
Czech Republic	520
Malaysia	519
Bulgaria	511
Latvia-LSS[2]	505
United States	502
England	496
New Zealand	491
Lithuania[3]	482
Italy	479
Cyprus	476
Romania	472
Moldova	469
Thailand	467
(Israel)	466
Tunisia	448
Macedonia, Republic of	447
Turkey	429
Jordan	428
Iran, Islamic Republic of	422
Indonesia	403
Chile	392
Philippines	345
Morocco	337
South Africa	275
International average of 38 nations	**487**

Science	
Nation	**Average**
Chinese Taipei	569
Singapore	568
Hungary	552
Japan	550
Korea, Republic of	549
Netherlands	545
Australia	540
Czech Republic	539
England	538
Finland	535
Slovak Republic	535
Belgium-Flemish	535
Slovenia	533
Canada	533
Hong Kong SAR	530
Russian Federation	529
Bulgaria	518
United States	515
New Zealand	510
Latvia-LSS[2]	503
Italy	493
Malaysia	492
Lithuania[3]	488
Thailand	482
Romania	472
(Israel)	468
Cyprus	460
Moldova	459
Macedonia, Republic of	458
Jordan	450
Iran, Islamic Republic of	448
Indonesia	435
Turkey	433
Tunisia	430
Chile	420
Philippines	345
Morocco	323
South Africa	243
International average of 38 nations	**488**

Average is significantly higher than the
U.S. average

Average is significantly lower than the
U.S. average

Average does not differ significantly from
the U.S. average

[1] The shading of Finland may appear incorrect; however, statistically, its placement is correct.

[2] Designated LSS because only Latvian-speaking schools were tested, which represents 61 percent of the population.

[3] Lithuania tested the same cohort of students as other nations, but later in 1999, at the beginning of the next school year.

NOTE: Eighth grade in most nations.
Parentheses indicate nations not meeting international sampling and/or other guidelines.
The international average is the average of the national averages of the 38 nations.

The academic failure–delinquency association is commonly found among chronic offenders. Those leaving school without a diploma are significantly more likely to become involved in chronic delinquency than graduates.[14] Only 9 percent of the chronic offenders in Wolfgang's Philadelphia cohort graduated from high school, compared with 74 percent of nonoffenders.[15] Chronic offenders also had significantly more disciplinary actions and remedial/disciplinary placements than nonoffenders.[16]

The relationship between school achievement and persistent offending is supported by surveys of prison inmates that indicate that only 40 percent of incarcerated felons had 12 or more years of education, compared with about 80 percent of the general population.[17]

School Failure and Delinquency

school failure Failing to achieve success in school can result in frustration, anger, and reduced self-esteem, which may contribute to delinquent behavior.

A CLOSER VIEW
Preventing school failure is critical because of its link to delinquency. To read about how one teacher approaches this task, go to Mary M. Wood, "Preventing School Failure: A Teacher's Current Conundrum," *Preventing School Failure* 45(2):52 (Winter 2001) on InfoTrac College Edition.

While there is general agreement that **school failure** and delinquency are related, some question exists over the nature and direction the relationship takes. One view is that the school experience is a *direct cause* of delinquent behavior. Children who fail at school soon feel frustrated, angry, and rejected. Believing they will never achieve success through conventional means, they seek like-minded companions and together engage in antisocial behaviors. Educational failure, beginning early in the life course, evokes negative responses from important people in the child's life, including teachers, parents, and prospective employers. These reactions help solidify feelings of social inadequacy and, in some cases, lead the underachieving student into a pattern of chronic delinquency.

A second view is that school failure leads to psychological and behavioral dysfunction, which are the actual cause of antisocial behavior. For example, academic failure reduces self-esteem; studies using a variety of measures of academic competence and self-esteem clearly demonstrate that good students have a better attitude about themselves than do poor students.[18] Reduced self-esteem has also been found to contribute to delinquent behavior.[19] The association then runs from school failure to low self-concept to delinquency. The school failure–delinquency association may be mediated then by efforts to stabilize or improve the self-image of academically challenged children.

A third view is that school failure and delinquency share a *common cause;* they are both part of the problem behavior syndrome (PBS). It would therefore be erroneous to conclude that school failure *precedes* antisocial behavior. The research evidence that the association between school failure and delinquency is a function of a PBS includes the issues described in Exhibit 9.1.[20]

Causes of School Failure

While disagreement still exists over the direction the relationship takes, there is little argument that delinquent behavior is linked to a child's educational experiences. A number of factors have been linked to the onset of school failure; the most prominent are discussed in some detail below.

Exhibit 9.1   Correlates of School Failure

- Delinquents may have lower IQs than nondelinquents, a factor that might also explain their poor academic achievement.
- Delinquent behavior has also been associated with a turbulent family life, a condition that most likely leads to academic underachievement.
- Delinquency has been associated with low self-control and impulsivity, traits that also may produce school failure.
- The adolescent who both fails at school and engages in delinquency may be experiencing drug use, depression, malnutrition, abuse, and disease, all symptoms of a generally troubled lifestyle.

Source: J. D. McKinney, "Longitudinal Research on the Behavioral Characteristics of Children with Learning Disabilities," *Journal of Learning Disabilities* 22:141–50 (1998).

Social Class and School Failure   During the 1950s, research by Albert Cohen indicated that delinquency was fundamentally a phenomenon of working-class students who were poorly equipped to function in middle-class schools. Cohen referred to this phenomenon as a failure to live up to "middle-class measuring rods," which were being used by teachers to assess the performance of lower-class youth.[21] It was claimed that the disadvantages lower-class children have in school (for example, lack of verbal skills, parental education, and motivation) are a direct result of their position in the social structure and implicitly foster their delinquency.[22] These views have been supported by the greater than average retention and dropout rates among lower-class children.

One reason that lower-class kids may do poorly in school is that economic problems require them to take part-time jobs to help support the family. Working while in school seems to lower commitment to educational achievement and is associated with higher levels of delinquent behavior.[23]

Some theorists contend that the high incidence of failure among lower-class youths is actually fostered by the schools themselves.[24] Kids from an impoverished background often find that the school experience can be a frightening one in which constant testing and the threat of failure are clear and ever-present dangers.[25] Research data confirm not only that such children begin school at lower levels of achievement but also that without help, their performance progressively deteriorates the longer they are in school. If this is true, the school itself becomes an active force in the generation of delinquency insofar as it is linked to failure.[26]

Not all experts, however, agree with the social class–school failure–delinquency hypothesis. A number of early research studies found that boys who do poorly in school, regardless of their socioeconomic background, are more likely to be delinquent than those who perform well.[27] There is evidence that affluent students are equally or even more deeply affected by school failure than lower-class kids and that middle-class youths who did poorly in school were actually more likely to become delinquent than their lower-class peers.[28] Arthur Stinchcombe's classic research on rebellion in a high school indicated that upper-class school failures were in fact more prone to be delinquent than lower-class **underachievers**.[29] Because lower-class youths are significantly less likely to indicate that getting good grades or going to college is important, they most likely feel less pressure to perform well and less strain if they fail.[30] School failure may cause more damage to more-affluent youth when their limited ability conflicts with their overinflated expectations (a finding that jibes with Agnew's General Strain Theory, as discussed in Chapter 4).[31]

underachievers   Those who do not achieve success in school at the level of their expectations.

Tracking

Placement in non-college tracks of the contemporary high school means consignment to an educational oblivion without apparent purpose or meaning.[32]

tracking   Dividing students into groups according to their ability and achievement levels.

Most researchers have looked at academic **tracking**—dividing students into groups according to ability and achievement level—as a contributor to delinquency.[33] Studies overwhelmingly indicate that compared with those in college tracks, noncollege preparatory students experience greater academic failure and progressive deterioration of achievement, participate less frequently in extracurricular activities, have an increased tendency to drop out, engage in more-frequent misbehavior in school, and commit more delinquent acts. These differences are at least partially caused by assignment to a low academic track, whereby the student is effectively locked out of a chance to achieve educational success. Some effects of tracking as it relates to delinquency are illustrated in Exhibit 9.2.[34]

Some school officials begin stereotyping and tracking students in the lowest grade levels.[35] Educators separate youths into special groups that have innocuous names (special enrichment program, for example) but may carry with them the taint

Exhibit 9.2   Effects of Tracking

- *Self-fulfilling prophecy:* Low-track students, from whom little achievement and more misbehavior are expected, tend to live up to these often unspoken assumptions about their behavior.
- *Stigma:* The labeling effect of placement in a low track leads to loss of self-esteem, which increases the potential for academic failure and troublemaking both in and out of school.
- *Student subculture:* Students segregated in lower tracks develop a value system that often rewards misbehavior, rather than the academic success they feel they can never achieve.
- *Teacher effectiveness:* Teachers of high-ability students make more of an effort to teach in an interesting and challenging manner than those who instruct lower-level students.
- *Future rewards:* Low-track students are less inclined to conform. Because they see no future rewards for their schooling, their futures are not threatened by a record of deviance or low academic achievement.
- *Grading policies:* Low-track students tend to receive lower grades than other students, even for work of equal quality, based on the rationale that students who are not college bound are "obviously" less bright and do not need good grades to get into college.

of failure and academic incompetence. Junior and senior high school students may be tracked within individual subjects based on their perceived ability. Classes may be labeled in descending order as advanced placement, academically enriched, average, basic, and remedial. It is common for students to have all their courses in only one or two tracks.[36]

The effects of negative school labels (for example, "failure," or "slow," or "special needs") accumulate over time. Thus, if a student fails academically, this often means that he or she is probably destined to fail again, and over time, the repeated instances of failure can help to produce the career of the "misfit," "delinquent," or "dropout."[37] Consequently, a tracking system keeps certain students from having any hope of achieving academic success, thereby causing a lack of motivation, failure, and rebellion, all of which may foster delinquent behavior.[38]

Another disturbing outcome of tracking is that students are often stigmatized as academically backward if they voluntarily attend a program or institution designed to help underachievers.[39] Teachers consider remedial reading programs to be dumping grounds for youths with a "bad attitude"; consequently, they expect youths who attended special-education programs to be disruptive in the classroom.[40] Those who oppose tracking also believe it retards the academic progress of many students, especially those in average and low groups.[41] Tracking may lead to lower self-esteem, promote school misbehavior and dropping out. Tracking also appears to lower the aspirations of students who are not in the top groups. And perhaps most important is that tracking separates students along socioeconomic lines, separating rich from poor, whites from minorities. The end result is that poor and minority children are found far more often than others in the bottom tracks. As a result, they are likely to suffer far more negative consequences of schooling than are their more fortunate peers.[42]

School Climate   School climate has also been related to crime and disorder in schools.[43] It is difficult to define *school climate,* but the term generally refers to a broad range of concepts that include the culture of the school, how the school is structured and administered, its design, and its rule structure.

Schools with a positive culture will maintain unwritten rules of conduct that encourage communication between students and also with faculty and administration. The schools norms should discourage negative actions such as bullying and discrimination.

Positive climate is enhanced by administrations that are sensitive to student needs. This can be manifested in curriculum designed to provide a relevant classroom experience—for example, English courses that include multicultural literature and/or technology courses that include Internet Web page design. Schools that can offer relevant courses with reasonable student-teacher ratios will produce a more positive culture than those that ignore such critical needs.

School climate is a critical determinant of delinquency within the schools. Even schools located in high-crime areas report relatively less crime when they maintain a positive and supportive climate. School stability then may help neutralize the delinquency-producing effect of neighborhood disorganization and high crime rates.

Student Alienation   Schools that do not maintain a positive school climate are at risk for producing large numbers of cynical, **alienated** students who report they neither like school nor care about their teachers' opinions. In contrast, kids who like school and report greater involvement in school activities are also less likely to engage in delinquent behaviors.[44] Commitment to school, coupled with the belief that their school is being fairly run and that school rules are being consistently applied, helps kids resist criminality.[45] Attachment to teachers also helps insulate high-risk adolescents from delinquency.[46] Some of the suspected causes of alienation are listed in Exhibit 9.3.

Alienated students attending isolated, impersonal schools that have curriculums irrelevant to their needs may become **dropouts,** and this may make them even more prone to antisocial behaviors, as can be seen in the Focus on Delinquency box entitled "Dropping Out."

A CLOSER VIEW

New approaches are now being tried to reduce student alienation. To read about one using general semantics, go to Martin H. Levinson, "A General Semantics Approach to Reducing Student Alienation," *ETC.: A Review of General Semantics* 58(3):258 (Fall 2001) on InfoTrac College Edition.

alienation   Feelings of separation and distance from mainstream society.

dropouts   Youths who leave school before completing their required program of education.

Exhibit 9.3   Sources of Student Alienation

- *School size:* Schools are getting larger because smaller school districts have been consolidated into multi-jurisdictional district schools. In 1900, there were 150,000 school districts; today there are approximately 16,000. Larger schools are often impersonal, and relatively few students can find avenues for meaningful participation. Teachers and other school personnel do not have the opportunity to deal with early indications of academic or behavior problems and thus act to prevent delinquency.
- *Irrelevant curriculum:* Some students may be unable to see the relevance or significance of what they are taught in school. The gap between their education and the real world leads them to feel that the school experience is little more than a waste of time.
- *Lack of payoff:* Many students, particularly those from low-income families, believe that school has no payoff in terms of their future. Because the legitimate channel of education appears to be meaningless, illegitimate alternatives become increasingly attractive for students who do not plan to attend college or to use their high school educations directly in their careers.
- *Middle- and upper-class bias:* The preeminent role of the college preparatory curriculum and the second-class position of vocational and technical programs in many school systems alienates some lower-class students. Furthermore, methods of instruction as well as curriculum materials reflect middle-class mores, language, and customs and have little meaning for the disadvantaged child.

Dropping Out

Though dropout rates are in decline, more than 10 percent of Americans ages 16 to 24 have left school permanently without a diploma; of these, more than 1 million withdrew before completing 10th grade.

Dropping out is a serious issue, because once kids leave school they are more likely to engage in drug abuse and antisocial behavior and to persist in criminal behavior throughout adulthood. For example, national surveys of substance-abuse levels among people who had been arrested by police find that juvenile arrestees who no longer attended school were more likely to abuse drugs than those who did attend school. Data from Phoenix, Arizona, show that 70 percent of male arrestees who had dropped out tested positively for drugs as compared to 57 percent who were still in school; among females, 70 percent of arrestees who had dropped out tested positive as compared to 36 percent who were still in school.

Why Do Kids Drop Out?

When surveyed, most dropouts say they left either because they did not like school or because they wanted to get a job. Others could not get along with teachers, had been expelled, or were under suspension. Almost half of all female dropouts left school because they were pregnant or had already given birth.

Poverty and family dysfunction increase the chances of dropping out among all racial and ethnic groups. Dropouts are more likely than graduates to have lived in single-parent families headed by parents who were educational underachievers.

Some youths have no choice but to drop out. They are pushed out of school because they lack attention or have poor attendance records. Teachers label them troublemakers, and school administrators use suspensions, transfers, and other means to "convince" them that leaving school is their only option. Because minority students often come from circumstances that interfere with their attendance, they are more likely to be labeled "disobedient."

Race and Dropping Out

Race-based disciplinary practices may help sustain high minority dropout rates. Although the African American dropout rate has declined faster than the white dropout rate over the past two decades, minority students still drop out at a high rate. About 14 percent of African Americans aged 16 to 24 are dropouts; the Hispanic dropout rate for this age group is 29 percent.

In his thoughtful book *Creating the Dropout,* Sherman Dorn shows that graduation rates have slowly but steadily risen during the twentieth century and that regional, racial, and ethnic differences in graduation rates declined. Nonetheless, Dorn argues that the relatively high dropout rate among minorities is the legacy of disciplinary policies instituted more than 40 years ago when educational administrators opposed to school desegregation employed a policy of race-based suspension and expulsion directed at convincing minority students to leave previously all-white high school districts. The legacy of these policies still infects contemporary school districts. Dorn believes that the dropout problem is a function of inequality of educational opportunity rather than the failure of individual students. The proportion of blacks who fail to graduate from high school remains high compared to the proportion of whites failing to graduate because the educational system still fails to provide minority group members with the services and support they need.

Not All Dropouts Are Equal

The reasons students choose to drop out may have a significant impact on their future law violations. Research by Roger Jarjoura shows

Delinquency within the School

A CLOSER VIEW
Jackson Toby has made the provocative suggestion that some kids would be better off by dropping out of school and so would their classmates and teachers. Read more about his views, in Jackson Toby, "Obsessive Compulsion," *National Review* 51(12):30 (June 28, 1999) on InfoTrac College Edition.

The nation was shocked when on March 24, 1998, a 13-year-old boy, who had vowed to kill all the girls who had broken up with him, and his 11-year-old cousin opened fire on students outside a middle school in Jonesboro, Arkansas, killing four girls and a teacher and wounding 11 other people.[47] The Jonesboro killings were premeditated murder: The two boys, dressed in camouflage clothing, apparently lay in wait in a wooded area near the school after setting off a fire alarm, forcing students and faculty members outside. There have been similar school shootings in the past few years, including well-publicized ones in West Paducah, Kentucky, and Pearl, Mississippi. (See Exhibit 9.4.) How is it possible that students so young have access to guns and feel free to carry them in school? These terrible incidents may be occurring because it is now commonplace for students to carry weapons in school. Research efforts have shown that students most likely to own guns and bring them to school are the ones who have engaged in other forms of deviant behavior, including selling drugs, and assault and battery.[48]

that youths who left school because of problems at home, for financial reasons, or because of poor grades were unlikely to increase their delinquent activity after leaving school. In contrast, those who dropped out to get married or because of pregnancy were more likely to increase their violent activities; this pattern may be linked to abuse. Those who were expelled did not increase their violent activity but were more likely to engage in theft and drug abuse.

Leaving school, then, is not a cause of misconduct per se, but youths with a history of misconduct in school often continue their antisocial behavior after dropping out. Dropouts engaged in more antisocial activity than graduates, but the reason youths dropped out influenced their offending patterns.

Dropping Out and School Policy

This debate has serious implications for educational policy. Evidence that delinquency rates decline after students leave school has caused some educators to question the wisdom of compulsory education. Some experts, such as Jackson Toby, argue that the effort to force teenagers to stay in school is counterproductive and that delinquency might be reduced by allowing them to assume a productive position in the workforce. For many youths, leaving school can have the effect of escape from a stressful situation. Toby proposes a radical solution: Make high schools voluntary, and require students to justify the expenses allocated for their education.

Critical Thinking

1. Do you believe that efforts to keep children in school, provide tutoring, and create programs conducive to educational achievement should be continued to lower both dropout and delinquency rates, or would the money be better spent on motivated students?

2. Do you believe that a free high school education is a privilege that must be earned, and therefore should nonmotivated

and/or disruptive students be asked to leave school before graduation?

InfoTrac College Edition Research

Is it possible that school climate is the cause behind both school failure and the likelihood that some students will drop out? To research this topic, use *school climate* as a subject guide on InfoTrac College Edition.

Sources: National Center for Education Statistics, "Drop Out Rates in the United States," (Washington, DC, 2000); Terence Thornberry, Melanie Moore, and R. L. Christenson, "The Effect of Dropping Out of High School on Subsequent Criminal Behavior," *Criminology* 23:3–18 (1985); Marvin Krohn, Terence Thornberry, Lori Collins-Hall, and Alan Lizotte, "School Dropout, Delinquent Behavior, and Drug Use," in Howard Kaplan, ed., *Drugs, Crime, and Other Deviant Adaptations: Longitudinal Studies* (New York: Plenum Press, 1995), pp. 163–83; ADAM, 1999 Annual Report on Drug Use among Adult and Juvenile Arrestees (Washington, DC: United States Government Printing Office, 2000); Howard Snyder and Melissa Sickmund, *Juvenile Offenders and Victims: A National Report* (Washington, DC: Office of Juvenile Justice and Delinquency Prevention, 1995), p. 15; Jay Teachman, Kathleen Paasch, and Karen Carver, "Social Capital and the Generation of Human Capital," *Social Forces* 75:1343–60 (1997); Michel Janosz, Marc Le Blanc, Bernard Boulerice, and Richard Tremblay, "What Information Is Really Needed to Predict School Dropout? A Replication on Two Longitudinal Samples" (University of Montreal, School of Psychoeducation, 1995); Christine Bowditch, "Getting Rid of Troublemakers: High School Disciplinary Procedures and the Production of Dropouts," *Social Problems* 40:493–508 (1993); Sherman Dorn, *Creating the Dropout* (New York: Praeger, 1996); G. Roger Jarjoura, "Does Dropping Out of School Enhance Delinquent Involvement? Results from a Large-Scale National Probability Sample," *Criminology* 31:149–72 (1993); Jackson Toby, "Getting Serious about School Discipline," *The Public Interest* 133:68–74 (1998).

Attention was first focused on school crime when more than 20 years ago, the federal government published its pioneering study of the school system, *Violent Schools—Safe Schools* (1977).[49] This survey found that although teenagers spend only 25 percent of their time in school, 40 percent of the robberies and 36 percent of the physical attacks involving this age group occur there. Two recent reports have highlighted the problem of school-based crime: the School Crime Victimization Survey and the School Substance Abuse Survey.

The School Crime Victimization Survey

The federal government's most recent School Crime Victimization Survey (2000) is a joint effort by the Justice Department and the Education Department.[50] In 1999, students ages 12 through 18 were victims of about 2.5 million total crimes at school. Of these, about 186,000 were serious violent crimes, such as rape, sexual assault, robbery, and aggravated assault. There were also 47 school-associated violent deaths

Exhibit 9.4 Recent School Shootings

- April 26, 2002. Eighteen teachers and students died when an expelled former student went on a shooting spree at his school in the eastern German city of Erfurt.
- March 5, 2001. A student in Santee, California, an alleged victim of schoolyard bullies, killed two students.
- February 29, 2000. A first-grader in Michigan shot and killed a fellow student, a 6-year-old girl with whom he had quarreled.
- May 20, 1999. A 15-year-old, upset over a broken romance, opened fire at Heritage High School in Conyers, Georgia, injuring six students.
- April 20, 1999. Two young men killed 13 students and injured 20 others before committing suicide at Columbine High School in Colorado.
- April 16, 1999. A high school sophomore fired two shotgun blasts in a school hallway in Notus, Idaho.
- May 21, 1998. Two teenagers were fatally shot and more than 20 people hurt when a 15-year-old boy allegedly opened fire at a high school in Springfield, Oregon. His parents were found slain at their home.
- May 19, 1998. Three days before his graduation, an 18-year-old honor student allegedly opened fire in a parking lot at a high school in Fayetteville, Tennessee, killing a classmate who was dating his ex-girlfriend.
- April 24, 1998. A science teacher was shot to death in front of students at the eighth-grade graduation dance in Edinboro, Pennsylvania.
- March 24, 1998. Four girls and a teacher were shot to death and 10 people wounded during a false fire alarm at a middle school in Jonesboro, Arkansas, when two boys, 11 and 13, opened fire from the woods.
- December 1, 1997. Three students were killed and five others wounded in a hallway at Heath High School in West Paducah, Kentucky.
- October 1, 1997. A 16-year-old boy in Pearl, Mississippi, was accused of killing his mother, then going to his high school and killing two students and wounding seven others.

in the United States between July 1, 1998, and June 30, 1999, including 38 homicides (33 involved school-aged children). (See Figure 9.2.)

While these numbers seem staggering, like the general delinquency rate, the total nonfatal victimization rate for students has declined over the last few years. Between 1995 and 1999, the percentage of students who reported being victims of crime at school decreased from 10 percent to 8 percent. (See Figure 9.3.) This decline was due in large part to the decrease in percentages of students in grades seven through nine who were victimized. Between 1995 and 1999, the prevalence of reported victimization dropped from 11 percent to 8 percent for seventh-graders, from 11 percent to 8 percent for eighth-graders, and from 12 percent to 9 percent for ninth-graders. However, the prevalence rates of some types of crimes at school have not changed. For example, between 1993 and 1999, the percentage of students in grades 9 through 12 who were threatened or injured with a weapon on school property in the previous 12 months remained constant—at about 7–8 percent.

As school crime has declined, perceptions of safety in school buildings increased. The percentage of students ages 12 through 18 who reported avoiding one or more places at school for their own safety decreased between 1995 and 1999—from 9 percent to 5 percent. Furthermore, the percentage of students who reported that street gangs were present at their schools decreased from 1995 to 1999.

While the decline in nonfatal school crime is encouraging, in 1999, students ages 12 through 18 were victims of about 186,000 serious violent crimes at school, and about 476,000 away from school.[51] About 7–8 percent of students in grades 9 to 12 reported being threatened or injured with a weapon such as a gun, knife, or club on school property in the previous 12 months. In 1999, about 7 percent of students carried a weapon such as a gun, knife, or club on school property in the past 30 days. So while the rate of school crime has been in decline, it is still a significant problem.

School Shootings

The nation has been rocked by a number of cases involving the most extreme form of school violence: deadly school shootings. Perhaps these incidents should not come as a surprise since so many students now routinely carry weapons and do not check them at the schoolhouse door. Kids who have been the victims of crime themselves and who hang with peers who carry weapons are the ones most likely to bring guns to school.[52]

Highly publicized incidents of fatal school shootings have helped focus attention on school crime. (Exhibit 9.4 lists some recent incidents of school-based shootings.) Though they have been the focus of much attention, there is as yet no single cause that links these incidents, nor is it possible to predict which student will become a school shooter.

Nature and Extent of Shootings   Social scientists are now conducting studies of these events in order to determine their trends and patterns. One recent study examined all school-related shootings occurring between July 1, 1994, through June 30, 1999.[53] A total of 220 incidents had occurred, resulting in 253 deaths. Of these, 202 involved a single victim and 18, multiple victims. Of the 220 shooting incidents, 172 were homicides, 30 were suicides, 11 were homicide-suicides, 5 were legal intervention deaths, and 2 were unintentional firearm-related deaths. While highly publicized in the media, the average annual incidence is only 0.068 per 100,000

Figure 9.2

Number of Nonfatal Crimes against Students Ages 12 through 18 Occurring at School or Going to or from School per 1,000 Students, by Type of Crime and Selected Student Characteristics, 1999

Note: Serious violent crimes include rape, sexual assault, robbery, and aggravated assault. Violent crimes include serious violent crimes and simple assault. Total crimes include violent crimes and theft. "At school" includes inside the school building, on school property, or on the way to or from school. Detail may not add to totals because of rounding. Source: U.S. Department of Justice, Bureau of Justice Statistics, *Indicators of School Crime & Safety*, 2001, p. 6.

Figure 9.3

Number of Nonfatal Crimes against Students Ages 12 through 18 per 1,000 Students, by Type of Crime and Location, 1992 to 1999

Note: Serious violent crimes include rape, sexual assault, robbery, and aggravated assault. Violent crimes include serious violent crimes and simple assault. Total crimes include violent crimes and theft. "At school" includes inside the school building, on school property, or on the way to or from school.
Source: U.S. Department of Justice, Bureau of Justice Statistics, *Indicators of School Crime & Safety*, 2001, p. 5.

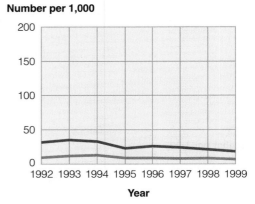

students. Between 1992 and 1999, the rate of single-victim student homicides decreased significantly, while multiple-victim incidents increased significantly.

The research found that most shooting incidents occur around the start of the school day, the lunch period, or the end of the school day. In most of the shootings (55%), a note, threat, or other action indicating risk for violence occurred before the event. Shooters were also likely to have expressed some form of suicidal behavior prior to the event and to report having been bullied by their peers. These patterns may help school officials one day to identify potential risk factors and respond in a timely fashion.

Who Is the School Shooter?   The U.S. Secret Service has developed a profile of school shootings and shooters after evaluating 41 school shooters who participated in 37 incidents.[54] They found that most attacks were neither spontaneous nor impulsive. Shooters typically developed a plan of attack well in advance; more than half had considered the attack for at least two weeks and had a plan for at least two days.

The attackers' mental anguish was well known, and they had come to the attention of someone (school officials, police, fellow students) because of their bizarre and disturbing behavior before the attack took place. One student told more than 20 friends beforehand about his plans, which included killing students and planting bombs. Threats were communicated in more than three-fourths of the cases, and in more than half the incidents, the attacker told more than one person. Some people knew detailed information, while others knew "something spectacular" was going to happen on a particular date. In less than one-fourth of the cases did the attacker make a direct threat to the target.

A CLOSER VIEW
To find out more about school shootings and other violent acts, use the term *school violence* as a subject guide on InfoTrac College Edition.

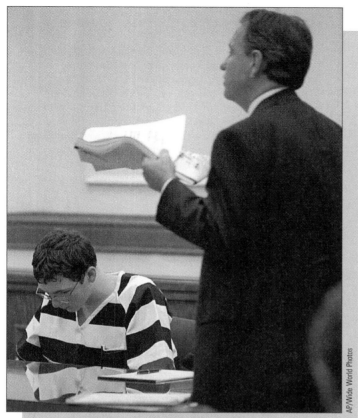

MICHAEL CARNEAL listens to his attorney during a court hearing. Carneal was on trial for 1997 shootings committed at Heath High School in West Paducah, Kentucky, in which three students died. The West Paducah killings, as well as the Columbine shootings, have focused the nation's attention on school violence. Numerous programs are now being designed to prevent similar incidents from occurring.

The Secret Service found that shooters came from such a wide variety of backgrounds that no accurate or useful profile of at-risk kids could be developed. They ranged in age from 11 to 21 and came from a wide variety of ethnic and racial backgrounds; about 25 percent of the shooters were minority-group members. Some lived in intact families with strong ties to the community, while others were reared in foster homes with histories of neglect. Some were excellent students, while others were poor academic performers. Shooters could not be characterized as isolated and alienated; some had many friends and were considered popular. There was no evidence that shootings were a result of the onset of mental disorder. Drugs and alcohol seemed to have little involvement in school violence.

What the Secret Service found was that many of the shooters had a history of feeling extremely depressed or desperate because they had been picked on or bullied. About three-fourths either threatened to kill themselves, made suicidal gestures, or tried to kill themselves before the attack; six of the students studied killed themselves during the incident. The most frequent motivation was revenge. More than three-fourths were known to hold a grievance, real or imagined, against the target and/or others. In most cases, this was the first violent act against the target. Two-thirds of the attackers described feeling persecuted, and in more than three-fourths of the incidents the attackers had difficulty coping with a major change in a significant relationship or a loss of status, such as a lost love or a humiliating failure. Not surprisingly, most shooters had experience with guns and weapons and had access to them at home. Some of the most important factors linked to extreme incidents of school violence are contained in Exhibit 9.5.

One factor that stands out in the profile of school shooters is that they were typically young boys who had been bullied or picked on in school. Because this issue of bullying is so important, it is the topic of the Focus on Delinquency box entitled "Bullying in School" on page 284.

The School Substance Abuse Survey

The national Center for Addiction and Substance Abuse (CASA) at Columbia University in New York conducts periodic surveys with students, parents, teachers, and principals about their attitudes toward cigarettes, alcohol, and illegal drugs (marijuana, heroin, cocaine, and acid) and their presence in schools.[55] The most recent survey finds that a majority (51%) of high school students say the drug problem is getting worse, and both middle and high school students say that drugs are their single biggest concern. The number of high school teens who report that drugs are used, sold, and kept at their schools is rising: from 72 percent in 1996 to 78 percent in 1998. By age 17, only 23 percent say their school is drug free, 54 percent say that alcohol was available at most parties they attended in the previous six months, and 35 percent say pot was available.

CASA lists seven signs of trouble in school: smoking, drinking, drugs, weapons, expulsion for drugs, student death in drug- or alcohol-related incidents, and students showing up in class drunk or stoned.[56] Considering these problems, it is not surprising that

Exhibit 9.5   Factors Linked to Children Who Engage in Serious School Violence

- *Social withdrawal.* In some situations, gradual and eventually complete withdrawal from social contacts. The withdrawal often stems from feelings of depression, rejection, persecution, unworthiness, and lack of confidence.
- *Excessive feelings of isolation and being alone.* Research indicates that in some cases feelings of isolation and not having friends are associated with children who behave aggressively and violently.
- *Excessive feelings of rejection.* Children who are troubled often are isolated from their mentally healthy peers. Some aggressive children who are rejected by nonaggressive peers seek out aggressive friends who, in turn, reinforce their violent tendencies.
- *Being a victim of violence.* Children who are victims of violence—including physical or sexual abuse in the community, at school, or at home—are sometimes at risk of becoming violent toward themselves or others.
- *Feelings of being picked on and persecuted.* The youth who feels constantly picked on, teased, bullied, singled out for ridicule, and humiliated at home or at school may initially withdraw socially.
- *Low school interest and poor academic performance.* In some situations—such as when the low achiever feels frustrated, unworthy, chastised, and denigrated—acting out and aggressive behaviors may occur.
- *Expression of violence in writings and drawings.* An overrepresentation of violence in writings and drawings that is consistently directed at specific individuals (family members, peers, other adults) over time, may signal emotional problems and the potential for violence.
- *Uncontrolled anger.* Patterns of impulsive and chronic hitting, intimidating, and bullying behaviors, if left

unattended, may later escalate into more serious behaviors.
- *History of discipline problems.* Chronic behavior and disciplinary problems, both in school and at home, may suggest that underlying emotional needs are not being met.
- *History of violent and aggressive behavior.* Unless provided with support and counseling, a youth who has a history of aggressive or violent behavior is likely to repeat those behaviors. Similarly, youths who engage in overt behaviors such as bullying, generalized aggression and defiance, and covert behaviors such as stealing, vandalism, lying, cheating, and fire setting also are at risk for more serious aggressive behavior.
- *Membership in hate groups or the willingness to victimize* individuals with disabilities or health problems is a precursor to violence.
- *Drug use and alcohol use.* Apart from being unhealthy behaviors, drug use and alcohol use reduce self-control and expose children and youths to violence, either as perpetrators or as victims, or both.
- *Inappropriate access to, possession of, and use of firearms.* Children and youths who inappropriately possess or have access to firearms can have an increased risk for violence or other emotional problems and should not have access to firearms and other weapons.
- *Serious threats of violence.* Recent incidents across the country clearly indicate that threats to commit violence against oneself or others should be taken very seriously. Steps must be taken to understand the nature of these threats and to prevent them from being carried out.

Source: Kevin Dwyer, *Early Warning, Timely Response: A Guide to Safe Schools* (Washington, DC: U.S. Department of Education, 1998), Section 3.

---

teens, parents, teachers, and principals support firm steps to keep drugs out of schools, including random locker searches, zero tolerance policies, and drug testing of student athletes. More than half of the students (52%) and principals (53%) support drug testing of all students, compared with 42 percent of parents and 38 percent of teachers.

The Community and School Crime

A number of researchers have observed that school crime is a function of the community in which the school is located. In other words, crime in schools does not occur in isolation from crime in the community.[57]

Poverty and Disorganization   Schools experiencing crime and drug abuse are most likely to be found in **socially disorganized neighborhoods** with a high proportion of students behind grade level in reading, with many students from families on welfare, and with high unemployment and poverty rates.[58] Neighborhoods with high population density and transient populations also have problem-prone schools.[59] In contrast, schools located in more stable areas, with high-achieving students, drug-free environments, and involved parents, have fewer behavioral problems within the student body.[60]

When Wayne Welsh, Robert Stokes, and Jack Greene studied community influences on school crime, they found that community influences may undermine school

socially disorganized neighborhood   Neighborhood or area marked by culture conflict, lack of cohesiveness, a transient population, and insufficient social organizations; these problems are reflected in the problems at schools in these areas.

stability and climate.[61] Poverty in a school's surrounding area influences the social characteristics of students. They may lack the readiness and interest to learn when compared with students from more affluent neighborhoods. Poor areas may find it difficult to hire and retain the most qualified faculty and/or provide students with the most up-to-date equipment and books. Because poor communities have lower tax bases, they are handcuffed when they want to provide remedial programs for students with learning issues, or conversely, enrichment programs for the gifted. Finally, parents and other students have neither the time nor resources to become involved in school activities or participate in governance. These factors may eventually undermine school climate and destabilize the educational environment, which leads to school crime and disorder.

Cross-national research efforts confirm the community influences on school crime. One study of violent crimes in the schools of Stockholm found that although only one-fifth of schools were located in areas of social instability and disorganization, almost a third of school crime happened in these schools.[62]

Neighborhood Crime There is also evidence that crime in schools reflects the patterns of antisocial behavior that exist in the surrounding neighborhood.[63] Schools in high-crime areas experience more crime than schools in safer areas. Students who report being afraid in school are actually more afraid of being in city parks, streets, or subways. Because of this fear, students in high-crime areas may carry weapons for self-protection as they go from their homes to school.[64]

Research also shows that many perpetrators of school crime have been victims of delinquency themselves.[65] It is possible that school-based crimes have "survival value"—striking back against a weaker victim is a method of regaining lost possessions or self-respect.[66] This would imply that areas with high crime rates that produce a large pool of student victims will also manifest high rates of school crime. This research suggests that it may be futile to attempt to eliminate school crime

SOME SCHOOLS ARE REALLY CRACKING DOWN in order to maintain school discipline. Here Leonard Lopez and his son, Vincent, sit at home surrounded by folders of newspaper clippings and legal papers on Feb. 15, 2000, in Arlington, Texas. Vincent was removed from his junior high school and placed into an alternative school for five days after one of his drawings was considered to show gang affiliation.

Bullying in School

Experts define bullying among children as repeated negative acts committed by one or more children against another. These negative acts may be physical or verbal in nature—for example, hitting or kicking, teasing or taunting—or they may involve indirect actions such as manipulating friendships or purposely excluding other children from activities. Implicit in this definition is an imbalance in real or perceived power between the bully and victim.

Recent research in the United States and abroad has documented that bullying is a common and potentially damaging form of violence among children. Not only does bullying harm both its intended victims and the perpetrators, it also may affect the climate of schools and, indirectly, the ability of all students to learn to the best of their abilities. There is also evidence of a link between bullying and later delinquent and criminal behavior.

Studies of individual school systems indicate that bullying is widespread and pervasive. In a study of 207 junior high and high school students from small Midwestern towns, 88 percent reported having observed bullying, and 77 percent indicated that they had been victims of bullying during their school careers. A study of 6,500 students in fourth to sixth grades in the rural South indicated that 1 in 4 students had been bullied with some regularity within the past three months and that 1 in 10 had been bullied at least once a week. Approximately 1 in 5 children admitted that they had bullied another child with some regularity in the previous three months.

Data collected on a national level as part of the most recent school safety survey (2000) indicate that about 5 percent of students ages 12 through 18 report that they had been bullied at school in the last six months. In general, females were as likely as males to report being bullied. While there are few racial differences in bullying, students in lower grades were more likely to be bullied than students in higher grades: About 10 percent of students in grades 6 and 7 reported being bullied, compared with about 5 percent of students in grades 8 and 9 and about 2 percent in grades 10 through 12.

Studies of bullying suggest that there are short- and long-term consequences for both the perpetrators and victims of bullying. Students who are chronic victims of bullying experience more physical and psychological problems than their peers who are not harassed by other children, and they tend not to grow out of the role of victim. Longitudinal studies have found that victims of bullying in early grades also reported being bullied several years later. Studies also suggest that chronically victimized students may as adults be at increased risk for depression, poor self-esteem, and other mental health problems, including schizophrenia.

It is not only victims who are at risk for short- and long-term problems; bullies also are at increased risk for negative outcomes. One researcher found that those elementary students who were bullies attended school less frequently and were more likely to drop out than other students. Several studies suggest that bullying in early childhood may be a critical risk factor for the development of future problems with violence and delinquency. For example, research conducted in Scandinavia found that in addition to threatening other children, bullies were several times more likely than their nonbullying peers to commit antisocial acts, including vandalism, fighting, theft, drunkenness, and truancy, and to have an arrest by young adulthood. Another study of more than 500 children found that aggressive behavior at the age of 8 was a powerful predictor of criminality and violent behavior at the age of 30.

Can Bullying Be Prevented?

The first and best-known intervention to reduce bullying among school children was launched by Dan Olweus in Norway and Sweden in the

---

without considering the impact of communities. The Welsh research found that schools that are stable and have a positive climate manifest lower rates of criminal activity on school grounds.

Reducing School Crime

Schools around the country have mounted a campaign to reduce the incidence of delinquency on campus. Nearly all states have developed some sort of crime-free, weapon-free, or safe-school zone statute.[67] Most have defined these zones to include school transportation and school-sponsored functions. Schools are also cooperating with court officials and probation officers to share information and monitor students who have criminal records. School districts are formulating crisis prevention and intervention policies and are directing individual schools to develop safe-school plans.

zero tolerance policy
Mandating specific consequences or punishments for delinquent acts and not allowing anyone to avoid these consequences.

Some schools have instituted strict controls over student activity—for example, making locker searches, preventing students from having lunch off campus, and using patrols to monitor drug use. According to the National Center survey on school violence (1998), a majority of schools have adopted a **zero tolerance policy** that man-early 1980s. Inspired by the suicides of several severely victimized children, Norway supported the development and implementation of a comprehensive program to address bullying among children in school. The program involved interventions at multiple levels:

- *Schoolwide interventions* A survey of bullying problems at each school, increased supervision, schoolwide assemblies, and teacher in-service training to raise the awareness of children and school staff regarding bullying.
- *Classroom-level interventions* The establishment of classroom rules against bullying, regular class meetings to discuss bullying at school, and meetings with all parents.
- *Individual-level interventions* Discussions with students identified as bullies and victims.

The program was found to be highly effective in reducing bullying and other antisocial behavior among students in primary and junior high schools. Within two years of implementation, both boys' and girls' self-reports indicated that bullying had decreased by half. These changes in behavior were more pronounced the longer the program was in effect. Moreover, students reported significant decreases in rates of truancy, vandalism, and theft and indicated that their school's climate was significantly more positive as a result of the program. Not surprisingly, those schools that had implemented more of the program's components experienced the most marked changes in behavior. The core components of the Olweus antibullying program have been adapted for use in several other cultures, including Canada, England, and the United States. Results of the antibullying efforts in these countries have been similar to the results experienced in the Scandinavian countries, with the efforts in Toronto schools showing somewhat more modest results. Again, as in the Scandinavian study, schools that were more active in implementing the program observed the most marked changes in reported behaviors.

Only one U.S. program has been based explicitly on the comprehensive model developed by Olweus. Gary B. Melton, Susan P. Limber, and colleagues at the Institute for Families in Society of the University of South Carolina in Columbia have adapted Olweus's model for use in rural middle schools in that state. Interventions are focused at the levels of the individual, classroom, school, and community at large. A comprehensive evaluation involving 6,500 children currently is under way to measure the effects of the program.

Critical Thinking

1. Would a no-tolerance policy that requires any aggressive act to be dealt with by suspension and a second act by expulsion help reduce schoolyard bullying? Do students have the right to be free from aggression while on school property?

InfoTrac College Edition Research

What are the long-term effects of bullying? Does it cause emotional problems even after the bullying has ceased? Read Lyndal Bond, John B. Carlin, Lyndal Thomas, Kerryn Rubin, George Patton, "Does Bullying Cause Emotional Problems? A Prospective Study of Young Teenagers," *British Medical Journal* 323(7311):480 (Sept 1, 2001).

Source: Adapted from Susan P. Limber and Maury M. Nation, "Bullying among Children and Youth," in June Arnette and Marjorie Walsleben, eds., *Combating Fear and Restoring Safety in Schools* (Washington, DC: Office of Juvenile Justice and Delinquency Prevention, 1998); see Dan Olweus, "Victimization by Peers: Antecedents and Long-Term Outcomes," in K. H. Rubin and J. B. Asendorf, eds., *Social Withdrawal, Inhibitions, and Shyness* (Hillsdale, NJ: Erlbaum, 1993), pp. 315–41; Phillip Kaufman et al., *Indicators of School Crime and Safety, 2000* (Washington, DC: National Center for Education Statistics, 2001).

> **The National School Safety** and Security Services is a Cleveland (Ohio)–based consulting firm specializing in school security and crisis-preparedness training, security assessments, and related safety consulting for K–12 schools, law enforcement, and other youth safety providers. Their site contains a lot of information on school security. Visit it at *http://www.schoolsecurity.org/* For an up-to-date list of Web links, go to *http://info.wadsworth.com/siegel*

dates predetermined consequences or punishments for specific offenses, most typically possession of drugs (88%), weapons (91%), or tobacco (79%), and/or engaging in violent behaviors (79%).[68]

School Security Efforts Almost every school has attempted to restrict entry of dangerous persons by having visitors sign in before entering; most close the campus for lunch in order to keep kids out of trouble off campus.[69] Schools have attempted to ensure the physical safety of students and school staff by using mechanical security devices such as surveillance cameras, electronic barriers to keep out intruders, and roving security guards. Law and order approaches have relied on such measures as metal detectors to identify gun-wielding students. About 4 percent of schools now use random metal detector checks, and 1 percent employ daily checks; metal detectors are much more common in large schools, especially where serious crime has taken place (15%).[70] One program in New York City uses random searches with inexpensive handheld detectors at the start of the school day; students report a greater sense of security, and attendance has increased.[71] Some districts have gone so far as to employ youthful undercover detectives on school grounds. These detectives pose as pupils, attend classes, mingle with students, contact drug dealers, make buys, and arrest campus dealers.[72]

Exhibit 9.6 Security Measures to Reduce School Crime

Outsiders on Campus

- Posted signs regarding penalties for trespassing
- Enclosed campus (fencing)
- Guard at main entry gate to campus
- Greeters in strategic locations
- Vehicle parking stickers
- Uniforms or dress codes
- Exterior doors locked from the outside
- A challenge procedure for anyone out of class
- Cameras in remote locations
- School laid out so all visitors must pass through front office
- Temporary "fading" badges issued to all visitors
- One main door entry to school, exits with push bars, all other doors to outside entry locked
- Bulletproof windows
- Closed-circuit video surveillance systems to reduce property crime such as break-ins, theft, vandalism, and assaults
- Landscaping that creates an inviting appearance without offering a hiding place for trespassers or criminals
- Motion-sensitive lights to illuminate dark corners in hallways or on campus
- Convex mirrors to monitor blind spots in school hallways
- Photo identification badges for students, teachers, and staff and identification cards for visitors on campus

Fights on Campus

- Cameras
- Duress alarms
- Whistles

Vandalism

- Graffiti-resistant sealers
- Glass-break sensors
- Aesthetically pleasing wall murals (these usually are not hit by graffiti)
- Law enforcement officers living on campus
- Eight-foot fencing
- Well-lit campus at night

Theft

- Interior intrusion detection sensors
- Property marking (including microdots) to deter theft
- Bars on windows, reinforced doors
- Elimination of access points to rooftops
- Cameras
- Doors with hingepins on secure side
- Computers and TVs bolted down, high-value assets located in interior rooms
- Key control
- Biometric entry into rooms with high-value assets
- Law enforcement officer living on campus

Drugs

- Drug detection swipes
- Hair analysis kits for drug use detection (intended for parental application)
- Drug search dogs
- Removal of lockers
- Random searches
- Vapor detection of drugs

Alcohol

- No open campus at lunch
- Breathalyzer® test equipment
- No access to vehicles
- No lockers
- Clear or open mesh backpacks
- Saliva test kits

Weapons

- Walk-through metal detectors
- Handheld metal detectors
- Vapor detection of gun powder
- Crimestopper hotline with rewards for information
- Gunpowder detection swipes
- Random locker, backpack, and vehicle searches
- X-ray inspection of bookbags and purses

Schools use a variety of security setups—some have independent security divisions, others hire private guards, while still others cooperate with local law enforcement agencies. For example, in cities such as Houston, it is routine to employ armed guards in full uniform during the day. Nor does security end in the evening. In San Diego, an elaborate security system makes use of infrared beams and silent alarms in order to protect school grounds from vandals and unwelcome visitors.[73] Rather than suspending violators, some school districts now send them to a separate center for evaluation and counseling so they are kept separate from the law-abiding students.[74] In New York City, the school board maintains a force of 3,200 officers in its Division of School Safety, who now patrol the more than 1,000 public schools armed only with handcuffs. The New York City Police Department is scheduled to take significant control over the recruitment, screening, and training of school security officers, though the assignment of regular police officers would be limited to the 130 schools they already help patrol at the invitation of principals.[75]

Malicious Acts

- Setback of all school buildings from vehicle areas
- Inaccessibility of air intake and water source
- All adults on campus required to have a badge
- Vehicle barriers near main entries and student gathering areas

Parking Lot Problems

- Cameras
- Parking decals
- Fencing
- Card ID systems for parking lot entry
- Parking lots sectioned off for different student schedules
- Sensors in parking areas that should have no access during school day
- Roving guards
- Bike patrol

False Fire Alarms

- Sophisticated alarm systems that allow assessment of alarms (and cancellation if false) before they become audible
- Boxes installed over alarm pulls that alarm locally (screamer boxes)

Bomb Threats

- Caller ID on phone system
- Crimestopper program with big rewards for information
- Recording of all phone calls, with a message regarding this at the beginning of each incoming call
- All incoming calls routed through a district office
- Phone company support
- No pay phones on campus
- Policy to extend the school year when plagued with bomb threats and subsequent evacuations

Bus Problems

- School bus drivers tested for drug and alcohol use
- Video cameras and recorders within enclosures on buses
- IDs required to get on school buses
- Security aides on buses
- Smaller buses
- Duress alarm system or radios for bus drivers

Teacher Safety

- Duress alarms
- Roving patrols
- Classroom doors left open during class
- Cameras in black boxes in classrooms
- Controlled access to classroom areas
- Classrooms equipped with intercom systems connected to the central school office
- Two-way radios for security patrols or campus staff members
- Cellular phones for use in crises or emergency situations

Campus Safety

- Neighborhood Watch programs in areas near schools
- Parents who provide safe houses along school routes and monitor "safe corridors" or walkways to and from school
- Parent volunteers who monitor hallways, cafeterias, playgrounds, and school walkways in order to increase visibility of responsible adults
- Block safety watch programs carried out by area residents at school bus stops as a crime deterrent for school children and area residents
- Fenced school grounds to secure campus perimeters
- Bathrooms with zigzag entrances, to make it easier to monitor sounds, and roll-down doors to secure bathrooms after hours

Sources: Adapted from *Mary W. Green Research Report: The Appropriate and Effective Use of Security Technologies in U.S. Schools* (Washington, DC: National Institute of Justice, 1999); June L. Arnette and Marjorie C. Walsleben, *Combating Fear and Restoring Safety in Schools* (Washington, DC: Office of Juvenile Justice and Delinquency Prevention, 1998).

Critics claim that even though these methods are effective, they reduce staff and student morale. Tighter security, stricter rule enforcement, and fortresslike alterations in a school's physical plant may reduce acts of crime and violence in school only to displace them to the community. Similarly, expelling or suspending troublemakers puts them on the street with nothing to do. Lowering the level of crime in schools may have no real impact on reducing the total amount of crime committed by young people. In fact, schools that employ strict controls are also the ones most likely to suffer increases in school-based victimization.[76] Exhibit 9.6 contains some of the most important security programs being used in schools today.

Reducing School Crime: Social Programs Rather than a strict security/law enforcement policy, it might also be possible to reduce school crime by improving school climate and increasing educational standards. Programs have been designed to improve the standards of the teaching staff and administrators and the educational climate in the school, increase the relevance of the curriculum, and provide law-related education classes.[77]

Controlling school crime is ultimately linked to the community and family conditions. When communities undergo such changes as increases in unemployment and the number of single-parent households, both school disruption and community crime rates may rise.[78] The school environment can be made safer only if community issues are addressed: for example, by taking steps to keep intruders out of school buildings, putting pressure on local police to develop community safety programs, increasing correctional services, strengthening laws on school safety, and making parents bear greater responsibility for their children's behavior.[79]

Schools must also use the resources of the community when controlling school crime. Most school districts refer problem students to social services outside the school. About 70 percent of public schools provide outside referrals for students with substance abuse problems, while 90 percent offer drug education within the school.[80]

Legal Rights within the School

As educational officials have attempted to restore order within schools, their actions have often run into opposition from the courts, which are concerned with maintaining the legal rights of minors. The U.S. Supreme Court has sought to balance the civil liberties of students with the school's mandate to provide a reasonable and safe educational environment. In some instances, the Court has sided with students, while in others, the balance has shifted toward the educational establishment. The main issues concerning the rights of children and the schools include compulsory attendance, free speech in school, and school discipline.

School Attendance

In the United States, compulsory school attendance statutes have been in effect for more than half a century.[81] Children are required by law to attend school until a given age, normally 16 or 17.[82] Violations of compulsory attendance laws generally result in complaints that can lead to court action. Often, however, children are truant because of emotional problems or learning disabilities. They are then brought into the court system for problems beyond their control. Many of them might be better off leaving school at an earlier age than the compulsory education law allows. On the other hand, emotionally disturbed and nonconforming children are pushed out of many school systems and thereby deprived of an education. Whether these children have a right to attend school is unclear. Many school systems ignore the difficult student, who may be classified as "bad" or "delinquent."

In 1925, the Supreme Court determined that compulsory education did not necessarily have to be provided by a public school system and that parochial schools could be a reasonable substitute.[83] From that time through the 1970s, the courts upheld the right of the state to make education compulsory. Then, in 1972, in the case of *Wisconsin v. Yoder*, the Supreme Court made an exception to the general compulsory education law by holding that traditional Amish culture was able to give its children the skills that would prepare them for adulthood within Amish society. Thus, the removal of Amish children from school after the completion of the eighth grade was justified.[84] It is not clear, however, whether this decision speaks directly to the issue of compulsory education or whether it is simply another instance of freedom of religion. Therefore, the state's role in requiring school attendance is still unsettled.

STUDENTS IN ROCHESTER, NEW YORK, are shown protesting a school ruling over the presence of metal detectors. The Supreme Court allows school officials to control student speech while on school premises if it interferes with the school's mission to implant "the shared values of a civilized social order." Student protest off-campus is still an open question. In the future, the courts may be asked to rule whether schools can control such forms of speech or whether they are shielded by the First Amendment.

Free Speech

Freedom of speech is granted and guaranteed in the First Amendment to the U.S. Constitution. The right has been divided into two major categories as it affects children in schools. The first category involves what is known as *passive speech,* a form of expression not associated with the actual speaking of words. Examples include wearing arm bands or political protest buttons. The most important U.S. Supreme Court decision concerning a student's right to passive speech was in 1969 in the case of *Tinker v. Des Moines Independent Community School District.*[85] This case involved the right to wear black arm bands to protest the war in Vietnam. Two high school students, aged 16 and 17, were told they would be suspended if they demonstrated their objections to the Vietnam War by wearing black arm bands. They attended school wearing the arm bands and were suspended. According to the Court, in order for the state (in the person of a school official) to justify prohibiting an expression of opinion, it must be able to show that its action was caused by something more than a mere desire to avoid the discomfort and unpleasantness that accompany the expression of an unpopular view. Unless it can be shown that the forbidden conduct will interfere with the discipline required to operate the school, the prohibition cannot be sustained. In the *Tinker* case, the Court said there was no evidence that the school authorities had reason to believe that the wearing of armbands would substantially interfere with the work of the school or infringe on the rights of the students.[86]

This decision is significant because it recognizes the child's right to free speech in a public school system. Justice Abe Fortas stated in his majority opinion, "Young people do not shed their constitutional rights at the schoolhouse door."[87] *Tinker* established two things: (1) A child is entitled to free speech in school under the First

Amendment of the U.S. Constitution, and (2) the test used to determine whether the child has gone beyond proper speech is whether he or she materially and substantially interferes with the requirements of appropriate discipline in the operation of the school.

The concept of free speech articulated in *Tinker* was used again in the 1986 case *Bethel School District No. 403 v. Fraser*.[88] This case upheld a school system's right to suspend or otherwise discipline a student who uses obscene or profane language and gestures. Matthew Fraser, a Bethel high school student, used sexual metaphors in making a speech nominating a friend for student office. His statement included these remarks:

> *I know a man who is firm—he's firm in his pants, he's firm in his shirt, his character is firm—but most . . . of all, his belief in you, the students of Bethel, is firm.*
>
> *Jeff Kuhlman is a man who takes his point and pounds it in. If necessary, he'll take an issue and nail it to the wall. He doesn't attack things in spurts—he drives hard, pushing and pushing until finally—he succeeds.*
>
> *Jeff is a man who will go to the very end—even the climax, for each and every one of you.*
>
> *So vote for Jeff for A.S.B. vice-president—he'll never come between you and the best our high school can be.*

The Court found that a school has the right to control lewd and offensive speech that undermines the educational mission. The Court drew a distinction between the sexual content of Fraser's remarks and the political nature of Tinker's arm band. It ruled that the pervasive sexual innuendo of the speech interfered with the school's mission to implant "the shared values of a civilized social order" in the student body.

In a 1988 case, *Hazelwood School District v. Kuhlmeier*, the Court extended the right of school officials to censor "active speech" when it ruled that the principal could censor articles in a student publication.[89] In this case, students had written about their personal experiences with pregnancy and parental divorce. The majority ruled that censorship was justified in this case because school-sponsored publications, activities, and productions were part of the curriculum and therefore designed to impart knowledge. Control over such school-supported activities could be differentiated from the action the Tinkers initiated on their own accord. In a dissent, Justice William J. Brennan accused school officials of favoring "thought control."

While the Court has dealt with of speech on campus, it may now be asked to address off-campus speech issues. Students have been suspended for posting messages on their Internet Web pages that school officials consider defamatory.[90] In the future, the Court may be asked to rule whether schools can control such forms of speech or whether they are shielded by the First Amendment.

School Prayer

One of the most divisive issues involving free speech is school prayer. While some religious-minded administrators, parents, and students want to have prayer sessions in schools or have religious convocations, others view the practice both as a violation of the principle of separation of church and state and as an infringement on the First Amendment caution against creating a state-approved religion. The 2000 case of *Santa Fe Independent School District, Petitioner v. Jane Doe* helps clarify the issue.[91]

Prior to 1995, the Santa Fe High School student who occupied the school's elective office of student council chaplain delivered a prayer over the public address system before each varsity football game for the entire season. After the practice was challenged in federal district court, the school district adopted a different policy that permitted, but did not require, prayer initiated and led by a student at all home games. The district court entered an order modifying that policy to permit only nonsectarian, nonproselytizing prayer. However, a federal appellate court held that even as modified, the football prayer policy was invalid. This decision was appealed to the U.S. Supreme Court, which ruled that prayers led by an "elected" student undermine the protection of minority viewpoints. Such a system encourages divisiveness along religious lines and threatens the students not desiring to participate in a religious exercise.

Though the Santa Fe case severely limits school-sanctioned prayer at public events, the Court has not totally ruled out the role of religion in schools. In its ruling in *Good News Club v. Milford Central School* (2001), the Supreme Court required an upstate New York school district to provide space for an after-school Bible club for elementary students.[92] The Court ruled that it was a violation of the First Amendment's free speech clause to deny the club access to the school's space on the ground that the club was religious in nature; the school routinely let secular groups use its space. The Court reasoned that because the club's meetings were to be held after school hours, not sponsored by the school, and open to any student who obtained parental consent, it could not be perceived that the school was endorsing the club or that students might feel coerced to participate in its activities. Finally, in 2001, the Court let stand a Virginia statute mandating that each school division in the state establish in its classrooms a "minute of silence" so that "each pupil may, in the exercise of his or her individual choice, meditate, pray, or engage in any other silent activity which does not interfere with, distract, or impede other pupils in the like exercise of individual choice."[93] The Court refused to hear an appeal filed by several Virginia students and their parents, which contended that a "moment of silence" establishes religion in violation of the First Amendment.[94]

School Discipline

Most states have statutes permitting teachers to use corporal punishment to discipline students in public school systems. Under the concept of *in loco parentis*, discipline is one of the assumed parental duties given to the school system. In two decisions, the Supreme Court upheld the school's right to use corporal punishment. In the case of *Baker v. Owen,* the Court stated:

> We hold that the Fourteenth Amendment embraces the right of parents generally to control the means and discipline of their children, but that the state has a countervailing interest in the maintenance of order in the schools... sufficient to sustain the right of teachers and school officials must accord to students minimal due process in the course of inflicting such punishment.[95]

In 1977, the Supreme Court again spoke on the issue of corporal punishment in school systems in the case of *Ingraham v. Wright,* which upheld the right of teachers to use corporal punishment.[96] In this case, students James Ingraham and Roosevelt Andrews sustained injuries as a result of paddling in the Charles Drew Junior High School in Dade County, Florida. The legal problems raised in the case were (1) whether corporal punishment by teachers was a violation in this case of the Eighth Amendment against cruel and unusual punishment and (2) whether the due process clause of the Fourteenth Amendment required that the students receive proper notice and a hearing before receiving corporal punishment. The Court held that neither the Eighth Amendment nor the Fourteenth Amendment were violated in this case. Even

A CLOSER VIEW
To find out more about the use of discipline in schools, use *school discipline* as a subject guide on InfoTrac College Edition.

though Ingraham suffered hematomas on his buttocks as a result of 20 blows with a wooden paddle and Andrews was hurt in the arm, the Supreme Court ruled that such punishment was not a constitutional violation. The Court established the standard that only reasonable discipline is allowed in school systems, but it excepted the degree of punishment administered in this case. The key principle in *Ingraham* is that the reasonableness standard that the Court articulated represents the judicial attitude that the scope of the school's right to discipline a child is by no means more restrictive than the rights of the child's own parents to impose corporal punishment. Today 24 states still use physical punishment.

Other issues involving the legal rights of students include their due process rights when interrogated, if corporal punishment is to be imposed, and when suspension and expulsion are threatened. When students are questioned by school personnel, no warning as to their legal rights to remain silent or right to counsel need be given. However, when school security guards, on-campus police officials, and public police officers question students, such constitutional warnings are required. In the area of corporal punishment, procedural due process established with the case of *Baker v. Owen* requires that students at least be forewarned about the possibility of corporal punishment as a discipline. In addition, the *Baker* case requires that there be a witness to the administration of corporal punishment and allows the student and the parent to elicit reasons for the punishment.

With regard to suspension and expulsion, the Supreme Court ruled in 1976 in the case of *Goss v. Lopez* that any time a student is to be suspended for up to a period of 10 days, he or she is entitled to a hearing.[97] The hearing would not include a right to counsel or a right to confront or cross-examine witnesses. The Court went on to state in *Goss* that the extent of the procedural due process requirements would be established on a case-by-case basis. That is, each case would represent its own facts and have its own procedural due process elements.

In sum, schools have the right to discipline students, but students are protected from unreasonable, excessive, and arbitrary discipline.

Privacy

Do students maintain the right to privacy while on school grounds, or can they be searched, tested, and questioned at the whim of teachers and school administrators? Are their school records private or part of the public record? These issues are discussed next.

The Right to Personal Privacy   One major issue is the right of school officials to search students and their possessions on school grounds. Drug abuse, theft, assault and battery, and racial conflicts in schools have increased the need to take action against troublemakers. School administrators have questioned students about their illegal activities, conducted searches of students' persons and possessions, and reported suspicious behavior to the police.

In 1984, in *New Jersey v. T.L.O.*, the Supreme Court helped clarify a vexing problem: whether the Fourth Amendment's prohibition against unreasonable searches and seizures applies to school officials as well as to police officers.[98] In this case, the Court found that students are in fact constitutionally protected from illegal searches but that school officials are not bound by the same restrictions as law-enforcement agents. Police need "probable cause" before they can conduct a search, but educators can legally search students when there are reasonable grounds to believe the students have violated the law or broken school rules. In creating this distinction, the Court recognized the needs of school officials to preserve an environment conducive to education and to secure the safety of students.

One question left unanswered by *New Jersey v. T.L.O.* is whether teachers and other school officials can search lockers and desks. Here, the law has been controlled by state decisions, and each jurisdiction may create its own standards. Some allow teachers a free hand in opening lockers and desks.[99]

Drug Testing   Another critical issue concerning privacy is the drug testing of students. In 1995, the Supreme Court extended schools' authority to search by legalizing a random drug-testing policy for student athletes. The Supreme Court's decision in *Vernonia School District 47J v. Acton* expanded the power of educators to ensure safe learning environments.[100]

As a result of *Vernonia,* schools may employ safe-school programs such as drug-testing procedures so long as the policies satisfy the reasonableness test. *Vernonia* may bring forth a spate of suspicionless searches in public schools across the country. Metal-detection procedures, the use of drug-sniffing dogs, and random locker searches will be easier to justify. In upholding random, suspicionless drug testing for student athletes, the Supreme Court extended one step further the schools' authority to search, despite court-imposed constitutional safeguards for children. Underlying this decision, like that of *New Jersey v. T.L.O.,* is a recognition that the use of drugs is a serious threat to public safety and to the rights of children to receive a decent and safe education.

Academic Privacy   Students have the right to expect that their records will be kept private. Although state laws govern the disclosure of information from juvenile court records, a 1974 federal law—the Family Educational Rights and Privacy Act (FERPA)—restricts disclosure of information from a student's education records without parental consent.[101] The act defines an education record to include all records, files, and other materials, such as photographs, containing information related to a student that an education agency maintains. In 1994, Congress passed the Improving America's Schools Act, which allowed educational systems to disclose education records under these circumstances: (1) State law authorizes the disclosure, (2) the disclosure is to a juvenile justice agency, (3) the disclosure relates to the justice system's ability to provide preadjudication services to a student, and (4) state or local officials certify in writing that the institution or individual receiving the information has agreed not to disclose it to a third party other than another juvenile justice system agency.[102]

The Role of the School in Delinquency Control Policy

Can the American school system, viewed by critics as overly conservative and archaic, play a significant role in delinquency prevention? Some experts contend that no significant change in the lives of youths is possible by merely changing the schools; the entire social and economic structure of society must be altered if schools are to help students realize their full potential.[103] Others suggest that smaller, alternative schools that create a positive learning environment with low student-teacher ratios, informal classroom structure, and individualized, self-paced learning may be the answer. While in theory such programs may help promote academic performance and reduce delinquency, evaluations suggest that attending alternative programs has little effect on delinquency rates.[104]

A danger also exists that the pressure being placed on schools to improve the educational experience of students can produce unforeseen problems for staff members.

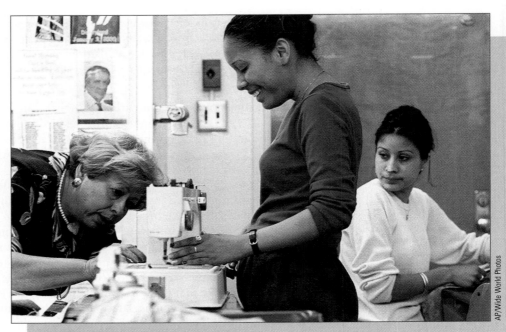

SCHOOLS HAVE ADOPTED a number of different delinquency prevention programs. This school is reaching out to troubled young women and helping them develop life skills that will shield them from delinquency and substance abuse. Ramona High School home economics teacher, Diane Sequine, helps student Lorena Herrera (center) repair a sewing machine as classmate Yulma Chavez watches.

For example, there have been recent reports of teachers being prosecuted for encouraging students to cheat on tests and providing them with answer sheets. The pressure to improve student performance on standardized tests was the motive for the faculty cheating.[105]

Education officials have instituted numerous programs to make schools more effective instruments of delinquency prevention.[106] Among the most prevalent strategies are

- *Cognitive:* Increase students' awareness about the dangers of drug abuse and delinquency.
- *Affective:* Improve students' psychological assets and self-image, giving them the resources to resist antisocial behavior.
- *Behavioral:* Train students in techniques to resist peer pressure.
- *Environmental:* Establish school management and disciplinary programs that deter crime, such as locker searches.
- *Therapeutic:* Treat youths who have already manifested problems.[107]

More specific suggestions include creating special classes or schools with individualized educational programs that foster success, rather than failure, for nonadjusting students.[108] Efforts can be made to help students learn to deal constructively with academic failure when it does occur. More personalized student-teacher relationships have been recommended. This effort to provide young persons with a caring, accepting adult role model will, it is hoped, strengthen the controls against delinquency.

It has been proposed that experiments be undertaken to integrate job training and experience with the usual classroom instruction so that students may see education as a meaningful and relevant prelude to their future careers. Job training programs could emphasize public service, so that students could gain a sense of attachment to their communities while they are acquiring useful vocational training.

Schools may not be able to reduce delinquency single-handedly, but a number of viable alternatives to their present operations could aid a communitywide effort to reduce the problem of juvenile crime. Because this issue is so critical, it is discussed in greater detail in Chapter 11.

SUMMARY

For several decades, criminologists have attempted to explain the relationship between schools and delinquency. Although no clear causal relationship has been established, research points to many definite links between the delinquent behavior of juveniles and their experiences within the educational system.

Contemporary youths spend much of their time in school because education has become increasingly important as a determinant of social and economic success. Educational institutions are one of the primary instruments of socialization, and it is believed that this role is bound to affect the amount of delinquent behavior by school-age children.

Those who claim a causal link between schools and delinquency cite two major factors in the relationship. The first is academic failure, which arises from a lack of aptitude, labeling, or class conflict and which results in tracking. The second factor is alienation from the educational experience, which is the result of the impersonal nature of schools, the traditionally passive role assigned

to students, and students' perception of their education as irrelevant to their future lives.

Student misbehavior, which may have its roots in the school experience itself, ranges from minor infractions of school rules (for example, smoking and loitering in halls) to serious crimes, such as assault, burglary, arson, drug abuse, and vandalism of school property.

Dissatisfaction with the educational experience frequently sets the stage for more serious forms of delinquency both in and out of school. Some dissatisfied students choose to drop out of school as soon as they reach the legal age, and research has shown a rapid decline in delinquency among those who do drop out.

School administrators have attempted to eliminate school crime and prevent delinquency. Among the measures taken are security squads, electronic surveillance, and teacher training. Curriculums are being significantly revised to make the school experience more meaningful.

KEY TERMS

academic achievement	underachievers	alienation	socially disorganized neighborhood
school failure	tracking	dropouts	
			zero tolerance policy

QUESTIONS FOR DISCUSSION

1. Was there a delinquency problem in your high school? If so, how was it dealt with?

2. Should disobedient youths be suspended from school? Does this solution hurt or help?

3. What can be done to improve the delinquency prevention capabilities of schools?

4. Is school failure responsible for delinquency, or are delinquents simply school failures?

VIEWPOINT

"I HATE BEING LAUGHED AT. But they won't laugh after they're scraping parts of their parents, sisters, brothers, and friends from the wall of my hate." These words were written in the journal of 15-year-old Kip Kinkel, who later killed both of his parents and then went into his high school in Springfield, Oregon, and shot more than two dozen students, two of them fatally.

The murders in Oregon were part of a wave of school shootings, spread far across the map of America, that triggered a national debate over methods to prevent similar tragedies from occurring. Physical security measures were investigated, discussed, and implemented. But another side of the debate focused on the motives behind the murders. Bullying was quickly identified as a prime suspect.

Because bullying can have such tragic consequences, there has been an ongoing effort to control its occurrence. What can be done? To find out, go to InfoTrac College Edition and read Peter Piazza, "Scourge of the Schoolyard: Technology Alone Isn't Enough. By Teaching Children—and Adults—to Fight Bullying, Schools Are Making Their Communities Safer," *Security Management* 45(11):68 (November 2001).

NOTES

1. *The People v. Randy G.*, Supreme Court of California (No. S089733, 2001).

2. Ibid.; for more on this case, Teresa Anderson, "School Security," *Security Management* 45:96–98 (2001).

3. *Justice and the Child in New Jersey*, report of the New Jersey Juvenile Delinquency Commission (1939), p. 110, cited in Paul H. Hahn, *The Juvenile Offender and the Law* (Cincinnati: Anderson, 1978).

4. U.S. Senate Subcommittee on Delinquency, *Challenge for the Third Century: Education in a Safe Environment* (Washington, DC: Government Printing Office, 1977), p. 1.

5. Delbert S. Eliott and Harwin L. Voss, *Delinquency and the Dropout* (Lexington, MA: Lexington Books, 1974), p. 204.

6. See, generally, Richard Lawrence, *School Crime and Juvenile Justice* (New York: Oxford University Press, 1998).

7. U.S. Office of Education, *Digest of Educational Statistics* (Washington, DC: Government Printing Office, 1969), p. 25.

8. Kenneth Polk and Walter E. Schafer, eds., *Schools and Delinquency* (Englewood Cliffs, NJ: Prentice-Hall, 1972), p. 13.

9. U.S. Department of Education, National Center for Education Statistics, *The Condition of Education 2000* (Washington, DC: U.S. Government Printing Office, 2000).

10. Simon Singer and Susyan Jou, "Specifying the SES/ Delinquency Relationship by Subjective and Objective Indicators of Parental and Youth Social Status." Paper presented at the annual meeting of the American Society of Criminology, New Orleans, November 1992.

11. For reviews see, Bruce Wolford and LaDonna Koebel, "Kentucky Model for Youths at Risk" *Criminal Justice* 9:5–55 (1995); J. David Hawkins et al., "The Seattle Social Development Project," in Joan McCord and Richard Tremblay, eds., *The Prevention of Antisocial Behavior in Children* (New York: Guilford, 1992), pp. 139–60.

12. Terence Thornberry, Alan Lizotte, Marvin Krohn, Margaret Farnworth, and Sung Joon Jang, "Testing Interactional Theory: An Examination of Reciprocal Causal Relationships among Family, School and Delinquency," *Journal of Criminal Law and Criminology* 82:3–35 (1991).

13. Carolyn Smith, Alan Lizotte, Terence Thornberry, and Marvin Krohn, "Resilience to Delinquency," *The Prevention Researcher* 4:4–7 (1997); Matthew Zingraff, Jeffrey Leiter, Matthew Johnsen, Kristen Myers, "The Mediating Effect of Good School Performance on the Maltreatment-Delinquency Relationship," *Journal of Research in Crime and Delinquency* 31:62–91 (1994).

14. Lyle Shannon, *Assessing the Relationship of Adult Criminal Careers to Juvenile Careers: A Summary* (Washington, DC: Government Printing Office, 1982).

15. Marvin Wolfgang, Robert Figlio, and Thorsten Sellin, *Delinquency in a Birth Cohort* (Chicago: University of Chicago Press, 1972).

16. Ibid., p. 94.

17. Bureau of Justice Statistics, *Prisons and Prisoners* (Washington, DC: Government Printing Office, 1982), p. 2.

18. Martin Gold, "School Experiences, Self-Esteem, and Delinquent Behavior: A Theory for Alternative Schools," *Crime and Delinquency* 24:294–95 (1978).

19. Ibid.

20. Michael Gottfredson and Travis Hirschi, *A General Theory of Crime* (Stanford, CA: Stanford University Press, 1990); J. D. McKinney, "Longitudinal Research on the Behavioral Characteristics of Children with Learning Disabilities," *Journal of Learning Disabilities* 22:141–50.

21. Albert K. Cohen, *Delinquent Boys* (New York: Free Press, 1955). See also Kenneth Polk, Dean Frease, and F. Lynn Richmond, "Social Class, School Experience, and Delinquency," *Criminology* 12:84–85 (1974).

22. Jackson Toby, "Orientation to Education as a Factor in the School Maladjustment of Lower-Class Children," *Social Forces* 35:259–66 (1957).

23. John Paul Wright, Francis Cullen, and Nicolas Williams, "Working While in School and Delinquent Involvement: Implications for Social Policy," *Crime and Delinquency* 43:203–21 (1997).

24. William Glaser, *Schools without Failure* (New York: Harper & Row, 1969).

25. Gold, "School Experiences, Self-Esteem, and Delinquent Behavior," p. 292.

26. Ibid., pp. 283–85.

27. Polk, Frease, and Richmond, "Social Class, School Experience, and Delinquency," p. 92.

28. Delos Kelly and Robert Balch, "Social Origins and School Failure," *Pacific Sociological Review* 14:413–30 (1971).

29. Arthur L. Stinchcombe, *Rebellion in a High School* (Chicago: Quadrangle Press, 1964), p. 70.

30. Singer and Jou, "Specifying the SES/Delinquency Relationship by Subjective and Objective Indicators of Parental and Youth Social Status," p. 11.

31. Robert Agnew, "Foundation for a General Strain Theory of Crime and Delinquency," *Criminology* 30:47–87 (1992), at 48.

32. Kenneth Polk, "Class, Strain, and Rebellion among Adolescents," in Kenneth Polk and Walter E. Schafer, eds., *Schools and Delinquency* (Englewood Cliffs, NJ: Prentice-Hall, 1972), p. 34.

33. For an opposing view, see Michael Waitrowski, Stephen Hansell, Charles Massey, and David Wilson, "Curriculum Tracking and Delinquency," *American Sociological Review* 47:151–60 (1982).

34. Based on Walter E. Schafer, Carol Olexa, and Kenneth Polk, "Programmed for Social Class: Tracking in High School," in Kenneth Polk and Walter E. Schafer, eds., *Schools and Delinquency* (Englewood Cliffs, NJ: Prentice-Hall, 1972), pp. 34–54.

35. Delos Kelly and William Pink, "School Crime and Individual Responsibility: The Perpetuation of a Myth," *Urban Review* 14:47–63 (1982).

36. Jeannie Oakes, *Keeping Track, How Schools Structure Inequality* (New Haven, CT: Yale University Press, 1985), p. 48.

37. Ibid., p. 57.

38. Delos Kelly, *Creating School Failure, Youth Crime, and Deviance* (Los Angeles: Trident Shop, 1982), p. 11.

39. Delos Kelly and W. Grove, "Teachers' Nominations and the Production of Academic Misfits," *Education* 101:246–63 (1981).

40. Delos Kelly, "The Role of Teacher's Nominations in the Perpetuation of Deviant Adolescent Careers," *Education* 96:209–17 (1976).

41. Oakes, *Keeping Track*, p. 48.

42. Ibid.

43. David Anderson, "Curriculum, Culture, and Community: The Challenge of School Violence," in Michael Tonry and Mark Moore, eds., *Youth Violence: Crime and Justice, An Annual Review of Research* (Chicago: University of Chicago Press, 1998), pp. 317–63.

44. Richard Lawrence, "Parents, Peers, School, and Delinquency." Paper presented at the American Society of Criminology meeting, Boston, November 1995.

45. Patricia Jenkins, "School Delinquency and the School Social Bond," *Journal of Research in Crime and Delinquency* 34:337–67 (1997).

46. Smith, Lizotte, Thornberry, and Krohn, "Resilience to Delinquency"; Matthew Zingraff, Jeffrey Leiter, Matthew Johnsen, and Kristen Myers, "The Mediating Effect of Good School Performance on the Maltreatment-Delinquency Relationship," *Journal of Research in Crime and Delinquency* 31:62–91 (1994).

47. Rick Bragg, "4 Girls and a Teacher Are Shot to Death in an Ambush at a Middle School in Arkansas," *New York Times,* 25 March 1998, p. 1.

48. Charles Callahan and Frederick Rivara, "Urban High School Youth and Handguns," *Journal of the American Medical Association* 267:3038–42 (1992).

49. National Institute of Education, U.S. Department of Health, Education and Welfare, *Violent Schools—Safe Schools: The Safe Schools Study Report to the Congress,* vol. 1 (Washington, DC: Government Printing Office, 1977).

50. Phillip Kaufman et al., *Indicators of School Crime and Safety, 2001* (Washington, DC: U.S. Department of Education and Bureau of Justice Statistics, 2001).

51. Callie Marie Rennison, *Criminal Victimization 2000, Changes 1999–2000 with Trends 1993–2000* (Washington, DC: Bureau of Justice Statistics, 2001).

52. Pamela Wilcox and Richard Clayton, "A Multilevel Analysis of School-Based Weapon Possession," *Justice Quarterly* 18:509–42 (2001).

53. Mark Anderson et al., "School-Associated Violent Deaths in the United States, 1994–1999," *Journal of the American Medical Association* 286:2695–2702 (2001).

54. Bryan Vossekuil, Marisa Reddy, Robert Fein, Randy Borum, and William Modzeleski, *Safe School Initiative, An Interim Report on the Prevention of Targeted Violence in Schools* (Washington, DC: United States Secret Service, 2000).

55. Joseph A. Califano, Jr., and Alyse Booth, *1998 CASA National Survey of Teens, Teachers, and Principals* (New York: The National Center for Addiction and Substance Abuse, Columbia University, 1998).

56. Luntz Research Companies and QEV Analytics, *Back to School 1997—The CASA National Survey of American Attitudes on Substance Abuse III: Teens and Their Parents, Teachers, and Principals* (New York: National Center for Addiction and Substance Abuse, Columbia University, 1998).

57. James Q. Wilson, "Crime in Society and Schools," in J. M. McPartland and E. L. McDill, eds., *Violence in Schools: Perspective, Programs and Positions* (Lexington, MA: D.C. Heath, 1977), p. 48.

58. Gary Gottfredson and Denise Gottfredson, *Victimization in Schools* (New York: Plenum Press, 1985), p. 18.

59. Daryl Hellman and Susan Beaton, "The Pattern of Violence in Urban Public Schools: The Influence of School and Community," *Journal of Research in Crime and Delinquency* 23:102–27 (1986).

60. Nancy Weishew and Samuel Peng, "Variables Predicting Students' Problem Behaviors," *Journal of Educational Research* 87:5–17 (1993).

61. Wayne Welsh, Robert Stokes, and Jack Greene, "A Macro-Level Model of School Disorder," *Journal of Research in Crime and Delinquency* 37:243–83 (2000).

62. Peter Lindstrom, "Patterns of School Crime: A Replication and Empirical Extension," *British Journal of Criminology* 37:121–31 (1997).

63. Richard Lawrence, *School Crime and Juvenile Justice* (New York: Oxford University Press, 1998).

64. Welsh, Stokes, and Greene, "A Macro-Level Model of School Disorder," p. 270.

65. Joan McDermott, "Crime in the School and in the Community: Offenders, Victims, and Fearful Youth," *Crime and Delinquency* 29:270–83 (1983).

66. Ibid.

67. June L. Arnette and Marjorie C. Walsleben, *Combating Fear and Restoring Safety in Schools* (Washington, DC: Office of Juvenile Justice and Delinquency Prevention, 1998).

68. Sheila Heaviside et al., *Violence and Discipline Problems in U.S. Public Schools: 1996–1997* (Washington, DC: United States Government Printing Office, 1998). Herein cited as National Violence Survey.

69. Ibid., p. 20

70. Ibid.

71. American Academy of Pediatrics Committee on School Health, "Violence in Schools: Current Status and Prevention," in *School Health: Policy and Practice* (Elk Grove Village, IL: American Academy of Pediatrics Committee on School Health), pp. 363–80 at 369.

72. Bruce Jacobs, "Anticipatory Undercover Targeting in High Schools," *Journal of Criminal Justice* 22:445–57 (1994).

73. Kevin Bushweller, "Guards with Guns," *The American School Board Journal* 180:34–36 (1993).

74. Bella English, "Hub Program to Counsel Violent Pupils," *Boston Globe*, 24 February 1987, p. 1.

75. Randal C. Archibold, "City Schools Tentatively Agree to Let the Police Run Security," *New York Times*, 29 August 1998.

76. Steven Lab and John Whitehead, *The School Environment and School Crime: Causes and Consequences* (Washington, DC: National Institute of Justice), p. 5.

77. Jackie Kimbrough, "School-Based Strategies for Delinquency Prevention," in Peter Greenwood, ed., *The Juvenile Rehabilitation Reader* (Santa Monica, CA: Rand Corp., 1985), pp. ix, 1–22.

78. Hellman and Beaton, "The Pattern of Violence in Public Schools," pp. 122–23.

79. Julius Menacker, Ward Weldon, and Emanuel Hurwitz, "Community Influences on School Crime and Violence," *Urban Education* 25:68–80 (1990).

80. Wendy Mansfield and Elizabeth Farris, *Public School Principal Survey on Safe, Disciplined and Drug Free Schools* (Washington, DC: U.S. GPO, 1992), p. iii.

81. S. Arons, "Compulsory Education: The Plain People Resist," *Saturday Review* 15:63–69 (1972).

82. Ibid.

83. See *Pierce v. Society of Sisters*, 268 U.S. 610, 45 S.Ct. 571, 69 L.Ed. 1070 (1925).

84. 406 U.S. 205, 92 S.Ct. 1526, 32 L.Ed.2d 15 (1972).

85. 393 U.S. 503, 89 S.Ct. 733 (1969).

86. Ibid.

87. Ibid., p. 741.

88. *Bethel School District No. 403 v. Fraser*, 478 U.S. 675, 106 S.Ct. 3159, 92 L.Ed.2d 549 (1986).

89. *Hazelwood School District v. Kuhlmeier*, 484 U.S. 260, 108 S.Ct. 562, 98 L.Ed.2d 592 (1988).

90. Terry McManus, "Home Web Sites Thrust Students into Censorship Disputes," *New York Times*, 13 August 1998, E9.

91. *Santa Fe Independent School District, Petitioner v. Jane Doe*, individually and as next friend for her minor children, Jane and John Doe, et al., No. 99-62 (June 19, 2000).

92. *Good News Club et al. v. Milford Central School No. 99—2036* (2001).

93. Va. Code Ann. S 22.1-203 (Michie 2000).

94. *Brown v. Gilmore*, 01-384 Case heard on October 29, 2001.

95. 423 U.S. 907, 96 S.Ct. 210, 46 L.Ed.2d 137 (1975).

96. 430 U.S. 651, 97 S.Ct. 1401 (1977).

97. 419 U.S. 565, 95 S.Ct. 729 (1976).

98. *New Jersey v. T.L.O.*, 469 U.S. 325, 105 S.Ct. 733 (1985).

99. *People v. Overton*, 24 N.Y.2d 522, 301 N.Y.S.2d 479, 249 N.E.2d 366 (1969); Brenda Walts, "*New Jersey v. T.L.O.*: Questions the Court Did Not Answer about School Searches," *Law and Education Journal* 14:421 (1985).

100. *Vernonia School District 47J v. Acton*, 115 S.Ct. 2394 (1995); Bernard James and Jonathan Pyatt, "Supreme Court Extends School's Authority to Search," *National School Safety Center News Journal* 26:29 (1995).

101. Michael Medaris, *A Guide to the Family Educational Rights and Privacy Act* (Washington, DC: Office of Juvenile Justice and Delinquency Prevention, 1998).

102. Ibid.

103. Alexander Liazos, "Schools, Alienation, and Delinquency," *Crime and Delinquency* 24:355–61 (1978).

104. Stephen Cox, William Davidson, and Timothy Bynum, "A Meta-Analytic Assessment of Delinquency-Related Outcomes of Alternative Education Programs," *Crime and Delinquency* 41:219–34 (1995).

105. Gary Putka, "Cheaters in Schools May Not Be Students but Their Teachers," *Wall Street Journal*, 2 November 1989, p. 1.

106. U.S. Senate Subcommittee on Delinquency, *Challenge for the Third Century*, p. 95.

107. William Bukoski, "School-Based Substance Abuse Prevention: A Review of Program Research," *Journal of Children in Contemporary Society* 18:95–116 (1985).

108. See, generally, J. David Hawkins and Denise Lishner, "Schooling and Delinquency," in E. H. Johnson, ed., *Handbook on Crime and Delinquency* (Westport, CO: Greenwood Press, 1987).

10 Drug Use and Delinquency

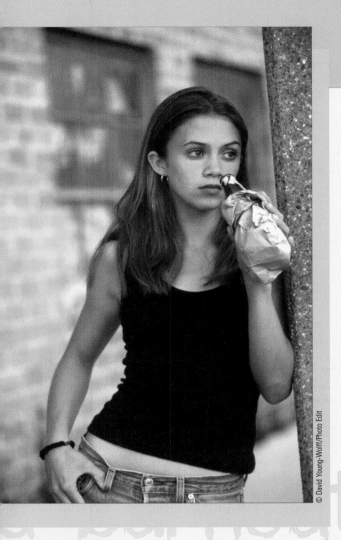
© David Young-Wolff/Photo Edit

The president has appointed you the new drug czar. You control $20 billion with which to wage a campaign against drugs. You know that drug use is unacceptably high, especially among poor inner-city kids, that a great deal of all criminal behavior is drug related, and that drug-dealing gangs are expanding around the United States.

At an open hearing, drug-control experts express their policy strategies. One group favors putting the money into hiring new law enforcement agents who will patrol borders, target large dealers, and make drug raids here and abroad. They also call for such get-tough measures as the creation of strict drug laws, the mandatory waiver of young drug dealers to the adult court system, and the death penalty for drug-related gang killings.

A second group believes that the best way to deal with drugs is to spend the money on community treatment programs, expanding the number of beds in drug detoxification units, and funding research on how to reduce drug dependency clinically.

A third group argues that neither punishment nor treatment can restrict teenage drug use and that the best course is to educate at-risk kids about the dangers of substance abuse and then legalize all drugs but control their distribution. This course of action will help to reduce crime and violence among drug users and also to balance the national debt, since drugs could be heavily taxed.

- Do you believe drugs should be legalized, and if so, what might be the negative consequences of legalization?

- Can any law enforcement strategies reduce drug consumption?

- Is treatment an effective drug-control technique?

A CLOSER VIEW
The United States is not alone when it comes to substance-abusing teens. To find out more about how other nations are dealing with this issue, use *international substance abuse* as keywords on InfoTrac College Edition.

For more information, use *teenage drug use* as a subject guide. CASCADE is a drug information service for young people that is run by young people in Great Britain. Visit their site at *http://www.cascade.u-net.com/home2.htm*
For an up-to-date list of Web links, go to *http://info.wadsworth.com/siegel*

There is little question that adolescent **substance abuse** and its association with delinquency are vexing problems. Almost every town, village, and city in the United States has confronted some type of teenage substance abuse problem.

Self-report surveys indicate that more than half of high school seniors have tried drugs and more than 80 percent use alcohol.[1] Adolescents at high risk for drug abuse often come from the most impoverished communities and experience a multitude of problems, including school failure and family conflict.[2] Equally troubling is the association between drug use and crime.[3] Research indicates that more than half of all juvenile arrestees in some cities test positive for cocaine.[4] Self-report surveys show that drug abusers are more likely to become delinquents than are nonabusers.[5] The pattern of drug use and crime makes teenage substance abuse a key national concern.[6]

This chapter addresses some important issues involving teenage substance abuse, beginning with a review of the kinds of drugs children and adolescents are using and how often they are using them. Then we discuss who uses drugs and what causes substance abuse. After describing the association between drug abuse and delinquent behavior, the chapter concludes with a review of efforts to control the use of drugs in the United States.

Frequently Abused Drugs

substance abuse Using drugs or alcohol in such a way as to cause physical, emotional and/or psychological harm to yourself.

A wide variety of substances referred to as "drugs" are used by teenagers. Some are addicting, others not. Some create hallucinations, others cause a depressed stupor, and a few give an immediate uplift. This section identifies the most widely used substances and discusses their effects. All of these drugs can be abused, and because of the danger they present, many have been banned from private use. Others are available legally only with a physician's supervision, and a few are available to adults but prohibited for children.

Marijuana and Hashish

hashish A concentrated form of cannabis made from unadulterated resin from the female cannabis plant.

marijuana The dried leaves of the cannabis plant.

Commonly called "pot" or "grass," marijuana is produced from the leaves of *Cannabis sativa*. **Hashish** (hash) is a concentrated form of cannabis made from unadulterated resin from the female plant. The main active ingredient in both marijuana and hashish is tetrahydrocannabinol (THC), a mild hallucinogen. **Marijuana** is the drug most commonly used by teenagers.

Smoking large amounts of pot or hash can cause distortions in auditory and visual perception, even producing hallucinatory effects. Small doses produce an early excitement ("high") that gives way to drowsiness. Pot use is also related to decreased activity, overestimation of time and space, and increased food consumption. When the user is alone, marijuana produces a dreamy state. In a group, users become giddy and lose perspective.

Marijuana is not physically addicting, but its long-term effects have been the subject of much debate. During the 1970s, it was reported that smoking pot caused a variety of physical and mental problems, including brain damage and mental illness. Although the dangers of pot and hash may have been overstated, use of these drugs does present some health risks, including an increased risk of lung cancer, chronic bronchitis, and other diseases. Marijuana smoking should be avoided by prospective parents because it lowers sperm count in male users, and females experience disrupted ovulation and a greater chance of miscarriage.[7]

A CLOSER VIEW
Is it possible that marijuana has some benefits that drug control advocates have overlooked? Read about its potential as a "wonder drug," on InfoTrac College Edition in Trevor Jackson, "Cannabis the Wonder Drug?" *British Medical Journal* 323(7321):1136 (November 10, 2001).

Cocaine and Crack

cocaine A powerful natural stimulant derived from the coca plant.

crack A highly addictive crystalline form of cocaine containing remnants of hydrochloride and sodium bicarbonate, which emits a crackling sound when smoked.

heroin A narcotic made from opium and then cut with sugar or some other neutral substance until it is only 1 to 4 percent pure.

addict A person with an overpowering physical or psychological need to continue taking a particular substance or drug.

Cocaine is an alkaloid derivative of the coca plant. When first isolated in 1860, it was considered a medicinal breakthrough that could relieve fatigue, depression, and other symptoms, and it quickly became a staple of patent medicines. When its addictive qualities and dangerous side effects became apparent, its use was controlled by the Pure Food and Drug Act of 1906.

Cocaine is the most powerful natural stimulant. Its use produces euphoria, restlessness, and excitement. Overdoses can cause delirium, violent manic behavior, and possible respiratory failure. The drug can be sniffed, or "snorted," into the nostrils, or it can be injected. The immediate feeling of euphoria, or "rush," is short-lived, and heavy users may snort coke as often as every 10 minutes. Another dangerous practice is "speedballing"—injecting a mixture of cocaine and heroin.

Crack is processed street cocaine. Its manufacture involves using ammonia or baking soda (sodium bicarbonate) to remove the hydrochlorides and create a crystalline form of cocaine that can be smoked. In fact, crack gets its name from the fact that the sodium bicarbonate often emits a crackling sound when the substance is smoked. Also referred to as "rock," "gravel," and "roxanne," crack gained popularity in the mid-1980s. It is relatively inexpensive, can provide a powerful high, and is highly addictive psychologically. Crack cocaine use has been in decline in recent years. Heavy criminal penalties, tight enforcement, and social disapproval have helped to lower crack use.

Heroin

Narcotic drugs have the ability to produce insensibility to pain and to free the mind of anxiety and emotion. Users experience relief from fear and apprehension, release of tension, and elevation of spirits. This short period of euphoria is followed by a period of apathy, during which users become drowsy and may nod off. Heroin, the most commonly used narcotic in the United States, is produced from opium, a drug derived from the opium poppy flower. Dealers cut the drug with neutral substances (sugar or lactose), and street heroin is often only 1 to 4 percent pure.

Heroin is probably the most dangerous commonly used drug. Users rapidly build up a tolerance for it, fueling the need for increased doses to obtain the desired effect. At first heroin is usually sniffed or snorted; as tolerance builds, it is "skin popped" (shot into skin, but not into a vein); and finally it is injected into a vein, or "mainlined."[8] Through this progressive use, the user becomes an **addict**—a person with an overpowering physical and psychological need to continue taking a particular substance by any means possible. If addicts cannot get enough heroin to satisfy their habit, they will suffer withdrawal symptoms, which include irritability, depression, extreme nervousness, and nausea.

Heroin use has stabilized in most of the country, although there are still hundreds of thousands of regular users in large cities.[9] Arrest data show that the most frequent users are older offenders who

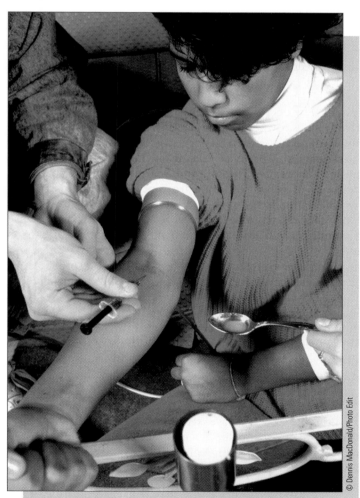

© Dennis MacDonald/Photo Edit

HEROIN, the most commonly used narcotic in the United States, is produced from opium, a drug derived from the opium poppy flower. Though street heroin is often only 1 to 4 percent pure, it can be highly addicting and produce a short period of euphoria followed by a period of apathy and lethargy.

started their heroin abuse decades ago. There is reason to believe heroin use is in decline among adolescents, possibly because it has acquired an extremely negative street image. Most youths know that heroin is addictive and destructive to health, and that needle sharing leads to HIV. Research conducted in New York City shows that most youths avoid heroin, shun users and dealers, and wish to avoid becoming addicts.[10]

Other Drug Categories

A CLOSER VIEW
InfoTrac College Edition has a significant amount of material on all aspects of heroin and its abuse. Use *heroin* as a keyword to gain access to this information.

anesthetic drugs Central nervous system depressants.

inhalants Volatile liquids that give off a vapor, which is inhaled, producing short-term excitement and euphoria followed by a period of disorientation.

sedatives Drugs of the barbiturate family that depress the central nervous system into a sleeplike condition.

tranquilizers Drugs that reduce anxiety and promote relaxation.

hallucinogens Natural or synthetic substances that produce vivid distortions of the senses without greatly disturbing consciousness.

stimulants Synthetic substances that produce an intense physical reaction by stimulating the central nervous system.

Anesthetic drugs are central nervous system (CNS) depressants. Local anesthetics block nervous system transmissions; general anesthetics act on the brain to produce loss of sensation, stupor, or unconsciousness. The most widely abused anesthetic drug is phencyclidine (PCP), known as "angel dust." Angel dust can be sprayed on marijuana or other leaves and smoked, drunk, or injected. Originally developed as an animal tranquilizer, PCP creates hallucinations and a spaced-out feeling that causes heavy users to engage in violent acts. The effects of PCP can last up to two days, and the danger of overdose is high.

Some youths inhale vapors from lighter fluid, paint thinner, cleaning fluid, or model airplane glue to reach a drowsy, dizzy state that is sometimes accompanied by hallucinations. **Inhalants** produce a short-term euphoria followed by a period of disorientation, slurred speech, and drowsiness. Amyl nitrite ("poppers") is a commonly used volatile liquid packaged in capsule form, which is inhaled when the capsule is broken open.

Sedatives, the most commonly used drugs of the barbiturate family, depress the central nervous system into a sleeplike condition. On the illegal market, sedatives are called "goofballs" or "downers" and are often known by the color of the capsules: "reds" (Seconal), "blue devils" (Amytal), and "rainbows" (Tuinal).

Sedatives can be prescribed by doctors as sleeping pills. Illegal users employ them to create relaxed, sociable feelings; overdoses can cause irritability, repellent behavior, and unconsciousness. Barbiturates are the major cause of drug-overdose deaths.

Tranquilizers reduce anxiety and promote relaxation. Legally prescribed tranquilizers, such as Ampazine, Thorazine, Pacatal, and Sparine, were originally designed to control the behavior of people suffering from psychoses, aggressiveness, and agitation. Less powerful tranquilizers, such as Valium, Librium, Miltown, and Equanil, are used to combat anxiety, tension, fast heart rate, and headaches. The use of illegally obtained tranquilizers can lead to addiction, and withdrawal can be painful and hazardous.

Hallucinogens, either natural or synthetic, produce vivid distortions of the senses without greatly disturbing the viewer's consciousness. Some produce hallucinations, and others cause psychotic behavior in otherwise normal people.

One common hallucinogen is mescaline, named after the Mescalero Apaches, who first discovered its potent effect. Mescaline occurs naturally in the peyote, a small cactus that grows in Mexico and the southwestern United States. After initial discomfort, mescaline produces vivid hallucinations and out-of-body sensations.

A second group of hallucinogens are synthetic alkaloid compounds, such as psilocybin. These can be transformed into lysergic acid diethylamide, commonly called LSD. This powerful substance stimulates cerebral sensory centers to produce visual hallucinations, intensify hearing, and increase sensitivity. Users often report a scrambling of sensations; they may "hear colors" and "smell music." Users also report feeling euphoric and mentally superior, although to an observer they appear disoriented. Anxiety and panic may occur, and overdoses can produce psychotic episodes, flashbacks, and even death.

Stimulants ("uppers," "speed," "pep pills," "crystal") are synthetic drugs that stimulate action in the central nervous system. They produce increased blood pressure, breathing rate, and bodily activity, and mood elevation. One widely used amphetamine produces psychological effects such as increased confidence, euphoria, impulsive behavior, and loss of appetite. Commonly used stimulants include Benzedrine ("bennies"), Dexedrine ("dex"), Dexamyl, Bephetamine ("whites"), and Methedrine ("meth," "speed," "crystal meth").

Methedrine is probably the most widely used and most dangerous amphetamine. Some people swallow it; heavy users inject it. Long-term heavy use can result in exhaustion, anxiety, prolonged depression, and hallucinations. A new form of methamphetamine is a crystallized substance with the street name of "ice" or "crystal." Smoking this crystal causes weight loss, kidney damage, heart and respiratory problems, and paranoia.[11]

anabolic steroids Drugs used by athletes and bodybuilders to gain muscle bulk and strength.

Teenagers use highly dangerous **anabolic steroids** to gain muscle bulk and strength.[12] Black-market sales of these drugs approach $1 billion annually. Although not physically addicting, steroids can become an "obsession" among teens who desire athletic success. Long-term users may spend up to $400 a week on steroids and may support their habit by dealing the drug.

Steroids are dangerous because of the health problems associated with their long-term use: liver ailments, tumors, kidney problems, sexual dysfunction, hypertension, and mental problems such as depression. Steroid use runs in cycles, and other drugs— Clomid, Teslac, and Halotestin, for example—that carry their own dangerous side effects are often used to curb the need for high dosages of steroids. Finally, steroid users often share needles, which puts them at high risk for contracting HIV, the virus that causes AIDS.

Club Drugs

club drugs Synthetic substances (such as ecstasy and Rohypnol) commonly used at nightclubs, bars, and raves.

Synthetic substances that are commonly used at nightclubs, bars, and raves are known as **club drugs.** Within this category are MDMA ("ecstasy"), GHB (gamma hydroxybutyrate), Rohypnol, OxyContin, DMT, 2c-B ("Nexus"), Ketamine, and methamphetamine. Rohypnol is a central nervous system depressant that has been connected with sexual assault, rape, and robbery. OxyContin (also known by its generic name, oxycodone) is widely used as a painkiller. Though it should be released slowly into

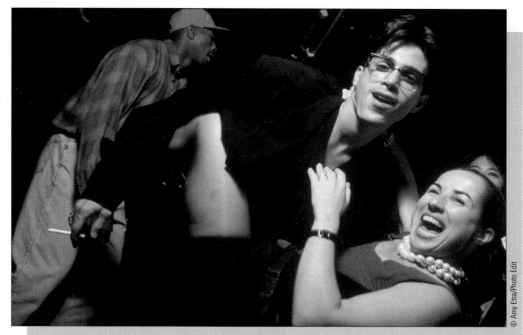

CLUB DRUGS are primarily synthetic substances commonly used at nightclubs, bars, and raves. The most widely used designer drug is ecstasy, or MDMA, which combines an amphetamine-like rush with hallucinogenic experiences. It produces mood swings, disturbs sleeping and eating habits, alters thinking processes, and creates aggressive behavior.

the system, abusers grind tablets into powder and snort or inject the drug to produce feelings of euphoria.

The most widely used club drug is MDMA, or ecstasy, a derivative of methamphetamine. It combines an amphetamine-like rush with hallucinogenic experiences. After being swallowed, snorted, injected, or smoked, ecstasy acts simultaneously as a stimulant and a hallucinogen, producing mood swings and disturbing sleeping and eating habits, which alter thinking processes. It can also create aggressive behavior, interfere with sexual function, affect sensitivity to pain, and increase blood pressure and heart rate. Teenage users taking ecstasy at raves have died from heat stroke because the drug can cause dehydration.

Despite their well-documented risks, club drugs, especially ecstasy, seem to be growing in popularity. The number of ecstasy-related cases reported to the Drug Abuse Warning Network (DAWN), an agency that monitors emergency room mentions of drugs, increased 295% from 1998 to 2000.[13] In 2000, the Drug Enforcement Administration (DEA) seized over 3 million tablets of ecstasy, compared to slightly over 1 million tablets in the previous year.[14]

A CLOSER VIEW
Research now appearing shows that ecstasy is a highly dangerous drug that produces long-term negative effects. Go to InfoTrac College Edition and read "Study: Ecstasy May Cause Long-Term Impairment in Memory," *Alcoholism & Drug Abuse Weekly* 13(40):7 (Oct 22, 2001); "Can Ecstasy's Effects Be Passed on to Offspring?" *Alcoholism & Drug Abuse Weekly* 13(18):3 (May 7, 2001).

Alcohol

alcohol Fermented or distilled liquids containing ethanol, an intoxicating substance.

The drug of choice for most teenagers continues to be **alcohol.** More than 70 percent of high school seniors reported using alcohol in the past year, and more than 80 percent say they have tried it at some time during their lifetime; by the 12th grade about two-thirds of American youth report that they have "been drunk."[15] More than 20 million Americans are estimated to be problem drinkers, and at least half of these are alcoholics.

Alcohol may be a factor in nearly half of all murders, suicides, and accidental deaths.[16] Alcohol-related deaths number 100,000 a year, far more than all other illegal drugs combined. About 1.5 million drivers are arrested each year for driving under the influence (including 14,000 teens), and more than 1 million more are arrested for other alcohol-related violations.[17] The economic cost is staggering. An estimated $117 billion is lost each year, including $18 billion from premature deaths, $66 billion in reduced work effort, and $13 billion for treatment.[18]

Considering these problems, why do so many youths drink to excess? Youths who use alcohol report that it reduces tension, enhances pleasure, improves social skills, and transforms experiences for the better.[19] Although these reactions may result from limited use of alcohol, alcohol in higher doses acts as a depressant. Long-term use has been linked with depression and physical ailments ranging from heart disease to cirrhosis of the liver. Many teens also think drinking stirs their romantic urges, but scientific evidence indicates that alcohol decreases sexual response.[20]

To learn more about the causes of alcoholism, go to the National Council on Alcoholism and Drug Dependence, Inc. (NCADD), a group that advocates prevention, intervention, research, and treatment of alcoholism and other drug addictions: *http://www.ncadd.org/* For an up-to-date list of Web links, go to *http://info.wadsworth.com/siegel*

Cigarettes

A decade-long effort to warn students about the dangers of smoking seems to be paying off. National surveys show that the daily use of cigarettes has been in decline.[21] Two possible reasons for the improvement: Disapproval of smoking is increasing; more kids view smoking as a "risky behavior." (See Figure 10.1.) Nonetheless, by the 12th grade approximately 20 percent of high school students smoke on a daily basis, and about 10 percent smoke at least a half pack per day or more.

Efforts to reduce teen smoking continue. Approximately 25 countries have established laws to prohibit the sale of cigarettes to minors. The reality, however, is that in many countries children and adolescents have easy access to tobacco products.[22] In the United States, the Synar Amendment, enacted in 1992, requires states to enact and enforce laws restricting the sale of tobacco products to youth under the age of 18. States are required to reduce illegal sales rates to minors to no more than 20 percent within several years. The FDA rules require age verification for anyone

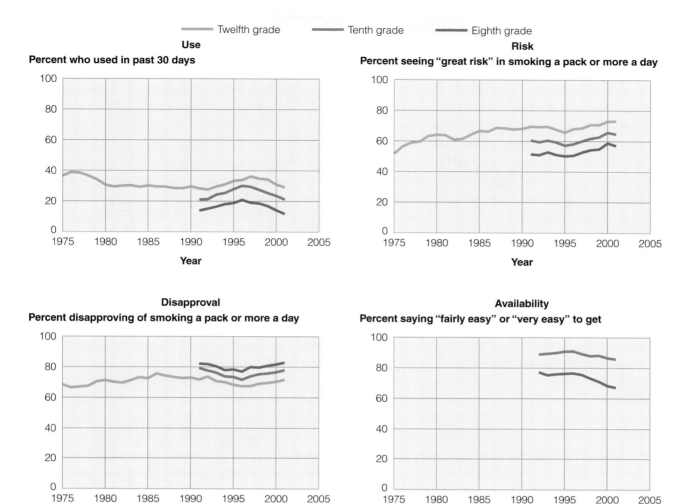

Legend: —— Twelfth grade   —— Tenth grade   —— Eighth grade

Use
Percent who used in past 30 days

Risk
Percent seeing "great risk" in smoking a pack or more a day

Disapproval
Percent disapproving of smoking a pack or more a day

Availability
Percent saying "fairly easy" or "very easy" to get

Figure 10.1
Cigarette Trends in Terms of 30-Day Use, Risk, Disapproval, and Availability
Source: *Monitoring the Future, 2001* (Ann Arbor, MI: Institute of Social Research, 2002).

under the age of 27 who is purchasing tobacco products. The FDA has also banned vending machines and self-service displays except in adults-only facilities.

Trends in Teenage Drug Use

Has America's decade-long war on drugs paid off? Has drug use declined, or is it on the upswing? A number of national surveys conduct annual reviews of teen drug use by interviewing samples of teens around the nation. What do national surveys tell us about the extent of drug use and what have been the recent trends in teen usage?

The Monitoring the Future (MTF) Survey

One of the most important and influential surveys of teen substance abuse is the annual Monitoring the Future survey conducted by the Institute for Social Research at

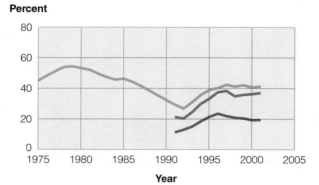

Use in the last twelve months

Percent

Figure 10.2
Trends in Annual Prevalence of an Illicit Drug Use Index
Source: *Monitoring the Future, 2001* (Ann Arbor, MI: Institute of Social Research, 2002).

the University of Michigan. In all, about 45,000 students located in 433 secondary schools participate in the study.[23]

The most recent MTF survey indicates that, with a few exceptions, drug use among American adolescents held steady in 2001, but declined from the recent peak levels reached in 1996 and 1997. As Figure 10.2 shows, drug use peaked in the late 1970s and early 1980s and then began a decade-long decline until showing an uptick in the mid-1990s; usage for most drugs has been stable or in decline since then. Especially encouraging has been a significant drop in the use of heroin and crack cocaine among students. There has also been a continuing decline in cigarette smoking and the use of smokeless tobacco products. Even the use of ecstasy, which has become quite popular because of its use at dance clubs and raves, has begun to slow.

It is possible that widely publicized overdose deaths of musicians and celebrities may have helped stabilize drug abuse, especially heroin and crack. Similarly, alcohol use among teens has been fairly stable over the past several years. Nonetheless, nearly one-quarter of 8th-graders, and half of 12th-graders, use alcohol regularly.

The PRIDE Survey

A second source of information on teen drug and alcohol abuse is the National Parents' Resource Institute for Drug Education (PRIDE) survey, which is also conducted annually. Typically, findings from the PRIDE survey correlate highly with the MTF drug survey. The most recent PRIDE survey (for the 1999–2000 school year) indicates decreases in drug activity in the last few years, specifically for marijuana, hallucinogens, cocaine, and inhalants. Students also reported decreasing their use of cigarettes and alcohol. About 14 percent of students in grades 6–12 claimed to have used drugs during the past year, down from just over 16 percent in 1998–1999 (Table 10.1). Cigarette smoking is also on a decline, from a high of almost 24 percent in 1999 to 19 percent today. The fact that two surveys generate the same pattern in drug abuse helps bolster their validity and give support to a decline in teenage substance abuse.

The National Household Survey of Drug Abuse

Conducted by the Department of Health and Human Services' National Institute on Drug Abuse (NIDA), the National Household Survey of Drug Abuse interviews approximately 70,000 people at home each year.[24] Like the MTF and PRIDE surveys, the Household survey shows that drug and alcohol use, though still a significant problem, has stabilized or declined.

Table 10.1 PRIDE Survey, Monthly Drug Use, 1998–99 vs. 1999–2000, Grades 6–12

	98–99	99–00	% rate of decrease
Cigarettes	23.5	18.8	20.0
Any alcohol	27.1	23.9	11.8
Any illicit drug	16.3	13.9	15.3

Source: PRIDE Survey, PRIDE Inc., 2001.

Although teen drug and alcohol use stabilized in recent years, it is still a significant problem. For example, heavy drinking was reported by 5.6 percent of the population aged 12 and older, or 12.6 million people; more than 40 percent of college students engaged in *binge drinking*, defined as having five or more alcoholic beverages at the same occasion.

Are the Survey Results Accurate?

Student drug surveys must be interpreted with caution. First, it may be overly optimistic to expect that heavy users are going to cooperate with a drug-use survey, especially one conducted by a government agency. Even if willing, these students are likely to be absent from school during testing periods. Also, drug abusers are more likely to be forgetful and to give inaccurate accounts of their substance abuse.

Another problem is the likelihood that the most drug-dependent portion of the adolescent population is omitted from the sample. More than half of all youths arrested dropped out of school before the 12th grade, and more than two-thirds of these arrestees are drug users.[25] Juvenile detainees (those arrested and held in a lockup) test positively for cocaine at a rate many times higher than those reporting recent use in the MTF survey.[26] The inclusion of eighth-graders in the MTF sample is one way of getting around the dropout problem. Nonetheless, high school surveys may be excluding some of the most drug-prone young people in the population.

There is evidence that the accuracy of reporting may be affected by social and personal traits: Girls are more willing than boys to admit taking drugs; kids from two-parent homes are less willing to admit taking drugs than kids growing up in single-parent homes. Julia Yun Soo Kim, Michael Fendrich, and Joseph Wislar speculate that it is culturally unacceptable for some subgroups in the population, such as Hispanic females, to use drugs, and therefore, in self-report surveys, they may underrepresent their involvement.[27]

While these problems are serious, they are consistent over time and therefore do not hinder the *measurement of change* or trends in drug usage. That is, prior surveys also omitted dropouts and other high-risk individuals and were biased because of cultural issues. However, since these problems are built into every wave of the surveys, any change recorded in the annual substance abuse rate is probably genuine. So, while the *validity* of these surveys may be questioned, they are probably *reliable* indicators of trends in substance abuse.

Why Do Youths Take Drugs?

Why do youths engage in an activity that is sure to bring them overwhelming problems? It is hard to imagine that even the youngest drug users are unaware of the problems associated with substance abuse. Although it is easy to understand dealers' desires for quick profits, how can we explain users' disregard for long- and short-term consequences?

Social Disorganization

One explanation for this dilemma ties drug abuse to poverty, social disorganization, and hopelessness. Drug use by young minority-group members has been tied to factors such as racial prejudice, low self-esteem, poor socioeconomic status, and the stress of living in a harsh urban environment.[28] The association between drug use, race, and poverty has been linked to the high level of mistrust and defiance found in lower socioeconomic areas.[29]

Despite a long association between social disorganization and drug use, the empirical data on the relationship between class and crime has been inconclusive. For example, the National Youth Survey (NYS), a longitudinal study of delinquent behavior conducted by Delbert Elliott and his associates, found little if any association between drug use and social class. The NYS found that drug use is higher among urban youths, but little evidence existed that minority youths or members of the lower class were more likely to abuse drugs than white youths and the more affluent.[30] Research by the Rand Corporation indicates that many drug-dealing youths had legitimate jobs at the time they were arrested for drug trafficking.[31] Therefore, it would be difficult to describe drug abusers simply as unemployed dropouts.

Peer Pressure

Research shows that adolescent drug abuse is highly correlated with the behavior of best friends, especially when parental supervision is weak.[32] Youths in inner-city areas where feelings of alienation run high often come in contact with drug users who teach them that drugs provide an answer to their feelings of inadequacy and stress.[33] Perhaps they join with peers to learn the techniques of drug use; their friendships with other drug-dependent youths give them social support for their habit. Empirical research efforts show that a youth's association with friends who are substance abusers increases the probability of drug use.[34] The relationship is reciprocal: Adolescent substance abusers seek friends who engage in these behaviors, and associating with drug abusers leads to increased levels of drug abuse.

Peer networks may be the most significant influence on long-term substance abuse. Shared feelings and a sense of intimacy lead youths to become enmeshed in what has been described as the "drug-use subculture."[35] Research indicates that drug users do in fact have warm relationships with substance-abusing peers who help support their behaviors.[36] This lifestyle provides users with a clear role, activities they enjoy, and an opportunity for attaining status among their peers.[37] One reason it is so difficult to treat hard-core users is that quitting drugs means leaving the fast life of the streets.

Family Factors

Poor family life is also offered as an explanation for drug use. Studies have found that the majority of drug users have had an unhappy childhood, which included harsh punishment and parental neglect.[38] The association between drug abuse and family quality may involve both racial and gender differences: Females and whites who were abused as children are more likely to have alcohol and drug arrests as adults; abuse was less likely to affect drug use in males and African Americans.[39] It is also common to find substance abusers within large families and with parents who are divorced, separated, or absent.[40]

Social psychologists suggest that drug-abuse patterns may also result from observation of parental drug use.[41] Youths who learn that drugs provide pleasurable sensations may be most likely to experiment with illegal substances; a habit may develop if the user experiences lower anxiety and fear.[42] Research shows, for example, that gang members raised in families with a history of drug use were more likely than other gang members to use cocaine and to use it seriously. Even among gang members, parental abuse was found to be a key factor in the onset of adolescent drug use.[43] Observing drug abuse may be a more important cause of drug abuse than other family-related problems.

Other family factors associated with teen drug abuse include parental conflict over childrearing practices, failure to set rules, and unrealistic demands followed by harsh punishments. Low parental attachment, rejection, and excessive family conflict have all been linked to adolescent substance abuse.[44]

Genetic Factors

The association between parental drug abuse and adolescent behavior may have a genetic basis. Research has shown that biological children of alcoholics reared by nonalcoholic adoptive parents develop alcohol problems more often than the natural children of the adoptive parents.[45] A number of studies comparing alcoholism among identical and fraternal twins have found that the degree of concordance (both siblings behaving identically) is twice as high among the identical twin groups.[46]

A genetic basis for drug abuse is also supported by evidence showing that future substance abuse problems can be predicted by behavior exhibited as early as 6 years of age. The traits predicting future abuse are independent from peer relations and environmental influences.[47]

Emotional Problems

Not all drug-abusing youths reside in lower-class urban areas. To explain drug abuse across social classes, some experts have linked drug use to emotional problems that can strike youths in any economic class. Psychodynamic explanations of substance abuse suggest that drugs help youths control or express unconscious needs. Some psychoanalysts believe adolescents who internalize their problems may use drugs to reduce their feelings of inadequacy. Introverted people may use drugs as an escape from real or imagined feelings of inferiority.[48] Another view is that adolescents who externalize their problems and blame others for their perceived failures are likely to engage in antisocial behaviors, including substance abuse. Research exists to support each of these positions.[49]

addiction-prone personality
A personality that has a compulsion for mood-altering drugs, believed by some to be the cause of substance abuse.

Drug abusers are also believed to exhibit psychopathic or sociopathic behavior characteristics, forming what is called an **addiction-prone personality.**[50] Drinking alcohol may reflect a teen's need to remain dependent on an overprotective mother or an effort to reduce the emotional turmoil of adolescence.[51]

Research on the psychological characteristics of narcotics abusers does, in fact, reveal the presence of a significant degree of pathology. Personality testing of users suggests that a significant percentage suffer from psychotic disorders. Studies have found that addicts suffer personality disorders characterized by a weak ego, a low frustration tolerance, and fantasies of omnipotence. Up to half of all drug abusers may also be diagnosed with antisocial personality disorder (ASPD), which is defined as a pervasive pattern of disregard for the rights of others.[52]

Problem Behavior Syndrome

For some adolescents, substance abuse is one of many problem behaviors that begin early in life and remain throughout the life course.[53] Longitudinal studies show that youths who abuse drugs are maladjusted, emotionally distressed, and have many social problems.[54] Having a deviant lifestyle means associating with delinquent peers, living in a family in which parents and siblings abuse drugs, being alienated from the dominant values of society, and engaging in delinquent behaviors at an early age.[55] Youths who abuse drugs lack commitment to religious values, disdain education, and spend most of their time in peer activities.[56] Youths who take drugs do poorly in school, have high dropout rates, and maintain their drug use after they leave school.[57] This view of adolescent drug taking is discussed in the Focus on Delinquency box entitled "Problem Behaviors and Substance Abuse."

Rational Choice

Youths may choose to use drugs because they want to get high, relax, improve their creativity, escape reality, or increase their sexual responsiveness. Research indicates that adolescent alcohol abusers believe getting high will increase their sexual performance

Problem Behaviors and Substance Abuse

According to the problem behavior syndrome model, substance abuse may be one of a constellation of social problems experienced by at-risk youth. There is significant evidence to substantiate the view that kids who abuse substances are also more likely to experience an array of social problems. For example, a recent study examined the relationship between adolescent illicit-drug use, physical abuse, and sexual abuse among a sample of Mexican-American and non-Hispanic white youths living in the southwestern United States. The research found that youths who report physical and/or sexual abuse are significantly more likely to report illicit drug use than those who have never been abused. About 40 percent of youths who have experienced physical abuse report using marijuana in the previous month, while only 28 percent of youths who have never been abused report using the drug within that time. These findings were independent of factors such as academic achievement and family structure, and they suggest that treatment directed at abused adolescents should include drug-use prevention, intervention, and education components (Figure A).

Kids who abuse drugs and alcohol are also more likely to have educational problems. A recent study of substance use among Texas students in grades 7 through 12 found that those who were absent 10 or more days during the previous school year were more likely to report alcohol, tobacco, and other drug use. For example, twice as many students with high absentee rates reported using marijuana in

Figure A
Percentage of Youths Reporting Past-Month Marijuana or Past-Year Cocaine Use, by Type of Abuse Suffered (N = 2,468)
Sources: Pérez, D. M. "The Relationship Between Physical Abuse, Sexual Victimization, and Adolescent Illicit Drug Use," *Journal of Drug Issues* 30:641–62 (2000).

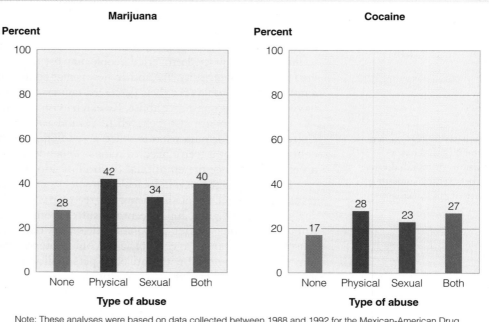

Note: These analyses were based on data collected between 1988 and 1992 for the Mexican-American Drug Use and Dropout Survey, a yearly survey of Mexican-American and non-Hispanic white school dropouts and a comparison group of enrolled students from one school district in each of three communities in the southwestern United States.

and facilitate their social behavior; they care little about negative consequences.[58] Substance abuse, then, may be a function of the rational, albeit mistaken, belief that substance abuse benefits the user.

Pathways to Drug Abuse

There is no single path to becoming a drug abuser, but it is generally believed that most users start at a young age using alcohol as a **gateway drug** to harder substances. That is, drug involvement begins with drinking alcohol at an early age, which pro-

Figure B
Percentage of Youths Aged 12 to 17 Reporting Dependence on Alcohol or Illicit Drugs, by Behavioral and Emotional Problem Scores, 1994–1996
Source: Substance Abuse and Mental Health Services Administration, Office of Applied Studies, "The Relationship between Mental Health and Substance Abuse among Adolescents," Analytic Series A-9, 1999.

Severity levels (high, intermediate, and low) for behavioral and emotional problem scales were determined using values set in the Youth Self-Report (YSR), an instrument extensively used in adolescent studies to assess psychological difficulties.

the previous month (29% vs. 14%, respectively) than students who did not miss school.

There is also a connection between substance abuse and serious behavioral and emotional problems. One national study found that behaviorally troubled youth are seven times more likely than those with less serious problems to report that they were dependent on alcohol or illicit drugs (17.1% vs. 2.3%). In addition, youths with serious emotional problems were nearly four times more likely to report dependence (13.2% vs. 3.4%) (Figure B).

Critical Thinking

1. These studies provide dramatic evidence that drug abuse is highly associated with other social problems—abuse, school failure, and emotional disorders. They imply that getting kids off drugs may take a lot more effort than relying on some simple solution like "Just Say No." What would it take to get kids to refrain from using drugs?

InfoTrac College Edition Research

There is significant evidence that kids who have a garden variety of social problems are at risk for drug abuse. To read one study examining this issue, go to Gavin D. Shoal and Peter R. Giancola, "Cognition, Negative Affectivity and Substance Use in Adolescent Boys with and without a Family History of a Substance Use Disorder," *Journal of Studies on Alcohol* 62(5):675 (September 2001).

Sources: Deanna Pérez, "The Relationship between Physical Abuse, Sexual Victimization, and Adolescent Illicit Drug Use," *Journal of Drug Issues* 30:641–62 (2000); Texas Commission on Alcohol and Drug Abuse, "Substance Use among Youths at High Risk of Dropping Out: Grades 7–12 in Texas, 1998," *Texas Commission on Alcohol and Drug Abuse Research Brief*, June 2000; Substance Abuse and Mental Health Services Administration, Office of Applied Studies, "The Relationship between Mental Health and Substance Abuse among Adolescents," Analytic Series: A-9, 1999. Data and tables supplied by the Center for Substance Abuse Research, University of Maryland, College Park (2001).

gateway drug A substance that leads to use of more serious drugs; alcohol use has long been thought to lead to more serious drug abuse.

gresses to experimentation with marijuana, and finally, to using cocaine and even heroin. Research on adolescent drug users in Miami found that youths who began their substance abuse careers early—by experimenting with alcohol at age 7, getting drunk at age 8, having alcohol with an adult present by age 9, and becoming regular drinkers by the time they were 11 years old—later became crack users.[59] Drinking with an adult present was a significant precursor of substance abuse and delinquency.[60]

Although the gateway concept is still being debated, there is little disagreement that serious drug users begin their involvement with alcohol.[61] Though most recreational users do not progress to "hard stuff," most addicts first experiment with recreational alcohol and recreational drugs before progressing to narcotics. By implication, if teen drinking could be reduced, the gateway to hard drugs would be narrowed.

ACCORDING TO THE GATEWAY MODEL OF DRUG ABUSE, drug involvement begins with drinking alcohol at an early age, which progresses to experimentation with recreational drugs such as marijuana, and finally, to using hard drugs such as cocaine and even heroin.

What are the patterns of teenage drug use? Are all abusers similar, or are there different types of drug involvement? Research indicates that drug-involved youths do take on different roles, lifestyles, and behavior patterns, some of which are described in the next sections.[62]

Adolescents Who Distribute Small Amounts of Drugs

Many adolescents who use and distribute small amounts of drugs do not commit any other serious delinquent acts. They occasionally sell marijuana, "crystal," and PCP to support their own drug use. Their customers include friends, relatives, and acquaintances. Deals are arranged over the phone, in school, or at public meeting places; however, the actual distribution takes place in more private arenas, such as at home or in cars.

Petty dealers do not consider themselves "seriously" involved in drugs. One girl commented, "I don't consider it dealing. I'll sell hits of speed to my friends, and joints and nickel bags [of marijuana] to my friends, but that's not dealing."

Petty dealers are insulated from the justice system because their activities rarely result in apprehension. In fact, few adults notice their activities because these adolescents are able to maintain a relatively conventional lifestyle. In several jurisdictions, however, agents of the justice system are cooperating in the development of educational programs to provide nonusers with the skills to resist the "sales pitch" of petty dealers.

Adolescents Who Frequently Sell Drugs

A small number of adolescents are high-rate dealers who bridge the gap between adult drug distributors and the adolescent user. Though many are daily users, they take part in many normal activities, including going to school and socializing with friends.

Frequent dealers often have adults who "front" for them—that is, sell them drugs for cash. The teenagers then distribute the drugs to friends and acquaintances. They return most of the proceeds to the supplier, keeping a commission for themselves. They may also keep drugs for their personal use, and, in fact, some consider their drug dealing as a way of "getting high for free." One young user, Winston, age 17, told investigators, "I sell the cracks for money and for cracks. The man, he give me this *much*. I sell most of it and I get the rest for me. I like this much. Every day I do this."[63] James Inciardi and his associates found that about 80 percent of the youths who dealt crack regularly were daily users.[64]

Frequent dealers are more likely to sell drugs in parks, schools, or other public places. Deals occur irregularly, so the chance of apprehension is not significant, nor is the payoff substantial. Robert MacCoun and Peter Reuter found that drug dealers make about $30 per hour when they are working and clear on average about $2,000 per month. These amounts are greater than most dealers could hope to have earned in legitimate jobs, but they are not enough to afford a steady stream of luxuries. Most small-time dealers also hold conventional jobs.[65]

Teenage Drug Dealers Who Commit Other Delinquent Acts

A more serious type of drug-involved youth is the one who distributes multiple substances and commits both property and violent crimes. These youngsters make up about 2 percent of the teenage population, but they may commit up to 40 percent of the robberies and assaults and about 60 percent of all teenage felony thefts and drug sales. Few gender or racial differences exist among these youths: Girls are as likely as boys to become persistent drug-involved offenders, white youths as likely as black youths, middle-class adolescents raised outside cities as likely as lower-class city children.[66]

In cities, these youths frequently are hired by older dealers to act as street-level drug runners. Each member of a crew of 3 to 12 youths will handle small quantities of drugs; the supplier receives 50 to 70 percent of the drug's street value. The crew members also act as lookouts, recruiters, and guards. Although they may be recreational drug users themselves, crew members refrain from using addictive drugs such as heroin. Between drug sales, the young dealers commit robberies, burglaries, and other thefts.

Most youngsters in the street drug trade either terminate their dealing or become drug dependent. A few, however, develop entrepreneurial skills. Those who are rarely apprehended by police advance in the drug business. They develop their own crews and may handle more than half a million dollars a year.

In many instances, these drug dealer–delinquents are members of teenage gangs. The gangs maintain "rock houses," or "stash houses," that receive drug shipments arranged by members who have the overseas connections and financial backing needed to wholesale drugs. The wholesalers pay the gang for permission to deal in their territory. Lower-echelon gang members help transport the drugs and work the houses, retailing cocaine and other drugs to neighborhood youths. Each member makes a profit for every ounce of rock sold. Police estimate that youths who work in rock houses will earn $700 and up for a 12-hour shift.[67]

Some experts question whether gangs are responsible for as much drug dealing as the media would have us believe. Some believe that the tightly organized "super" gangs are being replaced with loosely organized neighborhood groups. The turbulent environment of drug dealing is better handled by flexible organizations than by rigid, vertically organized gangs with a leader who is far removed from the action.[68]

Losers and Burnouts

Some drug-involved youths do not have the savvy to join gangs or groups and instead begin committing unplanned crimes that increase their chances of arrest. Their heavy drug use increases their risk of apprehension and decreases their value for organized drug distribution networks.

Drug-involved "losers" can earn a living by steering customers to a seller in a "copping" area, touting drug availability for a dealer, or acting as a lookout. However, they are not considered trustworthy or deft enough to handle drugs or money. Though these offenders get involved in drugs at an early age, they receive little attention from the justice system until they have developed an extensive arrest record. By then they are approaching the end of their minority and will either desist or become so entrapped in the drug-crime subculture that little can be done to deter their illegal activities.

Persistent Offenders

About two-thirds of substance-abusing youths continue to use drugs in adulthood, but about half desist from other criminal activities. Those who persist in both substance abuse and crime maintain these characteristics:

- They come from poor families.
- Other criminals are members of their families.
- They do poorly in school.
- They started using drugs and committing other delinquent acts at an early age.
- They use multiple types of drugs and commit crimes frequently.
- They have few opportunities in late adolescence to participate in legitimate and rewarding adult activities.[69]

Some evidence exists that these drug-using persisters have low nonverbal IQs and poor physical coordination. Nonetheless, there is little evidence to explain why some drug-abusing youths drop out of crime while others remain active.

Drug Use and Delinquency

An association between drug use and delinquency has been established, and this connection can take a number of forms. Crime may be an instrument of the drug trade: Violence erupts when rival gangs use weapons to settle differences and establish territorial monopolies. In New York City, authorities report that crack gangs will burn down their rival's headquarters. It is estimated that between 35 and 40 percent of New York's homicides are drug related.[70]

Drug users may also commit crimes to pay for their habits.[71] One study conducted in Miami found that 573 narcotics users *annually* committed more than 200,000 crimes to obtain cash. Similar research with a sample of 356 addicts accounted for 118,000 crimes annually.[72] If such proportions hold true, the nation's estimated 700,000 heroin addicts alone may be committing more than 100 million crimes each year.

Drug users may be more willing to take risks because their inhibitions are lowered by substance abuse. Cities with high rates of cocaine abuse are also more likely to experience higher levels of armed robbery. It is possible that crack and cocaine users are more willing to engage in a risky armed robbery to get immediate cash than a burglary, which requires more planning and effort.[73]

The relationship between alcohol and drug abuse and delinquency has been substantiated by a number of studies. Some have found that youths who abuse alcohol are most likely to engage in violence; as adults, those with long histories of drinking are more likely to report violent offending patterns.[74] For example, as part of the most recent National Household Survey on Drug Abuse, adolescents ages 12–17 were

Figure 10.3

Percentages of Youths Aged 12 to 17 Reporting Past-Month Alcohol Abuse, by Whether They Participated in Violent Behaviors during the Past Year

Source: *The NHSDA Report,* October 12, 2001. (Triangle Park, NC: Office of Applied Studies (OAS), SAMHSA, and by RTI).

Percent

Figure 10.4

Percentages of Youths Aged 12 to 17 Reporting Past-Month Illicit Drug Use, by Whether They Participated in Violent Behaviors during the Past Year

Source: *The NHSDA Report,* October 12, 2001. (Triangle Park, NC: Office of Applied Studies (OAS), SAMHSA, and by RTI).

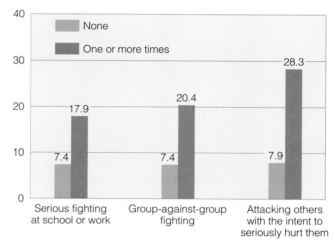

asked about their drug and alcohol use as well as their involvement in violence. As Figures 10.3 and 10.4 show, kids who say they drank and took drugs are almost twice as likely to engage in violent activity as those who abstain.[75]

The National Institute of Justice's Arrestee Drug Abuse Monitoring (ADAM) program tracks trends in drug use among arrestees in urban areas. Some of its 34 sites collect data on juveniles. The most recent data show 40 percent of juvenile male and 20 percent of juvenile female arrestees tested positive for marijuana, the most commonly used drug, and its prevalence was more than six times higher than cocaine use for both juvenile males and females.[76] In general, however, male detainees were more likely to test positive for the use of any drug than were female detainees. While males and minority-group members have somewhat higher positive test rates than females and Caucasians, drug use is prevalent among juvenile arrestees, reaffirming the close association between substance abuse and criminality.

There is evidence that incarcerated youths are much more likely to be involved in substance abuse than adolescents in the general population. For example, research by David Cantor on incarcerated youths in Washington, D.C., found their drug involvement more than double that of nonincarcerated area youths.[77]

Drugs and Chronic Offending

It is possible that most delinquents are not drug users but that police are more likely to apprehend muddle-headed substance abusers than clear-thinking abstainers. A second, more plausible, interpretation of the existing data is that the drug abuse–crime connection is so powerful because many delinquents are in fact substance abusers. Research by Bruce Johnson and his associates confirms this suspicion. Using data from a national self-report survey, these researchers found that less than 2 percent of the youths who responded to the survey (a) report using cocaine or heroin, and (b) commit two or more index crimes each year. However, these drug-abusing adolescents accounted for 40 to 60 percent of all the index crimes reported in the sample. Less than one-quarter of these delinquents committed crimes solely to support a drug habit. These data suggest that a small core of substance-abusing adolescents commits a significant proportion of all serious crimes. It is also evident that a behavior—drug abuse—that develops late in adolescence influences the extent of delinquent activity through the life course.[78]

The relationship between drug abuse and chronic offending is illustrated by Inciardi, Horowitz, and Pottieger's interviews with crack-involved youths in Miami. The 254 kids in their sample reported committing 223,439 criminal offenses during the 12 months prior to their interviews. It is not surprising that 87 percent of the sample had been arrested. The greater the involvement in the crack business, the greater the likelihood of committing violent crime. About 74 percent of the dealers committed robbery, and 17 percent engaged in assault. Only 12 percent of the nondealers committed robbery, and 4 percent engaged in assault.[79]

Explaining Drug Use and Delinquency

The association between delinquency and drug use has been established in a variety of cultures.[80] It is far from certain, however, whether (a) drug use *causes* delinquency, (b) delinquency *leads* youths to engage in substance abuse, or (c) both drug abuse and delinquency are *functions* of some other factor.[81]

Some of the most sophisticated research on this topic has been conducted by Delbert Elliott and his associates at the Institute of Behavioral Science at the University of Colorado.[82] Using data from the National Youth Survey, a longitudinal study of self-reported delinquency and drug use, Elliott and his colleagues David Huizinga and Scott Menard found a strong association between delinquency and drug use.[83] However, the direction of the relationship is unclear. As a general rule, drug abuse appears to be a *type* of delinquent behavior and not a *cause* of delinquency. Most youths become involved in delinquent acts *before* they are initiated into drugs; it is difficult, therefore, to conclude that drug use causes crime.

According to the Elliott research, both drug use and delinquency seem to reflect developmental problems; they are both part of a disturbed lifestyle. This research reveals some important associations between substance abuse and delinquency:

1. Alcohol abuse seems to be a cause of marijuana and other drug abuse because (a) most drug users started with alcohol, and (b) youths who abstain from alcohol almost never take drugs.
2. Marijuana use is a cause of multiple-drug use: About 95 percent of youths who use more serious drugs started on pot; only 5 percent of serious drug users never smoked pot.
3. Youths who commit felonies started off with minor delinquent acts. Few delinquents (1%) report committing felonies only.

The Elliott research has been supported by other studies also indicating that delinquency and substance abuse are part of a general pattern of deviance or problem behavior syndrome, such as association with an antisocial peer group and educational failure.[84] There seems to be a pattern in which troubled youths start by committing petty crimes and drinking alcohol and proceed to harder drugs and more serious crimes. Kids who drink at an early age later go on to engage in violent acts in their adolescence; violent adolescents increase their alcohol abuse as they mature.[85] Both their drug abuse and the delinquency are part of an urban underclass lifestyle involving limited education, few job skills, unstable families, few social skills, and patterns of law violations.[86]

Drug Control Strategies

To read more about the concept of addiction, go to the Psychedelic Library and read
http://www.psychedelic-library.org/davies/myth4.htm
For an up-to-date list of Web links, go to http://info.wadsworth.com/siegel

Billions of dollars are being spent each year to reduce the importation of drugs, deter drug dealers, and treat users. Yet, although the overall incidence of drug use has declined, drug use has concentrated in the nation's poorest neighborhoods, with a consequent association between substance abuse and crime.

A number of drug-control strategies have been tried. Some are designed to deter drug use by stopping the flow of drugs into the country, apprehending dealers, and cracking down on street-level drug deals. Another approach is to prevent drug use by educating would-be users and convincing them to "say no" to drugs. A third approach is to treat users so that they can terminate their addictions. Some of these efforts are discussed in the following sections.

Law Enforcement Efforts

Law enforcement strategies are aimed at reducing the supply of drugs and, at the same time, deterring would-be users from drug abuse.

Source Control One approach to drug control is to deter the sale of drugs through apprehension of large-volume drug dealers, coupled with enforcement of drug laws that carry heavy penalties. This approach is designed to punish known dealers and users and to deter those who are considering entering the drug trade.

A major effort has been made to cut off supplies of drugs by destroying overseas crops and arresting members of drug cartels; this approach is known as *source control*. The federal government has been encouraging exporting nations to step up efforts to destroy drug crops and to prosecute dealers. Three South American nations—Peru, Bolivia, and Colombia—have agreed to coordinate control efforts with the United States. However, translating words into deeds is a formidable task. Drug lords fight back through intimidation, violence, and corruption. The United States was forced to invade Panama with 20,000 troops in 1989 to stop its leader, General Manuel Noriega, from trafficking in cocaine.

To find out more about the federal government's drug control strategies, go to
http://206.6.118.10/CRACK/EXEC.HTM
For an up-to-date list of Web links, go to http://info.wadsworth.com/siegel

Even when efforts are successful in one area, production may shift to another. For example, between 1994 and 1999, enforcement efforts in Peru and Bolivia were so successful that they altered cocaine cultivation patterns. As a consequence, Colombia became the premier coca-cultivating country when the local drug cartels encouraged growers to cultivate coca plants. When the Colombian government mounted an effective eradication campaign in the traditional growing areas, the cartel linked up with rebel groups in remote parts of the country for their drug supply.[87] Leaders in neighboring countries expressed fear when, in August 2000, the United States announced $1.3 billion in military aid to fight Colombia's rural drug dealers/rebels, assuming that success would drive traffickers over the border.[88]

Border Control Law enforcement efforts have also been directed at interdicting drug supplies as they enter the country. Border patrols and military personnel have been involved in massive interdiction efforts, and many billion-dollar seizures have been made. It is estimated that between one-quarter and one-third of the annual cocaine supply shipped to the United States is seized by drug enforcement agencies. Yet U.S. borders are so vast and unprotected that meaningful interdiction is impossible; between 240 and 340 tons of cocaine and 33 tons of heroin are imported each year.[89]

If all importation were ended, homegrown marijuana and lab-made drugs such as ecstasy could become the drugs of choice. Even now, their easy availability and relatively low cost are increasing their popularity; they are a $10 billion business in the United States today.

Targeting Dealers Law enforcement agencies have also made a concerted effort to focus on drug trafficking. Efforts have been made to bust large-scale drug rings. The long-term consequence has been to decentralize drug dealing and to encourage teenage gangs to become major suppliers. Ironically, it has proven easier for federal agents to infiltrate traditional organized crime groups than to take on drug-dealing gangs.

Police can also intimidate and arrest street-level dealers and users in an effort to make drug use so much of a hassle that consumption is cut back. Some street-level enforcement efforts have had success, but others are considered failures. "Drug sweeps" have clogged correctional facilities with petty offenders while proving a drain on police resources. These sweeps are also suspected of creating a displacement effect: Stepped-up efforts to curb drug dealing in one area or city may encourage dealers to seek friendlier territory.[90] People arrested on drug-related charges are the fastest growing segment of both the juvenile and adult justice systems. National surveys have found that juvenile court judges are prone to use a get-tough approach on drug-involved offenders. These offenders are more likely to be adjudicated, waived to adult court, and receive out-of-home placements than other categories of delinquent offenders, including those who commit violent crimes.[91] Despite these efforts, juvenile drug use continues to grow, indicating that a get-tough policy is not sufficient to deter drug use.

A CLOSER VIEW
To get more information on law enforcement strategies being used to limit the supply of narcotics into the United States, use *narcotics, control of* as a subject guide on InfoTrac College Edition.

Education Strategies

Another approach to reducing teenage substance abuse relies on educational programs. Drug education now begins in kindergarten and extends through the 12th grade. More than 80 percent of public school districts include these components: teaching students about the causes and effects of alcohol, drug, and tobacco use; teaching students to resist peer pressure; and referring students for counseling and treatment.[92] Education programs such as Project ALERT, based in middle schools in California and Oregon, appear to be successful in training youths to avoid recreational drugs and to resist peer pressure to use cigarettes and alcohol.[93] Drug Abuse Resistance Education (D.A.R.E.) is an elementary school course designed to give students the skills for resisting peer pressure to experiment with tobacco, drugs, and alcohol. It is unique because it employs uniformed police officers to carry the antidrug message to the students before they enter junior high school. Critics question whether the program is actually as effective as advertised. Because of its importance, D.A.R.E. is discussed in the accompanying Policy and Practice box.

To go to the official site
of D.A.R.E., check out
http://www.dare.com
For an up-to-date list
of Web links, go to
http://info.wadsworth.com/siegel

Community Strategies

Another type of drug-control effort relies on local community groups. Representatives of local government agencies, churches, civic organizations, and similar institutions are being brought together to create drug-prevention programs. Their activities include drug-free school zones, which encourage police to keep drug dealers away from schools; Neighborhood Watch programs, which are geared to reporting drug

Drug Abuse Resistance Education (D.A.R.E.)

The most widely known drug education program, Drug Abuse Resistance Education (D.A.R.E.), is an elementary school course designed to give students the skills for resisting peer pressure to experiment with tobacco, drugs, and alcohol. It is unique because it employs uniformed police officers to carry the antidrug message to the students before they enter junior high school. The program focuses on five major areas:

1. Providing accurate information about tobacco, alcohol, and drugs
2. Teaching students techniques to resist peer pressure
3. Teaching students respect for the law and law enforcers
4. Giving students ideas for alternatives to drug use
5. Building the self-esteem of students

The D.A.R.E. program is based on the concept that the young students need specific analytical and social skills to resist peer pressure and "say no" to drugs. Instructors work with children to raise their self-esteem, provide them with decision-making tools, and help them identify positive alternatives to substance abuse.

The D.A.R.E. approach has been adopted so rapidly since its founding 18 years ago that it is now taught in 75 percent of school districts nationwide and in 54 other countries. Millions of students have already taken the D.A.R.E. program. More than 40 percent of all school districts incorporate assistance from local law enforcement agencies in their drug-prevention programming. New community policing strategies commonly incorporate the D.A.R.E. program within their efforts to provide services to local neighborhoods at the grassroots level.

Does D.A.R.E. Work?

While D.A.R.E. is popular with both schools and police agencies, national evaluations have not found it to have a big impact on student drug usage. For example, in a highly sophisticated evaluation of the program, Dennis Rosenbaum and his associates found that D.A.R.E. had only a marginal impact on student drug use and attitudes. Though D.A.R.E. may work better in some settings and with some groups than others, Rosenbaum found that it had little overall effect on substance abuse rates. One of the most critical reviews of D.A.R.E. was conducted by psychologist Donald Lynam and his colleagues. They followed a cohort of sixth-grade children attending a total of 31 schools. Twenty-three of the schools were randomly assigned to receive D.A.R.E. in the sixth grade, while the other eight received whatever drug education was routinely provided in their classes. The research team assessed the participants yearly through the 10th grade and then recontacted them when they were 20 years old. They found that D.A.R.E. had no effect on students' drug use at any time through 10th grade. The 10-year follow-up failed to find any hidden or "sleeper" effects that were delayed in developing. At age 20, there were no differences between those who received D.A.R.E. and those who did not in their use of cigarettes, alcohol, marijuana, or other drugs; the only difference was that those who received D.A.R.E. reported slightly lower levels of self-esteem at age 20, an effect that proponents were not aiming for.

Changing the D.A.R.E. Curriculum

While national evaluations have questioned the validity of D.A.R.E. and a few communities have discontinued its use, it is still widely employed in school districts around the United States. To meet criticism head on, D.A.R.E. began testing a new curriculum in 2001. The new program is aimed at older students and relies more on having them question their assumptions about drug use than on listening to lectures on the subject. The new program will work largely on changing social norms, teaching students to question whether they really have to use drugs to fit in with their peers. Emphasis will shift from fifth-grade students to those in the seventh grade, and will add a booster program in ninth grade, when kids are more likely to experiment with drugs. Police officers will now serve more as coaches than as lecturers, encouraging students to challenge the social norm of drug use in discussion groups. Students also do more role-playing in an effort to learn decision-making skills. There will also be an emphasis on the role of media and advertising in shaping behavior. The new curriculum is undergoing tests in 80 high schools and 176 middle schools—half the schools will continue using the curriculum they do now, and the other half will use the new D.A.R.E. program—so that the new curriculum may be scientifically evaluated.

Critical Thinking

1. Do you believe that an education program such as D.A.R.E. can turn kids from drugs, or are the reasons for teenage drug use so complex that a single school-based program is doomed to fail?
2. If you ran D.A.R.E., what experiences would you give to the children? Do you think it would be effective to have current or ex-addicts address classes about how drugs influenced their lives?

InfoTrac College Edition Research

Though D.A.R.E. remains controversial, it is still being used around the nation. For more information on this important program, use *D.A.R.E.* as a keyword on InfoTrac College Edition.

Sources: Kate Zernike, "Antidrug Program Says It Will Adopt a New Strategy," *New York Times,* 15 February 2001, p.1; Donald R. Lynam et al., "Project D.A.R.E.: No Effects at 10-Year Follow-Up," *Journal of Consulting and Clinical Psychology* 67:590–93 (1999); Dennis Rosenbaum, Robert Flewelling, Susan Bailey, Chris Ringwalt, and Deanna Wilkinson, "Cops in the Classroom: A Longitudinal Evaluation of Drug Abuse Resistance Education (D.A.R.E.)," *Journal of Research in Crime and Delinquency* 31:3–31(1994); David Carter, *Community Policing and D.A.R.E.: A Practitioner's Perspective* (Washington, DC: Bureau of Justice Assistance, 1995).

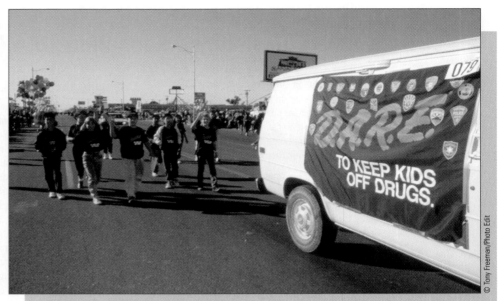

THE DRUG ABUSE RESISTANCE EDUCATION (D.A.R.E.) PROGRAM is an elementary school course designed to give students the skills for resisting peer pressure to experiment with tobacco, drugs, and alcohol. It employs uniformed police officers to carry the antidrug message to students before they enter junior high school. While reviews have been mixed, the program continues to be used around the nation.

For a Web-based antidrug education campaign, see Freevibe at *http://www.freevibe.com/ index.shtml* For an up-to-date list of Web links, go to *http://info.wadsworth.com/siegel*

dealers; citizen patrols, which frighten dealers away from public-housing projects; and community centers, which provide an alternative to the street culture.

Community-based programs reach out to high-risk youths, getting them involved in after-school programs; offering counseling; delivering clothing, food, and medical care when needed; and encouraging school achievement. Community programs also sponsor drug-free activities involving the arts, clubs, and athletics. Evaluations of community programs have shown that they may encourage antidrug attitudes and help insulate participating youths from an environment that encourages drugs.[94]

Treatment Strategies

multisystemic treatment (MST)
Addresses a variety of family, peer, and psychological problems by focusing on problem-solving and communication skills training.

Several approaches are available to treat users. Some efforts stem from the perspective that users have low self-esteem, and they use various techniques to build up the user's sense of self. Some use psychological counseling, and others, such as the **multisystemic treatment (MST)** technique developed by Scott Henggeler, direct attention to family, peer, and psychological problems by focusing on problem solving and communication skills.[95] Henggeler has found that adolescent abusers who have gone through MST programs are less likely to recidivate than youths in traditional counseling services.[96]

Another approach is to involve users in outdoor activities, wilderness training, and after-school community programs.[97] More intensive efforts use group therapy, in which leaders try to give users the skills and support that can help them reject the social pressure to use drugs. These programs are based on the Alcoholics Anonymous philosophy that users must find the strength to stay clean and that support from those who understand their experiences can be a successful way to achieve a drug-free life.

TYLER ANTER, 15, kisses his grandmother and teasingly puts on her hat. Anter is a successful participant in Clark County, Nevada's juvenile drug court program, the first in the nation when it began in 1985. Drug courts have proven so successful that there are more than 90 being used today.

Residential programs are used with more heavily involved drug abusers. Some are detoxification units that use medical procedures to wean patients from the more addicting drugs. Others are therapeutic communities that attempt to deal with the psychological causes of drug use. Hypnosis, aversion therapy (getting users to associate drugs with unpleasant sensations, such as nausea), counseling, biofeedback, and other techniques are often used.

Little evidence exists that these residential programs can efficiently terminate teenage substance abuse. Many are restricted to families whose health insurance will pay for short-term residential care; when the coverage ends, the children are released. Adolescents do not often enter these programs voluntarily, and most have little motivation to change.[98] A stay can stigmatize residents as addicts, even though they never used hard drugs; while in treatment, they may be introduced to hard-core users with whom they will associate upon release. Evaluations of residential programs show that drug abuse is sometimes curtailed during the residential phase of treatment, but once the offender is returned to the community, the abuse continues. Even programs that feature intensive aftercare show little evidence that substance abuse can be reversed through treatment.[99]

Balanced/Restorative Justice Model Another approach to treating drug-involved juveniles is referred to as the *balanced and restorative justice* (BARJ) method. This model integrates the traditional rehabilitative philosophy of the juvenile court with increasing societal concern about victims' rights and community safety.[100]

BARJ programs attempt to make offenders more accountable by having them make amends to the victim and community, while at the same time improving their competency development by changing their behaviors and improving functional skills. BARJ programs also focus on community safety and stress protecting the community by carefully monitoring the juvenile's behavior. BARJ has become the guiding philosophy in juvenile justice system change in at least 12 states. An important aspect of the BARJ philosophy is a system of graduated sanctions that hold juveniles accountable for their actions and reward them for positive progress toward rehabilitation: Good behavior results in increased freedom or other rewards, while negative behavior results in more severe restrictions or a more intensive therapeutic environment. If the offender lapses into alcohol or drug (AOD) use and/or delinquent behavior at any point in the treatment process, graduated sanctions involving placing the juvenile in a higher-security, more intense therapeutic environment are applied. This approach may be applied in a specialized juvenile drug court, where the juvenile's progress is generally monitored by a judge who relies on a variety of professionals in assessing needs, recommending services, monitoring behaviors, and applying sanctions when a lack of improvement is evident.

What Does the Future Hold?

The United States appears willing to go to great lengths to fight the drug war. Law enforcement efforts, along with prevention programs and treatment projects, have been stepped up. Yet all drug-control strategies are doomed to fail as long as youths want to take drugs and dealers find that selling drugs is a lucrative source of income. Prevention, deterrence, and treatment strategies ignore the core reasons for the drug problem: poverty, alienation, and family disruption. As the gap between rich and poor widens and the opportunities for legitimate advancement decrease, it should come as no surprise that adolescent drug use continues.

Despite all efforts, drug control is difficult because there is so much money to be made in drug trafficking. For example, the profits involved in the sale of a single drug such as ecstasy are enormous. Ecstasy, or MDMA, is manufactured clandestinely in western Europe, primarily in the Netherlands and Belgium. A typical clandestine laboratory is capable of producing 70,000 to 100,000 tablets per day; one laboratory raided by Dutch police was producing 350,000 tablets per day. The cost of producing a tablet runs as little as 50 cents, and they sell for up to about $2, giving the lab owners a potential profit of between $100,000 and $150,000 per day. Once the MDMA reaches the United States, a domestic cell distributor will charge from $6 to $8 per tablet. The MDMA retailer will, in turn, distribute the MDMA for $25 to $40 per tablet.[101]

legalization of drugs
Decriminalizing drug use to reduce the association between drug use and crime.

Some commentators have called for the **legalization of drugs.** This approach can have the short-term effect of reducing the association between drug use and crime (since, presumably, the cost of drugs would decrease), but it may have grave consequences. Drug use would most certainly increase, creating an overflow of unproductive people who must be cared for by the rest of society. The problems of teenage alcoholism should serve as a warning of what can happen when controlled substances are made readily available. However, the implications of criminalization should be further studied: What effect would a policy of partial criminalization (for example, legalizing small amounts of marijuana) have on drug-use rates? Does a get-tough policy on drugs "widen the net"? Are there alternatives to the criminalization of drugs that could help reduce their use?[102]

The Rand Corporation study of drug dealing in Washington, D.C., suggests that law enforcement efforts can have little influence on drug-abuse rates as long as dealers can earn more than the minimal salaries they might earn in the legitimate world. Only by giving youths legitimate future alternatives can hard-core users be made to forgo drug use willingly.[103]

SUMMARY

Drug abuse has been linked to juvenile delinquency. Among the most popular drugs are marijuana, cocaine and its derivative, crack, crystal, LSD, and PCP. However, the most commonly used drug is alcohol, which contributes to almost 100,000 deaths per year.

Self-report surveys indicate that, after years of decline, more teenagers are using drugs today than in the 1990s. Surveys of arrestees indicate that a significant proportion of teenagers are drug users and many of these are high school dropouts. The number of drug users may be even higher than surveys suggest, because surveys of teen abusers may be missing the most delinquent youths.

A variety of youths use drugs. Some are occasional users who might sell to friends. Others are seriously involved in both drug abuse and delinquency; many of these are gang members. There are also losers, who filter in and out of the justice system. A small percentage of teenage users remain involved with drugs into adulthood.

It is not certain whether drug abuse causes delinquency. Many adolescents who break the law later abuse drugs. Some experts believe there is a common cause for both delinquency and drug abuse—perhaps alienation and rage.

Many attempts have been made to control the drug trade. Some have attempted to inhibit the importation of drugs, others have been aimed at closing down major drug rings, and a few have tried to stop street-level dealing. There have also been attempts to treat users through rehabilitation programs and to reduce juvenile use by educational efforts. Communities have mounted grassroots drives to reduce drug abuse. So far, these efforts have not been totally successful, although overall use of drugs may have declined somewhat. It is difficult to eradicate drug abuse because there is so much profit to be made. One suggestion: Legalize drugs. Critics warn that such a step may produce greater numbers of substance abusers.

KEY TERMS

substance abuse	addict	stimulants	gateway drug
hashish	anesthetic drugs	anabolic steroids	multisystemic treatment (MST)
marijuana	inhalants	club drugs	
cocaine	sedatives	alcohol	legalization of drugs
crack	tranquilizers	addiction-prone personality	
heroin	hallucinogens		

QUESTIONS FOR DISCUSSION

1. Discuss the differences among the various categories and types of substances of abuse. Is the term *drugs* too broad to have real meaning?

2. Why do you think youths take drugs? Do you know anyone with an addiction-prone personality?

3. What policy might be the best strategy to reduce teenage drug use: source control? reliance on treatment? national education efforts? community-level enforcement?

4. Under what circumstances, if any, might the legalization or decriminalization of drugs be beneficial to society?

5. Do you consider alcohol a drug? Should greater control be placed on the sale of alcohol?

6. Do TV shows and films glorify drug usage and encourage youths to enter the drug trade? Should all images of drinking and smoking be banned from TV? What about advertisements that try to convince youths how much fun it is to drink beer or smoke cigarettes?

VIEWPOINT

"...[M]en control access to illicit drugs, and this may be seen as yet another way in which men limit women's social access and options. Moreover, the ways in which men obtain illicit drugs can be described as essentially secular, based, as they are, on the exchange of cash for a commodity. By contrast, the ways in which women obtain illicit drugs are almost always shown to revolve around some form of sexual manipulation or outright prostitution."

To read more about adolescent girls and their drug abuse on InfoTrac College Edition, go to Jessica Warner, Timothy R. Weber, and Ricardo Albanes, "Girls Are Retarded When They're Stoned: Marijuana and the Construction of Gender Roles among Adolescent Females," *Sex Roles: A Journal of Research* 4:25 (January 1999).

NOTES

1. Lloyd Johnston, Patrick O'Malley, and Jerald Bachman, "Rise in Ecstasy Use among American Teens Begins to Slow," news release, University of Michigan News and Information Services, Ann Arbor, MI (December 19, 2001).

2. Peter Greenwood, "Substance Abuse Problems among High-Risk Youth and Potential Interventions," *Crime and Delinquency* 38:444–58 (1992).

3. U.S. Department of Justice, *Drugs and Crime Facts, 1988* (Washington, DC: Bureau of Justice Statistics, 1989), pp. 3–4.

4. Thomas Feucht, Richard Stephens, and Michael Walker, "Drug Use among Juvenile Arrestees: A Comparison of Self-Report, Urinalysis, and Hair Assay," *Journal of Drug Issues* 24:99–116 (1994).

5. Mary Ellen Macksey-Amiti and Michael Fendrich, "Delinquent Behavior and Inhalant Use among High School Students." Paper presented at the American Society of Criminology meeting, Boston, November 1995.

6. National Institute on Drug Abuse, Community Epidemiology Work Group, *Epidemiological Trends in Drug Abuse* (Washington, DC: National Institute on Drug Abuse, 1997).

7. Dennis Coon, *Introduction to Psychology* (St. Paul, MN: West, 1992), p. 178.

8. Alan Neaigus et al., "Trends in the Noninjected Use of Heroin and Factors Associated with the Transition to Injecting," in James Inciardi and Lana Harrison, eds., *Heroin in the Age of Crack-Cocaine* (Thousand Oaks, CA: Sage, 1998), pp. 108–30.

9. Ibid., p. 10.

10. Bruce Johnson, George Thomas, and Andrew Golub, "Trends in Heroin Use among Manhattan Arrestees from the Heroin and Crack Era," in James Inciardi and Lana Harrison, eds., *Heroin in the Age of Crack-Cocaine* (Thousand Oaks, CA: Sage, 1998), pp. 108–30.

11. Mary Tabor, "'Ice' in an Island Paradise," *Boston Globe*, 8 December 1989, p. 3.

12. Paul Goldstein, "Anabolic Steroids: An Ethnographic Approach." Unpublished paper (Narcotics and Drug Research, Inc., March 1989).

13. Year-End 2000 Emergency Department Data from the Drug Abuse Warning Network, (Washington, DC: Department of Health and Human Services, 2001).

14. Donnie R. Marshall, DEA Congressional Testimony, Senate Caucus on International Narcotics Control, March 21, 2001.

15. Johnston, O'Malley, and Bachman, "Rise in Ecstasy Use among American Teens Begins to Slow."

16. Special Issue, "Drugs—The American Family in Crisis," *Juvenile and Family Court* 39:45–46 (1988).

17. Federal Bureau of Investigation, *Crime in the United States, 1999* (Washington, DC: U.S. Government Printing Office, 2000), Table 29.

18. Robyn Cohen, *Drunk Driving* (Washington, DC: Bureau of Justice Statistics, 1992), p. 2.

19. D.J. Rohsenow, "Drinking Habits and Expectancies about Alcohol's Effects for Self versus Others," *Journal of Consulting and Clinical Psychology* 51:75–76 (1983).

20. Spencer Rathus, *Psychology*, 4th ed. (New York: Holt, Rinehart & Winston, 1990), p. 161.

21. Institute for Social Research, "Cigarette Smoking among American Teens Declines Sharply in 2001," press release (Ann Arbor, MI, 12/19/01).

22. Centers for Disease Control, *Center Facts about Access to Tobacco by Minors* (Atlanta: Centers for Disease Control, May 23, 1997).

23. Johnston, O'Malley, and Bachman, "Rise in Ecstasy Use among American Teens Begins to Slow."

24. Data in this section come from Department of Health and Human Services, *The Household Survey on Drug Abuse, 2000* (Washington, DC: Department of Health and Human Services, 2000).

25. Joyce Ann O'Neil and Eric Wish, *Drug Use Forecasting, Cocaine Use* (Washington, DC: U.S. Government Printing Office, 1989), p. 7.

26. Eric Wish, "U.S. Drug Policy in the 1990s: Insights from New Data from Arrestees," *International Journal of the Addictions* 25:1–15 (1990).

27. Julia Yun Soo Kim, Michael Fendrich, and Joseph Wislar, "The Validity of Juvenile Arrestees' Drug Use Reporting: A Gender Comparison," *Journal of Research in Crime and Delinquency* 37:419–32 (2000).

28. G. E. Vallant, "Parent-Child Disparity and Drug Addiction," *Journal of Nervous and Mental Disease* 142:534–39 (1966).

29. Charles Winick, "Epidemiology of Narcotics Use," in D. Wilner and G. Kassenbaum, eds., *Narcotics* (New York: McGraw-Hill, 1965), pp. 3–18.

30. Delbert Elliott, David Huizinga, and Scott Menard, *Multiple Problem Youth: Delinquency, Substance Abuse and Mental Health Problems* (New York: Springer-Verlag, 1989).

31. Peter Reuter, Robert MacCoun, and Patrick Murphy, *Money from Crime: A Study of the Economics of Drug Dealing in Washington, D.C.* (Santa Monica: Rand, 1990).

32. Thomas Dishion, Deborah Capaldi, Kathleen Spracklen, and Fuzhong Li, "Peer Ecology of Male Adolescent Drug Use," *Development and Psychopathology* 7:803–24 (1995).

33. C. Bowden, "Determinants of Initial Use of Opioids," *Comprehensive Psychiatry* 12:136–40 (1971).

34. Terence Thornberry and Marvin Krohn, "Peers, Drug Use and Delinquency," in David Stoff, James Breiling, and Jack Maser, eds., *Handbook of Antisocial Behavior* (New York: Wiley, 1997), pp. 218–33.

35. R. Cloward and L. Ohlin, *Delinquency and Opportunity: A Theory of Delinquent Gangs* (Glencoe, IL: Free Press, 1960).

36. Denise Kandel and Mark Davies, "Friendship Networks, Intimacy and Illicit Drug Use in Young Adulthood: A Comparison of Two Competing Theories," *Criminology* 29:441–71 (1991).

37. James Inciardi, Ruth Horowitz, and Anne Pottieger, *Street Kids, Street Drugs, Street Crime: An Examination of Drug Use and Serious Delinquency in Miami* (Belmont, CA: Wadsworth, 1993), p. 43.

38. D. Baer and J. Corrado, "Heroin Addict Relationships with Parents during Childhood and Early Adolescent Years," *Journal of Genetic Psychology* 124:99–103 (1974).

39. Timothy Ireland and Cathy Spatz Widom, *Childhood Victimization and Risk for Alcohol and Drug Arrests* (Washington, DC: National Institute of Justice, 1995).

40. See S. F. Bucky, "The Relationship between Background and Extent of Heroin Use," *American Journal of Psychiatry* 130:709–10 (1973); I. Chien, D. L. Gerard, R. Lee, and E. Rosenfield, *The Road to H: Narcotics Delinquency and Social Policy* (New York: Basic Books, 1964).

41. J. S. Mio, G. Nanjundappa, D. E. Verlur, and M. D. DeRios, "Drug Abuse and the Adolescent Sex Offender: A Preliminary Analysis," *Journal of Psychoactive Drugs* 18:65–72 (1986).

42. G. T. Wilson, "Cognitive Studies in Alcoholism," *Journal of Consulting and Clinical Psychology* 55:325–31 (1987).

43. John Hagedorn, Jose Torres, and Greg Giglio, "Cocaine, Kicks, and Strain: Patterns of Substance Use in Milwaukee Gangs," *Contemporary Drug Problems* 25:113–45 (1998).

44. For a thorough review, see Karol Kumpfer, "Impact of Maternal Characteristics and Parenting Processes on Children of Drug Abusers." Paper presented at the American Society of Criminology meeting, Boston, November 1995.

45. D.W. Goodwin, "Alcoholism and Genetics," *Archives of General Psychiatry* 42:171–74 (1985).

46. Ibid.

47. Patricia Dobkin, Richard Tremblay, Louise Masse, and Frank Vitaro, "Individual and Peer Characteristics in Predicting Boys' Early Onset of Substance Abuse: A Seven-Year Longitudinal Study," *Child Development* 66:1198–1214 (1995).

48. Ric Steele, Rex Forehand, Lisa Armistead, and Gene Brody, "Predicting Alcohol and Drug Use in Early Adulthood: The Role of Internalizing and Externalizing Behavior Problems in Early Adolescence," *American Journal of Orthopsychiatry* 65:380–87 (1995).

49. Ibid., pp. 380–81.

50. Jerome Platt and Christina Platt, *Heroin Addiction* (New York: Wiley, 1976), p. 127.

51. Rathus, *Psychology*, p. 158.

52. Eric Strain, "Antisocial Personality Disorder, Misbehavior and Drug Abuse," *Journal of Nervous and Mental Disease* 163:162–65 (1995).

53. Dobkin, Tremblay, Masse, and Vitaro, "Individual and Peer Characteristics in Predicting Boys' Early Onset of Substance Abuse.

54. J. Shedler and J. Block, "Adolescent Drug Use and Psychological Health: A Longitudinal Inquiry," *American Psychologist* 45:612–30 (1990).

55. Greenwood, "Substance Abuse Problems among High-Risk Youth and Potential Interventions," p. 448.

56. John Wallace and Jerald Bachman, "Explaining Racial/ Ethnic Differences in Adolescent Drug Use: The Impact of Background and Lifestyle," *Social Problems* 38:333–57 (1991).

57. Marvin Krohn, Terence Thornberry, Lori Collins-Hall, and Alan Lizotte, "School Dropout, Delinquent Behavior, and Drug Use," in Howard Kaplan, ed., *Drugs, Crime and Other Deviant Adaptations: Longitudinal Studies* (New York: Plenum Press, 1995), pp. 163–83.

58. B. A. Christiansen, G. T. Smith, P. V. Roehling, and M. S. Goldman, "Using Alcohol Expectancies to Predict Adolescent Drinking Behavior after One Year," *Journal of Counseling and Clinical Psychology* 57:93–99 (1989).

59. Inciardi, Horowitz, and Pottieger, *Street Kids, Street Drugs, Street Crime*, p. 135.

60. Ibid., p. 136.

61. Mary Ellen Mackesy-Amiti, Michael Fendrich, and Paul Goldstein, "Sequence of Drug Use among Serious Drug Users: Typical vs. Atypical Progression," *Drug and Alcohol Dependence* 45:185–96 (1997).

62. The following sections lean heavily on Marcia Chaiken and Bruce Johnson, *Characteristics of Different Types of*

Drug-Involved Youth (Washington, DC: National Institute of Justice, 1988).

63. Ibid., p. 100.

64. Ibid., p. 101.

65. Robert MacCoun and Peter Reuter, "Are the Wages of Sin $30 an Hour? Economic Aspects of Street-Level Drug Dealing," *Crime and Delinquency* 38:477–91 (1992).

66. Chaiken and Johnson, *Characteristics of Different Types of Drug-Involved Youth*, p. 12.

67. Rick Graves and Ed Allen, *Narcotics and Black Gangs* (Los Angeles: Los Angeles County Sheriff's Department, n.d.).

68. John Hagedorn, "Neighborhoods, Markets, and Gang Drug Organization," *Journal of Research in Crime and Delinquency* 31:264–94 (1994).

69. Chaiken and Johnson, *Characteristics of Different Types of Drug-Involved Youth*, p. 14.

70. Eric Baumer, Janet Lauritsen, Richard Rosenfeld, and Richard Wright, "The Influence of Crack Cocaine on Robbery, Burglary, and Homicide Rates: A Cross-City, Longitudinal Analysis," *Journal of Research in Crime and Delinquency* 35:316–40 (1998).

71. Ibid.

72. James Inciardi, "Heroin Use and Street Crime," *Crime and Delinquency* 25:335–46 (1979); idem, *The War on Drugs* (Palo Alto, CA: Mayfield, 1986); see also W. McGlothlin, M. Anglin, and B. Wilson, "Narcotic Addiction and Crime," *Criminology* 16:293–311 (1978); George Speckart and M. Douglas Anglin, "Narcotics Use and Crime: An Overview of Recent Research Advances," *Contemporary Drug Problems* 13:741–69 (1986); Charles Faupel and Carl Klockars, "Drugs-Crime Connections: Elaborations from the Life Histories of Hard-Core Heroin Addicts," *Social Problems* 34:54–68 (1987).

73. Eric Baumer, "Poverty, Crack and Crime: A Cross-City Analysis," *Journal of Research in Crime and Delinquency* 31:311–27 (1994).

74. Marvin Dawkins, "Drug Use and Violent Crime among Adolescents," *Adolescence* 32:395–406 (1997); Robert Peralta, "The Relationship between Alcohol and Violence in an Adolescent Population: An Analysis of the Monitoring the Future Survey." Paper presented at the annual Society of Criminology meeting, San Diego, November 1997; Helene Raskin White and Stephen Hansell, "The Moderating Effects of Gender and Hostility on the Alcohol-Aggression Relationship," *Journal of Research in Crime and Delinquency* 33:450–70 (1996); D. Wayne Osgood, "Drugs, Alcohol, and Adolescent Violence." Paper presented at the annual meeting of the American Society of Criminology, Miami, 1994.

75. National Household Survey on Drug Abuse, NHSA Report, November 9, 2001, Washington, D.C.

76. National Institute of Justice, "Study Shows Substantial Levels of Drug Use Among Arrestees across the Nation," press release, July 20, 2000.

77. David Cantor, "Drug Involvement and Offending of Incarcerated Youth." Paper presented at the American Society of Criminology meeting, Boston, November 1995.

78. B. D. Hohnson, E. Wish, J. Schmeidler, and D. Huizinga, "Concentration of Delinquent Offending: Serious Drug Involvement and High Delinquency Rates," *Journal of Drug Issues* 21:205–29 (1991).

79. Inciardi, Horowitz, and Pottieger, *Street Kids, Street Drugs, Street Crime.*

80. W. David Watts and Lloyd Wright, "The Relationship of Alcohol, Tobacco, Marijuana, and Other Illegal Drug Use to Delinquency among Mexican-American, Black, and White Adolescent Males," *Adolescence* 25:38–54 (1990).

81. For a general review of this issue, see Helene Raskin White, "The Drug Use–Delinquency Connection in Adolescence," in Ralph Weisheit, ed., *Drugs, Crime and Criminal Justice* (Cincinnati: Anderson, 1990), pp. 215–56; Speckart and Anglin, "Narcotics Use and Crime"; Faupel and Klockars, "Drugs-Crime Connections."

82. Delbert Elliott, David Huizinga, and Susan Ageton, *Explaining Delinquency and Drug Abuse* (Beverly Hills: Sage, 1985).

83. David Huizinga, Scott Menard, and Delbert Elliott, "Delinquency and Drug Use: Temporal and Developmental Patterns," *Justice Quarterly* 6:419–55 (1989).

84. Helene Raskin White, Robert Padina, and Randy LaGrange, "Longitudinal Predictors of Serious Substance Use and Delinquency," *Criminology* 25:715–40 (1987).

85. Bu Huang, Helene White, Rick Kosterman, Richard Catalano, and J. David Hawkins, "Developmental Associations between Alcohol and Interpersonal Aggression during Adolescence," *Journal of Research in Crime and Delinquency* 38:64-83 (2001).

86. Wish, "U.S. Drug Policy in the 1990s."

87. U.S. Department of State, 1998 International Narcotics Control Strategy Report, February 1999.

88. Clifford Krauss, "Neighbors Worry about Colombian Aid," *New York Times,* 25 August 2000, A3.

89. William Rhodes et al., *What America's Users Spend on Illegal Drugs, 1988–1993* (Cambridge, MA: ABT Associates, 1995).

90. Mark Moore, *Drug Trafficking* (Washington, DC: National Institute of Justice, 1988).

91. Jeffrey Butts and Melissa Sickmund, *Offenders in Juvenile Court, 1989* (Washington, DC: Office of Juvenile Justice and Delinquency Prevention, 1992), p. 1.

92. Ibid.

93. Phyllis Ellickson and Robert Bell, *Prospects for Preventing Drug Use among Young Adolescents* (Santa Monica: Rand, 1990).

94. Wayne Lucan and Steven Gilham, "Impact of a Drug Use Prevention Program: An Empirical Assessment." Paper presented at the annual meeting of the American Society of Criminology, New Orleans, November 1992.

95. Scott Henggeler, *Delinquency and Adolescent Psychopathology: A Family–Ecological Systems Approach* (Littleton, MA: Wright-PSG, 1982).

96. Scott Henggeler, "Effects of Multisystemic Therapy on Drug Use and Abuse in Serious Juvenile Offenders: A Progress Report from Two Outcome Studies," *Family Dynamics of Addiction Quarterly* 1:40–51 (1991).

97. Eli Ginzberg, Howard Berliner, and Miriam Ostrow, *Young People at Risk: Is Prevention Possible?* (Boulder: Westview Press, 1988), p. 99.

98. Ibid.

99. Miriam Sealock, Denise Gottfredson, and Catherine Gallagher, "Addressing Drug Use and Recidivism in Delinquent Youth: An Examination of Residential and Aftercare Treatment Programs." Paper presented at the American Society of Criminology meeting, Boston, November 1995.

100. The following section is adapted from Curtis J. Vander Waal, Duane C. McBride, Yvonne M. Terry-McElrath, and Holly VanBuren, *Breaking the Juvenile Drug-Crime Cycle* (Washington, DC: National Institute of Justice, 2001).

101. Donnie R. Marshall, DEA congressional testimony, Senate Caucus on International Narcotics Control, March 21, 2001.

102. Kathryn Ann Farr, "Revitalizing the Drug Decriminalization Debate," *Crime and Delinquency* 36:223–37 (1990).

103. Reuter, MacCoun, and Murphy, *Money from Crime*, pp. 165–68.

11 Delinquency Prevention: Social and Developmental Perspectives

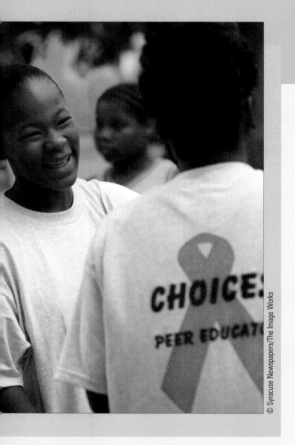

© Syracuse Newspapers/The Image Works

You are the mayor of a medium-sized city. Juvenile delinquency is on the rise, and there have been disturbing reports of increased gang activity. The police chief informs you that some urban gangs, seeking to migrate to your city, have sent members to recruit local youth. Their appeal appears to have been working, and several local chapters of the Crips, Bloods, and Latin Kings have now been formed. Street shootings, thefts of cars, and other serious delinquency problems have risen in recent weeks, and all have been linked to this new gang activity. The police, business groups in the downtown core of the city, and the public are all calling for you to take immediate action to deal with these problems.

When you meet with local community leaders they inform you that the gangs appeal to many local kids who come from troubled homes and have no real hope of success in the conventional world. Some are doing poorly in school and receive little educational support. Others who have left school have trouble finding jobs. The gangs also appeal to kids with emotional and developmental problems.

The police chief suggests that you cannot coddle these hoodlums. He tells you to put more police on the streets and hire more police officers. He also argues that you should lobby the governor and legislature to pass new laws making it mandatory that kids involved in gang violence are transferred to the adult court for trial.

In contrast, community advocates ask you to spend more money on disadvantaged families so they have access to childcare and health care. They suggest you beef up the educational budget to reduce class sizes, reduce dropout rates, and improve attendance rates.

- Would you spend more money on community-based services for young people, or would you order the chief to crack down on the gangs?

- If you choose to spend money on prevention, which programs would you support?

- When should prevention begin? Should kids be given special help even before they get in trouble with the law?

training

anti-gang
police task force

M ayors and other public officials faced with the problem of juvenile delinquency in their cities have many options. For some, it will be a clear choice of getting tough on juvenile delinquency and implementing punitive or justice-oriented measures. For others, it will be a matter of getting tough on the causes of juvenile delinquency and implementing prevention programs to ward off delinquency before it takes place. Still others will combine justice and nonjustice measures to combat the problem. Ideally, decisions about which approach or which combination of measures to use will be based on the needs of the community and the best available evidence on what works in preventing juvenile delinquency.

This chapter begins with a discussion of key features of delinquency prevention, which include the differences between prevention and other approaches to tackle delinquent behavior, the financial costs that delinquency imposes on society, and efforts to make sense of the many different types of prevention programs and measures. The history of delinquency prevention in the United States is also discussed. Next, we review the effectiveness of delinquency prevention programs that are provided in the childhood years. Daycare, preschool, and primary school programs are among the different types of prevention programs covered. This is followed by a review of the effectiveness of a wide range of delinquency prevention programs implemented in the teenage years, including school-based, after-school, and job training programs. The chapter concludes with a look at key issues to be faced in the ongoing efforts to prevent delinquency.

The Many Faces of Delinquency Prevention

delinquency control or delinquency repression Involves any justice program or policy designed to prevent the occurrence of a future delinquent act.

delinquency prevention Involves any nonjustice program or policy designed to prevent the occurrence of a future delinquent act.

Preventing juvenile delinquency means many different things to many different people. Programs or policies designed to prevent juvenile delinquency can include the police making an arrest as part of an operation to address gang problems, a juvenile court sanction to a secure correctional facility, or, in the extreme case, a death penalty sentence. These measures are often referred to as **delinquency control** or **delinquency repression.** More often though, **delinquency prevention** refers to intervening in young people's lives before they engage in delinquency in the first place; that is, preventing the first delinquent act. Both forms of delinquency prevention have a common goal of trying to prevent the occurrence of a future delinquent act; but what distinguishes delinquency prevention from delinquency control is that prevention typically does not involve the juvenile justice system. Instead, programs or policies designed to prevent delinquency involve daycare providers, nurses, teachers, social workers, recreation staff at the YMCA, counselors at Boys and Girls Clubs of America, other young people in school, and parents. This form of delinquency prevention is sometimes referred to as nonjustice delinquency prevention or alternative delinquency prevention. Exhibit 11.1 lists examples of programs to prevent and control delinquency.

Delinquency prevention programs are not designed with the intention of excluding juvenile justice personnel. Many types of delinquency prevention programs,

Exhibit 11.1   Delinquency Prevention vs. Control

Prevention	Control
Home Visitation	Anti-Gang Police Task Force
Preschool	Boot Camps
Child Skills Training	Wilderness Programs
Mentoring	Probation
After-School Recreation	Electronic Monitoring
Job Training	Secure Confinement

especially those that focus on adolescents, involve juvenile justice personnel such as the police. In these cases, the juvenile justice personnel work in close collaboration with those from such areas as education, health care, recreation, and social services. In this chapter, we focus on delinquency prevention programs that are driven or led by these non–juvenile justice agencies.

An important issue facing delinquency prevention is cost: Programs cost money to run. Expenses include staff salaries, equipment, and sometimes rent for the facilities in which programs take place. Though prevention programs can be costly, they are beneficial because they save money that would otherwise be spent in the justice system.

Costs of Delinquency: A Justification for Prevention

The impacts of juvenile delinquency on society, which include such things as damaged property, pain and suffering to victims, and the involvement of police and other agencies of the juvenile justice system, can be converted into dollars and cents. The damaged property will need to be repaired or replaced, and it is the victim who will often have to pay for this, as many crime victims do not have insurance. The pain and suffering inflicted on an individual from an assault or robbery can result not only in immediate costs of medical care and lost wages from missing work, but also in reduced quality of life from debilitating injuries or fear of being victimized again, which can result in not being able to go to work, long-term medical care, and counseling. Here again it is the crime victim and also the victim's family, employer, and many services, such as Medicaid, welfare, and mental health, that incur the dollar costs associated with these services. Victim costs resulting from an assault are as high as $9,400, and are even higher for rape and arson (Figure 11.1). The average murder costs around $3 million.[1] Then there is the cost of the involvement of the police, courts, and corrections agencies. While some of the costs incurred by the juvenile

THE FINANCIAL COSTS OF JUVENILE VIOLENCE are immense. One study estimates that juvenile violence costs the United States $158 billion each year. Costs to victims, including pain, suffering, and reduced quality of life, account for the majority of these costs. Here, teenage girls lay flowers on the coffin of a drive-by shooting victim in Glendora, California.

Figure 11.1
Costs to Crime Victims
Source: Adapted from Ted R. Miller, Mark A. Cohen, and Brian Wiersema, *Victim Costs and Consequences: A New Look* (Washington, DC: NIJ, 1996), p. 9, table 2.

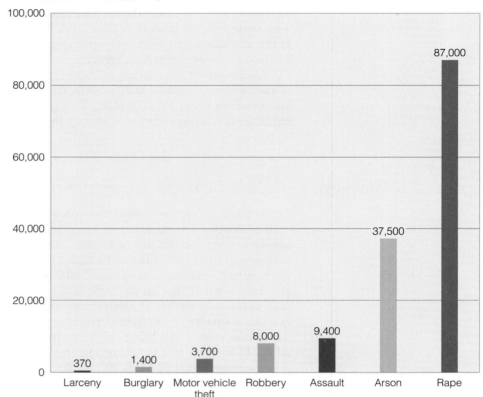

Costs to crime victims (dollars)

Type of crime: Larceny 370, Burglary 1,400, Motor vehicle theft 3,700, Robbery 8,000, Assault 9,400, Arson 37,500, Rape 87,000

justice system go toward addressing the needs of victims, such as follow-up interviews by police and court-based victim assistance programs, the majority of the costs are directed at the processing of offenders. Police arrest, public defender costs, court appearances, serving a sentence—whether it be probation or incarceration—and aftercare programs upon release into the community are all costly steps in the justice system. There are also costs incurred by society in efforts to prevent juvenile delinquency, through different types of prevention programs.

The typical criminal career over the juvenile (ages 14–17) and adult (ages 18–23) years costs society between $1.3 and $1.5 million.[2] Adding the costs of drug use and dropping out of high school brings the total cost to $1.7 to $2.3 million. Just focusing on juveniles, it has been estimated that a typical juvenile criminal career imposes costs on society in the range of $80,000 to $325,000.

Studies have looked at the costs of juvenile delinquency to different states and the nation as a whole.

State Costs   Ted Miller and his associates examined the costs of juvenile violence in the state of Pennsylvania.[3] The study was based on the violent offenses of murder, rape, robbery, assault, and physical and sexual abuse. Violence by juveniles was estimated to cost $2.6 billion in victim costs and $46 million in perpetrator costs per year. Juvenile perpetrator costs were made up of costs to the juvenile and adult justice systems, which included costs from probation, detention, juvenile treatment programs, and incarceration in adult prisons. Interestingly, this study also reported on the costs of violence against juveniles that was committed by adults and other juveniles. Compared to the victim costs of violence committed by juveniles, the victim costs of violence committed against juveniles was much higher: $4.5 billion versus $2.6 billion. The main reason for this difference was because juveniles suffered more sexual abuse—a very costly offense—at the hands of adults, but there was very little sexual abuse by juveniles against adults.

National Costs The only national estimate of the costs of juvenile delinquency focuses on juvenile violence. Violent crime by juveniles costs the United States $158 billion each year.[4] This estimate includes some of the costs incurred by federal, state, and local governments to assist victims of juvenile violence, such as medical treatment for injuries and services for victims. These tangible, or out-of-pocket, victim costs of juvenile violence came to $30 billion. But the majority of the costs of juvenile violence, the remaining $128 billion, were due to losses suffered by victims, such as lost wages, pain, suffering, and reduced quality of life. Missing from this $158 billion price tag of juvenile violence are the costs from society's response to juvenile violence, which include early prevention programs, services for juveniles, and the juvenile justice system. These costs are unknown.

Considering these costs, it is not surprising that there has been a long-standing effort to prevent juvenile delinquency.

To read more about the costs of juvenile violence in the United States, go to http://www.csneirc.org/pubs/tables/youth-viol.htm For an up-to-date list of Web links, go to http://info.wadsworth.com/siegel

A Brief History of Delinquency Prevention

The history of the prevention of juvenile delinquency in the United States is closely tied to the history of juvenile justice in this country. From the House of Refuge, which opened in New York in 1825, to more contemporary events, such as amendments to the federal Juvenile Justice and Delinquency Prevention Act of 1974, child saving organizations and lawmakers have had an interest in both the prevention and control of delinquency. However, many social scientists have noted that efforts to prevent juveniles from engaging in delinquency in the first place were secondary to and often overlooked in favor of interventions with juveniles who had already committed delinquent acts.[5] This imbalance between prevention and control of juvenile delinquency remains in place to this day.

Chicago Area Project One of the earliest juvenile delinquency prevention programs was the Chicago Area Project, which was started in 1933 by Clifford Shaw and

THE HOUSE OF REFUGE was one of the earliest juvenile institutions in the United States to offer residents vocational training.

Henry McKay.[6] (See also Chapter 4.) This project was designed to produce social change in communities that suffered from high delinquency rates and gang activity. As part of the project, qualified local leaders coordinated social service centers that promoted community solidarity and counteracted social disorganization. More than 20 different programs were developed, featuring discussion groups, counseling services, hobby groups, school-related activities, and recreation. There is still some question of whether these programs had a positive influence on the delinquency rate. Some evaluations indicated positive results, but others showed that the Chicago Area Project efforts did little to reduce juvenile delinquency.[7]

Cambridge-Somerville Youth Study   Another well-known delinquency prevention program that was implemented around the same time as the Chicago project was the Cambridge-Somerville (Massachusetts) Youth Study.[8] The focus of this program was more on improving individuals than their surroundings. One interesting feature of this program is that it was one of the first delinquency prevention programs to be evaluated using a **randomized experimental design.** Prior to the start of the program, 650 boys (325 matched pairs) were assigned to receive the program (the **experimental group**) or not to receive the program (the **control group**). The experimental group boys received regular friendly attention from counselors for an average of five years, and whatever medical and educational services were needed. The counselors talked to the boys, took them on trips and to recreational activities, tutored them in reading and arithmetic, played games with them at the project's center, encouraged them to attend church, and visited their families to give advice and general support. The program was to have continued for 10 years, but when America became involved in World War II, many of the adult counselors were drafted.[9] An evaluation of the program 30 years after it ended, when the men were 45 years old, found that those in the experimental group committed more crime than those in the control group.[10] One possible reason for this negative result was that the program was done in groups instead of one-on-one. The group format was thought to have resulted in minor delinquents being influenced by more involved or serious delinquents.[11]

Detached Street Workers   In the 1950s, a major focus of delinquency prevention programs was to reach out to youths who were unlikely to use community centers. Instead of having troubled youths come to them, detached street workers were sent into inner-city neighborhoods, creating close relationships with juvenile gangs and groups in their own milieu.[12] The best-known detached street worker program was Boston's Mid-City Project, which dispatched trained social workers to seek out and meet with youth gangs three to four times a week on the gangs' own turf. Their goal was to modify the organization of the gang and allow gang members a chance to engage in more conventional behaviors. The detached street workers tried to help gang members get jobs and educational opportunities. They acted as go-betweens for gang members with agents of the power structure—lawyers, judges, parole officers, and the like. Despite these efforts, an evaluation of the program by Walter Miller failed to show that it resulted in a significant reduction in criminal activity.[13]

Federally Funded Programs   The 1960s ushered in a tremendous interest in the prevention of delinquency. A great deal of this interest was in programs based on social structure theory. This approach seemed quite compatible with the rehabilitative policies of the Kennedy (New Frontier) and Johnson (Great Society/War on Poverty) administrations. Delinquency prevention programs received a great deal of federal funding. The most ambitious of these was the New York City–based Mobilization for Youth (MOBY). Funded by more than $50 million, MOBY attempted an integrated approach to community development. Based on Cloward and Ohlin's concept of providing opportunities for legitimate success, MOBY created employment opportunities in the community, coordinated social services, and sponsored social action groups such as tenants' committees, legal action services, and voter registra-

randomized experimental design Considered the "gold standard" of evaluation designs to measure the effect of a program on delinquency or other outcomes. Involves randomly assigning subjects either to receive the program (the experimental group) or not receive it (the control group).

experimental group The group of subjects that receives the program.

control group The comparison group of subjects that does not receive the program.

Head Start

Head Start is probably the best-known effort to help lower-class youths achieve proper socialization and, in so doing, reduce their potential for future criminality. Head Start programs were instituted in the 1960s as part of President Johnson's War on Poverty. In the beginning, Head Start was a two-month summer program for children who were about to enter a school that was aimed at embracing the "whole child." In embracing the whole child, the school offered comprehensive programming that helped improve physical health, enhance mental processes, and improve social and emotional development, self-image, and interpersonal relationships. Preschoolers were provided with an enriched educational environment to develop their learning and cognitive skills. They were given the opportunity to use pegs and pegboards, puzzles, toy animals, dolls, letters and numbers, and other materials that middle-class children take for granted. These opportunities provided the children a leg up in the educational process.

Today, with annual funding approaching $5 billion, the Head Start program is administered by the Head Start Bureau, the Administration on Children, Youth, and Families (ACYF), the Administration for Children and Families (ACF), and the Department of Health and Human Services (DHHS). Head Start teachers strive to provide a variety of learning experiences appropriate to the child's age and development. These experiences encourage the child to read books, to understand cultural diversity, to express feelings, and to play with and relate to peers in an appropriate fashion. Students are guided in developing gross and fine motor skills, and self-confidence. Health care is also an issue, and most children enrolled in the program receive comprehensive health screening, physical and dental examinations, and appropriate follow-up. Many programs provide meals, and in so doing help children receive proper nourishment.

Head Start programs now serve parents in addition to their preschoolers. Some programs allow parents to enroll in classes, which cover parenting, literacy, nutrition/weight loss, domestic violence prevention, and other social issues; social services, health, nutrition, and educational services are also available.

Considerable controversy has surrounded the success of the Head Start program. In 1970, the Westinghouse Learning Corporation issued a definitive evaluation of the Head Start effort and concluded that there was no evidence of lasting cognitive gains on the part of the participating children. Initial gains seemed to evaporate during the elementary school years, and by the third grade, the performance of the Head Start children was no different than their peers.

While disappointing, this evaluation focused on IQ levels and gave short shrift to improvement in social competence and other survival skills. More recent research has produced dramatically different results. One report found that by age 5, children who experienced the enriched daycare offered by Head Start averaged more than 10 points

higher on their IQ scores than their peers who did not participate in the program. Other research that carefully compared Head Start children to similar youngsters who did not attend the program found that the former made significant intellectual gains. Head Start children were less likely to have been retained in a grade or placed in classes for slow learners; they outperformed peers on achievement tests; and they were more likely to graduate from high school.

Head Start kids also made strides in nonacademic areas: They appear to have better health, immunization rates, nutrition, and enhanced emotional characteristics after leaving the program. Research also shows that the Head Start program can have important psychological benefits for the mothers of participants, such as decreasing depression and anxiety and increasing feelings of life satisfaction. While findings in some areas may be tentative, they are all in the same direction: Head Start enhances school readiness and has enduring effects on social competence.

If, as many experts believe, there is a close link between school performance, family life, and crime, programs such as Head Start can help some potentially criminal youths avoid problems with the law. By implication, their success indicates that programs that help socialize youngsters can be used to combat urban criminality. While some problems have been identified in individual centers, the government has shown its faith in Head Start as a socialization agent.

Critical Thinking

1. Head Start reaches only one-third of all children and families in need. In addition to spending more money, what does the U.S. government need to do to expand Head Start's reach?
2. What changes could be made to Head Start to make it more effective in improving the lives of children and families?

InfoTrac College Edition Research

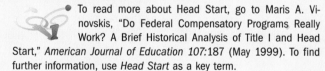

To read more about Head Start, go to Maris A. Vinovskis, "Do Federal Compensatory Programs Really Work? A Brief Historical Analysis of Title I and Head Start," *American Journal of Education* 107:187 (May 1999). To find further information, use *Head Start* as a key term.

Sources: Current information, personal contact, Head Start program, 2001; Edward Zigler and Sally Styfco, "Head Start, Criticisms in a Constructive Context," *American Psychologist* 49:127–32 (1994); Nancy Kassebaum, "Head Start, Only the Best for America's Children," *American Psychologist* 49:123–26 (1994); Faith Lamb Parker, Chaya Piorkowski, and Lenore Peay, "Head Start as Social Support for Mothers: The Psychological Benefits of Involvement," *American Journal of Orthopsychiatry* 57:220–33 (1987).

tion. But MOBY ended for lack of funding amid questions about its utility and use of funds.

Improving the socialization of lower-class youths to reduce their potential for future delinquency was also an important focus of other federally funded programs during the 1960s. The largest and best-known of these programs was Head Start, a national program for preschoolers that continues to this day. (See the accompanying Policy and Practice box.)

Contemporary Preventive Approaches The emphasis on large-scale federally funded programs aimed at the prevention of delinquency continued into the 1970s and 1980s, and these types of programs are still important today. But in recent years the focus of delinquency prevention efforts has shifted from neighborhood reclamation projects of the 1960s to more individualized, family-centered treatments.

Classifying Delinquency Prevention

Just as there are a number of different ways to define delinquency prevention and very little agreement on the best way to do so,[14] the organization or classification of delinquency prevention is equally diverse, and there is very little agreement on the most effective way to do this.

Public Health Approach One of the first efforts to classify the many different types of delinquency prevention activities drew upon the public health approach to preventing diseases and injuries.[15] This method divided delinquency prevention activities into three categories: primary prevention, secondary prevention, and tertiary prevention. Primary prevention focuses on improving the general well-being of individuals through such measures as access to health care services and general prevention education, and modifying conditions in the physical environment that are conducive to delinquency through such measures as removing abandoned vehicles and improving the appearance of buildings. Secondary prevention focuses on intervening with children and young people who are potentially at risk for becoming offenders, as well as the provision of neighborhood programs to deter known delinquent activity. Tertiary prevention focuses on intervening with adjudicated juvenile offenders through such measures as substance abuse treatment and imprisonment. Here, the goal is to reduce repeat offending or recidivism.

risk factor A negative prior factor in an individual's life that increases the risk of occurrence of a future delinquent act.

protective factor A positive prior factor in an individual's life that decreases the risk of occurrence of a future delinquent act.

Developmental Perspective Another popular approach to classifying delinquency prevention activities is the developmental perspective. Developmental prevention refers to interventions, especially those targeting **risk and protective factors,** designed to prevent the development of criminal potential in individuals.[16] Developmental prevention of juvenile delinquency is informed generally by motivational or human development theories on juvenile delinquency, and specifically by longitudinal studies that follow samples of young persons from their early childhood experiences to the peak of their involvement with delinquency in their teens and crime in their 20s.[17] The developmental perspective claims that delinquency in adolescence (and later criminal offending in adulthood) is influenced by "behavioral and attitudinal patterns that have been learned during an individual's development."[18] Exhibit 11.2 lists key features of the developmental perspective. From this perspective, prevention activities are organized around different stages of the life course; and we divide our discussion of developmental prevention of juvenile delinquency into two stages: childhood and adolescence.

For the most part, we have adopted the developmental perspective in discussing the effectiveness of different types of delinquency prevention programs in the rest of

---

Exhibit 11.2 Developmental Prevention of Delinquency—Key Features

- Informed by human development theories and longitudinal studies
- Designed to prevent the development of criminal potential in individuals
- Targeted at risk factors for delinquency and protective factors against delinquency
- Provided to children and families
- Implemented at different stages over the life course: childhood, early school years, adolescence, and transition to work

this chapter. This approach has several advantages: It allows for assessing the success of programs at different life-course stages; its coverage of the types of delinquency prevention programs that have been implemented is vast; and it is a well-recognized approach that has been used by other social scientists in reviews of the effectiveness of delinquency prevention.[19]

Early Prevention of Delinquency

In the effort to address juvenile delinquency, early childhood interventions—initiated before delinquency occurs—have received much interest and have come to be seen as an important part of an overall strategy to reduce the harm caused by juvenile delinquency. Early childhood delinquency prevention programs aim at positively influencing the early risk factors or "root causes" of delinquency and criminal offending that may continue into the adult years. These early risk factors are many, some of which include growing up in poverty, a high level of hyperactivity or impulsiveness, inadequate parental supervision, and harsh or inconsistent discipline. Early childhood interventions are often multidimensional, targeted at more than one risk factor, because they take a variety of different forms, including cognitive development, child skills training, and family support. The following sections examine early childhood delinquency prevention programs that have been implemented in the four most influential settings: home, daycare, preschool, and the school. Most of the programs have been carried out in the United States.

Home-Based Programs

In a supportive and loving home environment, parents care for their children's health and general well-being, help instill in their children positive values such as honesty and respect for others, and nurture prosocial behaviors. One of the most important types of home-based programs to prevent juvenile delinquency involves the provision of support for families. Support for families in their homes can take many different forms. A popular and effective form of family support is home visitation.[20]

Home Visitation One of the best-known home visitation programs is the Prenatal/Early Infancy Project (PEIP) that was started in Elmira, New York.[21] This program was designed with three broad objectives:

1. to improve the outcomes of pregnancy;
2. to improve the quality of care that parents provide to their children (and their children's subsequent health and development); and
3. to improve the women's own personal life-course development (completing their education, finding work, and planning future pregnancies).[22]

The program targeted first-time mothers-to-be who were under 19 years of age, unmarried, or poor. In all, 400 women were enrolled in the program. The mothers-to-be received home visits from nurses during pregnancy and during the first two years of the child's life. Each home visit lasted about one and one-quarter hours, and the mothers were visited on average every two weeks. The home visitors gave advice to the mothers about care of the child, infant development, and the importance of proper nutrition and avoiding smoking and drinking during pregnancy. Fifteen years after the program started, children of the mothers who received home visits had half as many arrests as children of mothers who received no home visits (the control group).[23] It was also found that these children, compared to those in the control group, had fewer convictions and violations of probation, were less likely to run away from home, and were less likely to drink alcohol. In addition to the program's success in preventing juvenile crime and other delinquent activities, it also produced a number of benefits for the mothers in the program, such as lower rates of child abuse and neglect, crime in general, and substance abuse, as well as less reliance on welfare and social services.[24] A Rand study found that these benefits translated into substantial cost savings for government and taxpayers.[25]

There are many other home visitation programs across the United States, such as one very similar to the Elmira program that was implemented in Memphis, Tennessee,[26] and the Hawaii Healthy Start program.[27] Because none have been around long enough to test their effectiveness in preventing juvenile delinquency, it is difficult to say with much certainty whether home visitation services achieve their goal. The claim can, however, be made that home visitation can be very effective in reducing child abuse and neglect and child injuries, and in improving the lives of families, particularly young mothers.[28]

A CLOSER VIEW
To read more about home visitation on InfoTrac College Edition, go to American Academy of Pediatrics Council on Child and Adolescent Health, "The Role of Home-Visitation Programs in Improving Health Outcomes for Children and Families," *Pediatrics 101*:486–89 (1998).

Improving Parenting Skills

Another form of family support that has shown some success in preventing juvenile delinquency is improving parenting skills. Although the main focus of parent training programs is on the parents, many of these programs also involve children with the aim of improving the parent-child bond.

Oregon Social Learning Center   The most widely cited parenting skills program is one created at the Oregon Social Learning Center (OSLC) by Gerald Patterson and his colleagues.[29] Patterson's research convinced him that poor parenting skills were associated with antisocial behavior in the home and at school. Family disruption and coercive exchanges between parents and children led to increased family tension, poor academic performance, and negative peer relations. The primary cause of the problem seemed to be that parents did not know how to deal effectively with their children. Parents sometimes ignored their children's behavior, but at other times the same actions would trigger explosive rage. Some parents would discipline their children for reasons that had little to do with the children's behavior, instead reflecting their own frustrations.

The children reacted in a regular progression, from learning to be noncompliant to learning to be assaultive. Their "coercive behavior," which included whining, yelling, and temper tantrums, would sometimes be acquired by other family members. Eventually family conflict would flow out of the home and into the school and social environment.

The OSLC program uses behavior modification techniques to help parents acquire proper disciplinary methods. Parents are asked to select several behaviors for change and to count the frequency of their occurrence. OSLC personnel teach social skills to reinforce positive behaviors, and constructive disciplinary methods to discourage negative ones. Incentive programs are initiated in which a child can earn points for desirable behaviors. Points can be exchanged for allowance, prizes, or privileges. Parents are also taught disciplinary techniques that stress firmness and consistency rather than "nattering" (low-intensity behaviors, such as scowling or scolding) or explosive discipline, such as hitting or screaming. One important technique is the "time out," in which the child is removed for brief isolation in a quiet room. Parents are taught the importance of setting rules and sticking to them. A number of evaluation studies carried out by Patterson and his colleagues showed that improving parenting skills can lead to reductions in juvenile delinquency.[30]

The parent training method used by the OSLC may be the most cost-effective method of early intervention. A Rand study found that parent training costs about one-twentieth what a home visit program costs and is more effective in preventing serious crimes. The study estimates that 501 serious crimes could be prevented for

To read more about the OSLC parenting skills program, go to *http://www.oslc.org*
For an up-to-date list of Web links, go to *http://info.wadsworth.com/siegel*

EARLY PREVENTION PROGRAMS that stress family support can reduce child abuse and neglect and juvenile delinquency. The most effective early family support programs provide infants with regular pediatrician checkups and provide parents with advice about care for the child, infant development, and local services. Here, Arlington, Texas, nurse practitioner Marilyn Graham gives 3-month-old Donovan Washington a checkup, as his father, Guy Washington, holds him.

every million dollars spent on parent training (or $2,000 per crime), a far cheaper solution than long-term incarceration, which would cost about $16,000 to prevent a single crime.[31]

Daycare Programs

Daycare services are available to children as young as 6 weeks old in the United States and other Western countries.[32] In addition to allowing parents to return to work, daycare serves to provide children with a number of important benefits, including social interaction with other children and stimulation of their cognitive, sensory, and motor control skills. The effectiveness of early childhood intervention has been studied in two programs described here—one in Syracuse, New York, and one in Houston, Texas.

Among the best-known of early childhood intervention programs that provides high-quality daycare services is the Syracuse University Family Development Research Program. This program involved high-risk women during the later stages of their pregnancies. After the women gave birth, paraprofessionals were assigned to work with them, encouraging sound parent-child relationships, providing nutrition information, and helping them establish relationships with social service agencies. In addition, the children received free full-time daycare, designed to develop their intellectual abilities, up to age 5. A 10-year follow-up compared children involved in the program with a control group and found that those who received the intervention were less likely to be referred to the juvenile court for delinquency offenses, more likely to express positive feelings about themselves, and able to take a more active role in dealing with personal problems. Girls seemed especially to benefit, doing better in school; parents were more likely to express prosocial attitudes.[33]

Another high-quality daycare program was that of the Houston Parent-Child Development Center. Like the Syracuse University program, both mothers and their children received services. In the first year of the program, the mothers received home visits from social service professionals, for the purpose of informing them about child development and parenting skills and helping them to develop prosocial bonds with their children. In the second year of the program, the mothers and their children attended a child development center four mornings a week. Here, children were provided with day services to foster cognitive skills and encourage positive interactions with other children. Mothers participated in classes on family communication and child management. Eight years after the program ended, children who received the program were less involved in fighting and other delinquent activities when compared to a control group.[34]

The success of these programs rests in their targeting of important individual- and family-level risk factors for delinquency, such as low intelligence, impulsiveness, and inconsistent and poor parenting. Social scientists point to a package of child- and parent-centered interventions targeted at multiple risk factors as a core ingredient of successful delinquency prevention programs.[35]

Preschool

Preschool programs differ from daycare programs in that preschool is geared more toward preparing children for school. Preschool is typically provided to children ages 3 to 5 years. These are the formative years of brain development; more learning takes place during this developmental stage than at any other stage over the life course. Low intelligence and school failure are important risk factors for juvenile delinquency.[36] (See Chapter 5 for why these are risk factors for juvenile delinquency.) For these reasons, highly structured, cognitive-based preschool programs give young children a positive start in life. A preschool in Michigan, a program in Chicago, and Head Start centers in Washington provide some positive findings on the benefits of early intervention.

Started in the mid-1960s, the Perry Preschool in Ypsilanti, Michigan, provided disadvantaged children with a program of educational enrichment supplemented with weekly home visits. The main hypothesis of the program was that "good preschool programs can help children in poverty make a better start in their transition from home to community and thereby set more of them on paths to becoming economically self-sufficient, socially responsible adults."[37] The main intervention was high-quality, active-learning preschool programming administered by professional teachers for two years. Preschool sessions were one-half day long and were provided 5 days a week for the duration of the 30-week school year. The educational approach focused on supporting the development of the children's cognitive and social skills through individualized teaching and learning.

A number of assessments were made of the program at important stages of development. The first assessment of juvenile delinquency, when the participants were age 15, found that those who received the program reported one-third fewer offenses than a control group.[38] By the age of 27, program participants had accumulated half the arrests of the control group. The researchers also found that the preschoolers had achieved many other significant benefits compared to their control group counterparts, including

- Higher monthly earnings (27% vs. 7% earning $2,000 or more per month)
- Higher percentages of home ownership (36% vs. 13%) and second car ownership (30% vs. 13%)
- A higher level of schooling completed (71% vs. 54% completing 12th grade or higher)
- A lower percentage receiving welfare benefits at some time in the previous 10 years (59% vs. 80%)[39]

All of these benefits translated into substantial dollar cost savings. It was estimated that for each dollar it cost to run and administer the program, more than $7 was saved to taxpayers, potential crime victims, and program participants.[40] An independent study by Rand also found that Perry Preschool was a very worthwhile investment.[41]

The Child-Parent Center (CPC) program in Chicago, like Perry Preschool, provided disadvantaged children, ages 3–4 years, with high-quality, active-learning preschool supplemented with family support. However, unlike Perry, CPC continued to provide the children with the educational enrichment component into elementary school, up to the age of 9 years. Just focusing on the effect of the preschool, it was found that, compared to a control group, those who received the program were less likely to be arrested for nonviolent offenses (17% vs. 25%) and violent offenses (9% vs. 15%) by the time they were 18. Preschool participants, compared to a control group, were also less likely to be arrested more than once (10% vs. 13%). Other significant benefits realized by the preschool participants compared to the control group, included

- A higher rate of high school completion (50% vs. 39%)
- More years of completed education (11 vs. 10)
- A lower rate of dropping out of school (47% vs. 55%)[42]

The success of the CPC program in preventing juvenile delinquency and improving other life-course outcomes produced substantial cost savings. For each dollar spent on the program, almost $8 was saved to taxpayers, potential crime victims, and program participants.[43]

Another early intervention that closely resembles these preschool programs is Head Start. (See the Policy and Practice box earlier in the chapter.) Head Start provides children with, among other things, an enriched educational environment to develop their learning and cognitive skills. One study of Head Start centers in Seattle, Washington, found that very young children who were enrolled in the program were less likely to misbehave than children in the control group.[44]

Overall, high-quality, intensive preschool programs show strong support for preventing delinquency and improving the lives of young people.[45] The provision of family support services combined with preschool programming likely adds to the strength of the Perry and CPC programs in preventing delinquency, but it is clear that preschool was the most important element. The intellectual enrichment component of preschool helps prepare children for the academic challenges of elementary and later grades; reducing the chances of school failure is a significant factor in reducing delinquency. Another notable point about the positive findings of Perry and CPC is that these two programs were implemented many years apart, yet the CPC, as a semi-replication of Perry, demonstrates that preschool programs today can still be effective in preventing delinquency.

School Programs in the Primary Grades

Schools are a critical social context for delinquency prevention efforts, from the early to later grades.[46] (See Chapter 9.) All schools work to produce vibrant and productive members of society. The school's role in preventing delinquency in general, which is the focus of this section, differs from measures taken to make the school a safer place. In this case, a school may adopt a greater security orientation and implement such measures as metal detectors, police in school, and closed circuit television cameras. A number of experimental programs have attempted to prevent or reduce delinquency by manipulating factors in the learning environment; two are discussed here.

The Seattle Social Development Project (SSDP) used a method in which teachers learn techniques that reward appropriate student behavior and minimize disruptive behavior. The program started in first grade and continued through sixth grade. Students were taught in small groups. Students were also provided with skills training to help them master problem-solving, communication, and conflict resolution skills. Family training classes were offered, teaching parents how to reward and encourage desirable behavior and provide negative consequences for undesirable behavior in a consistent fashion. Other parent training focused on improving their children's academic performance while reducing at-risk behaviors such as drug abuse. In short, the program was extremely comprehensive, targeting an array of important risk factors for delinquency.

To read more about SSDP, go to *http://depts.washington.edu/ssdp/* For an up-to-date list of Web links, go to *http://info.wadsworth.com/siegel*

A long-term evaluation of the Seattle program found that children who received the program reported more commitment and attachment to school, better academic achievement, less alcohol abuse, and fewer violent delinquent acts compared to a control group.[47] One study found that the program's success in preventing delinquency alone—not including the other important successes—produced cost savings to the criminal justice system and victims of crime that outweighed the costs of running the program.[48]

In Montreal, child psychologist Richard Tremblay set up an experiment to investigate the effects of an early preventive intervention program for 6-year-old boys who were aggressive and hyperactive and from poor neighborhoods. Known as the Montreal Longitudinal-Experimental Study, the program lasted for two years and had two components: school-based social skills training and home-based parent training. Social skills training for the children focused predominantly on improving social interactions with peers. The parent training component was based on the social learning principles of Gerald Patterson and involved training parents on how to provide positive reinforcement for desirable behavior, use nonpunitive and consistent discipline practices, and develop family crisis management techniques. The program was successful in reducing delinquency. By age 12, boys in the experimental group compared to those in the control group committed less burglary and theft and were less likely to be involved in fights. At every age from 10 to 15, self-reported delinquency was lower for the boys in the experimental group compared to those in the control group.[49]

Schools may not be able to reduce delinquency single-handedly, but a number of viable alternatives to their present operations could aid a community-wide effort to reduce the problem of juvenile crime. A recent review of school-based programs was conducted by Denise Gottfredson and her colleagues as part of a study to determine the best methods of delinquency prevention. Some of their findings are contained in Exhibit 11.3. The main difference between the programs that work and those that

---

Exhibit 11.3   School-Based Delinquency Prevention Programs that Work

What Works for Delinquency?

- Programs aimed at building school capacity to initiate and sustain innovation.
- Programs aimed at clarifying and communicating norms about behaviors—by establishing school rules, improving the consistency of their enforcement (particularly when they emphasize positive reinforcement of appropriate behavior), or communicating norms through schoolwide campaigns (for example, antibullying campaigns) or ceremonies.
- Comprehensive instructional programs that focus on a range of social competency skills (such as developing self-control and skills in stress management, responsible decision making, social problem solving, and communication) and that are delivered over a long period of time to continually reinforce skills.

What Does Not Work for Delinquency?

- Instructional programs that do not focus on social competency skills or do not make use of cognitive-behavioral teaching methods.

What Is Promising for Delinquency?

- Programs that group youths into smaller "schools-within-schools" to create smaller units, more supportive interactions, or greater flexibility in instruction.
- Classroom or instructional management.

Source: Denise C. Gottfredson, David B. Wilson, and Stacy Skroban Najaka, "School-Based Crime Prevention," in Lawrence W. Sherman, David P. Farrington, Brandon C. Welsh, and Doris Layton MacKenzie, eds., *Evidence-Based Crime Prevention* (London: Routledge, 2002).

do not is that successful programs target an array of important risk factors. Often it is not enough to improve only the school environment or only the family environment; for example, a youth who has a troubled family life may find it more difficult to do well at school, regardless of the improvements made at school. Another important ingredient of successful school-based programs is that they be intensive; two or three sessions a semester often does not cut it.

Prevention of Delinquency in the Teenage Years

Like early childhood interventions, delinquency prevention programs started in the teenage years also play an important role in an overall strategy to reduce juvenile delinquency. A wide range of non–juvenile justice delinquency prevention programs attempt to address such risk factors as parental conflict and separation, poor housing, dropping out of high school, and antisocial peers. The following sections examine the five main delinquency prevention approaches targeted at teenagers: mentoring, school-based programs, after-school programs, job training, and comprehensive community-based programs.

Mentoring

Mentoring programs usually involve nonprofessional volunteers spending time with young people at risk for delinquency, dropping out of school, school failure, and other social problems. Mentors behave in a supportive, nonjudgmental manner while acting as role models.[50] In recent years, there has been a large increase in the number of mentoring programs, many of which are aimed at preventing delinquency.[51]

Juvenile Mentoring Program   The Office of Juvenile Justice and Delinquency Prevention (OJJDP) has supported mentoring for many years in all parts of the United States, most notably through the Juvenile Mentoring Program (JUMP). The program relies on responsible and caring adults to volunteer their time as mentors to young people who are exposed to some risk factors, including delinquency, dropping out of school, and problems in school. The most common areas of increased risk, based on a large number of male and female youths enrolled in JUMP, are school and social/family domains. (See Table 11.1.) Mentors work one-on-one with young people.[52] Research has shown that mentoring and other types of delinquency prevention programs offered in group settings, particularly for high-risk youths, may end up causing more harm than good. By offering these types of programs in groups, young people who are more chronically involved in delinquency may negatively affect those who are marginally involved in delinquency.[53] OJJDP's two-year evaluation of JUMP suggests that strengthening the role of mentoring as a component of youth programming may pay handsome dividends in improved school performance and reduced antisocial behavior, including alcohol and other drug abuse.[54]

Quantum Opportunities Program   One of the most successful mentoring programs in preventing juvenile delinquency is the Quantum Opportunities Program (QOP). QOP was implemented in five sites across the country: Milwaukee, Oklahoma City, Philadelphia, Saginaw (Michigan), and San Antonio. At each of the five sites, 25 young people received the program, while another 25 young people served as the comparison group. The main goal of the program was to improve the life course opportunities of disadvantaged, at-risk youths during the high school years. The program ran for four years or up to grade 12, and was designed around the provision of three "quantum opportunities":

To read more about JUMP, go to *http://ojjdp.ncjrs.org/jump/*
For an up-to-date list of Web links, go to *http://info.wadsworth.com/siegel*

Table 11.1 **Risk Factors of Young People in the Juvenile Mentoring Program (JUMP)**

	Percentage of Enrolled Youth*	
Risk Domain	**Male (*n* = 3,592)**	**Female (*n* = 3,807)**
School Problems	74.6%	63.0%
School behavior	39.5	23.5
Poor grades	53.6	45.9
Truancy	10.4	9.1
Social/Family Problems	51.7	56.4
Delinquency	17.5	8.5
Fighting	12.8	6.3
Property crime	2.8	0.5
Gang activity	3.0	1.0
Weapons	1.1	0.4
Alcohol Use	3.2	1.5
Drug Use	4.0	1.8
Tobacco Use	2.3	1.9
Pregnancy/Early Parenting	0.2	1.5

*Percentage of total JUMP enrollment for each gender. For 23 youths, no gender was reported in the database.

Source: Laurence C. Novotney, Elizabeth Mertinko, James Lange, and Tara Kelly Baker, *Juvenile Mentoring Program: A Progress Review* (Washington, DC: *OJJDP Juvenile Justice Bulletin,* 2000), p. 5.

1. Educational activities (peer tutoring, computer-based instruction, homework assistance)
2. Service activities (volunteering with community projects)
3. Development activities (curricula focused on life and family skills, and college and career planning)

Incentives in the form of cash and college scholarships were also offered to students for work carried out in these three areas. These incentives served to provide short-run motivation for school completion and future academic and social achievement. Staff also received cash incentives and bonuses for keeping youths involved in the program.[55]

An evaluation of the program six months after it ended found that those who received the program were less likely to be arrested compared to the control group (17% vs. 58%). A number of other significant effects were observed. For example, compared to the control group, QOP group members were

- more likely to have graduated from high school (63% vs. 42%)
- more likely to be enrolled in some form of postsecondary education (42% vs. 16%)
- less likely to have dropped out of high school (23% vs. 50%)[56]

Despite the findings of these two mentoring programs, the overall evidence of the impact of mentoring on delinquency remains mixed.[57] Furthermore, other mentoring programs have not had success in other areas, such as academic achievement, school attendance, school dropout, and employment.[58] So, why do some mentoring programs work and not others? The biggest issue has to do with what the mentors actually do and how they do it. In JUMP and QOP, mentors are a source of support and guidance to help young people deal with a broad range of issues that have to do with their family, school, and future career. They work one-on-one with young people, in many cases forming strong bonds. Care is taken in matching the mentor and young person. For future mentoring programs to be successful they should follow the approaches adopted in JUMP and QOP.

A CLOSER VIEW
To read more about mentoring on InfoTrac College Edition, use *mentoring* and *delinquency-prevention* as key terms.

School Programs for Teens

Safety of students in middle schools and high schools takes on a much higher profile than in the early grades because of a larger number of school shootings and other violent incidents. However, the role of schools in the prevention of delinquency in the wider community remains prominent. A wide range of programs to deal with juvenile delinquency in the community have been set up in middle schools and high schools across the United States and in other countries. We review just a couple of the most influential school-based delinquency prevention programs.

Project PATHE   Positive Action Through Holistic Education, or PATHE, is a comprehensive program used in secondary schools that reduces school disorder and aims to improve the school environment. The goal is to enhance students' experiences and attitudes about school by increasing students' bonds to the school, increasing their self-concept, and improving educational and occupational attainment. These improvements will help reduce juvenile delinquency.

PATHE was operated in four middle schools and three high schools in South Carolina. It focused on four elements: strengthening students' commitment to school, providing successful school experiences, encouraging attachment to the educational community, and increasing participation in school activities. By increasing students' sense of belonging and usefulness, the project sought to promote a positive school experience. The PATHE program has undergone extensive evaluation by sociologist Denise Gottfredson, who found that the schools in which it was used experienced a moderate reduction in delinquency. Replications of the project are currently under development.[59]

Violence Prevention Curriculum for Adolescents   High school students in a number of locations across the country received this program through health education classes. The curriculum was designed to do five main things in the following order:

1. Provide statistical information on adolescent violence and homicide.
2. Present anger as a normal, potentially constructive emotion.
3. Create a need in the students for alternatives to fighting by discussing the potential gains and losses from fighting.
4. Have students analyze the precursors to a fight and practice avoiding fights using role-play and videotape.
5. Create a classroom ethos that is nonviolent and values violence prevention behavior.[60]

The curriculum was administered in 10 sessions. The sessions were very interactive between the teacher and the students, relying on many different techniques, including brainstorming and role-playing. Like many school-based delinquency prevention programs, the violence prevention curriculum was concerned with reducing delinquency, specifically fighting, in schools and in the larger community. An evaluation of the program in four major urban areas showed that fighting had been significantly reduced among the young people who attended the sessions compared to a control group that did not receive the curriculum.[61]

The review of what works in preventing delinquency in schools by Denise Gottfredson and her colleagues (see Exhibit 11.3) is not limited to the early grades, but also includes programs in middle schools and high schools. And the conclusion on the effectiveness of school-based delinquency prevention programs in the later grades is the same as for the early grades: Some programs work and some programs do not work. But what are the key features of successful school-based delinquency prevention programs? As with the successful school programs in the early grades, successful programs in the later grades are those that target a number of important risk factors. For the two programs described here, this meant a focus on reducing school disorder and improving the school environment. Two additional components of

A CLOSER VIEW
To read more about school-based programs for teens on InfoTrac College Edition, use *adolescence* and *delinquency-prevention* as key terms.

successful school-based delinquency prevention programs in the later grades are improving the family environment by engaging parents in helping the student to learn, and reducing negative peer influences through information about the downsides of gun carrying, drug use, and gang involvement.

After-School Programs

Because three out of four mothers with school-age children are employed, and two-thirds of them work full time, there is a growing need for after-school programs. Today, after-school options include childcare centers, tutoring programs at school, dance groups, basketball leagues, and drop-in clubs. State and federal budgets for education, public safety, delinquency prevention, and childcare provide some funding for after-school programs; in 1999, $200 million in federal grants were made to enable schools to establish after-school programs called Twenty-First Century Community Learning Centers. Research shows that younger children (ages 5 to 9) and those in low-income neighborhoods gain the most from after-school programs, showing improvement in work habits, behavior with peers and adults, and performance in school. Young teens who attend after-school activities achieve higher grades in school and engage in less risky behavior. These findings must be interpreted with caution. Because after-school programs are voluntary, participants may be the more motivated youngsters in a given population and the least likely to engage in antisocial behavior.[62]

Boys and Girls Clubs of America   One of the most successful after-school programs in preventing delinquency (and substance abuse) is provided by the Boys and Girls Clubs of America. Founded in 1902, the Boys and Girls Clubs of America is a nonprofit organization with a membership today of more than 1.3 million boys and girls nationwide. Boys and Girls Clubs (BGC) provide programs in six main areas:

- Cultural enrichment
- Health and physical education
- Social recreation
- Personal and educational development
- Citizenship and leadership development
- Environmental education[63]

One study examined the effectiveness of BGCs for high-risk youths in public housing developments at five sites across the United States. The usual services of BGCs, which include reading classes, sports, and homework assistance, were offered, as well as a program to prevent substance abuse, known as SMART Moves (Self-Management and Resistance Training). This program targets the specific pressures that young people face to try drugs and alcohol. It also provides education to parents and the community at large to assist young people in learning about the dangers of substance abuse and strategies for resisting the pressures to use drugs and alcohol.[64] Evaluation results showed that housing developments with BGCs, with and without SMART Moves, had fewer damaged units and less delinquency in general than housing developments without the clubs. There was also an overall reduction in substance abuse, drug trafficking, and other drug-related delinquency activity.[65]

Participate and Learn Skills   A Canadian program implemented in a public housing development in the nation's capital, Ottawa, recruited low-income young people to participate in after-school activities, such as sports (ice hockey), music, dance, and scouting. Known as Participate and Learn Skills (PALS), the program ran for almost three years and aimed to advance young people toward higher skill levels in

AFTER-SCHOOL PROGRAMS, like the Boys and Girls Club, provide young people with a wide range of services, including sports and cultural activities, help with homework, and educational programs. Some programs show that involvement in these and other positive activities with adult supervision can keep youth out of trouble during the after-school hours and improve school performance. Here, boys play basketball at the Boys and Girls Club of Greater Washington, D.C.

the activities they chose and to integrate them into activities in the wider community. PALS was based on the belief that skill development in sports, music, dance, and so on, could affect other areas of young people's lives, such as prosocial attitudes and behaviors, which in turn could help them avoid engaging in delinquent activities.

At the end of the program, it was found that those who participated in the after-school activities were much better off than their control counterparts on a range of measures. The strongest impact of the program was found for juvenile delinquency, with an 80 percent reduction in police arrests. This positive effect was diminished somewhat in the 16 months after the program ended. The researchers speculated that the effects of the program may wear off. Substantial gains were also observed in skill acquisition, as measured by the number of levels advanced in an activity, and in integration in the wider community. These benefits translated into impressive cost savings. For every dollar that was spent on the program, more than $2.50 was saved to the juvenile justice system (fewer arrests), the housing development (less need for private security services), and the city government.[66]

Overall, after-school recreation represents a promising approach to preventing juvenile delinquency. It works because it engages young people in productive, fun, and rewarding activities. For some young people, this is enough to keep them occupied and out of trouble. These programs are also successful in reducing delinquency because they instill in young people important messages about the downsides of drug use and gang membership.

Not enough of these programs have been evaluated to say that after-school recreation is a success, but it does deserve further testing.[67] The fact that violent juvenile

A CLOSER VIEW
To read more about after-school programs on InfoTrac College Edition, search on these key terms: *after-school, adolescence,* and *delinquency-prevention.*

delinquency is at its peak in the after-school hours[68] underscores the importance of high-quality after-school programs.

Job Training

Having a job means having money to pay for necessities as well as to spend on leisure activities. It can bring a sense of pride and accomplishment, and it can be a protective factor against involvement in delinquency. Job training programs improve the chances of obtaining jobs in the legal economy and thereby may reduce delinquency.[69] The developmental stage of transition to work is difficult for many young people. Coming from a disadvantaged background, having poor grades in school or perhaps dropping out of school, and having some involvement in delinquency can all pose difficulties in securing a steady, well-paying job in early adulthood. Programs like the two described here are concerned not only with providing young people with employable skills, but also with helping them overcome some of these immediate problems.

Job Corps The best-known and largest job training program in the United States is Job Corps, which was established in 1964 as a federal training program for disadvantaged, unemployed youths. The designers of the national program, the Department of Labor, were hopeful that spin-off benefits in the form of reduced dependence on social assistance and a reduction in delinquency would occur as a result of empowering at-risk youth to achieve stable, long-term employment opportunities. The program is still active today, operating out of 119 centers across the nation, and each year provides services to more than 60,000 new young people at a cost of over $1 billion.[70]

Job Corps' main goal is to improve the employability of participants by offering a comprehensive set of services that largely includes vocational skills training, basic education (the ability to obtain graduate equivalent degrees), and health care. Job Corps is provided to young people between the ages of 16 and 24 years. Most of the young people enrolled in the program are at high risk for substance abuse, delinquency, and social assistance dependency. Two out of five youths come from families on social assistance, four out of five have dropped out of school, and the average family income is $6,000 per year.[71] Almost all of the Job Corps centers require the participants to live there while taking the program.

A large-scale evaluation of Job Corps, involving almost 12,000 young people, found that the program was successful in reducing delinquency. Arrest rates were 16 percent lower for those who received the program compared to a comparison group. Program group members were less likely to be convicted and serve jail time upon conviction. Also, there were higher employment rates and greater earnings for those who received the program.[72] An earlier evaluation of Job Corps found it to be a worthwhile investment of public resources: For each dollar that was spent on the program, $1.45 was saved to government or taxpayers, crime victims, and program participants.[73]

To read more about Job Corps, go to http://www.jobcorps.org/ For an up-to-date list of Web links, go to http://info.wadsworth.com/siegel

YouthBuild U.S.A. Another job training program for disadvantaged, unemployed youths is YouthBuild U.S.A. Started in 1978 by a group of young people in New York City, YouthBuild has become a national program, serving more than 6,000 young people between the ages of 16 and 24 years in more than 100 locations across the country. The program's focus is on building or renovating affordable housing, and through this young people learn skills in carpentry and construction. Youth-Build also provides educational services—for example, to achieve a high school diploma or prepare for college—and promotes the development of leadership skills. The program's impact on delinquency is not known, but the program has proven tremendously successful, with a large percentage of participants finding work in the construction industry or attending college.[74]

Comprehensive Community-Based Programs

Experimentation with comprehensive community-based delinquency prevention programs began as early as the 1930s, with Shaw and McKay's Chicago Area Project. The Mobilization for Youth program of the 1960s is another example of this type of initiative to prevent juvenile delinquency. Neither of these programs was found to be overly successful in reducing delinquency, but few of these types of programs have been evaluated. Typically implemented in neighborhoods with high delinquency and crime rates, they are made up of a range of different types of interventions and usually involve an equally diverse group of community and government agencies that are concerned with the problem of juvenile delinquency, such as the YM/YWCA, Boys and Girls Clubs of America, social and health services. The three programs discussed here rely on a systematic approach or comprehensive planning model to develop preventive interventions. This includes analyzing the delinquency problem, identifying available resources in the community, developing priority delinquency problems, and identifying successful programs in other communities and tailoring them to local conditions and needs.[75] Not all comprehensive community-based prevention programs follow this model, but there is evidence to suggest that this approach will produce the greatest reductions in juvenile delinquency.[76] One of the main drawbacks of this approach is the difficulty of sustaining the level of resources and

PREVENTING DELINQUENCY ON A COMMUNITYWIDE SCALE requires a number of interventions targeted at an array of risk factors for delinquency. Some programs combine family support, mental health services, mentoring, and educational programs. Here, high school students discuss family and health issues as part of a self-help group.

multiagency cooperation necessary to lower the rates of juvenile delinquency across a large geographical area such as a city.

Children At Risk Program   One contemporary example of a comprehensive community-based delinquency prevention program that has been evaluated is the Children At Risk (CAR) program. CAR was set up to help improve the lives of young people at high risk for delinquency, gang involvement, substance abuse, and other problem behaviors. It was delivered to a large number of young people in poor and high-crime neighborhoods in five cities across the country. It involved a wide range of preventive measures, including case management and family counseling, family skills training, tutoring, mentoring, after-school activities, and community policing. The program was different in each neighborhood. A study of all five cities showed that one year after the program ended the young people who received the program, compared to a control group, were less likely to have committed violent delinquent acts and to have used or sold drugs. Other beneficial results for those in the program included less association with delinquent peers, less peer pressure to engage in delinquency, and more positive peer support.[77]

Communities That Care and the SafeFutures Initiative   Other large-scale comprehensive community-based delinquency prevention programs include Communities That Care (CTC)[78] and the SafeFutures Initiative.[79] Both programs are funded by OJJDP. The CTC strategy emphasizes the reduction of risk factors for delinquency and the enhancement of protective factors against delinquency for different developmental stages from birth through adolescence.[80] CTC follows a rigorous, multi-level planning process that includes drawing upon interventions that have previously demonstrated success and tailoring them to the needs of the community.[81]

The SafeFutures Initiative operates much like CTC; for example, by emphasizing the reduction of risk factors for delinquency and protective factors against delinquency, using what works, and following a rigorous planning model to implement different interventions. It also works to build or strengthen existing collaborations among the many community groups and government departments working to prevent delinquency. Unlike CTC, the SafeFutures Initiative is only targeted at youths who are both at high risk for delinquency and adjudicated offenders. (See Exhibit 11.4.)

To read more about SafeFutures, go to *http://ojjdp.ncjrs.org/safefutures/index.html* For an up-to-date list of Web links, go to *http://info.wadsworth.com/siegel*

A CLOSER VIEW
To read more about comprehensive community-based programs on InfoTrac College Edition, go to William H. Barton, Marie Watkins, and Roger Jarjoura, "Youths and Communities: Toward Comprehensive Strategies for Youth Development," *Adolescence* 42:483–93 (1997).

Exhibit 11.4   SafeFutures Program to Reduce Juvenile Delinquency and Youth Violence

SafeFutures is made up of nine program areas:

1. After-school programs

2. Juvenile mentoring programs (JUMP)

3. Family strengthening and support services

4. Mental health services for at-risk and adjudicated youth

5. Delinquency prevention programs in general

6. Comprehensive communitywide approaches to gang-free schools and communities

7. Community-based day treatment programs

8. Continuum-of-care services for at-risk and delinquent girls

9. Serious, violent, and chronic juvenile offender programs (with an emphasis on enhancing graduated sanctions)

Source: Elaine Morley, Shelli B. Rossman, Mary Kopczynski, Janeen Buck, and Caterina Gouvis, *Comprehensive Responses to Youth at Risk: Interim Findings from the SafeFutures Initiative* (Washington, DC: Office of Juvenile Justice and Delinquency Prevention, 2000), p. x.

Blueprints for Violence Prevention

In 1996 the Center for the Study and Prevention of Violence (CSPV) at the University of Colorado at Boulder launched the Blueprints for Violence Prevention initiative. The principal aim of the Blueprints initiative is to "identify and replicate effective youth violence prevention programs across the Nation." For programs to be labeled as effective, they must adhere to a set of strict scientific standards. The key standards include

- Statistical evidence of effectiveness in reducing violent behavior
- Evaluations using the most rigorous designs (for example, randomized experiment)
- Large sample size to allow for any changes to be detected
- Low attrition of subjects
- Use of reliable and accepted instruments to assess impact on violence
- Sustained reductions in violence for at least one year after the end of the program
- Replication: implementation of the program in at least two different sites

More than 500 programs have been reviewed. There are 11 model programs, or Blueprints, that have proven to be effective in reducing juvenile violence or risk factors for juvenile violence. Not all of the model programs are designed to prevent violence before it takes place; some are designed for offenders and involve the juvenile justice system. The 11 model programs are

1. Prenatal and infancy home visitation by nurses.
2. Promotion of social competence and reduction of child conduct problems.
3. Promotion of alternative thinking strategies.
4. Prevention of bullying.
5. Big Brothers and Big Sisters of America.
6. Life skills training.

7. Comprehensive substance abuse prevention.
8. Functional family therapy: brings together families and juvenile offenders to address family problems and unlearn aggressive behavior.
9. Multisystemic therapy: multiple component treatment for chronic and violent juvenile offenders, which may involve individual, family, peer, school, and community interventions.
10. Multidimensional treatment foster care: an alternative to incarceration that matches juvenile offenders with trained foster families.
11. Quantum Opportunities Program (QOP).

These model programs are distributed to communities and act like a prevention menu, allowing communities to select proven programs that are best suited to their needs.

Critical Thinking

1. What is the importance of replicating delinquency prevention programs in multiple sites?
2. How is the Blueprints initiative helpful to communities faced with a delinquency problem?

InfoTrac College Edition Research

 To read more about youth violence prevention on InfoTrac College Edition, use *violence-prevention* as a key term.

Source: Sharon Mihalic, Katherine Irwin, Delbert Elliott, Abigail Fagan, and Diane Hansen, *Blueprints for Violence Prevention* (Washington, DC: OJJDP Juvenile Justice Bulletin, 2001).

Future of Delinquency Prevention

The success of delinquency prevention is shown by evaluations of individual programs (as described throughout the chapter) and larger efforts to assess what works, such as the Blueprints for Violence Prevention initiative, discussed in the accompanying Policy and Practice box. Despite the success of many different types of delinquency prevention programs—from preschool to mentoring—these programs receive a fraction of what is spent on the juvenile justice system to deal with young people once they have broken the law.[82] This is also true in the adult criminal justice system.[83] To many juvenile justice officials, policy makers, and politicians, prevention is tantamount to being soft on crime, and delinquency prevention programs are often referred to as "pork," otherwise known as pork barrel, or wasteful, spending.[84] Aside from these views, delinquency prevention programs face a number of very real obstacles, including

- Ethical concerns about early intervention:[85] Is it right to intervene in the lives of children and young people using methods that may or may not be successful?

To learn more about the Blueprints program, go to *http://www.colorado.edu/cspv/ blueprints/Default.htm* For an up-to-date list of Web links, go to *http://info.wadsworth.com/siegel*

- Labeling and stigmatization associated with programs that target high-risk populations:[86] Children and families receiving support may be called hurtful names and/or looked down upon by fellow community members.
- Long delay before early childhood programs can have an impact on delinquency:[87] While the saying "pay now, save later" is true for early childhood delinquency prevention programs, the length of time for this benefit to be felt can act as a deterrent. In a society and political system that demand immediate results, the building of a juvenile corrections facility is often seen as a more tangible measure than the building of a preschool.

The future of preventive programs depends on educating the public and key decision makers about the value of preventing delinquency. One example of this is discussing the success of delinquency prevention programs in financial terms.[88] For the handful of programs that have measured costs and benefits, some of which are discussed in this chapter, the savings are rather substantial.[89] The costs of running prevention programs are low relative to the very costly nature of delinquency. Notwithstanding these important issues, the future of delinquency prevention is likely to be very bright. With many local efforts, state initiatives, and a growing list of national programs showing positive results, the prevention of delinquency is proving its worth.

SUMMARY

The costs of juvenile delinquency are considerable. These costs include the responses of the juvenile justice system, losses to victims of delinquent acts, and the financial impact on offenders and their families. One approach to reduce these costs that has garnered a great deal of attention in recent years is prevention.

Prevention is distinguished from control or repression in that prevention seeks to reduce the risk factors for delinquency before antisocial behavior or delinquency becomes a problem. Delinquency control programs, which involve the juvenile justice system, intervene in the lives of juvenile offenders with the aim of preventing the occurrence of future delinquent acts.

Many different types of delinquency prevention programs have been targeted at children, young people, and families, and many of these programs show positive results in reducing delinquency as well as other problem behaviors, such as substance abuse and truancy. They have also been shown to lead to improvements in other areas of life, such as educational achievement, health, and employment. These benefits often translate into substantial cost savings. But not all delinquency prevention programs work. Some programs do more harm than good, but fortunately these are rare.

Efforts to better understand what works in preventing delinquency and to address some of the concerns with prevention programs need more attention. Intervening in the lives of children, young people, and their families to prevent delinquency before it takes place is a key component of an overall strategy to address the problem of juvenile delinquency.

KEY TERMS

delinquency control or delinquency repression

delinquency prevention

randomized experimental design

experimental group

control group

risk factor

protective factor

QUESTIONS FOR DISCUSSION

1. Prevention and control are the two broad-based approaches that can be used to reduce delinquency. How do these approaches differ?

2. The costs of juvenile delinquency are wide-ranging and substantial. Do you think these costs justify spending money on delinquency prevention programs?

3. What are some of the benefits of implementing prevention programs in childhood compared to adolescence?

4. In addition to reducing delinquency, many prevention programs also have a positive impact on other social problems. Identify four of these problems, and give an example of a program that was successful in reducing each one of them.

5. What are comprehensive community-based delinquency prevention programs?

6. Many programs have been successful in preventing delinquency, but many have not been successful. What are some of the reasons why a program may fail to reduce delinquency?

VIEWPOINT

Following a rash of vandalism of homes and schools that was taking place during the after-school hours, community members in Mesa, Arizona, organized after-school programs to provide structured, positive alternatives to delinquency. The prevention of vandalism is one of the top priorities of the program, as well as the prevention of substance abuse.

To read more about after-school programs on InfoTrac College Edition, go to National Education Association of the United States, "Keeping Kids out of Trouble during After-School Hours," *NEA Today* 19:40 (Sept. 2000).

NOTES

1. Ted R. Miller, Mark A. Cohen, and Brian Wiersema, *Victim Costs and Consequences: A New Look* (Washington, DC: NIJ, 1996), p. 9, table 2.

2. Mark A. Cohen, "The Monetary Value of Saving a High-Risk Youth," *Journal of Quantitative Criminology* 14:5–33 (1998).

3. Ted R. Miller, Deborah A. Fisher, and Mark A. Cohen, "Costs of Juvenile Violence: Policy Implications," *Pediatrics* 107(1):1–7 (2001), http//www.pediatrics.org/cgi/content/full/107/1/e3. This study was based on a larger report: Joint State Government Commission, General Assembly of the Commonwealth of Pennsylvania, *The Cost of Juvenile Violence in Pennsylvania*, staff report to the Task Force to Study the Issues Surrounding Violence as a Public Health Concern (Harrisburg, PA: Author, January 1995).

4. Children's Safety Network Economics and Insurance Resource Center, "State Costs of Violence Perpetrated by Youth," http://www.csneirc.org/pubs/tables/youth-viol.htm (July 12, 2000).

5. Barry Krisberg and James Austin, *The Children of Ishmael: Critical Perspectives on Juvenile Justice* (Palo Alto, CA: Mayfield, 1978), pp. 7–45; Joseph G. Weis and J. David Hawkins, *Preventing Delinquency* (Washington, DC: Office of Juvenile Justice and Delinquency Prevention, 1981), pp. 1–6; Richard J. Lundam, *Prevention and Control of Juvenile Delinquency*, 3rd ed. (New York: Oxford University Press, 2001), pp. 23, 25.

6. Clifford R. Shaw and Henry D. McKay, *Juvenile Delinquency and Urban Areas: A Study of Rates of Delinquents in Relation to Differential Characteristics of Local Communities in American Cities* (Chicago: University of Chicago Press, 1942).

7. For an intensive look at the Chicago Area Project, see Steven Schlossman and Michael Sedlack, "The Chicago Area Project Revisited," *Crime and Delinquency* 29: 398–462 (1983).

8. Joan McCord and William McCord, "A Follow-Up Report on the Cambridge-Somerville Youth Study," *Annals of the American Academy of Political and Social Science* 322: 89–96 (1959).

9. Richard J. Lundman, *Prevention and Control of Juvenile Delinquency*, 3rd ed. (New York: Oxford University Press, 2001), p. 50.

10. Joan McCord, "A Thirty-Year Follow-Up of Treatment Effects," *American Psychologist* 33:284–89 (1978).

11. Thomas J. Dishion, Joan McCord, and François Poulin, "When Interventions Harm: Peer Groups and Problem Behavior," *American Psychologist* 54:755–64 (1999).

12. See New York City Youth Board, *Reaching the Fighting Gang* (New York: New York City Youth Board, 1960).

13. Walter Miller, "The Impact of a 'Total Community' Delinquency Control Project," *Social Problems* 10:168–91 (1962).

14. Trevor Bennett, "Crime Prevention," in Michael Tonry, ed., *The Handbook of Crime and Punishment* (New York: Oxford University Press, 1998).

15. Paul J. Brantingham and Frederick L. Faust, "A Conceptual Model of Crime Prevention," *Crime and Delinquency* 22:284–96 (1976).

16. David P. Farrington, "Early Developmental Prevention of Juvenile Delinquency," *Criminal Behaviour and Mental Health* 4:209–27 (1994).

17. David P. Farrington, "The Development of Offending and Antisocial Behaviour from Childhood: Key Findings from the Cambridge Study in Delinquent Development," *Journal of Child Psychology and Psychiatry* 36:929–64 (1995).

18. Richard E. Tremblay and Wendy M. Craig, "Developmental Crime Prevention," in Michael Tonry and David P. Farrington, eds., *Building a Safer Society: Strategic Approaches to Crime Prevention. Crime and Justice: A Review of Research*, volume 19 (Chicago: University of Chicago Press, 1995), p. 151.

19. Tremblay and Craig, "Developmental Crime Prevention"; Gail A. Wasserman and Laurie S. Miller, "The Prevention of Serious and Violent Juvenile Offending," in Rolf Loeber and David P. Farrington, eds., *Serious and Violent Juvenile Offenders: Risk Factors and Successful Interventions* (Thousand Oaks, CA: Sage, 1998); Joan McCord, Cathy Spatz Widom, and Nancy A. Crowell, eds., *Juvenile Crime, Juvenile Justice*. Panel on Juvenile Crime: Prevention, Treatment, and Control (Washington, DC: National Academy Press, 2001); Patrick Tolan, "Crime Prevention: Focus on Youth," in James Q. Wilson and Joan Petersilia, eds., *Crime: Public Policies for Crime Control* (Oakland, CA: Institute for Contemporary Studies, 2002).

20. Deanna S. Gomby, Patti L. Culross, and Richard E. Behrman, "Home Visiting: Recent Program Evaluations—Analysis and Recommendations," *The Future of Children* 9(1):4–26 (1999).

21. David L. Olds, Charles R. Henderson, Robert Chamberlin, and Robert Tatelbaum, "Preventing Child Abuse and Neglect: A Randomized Trial of Nurse Home Visitation," *Pediatrics* 78:65–78 (1986).

22. David L. Olds, Charles R. Henderson, Charles Phelps, Harriet Kitzman, and Carole Hanks, "Effects of Prenatal and Infancy Nurse Home Visitation on Government Spending," *Medical Care* 31:155–74 (1993).

23. David L. Olds et al., "Long-Term Effects of Nurse Home Visitation on Children's Criminal and Antisocial Behavior: 15-Year Follow-Up of a Randomized Controlled Trial," *Journal of the American Medical Association* 280:1238–44 (1998).

24. David L. Olds et al., "Long-Term Effects of Home Visitation on Maternal Life Course and Child Abuse and Neglect: Fifteen-Year Follow-Up of a Randomized Trial," *Journal of the American Medical Association* 278:637–43 (1997).

25. Lynn A. Karoly et al., *Investing in Our Children: What We Know and Don't Know about the Costs and Benefits of Early Childhood Interventions* (Santa Monica: Rand, 1998).

26. Harriet Kitzman et al., "Effect of Prenatal and Infancy Home Visitation by Nurses on Pregnancy Outcomes, Childhood Injuries, and Repeated Childbearing: A Randomized Controlled Trial," *Journal of the American Medical Association* 278:644–52 (1997).

27. Anne K. Duggan et al., "Evaluation of Hawaii's Healthy Start Program," *The Future of Children* 9(1):66–90 (1999).

28. David P. Farrington and Brandon C. Welsh, "Delinquency Prevention Using Family-Based Interventions," *Children and Society* 13:287–303 (1999); David P. Farrington and Brandon C. Welsh, "Family-Based Crime Prevention," in Lawrence W. Sherman, David P. Farrington, Brandon C. Welsh, and Doris Layton MacKenzie, eds., *Evidence-Based Crime Prevention* (London: Routledge, 2002).

29. See, generally, Gerald R. Patterson, "Performance Models for Antisocial Boys," *American Psychologist* 41:432–44 (1986); idem, *Coercive Family Process* (Eugene, OR: Castalia, 1982).

30. Gerald R. Patterson, Patricia Chamberlain, and John B. Reid, "A Comparative Evaluation of a Parent-Training Program," *Behavior Therapy* 13:638–50 (1982); Gerald R. Patterson, John B. Reid, and Thomas J. Dishion, *Antisocial Boys* (Eugene, OR: Castalia, 1992).

31. Peter W. Greenwood, Karyn E. Model, C. Peter Rydell, and James Chiesa, *Diverting Children from a Life of Crime: Measuring Costs and Benefits* (Santa Monica: Rand, 1996).

32. Sonya Michel, *Children's Interests/Mother's Rights: The Shaping of America's Child Care Policy* (New Haven, CT: Yale University Press, 1999).

33. J. Ronald Lally, Peter L. Mangione, and Alice S. Honig, "The Syracuse University Family Development Research Program: Long-Range Impact of an Early Intervention with Low-Income Children and their Families," in D. R. Powell, ed., *Parent Education as Early Childhood Intervention: Emerging Directions in Theory, Research and Practice* (Norwood, NJ: Ablex, 1988).

34. Dale L. Johnson and Todd Walker, "Primary Prevention of Behavior Problems in Mexican-American Children," *American Journal of Community Psychology* 15:375–85 (1987).

35. Tremblay and Craig, "Developmental Crime Prevention."

36. Farrington, "Early Developmental Prevention of Juvenile Delinquency," pp. 216–17.

37. Lawrence J. Schweinhart, Helen V. Barnes, and David P. Weikart, *Significant Benefits: The High/Scope Perry Preschool Study Through Age 27* (Ypsilanti, MI: High/Scope Press, 1993), p. 3.

38. Lawrence J. Schweinhart and David P. Weikart, *Young Children Grow Up: The Effects of the Perry Preschool Program through Age 15* (Ypsilanti, MI: High/Scope Press, 1980).

39. Schweinhart, Barnes, and Weikart, *Significant Benefits: The High/Scope Perry Preschool Study through Age 27*, p. xv.

40. W. Steven Barnett, *Lives in the Balance: Age 27 Benefit-Cost Analysis of the High/Scope Perry Preschool Program* (Ypsilanti, MI: High/Scope Press, 1996); idem, "Cost-Benefit Analysis,"in Schweinhart, Barnes, and Weikart, *Significant Benefits: The High/Scope Perry Preschool Study Through Age 27* (Ypsilanti, MI: High/Scope Press, 1993).

41. Karoly et al., *Investing in Our Children.*

42. Arthur J. Reynolds, Judy A. Temple, Dylan L. Robertson, and Emily A. Mann, "Long-Term Effects of an Early Childhood Intervention on Educational Achievement and Juvenile Arrest: A 15-Year Follow-up of Low-Income Children in Public Schools," *Journal of the American Medical Association* 285:2339–46 (2001).

43. Arthur J. Reynolds, Judy A. Temple, Dylan L. Robertson, and Emily A. Mann, "Long-Term Benefits of Participation in the Title 1 Chicago Child-Parent Centers." Paper presented at the Biennial Meeting of the Society for Research on Adolescence, Chicago, March 30–April 2, 2000.

44. Carolyn Webster-Stratton, "Preventing Conduct Problems in Head Start Children: Strengthening Parenting Competencies," *Journal of Consulting and Clinical Psychology* 66:715–30 (1998).

45. Edward Zigler and Sally J. Styfco, "Extended Childhood Intervention Prepares Children for School and Beyond," *Journal of the American Medical Association* 285:2378–80 (2001).

46. Delbert S. Elliott, Beatrix Hamburg, and Kirk R. Williams, "Violence in American Schools: An Overview," in Delbert S. Elliott, Beatrix Hamburg, and Kirk R. Williams, eds., *Violence in American Schools: A New Perspective* (New York: Cambridge University Press, 1998), p. 16.

47. J. David Hawkins, Richard F. Catalano, Rick Kosterman, Robert Abbott, and Karl G. Hill, "Preventing Adolescent Health-Risk Behaviors by Strengthening Protection during Childhood," *Archives of Pediatrics and Adolescent Medicine* 153:226–34 (1999).

48. Steve Aos, Polly Phipps, Robert Barnoski, and Roxanne Lieb, "The Comparative Costs and Benefits of Programs to Reduce Crime: A Review of Research Findings with Implications for Washington State," in Brandon C. Welsh, David P. Farrington, and Lawrence W. Sherman, eds., *Costs and Benefits of Preventing Crime* (Boulder: Westview Press, 2001).

49. Richard E. Tremblay et al., "Parent and Child Training to Prevent Early Onset of Delinquency: The Montréal Longitudinal-Experimental Study," in Joan McCord and Richard E. Tremblay, eds., *Preventing Antisocial Behavior: Interventions from Birth through Adolescence* (New York: Guilford, 1992); Richard E. Tremblay, Linda Pagani-Kurtz, Louise C. Mâsse, Frank Vitaro, and Robert O. Pihl, "A Bimodal Preventive Intervention for Disruptive Kindergarten Boys: Its Impact through Mid-Adolescence," *Journal of Consulting and Clinical Psychology* 63:560–568 (1995); Richard E. Tremblay, Louise C. Mâsse, Linda Pagani-Kurtz, and Frank Vitaro, "From Childhood Physical Aggression to Adolescent Maladjustment: The Montreal Prevention Experiment," in R. De V. Peters and R. J. McMahon, eds., *Preventing Childhood Disorders: Substance Abuse, and Delinquency* (Thousand Oaks, CA: Sage, 1996).

50. James C. Howell, ed., *Guide for Implementing the Comprehensive Strategy for Serious, Violent, and Chronic Juvenile Offenders* (Washington, DC: Office of Juvenile Justice and Delinquency Prevention, U.S. Department of Justice, 1995), p. 90.

51. Joan McCord, Cathy Spatz Widom, and Nancy A. Crowell, eds., *Juvenile Crime, Juvenile Justice*. Panel on Juvenile Crime: Prevention, Treatment, and Control (Washington, DC: National Academy Press, 2001), p. 147.

52. Laurence C. Novotney, Elizabeth Mertinko, James Lange, and Tara Kelly Baker, *Juvenile Mentoring Program: A Progress Review* (Washington, DC: OJJDP Juvenile Justice Bulletin, 2000).

53. Thomas J. Dishion, Joan McCord, and François Poulin, "When Interventions Harm: Peer Groups and Problem Behavior," *American Psychologist* 54:755–64 (1999).

54. Jean Grossman and Eileen Gary, *Mentoring—A Proven Delinquency Prevention Strategy* (Washington, DC: OJJDP Juvenile Justice Bulletin, 1997).

55. Andrew Hahn, "Extending the Time of Learning," in Douglas J. Besharov, ed., *America's Disconnected Youth: Toward a Preventive Strategy* (Washington, DC: Child Welfare League of America Press, 1999).

56. Andrew Hahn, *Evaluation of the Quantum Opportunities Program (QOP): Did the Program Work?* (Waltham, MA: Brandeis University, 1994).

57. Brandon C. Welsh and Akemi Hoshi, "Communities and Crime Prevention," in Lawrence W. Sherman, David P. Farrington, Brandon C. Welsh, and Doris Layton MacKenzie, eds., *Evidence-Based Crime Prevention* (London: Routledge, 2002); Joan McCord, Cathy Spatz Widom, and Nancy A. Crowell, eds., *Juvenile Crime, Juvenile Justice*.

58. McCord, Spatz Widom, and Crowell, eds., *Juvenile Crime, Juvenile Justice*, p. 147.

59. Denise C. Gottfredson, "An Empirical Test of School-Based Environmental and Individual Interventions to Reduce the Risk of Delinquent Behavior," *Criminology* 24:705–31 (1986); idem, "Changing School Structures to Benefit High-Risk Youth," in Peter Leone, ed., *Understanding Troubled and Troubling Youth* (Newbury Park, CA: Sage, 1990); Denise C. Gottfredson, *Schools and Delinquency* (New York: Cambridge University Press, 2001).

60. James Larson, "Violence Prevention in the Schools: A Review of Selected Programs and Procedures," *School Psychology Review* 23:151–64 (1994).

61. Ibid., p. 153.

62. Executive Summary, "When School Is Out," *The Future of Children* 9:Fall 1999 (Los Altos, CA: The David and Lucile Packard Foundation).

63. Steven P. Schinke, Mario A. Orlandi, and Kristin C. Cole, "Boys & Girls Clubs in Public Housing Developments: Prevention Services for Youth at Risk," *Journal of Community Psychology, Office of Substance Abuse Prevention Special Issue*:118–28 (1992).

64. Ibid., p. 120.

65. Ibid., pp. 125–27.

66. Marshall B. Jones and David R. Offord, "Reduction of Anti-Social Behaviour in Poor Children by Nonschool Skill Development," *Journal of Child Psychology and Psychiatry* 30:737–50 (1989).

67. Lawrence W. Sherman et al., *Preventing Crime: What Works, What Doesn't, What's Promising* (Washington, DC: NIJ, 1997); Lawrence W. Sherman et al., *Preventing Crime: What Works, What Doesn't, What's Promising* (Washington, DC: NIJ Research in Brief, 1998). (Note: The 1998 publication is a summary of the 1997 publication.)

68. Howard Snyder and Melissa Sickmund, *Juvenile Offenders and Victims: 1999 National Report* (Washington, DC: Office of Juvenile Justice and Delinquency Prevention, 1999).

69. McCord, Spatz Widom, and Crowell, eds., *Juvenile Crime, Juvenile Justice*, pp. 150–51.

70. Peter Z. Schochet, John Burghardt, and Steven Glazerman, *National Job Corps Study: The Short-Term Impacts of Job Corps on Participants' Employment and Related Outcomes: Executive Summary* (Princeton, NJ: Mathematica Policy Research, 2000), p. 3.

71. Lynn A. Curtis, *The State of Families: Family, Employment and Reconstruction: Policy Based on What Works* (Milwaukee, WI: Families International, 1995).

72. Schochet, Burghardt, and Glazerman, *National Job Corps Study*.

73. David A. Long, Charles D. Mallar, and Craig V. D. Thornton, "Evaluating the Benefits and Costs of the Job Corps," *Journal of Policy Analysis and Management* 1: 55–76 (1981).

74. Rudy Hernandez, *YouthBuild U.S.A.* (Washington, DC: OJJDP Youth in Action Fact Sheet, 2001).

75. J. David Hawkins, Richard F. Catalano, and Associates, *Communities That Care: Action for Drug Abuse* (San Francisco: Jossey-Bass, 1992).

76. Richard F. Catalano, Michael W. Arthur, J. David Hawkins, Lisa Berglund, and Jeffrey J. Olson, "Comprehensive Community- and School-Based Interventions to Prevent Antisocial Behavior," in Rolf Loeber and David P. Farrington, eds., *Serious and Violent Juvenile Offenders: Risk Factors and Successful Interventions* (Thousand Oaks, CA: Sage, 1998), p. 281.

77. Adele V. Harrell, Shannon E. Cavanagh, and Sanjeev Sridharan, *Evaluation of the Children At Risk Program: Results 1 Year after the End of the Program* (Washington, DC: NIJ Research in Brief, 1999).

78. Hawkins, Catalano, and Associates, *Communities That Care: Action for Drug Abuse Prevention*.

79. Elaine Morley, Shelli B. Rossman, Mary Kopczynski, Janeen Buck, and Caterina Gouvis, *Comprehensive*

Responses to Youth at Risk: Interim Findings from the SafeFutures Initiative (Washington, DC: Office of Juvenile Justice and Delinquency Prevention, 2000).

80. Catalano, Arthur, Hawkins, Berglund, and Olson, "Comprehensive Community- and School-Based Interventions to Prevent Antisocial Behavior."

81. James C. Howell and J. David Hawkins, "Prevention of Youth Violence," in Michael Tonry and Mark H. Moore, eds., *Youth Violence: Crime and Justice: A Review of Research,* vol. 24 (Chicago: University of Chicago Press, 1998), pp. 303–304.

82. Bryan J. Vila, "Human Nature and Crime Control: Improving the Feasibility of Nurturant Strategies," *Politics and the Life Sciences* 16:3–21 (1997).

83. Irvin Waller and Brandon C. Welsh, "International Trends in Crime Prevention: Cost-Effective Ways to Reduce Victimization," in Graeme Newman, ed., *Global Report on Crime and Justice* (New York: Oxford University Press, 1999).

84. Richard A. Mendel, *Prevention or Pork? A Hard-Headed Look at Youth-Oriented Anti-Crime Programs* (Washington, DC: American Youth Policy Forum, 1995), p. 1.

85. Thomas Gabor, "Prevention into the Twenty-First Century: Some Final Remarks," *Canadian Journal of Criminology* 32:197–212 (1990).

86. David R. Offord, Helena Chmura Kraemer, Alan E. Kazdin, Peter S. Jensen, and Richard Harrington, "Lowering the Burden of Suffering from Child Psychiatric Disorder: Trade-Offs Among Clinical, Targeted, and Universal Interventions," *Journal of the American Academy of Child and Adolescent Psychiatry* 37:686–94 (1998).

87. Farrington and Welsh, "Delinquency Prevention Using Family-Based Interventions."

88. National Crime Prevention Council, "Saving Money While Stopping Crime," *Topics in Crime Prevention* (Washington, DC: NCPC, Fall 1999).

89. Brandon C. Welsh, "Economic Costs and Benefits of Early Developmental Prevention," in Rolf Loeber and David P. Farrington, eds., *Child Delinquents: Development, Intervention, and Service Needs* (Thousand Oaks, CA: Sage, 2001); Brandon C. Welsh, David P. Farrington, and Lawrence W. Sherman, eds., *Costs and Benefits of Preventing Crime* (Boulder: Westview, 2001).

Part Four The Juvenile Justice System

Since 1900, a separate juvenile justice system has been developed that features its own rules, institutions, laws, and processes. The separation of juvenile and adult offenders reflects society's concern for the plight of children. Ideally, care, protection, and treatment are the bywords of the juvenile justice system. However, because of public fear of violent youth, there have been efforts to "toughen up" the juvenile justice system and treat some delinquents much more like adult offenders. Because of these concerns, the treatment of delinquents has become an American dilemma. Severe punishment seems to have little deterrent effect on teenagers—if anything, it may prepare them for a life of adult criminality. Many incarcerated adult felons report that they were institutionalized as youths. The juvenile justice system is caught between the futility of punishing juveniles and the public's demand that something be done about serious juvenile crime. Yet, the rehabilitative ideal of the juvenile justice system has not been totally lost. Even though the nation seems to be in the midst of a punishment cycle, juvenile justice experts continue to press for judicial fairness, rehabilitation, and innovative programs for juvenile offenders.

Part Four provides a general overview of the juvenile justice system, including its process, history, and legal rules. Chapter 12 reviews the history and development of juvenile justice and provides an overview of its major components, processes, goals, and institutions. Chapter 13 deals with police handling of delinquent and status offenders. It contains information on the police role, the organization of police services, legal rights of minors in police custody, and prevention efforts. Chapter 14 is concerned with the juvenile court process. It describes such issues and programs as diversion, the transfer of youths to adult courts, legal rights during trial, the role of the prosecutor, the juvenile court judge, and the defense attorney, and the sentencing of juvenile offenders.

Chapter 15 discusses efforts to treat juveniles who have been found to be delinquent. It reviews the history and practices of probation, community corrections, and juvenile institutions. Finally, Chapter 16 reviews international efforts to treat delinquent offenders. It compares how other nations organize their juvenile justice systems and treat juvenile offenders with methods used in the United States.

12 The History and Development of Juvenile Justice

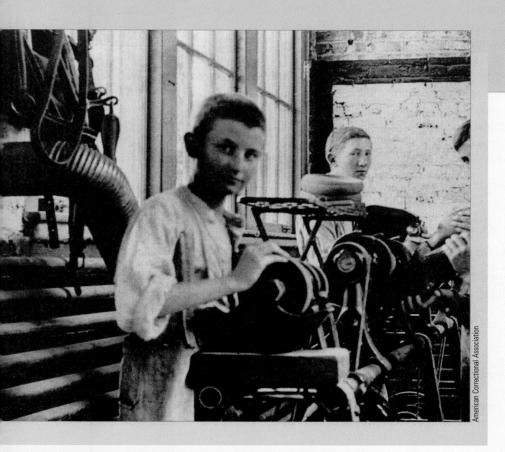

Fourteen-year-old Daphne A., a product of the city's best private schools, lives with her wealthy family in a luxury condo in a fashionable neighborhood. Her father is an executive at a local financial services conglomerate and earns close to a million dollars per year. Daphne, however, has a hidden, dark side. She is always in trouble at school, and teachers report she is impulsive and has poor self-control. At times she can be kind and warm, but on other occasions she is obnoxious, unpredictable, insecure, and demanding of attention. She is overly self-conscious about her body and has a drinking problem. Daphne attends AA meetings and is on the waiting list at High Cliff Village, a residential substance abuse treatment program. Her parents seem intimidated by her, confused by her complexities; her father filed a harassment complaint against her once, saying she slapped him.

Despite repeated promises to get her life together, Daphne likes to hang out at night in a local park, drinking with neighborhood kids. On more than one occasion she has gone to the park with her friend and confidant Christopher G., a quiet boy who has his own set of personal problems. His parents have separated, and he is prone to suffer severe anxiety attacks. Chris has been suspended from school and diagnosed with depression, for which he takes two drugs—Zoloft, an antidepressant, and Lorazepam, a sedative.

One night in the park, Daphne and Chris met up with Michael M., a 44-year-old man with a long history of problems with alcohol. After a night of drinking, a fight broke out and Michael was stabbed, his throat cut, and his body dumped in a pond. Soon after the attack, Daphne called 911, telling police that a friend "jumped in the lake and didn't come out." Police searched the area and found Michael's slashed and stabbed body in the water; he had been disemboweled by Chris and Daphne in an attempt to sink the body. When the authorities traced the call, Daphne was arrested; she confessed to police that she had helped Chris murder the victim.

During an interview with court psychiatrists, Daphne admits she participated in the killing but cannot articulate what caused her to get involved. She had been drinking and remembers little of the events. She said she was flirting with Michael, and Chris stabbed him in a jealous rage. She speaks in a flat, hollow voice and shows little remorse for her actions. It was a spur-of-the-moment thing, she claims, and after all, it was Chris who had the knife and not she. Later, Chris claims that Daphne instigated the fight, egged him on, taunting him that he was too scared to kill someone. Chris says that Daphne, while drunk, often talked of killing an adult because she hates older people, especially her parents.

Daphne's parents claim that, while she has been a burden with her mood swings and volatile behavior, she is still a child and can be helped with proper treatment. They are willing to supplement any state intervention with privately funded psychiatrists. They believe that given this is her first real offense and she is just 15, home confinement with intense treatment is the best course. If Daphne is tried as a juvenile, she can be kept in institutions until she is 17; the sentence could be expanded to age 21, but only if, while in custody, she has a behavior problem and demonstrates conclusive need for further secure treatment.

- Should the case of Daphne A. be dealt with in the juvenile court, even though the maximum possible sentence she can receive is two to six years?

- If not, over what kind of cases should the juvenile court have jurisdiction?

- How does the concept of *parens patriae* apply to cases such as Daphne A.?

- If you believe that the juvenile court is not equipped to handle cases of extremely violent youth, then should it be abolished?

To read stories describing the actual case, go to
http://www.echonyc.com/~hearst/otr/ma/archive/featherstone2.html
http://www.news-star.com/stories/040398/new_forgive.html
For an up-to-date list of Web links, go to http://info.wadsworth.com/siegel

In recent years many communities have seen significant declines in serious violent crime among teenagers. But even as rates of urban juvenile delinquency are declining, hundreds of thousands of cases like Daphne's (which is based on an actual New York City case) have rekindled debate over the juvenile justice system. According to some experts, the country has a long way to go before claiming victory over juvenile delinquency.[1] What kinds of punishment can society use to fit these crimes? How can such crimes be prevented? What reforms must be made in the juvenile justice system to rehabilitate adolescents such as Daphne? Or should we even try? Formulating effective policies to meet such challenges requires a clear understanding of the history and development of juvenile justice.

This chapter begins with a discussion of the major social changes leading to creation of the first modern juvenile court in Chicago in 1899. We then cover the reform efforts of the twentieth century, including the movement to grant children the procedural rights typically given to adult offenders. This discussion includes descriptions of some landmark Supreme Court decisions that have influenced present-day juvenile justice procedures.

The second part of this chapter presents an overview of the contemporary juvenile justice system and the various philosophies, processes, organizations, and legal constraints that dominate its operations. The chapter describes the process that takes a youthful offender through a series of steps, beginning with arrest and concluding with reentry into society. What happens to young people who violate the law? Do they have legal rights? How are they helped? How are they punished? Should juvenile killers be released from custody prior to their 18th birthday? Should the goal of the system be rehabilitation or punishment?

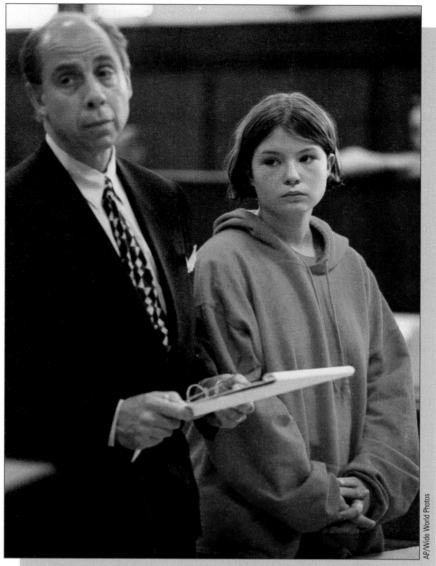

THE OPENING SCENARIO is based on a true story. Fifteen-year-old Daphne Abdela was a product of some of New York City's best private schools. Always in trouble, she had poor self-control, was overly self-conscious about her weight, and had a drinking problem. On March 11, 1998, Daphne pleaded guilty to manslaughter in the death of a drinking companion in Central Park. She received a sentence of 3⅓ to 10 years in prison.

To help address such questions, we have included a discussion of the similarities and differences between the adult and juvenile justice systems. This discussion draws attention to the principle that children are treated separately. By segregating delinquent children from adult offenders, society has placed greater importance on the delinquent being a *child* rather than being a *criminal*. Consequently, rehabilitation rather than punishment has traditionally been the goal. Today, with children committing more serious crimes, the juvenile justice system is having great difficulty handling these offenders.

In the final section, we discuss the need for a comprehensive juvenile justice strategy and the role of the federal government in juvenile justice reform—the key element in funding state juvenile justice and delinquency prevention efforts.

MC MicroCase® CORPORATION

Go to the Siegel/Welsh/Senna *Juvenile Delinquency* book-specific Web site for MicroCase exercises about this material:

http://info.wadsworth.com/siegel

A CLOSER VIEW
Child welfare is still an important social goal in contemporary society. Use it as a subject guide on InfoTrac College Edition to learn more about current efforts.

Urbanization

To learn more about this era, go to the Library of Congress Web page devoted to American history at *http://www.americaslibrary.gov/cgi-bin/page.cgi* For an up-to-date list of Web links, go to *http://info.wadsworth.com/siegel*

A CLOSER VIEW
To learn more about the growth of urbanization and its effect on society, use it as a keyword on InfoTrac College Edition.

At the beginning of the nineteenth century, delinquent, neglected, and runaway children in the United States were treated the same as adult criminal offenders.[2] Like children in England, when convicted of crimes they received harsh sentences similar to those imposed on adults. The adult criminal code applied to children, and no juvenile court existed.

Through the early nineteenth century, various pieces of legislation were introduced to humanize criminal procedures for children. The concept of probation, introduced in Massachusetts in 1841, was geared toward helping young people avoid imprisonment. Many books and reports written during this time heightened public interest in juvenile care.

Despite this interest, no special facilities existed for the care of youths in trouble with the law, nor were there separate laws or courts to control their behavior. Youths who committed petty crimes, such as stealing or vandalism, were viewed as wayward children or victims of neglect and were placed in community asylums or homes. Youths who were involved in more serious crimes were subject to the same punishments as adults—imprisonment, whipping, or death.

Several events led to reforms and nourished the eventual development of the juvenile justice system: (1) urbanization, (2) the child saving movement and growing interest in the concept of *parens patriae,* and (3) development of institutions for the care of delinquent and neglected children.

Especially during the first half of the nineteenth century, the United States experienced rapid population growth, primarily due to an increased birthrate and expanding immigration. The rural poor and immigrant groups were attracted to urban commercial centers that promised jobs in manufacturing. In 1790, 5 percent of the population lived in cities. By 1850, the share of the urban population had increased to 15 percent; it jumped to 40 percent in 1900, and 51 percent in 1920.[3] New York had more than quadrupled its population in the 30-year stretch between 1825 and 1855—from 166,000 in 1825 to 630,000 in 1855.[4]

Urbanization gave rise to increased numbers of young people at risk, who overwhelmed the existing system of work and training. To accommodate destitute youths, local jurisdictions developed poorhouses (almshouses) and workhouses. The poor, the insane, the diseased, and vagrant and destitute children were housed there in crowded and unhealthy conditions.

By the late eighteenth century, the family's ability to exert control over children began to be questioned. Villages developed into urban commercial centers, and work began to center around factories, not the home. Children of destitute families left home or were cast loose to make out as best they could; wealthy families could no longer absorb vagrant youth as apprentices or servants.[5] Chronic poverty became an American dilemma. The affluent began to voice concern over the increase in the number of people in what they considered the "dangerous classes"—the poor, single, criminal, mentally ill, and unemployed.

Urbanization and industrialization also generated the belief that certain segments of the population (youths in urban areas, immigrants) were susceptible to the influences of their decaying environment. The children of these classes were considered a group that might be "saved" by a combination of state and community intervention.[6] Intervention in the lives of these so-called dangerous classes became acceptable for wealthy, civic-minded citizens. Such efforts included *settlement houses,* a term used around the turn of the twentieth century to describe shelters, or nonsecure residential facilities for vagrant children.

Child Saving Movement

To read more about the child savers, go to http://www.ncjrs.org/criminal_justice2000/vol_2/02b2.pdf

For an up-to-date list of Web links, see http://info.wadsworth.com/siegel

The problems generated by urban growth sparked interest in the welfare of the "new" Americans, whose arrival fueled this expansion. In 1816, prominent New Yorkers formed the Society for the Prevention of Pauperism. Although they concerned themselves with attacking taverns, brothels, and gambling parlors, they also were concerned that the moral training of children of the dangerous classes was inadequate. Soon other groups concerned with the plight of poor children began to form. Their focus was on extending government control over youthful activities (drinking, vagrancy, and delinquency) that had previously been left to private or family control.

These activists became known as *child savers*. Prominent among them were penologist Enoch Wines; Judge Richard Tuthill; Lucy Flowers, of the Chicago Women's Association; Sara Cooper, of the National Conference of Charities and Corrections; and Sophia Minton, of the New York Committee on Children.[7] Poor children could become a financial burden, and the child savers believed these children presented a threat to the moral fabric of society. Child saving organizations influenced state legislatures to enact laws giving courts the power to commit children who were runaways or criminal offenders to specialized institutions.

House of Refuge

House of Refuge A care facility developed by the child savers to protect potential criminal youths by taking them off the street and providing a family-like environment.

The most prominent of the care facilities developed by child savers was the **House of Refuge**.[8] Its creation was effected by prominent Quakers and influential political leaders, such as Cadwallader Colden and Stephen Allen. In 1816, they formed the Society for the Prevention of Pauperism, which was devoted to the concept of protecting indigent youths who were at risk to crime by taking them off the streets and reforming them in a family-like environment.

The first House of Refuge, constructed in New York City, was the product of their reform efforts. Though privately managed, the state legislature began providing funds, partly through a head tax on arriving transatlantic passengers and seamen, plus the proceeds from license fees for New York City's taverns, theaters, and circuses. These revenue sources were deemed appropriate, since supporters blamed immigration, intemperance, and commercial entertainment for juvenile crime!

The reformatory opened January 1, 1825, with only six boys and three girls, but within the first decade of its operation 1,678 inmates were admitted. Most kids were sent because of vagrancy and petty crimes and were sentenced or committed indefinitely until they reached adulthood. Originally, the institution accepted inmates from across the state of New York, but when a Western House of Refuge was opened in Rochester, New York, in 1849, residents came mostly from the New York City environs.

Once a resident, the adolescent's daily schedule was devoted for the most part to supervised labor, which was regarded as beneficial to education and discipline. Inmate labor also supported operating expenses for the reformatory. Male inmates worked in shops that produced brushes, cane chairs, brass nails, and shoes. The female inmates sewed uniforms, did laundry, and carried out other domestic work. A badge system was used to segregate inmates according to their behavior. Although students received rudimentary educational skills, greater emphasis was placed on evangelical religious instruction; non-Protestant clergy were excluded. The reformatory had the authority to bind out inmates through indenture agreements to private employers; most males were farmworkers and females domestic laborers.

The Refuge Movement Spreads When the House of Refuge opened, the majority of children admitted were status offenders placed there because of vagrancy or neglect. Children were placed in the institution by court order, sometimes over parents' objections. Their length of stay depended on need, age, and skill. Critics complained that the institution was run like a prison, with strict discipline and absolute separation of the sexes. Such a harsh program drove many children to run away, and the House of Refuge was forced to take a more lenient approach. Despite criticism, the concept enjoyed expanding popularity. In 1826, the Boston City Council founded the House of Reformation for juvenile offenders.[9] The courts committed children found guilty of criminal violations, or found to be beyond the control of their parents, to these schools. Because the child savers considered parents of delinquent children to be as guilty as convicted offenders, they sought to have the reform schools establish control over the children. Refuge managers believed they were preventing poverty and crime by separating destitute and delinquent children from their parents and placing them in an institution.[10]

The earliest institutions resembled the New York House of Refuge and housed a small number of children in relatively small buildings. But by the 1850s, the number of incarcerated children began to climb, resulting in the construction of larger institutions removed from the urban environment. For example, in New York the number of youthful residents expanded from 9 at the outset to more than 1,000 housed on Randall's Island in the East River in an institution indistinguishable from an adult prison.[11]

Despite ongoing criticism and scandal, the Houses of Refuge hung on for more than 100 years. After the Civil War, the urban Refuge began to be replaced by state institutions located in rural areas. In 1935, the institution on Randall's Island closed forever.

Development of Juvenile Institutions

Children's Aid Society Child saving organization that took children from the streets of large cities and placed them with farm families on the prairie.

orphan trains The name for trains in which urban youths were sent West by the Children's Aid Society for adoption with local farm couples.

State intervention in the lives of children continued well into the twentieth century. The child savers influenced state and local governments to create special institutions, called *reform schools,* which would house delinquent youths who would have otherwise been sent to adult prisons. The first institutions opened in Westboro, Massachusetts, in 1848 and in Rochester, New York, in 1849.[12] Institutional programs began in Ohio in 1850 and in Maine, Rhode Island, and Michigan in 1906. The Houses of Refuge began to be replaced by rural facilities, which used cottages to house residents rather than large prisonlike facilities. In New York, for example, the legislature authorized a State Training School for Boys at Warwick for inmates under 16, and the State Vocational School at Coxsackie for those 16 to 19.[13]

Children spent their days working in the institution, learning a trade where possible, and receiving some basic education. They were racially and sexually segregated, discipline was harsh, and their physical care was poor. Some were labeled as criminal, but were in reality abused and neglected. They too were subject to harsh working conditions, strict discipline, and intensive labor.[14] Although some people viewed reform schools as humanitarian answers to poorhouses and prisons, many were opposed to such programs.

Children's Aid Society

To read more about the life of Charles Loring Brace, go to http://longman.awl.com/nash/primarysource_21_4.htm
For an up-to-date list of Web links, go to http://info.wadsworth.com/siegel

As an alternative to secure correctional facilities, New York philanthropist Charles Loring Brace helped develop the **Children's Aid Society** in 1853.[15] Brace's formula for dealing with delinquent youths was to rescue them from the harsh environment of the city and provide them with temporary shelter.

Deciding there were simply too many needy children to care for in New York City, and believing the urban environment was injurious to children, Brace devised what he called his *placing-out plan* to send these children to western farms where they could be cared for and find a home. They were placed on what became known as **orphan trains,** which made preannounced stops in western farming communities. Families wishing to take in children would meet the train, be briefly introduced to

THIS ENGRAVING depicts the work of the Children's Aid Society, founded in 1853.

Stock Montage, Inc.

A CLOSER VIEW

Use *orphan train* as a key term on InfoTrac College Edition.

the passengers, and leave with one of the children. Brace's plan was activated in 1854 and very soon copied by other childcare organizations. Though the majority of the children benefited from the plan and did find a new life, others were less successful, and some were exploited and harmed by the experience. By 1930, political opposition to Brace's plan, coupled with the negative effects of the economic depression, spelled the end of the orphan trains, but not before 150,000 children were placed in rural homesteads.

Society for the Prevention of Cruelty to Children (SPCC)

Society for the Prevention of Cruelty to Children (SPCC) First established in 1874, these organizations protected children subjected to cruelty and neglect at home or at school.

In 1874, the first **Society for the Prevention of Cruelty to Children (SPCC)** was established in New York. Agents of the society were granted power to remove children from their homes and arrest anyone who interfered with their work; they also assisted the court in making placement decisions.[16] By 1890, the society controlled the intake and disposition of an annual average of 15,000 poor and neglected children. By 1900 there were 300 such societies in the United States.[17]

Leaders of the SPCCs were concerned that abused boys would become lower-class criminals and that mistreated young girls might become sexually promiscuous women. A growing crime rate and concern about a rapidly changing population served to swell SPCC membership. In addition, these organizations protected children who had been subjected to cruelty and neglect at home and at school.

SPCC groups influenced state legislatures to pass statutes protecting children from parents who did not provide them with adequate food and clothing or made them beg or work in places where liquor was sold.[18] Criminal penalties were created for negligent parents, and provisions were established for removing children from the home. In some states, agents of the SPCC could actually arrest abusive parents; in others, they would inform the police about suspected abuse cases and accompany officers when they made an arrest.[19]

The organization and control of SPCCs varied widely. For example, the New York City SPCC was a city agency supported by municipal funds. It conducted investigations of delinquent and neglected children for the court. In contrast, the Boston SPCC emphasized delinquency prevention and worked with social welfare groups; the Philadelphia SPCC emphasized family unity and was involved with other charities.[20]

Were They Really Child Savers?

Debate continues over the true objectives of the early child savers. Some historians conclude that they were what they seemed—concerned citizens motivated by humanitarian ideals.[21] Modern scholars, however, have reappraised the child saving movement. In *The Child Savers*, Anthony Platt paints a picture of representatives of the ruling class who were galvanized by immigrants and the urban poor to take action to preserve their own way of life.[22] He claims

> *The child savers should not be considered humanists: (1) their reforms did not herald a new system of justice but rather expedited traditional policies which had been informally developed during the nineteenth century; (2) they implicitly assumed the natural dependence of adolescents and created a special court to impose sanctions on premature independence and behavior unbecoming to youth; (3) their attitudes toward delinquent youth were largely paternalistic and romantic but their commands were backed up by force; (4) they promoted correctional programs requiring longer terms of imprisonment, longer hours of labor, and militaristic discipline, and the inculcation of middle class values and lower class skills.[23]*

Other critical thinkers followed Platt in finding that child saving was motivated more by self-interest than by benevolence. For example, Randall Shelden and Lynn Osborne traced the child saving movement in Memphis, Tennessee, and found that its leaders were a small group of upper-class citizens who desired to control the behavior and lifestyles of lower-class youth. The outcome was ominous. Most cases petitioned to the juvenile court (which opened in 1910) were for petty crimes and status offenses, yet 25 percent of the youths were committed to some form of incarceration; more than 96 percent of the actions with which females were charged were status offenses.[24]

In summary, these scholars believe that the reformers applied the concept of *parens patriae* for their own purposes, including the continuance of middle- and upper-class values and the furtherance of a child labor system consisting of marginal and lower-class skilled workers.

In the course of "saving children" by turning them over to houses of refuge, the basic legal rights of children were violated: Children were simply not granted the same constitutional protections as adults.

A Century of Juvenile Justice

Although reform groups continued to lobby for government control over children, the committing of children under the doctrine of *parens patriae* without due process of law began to be questioned. Could the state incarcerate children who had not violated the criminal law? Should children be held in the same facilities that housed adults? Serious problems challenged the effectiveness of the existing system: Institutional deficiencies, the absence of due process for poor, ignorant, and noncriminal delinquents, and the treatment of these children by inadequate private organizations all spurred the argument that a juvenile court should be established.

Increasing delinquency rates also hastened the development of a juvenile court. Theodore Ferdinand's analysis of the Boston juvenile court found that in the 1820s and 1830s very few juveniles were charged with serious offenses. By 1850, juvenile delinquency was the fastest growing component of the local crime problem.[25] Ferdinand concluded that the flow of juvenile cases strengthened the argument that juveniles needed their own court.

The Illinois Juvenile Court Act and Its Legacy

The child saving movement culminated in passage of the Illinois Juvenile Court Act of 1899, which established the nation's first independent juvenile court. Interpretations of its intentions differ, but unquestionably the Illinois Juvenile Court Act established juvenile delinquency as a legal concept. For the first time the distinction was made between children who were neglected and those who were delinquent. Delinquent children were those under the age of 16 who violated the law. Most important, the act established a court and a probation program specifically for children. In addition, the legislation allowed children to be committed to institutions and reform programs under the control of the state. The key provisions of the act were these:

- A separate court was established for delinquent and neglected children.
- Special procedures were developed to govern the adjudication of juvenile matters.
- Children were to be separated from adults in courts and in institutional programs.
- Probation programs were to be developed to assist the court in making decisions in the best interests of the state and the child.

Following passage of the Illinois Juvenile Court Act, similar legislation was enacted throughout the nation. The special courts these laws created maintained jurisdiction over predelinquent (neglected and dependent) and delinquent children. Juvenile court jurisdiction was based primarily on a child's noncriminal actions and status, not strictly on a violation of criminal law. The *parens patriae* philosophy predominated, ushering in a form of personalized justice that still did not provide juvenile offenders with the full array of constitutional protections available to adult criminal offenders. The court's process was paternalistic rather than adversarial. Attorneys were not required, and hearsay evidence, inadmissible in criminal trials, was admissible in the adjudication of juvenile offenders. Verdicts were based on a *preponderance of the evidence* instead of the stricter standard used by criminal courts, *beyond a reasonable doubt*, and children were often not granted any right to appeal their convictions.

The principles motivating the Illinois reformers were these:

1. Children should not be held as accountable as adult transgressors;
2. The objective of the juvenile justice system is to treat and rehabilitate rather than punish;
3. Disposition should be predicated on analysis of the youth's special circumstances and needs; and
4. The system should avoid the trappings of the adult criminal process with all its confusing rules and procedures.

This was a major event in the juvenile justice movement. Its significance was such that by 1917, juvenile courts had been established in all but three states.

The Legacy of Illinois   Just what were the ramifications of passage of the Illinois Juvenile Court Act? The traditional interpretation is that the reformers were genuinely motivated to pass legislation that would serve the best interests of the child. U.S. Supreme Court Justice Abe Fortas took this position in the landmark 1967 *In re Gault* case:

> *The early reformers were appalled by adult procedures and penalties and by the fact that children could be given long prison sentences and mixed in jails with hardened criminals. They were profoundly convinced that society's duty to the child could not be confined by the concept of justice alone.... The child—essentially good, as they saw it—was to be made to feel that he was the object of the state's care and solicitude, not that he was under arrest or on trial.... The idea of crime and punishment was to be abandoned. The child was to be treated and rehabilitated and the procedures from apprehension through institutionalization were to be clinical rather than punitive.*[26]

The child savers believed that children were influenced by their environments. Society was to be concerned with what their problems were and how these problems could be handled in the interests of the children and the state.

Nowhere can this procedural informality be seen more fully than in the Denver Juvenile Court presided over by Judge Benjamin Lindsey.[27] He viewed the children who came before him as "his boys" who were fundamentally good human beings led astray by their social and psychological environment. While Lindsey had no specific statutory authority to do so, he adopted a social worker–friend approach to the children who had been petitioned to court. The need for formal adjudication of the charges was unimportant compared to an effort to treat and rehabilitate these wayward youth. He condemned the criminal justice system, which he saw operating as a "medieval torture chamber" that victimized children.[28]

The Early Juvenile Court   The major functions of the juvenile justice system were to prevent juvenile crime and to rehabilitate juvenile offenders. The roles of the judge and the probation staff were to diagnose the child's condition and prescribe programs to alleviate it; judgments about children's actions and consideration for their constitutional rights were secondary.

By the 1920s, noncriminal behavior in the form of incorrigibility and truancy from school was added to the jurisdiction of many juvenile court systems. Of particular interest was the sexual behavior of young girls, and the juvenile court enforced a strict moral code on working-class girls, not hesitating to incarcerate those who were sexually active.[29] Programs of all kinds, including individualized counseling and institutional care, were used to *cure* juvenile criminality.

By 1925, juvenile courts existed in virtually every jurisdiction in every state. Although the juvenile court concept expanded rapidly, it cannot be said that each state implemented it thoroughly. Some jurisdictions established elaborate juvenile court systems, whereas others passed legislation but provided no services. Some courts had trained juvenile court judges; others had nonlawyers sitting in juvenile cases. Some courts had extensive probation departments; others had untrained probation personnel. In 1920, a U.S. Children's Bureau survey found that only 16 percent of these new juvenile courts held separate calendars or hearings for children's cases or had an officially established probation service, and recorded social information about the children coming through the court. In 1926, it was reported that five out of six of these courts in the United States failed to meet the minimum standards of the Children's Bureau.[30]

Great diversity also marked juvenile institutions. Some maintained a lenient orientation, but others relied on harsh punishments, including beatings, straitjacket restraints, immersion in cold water, and solitary confinement with a diet of bread and water.

These conditions were exacerbated by the rapid growth in the juvenile institutional population. Between 1890 and 1920, the number of institutionalized youths jumped 112 percent, a rise that far exceeded the increase in the total number of adolescents in the United States.[31] Although social workers and court personnel deplored the increased institutionalization of youth, the growth was due in part to the successful efforts by reformers to close poorhouses, thereby creating a need for institutions to house their displaced populations. In addition, the lack of a coherent national policy on needy children allowed private entrepreneurs to fill the void.[32] Although the increase in institutionalization seemed contrary to the goal of rehabilitation, such an approach was preferable to the poorhouse and the streets.

Reforming the System

The Children's Bureau (CB) is the oldest federal agency for children and is located within the United States Department of Health and Human Services' Administration for Children and Families, Administration on Children, Youth and Families. It is responsible for assisting states in the delivery of child welfare services—services designed to protect children and strengthen families. To view their Web site: http://www.acf.dhhs.gov/programs/cb/ For an up-to-date list of Web links, go to http://info.wadsworth.com/siegel

Reform of this system was slow in coming. In 1912, the U.S. Children's Bureau was formed as the first federal child welfare agency. By the 1930s, the bureau began to investigate the state of juvenile institutions and tried to expose some of their more repressive aspects.[33] After World War II, critics such as Paul Tappan and Francis Allen began to identify problems in the juvenile justice system, among which were the neglect of procedural rights and the warehousing of youth in ineffective institutions. Status offenders commonly were housed with delinquents and given sentences that were more punitive than those given to delinquents.[34]

From its origin, the juvenile court system denied children procedural rights normally available to adult offenders. Due-process rights, such as representation by counsel, a jury trial, freedom from self-incrimination, and freedom from unreasonable search and seizure, were not considered essential for the juvenile court system because its primary purpose was not punishment but rehabilitation. However, the dream of trying to rehabilitate children was not achieved. Individual treatment approaches failed, and delinquency rates soared.

Reform efforts, begun in earnest in the 1960s, changed the face of the juvenile justice system. In 1962, New York passed legislation creating a family court system.[35] The new court assumed responsibility for all matters involving family life, with emphasis on delinquent and neglected children. In addition, the legislation established the PINS classification (person in need of supervision). This category included individuals involved in such actions as truancy and incorrigibility. By using labels like PINS and CHINS (children in need of supervision) to establish jurisdiction over children, juvenile courts expanded their role as social agencies. Because noncriminal children were now involved in the juvenile court system to a greater degree, many juvenile courts had to improve their social services. Efforts were made to personalize the system of justice for children. These reforms were soon followed by a due-process revolution, which ushered in an era of procedural rights for court-adjudicated youth.

In the 1960s and 1970s, the U.S. Supreme Court radically altered the juvenile justice system when it issued a series of decisions that established the right of juveniles to receive due process of law.[36] The Court established that juveniles had the same rights as adults in important areas of trial process, including the right to con-

Exhibit 12.1 Leading Constitutional Cases in Juvenile Justice

Kent v. United States (1965) determined that a child has due process rights, such as having an attorney present at waiver hearings.

In re Gault (1967) ruled that a minor has basic due process rights including: (1) notice of the charges with respect to their timeliness and specificity, (2) right to counsel, (3) right to confrontation and cross-examination, (4) privilege against self-incrimination, (5) right to a transcript of the trial record, and (6) right to appellate review.

McKiever v. Pennsylvania (1971) held that trial by jury in a juvenile court's adjudicative stage is not a constitutional requirement.

Breed v. Jones (1975) ruled that a child has the protection of the double-jeopardy clause of the Fifth Amendment and cannot be tried twice for the same crime.

Fare v. Michael C. (1979) held that a child's request to see his probation officer at the time of interrogation did not operate to invoke his Fifth Amendment right to remain silent. According to the Court, the probation officer cannot be expected to offer the type of advice that an accused would expect from an attorney. The landmark *Miranda v. Arizona* case ruled that a request for a lawyer is an immediate revocation of a person's right to silence, but this rule is not applicable for a request to see the probation officer.

Eddings v. Oklahoma (1982) ruled that a defendant's age should be a mitigating factor in deciding whether to apply the death penalty.

Schall v. Martin (1984) upheld a statute allowing for the placement of children in preventive detention before their adjudication. The Court concluded that it was not unreasonable to detain juveniles for their own protection.

New Jersey v. T.L.O. (1985) determined that the Fourth Amendment applies to school searches. The Court adopted a "reasonable suspicion" standard, as opposed to the stricter standard of "probable cause," to evaluate the legality of searches and seizures in a school setting.

Thompson v. Oklahoma (1988) ruled that imposing capital punishment on a juvenile murderer who was 15 years old at the time of the offense violated the Eighth Amendment's constitutional prohibition against cruel and unusual punishment.

Stanford v. Kentucky and *Wilkins v. Missouri* (1989) concluded that the imposition of the death penalty on a juvenile who committed a crime between the ages of 16 and 18 was not unconstitutional and that the Eighth Amendment's cruel and unusual punishment clause did not prohibit capital punishment.

Vernonia School District v. Acton (1995) held that the Fourth Amendment's guarantee against unreasonable searches is not violated by the suspicionless drug testing of all students choosing to participate in interscholastic athletics. The Supreme Court expanded power of public educators to ensure safe learning environments in schools.

United States v. Lopez (1995) ruled that Congress exceeded its authority under the Commerce Clause when it passed the Gun-Free School Zone Act, which made it a federal crime to possess a firearm within 1,000 feet of a school.

Sources: *Kent v. United States,* 383 U.S. 541, 86 S.Ct. 1045, 16 L.Ed.2d 84 (1966); *In re Gault,* 387 U.S. 1; 87 S.Ct. 1248 (1967); *McKeiver v. Pennsylvania,* 403 U.S. 528, 91 S.Ct. 1976 (1971); *Breed v. Jones,* 421 U.S. 519, 95 S.Ct. 1779 (1975); *Fare v. Michael C.,* 442 U.S. 707, 99 S.Ct. 2560 (1979); *Eddings v. Oklahoma,* 455 U.S. 104, 102 S.Ct. 869, 71 L.Ed.2d 1 (1982); *Schall v. Martin,* 467 U.S. 253, 104 S.Ct. 2403 (1984); *New Jersey v. T.L.O.,* 469 U.S. 325, 105 S.Ct. 733 (1985); *Thompson v. Oklahoma,* 487 U.S. 815, 108 S.Ct. 2687, 101 L.Ed.2d 702 (1988); *Stanford v. Kentucky,* 492 U.S. 361, 109 S.Ct. 2969 (1989); *Vernonia School District v. Acton,* 515 U.S. 646, 115 S.Ct. 2386, 132 L.Ed.2d 564 (1995); *Wilkins v. Missouri,* 492 U.S. 361, 109 S.Ct. 2969 (1989); *United States v. Lopez,* 115 S.Ct. 1624 (1995).

front witnesses, notice of charges, and the right to counsel. Exhibit 12.1 illustrates some of the most important legal cases bringing procedural due process to the juvenile justice process.

Federal Commissions In addition to the legal revolution brought about by the Supreme Court, a series of national commissions sponsored by the federal government helped change the shape of juvenile justice. In 1967, the President's Commission on Law Enforcement and the Administration of Justice, organized by President Lyndon Johnson, suggested that the juvenile justice system must provide underprivileged youths with opportunities for success, including jobs and education. The commission also recognized the need to develop effective law enforcement procedures to control hard-core offenders, while at the same time granting them due process. The commission's report acted as a catalyst for passage of the federal Juvenile Delinquency Prevention and Control (JDP) Act of 1968. This law created a Youth Development and Delinquency Prevention Administration, which concentrated on helping states develop new juvenile justice programs, particularly those involving diversion of youth, decriminalization, and decarceration. In 1968, Congress also passed the Omnibus Safe Streets and Crime Control Act.[37] Title I of this law established the **Law Enforcement Assistance Administration (LEAA)** to provide federal funds for improving the adult and juvenile justice systems. In 1972, Congress

Law Enforcement Assistance Administration (LEAA) Unit in the U.S. Department of Justice established by the Omnibus Crime Control and Safe Streets Act of 1968 to administer grants and provide guidance for crime prevention policy and programs.

amended the JDP Act to allow the LEAA to focus its funding on juvenile justice and delinquency prevention programs. State and local governments were required to develop and adopt comprehensive plans to obtain federal assistance.

Because crime continued to receive much publicity, a second effort called the National Advisory Commission on Criminal Justice Standards and Goals was established in 1973 by the Nixon administration.[38] Its report identified such strategies as (1) preventing delinquent behavior, (2) developing diversion activities, (3) establishing dispositional alternatives, (4) providing due process for all juveniles, and (5) controlling violent and chronic delinquents. This commission's recommendations formed the basis for the Juvenile Justice and Delinquency Prevention Act of 1974.[39] This act eliminated the Youth Development and Delinquency Prevention Administration and replaced it with the Office of Juvenile Justice and Delinquency Prevention (OJJDP) within the LEAA. In 1980, the LEAA was phased out, and the OJJDP became an independent agency in the Department of Justice. Throughout the 1970s, its two most important goals were (1) removing juveniles from detention in adult jails, and (2) eliminating the incarceration together of delinquents and status offenders. During this period, the OJJDP stressed the creation of formal diversion and restitution programs.

The latest effort was the Violent Crime Control and Law Enforcement Act of 1994.[40] The largest piece of crime legislation in the history of the United States, it provided 100,000 new police officers and billions of dollars for prisons and prevention programs for both adult and juvenile offenders. A revitalized juvenile justice system would need both a comprehensive strategy to prevent and control delinquency and a consistent program of federal funding.[41]

To read about the Juvenile Justice and Delinquency Prevention Act of 1974, go to *http://ojjdp.ncjrs.org/about/ ojjjact.txt* For an up-to-date list of Web links, go to *http://info.wadsworth.com/siegel*

Juvenile Justice Today

A CLOSER VIEW
How can using status offenses reduce crime in the community? To find out, go to InfoTrac College Edition: Robert J. Girod, "Operation Linebacker: Using Status Offenses to Reduce Crimes in Communities," *The FBI Law Enforcement Bulletin* 68(7):7 (July 1999).

Today the juvenile justice system exercises jurisdiction over two distinct categories of offenders—delinquents and status offenders.[42] *Delinquent children* are those who fall under a jurisdictional age limit, which varies from state to state, and who commit an act in violation of the penal code. *Status offenders* are commonly characterized in state statutes as persons or children in need of supervision (PINS or CHINS). Most states distinguish such behavior from delinquent conduct to reduce the effect of any stigma on children as a result of their involvement with the juvenile court. In addition, juvenile courts generally have jurisdiction over situations involving conduct directed at (rather than committed by) juveniles, such as parental neglect, deprivation, abandonment, and abuse.

The states have also set different maximum ages below which children come under the jurisdiction of the juvenile court. Many states include all children under 18, others set the upper limit at 17, and still others include children under 16.

Some states exclude certain classes of offenders or offenses from the juvenile justice system. For example, youths who commit serious violent offenses such as rape and/or murder may be automatically excluded from the juvenile justice system and treated as adults, on the premise that they stand little chance of rehabilitation within the confines of the juvenile system. Juvenile court judges may also transfer, or *waive*, repeat offenders who they deem untreatable by the juvenile authorities.

Today's juvenile justice system exists in all states by statute. Each jurisdiction has a juvenile code and a special court structure to accommodate children in trouble. Nationwide, the juvenile justice system consists of thousands of public and private agencies, with a total budget amounting to hundreds of millions of dollars. Most of the nation's police agencies have juvenile components, and there are more than 3,000 juvenile courts and about an equal number of juvenile correctional facilities.

Figure 12.1 depicts the numbers of juvenile offenders removed at various stages of the juvenile justice process. These figures do not take into account the large number of children who are referred to community diversion and mental health programs. There are thousands of these programs throughout the nation. This multitude of agencies and

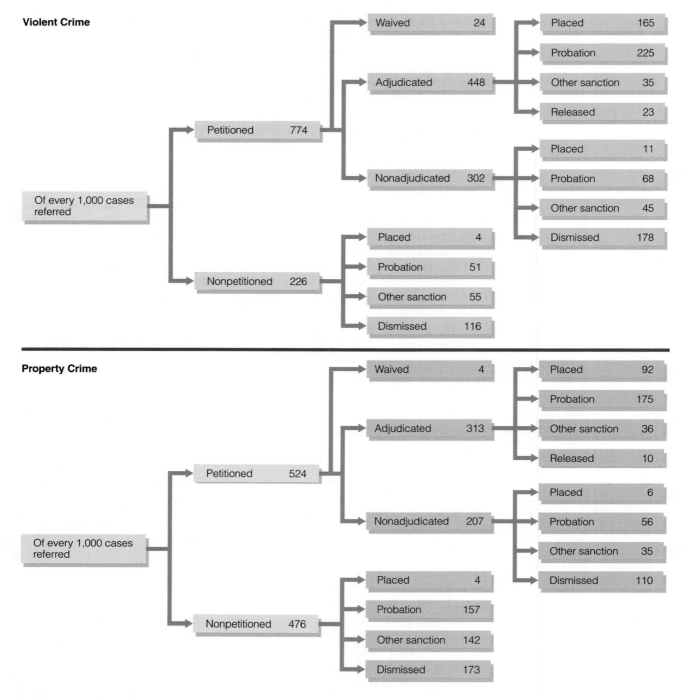

Violent Crime

Of every 1,000 cases referred
- Petitioned 774
  - Waived 24
  - Adjudicated 448
    - Placed 165
    - Probation 225
    - Other sanction 35
    - Released 23
  - Nonadjudicated 302
    - Placed 11
    - Probation 68
    - Other sanction 45
    - Dismissed 178
- Nonpetitioned 226
  - Placed 4
  - Probation 51
  - Other sanction 55
  - Dismissed 116

Property Crime

Of every 1,000 cases referred
- Petitioned 524
  - Waived 4
  - Adjudicated 313
    - Placed 92
    - Probation 175
    - Other sanction 36
    - Released 10
  - Nonadjudicated 207
    - Placed 6
    - Probation 56
    - Other sanction 35
    - Dismissed 110
- Nonpetitioned 476
  - Placed 4
  - Probation 157
  - Other sanction 142
  - Dismissed 173

Note: More than half (57%) of all formally processed cases in 1997 resulted in the youth being adjudicated delinquent. With the exception of criminal homicide, cases involving more serious offenses were more likely to be adjudicated than were other cases. The relatively low likelihood of adjudication for criminal homicide cases is because nearly one-third (31%) of these cases were judicially waived to criminal court for processing. As a result, petitioned criminal homicide cases were the most likely to receive a formal judicial response—either judicial waiver or adjudication.

The likelihood of adjudication also varied within the general offense categories. For example, within person offenses, 61% of petitioned robbery cases were adjudicated in 1997, compared with 51% of petitioned simple assault cases. In general, the more serious the charge, the more likely the case was to result in adjudication.

Figure 12.1
Case Processing of Typical Violent Crime and Property Crime in the Juvenile Justice System
Source: *Juvenile Court Statistics, 1997* (Washington, DC: Office of Juvenile Justice and Delinquency Prevention, 2000).

SOME STATES EXCLUDE CERTAIN CLASSES of offenders or offenses from the juvenile justice system—for example, youths who commit serious violent offenses such as rape and/or murder—while others retain even the most serious cases in the juvenile justice system. Here, 12-year-old Michael Nichols is led from an Arkansas court on July 25, 2000, after a juvenile court judge refused to consider an insanity defense in his case. Nichols was tried on charges of shooting a police officer who stopped him while he was heading toward his school with a shotgun.

juvenile justice process Under the paternal (*parens patriae*) philosophy, juvenile justice procedures are informal and nonadversarial, invoked for the juvenile offender rather than against him or her; a petition instead of a complaint is filed; courts make findings of involvement or adjudication of delinquency instead of convictions; and juvenile offenders receive dispositions instead of sentences.

detention hearing A hearing by a judicial officer of a juvenile court to determine whether a juvenile is to be detained or released while juvenile proceedings are pending in the case.

people dealing with juvenile delinquency has led to the development of what professionals view as an incredibly expansive and complex juvenile justice system.

The Juvenile Justice Process

How are children processed by the juvenile justice system?[43] Most children come into the justice system as a result of contact with a police officer. When a juvenile commits a serious crime, the police are empowered to make an arrest. Less-serious offenses may also require police action, but in these instances, instead of being arrested, the child may be warned or a referral may be made to a social service program. Only about half of all children arrested are referred to the juvenile court. Figure 12.2 outlines the **juvenile justice process**, and a detailed analysis of this process is presented in the next sections.

Police Investigation   When youths commit a crime, police have the authority to investigate the incident and decide whether to release the youths or commit them to the juvenile court. This is often a discretionary decision, based not only on the nature of the offense but also on conditions existing at the time of the arrest. Such factors as the seriousness of the offense, the child's past contacts with the police, and whether the child denies committing the crime determine whether a petition is filed. Juveniles in custody have constitutional rights similar to those of adult offenders. Children are protected against unreasonable search and seizure under the Fourth and Fourteenth Amendments of the Constitution. The Fifth Amendment places limitations on police interrogation procedures.

Detention   If the police decide to file a petition, the child is referred to juvenile court. The primary decision at this point is whether the child should remain in the community or be placed in a detention facility or shelter home. In the past, children were routinely held in detention facilities to await court appearances. Normally, a **detention hearing** is held to determine whether to remand the child to a shelter. At this point, the child has a right to counsel and other procedural safeguards. A child who is not detained is usually released to a parent or guardian. Most state juvenile-court acts provide for a child to return home to await further court action, except when it is necessary to protect the child, when the child presents a serious danger to the public, or when it is not certain that the child will return to court. In many cases the police will refer the child to a community service program instead of filing a formal charge.

Pretrial Procedures   In most jurisdictions, the adjudication process begins with some sort of hearing. At this hearing juvenile court rules normally require that juveniles be informed of their right to a trial, that the plea or admission be voluntary, and that they understand the charges and consequences of the plea. The case will often not be further adjudicated if a child admits to the crime at the initial hearing.

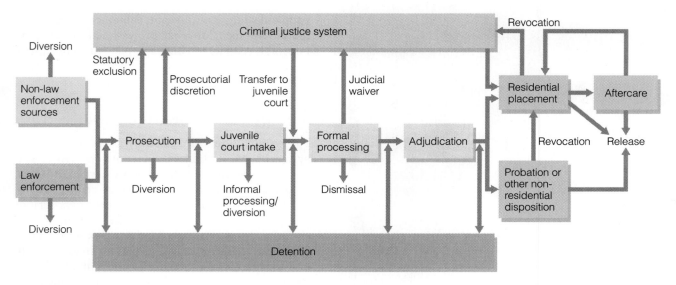

Figure 12.2
Case Flow through the Juvenile Justice Process
Source: This figure can be accessed online through the Office of Juvenile Justice and Delinquency
Prevention at http://www.ojjdp.ncjrs.org/facts/casejpg.html.

adjudicatory hearing The fact-finding process wherein the juvenile court determines whether there is sufficient evidence to sustain the allegations in a petition.

In some cases, youths may be detained at this stage pending a trial. Juveniles who are detained are eligible for bail in a handful of jurisdictions. Plea bargaining may also occur at any stage of the proceedings. A plea bargain is an agreement between the prosecution and the defense by which the juvenile agrees to plead guilty for certain considerations, such as a lenient sentence. This issue is explored more thoroughly in Chapter 14, which discusses pretrial procedures.

If the child denies the allegation of delinquency, an **adjudicatory hearing** or trial is scheduled. Under extraordinary circumstances, a juvenile who commits a serious crime may be transferred or waived to an adult court. Today, most jurisdictions have laws providing for such transfers. Whether such a transfer occurs depends on the type of offense, the youth's prior record, the availability of treatment services, and the likelihood that the youth will be rehabilitated in the juvenile court system.

Adjudication   The trial stage of the juvenile court process is known as adjudication. If the child does not admit guilt at the initial hearing and is not transferred to an adult court, an adjudication hearing is held to determine the facts of the case. The court hears evidence on the allegations in the delinquency petition. This is a trial on the merits (dealing with issues of law and facts), and rules of evidence similar to those of criminal proceedings generally apply. At this stage, the juvenile offender is entitled to many of the procedural guarantees given adult offenders. These include the right to counsel, freedom from self-incrimination, the right to confront and cross-examine witnesses, and, in certain instances, the right to a jury trial. In addition, many states have their own procedures concerning rules of evidence, competence of witnesses, pleadings, and pretrial motions. At the end of the adjudicatory hearing, the court enters a judgment against the juvenile.

bifurcated process The procedure of separating adjudicatory and dispositionary hearings so different levels of evidence can be heard at each.

disposition For juvenile offenders, the equivalent of sentencing for adult offenders; however, juvenile dispositions should be more rehabilitative than retributive.

Disposition   If the adjudication process finds the child delinquent, the court must decide what should be done to treat the child. Most juvenile court acts require a dispositional hearing separate from the adjudication. This two-stage decision is often referred to as a **bifurcated process**. The dispositional hearing is less formal than adjudication. Here, the judge imposes a **disposition** on the offender in light of the offense, the youth's prior record, and his or her family background. The judge can prescribe a wide range of dispositions, ranging from a reprimand to probation to institutional commitment. In theory, the judge's decision serves the best interests of the child, the family, and the community.

Treatment   After disposition in juvenile court, delinquent offenders may be placed in some form of correctional treatment. Probation is the most commonly used formal sentence for juvenile offenders, and many states require that a youth fail on probation before being sent to an institution (unless the criminal act is extremely serious). Probation involves placing the child under the supervision of the juvenile probation department for the purpose of community treatment. The most severe of the statutory dispositions available to the juvenile court involves commitment of the child to an institution. The committed child may be sent to a state training school or a private residential treatment facility. These are usually minimum-security facilities with small populations and an emphasis on treatment and education. Some states, however, maintain facilities with populations of over 1,000 youths. Currently there are more than 100,000 youths in some form of correctional institution.

Some jurisdictions allow for a program of juvenile aftercare or parole. A youth can be paroled from an institution and placed under the supervision of a parole officer. This means that he or she will complete the period of confinement in the community and receive assistance from the parole officer in the form of counseling, school referral, and vocational training.

Juveniles who are committed to programs of treatment and control have a legal right to treatment. States are required to provide suitable rehabilitation programs that include counseling, education, and vocational services. Appellate courts have ruled that if such minimum treatment is not provided, individuals must be released from confinement.

A CLOSER VIEW
To read a review of an innovative approach to treating juvenile offenders, go to InfoTrac College Edition: William Schossler and Mike Powers, "We Make House Calls: A Fresh Approach to Treating Juvenile Offenders," *Corrections Today* 61(2):112 (April 1999).

Conflicting Values in Juvenile Justice

This overview of the juvenile justice process hints at the often-conflicting values at the heart of the system. Efforts to ensure that juveniles are given appropriate treatment are consistent with the doctrine of *parens patriae* that predominated in the first half of the twentieth century. (See Exhibit 12.2 for a time line of ideologies of juvenile justice during the twentieth century.)

Exhibit 12.2   **Time Line of Juvenile Justice Ideology**

Time Frame	Activity
Prior to 1899	Juveniles treated similarly to adult offenders. No distinction by age or capacity to commit criminal acts.
From 1899 to 1950s	Children treated differently, beginning with the Illinois Juvenile Court Act of 1899. By 1925 juvenile court acts are established in virtually every state.
1950s to 1970s	Recognition by experts that the rehabilitation model and the protective nature of *parens patriae* have failed to prevent delinquency.
1960s to 1970s	Constitutional due process is introduced into the juvenile justice system. The concept of punishing children or protecting them under *parens patriae* is under attack by the courts.
1970s to 1980s	Failure of rehabilitation and due-process protections to control delinquency leads to a shift to a crime control and punishment philosophy similar to that of the adult criminal justice system.
Early 1990s	Mixed constitutional protections with some treatment. Uncertain goals and programs; the juvenile justice system relies on punishment and deterrence.
Mid-1990s to present	Attention given to strategy that focuses on reducing the threat of juvenile crime and expanding options for handling juvenile offenders. Emphasis is placed on "what works" and implementing the best intervention and control programs. Effort is made to utilize the restorative justice model, which involves balancing the needs of the victim, the community, and the juvenile.

Over the past century, the juvenile court struggled to provide treatment for juvenile offenders while guaranteeing them constitutional due process. But the system has been so overwhelmed by the increase in violent juvenile crime and family breakdown that some judges and politicians have suggested abolishing the juvenile system. Even those experts who want to retain an independent juvenile court have called for its restructuring. Crime-control advocates want to reduce the court's jurisdiction over juveniles charged with serious crimes and liberalize the prosecutor's ability to try them in adult courts. In contrast, child advocates suggest that the court scale back its judicial role and transfer its functions to community groups and social service agencies.[44]

It is not surprising, then, that the current system reflects a multiplicity of values and viewpoints. In many instances, juveniles are now granted the same due-process rights (for example, competent legal counsel) as adult offenders. There are also efforts under way to reduce the stigma of a juvenile delinquency label by diverting youths from the formal justice process and placing them in treatment-oriented programs. There are also conservative efforts at reform that have led both to a toughening of juvenile sentencing statutes and to restrictions on cases that can be handled in juvenile courts; cases involving extreme violence and multiple recidivists are now routinely sent to the adult system. As a result of these conflicting practices, no single ideology or program dominates the juvenile justice system.

Criminal Justice vs. Juvenile Justice

The components of the adult and juvenile criminal processes are similar. However, the juvenile system has a separate organizational structure. In many communities, juvenile justice is administered by people who bring special skills to the task. Also, more kinds of facilities and services are available to juveniles than to adults.

petition Document filed in juvenile court alleging that a juvenile is a delinquent, a status offender, or a dependent and asking that the court assume jurisdiction over the juvenile.

One concern of the juvenile court reform movement was to make certain that the stigma attached to a convicted offender would not be affixed to young people in juvenile proceedings. Thus, even the language used in the juvenile court differs from that used in the adult criminal court (Exhibit 12.3). Juveniles are not indicted for a crime; they have a **petition** filed against them. Secure pretrial holding facilities are called *detention centers* rather than jails. Similarly, the criminal trial is called a *hearing* in the juvenile justice system. Exhibit 12.4 compares the two systems.

Exhibit 12.3   Comparison of Terms Used in Adult and Juvenile Justice Systems

	Juvenile Terms	Adult Terms
The Person and the Act	Delinquent child	Criminal
	Delinquent act	Crime
Preadjudicatory Stage	Take into custody	Arrest
	Petition	Indictment
	Agree to a finding	Plead guilty
	Deny the petition	Plead not guilty
	Adjustment	Plea bargain
	Detention facility; childcare shelter	Jail
Adjudicatory Stage	Substitution	Reduction of charges
	Adjudication or fact-finding hearing	Trial
	Adjudication	Conviction
Postadjudicatory Stage	Dispositional hearing	Sentencing hearing
	Disposition	Sentence
	Commitment	Incarceration
	Youth development center; treatment; training school	Prison
	Residential childcare facility	Halfway house
	Aftercare	Parole

Similarities between the Juvenile and Adult Justice Systems	Differences between the Juvenile and Adult Justice Systems
Police officers, judges, and correctional personnel use discretion in decision making in both the adult and the juvenile systems.	The primary purpose of juvenile procedures is protection and treatment. With adults, the aim is to punish the guilty.
The right to receive Miranda warnings applies to juveniles as well as to adults.	Age determines the jurisdiction of the juvenile court. The nature of the offense determines jurisdiction in the adult system. Juveniles can be ordered to the criminal court for trial as adults.
Juveniles and adults are protected from prejudicial lineups or other identification procedures.	Juveniles can be apprehended for acts that would not be criminal if committed by an adult (status offenses).
Similar procedural safeguards protect juveniles and adults when they make an admission of guilt.	Juvenile proceedings are not considered criminal; adult proceedings are.
Prosecutors and defense attorneys play equally critical roles in juvenile and adult advocacy.	Juvenile court procedures are generally informal and private. Those of adult courts are more formal and are open to the public.
Juveniles and adults have the right to counsel at most key stages of the court process.	Courts cannot release identifying information about a juvenile to the press, but they must release information about an adult.
Pretrial motions are available in juvenile and criminal court proceedings.	Parents are highly involved in the juvenile process but not in the adult process.
Negotiations and plea bargaining exist for juvenile and adult offenders.	The standard of arrest is more stringent for adults than for juveniles.
Juveniles and adults have a right to a hearing and an appeal.	Juveniles are released into parental custody. Adults are generally given the opportunity for bail.
The standard of evidence in juvenile delinquency adjudications, as in adult criminal trials, is proof beyond a reasonable doubt.	Juveniles have no constitutional right to a jury trial. Adults have this right. Some state statutes provide juveniles with a jury trial.
Juveniles and adults can be placed on probation by the court.	Juveniles can be searched in school without probable cause or a warrant.
Both juveniles and adults can be placed in pretrial detention facilities.	A juvenile's record is generally sealed when the age of majority is reached. The record of an adult is permanent.
Juveniles and adults can be kept in detention without bail if they are considered dangerous.	A juvenile court cannot sentence juveniles to county jails or state prisons; these are reserved for adults.
After trial, both can be placed in community treatment programs.	The U.S. Supreme Court has declared that the Eighth Amendment does not prohibit the death penalty for crimes committed by juveniles ages 16 and 17, but it is not a sentence given to children under age 16.
Juveniles and adults can be required to undergo drug testing.	
Boot camp correctional facilities are now being used for both juveniles and adults.	

A Comprehensive Juvenile Justice Strategy

At a time when much attention is focused on serious juvenile offenders, a comprehensive strategy has been called for to deal with all aspects of juvenile crime. This strategy focuses on crime prevention and expanding options for handling juvenile offenders. It addresses the links between crime and poverty, child abuse, drugs, weapons, and school behavior. Programs are based on a continuum of care that begins in early childhood and progresses through late adolescence. The components of this strategy include (1) prevention in early childhood; (2) intervention for at-risk teenage youths; (3) graduated sanctions to hold juvenile offenders accountable for crimes; (4) proper utilization of detention and confinement; and (5) placement of serious juvenile offenders in adult courts.[45]

Prevention

Research has identified certain factors that may suggest future delinquency. For young children, these include abuse and neglect, domestic violence, educational under-achievement, and health problems. Early childhood services may prevent delinquency and make a child less vulnerable to future criminality. State legislatures are increasingly investing in state-funded early education programs like Head Start to reduce juvenile crime, and Smart Start is designed to make certain children are healthy before starting school. Home-visiting programs target families at risk because of child abuse and neglect. Chapter 11 discusses these programs in greater detail.

Intervention

Many jurisdictions are developing new intervention programs for teenage youths. An example is the Big Brother/Big Sister program, which matches a volunteer adult with a youngster. More and more cities are finding that night curfews can reduce gang violence and vandalism. Curfews may also contribute to a feeling of safety among residents in high-crime neighborhoods. Efforts are also being made to deter young people from becoming involved with gangs, because gang members ordinarily have higher rates of serious violent behavior.

Graduated Sanctions

Graduated sanction programs for juveniles are another solution being explored by states across the country. Types of graduated sanctions include (1) immediate sanctions for nonviolent offenders; (2) intermediate sanctions such as probation and electronic monitoring, which target repeat minor offenders and first-time serious offenders; and (3) secure institutional care, which is reserved for repeat serious offenders and violent offenders. A survey conducted on more than 3,000 intervention programs found that about 425 of these programs showed success in juvenile treatment and control.[46]

Institutional Programs

Another key to a comprehensive strategy is improving institutional programs. Many experts believe juvenile incarceration is overused, particularly for nonviolent offenders. That is why the concept of deinstitutionalization—removing as many youths from secure confinement as possible—was established by the Juvenile Justice and Delinquency Act of 1974. Considerable research supports the fact that warehousing juveniles without proper treatment does little to deter criminal behavior. The most effective secure corrections programs are those that provide individual services for a small number of participants.

Alternative Courts

drug courts Courts whose focus is providing treatment for youths accused of drug-related acts.

teen courts Courts that make use of peer juries to decide nonserious delinquency cases.

New venues of juvenile justice that provide special services to youth while helping to alleviate the case flow problems that plague overcrowded juvenile courts are being implemented around the United States. For example, there are more than 40 juvenile **drug courts,** which have jurisdiction over the burgeoning number of cases involving substance abuse and trafficking. The aim is to place nonviolent first offenders into intensive treatment programs rather than placing them in a custodial institution. The Policy and Practice box entitled "Teen Courts" discusses the alternative of **teen courts.**

Teen Courts

To relieve overcrowding and provide an alternative to traditional forms of juvenile courts, more than 300 jurisdictions are now experimenting with teen courts. These differ from other juvenile justice programs because young people rather than adults determine the disposition in a case. Cases handled in these courts typically involve young juveniles (ages 10 to 15) with no prior arrest records, who are being charged with minor law violations (shoplifting, vandalism, and disorderly conduct). Typically, young offenders are asked to volunteer to have their case heard in a teen court instead of the more formal court of the traditional juvenile justice system.

As in a regular juvenile court, teen court defendants may go through an intake process, a preliminary review of charges, a court hearing, and sentencing. In a teen court, however, other young people are responsible for much of the process. Charges may be presented to the court by a 15-year-old "prosecutor." Defendants may be represented by a 16-year-old "defense attorney." Other youths may serve as jurors, court clerks, and bailiffs. In some teen courts, a youth "judge" (or panel of youth judges) may choose the best disposition or sanction for each case. In a few teen courts, youths even determine whether the facts in a case have been proven by the prosecutor (similar to a finding of guilt). Offenders are often ordered to pay restitution or perform community service. Some teen courts require offenders to write formal apologies to their victims; others require offenders to serve on a subsequent teen court jury. Many courts use other innovative dispositions, such as requiring offenders to attend classes designed to improve their decision-making skills, enhance their awareness of victims, and deter them from future theft.

Though decisions are made by juveniles, adults are also involved in teen courts. They often administer the programs, and they are usually responsible for essential functions such as budgeting, planning, and personnel. In many programs, adults supervise the courtroom activities, and they often coordinate the community service placements, where youths work to fulfill the terms of their dispositions. In some programs, adults act as the judges while teens serve as attorneys and jurors.

Proponents of teen court argue that the process takes advantage of one of the most powerful forces in the life of an adolescent—the desire for peer approval and the reaction to peer pressure. According to this argument, youths respond better to prosocial peers than to adult authority figures. Thus, teen courts are seen as a potentially effective alternative to traditional juvenile courts that are staffed with paid professionals such as lawyers, judges, and probation officers. Teen court advocates also point out that the benefits extend beyond defendants. Teen courts may benefit the volunteer youth attorneys and judges, who probably learn more about the legal system than they ever could in a classroom. The presence of a teen court may also encourage the entire community to take a more active role in responding to juvenile crime. In sum, teen courts offer at least four potential benefits:

1. *Accountability:* Teen courts may help to ensure that young offenders are held accountable for their illegal behavior, even when their offenses are relatively minor and would not likely result in sanctions from the traditional juvenile justice system.

2. *Timeliness:* An effective teen court can move young offenders from arrest to sanctions within a matter of days rather than the months that may pass with traditional juvenile courts. This rapid response may increase the positive impact of court sanctions, regardless of their severity.

3. *Cost savings:* Teen courts usually depend heavily on youth and adult volunteers. If managed properly, they may handle a substantial number of offenders at relatively little cost to the community.

4. *Community cohesion:* A well-structured and expansive teen court program may affect the entire community by increasing public appreciation of the legal system, enhancing community-court relationships, encouraging greater respect for the law among youth, and promoting volunteerism among both adults and youth.

The teen court movement is just beginning, and its effectiveness is still a matter of debate. But currently there are over 300 of these courts in operation around the United States. Recent evaluations of teen courts have found that they did not "widen the net" of justice by handling cases that in the absence of the peer court would have been subject to a lesser level of processing. However, research by Kevin Minor and his associates of teen courts in Kentucky, and by Paige Harrison and her colleagues in New Mexico, indicates that recidivism levels range from 25 percent to 30 percent. Considering that these cases typically involve offenses of only moderate seriousness, the findings do not suggest that the program can play a significant role in reducing teenage crime rates.

Critical Thinking

1. Could teen courts be used to try serious criminal acts such as burglary and robbery?
2. Is a conflict of interest created when teens judge the behavior of other teens? Does the fact that they themselves may one day become defendants in a teen court influence decision making?

InfoTrac College Edition Research

To read more about teen courts, go to Kathiann M. Kowalski, "Courtroom Justice for Teens—by Teens" *Current Health 2,* a Weekly Reader publication, vol. 25(8):29 (April 1999).

Sources: Jeffrey A. Butts and Janeen Buck, "Teen Courts: A Focus on Research," *Juvenile Justice Bulletin* October (Washington, DC: Office of Juvenile Justice and Delinquency Prevention, 2000); Kevin Minor, James Wells, Irinia Soderstrom, Rachel Bingham, and Deborah Williamson, "Sentence Completion and Recidivism among Juveniles Referred to Teen Courts," *Crime and Delinquency* 45:467–80 (1999); Paige Harrison, James Maupin, and G. Larry Mays, "Are Teen Courts an Answer to Our Delinquency Problems?" *Juvenile and Family Court Journal* 51:27–33 (2000); Paige Harrison, James R. Maupin, and G. Larry Mays, "Teen Court: An Examination of Processes and Outcomes, *Crime and Delinquency,* 47:243–64 (2001).

Future of Juvenile Justice

The future of the juvenile court is now being debated. Some experts, including Barry Feld, believe that over the years the juvenile justice system has taken on more of the characteristics of the adult courts; he refers to this as the "criminalizing" of the juvenile court.[47]

Robert Dawson suggests that because the legal differences between the juvenile and criminal systems are narrower than they ever have been, it may be time to abolish the juvenile court.[48] This value conflict has led some experts to advocate the actual abolition of the juvenile court, a topic discussed in the accompanying Policy and Practice box.

These concerns reflect the change that has been ongoing in the juvenile justice system. There has been a nationwide effort to modify the system in response to the public's perceived fear of predatory juvenile offenders and the reaction to high-profile cases such as the Columbine tragedy. As a result, states have begun to institute policies that critics believe undermine the true purpose of the juvenile court movement.[49] Some have made it easier to transfer children to the adult courts. During the past five years, at least four states lowered the age limit for transfer to adult court, seven have added crimes, and four added or modified prior-record provisions. As a result, more juvenile offenders are being sentenced as adults and incarcerated in adult prisons.[50] Getting tough on juvenile crime is the primary motivation for moving cases to the adult criminal justice system. Some commentators argue that transferring juveniles is a statement that juvenile crime is taken seriously by society; others believe the fear of being transferred serves as a deterrent.[51] Some states, such as Arizona, have initiated legislation that significantly restricts eligibility for juvenile justice processing and criminalizing acts that heretofore would have fallen under the jurisdiction of the juvenile court (Exhibit 12.5).[52]

A CLOSER VIEW

To read more about Feld's views, go to InfoTrac College Edition: Barry C. Feld, "Abolish the Juvenile Court: Youthfulness, Criminal Responsibility, and Sentencing Policy," *Journal of Criminal Law and Criminology* 88(1):68–136 (Fall 1997).

PEER COURTS are becoming a popular alternative to traditional juvenile courts. Here, youth peer court prosecutor Dante Ballensky, a freshman at Mazama High School, confers with David Schutt, the court's judge and a Klamath County deputy district attorney, during a session of court in Klamath Falls, Oregon, on June 26, 2000.

Abolish the Juvenile Court?

In an important work, *Bad Kids: Race and the Transformation of the Juvenile Court,* legal expert Barry Feld makes the rather controversial suggestion that the juvenile court system should be discontinued and/or replaced by an alternative method of justice. He suggests that the current structure makes it almost impossible for the system to fulfill or achieve the purpose for which it was originally intended.

Feld maintains that the juvenile court was developed in an effort to create a more lenient atmosphere and process than the one used against adult criminals. Although a worthwhile goal, the juvenile court system was doomed to failure even from the beginning, because it was thrown into the role of providing child welfare at the same time that it was an instrument of law enforcement. These two missions are often at cross-purposes. During its history, various legal developments have further undermined its purpose—most notably the *In re Gault* ruling, which ultimately led to juveniles receiving similar legal protections as adults and led to children being treated like adults in all respects. The juvenile court's vision of leniency was further undercut by the fear and consequent racism created by postwar migration and economic trends that led to the development of large enclaves of poor and underemployed African Americans living in northern cities. Then in the 1980s, the sudden rise in gang membership, gun violence, and homicide committed by juveniles further undermined the juvenile court mission and resulted in legislation that created mandatory sentences for juvenile offenders and mandatory waiver to the adult court. As a result, the focus of the court has been on dealing with the offense rather than treating the offender. In Feld's words, the juvenile court has become a "deficient second-rate criminal court." The welfare and rehabilitative purposes of the juvenile court have been subordinated to its role of law enforcement agent.

Can juvenile courts be reformed? Feld maintains that it is impossible because of their conflicting purposes and shifting priorities. The money spent on serving the court and its large staff would be better spent on child welfare, which would target a larger audience and prevent children's antisocial acts before they occur. In lieu of juvenile court, youths who violate the law should receive full procedural protections in the criminal court system. The special protections given youths in the juvenile court could be provided by altering the criminal law and recognizing age as a factor in the creation of criminal liability. Because youths have had a limited opportunity to develop self-control, their criminal liability should also be curtailed or restricted.

Is Feld's rather dour assessment of the juvenile court valid, and should it in fact be abolished? Not so, according to John Johnson Kerbs, who suggests that Feld makes assumptions that may not be wedded to the reality of the American legal system. First, Kerbs finds that it is naïve to assume the criminal courts can provide the same or greater substantive and procedural protections as the juvenile court. Many juvenile court defendants are indigent, especially those coming from the minority community, and it may be impossible for them to obtain adequate legal defense in the adult system. Second, Feld's assumption that criminal courts will take a defendant's age into close consideration may be illusory. In this get-tough era, it is likely that criminal courts will provide harsher sentences, and the brunt of these draconian sentences will fall squarely on the shoulders of minority youth. Research efforts routinely show that African American adults are unduly punished in adult courts. Sending juvenile offenders to these venues will most likely further enmesh them in an already unfair system. Finally, Kerbs finds that the treatment benefits of the juvenile courts should not be overlooked or abandoned. There is ample research, he maintains, that shows that juvenile courts can create lower recidivism rates than criminal courts. Though the juvenile court is far from perfect and should be improved, it would be foolish to abandon a system aimed at helping kids find alternatives to crime. The alternative is one that produces higher recidivism rates, lowers their future prospects, and has a less than stellar record of providing due process and equal protection for the nation's most needy citizens.

Critical Thinking

1. What's your take on this issue? Should the juvenile court be abolished? Since the trend has been to transfer the most serious criminal cases to the adult court, is there still a purpose for an independent juvenile court? Should the juvenile court be reserved for nonserious first offenders?

InfoTrac College Edition Research

Before you make up your mind about the future of juvenile court, read Joseph V. Penn, "Justice for Youth? A History of the Juvenile and Family Court," *The Brown University Child and Adolescent Behavior Letter* 17(9):1 (September 2001).

Sources: Barry C. Feld, *Bad Kids: Race and the Transformation of the Juvenile Court* (New York: Oxford University Press, 1999); John Johnson Kerbs, "(Un)equal Justice: Juvenile Court Abolition and African Americans," *Annals, AAPSS, 564:*109–25 (1999).

There is other evidence of this get-tough movement. More states are now permitting juvenile court judges to commit a juvenile to the corrections department for a longer period of time than the court's original jurisdiction, typically to age 21. During the past five years, at least five states (Florida, Kansas, Kentucky, Montana, Tennessee) increased the age for extended juvenile court jurisdiction for serious and violent juvenile offenders.[53]

Exhibit 12.5   Recent Changes in the Arizona Juvenile Justice System

In November 1996, voters approved an amendment to the Arizona Constitution known as Proposition 102, the *Stop Juvenile Crime Initiative*. The amendment authorized the legislature or the people to enact by initiative or referendum substantive and procedural laws regarding all proceedings and matters affecting juveniles. The amendment was required so that new transfer laws would not be challenged for being unconstitutional. As a result, Senate Bill 1446, the Juvenile Justice Reform Act, became law effective July 21, 1997, and implemented many provisions of the initiative. Senate Bill 1446 created the following:

- Statutory exclusion for 15-, 16-, or 17-year-olds charged with violent crime (murder, sexual assault, armed robbery, drive-by shooting, discharging a firearm at a structure, and aggravated assault with serious injury or use of a deadly weapon) or if the juvenile had two prior felony adjudications and was charged with any third felony.
- Direct file for 14-year-olds charged with a violent crime or if arrested for any third felony. Chronic offender classification with procedures for notice of possible consequences, dispositions, and determination of whether prior offenses occurred.
- Reverse waiver, where, at a pretrial hearing, a juvenile does not qualify as a chronic felony offender.
- Once an adult, always an adult, where, if a juvenile was previously tried and convicted in criminal court, any future offenses involving that juvenile will be tried in adult court.
- Proceedings and records open to the public.
- Mandatory sentencing, where a juvenile age 14 and older adjudicated for any second felony in juvenile court must either serve mandated juvenile detention time, be incarcerated in the Arizona Department of Juvenile Corrections, or be placed under juvenile intensive supervision. The juvenile also may be tried as an adult.
- The appropriation of funds for the purpose of providing short-term detention for juveniles on intensive probation, for expanding the juvenile intensive supervision and progressively increasing sanction programs, and for investigating and prosecuting juvenile gang offenses.

Source: Patricia Torbet and Linda Szymanski, *State Legislative Responses to Violent Crime: 1996–97 Update* (Washington, DC: Office of Juvenile Justice and Delinquency Prevention, 1998).

These changes concern juvenile justice advocates such as Hunter Hurst, director of the National Center for Juvenile Justice, who warns

> *How could the wholesale criminalization of children possibly be a wise thing? If their vulnerability to predation in jails and prisons does not destroy them, won't the so-called taint of criminality that they carry with them for the rest of their lives be an impossible social burden for them and us? . . . Have our standards of decency devolved to the point where protection of children is no longer a compelling state interest? In may ways the answer is yes.*[54]

Those who support the juvenile justice concept believe that it is too soon to write off the rehabilitative ideal that has always underpinned the separate treatment of juvenile offenders. They note that fears of a juvenile crime wave are misplaced and that the actions of a few violent children should not mask the needs of millions who can benefit from solicitous treatment rather than harsh punishments. Alida Merlo, Peter Benekos, and William Cook note that a child is more likely to be hit by lightning than shot in a school.[55] Despite these differences, it is likely that the juvenile court will remain a critical social institution; there are few viable alternatives. The question is not *whether* there will be a juvenile court but what form it will take.

SUMMARY

The juvenile justice system was established at the turn of the twentieth century after decades of effort by child saving groups. These reformers sought to create an independent category of delinquent offender and keep their treatment separate from adults.

The juvenile justice process consists of a series of steps: the police investigation, the intake procedure in the juvenile court, the pretrial procedures used for juvenile offenders, and the adjudication, disposition, and post-dispositional procedures.

Over the past four decades, the U.S. Supreme Court and lower courts have granted juveniles procedural safeguards and the protection of due process in juvenile courts. Major court decisions have laid down the constitutional requirements for juvenile court proceedings. It is important to recognize that in years past the protections currently afforded to both adults and children were not available to children.

How the juvenile justice system deals with the adolescent is also determined by ever-changing theoretical perspectives and models. Elements of a comprehensive strategy for juvenile justice include (1) delinquency prevention, (2) intervention programs, (3) graduated sanctions, (4) improvement of institutional programs, and (5) treating juveniles like adults. New courts, such as drug courts and teen courts, are now in place.

It is doubtful any real progress in improving the juvenile justice system could be made without significant support from the federal government. By reauthorizing the Juvenile Justice and Delinquency Prevention Act of 1974 and by passing the Violent Crime Control and Law Enforcement Act of 1994, Congress has made a historic financial effort to address juvenile justice reform.

The future of the juvenile justice system is in doubt. A number of state jurisdictions are now revising their juvenile codes to restrict eligibility in the juvenile justice system and eliminate the most serious offenders.

KEY TERMS

House of Refuge

Children's Aid Society

orphan trains

Society for the Prevention of Cruelty to Children (SPCC)

Law Enforcement Assistance Administration (LEAA)

juvenile justice process

detention hearing

adjudicatory hearing

bifurcated process

disposition

petition

drug courts

teen courts

QUESTIONS FOR DISCUSSION

1. What factors precipitated the development of the Illinois Juvenile Court Act of 1899?

2. One of the most significant reforms in dealing with the juvenile offender was the opening of the New York House of Refuge in 1825. What were the social and judicial consequences of this reform on the juvenile justice system?

3. The "child savers" have been accused of wanting to control the lives of poor and immigrant children for their own benefit. Are there any parallels to the "child saving" movement in modern-day America?

4. Should there be a juvenile justice system, or should juveniles who commit serious crimes be treated as adults, while the others are handled by social welfare agencies?

5. The Supreme Court has made a number of major decisions in the area of juvenile justice. What are these decisions? What is their impact on the juvenile justice system?

6. What is the meaning of the term *procedural due process of law*? Explain why and how procedural due process has had an impact on juvenile justice.

7. The formal components of the criminal justice system are often considered to be the police, the court, and the correctional agency. How do these components relate to the major areas of the juvenile justice system? Is the operation of justice similar in the juvenile and adult systems?

8. How would each model of juvenile justice consider the use of capital punishment as a criminal sanction for first-degree murder by a juvenile offender?

9. What role has the federal government played in the juvenile justice system over the last 25 years?

VIEWPOINT

"The great majority of our little emigrants," claimed Charles Loring Brace, "are the 'waifs and strays' of the streets in a large city." When the Children's Aid Society opened its doors in March 1853, according to Brace, a "crowd of wandering little ones" immediately found their way to the small office on Amity Street. "Ragged young girls who had nowhere to lay their heads; children driven from drunkards' homes; orphans who slept where they could find a box or a stairway; boys cast out by step-mothers or step-fathers; newsboys, whose incessant answer to our question 'Where do you live?' rung in our ears, 'Don't live nowhere!' "

For a detailed review of Charles Loring Brace and the Children's Aid Society on InfoTrac College Edition, read Clay Gish, "Rescuing the 'Waifs and Strays' of the City: The Western Emigration Program of the Children's Aid Society," *Journal of Social History* 33:121 (1999).

NOTES

1. Timothy Egan, "From Adolescent Angst to Shooting Up Schools," *New York Times,* 14 June 1998, p. 1; James Alan Fox, "Again School Attacks Show Need for New Strategies," *Boston Sunday Globe,* 24 May 1998, pp. D1–2; Patricia King and Andrew Murr, "A Son Out of Control," *Newsweek,* 1 June 1998, pp. 32–33; Jerome Shestack, "What about Juvenile Justice?" *American Bar Association Journal* 84:8 (1998).

2. Robert M. Mennel, "Origins of the Juvenile Court: Changing Perspectives on the Legal Rights of Juvenile Delinquents," *Crime and Delinquency* 18:68–78 (1972).

3. Anthony Salerno, "The Child Saving Movement: Altruism or Conspiracy," *Juvenile and Family Court Journal* 42:37 (1991).

4. Frank J. Coppa and Philip C. Dolce, *Cities in Transition: From the Ancient World to Urban America* (Chicago: Nelson Hall, 1974), p. 220.

5. Robert Mennel, "Attitudes and Policies toward Juvenile Delinquency," *Crime and Justice,* vol. 5 (Chicago: University of Chicago Press, 1983), p. 198.

6. Anthony M. Platt, *The Child Savers: The Invention of Delinquency* (Chicago: University of Chicago Press, 1969).

7. See, generally, Anne Meis Knupfer, *Reform and Resistance: Gender, Delinquency, and America's First Juvenile Court* (London: Routledge, 2001).

8. This section is based on material from the New York State Archives, *The Greatest Reform School in the World: A Guide to the Records of the New York House of Refuge: A Brief History 1824–1857* (Albany, NY, 2001); Sanford J. Fox, "Juvenile Justice Reform: A Historical Perspective," *Stanford Law Review* 22:1187 (1970).

9. Robert S. Pickett, *House of Refuge—Origins of Juvenile Reform in New York State, 1815–1857* (Syracuse, NY: Syracuse University Press, 1969).

10. Mennel, "Origins of the Juvenile Court," pp. 69–70.

11. Sanford Fox, "The Early History of the Court" from *The Future of Children* (Los Altos, CA: David and Lucille Packard Foundation, 1996).

12. U.S. Department of Justice, Juvenile Justice and Delinquency Prevention, *Two Hundred Years of American Criminal Justice: An LEAA Bicentennial Study* (Washington, DC: LEAA, 1976).

13. New York State Law Ch. 412, Laws of 1929; Ch. 538, Laws of 1932.

14. Beverly Smith, "Female Admissions and Paroles of the Western House of Refuge in the 1880s, An Historical Example of Community Corrections," *Journal of Research in Crime and Delinquency* 26:36–66 (1989).

15. Fox, "Juvenile Justice Reform," p. 1229.

16. Fox, "The Early History of the Court."

17. Elizabeth Pleck, "Criminal Approaches to Family Violence, 1640–1980," in Lloyd Ohlin and Michael Tonry, eds., *Family Violence* (Chicago: University of Chicago Press, 1989), pp. 19–58.

18. Elizabeth Pleck, *Domestic Tyranny: The Making of Social Policy against Family Violence from Colonial Times to the Present* (New York: Oxford University Press, 1987), pp. 28–30.

19. Linda Gordon, *Family Violence and Social Control* (New York: Viking, 1988).

20. Kathleen Block and Donna Hale, "Turf Wars in the Progressive Era of Juvenile Justice: The Relationship of Private and Public Child Care Agencies," *Crime and Delinquency* 37:225–41 (1991).

21. Salerno, "The Child Saving Movement," p. 37.

22. Platt, *The Child Savers.*

23. Ibid., p. 116.

24. Randall Shelden and Lynn Osborne, " 'For Their Own Good': Class Interests and the Child Saving Movement in Memphis, Tennessee, 1900–1917," *Criminology* 27:747–67 (1989).

25. Theodore Ferdinand, "Juvenile Delinquency or Juvenile Justice: Which Came First?" *Criminology* 27:79–106 (1989).

26. *In re Gault,* 387 U.S. 1, 87 S.Ct. 1428, 18 L.Ed.2d 527 (1967).

27. Fox, "The Early History of the Court," p. 4.

28. Ibid.

29. Mary Odem and Steven Schlossman, "Guardians of Virtue: The Juvenile Court and Female Delinquency in Early 20th-Century Los Angeles," *Crime and Delinquency* 37:186–203 (1991).

30. Fox, "The Early History of the Court," p. 4.

31. John Sutton, "Bureaucrats and Entrepreneurs: Institutional Responses to Deviant Children in the United States, 1890–1920," *American Journal of Sociology 95:* 1367–1400 (1990).

32. Ibid., p. 1383.

33. Marguerite Rosenthal, "Reforming the Juvenile Correctional Institution: Efforts of the U.S. Children's Bureau in the 1930s," *Journal of Sociology and Social Welfare 14:*47–74 (1987); see also David Steinhart, "Status Offenses," The Center for the Future of Children, The Juvenile Court (Los Altos, CA: David and Lucille Packard Foundation, 1996).

34. For an overview of these developments, see Theodore Ferdinand, "History Overtakes the Juvenile Justice System," *Crime and Delinquency* 37:204–24 (1991).

35. N.Y. Fam.Ct. Act, Art. 7, Sec. 712 (Consol. 1962).

36. *Kent v. United States,* 383 U.S. 541, 86 S.Ct. 1045, 16 L.Ed.2d 84 (1966); *In re Gault,* 387 U.S. 1, 87 S.Ct. 1428, 18 L.Ed.2d 527 (1967): Juveniles have the right to notice, counsel, confrontation, and cross-examination, and to the privileges against self-incrimination in juvenile court proceedings. *In re Winship,* 397 U.S. 358, 90 S.Ct. 1068, 25 L.Ed.2d 368 (1970): Proof beyond a reasonable doubt is necessary for conviction in juvenile proceedings. *Breed v. Jones,* 421 U.S. 519, 95 S.Ct. 1779, 44 L.Ed.2d 346 (1975): Jeopardy attaches in a juvenile court adjudicatory hearing, thus barring subsequent prosecution for the same offense as an adult.

37. Public Law 90–351, Title I—Omnibus Safe Streets and Crime Control Act of 1968, 90th Congress, June 1968.

38. National Advisory Commission on Criminal Justice Standards and Goals, *A National Strategy to Reduce Crime* (Washington, DC: U.S. Government Printing Office, 1973).

39. Juvenile Justice and Delinquency Prevention Act of 1974, Public Law 93–415 (1974). For a critique of this legislation, see Ira Schwartz, *Justice for Juveniles—Rethinking the Best Interests of the Child* (Lexington, MA: D.C. Heath, 1989), p. 175.

40. For an extensive summary of the Violent Crime Control and Law Enforcement Act of 1994, see *Criminal Law Reporter* 55:2305–2430 (1994).

41. Shay Bilchik, "A Juvenile Justice System for the 21st Century," *Crime and Delinquency* 44:89 (1998).

42. For a comprehensive view of juvenile law, see, generally, Joseph J. Senna and Larry J. Siegel, *Juvenile Law: Cases and Comments,* 2nd ed. (St. Paul, MN: West, 1992).

43. For an excellent review of the juvenile process, see Adrienne Volenik, *Checklists for Use in Juvenile Delinquency Proceedings* (Washington, DC: American Bar Association, 1985); see also Jeffrey Butts and Gregory Halemba, *Waiting for Justice—Moving Young Offenders through the Juvenile Court Process* (Pittsburgh: National Center for Juvenile Justice, 1996).

44. Fox Butterfield, "Justice Besieged," *New York Times,* 21 July 1997, A16.

45. National Conference of State Legislatures, *A Legislator's Guide to Comprehensive Juvenile Justice, Juvenile Detention, and Corrections* (Denver: National Conference of State Legislators, 1996).

46. James Howell, ed., *Guide for Implementing the Comprehensive Strategy for Serious, Violent, and Chronic Juvenile Offenders* (Washington, DC: Office of Juvenile Justice and Delinquency Prevention, 1995).

47. Barry Feld, "Criminology and the Juvenile Court: A Research Agenda for the 1990s," in Ira M. Schwartz, *Juvenile Justice and Public Policy—Toward a National Agenda* (New York: Lexington Books, 1992), p. 59.

48. Robert O. Dawson, "The Future of Juvenile Justice: Is It Time to Abolish the System?" *Journal of Criminal Law and Criminology* 81:136–55 (1990); see also Leonard P. Edwards, "The Future of the Juvenile Court: Promising New Directions in the Center for the Future of Children," The Juvenile Court (Los Altos, CA: David and Lucille Packard Foundation, 1996).

49. Hunter Hurst, "Juvenile Court: As We Enter the Millennium," *Juvenile and Family Court Journal* 50:21–27 (1999).

50. Carol J. DeFrances and Kevin Strom, *Juveniles Prosecuted in the State Criminal Courts* (Washington, DC: Bureau of Justice Statistics, 1997).

51. Bilchik, "A Juvenile Justice System for the 21st Century."

52. Patricia Torbet and Linda Szymanski, *State Legislative Responses to Violent Crime: 1996–97 Update* (Washington, DC: Office of Juvenile Justice and Delinquency Prevention, 1998).

53. Ibid.

54. Hurst, "Juvenile Court: As We Enter the Millennium," p. 25.

55. Alida Merlo, Peter Benekos, and William Cook, "The Juvenile Court at 100 Years: Celebration or Wake?" *Juvenile and Family Court Journal* 50:1–9 at 7 (1999).

13 Police Work with Juveniles

© Cleve Bryant/Photo Edit

You are a new police officer assigned to a juvenile unit of a medium-sized urban police department. Wayne G. is an 18-year-old white male who was caught shoplifting with two male friends of the same age. Wayne attempted to leave a large department store with a $25 shirt and was apprehended by a police officer in front of the store.

Wayne seemed quite remorseful about the offense. He said several times that he didn't know why he did it and that he had not planned to do it. He seemed upset and scared and, while admitting the offense, did not want to go to court. Wayne had three previous contacts with the police as a juvenile: one for malicious mischief when he destroyed some property, another involving a minor assault of a boy, and a third involving another shoplifting charge. In all three cases, Wayne promised to refrain from ever committing such acts again, and as a result, he was not required to go to court. The other shoplifting involved a baseball worth three dollars.

Wayne appeared at the police department with his mother. His parents are divorced. His mother did not seem overly concerned about the case and felt that her son was not really to blame. She argued that he was always getting in trouble and she was not sure how to control him. She blamed most of his troubles with the law on his being in the wrong crowd. Besides, a $25 shirt was "no big deal," and she offered to pay back the store. The store had left matters in the hands of the police and would support any decision you make.

- Would you submit Wayne's case for prosecution, release him with a warning, or use some other tactic?

- Should police officers be forced to act as counselors for troubled youth?

and Seizure
system
probable cause

eciding what to do in a case like Wayne's is a routine activity for most police officers. When dealing with juveniles, they must consider not only the nature of the offense but also the needs of the juvenile. Police officers realize that the action they take can have a long-term effect on an adolescent's future. This chapter focuses on police work in juvenile justice. It first takes a brief look at the history of policing juveniles, from the time of the Norman conquest of England up to today. Community policing in modern times is the focus of the next section. Here the relationship between police and community efforts to prevent crime is explored. We then look at the roles and responsibilities of the police and the organization and management of police-juvenile operations. Legal aspects of police work, including the arrest procedure, search and seizure, and custodial interrogation, are reviewed. We also examine the concept of police discretion in light of the broad authority that police have in dealing with juveniles. The chapter ends with a review of police work and delinquency prevention. A wide range of police techniques in preventing delinquency are discussed, including those that rely on the deterrent powers of police and those that engage schools and the community.

History of Juvenile Policing

pledge system Early English system in which neighbors protected each other from thieves and warring groups.

watch system Replaced the pledge system in England; watchmen patrolled urban areas at night to provide protection from harm.

To gain a comprehensive history of the London Metropolitan Police from 1829 to 2000, go to http://www.met.police.uk/ police/mps/history/index.htm For an up-to-date list of Web links, go to http://info.wadsworth.com/siegel

Providing specialized police services for juveniles is a relatively recent phenomenon. At one time citizens were responsible for protecting themselves and maintaining order.

The origin of police agencies can be traced to early English society.[1] Before the Norman conquest of England, the **pledge system** assumed that neighbors would protect each other from thieves and warring groups. Individuals were entrusted with policing themselves and resolving minor problems. By the thirteenth century, however, the **watch system** was created to police larger communities. Men were organized in church parishes to patrol areas at night and guard against disturbances and breaches of the peace. This was followed by establishment of the constable, who was responsible for dealing with more serious crimes. By the seventeenth century, the constable, the justice of the peace, and the night watchman formed the nucleus of the police system.

When the Industrial Revolution brought thousands of people from the countryside to work in factories, the need for police protection increased. As a result, the first organized police force was established in London in 1829. The British "bobbies" (so-called after their founder, Sir Robert Peel) were not successful at stopping crime and were influenced by the wealthy for personal and political gain.[2]

In the American colonies, the local sheriff became the most important police official. By the mid-1800s, city police departments had formed in Boston, New York, and Philadelphia. Officers patrolled on foot, and conflicts often arose between untrained officers and the public.

By this time, children began to be treated as a distinguishable group (see Chapter 1). When children violated the law they were often treated the same as adult offenders. But even at this stage a belief existed that the enforcement of criminal law should be applied differently to children.

During the late nineteenth century and into the twentieth, the problems associated with growing numbers of unemployed and homeless youths increased. Groups such as the Wickersham Commission of 1931 and the International Association of Chiefs of Police became the leading voices for police reform.[3] Their efforts resulted in creation of specialized police units, known as delinquency control squads.

The most famous police reformer of the 1930s was August Vollmer. As the police chief of Berkeley, California, Vollmer instituted numerous reforms, including university training, modern management techniques, prevention programs, and juvenile aid bureaus.[4] These bureaus were the first organized police services for juvenile offenders.

In the 1960s, policing entered a turbulent period.[5] The U.S. Supreme Court handed down decisions designed to restrict police operations and discretion. Civil unrest produced growing tensions between police and the public. Urban police departments were unable to handle the growing crime rate. Federal funding from the Law Enforcement Assistance Administration (LEAA), an agency set up to fund justice-related programs, was a catalyst for developing hundreds of new police programs and enhancement of police services for children. By the 1980s, most urban police departments recognized that the problem of juvenile delinquency required special attention.

The role of the juvenile police officer (officer assigned to juvenile work) has taken on added importance, particularly with the increase in violent juvenile crime. Today the majority of the nation's urban law enforcement agencies have specialized juvenile police programs. Typically, such programs involve (1) prevention (Police Athletic Leagues (PALs)), D.A.R.E. programs, community outreach), and (2) law enforcement work (juvenile court, school policing, gang control). Other concerns of the programs include child abuse, domestic violence, and missing children.

Community Policing in the New Millennium

In the minds of most citizens, the primary responsibility of the police is to protect the public. While the image depicted in films, books, and TV shows is one of crime fighters who always get their man, since the 1960s, the public has become increasingly aware that the reality of police work is substantially different from its fictional glorification. When police departments failed to bring the crime rate down despite massive government subsidies, when citizens complained of civil rights violations, and when tales of police corruption became widespread, it was evident that a crisis was imminent in American policing.

Recently, a new view of policing has emerged. Discarding the image of crime fighters who track down serious criminals or stop armed robberies in progress, many police departments have adopted the concept that the police role should be to maintain order and be a visible and accessible component of the community. The argument is that police efforts can be successful only when conducted in partnership with concerned citizens. This movement is referred to as **community policing.**[6]

community policing Police strategy that emphasizes reducing fear, organizing the community, and maintaining order rather than fighting crime.

Interest in community policing does not mean that the crime control model of law enforcement is history. An ongoing effort is being made to improve the crime-fighting capability of police agencies and there are some indications that the effort is paying off. Research indicates that aggressive action by police can help reduce the incidence of repeat offending, and innovations such as computerized fingerprinting systems may bring about greater efficiency.[7] Nonetheless, little conclusive evidence exists that merely improving police officers' crime-fighting skills alone can lower crime rates.[8] Thus, the emergence of the community policing model of crime prevention, regarded as one of the most important changes in U.S. law enforcement, warrants further exploration.

Working with juvenile offenders presents a special challenge for police officers: The desire to help young people and to steer them away from crime seems to conflict with the traditional police duties of preventing crime and maintaining order that fall under the crime control model of law enforcement. The police address this conflict daily as they face the nationwide problems of adolescent drug use and renewed gang activity. While the need to help troubled youths may conflict with traditional police roles, it fits nicely with the emerging community policing models. Improving these relationships is critical because many juveniles do not have a high regard for the police; minority teens are especially critical of police performance.[9]

The Community Policing Model

The premise of the community policing model of crime prevention is that the police can carry out their duties more effectively by gaining the trust and assistance of concerned citizens. Under this model, the main police role is to increase feelings of community safety and encourage area residents to cooperate with their local police agencies.[10] Advocates of community policing regard the approach as useful in juvenile justice for a number of reasons:

1. Direct engagement with a community gives police more immediate information about problems unique to a neighborhood and better insight into their solutions.
2. Freeing officers from the emergency response system permits them to engage more directly in proactive crime prevention.
3. Making police operations more visible increases police accountability to the public.
4. Decentralizing operations allows officers to develop greater familiarity with the needs of various constituencies in the community and to adapt procedures to accommodate those needs.
5. Encouraging officers to view citizens as partners improves relations between police and the public.
6. Moving decision making to patrol officers places more authority in the hands of the people who best know the community's problems and expectations.[11]

A recent survey of community policing in the United States—the Law Enforcement Management and Administrative Statistics (LEMAS) survey—shows that the use of community policing is becoming more widespread. According to the survey there are almost 113,000 full-time community police officers.[12] This number represents a fivefold increase from 1997 to 1999 in full-time sworn police officers regularly engaged in community policing activities.[13] Other 1999 highlights of the survey include

- Sixty-four percent of local police departments serving 86 percent of all residents had full-time officers engaged in community policing activities.
- Eighty-seven percent of local police officers were employed by a department that provided community policing training for some or all new recruits.[14]

The community policing model has been translated into a number of policy initiatives. It has encouraged police departments to get officers out of patrol cars, where they were insulated from the community, and into the streets via foot patrol.[15] The LEMAS survey found that 63 percent of local police departments serving 85 percent of all residents used routine foot patrol and/or bicycle patrol.[16] In addition, the police have encouraged citizens to create neighborhood watches and crime prevention groups. One of the best known of these programs is the Philadelphia Block Watch, which cooperates with the police in delinquency control and victim-aid projects. Another is the Innovative Neighborhood-Oriented Policing (INOP) program.[17] The main objectives of the INOP program are to foster community policing initiatives and to implement drug-reduction efforts aimed at juveniles and adults.[18]

Another third community policing program, the Youth Firearms Violence Initiative (YFVI) of the federal Office of Community Oriented Policing Services (COPS), is running in 10 cities across the United States with the aim of reducing juvenile gun violence. Each city was provided with up to $1 million to pay for interventions that incorporated community policing strategies.[19] These strategies include:

- Working in partnership with other city agencies to promote education, prevention, and intervention programs related to handguns and their safety
- Developing community-based programs focused on youth handgun violence
- Developing programs involving and assisting families in addressing youth handgun problems[20]

A CLOSER VIEW
To read more about community outreach by police on InfoTrac College Edition, go to William Holley and Maria Fazalare, "The Community Outreach Program," *FBI Law Enforcement Bulletin* 69:6 (September 2000).

Table 13.1 Impact of YFVI Programs on Gun Crimes

	Number of Gun Crimes in 12-Month Period before YFVI Began	Number of Gun Crimes in 12-Month Period after YFVI Began	Change (%)
Baltimore, MD	8,764	8,581	–2
Cherry Hill	104	105	0
Park Heights	643	594	–8
Cleveland, OH	3,149	2,672	–15
Three RAPP houses*	26	16	–38
Inglewood, CA	945	730	–23
Darby-Dixon	43	22	–49
Salinas, CA			
Citywide	552	490	–11
San Antonio, TX	2,895	1,716	–41
Four target areas	523	328	–37

*RAPP = Residential Area Policing Program

Source: Adapted from Terence Dunworth, *National Evaluation of the Youth Firearms Violence Initiative* (Washington, DC: NIJ Research in Brief, 2000), p. 8, exhibit 6.

The YFVI programs also include some traditional law enforcement measures, such as new enforcement units within the police department and standard surveillance and intelligence-gathering techniques.

An evaluation of the YFVI was conducted in all 10 cities, but in only 5 cities was program effectiveness in reducing gun violence measured. Police-reported gun crimes were reduced in each of the five cities and in every target area of the cities, with the exception of Cherry Hill in Baltimore. (See Table 13.1 for the impact of the program on gun crimes.) The evaluation also examined the percentage change of gun crimes involving young people in the before and after periods. The results were not as encouraging. Only San Antonio demonstrated a significant reduction in the percentage of gun crimes involving youths, from 57 percent to 55 percent.

Efforts are being made by police departments to involve citizens in delinquency control. Community policing is a philosophy that promotes community, government, and police partnerships that address juvenile crime, as well as adult crime.[21] Although there is not a great deal of evidence that these efforts can lower crime rates, they do seem to be effective methods of improving perceptions of community safety and the quality of community life while involving citizens in the juvenile justice network. Under the community policing philosophy, prevention programs may become more effective crime control measures. Programs that combine the reintegration of youths into the community after institutionalization with police surveillance and increased communication are vital for improving police effectiveness with juveniles.[22]

To read more about COPS, go to
http://www.usdoj.gov/cops/home.htm
For an up-to-date list of Web links, go to
http://info.wadsworth.com/siegel

The Police and Juvenile Offenders

The alarming increase in serious juvenile crime in the past few years has made it obvious that the police can no longer neglect youthful antisocial behavior. Departments need to assign resources to the problem and have the proper organization for coping with it. The theory and practice of police organization have undergone many changes, and as a result, police departments are giving greater emphasis to the juvenile function. The organization of juvenile work depends on the size of the police department, the kind of community in which the department is located, and the amount and quality of resources available in the community.

Police Services

Police who work with juvenile offenders usually have skills and talents that go beyond those generally associated with regular police work. In large urban police departments, juvenile services are often established through a special unit. Ordinarily this unit is the responsibility of a command-level police officer, who assigns officers to deal with juvenile problems throughout the police department's jurisdiction. Police departments with very few officers have little need for an internal division with special functions. Most small departments make one officer responsible for handling juvenile matters for the entire community. A large proportion of justice agencies have written policy directives for handling juvenile offenders. Figure 13.1 illustrates the major elements of a police department organization dealing with juvenile offenders. However, in both large and small departments, officers assigned to work with juveniles will not necessarily be the only ones involved in handling juvenile offenses. When officers on patrol encounter a youngster committing a crime, they are responsible for dealing with the problem initially; they generally refer the case to the juvenile unit or to a juvenile police officer for follow-up.

Police Roles

juvenile officers Police officers who specialize in dealing with juvenile offenders; they may operate alone or as part of a juvenile police unit within the department.

Juvenile officers operate either as specialists within a police department or as part of the juvenile unit of a police department. Their role is similar to that of officers working with adult offenders: to intervene if the actions of a citizen produce public danger or disorder. Most juvenile officers are appointed after having had some general patrol experience. A desire to work with juveniles as well as an aptitude for the work are considered essential for the job. Officers must also have a thorough knowledge of the law, especially the constitutional protections available to juveniles.

Most officers regard the violations of juveniles as nonserious unless they are committed by chronic troublemakers or involve significant damage to persons or property. Police encounters with juveniles are generally the result of reports made by citizens, and the bulk of such encounters pertain to matters of minor legal consequence.[23] Of course, police must also deal with serious juvenile offenders whose criminal acts are similar to those of adults; these are a minority of the offender population. Thus, police who deal with delinquency must concentrate on being peacekeepers and crime preventers.[24]

role conflicts Conflicts police officers face that revolve around the requirement to perform their primary duty of law enforcement and a desire to aid in rehabilitating youthful offenders.

Handling juvenile offenders can produce major **role conflicts** for police. They may experience a tension between their desire to perform what they consider their primary duty, law enforcement, and the need to aid in the rehabilitation of youthful offenders. Police officers' actions in cases involving adults are usually controlled by the law and their own judgment or discretion. (The concept of discretion is discussed later in this chapter.) In contrast, a case involving a juvenile often demands that the officer consider the "best interests of the child" and how the officer's actions will influence the child's future well-being. Consequently, police are much less likely to refer juvenile offenders to courts. It is estimated that 30 percent of all juvenile arrests are

Prevention Programs		Juvenile Crimes
• Community Relations • Police Athletic League (PAL) • D.A.R.E. programs (drug prevention) • Officer Friendly		• Detective Bureau • Juvenile Court Processing • School Liaison • Gang Control Unit

Figure 13.1
Typical Urban Police Department Organization with Juvenile Justice Component

Figure 13.2

Police Response to Juvenile Crime
To understand how police deal with juvenile crime, picture a funnel, with the result shown here. For every 500 juveniles taken into custody, a little more than 70 percent are sent to juvenile court, and a little more than 20 percent are released.
Source: FBI, *Crime in the United States 2000* (Washington, DC: U.S. Government Printing Office, 2001), p. 273, table 68.

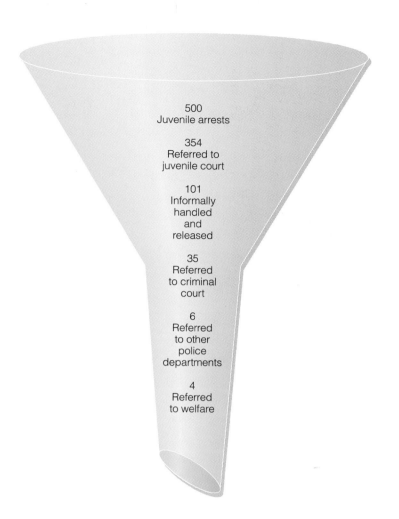

500
Juvenile arrests

354
Referred to
juvenile court

101
Informally
handled
and
released

35
Referred
to criminal
court

6
Referred
to other
police
departments

4
Referred
to welfare

handled informally within the police department or are referred to a community service agency (Figure 13.2). These informal dispositions are the result of the police officer's discretionary authority.[25]

Police intervention in situations involving juveniles can be difficult and emotional. The officer often encounters hostile behavior from the juvenile offender, as well as agitated witnesses. Overreaction by the officer can result in a violent incident. Even if the officer succeeds in quieting or dispersing the witnesses, they will probably reappear the next day, often in the same place.[26]

Role conflicts are common, because most police-juvenile encounters are brought about by loitering and rowdiness rather than by serious law violations. Public concern has risen about out-of-control youth. Yet, because of legal constraints and family interference, the police are often limited in the ways they can respond to such offenders.[27]

What role should the police play in mediating problems with youths—law enforcer, or delinquency prevention worker? The answer may lie somewhere in between. Most police departments operate juvenile programs that combine law enforcement and delinquency prevention roles, and the police work with the juvenile court to determine a role most suitable for their community.[28] Actually, police officers may also act as prosecutors in some rural courts when attorneys are not available. Thus, the police-juvenile role extends from the on-the-street encounter to the station house to the court. For juvenile matters involving minor criminal conduct or incorrigible behavior, the police ordinarily select the least restrictive alternative, which includes such measures as temporary assistance or referral to community agencies. In contrast, violent juvenile crime requires that the police arrest youths while providing constitutional safeguards similar to those available to adult offenders.

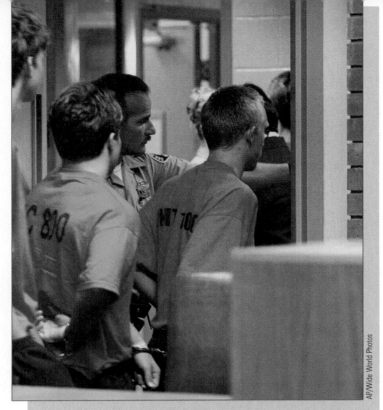

AP/Wide World Photos

POLICE OFFICERS MUST DEAL WITH serious offenders whose violent acts are similar to those of adults, but these are a small minority of the offender population. Here, San Diego Sheriff's deputies lead three of the seven teenage defendants from Juvenile Court Department 8 after an arraignment hearing in San Diego. The seven San Diego area youths are charged with attacks against several migrant workers. The victims, all men in their 60s, told police that a group of eight to ten young men fired at them with a BB gun, beat them with pipes, and stole money from them at a migrant workers' camp in northern San Diego.

Police and Violent Juvenile Crime

Violent juvenile offenders are defined as those adjudicated delinquent for crimes of homicide, rape, robbery, aggravated assault, and kidnapping. Juveniles typically account for nearly 20 percent of all violent crime arrests. Though the juvenile violence rate has recently declined, the future is uncertain. Some experts believe that a surge of violence will occur as the children of baby boomers enter their "prime crime" years. Some experts predict that juvenile arrests for violent crime will double by the year 2010.[29]

As a result of these predictions, police and other justice agencies are experimenting with different methods of controlling violent youth. Some of these methods, such as placing more officers on the beat, have existed for decades; others rely on state-of-the-art technology to pinpoint the locations of violent crimes and develop immediate countermeasures. Research shows that there are a number of effective policing practices, including increased directed patrols in street-corner hot spots of crime; proactive arrests of serious repeat offenders; and **problem-oriented policing**.[30] (See Exhibit 13.1, for a complete list of policing practices that work, do not work, or are promising.) These strategies address problems of community disorganization and can be effective deterrents when combined with other laws and policies, such as restricting the possession of firearms.[31] Although many of these policing strategies are not

problem-oriented policing Law enforcement that focuses on addressing the problems underlying incidents of juvenile delinquency rather than the incidents only.

new, implementing them as one element of an overall police plan may have an impact on preventing juvenile violence.

Finally, one key component of any innovative police program dealing with violent juvenile crime is improved communications between the police and the community.

Exhibit 13.1   Policing Programs That Work

What Works

- Increased directed patrols in street-corner hot spots of crime
- Proactive arrests of serious repeat offenders
- Proactive arrests of drunk drivers
- Arrests of employed suspects for domestic assault
- Problem-oriented policing

What Does Not Work

- Neighborhood block watch
- Arrests of some juveniles for minor offenses
- Arrests of unemployed suspects for domestic assault
- Drug market arrests
- Community policing that is not targeted at risk factors
- Adding extra police to cities with no regard to assignment or activity

What Is Promising

- Police traffic enforcement patrols targeting illegally carried handguns
- Community policing when the community is involved in setting priorities
- Community policing focused on improving police legitimacy
- Warrants for arrest of suspect absent when police respond to domestic violence

Source: Lawrence W. Sherman and John E. Eck, "Policing for Crime Prevention," in Lawrence W. Sherman, David P. Farrington, Brandon C. Welsh, and Doris Layton MacKenzie, eds., *Evidence-Based Crime Prevention* (London: Routledge, 2002), pp. 321–22.

Police and the Rule of Law

When police are involved with criminal activity of juvenile offenders, their actions are controlled by statute, constitutional case law, and judicial review. Police methods of investigation and control include (1) the arrest procedure, (2) search and seizure, and (3) custodial interrogation.

The Arrest Procedure

arrest Taking a person into the custody of the law to restrain the accused until he or she can be held accountable for the offense in court proceedings.

probable cause Reasonable ground to believe that an offense was committed and that the accused committed that offense.

When a juvenile is apprehended, the police must decide whether to release the youngster or make a referral to the juvenile court. Cases involving serious crimes against property or persons are often referred to court. Less serious cases, such as disputes between juveniles, petty shoplifting, runaways, and assaults of minors, are often diverted from court action.

Most states require that the law of **arrest** be the same for both adults and juveniles. To make a legal arrest, an officer must have probable cause to believe that an offense took place and that the suspect is the guilty party. **Probable cause** is usually defined as falling somewhere between a mere suspicion and absolute certainty. In misdemeanor cases the police officer must personally observe the crime in order to place a suspect in custody. For a felony, the police officer may make the arrest without having observed the crime if the officer has probable cause to believe the crime occurred and the person being arrested committed it.

The main difference between arrests of adult and juvenile offenders is the broader latitude police have to control youthful behavior. Most juvenile codes, for instance, provide broad authority for the police to take juveniles into custody.[32] Such statutes are designed to give the police the authority to act *in loco parentis* ("in place of the parent"). Accordingly, the broad power granted to police is consistent with the notion that a juvenile is not arrested but taken into custody, which implies a protective rather than a punitive form of detention.[33] Once a juvenile is arrested, however, the constitutional safeguards of the Fourth and Fifth Amendments available to adults apply to the juvenile as well.

Section 13 of the Uniform Juvenile Court Act is an example of the provisions used in state codes regarding juvenile arrest procedures (Exhibit 13.2). There is currently a trend toward treating juvenile offenders more like adults. Related to this trend are efforts by the police to provide a more legalistic and less informal approach to the arrest process, and a more balanced approach to case disposition.[34]

Exhibit 13.2   Uniform Juvenile Court Act, Section 13 (Taking into Custody)

a. A child may be taken into custody:
   1. pursuant to an order of the court under this Act;
   2. pursuant to the laws of arrest;
   3. by a law enforcement officer (or duly authorized officer of the court) if there are reasonable grounds to believe that the child is suffering from illness or injury or is in immediate danger from his surroundings, and that his removal is necessary; or
   4. by a law enforcement officer (or duly authorized officer of the court) if there are reasonable grounds to believe that the child has run away from his parents, guardian, or other custodian.

b. The taking of a child into custody is not an arrest, except for the purpose of determining its validity under the constitution of this State or of the United States.

Source: National Conference of Commissioners on Uniform State Laws, *Uniform Juvenile Court Act* (Chicago: National Conference on Uniform State Laws, 1968), Sect. 13.

Search and Seizure

search and seizure The U.S. Constitution protects citizens from any search and seizure by police without a lawfully obtained search warrant; such warrants are issued when there is probable cause to believe that an offense has been committed.

Do juveniles have the same right to be free from unreasonable **search and seizure** as adults? In general, a citizen's privacy is protected by the Fourth Amendment of the Constitution, which states

> The right of the people to be secure in their persons, houses, papers, and effects, against unreasonable searches and seizures, shall not be violated, and no warrants shall issue, but upon probable cause, supported by oaths or affirmation, and particularly describing the place to be searched, and the persons or things to be seized.[35]

Most courts have held that the Fourth Amendment ban against unreasonable search and seizure applies to juveniles and that illegally seized evidence is inadmissible in a juvenile trial. To exclude incriminating evidence, a juvenile's attorney makes a pretrial motion to suppress the evidence, the same procedure that is used in the adult criminal process.

A full discussion of search and seizure is beyond the scope of this book, but it is important to note that the Supreme Court has ruled that police may stop a suspect and search for evidence without a warrant under certain circumstances. A person may be searched after a legal arrest, but then only in the immediate area of the suspect's control. For example, after an arrest for possession of drugs, the pockets of a suspect's jacket may be searched;[36] an automobile may be searched if there is probable cause to believe a crime has taken place;[37] a suspect's outer garments may be frisked if police are suspicious of his or her activities;[38] and a search may be conducted if a person volunteers for the search.[39] These rules are usually applied to juveniles as well as to adults.

Custodial Interrogation

custodial interrogation Questions posed by the police to a suspect held in custody in the prejudicial stage of the juvenile justice process; juveniles have the same rights against self-incrimination as adults do when being questioned.

Miranda *warning* Supreme Court decisions require police officers to inform individuals under arrest of their constitutional rights; warning must also be given when suspicion begins to focus on an individual in the accusatory stage.

In years past, police often questioned juveniles without their parents or even an attorney present. Any incriminating statements arising from such **custodial interrogation** could be used at trial. However, in the 1966 Miranda case, the Supreme Court placed constitutional limitations on police interrogation procedures with adult offenders. Miranda held that persons in police custody must be told the following:

- They have the right to remain silent.
- Any statements they make can be used against them.
- They have the right to counsel.
- If they cannot afford counsel, it will be furnished at public expense.[40]

These **Miranda warnings** have been made applicable to juveniles taken into custody. The Supreme Court case of *in re Gault* stated that constitutional privileges against self-incrimination apply in juvenile as well as adult cases. Because *in re Gault* implies that *Miranda* applies to custodial interrogation in criminal procedures, state court jurisdictions apply the requirements of *Miranda* to juvenile proceedings as well. Since the *Gault* decision in 1967, virtually all courts that have ruled on the question of the *Miranda* warning have concluded that the warning does apply to the juvenile process.

One problem associated with custodial interrogation of juveniles has to do with waiver of *Miranda* rights: Under what circumstances can juveniles knowingly and willingly waive the rights given them by *Miranda v. Arizona*? Does a youngster, acting alone, have sufficient maturity to appreciate the right to remain silent?

Most courts have concluded that parents or attorneys need not be present for juveniles effectively to waive their rights.[41] In a frequently cited California case, *People v. Lara,* the court said that the question of a juvenile's waiver is to be determined by the totality of the circumstances doctrine.[42] This means that the validity of a waiver rests not only on the age of the youth but also on a combination of other factors,

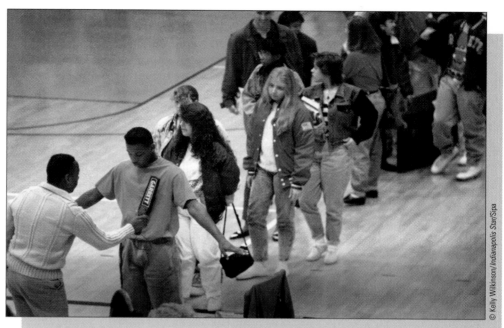

OFFICERS SEARCH STUDENTS AT A HIGH SCHOOL. The Supreme Court allows police officers and security agents greater latitude in searching students than they would have with other citizens, on the grounds that the campus must be a safe and crime-free environment.

including the education of the accused, the accused's knowledge of the charge, whether the youth was allowed to consult with family or friends, and the method of interrogation.[43] The general rule is that juveniles can waive their rights to protection from self-incrimination, but that the validity of this waiver is determined by the circumstances of each case.

The waiver of *Miranda* rights by a juvenile is one of the most controversial legal issues addressed in the state courts. It has also been the subject of federal constitutional review. In two cases, *Fare v. Michael C.* and *California v. Prysock*, the Supreme Court has attempted to clarify children's rights when they are interrogated by the police. In *Fare v. Michael C.*, the Court ruled that a child's asking to speak to his probation officer was not the equivalent of asking for an attorney; consequently, statements he made to the police absent legal counsel were admissible in court.[44] In *California v. Prysock*, the Court was asked to rule on the adequacy of a *Miranda* warning given to Randall Prysock, a youthful murder suspect.[45] After reviewing the taped exchange between the police interrogator and the boy, the Court upheld Prysock's conviction when it ruled that even though the *Miranda* warning was given in slightly different language and out of exact context, its meaning was easily understandable, even to a juvenile.

Taken together, *Fare* and *Prysock* make it seem indisputable that juveniles are at least entitled to receive the same *Miranda* rights as adults. *Miranda v. Arizona* is a historic decision that continues to protect the rights of all suspects placed in custody.[46]

To read more about the *Miranda* decision, go to http://www.rh.cc.ca.us/ departments/academic/ pubserv/leo/miranda.htm For an up-to-date list of Web links, go to http://info.wadsworth.com/siegel

Discretionary Justice

Today juvenile offenders receive nearly as much procedural protection as adult offenders. However, the police have broader authority in dealing with juveniles than with adults. Granting such **discretion** to juvenile officers raises some important questions: Under what circumstances should an officer arrest status offenders? Should a

discretion Use of personal decision making and choice in carrying out operations in the criminal justice system, such as deciding whether to make an arrest or when to accept a plea bargain.

summons be used in lieu of arrest? Under what conditions should a juvenile be taken into protective custody?

When police confront a case involving a juvenile offender, they rely on their discretion to choose an appropriate course of action. Police discretion is selective enforcement of the law by authorized police agents. Discretion gives officers a choice among possible courses of action within the limits on their power.[47] This is a prime example of *low-visibility decision making*—a public official making decisions that the public is not in a position to regulate or criticize.[48]

Discretion exists not only in the police function but also in prosecutorial decision making, judicial judgments, and corrections. Discretion results in the law being applied differently in similar situations. For example, two teenagers are caught in a stolen automobile; one is arrested, the other released. Two youths are drunk and disorderly; one is sent home, the other to juvenile court. A group of youngsters is involved in a gang fight; only a few are arrested, the others are released.

Much discretion is exercised in juvenile work because of the informality that has been built into the system in an attempt to individualize justice.[49] Furthermore, officials in the juvenile justice system make decisions that are often without oversight or review. The daily procedures of juvenile personnel are rarely subject to judicial review, except when they clearly violate a youth's constitutional rights. As a result, discretion sometimes deteriorates into discrimination and other abuses on the part of the police. The real danger in discretion is that it allows the law to discriminate against precisely those elements in the population—the poor, the ignorant, the unpopular—who are least able to draw attention to their plight.[50]

The problem of discretion in juvenile justice is one of extremes: Too little discretion provides insufficient flexibility to treat juvenile offenders as individuals. Too much discretion can lead to injustice. Guidelines and controls are needed to structure the use of discretion.

Generally, the first contact a youth has with the juvenile justice system is with the police.[51] In a classic 1963 study, Nathan Goldman examined the arrest records of more than 1,000 juveniles from four communities in Pennsylvania.[52] He concluded that more than 64 percent of police contacts with juveniles were handled informally. Subsequent research offered additional evidence of informal disposition of juvenile cases.[53] For example, in the 1970s, Paul Strasburg found that about 50 percent of all children who come in contact with the police do not get past the initial stage of the juvenile justice process.[54]

The most recent study analyzed juvenile data collected as part of the Project on Policing Neighborhoods—a comprehensive study of police patrols in Indianapolis, Indiana, and St. Petersburg, Florida indicates that police still use discretion.[55] The study found that 13 percent of police encounters with juveniles resulted in arrest.[56] As shown in Table 13.2, the most likely disposition of police encounters with juveniles is a command or threat to arrest (38%), the second most likely, search and/or interrogation of the suspects (24%). Furthermore, studies show that many juvenile offenders are never referred to the juvenile court.

To read about trends in juvenile arrests, go to *http://www.ncjrs.org/pdffiles1/ ojjdp/185236.pdf* For an up-to-date list of Web links, go to *http://info.wadsworth.com/siegel*

Table 13.2   Disposition of Police Encounters with Juveniles

Disposition	Juveniles (%)
Release	14
Advise	11
Search/interrogate	24
Command/threaten	38
Arrest	13

Source: Robert E. Worden and Stephanie M. Myers, *Police Encounters with Juvenile Suspects* (Albany, NY: Hindelang Criminal Justice Research Center and School of Criminal Justice, University at Albany, SUNY, 2001), Table 3.

The most current data show an increase in the number of cases referred to the juvenile court. The FBI estimates that about two-thirds of all juvenile arrests are referred to juvenile court.[57] Despite the variations between the estimates, these studies indicate that the police use significant discretion in their decisions regarding juvenile offenders. Research shows that differential decision making goes on without clear guidance.

If all police officers acted in a fair and just manner, the seriousness of the crime, the situation in which it occurred, and the legal record of the juvenile would be the factors that affect decision making. Research does show that police are much more likely to take formal action if the crime is serious and has been reported by a victim who is a respected member of the community, and if the offender is well known to them.[58] However, there are other factors that are believed to shape police discretion; they are discussed next.

Environmental Factors

How does a police officer decide what to do with a juvenile offender? The norms of the community are a factor in the decision. Some officers work in communities that tolerate a fair amount of personal freedom. In liberal environments, the police may be inclined to release juveniles rather than arrest them. Other officers work in conservative communities that expect a no-nonsense approach to police enforcement. Here, police may be more inclined to arrest a juvenile.

Police officers may be influenced by their perception of community alternatives to police intervention. Some officers may use arrest because they believe nothing else can be done.[59] Others may favor referring juveniles to social service agencies, particularly if they believe a community has a variety of good resources. These referrals save time and effort; records do not have to be filled out, and court appearances can be avoided. The availability of such options allows for greater latitude in police decision making.[60]

Police Policy

The policies and customs of the local police department also influence decisions. Juvenile officers may be pressured to make more arrests or to refrain from making arrests under certain circumstances. Directives instruct officers to be alert to certain types of juvenile violations. The chief of police might initiate policies governing the arrest practices of the juvenile department. For example, if local merchants complain that youths congregating in a shopping center parking lot are inhibiting business, police may be called on to make arrests. Under other circumstances, an informal warning might be given. Similarly, a rash of deaths caused by teenage drunk driving may galvanize the local media to demand police action. The mayor and the police chief, sensitive to possible voter dissatisfaction, may then demand that formal police action be taken in cases of drunk driving.

Another source of influence is pressure from supervisors. Some supervising officers may believe it is important to curtail disorderly conduct or drug use. In addition, officers may be influenced by the discretionary decisions made by their peers.

Situational Factors

In addition to the environment, a variety of situational factors affect a police officer's decisions. Situational factors are those attached to a particular crime, such as specific traits of offenders. Traditionally, it was believed that police officers rely heavily on the demeanor and appearance of the juvenile in making decisions. Some research shows that the decision to arrest is often based on factors such as dress, attitude, speech, and level of hostility toward the police.[61] Kids who display "attitude" were believed to be the ones more likely to be arrested than those who are respectful and contrite.[62] However, more recent research has challenged the influence of demeanor on police decision making, suggesting that it is delinquent behavior and actions that occur during police detention that influence the police decision to take formal action.[63] For example, a person who struggles or touches police during a confrontation is a likely candidate for arrest, but those who merely sport a bad attitude or negative demeanor are as likely to suffer an arrest as the polite and contrite.[64] It is possible that the earlier research reflected a time when police officers demanded absolute respect and were quick to take action when their authority was challenged. The more recent research may indicate that police, through training or experience, are now less sensitive to slights and confrontational behavior and view them as part of the job. Most studies conclude that the following variables are important in the police discretionary process:[65]

- The attitude of the complainant
- The type and seriousness of the offense
- The race, sex, and age of the offender
- The attitude of the offender
- The offender's prior contacts with the police
- The perceived willingness of the parents to assist in solving the problem (in the case of a child)
- The setting or location in which the incident occurs
- Whether the offender denies the actions or insists on a court hearing (in the case of a child)
- The likelihood that a child can be served by an agency in the community

Bias and Police Discretion

Do police allow bias to affect their decisions on whether to arrest youths? Do they routinely use "racial profiling" when they decide to make an arrest? A great deal of debate has been generated over this issue. Some experts believe that police decision making is deeply influenced by the offender's personal characteristics, whereas others maintain that crime-related variables are more significant.

Racial Bias   It has long been charged that police are more likely to act formally with African American suspects and use their discretion to benefit whites.[66] As Table 13.3 shows, African American youths are arrested at a rate disproportionate to their representation in the population. Research on this issue has yielded mixed conclusions. One view is that while discrimination may have existed in the past, there is no longer a need to worry about racial discrimination because minorities now possess sufficient political status to protect them within the justice system.[67] As Har-

Table 13.3 African American Representation in Arrest Statistics

Most Serious Offense	African American Juvenile Arrests in 2000 (%)
Murder	50
Forcible rape	35
Robbery	56
Aggravated assault	37
Burglary	25
Larceny-theft	26
Motor vehicle theft	41
Weapons	31
Drug abuse violations	28
Curfew and loitering	25
Runaways	18

Source: FBI, *Crime in the United States 2000* (Washington, DC: U.S. Government Printing Office, 2001), p. 235, table 43.

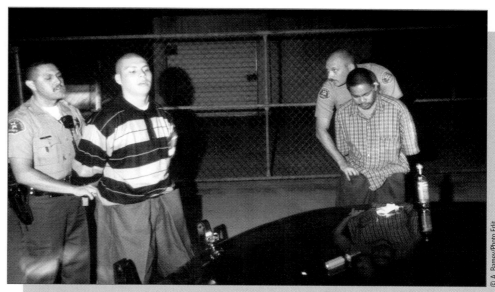

TWO TEENAGE GANG MEMBERS are arrested for possession of drugs and firearms by officers of the Los Angeles Police Department. Police have discretion to take formal action against youthful offenders, to release them with a warning, or take some other informal action.

vard University law professor Randall Kennedy forcefully argues, even if a law enforcement policy exists that disproportionately affects African American suspects, it might be justified as a "public good" because law-abiding African Americans are statistically more often victims of crimes committed by other African Americans.[68]

In contrast to these views, several research efforts do show evidence of police discrimination against African American youths.[69] Donna Bishop and Charles Frazier found that race can have a direct effect on decisions made at several junctures of the juvenile justice process.[70] According to Bishop and Frazier, African Americans are more likely than whites to be recommended for formal processing, referred to court, adjudicated delinquent, and given harsher dispositions for comparable offenses. In the arrest category, specifically, being African American increases the probability of formal police action.[71]

Similarly, a study by the National Council on Crime and Delinquency revealed significant overrepresentation by black youths at every point in the California juvenile justice system. Although they make up less than 9 percent of the state youth population, black youths accounted for 19 percent of juvenile arrests. According to the study, the causes for the disparity included (1) institutional racism, (2) environmental factors, (3) family dysfunction, (4) cultural barriers, and (5) school failure.[72]

In summary, studies of bias in police decision making have revealed the following:

1. Some researchers have concluded that the police discriminate against minority youths.
2. Other researchers do not find evidence of discrimination.
3. Racial disparity is most often seen at the arrest stage but probably exists at other stages.
4. The higher arrest rates of minorities are related to interpersonal, family, community, and organizational differences. Other influences may include police discretion, street crime visibility, and high crime rates within a particular group. Such factors, however, may also be linked to general societal discrimination.

For further information on racial bias in police decisions, see the Focus on Delinquency box entitled "Juvenile Race, Gender, and Ethnicity in Police Decision Making." Further research is needed to better understand and document what appears to be findings of disproportional arrests of minority juvenile offenders.[73]

Juvenile Race, Gender, and Ethnicity in Police Decision Making

Does police discretion work against the young, males, the poor, and minority group members, or does it favor special interest groups? Current research has uncovered information supporting both sides.

Although the police are involved in at least some discrimination against racial minorities who are juveniles, the frequency and scope of such discrimination may be less than anticipated. Some of today's literature shows that the police are likely to interfere with or arrest poor African American youths. The police frequently stop and question youths of color walking down the streets of their neighborhoods or hanging around street corners. If this is the case, then race plays a role in police discretion.

In contrast to these findings, data from other studies indicate that racial bias does not influence the decision to arrest and move a youngster through the juvenile justice system. The attitude of the youth, prior record, seriousness of crime, setting or location of the crime, and other variables control police discretion, not race, ethnicity, or gender. Another problem in determining the impact of race or gender on police discretion is that the victim's race, not the juvenile offender's, may be the key to racial bias. Police officers may take differential action when the victim is white rather than when the victim is a minority group member.

Police bias may also be a result of organizational and administrative directions as opposed to bias by an individual officer "on the beat" or in a cruiser. For example, the police departments have been found to use racial profiles for stopping and questioning suspects.

Obviously, not all officers operate unfairly or with a racial bias. Quite possibly the impact of juvenile race on police discretion varies from jurisdiction to jurisdiction and from one group of juveniles to another. Many African American youngsters, for example, view their gang affiliation as a means of survival. Teenage gang members and their families often feel frustrated about the lack of opportunities and their experiences as being targets of discrimination.

Despite all the research findings, uncertainty about the extent and degree of racial bias continues to plague the juvenile justice system. Unfortunately, minority youths are involved in a disproportionate percentage of all juvenile arrests. This often gives the impression that racial, gender, and ethnic bias exists in urban police departments.

Critical Thinking

1. What do you think? Do the police take race into account when making decisions to arrest juveniles suspected of violating the law?

InfoTrac College Edition Research

To read more about racial bias on the part of police toward juveniles, go to Jim Leitzel, "Race and Policing," *Society 38*:38 (March 2001).

Sources: For an extensive review of research on police discretion (adult and juvenile) since 1980, see Eric Riksheim and Steven Chermak, "Causes of Police Behavior Revisited," *Journal of Criminal Justice 21*:353–82 (1993); also William Brown, "The Fight for Survival: African American Gang Members and Their Families in a Segregated Society," *Juvenile and Family Court Journal 49*:1–15 (1998); Bohsui Wu, "The Effect of Race on Juvenile Justice Processing," *Juvenile and Family Court Journal 48*:43–53 (1997); Richard Sutphen, David Kurtz, and Martha Giddings, "The Influence of Juveniles' Race on Police Decision-Making: An Exploratory Study," *Juvenile and Family Court Journal 44*:69–78 (1997).

Gender Bias   Do the police treat male and female offenders differently? Some experts favor the *chivalry hypothesis*, which holds that police are likely to act paternally toward young girls and not arrest them. Others believe that police may be more likely to arrest female offenders because their actions violate officers' stereotypes of the female.

There is some research support for various forms of gender bias. The nature of this bias may vary according to the seriousness of the offense and the age of the offender. Studies offer a variety of conclusions, but there seems to be general agreement that police are less likely to process females for delinquent acts and that they discriminate against them by arresting them for status offenses. Examples of the conclusions reached by some of these studies follow:

- Police tend to be more lenient toward females than males with regard to acts of delinquency. Merry Morash found that boys who engage in "typical male" delinquent activities are much more likely to develop police records than females.[74]
- Females who have committed minor or status offenses seem to be referred to juvenile court more often than males. Meda Chesney-Lind has found that adolescent female status offenders are arrested for less-serious offenses than boys.[75]

- Recent evidence has confirmed earlier studies showing that the police, and most likely the courts, apply a double standard in dealing with male and female juvenile offenders. Bishop and Frazier found that both female status offenders and male delinquents are differently disadvantaged in the juvenile justice system in that, for status offenses, females are more likely to be arrested, and for other offenses, males are more likely to be arrested.[76]

Organizational Bias The policies of some police departments may result in biased practices. Research has found that police departments can be characterized by their professionalism (skills and knowledge) and bureaucratization.[77] Departments that are highly bureaucratized (high emphasis on rules and regulations) and at the same time unprofessional are most likely to be insulated from the communities they serve. Organizational policy may be influenced by the perceptions of police decision makers. A number of experts have found that law-enforcement administrators have a stereotyped view of the urban poor as troublemakers who must be kept under control.[78] Consequently, lower-class neighborhoods experience much greater police scrutiny than middle-class areas, and their residents face a proportionately greater chance of arrest. For example, a significant body of literature shows that police are more likely to "hassle" or arrest African American males in poor neighborhoods than white males in middle-class neighborhoods.[79] It is therefore not surprising, as criminologist Robert Sampson has found, that teenage residents of neighborhoods in low socioeconomic areas have a significantly greater chance of acquiring police records than youths living in higher socioeconomic areas, regardless of the actual crime rates in these areas.[80] Sampson's research indicates that although police officers may not discriminate on an individual level, departmental policy that focuses on lower-class areas may result in class and racial bias in the police processing of delinquent youth.

Not all experts believe there is rampant police organizational bias. For example, when Ronald Weitzer surveyed people in three Washington, D.C., neighborhoods, he found that residents in primarily African American neighborhoods value racially integrated police services.[81] Similarly, Thomas Priest and Deborah Brown Carter have found that the African American community is supportive of the local police, especially when they respond quickly to calls for service. It is unlikely that African Americans would appreciate rapid service, or the presence of white officers, if police routinely practiced racial discrimination.[82]

One reason for these contrasting views is that racial influences on police decision making are often quite subtle and hard to detect. For example, research consistently shows that the victim's race, and not the criminal's, is the key to racial bias; police officers are more likely to take formal action when the victim of crime is white than when the victim is a minority-group member. These data suggest that to be valid, any study of police discretion must take into account both victim and offender characteristics.

In summary, the policies, practices, and customs of the local police department influence discretion. Conditions vary from department to department and depend on the judgment of the chief and others in the organizational hierarchy. Because the police retain a large degree of discretionary power, the ideal of nondiscrimination is often difficult to achieve in practice. However, policies to limit police discretion can help eliminate bias.

A CLOSER VIEW
To read more about organizational bias on the part of police toward juveniles on InfoTrac College Edition, go to Michael Borrero, "The Widening Mistrust between Youth and Police," *Families in Society: The Journal of Contemporary Human Services* 82:399 (July 2001).

To read about what is being done to reduce racial profiling, go to *http://www.ncjrs.org/ txtfiles1/bja/184768.txt* For an up-to-date list of Web links, go to *http://info.wadsworth.com/siegel*

Limiting Police Discretion

A number of leading organizations have suggested the use of guidelines to limit police discretion. The American Bar Association (ABA) states, "Since individual police officers may make important decisions affecting police operations without discretion, with limited accountability and without any uniformity within a department, police discretion should be structured and controlled."[83] There is an almost unanimous opinion

Controls on Discretion
- Written rules
- Narrow laws
- Personnel training

Police discretion
decision

Situational
factors

Race and gender
bias

Organizational
bias

Environmental
factors

Figure 13.3
Discretionary Justice with Juveniles

that steps must be taken to provide better control and guidance over police discretion in street and station house adjustments of juvenile cases.

One leading exponent of police discretion is Kenneth Culp Davis, who has done much to raise the consciousness of criminal justice practitioners about discretionary decision making. Davis recommends controlling administrative discretion through (1) the use of more narrowly defined laws, (2) the development of written policies, and (3) the recording of decisions by criminal justice personnel.[84] Narrowing the scope of juvenile codes, for example, would limit and redefine the broad authority police officers currently have to take youths into custody for criminal and noncriminal behavior. Such practices would provide fair criteria for arrests, adjustment, and police referral of juvenile offenders and would help eliminate largely personal judgments based on race, attitude, or demeanor of the juvenile.[85] Discretionary decision making in juvenile police work can be better understood by examining Figure 13.3.

Police Work and Delinquency Prevention

Police have taken the lead in delinquency prevention. They have used a number of techniques; some rely on their deterrent powers, others on their relationship with schools and the community.

Aggressive Law Enforcement

One method of contemporary delinquency prevention relies on aggressive patrolling targeted at specific patterns of delinquency. Police departments in Chicago and Los Angeles have at one time used saturation patrol, targeting gang areas and arresting members for any law violations. These tactics have not proven to be effective against gangs. For example, in 1996 the Dallas Police Department initiated a successful gang-control effort that employed such tactics as saturating known gang areas with anti-gang units, as well as aggressive enforcement of curfew and truancy laws. Targeting truancy and curfew laws led to a significant reduction in gang activity, whereas the saturation patrols proved ineffective.[86]

Community-Based Policing Services

Some police departments are now replacing more aggressive measures with cooperative community-based efforts. Because police officers are responsible for the care of juveniles taken into custody, it is essential that they work closely with social service groups day by day. In addition, the police are assuming a leadership role in identifying the needs of children in the community and helping the community meet those needs. In helping to develop delinquency prevention programs, the police are working closely with youth service bureaus, schools, recreational facilities, welfare agencies, and employment programs.[87]

Using community services for juveniles has many advantages. Such services allow young people to avoid the stigma of being processed by a police agency. They also improve the community's awareness of the needs of young people and make it possible to restrict court referral to cases involving serious crime.

Curfews represent a community-based policing service. Curfew laws vary with respect to the locale affected, the time frame, and the sanctions. Most restrict minors to their homes or property between the hours of 11:00 P.M. and 6:00 A.M. Sanctions for curfew violations by youths range from fines to being charged with a misdemeanor violation, and may include participation in diversion programs or, in some jurisdictions, jail time for parents.

Curfew enforcement activities are implemented through regular law enforcement and special policing units. Studies of the impact of juvenile curfew ordinances are limited, but a recent assessment of the empirical evidence, including an evaluation of a curfew law in Charlotte, North Carolina, suggests that on their own, curfews are not effective in managing juveniles or reducing juvenile delinquency.[88]

Police in Schools

You can visit G.R.E.A.T.'s Web site at

http://www.atf.treas.gov/great/

For an up-to-date list of Web links, go to

http://info.wadsworth.com/siegel

A CLOSER VIEW

To read more about the prevention of juvenile gang crime on InfoTrac College Edition, go to "Reducing Gang Crime," *FBI Law Enforcement Bulletin* 68:20 (September 1999).

One of the most important institutions playing a role in delinquency prevention is the school. Liaison prevention programs between the police and schools have been implemented in many communities. Liaison officers from schools and police departments have played a leadership role in developing recreational programs for juveniles. In some instances, police have actually operated such programs. In others, they have encouraged community support for recreational activities, including Little League baseball, athletic clubs, camping outings, and police athletic and scouting programs.

The Gang Resistance Education and Training (G.R.E.A.T.) program is one example of a police and school partnership to reduce delinquency. Modeled after D.A.R.E. (Drug Abuse and Resistance Education; see Chapter 10), G.R.E.A.T. was developed among a number of Arizona police departments in an effort to reduce adolescent involvement in criminal behavior. Today the program is in school curricula in all 50 states and the District of Columbia.[89] The program has two main objectives: to reduce gang activity and to teach students about the negative consequences of becoming involved in a gang. Trained police officers administer the program in school classrooms about once a week. The program, which is designed for middle-school students, comprises eight main lessons, as described in Exhibit 13.3.

Evaluations of G.R.E.A.T. show mixed results in reducing delinquency and gang involvement. One evaluation found that students who complete the curriculum develop more prosocial attitudes and have lower rates of gang membership and delinquency than those in a comparison group who were not exposed to G.R.E.A.T.[90] A

Exhibit 13.3   The Eight Lessons of the G.R.E.A.T. Program

1. *Introduction:* Students get acquainted with the G.R.E.A.T. program and the presenting officer.

2. *Crime, Victims, and Your Rights:* Students learn about crimes, their victims, and their impact on school and neighborhood.

3. *Cultural Sensitivity and Prejudice:* Students explore how cultural differences affect their school and neighborhood.

4. *Conflict Resolution (two sessions):* Students are taught how to create an atmosphere of understanding that enables all parties to better address problems and work on solutions together.

5. *Meeting Basic Needs:* Students learn how to meet their basic needs without joining a gang.

6. *Drugs and Neighborhoods:* Students are educated about how drugs affect their school and neighborhood.

7. *Responsibility:* Students examine the diverse responsibilities of people in their school and neighborhood.

8. *Goal Setting:* Students learn the need for goal setting and how to establish short- and long-term goals.

Source: Finn-Aage Esbensen, D. Wayne Osgood, Terrance J. Taylor, Dana Peterson, and Adrienne Freng, "How Great Is G.R.E.A.T.? Results from a Longitudinal Quasi-Experimental Design," *Criminology and Public Policy* 1:87–118 (2001), p. 88.

more recent evaluation of the program, four years after students completed the curriculum, did not find any significant differences for gang membership or delinquency compared to a control group. The evaluation did find that those who took the program held more prosocial attitudes than those who did not.[91]

Integrated Policing Models

To read more about Operation Ceasefire in Boston, go to *http://www.ojjdp.ncjrs.org/ pubs/gun_violence/profile21.html* For an up-to-date list of Web links, go to *http://info.wadsworth.com/siegel*

In another approach to delinquency prevention, police work with other juvenile justice agencies as well as the community. One of the most successful of these delinquency prevention programs is Operation Ceasefire. Implemented in Boston, this problem-oriented policing program aims to reduce youth homicide victimization and youth gun violence.[92] Despite being a police-led program, Operation Ceasefire involves many other juvenile and criminal justice and social agencies, including probation and parole, Bureau of Alcohol, Tobacco, and Firearms (ATF), gang outreach and prevention streetworkers, and the Drug Enforcement Administration (DEA). This group of agencies has become known as the Ceasefire Working Group.

The program has two main elements:

1. a direct law enforcement focus on illicit gun traffickers who supply youth with guns, and
2. an attempt to generate a strong deterrent to gang violence.[93]

A wide range of measures have been used to reduce the flow of guns to youth, including pooling the resources of local, state, and federal justice authorities to track and seize illegal guns, and targeting traffickers of guns most used by gang members.

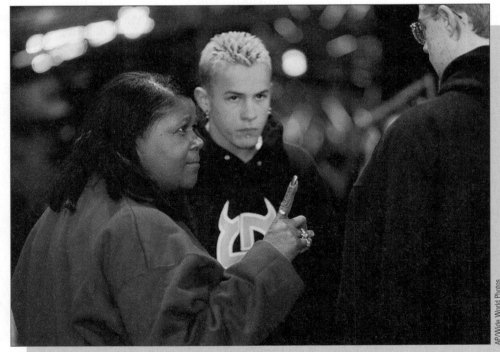

TO BE SUCCESSFUL, policing involving the community requires that citizens play a dynamic role in law enforcement. Sometimes this means taking an active role in delinquency prevention. Here, Lyn Jones (left), a member of the Mighty Moms, reminds a group of teenagers about the Mall of America's policy that children under 16 must be accompanied by an adult on weekend evenings. Jones is part of a team of 30 paid parents called Mighty Moms and Dedicated Dads, who walk among the thousands of visitors to the mall looking for unsupervised teens and helping to keep the peace.

FREDDIE CARDOZA

Problem:
Violent Gang Member

"Given his extensive criminal record,
if there was a Federal law against
jaywalking, we'd indict him for that."

—*Don Stern, U.S. Attorney*

Solution:
Armed Career Criminal Conviction

Arrested with one bullet
Sentence: 19 years, 7 months
No possibility of parole

Address:

Otisville Federal Correctional Institute
Maximum Security Facility, New York

Figure 13.4
Poster Created by the Gun Project Working Group
Source: David M. Kennedy, Anthony A. Braga, and Anne Morrison Piehl, "Developing and Implementing Operation Ceasefire," in *Reducing Gun Violence: The Boston Gun Project's Operation Ceasefire* (Washington, DC: NIJ Research Report, 2001), p. 38, Exhibit 1-6.

The response to gang violence has been to pull every deterrence "lever" available, including shutting down drug markets, serving warrants, enforcing probation restrictions, and making disorder arrests.[94] The Ceasefire Working Group delivered its message clearly to gang members: "We're ready, we're watching, we're waiting: Who wants to be next?"[95] An example of how the Working Group communicated this message to gang members is shown in Figure 13.4.

The SHIELD Program

The Westminster, California, police department designed the SHIELD program to accomplish two primary goals. First, it uses the contacts that police officers make in the course of their normal duties to identify youths who they think are likely to become involved in violent behavior, substance abuse, and gang activities. At-risk youths are identified as those who are exposed to family risk factors such as domestic violence and other criminal activities in the home. Second, SHIELD provides youths with services tailored to meet their individual needs by using a multidisciplinary team of representatives from the community, schools, and service agencies.

The SHIELD youth referral process gives officers a procedure for providing assistance to youths exposed to family risk factors. All patrol officers in Westminster receive the following orders as part of the youth referral protocol:

> Police personnel are required to obtain the name, age, and school attended of any minor youth living in a home where a report is filed involving the following police activity: family violence of any type, neglect or abandonment, gang activity, drug sales or usage, arrests made associated with alcohol abuse, or any other call for service where the welfare of minor youth is at risk due to the behavior of older siblings or adults living in, or frequenting, the home.

Whenever the SHIELD Resource Officer (SRO) receives a report from the officer on the scene, he or she screens the case to determine whether the circumstances make the youth appropriate for SHIELD intervention. If appropriate, a student referral report is created that contains a synopsis of the incident as it pertains to the youth, as well as demographic and personal information, including assessments of both risk and protective factors. The SRO then sends the student referral report to the Youth and Family Resource Team. This multidisciplinary team includes officials from the local school district, such as the pupil personnel administrator, the district nurse, a specialist in drug abuse prevention, and school principals; counseling staff from a community service provider; a county social worker; the Westminster Community Services Recreation Supervisor; the SRO; and a second officer formerly assigned to Drug Abuse Resistance Education (D.A.R.E.).

When they receive the student referral report, the members of the Youth and Family Resource Team consider a range of school- and community-based treatment options and make recommendations for treatment. The Youth and Family Resource Team reassesses the treat-

ment recommendations and progress of each youth three weeks after the initial recommendation. While a youth is involved in treatment, the service providers send monthly progress reports to the SHIELD staff at the Westminster Police Department. These reports allow for ongoing tracking and reassessment of the services provided to program youth.

The treatment delivery systems that SHIELD relies on are already in the community. The program works closely with all of the local schools and the local Boys and Girls Clubs. Individual and group counseling are commonly used in both school and community settings. Issues covered in counseling vary according to the circumstances of the individual case, but common themes include anger management, goal setting, pregnancy prevention, conflict resolution, and other coping skills. Informal school-based monitoring is also frequently included in treatment plans. When teachers and administrators are aware of the risk factors that a student faces outside the classroom and they are actively monitoring that student, they are more likely to detect and respond to early signs of problem behavior, abuse, or neglect.

To date, there has been no definitive evaluation of the SHIELD program. Nevertheless, the identification and referral activities stand as the central program elements of SHIELD, and these show great promise as a model for the mobilization of community resources to prevent delinquency.

Critical Thinking

1. What is the importance of having a multidisciplinary team as part of the program?
2. What are some of the advantages to the SHIELD program's use of treatment delivery systems that already exist in the community?

InfoTrac College Edition Research

To read more about police work and delinquency prevention, use *police-services-for-juveniles* as a key term.

Sources: Adapted from Phelan A. Wyrick, "Law Enforcement Referral of At-Risk Youth: The SHIELD Program," *Juvenile Justice Bulletin*, November 2000 (Washington, DC: Office of Juvenile Justice and Delinquency Prevention, 2000); personal communication with SHIELD program officers, 2001.

A CLOSER VIEW
To read more about problem-oriented policing and juvenile delinquency on InfoTrac College Edition, go to Terry Eisenberg and Bruce Glasscock, "Looking Inward with Problem-Oriented Policing," *FBI Law Enforcement Bulletin* 70:1 (July 2001).

An evaluation of the program from before it started to the time it ended showed a substantial reduction in youth homicide victims, youth gun assaults, and overall gang violence across the city. In a comparison with other New England cities and large cities across the United States, the majority of which also experienced a reduction in youth homicides over the same period, it was found that the significant reduction in youth homicides in Boston was due to Operation Ceasefire.

Following on the success of the Boston program, the Office of Juvenile Justice and Delinquency Prevention (OJJDP) launched a comprehensive initiative to reduce juvenile gun violence in four cities (Baton Rouge and Shreveport, Louisiana; Oakland, California; and Syracuse, New York). Called the Partnerships to Reduce Juvenile Gun Violence Program, problem-oriented policing strategies are at the center of the program, but other intervention strategies are also important. These include delinquency prevention (job training and mentoring), juvenile justice sanctions, and a public information campaign designed to communicate the dangers and consequences of gun violence to juveniles, families, and community residents.[96] An evaluation of the implementation of the program found that three of the four cities were successful in developing comprehensive strategies.[97] An evaluation of the effectiveness of the program in reducing juvenile gun violence is under way.[98] With a successful implementation and inclusion of many of the components of the Boston program, this program offers promise in reducing juvenile violence.

Today, many experts consider delinquency prevention efforts to be crucial to the development of a comprehensive approach to youth crime. Although such efforts cut across the entire juvenile justice system, police programs have become increasingly popular. See the Policy and Practice box entitled "The SHIELD Program," for more on this topic.

SUMMARY

As rates of delinquency have soared, the police have become more important to the juvenile justice system. It is almost always the police officer who has the initial contact with young people committing antisocial acts. This contact can have a significant impact on an offender's future.

The community policing philosophy, which emphasizes partnerships between police and citizens, has been applied to both adult and juvenile crime.

Numerous factors influence the decisions police make about juvenile offenders. They include the seriousness of the offense, the harm inflicted on the victim, and the likelihood that the juvenile will break the law again.

Police officers must be familiar with procedural law because their contact with young people includes the legal aspects of arrest, custodial interrogation, and lineups. Through the *Miranda v. Arizona* decision, the U.S.

Supreme Court established a clearly defined procedure for custodial interrogation. Such practices are applicable to juvenile suspects. Search and seizure actions, lineups, and other police procedures are also subject to court review.

Another important issue is police discretion in dealing with juvenile offenders. Discretion is a low-visibility decision made in the administration of adult and juvenile justice. Discretionary decisions are made without guidelines from the police administrator. Discretion is essential in providing individualized justice, but problems such as discrimination, unfairness, and bias toward particular groups of juveniles must be controlled.

New initiatives in law enforcement to reduce the incidence of youth crime include (1) involvement in prevention programs such as mentoring and after-school recreation, (2) gang membership prevention and control, and (3) firearm interventions.

KEY TERMS

pledge system	juvenile officers	arrest	custodial interrogation
watch system	role conflicts	probable cause	*Miranda* warning
community policing	problem-oriented policing	search and seizure	discretion

QUESTIONS FOR DISCUSSION

1. The term discretion is often defined as selective decision making by police and others in the juvenile justice system who are faced with alternative modes of action. Discuss some of the factors affecting the discretion of the police when dealing with juvenile offenders.

2. What role should police organizations play in delinquency prevention and control? Is it feasible to expect police departments to provide social services to children and families? How should police departments be better organized to provide for the control of juvenile delinquency?

3. What qualities should a police juvenile officer have? Should a college education be a requirement?

4. For the first time in a decade, arrests of juveniles for violent crime have declined. What do you believe caused this decline?

5. In light of the traditional and protective roles assumed by law enforcement personnel in juvenile justice, is there any reason to have a *Miranda* warning for youths taken into custody?

6. Can the police and community be truly effective in forming a partnership to reduce juvenile delinquency? Discuss the role of the juvenile police officer in preventing and investigating juvenile crime.

VIEWPOINT

Community policing is an important component of the day-to-day operations of the San Diego Police Department. In a high-crime area of the city known as City Heights, the police joined forces with community residents and organizers to address juvenile delinquency and drug-related problems. Mobilizing residents to participate in solving delinquency problems was an important goal of the group. Within a short time frame the group achieved a number of successes, including shutting down drug houses, improving community trust in the police, and getting youth involved in delinquency prevention programs.

To read more about community policing and juvenile delinquency on InfoTrac College Edition, go to Recheal Stewart-Brown, "Community Mobilization," *FBI Law Enforcement Bulletin* 70:9 (June 2001). To find further information, use community-policing as a key term.

NOTES

1. This section relies on sources such as Malcolm Sparrow, Mark Moore, and David Kennedy, *Beyond 911, A New Era for Policing* (New York: Basic Books, 1990); Daniel Devlin, *Police Procedure, Administration, and Organization* (London: Butterworth, 1966); Robert Fogelson, *Big City Police* (Cambridge: Harvard University Press, 1977); Roger Lane, *Policing the City, Boston 1822–1885* (Cambridge: Harvard University Press, 1967); Roger Lane, "Urban Police and Crime in Nineteenth-Century America," in Norval Morris and Michael Tonry, eds., *Crime and Justice,* vol. 2 (Chicago: University of Chicago Press, 1980), pp. 1–45; J. J. Tobias, *Crime and Industrial Society in the Nineteenth Century* (New York: Schocken, 1967); Samuel Walker, *A Critical History of Police Reform: The Emergence of Professionalism* (Lexington, MA: Lexington Books, 1977); idem, *Popular Justice* (New York: Oxford University Press, 1980); President's Commission on Law Enforcement and the Administration of Justice, *Task Force Report: The Police* (Washington, DC: U.S. Government Printing Office, 1967), pp. 1–9.

2. See, generally, Walker, *Popular Justice,* p. 61.

3. Law Enforcement Assistance Administration, *Two Hundred Years of American Criminal Justice* (Washington, DC: U.S. Government Printing Office, 1976).

4. August Vollmer, *The Police and Modern Society* (Berkeley: University of California Press, 1936).

5. O. W. Wilson, *Police Administration,* 2nd ed. (New York: McGraw-Hill, 1963).

6. Herman Goldstein, "Toward Community-Oriented Policing: Potential Basic Requirements and Threshold Questions," *Crime and Delinquency* 33:630 (1987); see also Janet Reno, "Taking America Back for Our Children," *Crime and Delinquency* 44:75 (1998).

7. Lawrence W. Sherman and Richard Berk, "The Specific Deterrent Effects of Arrest for Domestic Assault," *American Sociological Review* 49:261–72 (1984).

8. John E. Eck and Edward R. Maguire, "Have Changes in Policing Reduced Violent Crime? An Assessment of the Evidence," in Alfred Blumstein and Joel Wallman, eds., *The Crime Drop in America* (New York: Cambridge University Press, 2000); Lawrence W. Sherman, "Fair and Effective Policing," in James Q. Wilson and Joan Petersilia, eds., *Crime: Public Policies for Crime Control* (Oakland, CA: Institute for Contemporary Studies, 2002); Lawrence W. Sherman and John E. Eck, "Policing for Crime Prevention," in Lawrence W. Sherman, David P. Farrington, Brandon C. Welsh, and Doris Layton MacKenzie, eds., *Evidence-Based Crime Prevention* (London: Routledge, 2002).

9. Yolander Hurst, James Frank, and Sandra Lee Browning, "The Attitudes of Juveniles toward the Police: A Comparison of Black and White Youth," *Policing* 23:37–53 (2000).

10. For an analysis of this position, see George Kelling and James Q. Wilson, "Broken Windows: The Police and Neighborhood Safety," *Atlantic Monthly* 249:29–38 (1982).

11. U.S. Department of Justice, "Community Policing," *National Institute of Justice Journal* 225:1–32 (1992).

12. Matthew J. Hickman and Brian A. Reaves, *Community Policing in Local Police Departments, 1997 and 1999* (Washington, DC: Bureau of Justice Statistics Special Report, 2001).

13. Ibid., p. 1.

14. Ibid.

15. Robert Trojanowicz and Hazel Harden, *The Status of Contemporary Community Policing Programs* (East Lansing, MI: Michigan State University Neighborhood Foot Patrol Center, 1985).

16. Hickman and Reaves, *Community Policing in Local Police Departments, 1997 and 1999*, p. 1.

17. Peter Finn, "Block Watches Help Crime Victims in Philadelphia," *National Institute of Justice Reports*: 2–10 (December 1986).

18. James Q. Wilson, "Drugs and Crime," in Michael Tonry and James Q. Wilson, eds., *Crime and Justice—A Review of Research,* vol. 13 (Chicago: University of Chicago Press, 1990).

19. Terence Dunworth, *National Evaluation of the Youth Firearms Violence Initiative* (Washington, DC: NIJ Research in Brief, 2000), p. 1.

20. Ibid., p. 4.

21. Susan Guarino-Ghezzi, "Reintegrative Police Surveillance of Juvenile Offenders: Forging an Urban Model," *Crime and Delinquency* 40:131–53 (1994).

22. The President's Crime Prevention Council, *Preventing Crime and Promoting Responsibility: 50 Programs that Help Communities Help Their Youth* (Washington, DC: U.S. Government Printing Office, 1995).

23. Donald Black and Albert J. Reiss Jr., "Police Control of Juveniles," *American Sociological Review* 35:63 (1970); Richard Lundman, Richard Sykes, and John Clark, "Police Control of Juveniles: A Replication," *Journal of Research on Crime and Delinquency* 15:74 (1978).

24. American Bar Association, *Standards Relating to Police Handling of Juvenile Problems* (Cambridge, MA: Ballinger, 1977), p. 1.

25. FBI, *Uniform Crime Reports 2000* (Washington, DC: U.S. Government Printing Office, 2001).

26. Samuel Walker, *The Police of America* (New York: McGraw-Hill, 1983), p. 133.

27. Karen A. Joe, "The Dynamics of Running Away, Deinstitutionalization Policies and the Police," *Juvenile Family Court Journal* 46:43–45 (1995).

28. The President's Crime Prevention Council, *Preventing Crime and Promoting Responsibility.*

29. National Conference of State Legislatures, *A Legislator's Guide to Comprehensive Juvenile Justice, Interventions for Youth at Risk* (Denver: NCSL, 1996).

30. Sherman and Eck, "Policing for Crime Prevention," p. 321; for "hot spots" policing, see also Anthony A. Braga, "The Effects of Hot Spots Policing on Crime," in David P. Farrington and Brandon C. Welsh, "What Works in Preventing Crime? Systematic Reviews of Experimental and Quasi-Experimental Research," *Annals of the American Academy of Political and Social Science* 578:104–25 (2001).

31. See, for example, Edmund F. McGarrell, Steven Chermak, Alexander Weiss, and Jeremy Wilson, "Reducing Firearms Violence through Directed Police Patrol," *Criminology and Public Policy* 1:119-48 (2001).

32. Linda Szymanski, *Summary of Juvenile Code Purpose Clauses* (Pittsburgh: National Center for Juvenile Justice, 1988); see also, for example, GA Code Ann. 15; Iowa Code Ann. 232.2; Mass. Gen. Laws, ch. 119, 56.

33. Samuel M. Davis, *Rights of Juveniles—The Juvenile Justice System* (New York: Clark-Boardmen, rev. June 1989), Sec. 3.3.

34. National Council of Juvenile and Family Court Judges, *Juvenile and Family Law Digest* 29:1–2 (1997).

35. See Fourth Amendment, U.S. Constitution.

36. *Chimel v. Cal.,* 395 U.S. 752, 89 S.Ct. 2034 (1969).

37. *United States v. Ross,* 456 U.S. 798, 102 S.Ct. 2157 (1982).

38. *Terry v. Ohio,* 392 U.S.1, 88 S.Ct. 1868 (1968).

39. *Bumper v. North Carolina,* 391 U.S. 543, 88 S.Ct. 1788 (1968).

40. *Miranda v. Arizona,* 384 U.S. 436, 86 S.Ct. 1602 (1966).

41. *Commonwealth v. Gaskins,* 471 Pa. 238, 369 A.2d 1285 (1977); *In re E.T.C.,* 141 Vt. 375, 449 A.2d 937 (1982).

42. *People v. Lara,* 67 Cal.2d 365, 62 Cal.Rptr. 586, 432 P.2d 202 (1967).

43. *West v. United States,* 399 F.2d 467 (5th Cir. 1968).

44. *Fare v. Michael C.,* 442 U.S. 707, 99 S.Ct. 2560 (1979).

45. *California v. Prysock,* 453 U.S. 355, 101 S.Ct. 2806 (1981).

46. See, for example, Larry Holtz, "*Miranda* in a Juvenile Setting—A Child's Right to Silence," *Journal of Criminal Law and Criminology* 79:534–56 (1987).

47. Kenneth C. Davis, *Discretionary Justice: A Preliminary Inquiry* (Baton Rouge: Louisiana State University Press, 1969); H. Ted Rubin, *Juvenile Justice: Police, Practice and Law* (Santa Monica: Goodyear, 1979).

48. Joseph Goldstein, "Police Discretion Not to Invoke the Criminal Process: Low-Visibility Decisions in the Administration of Justice," *Yale Law Journal* 69:544 (1960).

49. Victor Streib, *Juvenile Justice in America* (Port Washington, NY: Kennikat, 1978).

50. Herbert Packer, *The Limits of the Criminal Sanction* (Palo Alto, CA: Stanford University Press, 1968).

51. Black and Reiss, "Police Control of Juveniles"; Richard J. Lundman, "Routine Police Arrest Practices," *Social Problems* 22:127–41 (1974); Robert E. Worden and Stephanie M. Myers, *Police Encounters with Juvenile Suspects* (Albany, NY: Hindelang Criminal Justice Research Center and School of Criminal Justice, University at Albany, SUNY, 2001).

52. Nathan Goldman, *The Differential Selection of Juvenile Offenders for Court Appearance* (Washington, DC: National Council on Crime and Delinquency, 1963).

53. Irving Piliavin and Scott Briar, "Police Encounters with Juveniles," *American Journal of Sociology* 70:206–14 (1964); Theodore Ferdinand and Elmer Luchterhand, "Inner-City Youth, the Police, Juvenile Court, and Justice," *Social Problems* 8:510–26 (1970).

54. Paul Strasburg, *Violent Delinquents: Report to Ford Foundation from Vera Institute of Justice* (New York: Monarch, 1978), p. 11; Robert Terry, "The Screening

of Juvenile Offenders," *Journal of Criminal Law, Criminology, and Police Science* 58:173–81 (1967).

55. Joan McCord, Cathy Spatz Widom, and Nancy A. Crowell, eds., *Juvenile Crime, Juvenile Justice.* Panel on Juvenile Crime: Prevention, Treatment, and Control (Washington, DC: National Academy Press, 2001), p. 163.

56. Worden and Myers, *Police Encounters with Juvenile Suspects.*

57. FBI, *Crime in the U.S.: Uniform Crime Reports, 2000* (Washington, DC: U.S. Government Printing Office, 2001).

58. Douglas Smith and Christy Visher, "Street-Level Justice: Situational Determinants of Police Arrest Decisions," *Social Problems* 29:167–78 (1981).

59. Douglas Smith and Jody Klein, "Police Control of Interpersonal Disputes," *Social Problems* 31:468–81 (1984).

60. Goldman, *The Differential Selection of Juvenile Offenders for Court Appearance,* p. 25; Norman Werner and Charles Willie, "Decisions of Juvenile Officers," *American Journal of Sociology* 77:199–214 (1971).

61. Aaron Cicourel, *The Social Organization of Juvenile Justice* (New York: Wiley, 1968).

62. Piliavin and Briar, "Police Encounters with Juveniles," p. 214.

63. David Klinger, "Demeanor or Crime? Why 'Hostile' Citizens Are More Likely to Be Arrested," *Criminology* 32:475–93 (1994).

64. Richard Lundman, "Demeanor or Crime? The Midwest City Police-Citizen Encounters Study," *Criminology* 32:631–53 (1994); Robert Worden and Robin Shepard, "On the Meaning, Measurement, and Estimated Effects of Suspects' Demeanor toward the Police." Paper presented at the American Society of Criminology meeting, Miami, November 1994.

65. James Fyfe, David Klinger, and Jeanne Flaving, "Differential Police Treatment of Male-on-Female Spousal Violence," *Criminology* 35:455–73 (1997).

66. Dale Dannefer and Russel Schutt, "Race and Juvenile Justice Processing in Police and Court Agencies," *American Journal of Sociology* 87:1113–32 (1982); Smith and Visher, "Street-Level Justice: Situational Determinants of Police Arrest Decisions"; also, Ronald Weitzer, "Racial Discrimination in the Criminal Justice System: Findings and Problems in the Literature," *Journal of Criminal Justice* 24:309–22 (1996).

67. Dan M. Kahan and Tracey L. Meares, "The Coming Crisis of Criminal Procedure," *Georgetown Law Journal* 86:1153–84 (2000).

68. Randall Kennedy, *Race, Crime and the Law* (New York: Vintage, 1998).

69. Terence Thornberry, "Race, Socioeconomic Status, and Sentencing in the Juvenile Justice System," *Journal of Criminal Law and Criminology* 70:164–71 (1979); Dannefer and Schutt, "Race and Juvenile Justice Processing in Police and Court Agencies"; Jeffrey Fagan, Ellen Slaughter, and Eliot Hartstone, "Blind Justice? The Impact of Race on the Juvenile Justice Process," *Crime and Delinquency* 33:224–58 (1987).

70. Donna M. Bishop and Charles E. Frazier, "The Influence of Race in Juvenile Justice Processing," *Journal of Research in Crime and Delinquency* 25:242–61 (1988).

71. Ibid., p. 258; see also Howard N. Snyder and Melissa Sickmund, *Juvenile Offenders and Victims: 1999 National Report* (Pittsburgh: National Center for Juvenile Justice, 1999), p. 192.

72. National Council on Crime and Delinquency, *The Over-Representation of Minority Youth in the California Juvenile Justice System* (San Francisco: NCCD, 1992).

73. See Samuel Walker, Cassie Spohn, and Miriam DeLone, *The Color of Justice: Race, Ethnicity, and Crime in America* (Belmont, CA: Wadsworth, 1996).

74. Merry Morash, "Establishment of a Juvenile Record: The Influence of Individual and Peer Group Characteristics," *Criminology* 22:97–112 (1984).

75. Meda Chesney-Lind, "Judicial Enforcement of the Female Sex Role: The Family Court and Female Delinquency Issues," *Criminology* 8:51–71 (1973); idem, "Young Women in the Arms of Law," in L. Bowker, ed., *Women, Crime, and the Criminal Justice System,* 2nd ed. (Lexington, MA: Lexington Books, 1978).

76. Donna Bishop and Charles Frazier, "Gender Bias in Juvenile Justice Processing: Implications of the JJDP Act," *Journal of Criminal Law and Criminology* 82:1162–86 (1992).

77. Douglas Smith, "The Organizational Context of Legal Control," *Criminology* 22:19–38 (1984); see also Stephen Mastrofski and Richard Ritti, "Police Training and the Effects of Organization on Drunk Driving Enforcement," *Justice Quarterly* 13:291–320 (1996).

78. John Irwin, *The Jail: Managing the Underclass in American Society* (Berkeley: University of California Press, 1985).

79. Darlene Conley, "Adding Color to a Black and White Picture: Using Qualitative Data to Explain Racial Disproportionality in the Juvenile Justice System," *Journal of Research in Crime and Delinquency* 31:135–48 (1994).

80. Robert Sampson, "Effects of Socioeconomic Context of Official Reaction to Juvenile Delinquency," *American Sociological Review* 51:876–85 (1986).

81. Ronald Weitzer, "White, Black, or Blue Cops? Race and Citizen Assessments of Police Officers," *Journal of Criminal Justice* 28:313–24 (2000).

82. Thomas Priest and Deborah Brown Carter, "Evaluations of Police Performance in an African American Sample," *Journal of Criminal Justice* 27:457–65 (1999); see also Matt De Lisi and Bob Regoli, "Race, Conventional Crime, and Criminal Justice: The Declining Importance of Skin Color," *Journal of Criminal Justice* 27:549–57 (1999).

83. American Bar Association, *Standards of Criminal Justice: Standards Relating to Urban Police Function* (New York: Institute of Judicial Administration, 1972), Standard 4.2, p. 121.

84. Kenneth C. Davis, *Police Discretion* (St. Paul, MN: West, 1975).

85. Robert Shepard Jr., ed., *Juvenile Justice Standards Annotated—A Balanced Approach* (Chicago: ABA, 1996).

86. Eric Fritsch, Tory Caeti, and Robert Taylor, "Gang Suppression through Saturation Patrol, Aggressive Curfew, and Truancy Enforcement: A Quasi-Experimental Test of the Dallas Anti-Gang Initiative," *Crime and Delinquency* 45:122–39 (1999).

87. Sherwood Norman, *The Youth Service Bureau—A Key to Delinquency Prevention* (Hackensack, NJ: National Council on Crime and Delinquency, 1972), p. 8.

88. J. David Hirschel, Charles W. Dean, and Doris Dumond, "Juvenile Curfews and Race: A Cautionary Note,"

Criminal Justice Policy Review 12:197–214 (2001), p. 209; see also McCord, Spatz Widom, and Crowell, eds., *Juvenile Crime, Juvenile Justice,* p. 145.

89. Finn-Aage Esbensen, D. Wayne Osgood, Terrance J. Taylor, Dana Peterson, and Adrienne Freng, "How Great Is G.R.E.A.T.? Results from a Longitudinal Quasi-Experimental Design," *Criminology and Public Policy* 1:87–118 (2001), p. 88.

90. Finn-Aage Esbensen and D.Wayne Osgood, "Gang Resistance Education and Training (G.R.E.A.T.): Results from the National Evaluation," *Journal of Research in Crime and Delinquency* 36:194–225 (1999).

91. Esbensen, Osgood, Taylor, Peterson, and Freng, "How Great Is G.R.E.A.T.?"

92. Anthony A. Braga, David M. Kennedy, Elin J. Waring, and Anne Morrison Piehl, "Problem-Oriented Policing Deterrence, and Youth Violence: An Evaluation of Boston's Operation Ceasefire," *Journal of Research in Crime and Delinquency* 38:195–225 (2001); David M. Kennedy, Anthony A. Braga, and Anne Morrison Piehl, "Developing and Implementing Operation Ceasefire," in *Reducing Gun Violence: The Boston Gun Project's Operation Ceasefire* (Washington, DC: NIJ Research Report, 2001).

93. Braga, Kennedy, Waring, and Morrison Piehl, "Problem-Oriented Policing Deterrence, and Youth Violence," p. 199.

94. David M. Kennedy, "Pulling Levers: Chronic Offenders, High-Crime Settings, and a Theory of Prevention," *Valparaiso University Law Review* 31:449–84 (1997).

95. Idem, "Pulling Levers: Getting Deterrence Right," *National Institute of Justice Journal* 2–8 (July 1998), p. 6.

96. David Sheppard, Heath Grant, Wendy Rowe, and Nancy Jacobs, *Fighting Juvenile Gun Violence* (Washington, DC: OJJDP Juvenile Justice Bulletin, 2000), p. 2.

97. Ibid., p. 10.

98. Alan Lizotte and David Sheppard, *Gun Use by Male Juveniles: Research and Prevention* (Washington, DC: OJJDP Juvenile Justice Bulletin, 2001), p. 7.

14 Juvenile Court Process: Pretrial, Trial, and Sentencing

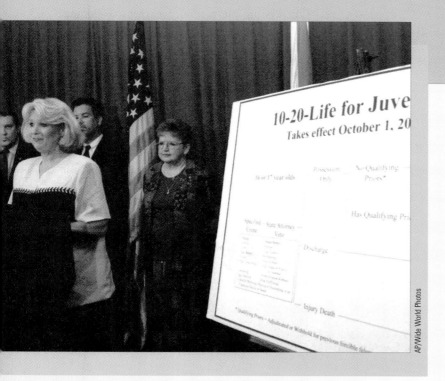

AP/Wide World Photos

As an experienced family court judge, you are often faced with difficult decisions, but few are more difficult than the case of John M., who was arrested at age 14 for robbery and rape. His victim, a young neighborhood girl, was seriously injured in the attack and needed extensive hospitalization; she is now in counseling. Even though the charges are serious, because of his age John can still be subject to the jurisdiction of the juvenile division of the state family court. However, the prosecutor has filed a petition to waive jurisdiction to the adult court. Under existing state law, a hearing must be held to determine whether there is sufficient evidence that John cannot be successfully treated in the juvenile justice system and therefore warrants transfer to the adult system; the final decision on the matter is yours alone.

At the waiver hearing, you discover that John is the oldest of three siblings living in a single-parent home. He has had no contact with his father for more than 10 years. His psychological evaluation showed hostility, anger toward females, and great feelings of frustration. His intelligence is below average, and his behavioral and academic records are poor. In addition, John seems to be involved with a local youth gang, although he denies any formal association with the group. This is John's first formal involvement with the juvenile court. Previous contact was limited to an informal complaint for disorderly conduct at age 13, which was dismissed by the court's intake department. During the hearing, John verbalizes what you interpret to be superficial remorse for his offenses.

To the prosecutor, John seems to be a youth with poor controls who is likely to commit future crimes. The defense attorney argues that there are effective treatment opportunities within the juvenile justice system that can meet John's needs. Her views are supported by an evaluation of the case conducted by the court's probation staff, which concludes that the case can be dealt with in the confines of juvenile corrections.

If the case remains in the juvenile court, John can be kept in custody in a juvenile facility until age 18; if the case is transferred to felony court, he could be sentenced to up to 20 years in a maximum-security prison. As the judge, you recognize the seriousness of the crimes committed by John and realize that it is very difficult to predict or assess John's future behavior and potential dangerousness.

- Would you authorize a waiver to adult court or keep the case in the juvenile justice system?

- Can 14-year-olds truly understand the seriousness of their behavior?

- When making a disposition decision, should a juvenile court judge consider the victim?

A CLOSER VIEW
To help you make up your mind in this case, go to InfoTrac College Edition and read James A. Gondles, Jr., "Kids Are Kids, Not Adults" *Corrections Today* 59(3):6 (June 1997).

Cases such as that of John M. are still all too common in the juvenile justice system. They require juvenile court judges to make decisions that will shape the rest of a child's life.

Because the judicial process is one of the most critical points in the juvenile justice process, it is covered here in some detail. We begin with a discussion of the juvenile court and its jurisdiction. We then turn to issues involving the preadjudicatory stage of juvenile justice: detention, intake, diversion, pretrial release, plea bargaining, and waiver. The trial stage is examined next, looking at the rights of the child at trial—particularly those rights dealing with counsel and trial by jury—through a detailed analysis of U.S. Supreme Court decisions. Procedural rules that govern the adjudicatory and dispositional hearings are also reviewed. We conclude with a discussion of dispositional alternatives and trends in sentencing.

The Juvenile Court and Its Jurisdiction

Today's juvenile delinquency cases are sometimes handled as part of a criminal trial court jurisdiction, or even within the probate court. However, in many jurisdictions they are treated within the structure of a family court or an independent juvenile court (14 states use more than one method to process juvenile cases).[1] The independent juvenile court is a specialized court for children, designed to promote rehabilitation of youths within a framework of procedural due process. It is concerned with acting both in the best interest of the child and in the best interest of public protection, two often-incompatible goals. Family courts, in contrast, have broad jurisdiction over a wide range of personal and household problems, including delinquency, paternity, child support, and custody issues. The major advantages of such a system are that it can serve sparsely populated areas, it permits judicial personnel and others to deal exclusively with children's matters, and it can obtain legislative funding more readily than other court systems.

Court Case Flow

The most recent data available indicate that U.S. juvenile courts process an estimated 1.8 million delinquency cases (cases involving juveniles charged with criminal law violations) each year. The number of delinquency cases handled by juvenile courts increased 44 percent during the 10-year period between 1989 and 1998 (the last data available). During this time, cases involving crimes against people (such as assaults and robberies) increased 88 percent; public order offenses (prostitution, traffic offenses) increased 73 percent, and property offense cases increased 11 percent.[2] There has also been a rapid increase in drug offenses, which more than doubled between 1993 and 1998; drug offense cases accounted for 11 percent of all delinquency cases in 1998, compared with 8 percent in 1994; the number of drug offense cases processed during 1998 was 108 percent greater than in 1993 and 148 percent greater than 1989.[3] Like the crime rate, the number of youths processed to juvenile court has stabilized, declining 3 percent between 1997 and 1998.[4]

There were distinct gender- and race-based differences in the juvenile court population during this same period. About three-quarters of all juvenile crime in 1998 involved a male. However, the number of females processed by juvenile courts has increased significantly during the past decade; in 1988, less than 20 percent of the cases involved female offenders. Similarly, about 30 percent of the juvenile court population was composed of African American youth, although they make up only about 15 percent of the general population.

The Actors in the Juvenile Courtroom

The key players in the juvenile court are prosecutors, judges, and defense attorneys.

The Defense Attorney   As a result of a series of Supreme Court decisions, the right of a delinquent youth to have counsel at state trials has become a fundamental part of the juvenile justice system.[5] Today, courts must provide counsel to indigent defendants who face the possibility of incarceration. Over the past three decades, the rules of juvenile justice administration have become extremely complex. Preparation of a case for juvenile court often involves detailed investigation of a crime, knowledge of court procedures, use of rules of evidence, and skills in trial advocacy. The right to counsel is essential if children are to have a fair chance of presenting their cases in court.

juvenile defense attorney
Represents children in juvenile court and plays an active role at all stages of the proceedings.

In many respects, the role of **juvenile defense attorney** is similar to that in the criminal and civil areas. Defense attorneys representing children in the juvenile court play an active and important part in virtually all stages of the proceedings. For example, the defense attorney helps to clarify jurisdictional problems and to decide whether there is sufficient evidence to warrant filing a formal petition. The defense attorney helps outline the child's position regarding detention hearings and bail, and explores the opportunities for informal adjustment of the case. If no adjustment or diversion occurs, the defense attorney represents the child at adjudication, presenting evidence and cross-examining witnesses to see that the child's position is made clear to the court. Defense attorneys also play a critical role in the dispositional hearing. They present evidence bearing on the treatment decision and help the court formulate alternative plans for the child's care. Finally, defense attorneys pursue any appeals from the trial, represent the child in probation revocation proceedings, and generally protect the child's right to treatment.

guardian ad litem   A court-appointed attorney who protects the interests of the child in cases involving the child's welfare.

In some cases, a **guardian *ad litem*** may be appointed by the court.[6] The guardian *ad litem*—ordinarily seen in abuse, neglect, and dependency cases—may be appointed in delinquency cases where there is a question of a need for a particular treatment

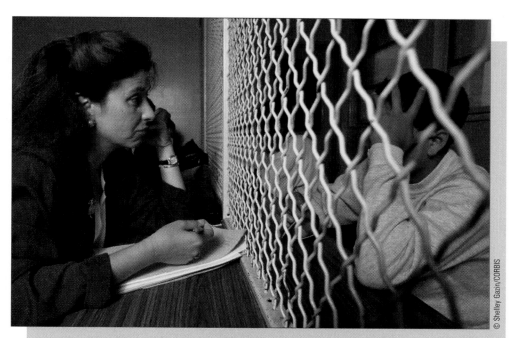

JUVENILE DEFENSE ATTORNEYS play an active and important part in virtually all stages of the juvenile court proceedings, ranging from representing youths in police custody to filing their final appeals.

(for example, placement in a mental health center), and offenders and their attorneys resist placement. The guardian *ad litem* may advocate for the commitment on the ground that it is in the child's best interests. The guardian *ad litem* fulfills many roles, ranging from legal advocate to concerned individual, who works with parents and human service professionals in developing a proper treatment plan that best serves the interests of the minor child.[7]

To read more about the CASA program, go to http://www.nationalcasa.org/ For an up-to-date list of Web links, go to http://info.wadsworth.com/siegel

Court Appointed Special Advocates (CASA) Court Appointed Special Advocates (CASA) employ volunteers who advise the juvenile court about child placement. The CASA programs (*casa* is Spanish for "home") have demonstrated that volunteers can investigate the needs of children and provide a vital link between the judge, the attorneys, and the child in protecting the juvenile's right to a safe placement.[8]

Public Defender Services for Children To satisfy the requirement that indigent children be provided with counsel, the federal government and the states have expanded **public defender** services. Three alternatives exist for providing children with legal counsel: (1) an all–public defender program, (2) an appointed private-counsel system, and (3) a combination system of public defenders and appointed private attorneys.

public defender An attorney who works in a public agency or under private contractual agreement as defense counsel to indigent defendants.

The public defender program is a statewide program established by legislation and funded by the state government to provide counsel to children at public expense. This program allows access to the expertise of lawyers, who spend a considerable amount of time representing juvenile offenders every day. Defender programs generally provide separate office space for juvenile court personnel, as well as support staff, and training programs for new lawyers.

In many rural areas, where individual public defender programs are not available, defense services are offered through appointed private counsel. Private lawyers are assigned to individual juvenile court cases, and they receive compensation for the time and services they provide. When private attorneys are used in large urban areas, they are generally selected from a list established by the court, and they often operate in conjunction with a public defender program. The weaknesses of a system of assigned private counsel include assignment to cases for which the lawyers are unqualified, inadequate compensation, and lack of supportive or supervisory services.

Though efforts have been made to supply juveniles with adequate legal representation, many juveniles still go to court unrepresented, or with an overworked lawyer who provides inadequate representation. Many juvenile court defense lawyers work on more than 500 cases per year, and more than half leave their jobs in under two years.[9] Other problems facing public defenders include (1) lack of resources for independent evaluations, expert witnesses, and investigatory support; (2) lack of computers, telephones, files, and adequate office space; (3) juvenile public defenders' inexperience, lack of training, low morale, and salaries lower than those of their counterparts who defend adults or serve as prosecutors; and (4) inability to keep up with rapidly changing juvenile codes.[10] With juvenile offenders facing the prospect of much longer sentences, mandatory minimum sentences, and time in adult prisons, the need for quality defense attorneys for juveniles has never been greater.

juvenile prosecutor Government attorney responsible for representing the interests of the state and bringing the case against the accused juvenile.

The Prosecutor in the Juvenile Court The juvenile prosecutor is the attorney responsible for bringing the state's case against the accused juvenile. Depending on the level of government and the jurisdiction, the prosecutor can be called a district attorney, a county attorney, a state attorney, or a United States attorney. Prosecutors are members of the bar selected for their positions by political appointment or popular election.

Ordinarily, the juvenile prosecutor is a staff member of the prosecuting attorney's office. If the office of the district attorney is of sufficient size, the juvenile prosecutor may work exclusively on juvenile and other family law matters. If the caseload of juvenile offenders is small, the juvenile prosecutor may also have criminal prosecution responsibilities.

For the first 60 years of its existence, the juvenile court did not include a prosecutor, because the concept of an adversary process was seen as inconsistent with the philosophy of treatment. The court followed a social service helping model, and informal proceedings were believed to be in the best interests of the child. Today, in a more legalistic juvenile court, almost all jurisdictions require by law that a prosecutor be present in the juvenile court.

A number of states have passed legislation giving prosecutors control over intake and waiver decisions. Some have passed concurrent-jurisdiction laws that allow prosecutors to decide in which court to bring serious juvenile cases. In some jurisdictions, it is the prosecutor and not the juvenile court judge who is entrusted with the decision of whether to transfer a case to adult court. Consequently, the role of juvenile court prosecutor is now critical in the juvenile justice process. Including a prosecutor in juvenile court balances the interests of the state, the defense attorney, the child, and the judge, preserving the independence of each party's functions and responsibilities.

The prosecutor has the power either to initiate or to discontinue delinquency or status offense allegations. Like police officers, prosecutors have broad discretion in the exercise of their duties. Because due-process rights have been extended to juveniles, the prosecutor's role in the juvenile court has in some ways become similar to the prosecutor's role in the adult court.

Because children are committing more serious crimes today and because the courts have granted juveniles constitutional safeguards, the prosecutor is likely to play an increasingly significant role in the juvenile court system. The prosecutor's involvement should result in a fairer, more just system for all parties. But prosecutors also require more information on such issues as (1) how to identify repeat offenders, (2) how to determine which programs are most effective, (3) how early childhood experiences relate to delinquency, and (4) what measures can be used in place of secure placements without reducing public safety.[11]

Today, prosecutors are addressing the problems associated with juvenile crime. A balanced approach has been recommended—one that emphasizes enforcement, prosecution, and detention of serious offenders and the use of proven prevention and intervention programs.[12]

To read more about the players in the court system, go to the Web site of the American Judicature Society, a nonpartisan organization with a membership of judges, lawyers, and nonlegally trained citizens interested in the administration of justice: *http://www.ajs.org/about.html* For an up-to-date list of Web links, go to *http://info.wadsworth.com/siegel*

juvenile court judge A judge elected or appointed to preside over juvenile cases and whose decisions can only be reviewed by a judge of a higher court.

The Juvenile Court Judge Even with the elevation of the prosecutor's role, the **juvenile court judge** is still the central character in a court of juvenile or family law. Her or his responsibilities have become far more extensive and complex in recent years. Juvenile or family court judges perform the functions listed in Exhibit 14.1.

In addition, judges often have extensive influence over other agencies of the court: probation, the court clerk, the law enforcement officer, and the office of the juvenile prosecutor. Juvenile court judges exercise considerable leadership in developing solutions to juvenile justice problems. In this role they must respond to the pressures the community places on juvenile court resources. According to the *parens patriae*

Exhibit 14.1 Duties of the Juvenile Court Judge

- Rule on pretrial motions involving such legal issues as arrest, search and seizure, interrogation, and lineup identification
- Make decisions about the continued detention of children prior to trial
- Make decisions about plea-bargaining agreements and the informal adjustment of juvenile cases
- Handle trials, rule on the appropriateness of conduct, settle questions of evidence and procedure, and guide the questioning of witnesses
- Assume responsibility for holding dispositional hearings and deciding on the treatment accorded the child
- Handle waiver proceedings
- Handle appeals where allowed by statute

philosophy, the juvenile judge must ensure that the necessary community resources are available so that the children and families who come before the court can receive the proper care and help.[13] This may be the most untraditional role for the juvenile court judge, but it may also be the most important.

In some jurisdictions juvenile court judges handle family-related cases exclusively. In others they preside over criminal and civil cases as well. Traditionally, juvenile court judges have been relegated to a lower status than other judges. Judges assigned to juvenile courts have not ordinarily been chosen from the highest levels of the legal profession. Such groups as the American Judicature Society have noted that the field of juvenile justice has often been shortchanged by the appointment of unqualified judges. In some jurisdictions, particularly major urban areas, juvenile court judges may be of the highest caliber, but many courts continue to function with mediocre judges.

Inducing the best-trained individuals to accept juvenile court judgeships is a very important goal. Where the juvenile court is part of the highest general court of trial jurisdiction, the problem of securing qualified personnel is not as great. However, if the juvenile court is of limited or specialized jurisdiction and has the authority to try only minor cases, it may attract only poorly trained personnel. Lawyers and judges who practice in juvenile court receive little respect. The juvenile court has a negative image, because even though what it does is of great importance to parents, children, and society in general, it has been placed at the lowest level of the judicial hierarchy.

The National Council of Juvenile and Family Court Judges is dedicated to serving the nation's children and families by improving the courts of juvenile and family jurisdictions. Their Web site can be found at http://www.ncjfcj.unr.edu/ index.html For an up-to-date list of Web links, go to http://info.wadsworth.com/siegel

Juvenile Court Process

Now that we have briefly described the setting of the juvenile court and the major players who control its operations, we turn to a discussion of the procedures that shape the contours of juvenile justice—the pretrial process and the juvenile trial and disposition. Many critical decisions are made at this stage in the juvenile justice system: whether to detain a youth or release the youth to the community; whether to waive youths to the adult court or retain them in the juvenile justice system; whether to treat them in the community or send them to a secure treatment center. Each of these can have a profound influence on the child, with effects lasting throughout the life course. What are these critical stages, and how are decisions made within them?

Release or Detain?

After a child has been taken into custody and a decision is made to treat the case formally (that is, with a juvenile court hearing), a decision must be made either to release the child into the custody of parents or to detain the child in the temporary care of the state, in physically restrictive facilities pending court disposition or transfer to another agency.[14] Nationally, about 70 percent of all states have detention centers administered at the county level; about 34 percent have state-level facilities, 16 percent have court-administered facilities, and 11 percent contract with private vendors to operate facilities.[15]

Detention can be a traumatic experience because many facilities are prisonlike, with locked doors and barred windows. Consequently, most experts in juvenile justice advocate that detention be limited to alleged offenders who require secure custody for the protection of themselves and others. However, children who are neglected and dependent, runaways, and those who are homeless may under some circumstances be placed in secure detention facilities along with violent and dangerous youths until more suitable placements can be found.[16] Others have had a trial but have not been sentenced, or are awaiting the imposition of their sentence. Some may have violated probation and are awaiting a hearing while being kept alongside a severely mentally ill adolescent for whom no appropriate placement can be found. Another group are adjudicated delinquents awaiting admittance to a correctional training school.[17] Consequently, it is possible for nonviolent status offenders to be housed in the same facility with delinquents who have committed felony-type offenses.

To remedy this situation, an ongoing effort has been made to remove status offenders and neglected or abused children from detention facilities that also house juvenile delinquents. In addition, alternatives to detention centers—temporary foster homes, detention boarding homes, and programs of neighborhood supervision—have been developed. These alternatives, referred to as **shelter care,** enable youths to live in a more homelike setting while the courts dispose of their cases.

shelter care A place for temporary care of children in physically unrestricting facilities.

National Detention Trends

Despite an ongoing effort to limit detention, juveniles are still being detained in about 20 percent of all delinquency cases, including drug law violations, violent offenses, and public order cases; detention is used less often in property offense cases.[18]

The typical delinquent detainee is male, over 15 years of age (Figure 14.1), and charged with a property crime; whereas the typical status offender is female, under 16 years of age, and a runaway.[19] Racial minorities are overrepresented in detention (Figure 14.2), especially those who are indigent and whose families may be receiving

Figure 14.1
Profile of Detainees by Age
Source: Paul Harms, *Detention in Delinquency Cases 1989–1998* (Washington, DC: Office of Juvenile Justice and Delinquency Prevention 2002).

Percent of cases detained

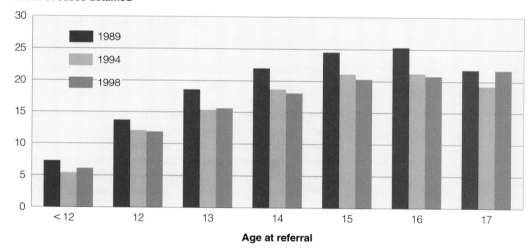

Age at referral

Figure 14.2
Cases Involving Detention of Black Juveniles vs. White Juveniles
Source: Paul Harms, *Detention in Delinquency Cases 1989–1998* (Washington, DC: Office of Juvenile Justice and Delinquency Prevention 2002).

Percent of cases detained

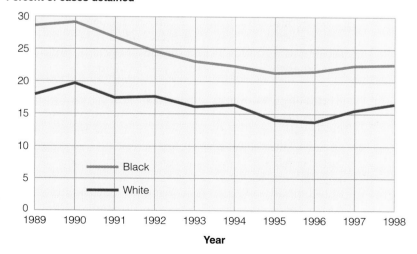

Year

public assistance. Minority overrepresentation is particularly vexing, considering that detention may increase the risk of a youth being adjudicated and eventually confined.[20]

Why Is Detention Increasing?   This rise in the juvenile detention rate is occurring at a time when the overall population of juvenile offenders is decreasing. Experts believe the steady increase in detention use may result from (1) a steady rise in the rate of serious juvenile offenses, (2) an increasing number of drug-related crimes, and (3) the involvement of younger children in the juvenile justice system.[21] However, some things about juvenile detention have not changed: There remains a serious problem of overrepresentation of minorities in secure detention.[22]

The Decision to Detain   The majority of children taken into custody by the police are released to their parents or guardians. Some are held overnight until their parents can be notified of the arrest. Police officers normally take a child to a place of detention only after other alternatives have been exhausted. Many juvenile courts in urban areas have staff members, such as intake probation officers, on duty 24 hours a day to screen detention admissions.

Ordinarily, delinquent children are detained if the police believe they are inclined to run away while awaiting trial, or if they are likely to commit an offense dangerous to the parent. There is evidence that some decision makers are more likely to detain minority youth, especially if they live in dangerous lower-class areas.[23]

Typically, children should not be held in a detention facility or shelter care unit for more than 24 hours without a formal petition (a written request to the court) being filed to extend the detention period. To detain a juvenile, there must be clear evidence of probable cause that the child has committed the offense and that he or she will flee if not detained. Although the requirements for detention hearings vary, most jurisdictions require that they occur almost immediately after the child's admission to a detention facility and provide the youth with notice and counsel.

New Approaches to Detention   Efforts have been ongoing to improve the process and conditions of detention. Experts maintain that detention facilities should provide youth with education, visitation, private communications, counseling, continuous supervision, medical and health care, nutrition, recreation, and reading. Detention should also include, or provide, a system for clinical observation and diagnosis that complements the wide range of helpful services.[24]

The consensus today is that juvenile detention centers should be reserved for youths who present a clear threat to the community. In some states, nonsecure facilities are being used to service juveniles for a limited period. Alternatives to secure detention include (1) in-home monitoring, (2) home detention, (3) day-center electronic monitoring, (4) high-intensity community supervision, and (5) comprehensive case management programs. (See the Policy and Practice box entitled "The Detention Diversion Advocacy Program.")

Undoubtedly, juveniles pose special detention problems, but some efforts are being made to improve programs and to reduce pretrial detention use, especially in secure settings. Of all the problems associated with detention, however, none is as critical as the issue of placing youths in adult jails.

Restricting Detention in Adult Jails   A significant problem in juvenile justice is placing youths in adult jails. This is usually done in rural areas where no other facility exists. Almost all experts agree that placing children under the age of 18 in any type of jail facility should be prohibited because youngsters can easily be victimized by other inmates and staff, be forced to live in squalid conditions, and be subject to physical and sexual abuse.

Until a few years ago, placing juveniles in adult facilities was common, but efforts have been made to change this situation. In 1989, the Juvenile Justice and Delinquency Prevention Act (JJDPA) of 1974 was amended to require that the states remove all juveniles from adult jails and lockups. According to federal guidelines, all

The Detention Diversion Advocacy Program

The concept behind the Detention Diversion Advocacy Program (DDAP) approach is case advocacy employing the efforts of a staff of laypersons or nonlegal experts acting on behalf of youthful offenders at disposition hearings. It relies on a case management strategy that involves coordination of human services, opportunities, or benefits. Case management efforts are designed to integrate services across a cluster of organizations, to ensure continuity of care, and to facilitate development of client skills (for example, job interviewing, or reading and writing skills) by involving a variety of social networks and service providers (social agencies that provide specific services to youth, like drug counseling and crisis intervention).

Detention advocacy involves identifying youths likely to be detained pending their adjudication. Detention Diversion Advocacy Program clients are identified primarily through referrals from the public defender's office, the probation department, community agencies, and parents. Admission to DDAP is restricted to youths currently held, or likely to be held, in secure detention. Once a potential client is identified, DDAP case managers present a release plan to the judge that includes a list of appropriate community services (tutoring, drug counseling, family counseling) that will be made available on the youth's behalf. Additionally, the plan includes specified objectives (improved grades, victim restitution, drug-free status) as a means of evaluating the youth's progress in the program. Emphasis is placed on allowing the youth to live at home while going through the program. If home placement is not a viable option, program staff will identify and secure a suitable alternative. If the judge deems the release plan acceptable, the youth is released to DDAP supervision.

The DDAP case management model provides frequent and consistent support and supervision to youths and their families. Case managers link youths to community-based services and closely monitor their progress. The DDAP program requires the case manager to have daily contact with the youth, the family, and significant others, including a minimum of three in-person meetings a week with the youth. The youth's family members, particularly parents and guardians,

are provided with additional services that typically include assistance in securing employment, daycare, drug treatment services, and income support (for example, food stamps).

Evaluations of the DDAP program have indicated that it is very successful:

- The overall recidivism rate of the DDAP group is 34 percent, compared with 60 percent for the comparison group.
- Fourteen percent of the DDAP group have two or more subsequent referrals, compared with 50 percent of the comparison group.
- Nine percent of the DDAP group return to court on a violent crime charge, compared with 25 percent of the comparison group.
- Five percent of the DDAP group have two or more subsequent petitions, compared with 22 percent of the comparison group.

Critical Thinking

1. Should adolescents be detained for nonviolent offenses such as substance abuse and/or theft?
2. Do you believe that the decision to detain a child is based on an evaluation of the child's behavior or his/her parent's behavior and ability to provide care and supervision? If the latter, is that a violation of due process? In other words, why should children be punished for the shortcomings of their parents?

InfoTrac College Edition Research

 To learn more about the concept of juvenile detention, use it as a subject guide on InfoTrac College Edition.

Source: Randall G. Shelden, "Detention Diversion Advocacy: An Evaluation," *Juvenile Justice Bulletin* (Washington, DC: Office of Juvenile Justice and Delinquency Prevention, 1999).

juveniles in state custody must be separated from adult offenders, or the state could lose federal juvenile justice funds. The OJJDP defines separation as the condition in which juvenile detainees have either totally independent facilities or shared facilities that are designed so that juveniles and adults neither have contact nor share programs or staff.[25]

Much debate has arisen over whether the initiative to remove juveniles from adult jails has succeeded. Most indications are that the number of youths being held in adult facilities has declined significantly from the almost 500,000 a year recorded in 1979.[26] Today, less than 100,000 juveniles are detained annually in adult jails. These figures may be misleading, however, because they do not include youths held in urban jails for under 6 hours, or in rural ones for under 24 hours; youths transferred to adult courts; or youths in states that consider anyone over 16 or 17 to be an adult.

With federal help, some progress appears to have been made in removing juveniles from adult facilities, but thousands each year continue to be held in close contact with adults, and thousands more are held in facilities that, although physically separate, put them in close proximity to adults. To the youths held within their walls, there may appear to be little difference between the juvenile detention facilities and the adult jail.

Removing Status Offenders   Along with removing all juveniles from adult jails, the OJJDP has made deinstitutionalization of status offenders a cornerstone of its policy. The Juvenile Justice and Delinquency Prevention Act of 1974 prohibits the placement of status offenders in secure detention facilities.

Removing status offenders from secure facilities serves two purposes: (1) It reduces interaction with serious offenders, and (2) it insulates status offenders from the stigma associated with being a detainee in a locked facility. Efforts appear to be working, and the number of status offenders being held in some sort of secure confinement has been on a two-decade decline. Nonetheless, the debate over the most effective way to handle juvenile status offenders continues, and some critics have argued that if the juvenile court is unable to take effective action in status offender cases, it should be stripped of jurisdiction over these youths. Most judges would prefer to retain jurisdiction so they can help children and families resolve problems that cause runaways, truancy, and other status offense behaviors.[27]

Bail for Children

bail   Amount of money that must be paid as a condition of pretrial release to ensure that the accused will return for subsequent proceedings; bail is normally set by the judge at the initial appearance, and if unable to make bail, the accused is detained in jail.

One critical pretrial issue is whether juveniles can be released on **bail**. Adults retain the right, via the Eighth Amendment to the Constitution, to reasonable bail in noncapital cases. Most states, however, refuse juveniles the right to bail. They argue that juvenile proceedings are civil, not criminal, and that detention is rehabilitative, not punitive. In addition, they argue that juveniles do not need a constitutional right to bail because statutory provisions allow children to be released into parental custody.

State juvenile bail statutes fall into three categories: (1) those guaranteeing the right to bail, (2) those that grant the court discretion to give bail, and (3) those that deny a juvenile the right to bail.[28] This disparity may be a function of the lack of legal guidance on the matter. The U.S. Supreme Court has never decided the issue of juvenile bail. Some courts have stated that bail provisions do not apply to juveniles. Others rely on the Eighth Amendment against cruel and unusual punishment, or on state constitutional provisions or statutes, and conclude that juveniles do have a right to bail.

preventive detention   Keeping the accused in custody prior to trial because the accused is suspected of being a danger to the community.

Preventive Detention   Even if the U.S. Supreme Court has not yet decided whether juveniles have a right to traditional money bail, they have concluded that the state has a right to detain dangerous youths until their trial, a practice called **preventive detention**. On June 4, 1984, the U.S. Supreme Court dealt with this issue in *Schall v. Martin,* when it upheld the State of New York's preventive detention statute.[29] Because this is a key case in juvenile justice, it is the subject of the accompanying Juvenile Law in Review. Today, most states allow "dangerous" youths to be held indefinitely before trial. Because preventive detention may attach a stigma of guilt to a child presumed innocent, the practice remains a highly controversial one, and the efficacy of such laws remains unknown.[30]

The Intake Process

intake   Process during which a juvenile referral is received and a decision is made to file a petition in juvenile court to release the juvenile, to place the juvenile under supervision, or to refer the juvenile elsewhere.

The term **intake** refers to the screening of cases by the juvenile court system. The child and his or her family are screened by intake officers to determine whether the services of the juvenile court are needed. Intake officers may (1) send the youth home with no further action, (2) divert the youth to a social agency, (3) petition the youth to the juvenile court, or (4) file a petition and hold the youth in detention. The intake process reduces demands on court resources, screens out cases that are not within the court's jurisdiction, and enables assistance to be obtained from community agencies without court intervention.

After reviewing the case, justice system authorities decide whether to dismiss, informally handle, or formally process the case by taking the matter before a judge.

Schall v. Martin

Facts

Gregory Martin was arrested in New York City on December 13, 1977, on charges of robbery, assault, and criminal possession of a weapon. Because he was arrested at 11:30 P.M. and lied about his residence, Martin was kept overnight in detention and brought to juvenile court the next day for an "initial appearance" accompanied by his grandmother. The family court judge, citing possession of a loaded weapon, the false address given to police, and the fact that Martin was left unsupervised late in the evening, ordered him detained before trial under section 320.5(3)(6) of the New York State code, which authorizes pretrial detention of an accused juvenile delinquent if "there is a substantial probability that he will not appear in court on the return date or there is a serious risk that he may before the return date commit an act which if committed by an adult would constitute a crime." Later, at trial, Martin was found to be a delinquent and sentenced to two years' probation.

While he was in pretrial detention, Martin's attorneys filed a class action on behalf of all youths subject to preventive detention in New York, charging that this form of detention was a denial of due-process rights under the Fifth and Fourteenth Amendments. The New York appellate courts upheld Martin's claim on the ground that because, at adjudication, most delinquents are released or placed on probation it was unfair to incarcerate them before trial. The prosecution brought the case to the U.S. Supreme Court for final judgment.

Decision

The U.S. Supreme Court upheld the state's right to place juveniles in preventive detention, holding that the practice serves the legitimate objective of protecting both the juvenile and society from pretrial crime. Pretrial detention need not be considered punishment merely because the juvenile is eventually released or put on probation. In addition, there are procedural safeguards, such as notice and a hearing, and a statement of facts that must be given to juveniles before they are placed in detention. The Court also found that detention based on prediction of future behavior was not a violation of due process. Many decisions are made in the justice system, such as the decision to sentence or grant parole, that are based in part on a prediction of future behavior, and these have all been accepted by the courts as legitimate exercises of state power.

Significance of the Case

Schall v. Martin established the right of juvenile court judges to deny youths pretrial release if they perceive them to be dangerous. However, the case also established a due-process standard for detention hearings that includes notice and a statement of substantial reasons for the detention. Despite these measures, opponents hold that preventive detention deprives offenders of their freedom because guilt has not been proven. It is also unfair, they claim, to punish people for what judicial authorities believe they may do in the future, as it is impossible to predict who will be a danger to the community. Moreover, because judges are able to use discretion in their detention decisions, an offender could unfairly be deprived of freedom without legal recourse.

Source: *Schall v. Martin*, 104 S.Ct. 2403 (1984).

About 19 percent (327,800) of all delinquency cases in 1998 were dismissed at intake, often for lack of legal sufficiency. Another 24 percent (429,300 cases) were processed informally, with the juvenile voluntarily agreeing to the recommended disposition (for example, probation). More than half (57% or 1,000,300) of delinquency cases in 1998 were processed formally and involved either an adjudicatory hearing or a hearing to consider waiving jurisdiction to the criminal (adult) court.[31]

Juvenile court intake is provided for by statute in almost all the states. Intake screening allows juvenile courts to enter into consent decrees with juveniles without filing petitions and without formal adjudication. (The consent decree is a court order authorizing disposition of the case without a formal label of delinquency. It is based on an agreement between the intake department of the court and the juvenile who is the subject of the complaint.)

Intake also has some problems. Although almost all state juvenile court systems provide intake and diversion programs, there are few formal criteria for selecting children for such alternatives. There are also legal problems associated with the intake process. Among them are whether the child has a right to counsel, whether the child is protected against self-incrimination, and to what degree the child needs to consent to nonjudicial disposition as recommended by the intake officer. Finally, intake dispositions are often determined by the prior record rather than by the seriousness of the offense or the social background of the child. This practice departs from the philosophy of *parens patriae*.[32]

The shift from rehabilitation has led to changes in the intake process. One trend has been the increased influence of prosecutors. Traditionally, the intake process has

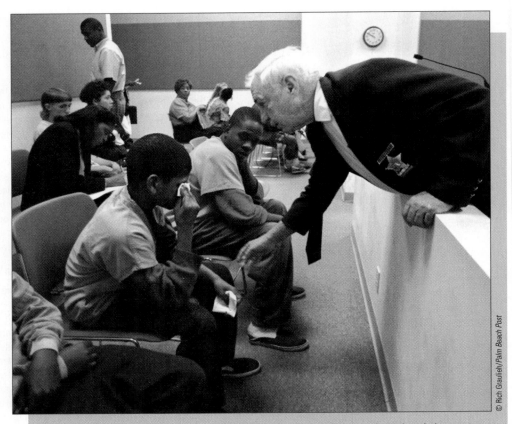

THE MAJORITY OF CHILDREN taken into custody by the police are released to their parents or guardians. Some are held overnight until their parents can be notified of the arrest. Police officers normally take a child to a place of detention only after other alternatives have been exhausted. Many juvenile courts in urban areas have staff members, such as intake probation officers, who are on duty twenty-four hours a day to screen detention admissions.

been controlled by probation personnel whose decisions influenced the judge's view of which cases to handle formally and which should be settled without court action. This approach to intake, in which probation personnel seek to dispense the least disruptive amount of rehabilitative justice, is being replaced in some jurisdictions by a model in which a prosecutor is the central figure. Some states now require that intake officers get approval from the prosecutor before either accepting or rejecting a delinquency petition. Other states allow the complaining party to appeal petitions rejected by intake officers to the prosecutor.[33]

Diversion

diversion Official halting or suspending of a formal criminal or juvenile justice proceeding at any legally prescribed processing point after a recorded justice system entry, and referral of that person to a treatment or care program or a recommendation that the person be released.

One of the most important alternatives chosen at intake is nonjudicial disposition or, as it is variously called, nonjudicial adjustment, handling, or processing; informal disposition, adjustment, or (most commonly) **diversion**. Juvenile diversion is the process of placing youths suspected of law-violating behavior into treatment-oriented programs prior to formal trial and disposition in order to minimize their penetration into the justice system and thereby avoid stigma and labeling.

Diversion implies more than simply screening out cases for which no additional treatment is needed. Screening involves abandoning efforts to apply coercive measures to a defendant. In contrast, diversion encourages an individual to participate in some specific program or activity to avoid further prosecution.

A CLOSER VIEW
Some legal experts consider the juvenile court as essentially a diversionary agency that shields adolescents from the criminal court process. To read more on this view, go to InfoTrac College Edition: Franklin E. Zimring, "The Common Thread: Diversion in Juvenile Justice," *California Law Review* 88(6):2477 (December 2000).

widening the net Phenomenon that occurs when programs created to divert youths from the justice system actually involve them more deeply in the official process.

Most court-based diversion programs employ a particular formula for choosing youths for diversion. Criteria such as being a first offender, a nonviolent offender, or a status offender, or being drug or alcohol dependent, are used to select clients. In some programs, youths will be asked to partake of services voluntarily in lieu of a court appearance. In other programs, prosecutors will agree to defer, and then dismiss, a case once a youth has completed a treatment program. Finally, some programs can be initiated by the juvenile court judge after an initial hearing.

In summary, diversion programs have been created to remove nonserious offenders from the justice system, provide them with nonpunitive treatment services, and help them avoid the stigma of a delinquent label.

Issues in Diversion: Widening the Net Diversion has been viewed as a promising alternative to official procedures, but over the years its basic premises have been questioned.[34] The most damaging criticism has been that diversion programs are involving children in the juvenile justice system who previously would have been released without official notice. This is referred to as **widening the net.** Various studies indicate that police and court personnel are likely to use diversion programs for youths who ordinarily would have been turned loose at the intake or arrest stage.[35] Why does net-widening occur? One explanation is that police and prosecutors find diversion a more attractive alternative than both official processing and outright release—diversion helps them resolve the conflict between doing too much and doing too little.

Diversion has also been criticized as ineffective; that is, youths being diverted make no better adjustment in the community than those who go through official channels. However, not all experts are critical of diversion. Some challenge the net-widening concept as naive: How do we know that diverted youths would have had less interface with the justice system if diversion didn't exist?[36] Even if juveniles escaped official labels for their current offense, might they not eventually fall into the hands of the police? The rehabilitative potential of diversion should not be overlooked.[37] Juvenile diversion programs represent one alternative to the traditional process.

The Petition

complaint Report made by the police or some other agency to the court that initiates the intake process.

A **complaint** is the report made by the police or some other agency to the court to initiate the intake process. Once the agency makes a decision that judicial disposition is required, a petition is filed. The petition is the formal complaint that initiates judicial action against a juvenile charged with delinquency or a status offense. The petition includes basic information such as the name, age, and residence of the child; the parents' names; and the facts alleging the child's delinquency. The police officer, a family member, or a social service agency can file a petition. If, after being given the right to counsel, the child admits the allegation in the petition, an initial hearing is scheduled for the child to make the admission before the court, and information is gathered to develop a treatment plan. If the child does not admit to any of the facts in the petition, a date is set for a hearing on the petition. This hearing, whose purpose is to determine the merits of the petition, is similar to the adult trial. Once a hearing date has been set, the probation department is normally asked to prepare a social study report. This predisposition report contains relevant information about the child, along with recommendations for treatment and service. When a date has been set for the hearing on the petition, parents or guardians and other persons associated with the petition (witnesses, the arresting police officer, and victims) are notified. On occasion, the court may issue a summons—a court order requiring the juvenile or others involved in the case to appear for the hearing. The statutes in a given jurisdiction govern the contents of the petition. Some jurisdictions, for instance, allow for a petition to be filed based on the information of the complainant alone. Others require that the petition be filed under oath or that an affidavit accompany the petition. Some jurisdictions authorize only one official, such as a probation officer or prosecutor, to file the petition. Others allow numerous officials, including family and social service agencies, to set forth facts in the petition.

The Plea and Plea Bargaining

plea bargaining The exchange of prosecutorial and judicial concessions for a guilty plea by the accused; plea bargaining usually results in a reduced charge or a more lenient sentence.

In the adult criminal justice system, the defendant normally enters a plea of guilty or not guilty. More than 90 percent of all adult defendants plead guilty. A large proportion of those pleas involve **plea bargaining,** the exchange of prosecutorial and judicial concessions for guilty pleas.[38] Plea bargaining permits a defendant to plead guilty to a less-serious charge in exchange for an agreement by the prosecutor to recommend a reduced sentence to the court. In the case of juvenile justice, it involves a discussion between the child's attorney and the prosecutor by which the child agrees to plead guilty to obtain a reduced charge or a lenient sentence.

Few juvenile codes require a guilty or not-guilty plea when a petition is filed against a child. In most jurisdictions an initial hearing is held at which the child either submits to a finding of the facts or denies the petition.[39] If the child admits to the facts, the court determines an appropriate disposition. If the child denies the allegations, the case normally proceeds to trial. When a child enters no plea, the court ordinarily imposes a denial of the charges. This may occur where a juvenile doesn't understand the nature of the complaint or isn't represented by an attorney.

A high percentage of juvenile offenders enter guilty pleas; that is, they admit to the facts of the petition. How many of these pleas involve plea bargaining is unknown. In the past it was believed that plea bargaining was unnecessary in the juvenile justice system because there was little incentive to bargain in a system that does not have jury trials or long sentences. In addition, because the court must dispose of cases in the best interests of the child, plea negotiation seemed unnecessary. Consequently, there has long been a debate over the appropriateness of plea bargaining in juvenile justice. The arguments in favor of plea bargaining include lower court costs and efficiency. Counterarguments hold that plea bargaining with juveniles is an unregulated and unethical process. When used, experts believe the process requires the highest standards of good faith by the prosecutor.[40]

Growing concern about violent juvenile crime has spurred attorneys increasingly to seek to negotiate a plea rather than accept the so-called good interests of the court judgment—a judgment that might result in harsher sanctions. The extension of the adversary process to children has led to an increase in plea bargaining, creating an informal trial process that parallels the adult system. Other factors in the trend toward juvenile plea bargaining include the use of prosecutors rather than probation personnel and police officers in juvenile courts, and the ever-increasing caseloads in such courts.

Plea bargaining negotiations generally involve one or more of the following: (1) reduction of a charge, (2) change in the proceedings from that of delinquency to a status offense, (3) elimination of possible waiver to the criminal court, and (4) agreements regarding dispositional programs for the child. In states where youths are subject to long mandatory sentences, reduction of the charges may have a significant impact on the outcome of the case. In states where youths may be waived to the adult court for committing certain serious crimes, a plea reduction may result in the juvenile courts maintaining jurisdiction.

Little clear evidence exists of how much plea bargaining there is in the juvenile justice system, but it is apparent that such negotiations do take place and seem to be increasing. Joseph Sanborn found that about 20 percent of the cases processed in Philadelphia resulted in a negotiated plea. Most were for reduced sentences, typically probation in lieu of incarceration. Sanborn found that plea bargaining was a complex process, depending in large measure on the philosophy of the judge and the court staff. In general, he found it to have greater benefit for the defendants than for the court.[41]

In summary, the majority of juvenile cases that are not adjudicated seem to be the result of admissions to the facts rather than actual plea bargaining. Plea bargaining is less common in juvenile courts than in adult courts because incentives such as dropping multiple charges or substituting a misdemeanor for a felony are unlikely. Nonetheless, plea bargaining is firmly entrenched in the juvenile process. Any plea bargain, however, must be entered into voluntarily and knowingly; otherwise, the conviction may be overturned on appeal.

Transfer to the Adult Court

transfer process Transfer of a juvenile offender from the jurisdiction of juvenile court to adult criminal court.

One of the most significant actions that can occur in the early court processing of a juvenile offender is the **transfer process**. Otherwise known as waiver, **bindover,** or **removal,** this process involves transferring a juvenile from the juvenile court to the adult criminal court. Virtually all state statutes allow for this kind of transfer.

For every 1,000 formally handled delinquency cases, 8 are waived to criminal court. In 1998, U.S. courts with juvenile jurisdiction handled nearly 1.8 million delinquency cases. More than half (57% or 1,000,300) of these cases were handled formally (that is, a petition was filed requesting an adjudication or waiver hearing). The number of delinquency cases judicially waived to criminal court peaked in 1994 with 12,100 cases, an increase of more than 50 percent over the number of cases waived in 1989 (8,000). Since 1994, however, the number of cases waived to criminal court has actually declined 33 percent to 8,100 cases, representing less than 1 percent of the formally processed delinquency caseload. One reason may be that the number of youths waived for drug cases is in decline, falling from 4.1 percent (1,800 cases) in 1991, and has declined since then (1.1% or 1,300 cases in 1998).[42]

Figure 14.3 shows the number of youths waived for personal, property, and drug crimes.

Waiver Procedures

Today, all states allow juveniles to be tried as adults in criminal courts in one of three ways:

- *Judicial waiver:* In a procedure known as *binding over,* or *certifying,* juvenile cases to criminal court, a hearing is held before a juvenile court judge, who then decides whether jurisdiction should be waived and the case transferred to criminal court.[43]
- *Direct file:* Also known as concurrent jurisdiction or prosecutor discretion, direct file is another increasingly prominent form of criminal court transfer. Direct file laws give prosecutors the discretion to prosecute juveniles either in juvenile or adult court. The popularity of direct file provisions has grown significantly; in 1982, just 8 states had direct file statutes; by 1997, there were 15 states with these laws. Colorado, for example, authorizes prosecutors to proceed directly to criminal court in any case involving a youth age 14 or older charged with a wide array of felony offenses. Louisiana gives prosecutors discretion to file criminal charges against any youth age 15 and older and charged with a second drug felony, a second aggravated burglary, and any violent felony.
- *Excluded offenses:* In about 28 states, certain offenses are automatically excluded from juvenile court. These offenses can be minor, such as traffic violations, or serious, such as murder or rape. Statutory exclusion accounts for the largest number of juveniles tried as adults.

Those states that have amended their waiver policies with statutory exclusion policies now exclude certain serious offenses from juvenile court jurisdiction. Judicial

Figure 14.3
Number of Youths Waived for Personal, Property, and Drug Crimes
Source: Charles M. Puzzanchera, *Delinquency Cases Waived to Criminal Court, 1989–1998* (Washington, DC: Bureau of Justice Statistics, 2001).

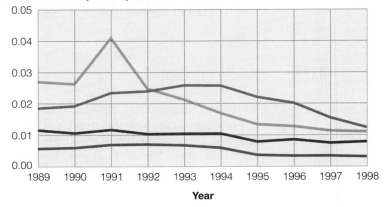

Since 1991, the use of judicial waiver has declined considerably for drug offense cases.

Number of cases judicially waived to criminal court

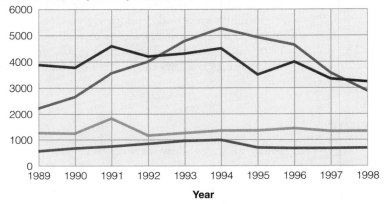

From 1993 to 1997, more person offense than property offense cases were judicially waived.

Number of cases judicially waived to criminal court

consent is unnecessary if a youth is at least a certain age and charged with a certain offense. For example, Indiana excludes cases involving 16- and 17-year-olds charged with kidnapping, rape, and robbery. In Illinois, youths ages 15 and 16 who are charged with murder, assault, or robbery with a firearm are automatically sent to criminal court; in Pennsylvania, any child accused of murder, regardless of age, is tried before the criminal court. Georgia excludes all juveniles age 13 and older from juvenile court if they are charged with one of several violent offenses such as murder, voluntary manslaughter, rape, or armed robbery with a firearm. Arizona automatically excludes juveniles charged with any felony if the youth was adjudicated for two or more prior felony offenses. About 28 states have passed legislation to exclude at least some juveniles from the juvenile court.[44] Other jurisdictions use exclusion to remove traffic offenses and public-ordinance violations.

The trend toward excluding serious violent offenses from juvenile court jurisdictions is growing in response to the demand to "get tough on crime." In addition, large numbers of youths under age 18 are tried as adults in states where the upper age of juvenile court jurisdiction is 15 or 16.

Due Process in the Juvenile Waiver Procedure

transfer hearing Preadjudicatory hearing in juvenile court for the purpose of determining whether juvenile court should be retained over a juvenile or waived and the juvenile transferred to adult court for prosecution.

Since 1966, the U.S. Supreme Court and other federal and state courts have attempted to ensure fairness in the judicial waiver process by handing down decisions that spell out the need for due process. Two Supreme Court decisions, *Kent v. United States* (1966) and *Breed v. Jones* (1975), are relevant.[45] (See the accompanying Juvenile Law in Review.) The *Kent* case declared a District of Columbia transfer statute unconstitutional and attacked the subsequent conviction of the child by granting him the specific due-process rights of having an attorney present at the hearing and access to the evidence that would be used in the case. In *Breed v. Jones,* the U.S. Supreme Court declared that the child was to be granted the protection of the double jeopardy clause of the Fifth Amendment after he was tried as a delinquent in the juvenile court: Once found to be a delinquent, the youth can no longer be tried as an adult.

Today, as a result of *Kent* and *Breed,* states that have **transfer hearings** provide (1) a legitimate transfer hearing, (2) sufficient notice to the child's family and defense attorney, (3) the right to counsel, and (4) a statement of the reason for the court order regarding transfer. These rights recognize that the transfer proceeding is critical in determining the statutory rights of the juvenile offender.

Should Youths Be Transferred to Adult Court?

Most juvenile justice experts oppose waiver because it clashes with the rehabilitative ideal. Basing waiver decisions on type and seriousness of offense rather than on the rehabilitative needs of the child has advanced the *criminalization* of the juvenile court and interfered with its traditional mission of treatment and rehabilitation.[46] And despite this sacrifice, there is little evidence that strict waiver policies can lower crime rates.[47] While it is true that some juvenile offenders commit crimes that deserve punishment, and that rehabilitation programs will not be effective with all juveniles, the fact remains that most kids who remain in the juvenile justice system do not become adult offenders.

Waiver can also create long-term harm. Waived children may be stigmatized by a conviction in the criminal court. Labeling children as adult offenders early in life may seriously impair their future educational, employment, and other opportunities. Youthful offenders convicted in adult courts are more likely to be incarcerated and to receive longer sentences than had they remained in the juvenile court. And these children may be incarcerated under conditions so extreme, and in institutions where they may be physically and sexually exploited, that they will become permanently damaged.[48]

Bucks County Courier Times © Jay Crawford

SOME KIDS who commit the most serious crimes are routinely waived to adult court. Here, 14-year-old Kareem Watts is led from court in Doylestown, Pennsylvania, where he was tried as an adult for the murder of a neighbor, Darlyne Jules. A troubled young man, Watts started hearing voices in his head at age 8 and began to self-medicate by smoking pot and snorting household chemicals at age 11. When he stabbed his neighbor, Jules, he was high on pot laced with embalming fluid. After his conviction, Watts was sent to a special unit within the juvenile justice system that houses young convicted offenders who need special psychiatric care. He will be released in seven years, on his 21st birthday, following an evaluation of his mental condition.

Kent v. United States and Breed v. Jones

Kent v. United States: Facts

Morris Kent was arrested at the age of 16 in connection with charges of housebreaking, robbery, and rape. As a juvenile, he was subject to the exclusive jurisdiction of the District of Columbia Juvenile Court. The District of Columbia statute declared that the court could transfer the petitioner "after full investigation" and remit him to trial in the U.S. District Court. Kent admitted his involvement in the offenses and was placed in a receiving home for children. Subsequently, his mother obtained counsel, and they discussed with the social service director the possibility that the juvenile court might waive its jurisdiction.

Kent was detained at the receiving home for almost a week. There was no arraignment, no hearing, and no hearing for petitioner's apprehension. Kent's counsel arranged for a psychiatric examination, and a motion requesting a hearing on the waiver was filed. The juvenile court judge did not rule on the motion and entered an order stating "After full investigation, the court waives its jurisdiction and directs that a trial be held under the regular proceedings of the criminal court." The judge made no finding and gave no reasons for his waiver decision. It appeared that the judge denied motions for a hearing, recommendations for hospitalization for psychiatric observation, requests for access to the social service file, and offers to prove that the petitioner was a fit subject for rehabilitation under the juvenile court.

After the juvenile court waived its jurisdiction, Kent was indicted by the grand jury and was subsequently found guilty of housebreaking and robbery and not guilty by reason of insanity on the charge of rape. Kent was sentenced to serve a period of 30 to 90 years on his conviction.

Decision

The petitioner's lawyer appealed the decision on the basis of the infirmity of the proceedings by which the juvenile court waived its jurisdiction. He further attacked the waiver on statutory and constitutional grounds, stating, "(1) no hearing occurred, (2) no findings were made, (3) no reasons were stated before the waiver, and (4) counsel was denied access to the social service file."

The U.S. Supreme Court found that the juvenile court order waiving jurisdiction and remitting the child to trial in the district court was invalid. Its arguments were based on the following criteria:

- The theory of the juvenile court act is rooted in social welfare procedures and treatments.
- The philosophy of the juvenile court, namely *parens patriae*, is not supposed to allow procedural unfairness.
- Waiver proceedings are critically important actions in the juvenile court.
- The juvenile court act requiring full investigation in the District of Columbia should be read in the context of constitutional principles relating to due process of law. These principles require at a minimum that the petitioner be entitled to a hearing, access to counsel, access by counsel to social service records, and a statement of the reason for the juvenile court decision.

Significance of the Case

This examined for the first time the substantial degree of discretion associated with a transfer proceeding in the District of Columbia. Thus, the Supreme Court significantly limited its holding to the statute involved but justified its reference to constitutional principles relating to due process and the assistance of counsel. In addition, it said that the juvenile court waiver hearings need to measure up to the essentials of due process and fair treatment. Furthermore, in an appendix to its opinion, the Court set up criteria concerning waiver of the jurisdictions. These are

The seriousness of the alleged offense to the community

Whether the alleged offense was committed in an aggressive, violent, or willful manner

---

Waivers don't always support the goal of increased public protection. Because juveniles may only serve a fraction of the prison sentence imposed by the criminal court, the actual treatment of delinquents in adult court is similar to what they might have received had they remained in the custody of juvenile authorities.[49] In the majority of cases involving transferred juveniles sentenced to incarceration, the length of sentence does not exceed three years, a length of time typically within the range of options available to juvenile courts.[50] Once they are released, waived juveniles have a higher recidivism rate than those kept in juvenile court. This has prompted some critics to ask, Why bother transferring these children?

Sometimes waiver can add an undue burden to youthful offenders. Studies have found that although transfer to criminal court was intended for the most serious juvenile offenders, many transferred juveniles were not violent offenders but repeat property offenders.[51] Cases involving waiver take significantly longer than a comparable juvenile court case, during which time the waived youth is more likely to be held in a **detention** center. This finding is vexing, considering that some research shows that many waived youths were no more dangerous than youths who remain in juvenile courts.[52]

detention Temporary care of a child alleged to be delinquent who requires secure custody in physically restricting facilities pending court disposition or execution of a court order.

Whether the alleged offense was committed against persons or against property

The prosecutive merit of the complaint

The sophistication and maturity of the juvenile

The record and previous history of the juvenile

Prospects for adequate protection of the public and the likelihood of reasonable rehabilitation

Breed v. Jones: Facts

In 1971, a petition in the juvenile court of California was filed against Jones, who was then 17, alleging that he had committed an offense that if committed by an adult, would constitute robbery. The petitioner was detained pending a hearing. At the hearing the juvenile court took testimony, found that the allegations were true, and sustained the petition. The proceedings were continued for a disposition hearing, at which point Jones was found unfit for treatment in the juvenile court. It was ordered that he be prosecuted as an adult offender. At a subsequent preliminary hearing, the petitioner was held for criminal trial, an information was filed against him for robbery, and he was tried and found guilty. He was committed to the California Youth Authority over objections that he was being subjected to double jeopardy.

Petitioner Jones sought an appeal in the federal district court on the basis of the double jeopardy argument that jeopardy attaches at the juvenile delinquency proceedings. The writ of habeas corpus was denied.

Decision

The U.S. Supreme Court held that the prosecution of Jones as an adult in the California Superior Court, after an adjudicatory finding in the juvenile court that he had violated a criminal statute and a subsequent finding that he was unfit for treatment as a juvenile, violated the double jeopardy clause of the Fifth Amendment to the U.S. Constitution as applied to the states through the Fourteenth Amendment. Thus,

Jones's trial in the California Superior Court for the same offense as that for which he was tried in the juvenile court violated the policy of the double jeopardy clause, even if he never faced the risk of more than one punishment. Double jeopardy refers to the risk or potential risk of trial and conviction, not punishment.

Significance of the Case

The *Breed* case provided answers on several important transfer issues: (1) *Breed* prohibits trying a child in an adult court when there has been a prior adjudicatory juvenile proceeding; (2) probable cause may exist at a transfer hearing, and this does not violate subsequent jeopardy if the child is transferred to the adult court; (3) because the same evidence is often used in both the transfer hearing and subsequent trial in either the juvenile or adult court, a different judge is often required for each hearing.

Critical Thinking

1. Do you believe that some cases should be automatically waived to the adult system, or should all juvenile offenders be evaluated for the possibility of treatment in the juvenile court before a waiver decision is made?

InfoTrac College Edition Research

 Use *juvenile waiver* as a subject guide on InfoTrac College Edition to find out more about this issue.

Sources: *Kent v. United States*, 383 U.S. 541, 86 S.Ct. 1045, 16 L.Ed.2d 84 (1966); *Breed v. Jones*, 421 U.S. 519, 95 S.Ct. 1779 (1975).

Transfer decisions are not always carried out fairly or equitably, and there is evidence that minorities are waived at a rate that is greater than their representation in the population.[53] About 40 percent of all waived youths are African Americans, even though they represent less than a third (31%) of the juvenile court population.[54]

In Support of Waiver Not all experts challenge the waiver concept. Waiver is attractive to conservatives because it jibes with the get-tough policy currently popular. Some have argued that the increased use of waiver can help get violent offenders off the streets and should be mandatory for juveniles committing serious violent crimes.[55] Others point to studies that show that, for the most part, transfer is reserved for the most serious cases and the most serious juvenile offenders. Kids are most likely to be transferred to criminal court if they have injured someone with a weapon or if they have a long juvenile court record.[56] Frank Zimring argues that, despite its faults, waiver is superior to alternative methods for handling the most serious juvenile offenders.[57] Some cases involving serious offenses, he argues, require a minimum criminal penalty greater than that available to the juvenile court. It is also possible that some juveniles take advantage of decisions to transfer them to the

A CLOSER VIEW

One argument against waiver is that treating juveniles as adults will reinforce their criminal tendencies throughout their adult lives. Read more about this view at InfoTrac College Edition: Eric K. Klein, "Dennis the Menace or Billy the Kid: An Analysis of the Role of Transfer to Criminal Court in Juvenile Justice, *American Criminal Law Review* 35(2):371–410 (Winter 1998).

adult court. Although the charge against a child may be considered serious in the juvenile court, the adult criminal court will not find it so; consequently, a child may have a better chance for dismissal of the charges, or acquittal after a jury trial.

In sum, though the use of waiver has been in decline, it is still an important strategy for attacking serious youth crime.[58] Its continued use can be attributed to the get-tough attitude toward the serious juvenile offender.

Juvenile Court Trial

If the case cannot be decided during the pretrial stage, it will be brought forth for a trial in the juvenile court. An adjudication hearing is held to determine the merits of the petition claiming that a child is either a delinquent youth or in need of court supervision. The judge is required to make a finding based on the evidence and arrive at a judgment. Adjudication is comparable to an adult trial. Rules of evidence in adult criminal proceedings are generally applicable in juvenile court, and the standard of proof used—*beyond a reasonable doubt*—similar to that used in adult trials.

State juvenile codes vary with regard to the basic requirements of due process and fairness. Most juvenile courts have bifurcated hearings—that is, separate hearings for adjudication and disposition (sentencing). At disposition hearings, evidence can be submitted that reflects nonlegal factors such as the child's home life.

To get information on juvenile courts, go to the Web site of the National Center for State Courts at *http://www.ncsc.dni.us/* For an up-to-date list of Web links, go to *http://info.wadsworth.com/siegel*

Most state juvenile codes provide specific rules of procedure, which have several purposes: They require that a written petition be submitted to the court, ensure the right of a child to have an attorney, provide that the adjudication proceedings be recorded, allow the petition to be amended, and provide that a child's plea be accepted. Where the child admits to the facts of the petition, the court generally seeks assurance that the plea is voluntary. If plea bargaining is used, prosecutors, defense counsel, and trial judges take steps to ensure the fairness of such negotiations.

At the end of the adjudication hearing, most juvenile court statutes require the judge to make a factual finding on the legal issues and evidence. In the criminal court, this finding is normally a prelude to reaching a verdict. In the juvenile court, however, the finding itself is the verdict—the case is resolved in one of three ways:

1. The juvenile court judge makes a finding of fact that the child or juvenile is not delinquent or in need of supervision.
2. The juvenile court judge makes a finding of fact that the juvenile is delinquent or in need of supervision.
3. The juvenile court judge dismisses the case because of insufficient or faulty evidence.

In some jurisdictions, informal alternatives are used, such as filing the case with no further consequences or continuing the case without a finding for a period of time, such as six months. If the juvenile does not get into further difficulty during that time, the case is dismissed. These alternatives involve no determination of delinquency or noncriminal behavior. Because of the philosophy of the juvenile court that emphasizes rehabilitation over punishment, a delinquency finding is not the same thing as a criminal conviction. The disabilities associated with conviction, such as disqualifications for employment or being barred from military service, do not apply in an adjudication of delinquency.

There are other differences between adult and juvenile proceedings. For instance, while adults are entitled to public trials by a jury of their peers, these rights are not extended to juveniles.[59] Because juvenile courts are treating some defendants similar to adult criminals, an argument can be made that the courts should extend to these youths the Sixth Amendment right to a public jury trial.[60] For the most part, however, state juvenile courts operate without recognizing a juvenile's constitutional right to a jury trial.

Constitutional Rights at Trial

due process Basic constitutional principle based on the concept of the primacy of the individual and the complementary concept of limitation on governmental power; safeguards the individual from unfair state procedures in judicial or administrative proceedings; due-process rights have been extended to juvenile trials.

For a review of due process issues in juvenile justice, go to http://www.ncjrs.org/txtfiles/fs9749.txt For an up-to-date list of Web links, go to http://info.wadsworth.com/siegel

In addition to mandating state juvenile code requirements, the U.S. Supreme Court has mandated the application of constitutional due-process standards to the juvenile trial. **Due process** is addressed in the Fifth and Fourteenth Amendments to the U.S. Constitution. It refers to the need for rules and procedures that protect individual rights. Having the right to due process means that no person can be deprived of life, liberty, or property without such protections as legal counsel, an open and fair hearing, and an opportunity to confront those making accusations against the person.

For many years, children were deprived of their due-process rights because the *parens patriae* philosophy governed their relationship to the juvenile justice system. Such rights as having counsel and confronting one's accusers were deemed unnecessary. After all, why should children need protection from the state when the state was seen as acting in their interest? As we have seen, this view changed in the 1960s, when the U.S. Supreme Court began to grant due-process rights and procedures to minors. The key case was that of Gerald Gault; it articulated the basic requirements of due process that must be satisfied in juvenile court proceedings. Because *Gault* remains the key constitutional case in the juvenile justice system, it is set forth in the accompanying Juvenile Law in Review.

The *Gault* decision reshaped the constitutional and philosophical nature of the juvenile court system and, with the addition of legal representation, made it more similar to the adult system.[61] Following the *Gault* case, the U.S. Supreme Court decided *in re Winship* that the amount of proof required in juvenile delinquency adjudications is "beyond a reasonable doubt," a level equal to the requirements in the adult system.[62]

Although the ways in which the juvenile court operates were altered by *Gault* and *Winship*, the trend toward increased rights for juveniles was somewhat curtailed by the U.S. Supreme Court's decision in *McKeiver v. Pennsylvania* (1971), which held that trial by jury in a juvenile court's adjudicative stage is not a constitutional

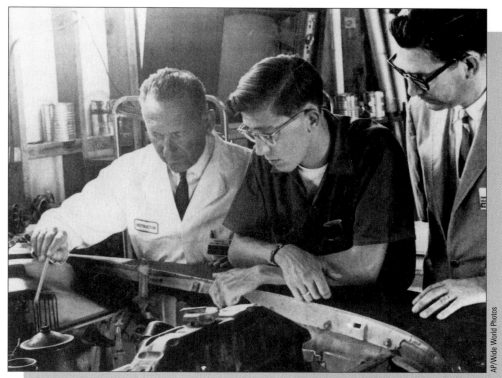

THE APPEAL OF GERALD GAULT (center) heralded in the due process revolution in juvenile justice.

In re Gault

Facts

Gerald Gault, 15 years of age, was taken into custody by the sheriff of Gila County, Arizona, because a woman complained that he and another boy had made an obscene telephone call to her. At the time, Gerald was under a six-month probation after being found delinquent for stealing a wallet. As a result of the woman's complaint, Gerald was taken to a children's home. His parents were not informed that he was being taken into custody. His mother appeared in the evening and was told by the superintendent of detention that a hearing would be held in the juvenile court the following day. On the day in question, the police officer who had taken Gerald into custody filed a petition alleging his delinquency. Gerald, his mother, and the police officer appeared before the judge in his chambers. Mrs. Cook, the complainant, was not at the hearing. Gerald was questioned about the telephone calls and was sent back to the detention home and subsequently released a few days later.

On the day of Gerald's release, Mrs. Gault received a letter indicating that a hearing would be held on Gerald's delinquency a few days later. A hearing was held, and the complainant again was not present. There was no transcript or recording of the proceedings, and the juvenile officer stated that Gerald had admitted making the lewd telephone calls. Neither the boy nor his parents were advised of any right to remain silent, right to be represented by counsel, or any other constitutional rights. At the conclusion of the hearing, the juvenile court committed Gerald as a juvenile delinquent to the state industrial school for the period of his minority.

This meant that at the age of 15, Gerald Gault was sentenced to remain in the state school until he reached the age of 21, unless he was discharged sooner. An adult charged with the same crime would have received a maximum punishment of no more than a $50 fine or two months in prison.

Decision

Gerald's attorneys filed a writ of habeas corpus, which was denied by the Superior Court of the State of Arizona. That decision was subsequently affirmed by the Arizona Supreme Court. On appeal to the U.S. Supreme Court, Gerald's counsel argued that the juvenile code of Arizona under which Gerald was found delinquent was invalid because it was contrary to the due-process clause of the Fourteenth Amendment. In addition, Gerald was denied the following basic due-process rights: (1) notice of the charges with respect to their timeliness and specificity, (2) right to counsel, (3) right to confrontation and cross-examination, (4) privilege against self-incrimination, (5) right to a transcript of the trial record, and (6) right to appellate review. In deciding the case, the U.S. Supreme Court had to determine whether procedural due process of law within the context of fundamental fairness under the Fourteenth Amendment applied to juvenile delinquency proceedings in which a child is committed to a state industrial school.

The Court, in a far-reaching opinion, agreed that Gerald's constitutional rights had been violated. Notice of charges was an essential ingredient of due process of law, as was the right to counsel, the right to cross-examine and to confront witnesses, and the privilege against self-incrimination. The questions of appellate review and a right to a transcript were not answered by the Court in this case.

Significance of the Case

The *Gault* case established that a child has the due-process constitutional rights listed here in delinquency adjudication proceedings, where the consequences were that the child could be committed to a state institution. It was confined to rulings at the adjudication state of the juvenile process.

This decision was significant not only because of the procedural reforms it initiated but also because of its far-reaching impact throughout the entire juvenile justice system. *Gault* instilled in juvenile proceedings the development of due-process standards at the pretrial, trial, and posttrial stages of the juvenile process. While recognizing the history and development of the juvenile court, it sought to accommodate the motives of rehabilitation and treatment with children's rights. It recognized the principle of fundamental fairness of the law for children as well as for adults. Judged in the context of today's juvenile justice system, *Gault* redefined the relationships between juveniles, their parents, and the state. It remains the single most significant constitutional case in the area of juvenile justice.

Critical Thinking

1. The *Gault* case is hailed as a milestone for giving juveniles due-process rights; does the provision of those rights actually harm youth? In other words, would it have been advisable to keep attorneys and legal process out of the juvenile court? Is it too late to transform the system so that it reflects its original ideals?

InfoTrac College Edition Research

How has the *Gault* case shaped the philosophy of the juvenile court? To find out, read Lise A. Young, "Suffer the Children: The Basic Principle of Juvenile Justice Is to Treat the Child, Not Punish the Offense," *America* 185(12):19 (October 22, 2001).

Source: *In re Gault*, 387 U.S. 1; 87 S.Ct. 1248 (1967).

requirement.[63] This decision does not prevent states from giving the juvenile a trial by jury, but in the majority of states a child has no such right.

Once an adjudicatory hearing has been completed, the court is normally required to enter a judgment or finding against the child. This may take the form of declaring the child delinquent, adjudging the child to be a ward of the court, or possibly even suspending judgment so as to avoid the stigma of a juvenile record. After a judgment has been entered, the court can begin its determination of possible dispositions.

Disposition

A CLOSER VIEW

Use *juvenile sentencing* as a key term on InfoTrac College Edition to learn more about this topic.

The sentencing step of the juvenile justice process is called disposition. At this point the court orders treatment for the juvenile.[64] According to prevailing juvenile justice philosophy, dispositions should be in the *best interest of the child,* which in this context means providing the help necessary to resolve or meet the adolescent's personal needs, while at the same time meeting society's needs for protection.

In most jurisdictions, adjudication and disposition hearings are separated, or bifurcated, so that evidence that could not be entered during the juvenile trial can be considered at the dispositional hearing. At the hearing, the defense counsel represents the child, helps the parents understand the court's decision, and influences the direction of the disposition. Others involved at the dispositional stage include representatives of social service agencies, psychologists, social workers, and probation personnel.

The Predisposition Report   After the child has admitted to the allegations, or the allegations have been proved in a trial, the judge normally orders the probation department to complete a predisposition report. The predisposition report, which is similar to the presentence report of the adult justice system, has a number of purposes:

- It helps the judge decide which disposition is best for the child.
- It aids the juvenile probation officer in developing treatment programs where the child is in need of counseling or community supervision.
- It helps the court develop a body of knowledge about the child that can aid others in treating the child.[65]

Sources of dispositional data include family members, school officials, and statements from the juvenile offenders themselves. The results of psychological testing, psychiatric evaluations, and intelligence testing may be relevant. Furthermore, the probation officer might include information about the juvenile's feelings concerning his or her case.

Some state statutes make the predisposition report mandatory. Other jurisdictions require the report only when there is a probability that the child will be institutionalized. Some appellate courts have reversed orders institutionalizing children where the juvenile court did not use a predisposition report in reaching its decision. Access to predisposition reports is an important legal issue.

In the final section of the predisposition report, the probation department recommends a disposition to the presiding judge. This is a critical aspect of the report because it has been estimated that the court follows more than 90 percent of all probation department recommendations.

Juvenile Court Dispositions   Historically, the juvenile court has had broad discretionary power to make dispositional decisions. The major categories of dispositional choices are (1) community release, (2) out-of-home placements, (3) fines or restitution, (4) community service, and (5) institutionalization. A more detailed list of the dispositions open to the juvenile court judge appears in Exhibit 14.2.[66]

Most state statutes allow the juvenile court judge to select whatever disposition seems best suited to the child's needs, including institutionalization. In some states the court determines commitment to a specific institution; in other states the youth corrections agency determines where the child will be placed. In addition to the dispositions in Exhibit 14.2, some states grant the court the power to order parents into treatment or to suspend a youth's driver's license.

Today it is common for juvenile court judges to employ a graduated sanction program for juveniles: (1) immediate sanctions for nonviolent offenders, which consist of community-based diversion and day treatment imposed on first-time nonviolent offenders; (2) intermediate sanctions, which target repeat minor offenders and first-time serious offenders; and (3) secure care, which is reserved for repeat serious offenders and violent offenders.[67]

In 1998, juveniles were adjudicated delinquent in 63 percent of the 1,000,300 cases brought before a judge. Once adjudicated, juveniles in 58 percent (365,100) of

Exhibit 14.2 Common Juvenile Dispositions

Disposition	Action Taken
Informal consent decree	In minor or first offenses, an informal hearing is held, and the judge will ask the youth and his or her guardian to agree to a treatment program, such as counseling. No formal trial or disposition hearing is held.
Probation	A youth is placed under the control of the county probation department and required to obey a set of probation rules and participate in a treatment program.
Home detention	A child is restricted to his or her home in lieu of a secure placement. Rules include regular school attendance, curfew observance, avoidance of alcohol and drugs, and notification of parents and the youth worker of the child's whereabouts.
Court-ordered school attendance	If truancy was the problem that brought the youth to court, a judge may order mandatory school attendance. Some courts have established court-operated day schools and court-based tutorial programs staffed by community volunteers.
Financial restitution	A judge can order the juvenile offender to make financial restitution to the victim. In most jurisdictions, restitution is part of probation (see Chapter 15), but in a few states, such as Maryland, restitution can be a sole order.
Fines	Some states allow fines to be levied against juveniles age 16 and over.
Community service	Courts in many jurisdictions require juveniles to spend time in the community working off their debt to society. Community service orders are usually reserved for victimless crimes, such as possession of drugs, or crimes against public order, such as vandalism of school property. Community service orders are usually carried out in schools, hospitals, or nursing homes.
Outpatient psychotherapy	Youths who are diagnosed with psychological disorders may be required to undergo therapy at a local mental health clinic.
Drug and alcohol treatment	Youths with drug- or alcohol-related problems may be allowed to remain in the community if they agree to undergo drug or alcohol therapy.
Commitment to secure treatment	In the most serious cases a judge may order an offender admitted to a long-term treatment center, such as a training school, camp, ranch, or group home. These may be either state- or privately run institutions, usually located in remote regions. Training schools provide educational, vocational, and rehabilitation programs in a secure environment (see Chapter 15).
Commitment to a residential community program	Youths who commit crimes of a less serious nature but who still need to be removed from their homes can be placed in community-based group homes or halfway houses. They attend school or work during the day and live in a controlled, therapeutic environment at night.
Foster home placement	Foster homes are usually used for dependent or neglected children and status offenders. Today judges are placing delinquents with insurmountable problems at home in state-licensed foster care homes.

the cases were placed on formal probation; in 26 percent (163,800) of the cases, juveniles were placed in a residential facility.

Eleven percent of adjudicated cases resulted in other dispositions, such as referral to an outside agency, community service, or restitution. Between 1989 and 1998, the number of cases in which the court ordered an adjudicated delinquent to be placed in a residential facility increased 37 percent, while the number of formal probation cases increased 73 percent (Figure 14.4).[68]

While the juvenile court has been under pressure to get tough on youth crime, probation is still the disposition of choice in even the most serious cases. For example, Table 14.1 shows the disposition patterns for robbery cases between 1989 and 1998. As the table shows, fewer youths are being waived to the adult court today

Figure 14.4
**Juvenile Court Placement
of Adjudicated Youths**
Source: Charles M. Puzzanchera,
*Juvenile Court Placement of Adjudi-
cated Youth, 1989–1998* (Washington, DC: Office of Juvenile Justice
and Delinquency Prevention, 2002).

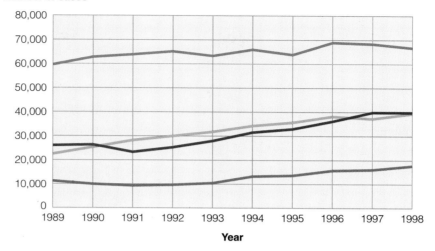

- In 1998, more than one in four adjudicated delinquency cases resulted in out-of-home placement (i.e., placement in a residential treatment center, juvenile corrections facility, foster home, or group home); 58% resulted in an order of probation; 11% resulted in some other disposition, such as restitution, fines, community service, or referral to other treatment agencies; and 5% were released at disposition without sanction.

- Placement cases grew 37% between 1989 and 1998.

- There were racial differences in out-of-home placements. About 24% of adjudicated cases involving white youth resulted in out-of-home placements, compared with 30% of cases involving black youth and 25% involving other minority youth.

Table 14.1   Characteristics of Robbery Cases Disposed by Juvenile Courts, by Gender, 1989 and 1998

	Males		Females	
	1989	**1998**	**1989**	**1998**
Cases disposed	20,900	26,700	2,000	2,800
Manner of handling				
Formal	87%	88%	86%	85%
Informal	13	12	14	15
Outcome of formal handling				
Waived	4%	4%	1%	2%
Adjudicated	59	63	65	61
Not adjudicated	37	34	34	37
Disposition of adjudicated cases				
Out-of-home placement	47%	43%	33%	38%
Formal probation	43	46	48	51

Note: Detail may not add to totals because of rounding.

Source: Paul Harms, *Robbery Cases in Juvenile Court* (Washington, DC: Office of Juvenile Justice and Delinquency Prevention, 2002).

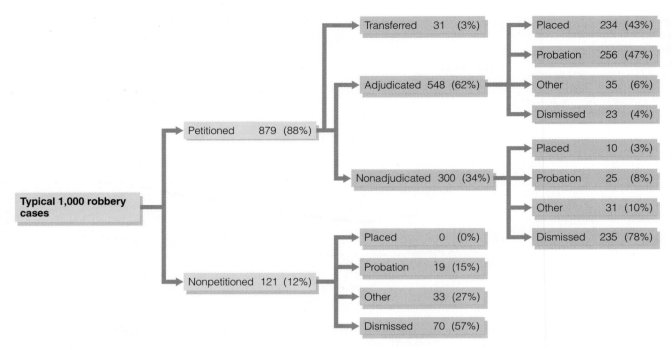

Figure 14.5
Juvenile Court Processing of a Typical 1,000 Robbery Cases, 1998
Source: Paul Harms, *Robbery Cases in Juvenile Court* (Washington, DC: Office of Juvenile Justice and Delinquency Prevention, 2002).

than a decade ago; conversely, more are being placed on probation. As Figure 14.5 shows, today, more juveniles are being placed on probation, rather than in an institution, for a serious crime such as robbery.[69]

Juvenile Sentencing Structures

For most of the juvenile court's history, disposition was based on the presumed needs of the child. Although critics have challenged the motivations of early reformers in championing rehabilitation, there is little question that the rhetoric of the juvenile court has promoted that ideal.[70] For example, in their classic work *Beyond the Best Interest of the Child,* Joseph Goldstein, Anna Freud, and Albert Solnit say that placement of children should be based on the **least detrimental alternative** available in order to foster the child's development.[71] Most states have adopted this ideal in their sentencing efforts, and state courts usually insist that the purpose of disposition must be rehabilitation and not punishment.[72] Consequently, it is common for state courts to require judges to justify their sentencing decisions if it means that juveniles are to be incarcerated in a residential treatment center: They must set forth in writing the reasons for the placement, address the danger the child poses to society, and explain why a less-restrictive alternative has not been used.[73]

Traditionally, states have used the **indeterminate sentence** in juvenile court. In about half of the states, this means having the judge place the offender with the state department of juvenile corrections until correctional authorities consider the youth ready to return to society or until the youth reaches legal majority. A preponderance of states consider 18 to be the age of release; others peg the termination age at 19; a few can retain minority status until their 21st birthday. In practice, few youths remain in custody for the entire statutory period, but juveniles are usually released if

least detrimental alternative
Choice of a program for the child that will best foster the child's growth and development.

indeterminate sentence Does not specify the length of time the juvenile must be held; rather, correctional authorities decide when the juvenile is ready to return to society.

individualized treatment model
Each sentence must be tailored to the individual needs of the child.

determinate sentence Specifies a fixed term of detention that must be served.

mandatory sentence Defined by a statutory requirement that states the penalty to be set for all cases of a specific offense.

their rehabilitation has been judged to have progressed satisfactorily. This practice is referred to as the **individualized treatment model.**

Another form of the indeterminate sentence allows judges to specify a maximum term. Under this form of sentencing, youths may be released if the corrections department considers them to be rehabilitated or they reach the automatic age of termination (usually 18 or 21). In states that stipulate a maximum sentence, the court may extend the sentence, depending on the youth's progress in the institutional facility.

A number of states have changed from an indeterminate to a **determinate sentence.** This means sentencing juvenile offenders to a fixed term of incarceration that must be served in its entirety. Other states have passed laws creating **mandatory sentences** for serious juvenile offenders. Juveniles receiving mandatory sentences are usually institutionalized for the full sentence and are not eligible for early parole. The difference between mandatory and determinate sentences is that the mandatory sentence carries a statutory requirement that a certain penalty be set in all cases on conviction for a specified offense.

Sentencing Reform

There have been a number of attempts to create rational sentencing within juvenile justice. In some instances the goal has been to reduce judicial discretion, in others to toughen sentencing practices and create mandatory periods of incarceration for juveniles who commit serious crimes. However, not all statutory changes have had the desired effect. For instance, New York State has implemented a juvenile offender law requiring that juveniles accused of violent offenses be tried in criminal court as a get-tough-on-crime measure; evaluations found many youths ended up receiving lighter sentences than they would have in the family court.[74]

Probably the best-known effort to reform sentencing in the juvenile court is the state of Washington's Juvenile Justice Reform Act of 1977. This act created a mandatory sentencing policy requiring juveniles ages 8 to 17 who are adjudicated delinquent to be confined in an institution for a minimum time.[75] The intent of the act was to make juveniles accountable for criminal behavior and to provide for punishment commensurate with the (1) age, (2) crime, and (3) prior history of the offender. Washington's approach is based on the principle of *proportionality.* How much time a youth must spend in confinement is established by the Juvenile Dispositions Standards Commission, based on the three stated criteria. The introduction of such mandatory-sentencing procedures reduces disparity in the length of sentences, according to advocates of a get-tough juvenile justice system.

The growing realization that the juvenile crime rate has stabilized may slow the tide of legislative change in juvenile justice. What is more likely is that states will continue to pass legislation making it easier to transfer youths to the adult court or giving the adult court original jurisdiction over serious cases. Thus, rather than toughening juvenile law for everyone, the system may reserve the harshest measures for the few more serious cases.

Blended Sentences   State sentencing trends indicate that punishment and accountability, in addition to rehabilitation, have become equally important in juvenile justice policy. As a result, many states have created blended sentencing structures for cases involving serious offenders. Blended sentencing allows the imposition of juvenile and adult sanctions for juvenile offenders adjudicated in juvenile court or convicted in criminal court. In other words, this expanded sentencing authority allows criminal and juvenile courts to impose either a juvenile or an adult sentence, or both, in cases involving juvenile offenders. When both sentences are imposed simultaneously, the court suspends the adult sanction. If the youth follows the conditions of the juvenile sentence and commits no further violation, the adult sentence is revoked. This type of statute has become popular in recent years, with Connecticut, Kentucky, and Minnesota among the states adopting it since 1994.[76]

The Death Penalty for Juveniles

Juveniles who have been waived to adult court can receive the death penalty. The execution of minor children has not been uncommon in our nation's history; about 350 juvenile offenders have been executed since 1642. This represents about 2 percent of the total of more than 18,000 executions carried out since colonial times.

During the past 20 years, 196 juvenile death sentences have been imposed (about 3 percent of the almost 6,900 total U.S. death sentences). Approximately two-thirds of these have been imposed on 17-year-olds and nearly one-third on 15- and 16-year-olds.[77] More than 170 offenders are now on death row in 16 different states. All are male; 73 percent committed their crimes at age 17; 63 percent are minorities. Texas, with 24 juvenile offenders on death row, held 34 percent of the national total of such offenders.[78]

Legal Issues In *Thompson v. Oklahoma* (1988), the U.S. Supreme Court prohibited the execution of persons *under age 16,* but left open the age at which execution would be legally appropriate.[79] They then answered this question in two 1989 cases, *Wilkins v. Missouri* and *Stanford v. Kentucky,* in which they ruled that states were free to impose the death penalty for murderers who committed their crimes after they reached age 16 or 17.[80] According to the majority opinion, society has not formed a consensus that the execution of such minors constitutes a cruel and unusual punishment.

Those who oppose the death penalty for children find that it has little deterrent effect on youngsters who are impulsive and do not have a realistic view of the destructiveness of their misdeeds or their consequences. Victor Streib, the leading critic of the death penalty for children, argues that such a practice is cruel and unusual punishment because (1) the condemnation of children makes no measurable contribution to the legitimate goals of punishment; (2) condemning any minor to death violates contemporary standards of decency; (3) the capacity of the young for change, growth, and rehabilitation makes the death penalty particularly harsh and inappropriate; and (4) both legislative attitudes and public opinion reject juvenile executions.[81] Supporters of the death penalty hold that people, regardless of their age, can form criminal intent and therefore should be responsible for their actions. If the death penalty is legal for adults, they argue, then it can also be used for children who commit serious crimes.

The fact that the United States is not alone in executing criminals appears to support retention of the death penalty. However, the fact that many countries have abolished capital punishment encourages those who want capital punishment to be abandoned.

The Child's Right to Appeal

final order Order that ends litigation between two parties by determining all their rights and disposing of all the issues.

Regardless of the sentence imposed, juveniles may want to appeal the decision made by the juvenile court judge. Juvenile court statutes normally restrict appeals to cases where the juvenile seeks review of a **final order,** one that ends the litigation between two parties by determining all their rights and disposing of all the issues.[82] The **appellate process** gives the juvenile the opportunity to have the case brought before a reviewing court after it has been heard in the juvenile or family court. Today, the law does not recognize a federal constitutional right of appeal. In other words, the U.S.

appellate process Allows the juvenile an opportunity to have the case brought before a reviewing court after it has been heard in juvenile or family court.

Constitution does not require any state to furnish an appeal to a juvenile charged and found to be delinquent in a juvenile or family court. Consequently, appellate review of a juvenile case is a matter of statutory right in each jurisdiction. However, the majority of states do provide juveniles with some method of statutory appeal.

The appeal process was not always part of the juvenile law system. In 1965, few states extended the right of appeal to juveniles.[83] Even in the *Gault* case in 1967, the U.S. Supreme Court refused to review the Arizona juvenile code, which provided no appellate review in juvenile matters. It further rejected the right of a juvenile to a transcript of the original trial record.[84] Today, however, most jurisdictions that provide a child with some form of appeal also provide for counsel and for securing a record and transcript, which are crucial to the success of any appeal.

Because juvenile appellate review is defined by individual statutes, each jurisdiction determines for itself what method of review will be used. There are two basic methods of appeal: the direct appeal and the collateral attack.

The *direct appeal* normally involves an appellate court review to determine whether, based on the evidence presented at the trial, the rulings of law and the judgment of the court were correct. The second major area of review involves the collateral attack of a case. The term *collateral* implies a secondary or indirect method of attacking a final judgment. Instead of appealing the juvenile trial because of errors, prejudice, or lack of evidence, *collateral review* uses extraordinary legal writs to challenge the lower-court position. One such procedural device is the writ of habeas corpus. Known as the *Great Writ*, the **writ of habeas corpus** refers to a procedure for determining the validity of a person's custody. In the context of the juvenile court, it is used to challenge the custody of a child in detention or in an institution. This writ is often the method by which the Supreme Court exercises its discretionary authority to hear cases regarding constitutional issues. Even though there is no constitutional right to appeal a juvenile case and each jurisdiction provides for appeals differently, juveniles have a far greater opportunity for appellate review today than in years past.

writ of habeas corpus Judicial order requesting that a person detaining another produce the body of the prisoner and give reasons for his or her capture and detention.

Confidentiality in Juvenile Proceedings

confidentiality Restriction of information in juvenile court proceedings in the interest of protecting the privacy of the juvenile.

Along with the rights of juveniles at adjudication and disposition, the issue of **confidentiality** in juvenile proceedings has also received attention in recent years. The debate on confidentiality in the juvenile court deals with two areas: (1) open versus closed hearings, and (2) privacy of juvenile records. Confidentiality has become moot in some respects, as many legislatures have broadened access to juvenile records.

Open vs. Closed Hearings   Generally, juvenile trials are closed to the public and the press, and the names of the offenders are kept secret. The U.S. Supreme Court has ruled on the issue of privacy in three important decisions. In *Davis v. Alaska*, the Court concluded that any injury resulting from the disclosure of a juvenile's record is outweighed by the right to completely cross-examine an adverse witness.[85] The *Davis* case involved an effort to obtain testimony from a juvenile probationer who was a witness in a criminal trial. The Supreme Court held that a juvenile's interest in confidentiality was secondary to the constitutional right to confront adverse witnesses.

The decisions in two subsequent cases, *Oklahoma Publishing Co. v. District Court* and *Smith v. Daily Mail Publishing Co.*, sought to balance juvenile privacy with freedom of the press. In the *Oklahoma* case, the Supreme Court ruled that a state court was not allowed to prohibit the publication of information obtained in an open juvenile proceeding.[86] The case involved an 11-year-old boy suspected of homicide, who appeared at a detention hearing where photographs were taken and published in local newspapers. When the local district court prohibited further disclosure, the publishing company claimed that the court order was a restraint in violation of the First Amendment, and the Supreme Court agreed.

The *Smith* case involved the discovery and publication of the identity of a juvenile suspect in violation of a state statute prohibiting publication. The Supreme Court, however, declared the statute unconstitutional because the Court believed the state's interest in protecting the child's identity was not of such a magnitude as to justify the use of such a statute.[87] Therefore, if newspapers lawfully obtain pictures or names of juveniles, they may publish them. Based on these decisions, it appears that the Supreme Court favors the constitutional rights of the press over the right to privacy of the juvenile offender.

None of the decisions, however, give the press or public access to juvenile trials. Some jurisdictions still bar the press from juvenile proceedings unless they show at a hearing that their presence will not harm the youth. However, the trend has been to make it easier for the press and the public to have open access to juvenile trials. For example, in 1995 Georgia amended its juvenile code to allow the public access to juvenile hearings in cases in which a juvenile is charged with certain designated felonies, such as kidnapping and attempted murder. Also in 1995, Missouri passed legislation that "removes the veil of secrecy that once kept juvenile court proceedings private—in the hope that allowing names and photos in newspapers will discourage teen crime and alert school officials." Michigan has granted public access to court proceedings and documents in cases involving delinquents, truants, runaways, and abuse victims. During the past decade 17 jurisdictions have amended their laws to provide for greater openness in juvenile courts.[88]

A CLOSER VIEW
Should the press have access to juvenile court proceedings, and should they write articles about cases? On InfoTrac College Edition, read M. L. Stein, "Penetrating Juvenile Courts," *Editor & Publisher* *130*(28):8 (July 12, 1997).

Privacy of Juvenile Records   For most of the twentieth century, juvenile records were kept confidential.[89] Today, however, the record itself, or information contained in it, can be opened by court order in many jurisdictions on the basis of statutory exception. The following groups can ordinarily gain access to juvenile records: (1) law enforcement personnel, (2) the child's attorney, (3) the parents or guardians, (4) military personnel, and (5) public agencies such as schools, court-related organizations, and correctional institutions.

Many states have enacted laws authorizing a central repository for juvenile arrest records. About 30 states have enacted provisions to allow open hearings in at least some juvenile cases. Forty-two states have enacted legislation authorizing the release and publication of the names and addresses of juvenile offenders in some cases. States also began to allow more juveniles to be fingerprinted and photographed. Nearly all states now allow juvenile fingerprints to be included in criminal history records, and nearly all states authorize juveniles to be photographed for later identification.[90] Some states allow a juvenile adjudication for a criminal act to be used as evidence in an adult criminal proceeding for the same act, to show predisposition or criminal nature.

Today, most states recognize the importance of juvenile records in sentencing. Many first-time adult offenders committed numerous crimes as juveniles, and evidence of these crimes may not be available to sentencing for the adult offenses unless states pass statutes allowing access. Knowledge of a defendant's juvenile record may help prosecutors and judges determine appropriate sentencing for offenders ages 18 to 24, the age group most likely to be involved in violent crime.

According to experts such as Ira Schwartz, the need for confidentiality to protect juveniles is far less than the need to open up the courts to public scrutiny.[91] The problem of maintaining confidentiality of juvenile records will become more acute in the future as electronic information storage makes these records both more durable and more accessible.

In conclusion, virtually every state provides prosecutors and judges access to the juvenile records of adult offenders. There is great diversity, however, regarding provisions for the collection and retention of juvenile records.[92]

SUMMARY

Many decisions about what happens to a child may occur prior to adjudication. Detention in secure facilities for those charged with juvenile delinquency and involuntary placement in shelter care for those involved in noncriminal behavior place severe limitations on the rights of the child and the parents. There has been a major effort to remove juveniles from detention in adult jails and to make sure status offenders are not placed in secure detention facilities.

Most statutes require a hearing if the initial decision is to keep the child in custody. The child has a right to counsel and is generally given other procedural due-process safeguards, notably the privilege against self-incrimination and the right to confront and cross-examine witnesses.

In addition, most juvenile court procedures provide criteria to be used in deciding whether to detain a child. These include (1) the need to protect the child, (2) the likelihood that the child presents a serious danger to the public, and (3) the likelihood that the child will return to court for adjudication.

The intake stage is a screening process. The law enforcement officer is required to make decisions about court action or referral to social agencies. In addition, it is important for law enforcement agencies and the juvenile courts to have sound working relationships. Their objective is the same: to protect the child and the community.

In the last decade, juvenile justice practitioners have made efforts to divert as many children as possible from the juvenile courts and place them in nonsecure treatment programs. Critics charge that diversion programs actually involve more youths in the justice system than would be the case had the programs not been in operation, a concept referred to as widening the net. Moreover, the effectiveness of diversion as a crime-reducing policy has been questioned.

Those who are held for trial are generally released to their parents, on bail, or through other means. Because the juvenile justice system is not able to try every child accused of a crime or a status offense due to personnel limitations, diversion programs seem to hold greater hope for the control of delinquency. As a result, such subsystems as diversion, statutory intake proceedings, plea bargaining, and other informal adjustments are essential ingredients in the administration of the juvenile justice system.

An issue related to bail is preventive detention, which refers to the right of a judge to deny persons release before trial on the grounds that they may be dangerous to themselves or others. Advocates of preventive detention argue that dangerous juvenile offenders should not be granted bail and pretrial release because they would then have an opportunity to intimidate witnesses and commit further crimes. Opponents retaliate that defendants are *innocent until proven guilty* and therefore should be allowed freedom before trial.

Prior to the creation of the first juvenile court in 1899, juveniles were tried in adult courts. However, even with the development of the juvenile court system, it is recognized that certain crimes require that children be tried as adults.

Each year, thousands of youths are transferred to adult courts because of the serious nature of their crimes. This process, known as waiver, is an effort to remove serious offenders from the juvenile process and into the more punitive adult system. Despite controversy surrounding this practice, most states have modified their laws, making it easier to prosecute juveniles in criminal court. Today, virtually all jurisdictions provide for waiver of juvenile offenders to the criminal courts. The number of juveniles transferred to criminal court has actually declined in recent years. More research is needed on the impact of transferring juveniles to the adult justice system.

Most jurisdictions have a bifurcated juvenile code system that separates the adjudication hearing from the dispositional hearing. Juveniles alleged to be delinquent have virtually all the rights given a criminal defendant at trial—except possibly the right to a trial by jury. In addition, juvenile proceedings are generally closed to the public.

Types of dispositional orders include dismissal, fine, probation, and institutionalization. The use of such dispositions has not curtailed the rising rate of juvenile crime, however. As a result, legislatures and national commissions have begun to take a tougher position with regard to the sentencing of some juvenile offenders. The traditional notion of rehabilitation and treatment as the proper goals for disposition is being questioned, and some jurisdictions have replaced it with proportionality and determinacy in sentencing procedures. However, many juvenile codes do require that the court consider the *least-restrictive* alternative.

The predisposition report is the primary informational source for assisting the court in making a judgment. Once a juvenile is found delinquent, or in need of supervision, the juvenile court is empowered to make fundamental changes in the child's life. In recent years a number of states have made drastic changes in juvenile sentencing law, moving away from the indeterminate sentence and embracing more determinate forms of disposition. States have passed laws allowing judges to hand down blended sentences to children found guilty of serious crimes: a juvenile sentence that remains in effect until the defendant turns 21 and a suspended adult sentence that can be reinstated if the juvenile has any further brushes with the law.

The most extreme form of punishment is the death penalty, which in some states can be administered to children as young as 16. The use of capital punishment has been the subject of much debate, but at present 67 persons remain on death row for crimes committed as juveniles.

Finally, many state statutes require that juvenile hearings be closed and that the privacy of juvenile records be maintained to protect the child from public scrutiny and to provide a greater opportunity for rehabilitation. This approach may be inconsistent with the public's interest in taking a closer look at the juvenile justice system.

KEY TERMS

juvenile defense attorney	preventive detention	transfer hearing	determinate sentence
guardian *ad litem*	intake	detention	mandatory sentence
public defender	diversion	due process	final order
juvenile prosecutor	widening the net	least detrimental alternative	appellate process
juvenile court judge	complaint	indeterminate sentence	writ of habeas corpus
shelter care	plea bargaining	individualized treatment model	confidentiality
bail	transfer process		

QUESTIONS FOR DISCUSSION

1. Discuss and identify the major participants in the juvenile adjudication process. What are each person's role and responsibilities in the course of a juvenile trial?

2. The criminal justice system in the United States is based on the adversarial process. Should the same adversary principle apply in the juvenile justice system?

3. Children have certain constitutional rights at adjudication, such as the right to an attorney and the right to confront and cross-examine witnesses. But they do not have the right to a trial by jury. Should juvenile offenders have a constitutional right to a jury trial? Should each state make that determination? Discuss the legal decision that addresses this issue.

4. What is the point of obtaining a predisposition report in the juvenile court? Is it of any value in cases where the child is released to the community? Does it have a significant value in serious juvenile crime cases?

5. The standard of proof in juvenile adjudication is to show that the child is guilty beyond a reasonable doubt. Explain the meaning of this standard of proof in the U.S. judicial system.

6. Should states adopt get-tough sentences in juvenile justice or adhere to the individualized treatment model?

7. Do you agree with the principle of imposing the death penalty on juveniles found to have committed certain capital crimes?

8. What are blended sentences?

9. Should individuals who committed murder while under age 16 be legally executed?

VIEWPOINT

Three teenagers are arraigned on hate-crime charges in a U.S. district court. The judge refuses to let reporters attend any hearings in the case and orders that any information that could identify the juveniles be deleted from case records before they are released to the press. A newspaper appeals the judge's order, but a federal appeals court affirms the decision and declares that juvenile proceedings in federal court are presumptively closed. Believing that important rights are at stake, the newspaper petitions for U.S. Supreme Court review, arguing that the First Amendment creates a right of public access to juvenile court proceedings.

This is precisely what happened in United States v. Three Juveniles, *a case involving* The Boston Globe. *The* Globe Newspaper Co. *filed a petition for writ of certiorari in November 1995, and the U.S. Supreme Court denied review on April 29, 1996.*

To read more about the issue of open access to juvenile trials, go to the following article on InfoTrac College Edition: Thomas A. Hughes, "Opening the Doors to Juvenile Court: Is There an Emerging Right of Public Access?" *Communications and the Law* 19:1–50 (1997).

NOTES

1. Kelly Dedel, "National Profile of the Organization of State Juvenile Corrections Systems," *Crime and Delinquency* 44:507–25 (1998). Herein cited as National Profile.

2. Anne L. Stahl, *Delinquency Cases in Juvenile Courts, 1998* (Washington, DC: Office of Juvenile Justice and Delinquency Prevention, 2001).

3. Anne L. Stahl, *Drug Offense Cases in Juvenile Courts, 1989–1998* (Washington, DC: Office of Juvenile Justice and Delinquency Prevention, 2001).

4. Stahl, *Delinquency Cases in Juvenile Courts, 1998.*

5. *Powell v. Alabama* 287 U.S. 45, 53 S.Ct. 55, 77, L.Ed.2d 158 (1932); *Gideon v. Wainwright* 372 U.S. 335, 83 S.Ct. 792, 9 L.Ed.2d 799 (1963); *Argersinger v. Hamlin* 407 U.S. 25, 92 S.Ct. 2006, 32 L.Ed.2d 530 (1972).

6. Howard Davidson, "The Guardian *ad Litem*: An Important Approach to the Protection of Children," *Children Today* 10:23 (1981); Daniel Golden, "Who Guards the Children?" *Boston Globe Magazine*, 27 December 1992, p. 12.

7. Chester Harhut, "An Expanded Role for the Guardian ad Litem," *Juvenile and Family Court Journal* 51:31–35 (2000).

8. Steve Riddell, "CASA, Child's Voice in Court," *Juvenile and Family Justice Today* 7:13–14 (1998).

9. American Bar Association, *A Call for Justice: An Assessment of Access to Counsel and Quality of Representation in Delinquency Proceedings* (Washington, DC: ABA Juvenile Justice Center, 1995).

10. Douglas C. Dodge, *Due Process Advocacy* (Washington, DC: Office of Juvenile Justice and Delinquency Prevention, 1997).

11. James Shine and Dwight Price, "Prosecutor and Juvenile Justice: New Roles and Perspectives," in Ira Schwartz, ed., *Juvenile Justice and Public Policy* (New York: Lexington Books, 1992), pp. 101–33.

12. James Backstrom and Gary Walker, "A Balanced Approach to Juvenile Justice: The Work of the Juvenile Justice Advisory Committee," *The Prosecutor* 32:37–39 (1988); see also *Prosecutors' Policy Recommendations on Serious, Violent, and Habitual Youthful Offenders* (Alexandria, VA: American Prosecutors' Institute, 1997).

13. Leonard P. Edwards, "The Juvenile Court and the Role of the Juvenile Court Judge," *Juvenile and Family Court Journal* 43:3–45 (1992); Lois Haight, "Why I Choose to Be a Juvenile Court Judge," *Juvenile and Family Justice Today* 7:7 (1998).

14. American Correctional Association, *Standards for Juvenile Detention Facilities* (Laurel, MD: ACA, 1991).

15. National Profile, p. 514.

16. Madeline Wordes and Sharon Jones, "Trends in Juvenile Detention and Steps Toward Reform," *Crime and Delinquency* 44:544–60 (1998).

17. Robert Shepard, *Juvenile Justice Standards Annotated: A Balanced Approach* (Chicago: ABA, 1997).

18. Stahl, *Delinquency Cases in Juvenile Courts, 1998.*

19. Paul Harms, *Detention in Delinquency Cases, 1989–1998* (Washington, DC: Office of Juvenile Justice and Delinquency Prevention, 2002).

20. Bohsiu Wu and Angel Ilarraza Fuentes, "The Entangled Effects of Race and Urban Poverty," *Juvenile and Family Court Journal* 49:41–51 (1998).

21. Edward J. Loughran, "How to Stop Our Kids from Going Bad," *Boston Globe*, 11 February 1990, p. 42.

22. Ira M. Schwartz and William H. Barton, eds., *Reforming Juvenile Detention—No More Hidden Closets* (Columbus: Ohio State University Press, 1994), p. 176.

23. James Maupin and Lis Bond-Maupin, "Detention Decision-Making in a Predominantly Hispanic Region: Rural and Non-Rural Differences," *Juvenile and Family Court Journal* 50:11–21 (1999).

24. Earl Dunlap and David Roush, "Juvenile Detention as Process and Place," *Juvenile and Family Court Journal* 46:1–16 (1995).

25. "OJJDP Helps States Remove Juveniles from Jails," *Juvenile Justice Bulletin* (Washington, DC: U.S. Department of Justice, 1990).

26. Community Research Associates, *The Jail Removal Initiative: A Summary Report* (Champaign, IL: Community Research Associates, 1987).

27. David Steinhart, "Status Offenders," *The Future of Children—The Juvenile Court*, 1996, p. 96.

28. Mark Soler et al., *Representing the Child Client* (New York: Matthew Bender, 1989), Sec. 5.03b.

29. *Schall v. Martin*, 467 U.S. 253, (1984).

30. Jeffrey Fagan and Martin Guggenheim, "Preventive Detention for Juveniles: A Natural Experiment," *Journal of Criminal Law and Criminology*, 86:415–28 (1996).

31. Stahl, *Delinquency Cases in Juvenile Courts, 1998.*

32. Leona Lee, "Factors Influencing Intake Disposition in a Juvenile Court," *Juvenile and Family Court Journal* 46:43–62 (1995).

33. H. Ted Rubin, "The Emerging Prosecutor Dominance of the Juvenile Court Intake Process," *Crime and Delinquency* 26:299–318 (1980).

34. Edwin E. Lemert, "Diversion in Juvenile Justice: What Hath Been Wrought?" *Journal of Research in Crime and Delinquency* 18:34–46 (1981).

35. Don C. Gibbons and Gerald F. Blake, "Evaluating the Impact of Juvenile Diversion Programs," *Crime and Delinquency Journal* 22:411–19 (1976); Richard J. Lundman, "Will Diversion Reduce Recidivism?" *Crime and Delinquency Journal* 22:428–37 (1976); B. Bullington, J. Sprowls, D. Katkin, and M. Phillips, "A Critique of

Diversionary Juvenile Justice," *Crime and Delinquency* 24:59–71 (1978); Thomas Blomberg, "Diversion and Accelerated Social Control," *Journal of Criminal Law and Criminology* 68:274–82 (1977); Sharla Rausch and Charles Logan, "Diversion from Juvenile Court: Panacea or Pandora's Box," in J. Klugel, ed., *Evaluating Juvenile Justice* (Beverly Hills: Sage, 1983), pp. 19–30.

36. Arnold Binder and Gilbert Geis, "Ad Populum Argumentation in Criminology: Juvenile Diversion as Rhetoric," *Criminology* 30:309–33 (1984).

37. Mark Ezell, "Juvenile Diversion: The Ongoing Search for Alternatives," in Ira M. Schwartz, ed., *Juvenile Justice and Public Policy* (New York: Lexington Books, 1992), pp. 45–59.

38. Albert W. Alschuler, "The Prosecutor's Role in Plea Bargaining," *University of Chicago Law Review* 36:50–112 (1968); Joyce Dougherty, "A Comparison of Adult Plea Bargaining and Juvenile Intake," *Federal Probation* June:72–79 (1988).

39. Sanford Fox, *Juvenile Courts in a Nutshell* (St. Paul, MN: West, 1985), pp. 154–56.

40. See Darlene Ewing, "Juvenile Plea Bargaining: A Case Study," *American Journal of Criminal Law* 6:167 (1978); Adrienne Volenik, *Checklists for Use in Juvenile Delinquency Proceedings* (Chicago: American Bar Association, 1985); Bruce Green, "Package Plea Bargaining and the Prosecutor's Duty of Good Faith," *Criminal Law Bulletin* 25:507–50 (1989).

41. Joseph Sanborn, *Plea Negotiations in Juvenile Court* (Ph.D. thesis, State University of New York at Albany, 1984); Joseph Sanborn, "Philosophical, Legal, and Systematic Aspects of Juvenile Court Plea Bargaining," *Crime and Delinquency* 39:509–27 (1993).

42. Charles M. Puzzanchera, *Delinquency Cases Waived to Criminal Court, 1989–1998* (Washington, DC: Office of Juvenile Justice and Delinquency Prevention, 2001).

43. Ibid.

44. Ind. Code Ann. 31-6-2(d) 1987; Ill.Ann.Stat. Ch. 37 Sec. 805 (1988); Penn.Stat.Ann.Title 42 6355(a) (1982); Patrick Griffin et al., *Trying Juveniles as Adults in Criminal Court: An Analysis of State Transfer Provisions* (Washington, DC: OJJDP, 1998).

45. *Kent v. United States*, 383 U.S. 541, 86 S.Ct. 1045, 16 L.Ed.2d 84 (1966); *Breed v. Jones*, 421 U.S. 519, 95 S.Ct. 1179, 44 L.Ed.2d 346 (1975).

46. Barry Feld, "The Juvenile Court Meets the Principle of the Offense: Legislative Changes in Juvenile Waiver Statutes," *Journal of Criminal Law and Criminology* 78:471–534 (1987); Paul Marcotte, "Criminal Kids," *American Bar Association Journal* 76:60–66 (1990); Dale Parent et al., *Transferring Serious Juvenile Offenders to Adult Courts* (Washington, DC: U.S. Department of Justice, National Institute of Justice, 1997).

47. Richard Redding, "Juvenile Offenders in Criminal Court and Adult Prison: Legal, Psychological and Behavioral Outcomes," *Juvenile and Family Court Journal* 50:1–15 (1999).

48. Ibid., p. 11.

49. Ibid.

50. Snyder and Sickmund, *Juvenile Offenders and Victims: A National Report*, p. 157; Eric Fritsch, Tory Caeti, and Craig Hemmens, "Spare the Needle but Not the Punishment: The Incarceration of Waived Youth in Texas Prisons," *Crime and Delinquency,* 42:593–610 (1996).

51. James Howell, "Juvenile Transfers to the Criminal Justice System: State of the Art," *Law & Policy* 18:17–60 (1996).

52. M. A. Bortner, "Traditional Rhetoric, Organizational Realities: Remand of Juveniles to Adult Court," *Crime and Delinquency* 32:53–73 (1986).

53. Puzzanchera, *Delinquency Cases Waived to Criminal Court, 1988–1998*; Jeffrey Fagan, Martin Forst, and T. Scott Vivona, "Racial Determinants of the Judicial Transfer Decision: Prosecuting Violent Youth in Criminal Court," *Crime and Delinquency* 33:359–86 (1987); J. Fagan, E. Slaughter, and E. Hartstone, "Blind Justice: The Impact of Race on the Juvenile Justice Process," *Crime and Delinquency* 53:224–58 (1987); J. Fagan and E. P. Deschenes, "Determinants of Judicial Waiver Decisions for Violent Juvenile Offenders," *Journal of Criminal Law and Criminology* 81:314–47 (1990); see also James Howell, "Juvenile Transfers to Criminal Court," *Juvenile and Family Justice Journal* 6:12–14 (1997).

54. Anne L. Stahl, *Delinquency Cases in Juvenile Courts, 1997* (Washington, DC: Office of Juvenile Justice and Delinquency Prevention, 2000); Puzzanchera, *Delinquency Cases Waived to Criminal Court, 1988–1998.*

55. Barry Feld, "Delinquent Careers and Criminal Policy," *Criminology* 21:195–212 (1983).

56. Howard N. Snyder, Melissa Sickmund, Eileen Poe-Yamagata, *Juvenile Transfers to Criminal Court in the 1990s: Lessons Learned from Four Studies* (Washington, DC: Office of Juvenile Justice and Delinquency Prevention, 2000).

57. Frank Zimring, "Treatment of Hard Cases in American Juvenile Justice: In Defense of the Discretionary Waiver," *Notre Dame Journal of Law, Ethics and Policy* 5:267–80 (1991); Lawrence Winner, Lonn Kaduce, Donna Bishop, and Charles Frazier, "The Transfer of Juveniles to Criminal Courts: Reexamining Recidivism over the Long Term," *Crime and Delinquency* 43:548–64 (1997).

58. Robert Shepard, "The Rush to Waive Children to Adult Courts," *American Bar Association Journal of Criminal Justice* 10:39–42 (1995); see also Kevin Strom and Steven Smith, *Juvenile Felony Defendants in Criminal Courts* (Washington, DC: Bureau of Justice Statistics, 1998).

59. Institute of Judicial Administration, American Bar Association Joint Commission on Juvenile Justice Standards, *Standards Relating to Adjudication* (Cambridge, MA: Ballinger, 1980).

60. Joseph B. Sanborn Jr., "The Right to a Public Jury Trial—A Need for Today's Juvenile Court," *Judicature* 76:230–38 (1993).

61. Linda Szymanski, *Juvenile Delinquents' Right to Counsel* (Pittsburgh: National Center for Juvenile Justice, 1988).

62. *In re Winship*, 397 U.S. 358, 90 S.Ct. 1068 (1970).

63. *McKeiver v. Pennsylvania*, 403 U.S. 528, 91 S.Ct. 1976 (1971).

64. See, generally, R. T. Powell, "Disposition Concepts," *Juvenile and Family Court Journal* 34:7–18 (1983).

65. Sanford Fox, *Juvenile Courts in a Nutshell* (St. Paul, MN: West, 1984), p. 221.

66. This section is adapted from Jack Haynes and Eugene Moore, "Particular Dispositions," *Juvenile and Family Court Journal* 34:41–48 (1983); see also Grant Grissom, "Dispositional Authority and the Future of the Juvenile Justice System," *Juvenile and Family Court Journal* 42:25–34 (1991).

67. Barry Krisberg, Elliot Currie, and David Onek, "What Works with Juvenile Offenders," *American Bar Association Journal on Criminal Justice* 10:20–24 (1995).

68. Stahl, *Delinquency Cases in Juvenile Courts, 1998.*

69. Paul Harms, *Robbery Cases in Juvenile Court, 1989–1998* (Washington, DC: Office of Juvenile Justice and Delinquency Prevention, 2002).

70. Anthony Platt, *The Child Savers: The Invention of Delinquency* (Chicago: University of Chicago Press, 1969); David Rothman, *Conscience and Convenience: The Asylum and the Alternative in Progressive America* (Boston: Little, Brown, 1980).

71. Joseph Goldstein, Anna Freud, and Albert Solnit, *Beyond the Best Interests of the Child* (New York: Free Press, 1973).

72. See, for example, *in Interest on M.P.* 697 N.E.2d 1153 (Il. App. 1998); *Matter of Welfare of CAW* 579 N.W.2d 494 (MN. App. 1998).

73. See, for example, *Matter of Willis Alvin M.* 479 S.E.2d. 871 (WV 1996).

74. Simon Singer and David McDowall, "Criminalizing Delinquency: The Deterrent Effects of NYJO Law," *Law and Society Review* 22:Sections 21–37 (1988).

75. Washington Juvenile Justice Reform Act of 1977, Chap. 291; Wash.Rev.Code Ann. Title 9A, Sec. 1–91 (1977).

76. National Criminal Justice Association, *Juvenile Justice Reform Initiatives in the States, 1994–1996* (Washington, DC: U.S. Department of Justice, 1997).

77. Lynn Cothern, *Juveniles and the Death Penalty* (Washington, DC: Office of Juvenile Justice and Delinquency Prevention, 2000).

78. Victor Streib, *The Juvenile Death Penalty Today: Death Sentences and Executions for Juvenile Crimes, January 1, 1973–June 30, 2000* (Ada, OH: Ohio Northern University Claude W. Pettit College of Law 2000); idem, *Death Penalty for Juveniles* (Bloomington: Indiana University Press, 1987); Paul Reidinger, "The Death Row Kids," *American Bar Association Journal* April:78 (1989); Victor Streib, *The Juvenile Death Penalty Today: Present Death Row Inmates under Juvenile Death Sentences* (Cleveland: Cleveland State University, August 25, 1992); see also Sam Verhovek, "A Legislator Proposes Death Penalty for Murderers as Young as Eleven," *New York Times,* 18 April 1998, p. B10.

79. Steven Gerstein, "The Constitutionality of Executing Juvenile Offenders, *Thompson v. Oklahoma,*" *Criminal Law Bulletin* 24:91–98 (1988); *Thompson v. Oklahoma,* 108 S.Ct. 2687 (1988).

80. 109 S.Ct. 2969 (1989); for a recent analysis of the *Wilkins* and *Stanford* cases, see the note in "*Stanford v. Kentucky* and *Wilkins v. Missouri*: Juveniles, Capital Crime, and Death Penalty," *Criminal Justice Journal* 11:240–66 (1989).

81. Victor Streib, "Excluding Juveniles from New York's Impendent Death Penalty," *Albany Law Review* 54:625–79 (1990).

82. Paul Piersma, Jeanette Ganousis, Adrienne E. Volenik, Harry F. Swanger, and Patricia Connell, *Law and Tactics in Juvenile Cases* (Philadelphia: American Law Institute, American Bar Association, Committee on Continuing Education, 1977), p. 397.

83. J. Addison Bowman, "Appeals from Juvenile Courts," *Crime and Delinquency Journal* 11:63–77 (1965).

84. *In re Gault,* 387 U.S. 1 87 S.Ct. 1428 (1967).

85. *Davis v. Alaska,* 415 U.S. 308 (1974); 94 S.Ct. 1105.

86. *Oklahoma Publishing Co. v. District Court,* 430 U.S. 97 (1977); 97 S.Ct. 1045.

87. *Smith v. Daily Mail Publishing Co.,* 443 U.S. 97, 99 S.Ct. 2667, 61 L.Ed.2d 399 (1979).

88. Thomas Hughes, "Opening the Doors to Juvenile Court: Is There an Emerging Right of Public Access," *Communications and the Law,* 19:1–50 (1997).

89. Linda Szymanski, *Confidentiality of Juvenile Court Records* (Pittsburgh: National Center for Juvenile Justice, 1989).

90. Jeffrey A. Butts, *Can We Do Without Juvenile Justice?* (Washington, DC; Urban Institute, 2000).

91. Ira M. Schwartz, *Justice for Juveniles: Rethinking the Best Interests of the Child* (Lexington, MA: D. C. Heath, 1989), p. 172.

92. National Institute of Justice Update, "State Laws on Prosecutors' and Judges' Use of Juvenile Records" (Washington, DC: Office of Justice Programs, 1995).

15 Juvenile Corrections: Probation, Community Treatment, and Institutionalization

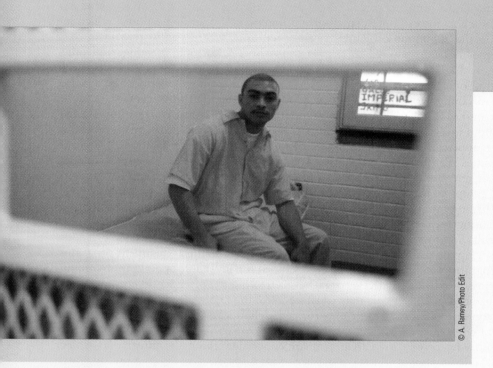

As a local juvenile court judge you have been assigned the case of Jim Butler, a 13-year-old juvenile so short he can barely see over the bench. On trial for armed robbery, Jim has been accused of threatening a woman with a knife and stealing her purse. Barely a teenager, Jim has already had a long history of involvement with the law. At age 11 he was arrested for drug possession and placed on probation; soon after, he stole a car. At age 12 he was arrested for shoplifting. Jim is accompanied by his legal guardian, his maternal grandmother. His parents are unavailable because his father abandoned the family years ago and his mother is currently undergoing inpatient treatment at a local drug clinic. After talking with his attorney, Jim decides to admit to the armed robbery. At a dispositional hearing, his court-appointed attorney tells you of the tough life Jim has been forced to endure. His grandmother states that, while she loves the boy, her advanced age makes it impossible for her to provide the care he needs to stay out of further trouble. She tells you that Jim is a good boy who has developed a set of bad companions; his current scrape was precipitated by his ill-chosen friends. A representative of the school system testifies that Jim has above-average intelligence and is actually respectful of teachers. He has potential, but his life circumstances have short-circuited his academic success. Jim himself shows remorse and appears to be a sensitive youngster who is easily led astray by older youths.

You must now make a decision in the case. You can place Jim on probation and allow him to live with his grandmother while being monitored by county probation staff. You can place him in a secure incarceration facility for up to three years. You could also put him into an intermediate program such as a community-based facility, which would allow him to attend school during the day while residing in a halfway house and receiving group treatment in the evenings. Your decision is difficult because, while Jim appears salvageable, his crime was serious and involved the use of a weapon. If he remains in the community, he may offend again; if he is sent to a correctional facility, he will interact with older, tougher kids.

- Would you place Jim on probation and allow him to live with his grandmother while being monitored by county probation staff?

- Would you send him to a secure incarceration facility for up to three years?

- Would you put him into an intermediate program such as a community-based facility, which would allow him to attend school during the day while residing in a halfway house and receiving group treatment in the evenings?

community treatment Using nonsecure and noninstitutional residences, counseling services, victim restitution programs, and other community services to treat juveniles in their own communities.

There is a wide choice of correctional treatments available for juveniles, which can be subdivided into two major categories: community treatment and institutional treatment. **Community treatment** refers to efforts to provide care, protection, and treatment for juveniles in need. These efforts include probation, treatment services (such as individual and group counseling), restitution, and other programs. Community treatment also refers to the use of privately maintained residences, such as foster homes, small-group homes, and boarding schools, which are located in the community. Nonresidential programs, where youths remain in their own homes but are required to receive counseling, vocational training, and other services, also fall under the rubric of community treatment.

Institutional treatment facilities are correctional centers operated by federal, state, and county governments; these facilities restrict the movement of residents through staff monitoring, locked exits, and interior fence controls. A variety of functions within juvenile corrections are served by these facilities, including (1) reception centers that screen juveniles and assign them to an appropriate facility; (2) specialized facilities that provide specific types of care, such as drug treatment; (3) training schools or reformatories for youths needing a long-term secure setting; (4) ranch or forestry camps that provide long-term residential care; and (5) boot camps, which seek to rehabilitate youths through the application of rigorous physical training.

Choosing between community and institutional modes of juvenile corrections can be difficult. Some experts believe that any hope for rehabilitating juvenile offenders and resolving the problems of juvenile crime lies in community treatment programs. Such programs are smaller than secure facilities for juveniles, operate in a community setting, and offer creative approaches to treating the offender. In contrast, institutionalizing young offenders may do more harm than good. It exposes them to prisonlike conditions and to more-experienced delinquents without giving them the benefit of constructive treatment programs.

Those who favor secure treatment are concerned about the threat that violent young offenders present to the community and believe that a stay in a juvenile insti-

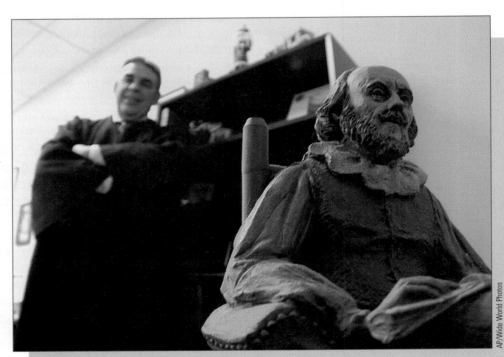

SOME COMMUNITY SENTENCES for juveniles are quite innovative. Juvenile Court Judge Paul Perachi stands in his office next to a small statue of William Shakespeare, December 12, 2000, in Pittsfield, Massachusetts. Perachi is working with the Massachusetts-based Shakespeare and Company, sending troubled youth to serve sentences in Shakespeare plays.

suppression effect A reduction in the number of arrests per year for youths who have been incarcerated or otherwise punished.

tution may have a long-term deterrent effect. They point to the findings of Charles Murray and Louis B. Cox, who uncovered what they call a **suppression effect**—a reduction in the number of arrests per year following release from a secure facility—which is not achieved when juveniles are placed in less-punitive programs.[1] Murray and Cox concluded that the justice system must choose which outcome its programs are aimed at achieving: prevention of delinquency, or the care and protection of needy youths. If the former is a proper goal, institutionalization or the threat of institutionalization is desirable. Not surprisingly, secure treatment is still being used extensively, and the populations of these facilities continue to grow as state legislators pass more stringent and punitive sentencing packages aimed at repeat juvenile offenders.

We begin this chapter with a detailed discussion of community treatment, examining both traditional probation and new approaches for providing probation services to juvenile offenders. Next, we trace the development of alternatives to incarceration, including community-based, nonsecure treatment programs and graduated sanctions (programs that provide community-based options while reserving secure care for violent offenders). The current state of secure juvenile corrections is then reviewed, beginning with some historical background, followed by a discussion of life in institutions, treatment issues, legal rights, and aftercare programs.

Juvenile Probation

probation Nonpunitive, legal disposition for juveniles emphasizing community treatment in which the juvenile is closely supervised by an officer of the court and must adhere to a strict set of rules to avoid incarceration.

Probation and other forms of community treatment generally refer to nonpunitive legal disposition for delinquent youths, emphasizing treatment without incarceration. Probation is the primary form of community treatment used by the juvenile justice system. A juvenile who is on probation is maintained in the community under the supervision of an officer of the court. Probation also encompasses a set of rules and conditions that must be met for the offender to remain in the community. Juveniles on probation may be placed in a wide variety of community-based treatment programs that provide services ranging from group counseling to drug treatment.

Community treatment is based on the idea that the juvenile offender is not a danger to the community and has a better chance of being rehabilitated within the community. It provides offenders with the opportunity to be supervised by trained personnel who can help them reestablish forms of acceptable behavior in a community setting. When applied correctly, community treatment (1) maximizes the liberty of the individual while vindicating the authority of the law and protecting the public; (2) promotes rehabilitation by maintaining normal community contacts; (3) avoids the negative effects of confinement, which often severely complicate the reintegration of the offender into the community; and (4) greatly reduces the financial cost to the public.[2]

Historical Development

Although the major developments in community treatment have occurred in the twentieth century, its roots go back much farther. In England specialized procedures for dealing with youthful offenders were recorded as early as 1820, when the magistrates of the Warwickshire quarter sessions (periodic court hearings held in a county, or shire, of England) adopted the practice of sentencing youthful criminals to prison terms of one day, then releasing them conditionally under the supervision of their parents or masters.[3]

In the United States, juvenile probation developed as part of the wave of social reform characterizing the latter half of the nineteenth century. Massachusetts took the first step. Under an act passed in 1869, an agent of the state board of charities was authorized to appear in criminal trials involving juveniles, to find them suitable homes, and to visit them periodically. These services were soon broadened, so that by 1890 probation had become a mandatory part of the court structure.[4]

Probation was a cornerstone in the development of the juvenile court system. In fact, in some states, supporters of the juvenile court movement viewed probation as the first step toward achieving the benefits that the new court was intended to provide. The rapid spread of juvenile courts during the first decades of the twentieth century encouraged the further development of probation. The two were closely related and, to a large degree, both sprang from the conviction that the young could be rehabilitated and that the public was responsible for protecting them.

Expanding Community Treatment

By the mid-1960s, juvenile probation had become a complex institution that touched the lives of an enormous number of children. To many experts, institutionalization of even the most serious delinquent youths is a mistake. Reformers believed that confinement in a high-security institution could not solve the problems that brought a youth into a delinquent way of life, and that the experience could actually help amplify delinquency once the youth returned to the community.[5] Surveys indicating that 30 to 40 percent of adult prison inmates had prior experience with the juvenile court, and that many had been institutionalized as youths, gave little support to the argument that an institutional experience can be beneficial or reduce recidivism.[6]

The Massachusetts Experience The expansion of community programs was energized by correctional reform in the state of Massachusetts. Since the early 1970s, Massachusetts has led the movement to keep juvenile offenders in the community. After decades of documenting the failures of the youth correctional system, Massachusetts, led by its juvenile correctional commissioner Jerome Miller, closed most of its secure juvenile facilities.[7] Today, 30 years later, the Massachusetts Department of Youth Services still operates a community-based correctional system. The majority of youths are serviced in nonsecure community settings, and only a few dangerous or unmanageable youths are placed in some type of secure facilities.

Many of the early programs suffered from residential isolation and limited services. Over time, however, many of the group homes and unlocked structured residential settings were relocated in residential community environments and became highly successful in addressing the needs of juveniles, while presenting little or no security risk to themselves or others. For example, the Roxbury Youthworks is an inner-city program in Boston that aims to control delinquency through a comprehensive range of resources that include (1) evaluation and counseling at a local court clinic, (2) employment and training, (3) detention diversion, and (4) outreach and tracking to help youths reenter the community. Contracting with the state, Roxbury Youthworks provides intensive community supervision for almost 90 percent of the youths under its jurisdiction.[8]

Though the efforts to turn juvenile corrections into a purely community-based system has not been adopted elsewhere, the Massachusetts model encouraged development of nonpunitive programs, which have proliferated across the nation. The concept of probation has been expanded, and new programs have been created.

Contemporary Juvenile Probation

Traditional probation is still the backbone of community-based corrections. As Figure 15.1 shows, more than 350,000 juveniles are currently being placed on formal probation each year, which amounts to more than 50 percent of all juvenile dispositions. The use of probation has increased significantly since 1989, when a little more than 200,000 adjudicated youths were being placed on probation.[9] These figures show that regardless of public sentiment, probation continues to be a popular dispositional alternative for judges. Here are the arguments in favor of probation:

Figure 15.1
**Probation and Correctional
Population Trends**
Source: Adapted from Charles M.
Puzzanchera et al., *Juvenile Court
Statistics, 1998* (Washington, DC:
Office of Juvenile Justice and
Delinquency Prevention, 2001).

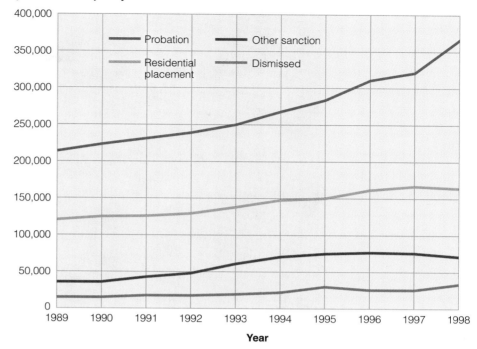

Adjudicated delinquency cases

Note: There has been a substantial increase in the number of cases in which the youth was placed on probation or ordered to a residential facility between 1989 and 1998.

1. For youths who can be supervised in the community, probation represents an appropriate disposition.
2. Probation allows the court to tailor a program to each juvenile offender, including those involved in person-oriented offenses.
3. The justice system continues to have confidence in rehabilitation, while accommodating demands for legal controls and public protection, even when caseloads may include many more serious offenders than in the past.
4. Probation is often the disposition of choice, particularly for status offenders.[10]

The Nature of Probation In the majority of jurisdictions, probation is a direct judicial order that allows a youth who is found to be a delinquent or status offender to remain in the community under court-ordered supervision. A probation sentence implies a contract between the court and the juvenile. The court promises to hold a period of institutionalization in abeyance; the juvenile promises to adhere to a set of rules mandated by the court. If the rules are violated—and especially if the juvenile commits another offense—the probation may be revoked. In that case, the contract is terminated and the original commitment order may be enforced. The rules of probation vary, but they typically involve conditions such as attending school or work, keeping regular hours, remaining in the jurisdiction, and staying out of trouble.

In the juvenile court, probation is often ordered for an indefinite period. Depending on the statutes of the jurisdiction, the seriousness of the offense, and the juvenile's adjustment on probation, youths can remain under supervision until the court no longer has jurisdiction over them (that is, when they reach the age of majority). State statutes determine whether a judge can specify how long a juvenile may be placed under an order of probation. In most jurisdictions, the status of probation is reviewed regularly to ensure that a juvenile is not kept on probation needlessly. Generally, discretion lies with the probation officer to discharge youths who are adjusting to the treatment plan.

JUVENILE PROBATION OFFICERS provide supervision and treatment in the community. The treatment plan is a product of the intake, diagnostic, and investigative aspects of probation. Treatment plans vary in terms of approach and structure. Some juveniles simply report to the probation officer and follow the conditions of probation. In other cases, juvenile probation officers will supervise young people more intensely, monitor their daily activities, and work with them in directed treatment programs. Here, a juvenile probation officer and police officer talk with Crips gang members in California.

Conditions of Probation   Probation conditions are rules mandating that a juvenile on probation behave in a particular way. They can include restitution or reparation, intensive supervision, intensive counseling, participation in a therapeutic program, or participation in an educational or vocational training program. In addition to these specific conditions, state statutes generally allow courts to insist that probationers lead law-abiding lives, maintain a residence in a family setting, refrain from associating with certain types of people, and remain in a particular area unless they have permission to leave. (See Figure 15.2 for different probation options.)

Probation conditions vary, but they are never supposed to be capricious, cruel, or beyond the capacity of the juvenile to satisfy. Furthermore, conditions of probation should relate to the crime that was committed and to the conduct of the youth.

Courts have invalidated probation conditions that were harmful or that violated the juvenile's due-process rights. Restricting a young person's movement, insisting on a mandatory program of treatment, ordering indefinite terms of probation, and demanding financial reparation where this is impossible are all grounds for appellate court review. For example, it would not be appropriate for a probation order to bar a youth from visiting his girlfriend (unless he had threatened or harmed her) merely because her parents objected to the relationship.[11] However, courts have ruled that it is permissible to bar juveniles from such sources of danger as a "known gang area" in order to protect them from harm.[12]

If a youth violates the conditions of probation or breaks the law again, the court can revoke probation. The juvenile court ordinarily handles a decision to revoke probation upon recommendation of the probation officer. Today, as a result of Supreme Court decisions dealing with the rights of adult probationers, a juvenile is normally entitled to legal representation and a hearing when a violation of probation occurs.[13]

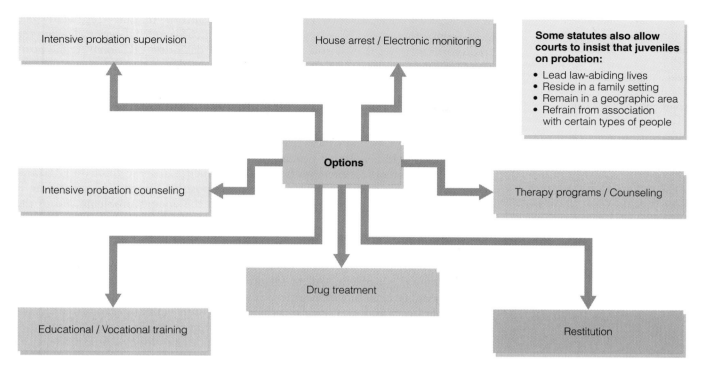

Figure 15.2
Conditions of Probation

Organization and Administration

Probation services are administered by the local juvenile court, or by the state administrative office of courts, in 23 states and the District of Columbia. In another 14 states, juvenile probation services are split, with the juvenile court having control in urban counties and a state executive serving in smaller counties. About 10 states have a statewide office of juvenile probation located in the executive branch. In 3 states, county executives administer probation.[14] These agencies employ an estimated 18,000 juvenile probation officers throughout the United States.

In the typical juvenile probation department, the chief probation officer is central to its effective operation. In addition, large probation departments include one or more assistant chiefs, each of whom is responsible for one aspect of probation service. One assistant chief might oversee training, another might supervise special offender groups, and still another might act as liaison with police or community-service agencies.

Although juvenile probation services continue to be predominantly organized under the judiciary, recent legislative activity has been in the direction of transferring those services from the local juvenile court judge to a state court administrative office. Whether local juvenile courts or state agencies should administer juvenile probation services is debatable. In years past, the organization of probation services depended primarily on the size of the program and the number of juveniles under its supervision. Because of this momentum to develop unified court systems, many juvenile court services are being consolidated into state court systems.

Duties of Juvenile Probation Officers

The **juvenile probation officer** plays an important role in the justice process, beginning with intake and continuing throughout the period in which a juvenile is under court supervision. Probation officers are involved at four stages of the court process.

juvenile probation officer
Officer of the court involved in all four stages of the court process—intake, predisposition, postadjudication, and postdisposition—who assists the court and supervises juveniles placed on probation.

social investigation report, predisposition report Developed by the juvenile probation officer, this report consists of a clinical diagnosis of the juvenile and his or her need for court assistance, relevant environmental and personality factors, and any other information that would assist the court in developing a treatment plan for the juvenile.

conditions of probation The rules and regulations mandating that a juvenile on probation behave in a particular way.

At *intake,* they screen complaints by deciding to adjust the matter, refer the juvenile to an agency for service, or refer the case to the court for judicial action. During the *predisposition* stage, they participate in release or detention decisions. At the *postadjudication* stage, they assist the court in reaching its dispositional decision. During *postdisposition,* they supervise juveniles placed on probation.

At intake, the probation staff has preliminary discussions with the juvenile and the family to determine whether court intervention is necessary or whether the matter can be better resolved by some form of social service. If the juvenile is placed in a detention facility, the probation officer helps the court decide whether the juvenile should continue to be held or released pending the adjudication and disposition of the case.

The probation officer exercises tremendous influence over the youth and the family by developing a **social investigation**, or **predisposition**, **report** and submitting it to the court. This report is a clinical diagnosis of the youth's problems and of the need for court assistance based on an evaluation of social functioning, personality, and environmental issues. The report includes an analysis of the child's feelings about the violations and his or her capacity for change. It also examines the influence of family members, peers, and other environmental influences in producing and possibly resolving the problems. All of this information is brought together in a complex but meaningful picture of the offender's personality, problems, and environment.

Juvenile probation officers also provide the youth with supervision and treatment in the community. Treatment plans vary in terms of approach and structure. Some juveniles simply report to the probation officer and follow the **conditions of probation.** In other cases, the probation officer may need to provide extensive counseling to the youth and family or, more typically, refer them to other social service agencies, such as a drug treatment center. Figure 15.3 provides an overview of the juvenile probation officer's sphere of influence. Exhibit 15.1 summarizes the probation officer's role. Performance of such a broad range of functions requires thorough

Figure 15.3
The Juvenile Probation Officer's Influence

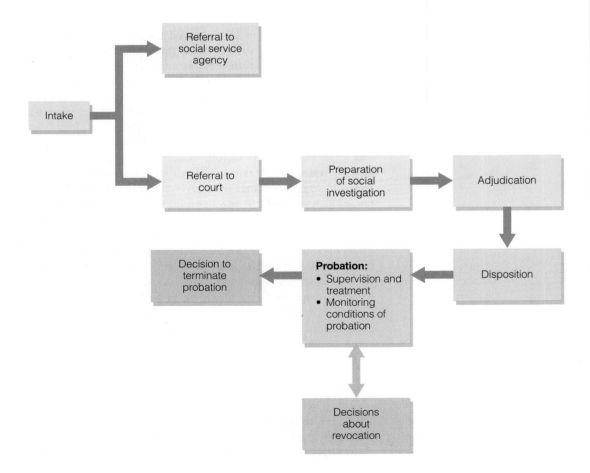

Exhibit 15.1 Duties of the Juvenile Probation Officer

- Providing direct counseling and casework services
- Interviewing and collecting social service data
- Making diagnostic recommendations
- Maintaining working relationships with law enforcement agencies
- Using community resources and services
- Directing volunteer case aides
- Writing predisposition or social investigation reports
- Working with families of children under supervision
- Providing specialized services, such as group therapy
- Supervising specialized caseloads involving children with special problems
- Making decisions about the revocation of probation and its termination

training. Today, juvenile probation officers have legal or social-work backgrounds or special counseling skills.

Probation Innovations

Community corrections have traditionally emphasized offender rehabilitation. The probation officer has been viewed as a caseworker or counselor, whose primary job is to help the offender adjust to society. Offender surveillance and control has seemed more appropriate for law enforcement, jails, and prisons than for community corrections.[15] Since 1980, a more conservative justice system has reoriented toward social control. While the rehabilitative ideals of probation have not been abandoned, new programs have been developed that add a control dimension to community corrections. These programs can be viewed as "probation plus," since they add restrictive penalties and conditions to community-service orders. More punitive than probation, intermediate sanctions can be politically attractive to conservatives, while still appealing to liberals as alternatives to incarceration. What are some of these new alternative sanctions?

Intensive Supervision

juvenile intensive probation supervision (JIPS) A true alternative to incarceration that involves almost daily supervision of the juvenile by the probation officer assigned to the case.

Juvenile intensive probation supervision (JIPS) involves treating offenders who would normally have been sent to a secure treatment facility as part of a very small probation caseload that receives almost daily scrutiny.[16] The primary goal of JIPS is *decarceration*; without intensive supervision, youngsters would normally be sent to secure juvenile facilities that are already overcrowded. The second goal is control: High-risk juvenile offenders can be maintained in the community under much closer security than traditional probation efforts can provide. A third goal is maintaining community ties and reintegration: Offenders can remain in the community and complete their education while avoiding the pains of imprisonment.

Intensive probation programs get mixed reviews. Some jurisdictions find that they are more successful than traditional probation supervision and come at a much cheaper cost than incarceration.[17] However, most research indicates that the failure rate is high and that younger offenders who commit petty crimes are the most likely to fail when placed in intensive supervision programs.[18] It is not surprising that intensive probation clients fail more often because, after all, they are more serious offenders who might otherwise have been incarcerated and are now being watched and supervised more closely than probationers.

An innovative experiment in three Mississippi counties examined the differential effects on juvenile justice costs for intensive supervision and monitoring, regular probation, and cognitive behavioral treatment, which involved sessions on problem solving, social skills, negotiation skills, the management of emotion, and values enhancement, to improve the thinking and reasoning ability of juvenile offenders. After one year of the program the intensive supervision treatment was found to be less cost effective than the other two treatments, with the cognitive behavioral treatment imposing the fewest costs on the juvenile justice system.[19]

Electronic Monitoring

house arrest An offender is required to stay at home during specific periods of time; monitoring is done by random phone calls and visits or by electronic devices.

electronic monitoring Active monitoring systems consist of a radio transmitter worn by the offender that sends a continuous signal to the probation department computer, alerting officials if the offender leaves his or her place of confinement. Passive systems employ computer-generated random phone calls that must be responded to in a certain period of time from a particular phone or other device.

Another program, which has been used with adult offenders and is finding its way into the juvenile justice system, is **house arrest,** which is often coupled with **electronic monitoring.** This program allows offenders sentenced to probation to remain in the community on condition that they stay at home during specific periods (for example, after school or work, on weekends, and in the evenings). Offenders may be monitored through random phone calls, visits, or, in some jurisdictions, electronic devices.

Two types of electronic systems are used: active and passive. *Active systems* monitor the offender by continuously sending a signal back to the central office. If an offender leaves home at an unauthorized time, the signal is broken and the failure recorded. In some cases, the control officer is automatically notified through a beeper. In contrast, *passive systems* usually involve random phone calls generated by computers to which the juvenile offender must respond within a particular time (for example, 30 seconds). Some passive systems require the offender to place the monitoring device in a verifier box that sends a signal back to the control computer; another approach is to have the arrestee repeat words that are analyzed by a voice verifier and compared with tapes of the juvenile's voice.

Most systems employ radio transmitters that receive a signal from a device worn by the offender and relay it back to the computer via telephone lines. Probationers are fitted with an unremovable monitoring device that alerts the probation department's computers if they leave their place of confinement.[20]

Joseph B. Vaughn conducted one of the first surveys of juvenile electronic monitoring in 1989, examining eight programs in five different probation departments.[21] Vaughn found that all the programs adopted electronic monitoring to reduce institutional overcrowding and that most agencies reported success in reducing the number of days juveniles spent in detention. In addition, the programs allowed the youths, who would otherwise be detained, to remain in the home and participate in counseling, educational, or vocational activities. Of particular benefit to pretrial detainees was the opportunity to remain in a home environment with supervision. This experience provided the court with a much clearer picture of how the juvenile would eventually reintegrate into society. However, Vaughn found that none of the benefits of the treatment objective in the programs had been empirically validated. The potential for behavior modification and the lasting effects of any personal changes remain unknown.

Recent indications are that electronic monitoring can be effective. Evaluations show that recidivism rates are no higher than in traditional programs, costs are lower, and overcrowding is reduced. Also, electronic monitoring seems to work better with some individuals than others: Serious felony offenders, substance abusers, repeat offenders, and people serving the longest sentences are the most likely to fail.[22]

Electronic monitoring combined with house arrest is being hailed as one of the most important developments in correctional policy. Its supporters claim that it has the benefits of relatively low cost and high security, while at the same time it helps offenders avoid imprisonment in overcrowded, dangerous state facilities. Furthermore, fewer supervisory officers are needed to handle large numbers of offenders.

Despite these strengths, electronic monitoring has its drawbacks:

- Existing systems can be affected by faulty telephone equipment.
- Most electronic monitoring/house arrest programs do not provide rehabilitation services.
- Some believe electronic monitoring is contrary to a citizen's right to privacy.[23]

Balanced Probation

balanced probation Programs that integrate community protection, accountability of the juvenile offender, competency, and individualized attention to the juvenile offender; based on the principle that juvenile offenders must accept responsibility for their behavior.

Figure 15.4
Balanced Approach Mission
Source: Gordon Bazemore and Mark Umbreit, *Balanced and Restorative Justice for Juveniles—A Framework for Juvenile Justice in the 21st Century* (Washington, DC: Office of Juvenile Justice and Delinquency Prevention, 1997), p. 14.

In recent years some jurisdictions have turned to a **balanced probation** approach in an effort to enhance the success of probation.[24] Balanced probation systems integrate community protection, the accountability of the juvenile offender, and individualized attention to the offender (see Figure 15.4). These programs are based on the view that juveniles are responsible for their actions and have an obligation to society whenever they commit an offense. The probation officer establishes a program tailored to the offender while helping the offender accept responsibility for his or her actions. The balanced approach is promising because it specifies a distinctive role for the juvenile probation system.[25] The balanced approach has been implemented with some success, as these examples demonstrate:

- In Pittsburgh, probationers in an intensive day treatment program solicit suggestions from community organizations about service projects they would like to see completed. They work with community residents on projects such as home repair and gardening for the elderly, voter registration, painting homes and public buildings, and cultivating community gardens.
- In Florida, in a program sponsored by the Florida Department of Juvenile Justice and supervised by The 100 Black Men of Palm Beach County, Inc., offenders create shelters for abused, abandoned, and HIV-positive infants. Victims' rights advocates also train juvenile justice staff on sensitivity in their interaction with victims and help prepare victim awareness curriculums for youths in residential programs.
- In cities and towns in Pennsylvania, Montana, and Minnesota, family members and other citizens acquainted with a juvenile offender, or the victim of a juvenile crime, gather to determine the best response to the offense. Held in schools, churches, or other community facilities, these conferences ensure that offenders hear community disapproval of their behavior. Participants develop an agreement for repairing the damage to the victim and the community and define a plan for reintegrating the offender.[26]

Another promising program that adheres to a balanced probation approach is the California 8% Solution, which is run by the Orange County Probation Department. The "8%" refers to the percentage of juvenile offenders who are responsible for the majority of crime: In the case of Orange County, 8 percent of first-time offenders were responsible for 55 percent of repeat cases over a three-year period. This 8 percent problem has become the 8 percent solution, by the Probation Department initiating a comprehensive, multiagency program targeting this group of offenders.[27]

Once the probation officer identifies an offender for the program—the 8% Early Intervention Program—the youth is referred to the Youth and Family Resource Center. Here the youth's needs are assessed and an appropriate treatment plan is developed. Some of the services provided to youths include

- An outside school for students in junior and senior high school
- Transportation to and from home
- Counseling for drug and alcohol abuse
- Employment preparation and job placement services
- At-home, intensive family counseling for families[28]

Although balanced probation programs are still in their infancy and their effectiveness remains to be tested, they have generated great interest because of their potential for relieving overcrowded correctional facilities and reducing the pain and stigma of incarceration. There seems to be little question that the use of these innovations, and juvenile probation in general, will increase in the years ahead. Given the $40,000 cost of a year's commitment to a typical residential facility, it should not be a great burden to develop additional probation services.

BALANCED PROBATION SYSTEMS integrate community protection, accountability of the juvenile offender, and individualized attention to the offender. Here, Charley Cobb (right), a teenager who accidentally killed her newborn baby in January 1999, talks with her lawyer, Jennifer Sobel, in Grafton County Superior Court in Haverhill, New Hampshire, May 8, 2000. Cobb fell behind in her community service work, but told the judge that she has completed 70 hours of her 500 hours community service, attends counseling regularly, and expects to graduate from high school later this month. The judge added six months to Cobb's probation.

Restitution

monetary restitution A requirement that juvenile offenders compensate crime victims for out-of-pocket losses caused by the crime, including property damage, lost wages, and medical expenses.

victim service restitution The juvenile offender is required to provide some service directly to the crime victim.

community service restitution The juvenile offender is required to assist some worthwhile community organization for a period of time.

Victim restitution is another widely used method of community treatment. In most jurisdictions, restitution is part of a probationary sentence and is administered by the county probation staff. In many jurisdictions, independent restitution programs have been set up by local governments; in others, restitution is administered by a private nonprofit organization.[29]

Restitution can take several forms. A juvenile can reimburse the victim of the crime or donate money to a charity or public cause; this is referred to as **monetary restitution**. In other instances, a juvenile may be required to provide some service directly to the victim (**victim service restitution**) or to assist a community organization (**community service restitution**).

Requiring youths to reimburse the victims of their crimes is the most widely used method of restitution in the United States. Less widely used, but more common in Europe, is restitution to a charity. In the past few years numerous programs have been set up for the juvenile offender to provide service to the victim or to participate in community programs—for example, working in schools for retarded children. In some cases, juveniles are required to contribute both money and community service. Other programs emphasize employment.[30]

Restitution programs can be employed at various stages of the juvenile justice process. They can be part of a diversion program prior to conviction, a method of informal adjustment at intake, or a condition of probation. Restitution has a number of advantages: It provides alternative sentencing options; it offers monetary compensation or service to crime victims; it allows the juvenile the opportunity to compensate the victim and take a step toward becoming a productive member of society; it helps relieve overcrowded juvenile courts, probation caseloads, and detention facilities. Finally, like other alternatives to incarceration, restitution has the potential for allowing vast savings in the operation of the juvenile justice system. Monetary restitution programs in particular may improve the public's attitude toward juvenile justice by offering equity to the victims of crime and ensuring that offenders take responsibility for their actions.

Despite its many advantages, some believe restitution supports retribution rather than rehabilitation because it emphasizes justice for the victim and criminal responsibility for illegal acts. There is some concern that restitution creates penalties for juvenile offenders where none existed before.

The use of restitution is increasing. In 1977 there were fewer than 15 formal restitution programs around the United States. By 1985, formal programs existed in 400 jurisdictions, and 35 states had statutory provisions that gave courts the authority to order juvenile restitution.[31] Today, all 50 states, as well as the District of Columbia, have statutory restitution programs.

Does Restitution Work?   How successful is restitution as a treatment alternative? Most evaluations have shown that it is reasonably effective, and should be expanded.[32] In an analysis of federally sponsored restitution programs, Peter Schneider and his associates found that about 95 percent of youths who received restitution as a condition of probation successfully completed their orders.[33] Factors related to success were family income, good school attendance, few prior offenses, minor current offense, and size of restitution order. Schneider found that the youths who received restitution as a sole sanction (without probation) were those originally viewed by juvenile court judges as the better risks, and consequently they had lower failure and recidivism rates than youths ordered to make restitution after being placed on probation.

Anne Schneider conducted a thorough analysis of restitution programs in four different states and found that participants had lower recidivism rates than youths in control groups (regular probation caseloads).[34] Although Schneider's data indicate that restitution may reduce recidivism, the number of youths who had subsequent involvement in the justice system still seemed high. In short, there is evidence that most restitution orders are successfully completed and that youths who make restitution are less likely to become recidivists. However, the number of repeat offenses committed by juveniles who made restitution suggests that, by itself, restitution is not the answer to the delinquency problem.

Restitution programs may be difficult to implement in some circumstances. Offenders may find it difficult to make monetary restitution without securing new employment, which can be difficult during periods of high unemployment. Problems also arise when offenders who need jobs suffer from drug abuse or emotional problems. Public and private agencies are likely sites for community service restitution, but their directors are sometimes reluctant to allow delinquent youths access to their organizations. Beyond these problems, some juvenile probation officers view restitution programs as a threat to their authority and to the autonomy of their organizations.

Another criticism of restitution programs is that they foster involuntary servitude. Indigent clients may be unfairly punished when they are unable to make restitution payments or face probation violations. To avoid such bias, probation officers should first determine why payment has stopped and then suggest appropriate action, rather than simply treating nonpayment as a matter of law enforcement.

Finally, restitution orders are subject to the same abuses as traditional sentencing methods. Restitution orders given to one delinquent offender may be quite different from those given another in a comparable case. To remedy this situation, a number of jurisdictions have been using guidelines to encourage standardization of orders.

Restitution programs may be an important alternative to incarceration, benefiting the child, the victim, and the juvenile justice system. H. Ted Rubin, a leading juvenile justice expert, even advocates that courts placing juveniles in day treatment and community-based residential programs also include restitution requirements in their orders and expect that these requirements be fulfilled during placement.[35] However, all restitution programs should be evaluated carefully to answer these questions:

- What type of offenders would be most likely to benefit from restitution?
- When is monetary restitution more desirable than community service?
- What is the best point in the juvenile justice process to impose restitution?
- What is the effect of restitution on the juvenile justice system?
- How successful are restitution programs?

Residential Community Treatment

As noted earlier, many experts believe that institutionalization of even the most serious delinquent youths is a mistake. Confinement in a high-security institution usually cannot solve the problems that brought a youth into a delinquent way of life, and the experience may actually amplify delinquency once the youth returns to the community. Many agree that warehousing juveniles without attention to their treatment needs does little to prevent their return to criminal behavior. Research has shown that the most effective secure-corrections programs provided individualized services for a small number of participants. Large training schools have not proved to be effective.[36] This realization has produced a wide variety of residential community treatment programs to service youths who need a more secure environment than can be provided by probation services, but who do not require placement in a state-run juvenile correctional facility.

How are community corrections implemented? In some cases, youths are placed under probation supervision, and the probation department maintains a residential treatment facility. Placement can also be made to the department of social services or juvenile corrections with the direction that the youth be placed in a residential facility. **Residential programs** are typically divided into four major categories: (1) group homes, including boarding schools and apartment-type settings; (2) foster homes; (3) family group homes; and (4) rural programs.

Group homes are nonsecure residences that provide counseling, education, job training, and family living. They are staffed by a small number of qualified persons, and generally house 12–15 youngsters. The institutional quality of the environment is minimized, and youths are given the opportunity to build a close relationship with the staff. Youths reside in the home, attend public schools, and participate in community activities in the area.

Foster care programs involve one or two juveniles who live with a family—usually a husband and wife who serve as surrogate parents. The juveniles enter into a close relationship with the foster parents and receive the attention and care they did not receive at home. The quality of the foster home experience depends on the foster parents. Foster care for adjudicated juvenile offenders has not been extensive in the United States. Welfare departments generally handle foster placements, and funding of this treatment option has been a problem for the juvenile justice system. However, foster home services have expanded as a community treatment approach.

One example of a successful foster care program is the multidimensional treatment foster care (MTFC) program, developed by social scientists at the Oregon Social Learning Center. Designed for the most serious and chronic male young offenders, this program combines individual therapy such as skill building in problem solving for the youths, and family therapy for the biological or adoptive parents. The foster care families receive training by program staff so they can provide the young people with close supervision, fair and consistent limits and consequences, and a supportive relationship with an adult.[37] Foster care families also receive close supervision and are consulted regularly on the progress of the youth by program staff. An

residential programs Placement of a juvenile offender in a residential, nonsecure facility such as a group home, foster home, family group home, or rural home where the juvenile can be closely monitored and develop close relationships with staff members.

group homes Nonsecured, structured residences that provide counseling, education, job training, and family living.

foster care programs Juveniles who are orphans or whose parents cannot care for them are placed with families who provide the attention, guidance, and care they did not receive at home.

experiment of MTFC found that one year after the completion of the program, participating youths were significantly less likely to be arrested than a control group.[38]

Family group homes combine elements of foster care and group home placements. Juveniles are placed in a group home that is run by a family rather than by a professional staff. Troubled youths have an opportunity to learn to get along in a family-like situation, and at the same time the state avoids the startup costs and neighborhood opposition often associated with establishing a public institution.

Rural programs include forestry camps, ranches, and farms that provide recreational activities or work for juveniles. Programs typically handle from 30 to 50 youths. Such programs have the disadvantage of isolating juveniles from the community, but reintegration can be achieved if the youth's stay is short and if family and friends are allowed to visit.

Most residential programs use group counseling as the major treatment tool. Although group facilities have been used less often than institutional placements, there is a trend toward developing community-based residential facilities.

family group homes A combination of foster care and a group home in which a juvenile is placed in a private group home run by a single family rather than by professional staff.

rural programs Specific recreational and work opportunities provided for juveniles in a rural setting such as a forestry camp, a farm, or a ranch.

Nonresidential Community Treatment

nonresidential programs Juveniles remain in their own homes but receive counseling, education, employment, diagnostic, and casework services through an intensive support system.

In **nonresidential programs** youths remain in their homes and receive counseling, education, employment, diagnostic, and casework services. A counselor or probation officer gives innovative and intensive support to help the youth remain at home. Family therapy, educational tutoring, and job placement may all be part of the program.

Nonresidential programs are often modeled on the Provo experiment, begun in 1959 in Utah, and on the Essexfields Rehabilitation Project, started in the early 1960s in Essex County, New Jersey.[39] Today, one of the best-known approaches is Project New Pride, which has been replicated at a number of sites around the United States. Project New Pride and two other innovative programs are the subject of the Policy and Practice box entitled "Three Model Nonresidential Programs."

Pros and Cons of Residential Community Treatment   The community treatment approach has limitations. The public may have a negative impression of community treatment, especially when it is offered to juvenile offenders who pose a threat to society. Institutionalization may be the only answer for violent, chronic offenders. Even if the juvenile crime problem abates, society may be unwilling to accept the outcomes of reform-minded policies and practices. For example, it is not uncommon for neighborhood groups to oppose the location of corrections programs in their community. But is their fear realistic?

Much of the early criticism of community treatment was based on poor delivery of services, shabby operation, and haphazard management, follow-up, and planning. In the early 1970s, when Massachusetts deinstitutionalized its juvenile correction system, a torrent of reports revealed the inadequate operation of community treatment programs, based in part on the absence of uniform policies and procedures and the lack of accountability. The development of needed programs was hampered, and available resources were misplaced. Today's community treatment programs have generally overcome their early deficiencies and operate more efficiently than in the past.

Despite such criticisms, community-based programs continue to present the most promising alternative to the poor results of reform schools for these reasons:

1. Some states have found that residential and nonresidential settings produce comparable or lower recidivism rates. Some researchers have found that youths in nonsecure settings are less likely to become recidivists than those placed in more secure settings (although this has not been proven conclusively).
2. Community-based programs have lower costs and are especially appropriate for large numbers of nonviolent juveniles and those guilty of lesser offenses.
3. Public opinion of community corrections remains positive. Many citizens prefer community-based programs for all but the most serious juvenile offenders.[40]

Three Model Nonresidential Programs

Project New Pride

One of the best-known community-based treatment programs is Project New Pride. Begun in 1973 in Denver, Colorado, it has been a model for similar programs around the country.

The target group for Project New Pride is serious or violent youthful offenders from 14 to 17 years of age who have at least two prior convictions for serious misdemeanors or felonies and are formally charged or convicted of another offense when they are referred to New Pride. The only youths not eligible for participation are those who have committed forcible rape or are diagnosed as severely psychotic. New Pride believes this restriction is necessary in the interest of the safety of the community and of the youths themselves.

The project's specific goals are to steer these hard-core offenders back into the mainstream of their communities and to reduce the number of rearrests. Generally, reintegration into the community means enrolling in school, getting a job, or both. The success of this program revolves around four ideas:

1. *Schooling:* New Pride youths receive alternative schooling and are then reintegrated into the public school system or directed toward vocational training. Some youths get jobs and pursue a general equivalency diploma (GED). Some of them complete high school in the alternative school (certified by the public school system).
2. *Jobs:* New Pride emphasizes vocational training. The staff recognizes that money is the key to independence for these youths, and the most socially acceptable way to get money is to work for it.
3. *Family:* Not only do the youths benefit from intensive counseling but their families also have access to counselors. New Pride encourages family members to visit the project facility to observe the daily operations, involve themselves in their child's treatment, and get to know staff.
4. *Cost-effectiveness:* New Pride community-based programs are extremely cost effective when compared with the cost of placing a child in an institution. In Colorado and New Jersey, for example, it costs approximately $28,000 per year to incarcerate a youth; the cost for placing a youth in Denver New Pride is approximately $4,500.

Each participant in New Pride has six months of intensive involvement and a six-month follow-up period during which the youth slowly reintegrates into the community. During the follow-up period, the youth continues to receive as many services as necessary, such as schooling and job placement, and works closely with counselors.

The Bethesda Day Treatment Center Program

The Bethesda Day Treatment Center Program in West Milton, Pennsylvania, is another model day-treatment program. The center's services include intensive supervision, counseling, and coordination of a range of services necessary for youths to develop skills to function effectively in the community. The program provides delinquent and dependent youths, ages 10 to 17, with up to 55 hours of services a week without removing them from their homes. A unique program feature requires work experience for all working-age clients, with 75 percent of their paychecks directed toward payment of fines, court costs, and restitution. A preliminary study revealed recidivism rates far lower than state and national norms.

Multisystemic Therapy

Multisystemic Therapy (MST), a nonresidential delinquency treatment program developed by Dr. Scott Henggeler of the Medical University of South Carolina, views individuals as being "nested" within a complex of interconnected systems, including the family, community, school, and peers. The MST treatment team may target problems in any of these systems for change and use the individual's strengths in these systems to effect that change. Treatment teams, which usually include three counselors, provide services over a four-month period for about 50 families per year. In one evaluation the rearrest rate for the MST group was found to be about half that of the group receiving traditional services. In another, the recidivism rate four years after treatment was 22 percent for MST youths, 72 percent for youths receiving individual counseling, and 87 percent for youths who refused either treatment. These evaluation results are a strong indicator of program effectiveness.

Critical Thinking

1. What are some of the differences between residential and nonresidential treatment programs for juvenile offenders?
2. What are the features that are characteristic of all three of these successful nonresidential treatment programs?

InfoTrac College Edition Research

To read more about nonresidential programs for juvenile offenders, go to Diane Hirth, "Early Intensive Help for High-Risk Juveniles," *Corrections Today* 63:80 (December 2001). To find further information, use *juvenile corrections* as a key term.

Sources: Project New Pride (Washington, DC: U.S. Government Printing Office, 1985); Shay Bilchik, *A Juvenile Justice System for the 21st Century* (Washington, DC: Office of Juvenile Justice and Delinquency Prevention, 1998).

As jurisdictions continue to face high rates of violent juvenile crime and ever-increasing costs for juvenile justice services, community-based programs will play an important role in providing rehabilitation of juvenile offenders and ensuring public safety.

Experts have confirmed the decline of rehabilitation in juvenile justice throughout much of the United States over the last 25 years.[41] But several recent **meta-analysis**

meta-analysis An analysis technique that synthesizes results across many programs over time.

studies have refuted the claim that "nothing works" with juvenile offenders and have given support to community rehabilitation.[42] According to Barry Krisberg and his associates, the most successful community-based programs seem to share at least some of these characteristics: (1) comprehensiveness, dealing with many aspects of youths' lives; (2) intensivity, involving multiple contacts; (3) operation outside the justice system; (4) foundation upon youths' strengths; and (5) adoption of a socially grounded approach to understanding a juvenile's situation rather than an individual-level (medical or therapeutic) approach.[43]

Secure Corrections

When the court determines that community treatment can't meet the special needs of a delinquent youth, a judge may refer the juvenile to a secure treatment program. Today, correctional institutions operated by federal, state, and county governments are generally classified as either secure or open facilities. Secure facilities restrict the movement of residents through staff monitoring, locked exits, and interior fence controls. Open institutions generally do not restrict the movement of the residents and allow much greater freedom of access to the facility.[44] In the following sections, we analyze the state of secure juvenile corrections, beginning with some historical background. This is followed by a discussion of life in institutions, the juvenile client, treatment issues, legal rights, and aftercare programs.

History of Juvenile Institutions

reform schools Institutions in which educational and psychological services are used in an effort to improve the conduct of juveniles who are forcibly detained.

cottage system Housing juveniles in a compound containing a series of small cottages, each of which accommodates 20 to 40 children and is run by a set of cottage parents who create a homelike atmosphere.

Until the early 1800s, juvenile offenders, as well as neglected and dependent children, were confined in adult prisons. The inhumane conditions in these institutions were among the factors that led social reformers to create a separate children's court system in 1899.[45] Early juvenile institutions were industrial schools modeled after adult prisons but designed to protect children from the evil influences in adult facilities. The first was the New York House of Refuge, established in 1825. Not long after this, states began to establish **reform schools** for juveniles. Massachusetts was the first, opening the Lyman School for Boys in Westborough in 1846. New York opened the State Agricultural and Industrial School in 1849, and Maine opened the Maine Boys' Training School in 1853. By 1900, 36 states had reform schools.[46] Although it is difficult to determine exact populations of these institutions, by 1880 there were approximately 11,000 youths in correctional facilities, a number that more than quadrupled by 1980.[47] Early reform schools were generally punitive in nature and were based on the concept of rehabilitation (or reform) through hard work and discipline.

In the second half of the nineteenth century, emphasis shifted to the **cottage system.** Juvenile offenders were housed in compounds of cottages, each of which could accommodate 20–40 children. A set of parents ran each cottage, creating a homelike atmosphere. This setup was believed to be more conducive to rehabilitation.

The first cottage system was established in Massachusetts in 1855, the second in Ohio in 1858.[48] The system was held to be a great improvement over training schools. The belief was that by moving away from punishment and toward rehabilitation, not only could offenders be rehabilitated, but also crime among unruly children could be prevented.[49]

Twentieth-Century Developments The early twentieth century witnessed important changes in juvenile corrections. Because of the influence of World War I, reform schools began to adopt a militaristic style. Living units became barracks; cottage groups became companies; house fathers became captains; and superintendents became majors or colonels. Military-style uniforms were standard wear.

In addition, the establishment of the first juvenile court in 1899 reflected the expanded use of confinement for delinquent children. As the number of juvenile offenders increased, the forms of juvenile institutions varied to include forestry camps, ranches, and vocational schools. Beginning in the 1930s, camps modeled after those run by the Civilian Conservation Corps became a part of the juvenile correctional system. These camps centered on conservation activities and work as a means of rehabilitation.

Los Angeles County was the first to use camps during this period.[50] Southern California was experiencing problems with transient youths who came to California with no money and then got into trouble with the law. Rather than filling up the jails, the county placed these offenders in conservation camps, paid them low wages, and released them when they had earned enough money to return home. The camps proved more rehabilitative than training schools, and by 1935 California had established a network of forestry camps for delinquent boys. The idea soon spread to other states.[51]

Also during the 1930s, the U.S. Children's Bureau sought to reform juvenile corrections. The bureau conducted studies to determine the effectiveness of the training school concept. Little was learned from these programs because of limited funding and bureaucratic ineptitude, and the Children's Bureau failed to achieve any significant change. But such efforts recognized the important role of positive institutional care.[52]

Another innovation came in the 1940s with passage of the American Law Institute's Model Youth Correction Authority Act. This act emphasized reception/classification centers. California was the first to try out this idea, opening the Northern Reception Center and Clinic in Sacramento in 1947. Today, there are many such centers scattered around the United States.

Since the 1970s, a major change in institutionalization has been the effort to remove status offenders from institutions housing juvenile delinquents. This includes removing status offenders from detention centers and removing all juveniles from contact with adults in jails. This *decarceration* policy mandates that courts use the **least restrictive alternative** in providing services for status offenders. A noncriminal youth should not be put in a secure facility if a community-based program is available. In addition, the federal government prohibits states from placing status offenders in separate facilities that are similar in form and function to those used for delinquent offenders. This is to prevent states from merely shifting their institutionalized population around so that one training school houses all delinquents and another houses all status offenders, but actual conditions remain the same.

Throughout the 1980s and into the 1990s, admissions to juvenile correctional facilities grew substantially.[53] Capacities of juvenile facilities also increased, but not enough to avoid overcrowding. Training schools became seriously overcrowded in some states, causing private facilities to play an increased role in juvenile corrections. Reliance on incarceration became costly to states: Inflation-controlled juvenile corrections expenditures for public facilities grew to more than $2 billion in 1995, an increase of 20 percent from 1982.[54] A 1994 report issued by the OJJDP said that crowding, inadequate health care, lack of security, and poor control of suicidal behavior was widespread in juvenile corrections facilities. Despite new construction, crowding persisted in more than half the states.[55]

least restrictive alternative
Choosing a program with the least restrictive or secure setting that will best benefit the child.

Juvenile Institutions Today: Public and Private

Most juveniles are housed in public institutions administered by state agencies: child and youth services, health and social services, corrections, or child welfare.[56] In some states these institutions fall under a centralized system that covers adults as well as juveniles. Recently, a number of states have removed juvenile corrections from an existing adult corrections department or mental health agency. However, the majority of states still place responsibility for the administration of juvenile corrections within social service departments.

Supplementing publicly funded institutions are private facilities that are maintained and operated by private agencies funded or chartered by state authorities. The majority of today's private institutions are relatively small facilities holding fewer than 30 youths. Many have a specific mission or focus (for example, treating females who display serious emotional problems). Although about 80 percent of public institutions can be characterized as secure, only 20 percent of private institutions are high-security facilities.

Population Trends

Whereas most delinquents are held in public facilities, most status offenders are held in private facilities. At last count, there were almost 110,000 juveniles being held in public (70%) and private (30%) facilities in the United States.[57] The juvenile custody rate varies widely among states: The District of Columbia makes the greatest use of custodial treatment, incarcerating just over 700 delinquents in public and private facilities per 100,000 juveniles in the general population. In contrast, about half of the states had rates of about 300 juveniles per 100,000. Some states rely heavily on privately run facilities, while others place many youths in out-of-state facilities.

Although the number of institutionalized youths appears to have stabilized in the last few years, the data may reveal only the tip of the iceberg. The data do not include many minors who are incarcerated after they are waived to adult courts or who have been tried as adults because of exclusion statutes. Most states place under-age juveniles convicted of adult charges in youth centers until they reach the age of majority, whereupon they are transferred to an adult facility. In addition, there may be a hidden, or subterranean, correctional system that places wayward youths in private mental hospitals and substance abuse clinics for behaviors that might otherwise have brought them a stay in a correctional facility or community-based program.[58] These data suggest that the number of institutionalized children may be far greater than reported in the official statistics.[59]

Physical Conditions

The physical plants of juvenile institutions vary in size and quality. Many older training schools still place all offenders in a single building, regardless of the offense. More acceptable structures include a reception unit with an infirmary, a security unit, and dormitory units or cottages. Planners have concluded that the most effective design for training schools is to have facilities located around a community square. The facilities generally include a dining hall and kitchen area, a storage warehouse, academic and vocational training rooms, a library, an auditorium, a gymnasium, an administration building, and other basic facilities.

The individual living areas also vary, depending on the type of facility and the progressiveness of its administration. Most traditional training school conditions were appalling. Today, however, most institutions provide toilet and bath facilities, beds, desks, lamps, and tables. New facilities usually provide a single room for each individual.

Most experts recommend that juvenile facilities have leisure areas, libraries, education spaces, chapels, facilities where youths can meet with their visitors, windows in all sleeping accommodations, and fire-safety equipment and procedures. Because institutions for delinquent youths vary in purpose, it is not necessary that they meet identical standards. Security measures used in some closed institutions, for instance, may not be required in a residential program.

The physical conditions of secure facilities for juveniles have come a long way from the training schools of the turn of the century. However, many administrators

A CLOSER VIEW

To read more about improvements in the physical conditions of juvenile institutions on InfoTrac College Edition, go to Gary Karst and James Frazier, "Reshaping the Design of Juvenile Facilities in Kansas," *Corrections Today* 62:84 (July 2000).

THE PHYSICAL CONDITION of some juvenile facilities is far less than ideal. An inmate looks out the window of his cell at the New Jersey Training School for Boys. The state budget includes a special $1 million appropriation to renovate cells for suicide prevention due to a growing problem of mentally ill inmates. The toilet and sink will be replaced with safer versions as part of the numerous changes being made during the renovation.

realize that more modernization is necessary to comply with national standards for juvenile institutions. Correctional administrators have described conditions as horrendous, and health officials have cited institutions for violations such as pollution by vermin and asbestos.[60] Although some improvements have been made, there are still enormous problems to overcome.

The Institutionalized Juvenile

To read about life in a secure Canadian facility, go to the Web site maintained by the Prince George Youth Custody Center in British Columbia, a secure facility providing a range of programs to allow youths to make maximal constructive use of their time while in custody: *http://members.pgonline.com/ ~pgycc/index.html#mainmenu* For an up-to-date list of Web links, go to *http://info.wadsworth.com/siegel*

The typical resident of a juvenile facility is a 15- to 16-year-old white male incarcerated for an average stay of five months in a public facility or six months in a private facility. Private facilities tend to house younger children, while public institutions provide custodial care for older children, including a small percentage of youths between 18 and 21 years of age. Most incarcerated youths are person, property, or drug offenders.

Minority youths are incarcerated at a rate two to five times that of white youths. The difference is greatest for black youths, with a custody rate of 1,004 per 100,000 juveniles; for white youths the rate is 212.[61] Research has found that this overrepresentation is not a result of differentials in arrest rates, but often stems from disparity at early stages of case processing.[62] Of equal importance, minorities are more likely to be confined in secure public facilities rather than in open private facilities that might provide more costly and effective treatment.[63]

Minority youths accused of delinquent acts are less likely than white youths to be diverted from the court system into informal sanctions and are more likely to receive sentences involving incarceration. Racial disparity in juvenile disposition is a growing problem that demands immediate public scrutiny.[64] In response, some jurisdictions have initiated studies of racial disproportion in their juvenile justice systems.[65] Today, more than 6 in 10 juveniles in custody belong to racial or ethnic minorities, and 7 in 10 youths held in custody for a violent crime are minorities.[66]

More than two decades ago, shocking exposés focused public attention on the problems of juvenile corrections. Today, some critics believe public scrutiny has improved conditions within training schools. There is greater professionalism among the staff, and staff brutality seems to have diminished. Status offenders and delinquents are, for the most part, held in separate facilities. Confinement length is shorter, and rehabilitative programming has increased. However, there are significant differences in the experiences of male and female delinquents within the institution.

Male Inmates

Males make up the great bulk of institutionalized youth, and most programs are directed toward their needs. In many ways their experiences mirror those of adult offenders. In an important paper, Clement Bartollas and his associates identified an inmate value system that they believed was common in juvenile institutions:

> Exploit whomever you can.
> Don't play up to staff.
> Don't rat on your peers.
> Don't give in to others.[67]

In addition to these general rules, the researchers found that there were separate norms for African American inmates ("exploit whites; no forcing sex on blacks; defend your brother") and for whites ("don't trust anyone; everybody for himself").

Other research efforts confirm the notion that residents do in fact form cohesive groups and adhere to an informal inmate culture.[68] The more serious the youth's record and the more secure the institution, the greater the adherence to the inmate social code. Male delinquents are more likely to form allegiances with members of their own racial group and to attempt to exploit those outside the group. They also scheme to manipulate staff and take advantage of weaker peers. However, in institutions that are treatment oriented, and where staff-inmate relationships are more intimate, residents are less likely to adhere to a negativistic inmate code.

Female Inmates

The growing involvement of girls in criminal behavior and the influence of the feminist movement have drawn more attention to the female juvenile offender. This attention has revealed a double standard of justice. For example, girls are more likely than boys to be incarcerated for status offenses. Institutions for girls are generally more restrictive than those for boys, and they have fewer educational and vocational programs and fewer services. Institutions for girls also do a less-than-adequate job of rehabilitation. It has been suggested that this double standard operates because of a male-dominated justice system that seeks to "protect" young girls from their own sexuality.[69]

Over the years, the number of females held in public institutions has declined. This represents the continuation of a long-term trend to remove girls, many of whom are nonserious offenders, from closed institutions and place them in private or community-based facilities. So, although a majority of males are housed in public facilities today, most female delinquents reside in private facilities.

The same double standard that brings a girl into an institution continues to exist once she is in custody. Females tend to be incarcerated for longer terms than males. In addition, institutional programs for girls tend to be oriented toward reinforcing traditional roles for women. How well these programs rehabilitate girls is questionable.

Many of the characteristics of juvenile female offenders are similar to those of their male counterparts, including poor social skills and low self-esteem. Other problems are more specific to the female juvenile offender (sexual abuse issues, victimization histories, lack of placement options). In addition, there have been numerous allegations of emotional and sexual abuse by correctional workers, who either exploit vulnerable young women or callously disregard their emotional needs. A recent (1998) interview survey conducted by the National Council on Crime and Delinquency uncovered numerous incidents of abuse, and bitter resentment by the young women over the brutality of their custodial treatment.[70]

Although there are more coed institutions for juveniles than in the past, most girls remain incarcerated in single-sex institutions that are isolated in rural areas and rarely offer adequate rehabilitative services. Several factors account for the different treatment of girls. One is sexual stereotyping by administrators, who believe that teaching girls "appropriate" sex roles will help them function effectively in society. These beliefs are often held by the staff as well, many of whom hold highly sexist ideas of what is appropriate behavior for adolescent girls. Girls' institutions tend to be smaller than boys' institutions and lack the money to offer as many programs and services as do the larger male institutions.[71]

It appears that although society is more concerned about protecting girls who act out, it is less concerned about rehabilitating them because the crimes they commit are not serious. These attitudes translate into fewer staff, older facilities, and poorer educational and recreational programs than those found in boys' institutions.[72]

A CLOSER VIEW
To read more about treatment programs for female juvenile offenders on InfoTrac College Edition, go to Al Palomino, "The Ventura Youth Correctional Facility Provides Needed Treatment Programs to Youthful Female Offenders," *Corrections Today* 63:82 (February 2001).

Correctional Treatment for Juveniles

Nearly all juvenile institutions implement some form of treatment program: counseling, vocational and educational training, recreational programs, and religious counseling. In addition, most institutions provide medical programs as well as occasional legal service programs. Generally, the larger the institution, the greater the number of programs and services offered.

The purpose of these programs is to rehabilitate youths to become well-adjusted individuals and send them back into the community to be productive citizens. Despite good intentions, however, the goal of rehabilitation is rarely attained, due in large part to programs being poorly implemented.[73] A significant number of juvenile offenders commit more crimes after release and some experts believe that correctional treatment has little effect on recidivism.[74] However, a careful evaluation of both community-based and institutional treatment services found that juveniles who receive treatment have recidivism rates about 10 percent lower than untreated juveniles, and that the best programs reduced recidivism between 20 and 30 percent.[75] The most successful programs provide training designed to improve interpersonal skills, self-control, and school achievement. These programs also tend to be the most intensive in terms of the amount and duration of attention to youths. Programs of a more psychological orientation, such as individual, family, and group counseling, showed only moderate positive effects on delinquents. Education, vocational training, and specific counseling strategies can be effective if they are intensive, relate to program goals, and meet the youth's individual needs.[76]

What are the drawbacks to correctional rehabilitation? One of the most common problems in efforts to rehabilitate juveniles is a lack of well-trained staff members. Budgetary limitations are a primary concern. It costs a substantial amount of money per year to keep a child in an institution, which explains why institutions generally do not employ large professional staffs.

The most glaring problem with treatment programs is that they are not being administered as intended. Although the official goals of many institutions may be treat-

If you want to learn more about improving the conditions of children in custody, go to *http://www.ojjdp.ncjrs.org/pubs/walls/contents.html* For an up-to-date list of Web links, go to *http://info.wadsworth.com/siegel*

ment and rehabilitation, the actual programs may center around security and punishment. The next sections describe some treatment approaches that aim to rehabilitate offenders.

Individual Treatment Techniques: Past and Present

individual counseling
Counselors help juveniles understand and solve their current adjustment problems.

In general, effective individual treatment programs are built around combinations of psychotherapy, reality therapy, and behavior modification. **Individual counseling** is one of the most common treatment approaches, and virtually all juvenile institutions use it to some extent. This is not surprising, as psychological problems such as depression are prevalent in juvenile institutions.[77] The goal of individual counseling is not to change a youth's personality; rather, it is to help individuals understand and solve their current adjustment problems. Some institutions employ counselors who are not professionally qualified, which subjects offenders to a superficial form of counseling.

psychotherapy Highly structured counseling in which a skilled therapist helps a juvenile solve conflicts and make a more positive adjustment to society.

reality therapy A form of counseling that emphasizes current behavior and that requires the individual to accept responsibility for all of his or her actions.

behavior modification A technique for shaping desired behaviors through a system of rewards and punishments.

Professional counseling may be based on **psychotherapy**, which requires extensive analysis of the individual's childhood experiences. A skilled therapist attempts to help the individual make a more positive adjustment to society by altering negative behavior patterns learned in childhood. Another frequently used treatment is **reality therapy**.[78] This approach, developed by William Glasser during the 1970s, emphasizes current, rather than past, behavior by stressing that offenders are completely responsible for their own actions. The object of reality therapy is to make individuals more responsible people. This is accomplished by giving youths confidence through developing their ability to follow a set of expectations as closely as possible. The success of reality therapy depends greatly on the warmth and concern of the counselor. Many institutions rely heavily on this type of therapy because they believe trained professionals aren't needed to administer it. Actually, a skilled therapist is essential to the success of this form of treatment.

Behavior modification is used in many institutions.[79] It is based on the theory that all behavior is learned and that current behavior can be shaped through rewards and punishments. This type of program is easily used in an institutional setting that offers privileges as rewards for behaviors such as work, study, or the development of skills. It is reasonably effective, especially when a contract is formed with the youth to modify certain behaviors. When youths know what is expected of them, they plan their actions to meet these expectations and then experience the anticipated consequences. In this way, youths can be motivated to change. Behavior modification is effective in controlled settings where a counselor can manipulate the situation, but once the youth is back in the real world it becomes difficult to use.

To learn more about reality therapy, go to William Glasser's Web site at *http://www.wglasserinst.com/* For an up-to-date list of Web links, go to *http://info.wadsworth.com/siegel*

Group Treatment Techniques

group therapy Counseling several individuals together in a group session; individuals can obtain support from other group members as they work through similar problems.

Group therapy is more economical than individual therapy because one therapist can counsel more than one individual at a time. Also, the support of the group is often valuable to individuals in the group, and individuals derive hope from other members of the group who have survived similar experiences. Another advantage of group therapy is that a group can often solve a problem more effectively than an individual.

One disadvantage of group therapy is that it provides little individual attention. Everyone is different, and some group members may need more individualized treatment. Others may be afraid to speak up in the group and thus fail to receive the benefits of the group experience. Conversely, some individuals may dominate group interaction, making it difficult for the leader to conduct an effective session. In addition, group condemnation may seriously hurt a participant. Finally, there is also the concern that by providing therapy in a group format, those who are more chronically involved in delinquency may negatively affect those who are marginally involved in delinquency.[80] This can also happen with non–juvenile justice delinquency prevention programs (see Chapter 11).

More than any other group treatment technique, group psychotherapy probes into an individual's personality and attempts to restructure it. Relationships in these groups tend to be intense. The group is used to facilitate expression of feelings, solve problems, and teach members to empathize with one another.

Unfortunately, the ingredients for an effective group session—interaction, cooperation, and tolerance—are in conflict with the antisocial and antagonistic orientation of delinquents. This technique can be effective when the members of the group are in attendance voluntarily, but such is not the case with institutionalized delinquents. Consequently, the effectiveness of these programs is questionable.

Guided group interaction (**GGI**) is a fairly common method of group treatment. It is based on the theory that through group interactions, a delinquent can acknowledge and solve personal problems. A leader facilitates interaction, and a group culture develops. Individual members can be mutually supportive and can reinforce acceptable behavior. In the 1980s, a version of GGI called **positive peer culture** (**PPC**) became popular. These programs used groups in which peer leaders encourage other youths to conform to conventional behaviors. The rationale is that if negative peer influence can encourage youths to engage in delinquent behavior, then positive peer influence can help them conform.[81] Though research results are inconclusive, there is evidence that PPC may facilitate communication ability for incarcerated youth.[82]

Another common group treatment approach, **milieu therapy**, seeks to make all aspects of the inmates' environment part of their treatment and to minimize differences between custodial staff and treatment personnel. Based on psychoanalytic theory, milieu therapy was developed during the late 1940s and early 1950s by Bruno Bettelheim.[83] This therapy attempted to create a conscience, or superego, in delinquent youths by getting them to depend on their therapists to a great extent and then threatening them with loss of the caring relationship if they failed to control their behavior. Today, milieu therapy more often makes use of peer interactions and attempts to create an environment that encourages meaningful change, growth, and satisfactory adjustment. This is often accomplished through peer pressure to conform to group norms.

Today, group counseling often focuses on drug and alcohol issues, self-esteem development, or role-model support. In addition, because greater numbers of violent juveniles are entering the system than in years past, group sessions often deal with appropriate expressions of anger and methods for controlling such behavior.

guided group interaction (GGI)
Through group interactions a delinquent can acknowledge and solve personal problems with support from other group members.

positive peer culture (PPC)
Counseling program in which peer leaders encourage other group members to modify their behavior, and peers help reinforce acceptable behaviors.

milieu therapy All aspects of the environment are part of the treatment, and meaningful change, increased growth, and satisfactory adjustment are encouraged; this is often accomplished through peer pressure to conform to the group norms.

> **To see how positive peer** culture can be used effectively, go to
> http://www.nida.nih.gov/MeetSum/CODA/Youth.html
> For an up-to-date list of Web links, go to
> http://info.wadsworth.com/siegel

Educational, Vocational, and Recreational Programs

Because educational programs are an important part of social development and have therapeutic as well as instructional value, they are an essential part of most treatment programs. What takes place through education is related to all other aspects of the institutional program—work activities, cottage life, recreation, and clinical services.

Educational programs are probably the best-staffed programs in training schools, but even at their best, most are inadequate. Training programs must contend with a myriad of problems. Many of the youths coming into these institutions are mentally challenged, have learning disabilities, and are far behind their grade levels in basic academics. Most have become frustrated with the educational experience, dislike school, and become bored with any type of educational program. Their sense of frustration often leads to disciplinary problems.

Ideally, institutions should allow the inmates to attend a school in the community or offer programs that lead to a high school diploma or GED. Unfortunately, not all institutions offer these types of programs. Secure institutions, because of their large size, are more likely than group homes or day treatment centers to offer programs such as remedial reading, physical education, and tutoring. Some offer computer-based learning and programmed learning modules.

A CLOSER VIEW
To read more about education programs for juvenile offenders on InfoTrac College Edition, go to Bruce I. Wolford, "Youth Education in the Juvenile Justice System," *Corrections Today* 62:128 (August 2000).

wilderness probation Programs involving outdoor expeditions that provide opportunities for juveniles to confront the difficulties of their lives while achieving positive personal satisfaction.

Vocational training has long been used as a treatment technique for juveniles. Early institutions were even referred to as "industrial schools." Today, vocational programs in institutions include auto repair, printing, woodworking, mechanical drawing, food service, cosmetology, secretarial training, and data processing. A common drawback of vocational training programs is sex-typing. The recent trend has been to allow equal access to all programs offered in institutions that house girls and boys. Sex-typing is more difficult to avoid in single-sex institutions, because funds aren't usually available for all types of training.

These programs alone are not panaceas. Youths need to acquire the kinds of skills that will give them hope for advancement. The Ventura School for Female Juvenile Offenders, established under the California Youth Authority, has been a pioneer in the work placement concept. Private industry contracts with the Youth Authority to establish businesses on the institution's grounds. The businesses hire, train, and pay for work. Wages are divided into a victim's restitution fund, room and board fees, and forced savings, with a portion given to the juvenile to purchase canteen items.[84] A study by the National Youth Employment Coalition (NYEC) finds that employment- and career-focused programs can do a great deal to prepare youths involved in the juvenile justice system for a successful transition to the workforce as long as they are comprehensive, last for a relatively long time, and are connected to further education or long-term career opportunities.[85]

Recreational activity is also an important way to help relieve adolescent aggressions, as evidenced by the many programs that focus on recreation as the primary treatment technique.

In summary, treatment programs that seem to be most effective for rehabilitating juvenile offenders are those that use a combination of techniques. Programs that are comprehensive, build on a juvenile's strengths, and adopt a socially grounded position have a much greater chance for success. Successful programs address issues relating to school, peers, work, and community.

AP/Wide World Photos

Wilderness Programs

Wilderness probation programs involve troubled youths in outdoor activities as a mechanism to improve their social skills, self-concept, and self-control. Typically, wilderness programs maintain exposure to a wholesome environment; where the concepts of education and the work ethic are taught and embodied in adult role models, troubled youth can regain a measure of self-worth. One such program, which is privately funded and takes cases that might otherwise go to a state correctional facility, is the Turn About Ranch (Exhibit 15.2).

Few wilderness programs for juvenile offenders have been evaluated for their effects on recidivism. In a detailed review of the effects of wilderness programs on recidivism, Doris MacKenzie concludes that these programs do not work.[86] While some of the programs

WILDERNESS PROGRAMS help give young people a sense of confidence and purpose by involving them in outdoor expeditions. They provide an opportunity for juveniles to confront the difficulties in their lives while achieving positive personal satisfaction. Here, a group of young people at the Piedmont Wilderness Institute in Clinton, South Carolina, learn team building as they work together to accomplish the task of getting eight of them onto the platform without spilling the water in the can.

Exhibit 15.2 Turn About Ranch

Turn About Ranch is a private, short-term, high-impact therapy program that emphasizes family values and relationships. Its clientele are 27 boys and girls from 12 to 18 years of age, who spend at least 60 days (90 days is the average) at its facility in the southern Utah canyonlands country. The objective of Turn About Ranch is to provide troubled teens with a tough, hard-hitting, high-impact program that helps remold their lives. The program objectives are facilitated through the environment of a historic, real-life cow-calf ranch, utilizing old-time values and morals such as honesty, respect, teamwork, and accountability. No smoking, drinking, tobacco, drugs, sex, or swearing is allowed. Turn About Ranch employs a behavior modification program that promotes positive behavioral changes; counselors are with the youths 24 hours a day. Problems are dealt with swiftly and fairly. Through this consistent correction and positive direction, day after day, in a hard-working, real-life, down-to-earth ranch environment, the seed of life being "turned-about" begins to emerge.

Source: Personal communication with Annette Ormond, administrative assistant, January 4, 2001; program descriptions may be obtained from Turn About Ranch, 280 North 300 East, P.O. Box 345, Escalante, UT 84726.

A CLOSER VIEW
To read more about wilderness programs for juvenile offenders on InfoTrac College Edition, go to Magdalena Rosol, "Wilderness Therapy for Youth-at-Risk," *Parks & Recreation* 35:42 (September 2000).

show success, such as the Spectrum Wilderness Program in Illinois,[87] others had negative effects; that is, the group that received the program had higher arrest rates than the comparison group that did not receive the program. Taken together, the programs suffered from

- Poor implementation
- Weak evaluation designs or problems with too few subjects or large dropout rates
- Failure to adhere to principles of successful rehabilitation, such as targeting high-risk youths and lasting for a moderate period of time[88]

Juvenile Boot Camps

boot camps Juvenile programs that combine get-tough elements from adult programs with education, substance abuse treatment, and social skills training.

Correctional **boot camps** combine the get-tough elements of adult programs with education, substance abuse treatment, and social skills training. The American Correctional Association's Juvenile Project sees merit in well-run boot camp programs provided they incorporate these elements: (1) a focus on concrete feelings and increasing self-esteem, (2) discipline through physical conditioning, and (3) programming in literacy as well as academic and vocational education.[89]

In theory, a successful boot camp program should rehabilitate juvenile offenders, reduce the number of beds needed in secure institutional programs, and thus reduce the overall cost of care. The Alabama boot camp program for youthful offenders estimated savings of $1 million annually when compared with traditional institutional sentences.[90] However, no one seems convinced that participants in these programs have lower recidivism rates than those who serve normal sentences. Ronald Corbett and Joan Petersilia do note, however, that boot camp participants seem to be less antisocial upon returning to society.[91]

Some juvenile corrections agencies feature shock incarceration programs, with high-intensity military discipline and physical training for short periods. The expectation is that the offender will be "shocked" into going straight. These programs are being used with young adult offenders and juveniles who have been waived to the adult system in many jurisdictions.

Some experts point out that (1) boot camps cannot save money unless they have hundreds of beds and the stay is limited to three months, conditions that would make the programs pointless; (2) boot camps often keep costs down by leaving aftercare to overloaded parole officers; and (3) no documentation exists that boot camps decrease delinquency.[92]

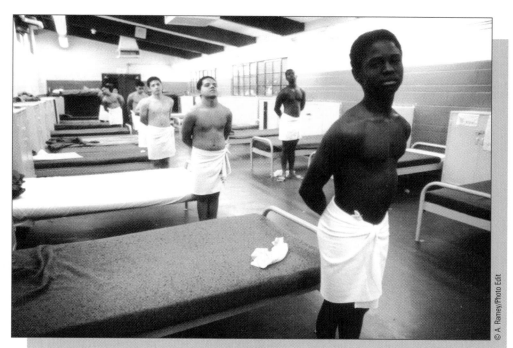

JUVENILE BOOT CAMPS apply rigorous, military-style training and discipline in an attempt to reshape the attitudes and behavior of unruly youth. Here, juveniles in Camp Holton, California, stand at attention as they wait to be inspected by boot camp officers.

To read more about boot camps, go to
http://www.ncjrs.org/ txtfiles/164258.txt
For an up-to-date list of Web links, go to *http://info.wadsworth.com/siegel*

Bootcamp Evaluation In 1992 OJJDP funded three juvenile boot camps designed to overcome these objections and meet the special needs of adolescent offenders. The programs were conducted in Cleveland, Ohio; Denver, Colorado; and Mobile, Alabama.[93] Focusing on nonviolent offenders under the age of 18, the highly structured, three-month residential programs were followed by six to nine months of community-based aftercare. During the aftercare period, youths were to pursue academic and vocational training or employment while under progressively diminishing supervision.

The Office of Juvenile Justice and Delinquency Prevention undertook evaluations for all three sites, comparing recidivism rates for juveniles who participated in the programs with those of control groups. The evaluations also compared the cost-effectiveness of juvenile boot camps with other dispositional alternatives. The findings indicated these successes:

- Most participants completed the residential program and graduated to aftercare. Program completion rates were 96 percent in Cleveland, 87 percent in Mobile, and 76 percent in Denver.
- At the two sites where educational gains were measured, substantial improvements in academic skills were noted. In Mobile, approximately three-quarters of the participants improved their performance in reading, spelling, language, and math by one grade level or more. In Cleveland, the average participant improved reading, spelling, and math skills by approximately one grade level.
- Where employment records were available, a significant number of participants found jobs while in aftercare. The pilot programs, however, did not demonstrate a reduction in recidivism. In Denver and Mobile no statistically significant difference could be found between the recidivism rates of boot camp participants and those of the control groups (youths confined in state or county institutions or released on probation). In Cleveland, program participants evidenced a higher recidivism rate than offenders confined in traditional juvenile correctional facilities.

Other successes of juvenile boot camps are revealed in a national study comparing the environments of boot camps with more traditional secure correctional facilities for juveniles. Some of the main findings include

- Boot camp youths report more positive attitudes to their environment.
- Initial levels of depression are lower for boot camp youths, but initial levels of anxiety are higher; both of these declined over time for youths in both facilities.
- Staff at boot camps report more favorable working conditions, such as less stress and better communication among staff.[94]

However, the bottom line for juvenile boot camps, like other correctional sanctions, is whether or not they reduce recidivism. A recent meta-analysis of the effects of juvenile boot camps on recidivism found this to be an ineffective correctional approach to reducing recidivism; from the 16 different program samples, the control groups had, on average, lower recidivism rates than the treatment groups.[95] Interestingly, when compared to the effects of 28 program samples of boot camps for adults, the juvenile boot camps had a higher average recidivism rate, although the difference was not significant.[96]

Why do boot camps for juveniles fail to reduce future offending? The main reason is that they provide little in the way of therapy or treatment to correct offending behavior. Experts have also suggested that part of the reason for not finding differences in recidivism between boot camps and other correctional alternatives (the control groups) may be due to juveniles in the control groups receiving enhanced treatment while juveniles in the boot camps are spending more time on physical activities.[97]

In spite of these findings, more than 75 boot camps are now in operation in more than 30 states. They appear to have a place among the array of sentencing options, if for no other reason than to appease the public with the promise of tougher sentences and lower costs.[98] If boot camps are to become a viable alternative for juvenile corrections, they must be seen, not as a panacea that provides an easy solution to the problems of delinquency, but as part of a comprehensive approach to juvenile care that is appropriate to a select group of adolescents.[99]

The Legal Right to Treatment

right to treatment Philosophy espoused by many courts that juvenile offenders have a statutory right to treatment while under the jurisdiction of the courts.

The primary goal of placing juveniles in institutions is to help them reenter the community successfully. Therefore, lawyers claim that children in state-run institutions have a legal right to treatment.

The concept of a **right to treatment** was introduced to the mental health field in 1960 by Morton Birnbaum, who argued that individuals deprived of their liberty because of a mental illness are entitled to treatment to correct that condition.[100] The right to treatment has expanded to include the juvenile justice system, an expansion bolstered by court rulings that mandate that rehabilitation and not punishment or retribution be the basis of juvenile court dispositions.[101] It stands to reason then, that if incarcerated, juveniles are entitled to the appropriate social services that will promote their rehabilitation.

One of the first cases to highlight this issue was *Inmates of the Boys' Training School v. Affleck* in 1972.[102] In its decision, a federal court argued that rehabilitation is the true purpose of the juvenile court and that without that goal, due-process guarantees are violated. It condemned such devices as solitary confinement, strip cells, and lack of educational opportunities, and held that juveniles have a statutory right to treatment. The court also established the following minimum standards for all juveniles confined in training schools:

- A room equipped with lighting sufficient for an inmate to read until 10:00 P.M.
- Sufficient clothing to meet seasonal needs

- Bedding, including blankets, sheets, pillows, pillowcases, and mattresses, to be changed once a week
- Personal hygiene supplies, including soap, toothpaste, towels, toilet paper, and toothbrush
- A change of undergarments and socks every day
- Minimum writing materials: pen, pencil, paper, and envelopes
- Prescription eyeglasses, if needed
- Equal access to all books, periodicals, and other reading materials located in the training school
- Daily showers
- Daily access to medical facilities, including provision of a 24-hour nursing service
- General correspondence privileges[103]

In 1974, in the case of *Nelson v. Heyne,* the First Federal Appellate Court affirmed that juveniles have a right to treatment and condemned the use of corporal punishment in juvenile institutions.[104] In *Morales v. Turman,* the court held that all juveniles confined in training schools in Texas have a right to treatment, including development of education skills, delivery of vocational education, medical and psychiatric treatment, and adequate living conditions.[105] In a more recent case, *Pena v. New York State Division for Youth,* the court held that the use of isolation, hand restraints, and tranquilizing drugs at Goshen Annex Center violated the Fourteenth Amendment right to due process and the Eighth Amendment right to protection against cruel and unusual punishment.[106]

The right to treatment has also been limited. For example, in *Ralston v. Robinson,* the Supreme Court rejected a youth's claim that he should continue to be given treatment after he was sentenced to a consecutive term in an adult prison for crimes committed while in a juvenile institution.[107] In the *Ralston* case, the offender's proven dangerousness outweighed the possible effects of rehabilitation. Similarly, in *Santana v. Callazo,* the U.S. First Circuit Court of Appeals rejected a suit brought by residents at the Maricao Juvenile Camp in Puerto Rico on the ground that the administration had failed to provide them with an individualized rehabilitation plan or adequate treatment. The circuit court concluded that it was a legitimate exercise of state authority to incarcerate juveniles solely to protect society if they are dangerous.

The Struggle for Basic Civil Rights

Several court cases have led federal, state, and private groups—for example, the American Bar Association, the American Correctional Association, and the National Council on Crime and Delinquency—to develop standards for the juvenile justice system. These standards provide guidelines for conditions and practices in juvenile institutions and call on administrators to maintain a safe and healthy environment for incarcerated youths.

For the most part, state-sponsored brutality has been outlawed, although the use of restraints, solitary confinement, and even medication for unruly residents has not been eliminated. The courts have ruled that corporal punishment in any form violates standards of decency and human dignity.

There are a number of mechanisms for enforcing these standards. For example, the federal government's Civil Rights of Institutionalized Persons Act (CRIPA) gives the Civil Rights Division of the U.S. Department of Justice (DOJ) the power to bring actions against state or local governments for violating the civil rights of persons institutionalized in publicly operated facilities.[108] CRIPA does not create any new substantive rights; it simply confers power on the U.S. Attorney General to bring action to enforce previously established constitutional or statutory rights of institutionalized persons. About 25 percent of cases involve juvenile detention and correctional facilities. There are many examples in which CRIPA-based litigation has helped insure that incarcerated adolescents obtain their basic civil rights. For example, in November

1995, a federal court in Kentucky ordered state officials to remedy serious deficiencies in Kentucky's 13 juvenile treatment facilities. The decree required the state to take a number of steps to protect juveniles from abuse, mistreatment, and injury; to ensure adequate medical and mental health care; and to provide adequate educational, vocational, and aftercare services. Another CRIPA consent decree, ordered by a federal court in Puerto Rico in October 1994, addressed life-threatening conditions at eight juvenile detention and correction facilities. These dire conditions included juveniles committing and attempting suicide without staff intervention or treatment, widespread infection-control problems caused by rats and other vermin, and defective plumbing that forced juveniles to drink from their toilet bowls.

What provisions does the juvenile justice system make to help institutionalized offenders return to society? The remainder of this chapter is devoted to this topic.

A CLOSER VIEW
To read more about the importance of mental health care for juvenile offenders on InfoTrac College Edition, go to Lisa Melanie Boesky, "Mental Health Training in Juvenile Justice: A Necessity," *Corrections Today* 63:98 (August 2001).

Juvenile Aftercare

aftercare Transitional assistance to juveniles, equivalent to adult parole, to help youths adjust to community life.

Aftercare in the juvenile justice system is the equivalent of parole in the adult criminal justice system. When juveniles are released from an institution, they may be placed in an aftercare program of some kind, so that youths who have been institutionalized are not simply returned to the community without some transitional assistance. Whether individuals who are in aftercare as part of an indeterminate sentence remain in the community or return to the institution for further rehabilitation depends on their actions during the aftercare period. Aftercare is an extremely important stage in the juvenile justice process because few juveniles age out of custody.[109]

In a number of jurisdictions, a paroling authority, which may be an independent body or part of the corrections department or some other branch of state services, makes the release decision. Juvenile aftercare authorities, like adult parole officers, review the youth's adjustment within the institution, whether there is chemical dependence, what the crime was, and other specifics of the case. Some juvenile authorities are even making use of **parole guidelines** first developed with adult parolees. Each youth who enters a secure facility is given a recommended length of confinement that is explained at the initial interview with parole authorities. The stay is computed on the basis of the offense record, influenced by aggravating and mitigating factors. The parole authority is not required to follow the recommended sentence but uses it as a tool in making parole decisions.[110] Whatever approach is used, several primary factors are considered by virtually all jurisdictions when recommending a juvenile for release: (1) institutional adjustment, (2) length of stay and general attitude, and (3) likelihood of success in the community.

parole guidelines Recommended length of confinement and kinds of aftercare assistance most effective for a juvenile who committed a specific offense.

Risk classifications have also been designed to help parole officers make decisions about which juveniles should receive aftercare services.[111] The risk-based system uses an empirically derived risk scale to classify youths. Juveniles are identified as most likely or least likely to commit a new offense based on factors such as prior record, type of offense, and degree of institutional adjustment.

Supervision

One purpose of aftercare is to provide support during the readjustment period following release. First, individuals whose activities have been regimented for some time may not find it easy to make independent decisions. Second, offenders may perceive themselves as scapegoats, cast out by society. Finally, the community may view the returning minor with a good deal of prejudice; adjustment problems may reinforce a preexisting need to engage in deviant behavior.

Juveniles in aftercare programs are supervised by parole caseworkers or counselors whose job is to maintain contact with the juvenile, make sure that a corrections plan is followed, and show interest and caring. The counselor also keeps the youth informed of services that may assist in reintegration and counsels the youth and his or her family. Unfortunately, aftercare caseworkers, like probation officers, often carry such large caseloads that their jobs are next to impossible to do adequately.

Recent state legislation underscores the importance of aftercare for juvenile offenders. For example, the Texas Youth Commission operates an "independent living program" that provides prerelease and transition assistance to male and female offenders ages 16 to 18 who are returning to the community; an aftercare program in Cuyahoga County, Ohio, begins with education and employment training while a youth is incarcerated and continues after the youth is released; a reintegration program for youths released from the New Mexico Boys' School has been successful because clients spend less time in secure correction.[112]

Intensive Aftercare Program (IAP)
A balanced, highly structured, comprehensive continuum of intervention for serious and violent juvenile offenders returning to the community.

The Intensive Aftercare Program (IAP) Model New models of aftercare have been aimed at the chronic and/or violent offender. The **Intensive Aftercare Program (IAP)** model developed by David Altschuler and Troy Armstrong offers a continuum of intervention for serious juvenile offenders returning to the community following placement. The IAP model begins by drawing attention to five basic principles, which collectively establish a set of fundamental operational goals:

1. Preparing youth for progressively increased responsibility and freedom in the community
2. Facilitating youth-community interaction and involvement
3. Working with both the offender and targeted community support systems (families, peers, schools, employers) on qualities needed for constructive interaction and the youth's successful community adjustment
4. Developing new resources and supports where needed
5. Monitoring and testing the youth and the community on their ability to deal with each other productively

These basic goals are then translated into practice, which incorporates individual case planning with a family and community perspective. The program stresses a mix of intensive surveillance and services and a balance of incentives and graduated consequences coupled with the imposition of realistic, enforceable conditions. There is also "service brokerage," in which community resources are used and linkage with social networks established.[113]

The IAP initiative was designed to help correctional agencies implement effective aftercare programs for chronic and serious juvenile offenders. After more than 12 years of testing, the program is now being aimed at determining how juveniles are prepared for reentry into their communities, how the transition is handled, and how the aftercare in the community is provided.[114] The Policy and Practice box entitled "Using the Intensive Aftercare Program (IAP) Model" illustrates how the model is being used in three state jurisdictions.

Aftercare Revocation Procedures

Juvenile parolees are required to meet set standards of behavior, which typically include but are not limited to the following:

- Adhere to a reasonable curfew set by youth worker or parent.
- Refrain from associating with persons whose influence would be detrimental.
- Attend school in accordance with the law.
- Abstain from drugs and alcohol.
- Report to the youth worker when required.
- Refrain from acts that would be crimes if committed by an adult.
- Refrain from operating an automobile without permission of the youth worker or parent.
- Refrain from being habitually disobedient and beyond the lawful control of parent or other legal authority.

Using the Intensive Aftercare Program (IAP) Model

Programs in Colorado, Nevada, and Virginia are representative of how the IAP model has been used around the nation.

Colorado

While adolescents are still institutionalized, community-based providers begin weekly services (including multifamily counseling and life-skills services) that continue during aftercare. Sixty days prior to release, IAP youths begin a series of step-down measures, including supervised trips to the community and, 30 days before release, overnight or weekend home passes. Upon release to parole, most program youths go through several months of day treatment programming that, in addition to services, provides a high level of structure during the day. Trackers provide evening and weekend monitoring during this period of reentry. As a youth's progress warrants, the frequency of supervision decreases. The planned frequency of contact is once a week during the first few months of supervision, with gradual reductions to once a month in later stages of supervision.

Nevada

Once the parole plan is finalized, all IAP youths begin a 30-day pre-release phase, during which IAP staff provide a series of services that continue through the early months of parole. These consist primarily of two structured curriculums on life skills (Jettstream) and substance abuse (Rational Recovery). In addition, a money management program (The Money Program) is initiated. Youths are provided with mock checking accounts from which "bills" must be paid for rent, food, insurance, and other necessities. Youths can also use their accounts to purchase recreation and other privileges, but each youth must have a balance of at least $50 at the end of the 30 days to purchase his bus ticket home. The initial 30 days of release are considered an institutional furlough (youths are still on the institutional rolls) that involves intensive supervision and service; any time during this period the youth may be returned to the institution for significant program infractions. During furlough, youths are involved in day programming and are subject to frequent drug testing and evening and weekend surveillance. Upon successful completion of the furlough, the IAP transition continues through the use of phased levels of supervision. During the first

three months, three contacts per week with the case manager or field agent are required. This level of supervision is reduced to two contacts per week for the next two months, and then to once per week during the last month of parole.

Virginia

Virginia's transition differs from the other two sites in that its central feature is the use of group home placements as a bridge between the institution and the community. Immediately after release from the institution, youths enter one of two group homes for a 30- to 60-day period. The programs and services in which they will be involved in the community are initiated shortly after placement in the group home. Virginia uses a formal step-down system to ease the intensity of parole supervision gradually. In the two months following the youth's release from the group home, staff are required to contact him five to seven times per week. This is reduced to three to five times per week during the next two months, and again to three times per week during the final 30 days.

Critical Thinking

1. What is the importance of reducing the number of supervision contacts with the juvenile offender toward the end of the aftercare program?
2. Should juvenile offenders who have committed less serious offenses also have to go through intensive aftercare programs?

InfoTrac College Edition Research

 To read more about aftercare programs for juvenile offenders, go to Kit Glover and Kurt Bumby, "Re-Entry at the Point of Entry," *Corrections Today* 63:68 (December 2001). To find further information, use *juvenile corrections* as a key term.

Source: Richard G. Wiebush, Betsie McNulty, and Thao Le, "Implementation of the Intensive Community-Based Aftercare Program," *Juvenile Justice Bulletin* (Washington, DC: Office of Juvenile Justice and Delinquency Prevention, 2000).

- Refrain from running away from the lawful custody of parent or other lawful authority.

If these rules are violated, the juvenile may have his parole revoked and be returned to the institution. Most states have extended the same legal rights enjoyed by adults at parole revocation hearings to juveniles who are in danger of losing their aftercare privileges, as follows:

- Juveniles must be informed of the conditions of parole and receive notice of any obligations.
- Juveniles have the right to legal counsel at state expense if necessary.
- They maintain the right to confront and cross-examine witnesses against them.
- They have the right to introduce documentary evidence and witnesses.
- They have the right to a hearing before an officer who shall be an attorney but not an employee of the revoking agency.[115]

SUMMARY

Community treatment encompasses efforts to keep offenders in the community and spare them the pain and stigma of incarceration. Its primary purpose is to address the needs of juveniles in a nonrestrictive or home setting, employing educational, vocational, counseling, and employment services.

The most widely used method of community treatment is probation. Youths on probation must obey rules given to them by the court and participate in some form of treatment program. Their behavior is monitored by probation officers. If rules are violated, youths can have their probation revoked.

It is now common to enhance probation with more restrictive forms of treatment, such as intensive supervision and house arrest with electronic monitoring. Restitution programs involve having juvenile offenders either reimburse their victims or do community service. Some community programs allow youths to live at home while receiving treatment in a nonpunitive, community-based center. There are also residential programs that require that youths reside in group homes while receiving treatment.

The secure juvenile institution was developed in the mid-nineteenth century as an alternative to placing youths in adult prisons. Youth institutions evolved from large, closed institutions to cottage-based education- and rehabilitation-oriented institutions. Today most institutions for youths are low-security facilities.

The juvenile institutional population has increased in recent years despite efforts to decarcerate status offenders and petty delinquent offenders. In addition, in-creasing numbers of youths are "hidden" in private medical centers and drug treatment clinics. A disproportionate number of minorities are being incarcerated in more secure, state-run youth facilities.

Most institutions maintain intensive treatment programs featuring individual or group therapy. Although a variety of techniques are used, little evidence has been found that any single method is effective in reducing recidivism. Yet rehabilitation remains an important goal of juvenile practitioners. Recent studies indicate that some programs do work.

The right to treatment is an important issue in juvenile justice. Legal decisions have mandated that a juvenile cannot simply be warehoused in a correctional center but must receive proper care and treatment to aid rehabilitation. What constitutes proper care is still being debated, however, and recent court decisions have backed off from the belief that every youth can be rehabilitated.

Juveniles released from institutions are often placed on parole or aftercare. However, there is little evidence that community supervision is more beneficial than simply releasing youths. Many jurisdictions are experiencing success with halfway houses and reintegration centers.

Deciding when to use secure incarceration and providing appropriate programs for serious offenders that include aftercare are key components to a comprehensive system of juvenile justice. At a time when the amount of juvenile crime is significant, strengthening and defining the use of juvenile corrections is vital.

KEY TERMS

community treatment	electronic monitoring	nonresidential programs	guided group interaction (GGI)
suppression effect	balanced probation	meta-analysis	positive peer culture (PPC)
probation	monetary restitution	reform schools	milieu therapy
juvenile probation officer	victim service restitution	cottage system	wilderness probation
social investigation report, predisposition report	community service restitution	least restrictive alternative	boot camps
conditions of probation	residential programs	individual counseling	right to treatment
juvenile intensive probation supervision (JIPS)	group homes	psychotherapy	aftercare
	foster care programs	reality therapy	parole guidelines
house arrest	family group homes	behavior modification	Intensive Aftercare Program (IAP)
	rural programs	group therapy	

QUESTIONS FOR DISCUSSION

1. Would you want a community treatment program in your neighborhood? Why or why not?

2. Is widening the net a real danger, or are treatment-oriented programs simply a method of helping troubled youths?

3. If youths violate the rules of probation, should they be placed in a secure institution?

4. Is juvenile restitution fair? Should a poor young person have to pay back a wealthy victim, such as a store owner?

5. What are the most important advantages to community treatment for juvenile offenders?

6. What is the purpose of juvenile probation? Identify some conditions of probation and discuss the responsibilities of the juvenile probation officer.

7. What are graduated sanctions?

8. Has community treatment generally proven successful?

VIEWPOINT

D. H., 17, hanged himself with a bed sheet tied to the cell door at a juvenile detention facility in a southern state on Jan. 6, 2000. M. S., 14, hanged herself with a bed sheet tied to a shower brace at a public juvenile training school in a western state on Dec. 22, 1999. J. S., 16, hanged himself with a bed sheet tied to a sprinkler head on the ceiling of his room at a county juvenile boot camp in an eastern state on Nov. 2, 1999. K. T., 13, hanged himself with a bed sheet tied to a ceiling grate at a private juvenile training school in a northwestern state on Oct. 15, 1999.

These deaths represent only a handful of the unknown number of suicides that occur each year in juvenile facilities across the country. Youth suicide in the general population is a major public health problem. According to the Centers for Disease Control, as of 1995 the suicide rate of adolescents (ages 15 to 19) has quadrupled from 2.7 per 100,000 in 1950 to 10.8 per 100,000 in 1992. More teenagers die from suicide than from cancer, heart disease, AIDS, birth defects, stroke, pneumonia and influenza, and chronic lung disease combined, according to the U.S. Department of Health and Human Services.

Suicide in youth correctional institutions is of major concern to juvenile justice administrators. To learn more about this issue, go to InfoTrac College Edition and read Lindsay M. Hayes, "Juvenile Suicide in Confinement: A National Survey," *Corrections Today* 62:26 (July 2000). For more information, use *juvenile corrections* as a key term.

NOTES

1. Charles Murray and Louis B. Cox, *Beyond Probation* (Beverly Hills, CA: Sage, 1979).

2. Robert Shepard Jr., ed., *Juvenile Justice Standards, A Balanced Approach* (Chicago: ABA, 1996).

3. George Killinger, Hazel Kerper, and Paul F. Cromwell Jr., *Probation and Parole in the Criminal Justice System* (St. Paul, MN: West, 1976), p. 45; National Advisory Commission on Criminal Justice Standards and Goals, *Corrections* (Washington, DC: U.S. Government Printing Office, 1983), p. 75.

4. Ibid.

5. Jerome Miller, *Last One over the Wall: The Massachusetts Experiment in Closing Reform Schools* (Columbus: Ohio State University Press, 1998).

6. Bureau of Justice Statistics, *Report to the Nation on Crime and Justice* (Washington, DC: U.S. Government Printing Office, 1988), pp. 44–45; Peter Greenwood, "What Works with Juvenile Offenders: A Synthesis of the Literature and Experience," *Federal Probation* 58:63–67 (1994).

7. Robert Coates, Alden Miller, and Lloyd Ohlin, *Diversity in a Youth Correctional System* (Cambridge, MA: Ballinger, 1978); Barry Krisberg, James Austin, and Patricia Steele, *Unlocking Juvenile Corrections* (San Francisco: National Council on Crime and Delinquency, 1989).

8. Personal correspondence, Taneekah Freeman, executive assistant, January 3, 2001; "Roxbury Agency Offers a Map for Youths at the Crossroads," *Boston Globe*, 18 February 1990, p. 32.

9. Adapted from Charles M. Puzzanchera et al., *Juvenile Court Statistics 1998* (Washington, DC: Office of Juvenile Justice and Delinquency Prevention, 2001).

10. Ibid.

11. *In re J.G.* 692 N.E.2d 1226 (Ill.App. 1998).

12. *In re Michael D*, 264 CA Rptr 476 (CA App. 1989).

13. *Morrissey v. Brewer,* 408 U.S. 471, 92 S.Ct. 2593, 33 L.Ed.2d 484 (1972); *Gagnon v. Scarpelli*, 411 U.S. 778, 93 S.Ct. 1756, 36 L.Ed.2d 655 (1973).

14. Patricia McFall Torbet, *Juvenile Probation: The Workhorse of the Juvenile Justice System* (Washington, DC: Office of Juvenile Justice and Delinquency Prevention, 1996).

15. Richard Lawrence, "Reexamining Community Corrections Models," *Crime and Delinquency* 37:449–64 (1991).

16. See Richard G. Wiebush, "Juvenile Intensive Supervision: The Impact on Felony Offenders Diverted from Institutional Placement," *Crime and Delinquency* 39:68–89 (1993); James Byrne, "The Control Controversy: A Preliminary Examination of Intensive Probation Supervision Programs in the United States," *Federal Probation* 50:4–16 (1986).

17. For a review of these programs, see James Byrne, ed., "Introduction," *Federal Probation* 50:2 (1986); see also Emily Walker, "The Community Intensive Treatment for Youth Program: A Specialized Community-Based Program for High-Risk Youth in Alabama," *Law and Psychology Review* 13:175–99 (1989).

18. James Ryan, "Who Gets Revoked? A Comparison of Intensive Supervision Successes and Failures in Vermont," *Crime and Delinquency* 43:104–18 (1997).

19. Angela A. Robertson, Paul W. Grimes, and Kevin E. Rogers, "A Short-Run Cost-Benefit Analysis of Community-Based Interventions for Juvenile Offenders," *Crime and Delinquency* 47:265–84 (2001).

20. Richard Ball and J. Robert Lilly, "A Theoretical Examination of Home Incarceration," *Federal Probation* 50:17–25 (1986); Joan Petersilia, "Exploring the Option of House Arrest," *Federal Probation* 50:50–56 (1986); Annesley Schmidt, "Electronic Monitors," *Federal Probation* 50: 56–60 (1986); Michael Charles, "The Development of a Juvenile Electronic Monitoring Program," *Federal Probation* 53:3–12 (1989).

21. Joseph B. Vaughn, "A Survey of Juvenile Electronic Monitoring and Home Confinement Programs," *Juvenile and Family Court Journal* 40:1–36 (1989).

22. Sudipto Roy, "Five Years of Electronic Monitoring of Adults and Juveniles in Lake County, Indiana: A Comparative Study on Factors Related to Failure," *Journal of Crime and Justice* 20:141–60 (1997).

23. Joseph Papy and Richard Nimer, "Electronic Monitoring in Florida," *Federal Probation* 55:31–33 (1991); Annesley Schmidt, "Electronic Monitors—Realistically, What Can Be Expected?" *Federal Probation* 55:47–53 (1991).

24. Dennis Mahoney, Dennis Romig, and Troy Armstrong, "Juvenile Probation: The Balanced Approach," *Juvenile and Family Court Journal* 39:1–59 (1988).

25. Gordon Bazemore, "On Mission Statements and Reform in Juvenile Justice: The Case of the Balanced Approach," *Federal Probation* 61:64–70 (1992); Gordon Bazemore and Mark Umbreit, *Balanced and Restorative Justice* (Washington, DC: Office of Juvenile Justice and Delinquency Prevention, 1994).

26. Gordon Bazemore, *Guide for Implementing the Balanced and Restorative Justice Model* (Washington, DC: Office of Juvenile Justice and Delinquency Prevention, 1998).

27. Office of Juvenile Justice and Delinquency Prevention, *The 8% Solution* (Washington, DC: OJJDP Fact Sheet, 2001).

28. Ibid., pp. 1–2.

29. Anne L. Schneider, ed., *Guide to Juvenile Restitution* (Washington, DC: Department of Justice, 1985); Anne Schneider and Jean Warner, *National Trends in Juvenile Restitution Programming* (Washington, DC: U.S. Government Printing Office, 1989).

30. Gordon Bazemore, "New Concepts and Alternative Practice in Community Supervision of Juvenile Offenders: Rediscovering Work Experience and Competency Development," *Journal of Crime and Justice* 14:27–45 (1991); Jeffrey Butts and Howard Snyder, *Restitution and Juvenile Recidivism* (Washington, DC: Department of Justice, 1992).

31. Anne Schneider, "Restitution and Recidivism Rates of Juvenile Offenders: Results from Four Experimental Studies," *Criminology* 24:533–52 (1986).

32. Shay Bilchik, *A Juvenile Justice System for the 21st Century* (Washington, DC: Office of Juvenile Justice and Delinquency Prevention, 1998).

33. Peter Schneider, William Griffith, and Anne Schneider, *Juvenile Restitution as a Sole Sanction or Condition of Probation: An Empirical Analysis* (Eugene, OR: Institute for Policy Analysis, 1980); S. Roy, "Juvenile Restitution and Recidivism in a Midwestern County," *Federal Probation* 57:55–62 (1995).

34. Anne Schneider, "Restitution and Recidivism Rates of Juvenile Offenders," *Directory of Restitution Programs* (Washington, DC: OJJDP Juvenile Justice Clearinghouse, 1996). This directory contains information on more than 500 restitution programs across the country.

35. H. Ted Rubin, "Fulfilling Juvenile Restitution Requirements in Community Correctional Programs," *Federal Probation* 52:32–43 (1988).

36. Peter Greenwood, "What Works with Juvenile Offenders: A Synthesis of the Literature and Experience," *Federal Probation* 58:63–67 (1994).

37. Sharon Mihalic, Katherine Irwin, Delbert Elliott, Abigail Fagan, and Dianne Hansen, *Blueprints for Violence Prevention* (Washington, DC: OJJDP Juvenile Justice Bulletin, 2001), p. 10.

38. Patricia Chamberlain and John B. Reid, "Comparison of Two Community Alternatives to Incarceration," *Journal of Consulting and Clinical Psychology* 66:624–33 (1998).

39. Lamar T. Empey and Maynard Erickson, *The Provo Experiment* (Lexington, MA: D.C. Heath, 1972); Paul Pilnick, Albert Elias, and Neale Clapp, "The Essexfields Concept: A New Approach to the Social Treatment of Juvenile Delinquents," *Journal of Applied Behavioral Sciences* 2:109–21 (1966); Yitzhak Bakal, "Reflections: A Quarter Century of Reform in Massachusetts Youth Corrections," *Crime and Delinquency* 40:110–17 (1998).

40. Ira Schwartz, *Juvenile Justice and Public Policy* (New York: Lexington Books, 1992), p. 217.

41. Dan Macallair, "Reaffirming Rehabilitation in Juvenile Justice," *Youth and Society* 25:104–23 (1993).

42. Mark W. Lipsey, "Juvenile Delinquency Treatment: A Meta-Analytic Inquiry into the Variability of Effects," in Thomas D. Cook et al., eds., *Meta-Analysis for Explanation: A Casebook* (San Francisco: Russell Sage Foundation, 1991); Carol Garrett, "Effects of Residential Treatment on

Adjudicated Delinquents: A Meta-Analysis," *Crime and Delinquency* 22:287–308 (1985); Ted Palmer, *The Re-Emergence of Correctional Interventions* (Newbury Park, CA: Russell Sage Foundation, 1992), p. 69.

43. Barry Krisberg, Elliot Currie, and David Onek, "New Approaches in Corrections," *American Bar Association Journal of Criminal Justice* 10:51 (1995).

44. U.S. Department of Justice, *Children in Custody 1975–85: Census of Public and Private Juvenile Detention, Correctional, and Shelter Facilities* (Washington, DC: U.S. Department of Justice, 1989), p. 4.

45. For a detailed description of juvenile delinquency in the 1800s, see J. Hawes, *Children in Urban Society: Juvenile Delinquency in Nineteenth Century America* (New York: Oxford University Press, 1971).

46. D. Jarvis, *Institutional Treatment of the Offender* (New York: McGraw-Hill, 1978), p. 101.

47. Margaret Werner Cahalan, *Historical Corrections Statistics in the United States, 1850–1984* (Washington, DC: U.S. Department of Justice, 1986), pp. 104–105.

48. Clemons Bartollas, Stuart J. Miller, and Simon Dinitiz, *Juvenile Victimization: The Institutional Paradox* (New York: Wiley, 1976), p. 6.

49. LaMar T. Empey, *American Delinquency—Its Meaning and Construction* (Homewood, IL: Dorsey, 1978), p. 515.

50. Edward Eldefonso and Walter Hartinger, *Control, Treatment, and Rehabilitation of Juvenile Offenders* (Beverly Hills: Glencoe, 1976), p. 151.

51. Ibid., p. 152.

52. M. Rosenthal, "Reforming the Justice Correctional Institution: Efforts of U.S. Children's Bureau in the 1930s," *Journal of Sociology and Social Welfare* 14:47–73 (1987).

53. Bureau of Justice Statistics, *Fact Sheet on Children in Custody* (Washington, DC: U.S. Department of Justice, 1989); Barbara Allen-Hagen, *Public Juvenile Facilities—Children in Custody, 1989* (Washington, DC: Office of Juvenile Justice and Delinquency Prevention, 1991); James Austin et al., *Juveniles Taken into Custody, 1993* (Washington, DC: Office of Juvenile Justice and Delinquency Prevention, 1995).

54. National Conference of State Legislatures, *A Legislator's Guide to Comprehensive Juvenile Justice, Juvenile Detention and Corrections* (Denver: National Conference of State Legislators, 1996).

55. Ibid.

56. Hunter Hurst and Patricia Torbet, *Organization and Administration of Juvenile Services: Probation, Aftercare, and State Delinquent Institutions* (Pittsburgh: National Center for Juvenile Justice, 1993), p. 4.

57. Melissa Sickmund and Yi-chun Wan, "Census of Juveniles in Residential Placement Databook" (2001). Online available at http://www.ojjdp.ncjrs.org/ojstatbb/cjrp.

58. Ira Schwartz, Marilyn Jackson-Beck, and Roger Anderson, "The 'Hidden' System of Juvenile Control," *Crime and Delinquency* 30:371–85 (1984).

59. Rebecca Craig and Andrea Paterson, "State Involuntary Commitment Laws: Beyond Deinstitutionalization," *National Conference of State Legislative Reports* 13:1–10 (1988).

60. Alan Breed and Barry Krisberg, "Is There a Future?" *Corrections Today* 48:14–26 (1986).

61. Melissa Sickmund and Yi-chun Wan, "Census of Juveniles in Residential Placement Databook."

62. Howard N. Snyder and Melissa Sickmund, *Juvenile Offenders and Victims: 1999 National Report* (Pittsburgh: National Center for Juvenile Justice, 1999), p. 192.

63. Ibid., p. 195.

64. Barry Krisberg, Ira Schwartz, G. Fishman, Z. Eisikovits, and E. Gitman, "The Incarceration of Minority Youth," *Crime and Delinquency* 33:173–205 (1987).

65. Craig Fischer, ed., "Washington State Moves to End Juvenile Justice Race Disparity," *Criminal Justice Newsletter* 27:1–8 (1996).

66. Snyder and Sickmund, *Juvenile Offenders and Victims: 1999 National Report*, p. 195.

67. Bartollas, Miller, and Dinitz, *Juvenile Victimization*.

68. Christopher Sieverdes and Clemens Bartollas, "Security Level and Adjustment Patterns in Juvenile Institutions," *Journal of Criminal Justice* 14:135–45 (1986).

69. Several authors have written of this sexual double standard. See E. A. Anderson, "The Chivalrous Treatment of the Female Offender in the Arms of the Criminal Justice System: A Review of the Literature," *Social Problems* 23:350–57 (1976); G. Armstrong, "Females under the Law: Protected but Unequal," *Crime and Delinquency* 23:109–20 (1977); M. Chesney-Lind, "Judicial Enforcement of the Female Sex Role: The Family Court and the Female Delinquent," *Issues in Criminology* 8:51–59 (1973); idem, "Juvenile Delinquency: The Sexualization of Female Crime," *Psychology Today* 19:43–46 (1974); Allan Conway and Carol Bogdan, "Sexual Delinquency: The Persistence of a Double Standard," *Crime and Delinquency* 23:13–135 (1977); M. Chesney-Lind, *Girls, Delinquency and the Juvenile Justice System* (Pacific Grove, CA: Brooks/Cole, 1991).

70. Leslie Acoca, "Outside/Inside: The Violation of American Girls at Home, on the Streets, and in the Juvenile Justice System," *Crime and Delinquency* 44:561–89 (1998).

71. For a historical analysis of a girls' reformatory, see Barbara Brenzel, *Daughters of the State* (Cambridge, MA: MIT Press, 1983).

72. Ilene R. Bergsmann, "The Forgotten Few Juvenile Female Offenders," *Federal Probation* 53:73–79 (1989).

73. Doris Layton MacKenzie, "Reducing the Criminal Activities of Known Offenders and Delinquents: Crime Prevention in the Courts and Corrections," in Lawrence W. Sherman, David P. Farrington, Brandon C. Welsh, and Doris Layton MacKenzie, eds., *Evidence-Based Crime Prevention* (London: Routledge, 2002), p. 352.

74. For an interesting article highlighting the debate over the effectiveness of correctional treatment, see John Whitehead and Steven Lab, "Meta-Analysis of Juvenile Correctional Treatment," *Journal of Research in Crime and Delinquency* 26:276–95 (1989).

75. National Conference of State Legislatures, *A Legislator's Guide to Comprehensive Juvenile Justice*, 1996.

76. Robert Shepard Jr., "State Pen or Playpen? Is Prevention 'Pork' or Simply Good Sense?" *American Bar Association Journal of Criminal Justice* 10:34–37 (1995); James Howell, ed., *Guide for Implementing the Comprehensive Strategy for Serious, Violent and Chronic Juvenile Offenders* (Washington, DC: OJJDP, 1995).

77. Louise Sas and Peter Jaffe, "Understanding Depression in Juvenile Delinquency: Implications for Institutional Admission Policies and Treatment Programs," *Juvenile and Family Court Journal* 37:49–58 (1985–1986).

78. See, generally, William Glasser, "Reality Therapy: A Realistic Approach to the Young Offender," in Robert Schaste and Jo Wallach, eds., *Readings in Delinquency and Treatment* (Los Angeles: Delinquency Prevention Training Project, Youth Studies Center, University of Southern California, 1965); see also Richard Rachin, "Reality Therapy: Helping People Help Themselves," *Crime and Delinquency* 16:143 (1974).

79. Helen A. Klein, "Toward More Effective Behavior Programs for Juvenile Offenders," *Federal Probation* 41:45–50 (1977); Albert Bandura, *Principles of Behavior Modification* (New York: Holt, Rinehart & Winston, 1969); H. A. Klein, "Behavior Modification as Therapeutic Paradox," *American Journal of Orthopsychiatry* 44:353 (1974).

80. Thomas J. Dishion, Joan McCord, and François Poulin, "When Interventions Harm: Peer Groups and Problem Behavior," *American Psychologist* 54:755–64 (1999).

81. Larry Brendtero and Arlin Ness, "Perspectives on Peer Group Treatment: The Use and Abuses of Guided Group Interaction/Positive Peer Culture," *Child and Youth Services Review* 4:307–24 (1982).

82. Elaine Traynelis-Yurek and George A. Giacobbe, "Communication Rehabilitation Regime for Incarcerated Youth: Positive Peer Culture," *Journal of Offender Rehabilitation* 26:157–67 (1998).

83. Bruno Bettelheim, *The Empty Fortress* (New York: Free Press, 1967).

84. California Youth Authority, "Ventura School for Juvenile Female Offenders," *CYA Newsletter* (Ventura, CA: author, 1988).

85. Kate O'Sullivan, Nancy Rose, and Thomas Murphy, *PEPNet: Connecting Juvenile Offenders to Education and Employment* (Washington, DC: OJJDP Fact Sheet, 2001), p. 1.

86. Doris Layton MacKenzie, "Reducing the Criminal Activities of Known Offenders and Delinquents, p. 355; idem, "Evidence-Based Corrections: Identifying What Works," *Crime and Delinquency* 46:457–71 (2000), p. 466.

87. Thomas Castellano and Irina Soderstrom, "Therapeutic Wilderness Programs and Juvenile Recidivism: A Program Evaluation," *Journal of Offender Rehabilitation* 17:19–46 (1992).

88. MacKenzie, "Reducing the Criminal Activities of Known Offenders and Delinquents, p. 355.

89. William J. Taylor, "Tailoring Boot Camps to Juveniles," *Corrections Today*:124 (July 1992).

90. Jerald Burns and Gennaro Vito, "An Impact Analysis of the Alabama Boot Camp Program," *Federal Probation* 59:63–67 (1995).

91. Ronald Corbett and Joan Petersilia, eds., "The Results of a Multi-Site Study of Boot Camps," *Federal Probation* 58:60–66 (1995).

92. Margaret Beyer, "Juvenile Boot Camps Don't Make Sense," *American Bar Association Journal of Criminal Justice* 10:20–21 (1996).

93. Eric Peterson, *Juvenile Boot Camps: Lessons Learned* (Washington, DC: Office of Juvenile Justice and Delinquency Prevention, 1996); Michael Peters et al., *Boot Camps for Juvenile Offenders* (Washington, DC: Office of Juvenile Justice and Delinquency Prevention, 1997).

94. Doris Layton MacKenzie, Angela R. Gover, Gaylene Styve Armstrong, and Ojmarrh Mitchell, *A National Study Comparing the Environments of Boot Camps with Traditional Facilities for Juvenile Offenders* (Washington, DC: NIJ Research in Brief, 2001), pp. 1–2.

95. Doris Layton MacKenzie, David B. Wilson, and Suzanne B. Kider, "Effects of Correctional Boot Camps on Offending," in David P. Farrington and Brandon C. Welsh, eds., "What Works in Preventing Crime? Systematic Reviews of Experimental and Quasi-Experimental Research," *Annals of the American Academy of Political and Social Science* 578:126–143 (2001).

96. Ibid., p. 134.

97. MacKenzie, "Reducing the Criminal Activities of Known Offenders and Delinquents," p. 348.

98. Anthony Salerno, "Boot Camps—A Critique and Proposed Alternative," *Journal of Offender Rehabilitation* 20:147–58 (1994).

99. Joanne Ardovini-Brooker and Lewis Walker, "Juvenile Boot Camps and the Reclamation of Our Youth: Some Food for Thought," *Juvenile and Family Court Journal* 51:12–28 (2000).

100. Morton Birnbaum, "The Right to Treatment," *American Bar Association Journal* 46:499 (1960).

101. See, for example, *Matter of Welfare of CAW* 579 N.W.2d 494 (MN App. 1998).

102. *Inmates of the Boys' Training School v. Affleck*, 346 F. Supp. 1354 (D.R.I. 1972).

103. Ibid., p. 1343.

104. *Nelson v. Heyne*, 491. F.2d 353 (1974).

105. *Morales v. Turman*, 383 F.Supp. 53 (E.D. Texas 1974).

106. *Pena v. New York State Division for Youth*, 419 F. Supp. 203 (S.D.N.Y. 1976).

107. *Ralston v. Robinson*, 102 S.Ct. 233 (1981).

108. Patricia Puritz and Mary Ann Scali, *Beyond the Walls: Improving Conditions of Confinement for Youth in Custody* (Washington, DC: Office of Juvenile Justice and Delinquency Prevention, 1998).

109. Joan McCord, Cathy Spatz Widom, and Nancy A. Crowell, *Juvenile Crime, Juvenile Justice*, Panel on Juvenile Crime: Prevention, Treatment, and Control (Washington, DC: National Academy Press, 2001), p. 194.

110. Michael Norman, "Discretionary Justice: Decision Making in a State Juvenile Parole Board," *Juvenile and Family Court Journal* 37:19–26 (1985–1986).

111. James Maupin, "Risk Classification Systems and the Provisions of Juvenile Aftercare," *Crime and Delinquency* 39:90–105 (1993).

112. National Conference of State Legislatures, *A Legislator's Guide to Comprehensive Juvenile Justice*.

113. David M. Altschuler, "Intensive Aftercare for High-Risk Juvenile Parolees: Overview" (Washington, DC: Office of Juvenile Justice and Delinquency Prevention, n.d.).

114. David M. Altschuler and Troy Armstrong, "Reintegrating Juvenile Offenders: Translating the Intensive Aftercare Program Model into Performance Standards." Paper presented at the American Society of Criminology meeting, San Francisco, November 2000.

115. See *Morrissey v. Brewer*, 408 U.S. 471, 92 S.Ct. 2593, 33 L.Ed.2d 484 (1972).

16 Delinquency and Juvenile Justice Abroad

Delinquency around the World
- **Europe**
- **The Americas**
- **Australia and New Zealand**
- **Asia**
- **Africa**

International Comparisons
- **Problems of Cross-National Research**
- **Benefits of Cross-National Research**
- **Juvenile Violence**
- **Juvenile Property Crime**
- **Juvenile Drug Use**
- **Conclusion: What Do the Trends Tell Us?**

Juvenile Justice Systems across Countries
- **Juvenile Policing**
- **Age of Criminal Responsibility: Minimum and Maximum**
- **Presence of Juvenile Court**
- **Transfers to Adult Court**
- **Sentencing Policies**
- **Incarcerated Juveniles**
- **Aftercare**

A Profile of Juvenile Justice in England
- **Apprehension and Charge**
- **Bail**
- **Precourt Diversion**
- **Prosecution**
- **Youth Court**
- **Sentencing**

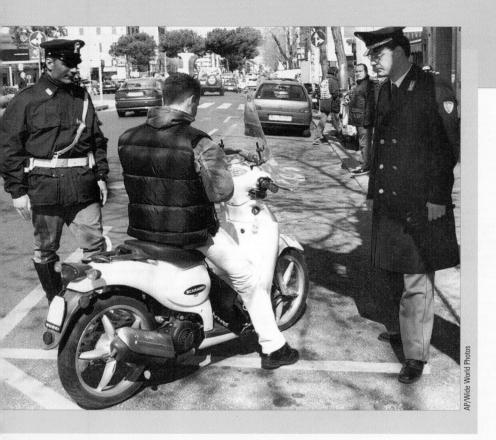
AP/Wide World Photos

As the recently elected prime minister of England you are faced with having to deal with national and international implications arising from the following case. In August 2001, two British teenagers, Jon Venables and Robert Thompson, were granted parole after serving eight years for the brutal murder of 2-year-old James Bulger. On February 12, 1993, these two boys, then 10 years old, abducted James from a mall just outside Liverpool, England. James's mother stopped to look at a display window of one of the stores, letting go of James's hand for a few seconds. When she turned around James was gone. The whole event was caught on the mall's surveillance system. The horrifying video showed the two boys walking up to James and calmly leading him out of the mall. The 2-year-old's badly beaten body was found a short time later near railway tracks, a short distance from the mall. Because of the video, the two child killers were quickly apprehended and taken into custody. Throughout England there was a kind of collective agony for the death of the boy and the mother's loss of her infant son.

The capture and subsequent trial of these two boys sparked national and international attention and debate. Immediately, England and other countries began to reconsider the minimum age when children can be held responsible for their delinquent or criminal actions. Fortunately for England, the minimum age was 10 years. But in other countries like Canada, Italy, Japan, and Russia, the minimum age is much higher.

Like the capture and trial of these child killers, their release and events leading up to it caused national and international debate over the administration of juvenile justice. In January 1994, it was learned that the decision of Lord Justice Morland to detain the boys at Her Majesty's Pleasure—the equivalent of a life sentence—had been recommended to be no higher than eight years. As a discretionary sentence, this was legal, but was it too lenient for the crime? England and other countries were soon contemplating mandatory minimum sentences for juvenile offenders, and in England the then home secretary, Michael Howard, tried unsuccessfully to have the boys serve a minimum of 15 years. Then, in the early months of 2001, the public learned that the two boys were to be paroled sometime in the summer. In addition, their identities were to be changed to protect them from reprisal from the public, and there were rumors about them being sent to another country.

These events put England's juvenile offender laws and juvenile justice system to an extreme test in trying to balance the rights of the offender with the rights of the community and the moral and public outrage caused by this violent act. The international implications of these events were wide reaching, causing some countries to re-examine their juvenile offender laws and how they deal with violent juvenile offenders. As prime minister, how would you answer these questions from the media?

- Did the English juvenile justice system fail the victim's family and society as a whole?

- Should England have done more to keep these juveniles locked up for a longer time, or was the sentence appropriate?

- What can England do to try to prevent this from happening again?

- How should other countries react to this terrible crime? Should they change their juvenile offender laws and policies?

The Bulger case, which is a real case, aptly illustrates that the issues of juvenile violence and delinquency are not unique to the United States. Many nations around the world are experiencing an upsurge in juvenile problem behavior, including gang violence, prostitution, and drug abuse. In response to the growing number of delinquent acts, some nations are now in the process of revamping their juvenile justice systems in an effort to increase their effectiveness and efficiency. This chapter addresses these issues by looking at international perspectives of delinquency and juvenile justice systems. The chapter begins by providing a snapshot of juvenile delinquency around the world. We discuss the challenges and benefits of making com-

JON VENABLES POSES FOR A POLICE PHOTOGRAPH, which was taken eight days after he and Robert Thompson, both 10 years old, abducted and brutally murdered 2-year-old James Bulger in northern England. This picture was released to the media on June 22, 2001, the day the British government announced that the two child killers, now 18, would be released from prison and given new identities. This case sparked national and international attention over the administration of juvenile justice, with some countries reexamining the minimum age at which children can be held responsible for their delinquent or criminal actions and the maximum sentence length for serious offenses.

developed countries Recognized by the United Nations as the richest countries in the world.

parisons across nations and examine trends in delinquency rates in different countries compared with the United States. Next we provide a review of juvenile justice systems in **developed countries,** organized around important issues facing juvenile justice today, such as minimum age of criminal responsibility, transfers to adult court, and maximum length of sentence for incarcerated juveniles. The chapter concludes with a profile of the juvenile justice system in England, examining the many different stages that juveniles may face as they go through the system.

Delinquency around the World

There has been a noted upswing in juvenile delinquency around the world. Where has this occurred, and what has been the cause? Examples are found in all major areas of the world, and though there are many reasons, some common themes emerge.

Europe

Teen crime has been on the rise in Europe. One of the most alarming developments has been the involvement of children in the international sex trade. Russia is plagued with Internet sex rings that involve youths in pornographic pictures. In May 2001, more than 800 tapes and videos were seized in Moscow during Operation Blue Orchid, a joint operation conducted by Russian police and U.S. Customs agents.[1] Operation Blue Orchid led to criminal investigations against people who ordered child pornography in more than 20 nations. Equally disturbing has been the involvement of European youths in global prostitution rings. Desperate young girls and boys in war-torn areas such as the former Yugoslavia and in impoverished areas such as Eastern Europe have become involved with gangs that ship them around the world. In one case, an organized crime group involved in wildlife smuggling of tiger bones and skins to Asian markets began a sideline of supplying sex clubs with young Russian women.[2]

Western Europe has also experienced a surprising amount of teen violence. On April 26, 2002, in Erfurt, Germany, a 19-year-old male, armed with a pump-action shotgun and a handgun, entered his high school and shot dead 14 teachers, two students, and a police officer; he then took his own life. The youth had just been expelled from the school. It was the worst mass killing in Germany since World War II. In May 2001, race riots broke out in England when young native-born Britons attacked groups of Asian immigrants. The young rioters were the sons of mill workers whose livelihoods were disrupted when the mills closed, leaving them with little chance of advancement.[3]

Violent hate crimes are not unique to England. Germany has been plagued with skinhead violence since reunification in 1989. Most German skinheads are social misfits, with minimal education and few employment opportunities. Because unemployment is high, they feel helpless and hopeless regarding their future, and many resort to physical violence in reaction to their plight.[4] Most of the increase in German youth violence has been encountered in what was Communist East Germany before the reunification. Youth violence in the East is 70 percent higher than in the West, a factor linked to the exposure of Eastern youth to greater poverty and unemployment than their West German peers.[5]

What has fueled this increase in teen violence? Although each nation is quite different, all share an explosive mix of racial tension, poverty, envy, drug abuse, broken families, unemployment, and alienation. Some of the areas hardest hit have been undergoing rapid social and economic change—the fall of communism, the end of the Cold War, the effects of the global economy, an influx of multinational immigration—as they move toward increased economic integration, privatization, and diminished social services. In Europe, the main reason for skyrocketing teen violence is believed to be the tremendous growth in immigrant youth populations. This is not because immigrants are more prone to violence, but rather because of the relative poverty and social disintegration they face upon arriving in very homogenous countries such as Sweden and the Netherlands.[6] This view has also been advanced as one of the main reasons for the growth in rates of total violent crime (adult plus juvenile) in Europe during the early to mid-1990s.[7] The result of these rapid changes has been the development of personal alienation in an anomic environment. (See Chapter 4 for more on the effect of anomie.) Kids become susceptible to violence when institutional and interpersonal sources of stability, such as schools and parents, are weak and/or absent.[8]

The Americas

Shocking stories of teen violence are also not uncommon in North America and South America. In Canada, there has been a rash of school shootings in recent years. Many have resulted in death and serious injury of other students and teachers. School shootings in Canada increased substantially following the massacre at Columbine High School in the United States in 1999, prompting some Canadian social scientists to speculate that these were copycat crimes. But other research points to the growing number of students who have access to guns and carry them to school,[9] as well as an increase in school violence in general.[10]

In Mexico, violent crime is one of the biggest problems facing the country. One study found more than 1,500 street gangs in Mexico City, the country's capital. Gang names include "Verdugos" (Executioners), "Malditos Ratas" (Wicked Punks), "Niños Podridos" (Bad Boys), and "Cerdos" (Pigs). Most of the gangs are made up of teenagers, and each gang is accompanied by what is referred to as their "diaper brigade," the equivalent of a "minor league" for children under age 12.[11]

South America has a long history of violent uprisings, police abuse, and political unrest. Some countries are more violent than others. In Brazil, violence is the second leading cause of death behind heart disease; there are more deaths each year by murder than by cancer. Young people are responsible for a disproportionate amount of these homicides.[12]

death squads Common to South America, organized government or criminal groups that selectively kill members of opposing groups and incite fear in those groups and among their supporters.

Among the more recent atrocities in South America are the killings of street children. These are children who leave home at a very young age because of abuse, neglect, or the loss of their parents, and earn their living largely by committing petty delinquent acts, begging, and selling garbage. In the Brazilian city of Rio de Janeiro, killings of street children are commonplace. **Death squads,** drug lords, juvenile gangs, and sometimes the police are behind these killings.[13]

Australia and New Zealand

Although not normally associated with high crime and delinquency rates, these island nations have had their share of youth crime, ranging from graffiti to homicide. In fact, the graffiti problem has become so serious in New Zealand that some police departments have been forced to use photographs to prepare victim damage estimates. In one police office, 135 different incidents were investigated before the culprits, a youth group, were finally arrested.[14]

Australia has experienced a wide range of juvenile crime. Like Europe, child prostitution has become a significant problem, and an estimated 4,000 children, some as young as 10 years old, are involved in selling sex for money and drugs.[15] Australia has also experienced juvenile violence. Youths are the offenders (and/or victims) in about one-third of all the murders occurring in Australia.[16] Youth homicides tend to occur among strangers, with the youngest offenders (10–14 years) killing people they had never met before and older teens victimizing acquaintances. One reason for this trend is that the Australian juvenile is more likely to kill while committing another crime such as a robbery. Juveniles were more likely to kill for revenge than were adults.

Asia

In December 2001, police in the Fukushima Prefecture, located north of Tokyo, arrested a 15-year-old boy for killing his father. The 15-year-old punched his 61-year-old father in the face and stomped on his stomach until he was dead. The incident was extremely shocking because it occurred one day after a 13-year-old was arrested for beating his mother to death because he objected to the meal she had cooked![17] Japanese teen violence is at its highest level in more than 30 years, and the term "hikikomori' (those who isolate themselves) has been coined to describe troubled youth who commit crimes and engage in other antisocial acts.[18] The Japanese experience with delinquency and youth violence is the topic of the accompanying Focus on Delinquency.

Japan is not the only Asian nation experiencing an uptick in juvenile crime. Chinese authorities have found that juvenile delinquency has been on the increase for several years, though it is still relatively lower than adult crime.[19] The rise in delinquency has been linked to China's ongoing social and economic upheaval that began in 1979 when the country first adopted its reform policies and embraced the outside world. While the rapid economic growth has transformed society, rapid change has strained traditional norms, values, and ethics. While China is often known for its ruthless suppression of crime and liberal use of the death penalty, the government has adopted a more humane approach to treating delinquents. The aim is to act as a wise and concerned pseudoparent and stress prevention and education and not punishment and repression.

Africa

Juvenile crime and gang violence are growing problems in many African countries. In the city of Dakar, Senegal, on the western coast of the continent, youth gang problems are out of control. Youth gangs here, with English names taken from American television and movies, like "The Hooligan Boys," "The Mafia Boys," and "The Eagles," prey on different segments of the population. The Hooligans, for example, are best known for the violence they inflict at dance parties organized by other young people. This gang has also developed a type of violence market in which they "buy a fight." This involves gang members offering to take over a fight that has already started and then fighting the weaker of the two parties. Many of the younger boys growing up in Dakar look up to gang members; this admiration serves as an important tool in recruiting future gang members.[20]

Abject poverty, ethnic tensions, and an ever-growing gap between the haves and have-nots underlie much of the violence throughout Africa. In Nairobi, the capital of Kenya and one of the largest cities in Africa, up to 70 percent of residents live in slums on the outskirts of the city; 80 percent of residents are low-income earners; the rich occupy 60 percent of the city's land; and two-thirds of the population does not have access to clean water.[21]

International Comparisons

How does youth crime around the world compare to what we are experiencing here in the United States? There have been numerous efforts to compare delinquency across different countries.[22] Social scientists have carried out international comparisons for many reasons, including to test theories of delinquency; to compare delinquency and punishment over long periods of time; to investigate the effects of government policies on delinquency, such as gun control or child welfare benefits; to examine why some countries have very low delinquency rates; or just for general

Youth Violence on the Rise in Japan

Japan has long been considered a low-crime country. Despite its industrial might and highly urbanized population—trademarks of high-crime countries in the developed world—Japan has maintained extremely low delinquency and crime rates in the post–World War II era. But in recent years this trend has changed, with a dramatic upsurge in violence among young people. As shown in Figure A, police arrests of 15- to 19-year-olds for violent offenses started to climb in 1996, following years of stability. (Although these figures are not expressed as rates per juvenile population, the increase in arrests between 1995 and 1998 far surpasses any increase in the juvenile population.) In 1997, the peak year, 2,300 arrests were made for juvenile violence.

Shocking events, rarely experienced before in Japan, are starting to become more common. Japanese youth gangs have started to carry out what they call "uncle hunting," whereby four or five gang members single out a lone businessman walking home and beat him to the ground. Victim reports claim that gangs are not only doing this for the money, but also for the thrill of inflicting pain on others. Other events include a 13-year-old boy murdering his female schoolteacher and a 16-year-old boy stabbing his girlfriend when she tried to end the relationship.

So what is causing this rise in youth violence in Japan? Japanese social scientists, politicians, leaders of business, and the public are all weighing in on the debate. One of the more controversial views is that the increase in juvenile violence and crime in general is being fueled by an increase in the number of multinational immigrants, which are overwhelmingly other Asians, who have come to find work in Japan. As in Europe, it is not that these new populations are more prone to violence, but rather that they are less well off financially, due in part to work being scarce, and are disconnected from familial and social groups.

Other views point to a decline in cultural values and societal norms, which are widely regarded as being fundamental to the economic success and crime-free lifestyle that Japan has long enjoyed. Conformity, sense of community, belonging to a group, honor or "face," and respect for authority are all believed to have declined in recent years, especially among young people. Economic stagnation has also played a role in the rise in youth violence. A higher unemployment rate and fewer opportunities have left many young people feeling marginalized and frustrated. It is also estimated that 45 percent of all crimes in Japan are committed by people under age 20, about double what it is in the United States. Because so much of Japanese crime is committed by youths and the rate of juvenile crime and violence is escalating, experts predict no slowdown in the present trends in youth violence.

Critical Thinking

1. What are some other possible reasons for Japan's increase in youth violence?
2. What type of action should Japan take to address this rise in youth violence? And how can young people be part of the solution?

InfoTrac College Edition Research

 To read more about changes in youth violence in Japan, go to Raymond Lamont-Brown, "Violence among Japanese Youth," *Contemporary Review* 277:86 (August 2000). To find further information, use *delinquency-international* as a key term.

Sources: Calvin Sims, "Shaken Japan Tries to Face Aftermath of School Attack," *New York Times,* New England edition, 10 June 2001; Erika Fairchild and Harry R. Dammer, *Comparative Criminal Justice Systems,* 2nd ed. (Belmont, CA: Wadsworth, 2001), pp. 37–38; Doug Struck, "Surge in Violent Crime Worries Japan," *Washington Post,* 10 February 2000; Nobuo Komiya, "A Cultural Study of the Low Crime Rate in Japan," *British Journal of Criminology* 39:369–90 (1999); Howard W. French, "Japan's Teen Crime Wave," *New York Times Upfront* 132:12 (November 15, 1999); Minoru Yokoyama, "Juvenile Justice: An Overview of Japan," in John Winterdyk, ed., *Juvenile Justice Systems: International Perspectives* (Toronto: Canadian Scholars' Press, 1997), pp. 1–28; Hans Joachim Schneider, "Crime and Its Control in Japan and the Federal Republic of Germany," *International Journal of Offender Therapy and Comparative Criminology* 36:307–21 (1992); Freda Adler, *Nations Not Obsessed with Crime* (Littleton, CO: Rothman, 1983).

Figure A
Arrests for Violent Offenses, 1988–1998

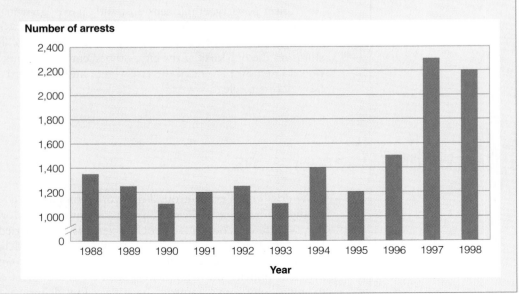

interest.[23] Advocacy organizations as well as governments sometimes point to events or trends in other countries to show how the United States is doing better or sometimes worse than other countries.

Problems of Cross-National Research

Unlike comparisons of delinquency in different cities or parts of the same country, international comparisons involving two or more countries demand that researchers pay a great deal more attention to what is being compared, what countries are being compared, and so on.[24] Comparing delinquency rates across countries can be difficult because of three main problems:

- The legal definitions of juvenile crime vary from country to country.[25]
- The measurement of juvenile crime varies across countries. In the United States, arrests are used to measure juvenile crime, while in many European countries, the number of cases solved by the police measures crime.[26]
- The age group defined as "juvenile" is not always the same.[27]

Despite these problems, valid comparisons of delinquency across different countries can still be made. The key is to acquire valid data and then make comparisons between nations that utilize similar methods of measuring youth crime. The best data sources are listed in Table 16.1.[28]

The United Nations Survey of Crime Trends and Operations of Criminal Justice Systems (UNCJS) provides data on juvenile delinquency and adult crime, as well as data on juvenile justice and criminal justice systems. Conducted every five years since 1977, the UNCJS survey makes it possible to look at changes over time, and for a very large number of countries around the world. However, because the data are a collection of statistics sent to the U.N. by individual countries, they are really no better than using official data provided by individual countries. The *European Sourcebook of Crime and Criminal Justice Statistics,* an initiative of the Council of Europe, is very similar to the UNCJS, but is limited to official statistics from Europe. Where the two data sources differ is that the Council of Europe is trying to develop a uni-

To read more about the U.N., go to
http://www.un.org
For an up-to-date list of Web links, go to
http://info.wadsworth.com/siegel

Table 16.1 International Sources of Delinquency Data

Data Source	Type of Delinquency Data Collected	Organization in Charge of Data Collection	Number of Countries Represented	Frequency of Data Collection
UNCJS	Police statistics	United Nations	103	Every five years (since 1977)
INTERPOL	Police statistics	International Criminal Police Organization	179	Annually
WHO	Medical certified homicides	World Health Organization	191	Annually
European Sourcebook of Crime and Criminal Justice Statistics	Police statistics	Council of Europe	36 European countries	Annually (latest data is for 1996)
International Self-Report Delinquency Study	Self-reports	Netherlands Ministry of Justice	12	One time only (early 1990s)

Sources: Josine Junger-Tas, Gert-Jan Terlouw, and Malcolm W. Klein, eds., *Delinquent Behavior among Young People in the Western World: First Results of the International Self-Report Delinquency Study* (New York: Kugler Publications, 1994); Graeme Newman and Gregory J. Howard, "Introduction: Data Sources and Their Use," in Graeme Newman, ed., *Global Report on Crime and Justice* (New York: Oxford University Press, 1999), pp. 3–12; European Committee on Crime Problems, *European Sourcebook of Crime and Criminal Justice Statistics* (Strasbourg, Germany: Council of Europe, 1999); Martin Killias and Marcelo F. Aebi, "Crime Trends in Europe from 1990 to 1996: How Europe Illustrates the Limits of the American Experience," *European Journal on Criminal Policy and Research* 8:43–63 (2000).

To read more about INTERPOL, go to *http://www.interpol.com/* For an up-to-date list of Web links, go to *http://info.wadsworth.com/siegel*

A CLOSER VIEW
To read more about different data sources on juvenile delinquency on InfoTrac College Edition, go to Thomas Gabor, "Trends in Youth Crime: Some Evidence Pointing to Increases in the Severity and Volume of Violence on the Part of Young People," *Canadian Journal of Criminology* 41:385–92 (1999).

form system in the way official statistics on delinquency and crime are collected and reported.

The International Criminal Police Organization (INTERPOL) and the World Health Organization (WHO) are two other sources of official statistics on delinquency and crime at the international level. The two sources differ in a number of ways. INTERPOL compiles police crime statistics (completions and attempts) received from countries that are members of the organization. WHO, on the other hand, compiles homicide statistics (completions only) based on medical records received from countries that are affiliated with the organization. WHO's measure of homicide, which is based on the "classification of causes of death worldwide" and determined by medical practitioners,[29] is considered the most accurate source of homicide statistics[30] and is used in many international studies of homicide.[31] The main reason for WHO being the most accurate source of homicide data is that medical doctors and coroners are trained to determine cause of death.

The International Self-Report Delinquency (ISRD) study, which was carried out in 12 developed countries in the early 1990s, was the first attempt to measure self-reported delinquency at an international level using a standard questionnaire.[32] Because the same questionnaire was used for all subjects, delinquency rates could be compared in a more valid way across countries. Disappointingly, the study has never been repeated, so it is not possible to look at changes over time.

Benefits of Cross-National Research

Are juvenile offenders in the United States more violent than those in Japan? Are delinquents in Western Europe more likely to steal cars? How does Australia's juvenile justice system differ from that of the United States? Knowledge of the nature of juvenile delinquency and how juvenile justice systems operate in other countries is not only beneficial for the concerned citizen, but also important to social scientists and government policy makers. Investigating whether juvenile offenders in the United States are more violent than, say, juveniles in Canada may lead to important discoveries to help explain any difference that exists. These discoveries may in turn be useful to policy makers and lead to action; for example, more funding for aggressive policing tactics to reduce gun violence by juveniles. (See Chapter 13 for examples of police efforts to reduce juvenile gun violence.)

Another value served by cross-national comparisons, whether it is delinquency rates or the treatment of incarcerated juvenile offenders, is to let a country know how well or how poorly it is doing relative to other countries. On the one hand, a poor international rating for the United States on juvenile homicides by an international agency, such as the United Nations, may prompt the U.S. government to take action to address this problem. On the other hand, a good international rating on, say, the legal rights afforded to detained juveniles demonstrates that the United States is on the right track. This, in turn, could lead to other countries making changes to follow the U.S. example.

Other benefits from cross-national comparisons can come from studying low-crime countries.[33] Examining these countries to find out how they maintain low delinquency rates may yield important insights for countries with higher delinquency rates.

According to Erika Fairchild and Harry Dammer, another good reason to make cross-national comparisons is the need to address **transnational** and **international crime** problems.[34] Transnational crimes are those activities that extend into two or more countries and violate the laws of those countries, such as illegal migration, trafficking in body parts, trafficking in illegal drugs and weapons, and theft and trafficking in automobiles.[35] Through the National Institute of Justice's International Center, the United States is playing an important role in addressing transnational crime problems.[36]

International crimes are those that are recognized by international law, such as war crimes.[37] Criminal activities that take place across borders have grown consid-

transnational crime Crime that is carried out across the borders of two or more countries and violates the laws of those countries.

international crime Crime that is punishable under international law.

A CLOSER VIEW
To read more about the globalization of delinquency and crime on InfoTrac College Edition, go to Nikos Passas, "Global Anomie, Dysnomie, and Economic Crime: Hidden Consequences of Neoliberalism and Globalization in Russia and around the World," *Social Justice* 27:16 (Summer 2000).

To read more about the National Institute of Justice's International Center, go to *http://www.ojp.usdoj.gov/nij/ international*
For an up-to-date list of Web links, go to *http://info.wadsworth.com/siegel*

erably in the last two decades. "The end of the Cold War, the collapse of state authority in some countries and regions, and the process of globalization—of trade, finance, communications and information—have all provided an environment in which many criminal organizations find it more profitable and preferable to operate across national borders than confine their activities to one country."[38] This phenomenon has become known as the globalization of delinquency and crime.[39]

The best method of comparing the level of delinquency across countries is to use data that have been collected in a uniform way; for example, using a standard questionnaire that asks young people in different countries the same questions about their involvement in delinquency. At present, the best and most up-to-date source of delinquency rates is police statistics available from individual countries.

German social scientist Christian Pfeiffer examined trends in juvenile crime and violence in 10 European countries and the United States.[40] The 10 European countries were England, Sweden, Germany, the Netherlands, Italy, Austria, France, Denmark, Switzerland, and Poland. Delinquency data were available from police statistics from the mid-1980s to the mid-1990s. Three main findings emerged from the study:

1. Juvenile violence, especially robbery and offenses involving serious bodily harm, increased substantially over this period of time in almost all of the countries.
2. Total juvenile crime, which includes burglary, motor vehicle theft, larceny, and vandalism, increased very little over this period of time, with some countries showing no increase or an actual decrease.
3. Crimes of violence committed by young adults (18–20) or by adults in general have increased far less rapidly since the mid-1980s than have those committed by juveniles, and in some countries they have not increased at all.[41]

What does this international data tell us about the differences in delinquency trends between the United States and similar nations?

Juvenile Violence

The increase in juvenile violence between the mid-1980s and the mid-1990s was greater in most European countries than it was in the United States. (See Table 16.2.) Canada, the other North American country for which data was available to add to this comparison, showed a substantial increase in juvenile violence over this period. Between 1986 and 1995, the rates of all categories of youth violence in Canada increased substantially: homicide, +50 percent; assault, +150 percent; sexual assault, +40 percent; and robbery, +160 percent.[42]

This substantial increase in all violence categories was not the case in all of the European countries, with the increase in juvenile violence rates being largely driven by robbery and offenses involving serious bodily harm.[43] For example, in the Netherlands, increases in the rates of robbery (+297 percent) and violence

JUVENILE VIOLENCE IS A PROBLEM in all parts of the world. Here, two American teens, covering their faces on the tables, sit by their lawyers in the Darmstadt, Germany, state court before hearing their sentence. The teenagers were convicted of murder for dropping stones from a highway overpass onto passing cars. Two women were killed, and four other motorists were injured.

Table 16.2   Juvenile Violence in Europe and North America

Country	Years	Age of Juveniles (years)	Percentage Change in Rate
England	1986–1994	10–16	+53%
Germany	1984–1995	14–17	+150%
Netherlands	1986–1995	12–17	+163
Italy	1986–1993	14–17	+175%
Austria	1991–1995	14–18	+20%
France	1984–1994	10–17	+87%
Denmark	1980–1994	15–17	+146%
Switzerland	1980–1995	15–17	+200%
United States	1985–1994	10–17	+75%
Canada	1986–1995	12–17	+130%

Sources: Rebecca Kong, *Canadian Crime Statistics, 1996* (Ottawa: Canadian Centre for Justice Statistics Juristat, 1997), p. 17, Table 4; Christian Pfeiffer, "Juvenile Crime and Violence in Europe," in Michael Tonry, ed., *Crime and Justice: A Review of Research*, volume 23 (Chicago: University of Chicago Press, 1998), pp. 263–91.

Table 16.3   Juvenile Property Crime in Europe and North America

Country	Years	Age of Juveniles (years)	Percentage Change in Rate
England	1986–1994	10–16	–9%
Germany	1984–1995	14–17	+75%
Netherlands	1985–1995	12–17	+4
Italy	1986–1993	14–17	+140%
Austria	1991–1995	14–18	+31%
France	1974–1992	10–18	+30%
Denmark	1980–1994	15–19	–30%
Switzerland	1980–1995	15–17	0
United States	1985–1994	10–17	+28%
Canada	1986–1995	12–17	+5%

Sources: Rebecca Kong, *Canadian Crime Statistics, 1996* (Ottawa: Canadian Centre for Justice Statistics Juristat, 1997), p. 17, Table 4; Christian Pfeiffer, "Juvenile Crime and Violence in Europe," in Michael Tonry, ed., *Crime and Justice: A Review of Research*, volume 23 (Chicago: University of Chicago Press, 1998), pp. 263–91.

against the person (+123 percent) were the driving forces behind the substantial increase in juvenile violence.[44] Russia too has experienced a significant increase in juvenile violence over this period of time.[45]

Juvenile Property Crime

Juvenile property crime rates (including burglary, motor vehicle theft, larceny, and vandalism) increased very little in Europe and North America from the mid-1980s to the mid-1990s, and in the case of England, Denmark, and Switzerland, rates decreased or did not change at all (Table 16.3). On the other hand, like juvenile violence, property crime rates increased substantially in two countries during this period of time: Germany with a 75 percent increase and Italy with a 140 percent increase. It is not altogether clear why total juvenile crime rates in these two countries increased as much as this. Perhaps the factors that were driving the increases in juvenile violence in these countries were also having an effect on less serious forms of delinquency, such as theft, burglary, and motor vehicle theft.

Juvenile Drug Use

The first comparative study of teenage drug use in the United States and Europe found that 1 in 4 American students compared to 1 in 10 European students had used illicit drugs over their lifetime.[46] Comparisons across European countries of the percentage of students who have ever used illicit drugs are just as striking, ranging from a low of 2 percent in Finland and Cyprus to a high of 12 percent in the United Kingdom (Figure 16.1). Carried out in conjunction with the Council of Europe and the University of Michigan's "Monitoring the Future" project, about 14,000 10th-grade students in the United States and approximately 95,000 10th-grade students in 30 European countries responded to the survey.

Although American students are more likely to use marijuana and other illicit drugs over their lifetime, European students are more likely to smoke cigarettes and use alcohol in the previous month. In the United States, 40 percent of students report any alcohol use in the previous month, while in Denmark, the country with the highest rate, 85 percent of students report using alcohol in the previous month. Of the 31 countries, the United States has the second lowest rate of teenage alcohol use and the third lowest rate of cigarette smoking.[47]

Past studies of teenage drug use in Europe show rates climbing (between 1995 and 1999), particularly in Eastern European countries,[48] while in the United States, the rate of teenage drug use held steady in 2000, but declined from the recent peak years of 1996 and 1997.

A CLOSER VIEW
To read more about delinquency in Europe on InfoTrac College Edition, go to Estrella Romero, Jorge Sobral, M. Angeles Luengo, and Jose A. Marzoa, "Values and Antisocial Behavior among Spanish Adolescents," *Journal of Genetic Psychology* 162:20 (March 2001).

Conclusion: What Do the Trends Tell Us?

Throughout the world, juvenile delinquency is a serious problem. Although there are many differences in the nature and character of juvenile delinquency in the different regions and countries of the world, there are a number of common threads. One is that juveniles account for a disproportionate amount of total crime. A second is the presence of violent youth gangs. The most important commonality is that a good number of countries report that juvenile delinquency, especially violence, is much higher in recent years than it was a decade ago. The question of greatest interest is why has this occurred?

As noted above, all countries share an explosive mix of racial tension, poverty, envy, drug abuse, broken families, unemployment, and alienation. Some countries are also feeling the impacts of rapid social and economic change. The end of apartheid in South Africa has left many broken promises for its youth, with access to education being severely limited and unemployment at an all-time high. The transition from communism to democracy in many Eastern European countries has had profound effects. For example, neighboring countries have had to cope with a tremendous increase in immigrant youth populations in search of jobs and better lives, but because of difficulties in finding jobs and social isolation from family and friends, many of these youths turn to delinquency. Over the same period of time in the United States, rates of juvenile violence increased, but not as much as in most European countries. One possible explanation for this is that the United States did not experience some of the rapid social and economic changes that took place in Europe.

To read more about delinquency across countries and what is being done to prevent it, go to *http://www.crime-prevention-intl. org/english/* For an up-to-date list of Web links, go to *http://info.wadsworth.com/siegel*

Figure 16.1

Lifetime Teenage Illicit Drug Use (Other Than Marijuana) in the United States and Europe
Source: Thor Bjarnason, "European School Survey Project on Alcohol and Drugs," press release issued by the State University of New York at Albany, 20 February 2001, Figure 8.

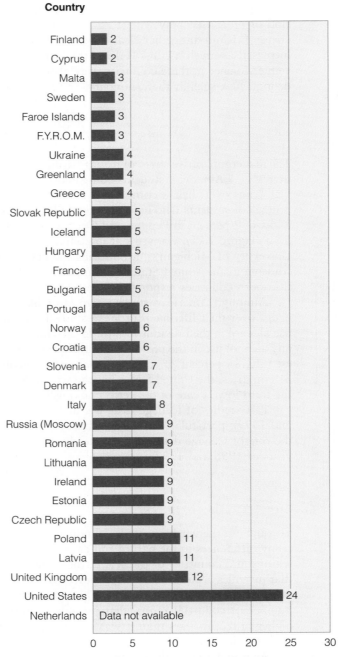

Country

Country	
Finland	2
Cyprus	2
Malta	3
Sweden	3
Faroe Islands	3
F.Y.R.O.M.	3
Ukraine	4
Greenland	4
Greece	4
Slovak Republic	5
Iceland	5
Hungary	5
France	5
Bulgaria	5
Portugal	6
Norway	6
Croatia	6
Slovenia	7
Denmark	7
Italy	8
Russia (Moscow)	9
Romania	9
Lithuania	9
Ireland	9
Estonia	9
Czech Republic	9
Poland	11
Latvia	11
United Kingdom	12
United States	24
Netherlands	Data not available

Percentage of respondents who had used illicit drugs over their lifetime

It is very likely that these trends in delinquency will continue unless governments are willing to tackle the many causal factors that give rise to juvenile delinquency. In some cases, this will mean countries working together to control the flow of immigration and providing assistance to new populations. In other cases, this will mean investing greater resources in education, employment training programs, and assistance programs for unemployed young people. It will also be important for countries to have effective and fair juvenile justice systems. In the next section we look at juvenile justice systems in different countries.

Juvenile Justice Systems across Countries

developing countries Recognized by the U.N. as countries that are showing signs of improved economic growth and are making the transition from low income to high income.

least developed countries Recognized by the U.N. as being the poorest countries in the world and suffering from long-term barriers to economic growth.

Many countries in the world have formal juvenile justice systems, but many do not. The presence of juvenile justice systems is strongly associated with a country's level of development; that is, developed or industrialized countries all have juvenile justice systems, while a smaller number of **developing** or **least developed countries** have juvenile justice systems. Part of the reason for countries not having separate justice systems to deal with juvenile delinquency and adult crime is the lack of importance placed on the special needs of juveniles who come in conflict with the law. Another reason is that developing and least developed countries have fewer financial resources to spend on a juvenile justice system, especially the building of separate correctional facilities.

In an effort to get more countries around the world to develop juvenile justice systems and improve the administration of juvenile justice, the United Nations, in 1985, adopted the "Standard Minimum Rules for the Administration of Juvenile Justice" (Exhibit 16.1). Also known as the "Beijing Rules" of juvenile justice because they were developed at a meeting in Beijing, these rules set out minimum standards for countries to follow in the administration of juvenile justice.[49]

There are many features of juvenile justice that are of interest to compare across countries. This section looks at the key features of juvenile justice systems in a number of developed countries: specialized police services for juveniles, age of criminal responsibility, presence of juvenile court, transfers to adult court, sentencing, treatment of incarcerated juveniles, and aftercare services.

Juvenile Policing

Specialized policing services for juveniles is an important but relatively recent addition to the repertoire of services offered by juvenile justice systems in many developed countries. The number of police officers assigned to juvenile work has increased in recent years. The International Association of Chiefs of Police found that approximately 500 departments, of the 1,400 surveyed in 1960, had juvenile units. By 1970, the number of police departments with a juvenile specialist doubled.[50] Few developing or least developed countries have police officers trained specifically to deal with juvenile offenders.

In the United States, juvenile officers operate either as specialists within a police department or as part of the juvenile unit of a police department. Their role is similar to that of officers working with adult offenders: To intervene if the actions of a citizen produce public danger or disorder. (See Chapter 13 for more information on juvenile policing in the United States.) In Austria an innovative delinquency prevention project involves specially trained police to deal with violent juvenile gangs. The gang unit works to establish an open dialogue with juvenile gangs to help get leaders of opposing gangs to meet and work out their conflicts in a nonviolent way. A four-year assessment of the program found that it was extremely successful in reducing juvenile violence.[51]

Canada has also developed special juvenile gang units as part of police departments. Juvenile gang units exist in all of the police departments of the biggest Canadian cities, such as Montreal, Toronto, Vancouver, and Halifax, as well as in many medium-sized and smaller cities and towns.[52] In Japan, police boxes (Koban) in urban areas and police houses (Chuzaisho) in rural areas have special officers who deal with juvenile delinquency. Because of the sheer number of these police stations in the country—about 6,500 Kobans and 8,700 Chuzaishos—the police have a very good understanding of conditions that might give rise to juvenile delinquency and violence problems in the community. This knowledge assists them in intervening before prob-

These rules were adopted by the U.N. General Assembly on November 29, 1985, on the recommendation of the Seventh U.N. Congress on the Prevention of Crime and the Treatment of Offenders (resolution 40/33).

Part 1: General Principles

Member states shall seek to further the well-being of juveniles and their families.

Member states shall try to develop conditions to ensure meaningful lives in the community for juveniles.

Sufficient attention should be given to positive measures involving mobilization of resources, such as the family, volunteers and community groups, to promote the well-being of juveniles.

Juvenile justice shall be an integral part of the national development process of each country.

In legal systems recognizing the concept of an age of criminal responsibility for juveniles, such an age level shall not be fixed too low, bearing in mind emotional, mental and physical maturity.

Any reaction by the juvenile justice system to juvenile offenders shall be in proportion to both the offenders and the offense.

Appropriate scope for the exercise of discretionary powers shall be allowed at all stages of legal processing affecting juveniles.

Efforts shall be made to ensure sufficient accountability at all stages in the exercise of such discretion.

Basic procedural safeguards, such as the presumption of innocence, the right to be notified of charges, the right to remain silent, the right to counsel, the right to the presence of a parent or guardian, the right to confront and cross-examine witnesses and the right to appeal, shall be guaranteed at all stages of proceedings.

The juvenile's right to privacy shall be respected at all stages.

Part 2: Investigation and Prosecution

Upon the apprehension of a juvenile, parents or guardians shall be notified as soon as possible.

Consideration shall be given to dealing with juvenile offenders without resort to trial, and any diversion to appropriate community or other services shall require consent of the juvenile or parents.

Part 3: Adjudication and Disposition

The placement of a juvenile in an institution shall always be a disposition of last resort and for the minimum necessary period.

Part 4: Non-Institutional Treatment

Efforts shall be made to provide necessary assistance, such as lodging, education, vocational training and employment, to facilitate the rehabilitation process.

Part 5: Institutional Treatment

Juveniles in institutions shall be kept separate from adults, and special attention shall be used to the greatest extent possible.

Part 6: Aftercare

Efforts shall be made to provide semi-institutional arrangements, such as halfway houses, educational homes and daytime training centers, to assist juveniles in their reintegration into society.

Source: Abridged from United Nations, *The United Nations and Crime Prevention: Seeking Security and Justice for All* (New York: United Nations, 1996), pp. 78–82.

lems get out of control. In addition to juvenile police officers, there is a police-established system of volunteers to aid the police in dealing with juvenile delinquency. There are three types of voluntary systems:

- Guidance volunteer
- Police helper for juveniles
- Instructors for juveniles

Guidance volunteers work with the police in providing advice to young people about the dangers of being involved in gangs or using drugs; they also provide some counseling services to young people in trouble with the law. Police helpers are mostly retired police officers in charge of dispersing large groups of juvenile delinquents, such as gangs. They are not a riot squad, but simply assist the police in dealing with large groups of young people who may be looking for trouble or are involved in delinquent acts. Instructors are authorized by the 1985 Law on Regulation of Business Affecting Public Morals to protect juveniles from unsafe environments; that is, where young people are being abused or neglected.[53] In many ways, these individuals act as child or juvenile protection agents.

Age of Criminal Responsibility: Minimum and Maximum

Across the world there is a great deal of variation in the minimum age a person can be held responsible for his or her criminal actions, ranging from a low of 6 years in Sri Lanka to a high of under 21 years in Indonesia. In the majority of countries across the world, full adult criminal responsibility begins at age 18 years or older.[54] This general pattern is the same for the developed countries listed in Table 16.4. Switzerland has the lowest minimum age of criminal responsibility at 7 years, and Belgium has the highest at 16–18 years. Interestingly, in the United States, 36 states have no set minimum age that a young person can be held criminally responsible. By common law, states may use 7 years as the minimum, but in practice children under the age of 10 are rarely brought before a juvenile court.[55]

In those countries in which the minimum age is quite high, such as Belgium (16 to 18 years), Denmark (15 years), or Sweden (15 years), what happens to young people below the minimum age who commit delinquent acts? Doing nothing is not an option in any of the developed countries. Instead, these young people are dealt with under various forms of child or social welfare or child protection legislation. Under these laws young people may be placed in state-run homes, undergo counseling, or report to a social worker on a regular basis.

In some countries the minimum age can be lowered. This is typically done when the offense is very serious; for example, in New Zealand, the minimum age is 14, but if the offense is murder or manslaughter, the minimum age becomes 10. In Romania, the minimum age can be dropped from 16 to 14 if the young person is capable of understanding right from wrong.[56]

Presence of Juvenile Court

The majority of the developed countries have courts specifically for juveniles (Table 16.4), and they operate pretrial diversion programs. (See the Policy and Practice box entitled "Precourt Diversion Programs around the World.") Only Denmark, Russia, and Sweden do not have juvenile courts. In each of these countries, juveniles appear before regular adult criminal courts. However, in Denmark, the Administration of Justice Act provides special rights for juveniles who appear in court; for example, closing the proceedings to the public and press.[57] Swedish courts also try to protect the identity of juvenile offenders if the court believes that publicity may be harmful to the juvenile.[58] In Russia too there are some protections afforded the juvenile: Age must be taken into account as a mitigating factor, the juvenile's living conditions must be considered, and whether or not the offense was committed with an adult must be considered.[59]

Transfers to Adult Court

Transfers of juvenile offenders to adult court are a widely accepted practice in developed countries (Table 16.4). In all of the countries in which transfers are allowed, the main criterion is that the offense was of a very serious or violent nature. Other criteria can include the youth's record of delinquency and the use of weapons. But in these cases, the evidence must be particularly strong for a transfer to take place.

In Canada, there are a few twists to transferring youths to adult court. There, the minimum age of criminal responsibility is 12 years, but transfers to adult court can only be made if the youth is 14 years or older. If the youth is then convicted in adult court, he or she cannot be subject to an adult sentence—25 years in the case of murder—until the age of 16, but will instead face the possibility of a maximum sentence of 10 years.[60] So it is conceivable that a 15-year-old convicted of murder in Canada could receive a sentence of 10 years or less. In other developed countries like Austria, France, Hungary, Italy, and Switzerland, transfers of juveniles to adult court are not permissible.

Table 16.4 International Comparisons of Juvenile Justice Systems

Country	Minimum Age of Criminal Responsibility	Age of Adult Criminal Responsibility	Court That Handles Juveniles	Transfer to Adult Court Allowable?	Maximum Length of Sentence for a Juvenile	Separation of Incarcerated Juveniles from Adults
Australia	10*	16–17**	Children's courts	Yes, for serious felonies	2–7 years	Not mandatory, generally separated in practice
Austria	14	19	Special sections in local and regional courts; youth courts	No	Half of adult sentence	Yes
Belgium	16–18	18	Special juvenile courts	Yes	No juvenile incarcerations in juvenile court	Not mandatory, generally separated in practice
Canada	12	18	Youth courts	Yes	10 years	Yes
Denmark	15	18	No juvenile court	N/A	8 years	Yes
England	10	18	Youth courts	Yes	2 years	Yes
France	13 (unofficial)	18	Children's tribunals; youth courts of assizes	No	Half of adult sentence	Yes
Germany	14	18	Single sitting judge; juvenile court; juvenile chamber	Yes	10 years	Yes
Hungary	14	18	Special sections of regular court	No	15 years	Yes
Italy	14	18	Separate juvenile courts	No	One-third adult sentence	Yes
Japan	14	20	Family courts	Yes	Lifetime sentence	Yes
The Netherlands	12	18	Special juvenile courts	Yes	Lifetime sentence	Yes
New Zealand	14; 10 for murder and manslaughter	18	Youth courts	Yes	No juvenile incarcerations in youth court	No (some exceptions)
Russia	16; 14 for certain crimes	18	No juvenile court	N/A	10 years	Yes
Sweden	15	18	No juvenile court	N/A	No lifetime sentence	Yes
Switzerland	7	18	Special juvenile courts and/or juvenile prosecutors	No	One year	Yes
United States	6–10 for 14 states; 36 other states have no set minimum but may use age 7	15 for 3 states; 16 for 10 states; 17 for 37 states	Juvenile courts	Yes	Lifetime, death penalty sentences	Yes

Notes: *The lower age limit is 7 in Tasmania; ** Age of full criminal responsibility differs by state; N/A = not available.

Sources: Adapted from Joan McCord, Cathy Spatz Widom, and Nancy Crowell, eds., *Juvenile Crime, Juvenile Justice.* Panel on Juvenile Crime: Prevention, Treatment, and Control (Washington, DC: National Academy Press, 2001), pp. 18–20, table 1-1. Canadian data adapted from Brandon C. Welsh and Mark H. Irving, "Crime and Punishment in Canada, 1981–1999," in David P. Farrington and Michael Tonry, eds., *Cross-National Studies in Crime and Justice. Crime and Justice: A Review of Research* (Chicago: University of Chicago Press, 2001). U.S. data adapted from Janet K. Wig, "Legal Issues," in Rolf Loeber and David P. Farrington, eds., *Child Delinquents: Development, Intervention, and Service Needs* (Thousand Oaks, CA: Sage, 2001), p. 324.

Precourt Diversion Programs around the World

Keeping youths who have become involved in minor delinquent acts from being formally processed through the juvenile justice system is a top priority of many countries around the world. This is because they recognize the need to protect young people against the stigma and labeling that can occur from being "processed" through a juvenile court. In many ways, entering the juvenile justice system is viewed as a last resort to dealing with juvenile delinquency. Informal processing or precourt diversion programs, which vary from country to country, also represent a cost savings from the expense of paying for juvenile court judges, prosecutors, public defenders, and other justice personnel and administrative costs. These alternative approaches are more often used in European, particularly Western European, countries than in the United States. These programs are also very popular in Australia and New Zealand. Part of the reason for the greater use of these programs outside of the United States is that these countries are less punitive toward juvenile offenders than the United States. What follows are profiles of the use of precourt diversion programs in the Netherlands, France, and Australia.

Netherlands

In response to a sharp rise in juvenile vandalism and its associated costs, the government of the Netherlands implemented a precourt diversion program called HALT, or *Het Alternatief,* which means "stop" in Dutch. Begun in the 1970s in the city of Rotterdam, the program quickly spread throughout the country and is now a national program in 60 locations. Accountability and assistance are at the center of the program. Young people aged 12–18 years caught for the first or second time committing an act of vandalism are offered the chance to avoid formal prosecution by participating in the program. Juveniles who go through the program must repair the vandalism damage they have caused, and counselors work with the young people to assist them with employment, housing, and education issues. If the program is successfully completed, police charges are dropped and the case is dismissed, and in those cases that are not successful, an official report is sent to the prosecutor. An evaluation of the program in three cities (Rotterdam, Eindoven, and Dordrecht) found the program to be very effective in reducing future acts of vandalism: Juvenile offenders in the treatment group were 63 percent less likely to be rearrested versus a comparison group that were 25 percent less likely to be rearrested.

France

Maisons de justice, or community justice centers, is one of the most well known pretrial diversion programs for juvenile offenders in France. Set up by the Ministry of Justice and community associations across the country, the centers address minor offenses and other legal problems through alternative justice approaches. One of these alternative approaches is victim-offender mediation, whereby a trained staff member works with the offender, the victim, and sometimes the victim's family to settle a dispute without the need for formal justice proceedings. An apology or an order of restitution or compensation is commonly reached as part of victim-offender mediation. Although there has been no formal evaluation of community justice centers, they are widely credited as helping to relieve some of the backlog in the courts and to settle cases much faster than traditional means.

Australia

Precourt diversion programs have gone through extensive changes in Australia in recent years. Up to the early 1990s, there were two types of juvenile diversion programs: police cautions, which involve the police more or less warning offenders that the next time they are caught, formal action will be taken; and children's panels, made up of police and social workers who admonish a young person for his or her delinquent behavior. Today, precourt diversion programs for juvenile offenders include an expanded use of police cautions and the addition of restorative justice–based programs known as "family group conferences." Family group conferences (FGCs) bring together the juvenile offender and his or her family, the victim, and a professional coordinator to discuss the problem caused by the juvenile offender and to agree on a mutually acceptable resolution that will benefit all parties and the wider community. FGCs attempt to provide the victim with restoration and restitution and the offender with rehabilitation and reintegration. An evaluation of an FGC program in South Australia showed that the overwhelming majority of offenders complied with the program, and more than 9 out of 10 victims were pleased with the process of FGCs and the resulting resolutions.

Critical Thinking

1. What are some of the problems with precourt diversion programs?
2. Should these programs also be used for serious and violent juvenile offenders? Explain.

InfoTrac College Edition Research

 To read more about pretrial diversion programs for juvenile offenders, use *juvenile-corrections* as a key term.

Sources: Irvin Waller and Brandon C. Welsh, "International Trends in Crime Prevention: Cost-Effective Ways to Reduce Victimization," in Graeme Newman, ed., *Global Report on Crime and Justice* (New York: Oxford University Press, 1999); Lynn Atkinson, "Juvenile Justice in Australia," in John A. Winterdyk, ed., *Juvenile Justice Systems: International Perspectives* (Toronto: Canadian Scholars' Press, 1997); Josine Junger-Tas, "Juvenile Delinquency and Juvenile Justice in the Netherlands," in John A. Winterdyk, ed., *Juvenile Justice Systems: International Perspectives* (Toronto: Canadian Scholars' Press, 1997).

Sentencing Policies

The maximum sentence length for juvenile offenders varies considerably across developed countries (Table 16.4). In Belgium and New Zealand there can be no sentence of incarceration for youths that appear before juvenile court; instead, youths must be transferred to adult court to receive custodial sentences. Some countries, such as Austria, France, and Italy, specify that sentences can only be for one-half or one-third of what an adult would receive for a similar offense. In Italy, juveniles who are sentenced to custody can receive up to one-third of the same sentence for adults but, unlike adults, can be conditionally released at any stage of the sentence regardless of the amount of time spent in custody.[61]

The country with the harshest sentence for juvenile offenders is the United States; here, juvenile offenders can be sentenced to death. Japan and the Netherlands have the next harshest sentences for juvenile offenders: lifetime sentences. In Japan, a life sentence may mean spending between 10 and 15 years in a correctional facility with or without forced labor, while in the Netherlands, a life sentence may mean serving as much as 20 years.[62] Switzerland, on the other hand, is the most lenient country: One year is the longest period of time that a juvenile offender can be sentenced to custody, and transfers to adult court are not allowed.

A CLOSER VIEW
To read more about alternative treatment approaches to incarcerating juveniles in Hong Kong on InfoTrac College Edition, go to Jon Vagg, "Delinquency and Shame: Data from Hong Kong," *British Journal of Criminology* 38:247 (Spring 1998).

Incarcerated Juveniles

The separation of juveniles from adults in correctional facilities is an important rule under the U.N.'s "Standard Minimum Rules for the Administration of Juvenile Justice" because juveniles are susceptible to negative influences of more seasoned and crime-prone adult offenders. In many ways, juvenile offenders become the apprentices of adult offenders, learning about new techniques to commit delinquent and criminal acts. Another reason for separating adults and juveniles in correctional institutions is for the physical safety of juveniles. With the average juvenile offender having less physical strength than the average adult offender, adults often prey upon juveniles.

In almost all of the developed countries, incarcerated juveniles are kept separate from incarcerated adults. In Australia and Belgium, separate incarceration is not mandatory, but in practice this is generally done. In New Zealand, the practice differs from all of the other countries. Incarcerated juveniles are not separated from incarcerated adults. But there are a few exceptions. For example, a juvenile offender that has been transferred to adult court and sentenced to a term of imprisonment may be held at the discretion of the Director General of Social Welfare and the Secretary for Justice in a social welfare facility until age 17. The reason for the government generally not housing juvenile and adult inmates in separate facilities is that there are no separate correctional facilities for juvenile offenders. The government claims that the country is too small and there are too few juvenile inmates to justify building a separate correctional facility.[63]

To read more about juvenile justice in Australia, go to *http://www.aic.gov.au/* For an up-to-date list of Web links, go to *http://info.wadsworth.com/siegel*

Aftercare

When juveniles are released from an institution, they may be placed in an aftercare program of some kind, rather than simply returned to the community without transitional assistance. This transitional assistance can take the form of halfway houses, educational homes, and daytime training centers. The U.N.'s "Standard Minimum Rules for the Administration of Juvenile Justice" recommends that all countries implement aftercare programs to help juveniles prepare for their return to the community.

All developed countries provide juveniles with a wide range of aftercare programs. In Hong Kong, now part of the People's Republic of China, supervision orders are the most commonly used aftercare program to help juvenile offenders make a successful transition from the correctional institution to their community. Juveniles are first granted early release from a correctional facility, with the provision that they must abide by a number of conditions. These conditions differ according to the nature of the delinquent act they committed, but almost always involve regular visits with their parole officer. Some juveniles will have to attend drug addiction treatment centers.[64]

In Canada, the replacement of the Young Offenders Act with the Youth Criminal Justice Act in 2002 greatly expanded aftercare programs for juvenile offenders. For example, it is now mandatory that all periods of time spent in an institution be followed by a period of intensive supervision in the community. The length of time of supervision is also stipulated in the law: It must be no less than half the time spent in custody. Thus, a juvenile offender who spends 12 months in an institution must then spend 6 months in intensive supervision while in the community. Under the old law, there were no requirements for supervision following a custodial sentence. Another important change to the juvenile aftercare system introduced by the new law is that there are a number of conditions, both mandatory and optional, that the judge can impose on the youth as part of supervision orders. Mandatory conditions include keeping the peace and reporting to authorities. Optional conditions include attending school, getting a job, adhering to a curfew, abstaining from alcohol and drugs, and not associating with gang members.[65]

In many developed countries, juvenile offenders are eligible for early release or parole much earlier than adult offenders sentenced to the same amount of time in institutions. In Germany, for example, a juvenile may be released to the community upon serving one-third of his or her sentence, while an adult must serve at least half of the sentence before being paroled.[66]

The next section profiles the juvenile justice system in England. It looks at the many different stages that juveniles may face as they go through the system, from arrest through sentencing. Comparisons are made with the U.S. juvenile justice system. One reason for making England the subject of this profile is that like the United States, it is a highly developed industrialized country and so comparisons are more meaningful. Another reason is the long-standing shared history between the two countries: Much of U.S. common law is derived from England.

A Profile of Juvenile Justice in England

In 1908 England passed legislation that established for the first time that young offenders were to be treated separately from adult offenders; the law was known as the Children Act. Like the United States, England adheres to the *parens patriae* treatment philosophy, which recognizes that youth are in need of special consideration and assistance. The Children Act was founded on three main principles:

1. Juvenile offenders should be kept *separate* from adult criminals and should receive *treatment* differentiated to suit their special needs.
2. Parents should be made more responsible for the wrongdoing of their children.
3. The imprisonment of juveniles should be abolished.[67]

Many changes have since taken place in juvenile justice in England. The following discussion of the different stages that juveniles may face as they go through the system reflects the way things are today. (See Figure 16.2.)

Apprehension and Charge

The process of juvenile justice begins when police apprehend and charge a young person suspected of committing a delinquent act. The police are not the only ones involved at this stage. Parents or guardians of the young person are contacted and requested to attend the police station. If they cannot attend, social workers may offer

Parents are expected to attend the police station. If they do not, social workers may intervene following an arrest to act as an "appropriate adult" during police interviews to protect the rights of young people.

Apprehension and charge

The police apprehend or have reported to them young people suspected of committing criminal offenses.

No national data is available on the numbers of such referrals or apprehensions.

Social workers or probation officers may intervene to try to secure the release of a young person on bail.

Intervention may include the provision of "bail support" (i.e., temporary accommodation and/or short-term supervision).

Bail

Most young offenders who are arrested are bailed by the police (i.e., they return home).

Some young people are remanded to custody (national facilities: age 15+ only) or local authority accommodation, which may be secure accommodation (local facilities).

Most local areas have established multiagency diversion panels to advise the police whether a formal prosecution is necessary.

Probation officers, social workers, and education welfare officers (but not parents or victims) are commonly involved in multiagency diversion panels.

Diversion

The police decide whether to prosecute or to divert a young person from prosecution. Over 90% of known 10–13-year-old offenders are formally cautioned by the police. Over 60% of known 14–17-year-old offenders are formally cautioned.

Young people in need (including offenders) may be referred to social workers as welfare cases. Most such young people are dealt with under a voluntary agreement between the family and the SSD, but some cases may be taken to the family proceedings court.

Prosecution

Instead of a formal caution, a young person may be given an "informal warning" or "no further action" may be taken. No national data is available on the use of these other disposals.

Parents are required to attend the youth court.

The probation service or the social services department may be asked to complete a Presentence Report.

Youth court

If (and only if) the police decide it would be right to prosecute, papers are passed to the Crown Prosecution Service (CPS). Of those young people referred to the CPS by the police for prosecution, over 25% are discontinued (on evidential insufficiency or public interest grounds).

Many young people appear in court on two or three occasions before sentence. Between court appearances, the young person may be bailed or remanded to local authority accommodation or custody (see above).

Legal representation is allowed, and is standard practice in more serious cases.

Sentence

Community Sentences

Custodial sentences
- Detention in a young offender institution
- 15 years+ only
- Secure Training Orders
- 12–14 year olds

Probation services
- Probation Orders*
- Supervision Orders*
- Community Service Orders
- Combination Orders
- 16–17 year olds

Social Services Department (SSD)
- Supervision Orders*
- 10–17 year olds

Other bodies
- Attendance Centers
- 10–17 year olds
- Curfew Orders
- 16–17 year olds

Other sentences
- Fines
- Absolute or conditional discharge
- Bind Over
- Compensation
- 10–17 year olds

*May contain additional specified requirements.

Figure 16.2
The Juvenile Justice System in England
Source: Anthony E. Bottoms, Kevin Haines, and David O'Mahony, "England and Wales," in Jill Mehlbye and Lode Walgrave, eds., *Confronting Youth in Europe: Juvenile Crime and Juvenile Justice* (Copenhagen: AKF, 1998), as cited in Loraine Gelsthorpe and Mark Fenwick, "Comparative Juvenile Justice: England and Wales," in John Winterdyk, ed., *Juvenile Justice Systems: International Perspectives* (Toronto: Canadian Scholars' Press, 1997), p. 108, figure 4.3.

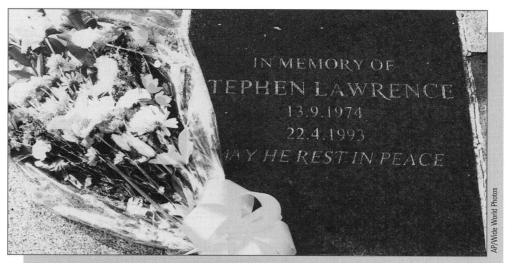

ENGLAND'S JUVENILE JUSTICE SYSTEM is facing mounting pressure to deal with an increase in the number of serious juvenile crimes, such as murder and hate crimes. Here, flowers rest on the memorial plaque to the black teenager, Stephen Lawrence, killed in 1993 in London by members of a racist group. The plaque is near the spot where Lawrence died.

assistance to the juvenile once an arrest has been made. The role of social workers at this stage is to act as an "appropriate adult" to help safeguard the legal rights of the juvenile. Alternatively, the juvenile may be represented by a defense attorney. The right to have legal representation exists throughout all stages of the juvenile justice system.[68] This is the same as in the U.S. juvenile justice system.

Bail

Once a decision has been made by the police to charge the juvenile, a bail hearing must take place to determine whether the juvenile can go home or be remanded in custody. This differs from the practice in the United States, where relatively few juveniles hold the right to be released on bail; in fact, most states refuse juveniles the right to bail. This is because detention is seen as rehabilitative, not punitive, and statutory provisions allow juveniles to be released into the custody of their parents. (See Chapter 14 for more information on bail for juveniles in the United States.)

In England, most juvenile offenders who are arrested are granted bail. For those who are denied bail, there are two options for where they will be held. National custody facilities can be used for juveniles 15 years and older, or local authority (local government) facilities may be used. For juveniles without legal representation, social workers or probation officers may assist the juvenile to be released on bail.

Precourt Diversion

Police "cautions"—the police issuing a warning to a young person involved or suspected of being involved in a delinquent act—is by far the most widely used and important precourt diversion measure in England. Begun in the 1970s, police cautions quickly became an essential component of the juvenile justice system. Although important administratively, so as to avoid the youth courts from becoming backlogged, police cautions were designed first and foremost with the best interests of the young person in mind: "Prosecution should not occur unless it was 'absolutely necessary' or as 'a last resort' and that the prosecution of first-time offenders where the offence was not serious was unlikely to be 'justifiable' unless there were 'exceptional circumstances.' Prosecution was to be regarded as a 'severe step.'"[69]

Between 1980 and 1990, the proportion of 16-year-old males given formal cautions for indictable offenses (the equivalent of felony offenses) increased from 34 percent to 69 percent, and for 10- to 13-year-old males, the proportions were even higher: 65 percent and 90 percent, respectively.[70] This trend has changed very little in more recent years.

Instead of formal cautions the police may issue "informal warnings" or "no further action" to a suspected juvenile delinquent. These involve the police merely making a verbal admonition. They may go something like this: "I want you to behave properly from now on and do not get yourself involved in anything that requires us to bring you down to the station." These are not recorded by police and, therefore, cannot be used in court.

In the United States, police do not use a system of formal or other cautions per se; instead, they must rely on their discretionary authority. (See Chapter 13 for more details.) Upon the arrest of a juvenile, the police have the following options: refer to juvenile court; handle informally and release; refer to criminal court; refer to welfare; or refer to another police department. It is estimated that 30 percent of all juvenile arrests are handled informally within the police department or are referred to a community service agency.

Prosecution

In England the prosecution of a juvenile offender is the mandate of the **Crown Prosecution Service**. The CPS is a national agency established by statute in 1985. It is headed by the director of public prosecutions, who is accountable to the attorney general.[71] In the United States, each jurisdiction has its own prosecuting attorney who oversees public prosecutions; with England having a central government system (there are no states), the reporting structure is somewhat different.

Importantly, in England a prosecution can only take place once the police have recommended to the CPS that it be done. This differs slightly from the practice in the United States in that the prosecutor has the power either to initiate or discontinue allegations against a juvenile. In England the prosecutor does, however, have the right to dismiss a case (allegation), and this is done in more than 25 percent of the cases that the police recommend to the CPS. There are two reasons that a prosecutor may dismiss a case: (1) There is insufficient evidence, or (2) it is not in the public interest. The latter is done when it is felt that the harm to the offender that comes from prosecuting him or her will outweigh any benefit to society from doing so. In the event that the prosecution dismisses a case because it is not in the public interest, the prosecution may recommend to the police that they issue a formal caution.[72]

Youth Court

Like the United States and most other developed countries, England has a special court that handles juveniles; it is called a youth court. Even before the commencement of trial a juvenile may have already had a number of hearings before youth court, such as a bail hearing or a hearing on transfer to adult court. In most instances, trials of juveniles are presided over by a three-member panel of youth court lay magistrates or judges. In urban areas it is common for a trial to be presided over by a single professional or more qualified judge. Juries are not used in English youth courts. The lay or nonprofessional youth court judges are elected to a three-year term by and from the court district in which they presently serve. These judges receive special training in the juvenile offender laws. During trials they are often assisted by a legally trained court clerk.[73]

In the United States only one juvenile court judge presides over a trial in the juvenile courtroom. Judges are assisted by court clerks, but unlike in England, court clerks in the United States rarely have law degrees and do not advise judges on legal matters. In the United States, juvenile court judges are either elected or appointed to that position, but when they are elected, it is by the public, not their fellow judges, as in England. In the United States, trial by jury in a juvenile court is seldom used; the majority of states do not allow for it.

Social workers and probation officers are other important actors in the English juvenile courtroom. Once a finding of guilt has been rendered, either party may be asked by the court to prepare a presentence report to assist the judge in sentencing. This is similar to a predisposition report in the U.S. juvenile justice system. As in the United States, plea bargaining is allowed for juveniles in England and is used extensively.

As in the United States, juveniles in England can be transferred to adult court—what is referred to as **Crown Court**. A juvenile can be transferred to Crown Court for two main reasons: (1) The juvenile is charged with a heinous crime, such as murder, or (2) the juvenile is charged with a serious crime in conjunction with an adult.[74]

Crown Court In England, the criminal court that deals with adult offenders or juveniles who have been transferred from youth court.

Sentencing

Once the juvenile has been convicted, the youth court judge passes sentence, either immediately following conviction or at a special hearing a short time later. As in the United States, sentences for juvenile offenders are much more punitive in England today than they were 10 or 20 years ago. In the early 1980s, England changed its approach to the sentencing of juvenile offenders dramatically, moving away from a focus on institutional placements toward community-based sanctions. The murder of James Bulger by two 10-year-olds and an upsurge of juvenile violence in the country led to the passage of the Criminal Justice and Public Order Act in 1994. This made incarceration of juvenile offenders the preferred choice once again; it also increased the maximum sentence length and made it easier for very young juvenile offenders to be placed in correctional facilities. This punitive approach to dealing with juvenile offending, especially serious and violent juvenile offending, was continued with the passage of the Crime and Disorder Act in 1998.

As shown in Figure 16.2, a wide range of sentencing options is available to the youth court judge, including custodial sentences, community sentences, and a general category of other sentences, which includes fines and compensation. Interestingly, boot camps modeled on the U.S. experience have received some interest in England, with one being introduced on a demonstration basis. The program showed favorable results, but public support for more boot camps was unfavorable, and the program was shut down.

England's punitive approach to juvenile offending is somewhat tempered by the availability of a wide range of community sentences like probation and aftercare services. For example, attendance center orders require juvenile offenders to report to a specified place in the community once a week for a range of activities, including recreation, social skills training, and vocational skills training. There are also community service orders, which require juvenile offenders to perform various work-related activities in the community, and combination orders that combine community service with increased supervision.[75]

In recent years, many developed countries have taken measures to "get tough" on juvenile offending. In some cases, this is being done because of a real increase in delinquency, particularly violence. In other cases, this is being done because of a perceived increase in delinquency coupled with a heightened level of public and political pressure. While more punitive juvenile justice systems seem to be the future for many countries, these countries are also making concerted efforts to reserve punitive sanctions for only the most serious and violent juvenile offenders and to provide more effective treatment and aftercare services.

A CLOSER VIEW
To read more about innovative probation programs for juvenile offenders in England on InfoTrac College Edition, go to "Straw Extends E-Surveillance," *Computer Weekly:* 10 (September 28, 2000).

SUMMARY

There is a long history of comparing delinquency and juvenile justice systems across different countries, but many important issues need to be considered in making international comparisons. Differences in legal systems, culture, language, and so on, demand that close attention be paid to what is being compared and what countries are being compared.

Knowledge of the nature of juvenile delinquency and how juvenile justice systems operate in other countries can be useful for concerned citizens, social scientists, and policy makers. Comparing delinquency rates across countries has three main challenges: (1) The legal definitions of juvenile crime vary from country to country; (2) the measurement of juvenile crime varies across countries; and (3) the age group defined as "juvenile" is not always the same.

Juvenile delinquency poses a serious problem to all regions of the world. Juvenile violence in Europe and North America increased substantially between the mid-1980s and the mid-1990s. During this same period, juvenile property crime increased very little, with some countries showing no increase or an actual decrease. More recent figures for teenage drug use show rates to be on the rise in Europe, but holding steady in the United States. Explanations for the increase in teen violence include an explosive mix of racial tension, poverty, envy, drug abuse, broken families, unemployment, and alienation.

Many countries in the world have formal juvenile justice systems, but many do not. In an effort to get more countries around the world to develop juvenile justice systems and improve the administration of juvenile justice, the United Nations, in 1985, adopted the "Standard Minimum Rules for the Administration of Juvenile Justice." Juvenile justice systems in developed countries have many commonalities but also differ in many respects. Examined are juvenile policing, age of criminal responsibility, presence of juvenile court, transfers to adult court, sentencing, treatment of incarcerated juveniles, and aftercare programs.

The juvenile justice system in England was developed at the beginning of the twentieth century. Like the United States, England adheres to the treatment philosophy known as *parens patriae*, which recognizes that youth are in need of special consideration and assistance. There are many similarities between the British and U.S. juvenile justice systems, such as the use of bail hearings, plea bargaining, and the ability to transfer youths to adult court. There are also a number of important differences. As in the United States, sentences for juvenile offenders are much more punitive in England today than they were 10 or 20 years ago.

KEY TERMS

developed countries	transnational crime	developing countries	Crown Prosecution Service
death squads	international crime	least developed countries	Crown Court

QUESTIONS FOR DISCUSSION

1. International comparisons of delinquency and juvenile justice systems are best done "like-with-like." What are some of the things that need to be considered in order to produce valid comparisons across countries?

2. What are some of the benefits and challenges in making international comparisons of delinquency?

3. Between the mid-1980s and the mid-1990s, juvenile violence increased substantially in most developed countries. What are some of the reasons for this rise in juvenile violence?

4. Across the world there is a great deal of variation in the minimum age a person can be held responsible for his or her criminal actions. What are the advantages and disadvantages of having a low minimum age?

5. Which developed countries appear to be the most lenient in their treatment of juvenile offenders, and which appear to be the most punitive?

6. What are some of the differences between juvenile justice systems in the United States and England? Identify two or three key differences and discuss how these differences could benefit the other country.

VIEWPOINT

While violence by juveniles represents a pressing problem in many countries across the world, so does violence against juveniles, also known as juvenile victimization. It is known that many juveniles who engage in violence are also victims of violence, either in their past as children or in their present lifestyle as gang members, drug dealers, and so on. A study of juvenile violence and victimization in the United States found that the costs of violence against juveniles (by adults) was substantially more than the costs of violence by juveniles.

To read more about juvenile victimization on InfoTrac College Edition, go to Joanne J. Paetsch and Lorne D. Bertrand, "Victimization and Delinquency among Canadian Youth," *Adolescence* 34:351 (Summer 1999). To find further information, use *delinquency-international* as a key term.

NOTES

1. "Pornography Cartel Broken," *Crime and Justice International* 17:13 (2001).

2. Sarah Shannon, "The Global Sex Trade: Humans as the Ultimate Commodity," *Crime and Justice International* 17:5–7 (2001).

3. Edmund L. Andrews, "Deep Shock in Germany, Where Guns Are Rare," *New York Times,* New England edition, 28 April 2002; "Race Riots," *Crime and Justice International* 17:17 (2001).

4. Stephan Lhotzky, "Will Kai Become a Skinhead? Cultures of Hate Germany the New Europe," *Reclaiming Children and Youth* 10:86–91 (2001).

5. Christian Pfeiffer, "The Impoverishment of the Lower Classes Is Increasing Juvenile Aggressivity," *European Education* 32:95–100 (2000).

6. Idem, "Juvenile Crime and Violence in Europe," in Michael Tonry, ed., *Crime and Justice: A Review of Research,* volume 23 (Chicago: University of Chicago Press, 1998), p. 300.

7. Martin Killias and Marcelo F. Aebi, "Crime Trends in Europe from 1990 to 1996: How Europe Illustrates the Limits of the American Experience," *European Journal on Criminal Policy and Research* 8:43–63 (2000).

8. John Hagan, Hans Merkens, and Klaus Boehnke, "Delinquency and Disdain: Social Capital and the Control of Right-Wing Extremism among East and West Berlin Youth," *The American Journal of Sociology* 100:1028–53 (1995).

9. Sandra Gail Walker, *Weapons Use in Canadian Schools* (Ottawa: Solicitor General Canada, 1994).

10. Thomas Gabor, *Responding to School Violence: An Assessment of Zero Tolerance and Related Policies* (Ottawa: Solicitor General Canada, 1995).

11. Héctor Castillo Berthier, "Popular Culture among Mexican Teenagers," *The Urban Age* 1:14–15 (Summer 1993).

12. Franz Vanderschueren, "From Violence to Justice and Security in Cities," *Environment and Urbanization* 8: 93–112 (1996).

13. José Carvalho de Noronha, "Drug Markets and Urban Violence in Rio de Janeiro: A Call for Action," *The Urban Age* 1:9 (Summer 1993).

14. "Graffiti, New York to New Zealand," *Crime and Justice International* 14:22 (1998).

15. "Child Prostitution on the Rise," *Crime and Justice International* 18:21 (2002).

16. Carlos Carcach, "Youth as Victims and Offenders of Homicide," *Crime and Justice International* 14:10–14 (1998).

17. "Japan Again Hit by Incidents of Violent Teen Crime," *Crime and Justice International* 17:15 (2001).

18. Horace Lyons, "Hikikomori and Youth Crime," *Crime and Justice International* 17:9–10 (2001).

19. Dai Yisheng, "Are the 'Wolves' Really Coming? An Alternative View of Juvenile Delinquency," *Crime and Justice International* 14:13–14 (1998).

20. Mademba Ndiaye, "Dakar: Youth Groups and the Slide toward Violence," *The Urban Age* 1:7–8 (Summer 1993).

21. Otula Owuor, "City Residents Meet in Nairobi," *The Urban Age* 1:8 (Summer 1993).

22. For a general overview, see Piers Beirne, "Cultural Relativism and Comparative Criminology," *Contemporary Crises* 7:371–91 (1983); James Lynch, "Crime in International Perspective," in James Q. Wilson and Joan Petersilia, eds., *Crime: Public Policies for Crime Control* (Oakland, CA: Institute for Contemporary Studies, 2002).

23. John Henry Sloan et al., "Handgun Regulation, Crime, Assaults, and Homicide: A Tale of Two Cities," *New England Journal of Medicine* 319:1256–62 (1988); Martin Killias, John van Kesteren, and Martin Rindlisbacher, "Guns, Violent Crime, and Suicide in 21 Countries," *Canadian Journal of Criminology* 43:429–48 (2001); Richard R. Bennett, "Constructing Cross-Cultural Theories in Criminology," *Criminology* 18:252–68 (1980); David Shichor, "Crime Patterns and Socioeconomic Development: A Cross-National Analysis," *Criminal Justice Review* 15:64–77 (1990); David P. Farrington, Patrick A. Langan,

and Per-Olof H. Wikström, "Changes in Crime and Punishment in America, England and Sweden between the 1980s and the 1990s," *Studies on Crime and Crime Prevention* 3:104–31 (1994); Patrick A. Langan and David P. Farrington, *Crime and Justice in the United States and in England and Wales, 1981–96* (Washington, DC: Bureau of Justice Statistics, 1998); Joanne Savage and Bryan Vila, "Lagged Effects of Nurturance on Crime: A Cross-National Comparison," *Studies on Crime and Crime Prevention* 6:101–20 (1997); Marshall B. Clinard, *Cities with Little Crime: The Case of Switzerland* (New York: Cambridge University Press, 1978); Freda Adler, *Nations Not Obsessed with Crime* (Littleton, CO: Rothman, 1983).

24. Graeme Newman and Gregory J. Howard, "Introduction: Data Sources and Their Use," in Graeme Newman, ed., *Global Report on Crime and Justice* (New York: Oxford University Press, 1999), p. 18.

25. Jan van Dijk and Kristiina Kangaspunta, "Piecing Together the Cross-National Crime Puzzle," *National Institute of Justice Journal*:34–41 (January 2000).

26. Joan McCord, Cathy Spatz Widom, and Nancy Crowell, eds., *Juvenile Crime, Juvenile Justice*. Panel on Juvenile Crime: Prevention, Treatment, and Control (Washington, DC: National Academy Press, 2001), p. 17.

27. Pfeiffer, "Juvenile Crime and Violence in Europe," p. 261.

28. For more detail on the different international sources, see Gregory J. Howard, Graeme Newman, and William Alex Pridemore, "Theory, Method, and Data in Comparative Criminology," in David Duffee, ed., *Measurement and Analysis of Crime and Justice: Volume 4. Criminal Justice 2000* (Washington, DC: National Institute of Justice, 2000).

29. Newman and Howard, "Introduction: Data Sources and Their Use."

30. Gary LaFree, *Losing Legitimacy: Street Crime and the Decline of Social Institutions in America* (Boulder: Westview Press, 1997), p. 29.

31. See, for example, Franklin E. Zimring and Gordon Hawkins, *Crime Is Not the Problem: Lethal Violence in America* (New York: Oxford University Press, 1997).

32. Josine Junger-Tas, Gert-Jan Terlouw, and Malcolm W. Klein, eds., *Delinquent Behavior among Young People in the Western World: First Results of the International Self-Report Delinquency Study* (New York: Kugler Publications, 1994).

33. See, for example, Clinard, *Cities with Little Crime: The Case of Switzerland*; Adler, *Nations Not Obsessed with Crime*.

34. Erika Fairchild and Harry R. Dammer, *Comparative Criminal Justice Systems*, 2nd ed. (Belmont, CA: Wadsworth, 2001), p. 9.

35. Phil Williams, "Emerging Issues: Transnational Crime and Its Control," in Graeme Newman, ed., *Global Report on Crime and Justice* (New York: Oxford University Press, 1999), p. 222.

36. James O. Finckenauer, "Meeting the Challenge of Transnational Crime," *National Institute of Justice Journal*:2–7 (July 2000).

37. Williams, "Emerging Issues: Transnational Crime and Its Control," p. 222.

38. Ibid., p. 221.

39. Mark Findlay, *The Globalisation of Crime: Understanding Transnational Relationships in Context* (Cambridge, England: Cambridge University Press, 1999).

40. Pfeiffer, "Juvenile Crime and Violence in Europe."

41. Ibid., p. 256.

42. Rebecca Kong, *Canadian Crime Statistics, 1996* (Ottawa: Canadian Centre for Justice Statistics Juristat, 1997), p. 17, Table 4.

43. Pfeiffer, "Juvenile Crime and Violence in Europe," p. 256.

44. Ibid., p. 279.

45. James O. Finckenauer, *Russian Youth: Law, Deviance, and the Pursuit of Freedom* (New Brunswick, NJ: Transaction Publishers, 1995), pp. 71–73.

46. Kate Zernike, "Study Finds Teenage Drug Use Higher in U.S. Than in Europe," *New York Times*, New England edition, 21 February 2001.

47. Thor Bjarnason, "European School Survey Project on Alcohol and Drugs," press release issued by the State University of New York at Albany, 20 February 2001.

48. Zernike, "Study Finds Teenage Drug Use Higher in U.S. Than in Europe."

49. Elmar G. M. Weitekamp, Hans-Juergen Kerner, and Gernot Trueg, *International Comparison of Juvenile Justice Systems: Report to the National Academy of Sciences Commission on Behavioral and Social Sciences and Education* (Tuebingen, German: Institute of Criminology, University of Tuebingen, July 1999), p. 13.

50. National Advisory Commission on Criminal Justice Standards and Goals, *Task Force Report on Juvenile Justice and Delinquency Prevention* (Washington DC: Law Enforcement Assistance Administration, 1976), p. 258.

51. Pfeiffer, "Juvenile Crime and Violence in Europe," p. 314.

52. John Winterdyk, "Juvenile Justice and Young Offenders: An Overview of Canada," in John Winterdyk, ed., *Juvenile Justice Systems: International Perspectives* (Toronto: Canadian Scholars' Press, 1997), p. 167.

53. Minoru Yokoyama, "Juvenile Justice: An Overview of Japan," in John Winterdyk, ed., *Juvenile Justice Systems: International Perspectives* (Toronto: Canadian Scholars' Press, 1997), p. 15.

54. Satyanshu Mukherjee and Philip Reichel, "Bringing to Justice," in Graeme Newman, ed., *Global Report on Crime and Justice* (New York: Oxford University Press, 1999), p. 79.

55. McCord, Spatz Widom, and Crowell, eds., *Juvenile Crime, Juvenile Justice*, p. 20.

56. Winterdyk, ed., *Juvenile Justice Systems: International Perspectives*, p. x.

57. Weitekamp, Kerner, and Trueg, *International Comparison of Juvenile Justice Systems*, p. 83.

58. Ibid., p. 268.

59. Ibid., p. 253.

60. Department of Justice Canada, "Fact Sheets: *Youth Criminal Justice Act*" (Ottawa: Department of Justice, March 1999), p. 2.

61. Uberto Gatti and Alfredo Verde, "Comparative Juvenile Justice: An Overview of Italy," in John Winterdyk, ed., *Juvenile Justice Systems: International Perspectives* (Toronto: Canadian Scholars' Press, 1997), p. 186.

62. Weitekamp, Kerner, and Trueg, *International Comparison of Juvenile Justice Systems*, pp. 208, 223.

63. Ibid., p. 243.

64. Harold Traver, "Juvenile Delinquency in Hong Kong," in John Winterdyk, ed., *Juvenile Justice Systems: International Perspectives* (Toronto: Canadian Scholars' Press, 1997), p. 117.

65. Department of Justice Canada, "Fact Sheets: *Youth Criminal Justice Act.*"

66. Hans-Jörg Albrecht, "Juvenile Crime and Juvenile Law in the Federal Republic of Germany," in John Winterdyk, ed., *Juvenile Justice Systems: International Perspectives* (Toronto: Canadian Scholars' Press, 1997), p. 255.

67. Loraine Gelsthorpe and Mark Fenwick, "Comparative Juvenile Justice: England and Wales," in John Winterdyk, ed., *Juvenile Justice Systems: International Perspectives* (Toronto: Canadian Scholars' Press, 1997), p. 79.

68. Weitekamp, Kerner, and Trueg, *International Comparison of Juvenile Justice Systems*, p. 90.

69. Gelsthorpe and Fenwick, "Comparative Juvenile Justice: England and Wales," p. 88.

70. Ibid.

71. Weitekamp, Kerner, and Trueg, *International Comparison of Juvenile Justice Systems*, p. 90.

72. Ibid., p. 103.

73. Ibid., p. 100.

74. Ibid., p. 90.

75. Gelsthorpe and Fenwick, "Comparative Juvenile Justice: England and Wales," p. 99.

Concluding Notes: American Delinquency

We have reviewed in this text the current knowledge of the nature, causes, and correlates of juvenile delinquency and society's efforts to bring about its elimination and control. We have analyzed research programs, theoretical models, governmental policies, and legal cases. Taken in sum, this information presents a rather broad and complex picture of the youth crime problem and the most critical issues confronting the juvenile justice system. Delinquents come from a broad spectrum of society: kids of every race, gender, class, region, family type, and culture are involved in delinquent behaviors. To combat law violations by youth, society has tried a variety of intervention and control strategies: tough law enforcement; counseling, treatment, and rehabilitation; provision of legal rights; community action; educational programs; family change strategies. Yet, despite decades of intense effort and study, it is still unclear why delinquency occurs and what, if anything, can be done to control its occurrence. One thing is certain, juvenile crime is one of the most serious domestic problems faced by Americans.

Though uncertainty prevails, it is possible to draw some inferences about youth crime and its control. After reviewing the material contained in this volume, certain conclusions seem self-evident. Some involve social facts; that is, particular empirical relationships and associations have been established that have withstood multiple testing and verification efforts. Other conclusions involve social questions; there are issues that need clarification, and the uncertainty surrounding them has hampered progress in combating delinquency and treating known delinquents.

In sum, we have reviewed some of the most important social facts concerning delinquent behavior and posed some of the critical questions that still remain to be answered.

The statutory concept of juvenile delinquency is in need of review and modification.

Today, the legal definition of a juvenile delinquent is a minor child, usually under 17 or 18 years of age, who has been found to have violated the criminal law (juvenile code). The concept of juvenile delinquency still occupies a legal position falling somewhere between criminal and civil law; juveniles still enjoy more rights, protections, and privileges than adults. Nonetheless, concerns about teen violence have encouraged some commentators to call for the abolition of a separate juvenile justice system. If kids are as violent as adults, or even more violent, why should they be given a special legal status consideration? Pressure for abolition may have subsided in the wake of reduced levels of delinquent behavior. If the teen violence rate begins to rise again, so too may calls for the abolition of a separate juvenile justice system.

The concept of the status offender (PINS, CHINS, and MINS) may be in for revision.

Special treatment for the status offender conforms with the *parens patriae* roots of the juvenile justice system. Granting the state the authority to institutionalize noncriminal youth in order "to protect the best interest of the child" cannot be considered an abuse of state authority. While it is likely that the current system of control will remain in place for the near future, it is not beyond the realm of possibility to see the eventual restructuring of the definition of status offenders, with jurisdiction of "pure" noncriminal first offenders turned over to a department of social services, and chronic status offenders and those with prior records of delinquency petitioned to juvenile court as delinquency cases.

The epidemic of juvenile violence seems to have abated.

Official delinquency data suggest that the decade-long rise in the juvenile violence rate has abated. The most recent data indicate that the juvenile murder rate is in decline. While this is welcome news, some forecasters suggest that an increasing juvenile population portends a long-term increase in the overall violence rate.

Easy availability of guns is a significant contributor to teen violence.

Research indicates a close tie between gun use, control of drug markets, and teen violence. Some new programs designed to control the spread of handguns or deter handgun use seem to be working.

The chronic violent juvenile offender is a serious social problem for society and the juvenile justice system.

Chronic male delinquent offenders commit a disproportionate amount of violent behavior, including a significant amount of the most serious juvenile crimes, such as homicides, rapes, robberies, and aggravated assaults. Many chronic offenders become adult criminals and eventually end up in the criminal court system. How to deal effectively with chronic juvenile offenders and drug users remains a high priority for the juvenile justice system.

Chronic juvenile delinquency has unquestionably become a major concept within the field. The best approach to dealing with chronic offenders remains uncertain, but concern about such offenders has shifted juvenile justice policy toward a punishment-oriented philosophy.

There is still debate about whether the propensity to commit crime changes as people mature.

Delinquency experts are now researching such issues as the onset, escalation, termination, and continuation of a delinquent career. There is an ongoing debate concerning change in delinquent behavior patterns. One position is that people do not change—conditions and opportunities do. A second view is that real human change is conditioned by life events. If the former position holds true, there is little hope of using treatment strategies to change known offenders; a more productive approach would be to limit their criminal opportunities through the use of long-term incarceration. If the latter position is accurate, effective treatment and provision of legitimate opportunities might produce real behavioral changes.

Female delinquency has been increasing at a faster pace than male delinquency.

The nature and extent of female delinquent activities changed in the late 1980s, and for more than a decade the female delinquency rate increased at a far higher pace than the male delinquency rate. Now it appears that the offending rate of both males and females is in decline. However, over the past five years, while the juvenile female arrest rate has declined, it has done so at a significantly lower rate than the decline in male delinquency. Although gender differences persist in the rate of the most serious crimes such as murder, it is possible that further convergence will occur in the near future.

There is little question that family environment affects patterns of juvenile behavior.

Family relationships have been linked to the problem of juvenile delinquency by many experts. Broken homes, for instance, are not in and of themselves a cause of delinquency, but some evidence indicates that single-parent households are more inclined to contain children who manifest behavioral problems. Limited resource allocations limit the single parent's ability to control and supervise children. In addition, there seems to be a strong association in family relationships between child abuse and delinquency. Cases of abuse and neglect have been found in every level of the economic strata, and a number of studies have linked child abuse and neglect to juvenile delinquency. While the evidence is not conclusive, it does suggest that a strong relationship exists between child abuse and subsequent delinquent behavior. This relationship does not bode well for delinquency rates because the extent of reported child abuse is on the increase. Some experts believe a major effort is needed to reestablish parental accountability and responsibility.

Juvenile gangs have become a serious and growing problem in many major metropolitan areas throughout the United States.

Ethnic youth gangs, mostly males aged 14 to 21, appear to be increasing in such areas as Los Angeles, Chicago, Boston, and New York. National surveys of gang activity now estimate that there are more than 750,000 members in the United States, up sharply over the previous 20 years. One view of gang development is that such groups serve as a bridge between adolescence and adulthood in communities where adult social control is not available. Another view suggests that gangs are a product of lower-class social disorganization and that they serve as an alternative means of economic advancement for poorly motivated and uneducated youth. Today's gangs are more often commercially than culturally oriented, and the profit motive may be behind increasing memberships. It is unlikely that gang control strategies can be successful as long as legitimate economic alternatives are lacking. If the economy declines, look for rapid growth in gang activity when the current adolescent population matures and limited job opportunities encourage gang members to prolong their involvement in illegal activities.

Many of the underlying problems of youth crime and delinquency are directly related to education.

Numerous empirical studies have confirmed that lack of educational success is an important contributing factor in delinquency; experts generally agree that chronic offenders have had a long history of school failure. Dropping out of school is now being associated with long-term antisocial behavior. About 10 percent of all victimizations occur on school grounds. School-based crime control projects have not been very successful, and a great deal more effort is needed in this critical area of school-delinquency prevention.

Substance abuse is closely associated with juvenile crime and delinquency.

Surveys of arrested juveniles indicate that sizable numbers of young people are substance abusers. Most efforts in the juvenile justice system to treat young offenders involved with substance abuse seem to be unsuccessful. Traditional prevention efforts and education programs have not had encouraging results.

The costs of delinquency are immense and wide ranging.

It is estimated that juvenile violence costs the United States $158 billion each year. The majority of this cost is due to losses suffered by victims, such as lost wages, pain, suffering, and reduced quality of life. Also included are costs incurred by federal, state, and local governments to assist victims of juvenile violence, such as medical treatment for injuries and services for victims. Missing from this estimate are the costs from society's response to juvenile violence, which include early prevention programs, services for juveniles, and the juvenile justice system. These costs are unknown. Many experts argue that the financial cost of juvenile delinquency is an important justification for greater delinquency prevention measures.

Prevention is a key component of an overall strategy to address the problem of juvenile delinquency.

In recent years, many different types of delinquency prevention programs have been targeted at children, young people, and families, and many of these programs show positive results in reducing delinquency as well as other problem behaviors, such as substance abuse and truancy. They have also been shown to lead to improvements in other areas of life, such as educational achievement, health, and employment. These benefits often translate into substantial cost savings. But not all delinquency prevention programs work. Some programs do more harm than good, but fortunately these are rare.

An analysis of the history of juvenile justice over the past 100 years shows how our policy regarding delinquency has gone through cycles of reform.

Many years ago, society focused primarily on the treatment of youths who committed criminal behavior, often through no fault of their own. Early in the nineteenth century, juveniles were tried in criminal courts, like everyone else. Reformers developed the idea of establishing separate institutions for juvenile offenders in which the rehabilitation idea could proceed without involvement with criminal adults. As a result, the House of Refuge Movement was born. By the late 1890s the system proved unworkable, because delinquent juveniles, minor offenders, and neglected children weren't benefiting from institutional placement. The 1899 Illinois Juvenile Court Act was an effort to regulate the treatment of children and secure institutional reform. *Parens patriae* was the justification to ignore legal formalities in the juvenile courts up until the early twentieth century. In the 1960s, the *Gault* decision heralded the promise of legal rights for children and interrupted the goal of individualized rehabilitation. The 1970s yielded progress in the form of the Juvenile Justice and Delinquency Prevention Act. Throughout the 1980s and 1990s, the juvenile justice system seemed suspended between the assurance of due process and efforts to provide services for delinquent children and their families. Today, society is concerned with the control of serious juvenile offenders and the development of firm sentencing provisions in the juvenile courts. These cycles represent the shifting philosophies of the juvenile justice system.

Today, no single ideology or view dominates the direction, programs, and policies of the juvenile justice system.

Throughout the past decade, numerous competing positions regarding juvenile justice have emerged. As the liberal program of the 1970s has faltered, more restrictive sanctions have been imposed. The "crime control" position seems most formidable as we enter the new millennium. However, there remains a great deal of confusion over what the juvenile justice system does, what it should do, and how it should deal with youthful antisocial behavior. The juvenile justice system operates on distinctly different yet parallel tracks. On the one hand, significant funding is available for prevention and treatment strategies. At the same time, states are responding to anxiety about youth crime by devising more punitive measures.

Today's problems in the juvenile justice system can often be traced to the uncertainty of its founders, the "child savers."

Such early twentieth-century groups formed the juvenile justice system on the misguided principle of reforming wayward youth and remodeling their behavior. The "best interest of the child" standard has long been the guiding light in juvenile proceedings, calling for the strongest available rehabilitative services. Today's juvenile justice system is often torn between playing the role of social versus crime control agent.

In recent years, the juvenile justice system has become more legalistic by virtue of Supreme Court decisions that have granted children procedural safeguards in various court proceedings.

The case of *In re Gault* of the 1960s motivated state legislators to revamp their legal procedures for juvenile court. Today, the Supreme Court continues to struggle with making distinctions between the legal rights of adults and those of minors. Recent Court decisions that allow children to be searched by teachers and deny their right to a jury trial show that the Court continues to recognize a legal separation between adult and juvenile offenders.

Despite some dramatic distinctions, juveniles have gained many of the legal due-process rights enjoyed by adults.

Among the more significant elements of due process are the right to counsel, evidence efficiency, protection from double jeopardy and self-incrimination, and the right to appeal. While the general public continues to favor providing juveniles with the same due-process and procedural guarantees accorded to adults, it is likely that constitutional protections that adults receive are not actually provided to juvenile offenders. High caseloads, poor pretrial preparation and trial performance, and the lack of dispositional representation are issues where juveniles are being denied due process of law. More resources are needed to implement constitutional procedures so that legal protections are not discarded.

The key area in which due process is required by *Gault* is the right to counsel. While progress has been made in improving the availability and quality of legal counsel afforded youths in delinquency proceedings in the three decades since *Gault*, much remains to be done.

States are increasingly taking legislative action to ensure that juvenile arrest and disposition records are available to prosecutors and judges.

Knowledge of defendants' juvenile records may help determine appropriate sentencing for offenders aged 18 to 24, the age group most likely to be involved in violent crime. Laws that are being passed include (1) police fingerprinting of juveniles charged with crimes that are felonies if committed by an adult; (2) centralized juvenile arrest and disposition record-holding and dissemination statutes; (3) prosecutor and court access to juvenile disposition records; and (4) limitations on expungement of juvenile records when there are subsequent adult convictions.

The juvenile court is the focal point of the contemporary juvenile justice system.

Created at the turn of the twentieth century, juvenile court was adopted as an innovative solution to the prob-lem of wayward youth. In the first half of the century, these courts (organized by the states and based on the historic notion of *parens patriae*) were committed to the treatment of the child. They functioned without procedures employed in the adult criminal courts. When the system was reviewed by the U.S. Supreme Court in 1966, due process was imposed on the juvenile court system. More than 30 years have since passed, and numerous reform efforts have been undertaken. But the statement of Judge Abe Fortas, "that the child receives the worst of both worlds—neither the protection afforded adults nor the treatment needed for children," still rings true. Reform efforts have been disappointing.

What are the remedies for the current juvenile court system?

Some suggest abolishing the delinquency-status jurisdiction of the courts. This is difficult to do because the organization of the courts is governed by state law. Others want to strengthen the legal rights of juveniles by improving the quality of services of legal counsel. The majority of experts believe there is an urgent need to develop meaningful dispositional programs and expand treatment services. Over the last 50 years, the juvenile court system has been transformed from a rehabilitative to a quasi-criminal court. With limited resources and procedural deficiencies, there is little likelihood of much change in the near future. One area of change has been the development of specialized courts, such as drug courts, which focus attention on specific problems, and teen courts, which use peer jurors to settle nonserious matters.

The death penalty for children has been upheld by the Supreme Court.

According to the *Wilkens v. Missouri* and *Standford v. Kentucky* cases in 1989, the Supreme Court concluded that states are free to impose the death penalty for murderers who commit their crimes while age 16 or 17. According to the majority decision written by Justice Antonin Scalia, society has not formed a consensus that such executions are a violation of the cruel and unusual punishment clause of the Eighth Amendment.

New approaches to policing juvenile delinquency show promising results in reducing serious offenses, such as gang activity and gun crimes.

Some of these new approaches include aggressive law enforcement, community-based policing services, and police in schools. One of the most successful approaches has involved the police working closely with other juvenile justice agencies and the community. Operation Ceasefire in Boston, which brought together a broad range of juvenile justice and social agencies and community groups, produced substantial reductions in youth homicide victims, youth gun assaults, and gang violence across the city. Versions of this successful program are now being replicated in other cities across the country.

The use of detention in the juvenile justice system continues to be a widespread problem.

After almost three decades of work, virtually all jurisdictions have passed laws requiring that status offenders be placed in shelter care programs rather than detention facilities. Another serious problem related to the use of juvenile detention is the need to remove young people from lockups in adult jails. The Office of Juvenile Justice and Delinquency Prevention continues to give millions of dollars in aid to encourage the removal of juveniles from such adult lockups. But eliminating the confinement of children in adult institutions remains an enormously difficult task in the juvenile justice system. Although most delinquency cases do not involve detention, its use is more common for cases involving males, minorities, and older juveniles. Juvenile detention is one of the most important elements of the justice system and one of the most difficult to administer. It is experiencing a renewed emphasis on programs linked to short-term confinement.

The use of waiver, bind-over, and transfer provisions in juvenile court statutes is now common.

This trend has led toward a criminalization of the juvenile system. Because there are major differences between the adult and juvenile court systems, transfer to an adult court exposes youths to more serious consequences of their antisocial behavior and is a strong recommendation of those favoring a crime control model. Waiver of serious offenders is one of the most significant developments in the trend to criminalize the juvenile court. According to the National Conference of State Legislatures, every state has transfer proceedings. Many states are considering legislation that makes it easier to transfer juveniles into adult courts. States continue to modify age and offense criteria, allowing more serious offenders to be tried as criminals; some are considering new transfer laws, such as mandatory and presumptive waiver provisions.

The role of the attorney in the juvenile justice process requires further research and analysis.

Most attorneys appear to be uncertain whether they should act as adversaries or advocates in the juvenile process. In addition, the role of the juvenile prosecutor has become more significant as a result of new and more serious statutory sentencing provisions, as well as legal standards promulgated by such organizations as the American Bar Association and the National District Attorneys Association. Juvenile defendants also need and are entitled to effective legal representation. Through cre-

ative and resourceful strategies, many more states are providing comprehensive representation for delinquent youth. These programs include law internships, attorney mentoring, and neighborhood defender services.

Juvenile sentencing procedures now reflect the desire to create uniformity and limited discretion in the juvenile court, and this trend is likely to continue.

Many states have now developed programs such as mandatory sentences, sentencing guidelines, and limited-discretion sentencing to bring uniformity into the juvenile justice system. As a result of the public's fear about serious juvenile crime, legislators have amended juvenile codes to tighten up juvenile sentencing provisions. Graduated sanctions are the latest type of sentencing solution being explored by states. The most popular piece of juvenile crime legislation in the near future will be tougher sentences for violent and repeat offenders. Perhaps the most dramatic impact on sentencing will be felt by the imposition of "blended sentences" that combine juvenile and adult sentences. Today, more than a dozen states now use blended sentencing statutes, which allow courts to impose juvenile and/or adult correctional sanctions on certain young offenders.

In the area of community sentencing, new forms of probation supervision have received greater attention in recent years.

Intensive probation supervision, balanced probation, wilderness probation, and electronic monitoring have become important community-based alternatives over the last few years. Some studies report mixed results for these new forms of probation, but more experimentation is needed. Probation continues to be the single most significant intermediate sanction available to the juvenile court system.

Restorative community juvenile justice is a new designation that refers to a preference for neighborhood-based, more accessible, and less formal juvenile services.

The restorative justice idea focuses on the relationship between the victim, the community, and the offender. For the victim, restorative justice offers the hope of restitution or other forms of reparation, information about the case, support for healing, the opportunity to be heard, and input into the case, as well as expanded opportunities for involvement and influence. For the community, there is the promise of reduced fear and safer neighborhoods, a more accessible justice process, and accountability, as well as the obligation for involvement and participation in sanctioning crime, supporting victim restoration, reintegrating offenders, and crime prevention and control. For the offender, restorative justice requires accountability in the form of obligations to repair the harm to individual victims and victimized communities, and the opportunity to develop new competencies, social skills, and the capacity to avoid future crime.

Deinstitutionalization has become an important goal of the juvenile justice system.

The Office of Juvenile Justice and Delinquency Prevention has provided funds to encourage deinstitutionalization. In the early 1980s, the deinstitutionalization movement seemed to be partially successful. Admissions to public juvenile correctional facilities declined in the late 1970s and early 1980s. In addition, the number of status offenders being held within the juvenile justice system was reduced. However, the number of institutionalized children in the 1990s and in the early part of the 2000s has increased, and the deinstitutionalization movement has failed to meet all of its optimistic goals. Nonetheless, the majority of states have achieved compliance with the DSO mandate (Deinstitutionalizing Status Offenders). Because juvenile crime is a high priority, the challenge to the states will be to retain a focus on prevention despite societal pressures for more punitive approaches. If that can be achieved, then deinstitutionalization will remain a central theme in the juvenile justice system.

The number of incarcerated youths continues to rise.

Today, there are close to 110,000 youths in some type of correctional institution. The juvenile courts seem to be using the most severe of the statutory dispositions, that is, commitment to the juvenile institution, rather than the "least restrictive statutory alternative." There is also wide variation in juvenile custody rates across the nation. The District of Columbia has the highest juvenile incarceration rate at over 700 per 100,000 juveniles; about half of the states have rates around 300.

Minority youths have higher incarceration rates.

A disproportionate number of minority youths are incarcerated in youth facilities. The difference is greatest for black youths, with the incarceration rate being almost five times greater than that for whites. Of equal importance, minorities are more likely to be placed in secure public facilities rather than in open private facilities that might provide more costly and effective treatment. The OJJDP is committed to ensuring that the country address situations where there is disproportionate confinement of minority offenders in the nation's juvenile justice system.

Juvenile boot camps don't work.

Correctional boot camps, which combine get-tough elements of adult programs with education, substance abuse treatment, and social skills training, are used to shock the offender into going straight. Systematic reviews and meta-analyses of the research evidence show that juvenile boot camps fail to reduce future offending. Despite their poor results, many states continue to use boot camps as a correctional option for juvenile offenders.

The future of the legal right to treatment for juveniles remains uncertain.

The appellate courts have established minimum standards of care and treatment on a case-by-case basis, but it does not appear that the courts can be persuaded today to expand this constitutional theory to mandate that incarcerated children receive adequate treatment. Eventually, this issue must be clarified by the Supreme Court. Reforms in state juvenile institutions often result from class-action lawsuits filed on behalf of incarcerated youth.

A serious crisis exists in the U.S. juvenile justice system.

How to cope with the needs of large numbers of children in trouble remains one of the most controversial and frustrating issues in our society. The magnitude of the problem is such that over 2 million youths are arrested each year; over 1.5 million delinquency dispositions and 150,000 status offense cases are heard in court; and drug abuse is a significant factor in more than 60 percent of all the cases referred to the juvenile courts. Today, the system and the process seem more concerned with crime control and more willing to ignore the rehabilitative ideal. Perhaps the answer lies outside the courtroom in the form of greater job opportunities, improved family relationships, and more effective education. Much needs to be done in delinquency prevention. One fact is also certain: according to many experts, the problem of violent juvenile crime is a national crisis. While the good news is that the juvenile crime rate declined in recent years, violence by juveniles is still too prevalent and remains an issue of great concern. Developing programs to fight juvenile violence seems to overshadow all other juvenile justice objectives.

Federal funding for juvenile delinquency is essential to improving state practices and programs.

The Juvenile Justice and Delinquency Prevention Act of 1974 has had a tremendous impact on America's juvenile justice system. Its mandates to deinstitutionalize status offenders and remove juveniles from adult jails have spurred change for over two decades. The survival of many state programs will likely depend on this federal legislation. Because the Act has contributed to a wide range of improvements, Congress will most likely approve future financial incentives. Reauthorization of JJDPA through 2002 was approved in the 106th Congress (1999).

Today, the juvenile justice system and court of 100 years is under attack more than ever before.

Yet the system has weathered criticism for failing to control and rehabilitate juveniles. It is a unique American institution duplicated in many other countries as being the best model for handling juveniles who commit crime. The major recommendations of such important organizations as the National Council of Juvenile Court Judges, the American Bar Association, and the Office of Juvenile Justice and Delinquency Prevention for the new century are (1) the court should be a leader for juvenile justice in the community; (2) people (judges, attorneys, and probation officers) are the key to the health of the juvenile justice system; (3) public safety and rehabilitation are the goals of the juvenile justice system; (4) juvenile court workloads are shaped today and in the future by the increase of substance abuse cases that must be resolved; and (5) the greatest future needs of the juvenile court in particular are resources and funding for more services, more staff, and more facilities.

Juvenile delinquency is not just a problem in the United States.

Juvenile delinquency poses a serious problem to all regions of the world. Many nations are experiencing an upsurge in juvenile problem behavior, including gang violence, prostitution, and drug abuse. Although each nation is quite different, all share an explosive mix of racial tension, poverty, envy, drug abuse, broken families, unemployment, and alienation. Some of the areas hardest hit have been undergoing rapid social and economic change—the fall of Communism, the end of the Cold War, the effects of the global economy, an influx of multi-national immigration—as they move toward increased economic integration, privatization, and diminished social services.

Many countries in the world have formal juvenile justice systems, but many do not.

The United Nations' "Standard Minimum Rules for the Administration of Juvenile Justice" was initiated in 1985 to encourage more countries around the world to develop juvenile justice systems and improve the administration of juvenile justice. Despite some differences, all industrialized nations have separate justice systems for juvenile and adult offenders. In response to a growing number of delinquent acts, some nations are now in the process of revamping their juvenile justice systems in an effort to increase their effectiveness and efficiency.

Appendix: Excerpts from the U.S. Constitution

Amendment I (1791)
Congress shall make no law respecting an establishment of religion, or prohibiting the free exercise thereof; or abridging the freedom of speech, or of the press; or the right of the people peaceably to assemble, and to petition the government for a redress of grievances.

Amendment II (1791)
A well regulated militia, being necessary to the security of a free state, the right of the people to keep and bear arms, shall not be infringed.

Amendment III (1791)
No soldier shall, in time of peace, be quartered in any house, without the consent of the owner, nor in time of war, but in a manner to be prescribed by law.

Amendment IV (1791)
The right of the people to be secure in their persons, houses, papers, and effects, against unreasonable searches and seizures, shall not be violated, and no warrants shall issue, but upon probable cause, supported by oath or affirmation, and particularly describing the place to be searched, and the persons or things to be seized.

Amendment V (1791)
No person shall be held to answer for a capital, or otherwise infamous, crime unless on a presentment or indictment of a grand jury, except in cases arising in the land or naval forces, or in the militia, when in actual service in time of war or public danger; nor shall any person be subject for the same offense to be twice put in jeopardy of life or limb; nor shall be compelled in any criminal case to be a witness against himself, nor be deprived of life, liberty, or property; without due process of law; nor shall private property be taken for public use without just compensation.

Amendment VI (1791)
In all criminal prosecutions, the accused shall enjoy the right to a speedy and public trial, by an impartial jury of the state and district wherein the crime shall have been committed, which district shall have been previously ascertained by law, and to be informed of the nature and cause of the accusation; to be confronted with the witnesses against him; to have compulsory process for obtaining witnesses in his favor, and to have the assistance of counsel for his defense.

Amendment VII (1791)
In suits at common law, where the value in controversy shall exceed twenty dollars, the right of trial by jury shall be preserved, and no fact tried by a jury shall be otherwise reexamined in any court of the United States, than according to the rules of common law.

Amendment VIII (1791)
Excessive bail shall not be required, nor excessive fines imposed, nor cruel and unusual punishment inflicted.

Amendment IX (1791)
The enumeration in the Constitution of certain rights shall not be construed to deny or disparage others retained by the people.

Amendment X (1791)
The powers not delegated to the United States by the Constitution, nor prohibited by it to the states, are reserved to the states respectively, or to the people.

Amendment XIV (1868)
Section I. All persons born or naturalized in the United States, and subject to the jurisdiction thereof, are citizens of the United States and of the state wherein they reside. No state shall make or enforce any laws which abridge the privilege or immunities of citizens of the United States; nor shall any state deprive any person of life, liberty, or property, without due process of law; nor deny to any person within its jurisdiction the equal protection of the laws.

Glossary

abandonment Parents physically leave their children with the intention of completely severing the parent-child relationship.

academic achievement Being successful in a school environment.

active speech Expressing an opinion by speaking or writing; freedom of speech is a protected right under the First Amendment to the U.S. Constitution.

addict A person with an overpowering physical or psychological need to continue taking a particular substance or drug.

addiction-prone personality The view that the cause of substance abuse can be traced to a personality that has a compulsion for mood-altering drugs.

adjudicatory hearing The fact-finding process wherein the juvenile court determines whether there is sufficient evidence to sustain the allegations in a petition.

adolescent-limiteds Delinquent youth who begin their offending career in their late teens and soon desist from crime.

advisement hearing A preliminary protective or temporary custody hearing in which the court will review the facts and determine whether removal of the child is justified and notify parents of the charges against them.

aftercare Transitional assistance to juveniles, equivalent to adult parole, to help youths adjust to community life.

age-graded theory Identifies turning points (such as marriage and career) that can cause delinquents to reverse course and desist from further criminal behavior.

age of consent Age at which youths are legally adults and may be independent of parental control. When an adolescent reaches the age of consent, he or she may engage in sexual behaviors prohibited to youths.

age of onset Age at which youths begin their delinquent careers; early onset is believed to be linked with chronic offending patterns.

aging-out process (also known as **desistance** or **spontaneous remission**) The tendency for youths to reduce the frequency of their offending behavior as they age; aging out is thought to occur among all groups of offenders.

alcohol Fermented or distilled liquids containing ethanol, an intoxicating substance.

alienation Feelings of separation and distance from mainstream society.

Alternative Work Sentencing Program (Earn-It) A Massachusetts program that brings together the juvenile and the crime victim to develop an equitable work program to provide restitution to the crime victim.

anabolic steroids Drugs used by athletes and bodybuilders to gain muscle bulk and strength.

androgen The principal male sex hormone.

anesthetic drugs Central nervous system depressants.

anomie Normlessness produced by rapidly shifting moral values; according to Merton, anomie occurs when personal goals cannot be achieved using available means.

appellate process Allows the juvenile an opportunity to have the case brought before a reviewing court after it has been heard in juvenile or family court.

arousal theorists Delinquency experts who believe that aggression is a function of the level of an individual's need for stimulation or arousal from the environment. Those who require more stimulation may act in an aggressive manner to meet their needs.

arrest Taking a person into the custody of the law to restrain the accused until he or she can be held accountable for the offense in court proceedings.

at-risk youths Young people who are extremely vulnerable to the negative consequences of school failure, substance abuse, and early sexuality.

authority-conflict pathway The developmental path taken to delinquency that begins with stubborn and defiant behavior.

bail Amount of money that must be paid as a condition of pretrial release to ensure that the accused will return for subsequent proceedings; bail is normally set by the judge at the initial appearance, and if unable to make bail the accused is detained in jail.

balanced probation Programs that integrate community protection, accountability of the juvenile offender, competency, and individualized attention to the juvenile offender; based on the principle that juvenile offenders must accept responsibility for their behavior.

balancing-of-the-interest approach Efforts of the courts to balance the parents' natural right to raise a child with the child's right to grow into adulthood free from physical abuse or emotional harm.

barrio A Latino term meaning neighborhood.

battered child syndrome Nonaccidental physical injury of children by their parents or guardians.

behaviorism Branch of psychology concerned with the study of observable behavior rather than unconscious processes; focuses on particular stimuli and responses to them.

behavior modification A technique for shaping desired behaviors through a system of rewards and punishments.

best interests of the child A philosophical viewpoint that encourages the state to take control of wayward children and provide care, custody, and treatment to remedy delinquent behavior.

bifurcated process The procedure of separating adjudicatory and dispositionary hearings so different levels of evidence can be heard at each.

bindover *See* waiver.

biosocial theory The view that both thought and behavior have biological and social bases.

blended families Nuclear families that are the product of divorce and remarriage; blending one parent from each of two families and their combined children into one family unit.

boot camps Juvenile programs that combine get-tough elements from adult programs with education, substance abuse treatment, and social skills training.

broken home Home in which one or both parents is absent due to divorce or separation; children in such an environment may be prone to antisocial behavior.

capital punishment Use of the death penalty to punish offenders.

chancery courts Court proceedings created in fifteenth-century England to oversee the lives of high-born minors who were orphaned or otherwise could not care for themselves.

child abuse Any physical, emotional, or sexual trauma to a child, including neglecting to give proper care and attention, for which no reasonable explanation can be found.

Children's Aid Society Child-saving organization that took children from the streets of large cities and placed them with farm families on the prairie.

child savers Nineteenth-century reformers who developed programs for troubled youth and influenced legislation creating the juvenile justice system; today some critics view them as being more concerned with control of the poor than with their welfare.

chivalry hypothesis (also known as **paternalism hypothesis**) View that low female crime and delinquency rates are a reflection of the leniency with which police treat female offenders.

choice theory Holds that youths will engage in delinquent and criminal behavior after weighing the consequences and benefits of their actions; delinquent behavior is a rational choice made by a motivated offender who perceives that the chances of gain outweigh any possible punishment or loss.

chronic delinquent offenders *See* chronic juvenile offender.

cholo A member of the Hispanic subculture of marginalized, antisocial youth.

chronic delinquents *See* chronic juvenile offender.

chronic juvenile offender (also known as **chronic delinquent offenders, chronic delinquents,** or **chronic recidivists**) Youths who have been arrested four or more times during their minority and perpetuate a striking majority of serious criminal acts; this small group, known as the "chronic 6 percent," is believed to engage in a significant portion of all delinquent behavior; these youths do not age out of crime but continue their criminal behavior into adulthood.

chronic recidivists *See* chronic juvenile offender.

classical criminology Holds that decisions to violate the law are weighed against possible punishments and to deter crime the pain of punishment must outweigh the benefit of illegal gain; led to graduated punishments based on seriousness of the crime (let the punishment fit the crime).

cliques Small groups of friends who share intimate knowledge and confidences.

club drugs Synthetic substances (such as ecstasy and Rohypnol) commonly used at nightclubs, bars, and raves.

cocaine A powerful natural stimulant derived from the coca plant.

cognitive theory The branch of psychology that studies the perception of reality and the mental processes required to understand the world we live in.

collective efficacy The ability of communities to regulate the behavior of their residents through the influence of community institutions, such as the family and school. Residents in these communities share mutual trust and a willingness to intervene in the supervision of children and the maintenance of public order.

college boy Strives to conform to middle-class values and to move up the social ladder, but is ill-equipped to succeed and fated to become frustrated and disappointed.

commitment to conformity The strength of the ties of youths to conventional social institutions predicts their likely behavior; those with poor or negative ties are more likely to indulge in delinquent acts.

community policing Police strategy that emphasizes fear reduction, community organization, and order maintenance rather than crime fighting.

community service restitution The juvenile offender is required to assist some worthwhile community organization for a period of time.

community services Local delinquency prevention services such as recreational programs and drug and alcohol information programs in schools that help meet the community's needs for youths.

community treatment Using nonsecure and noninstitutional residences, counseling services, victim restitution programs, and other community services to treat juveniles in their own communities.

complaint Report made by the police or some other agency to the court that initiates the intake process.

concurrent jurisdiction More than one court has jurisdiction; the prosecutor then has the discretion of filing charges in either juvenile or adult court.

conditions of probation The rules and regulations mandating that a juvenile on probation behave in a particular way.

confidentiality Restricting information in juvenile court proceedings in the interest of protecting the privacy of the juvenile.

contagion effect The negative, crime-promoting influence of deviant siblings on their brothers and sisters.

containment theory Asserts that a strong self-image insulates youths from the pressure to engage in illegal acts; youths with poor self-concepts and low self-esteem are more likely to engage in crime.

continuity of crime The idea that chronic juvenile offenders are likely to continue violating the law as adults.

control group The comparison group of subjects that does not receive the program.

control theories Suggest that many forms of delinquent behavior are attractive to all teenagers, but only those who have few social supports (through family, friends, and teachers) feel free to violate the law.

co-offending Committing criminal acts in groups.

corner boy Not a delinquent but may engage in marginal behavior; eventually will marry a local girl and obtain a menial job with few prospects for advancement or success.

cottage system Housing juveniles in a compound containing a series of small cottages, each of which accommodates twenty to forty children and is run by a set of cottage parents who create a home-like atmosphere.

Court Appointed Special Advocates (CASA) Volunteers appointed by the court to investigate the needs of the child and help officers of the court ensure a safe placement for the child.

covert pathway The developmental path taken to delinquency that begins with sneaky, deceitful, and underhanded behavior.

crack A highly addictive crystalline form of cocaine containing remnants of hydrochloride and sodium bicarbonate, which emits a crackling sound when smoked.

crack down A law enforcement operation that is designed to reduce or eliminate a particular criminal activity through the application of aggressive police tactics, typically involving a larger than usual contingent of police officers.

criminal atavism The idea that delinquents manifest physical anomalies that make them biologically and physiologically similar to our primitive ancestors, savage throwbacks to an earlier stage of human evolution.

critical criminologists Analysts who review historical and current developments in law and order to expose the interests of the power elite and ruling classes.

crowds Loosely organized groups who share interests and activities.

Crown Prosecution Service The national agency in England that is in charge of all criminal prosecutions of juveniles and adults.

Crown Court In England, the criminal court that deals with adult offenders or juveniles who have been transferred from youth court.

cultural deviance theory Links delinquent acts to the formation of independent subcultures with a unique set of values that clash with the mainstream culture.

cultural transmission Cultural norms and values that are passed down from one generation to the next.

culture conflict When the values of a subculture clash with those of the dominant culture.

culture of poverty View that lower-class people form a separate culture with their own values and norms, which are sometimes in conflict with conventional society.

custodial interrogation Questions posed by the police to a suspect held in custody in the prejudicial stage of the juvenile justice process; juveniles have the same rights against self-incrimination as adults do when being questioned.

D.A.R.E. (Drug Abuse Resistance Education) An elementary school program designed to prevent teenage drug abuse by giving youths the skills they need to resist peer pressure to experiment with drugs.

dark figures of crime Incidents of crime and delinquency that go undetected by police.

death squads Common to South America, organized government or criminal groups that selectively kill members of opposing groups and incite fear in those groups and among their supporters.

degradation ceremony Going to court, being scolded by a judge, or being found delinquent after a trial are examples of public ceremonies that can transform youthful offenders by degrading their self-image.

deinstitutionalization Removing juveniles from adult jails and placing them in community-based programs to avoid the stigma attached to these facilities.

delinquency prevention Involves any nonjustice program or policy designed to prevent the occurrence of a future delinquent act.

delinquency repression or **delinquency control** Involves any justice program or policy designed to prevent the occurrence of a future delinquent act.

delinquent Juvenile who has been adjudicated by a judicial officer of a juvenile court as having committed a delinquent act.

delinquent boy Adopts a set of norms and values in direct opposition to middle-class society and resists control efforts by authority figures.

designer drugs Lab-made drugs designed to avoid existing drug laws.

desistance *See* aging-out process.

detached street workers Social workers who go out into the community and establish close relationships with juvenile gangs with the goal of modifying gang behavior to conform to conventional behaviors and to help gang members get jobs and educational opportunities.

detention Temporary care of a child alleged to be delinquent who requires secure custody in physically restricting facilities pending court disposition or execution of a court order.

detention hearing A hearing by a judicial officer of a juvenile court to determine whether a juvenile is to be detained or released while juvenile proceedings are pending in the case.

determinate sentence Sentence that specifies a fixed term of detention that must be served.

developed countries Recognized by the United Nations as the richest countries in the world.

developing countries Recognized by the U.N. as countries that are showing signs of improved economic growth and are making the transition from low income to high income.

developmental process At different stages of the life course a variety of factors can influence behavior; factors influential at one stage of life may not be significant at a later stage.

developmental theories Assert that personal characteristics guide human development and influence behavioral choices but that these choices may change over the life course.

developmental view The view that factors present at birth and events that unfold over a person's lifetime influence behavior; developmental theory focuses on the onset, escalation, desistance, and amplification of delinquent behaviors.

differential association theory Asserts that criminal behavior is learned primarily within interpersonal groups and that youths will become delinquent if definitions they have learned favorable to violating the law exceed definitions favorable to obeying the law within that group.

differential reinforcement theory A refinement of differential association theory that asserts that behavior is shaped by the reactions of others to that behavior; youths who receive more rewards than punishments for conforming behavior will be the most likely to remain nondelinquent.

disaggregated Analyzing the relationship between two or more independent variables (such as murder convictions and death sentence) while controlling for the influence of a dependent variable (such as race).

discretion Use of personal decision making and choice in carrying out operations in the criminal justice system, such as deciding whether to make an arrest or when to accept a plea bargain.

disorganized neighborhood Inner-city areas of extreme poverty where the critical social control mechanisms have broken down.

disposition For juvenile offenders, the equivalent of sentencing for adult offenders; however, juvenile dispositions should be more rehabilitative than retributive.

disposition hearing The social service agency presents its case plan and recommendations for care of the child and treatment of the parents, including incarceration and counseling or other treatments.

diversion Officially halting or suspending a formal criminal or juvenile justice proceeding at any legally prescribed processing point after a recorded justice system entry, and referral of that person to a treatment or care program or a recommendation that the person be released.

dramatization of evil The process of social typing that transforms an offender's identity from a doer of evil to an evil person.

drift Idea that youths move in and out of delinquency and that their lifestyles can embrace both conventional and deviant values.

dropouts Youths who leave school before completing their required program of education.

drug courts Courts whose focus is providing treatment for youths accused of drug-related acts.

due process Basic constitutional principle based on the concept of the primacy of the individual and the complementary concept of limitation on governmental power; safeguards the individual from unfair state procedures in judicial or administrative proceedings; due process rights have been extended to juvenile trials.

early onset The outbreak of deviant or delinquent behavior in preadolescence, which is generally viewed as a precursor of chronic offending in adolescence and which generally continues into adulthood.

egalitarian families Husband and wife share power at home; daughters gain a kind of freedom similar to that of sons and their law-violating behaviors mirror those of their brothers.

ego identity According to Erik Erikson, ego identity is formed when persons develop a firm sense of who they are and what they stand for.

electronic monitoring Active monitoring systems consist of a radio transmitter worn by the offender that sends a continuous signal to the probation department computer, alerting officials if the offender leaves his or her place of confinement; passive systems employ computer-generated random phone calls that must be responded to in a certain period of time from a particular phone or other device.

equipotentiality View that all people are equal at birth and are thereafter influenced by their environment.

evolutionary theory Explaining the existence of aggression and violent behavior as positive adaptive behaviors in human evolution; these traits allowed their bearers to reproduce disproportionately, which has had an effect on the human gene pool.

excluded offenses Offenses, some minor and others very serious, that are automatically excluded from juvenile court.

experimental group The group of subjects that receives the program.

extravert A person who behaves impulsively and doesn't have the ability to examine motives and behavior.

familicide Mass murders in which a spouse and one or more children are slain.

family group homes A combination of foster care and a group home in which a juvenile is placed in a private group home run by a single family rather than by professional staff.

Federal Bureau of Investigation (FBI) Arm of the U.S. Department of Justice that investigates violations of federal law, gathers crime statistics, runs a comprehensive crime laboratory, and helps train local law enforcement officers.

feminist theory Asserts that the patriarchal social system oppresses women, creating gender bias and encouraging violence against women.

final order Order that ends litigation between two parties by determining all their rights and disposing of all the issues.

focal concerns The value orientation of lower-class culture that is characterized by a need for excitement, trouble, smartness, fate, and personal autonomy.

foot patrol Police patrolling an area by walking around the community rather than driving about in patrol cars.

foster care programs Juveniles who are orphans or whose parents cannot care for them are placed with families who provide the attention, guidance, and care they did not receive at home.

freebase Purified cocaine crystals that are crushed and smoked to provide a more powerful high than cocaine.

free will View that youths are in charge of their own destinies and are free to make personal behavior choices unencumbered by environmental factors.

gangs Groups of youths who collectively engage in delinquent behaviors.

gateway drug A substance that leads to use of more serious drugs; alcohol use has long been thought to lead to more serious drug abuse.

gender identity The gender characteristics individuals identify in their own behaviors; members of both sexes who identify with "masculine" traits are more likely to engage in delinquent acts.

gender-schema theory Asserts that our culture polarizes males and females, forcing them into exclusive gender roles of "feminine" or "masculine"; these gender scripts provide the basis for deviant behaviors.

general deterrence Crime control policies that depend on the fear of criminal penalties, such as long prison sentences for violent crimes; aim is to convince law violator that the pain outweighs the benefit of criminal activity.

gentrified The process of transforming a lower-class area into a middle-class enclave through property rehabilitation.

graffiti Inscriptions or drawings made on a wall or structure and used by delinquents for gang messages and turf definition.

group autonomy Maintaining subcultural values and attitudes that reinforce the independence of the group and separate it from other cultural groups.

group homes Nonsecured, structured residences that provide counseling, education, job training, and family living.

group therapy Counseling several individuals together in a group session; individuals can obtain support from other group members as they work through similar problems.

guardian *ad litem* A court-appointed attorney who protects the interests of the child in cases involving the child's welfare.

guided group interaction (GGI) Through group interactions a delinquent can acknowledge and solve personal problems with support from other group members.

hallucinogens Natural or synthetic substances that produce vivid distortions of the senses without greatly disturbing consciousness.

hashish A concentrated form of cannabis made from unadulterated resin from the female cannabis plant.

hearsay Out-of-court statements made by one person and recounted in court by another; such statements are generally not allowed as evidence except in child abuse cases wherein a child's statements to social workers, teachers, or police may be admissible.

heroin A narcotic made from opium and then cut with sugar or some other neutral substance until it is only 1 to 4 percent pure.

hot spot A particular location or address that is the site of repeated and frequent criminal activity.

house arrest An offender is required to stay at home during specific periods of time; monitoring is done by random phone calls and visits or by electronic devices.

House of Refuge A care facility developed by the child savers to protect potential criminal youths by taking them off the street and providing a family-like environment.

identity crisis Psychological state, identified by Erikson, in which youth face inner turmoil and uncertainty about life roles.

Illinois Juvenile Court Act of 1899 A major event in the history of juvenile justice, this act served as a model for other states, establishing the special status of juveniles and the emphasis on helping to treat rather than punish young offenders.

indeterminate sentence Does not specify the length of time the juvenile must be held; rather, correctional authorities decide when the juvenile is ready to return to society.

index crime *See* Part I offenses.

individual counseling Counselors help juveniles understand and solve their current adjustment problems.

individualized treatment model Each sentence must be tailored to the individual needs of the child.

inhalants Volatile liquids that give off a vapor, which is inhaled, producing short-term excitement and euphoria followed by a period of disorientation.

inheritance school An early form of biological theory that held that deviant behavior was inherited and therefore ran in families, being passed on from generation to generation.

in loco parentis In the place of the parent; rights given to schools that allow them to assume parental duties in disciplining students.

intake Process during which a juvenile referral is received and a decision is made to file a petition in juvenile court to release the juvenile, to place the juvenile under supervision, or to refer the juvenile elsewhere.

Intensive Aftercare Program (IAP) A balanced, highly structured, comprehensive continuum of intervention for serious and violent juvenile offenders returning to the community.

interactional theory Asserts that youths' interactions with institutions and events over the life course determine criminal behavior patterns and that these patterns of behavior evolve over time.

international crime Crime that is punishable under international law.

interstitial group Delinquent group that fills a crack in the social fabric and maintains standard group practices.

intrafamily conflict An environment of discord and conflict within the family; children who grow up in dysfunctional homes often exhibit delinquent behaviors, having learned at a young age that aggression pays off.

judicial waiver When the juvenile court waives its jurisdiction over a juvenile and transfers the case to adult criminal court.

jurisdiction Every kind of judicial action; the authority of courts and judicial officers to decide cases.

juvenile court Court that has original jurisdiction over persons defined by statute as juveniles and alleged to be delinquents, status offenders, or dependents.

juvenile court judge A judge elected or appointed to preside over juvenile cases and whose decisions can only be reviewed by a judge of a higher court.

juvenile defense attorneys Represent children in juvenile court and play an active role at all stages of the proceedings.

juvenile delinquency Participation in illegal behavior by a minor who falls under a statutory age limit.

juvenile intensive probation supervision (JIPS) A true alternative to incarceration that involves almost daily supervision of the juvenile by the probation officer assigned to the case.

Juvenile Justice and Delinquency Prevention Act of 1974 This act established the OJJDP as an independent agency charged with developing and implementing programs to prevent and reduce juvenile crime.

juvenile justice process Under the paternal (*parens patriae*) philosophy, juvenile justice procedures are informal and nonadversarial, invoked for the juvenile offender rather than against him or her; a petition instead of a complaint is filed; courts make findings of involvement or adjudication of delinquency instead of convictions; and juvenile offenders receive dispositions instead of sentences.

Juvenile Justice Reform Act of 1977 A Washington state statute that created mandatory sentencing for juvenile offenders based on their age, the crime, and their prior history as an offender.

juvenile justice system The segment of the justice system including law enforcement officers, the courts, and correctional agencies, designed to treat youthful offenders.

juvenile officers Police officers who specialize in dealing with juvenile offenders; they may operate alone or as part of a juvenile police unit within the department.

juvenile probation officer Officer of the court involved in all four stages of the court process—intake, predisposition, postadjudication, and postdisposition—who assists the court and supervises juveniles placed on probation.

juvenile prosecutor Government attorney responsible for representing the interests of the state and bringing the case against the accused juvenile.

klikas Subgroups of same-aged youths in Hispanic gangs that remain together and have separate names and a unique identity within the gang.

labeling theory Posits that society creates deviance through a system of social control agencies that designate (or label) certain individuals as delinquent, thereby stigmatizing youths and encouraging them to accept this negative personal identity.

latchkey children Children left unsupervised after school by working parents.

latent delinquents Youths whose troubled family life leads them to seek immediate gratification without consideration of right and wrong or the feelings of others.

latent trait view The view that a master trait, developed at birth or soon after, influences behavior across the life course. People who have this trait are crime-prone throughout their lives.

law enforcement The primary duty of all police officers to fight crime and keep the peace.

Law Enforcement Assistance Administration (LEAA) Unit in the U.S. Department of Justice established by the Omnibus Crime Control and Safe Streets Act of 1968 to administer grants and provide guidance for crime prevention policy and programs.

learning disability (LD) Neurological dysfunction that prevents an individual from learning to his or her potential.

learning theory Posits that delinquency is learned through close relationships with others; asserts that children are born "good" and learn to be "bad" from others.

least detrimental alternative Choosing a program for the child that will best foster a child's growth and development.

least developed countries Recognized by the U.N. as being the poorest countries in the world and suffering from long-term barriers to economic growth.

least restrictive alternative Choosing a program with the least restrictive or secure setting that will benefit the child.

left realism Asserts that crime is a function of relative deprivation and that criminals prey on the poor.

legalization of drugs Decriminalizing drug use to reduce the association between drug use and crime.

liberal feminism Asserts that females are less delinquent than males because their social roles provide them with fewer opportunities to commit crimes; as the roles of girls and women become more similar to those of boys and men, so too will their crime patterns.

life-course persisters Delinquent youth who begin their offending career quite early and persist into their adulthood.

life-course theory The view that people change as they mature and that the quality of their personal development shapes their behavior choices.

lifestyle violent juveniles Juveniles who become more violent when exposed to more serious offenders in institutions.

longitudinal studies A research design that entails repeated measures over time; for example, a cohort may be measured at several points over their life course to determine risk factors for chronic offending.

low-visibility decision making Decisions made by public officials in the criminal or juvenile justice system that the public is not in a position to understand, regulate, or criticize.

mandatory sentence Sentence is defined by a statutory requirement that states the penalty to be set for all cases of a specific offense.

marijuana The dried leaves of the cannabis plant.

Marxist feminists *See* radical feminists.

masculinity hypothesis View that women who commit crimes have biological and psychological traits similar to those of men.

meta-analysis An analysis technique that synthesizes results across many programs over time.

middle-class measuring rods Standards by which teachers and other representatives of state authority evaluate students' behavior; when lower-class youths cannot meet these standards they are subject to failure, which brings on frustration and anger at conventional society.

milieu therapy All aspects of the environment are part of the treatment, and meaningful change, increased growth, and satisfactory adjustment are encouraged; this is often accomplished through peer pressure to conform to the group norms.

minimal brain dysfunction (MBD) Damage to the brain itself that causes antisocial behavior injurious to the individual's lifestyle and social adjustment.

Miranda warning Supreme Court decisions require police officers to inform individuals under arrest of their constitutional rights; warnings must also be given when suspicion begins to focus on an individual in the accusatory stage.

Missouri Plan Sets out how juvenile court judges are chosen and specifies that a commission should nominate candidates, an elected official should make the appointment, and the incumbent judge should run uncontested on his or her record in a nonpartisan election, usually every three years.

monetary restitution A requirement that juvenile offenders compensate crime victims for out-of-pocket losses caused by the crime, including property damage, lost wages, and medical expenses.

moral entrepreneurs Interest groups that attempt to control social life by promoting their own personal set of moral values and establishing them as law.

multisystemic treatment (MST) Addresses a variety of family, peer, and psychological problems by focusing on problem solving and communication skills training.

National Advisory Commission on Criminal Justice Standards and Goals Established in 1973, the commission's report identified major strategies for juvenile justice and delinquency prevention.

National Council of Juvenile and Family Court Judges An organization that sponsors research and continuing legal education to help juvenile court judges master their field of expertise.

natural areas for crime Inner-city areas of extreme poverty where the critical social control mechanisms have broken down.

nature theory Holds that low intelligence is genetically determined and inherited.

near groups Relatively unstructured short-term groups with fluid membership.

need for treatment The criteria on which juvenile sentencing is based. Ideally, juveniles are treated according to their need for treatment and not the seriousness of the delinquent act they committed.

negative affective states Anger, depression, disappointment, fear, and other adverse emotions that derive from strain.

neglect Passive neglect by a parent or guardian, depriving children of food, shelter, health care, and love.

neurological The brain and nervous system structure.

neuroticism A personality trait marked by unfounded anxiety, tension, and emotional instability.

neutralization techniques A set of attitudes or beliefs that allow would-be delinquents to negate any moral apprehension they may have about committing crime so that they may freely engage in antisocial behavior without regret.

neutralization theory Holds that youths adhere to conventional values while "drifting" into periods of illegal behavior; for drift to occur, youths must first neutralize conventional legal and moral values.

nonresidential programs Juveniles remain in their own homes but receive counseling, education, employment, diagnostic, and casework services through an intensive support system.

nuclear family A family unit composed of parents and their children; this smaller family structure is subject to great stress due to the intense, close contact between parents and children.

nurture theory Holds that intelligence is partly biological but mostly sociological; negative environmental factors encourage delinquent behavior and depress intelligence scores for many youths.

Office of Juvenile Justice and Delinquency Prevention (OJJDP) Branch of the U.S. Justice Department charged with shaping national juvenile justice policy through disbursement of federal aid and research funds.

official delinquency Delinquent acts that result in arrest by local police. These are included in the FBI's arrest data.

orphan train A practice of the Children's Aid Society in which urban youths were sent West on trains for adoption with local farm couples.

overt pathway The developmental path taken to delinquency that begins with violent outbursts and bullying.

parens patriae Power of the state to act in behalf of the child and provide care and protection equivalent to that of a parent.

parental efficacy The ability of parents to effectively raise their children in a noncoercive fashion.

parole guidelines Recommended length of confinement and kinds of aftercare assistance most effective for a juvenile who committed a specific offense.

Part I offenses (also known as **index crimes**) Offenses including homicide and nonnegligent manslaughter, forcible rape, robbery, aggravated assault, burglary, larceny, arson, and motor vehicle theft; recorded by local law enforcement officers, these crimes are tallied quarterly and sent to the FBI for inclusion in the UCR.

Part II offenses All crimes other than Part I offenses; recorded by local law enforcement officers, arrests for these crimes are tallied quarterly and sent to the FBI for inclusion in the UCR.

passive speech A form of expression protected by the First Amendment but not associated with actually speaking words; examples include wearing symbols or protest messages on buttons or signs.

paternalism hypothesis *See* chivalry hypothesis.

paternalistic family A family style wherein the father is the final authority on all family matters and exercises complete control over his wife and children.

peacemakers Assert that peace and humanism can reduce crime and offers a new approach to crime control through mediation.

penis envy According to Freud, women are envious of the male sex organ and unconsciously wish that they were men.

persistence The process by which juvenile offenders continue to persist in their delinquent careers rather than aging out of crime.

petition Document filed in juvenile court alleging that a juvenile is a delinquent, a status offender, or a dependent and asking that the court assume jurisdiction over the juvenile.

plea bargaining The exchange of prosecutorial and judicial concessions for a guilty plea by the accused; plea bargaining usually results in a reduced charge or a more lenient sentence.

pledge system Early English system in which neighbors protected each other from thieves and warring groups.

Poor Laws English statutes that allowed the courts to appoint overseers over destitute and neglected children, allowing placement of these children as servants in the homes of the affluent.

positive peer culture (PPC) Counseling program in which peer leaders encourage other group members to modify their behavior and peers help reinforce acceptable behaviors.

power-control theory Holds that gender differences in the delinquency rate are a function of class differences and economic conditions that influence the structure of family life.

precocious sexuality Sexual experimentation in early adolescence.

predatory crimes Violent crimes against persons and crimes in which an offender attempts to steal an object directly from its holder.

predispositional investigation An investigation usually carried out by a member of the probationary staff to acquire information about the child that will allow the judge to make a decision in the best interest of the child.

predisposition report *See* social investigation report.

premenstrual syndrome (PMS) A set of symptoms related to hormonal changes just prior to menstruation that may contribute to mood swings in women.

President's Commission on Law Enforcement and the Administration of Justice This 1967 commission suggested that we must provide juveniles with opportunities for success, including jobs and education, and that we must develop effective law enforcement procedures to control hard-core youthful offenders.

prestige crimes Stealing or assaulting someone to gain prestige in the neighborhood; often part of gang initiation rites.

pretrial conference The attorney for the social services agency presents an overview of the case and a plea bargain or negotiated settlement can be agreed to in a consent decree.

preventive detention Keeping the accused in custody prior to trial because the accused is suspected of being a danger to the community.

primary deviance Deviant acts that do not redefine the self- and public-image of the offender.

primary sociopaths Individuals with an inherited trait that predisposes them to antisocial behavior.

primogeniture During the Middle Ages, the right of the first-born sons to inherit lands and titles, leaving their brothers the option of a military or religious career.

probable cause Reasonable ground to believe the existence of facts that an offense was committed and that the accused committed that offense.

probation Nonpunitive, legal disposition of juveniles emphasizing community treatment in which the juvenile is closely supervised by an officer of the court and must adhere to a strict set of rules to avoid incarceration.

problem behavior syndrome (PBS) Convergence of a variety of psychological problems and family dysfunctions including substance abuse and criminality.

problem-oriented policing Law enforcement that focuses on addressing the problems underlying incidents of juvenile delinquency rather than the incidents only.

prosecutorial discretion Allowing the prosecutor to determine the jurisdiction by selecting the charge to be filed or by choosing to file the complaint in either juvenile or adult court.

pro-social bonds The attachment a child has with positive elements of society such as schools, parents, and peers.

protective factor A positive prior factor in an individual's life that decreases the risk of occurrence of a future delinquent act.

psychodynamic theory Branch of psychology that holds that the human personality is controlled by unconscious mental processes developed early in childhood.

psychopathic personality (also known as **sociopathic personality**) A person lacking in warmth and affection, exhibiting inappropriate behavior responses, and unable to learn from experience.

psychotherapy Highly structured counseling in which a skilled therapist helps a juvenile solve conflicts and make a more positive adjustment to society.

public defender An attorney who works in a public agency or under private contractual agreement as defense counsel to indigent defendants.

radical feminists (also known as **Marxist feminists**) Hold that gender inequality stems from the unequal power of men and women and the subsequent exploitation of women by men; the cause of female delinquency originates with the onset of male supremacy and the efforts of males to control females' sexuality.

randomized experimental design Considered the "gold standard" of evaluation designs to measure the effect of a program on delinquency or other outcomes. Involves randomly assigning subjects either to receive the program (the experimental group) or not receive it (the control group).

reaction formation Rejecting conventional goals and standards that seem impossible to attain.

reality therapy A form of counseling that emphasizes current behavior and that requires the individual to accept responsibility for all of his or her actions.

reflective role-taking A process whereby youths take on antisocial roles assigned to them by others.

reform schools Institutions in which educational and psychological services are used in an effort to improve the conduct of juveniles who are forcibly detained.

relative deprivation Condition that exists when people of wealth and poverty live in close proximity to one another; the relatively deprived are apt to have feelings of anger and hostility, which may produce criminal behavior.

removal *See* waiver.

representing Tossing or flashing gang signs in the presence of rivals, often escalating into a verbal or physical confrontation.

residential programs Placement of a juvenile offender in a residential, nonsecure facility such as a group home, foster home, family group home, or rural home where the juvenile can be closely monitored and develop close relationships with staff members.

resource dilution As the number of children in a family increases, the social and economic resources available to raise them are spread thinner and become less effective.

restorative justice Nonpunitive strategies for dealing with juvenile offenders that make the justice system a healing process rather than a punishment process.

retreatists Gangs whose members actively engage in substance abuse.

review hearing Periodic meetings to determine whether the conditions of the case plan for an abused child are being met by the parents or guardians of the child.

right to treatment Philosophy espoused by many courts that juvenile offenders have a statutory right to treatment while under the jurisdiction of the courts.

risk factor A negative prior factor in an individual's life that increases the risk of occurrence of a future delinquent act.

role conflicts Conflicts police officers face that revolve around the requirement to perform their primary duty of law enforcement and a desire to aid in rehabilitating youthful offenders.

role diffusion According to Erik Erikson, role diffusion occurs when youths spread themselves too thin, experience personal uncertainty, and place themselves at the mercy of leaders who promise to give them a sense of identity they cannot develop for themselves.

routine activities theory View that crime is a "normal" function of the routine activities of modern living; offenses can be expected if there is a motivated offender and a suitable target that is not protected by capable guardians.

rural programs Specific recreational and work opportunities provided for juveniles in a rural setting such as a forestry camp, a farm, or a ranch.

school failure Failing to achieve success in school can result in frustration, anger, and reduced self-esteem, which may contribute to delinquent behavior.

search and seizure The U.S. Constitution protects citizens from any search and seizure by police without a lawfully obtained search warrant; such warrants are issued when there is probable cause to believe that an offense has been committed.

secondary deviance Deviant acts that redefine the offender's self- and public image, forming the basis for the youth's self-concept.

secondary prevention (also known as **special prevention**) Psychological counseling, psychotropic medications, and other rehabilitation treatment programs designed to prevent repeat offenses.

secondary sociopaths Individuals who are biologically normal but exhibit antisocial behavior due to negative life experiences.

sedatives Drugs of the barbiturate family that depress the central nervous system into a sleep-like condition.

self-control Ability to control impulsive and often imprudent behaviors that offer immediate short-term gratification.

self-fulfilling prophecy Deviant behavior patterns that are a response to an earlier labeling experience; youths act out these social roles even if they were falsely bestowed.

self-labeling The process in which a person who has been negatively labeled accepts the label as a personal role or identity.

self-reports Questionnaire or survey technique that asks subjects to reveal their own participation in delinquent or criminal acts.

shelter care A place for temporary care of children in physically unrestricting facilities.

skinhead Member of white supremacist gang, identified by a shaved skull and Nazi or Ku Klux Klan markings.

situational crime prevention A crime prevention method that relies on reducing the opportunity to commit criminal acts by (1) making them more difficult to perform, (2) reducing their reward and (3) increasing their risks.

social bond Ties a person to the institutions and processes of society; elements of the bond include attachment, commitment, involvement, and belief.

social capital The positive relationships a person develops that help them succeed in life and avoid criminal behaviors.

social conflict theory Asserts that society is in a state of constant internal conflict, and focuses on the role of social and governmental institutions as mechanisms for social control.

social control Ability of social institutions to influence human behavior; the justice system is the primary agency of formal social control.

social development model (SDM) An array of personal, psychological, and community-level risk factors that make some children susceptible to development of antisocial behaviors.

social disorganization Neighborhood or area marked by culture conflict, lack of cohesiveness, a transient population, and insufficient social organizations; these problems are reflected in the problems at schools in these areas.

social disorganization theory Posits that delinquency is a product of the social forces existing in inner-city, low-income areas.

social ecology Theory focuses attention on the influence social institutions have on individual behavior and suggests that law-violating behavior is a response to social rather than individual forces operating in an urban environment.

social investigation report (also known as **predisposition report**) Developed by the juvenile probation officer, this report consists of a clinical diagnosis of the juvenile and his or her need for court assistance, relevant environmental and personality factors, and any other information that would assist the court in developing a treatment plan for the juvenile.

socialization The process of learning the values and norms of the society or the subculture to which the individual belongs.

social learning theory The view that behavior is modeled through observation either directly through intimate contact with others or indirectly through media; interactions that are rewarded are copied, whereas those that are punished are avoided.

socially disorganized neighborhood Neighborhood or area marked by culture conflict, lack of cohesiveness, a transient population, and insufficient social organizations; these problems are reflected in the problems at schools in these areas.

social process theories Posit that the interactions a person has with key elements of the socialization process determine his or her future behavior.

social structure theories Explain delinquency using socioeconomic conditions and cultural values.

Society for the Prevention of Cruelty to Children (SPCC) First established in 1874, these organizations protected children subjected to cruelty and neglect at home or at school.

sociopathic personality *See* psychopathic personality.

somatotype school Argued that delinquents manifest distinct physiques that make them susceptible to particular types of delinquent behavior.

special prevention *See* secondary prevention.

specific deterrence Sending convicted offenders to secure incarceration facilities so that punishment is severe enough to convince offenders not to repeat their criminal activity.

spontaneous remission *See* aging-out process.

stable slum A neighborhood where population shifts have slowed down, permitting patterns of behavior and traditions to develop over a number of years.

status offense Conduct that is illegal only because the child is under age.

stimulants Synthetic substances that produce an intense physical reaction by stimulating the central nervous system.

strain theory Links delinquency to the strain of being locked out of the economic mainstream, which creates the anger and frustration that lead to delinquent acts.

stratification Grouping society into classes based on the unequal distribution of scarce resources.

stigmatized People who have been negatively labeled because of their participation, or alleged participation, in deviant or outlawed behaviors.

subculture of violence An identified urban-based subculture in which young males are expected to respond with violence to the slightest provocation.

subcultures Groups that are loosely part of the dominant culture but that maintain a unique set of values, beliefs, and traditions.

substance abuse Using drugs or alcohol in such a way as to cause physical, emotional and/or psychological harm to yourself.

subterranean values The ability of youthful law violators to repress social norms.

suppression effect A reduction in the number of arrests per year for youths who have been incarcerated or otherwise punished.

swaddling The practice during the Middle Ages of completely wrapping newborns in long bandage-like clothes in order to restrict their movements and make them easier to manage.

target-hardening technique Crime prevention technique that makes it more difficult for a would-be delinquent to carry out the illegal act, for example, by a security device in a home.

teen courts Courts that make use of peer juries to decide nonserious delinquency cases.

TOP program Police and community prevention effort in which teens are hired to patrol the city's parks and recreation areas.

totality of the circumstances doctrine Legal doctrine that mandates that a decision maker consider all the issues and circumstances of a case before judging the outcome; the suspect's age, intelligence, and competency may be issues that influence his or her understanding and judgment.

tracking Dividing students into groups according to their ability and achievement levels.

trait theory Holds that youths engage in delinquent or criminal behavior due to aberrant physical or psychological traits that govern behavioral choices; delinquent actions are impulsive or instinctual rather than rational choices.

tranquilizers Drugs that reduce anxiety and promote relaxation.

transfer hearing Preadjudicatory hearing in juvenile court for the purpose of determining whether juvenile court should be retained over a juvenile or waived and the juvenile transferred to adult court for prosecution.

transfer process Transferring a juvenile offender from the jurisdiction of juvenile court to adult criminal court.

transitional neighborhood Area undergoing a shift in population and structure, usually from middle-class residential to lower-class mixed use.

transnational crime Crime that is carried out across the borders of two or more countries and violates the laws of those countries.

trial de novo A review procedure in which there is a complete retrial of the original case.

truancy Staying out of school without permission.

truly disadvantaged According to William Julius Wilson, those people who are left out of the economic mainstream and reduced to living in the most deteriorated inner-city areas.

turning points According to Laub and Sampson, life events, such as marriage, that help a person desist from crime.

underachievers Those who do not achieve success in school at the level of their expectations.

underclass Group of urban poor whose members have little chance of upward mobility or improvement.

Uniform Crime Report (UCR) Compiled by the FBI, the UCR is the most widely used source of national crime and delinquency statistics.

utilitarians Those who believe that people weigh the benefits and consequences of their future actions before deciding on a course of behavior.

victimizations The number of people who are victims of criminal acts; young teens are fifteen times more likely than older adults (age 65 and over) to be victims of crimes.

victim service restitution The juvenile offender is required to provide some service directly to the crime victim.

Violent Crime Control and Law Enforcement Act of 1994 This act made available increased funding for juvenile justice and delinquency prevention.

Violent Juvenile Offender (VJO) program Specialized programs in small, secure settings where youths are gradually reintegrated into the community with intensive supervision.

waiver (also known as **bindover** or **removal**) Transferring legal jurisdiction over the most serious and experienced juvenile offenders to the adult court for criminal prosecution.

watch system Replaced the pledge system in England; watchmen patrolled urban areas at night to provide protection from harm.

wayward minors Early legal designation of youths who violate the law because of their minority status; now referred to as status offenders.

widening the net Phenomenon that occurs when programs created to divert youths from the justice system actually involve them more deeply in the official process.

wilderness probation Programs involving outdoor expeditions that provide opportunities for juveniles to confront the difficulties of their lives while achieving positive personal satisfaction.

writ of certiorari Order of a superior court requesting that the record of an inferior court (or administrative body) be brought forward for review or inspection.

writ of habeus corpus Judicial order requesting that a person detaining another produce the body of the prisoner and give reasons for his or her capture and detention.

zero tolerance policy Mandating specific consequences or punishments for delinquent acts and not allowing anyone to avoid these consequences.

Table of Cases

Name Index

Daly, Martin, 101, 133, 134, 224
Dammer, Harry R., 516
Daniele, Atonietta, 224
Dannefer, Dale, 414
Daro, Deborah, 224
Datesman, Susan, 28
Davidson, Howard, 449
Davidson, William, 298
Davies, Mark, 135, 327
Davies-Netley, Sally, 225
Davis, Kenneth C., 413, 414
Davis, Samuel M., 413
Davison, Elizabeth, 98
Dawkins, Eric, 328
Dawley, David, 262
Dawson, Robert O., 387
Day, H. D., 103
Dean, Charles W., 159, 160, 188, 414
DeBaryshe, Barbara, 159
Decker, Scott, 263, 264
Dedel, Kelly, 449
DeFrances, Carol J., 387
De Haan, Laura G., 133
DeJong, Christina, 55, 99, 222
DeKeseredy, Walter, 189
Delany-Shabazz, Robin V., 224
De Li, Spencer, 135
De Lisi, Matt, 414
DeLone, Miriam, 55, 414
Deng, Xiaogang, 162
Denno, Deborah, 103
Dentler, Robert, 55
DeRios, M. D., 327
Derzon, James, 160
Deschenes, E. P., 450
Devine, F. E., 98
Devlin, Daniel, 412
De Witt, Charles, 223
DiLalla, Lisabeth Fisher, 100
Dinitz, Simon, 56, 99, 488
Dishion, Thomas J., 223, 262, 327, 355, 356, 357, 489
Dobbin, Shirley, 224
Dobkin, Patricia, 327
Dodge, Douglas C., 449
Dodge, K. A., 102
Dolce, Philip C., 386
Donnerstein, Edward, 101
Donovan, John, 159
Dornfeld, Maude, 224
Dougherty, Joyce, 450
Downey, Douglas, 133, 223
Downs, William, 223, 225
Draper, Patricia, 224
Driver, Edward, 99
Droegemueller, W., 223
Duggan, Anne K., 356
Dumond, Doris, 414
Dunaway, R. Gregory, 55, 135, 189
Duncan, Greg J., 133
D'Unger, Amy, 56, 160
Dunlap, Earl, 449
Dunn, Melissa, 190, 191
Dunworth, Terence, 413
Dussault, Monique, 101
Dwiggins, Donna, 188
Dwing, Darlene, 450

E

Earls, Felton, 56, 134
Eccles, Jacquelynne, 99, 189, 190
Eck, John E., 225, 412, 413
Eckert, Penelope, 262
Edler, Rob, 98
Edwards, Leonard, 225, 387, 449
Eels, Kenneth, 102
Egan, Timothy, 386
Eggebeen, David, 223
Eggleston, Carolyn, 188
Egley, Arlen, Jr., 263
Eisikovits, Z., 488
Eldefonso, Edward, 488
Elias, Albert, 487
Ellickson, Phyllis, 328
Elliott, Delbert, 55, 162, 296, 327, 328, 356, 487
Ellis, Lee, 99, 100, 101, 103, 135, 161, 189, 190
Ellison, Christopher, 222
Empey, LaMar, 54, 487, 488
English, Bella, 298
Ennett, Susan, 55
Erickson, Erik, 101
Erickson, Maynard, 54, 99, 487
Erlenmeyer-Kimling, L., 100
Eron, L., 102
Esbensen, Finn-Aage, 263, 264, 265, 415
Evans, T. David, 55, 134, 135, 189
Eve, Raymond, 55, 191
Eysenck, Hans, 102
Eysenck, M. W., 102
Ezell, Mark, 450
Ezell, Michael, 56

F

Fadern, James, 56
Fagan, Abigail, 487
Fagan, Jeffrey, 55, 56, 263, 414, 449, 450
Fairchild, Erika, 516
Farnworth, Margaret, 56, 135, 161, 262, 296
Farr, Kathryn Ann, 329
Farrington, David P., 56, 57, 102, 103, 159, 160, 190, 221, 223, 262, 355, 356, 357, 358, 412, 413, 488, 489, 515, 516
Farris, Elizabeth, 298
Faupel, Charles, 328
Faust, Frederick L., 355
Fein, Robert, 297
Feingold, Alan, 162
Fejes-Mendoza, Kathy, 188
Feld, Barry, 28, 387, 450
Feldman, Marilyn, 100
Felson, Marcus, 98, 99
Fendrich, Michael, 222, 327
Fenwick, Mark, 517
Ferdinand, Theodore, 386, 387, 413
Fergusson, David, 135, 160
Ferrero, William, 188, 189
Feucht, Thomas, 326
Feyerherm, William, 55, 189
Field, Diane, 101

Figlio, Robert, 55, 56, 97, 296
Figuerdo, Aurelio Jose, 101
Finckenauer, James O., 516
Findlay, Mark, 516
Finkelhor, David, 57, 223, 224
Finn, Peter, 413
Firestone, Philip, 101
Fischer, Craig, 488
Fishbein, Diana, 99, 100, 190
Fisher, Bonnie, 57
Fisher, Deborah A., 355
Fishman, G., 488
Fisk, Wendy, 224
Flannery, Daniel, 161, 189
Flaving, Jeanne, 414
Flewelling, Robert, 54, 55
Fogelson, Robert, 412
Foglia, Wanda, 98, 99
Fontana, Vincent J., 224
Forde, David, 98, 161
Forehand, Rex, 327
Fowles, Richard, 133
Fox, James, 54, 386, 387
Fox, Robert J., 261
Fox, Sanford J., 386, 450
Frank, James, 412
Franklin, J. M., 103
Fraser, Brian G., 223
Frazee, Sharon Glave, 98
Frazier, Charles, 55, 414, 450
Frease, Dean, 297
Fredrich, Michael, 326
Freedman, Jonathan, 102
Freeman, Taneekah, 486
Frehsee, D., 224
Freitag, Raelene, 225
Freng, Adrienne, 415
Freud, Anna, 451
Freud, Sigmund, 101, 189
Friedrich-Cofer, Lynette, 101
Fritsch, Eric, 414, 450
Frodi, Ann, 190
Frost, Laurie, 102
Fuentes, Ilarraza, 449
Fukurai, Hiroshi, 136
Fyfe, James, 414

G

Gabor, Thomas, 358, 515
Gabrielli, William, 101, 103
Gadow, Kenneth, 101
Gallagher, Catherine, 329
Ganousis, Jeanette, 451
Garcia, Robert, 263
Garfinkel, Harold, 136
Garofalo, James, 98
Garrett, Carol, 487
Gary, Eileen, 357
Gatowski, Sophia, 224
Gatti, Uberto, 516
Geis, Gilbert, 450
Gelles, Richard, 223, 224, 225
Gelsthorpe, Loraine, 517
Gerard, D. L., 327
Gerstein, Dean, 160, 222
Gerstein, Steven, 451

Lorch, Elizabeth Pugzles, 101
Lorenz, Frederick, 160
Lotke, Eric, 133
Loughran, Edward J., 449
Lu, Chunmeng, 57
Lucan, Wayne, 328
Luchterhand, Elmer, 413
Lundman, Richard J., 355, 413, 414, 449
Lykken, D. T., 101
Lyman, Donald, 189
Lynch, James, 515
Lynch, Michael, 99
Lyons, Horace, 515

M

Macallair, Dan, 487
Maccauley, J., 190
MacCoby, Eleanor, 189, 190
MacCoun, Robert, 327, 328, 329
MacDermid, Shelley, 133
MacDonald, John, 191, 264
Machalek, Richard, 101
MacKenzie, Doris Layton, 225, 357, 412, 488, 489
Macksey-Amiti, Mary Ellen, 326, 327
MacMillan, Ross, 161
Maguire, Brendan, 137
Maguire, Edward R., 412
Mahan, Sue, 189
Mahoney, Anne R., 136
Mahoney, Dennis, 487
Maitland, Angela, 160
Mallar, Charles D., 357
Mallory, W. A., 100
Mangione, Peter L., 356
Manheim, Herman, 99
Mann, Emily A., 356
Mansfield, Wendy, 298
Marcotte, Paul, 450
Markle, Gerald, 222
Markman, Howard, 221
Markowitz, Fred, 134
Marshall, Chris, 29
Marshall, D. D., 103
Marshall, Donnie R., 326, 329
Marshall, Ineke, 29
Marshall, Paul, 99
Martin, Jamie, 162, 189
Martin, Lawrence, 28
Martin, LeRoy, 263
Martin, Randy, 99
Maser, Jack, 262, 327
Mason, Robert, 224
Massey, Charles, 297
Massey, James, 98, 99
Mastrofski, Stephen, 414
Mathur, Anita K., 224
Matsueda, Ross, 136, 161
Matza, David, 135, 136
Maume, David, 98
Maupin, James, 449, 489
Maxfield, Michael, 225
Maxson, Cheryl, 263
Maxwell, Christopher, 160
Maxwell, Sheila Royo, 160
Mays, G. Larry, 265
Mazerolle, Paul, 134, 159, 160, 188

McBride, Duane C., 329
McCall, Patricia, 160
McCall, Robert, 103
McCarthy, Bill, 222
McCord, Joan, 221, 296, 355, 356, 357, 414, 489, 516
McCord, William, 355
McCorkle, Richard, 263
McDermott, Joan, 298
McDill, E. L., 298
McDowall, David, 28, 97, 135, 451
Mcentire, Ranee, 134
McFall, Richard, 102-3
McGahey, Richard, 133
McGarrell, Edmund F., 413
McGee, Rob, 102
McGlothlin, W., 328
McGrath, John, 134
McGue, D. T., 101
McKay, Henry D., 222, 355
McKinney, J. D., 297
McLanahan, Sara, 222
McMahon, R. J., 357
McManus, Terry, 298
McMillan, Dean, 225
McMillan, Richard, 133
McNeill, Richard, 134
McNulty, Thomas, 134
McPartland, J. M., 298
Mealey, Linda, 102
Meares, Tracey L., 414
Mears, Daniel, 189
Medaris, Michael, 298
Mednick, Brigitte, 100
Mednick, Sarnoff, 56, 100, 101, 103, 222
Menacker, Julius, 298
Menard, Scott, 162, 327, 328
Mendel, Richard A., 358
Menlove, Frances, 101
Mennel, Robert, 28, 386
Merkens, Hans, 515
Merlo, Alida, 387
Mero, Richard, 161
Mertinko, Elizabeth, 357
Merton, Robert, 134
Merva, Mary, 133
Meseck-Bushey, Sylvia, 100, 223
MÎsse, Louise C., 327, 357
Messerschmidt, James, 188, 189, 191
Messner, Steven, 55, 98, 102, 132, 133, 134
Metsger, Linda, 99
Meyer, Linda, 223
Michel, Sonya, 356
Middleton, Warren, 189
Miethe, Terance, 263
Mihalic, Sharon, 487
Milich, Richard, 136
Miller, Alden, 486
Miller, Brenda, 223, 225
Miller, Darcy, 188
Miller, Jerome, 486
Miller, Laurie S., 356
Miller, Marc, 28
Miller, Stuart J., 488
Miller, Ted, 57, 355
Miller, Todd, 160
Miller, Walter B., 262, 263, 264, 355
Mio, J. S., 327

Mirowsky, John, 134, 188
Mischel, Walter, 102
Model, Karyn E., 356
Modzeleski, William, 297
Moffitt, Terrie, 56, 99, 100, 102, 103, 160, 161, 162, 189
Monahan, Thomas, 222
Monroe, Lawrence, 55
Monti, Daniel, 261
Mooney, Margaret, 189
Moore, Eugene, 450
Moore, Joan, 190, 263, 264
Moore, Mark H., 265, 297, 328, 358, 412
Moore, Melinda, 55
Morash, Merry, 414
Morenoff, Jeffrey, 133, 134
Morley, Elaine, 357
Morris, Allison, 188
Morris, E., 161
Morris, Norval, 56, 98, 100, 101, 159, 221, 262, 412
Morris, Ruth, 190, 222
Morse, Stephen J., 28
Morselli, Carlo, 97
Mueller, David, 265
Mukherjee, Satanshu, 516
Mulvey, Edward, 56
Murcheson, C., 102
Murphy, Fred, 54
Murphy, Patrick, 327, 329
Murphy, Thomas, 489
Murr, Andrew, 386
Murray, Charles, 99, 100, 136, 486
Murray, Ellen, 99
Mutchnick, Robert, 99
Myers, Kristen, 296, 297
Myers, Stephanie M., 413, 414

N

Nagin, Daniel, 98, 135, 160, 161
Nalla, Mahesh, 135
Nanjundappa, G., 327
Napier, Susan, 224
Nathan, John, 101
Ndiaye, Mademba, 515
Neaigus, Alan, 326
Needle, Jerome, 263, 265
Nelson, Gordon K., 221
Ness, Arlin, 489
New, Michelle, 225
Newcomb, Michael, 160
Newman, Graeme, 28, 358, 516
Nicewander, W. Alan, 161
Niederhoffer, Arthur, 264
Nimer, Richard, 487
Nobiling, Tracy, 55
Nofziger, Stacey, 189
Norman, Michael, 489
Norman, Sherwood, 414
Novotney, Laurence C., 357
Nurco, David, 159
Nye, F. Ivan, 54, 55, 57, 222, 223

O

Oakes, Jeannie, 297
O'Brien, Robert, 98

Rowe, Wendy, 415
Roy, Sudipto, 487
Ruben, Douglas, 224
Rubin, H. Ted, 449, 487
Rudolph, Jennifer, 134
Russell, Diana, 223, 224
Ryan, James, 487
Ryan, Kimberly, 57
Rydell, C. Peter, 356

S

Sack, William, 224
Sagatun, Inger, 225
Salerno, Anthony, 386, 489
Sampson, Robert, 56, 133, 134, 159, 161, 222, 223, 414
Samuelson, Leslie, 136
Sanborn, Joseph B., Jr., 450
Sanchez-Jankowski, Martin, 98, 265
Sanders, Wiley B., 28
Sansone, Lori, 225
Sansone, Randy, 225
Sas, Louise, 488
Saunders, Frank, 190
Savage, Joanne, 516
Savolainen, Jukka, 222
Scali, Mary Ann, 489
Schafer, Walter E., 296, 297
Scharf, P., 102
Schaste, Robert, 489
Schauss, Alexander, 99
Scheuerman, Leo, 133
Schichor, D., 29
Schiff, Mara, 137
Schinke, Steven P., 357
Schlossman, Seven, 355
Schmeidler, J., 328
Schmidt, Annesley, 487
Schneider, Anne L., 487
Schneider, Peter, 487
Schochet, Peter Z., 357
Schulsinger, Fini, 103
Schumacher, Michael, 56
Schur, Edwin, 103
Schuster, Richard, 56
Schutt, Russel, 414
Schwartz, Ira, 28, 29, 265, 387, 449, 450, 451, 487, 488
Schwartz, Joseph, 133
Schwartz, Martin, 189
Schweinhart, Lawrence J., 356
Schwendinger, Herman, 136, 191
Schwendinger, Julia, 136, 191
Sealock, Miriam, 55, 189, 191, 329
Sedlack, Michael, 355
Segal, Nancy, 100, 101
Seguin, Jean, 100
Selke, William, 136
Sellin, Thorsten, 56, 97, 99, 296
Seng, Magnus, 223
Senna, Joseph J., 387
Shannon, Lyle, 296
Shannon, Sarah, 515
Shantz, David, 99
Shaw, Clifford R., 133, 222, 355
Shedler, J., 327
Shelden, Randall, 29, 55, 386

Sheley, Joseph, 264
Shelton, Kelly, 161
Shepard, Robert, Jr., 414, 449, 450, 486, 488
Shepard, Robin, 414
Sheppard, David, 264, 415
Sherkat, Darren, 222
Sherman, Lawrence W., 225, 356, 357, 358, 412, 413, 488
Shestack, Jerome, 386
Shichor, D., 99
Shichor, David, 515
Shin, Hee-Choon, 160
Shine, James, 449
Shirley, Mary, 54
Shlossman, Steven, 387
Short, James, 55, 135, 262
Shover, Neal, 56
Sickmund, Melissa, 54, 328, 357, 414, 450, 488
Siegel, Jane, 191, 225
Siegel, Larry J., 387
Sieverdes, Christopher, 488
Silva, Phil, 56, 102, 161, 162, 189
Silver, H. K., 223
Silverman, F. N., 223
Silverman, Mitchell, 224
Simcha-Fagan, Ora, 133
Simon, Lenore, 223
Simon, Rita James, 188, 189, 190
Simons, Ronald, 135, 160, 222
Simpson, John, 191
Simpson, Sally, 55, 189, 191
Singer, Simon, 191, 296, 297, 451
Skogan, Wesley, 134
Skuse, David, 225
Slater, E., 189, 190
Slaughter, Ellen, 414, 450
Slawson, John, 102
Sloan, John, 57, 515
Sluder, Richard, 160
Small, John, 190
Smart, Carol, 191
Smart, Nicola, 225
Smetena, Judith, 222
Smith, Anne H.W., 225
Smith, Beverly, 386
Smith, Carolyn, 28, 135, 160, 189, 191, 221, 222, 223, 225, 296, 297
Smith, Douglas, 55, 189, 414
Smith, G. T., 327
Smith, Judith, 133
Smith, Steven, 450
Smith, Timothy, 160
Smith, William, 98
Snyder, Howard, 28, 54, 56, 357, 414, 450, 487, 488
Snyder, Phyllis, 28
Soderstrom, Irina, 489
Soler, Mark, 449
Solnit, Albert, 451
Somerville, Dora, 190
Sorenson, Ann Marie, 161, 264
Sorrells, James, 101
South, Scott, 134
Sparrow, Malcolm, 412
Speckart, George, 328
Spergel, Irving, 135, 262, 263, 264, 265

Spohn, Cassie, 55, 414
Spracklen, Kathleen, 262, 327
Sprafkin, Joyce, 101
Sprague, John, 98
Springate, Margaret, 224
Sprowls, J., 449
Spunt, Barry, 191
Sridharan, Sanjeev, 357
Stack, Susan, 56
Stahl, Anne L., 449, 450, 451
Stairs, Jayne, 55
Stapleton, W. Vaughan, 263, 265
Steele, Brandt F., 223, 224
Steele, Patricia, 486
Steele, Ric, 327
Steffensmeier, Darrell, 55, 56, 132, 191
Steinhart, David, 387, 449
Steinharthe, David J., 28
Steinmentz, Suzanne, 223
Stephens, Gene, 137
Stephens, Richard, 326
Stern, Susan, 222
Stevenson, Jim, 225
Stiles, Beverly, 134
Stinchcombe, Arthur L., 297
Stoff, David, 262, 327
Stokes, Robert, 298
Stone, Daryl, 261
Stone, Lawrence, 28
Stouhamer-Loeber, Magda, 159, 160, 221, 222, 262
Strachey, James, 101
Strain, Eric, 327
Strasburg, Paul, 413
Straus, Murray A., 221, 222, 223, 224, 225
Streib, Victor, 413, 451
Streifel, Cathy, 56
Stretesky, Paul, 99
Strodtbeck, Fred, 262
Strom, Kevin, 387, 450
Styfco, Sally J., 356
Su, S. Susan, 160
Sullivan, Mercer, 265
Sutherland, Edwin, 102, 135
Sutton, John, 28, 387
Swanger, Harry F., 451
Sykes, Gresham, 135, 136
Sykes, Richard, 413
Szymanski, Linda, 387, 413, 450, 451

T

Tabor, Mary, 326
Tamara, Hareven, 28
Tardiff, Kenneth, 98
Tatelbaum, Robert, 356
Taussig, Cara, 225
Taylor, Carl, 263
Taylor, Ralph, 133
Taylor, Robert, 414
Taylor, Terrance J., 415
Taylor, William J., 489
Tellegen A., 101
Temple, Judy A., 356
Terlouw, Gert-Jan, 516
Terman, L. M., 102
Terry, Robert, 262, 413

Wolfe, David, 222
Wolfgang, Marvin, 55, 56, 97, 99, 296
Wolford, Bruce, 296
Wolraich, Mark, 99
Wonders, Jerome, 263
Wong, Frank, 101
Wood, Peter, 103, 161
Wood, Wendy, 101
Woods, Kristi, 263
Wooton, Barbara, 223
Worden, Robert E., 413, 414
Wordes, Madeline, 449
Wormith, J. Stephen, 102
Wright, Bradley, 135, 161, 162
Wright, Claudia, 28
Wright, James, 264
Wright, John Paul, 135, 222, 223, 297

Wright, Lloyd, 328
Wright, Richard, 328
Wu, Bohsiu, 449
Wu, Chyi-In, 135, 160
Wu, Lawrence, 135

Y

Yablonsky, Lewis, 102, 265
Yardley, Jim, 54
Yeisley, Mark, 134
Yeung, W. Jean, 133
Yisheng, Dai, 515
Yoerger, Karen, 159, 160
Yokoyama, Minoru, 516
Young, Kimball, 102
Yun, Steve Chong, 264

Z

Zak, Lydia, 222
Zatz, Marjorie, 262
Zeeb, Linda, 221
Zernike, Kate, 516
Zhang, Joshua, 264
Zhang, Lening, 57, 162
Zhang, Quanwu, 262
Zigler, Edward, 225, 356
Zimmerman, Joel, 100
Zimring, Franklin E., 450, 516
Zingraff, Matthew, 225, 296, 297
Zlotnick, S. Jack, 101

Subject Index

Civil Rights Division (Justice Department), 481
Civil Rights of Institutionalized Persons Act (CRIPA), 481–482
classical criminology, 62, 63
class issues
    anomie/strain, 114–118
    child abuse, 210
    drug use, 311
    peer relations, 228
    power-control theory, 184
    school failure, 271–273
    social conflict theory, 106, 127–131
    see also social structure theories
Cleveland, Ohio, 479
cliques, 228, 241–242
closed-circuit television (CCTV), 215, 216, 220
club drugs, 305–306
cocaine, 303, 312, 316, 317
cognitive behavioral treatment, 462
cognitive differences, 167–168
cognitive psychology, 88–90, 96
cognitive strategies, 294
collateral review, 445
collective efficacy, 113
collective gang, 237
Colorado, 24, 25, 52, 217, 484
Columbia University, 77, 281
Columbine High School, 278, 494
commitment, 123
commitment to conformity, 122
communications, in gangs, 243–245
Communities That Care (CTC), 352
community, 147
    delinquency prevention programs, 351–353
    institutions of, 112–113
    school crime and, 282–288
    see also neighborhoods
community centers, 111, 336
community justice centers, 507
community policing, 129, 391–393, 412
community release, 439
community sentences, 510
community service, 439, 440, 461, 485, 513
community service restitution, 464
community treatment, 454, 485
    see also probation
complaint, 213, 429
comprehensive case management programs, 424
Comprehensive Employment Training Act, 130
compressed gang, 237
concentric zones maps, 110
concept of delinquency, 1, 3–4, 16–18, 26
    as adolescent dilemma, 5–9
    development of childhood, 11–16
    study of delinquency, 9–11
    see also childhood; status offenders
conduct disorders, 80
confidentiality, 445–446
conflict theory. see social conflict theory
Connecticut, 15, 444
conscientiousness, 91
Constitution, 212, 215

constitutional rights, 437–438
consumerism, 8
contagion effect, 203
contempt of court, 20–21
continuity of crime and delinquency, 145–146
control
    drug use strategies, 319–324
    in early America, 16
    evaluation of theories, 123–124
    of gangs, 163, 233, 255–260
    perceived, 64
    power-control theory, 183–184, 187
    prevention vs., 332–333
    school policy, 293–295
    social conflict theory, 128, 129
    social control, 24–25, 111–113, 217
    theories, 120, 122–124, 131, 229
control group, 336
controllo, 244
co-offending, 229
COPS (Office of Community Oriented Policing Services), 392
corporal punishment, 201, 207, 291–292
corrections, 453–455
    aftercare, 482–484
    boot camp, 478–480
    community treatment, 454–461, 485
    correctional treatment for juveniles, 474–480
    educational, vocational, and recreational programs, 476–477
    institutionalized juvenile, 472–474
    legal right to treatment, 480–482
    secure, 20, 71–72, 469–470
    struggle for basic civil rights, 481–482
    wilderness programs, 477–478
    see also institutionalization; probation; treatment
cottage system, 469, 485
Council of Europe, 497–498, 501
counseling, 475
Court Appointed Special Advocates (CASA), 420
court-ordered school attendance, 440
courtroom actors, 419–422, 427–428
covert pathway, 143
CPC (Child-Parent Center), 343
CPS (child protection services), 208
CPS (Crown Prosecution Service), 512
crack, 303, 316
CRC (Children's Rights Council), 6
crime
    as business enterprise, 111, 234, 237, 257
    continuity of with delinquency, 145–146
    gangs and, 245–248, 257
    General Theory of, 154–157
    index crimes, 32
    international, 498–499
    opportunity to commit, 66, 154–155, 180
    pathways to, 143–144, 158
    propensity to commit, 154
    schools and, 279–280, 283–288
    as seductive, 66
    situational crime prevention, 69, 71–73

transnational, 498
    see also crime rate; delinquency prevention; deterrence-based punishment; police; violence
Crime and Disorder Act (England), 513
Crime and Human Nature (Wilson and Herrnstein), 93
Crime and the American Dream (Messner and Rosenfeld), 115
Crime Index, 33
Crime in the Making (Sampson and Laub), 150
crime rate, 33–36
    choice theory, 66
    gender differences, 169–170, 180–183
    ISR data, 38–39
    see also crime
Crimes Against Children Research Center, 209
criminal areas, 111
criminal atavism, 74, 171
criminal career, 114, 118, 334
criminality, definition, 65
Criminality of Women, The (Pollack), 171–172
criminalization of juvenile court, 433
Criminal Justice and Public Order Act (England), 513
criminal laws, 17
CRIPA (Civil Rights of Institutionalized Persons Act), 481–482
Crips, 234, 236, 249
crowds, 228
Crown Court, 513
Crown Prosecution Service (CPS), 512
CSPV (Center for the Study and Prevention of Violence), 353
CTC (Communities That Care), 352
cultural deviance theory, 118, 131
cultural transmission, 110, 111
culture conflicts, 118
culture of poverty, 107
curfews, 24, 380, 406–407
custodial interrogation, 398–399
custody, 397
cycle of secondary deviance, 126

D

Dallas Police Department, 406
D.A.R.E. (Drug Abuse Resistance Education), 320–322, 407, 410
dark figures of crime, 33
DAWN (Drug Abuse Warning Network), 306
daycare programs, 195, 341–342
day-center electronic monitoring, 424
DDAP (Detention Diversion Advocacy Program), 425
DEA (Drug Enforcement Administration), 306, 408
death penalty, 70, 379, 444, 448
death squads, 494
decarceration, 461, 470
defense attorneys, 419–420
degradation ceremonies, 126
deinstitutionalization, 130
Delaware, 23

I

IAP (Intensive Aftercare Program), 483, 484
id, 84
Idaho, 23, 24
identity crisis, 85
Illinois, 18–19, 215, 478
    see also Chicago
Illinois Juvenile Court Act, 369–371, 377
immigration, 16, 253
    multinational, 490–494, 496
imprisonment boom, 112
Improving America's Schools Act, 293
impulsivity, 18, 73, 79, 91, 155, 272
incarceration. *see* corrections;
    institutionalization
incentive programs, 340, 346
incest, 178
income, 127, 342
in-court statements, 215–216
indeterminate sentence, 442–443
index crimes, 32
individual, 62
individual counseling, 475
individualism, 8, 255
individualized treatment model, 443
individual theories, 59, 61–62, 106
    choice theory, 62–73
    critique, 94–95
    preventing delinquency, 69–73
    rational delinquent, 63–65
    see also trait theories
Indonesia, 505
industrialization, 364
Industrial Revolution, 390
infant mortality rate, 8
informal consent decree, 440
information processing, 84, 89–90, 96
inhalants, 304
in-home monitoring, 424
initiation, 252–253
in loco parentis, 291, 397
Innovative Neighborhood-Oriented
    Policing (INOP), 392
Institute for Families and Society, 285
Institute for Social Research (ISR), 38–39,
    49–50, 307–308
Institute of Behavioral Science, 318
institutionalization, 439, 454
    decarceration, 461, 470
    economic issues and, 115
    female inmates, 473–474
    history of, 469–470
    institutionalized juvenile, 472–474
    international, 504
    juvenile justice system, 364, 366
    male inmates, 473
    physical conditions, 471–472
    population trends, 471
    public and private, 470–472
    secure corrections, 20, 71–72, 469–470
institutions, community, 112–113
instructors, 504
instrumental gangs, 237
intake, 213, 421, 426–428, 447, 460
intelligence, 46, 74–75, 92–94, 96, 140,
    147

Intensive Aftercare Program (IAP), 483, 484
intensive supervision, 461–462, 485
interactional theory, 149–150, 158
interactive kids, 229
intermediate sanctions, 439
International Association of Chiefs of
    Police, 390, 503
International Center, 498
international crime, 498–499
International Criminal Police Organization
    (INTERPOL), 497, 498
international delinquency, 491–493
    Africa, 495
    age of criminal responsibility, 505
    Americas, 494
    Asia, 495
    Australia and New Zealand, 494
    benefits of cross-national research,
        498–499
    comparisons, 495–502
    drug use, 501, 502
    England, 509–513
    Europe, 493–494
    international crime, 498–499
    juvenile court, 505
    juvenile justice systems, 503–509, 506
    juvenile policing, 503–504
    juvenile property crime, 500–501
    juvenile violence, 499–500
    problems of cross-national research,
        497–498
    prostitution, 493, 494
    sentencing, 508, 510, 513
    violence, 499–500
International Self-Report Delinquency
    Study (ISRD), 497, 498
Internet victimization, 50, 51
INTERPOL (International Criminal Police
    Organization), 497, 498
interrogation, 398–399
interstitial group, 231, 232
intervention, 95, 129–130, 285, 380
    juvenile justice system, 380
    schools, 285
    see also delinquency prevention;
        treatment
intrafamily conflict, 198
involvement, 123
IQ scores, 77, 92–94, 96, 218, 272, 337
iron deficiency, 109
Islands in the Street (Sanchez-Jankowski),
    255
ISR. *see* Institute for Social Research
ISRD (International Self-Report
    Delinquency Study), 497, 498
Italy, 501, 508

J

Jacksonville State Attorney's Office, 22
Japan, 495, 496, 503, 508
JIPS (juvenile intensive probation
    supervision), 461–462
Job Corps, 350
job training, 294–295, 350–351, 411
Joe Boys, 250–251

jointure, 12
Jonesboro killings, 276
judge, 421–422
JUMP (Juvenile Mentoring Program), 345,
    346, 352
Justice Department, 48, 257, 277, 481
juvenile court process, 417–418
    actors in courtroom, 419–422,
        427–428
    bail, 426
    confidentiality, 445–446
    court case flow, 418, 430
    diversion, 428–429
    intake process, 426–428
    jurisdiction of court, 418–422
    petition, 429–430
    plea bargaining, 430–431
    procedures, 422–431
    release *vs.* detention, 422–426
    sentencing, 442–444
    Supreme Court cases, 418–419,
        433–435, 437–438, 445–449
    transfer to adult court, 431–436
    see also juvenile justice system
Juvenile Delinquency Prevention and
    Control (JDP) Act of 1968,
    372–373
juvenile delinquent, as label, 125
Juvenile Disposition Standards
    Commission, 443
Juvenile Gangs in Context (Klein), 233
juvenile intensive probation supervision
    (JIPS), 461–462
Juvenile Justice and Delinquency
    Prevention Act (JJDPA) of 1974,
    335, 373, 380, 385, 424, 426
Juvenile Justice Reform Act of 1977
    (Washington), 443
Juvenile Justice Reform Act (Senate Bill
    1446), 384
juvenile justice system, 4, 10, 26, 37,
    359–363
    alternative courts, 380–381, 382
    case flow, 374, 376
    case processing, 373–374
    comprehensive strategy, 379–381, 385
    conflicting values, 377–378
    criminal justice *vs.* juvenile justice,
        378–379
    current status, 373–379
    deterrence strategy, 69–70
    double standard, 185, 473
    England, 364, 509–513
    federal commissions, 372–373
    future prospects, 382–384
    gender issues, 185–187, 473
    graduated sanctions, 380
    historical timeframe, 377
    Illinois Juvenile Court Act, 369–371,
        377
    institutional programs, 380
    international delinquency, 503–509
    intervention, 380
    nineteenth century, 364–369
    placement of adjudicated youths, 441
    prevention, 380
    process, 375–377, 385

juvenile justice system (*continued*)
    reforming system, 371–373
    status offender in, 20–22
    Supreme Court cases, 362, 370, 371, 385
    teen courts, 380–381
    terminology, 378
    see also institutionalization; juvenile court process
Juvenile Mentoring Program (JUMP), 345, 346, 352
juvenile officers, 394
Juvenile Project (American Correctional Association), 470

K

Kentucky, 444
Kenya, 495
Kids at Risk programs, 257
klikas, 241–242
knifing-off effect, 153
Kobans, 503
Ko-Lin Chin, 251

L

labeling, 295, 433
    ceremonies, 125, 126
    effect of, 124–125
    juvenile justice system and, 126–127
    school and, 273–274
    theories, 124, 126–127
latent delinquents, 85
latent trait view, 140, 154–158
Latin Kings, 243
Latin Queens, 243
law and justice, 127–128
law enforcement. *see* police
Law Enforcement Assistance Administration (LEAA), 372–373, 391
Law Enforcement Management and Administrative Statistics (LEMAS) survey, 392
Law on Regulation of Business Affecting Public Morals, 504
LD. *see* learning disabilities
LEAA (Law Enforcement Assistance Administration), 372–373, 391
lead poisoning, 109
learning disabilities (LD), 78–80, 173
learning processes, 84
learning theories, 120–122, 131
    social learning, 86–87, 96, 217, 340–341, 344
least detrimental alternative, 442
least developed countries, 503
least restrictive alternative, 395, 447
legal responsibility of youth, 17–18
legal rights, 288–293, 480–482
legislation, 69–70
legits, 240
LEMAS (Law Enforcement Management and Administrative Statistics) survey, 392
Lemert's cycle of secondary deviance, 126
liaison prevention programs, 407

liberal feminist view, 166, 180–183
life-course persisters, 145
life-course theories, 140, 157
life expectancy, 112
lifestyle. *see* risky behavior
life transitions, 141–142
Lindsey, Benjamin, 370
loco, 244
LoJack Corporation, 72
lone wolves, 124
longitudinal studies, 140, 284, 311, 318
Los Angeles, California, 406
    gangs, 234, 236, 238, 242, 245, 248–249, 251, 257
losers and burnouts, 315–316, 325
Louisiana, 213
low-birthweight children, 77, 78, 107, 109
low-visibility decision making, 400
loyalty, 250
LSD, 304
Lyman School for Boys, 469

M

machismo, 250
Maine, 23
Maine Boys' Training School, 469
mandatory sentencing, 71–72, 96, 384, 430, 443
Manhattan Institute, 6
Maricao Juvenile Camp, 481
marijuana, 302, 312–313, 317
marriage
    African American community, 42
    desistance and, 146, 150, 151
    divorce, 7, 177, 195–199, 220
    Middle Ages, 12–13
    see also family
Marxism, 182–183
Maryland, 15, 24, 440
    child abuse laws, 213, 216
Maryland Court of Appeals, 216
masculinity hypothesis, 166, 187
Massachusetts, 15, 336, 456, 469
Massachusetts Department of Youth Services, 456
MBD (minimal brain dysfunction), 77, 80
McMartin Day Care case, 214
MDMA (ecstasy), 305–306, 324
media, 87–88
    violence, 96, 97, 106
Memphis, Tennessee, 368
mental illness, 77, 140
    child abuse and, 216, 217, 218
mentoring, 345–346, 411
Mesa Gang Intervention Project (MGIP), 259
mescaline, 304
meta-analysis, 468–469
metal detector checks, 285
methedrine, 305
methodology, 94–95
Mexico, 494
MGIP (Mesa Gang Intervention Project), 259
Miami, Florida, 250
Michigan, 342, 446

Mid-City Project (Boston), 336
Middle Ages, 11–13
middle-class areas, 238
middle-class delinquency, 129, 273
Mighty Moms and Dedicated Dads, 408
milieu therapy, 476
military service, 153
Milwaukee, Wisconsin, 238–239, 240, 242, 243
minimal brain dysfunction (MBD), 77, 80
Minnesota, 444
Minnesota study of twins, 81–82
minor child, 17
Miranda warning, 379, 398
Mississippi, 461–462
Missouri, 24, 446
Mobile, Alabama, 479
Mobilization for Youth (MOBY), 336–337
Model Youth Correction Authority Act, 470
monetary restitution, 464
Monitoring the Future (MTF) survey, 38–39, 40, 41, 307–308, 309, 501
    victimization studies, 49–50
monozygotic twins (MZ), 81–82
Montreal Longitudinal-Experimental Study, 344
moral development, 88, 89, 96, 169
moral ruin, 186
mothers, 112, 194–195, 208
motivated offenders, 66–69, 72
MPD (multiple personality disorder), 216
MST (multisystemic treatment), 322, 353, 468
MTF. *see* Monitoring the Future
MTFC (multidimensional treatment foster care), 466–467
MTF (Monitoring the Future) survey, 307–308, 309
multidimensional treatment foster care (MTFC), 466–467
multiple marginality, 253
multiple personality disorder (MPD), 216
multisystemic treatment (MST), 322, 353, 468
MZ (monozygotic twins), 81–82

N

National Advisory Commission on Criminal Justice Standards and Goals, 22, 373
National Advisory Committee on Handicapped Children, 78
National Assessment, 256
National Center, 284–285
National Center for Juvenile Justice, 187, 384
National Center for Prosecution of Child Abuse, 216
National Center on Addiction and Substance Abuse, 77
National Council on Crime and Delinquency, 22, 403, 474
National Crime Victimization Survey (NCVS), 32, 48–50, 53
National District Attorneys Association, 216

National Gang Crime Research Center, 239
National Household Survey of Drug Abuse, 308–309, 316–317
National Institute of Justice, 317, 498
National Institute of Mental Health, 88
National Institute on Drug Abuse (NIDA), 308
National Juvenile Justice Standards Project, 22–23
National Organization for Women (NOW), 181
National Survey of Child Protective Services, 208
National Youth Employment Coalition (NYEC), 477
National Youth Gang Survey, 238, 245, 248
National Youth Survey (NYS), 310
nature and extent of delinquency, 31–32
    age and delinquency, 43–45
    chronic offenders, 45–48
    crime trends, 33–36
    gender and delinquency, 39–40, 53
    measuring official delinquency, 33–35
    official statistics, 32–36
    policy implications, 47–48
    racial issues, 40–42, 53
    self-report data, 32, 36–40
    social class and, 42–43, 53
    victimization of juveniles, 48–53
Nature Assumption, The (Harris), 204
nature theory, 92
NCVS. *see* National Crime Victimization Survey
negative affect, 64
negative affective states, 116, 117, 131, 217
neglect, 193, 200–216
    definition, 205
neighborhoods, 110, 128, 131
    location of gangs, 237–239
    reactions to gangs, 238–239
    restoration, 111, 129
    school crime and, 283–284
    see also community; social disorganization theory
neotraditional gang, 237
Netherlands, 494, 507, 508
neuroendocrine system, 77
neurological arousal, 80–81
neurological dysfunction, 75, 76–81, 83
    alcoholism and, 202–203
    domestic abuse link, 201
    gender differences, 168
neuroses, 84–85, 91
neurotics, 84
neutralization techniques, 122
Neutral Zone, 258
Nevada, 217, 484
New Jacks, 240
New Jersey, 292–293
New Jersey Delinquency Commission, 268
New Mexico Boys' School, 483
New York, 23, 76, 88, 218, 469, 481
    child saving movement, 204–205, 365–366, 368
    delinquency prevention programs, 341–342

gangs, 233, 237–238, 245, 247–248, 251, 254
    juvenile court process, 433
    MOBY, 336–337
    schools, 285, 286
New York City Department of Charities, 204
New Zealand, 494, 505, 507, 508
NIDA (National Institute on Drug Abuse), 308
nonchronic recidivists, 45
noncriminal behavior, 1
    see also status offenders
nonintervention movement, 130
nonjudicial disposition, 428–429
nonoffenders, 146
nonresidential community treatment, 467–469
nonresidential programs, 454
nonserious crime, incarceration for, 71–72
norms, 114
North Carolina, 213, 407
Norway, 284–285
NOW (National Organization for Women), 181
nuclear family, 194
nurture theory, 93
nutrition. *see* diet
NYEC (National Youth Employment Coalition), 477
NYS (National Youth Survey), 310

O

Office of Community Oriented Policing Services (COPS), 392
Office of Juvenile Justice and Delinquency Prevention (OJJDP), 20–21, 159, 216, 345, 352, 373, 410, 424, 470, 479
official delinquency, 33
OJJDP. *see* Office of Juvenile Justice and Delinquency Prevention
Oklahoma, 24
old heads, 239
Omnibus Safe Streets and Crime Control Act, 372
Operation Blue Orchid, 493
Operation Ceasefire, 408–410
Operation Night Light, 257
Operation Weed and Seed, 129
opium, 303
opportunity to commit crime, 66, 154–155, 180
oppression, 86
Orange County Probation Department, 463
Oregon Social Learning Center (OSLC), 340–341, 466
organized/corporate gang, 236, 237
organized crime families, 234–235
orphan trains, 366–367
OSLC (Oregon Social Learning Center), 340–341, 466
outcome expectancies, 65
out-of-home placements, 439
outreach programs, 129–130
oversensitivity, 89

overt pathway, 143
OxyContin, 305–306

P

pachuco, 250
PALS (Participate and Learn Skills), 348–349
pardons, 3–4
parens patriae, 26, 69, 197, 364
    chancery court, 14–15
    delinquency and, 16–17
    England, 509, 514
    juvenile court process and, 421–422, 427
    juvenile justice system, 368–369, 375, 377
    legal responsibility of youth, 17–18
parental efficacy, 119–120, 200–201
parental responsibility laws, 24–25
parents
    abuse in childhood of, 209–210, 220
    adolescents as, 142–143
    control, 156, 176
    deviant behavior, 120
    drug use by, 310
    as gang members, 252
    improving skills, 340–341, 344, 352
    incarcerated, 112
    mothers, 112, 194–195, 208
    parenting skills, 198
    stepparents, 210
    supervision by, 147
    see also family
Parents' Resource Institute for Drug Education (PRIDE), 308
parole, 482, 485, 509
Participate and Learn Skills (PALS), 348–349
Part I offenses, 32
Part II offenses, 32, 33
Partnerships to Reduce Juvenile Gun Violence Program, 410
party gang, 236
passive speech, 289
passive systems monitoring, 462
paternalism hypothesis, 171–172
paternalistic family, 11
PATHE (Positive Action through Holistic Education), 347
pathways to crime and delinquency, 143–144, 158
    drug use, 312–316
patriarchal capitalism, 183
PBS. *see* problem behavior syndrome
PCP (phencyclidine), 304
Peel, Robert, 390
peer relations, 117, 120, 145, 147, 149–150
    class issues, 228
    delinquency and, 229
    drug use, 124, 230, 310
    impact of, 229–230
    self-rejection and, 125
    see also gangs; socialization
PEIP (Prenatal/Early Infancy Project), 339
penis envy, 172
Pennsylvania, 173, 213, 240

Perry Preschool, 342
persistence, 10, 145, 153
    see also chronic offenders
personality, 90–93, 147, 168, 216
person in need of supervision (PINS), 371, 373
petition, 378, 429–430
phencyclidine (PCP), 304
Philadelphia Block Watch, 392
Philadelphia Collaborative Perinatal Project, 173
physical abuse, 206
physical factors, 140
physical neglect, 206
    see also neglect
Piedmont Wilderness Institute, 477
PINS (person in need of supervision), 371, 373
Pittsburgh Youth Study, 52
placasos/placa, 244
placing-out plan, 366
plea, 430–431
plea bargaining, 421, 447
pledge system, 390
police, 389–390
    aggressive law enforcement, 406
    arrest procedure, 397
    bias, 402–405
    child abuse reports, 208–209
    community-based services, 406–407
    community policing, 129, 391–393, 412
    control of gangs, 256–257
    custodial interrogation, 398–399
    delinquency prevention work, 406–411
    department organization, 394
    discretionary justice, 399–401, 405–406, 411
    disposition of encounters, 400
    drug control strategies, 319–320
    environmental factors, 401
    gangs and, 239, 256–257, 406, 503
    gender bias, 404–405
    history of juvenile policing, 390–391
    integrated models, 408–411
    international delinquency and, 503–504
    investigation, 375
    juvenile offenders and, 393–396
    limiting discretion, 405–406
    policy, 401, 405
    programs that work, 396
    as prosecutors, 395
    records, 35, 208–209
    response to juvenile crime, 395
    roles, 394–395
    rule of law and, 397–399
    in schools, 25, 286, 292–293, 407–408
    search and seizure, 398
    services, 394
    situational factors, 401–402
    Supreme Court cases, 391, 411
    violent juvenile crime and, 396
    see also arrest data
police chief, 401
police helpers, 504

police misbehavior, 127–128
political power, 110–111
Poor Laws, 14, 26
population trends, 35
por vida (p/v), 244
Positive Action through Holistic Education (PATHE), 347
positive peer culture (PPC), 476
positivism, 73
possessiveness, 175
postadjudicatory stage, 378, 460
postdisposition, 460
post-traumatic stress disorder (PTSD), 206, 211
poverty, 6–7, 9, 36, 106
    child poverty, 107–108
    culture of, 107
    racial issues, 108, 111
    school crime and, 282–283
    strain theory, 114–118
    see also sociological theories
poverty concentration effect, 111
power, 110–111, 128
power-control theory, 183–184, 187
PPC (positive peer culture), 476
prayer in school, 290–291
preadjudicatory stage, 378
precocious sexuality, 172–174
predatory crimes, 67
predatory gangs, 237
predisposition report, 429, 439, 460
pregnancy, 8–9, 37, 142, 147, 171, 173
premenstrual syndrome (PMS), 174–175
Prenatal/Early Infancy Project (PEIP), 339
preponderance of the evidence, 369–370
preschool, 342–343
prestige crimes, 248
pretrial conference, 213, 214
pretrial motions, 421
pretrial procedures, 375–376, 379
prevention, 119, 129–130
    see also delinquency prevention
preventive detention, 426, 447
PRIDE (Parents' Resource Institute for Drug Education), 308
primogeniture, 11, 26
Principles of Criminology (Sutherland), 121
privacy, 292–293, 445–446
probable cause, 292, 397
probation, 364, 379, 440, 455–461, 485
    balanced, 463–464
    conditions of, 458–459, 460
    contemporary, 456–455
    due process and, 458
    electronic monitoring, 459, 462
    expanding community treatment, 456
    historical development, 455–456
    innovations, 461–469
    intensive supervision, 461–462
    nature of, 457
    nonresidential community treatment, 467–469
    organization and administration, 459
    residential community treatment, 466–467
    restitution, 464–466
    wilderness probation, 477–478

probation counseling, 459
probation monitoring, 130
probation officers, 399, 458, 459–461
problem behavior syndrome (PBS), 142–143
    drug use, 311–313, 318–319
problem-oriented policing, 396
problem-solving, delinquency as, 64
problem-solving alternatives, 65
progression, 84
Project ALERT, 320
Project New Pride, 467, 468
Project on Policing Neighborhoods, 400
propensity to commit crime, 154
proportionality, 443
Proposition 102, 384
prosecution, 504, 510, 512
prosecutors, 420–421, 427–428, 430
    police as, 395
prosocial bonds, 148–149
prostitution rings, 207
protective factor, 338
Provo experiment, 467
pseudomaturity, 145
psychodynamic theory, 84–86, 172, 311
psychological theories, 83–95
    behavioral theory, 86–88, 96
    cognitive theory, 88–90, 96
    gangs, view of, 254
    gender differences, 172, 176–177
    intelligence, 92–94
    personality, 90–93
    psychodynamic theory, 84–86, 172, 311
psychopathy, 91–92
psychosis, 84–85
psychotherapy, 440, 459, 475
psychotics, 84–85
psychotropic medication, 95, 96
PTSD (post-traumatic stress disorder), 206, 211
puberty, 6, 176–177
public defenders, 420
Puerto Rican gangs, 243
Puerto Rico, 481, 482
punishment, 63
    see also deterrence-based punishment
punkers, 251
Pure Food and Drug Act of 1906, 303

Q
QOP (Quantum Opportunities Program), 345–346, 353
Quantum Opportunities Program (QOP), 345–346, 353

R
racial issues
    arrest rates, 40–42, 53
    composition of gangs, 248–251
    detention and, 423–424
    economic disparity, 108–109
    police bias, 402–404
    poverty, 108, 111
    victimization and, 49
    see also African Americans; Asian Americans; Hispanic Americans

social, community, and environmental relations, 163
social bonds, 122–124, 155
    interactional theory, 149–150
    prosocial bonds, 148–149
social capital, 151–152
social class. see class issues
social conflict theory, 106, 127–131
    law and justice, 127–128
    social policy, 130–131
social control, 24–25, 111–113, 151, 217
social development model (SDM), 147–149
social disorganization theory
    community fear, 112, 131
    consequences of disorganization, 110–111
    drug use, 309–310
    gangs and, 253
    neighborhood instability, 110–114
    school crime and, 282–283
    social controls, 111, 112–113
    summary, 113–114
social gang, 236
social hygiene campaign, 186
social incivility, 112
social investigation report, 460
socialization, 118
    crime and, 119–120
    gender differences, 166–169, 175–178, 187
    interactions and processes, 148–149
    peer relations, 228
    schools and, 268, 269–270, 295
    social policy and, 129–130
    theories of, 120–124
    see also peer relations
social kids, 229
social learning, 86–87, 96, 217, 340–341, 344
social policy, 129–131
social problems, 36, 107–109
    see also class issues; poverty; racial issues
social process theories, 106, 118–124, 131
social reaction theories, 106
    effect of labeling, 124–125
    labeling ceremonies, 125, 126
    social policy, 130
social structure, 107–109
social structure theories, 106, 107–118
    social policy and, 129
    social problems, 107–109
    structure, culture, and delinquency, 109–110
    see also class issues
Society for the Prevention of Cruelty to Animals (SPCA), 204–205
Society for the Prevention of Cruelty to Children (SPCC), 368
Society for the Prevention of Pauperism, 365
sociobiology, 74
sociological theories, 105–106
    conflict concept of delinquency, 128–129
    control theories, 120, 122–124, 131

cultural deviance theory, 118, 131
juvenile justice process and labeling, 126–127
learning theories, 120–122, 131
social conflict theory, 106, 127–131
socialization, theories of, 119–124
social policy and, 129–131
social process theories, 106, 118–124
social reaction theories, 106, 124–127
social structure theories, 106, 107–118
see also social disorganization; socialization
sociopathic personality, 91–93, 311
sociopathic youth, 254
source control, 319
South Africa, 501
South Carolina, 477
Soviet Union, 253
SPCA (Society for the Prevention of Cruelty to Animals), 204–205
SPCC (Society for the Prevention of Cruelty to Children), 368
special education, 273–274
specialized facilities, 454
specialty gang, 237
specific deterrence, 69, 71, 73, 96
Spectrum Wilderness Program, 470
speedballing, 303
spontaneous remission, 43–45
Sri Lanka, 505
SSDP (Seattle Social Development Project), 343–344
stable slum, 237–238
Standard Minimum Rules for the Administration of Juvenile Justice, (Beijing Rules), 503, 504, 508, 514
State Agricultural and Industrial School, 469
status offenders, 18–20, 373
    categories, 25
    detention and, 426
    in juvenile justice system, 20–22
status offense laws, 1, 18, 21–24
step-down system, 484
stepparents, 210
steroids, 305
stigmatization, 23, 26, 95, 112, 124, 132, 274, 433
stimulants, 304–305
stimuli, 116, 131
stoners, 251
Stop Juvenile Crime Initiative, 384
strain, 123–124
strain theory, 114–118, 166
stress, 5–6
stubborn child laws, 16
Study Group on Serious and Violent Juvenile Offenders (OJJDP), 159
study of juvenile delinquency, 9–11
subcultures, 118, 121, 274, 310
substance abuse, 302
    see also drug use
Suffolk County Probation Department, 23
suicide, 472, 486
suitable targets, 67, 68
superego, 84

supervision, 147, 424
    aftercare, 482–483
    CHINS, 19, 371, 373
    intensive, 461–462, 485
suppression effect, 455
Supreme Court, 70, 212, 220
    corrections cases, 480–481
    juvenile court process cases, 418–419, 433–435, 437–438, 445–449
    juvenile justice cases, 362, 370, 371, 385
    police cases, 391, 398–399, 411
    probation cases, 458
    school cases, 288–293
surveillance systems, 72, 285, 286
susceptibility rationale, 78
swaddling, 13
Sweden, 494, 505
Switzerland, 505, 508
Synar Amendment, 306
Syracuse University Family Development Research Program, 341–342

T

target-hardening technique, 72
teacher effectiveness, 274
technology, 106, 108
teen courts, 380–381
Teen Summer Academy, 257
television
    closed-circuit (CCTV), 215, 216, 220
    violence, 5, 87–88, 96–97, 106
terminology, 17, 378
tetrahydrocannabinol (THC), 302
Texas, 23, 25, 286, 444, 481, 483
Texas Youth Commission, 483
theory, defined, 59
therapeutic strategies, 294
Third International Mathematics and Science Study (TIMSS), 270, 271
time out, 340
TIMSS (Third International Mathematics and Science Study), 270, 271
tips, 244
toxic substances, 76
tracking, 273–274
tracking systems, 72
traditional gang, 237
training schools, 454
trait theories, 62, 72–73, 96
    gender and, 166, 170–175
    latent trait view, 140, 154–158
    origins of, 74
    prevention and, 95
    see also biosocial theories; psychological theories
tranquilizers, 304
transcript of trial record, 445
transfer hearing, 433
transfer process, 431
transitional neighborhoods, 110, 111
transnational crime, 498
treatment, 17–18, 95, 129, 474–480
    for child abuse, 212–213, 219–220
    community treatment, 454–461, 485
    for drug use, 322–324, 440, 459
    group treatment techniques, 475–476

Photograph Credits

Juvenile Delinquency and Children's Rights in the United States and Abroad

[c o n t i n u e d]

1970

In re Winship establishes that proof beyond a reasonable doubt is necessary in the adjudicatory phase of a juvenile hearing. A juvenile can appeal on the ground of insufficiency of the evidence if the offense alleged is an act that would be a crime in an adult court.

White House Conference on Children

1971

Mckeiver v. Pennsylvania establishes that a jury trial is not constitutionally required in a juvile hearing but states can permit one if they wish.

The Twenty-Sixth Amendment to the Constitution is passed, granting the right to vote to 18-year-olds.

1972

Wisconsin v. Yoder gives parents the right to impose their religion on their children.

Wolfgang publishes *Delinquency in a Birth Cohort*.

1954

Brown v. Board of Education, a major school desegregation decision

1973

In re Snyder gives minors the right to bring proceedings against their parents.

San Antonio Independent School District v. Rodriguez establishes that differences in education based on wealth were not necessarily discriminatory.

1959

Standard Family Court Act of National Council on Crime and Delinquency establishes that juvenile hearings are to be informal.

1974

Federal Child Abuse Prevention Act

Buckley Amendment to the Education Act of 1974, the Family Education Rights and Privacy Act. Students have the right to see their own files with parental consent.

Juvenile Justice and Delinquency Prevention Act

1966

Kent v. United States—initial decision to establish due process protections for juvenile at transfer proceedings.

1967

President's Commission on Law Enforcement recognizes the problems of the juvenile justice system.

In re Gault, a U.S. Supreme Court decision establishes juveniles have the right to counsel, notice, confrontation of witnesses, and the avoidance of self-incrimination. In general, the court holds that Fourteenth Amendment due process applies to the juvenile justice system, specifically in adjudicatory hearings.

1968

Ginsberg v. New York establishes that it is unlawful to sell pornography to a minor.

1969

Tinker v. Des Moines School District establishes that the First Amendment applies to juveniles and protects their constitutional right to free speech.

continued from front inside cover ...

1950   1960   1970